SUPPLEMENTS

P R E V I E W

TABLE OF CONTENTS

WE ARE PROUD TO BRING YOU THE

Fifth Edition of Lynn Quitman Troyka's *Simon & Schuster Handbook for Writers.*

In addition to its bold new design and color-coded organization, the Fifth Edition of this comprehensive yet easy-to-use handbook features updated MLA and APA documentation and offers a new MLA-style research paper. Revised coverage of research includes finding, evaluating, and documenting traditional and electronic sources. Newly combined "Parts" ensure a concise presentation of material in the new edition. The Annotations in the Instructor's Edition have also been completely revised, which makes this teaching tool invaluable for new and experienced instructors.

Please read on to learn about the Fifth Edition's fully integrated print and multimedia supplements package.

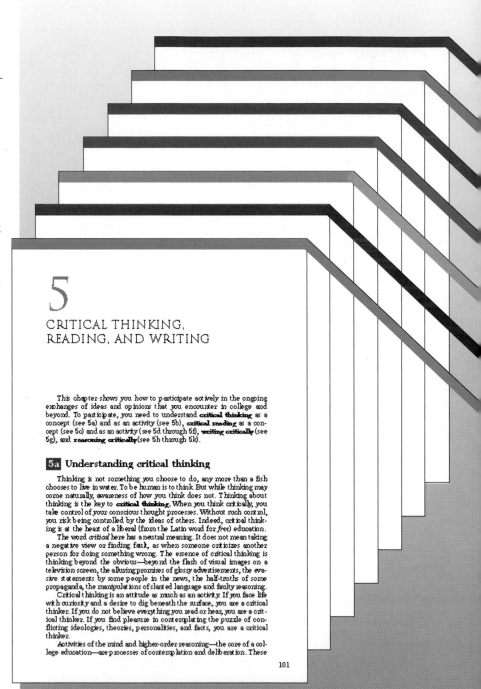

5

CRITICAL THINKING, READING, AND WRITING

This chapter shows you how to participate actively in the ongoing exchanges of ideas and opinions that you encounter in college and beyond. To participate, you need to understand **critical thinking** as a concept (see 5a) and as an activity (see 5b), **critical reading** as a concept (see 5c) and as an activity (see 5d through 5f), **writing critically** (see 5g), and **reasoning critically** (see 5h through 5k).

5a Understanding critical thinking

Thinking is not something you choose to do, any more than a fish chooses to live in water. To be human is to think. But while thinking may come naturally, awareness of how you think does not. Thinking about thinking is the key to **critical thinking**. When you think critically, you take control of your conscious thought processes. Without such control, you risk being controlled by the ideas of others. Indeed, critical thinking is at the heart of a liberal (from the Latin word for *free*) education.

The word *critical* here has a neutral meaning. It does not mean taking a negative view or finding fault, as when someone criticizes another person for doing something wrong. The essence of critical thinking is thinking beyond the obvious—beyond the flash of visual images on a television screen, the alluring promises of glossy advertisements, the evasive statements by some people in the news, the half-truths of some propaganda, the manipulations of slanted language and faulty reasoning.

Critical thinking is an attitude as much as an activity. If you face life with curiosity and a desire to dig beneath the surface, you are a critical thinker. If you do not believe everything you read or hear, you are a critical thinker. If you find pleasure in contemplating the puzzle of conflicting ideologies, theories, personalities, and facts, you are a critical thinker.

Activities of the mind and higher-order reasoning—the core of a college education—are processes of contemplation and deliberation. These

101

COLOR CODED ORGANIZATION

PART VII:
WRITING WHEN ENGLISH IS A SECOND LANGUAGE

PART VI:
WRITING ACROSS THE CURRICULUM

PART V:
WRITING RESEARCH

PART IV:
USING PUNCTUATION AND MECHANICS

PART III:
WRITING EFFECTIVELY

PART II:
UNDERSTANDING GRAMMAR AND WRITING CORRECT SENTENCES

PART I:
WRITING AN ESSAY

VISUAL ICONS

SUMMARY

CHECKLIST

GRAMMAR PATTERNS

COLOR CODED ORGANIZATION AND VISUAL ICONS.

COLOR CODING (shown at far left) creates a new, easy route to information! Each part of this handbook now features a distinctive color bar at the top of its pages—visible even when the book is closed—providing users with a simple way to learn and remember where to find information…FAST! This bold new edition also features updated 1998 MLA and APA documentation guidelines.

THREE COLORFUL ICONS (shown at left) in the Fifth Edition carry visual impact throughout the handbook, acting as concise navigation tools for students looking for summary, checklist, or grammar pattern charts.

These graphic elements give your students an impressive advantage: students will find the Fifth Edition of the *Simon & Schuster Handbook for Writers* both easier to use and more visually appealing than any other handbook on the market today.

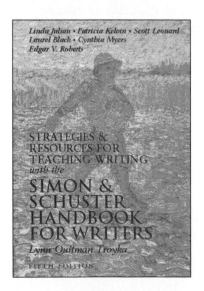

Annotated Instructor's Edition, Fifth Edition

Thoroughly revised by Lynn Quitman Troyka, this exceptional teaching tool features a section of essays written by specialists in their fields: *"Teaching at the Crossroads: Choices and Challenges in College Composition"* by Valerie Zimbaro; *"The History of Rhetoric: An Overview"* by William F. Woods, revised and updated by Catherine L. Hobbs; *"Portfolios in the Teaching and Assessing of Writing"* by Irwin Weiser; *"Writing Across the Curriculum: An Overview and Update"* by Margot I. Soven; and *"Teaching Composition to Speakers of Other Languages"* by Joy Reid. Also featured are marginal annotations that include quotations, cues to other supplements, answers to exercises, and more.

0-13-095512-4

Strategies and Resources for Teaching Writing, Fifth Edition

by LINDA JULIAN, PATRICIA KELVIN, SCOTT LEONARD, LAUREL BLACK, CYNTHIA MYERS, and EDGAR V. ROBERTS

A spiral-bound book featuring essays on collaborative writing by Patricia Kelvin & Scott Leonard, portfolios by Laurel Black, ESL by Cindy Myers, reading and writing about literature by Edgar V. Roberts, workplace writing by Linda Julian; strategies for teaching writing with the *Simon & Schuster Handbook for Writers*, Fifth Edition; and answers to exercises in the text.

0-13-081659-0

Diagnostic and Competency Tests

This valuable set of more than 500 test items is designed for use as pre-, mid-, or post-tests, and it is available in both printed and computerized format. Also featured are ESL diagnostic tests. Answers to test items are keyed to sections of the handbook.

0-13-081665-5

Preparing for the TASP

Designed for instructors whose students must take the Texas Academic Skills Program exam, this booklet offers sample exams that follow the actual TASP format. This guide may be copied free upon adoption of the handbook, or students can purchase it for a nominal price.

0-13-081640-X

Preparing for the CLAST

Designed for instructors whose students must take Florida's College Level Academic Skills Test, this booklet offers sample exams that follow the actual CLAST format. This guide may be copied free upon adoption of the handbook, or students can purchase it for a nominal price.

0-13-081649-3

SUPPLEMENTS FOR INSTRUCTORS

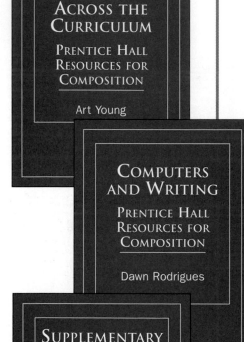

Teaching Writing Across the Curriculum

by ART YOUNG–Clemson University

Written for college teachers in all disciplines, this booklet provides useful advice on writing across the curriculum— on teaching, on using writing as a tool for learning the subjects being studied, and as a strategy for improving the confidence and the ability of students to communicate effectively.

0-13-493065-7

Computers and Writing

by DAWN RODRIGUES–University of Texas at Brownsville

For instructors who want to integrate computers into the composition classroom, this brief guide is invaluable. It provides an overview of possible pitfalls and advantages of technology and outlines clear strategies for successful computer use.

0-13-435934-8

Supplementary Essays for Writers

by GARY D. SCHMIDT

This 176-page, rhetorically arranged reader provides a collection of 31 classic essays, with questions. It is available free to adopters of the handbook, including permission to copy individual essays for students, and students can purchase it for a nominal price.

0-13-101338-6

Teaching Writing

by PHYLLIS HASTINGS—Saginaw Valley State University

This 120-page manual provides guidance on teaching writing for both new and experienced teachers. Topics include student-teacher interaction, class dynamics, course plans, and the evaluation of students' work. Available free to adopters.

0-13-435942-9

Portfolios

by PAT BELANOFF—State University of New York, Stony Brook

This booklet elaborates on the potential benefits and drawbacks of portfolio use across classes, departments, or institutions.

0-13-572322-1

Journals

by CHRISTOPHER C. BURNHAM—New Mexico State University

This booklet offers two examples of journal programs and exercises, including extensive instructions for students. Burnham addresses problems with evaluation and administration, including student privacy issues and the instructor's legal responsibilities.

0-13-572348-5

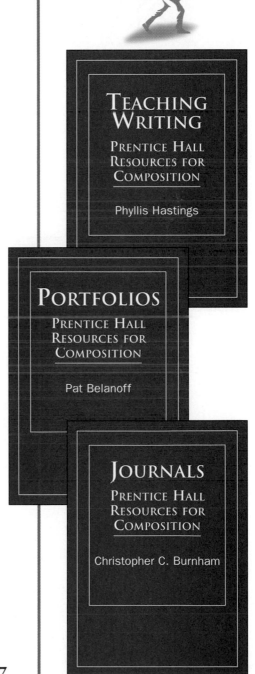

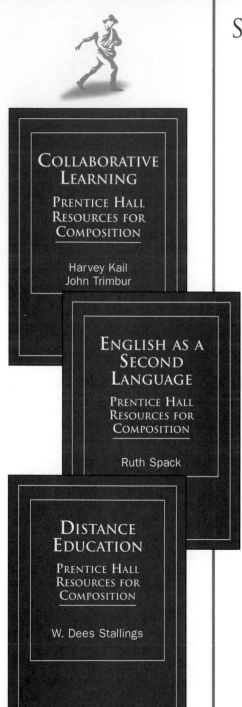

SUPPLEMENTS FOR INSTRUCTORS

Collaborative Learning

by HARVEY KAIL—University of Maine, and
    JOHN TRIMBUR—Worcester Polytechnic Institute

This booklet discusses how collaborative learning classrooms differ from traditional classrooms, and how to use and maintain a collaborative writing environment in the teaching of writing.

0-13-572371-X

English as a Second Language

by RUTH SPACK—Tufts University

This booklet offers strategies for teaching ESL, and considers how the adjustments made to help second language learners can lead to effective teaching and learning in the classroom.

0-13-572389-2

Distance Education

by W. DEES STALLINGS—University of Maryland, University College

This booklet illustrates the dynamics of writing instruction in the distance learning environment, and offers guidance on how to use the distance learning techniques described.

0-13-572314-0

SUPPLEMENTS FOR STUDENTS

Simon & Schuster Workbook for Writers, Fifth Edition

by LYNN QUITMAN TROYKA

This extremely useful workbook is organized to complement the handbook. Whether it is used to accompany the handbook or as a primary text for freshman composition or basic writing courses, this workbook is geared toward writers who need additional grammar practice. It offers instruction and exercises on a wide range of helpful topics from punctuation to planning an essay and ESL coverage.

0-13-081424-5

This workbook is salable to students. A separate *Answer Key* is available free to instructors using the workbook.

Prentice Hall Guide to Research and Documentation

This useful booklet provides students with research and documentation in a paperback format designed for ease of use and portability. A handy guide, it features the most recent information in MLA, APA, CBE, and CM formats, and covers the research process.

This supplement is available to students for a nominal fee.

0-13-438433-4

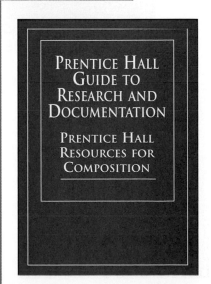

SUPPLEMENTS FOR STUDENTS

The Prentice Hall / *Themes of the Times* Program

This newspaper supplement features recent articles from *The New York Times* designed to inspire writing ideas with relevant examples to which students can relate.

Free to adopters of this handbook, this *Themes of the Times* program is available to instructors in student quantities.

0-13-690181-6

The Research Organizer, Second Edition
by SUE D. HOPKE—Broward Community College

This booklet is designed to help students to organize their notes, jot down quotes, organize their thoughts, and keep their drafts together as they progress throughout the entire research writing process.

0-13-813957-1

Rough Drafts: An Activity Book to Accompany the Simon & Schuster Handbook for Writers, Fifth Edition
by KATHLEEN SHINE CAIN, Merrimack College

Designed to provide practice with writing process skills, this book offers invention exercises, and then provides rough drafts for students to revise.

Professors may copy this supplement or parts of it free, or students may purchase it at a nominal cost.

0-13-081648-5

 ## English on the Internet: A Prentice Hall Guide 1998-1999

This brief paperback guide helps students navigate the journey through cyberspace. Completely updated to include the 1998 MLA and APA documentation guidelines, this guide is available to students free when packaged with this handbook.

Package ISBN: 0-13-983669-1

 ## Webster's Dictionary Offers

Either of the following dictionaries may be shrinkwrapped to this text at a discounted rate. The *Webster's New World™ Dictionary,* Third College Edition contains more than 11,000 American words and over 17,000 entries.

The *Webster's New World™ Compact Dictionary School and Office Dictionary,* Third Edition contains over 56,000 entries and assistance in pronunciation and spelling.

Model Student Essays

This anthology features 25 student essays collected from around the country and organized into three broad categories: personal experience, explanatory, and persuasive.

This supplement is available free to students when packaged with this handbook.

0-13-645516-6

MULTIMEDIA SUPPLEMENTS

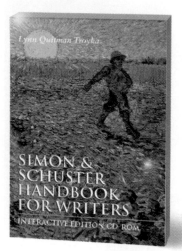

Simon & Schuster Handbook for Writers, Interactive Edition CD-ROM

(CD-ROM for Microsoft® Windows)

Designed for ease of use and accessibility, the *Simon & Schuster Handbook For Writers Interactive Edition* CD-ROM presents an all-in-one reference tool for today's student writers, and works in tandem with the most popular word-processors. While writing any document, users have the ability to search the entire contents of the *Simon & Schuster Handbook for Writers,* Fifth Edition quickly and easily for help with grammar, style, punctuation, organization, and all other aspects of writing, from the draft stage through final revisions. Students can also fine-tune their writing skills by working through numerous exercises. Additionally, this CD-ROM offers access to a complete dictionary, a comprehensive thesaurus, and a full encyclopedia of literature.

0-13-099690-4

World Wide Web site: http://www.prenhall.com/troyka

This content-rich WWW online companion web site includes completely interactive exercises on grammar and punctuation sections of the handbook, plus self-graded quizzes with references keyed back to the text. Relevant links to appropriate resources in English Composition direct students to helpful sources available to them on the Internet. This site also features special coverage of the writing process, research and documentation, and writing across the curriculum.

Blue Pencil Software

by Bob Bator

This interactive editing program allows students to practice their writing skills by making revisions in paragraph-length passages on their computer screen, complete with instant feedback on various skill categories and an on-screen counter to track remaining corrections.

SKILL CATEGORIES:
  A. Capitalization and Internal Punctuation
  B. Commas
  C. Fragments, Comma Splices
  D. Modifiers
  E. Pronouns
  F. Quotation Marks and End Punctuation
  G. Subject-Verb Agreement
  H. Usage
  I. Verbs
  J. Final Review

Blue Pencil is free to adopters of this handbook, with permission to make multiple student copies. A site license is available for computer labs.

0-13-081664-7

Visit EnglishCentral on the World Wide Web for more information about Prentice Hall English titles!

http://www.prenhall.com/english

On-line Handbook

This reference software allows students to access explanations and material on grammar, punctuation, and mechanics through a word-processing program, and is directly available by clicking an icon or at the touch of a hotkey. The main menu parallels the main parts of this handbook, and the sub-menus correspond to chapters within parts of the text.

This software is available free to qualified adopters of this handbook, with permission to use in a networked environment or to copy for students. It is available in two formats:

Macintosh®: 0-13-081662-0
Microsoft® Windows: 0-13-081663-9

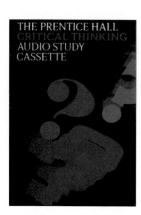

The Prentice Hall Critical Thinking Audio Study Cassette

This 60-minute cassette helps students develop critical thinking skills, from asking the right questions to studying, note-taking, and effective learning.

This cassette is free to qualified adopters of this handbook, and can be shrinkwrapped to the text for students at a nominal cost.

0-13-678335-X

ABC News/Prentice Hall Video Library: Composition, Volume 2

This collection of thematically arranged video clips from various ABC News programs can be used to inspire classroom discussion, critical thinking, and writing assignments.

VIDEO CLIPS
1. Lyme Disease—Nightline 7/13/89, *20:56*
2. Jack Smith's Vietnam Diary—Nightline, 1/21/94, *9:30*
3. Prozac—American Agenda, 1/4/94, *5:03*
4. Smart Cars and Highways are Keys to Environment's Future—American Agenda, 11/24/92, *4:05*
5. Teaching Values in the Schools—American Agenda, 9/8/93, *4:55*
6. Teens Confront Prejudices American Agenda, 12/14/93, *5:01*
7. Political Correctness on US Campuses—Nightline, 5/13/91, *7:56*
8. Maya Angelou, Inaugural Poetess—World News Tonight, 1/22/93, *4:48*
9. Crime and Punishment Issues and Politics—Nightline, 1/26/94, *8:18*

This video is free to qualified adopters of this handbook.

0-13-149030-3

ABCNEWS

MULTIMEDIA SUPPLEMENTS

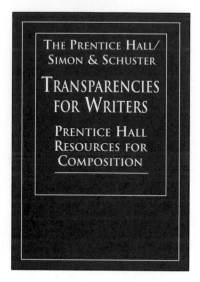

The Prentice Hall / Simon & Schuster Transparencies for Writers

This set of 100 two-and four-color transparencies features exercises, examples, and suggestions for writers that focus on all aspects of the writing process, from generating ideas to shaping an outline, drafting, revising, and editing work. Fine art selections are integrated to inspire ideas.

This set is available free to qualified adopters of this handbook.
0-13-703209-9

"Profiles of a Writer" Video Series

A professionally produced video series which documents the individual lives and work of seven renowned authors:

- Norman Mailer, *57 minutes*
- Jorge Luis Borges: Borges and I, *76 minutes*
- Gore Vidal, *58 minutes*
- Toni Morrison, *52 minutes*
- Agatha Christie, How Did She Do It? *51 minutes*
- Jean Cocteau, Autobiography of an Unknown, *58 minutes*
- Gabriel García Márquez, Tales Beyond Solitude, *59 minutes*

CONTACT YOUR PRENTICE HALL REPRESENTATIVE FOR ORDERING DETAILS AND AVAILABILITY.

Writer's Helper

by WILLIAM WRESCH—University of Wisconsin, Stevens Point

This new version of the award-winning disk-based program, *Writer's Helper*, now offers an innovative collection of 19 prewriting activities and 18 revising tools designed to help students work easily and creatively through all stages of the writing process. From essay assignments to memos and formal reports, business writing, and more, *Writer's Helper* software helps users convey their thoughts in a clear, concise style in these crucial stages of the writing process:

- PREWRITING. Students use the Prewriting Activities to find an idea, explore a topic, and organize information in a paper.

- DRAFTING. Using their favorite word processors, students use the ideas generated in the Prewriting Activities to write papers.

- REVISING. Returning to *Writer's Helper,* students import their drafts and use the Revising Tools to analyze and review their documents.

Macintosh®Version 4.0: 0-13-615014-4

Microsoft® Windows Version 4.0: 0-13-615254-6

FOR A LIMITED TIME

Prentice Hall is offering this software for $10 when shrinkwrapped with the *Simon & Schuster Handbook for Writers,* Fifth Edition. Contact your local Prentice Hall sales representative for ordering details and site license information.

INDEX OF TITLES

ANNOTATED INSTRUCTOR'S EDITION

FIFTH EDITION

SIMON & SCHUSTER HANDBOOK FOR WRITERS

Lynn Quitman Troyka

PRENTICE HALL
Upper Saddle River, New Jersey 07458

Editorial Director: Charlyce Jones Owen
Editor in Chief: Leah Jewell
Senior Development Editor: Joyce Perkins
Assistant Vice President of Humanities and Social Science: Barbara Kittle
Senior Managing Editor: Bonnie Biller
Senior Project Manager: Shelly Kupperman
Manufacturing Manager: Nick Sklitsis
Prepress and Manufacturing Buyer: Mary Ann Gloriande
Creative Design Director: Leslie Osher
Interior and Cover Designer: Ximena P. Tamvakopoulos
Manager, Production Services: John J. Jordan
Electronic Page Layout: Lori Clinton
Art: Mirella Signoretto, Michael D'Angelo
Marketing Director: Gina Sluss
Editorial Assistant: Patricia Castiglione

For permission to use copyrighted material, grateful acknowledgment is made to the copyright holders on pages xxvii-xxviii, which is considered an extension of this copyright page.

This book was set in 10/11 New Caledonia by Prentice Hall Production Services and printed and bound by World Color. The cover was printed by The Lehigh Press, Inc.

Printed in the United States of America

10   9   8   7   6   5   4   3   2   1

ISBN 0-13-079783-9 (student version)
ISBN 0-13-095512-4 (professional version)

Prentice-Hall International (UK) Limited, *London*
Prentice-Hall of Australia Pty. Limited, *Sydney*
Prentice-Hall Canada Inc., *Toronto*
Prentice-Hall Hispanoamericana, S.A., *Mexico*
Prentice-Hall of India Private Limited, *New Delhi*
Prentice-Hall of Japan, Inc., *Tokyo*
Simon & Schuster Asian Pte. Ltd., *Singapore*
Editora Prentice-Hall do Brasil, Ltda., *Rio de Janeiro*

CONTENTS

Brief Contents of the Student Edition

PREFACE TO THE ANNOTATED INSTRUCTOR'S EDITION

Over the recent months, I have personally updated, added to, and revised the Annotated Instructor's Edition (AIE) for the *Simon & Schuster Handbook for Writers,* Fifth Edition. My goal is to offer a collection of extensively overhauled and freshened material to support writing teachers, including full- and part-time contract faculty, along with adjuncts and teaching assistants.

Successful teaching, I feel, does not consist of a "grab bag of what works Monday morning." It results from a cohesive vision of goals and strategies shaped by informed access to the best of traditional and modern theories in rhetoric, language, and research. But many writing teachers today have too little time to keep pace with the large body of knowledge that emerges yearly. That's where this AIE comes in.

The AIE margins are filled with information for teachers, in annotations running beside each exactly duplicated page of the student edition. I chose information to help teachers stay abreast of developments in the theory and practice of teaching composition. I include teaching tips based on research-proven practice; detailed bibliographic citations from major journals in composition; thought-provoking quotations about writing, reading, and research; and descriptive cross-references to the rich bank of supplements provided by Simon & Schuster/Prentice Hall. Also, answers to exercises along with a text reference for each exercise item are available to help teachers see at a glance each student's strengths and weaknesses.

Even more important, I feel, is a feature unique to my AIE: the collection of specially commissioned, comprehensive bibliographic essays that set forth the theoretical grounding of my *Simon & Schuster Handbook for Writers,* Fifth Edition. They are placed intentionally before the student edition begins. The essays support the structure, content, and approaches I used to make each decision as I composed this *Handbook.*

The essays are "Teaching at the Crossroads: Choices and Challenges in College Composition"; "The History of Rhetoric: Overview and Update"; "Portfolios in the Teaching and Assessing of Writing"; "Writing Across the Curriculum: Overview and Update"; and "Teaching Composition to Speakers of Other Languages." I am indebted to the author of each essay for undertaking the specially commissioned research and for the writing entailed, for as a group these essays help me deliver my message that the teaching of writing relies on an intellectual tradition and current knowledge about language and learning.

For sharing their expertise for annotations in Part Five, I am especially grateful to Paulette Smith and D. J. Henry. For their fine work on previous editions of this AIE, I want to thank Ann B. Dobie, University of Southwestern Louisiana; Emily R. Gordon, Queensborough Community College; James MacDonald, University of Southwestern Louisiana; Patricia Morgan, Louisiana State University; and Judith A. Stanford, Rivier College.

At Prentice Hall/Simon & Schuster, I was fortunate to work with a top team. Leah Jewell, Editor in Chief, spearheaded the editorial effort with a strong, hands-on commitment to quality and innovation; Joyce F. Perkins, Senior Development Editor, kept her keen eye on the project with comforting good will; Shelly Kupperman, Senior Project Manager, brought order and efficiency to a production challenge on a dauntingly tight schedule. Others whose support were indispensable include Phil Miller, President of Humanities and Social Sciences; Charlyce Jones Owen, Editorial Director; Gina Sluss, Director of Marketing; Leslie Osher, Creative Design Director; Ximena P. Tamvakopoulos, Designer; Lori Clinton, Page Formatter; Mary Ann Gloriande, Manufacturing Buyer; and Patricia Castiglione, Editorial Assistant.

Lynn Quitman Troyka

TEACHING AT THE CROSSROADS: CHOICES AND CHALLENGES IN COLLEGE COMPOSITION

Valerie P. Zimbaro

Product or process? Convention or culture? Tradition or transformation? Which road should we choose as we teach composition into the next century? The veteran instructors among us are likely to have faced such dilemmas in the past; new teachers in the field are certain to explore these issues throughout their careers. Regardless of our levels of experience, we all share one common sentiment: We're anxious about the future of college composition. Fortunately, the anxiety we feel during this end of a century and of a cycle is both natural and necessary for the process of growth. Such has clearly been the case, over the past several decades, in the evolution of what we know as the "writing process." Donald A. Daiker urges our using a historical perspective when viewing cycles of instruction. He notes that "in times of upheaval" or when there has been a "perceived . . . 'crisis,' " "conflicting energies" have always resulted in calls for literacy reform [10]. This essay will review the crises that have shaped the most influential reform movements of the past fifty years. It will point to possible paths we may take in the future as teachers of writing. Most important, it will challenge all teachers to choose both their purpose and their place in a profession that will enable us all to live and work in a new century.

Origins of the Writing Process Movement

Prior to the 1950s, the term *composition* referred primarily to a product: a correct and predictable standardized theme. Yet as early as 1953, Barriss Mills vilified teachers who employed rote instructional methods, citing that their students' written products were often "static, atomistic, [and] non-functional" [9]. A few years later, traditional methods of teaching composition were again questioned, but this time for more practical reasons. Essentially, in the late 1950s, the influx of students returning to school on the G.I. Bill had significantly increased the workload of composition faculty. In an effort to solve this problem, proponents of the so-called Oregon Plan recommended the "adoption of peer workshops and small-group conferencing, not on intellectual grounds, but on pragmatic ones" [9].

Although such creative efforts were accepted and are still employed to date, at the time they posed no widespread threat to academic convention. The year 1964, however, marked a change in the profession when D. Gordon Rohman and Albert O. Wlecke introduced the concept of *prewriting* in their seminal cooperative research project. In this study, Rohman and Wlecke presented writing as a "process," and their findings presaged what is now known as the *stage model theory*. The theory suggests that a person must "assimilate his 'subject' to himself" through a series of creative stages before producing an effectively written composition [28].

While Rohman and Wlecke sparked the process-versus-product controversy, others fueled the fire with similar research. It is now widely acknowledged that one such effort, Janet Emig's 1971 study of the composing process, had a significant impact on the writing movement in both practice and pedagogy throughout the next two decades [13]. Her research, based largely on Jerome Bruner's studies on creativity [8], reflected the changing social climate of the early 1970s. During that time, a collective celebration of individuality and art, other theorists also began to shape composition study through their own versions of stage model work.

Such theorists include Ken Macrorie, Peter Elbow, and Donald Murray. Macrorie, for example, introduced the concept of recording one's uncensored thoughts on paper in his text *Searching Writing* [22]. His method of writing without stopping reflects the dynamic nature of interior monologue and clearly illustrates how cogent composition can often be rooted in chaos. In *Writing Without Teachers* [11] and later in *A Community of Writers* [12], Elbow echoed Macrorie's thoughts and endorsed freewriting as a way for students to "get the chaos out" of their heads before attempting coherence in their compositions [12]. Similarly, Murray, in *A Writer Teaches Writing* [25], encouraged expressive invention; nev-

---

Valerie Zimbaro is the Department Chair of Communications for the West Campus of Valencia Community College in Orlando, Florida. Previously, she has served as a professor of English, an online course designer, and the Director of Distance Learning at St. Petersburg Junior College. As a specialist in higher education curriculum development, she has also authored numerous teachers' guides, articles, and reference books in composition and in literature. Her most recent book is The Encyclopedia of Apocalyptic Literature *(ABC-Clio, 1997).*

ertheless, he emphasized the discovery of a clear writing plan through successive revisions of developmental drafts.

This call for planning in writing heralded the next evolution in the process movement. While most rhetoricians understood the obvious merit of unbridled creativity in the expression of ideas, many scholars, including James Moffett, Linda Flower, and John R. Hayes, stressed the importance of understanding cognitive processes in the teaching of writing. Moffett, in particular, relied on Jean Piaget's stages of intellectual development to show how writers develop habits to help them proceed throughout the stages of writing [24]. Flower and Hayes concurred with this research and suggested specific goal-directed strategies or "protocols" to help students move successfully from one writing stage to another [18]. But critics of this approach, such as David Bartholomae, argue that the goal of writing teachers must always be more than "the efficient production of text" [2]. Teachers should encourage writing as a collaborative mode of learning.

The Emergence of Writing Communities

If the 1970s marked the decade of individual expression in writing, the 1980s introduced the idea of writing as a social act. Noted proponents of the "social constructionist theory" include Bartholomae as well as Richard Gebhardt [16], Maxine Hairston [17], and Patricia Bizzell [5]. According to their shared views, students must learn to understand how their native communities influence both how and what they write; moreover, they must learn to use their unique writing voices to influence others within communities much broader than their own.

Xiao-Ming Li illustrates the particular challenge this creates for teachers whose students have English as their second language. She stresses a shared awareness of how culture, politics, and religious affiliations inevitably influence writers as they proceed through the composition process. Further, she urges teachers to use this awareness in a careful, nonbiased evaluation of their students' writing [21]. Additional research suggests that such insights must also extend to the growing body of students whose underpreparedness may have left them academically at risk.

Sylvia Holladay emphasizes that this problem exists in many colleges, but it proliferates, more often, in open-admission institutions where students enter college both because and in spite of their otherwise "chaotic, crisis-driven lives" [19]. Peter Elbow acknowledges the obvious when he explains how students from such backgrounds may initially react negatively, with "anger and disbelief," at having been placed in remedial classes. Such discouragement, he suggests, may be

countered by a supportive writing environment that will not only promote creativity but also encourage the risk taking that is necessary for "good learning" [27].

Writing as Revolution

Within the past decade, teachers of writing have been similarly challenged to take risks as a result of the "digital revolution." Lester Faigley cites the current technological transformation as one of the largest "forces of change" that will affect how we as teachers "see ourselves and what we do" [14]. On the most elementary level, computer-assisted writing makes it easier for students to improve their writing, in a variety of ways, which include spelling checks, grammar correction, and methods for simple revision. On a more sophisticated level, the use of both wide and local area networks has also made it possible for writers to participate in a global writing community. On local networks, for example, teachers may now conduct simultaneous instruction across multiple campuses by using networked software and prepared course materials. Course syllabi, class lectures, and sample papers are readily available for student access at their own convenience [26]. Though some cynics might consider these innovations little more than the next evolution of "canned" instruction, in truth, computer networks encourage diverse, spontaneous thought and enable students and teachers to communicate, both formally and informally, through chat rooms, newsgroups, and electronic mail correspondence. Rather than lamenting this change, many theorists, such as Peter Elbow, have been encouraged by these efforts because they create forums for freewriting wherein students have yet another way to move their thoughts into words [26]. This new community of writers, however, is not limited to classrooms; rather, it breaks all boundaries of traditional instruction and empowers students to set the limits of their own learning. The Internet, in particular, has provided today's writers with virtual access to information from the entire world. Cross-cultural conversations have become commonplace, specialized research is now conducted from home, and students have access to their instructors literally twenty-four hours a day [7]. This freedom, Faigley notes, has already initiated a "renegotiation of pedagogy and authority" that will continue to affect the nature of learning as well as that of our professional lives [14].

The Challenge of the Future

Even if some of us fear that traditional writing instruction may be compromised by this shift in the academic balance of power, none of us can afford to be Luddite in our views. Clearly, technology is linked with the future of composition. Most certainly, students will continue using it to improve the quality of both their lives and their work. We must help them harness its power. We must also help them recognize technology as merely a tool. In spite of our fears, it cannot replace reflective thinking, nor can it produce original writing. It can neither inspire greatness nor soothe a searching soul. But *we* can do all of that and more. If we are truly committed to our calling, we can use what we know about cognition, culture, composition, and even computers, to help our students become active learners and effective writers. In the end, we can show them ways to use their earned knowledge to make their lives more free and our world more humane [19]. As a professional educator, this is your charge; as a teacher of writing, this is your challenge. As a single individual, this is your choice. Choose well.

Annotated Bibliography: Suggested Reading

The following is a list of works related to the writing process. Some of these works have been cited in the text of this article; all have had an impact our profession as we know it. Though not a comprehensive bibliography on the subject, it will serve as a foundation for further study in the field.

1. Bartholmae, David. "Inventing the University." *When a Writer Can't Write: Studies in Writer's Block and Other Composing Problems*. Ed. Mike Rose. New York: Guilford, 1985. 134–65.
   Explains how students develop communication skills to help them bridge the gap between their personal histories, their high school experiences, and the required conventions of higher education.

2. ———. "What Is Composition and (If You Know What That Is) Why Do We Teach It? *Composition in the Twenty-First Century: Crisis and Change*. Ed. Lynn Z. Bloom, Donald A. Daiker, and Edward M. White. Carbondale: Southern Illinois UP, 1996. 11–28.
   Provides historical perspectives on the topic of composition as a course of study, a theory-based curriculum, a source of methodological criticism, and a career choice.

3. Berlin, James A. *Rhetoric and Reality: Writing Instruction in American Colleges, 1900–1985*. Carbondale: Southern Illinois UP, 1987.
   One of the first to notice the great significance of Janet Emig's 1971 study of composition process as experienced by twelfth-grade writers.

4. ———. "Cognition, Convention, and Certainty: What We Need to Know About Writing." *Pre/Text* 3 (1983): 213–43.
   Offers critiques of various theoretical approaches to writing, then presents one of the earliest statements of how social constructionists plan to transform studies in composition.

5. Bizzell, Patricia. "Contact Zones and English Studies." *College English* 56 (1994): 163–69.
   Demonstrates how English instructors can use the "social space" created by conflicting cultures within a classroom to help students comprehend and communicate their differences.

6. Bloom, Lynn Z., Donald A. Daiker, and Edward M. White, eds. *Composition in the Twenty-First Century: Crisis and Change*. Carbondale: Southern Illinois UP, 1996.
   A valuable collection of essays examining current and future trends in the theory and practice of writing instruction. Notable figures such as David Bartholomae, Peter Elbow, and Linda Flower reflect their positions in the existing pedagogical debate and cite implications for the field.

7. Bradshaw, Allen. "Designing a Virtual Classroom for Distance Learning Students through the Internet." *Walking the Tightrope: The Balance between Innovation and Leadership*. Proceedings of the Annual International Conference of the Chair Academy, Feb. 12–15, 1997.
   Enumerates the advantages of using the Internet for lectures, instruction, research, and e-mail.

8. Bruner, Jerome. *On Knowing: Essays for the Left Hand*. Cambridge, MA.: Bellknap, 1962.
   Provides an in-depth study of creativity and the processes that precede it. This work inspired Rohman and Wlecke to apply a similar theoretical approach to the writing process wherein writers must first process ideas through the self before attempting to respond to the structures of their writing environment.

9. Crowley, Sharon. "Around 1971: Current-Traditional Rhetoric and Process Models of Composing." *Composition in the Twenty-First Century: Crisis and Change*. Ed. Lynn Z. Bloom, Donald A. Daiker, and Edward M. White. Carbondale: Southern Illinois UP, 1996. 64–74.
   Provides a concise history of writing instruction from 1971 when product writing was overtaken by process writing as the predominant instructional mode. Examines key figures in the movement and questions whether their efforts had actually improved on those of the early traditionalists.

10. Daiker, Donald A. "Introduction: The New Geography of Composition." *Composition in the Twenty-First Century: Crisis and Change*. Ed. Lynn Z. Bloom, Donald A. Daiker, and Edward M. White. Carbondale: Southern Illinois UP, 1996: 1–7.
    Introduces the concept of the "new geography" of composition and the role of teachers as liberators for students who have struggled under the influence of elitism and injustice.

11. Elbow, Peter. *Writing without Teachers*. New York: Oxford UP, 1973.
    Urges writers to break the barriers of traditional writing process restrictions such as outlines. In their place, students

should focus on freewriting and other prewriting methods to develop their ideas.

12. ———, and Pat Belanoff. *A Community of Writers: A Workshop Course in Writing*. New York: Random, 1989.

13. Emig, Janet. *The Composing Processes of Twelfth Graders*. NCTE Research Report No. 13. Urbana: National Council of Teachers of English, 1971.
Perhaps the most influential study on the writing process movement, greatly responsible for generating nearly two decades of composition theory and pedagogy.

14. Faigley, Lester. "Literature after the Revolution." *College English* 58 (1997): 30–43.
Two significant forces, the "digital revolution" and "the revolution of the rich," have already begun to change writing pedagogy and practice. This article suggests how teachers must prepare themselves to renegotiate "traditional lines of authority" by understanding technology and its transformation of the writing community.

15. ———, et al. *Assessing Writers' Knowledge and Processes of Composing*. Norwood, NJ: Ablex, 1985.
Examines the cognitive backgrounds of the composition process and projects Faigley's assumptions in knowledge pedagogy and theory.

16. Gebhardt, Richard C. "Initial Plans and Spontaneous Composition: Toward a Comprehensive Theory of the Writing Process." *College English* 44 (1982): 620–27.
Examines two primary composing processes. The first shows how writers manage information they already know, and the second shows how they discover new information that they need.

17. Hairston, Maxine. "Different Products, Different Processes." *College Composition and Communication* 37 (1986): 442–54.
Defines and illustrates examples of three types of composing processes. One is based on the writer's purpose, another is based on the audience the writer wishes to influence, and a third focuses on the information that the writer seeks to gain.

18. Hayes, John R., and Linda Flower. "Writing Research and the Writer." *American Psychologist* 41 (1986): 1106–13.
A comprehensive discussion of earlier research in the area of writing "protocols" or strategic plans for helping writers move quickly from one writing stage to another.

19. Holladay, Sylvia A. "Order Out of Chaos: Voices from the Community College." *Composition in the Twenty-First Century: Crisis and Change*. Ed. Lynn Z. Bloom, Donald A. Daiker, and Edward M. White. Carbondale: Southern Illinois UP, 1996. 29–38.
Asserts that community college students live "chaotic, crisis-driven lives" that often interfere with their ability to write and proposes that such students can and often do learn to write well

and that this skill gives them freedom to make intelligent choices that will improve their lives in the future.

20. Jensen, George H., and John K. Di Tiberio. *Personality and the Teaching of Composition*. Norwood, NJ: Ablex, 1989.
Examines Carl Jung's theory of personality types and its impact on the development of the Myers-Briggs Type Indicator. Demonstrates how the MBTI can be used to identify cognitive styles and to predict their influence on students throughout the writing process.

21. Li, Xiao-Ming. *"Good Writing" in Cross-Cultural Context*. Albany: State U of New York P, 1996.
Case studies of writing teachers from America and China. This research examines the complex problems of assessment and the ways that an instructor's gender, age, race, and other factors influence the evaluation of student writing.

22. Macrorie, Ken. *Searching Writing*. Rochelle Park, NJ: Hayden, 1980.
Advocates the free flow of writing uninterrupted words on paper. This continuous outpouring of emotion leads writers to find central truths that will later serve as the core for improved writing.

23. McSpadden, Holly. "Which Fork? Cultural Mystifications and Classroom Expectations." *Teaching English in the Two-Year College* 23 (1996): 88–94.
Examines the first-year composition course as a diverse community in which students can learn to demystify institutional expectations, decrease academic anxiety, and gain personal power through writing.

24. Moffett, James. *Teaching the Universe of Discourse*. Boston: Houghton, 1968.
Explores the relationship between writer and audience and between writer and subject. This discourse focuses on students' cognitive development from concrete ideas to abstract representation.

25. Murray, Donald M. *A Writer Teaches Writing*. 2nd ed. Boston: Houghton, 1985.
Encourages writers and teachers of writing to examine their own approaches to the process. Stresses the importance of each stage of writing, and offers practical teaching strategies for each stage.

26. Peha, Jon M. "Debates via Computer Networks: Improving Writing and Bridging Classrooms." *T.H.E. Journal* 24.9 (1997): 65–68.
Describes the Electronic Issue Forum, a tool designed to provide students with experience in writing persuasive and topically balanced papers.

27. Peinado, Kelly. "An Interview with Peter Elbow." *Teaching English in the Two-Year College* 24 (1997): 199–204.
Revisits a process theorist and proponent of the freewriting movement and encourages him to share his views about under-

prepared students, the current obsession with evaluation and assessment, and the use of the Internet as a safe environment for a new technological community of writers.

28. Rohman, D. Gordon, and Albert O. Wlecke. *Pre-Writing: The Construction and Application of Models for Concept-Formation in Writing.* USOE Cooperative Research Project No. 2174. East Lansing: Michigan State U, 1964.
A seminal work that introduced the "stage model theory" at the center of the writing process. Explains why the three distinct stages of the process—prewriting, writing, and revising—are necessary for coherent products.

29. Shaughnessy, Mina P. *Errors and Expectations: A Guide for Teachers of Basic Writing.* New York: Oxford UP, 1977.
A seminal study explaining how teachers can identify typical error patterns in the writing of first-time college students and use them as pivotal points of instruction.

30. Tobin, Lad, and Thomas Newkirk, eds. *Taking Stock: The Writing Process Movement in the '90s.* Portsmouth, N.H.: Boynton/Cook-Heinemann, 1994.
A collection of articles reflecting key issues in the ongoing debate between proponents of the 1970s process movement and advocates of social constructionism.

THE HISTORY OF RHETORIC: OVERVIEW AND UPDATE

William F. Woods
Revised and updated
by Catherine L. Hobbs

From its beginnings in Sicily early in the fifth century B.C.E, rhetoric has been known as the art or "science" of persuasive discourse, the theory and practice of how to use available means of persuasion to affect the opinions of an audience. The earliest known treatises on rhetoric, by Corax and Tisias, responded to citizens' need to speak well before judges and large popular juries in litigations over land rights. However, as Barilli notes, a rhetoric of public decision making must also have emerged quite early [1].

A little more than a century later, Aristotle wrote his famous *Rhetoric* [13], a work based on a systematic description of public persuasive oratory as it was practiced in the law courts, the deliberative assembly, and the ceremonial gatherings of Athens. Thus from the start, rhetoric served to help a general audience interpret and react to practical affairs in the everyday world. Aristotle, especially in dialogue with his teacher Plato and his rival Isocrates, still serves as a rich and provocative starting point for the study of rhetoric [18, 20].

William F. Woods is Professor of English at Wichita State University, where he teaches medieval literature and the history of rhetoric. His published articles include "The Reform Tradition in Nineteenth-Century Composition Teaching," Written Communication *2 (1985): 377–90; "The Cultural Tradition of Nineteenth-Century Traditional Grammar Teaching,"* Rhetoric Society Quarterly *15 (1985): 3–12; and "Nineteenth-Century Psychology and the Teaching of Writing,"* College Composition and Communication *36 (1985): 20–41. Catherine Hobbs is Associate Professor of rhetoric/cultural studies in English at the University of Oklahoma, where she writes historical studies of eighteenth- and nineteenth-century rhetoric. She edited* Nineteenth-Century Women Learn to Write *(Charlottesville: University Press of Virginia, 1995).*

The key to Aristotle's approach to persuasion is *probability*. Philosophical logic can formally demonstrate a truth, but rhetoric can show that a position is worthy of belief—that it has a high probability of being true. Thus, while logical proofs are to be preferred in philosophical or scientific works, the persuasiveness of rhetoric is more effective in speaking or writing about practical affairs for a general audience.

Aristotle's *Rhetoric* discusses three modes of appeal that can be used to reach an audience: the appeal to logical arguments (*logos*, in the Greek), the appeal to emotions, attitudes, and values (*pathos*), and the appeal based on the moral or ethical character (*ethos*). In themselves, these modes are only guidelines—ways of orienting the speaker to the task. However, each of the modes was also associated with certain kinds of discourse, as well as with the rhetorical devices proper to that sort of appeal. Perhaps the easiest way to give the flavor of Aristotle's rhetoric is to describe some of the devices he suggests for appealing to the mind, heart, and moral character of an audience.

As Aristotle saw it, the appeal based on reasoned argument (*logos*) involved the use of certain basic concepts—fundamental, generally recognized strategies for thinking and expressing thought. Aristotle calls them the "common topics" because they are the commonplaces of thought. *Definition*, for example, is the classification of a subject, which in practice means identifying it by placing it in a class (for example, *rhetoric* is an ability or power) and then further defining it by pointing out characteristics (*differentiae*) that distinguish it from the other things in that class (*rhetoric* is the ability to see in each particular case the available means of persuasion) [13]. The other topics that belong to the appeal to reason are as familiar and essential to us as definition. *Comparison* brings out the similarity, the difference, and the degree of difference between two subjects. *Relationship* refers to patterns such as cause and effect, antecedent and consequence, contraries, and contradictions. *Circumstance* refers to the process we go through in deciding whether something is or was possible or impossible, given the particular circumstances; here we are defining the subject in relation to its occasion, or context.

Aristotle did not originate these common topics, of course. He merely gave them names, grouped them, and showed how they function in persuasive discourse. In the history of rhetoric since Aristotle, however, the topics have been one of the most useful and enduring parts of classical rhetorical theory. Aristotle primarily identifies the topics as aids to *invention*, or the *discovery* of arguments for or against a position. As with the other arts from classical rhetoric, contradictory interpretations exist. Are topics merely forms or a system of pigeonholes or categories for discourse, or are they strategies that can help a speaker or writer arrive at a judgment about a matter? Contemporary scholars believe that the inventional arts were more than devices to organize or manage language, that topics served as a basis for rhetorical thought leading to probable judgments [13; see also Enos and Lauer in 50]. Aristotle also described the *enthymeme*—a type of syllogism, or a statement with its supporting reasons or corollary—as a center of rhetorical logic. He presented reasoning drawn from examples as another slightly less valuable form of rhetorical invention.

The second mode of appeal Aristotle talks about (*pathos*) is the appeal to the emotions, attitudes, and values—to the heart. Aristotle recognized that the most powerful appeals are those that harness the primal human emotions, our tendencies to feel protectiveness, anger, envy, pride, fear, desire. Aristotle and the rhetoricians who came after him devoted considerable thought to what we would call "audience psychology"—the types of emotions and the types of people who experience them—but they also tried to identify the kinds of subjects that would evoke such an emotional response. What are the types of description, they asked, that powerfully involve an audience by helping them place themselves within an imagined experience? What are the phrases and the words associated with deeply felt issues? And then there were the stylistic effects associated with emotional states. The periodic or suspended sentence, for instance, was thought to create tension and a feeling of building to climax. The "rhetorical" question had its place here, as did the use of exaggeration (hyperbole), metaphor, and various other figures of speech. The study of style has always been closely connected with the appeal to the emotions. That is why both the first and later Sophists—the earliest rhetors before Plato and Aristotle, as well as later professional orators who flourished about the second century A.D.—were both praised and condemned. The orators of the "Second Sophistic" were known for their panegyrics (elaborate eulogies and other ceremonial speeches), which appealed to the emotions but were not always calculated to inspire sound judgments.

The third mode of appeal (*ethos*) is best described as a perceived relationship between the character of the speaker or writer and the social and ethical beliefs of the audience. It is an appeal to ethical values, perhaps, but it also has much to do with the ability of the audience to *identify* with the speaker, to accept him or her as someone who speaks for *them*. This appeal often derives as much from the personal qualities of a speaker or writer as it does from the overt content of the discourse. "Is this someone like us, who shares our values and whose opinion can be trusted?" These are the sorts of ques-

tions addressed by the ethical appeal, which has a great deal to do with the *tone* of a piece of writing and therefore with its syntax and choice of words. Tone also depends on the purpose of the discourse (to explain, persuade, entertain, etc.) and on the level of style adopted by the writer or speaker. Classical rhetoricians after Aristotle liked to identify three levels of style: (1) the high, or grand, style (appropriate for epics and for the sublime, high-flown passages of persuasive oratory); (2) the middle ("pleasing," ornate) style associated with literary works and with ceremonial oratory; and (3) the low, or plain, style associated with the language of instruction and everyday affairs. The New Rhetoric of the 1970s and 1980s focused attention once more on studies of style.

It is worth noting that the three modes of appeal—*logos*, *pathos*, and *ethos*—reflect a basic way in which Western culture has conceived or "pictured" the mind ever since the days of Plato. We say *mind, body*, and *spirit*—or *reason, memory*, and *imagination*—as if thought and substance were somehow united by a perceptive consciousness, our bond with the world outside us, and the source of our state of being. Somewhat paralleling this trinity, composition as classical rhetoricians described it also had three essential phases: invention, arrangement (organization), and style. Two other phases, or "departments," of rhetoric comprised the arts of memory and techniques of delivery, the final stages of producing a speech. These last two have not been directly involved in what we in our industrial age call the "process" of writing until quite recently. However, with the advent of computer techology and new electronic media, a resurgence of thought about memory, both human and artificial, and delivery, including publishing media, has reinvigorated these old arts [40, 49].

As oratory gave way to written rhetoric in the seventeenth and eighteenth centuries (a recurrent trend in the history of rhetoric), it became common to characterize discourse by its literary form rather than by the situation in which it occurred or its appeal to an audience. Whereas ancient oratory had been divided into deliberative (legislative), judicial (courtroom), and epideictic (ceremonial) oratory, the rhetorical spectrum by the 1700s had shifted to focus on formal letters (epistles), history, argument, narration, description, persuasion, and poetry. Since written discourse was now much more prevalent, it became customary to describe this as the art of "rhetoric and *belles lettres*" (borrowing a term from French literary criticism, which was then enjoying a period of authority) [22, 23]. With the successes of the new scientific method and theory, the method and theory of rhetoric was also changing. Rhetoric came to have two often-intertwining strands: a logical strand concerned with correctness, clarity, argument, and exposition, and a belletristic strand concerned with literary style, taste, and the expression of feelings. Rhetoricians appropriated theories of empiricist philosophers such as John Locke in assuming that language and thought reflected impressions from the senses, especially sight. Eighteenth-century writers such as the Scottish rhetorician George Campbell investigated how different forms of discourse engaged the four "faculties" of the mind: memory, imagination, intellect or understanding, and the will [23].

Later thinkers came to assume that the forms of discourse must derive from the different patterns of language we use to record our perceptions, to form a "point of view," and to influence the opinions (views) of others. For example, we record our perceptions of things (thus, *descriptive* writing); we record our perceptions of events, or "things in action" (*narrative* writing); we interpret the pattern, or "logic," of relationships in the things and events perceived (*expository*, or explanatory, writing); finally, we arrange our perceptions as proof in support of our point of view (*argumentative* writing; "persuasion" generally meant oral discourse). Authors of nineteenth-century textbooks on written rhetoric ("composition") found in these four terms, and in the kinds of writing they implied, a comprehensive schema for describing the teaching of writing. These four "modes of discourse" [6] (which had little or nothing to do with Aristotle's modes of appeal) were a typical feature of composition textbooks after 1850; they continued to shape teachers' approaches to English composition for at least the next hundred years. Rightly or wrongly, the four modes are now associated with the more conservative side of nineteenth-century composition teaching, which borrowed much from traditional methods of teaching English (and before that, Latin) grammar. There were other emphases, other theories at work in nineteenth-century composition teaching, but that period is remembered mainly for its drills, for the practice of having students memorize principles of grammar and style, for its increasing tendency to stress exposition (essay writing), and for giving first priority to a building-block structuring of words, sentences, paragraphs, and essays. This was also a pedagogy associated with the rigorous methods and the sometimes endearing eccentricities of writing masters and textbooks writers like Alexander Bain, George Quackenbos, and Adams Sherman Hill [3].

But while the main thrust of nineteenth-century rhetoric and composition teaching was on style and structure, the *character* of the speaker or writer was beginning to receive a new emphasis. In a time when political, religious, and artistic individualism was much respected, the mental nature of the individual thinker, writer, and student became a serious subject of inquiry. This expressivist strand of thought had begun in the eighteenth century, culminating in Rousseau and theorists of pedagogy, language learning, and child development such as Pestalozzi. The ultimate results of this spirit of romantic individualism, along with the studies of child nature that accompanied it, can be seen in the contemporary work of James Britton [29], a British educator who specialized in research on student writing. Britton's central insight, which owes much to his studies of the early-twentieth-century linguist Roman Jakobson, was that written discourse can be described in terms of "function categories" (see Figure 1) that represent what the writer is doing, in each case, in the act of writing. Writing is no longer seen as reflecting structures of the mind; rather, writing is assumed to represent three basic types of observed language behavior in a school setting (which may, of course, reflect three types of mental activity).

In Britton's first function category, the *transactional*, students participate in a problem, discussion, or other event: They get things done with words. The language relates closely to the needs of the audience and to the features of the task at hand. Language here is seen as a means to an end. In the second category, the *expressive*, students express their responses to an outside situation in language that relates closely to their own points of view or inner experiences of the situation. Here, the language is less a way of getting things done than it is a way of putting feelings into intelligible form; thus, expressive discourse probably serves the writer's needs more than it does the needs of the audience or the demands of the task at hand. In the third category, the *poetic*, the writer is a spectator to the problem or situation at hand and uses language that relates closely to the overall concept or "global context" of what is being done, created, or argued. Here, the writer is more a disinterested analyst than a participant in an interactive task or someone trying to verbalize an inner experience.

Figure 1

One striking difference between Britton's system and traditional rhetorics is the centrality of the expressive, or personal, aspect of writing in emergent literacy. Britton assumes that child language *begins* as expressive discourse and diversifies as the child grows older; the transactional and poetic modes are gradually acquired, and the resources of the expressive mode are further developed. So whereas Aristotle's modes of appeal were intended as ways of describing the impact of discourse on an audience, Britton's function categories are ways of identifying the kinds of discourse that emerge from three kinds of writing behavior and purpose. To put it another way, Aristotle's modes are reader-oriented, whereas Britton's are writer-oriented, since they describe discourse as the reflection of mental processes associated with certain adaptive social behaviors. Because of this emphasis on behavior, Britton's discussions were to help teachers trying to figure out "where students are coming from" in each of the various assignments that they write. Britton's work also served as a corrective influence on those who viewed expressive discourse as a sloppy aberration from expository writing or believed it should surface only in creative writing courses. This played a role in the valorization of expressive writing in the classroom [31]. In the 1980s, expressivism became a vital approach to composition, although it was early on a part of U.S. writing studies [2].

Despite some real differences in theoretical orientation, however, Aristotle and Britton or later expressivists are not mutually exclusive. Teachers who have studied Aristotle's account of the appeals to the reason and the emotions will probably arrive at a better appreciation of Britton's transactional and poetic functions than those who come to Britton with no preparation in rhetoric. In fact, even though social and historical conditions are vastly different now from what they were in ancient Greece, Aristotle's *Rhetoric* continues to stimulate and provoke scholars, for the truth is that there have been no modern Aristotles, and no modern rhetoric has made the impact on rhetorical tradition that Aristotle (and Cicero) did. In the 1960s, James Kinneavy [34] came as close to that goal as anyone, perhaps, in his attempt to write a comprehensive modern theory of rhetoric, or "discourse," as he calls it, to allow for the enlarged role of writing in modern communication [see also 36].

Influenced by Jakobson and linguistics, Kinneavy distinguished basic aims of discourse and described the processes and characteristics essential to each of them. He derived four aims of discourse from both ancient rhetorical and modern theory of communication, plotted on the familiar "communication triangle" (see Figure 2). The three points of the triangle refer to the *writer*, the *audience*, and the *subject* of

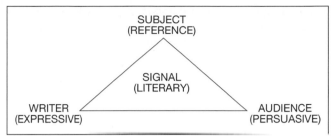

Figure 2 (adapted from Kinneavy)

discourse, while the body of the triangle refers to the *signal*, in this case, the written language of the message. Each of these four terms is the point of origin for one of the four *aims*, the purposes for which we produce discourse: Discourse that derives from the point of view or "inner experience" of the writer attempting to give it form is *expressive* (as in Britton's function theory). Discourse that is oriented more toward channeling or intensifying an audience's concerns, ideas, and feelings is called *persuasive* (as in Aristotle's theory of rhetoric). Discourse that is meant to represent accurately a subject of investigation is called *reference* discourse—this aim includes the nonpersuasive aspects of most academic and scientific writing, as well as what we call *expository* prose. And discourse that is self-referential or mimetic in purpose and that aims to be used or enjoyed for its own sake is called *literary* discourse or literature (similar to Britton's *poetic* function category but not synonymous with it).

Unlike Britton, Kinneavy was not concerned mainly with the development of students' discourse toward maturity. Rather, his emphasis was on taxonomizing and describing the aims and forms of discourse and their use. We can generalize by calling Kinneavy's work a comprehensive, painstaking description of the ways prose writing is used or understood in the twentieth century. In this sense, his work is reminiscent of Aristotle's systematic, analytical description of persuasive oratory in fourth-century B.C.E. Athens. A basic understanding of Kinneavy's four aims lends a structural perspective on written communication; moreover, his situating of English departments and composition within a linguistic pragmatic framework lent a new and influential way of thinking about the entire profession of teaching writing. For those who wish to backtrack Kinneavy's research and pursue their own investigations in one direction or another, full bibliographies are appended to each chapter of his book [34].

At the far end of our history lies rhetoric's growing edge, the gradual assimilation of modern theory and contemporary research into the body of the discipline. Slowly, the ideas of major theorists like I. A. Richards [37], Kenneth Burke [30], Richard McKeon (whose work is just now being republished), Chaim Perelman and Lucie Olbrechts-Tyteca [36], and Stephen Toulmin [39], have entered our shared assumptions about written rhetoric. Scholars using feminist- and gender-studies approaches have revised the very foundations of rhetoric and its history as they challenge the male-centeredness of its constructions (see especially Glenn [7] and Lunsford [48]). Research findings derived from multiple methodologies have begun to shape our teaching methods [see Lauer in 43]. But the central concerns, and thus the distinguishing traits of today's rhetoric, have more to do with our students—a varied lot, they reflect, in their challenging array of needs and abilities, the fragmentation that characterizes not only our own profession but academia at large and the arenas of national and international politics.

Responding to social changes beginning with immigration and urbanization early in the twentieth century, rhetoric teaching has recurrently transformed itself, deepening its resources and broadening its scope to provide effective instruction for nontraditional students. The crisis-related efforts that produced, for example, Sterling A. Leonard's *English Composition as a Social Problem* (1917), William Labov's *Study of Non-Standard English* (1970), or Mina P. Shaughnessy's *Errors and Expectations* (1977), have enabled significant pedagogical advances, and they remind us that divergence and difference can also mean growth. The emphasis on writing across the curriculum, with its implied sensitivity to differences in the situations of discourse and audiences, has been one broader, organizational response to this centurylong groundswell of diversity, and the debates over "discourse communities" has been one response at the level of theory.

What is a discourse community? It has been a useful phrase, a serviceable metaphor, because it gives form to our ambivalent thoughts about rhetoric's fractured audience. If doctors (or sociologists, literary critics, or street people) share a specialized body of knowledge, a common jargon, and a rhetoric that specifies the kinds of arguments acceptable within that group, they belong to a community of shared discourse features. These communities are, in effect, political entities that tend to overflow social, economic, and geographical boundaries. They are "city-states of language," and as such, Aristotle would have understood them well, even though his rhetoric served a smaller, more unified world, and ours must speak to so many, once again both orally and in print, where text and graphics more and more frequently work together and "interanimate" each other. The global rhetorical situation, brought about by and further complicated by the continuing transformations of electronic communication technology, has led rhetoric and composition to begin to adopt an anthropological perspective on writing and culture [28, 32, 33]. This means that researchers of rhetoric, composition, and literacy today study how writing emerged, emerges, or functions in diverse groups and cultures with their interacting ethnicities, classes, genders, and so on, in our local classrooms and communities, nation, ever-more-present hemisphere, and around the globe.

If there is a moral to be drawn from this lightning sketch of a few exemplary works on rhetoric, composition, and literacy, it is that a little knowledge is not a dangerous thing but rather our only salvation. Not one of us has the time or dedication to absorb over two thousand years of rhetorical treatises, debates, and biases; even to desire such a thing is to miss the point badly. Our goal as teachers of writing is rather, by knowing something of the needs, ideas, and practices of former times, to understand more deeply and truly what we are engaged in doing and where we are tending. Neither Aristotle nor Kinneavy, Corbett nor Crowley, Peter Elbow nor Erika Lindemann should be adopted as models of rigidly prescribed methods for teachers. Their books, as well as the others that we have mentioned or that are listed in the bibliography, are parts of the history of our profession and should be sampled, experimented with, and pondered as we proceed with our own teaching, in our own places and times, in our own reflective ways. To do so is to use history well; in so doing, we become rhetoricians—and enter history.

Annotated Bibliography: Suggested Reading

I. HISTORIES OF RHETORIC AND WRITING INSTRUCTION

1. Barilli, Renato. *Rhetoric*. Trans. Giuliana Menozzi. Minneapolis: U of Minnesota P, 1989.

2. Berlin, James, A. *Writing Instruction in Nineteenth-Century American Colleges*. Carbondale: Southern Illinois UP, 1984. Brief and helpful overview of the century's writing instruction. Along with Berlin's *Rhetoric and Reality: Writing Instruction in American Colleges, 1900–1985* (Carbondale: Southern Illinois UP, 1987), the best introduction to the history of U.S. writing instruction.

3. Bizzell, Patricia, and Bruce Herzberg, eds. *The Rhetorical Tradition: Readings from Classical Times to the Present*. New York: St. Martin's, 1990.

A superb anthology; the introductions and headnotes are in effect a substantial history of rhetoric.

4. Brereton, John C., ed. *The Origins of Composition Studies in the American Colleges, 1875–1925: A Documentary History.* Pittsburgh: U of Pittsburgh P, 1995.

5. Clark, Gregory, and S. Michael Halloran. *Oratorical Culture in Nineteenth-Century America: Transformations in the Theory and Practice of Rhetoric.* Carbondale: Southern Illinois UP, 1993.

6. Crowley, Sharon. *The Methodical Memory: Invention in Current-Traditional Rhetoric.* Carbondale: Southern Illinois UP, 1991.

7. Glenn, Cheryl. *Rhetoric Retold: Regendering the Tradition from Antiquity through the Renaissance.* Carbondale: Southern Illinois UP, 1998.

8. Howell, Wilbur Samuel. *Eighteenth-Century British Logic and Rhetoric.* Princeton: Princeton UP 1971.
   This classic study and *Logic and Rhetoric in England, 1500–1700* (Princeton: Princeton UP, 1956) catalog the changes rhetoric went through in response to the birth of empirical science and the resurgence of classical learning in the period between the early English Renaissance and the end of the seventeenth century.

9. Johnson, Nan. *Nineteenth-Century Rhetoric in North America.* Carbondale: Southern Illinois UP, 1991.

10. Kennedy, George A. *A New History of Classical Rhetoric.* Princeton: Princeton UP, 1994.
    Kennedy offers reliable overviews of rhetoric in its cultural tradition in this and in his *Classical Rhetoric and Its Christian and Secular Tradition from Ancient to Modern Times* (Berkeley: U of California P, 1980). Kennedy's specialized works are standard sources in Greek, Roman, and early Christian rhetoric.

11. Murphy, James J. *Rhetoric in the Middle Ages.* Berkeley: U of California P, 1974.
    The best survey of medieval rhetoric now available. Also see his *Renaissance Eloquence* (1983) and edited collection *A Short History of Writing Instruction,* new edition forthcoming.

12. Vickers, Brian. *In Defense of Rhetoric.* New York: Oxford UP, 1988.
    Excellent chapters on various periods in the history of rhetoric with an emphasis on style in rhetoric.

II. CLASSICAL AND MEDIEVAL THEORIES OF RHETORIC

13. *Aristotle on Rhetoric: A Theory of Civic Discourse.* Trans. George A. Kennedy. New York: Oxford UP, 1991.

A valuable resource making the knowledge of a classical scholar accessible to nonspecialists, with helpful introduction, notes, and appendixes by Kennedy.

14. Augustine of Hippo. *De Doctrina Christiana.* Trans. D. W. Robertson Jr. Indianapolis: Bobbs-Merrill, 1958.
    Books I–III of this treatise are a guide to the reading and interpretation of the scriptures. Book IV (on preaching) is probably the most important statement of rhetorical theory in the Middle Ages.

15. Cicero. *De Oratore.* Trans. E. W. Sutton and H. Rackham. 2 vols. Loeb Classical Library. Cambridge: Harvard UP, 1976.
    The comprehensive treatise that represents Cicero's mature rhetorical theory.

16. Corbett, Edward J. P. *Classical Rhetoric for the Modern Student.* 3rd ed. New York: Oxford UP, 1990.
    The first of the modern textbooks that make classical rhetorical theory and pedagogy available to teachers and upper-level students of English composition.

17. Enos, Richard Leo. *Greek Rhetoric Before Aristotle.* Prospect Heights, IL: Waveland P, 1993.

18. Isocrates. *Isocrates in Three Volumes.* Vols. 1 and 2, trans. George Norlin. Vol. 3, trans. Larue Van Hook. Cambridge: Harvard UP, 1930, 1932, 1945.

19. Quintilian. *Institutio Oratoria.* Trans. H. E. Butler. 4 vols. Loeb Classical Library. Cambridge: Harvard UP, 1980. See also Murphy's edition of Books 1, 2, and 10: *Quintilian on the Art of Speaking and Writing.* Carbondale: Southern Illinois UP, 1987.
    Quintilian was a teacher of rhetoric in Rome, under the empire. His "Institute" of rhetoric is a thoroughgoing description of the art as it was practiced and taught during his times.

20. *Rhetorica ad Herennium.* Trans. Harry Caplan. 2 vols. Loeb Classical Library. Cambridge: Harvard UP, 1981.
    This relatively brief manual, and Cicero's early work (*De Inventione (On Rhetorical Invention)*) were the classical Roman treatises that most influenced medieval rhetoric.

III. RENAISSANCE AND EARLY MODERN THEORIES OF RHETORIC

21. Erasmus, Desiderius. *On Copia of Words and Ideas (De Utraque Verborem ac Rerum Copia).* Trans. Donald B. King and H. David Rix. Milwaukee: Marquette UP, 1963.
    A much imitated treatise on the art of writing an "amplified," or richly developed, style, a major emphasis in Renaissance rhetoric.

22. Fénelon, François. *Fénelon's Dialogues on Eloquence.* Trans. Wilbur Samuel Howell. Princeton: Princeton UP, 1951.

"The greatest work on classical rhetoric written in French and the finest statement of the philosophical strand of the tradition since antiquity" (Kennedy).

23. Golden, James, and Edward P. J. Corbett, eds. *The Rhetoric of Blair, Campbell, and Whately.* Carbondale: Southern Illinois UP, 1990.

    Blair, Campbell, and Whately—sometimes called the "Scottish rhetoricians"—reflect the influence of empirical philosophy (e.g., Hume, Locke) on rhetorical theory; they also foreshadow the nineteenth-century shift in emphasis from spoken to written rhetoric (or "composition").

24. Harwood, John T. *The Rhetorics of Thomas Hobbes and Bernard Lamy.* Carbondale: Southern Illinois UP, 1986.

IV. NINETEENTH-CENTURY THEORIES OF RHETORIC

25. Adams, John Quincy. *Lectures on Rhetoric and Oratory, Delivered to the Classes of Senior and Junior Sophisters in Harvard University.* 2 vols. 1810. New York: Russell and Russell, 1962.

26. Channing, Edward T. *Lectures Read to the Seniors at Harvard College.* 1856. Carbondale: Southern Illinois UP, 1968.

27. De Quincey, Thomas. *Essays on Rhetoric.* Ed. Frederick Burwick. Carbondale: Southern Illinois UP, 1967.

V. MODERN THEORIES OF RHETORIC AND DISCOURSE

28. Berlin, James A. *Rhetorics, Poetics, and Culture.* Urbana, IL: NCTE, 1996.

29. Britton, James, et al. *The Development of Writing Abilities (11–18).* London: Macmillan, 1975.

    Considered the best of the early studies of how writing skills develop in young students. Britton offers a theory of composition based on extensive surveys of children's writing.

30. Burke, Kenneth. *A Grammar of Motives.* 1945. Berkeley: U of California P, 1969.

    Burke's original, syncretic thought drew on philosophical language study and a social view of traditional rhetorics. See also his *Rhetoric of Motives* (1950) and *Language as Symbolic Action* (1966).

31. Elbow, Peter. *Writing with Power.* New York: Oxford UP, 1987.

32. Faigley, Lester. *Fragments of Rationality: Postmodernity and the Subject of Composition.* Pittsburgh: Pittsburgh UP, 1992.

33. Kennedy, George, A. *Comparative Rhetorics.* New York: Oxford UP, 1998.

    A cultural approach to studying rhetorics from different historical periods and places that challenges universal statements made on behalf of rhetoric based on exclusively male, Western evidence.

34. Kinneavy, James, L. *A Theory of Discourse.* 1971. New York: Norton, 1980.

    Classifies the kinds of discourse according to purpose and describes the features associated with each of these purposes, or "aims." Grounded in the scholarship of linguistics, literature, communications, and philosophy, Kinneavy's became the reigning theory of discourse.

35. Moffett, James. *Teaching the Universe of Discourse.* 1956. Portsmouth, NH: Boynton/Cook, 1987.

    Helpful in understanding the neo-progressive or student-centered attitudes toward teaching writing that dominated the Dartmouth Conference (1966) and later produced the "open classroom."

36. Perelman, Chaim, and Lucie Olbrechts-Tyteca. *The New Rhetoric: A Treatise on Argumentation.* Notre Dame, IN: U of Notre Dame P, 1969.

    An Aristotle-like attempt to give a comprehensive account of everyday argument.

37. Richards, I. A. *The Philosophy of Rhetoric.* New York: Oxford UP, 1936. See also Berthoff, Ann E. *Richards on Rhetoric: I. A. Richards, Selected Essays, 1929–1974.* New York: Oxford UP, 1991.

38. Swearingen, C. Jan. *Rhetoric and Irony.* New York: Oxford UP, 1991.

39. Toulmin, Stephen E. *The Uses of Argument.* Cambridge: Cambridge UP, 1958.

40. Welch, Kathleen E. *The Contemporary Reception of Classical Rhetoric: Appropriations of Ancient Discourse.* Hillsdale, NJ: Erlbaum, 1990.

VI. COLLECTIONS ON RHETORIC AND PEDAGOGY

41. Baumlin, James S., and Tita French Baumlin, eds. *Ethos: New Essays in Rhetoric and Critical Theory.* Dallas: Southern Methodist UP, 1994.

42. Covino, William A., and David A. Joliffe, eds. *Rhetoric: Concepts, Definitions, Boundaries.* Boston: Allyn and Bacon, 1995.

43. Enos, Theresa, ed. *Learning from the Histories of Rhetoric: Essays in Honor of Winifred Bryan Horner.* Carbondale: Southern Illinois UP, 1993

44. ———, and Stuart C. Brown, eds. *Defining the New Rhetorics.* Newbury Park, CA: Sage, 1993.

45. Harkin, Patricia, and John Schilb, eds. *Contending with Words: Composition and Rhetoric in a Postmodern Age.* New York: MLA, 1991.

46. Horner, Winifred Bryan and Michael Leff, eds. *Rhetoric and Pedagogy: Its History, Philosophy, and Practice: Essays in Honor of James J. Murphy*. Hillsdale, NJ: Erlbaum, 1995.

47. Kintgen, Eugene R., Barry M. Kroll, and Mike Rose. *Perspectives on Literacy*. Carbondale: Southern Illinois UP, 1988.

48. Lunsford, Andrea A., ed. *Reclaiming Rhetorica: Women in the Rhetorical Tradition*. Pittsburgh: U of Pittsburgh P, 1995.

49. Selfe, Cynthia, and Susan Hilligoss, *Literacy and Computers: The Complications of Teaching and Learning with Technology*. New York: MLA, 1994.

50. Witte, Stephen P., Neil Nakadate, and Roger D. Cherry, eds. *A Rhetoric of Doing: Essays on Written Discourse in Honor of James L. Kinneavy*. Carbondale: Southern Illinois UP, 1992.

VII. REFERENCE WORKS

51. *CCCC (Conference on College Composition and Communication) Bibliography of Composition and Rhetoric*. 1991–. Annual bibliography in the field. See also the *Communication Index, Communication Abstracts,* and *Modern Language Association* bibliographies.

52. *Encyclopedia of English Studies and Language Arts*. Ed. Alan C. Purves. Urbana, IL: NCTE, 1994.

53. *Encyclopedia of Rhetoric and Composition: Communication from Ancient Times to the Information Age*. Ed. Theresa Enos. New York: Garland, 1996.

54. Lauer, Janice M., and J. William Asher. *Composition Research: Empirical Designs*. New York: Oxford UP, 1988.

55. Horner, Winifred Bryan, ed. *The Present State of Scholarship in Historical and Contemporary Rhetoric*. Rev. ed. Columbia: U of Missouri P, 1990.
Still the best starting point for historical research. See also Horner's *Historical Rhetoric: An Annotated Bibliography of Selected Sources in English*. (Boston: Hall, 1980).

56. Lindemann, Erika, and Gary Tate, eds. *An Introduction to Composition Studies*. New York: Oxford UP, 1990.

57. Mortensen, Peter, and Gesa E. Kirsch, eds. *Ethics and Representation in Qualitative Studies of Literacy*. Urbana: NCTE, 1996.

58. Olson, Gary A., and Todd W. Taylor, eds. *Publishing in Rhetoric and Composition*. Albany: State U of New York P, 1997.
Helpful advice on entering the conversation in published research in rhetoric and composition.

PORTFOLIOS IN THE TEACHING AND ASSESSING OF WRITING

Irwin Weiser

Though portfolios have been used for the assessment of writing for over twenty years, the past decade has seen interest in portfolios of student writing increase dramatically. I want to explore some of the reasons for this interest, outline some common features of portfolios, discuss various ways portfolios are being used, and raise some issues teachers and administrators wanting to implement portfolio grading assessment programs should plan to consider. While portfolios are being used in a variety of educational settings, from elementary schools through graduate programs [33, 35], and for subjects other than English and composition, my primary focus will be on portfolios of student writing in postsecondary settings. My goal is to provide composition teachers and administrators with an introduction to portfolios that will them to make informed decisions about whether portfolios are appropriate for their individual situations. This point is particularly important, since one of the central issues in any assessment program should be its fit with specific local conditions.

Indeed, one of the reasons that portfolios have become so popular is that they are consistent with newer assessment theories and practices that emphasize contextualized, authentic, local assessment and challenge, indirect, top-down externally developed assessment of student writing. Portfolios, as Edward White points out, are a natural extension of the movement away from indirect measures of writing ability such as multiple-choice tests of usage and vocabulary, toward the direct evaluation of written discourse [28]. The same arguments that led to the advocacy and development of essays as

Irwin Weiser is Professor of English at Purdue University where he serves as Director of Composition. He teaches undergraduate writing courses and graduate courses in Writing Across the Curriculum and Composition Research. A long-time advocate of portfolio evaluation, his most recent publication in this area is Situating Portfolios, *a collection of essays on portfolio use he co-edited with Kathleen Blake Yancey.*

components of the CLEP and TSWE and the use of analytical, primary trait, and holistic scoring for student writing—namely, that writing ability should be assessed by evaluating actual written texts rather than by indirect measures such as usage, grammar, or vocabulary tests—support the use of portfolios as providing more accurate and valid evidence of writing ability [5, 13]. Further, because portfolios often have been developed in response to local educational concerns, they are responsive to the specific needs and goals of particular contexts [15, 16, 26]. Teachers and writing program administrators can tailor portfolio requirements to their own classroom, program, or institutional needs.

A second reason portfolios have generated so much interest, one related to their usefulness in assessing writing ability, is their compatibility with theories of writing as a process and the pedagogical emphasis on teaching strategies of invention, drafting, revising, and editing that has become a common feature of many composition classes. Because in most approaches to classroom-based portfolio evaluation, student writing is not graded until near the end of the course, when it is submitted in the portfolio, teachers can emphasize the importance of continued improvement over the term and can encourage students to continue to rethink and revise pieces of writing begun earlier in the course. No longer are students penalized by receiving low grades on work submitted early in a writing course, before they have had the opportunity to practice and develop new strategies and skills. Nor do instructors face the dilemma of how to evaluate early work that does not reflect the writing ability students will develop during the course [26]. Instead, portfolios allow instructors and students to concentrate on improvement, uninfluenced by grades on individual papers—both the discouragement that low grades can lead to and the complacency that sometimes comes when students are satisfied with the grades they receive. Further, portfolios allow instructors to shift the focus of their responses to student writing in progress and away from summative commentary, which tends to treat a text as a completed product, highlighting its strengths and weakness and to some extent justifying the grade assigned it. Instead, portfolios support formative responses, responses that suggest, raise questions, and encourage further thinking and revision. Thus, portfolios allow for an emphasis on the accumulation of writing abilities, an emphasis consistent with our understanding that the development of writing ability occurs gradually.

Common Features of Portfolios

As I said earlier, one of the strengths of portfolios for the assessment of student writing is that they can be developed in response to local contexts and needs—as local as a single class-room, a single course, or a single institution. Hence, I begin this description of some common features of portfolios with the caveat that these features should not be interpreted as "rules" for portfolios. Nevertheless, most approaches to port-folios share these five features: collection, selection, reflec-tion, revision, and evaluation.

Collection is a fundamental aspect of portfolio use. The fact that a portfolio includes multiple samples of writing is a major part of its appeal as an assessment instrument. Writers are not judged by a single piece of writing, so their evaluation is not limited by the various constraints that may be imposed by single writing samples: ability to write a certain genre or discourse type, prior knowledge of or interest in the subject, and so on. Thus, at its simplest, a portfolio might be defined as any collection of work, so a writing portfolio could be a folder or file in which students keep all of the notes, plans, drafts, revisions, and final papers they produce in a course. Such a portfolio might be called a working portfolio, useful, as I will discuss later, as a resource from which more specific portfolios are drawn.

However, portfolios serve teaching and learning better when they are defined not just as collections but as collections of work selected for a specific purpose. For example, the guidelines for the portfolios that students are invited to submit for placement into composition courses at Miami University stipulates that stu-dents select one piece of writing that tells a story or describes; one "explanatory, exploratory, or persuasive essay"; a "response to a written text"; and to a reflective letter [11]. The intention here is for students to demonstrate their ability to write the kinds of papers that parallel writing assignments they would have at the university—papers that show their preparedness for specific courses at Miami. The selection of materials for a portfolio designed to demonstrate development or growth in writing might be quite different. Students might select, for example, early work that is not as a successful as writing they have done more recently in order to demonstrate how they have learned to address particular difficulties or how they have developed more sophistication and skill. Institutions with writing across the curriculum programs might determine that they would like stu-dents to develop portfolios that demonstrate their ability to write for a variety of academic disciplines. As these examples suggest, the criteria of what should be in a portfolio will not only differ according to its purpose but may also be determined in part by someone other than the writer—by administrators developing a placement procedure, by an instructor wanting to evaluate stu-dents' development in writing, and so on.

Reflection is a third feature of most portfolios, one that

many portfolio advocates argue is vital [14, 32]. Since it is cer-tainly a goal of writing courses not only to help students become better writers but also to help them become more independent and confident writers (in the sense that they are able to assess whether or not they are doing a good job with a writing assignment), a student's ability to reflect on what he or she has accomplished in a collection of work is both rele-vant to the assessment of a portfolio and reflective of the stu-dent as writer. A typical kind of reflection is a letter of the kind required by Miami University. In it, students are asked to evaluate their work, perhaps in terms of the content of the portfolio itself or perhaps in terms of how the pieces in the portfolio reflect their accomplishments or growth as writers (see also descriptions of reflective 15 and 17). While the abil-ity of students to assess their own work is certainly a valuable aspect of their learning, several scholars have pointed out that the reflective writing that usually introduces a portfolio may have an undue influence on those evaluating the portfolio [10, 24]. In a recent piece, I have discussed the "schmooze" factor, similar to the "glow" effect discussed by Sommers et al. [24]. "Glow" refers to the positive effect a single piece of writing in a portfolio may have on the overall rating of that portfolio, and Sommers and colleagues use as an example a reflective letter that ends like this:

> Over the past few years, I've developed new attitudes toward writing, enjoying it rather than dreading it, and viewing each piece not as one completed but as a work-in-progress. There is always a more appropriate word (most often, the one that awakens me out of a sound sleep at 4 a.m. the day after the deadline), a better phrase, room for improvement. I find this stimulating, not frustrating.

"Schmooze," as I've explained elsewhere [27], "is the often indistinguishable evil twin of 'glow,' the telling-the-teacher-what-she-wants-to-hear that students may very well write in their reflective letters to set the stage for a positive evalua-tion." "Glow" and "schmooze" aside, the goal of encouraging students to reflect on their writing remains, and should remain, an integral part of any portfolio system. And reflec-tive letters or portfolio introductions are not the only way in which portfolios encourage refection. Selecting the pieces to be included in a portfolio is a reflective act, though one that may not yield any written traces. And the decisions that underlie the next feature of portfolios I'll discuss, revision, are also reflections.

As the earlier discussion of the relationship between process pedagogy and portfolio evaluation suggests, the suc-cess with which students are able to revise their writing is often considered when portfolios are evaluated. Students may be asked to include the earlier drafts of one or more of the papers or to reflect on the changes they made as they reconsidered and revised their work. However, not all portfolios demonstrate revision; that is, not all portfolios require that earlier drafts of papers be included. Similarly, not all pieces in a portfolio need to be revisions of earlier work. Portfolios may contain unrevised pieces of writing such as journal entries or in-class writing (in fact, one piece of in-class writing is sometimes required in portfolios used as part of program or course assessments as a kind of touchstone [see 15, 23]. In the case of revision, as in all aspects of developing useful, appropriate portfolios, instructors and administrators need to consider what best suits their purposes for using portfolios.

The final feature of portfolio practice is evaluation. Though I have already mentioned a number of issues related to the evaluation of portfolios, I want to emphasize that how portfolios are evaluated and by whom is once more related to the particular context in which they are being used. The criteria for evaluation and the approaches to evaluation must be local, worked out by the particular instructor, faculty, program, department, institution, or agency responsible for the use of the portfolios. Locally developed criteria help lead to evaluation that is valid—that is, evaluation that measures what it intends to—since the people most intimately involved with the evaluation determine how the writing in the portfolios is to be evaluated. This point is made again and again in the portfolio literature, with respect to both positive [15, 22, 25] and negative [7, 20] experiences with portfolios.

Uses and Contexts for Portfolios

As I have suggested, portfolios may be used for a variety of purposes and in a variety of contexts, Classroom teachers may choose to use portfolios rather than to grade individual writing assignments. Such a decision is frequently based on the teacher's belief that to grade individual writing assignments or every writing assignment not only conflicts with the developmental nature of learning but is also inconsistent with a process approach to teaching writing. The teacher may also wish to deemphasize grades and emphasize progress. Portfolios enable this because since there are no grades on individual papers, students must be more attentive to the comments and advice they receive. Writing programs may choose to incorporate portfolio evaluation for similar reasons, as well as for some of the purposes alluded to earlier: to determine placement or proficiency, to assess the success of the writing program, to meet institutional assessment requirements. Port-

folios are useful for institutions that wish to provide evidence of student learning over time: Students may be required to keep portfolios throughout their enrollment in a high school or college. Portfolios have been used in large-scale assessment programs as well, to meet statewide assessment demands, Susan Callahan's "Portfolio Expectations: Possibilities and Limits" [8] provides an excellent overview of the range of contexts and uses for portfolios.

Although much of the preceding discussion has suggested that the major reason for using portfolios is that they provide an approach to evaluating writing that is more consistent both with current assessment theories and practices and with process-based approaches to teaching writing, it is important to mention that portfolios are being used in contexts other than composition classes or in writing across the curriculum programs. In particular, and also relevant to writing program administrators and postsecondary writing teachers, is the rich literature on teaching and teacher portfolios. In a teaching portfolio, teachers select, and reflect on materials that demonstrate their approaches to teaching. Such portfolios may include teaching philosophies, course descriptions and syllabi, original teaching materials, and teaching evaluations. Like student portfolios, teaching portfolios allow their creators to represent themselves, perhaps for the purpose of obtaining a new teaching position or in place of other kinds of evaluation [see 1, 12]. Equally interesting is the increased use of teacher portfolios—portfolios put together by prospective teachers to serve as both indications of what they are learning about teaching and as resources to draw from as they begin to teach. Such portfolios encourage prospective teachers to see themselves as practitioners, often prior to their initial teaching experiences. Though most of the work with teacher portfolios has focused on people preparing to teach secondary school, it has clear applications for the preparation of new teachers of college writing as well [6, 30, 34].

Implementing Portfolios:
Some Cautionary Words

By now it has become clear that there is no single model for portfolios. Rather, to be effective, portfolios must be developed in response to specific teaching and assessment goals. It is even possible that students (and teachers) will keep more than one type of portfolio. For example, the working portfolio mentioned earlier may be a repository of notes, drafts, and revisions, with little selection guiding what it holds. What might be called a showcase portfolio might consist of a collection of finished works selected for a specific purpose to represent specific achievements or abilities. Such a portfolio is dynamic, changing for the occasion, analogous to the portfolio an artist or architect might assemble to demonstrate either a range of abilities or a particular focus on accomplishments. Assessment portfolios used, as discussed earlier, to demonstrate development or proficiency or to determine placement are often drawn from larger working portfolios. Thus, a first consideration for people planning to use portfolios in their classes, programs, or institutions is the kinds of portfolios they want students to develop, since the purpose of the portfolio will determine what it contains.

A second consideration for classroom teachers is how to deal with gradelessness. Students and teachers alike are used to grades. Often, grades motivate students when learning doesn't, and some students may be extremely nervous about not knowing where they stand. As teachers, we find it convenient to rely on a grade to send students clear messages about the quality of their work. Several strategies may help address gradelessness. First, when students are introduced to portfolios in a classroom, it is important to stress the benefit that students are not being graded before they have had the opportunity to learn. This is particularly true in courses in which students are introduced to and practice writing strategies gradually throughout the course and is certainly one reason portfolios are especially appropriate in basic writing courses [26]. Second, it helps alleviate students' anxiety about grades to offer them opportunities to receive a tentative grade: Many instructors tell students that at any time during the course, they may request a tentative grade on one assignment, though the grade is nonbinding and not recorded. Another strategy is to confer with students midway through the course to talk about their progress so far and to tell them what their midterm grade would be, were the instructor required to give one. Such conferences also provide opportunities to talk with students about what they need to do to improve. Some instructors use dual portfolios, one that is submitted and graded at midterm and one that is graded at the end of the course. Such an approach is particularly appropriate if students do receive midterm grades or if the course material divides itself logically—for example, in a course that emphasizes personal writing for half the term and argument for the second. Third, students need very specific feedback on their work when it is not accompanied by a grade. Comments need to point to specific strengths and weaknesses. Instructors who typically rely on positive comments to encourage students, knowing that they will be tempered by the accompanying grade, may find themselves having to find a more accurate—and perhaps more blunt—vocabulary for assessing students' work. Fourth, it is

important that students know how much of their grade is determined by the portfolio and how much is determined by other factors such as examinations, attendance, participation, and assignments that do not contribute to the portfolio.

A third consideration in implementing portfolios is explaining to students—and reminding them about—what the portfolio will contain, what format requirements they must meet, and other prerequisites. Students need to know at the outset of the course that they have to collect, select, revise, and reflect according to a specific set of expectations. They also need to be reminded about the content and format of the portfolio a week or two prior to its submission.

Fourth, teachers, program administrators, and others responsible for implementing a portfolio evaluation system must consider how to best handle the evaluation of the portfolios. There is no consensus about whether portfolios add huge amounts of time to teachers' work or not, but it's fair to say that whether they do or not, a stack of portfolios to be evaluated is daunting. Often, instructors collect portfolios a week or two before the end of the term to give themselves extra time to read and evaluate them. During those last weeks, students work on a final project that is graded separately. And although it takes time to read and evaluate portfolios, it is also true that instructors typically spend less time marking and commenting on the work, since students will not have the opportunity to revise and resubmit it. The more time-consuming commenting will have taken place earlier in the term. Some different evaluation concerns come into play when portfolios are read and evaluated by people other than or in addition to the classroom instructor. Much of the literature on portfolio evaluation for program and institutional contexts raises issues that parallel those for any large-scale evaluation of writing: collecting sample portfolios, both for developing scoring guidelines and for training raters (this is especially important for establishing reliability among raters); making decisions about cutoff points for passing and for demonstrating proficiency and specific skills; and deciding how to reconcile diverse evaluations of the same portfolio and how and if the portfolio evaluation relates to grades students receive in writing courses or credit they are awarded for courses they are not required to take. Discussions of some of these issues and descriptions of implementing large-scale portfolio assessments can be found elsewhere [3, 8, 9, 15, 18, 20, 28].

Some Concluding Portfolios

Portfolios offer teachers, writing program administrators, and others responsible for the teaching and evaluation of writing many advantages over more traditional approaches. As I've indicated in this essay, portfolio assessment meets many of the criteria for valid, reliable, authentic assessment advocated by teachers of writing and assessment specialists. In particular, portfolios allow for assessment that is more consistent with theories about how people compose and how people learn to write than indirect tests of writing or single-writing sample assessments are. They allow students to represent their abilities with multiple samples of their work and to serve, through their reflective writing, as advocates for what their writing demonstrates about them as writers and thinkers. In classroom settings, portfolios allow instructors to deemphasize grades and emphasize improvement in writing. Portfolios may even create more student-centered classes if students make decisions about which pieces of writing to include in their portfolios and participate in developing the criteria by which their work is evaluated. But portfolios, despite their many advantages, are not appropriate for every assessment of writing, nor are they without problems of their own. Some of the latter I have mentioned: the influence of "glow" and "schmooze," the anxiety some students (and some instructors) may feel about not using grades as easy touchstones for performance, the sometimes daunting amount of work and time required to read large numbers of portfolios. In addition, when portfolio evaluation is imposed on teachers, writing programs, or institutions, portfolios lose the local, contextualized features that lend them much of their validity [8, 14, 15, 19, 20, 21]. Kathleen Yancey, among the strongest proponents of portfolios for a variety of purposes, cautions that portfolios may not be appropriate for new teachers of writing if the conditions for introducing these teachers to portfolio practices are not right [31]. Nevertheless, the value of portfolios appears to outweigh their limitations and potential problems. Fortunately, anyone planning to begin using portfolios to evaluate writing can benefit from the experience of teachers, scholars, and assessment experts who have used, studied, and written about them. The books and articles in the bibliography are but a sampling of the wealth of information available.

Annotated Bibliography: Suggested Reading

1. Anson, Chris M. "Portfolios for Teachers: Writing Our Way to Reflective Practice." *New Directions in Portfolio Assessment: Reflective Practice, Critical Theory, and Large-Scale Scoring*. Ed. Laurel Black, Donald A. Daiker, Jeffrey Sommers, and Gail Stygall. Portsmouth, NH: Boynton/Cook-Heinemann, 1994. 185–200.
    Describes teaching portfolios and discusses how they contribute to teachers' development as writers, scholars, and professionals. Anson argues that teaching portfolios must be adapted to the specific contexts of their use and offers insights into what he refers to as "the problem of assessment."

2. Belanoff, Pat, and Marcia Dickson, eds. *Portfolios: Process and Product*. Portsmouth, NH: Boynton/Cook-Heinemann, 1991. Twenty-three chapters, on a variety of applications of portfolios, organized into four sections: portfolios for proficiency testing, program assessment, classroom portfolios, and political issues.

3. Bishop, Wendy. "Going up the Creek without a Canoe: Using Portfolios to Train New Teachers of College Writing." *Portfolios: Process and Product*. Ed. Pat Belanoff and Marcia Dickson. Portsmouth, NH: Boynton/Cook-Heinemann, 1991. 215–227.
    A detailed discussion of procedures followed and lessons learned in implementing a portfolio evaluation system as a response to an anticipated proficiency testing program. Bishop explains how she and the composition director introduced portfolios to new teaching assistants and, quoting from the teaching assistants' teaching journals, provides insights into their reactions to portfolio evaluation.

4. Black, Laurel, Donald A. Daiker, Jeffrey Sommers, and Gail Stygall, eds. *New Directions in Portfolio Assessment: Reflective Practice, Critical Theory, and Large-Scale Scoring*. Portsmouth, NH: Boynton/Cook-Heinemann, 1994.
    Twenty-six chapters, each based on a paper delivered at the 1992 Miami University conference New Directions in Portfolio Assessment.

5. Black, Laurel, Edwina Helton, and Jeffrey Sommers. "Connecting Current Research on Authentic and Performance Assessment through Portfolios." *Assessing Writing* 1 (1994): 247–266.
    Discusses three alternative approaches to traditional assessment—authentic assessment, performance assessment, and portfolio assessment—and the connections among them.

6. Burch, C. Beth. "Finding Out What's in Their Heads: Using Teaching Portfolios to Assess English Education Students—and Programs." *Situating Portfolios: Four Perspectives*. Ed. Kathleen Blake Yancey and Irwin Weiser. Logan: Utah State UP, 1997. 263–277.
    Describes the use of portfolios in a Teaching Secondary English methods class. Burch discusses her ethnographic study of the documents comprising the portfolios, the reflective pieces introducing them, and other documents in an attempt to learn "what my preservice students as a whole know about English and how they conceptualized the discipline" (264).

7. Callahan, Susan. "Kentucky's State-Mandated Writing Portfolios and Teacher Accountability." *Situating Portfolios: Four Perspectives*. Ed. Kathleen Blake Yancey and Irwin Weiser. Logan: Utah State UP, 1997. 57–71.
    Using the portfolios mandated by the state of Kentucky as part of a larger school reform movement as her example, points out

the problems of top-down mandated portfolio assessment, particularly when the assessment program does not involve teachers from the outset.

8. ———. "Portfolio Expectations: Possibilities and Limits." *Assessing Writing* 2(1995): 117–152.

A concise yet thorough history of writing portfolios that includes a discussion of the important differences between portfolios designed for instructional purposes and those designed for testing.

9. Condon, William, and Liz Hamp-Lyons. "Introducing a Portfolio-Based Writing Assessment: Progress through Problems." *Portfolios: Process and Product*. Ed. Pat Belanoff and Marcia Dickson. Portsmouth, NH: Boynton/Cook-Heinemann, 1991. 231–247.

Traces the evolution at the University of Michigan from a timed, impromptu exit essay to a portfolio-based exit assessment. The authors describe the decisions underlying the change and the obstacles they encountered and reflect on the first two years of the portfolio assessment.

10. Conway, Glenda. "Portfolio Cover Letters, Students' Self-Presentation, and Teachers' Ethics." *New Directions in Portfolio Assessment: Reflective Practice, Critical Theory, and Large-Scale Scoring*. Ed. Laurel Black, Donald A. Daiker, Jeffrey Sommers, and Gail Stygall. Portsmouth, NH: Boynton/Cook-Heinemann, 1994. 83–92.

Addresses the rhetorical power of reflective cover letters that introduce portfolios. Conway acknowledges that although such letters may be written merely to fulfill an assignment, they can encourage "students to think substantively about their writing processes" (92). She cautions, however, against using the cover letter as the only reflection of the semester's work, arguing that required reflection must be an ongoing part of the course.

11. Daiker, Donald A., Jeffrey Sommers, and Gail Stygall. "The Pedagogical Implications of a College Placement Portfolio." *Assessment of Writing: Politics, Policies, Practices*. Ed. Edward M. White, William D. Lutz, and Sandra Kamusikiri. New York: MLA, 1996. 257–270.

Covers a wide range of issues concerning portfolio use while discussing the placement portfolios used at Miami University. Among the topics covered are the effects of these portfolios on high school writing programs in Ohio, the teaching of revision, self-assessment, and gender.

12. Edgerton, Russell, Patricia Hutchings, and Kathleen Quinlan. *The Teaching Portfolio: Capturing the Scholarship in Teaching*. Washington, DC: American Association of Higher Education, 1991.

A detailed discussion of and argument for the use of teaching portfolios. The authors argue that teaching portfolios enable teachers to represent the often overlooked scholarship that underlies their teaching.

13. Elbow, Peter. "Foreword." *Portfolios: Process and Product*. Ed. Pat Belanoff and Marcia Dickson. Portsmouth, NH: Boynton/Cook-Heinemann, 1991. ix–xvi.

Reflects on the increasing attractiveness of portfolios as assessment instruments, arguing that a major advantage of portfolios to other kinds of writing assessment is the increased validity achieved by using multiple writing samples. Elbow also suggests that portfolios create an inevitable and healthy tension between validity and reliability, a claim disputed by other assessment experts such as White [28].

14. ———. "Will the Virtues of Portfolios Blind Us to Their Potential Dangers?" *New Directions in Portfolio Assessment: Reflective Practice, Critical Theory, and Large-Scale Scoring*. Ed. Laurel Black, Donald A. Daiker, Jeffrey Sommers, and Gail Stygall. Portsmouth, NH: Boynton/Cook-Heinemann, 1994. 40–55.

Keynote address at the 1992 Miami University conference on portfolios; Elbow argues for the value of portfolios but also suggests some potential problems portfolios may produce, including an overemphasis on evaluation.

15. ———, and Pat Belanoff "State University of New York at Stony Brook Portfolio-Based Evaluation Program." *Portfolios: Process and Product*. Ed. Pat Belanoff and Marcia Dickson. Portsmouth, NH: Boynton/Cook-Heinemann, 1991. 3–16.

Details one of the earliest portfolio evaluation systems used as a substitute for an exit examination. Description covers portfolio contents, how they are evaluated, and how the system may contribute to the development of a teaching community.

16. Ford, James E., and Gregory Larkin. "The Portfolio System: An End to Backsliding Writing Standards." *College English* 39 (1978): 950–955.

One of the earliest pieces published on portfolios.

17. Gay, Pamela. "A Portfolio Approach to Teaching a Biology-Linked Basic Writing Class." *Portfolios: Process and Product*. Ed. Pat Belanoff and Marcia Dickson. Portsmouth, NH: Boynton/Cook-Heinemann, 1991. 182–193.

Describes use of portfolios in a summer EOP program for non-Anglo urban basic writers. Gay argues that portfolios support her goals of encouraging basic writers to think of themselves as developing writers.

18. Huot, Brian. "Beyond the Classroom: Using Portfolios to Assess Writing." *New Directions in Portfolio Assessment: Reflective Practice, Critical Theory, and Large-Scale Scoring*. Ed. Laurel Black, Donald A. Daiker, Jeffrey Sommers, and Gail Stygall. Portsmouth, NH: Boynton/Cook-Heinemann, 1994. 325–333.

Calls for a systematic examination of writing portfolios as tools for writing assessment beyond the classroom; in the early 1990s, much of the support for their use was based either on classroom applications or on anecdotal reports.

19. ———, and Michael M. Williamson. "Rethinking Portfolios for Evaluating Writing: Issues of Assessment and Power." *Situating Portfolios: Four Perspectives*. Ed. Kathleen Blake Yancey and Irwin Weiser. Logan: Utah State UP, 1997. 43–56. Focuses on the power relationships in assessment as they apply to portfolios, particularly in large-scale, non-classroom-based contexts.

20. Murphy, Sandra. "Teachers and Students: Reclaiming Assessment via Portfolios." *Situating Portfolios: Four Perspectives*. Ed. Kathleen Blake Yancey and Irwin Weiser. Utah State UP, 1997. 72–88. Referring to several portfolios projects used in California public schools, discusses alternatives to the "teacher as technician," top-down approach to evaluation that well-designed portfolio projects can offer. Emphasizes that portfolio systems that are initiated and developed by teachers and are evaluated by teachers promote teacher professionalism. Also addresses the contribution portfolios can make to students' development as independent learners.

21. ———, and Barbara Grant. "Portfolio Approaches to Assessment: Breakthrough or More of the Same?" *Assessment of Writing: Politics, Policies, Practices*. Ed. Edward M. White, William D. Lutz, and Sandra Kamusikiri. New York: MLA, 1996. 284–300. Discusses two perspectives on assessment, positivist and constructivist. The first leads to standardized, top-down assessments, whereas the second promotes collaborative, contextualized assessment. The authors offer suggestions for developing and using portfolios in ways consistent with constructivist assessment.

22. Rosenberg, Roberta. "Using the Portfolio to Meet State-Mandated Assessment: A Case Study." *Portfolios: Process and Product*. Ed. Pat Belanoff and Marcia Dickson. Portsmouth, NH: Boynton/Cook-Heinemann, 1991. 69–79. Describes the portfolio system used at Christopher Newport College to meet Virginia's state mandated assessment. Rosenberg points out that portfolios can be "good alternatives to standardized tests that may not reflect the goals or curriculum" (77).

23. Smit, David, Patricia Kolonosky, and Kathryn Seltzer. "Implementing a Portfolio System." *Portfolios: Process and Product*. Ed. Pat Belanoff and Marcia Dickson. Portsmouth, NH: Boynton/Cook-Heinemann, 1991. 46–56. A detailed description of the implementation of a portfolio system designed to establish more uniform grading standards at Kansas State University.

24. Sommers, Jeffrey, Laurel Black, Donald A. Daiker, and Gail Stygall. "The Challenge of Rating Portfolios: What WPAs Can Expect." *Writing Program Administration* 17 (1993): 7–29. Focuses on the scoring of portfolios, based on the authors' experience with the Miami University placement portfolio project. They address two main issues: reliability in scoring portfolios versus single essays and challenges in redefining holistic scoring for use in rating portfolios.

25. Wauters, Joan K. "Evaluation for Empowerment: A Portfolio Proposal for Alaska." *Portfolios: Process and Product*. Ed. Pat Belanoff and Marcia Dickson. Portsmouth, NH: Boynton/Cook-Heinemann, 1991. 57–68. Describes how the decision was made at the University of Alaska Southeast to develop a portfolio system to address calls for assessment and accountability. Discusses the development of the assessment goals, the pilot projects, faculty training, and future plans.

26. Weiser, Irwin. "Portfolio Practice and Assessment for Collegiate Basic Writers." *Portfolios in the Writing Classroom: An Introduction*. Ed. Kathleen Blake Yancey. Urbana, IL: NCTE, 1992. 89–101. Argues for the appropriateness of portfolio assessment for basic writing students and describes the approach to portfolio system implemented at Purdue University in the early 1980s. Addresses advantages to students and teachers of using portfolios as well as potential problems.

27. ———. "Revising Our Practices: How Portfolios Help Teachers Learn." *Situating Portfolios: Four Perspectives*. Ed. Kathleen Blake Yancey and Irwin Weiser. Logan: Utah State UP, 1997. 293–301. Argues that portfolios can play an important part in the preparation of new teachers of writing. Explains how portfolios can encourage reflective practice for new teachers and can help them learn to comment effectively on student writing.

28. White, Edward M. "Portfolios as an Assessment Concept." *New Directions in Portfolio Assessment: Reflective Practice, Critical Theory, and Large-Scale Scoring*. Ed. Laurel Black, Donald A. Daiker, Jeffrey Sommers, and Gail Stygall. Portsmouth, NH: Boynton/Cook-Heinemann, 1994. 25–39. Addresses some of the benefits and problems of portfolios as assessment instruments. White makes the case for the value of portfolios as direct measures of a broad range of student writing abilities. He also discusses problems of validity and reliability in writing assessment.

29. ———, William D. Lutz, and Sandra Kamusikiri, eds. *Assessment of Writing: Politics, Policies, Practices*. New York: MLA, 1996. Twenty-one essays on a range of issues surrounding the assessment of writing, including three chapters that focus specifically on portfolios.

30. Yagelski, Robert P. "Portfolios as a Way to Encourage Reflective Practice among Preservice English Teachers." *Situating*

Portfolios: Four Perspectives. Ed. Kathleen Blake Yancey and Irwin Weiser. Logan: Utah State UP, 1997. 225–244.

Describes a portfolio system developed by a team of university and high school teachers of English to encourage preservice English teachers to engage in self-assessment and reflection.

31. Yancey, Kathleen Blake. "Make Haste Slowly: Graduate Teaching Assistants and Portfolios." *New Directions in Portfolio Assessment: Reflective Practice, Critical Theory, and Large-Scale Scoring*. Ed. Laurel Black, Donald A. Daiker, Jeffrey Sommers, and Gail Stygall. Portsmouth, NH: Boynton/Cook-Heinemann, 1994. 210–218.

Acknowledges that carefully designed portfolio systems can be beneficial to new teachers of writing but suggests that it might be beneficial to new teachers to wait until they have some experience in the classroom before they adopt a portfolio system.

32. ———. "Portfolios in the Writing Classroom: A Final Reflection." *Portfolios in the Writing Classroom: An Introduction*. Ed. Kathleen Blake Yancey. Urbana, IL: NCTE, 1992. 102–116.

Provides an overview of the state of portfolio use in 1992, including characteristics of portfolios and various contexts in which they are used. Also raises questions about the future of portfolio assessment.

33. ———, ed. *Portfolios in the Writing Classroom: An Introduction*. Urbana, IL: NCTE, 1992.

Ten essays by English educators, assessment specialists, college and university faculty, and secondary school teachers, offering an introduction to a variety of portfolio practices in a wide range of educational settings.

34. ———. "Teacher Portfolios: Lessons in Resistance, Readiness, and Reflection." *Situating Portfolios: Four Perspectives*. Ed. Kathleen Blake Yancey and Irwin Weiser. Logan: Utah State UP, 1997, 244–262.

Presents and analyzes excerpts from students' portfolios, showing how to encourage students to reflect on what it means to be a teacher through elements designed to demonstrate concepts they have learned, applications of those concepts, development, and critical self-reflection.

35. ———, and Irwin Weiser, eds. *Situating Portfolios: Four Perspectives*. Logan: Utah State UP, 1997.

Twenty-four chapters by teachers from elementary schools through universities and by scholars and researchers who specialize in writing assessment. Of special interest are five essays discussing portfolios and technology, including hypertext portfolios..

WRITING ACROSS THE CURRICULUM: AN OVERVIEW AND UPDATE

Margot Soven

Writing across the curriculum (WAC) has just celebrated its twenty-fifth anniversary. As an educational "happening," WAC has had remarkable staying power. Despite ominous predictions about its impending demise, in an era when educators at all levels are struggling to do more with less, when demands for accountability threaten many programs, WAC survives. In the 1970s WAC enjoyed funding from outside sources, such as the National Endowment for the Humanities. In the 1980s, as public funding was channeled in new directions, many schools took on the challenge of paying for WAC-related activities, such as faculty workshops and peer tutoring programs. As we approach the end of the 1990s and look toward the new century, the financial demands on schools at all levels grow even greater. WAC must compete for funding with plans to implement educational technology, new programs such as service learning, and ESL.

The reason for WAC's continued survival during this time of downsizing and fiscal constraint is simple. WAC has won over the faculty. They no longer need to be convinced of the importance of writing. WAC has arrived. The principles associated with WAC are now integral to the culture of schooling. Although not all faculty in all disciplines state, as I do in my course descriptions, "Writing is as important as reading in this class," many faculty recognize the importance of writing as a means for facilitating learning and agree that writing is a skill that requires practice in classes other than English if students are to become competent writers. The potential benefits of using writing as a way of learning summarized by Allan Glatthorn in 1983 have been realized in many classrooms [12]:

1. The act of writing enhances knowing: Retrieving information, organizing it, and expressing it in writing seems to improve understanding and retention.

2. Writing is an active learning process, and active learning seems to be more effective than passive reception.

3. Writing is a way of making knowledge personal. The writer brings to bear a subjective point of view and reinterprets personally what has been learned.

4. Writing focuses attention: Students who know they are expected to write tend to be more attentive.

5. Writing seems to facilitate thinking about a subject. The act of writing enables the writer to discern new relationships and make new connections.

6. Writing is a way of sharing what is known. Students can use writing to share with classmates what they have learned.

7. Writing provides immediate feedback to the learner and to the teacher about what has been learned—and what has not been learned.

8. Writing is a self-paced mode of learning; the pace of writing seems to match the pace of learning better, slowing down the process of students who might be inclined to finish a learning task too quickly.

9. Each discipline has its own way of knowing and its own modes of communicating knowledge; students should have a broad knowledge of how writing is used in several disciplines. For example, a scientist reporting the results of a scientific experiment uses objective language to communicate results; a literary critic evaluating a novel writes using more subjective language to discuss reactions.

"Writing to learn" is no longer controversial on many campuses. Furthermore, whereas in the past, faculty might try to avoid the unpleasant experience of reading poorly written papers by not assigning writing, today more of them give writing assignments and help their students write better papers by

Margot Soven is Professor of English at La Salle University. She holds a doctorate with a specialization in the teaching of writing from the University of Pennsylvania. At La Salle, she is codirector of the Freshman Composition Program and director of the Writing Across the Curriculum Program and the Writing Fellows Program. Her essays and book reviews have appeared in such journals as College Composition and Communication, Journal of the Council of Writing Program Administrators, *and the* Journal of Teaching Writing, *and* Freshman English News. *She has written several chapters for texts on the teaching of writing and is the author of* Write to Learn: A Guide to Writing Across the Curriculum (*Southwestern Publishing, 1995) and* Teaching Writing in Middle and Secondary Schools (*in press, Allyn & Bacon). She is coeditor of* Writing Across the Curriculum: A Guide to Developing Programs (*SAGE Press, 1992) and* Writings from the Workplace (*Allyn & Bacon, 1995*).

reading drafts and encouraging revision. The attitudes expressed by the four professors from four disciplines (psychology, sociology, philosophy, and health and physical education) who participated in "Interchange: A Conversation Among the Disciplines" are typical of faculty in schools that have WAC programs [1]:

> Recognizing the value of personalized writing as a first stage to professional writing, enhancing communication between teacher and student, structuring the process for developing clear, organized thinking on paper, and providing a venue for self-expression, these seem to be the major reason why the four of us incorporate WAC in our classrooms.

Writing Across the Curriculum: Research and New Directions

Today, WAC faces a threefold challenge: to continue to provide faculty with the latest and best research on writing in the disciplines, to translate that research into teaching practices, and to demonstrate how writing can be used to support the goals of new programs and new curricula in the university. New directions in theory, research, and methodology will help us meet these goals. In addition, WAC must incorporate the new technologies for writing and research available to the campus community. For example, e-mail and the World Wide Web are rapidly becoming a part of the writing culture in the academy. Students are e-mailing drafts of their formal papers and daily journal entries to their classmates and instructors. Laura Mandell explains how e-mail has transformed the dynamics of her classroom [19]. "Screen conversations" seem especially liberating for students who lack confidence in their discussion and writing skills.

Writing in the Disciplines and Writing Assignments

Studies on the nature of writing in different disciplines grow more numerous. Many studies examine the relation between writing and specific disciplines [15, 16, 22]. Some studies, such as Hedley and Parker's [14], focus on the similarities of the writing assignments in various courses. Their research suggests that at four-year liberal arts colleges, the kinds of papers students write for different courses are strikingly similar. They argue that college teachers should stress generic skills such as "inquiry" rather than the discourse conventions of different disciplines. Other studies such as Langer's [17], point out that teachers' different responses to

writing in different disciplines reflect significant differences in the way they view writing. In Langer's study, the science teachers' concerns about presentation were quite different from the English teachers' concerns. Langer states: "Instead of encouraging students to formulate their own understanding and structure their explanations, [the science teacher] sees good writing (in this instance) as the ability to select relevant information from lab notes and place it in the proper category, according to his instructions."

As we develop a better understanding of the kinds of writing instructors see as valuable to their students, we are better able to devise clear guidelines for writing assignments. An assignment often fails because the instructions for the assignment are misleading. Walvoord and McCarthy's study of writing in a business course makes this point [22]. After exploring how students' difficulties with an assignment were related to the teachers' methods and students' strategies, Walvoord and McCarthy concluded that one of the most important changes the teacher could make in his strategies would be to "clarify his assignment sheet." Peer tutors in writing at my own institution report that a lot of writing problems are related to misunderstanding the assignment. After reviewing the drafts of many students in one class, they commented that most of the papers were missing at least one piece of the assignment. Their observations are not surprising in view of Langer's observation that "the overwhelming characteristic of teachers' discussions about the thinking patterns and conventions in the writing in their disciplines was their inexplicitness."

Faculty interested in improving assignment guidelines can turn to an increasing number of textbooks on writing in the disciplines. These texts include descriptions of both assignments common to many disciplines and assignments that are discipline-specific. Many of these books are designed for freshman composition courses. For example, *The Informed Writer: Using Sources in the Disciplines* has four parts: "Writing About Reading," "Writing Using Reading," "Writing in the Disciplines" and "The Craft of Writing" [3]. *Writing and Reading Across the Curriculum* introduces students to the skills necessary for all academic writing: summary, analysis, synthesis, and critique [4]. Other books are intended for courses in the disciplines [5, 6, 7]. My own text, *Write to Learn: A Guide to Writing Across the Curriculum*, provides checklists for evaluating writing and model assignments developed by La Salle University faculty in a variety of departments [20]. A list of these textbooks appears in *Writing Across the Curriculum: An Annotated Bibliography* [2].

WAC research has also focused on nontraditional assignments, appearing with increased frequency across the disciplines. In 1984, Bridgeman and Carlsen found that despite evidence of more creative and expressive forms in elementary grades in American schools, these forms were rare in college [8]. But the situation may be changing. For example, in an introductory class in psychology that included poetry and short story writing as well as more traditional assignments, the teachers concluded that poetic writing can enhance learning in classes other than English and that a mix of poetic and other kinds of writing stimulates exploration and imagination to a greater extent than traditional assignments [13]. They found that writing a poem from the point of view of a schizophrenic person helps students identify with the traumas of a patient who suffers from this mental condition, an important goal for the course.

Toby Fulwiler implemented various kinds of writing assignments to facilitate new goals for his American literature course [11]. He wanted to create a "community of learners" to make "reading and writing more fun" and "avoid training literary critics, but make the study of literature both serious and exciting at the same time." His students wrote journal entries daily "to encourage them to explore personally and react to the readings, essays to shape some of their reactions into finished pieces, and short stories to place themselves in the role of the authors." Fulwiler believes that he accomplished the goals he set for the course with the aid of writing.

At my own institution, the use of nontraditional assignments is becoming more widespread. A professor in our religion department who teaches an introductory course in the Bible uses writing to encourage his students to treat the Bible as literature rather than sacred text, a difficult task at a Catholic university. Students write personal response papers expressing their reaction to the Bible as a literary text and journalistic accounts of biblical narratives. A professor in the philosophy department finds that writing letters to their parents about the philosophers they are studying reduces students' apprehension about writing in philosophy.

Also, freshman composition programs are making room for other kinds of writing besides the expository essay. Lovitt and Young challenge the idea that teaching students how to write reports reduces the value of assignments as vehicles for learning [18]. They argue that "dismissing the teaching of reports as inimical to a liberal arts education may ironically disadvantage our students." Students will most likely be required to write reports more frequently than they will be called on to write essays, both in school and at work. Furthermore, they point out that "the teaching of the report can be as intellectually and academically challenging as teaching the essay."

Greater acceptance of nontraditional forms of writing in various disciplines should be no surprise given the findings of a study of the long-term effect of writing across the curriculum on faculty at three institutions. Barbara Walvoord and her colleagues found that the greatest effect experienced by faculty was a change in teaching philosophy, a "realization of how learners need to be involved in learning and of the many roles that writing can play in learning" [23].

WAC and Peer Tutoring Programs

Until the mid-1980s, faculty development workshops were the centerpiece of WAC programs, especially at small and medium-sized institutions. Now, approximately ten years later, peer tutoring programs not only augment faculty development but add a new and much valued student-centered dimension to WAC. At some Ivy League schools, these are often the mainstay of the WAC program. Peer tutors help teach writing in writing centers and through writing fellows programs, sometimes called curriculum-based peer tutoring programs. At schools that have such programs, the peer tutor is assigned to a specific course and helps all the students in that course with their drafts. Students in these courses learn that everyone can benefit from peer review and that revision is a natural part of the writing process. Peer tutors, to quote Ken Bruffee, "are potentially among the most powerful agents of change" in the university, because they learn the most important tool for effecting change, "the art of translation, the art of conversation at the boundaries of communities" [9]. In a presentation at a conference for peer tutors, Bruffee said, "What you do as a peer tutor, as I understand it, is to help a tutee cross the boundary between one knowledge community and another."

WAC and the Curriculum: Service Learning

Writing has become a means for achieving the objectives of curriculum initiatives such as service learning. An increasing number of schools are adding a service learning requirement, acknowledging the role of the university to create good citizens as well as knowledgeable ones. Students work at government agencies, charitable organizations, or community groups. Sometimes, this requirement is attached to specific courses. At other schools, such as Michigan State University, the service is a part of the composition program. Writing is used to help students integrate academic work with service learning. In some programs, students complete a writing project for the agency in which they are placed. They may produce a "working document" to solve a problem they identify in the agency or develop a brochure or a Web site. They often write reports reflecting about and evaluating their service learning experience.

What Might English Faculty Do?

English teachers are frequently called on to help their colleagues in other disciplines translate the latest research in composition into teaching practices related to writing. It is our task to keep abreast of this research and to use our own classrooms as laboratories for experimenting with new techniques and strategies. Writing across the curriculum is a concept that connects us to our colleagues through a shared interest: teaching our students the value of writing and helping them develop good writing skills.

Annotated Bibliography: Selected Reading

1. Abbott, Michael M., Pearl W. Bartelt, Stephen Fishman, and Charlotte Honda. "Interchange: A Conversation among the Disciplines." *Writing and Teaching in the Disciplines*. Ed. Anne Herrington and Charles Moran. New York: MLA, 1992. Answers to the question "Why do you use writing in your teaching?" by four instructors in different disciplines.

2. Anson, Chris M., John E. Schwiebert, and Michael M. Williamson. *Writing across the Curriculum: An Annotated Bibliography*. Westport, CT: Greenwood, 1993. An annotated bibliography on writing across the curriculum divided into two parts, "Scholarship" and "Pedagogy."

3. Bazerman, Charles. *The Informed Writer: Using Sources in the Disciplines*. 2nd ed. Boston: Houghton, 1985. Introduces students to the forms and conventions of writing in the disciplines.

4. Behrens, Laurence, and Leonard J. Rosen. *Writing and Reading across the* Curriculum. 4th ed. New York: Harper, 1991. Introduces to students the skills needed for writing about written texts: summary, synthesis, and critique skills. Includes readings representing the perspectives of various disciplines on different topics.

5. Biddle, Arthur W., and Toby Fulwiler. *Reading, Writing, and the Study of Literature*. New York: Random, 1989. Addresses the conventions of literary study from the viewpoint of both reading and writing.

6. Biddle, Arthur W., and A. S. Magistrale (with Toby Fulwiler). *Writers Guide: Political Science*. Lexington, MA: Heath, 1987. A guide for writing papers in political science.

7. ———— *Writers Guide: Psychology*. Lexington, MA: Heath, 1987. A guide for writing papers in psychology.

8. Bridgeman, Brent, and Sybil Carlson. "Survey of Academic Writing Tasks." *Written Communication* 1 (1984): 247–280. A study to determine the writing tasks faced by beginning and graduate students in 190 academic departments.

9. Bruffee, Kenneth. *Collaborative Learning: Higher Education, Interdependence, and the Authority of Knowledge*. Baltimore: John Hopkins UP, 1993. Discusses how collaborative learning activities, including peer tutoring, can transform the university.

10. Cooper, David D., and Laura Juliei, eds. *Writing in the Public Interest: Service Learning and the Writing Classroom*. East Lansing: Writing Center, Michigan State U, 1995. Describes the Service Learning Writing Project at Michigan State University.

11. Fulwiler, Toby. "Writing and Learning in American Literature." *Writing, Teaching, and Learning in the Disciplines*. Ed. Anne Herrington and Charles Moran. New York: MLA, 1992. Describes a series of writing assignments in a literature class designed to encourage students to explore personal reactions to readings, to analyze readings, and to place students in the role of authors.

12. Glatthorn, Allan. "A Review of Research, Theory, and Practice." (Unpublished materials.) U of Pennsylvania, 1983.

13. Gorman, Michael E., and Art Young. "Poetic Writing in Psychology." *Writing across the Disciplines*. Ed. Art Young and Toby Fulwiler. Portsmouth, NH: Boynton/Cook-Heinemann, 1986. Concludes that poetry and short story writing can enhance learning in classes other than English.

14. Hedley, Jane, and JoEllen Parker. "Writing across the Curriculum: The Vantage of the Liberal Arts." *ADE Bulletin* 98 (1991): 22–28. Argues that writing assignments should emphasize general inquiry skills associated with academic thinking rather than the learning of specialized discourse conventions.

15. Herrington, Anne, and Charles Moran, eds. *Writing, Teaching, and Learning in the Disciplines*. New York: MLA, 1992. A collection of essays on writing in the disciplines grouped in these categories: "Historical Perspectives," "Disciplinary and Predisciplinary Theory," "Teachers' Voices: Reflections on Practice," "Studies in the Classroom," "Disciplinary Values, Discourse Practices, and Teaching," and "Writing in the Disciplines: A Prospect."

16. Jollife, David, ed. *Advances in Writing Research*: Vol. 2. *Writing in Academic Disciplines*. Norwood, NJ: Ablex, 1988. A collection of essays on theoretical models for research related to WAC and studies on writing in different disciplines.

17. Langer. Judith. "Speaking of Knowing: Conceptions of Understanding in Academic Disciplines." *Writing, Teaching,*

and Learning in the Disciplines. Ed. Anne Herrington and Charles Moran. New York: MLA, 1992.
Explores the relationship between thinking and academic writing in various disciplines.

18. Lovitt, Carl, and Art Young. "Rethinking Genre in the First-Year Composition Course." *Profession 97*. New York: MLA, 1997. 113–126.
Discusses the value of report writing in the freshman composition class.

19. Mandell, Laura. "Virtual Encounters: Using an Electronic Mailing List in the Literature Classroom." *Profession 97*. New York: MLA, 1997. 126–133.
Demonstrates how e-mail had a transforming effect on the dynamics of communication in a literature classroom.

20. Soven, Margot. *Write to Learn: A Guide to Writing across the Curriculum*. Cincinnati: South-Western, 1996.

Includes instructions and models for academic assignments.

21. Walvoord, Barbara E., Linda Lawrence Hunt, H. Fil Dowling Jr., and Joan McMahon. *In the Long Run: A Study of Faculty in Three Writing across the Curriculum Programs*. Urbana, IL: NCTE, 1997.
Reports the long-term impact on faculty of writing across the curriculum programs.

22. Walvoord, Barbara E., and Lucille P. McCarthy. *Thinking and Writing in College: A Naturalistic Study of Students in Four Disciplines*. Urbana, IL: NCTE, 1991.
Presents the results of research on writing and thinking in four classes (in business, history, psychology and biology) taught by members of the research team. Illustrates a model of collaborative, naturalistic classroom research in a college setting.

TEACHING COMPOSITION TO SPEAKERS OF OTHER LANGUAGES: AN OVERVIEW

Joy Reid

Even experienced teachers of composition whose students are generally native English speakers may experience discomfort and puzzlement when they find nonnative speakers of English (ESL students)* in their classes—even before those ESL students submit their first writing assignment. New or less experienced composition teachers of native English speakers may face those same feelings as they first begin to teach, but they usually have the advantage that, at the very least, *they* have been native English-speaking students before they became teachers. Their experiences as students in U.S. classrooms have prepared them to understand both the expectations of their students and the nonverbal clues that native English speakers (NESs) offer in the classroom: heads nodding, notetaking, raised eyebrows, shifting in seats, shrugged shoulders, and the like. In contrast, teachers who encounter ESL students may have only limited knowledge about and experience with diverse cultures.† The expected protocols for asking questions, teacher-student exchanges, indicating understanding, and even group work that seem so "normal" in a class of NESs may be foreign to ESL students.

When composition teachers encounter the writing of their ESL students, their confusion and irritation may increase. A single ESL student paper may contain word- and sentence-level errors that differ in kind (if not in number or level of severity) from NES errors. In addition, there may be differences in the writer's perceptions of the effective presentation of ideas in an academic setting. These differences between ESL and NES errors and perceptions may well make the ESL errors more visible (in the words of one teacher, "They seem to jump off the page") and so seem even more egregious to the teacher-evaluator. This essay discusses several major areas

in which the needs of ESL students differ from those of NESs; it also provides information from experienced ESL composition teachers concerning the identification of typical ESL writing problems and suggests some solutions.

"Ear" Learners and "Eye" Learners

In much the same way that NESs differ in background knowledge, motivation, and perspective, it is important to realize that ESL students are not a homogeneous group. In addition to the clear diversity in language and cultural backgrounds, ESL students in U.S. colleges and universities can also be described in terms of the scenarios in which they acquired their second language. Specifically, most of the international (or "visa") students—students who travel to the United States from their homelands to attend postsecondary institutions—differ from ESL students who have grown up in the United States, who have graduated from U.S. high schools, and may be permanent U.S. residents or citizens.

Students who have studied English as a second language outside the United States and have entered postsecondary institutions here have, for the most part, acquired English *visually*: They have read and studied about the structures of the language. However, their practice in producing written English has been limited to occasional tests and papers in the classroom. Moreover, because cultures evolve writing styles appropriate to their own histories and the needs of their soci-

---

* Students for whom English is not a first language are called "English as a second language" (ESL) students in this essay, although of course English may be their third or fourth language.
† Samovar and Porter describe culture as the overall system of perceptions and beliefs, values, and patterns of thought that direct and constrain a social group, from the way the group uses space to the meaning of widened eyes and from the way members of the group approach relationships to the ways they view the world [23]. Language—verbal, nonverbal, and written communication—is an integral part of culture.

Joy Reid teaches in the University of Wyoming English Department and coordinates the ESL support program. She has published a three book ESL composition series: The Process of Composition *(Prentice Hall Regents, 3rd ed., 1998),* The Process of Paragraph Writing *(Prentice Hall Regents, 2nd ed., 1994), and* Basic Writing *(Prentice Hall Regents, 2nd ed., 1996), as well as coedited a four-level writing-grammar series,* Looking Ahead *(Heinle and Heinle, 1998). In addition, she has published teacher resource books:* Teaching ESL Writing *(Prentice Hall Regents, 1993),* Learning Styles in the ESL/EFL Classroom *(ed., Heinle and Heinle, 1995),* Grammar in the Composition Classroom *(with Pat Byrd, Heinle and Heinle, 1998), and* Understanding Learning Styles in the Second Language Classroom *(ed., Prentice Hall Regents, 1998). Her research articles and books on discourse analysis, computers and composition, learning styles, the writing-reading connection, and the change process are published in a variety of journals.*

eties, many international students have assumptions about the presentation of written ideas that are appropriate for their native discourse communities but not necessarily to the United States. A great majority of the students have not articulated or even considered those assumptions. As Ilona Leki [20] points out, not many educational systems appear to teach rhetorical patterns or the use of specific language structures for different communication purposes directly in the school setting. Indeed, in most countries outside the United States, there are virtually no courses in writing. Therefore, many international students have limited awareness of their writing strategies and underdeveloped rhetorical skills, even in their first languages.

In contrast, U.S. residents (that is, ESL students who have lived and attended secondary schools in the United States) have acquired much of their English through their *ears*. Although they may have had ESL classes alongside their regular public school work, their English has been learned mainly through immersion in the language.* As a result of this aural basis, their spoken language may be fluent and comprehensible, and their writing may appear fluent. However, because these students have limited knowledge of the structures of English, their writing may appear more or less phonetic, with limited and perhaps incorrect use of the structures (verb tenses, prepositions, word forms) of the language.

This single difference between international and U.S.-resident ESL students—whether they acquired their English principally through their ears or their eyes—bears directly on the strengths and weaknesses these students brings to their writing classes and significantly affects the ways teachers can approach writing processes with the ESL students in each group.†

Intercultural Communication in the Classroom

Initially, the experience of teaching ESL students may parallel the "blind-random" setting on an exercise step machine. At this setting, the rhythm of the stepping slows and speeds up automatically and randomly, and so the stepper is "blind," not knowing when the rhythm will change or in what direction.‡ Almost certainly, the inexperienced teacher of ESL students encounters periods of "randomness," of surprising incidents, time frames, and rhythms. Furthermore, because of the cultural differences between teacher and students and among the students themselves, the randomness is frequently not preceded by any clues—it occurs "blindly." The results: frustration and misperceptions for both teachers and students.

At the same time as composition teachers are struggling to accommodate their ESL students' needs, the ESL students may also be struggling to adjust their perceptions to a "foreign" classroom environment; that is, "blind-random" occurs on both sides of the desk. Even ESL students who have attended U.S. public schools and have lived in the United States most of their lives carry many of their first-culture values, needs, and expectations into their second-language classrooms. Researchers have shown that cultural differences between (and among) ESL students and their teachers may involve how students view teachers and student attitudes toward teaching and learning [1, 2, 12]. The degree of authority invested in and expected from the teacher, as well as the degree to which the teacher directs and dominates class activities, depends to a large extent on culture. For example, many Asian cultures (both in North American populations and in Asia) have a tradition of deference: questioning a person in authority—a parent, a teacher—is disrespectful, and receptive, as opposed to proactive, learning is the key to success. In a U.S. college composition class, however, such behavior may be seen as inappropriately nonparticipatory.

In contrast, the strong cooperative values and high level of social responsibility of many Latin societies (in both North America and South America) make the highly individualized and competitive values of many U.S. students seem unpleasantly aggressive. For the newly arrived international student, the adjustment may, be even more jarring: A class in the United States must seem a structureless, anarchical situation for learning. In the United States, composition students are expected to take an active part in the learning process, asking questions, challenging each other and their teachers, working (often loudly) in small groups with peers they know only slightly. Consequently, many ESL students must identify and practice a variety of learning behaviors. In fact, a truly multi-

---

* In some cases, the acquisition of ESL immigrant students' first language may have been similar, particularly if they are refugees who were forced to leave their countries and may have gaps in their schooling: Although they speak that language fluently, they may not read or write it fluently.

†Note that these ESL students, in actuality, exist along a continuum: from immigrant families whose prior first-language education was substantial and who may have studied ESL as well to an international student who has never studied English. Variables such as parental attitudes toward education, cultural constraints, and individual student learning styles and strategies also account for variations in student profiles.

‡My thanks to my English-teacher daughter, Shelley, for this analogy, gleaned during her first summer as an ESL teacher.

cultural class can result in substantial classroom imbalance in perspectives and even cross-cultural tensions as students and teachers struggle to develop appropriate roles and interactions.

Contrastive Rhetoric and the Composition Teacher

Robert Kaplan first defined contrastive rhetoric when he sought to discover whether organizational patterns of written material vary from culture to culture [16]. In his investigation of six hundred student expository paragraphs, written in English by native speakers of many non-English-language backgrounds, Kaplan used philosophical, psychological, anthropological, and linguistic insights to describe the differences between the essentially linear English paragraph, which does not tolerate digression or repetition, and paragraphs that he classified generally as Semitic, Oriental, Romance, and Russian. He represented the differences graphically (Figure 1); at the same time, he cautioned that "much more detailed and more accurate descriptions are required before any meaningful contrastive system can be elaborated."

Since the appearance of Kaplan's article, the notion of contrastive rhetoric, along with the issues surrounding the transfer of rhetorical patterns in second-language writing, has grown into an area of study. Research reported by proponents of this theory, published in a collection edited by Kaplan [15] and a resource book by Ulla Connor [6] demonstrate that the style in which each culture organizes and presents written material reflects the preferences of that particular culture. As a result, ESL writers often intuitively employ a rhetoric and a sequence of thought that violate the expectations of the native reader. When they write for readers in another culture, they often have problems with identifying audience expectations and communicating effectively with different discourse communities.

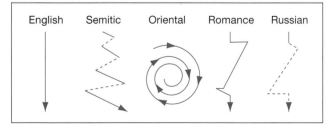

Kaplan's Contrastive Rhetoric Diagram

Even *within* a language, there appear to be different rhetorical rules and conventions that govern different categories of texts. Leki [20] and John Swales [24] indicate that in U.S. academic classes, discipline-specific writing conventions differ in such diverse areas as length of sentences, choice of vocabulary, acceptability of using first person, extent of using passive voice, decree to which writers are permitted to interpret, and amount of metaphorical language accepted. According to William Grabe and Robert Kaplan [12], the ESL writer is also likely to have a different notion of what constitutes evidence, of the order in which evidence should best be presented, and of the amount of evidence needed to explain a topic or persuade the reader.

Background Information in the Composition Classroom

Successful communication rests on background knowledge and experience that is shared by writers and readers; that is, the prior knowledge of student writers necessarily influences what, and how, they write. Consequently, ESL students can face misunderstanding and even failure in their academic written work not just because of second-language errors but also because they are often unaware of the content expectations and of the rhetorical problems in their prose.

Unfortunately, there is no reason to assume that ESL writers will acquire the conventions of written academic English without assistance. Because ESL writers often organize and present material in ways that are different from NESs, providing necessary cultural information about the rhetorical organization of U.S. academic expository text and audience expectations of such text will help ESL students' writing be more effective. In other words, teachers must help their ESL writing students acquire appropriate linguistic, content, and rhetorical background knowledge.

For ESL students, then, the composition course is much more than a skills course; it is also a *content* course in which they need to learn about audience and purpose, levels of content specificity, general writing strategies, and academic formats, perhaps for the first time. The students need to know that writing involves not only linguistic processes but social and cognitive processes as well: when it is appropriate to write, what is appropriate to write for an identified audience in a specific situation, and how to organize ideas appropriately for that audience and purpose. In addition, ESL students (and less experienced NES writers as well) need to learn repertoires of strategies to generate ideas, draft pieces of writing, and encounter feedback from peers and teachers. To assist their ESL students toward those goals, composition teachers may well need to be more didactic; certainly they must become cultural informants for their students, by doing all of the following:

- Identifying and explaining the rhetorical and contextual variables in U.S. academic writing

- *Researching* U.S. academic writing assignments and the expectations of the discourse communities that design, assign, and evaluate those assignments

- Investigating and discussing the writing conventions of U.S. academic discourse genres

- Providing opportunities for students to practice and experiment with the rhetoric and language that fulfills the expectations of U.S. academic readers

Recognize that although such differences between ESL and NES writers may affect communication in a U.S. academic discourse community, they should not be stigmatized as deficiencies. As Alan Purves and his colleagues reported, differences among rhetorical patterns do not represent differences in cognitive ability but rather differences in cognitive style [22]. After all, arrangement and presentation of ideas, as well as style, can all be defined, practiced, and valued in many ways. However, ESL writers (like NESs) must acquire the background knowledge necessary to identify and fulfill the expectations of the U.S. academic audience; knowledge about appropriate language use, content, and genre can empower ESL students.

Accuracy, Fluency, and the Issue of Error

Teachers of ESL writers will almost certainly face student essays with linguistic and rhetorical problems that are related to the first languages of the students or "developmental" problems that are the result of limitations in students' previous education. Barbara Kroll describes a useful way in which ESL writing proficiency can be broadly divided into categories: *plus-syntax* and *minus-syntax, plus-rhetoric* and *minus-rhetoric* [17]. "One paper can provide insightful commentary on a substantive topic while replete with problems in spelling and punctuation [+rhetoric and –syntax]. Another paper can exhibit wide range of sentence structures, flawless syntax, adherence to mechanics, yet lack development and support of its central thesis [–rhetoric and +syntax]." Still another paper may be hard to read because it contains both second-language errors and a lack of coherence [–rhetoric and –syntax]. In terms of the two broad categories of ESL students described in this essay, typical international student ("eye" learner) writing, will demonstrate limited coherence, particularly a limited knowledge of academic forms and audience expectations [–rhetoric]. In contrast, typical resident student ("ear" learner) writing will often demonstrate some knowledge of expected U.S. rhetorical forms and fluency but may also contain many language errors [–syntax].

The perceived dichotomy between fluency and accuracy has been discussed in language teaching for decades: Should the language teacher concentrate on one or the other? Traditionally, accuracy has been defined as the focus on discrete elements of the rules of language, while fluency has been defined as the focus on the communication of ideas without consideration of discrete language elements. This is probably a false dichotomy. A focus on fluency does not necessarily exclude consideration of the systematic properties of language; after all, it is not possible to communicate successfully without some knowledge and monitoring of the language of the message. Similarly, a focus on accuracy demands concentration on discrete points of language but does not necessarily curb creativity and self-expression, ignore cognitive processes, or overlook personality traits of the learner.

At the basis of the accuracy-fluency controversy is the question of error. Once thought to be deviant behavior, error—in both first- and second-language acquisition—is now regarded as a natural phenomenon. Research has demonstrated clearly that ESL errors are generally neither random nor sporadic nor deviant. Instead, they are systematic, regular, and rule-governed, the result of intelligence, not stupidity. ESL errors come from a conscious or unconscious attempt by students to use what they have learned.

The Foundations of Error

Of course, errors in written language can be due to inattention, memory lapse, or indifference. Moreover, in an in-class writing situation, NESs as well as ESL students will make hasty "performance errors" that they may have neither the time nor the ability to monitor. More serious errors that interfere with clear communication are unacceptable in both NES and ESL writing. However, an understanding of the logical bases for second-language error in writing may mitigate the visceral reaction that excludes other components of the student writing.

For many ESL "ear" learners, error can occur as a result of often unconscious rule formation that is based on their oral-aural experiences or of their misinterpretation of a rule half-learned. Some of these "rules" may be partially correct; others may be incorrect. Following are examples of incorrect "rules" cited by U.S. resident ESL students:

- Capitalize all nouns.
- Always put a comma after *but*.
- All the verbs in a paragraph have to be in the same tense.

In addition, these oral-aural acquirers of English often mix formal and informal language and use ear-based (phonetic) spellings that may involve, say, omitting verb inflections. Here are some examples, with informal language in **boldface** and incorrect spelling/word forms in *italics*:

> Young folks usually get a better **kick out of** trips than older people.
> It is imperative to **hang around** a large number of **kids.**
> They will want to **take off ASAP**.
> The students are *taken* their time.
> Some of the reasons *while* **guys** *getting* jobs.
> Students are *awared* of these matters.

In many ways, these "ear" learners are doubly disadvantaged in their writing. First, because their "eye" study of English has been limited, they may not have the necessary background knowledge to frame the structures of the language or even to talk about and understand the structures they are using. In addition, the "rules" they have used to categorize their language experiences must be analyzed, "unlearned," then relearned and habituated, a time-consuming and often frustrating experience.

Many NESs have experienced the process of unlearning and relearning a language structure on a much smaller scale. Consider the NES child raised in a relatively standard American English atmosphere who, as an adult and an English teacher, learns that she uses one English structure incorrectly: *lay/lie*. Having habituated that error for a quarter of a century, she spends the next twenty-five years "monitoring" for that error, thinking about the rules governing *lay* and *lie* before she uses those words, "unlearning," relearning, practicing, and, more often than not, avoiding that structure. Such habituated or "fossilized" language behavior, whether a single grammatical structure or an inappropriate oral response, are easy to identify but difficult to monitor, and that behavior is nearly impossible to change permanently, at least in a short period of time. For the ESL student (and especially for the "ear" learner), with not one but dozens of habituated language errors, writing flawless English prose is at best an overwhelming prospect.

Yet for many international students, grammatical error may come not so much from unconscious rule formation as from overgeneralization of rules they have learned through their eyes. That is, international ESL students may hypothesize, consciously or subconsciously, about a language form by extending the use of a rule they have learned in the second language. For instance, if the rule says that third-person singular verbs must take an *-s* ("he *runs*"), ESL students may overgeneralize the rule to include second-person singular verbs ("you *runs*"). The hypothesis is incorrect, but it does reflect the systematic application of a rule. In these cases, students who can identify or monitor for language errors can learn to reformulate new hypotheses and adopt new learning strategies to correct the errors.

When ESL students who have studied the structure of English encounter a language form, they often infer rules from previous knowledge of their first language; they "transfer" that knowledge into a hypothesis about the second language. For that reason, students from the same language background may well make some of the same types of errors, though their hypotheses (and therefore the resulting language) may not be exactly the same. For example, native speakers of Spanish may use adjectives that have both gender and number and that follow, rather than precede, the verb ("the flowers *reds*") because those rules apply in Spanish.* Such first-language transfer occurs not only with grammatical structures but with first-language writing skills and strategies as well; ESL writers often transfer both good and weak writing skills from their first language into English, and many ESL students who have not developed good strategies for writing in their first language will not have appropriate strategies to transfer to their second language.

Next, if a language rule is particularly obscure, complex, or difficult, students may make errors as they attempt to construct the language form, or they may avoid the form altogether. For example, why is one of these sentences incorrect?

- People, who are against the English-only movement, might say that . . .
- Anne, who is against the English-only movement, might say that . . .

Level of difficulty is a complicated concept, for it is in part dependent on both first-language differences and prior stu-

---

*For more information about contrastive analysis of grammatical differences between English and other languages, see [25] and [26].

dent experience. For example, while English is a subject-verb-object (SVO) language, Korean is a subject-object-verb (SOV) language, and word order is relatively free. A sentence in English, translated into Korean and then retranslated, word for word, into English, shows the differences:

English: Even though I told John not to take the chemistry class, he took it.

Korean: Even though I John chemistry class not to take told, John it took.

In addition to word order, many Asian languages are "tonal." That is, they have few or no inflections (such as verb tense and plural markers). Chinese, for instance, is a language that has no verb tenses and no articles; learning the complex rules for English verb tenses is an enormous task, and implementing those rules expands the task geometrically. Article use in English is often arbitrary and filled with exceptions; consequently, correct use of articles for an ESL student whose native language does not have articles is extremely difficult. For instance, try formulating the rules needed for the following examples, and consider the consequent decisions Asian ESL students must make. (X) indicates that no article is needed.

She considered him (a) genius.
(X) (The) number seven is lucky.
(The) only girl at (the) party was Nan.
(A/The) funny picture on (a/the) page

going to (a/the) church	versus	going to (X) church
going to (a/the) store	versus	going (X) (X) home
going on (a/the) journey	versus	going to (X) work

Some English-language structures are more difficult for learners of one second language than another. For Arabic speakers, relative clauses are easier to use than auxiliary verbs in English because relative clauses in Arabic parallel use in English (though in Arabic, the relative clause requires the use of a personal pronoun, resulting in such structures as "The man who likes coffee *he* . . ."). In contrast, there are no auxiliary verbs in Arabic, so a structure like "She *taking* a class" is a common error. And native Chinese speakers tend to avoid relative clauses in their writing because that structure does not occur in their language. In short, ESL students are similar to NES students of foreign languages: nativelike accuracy in nonnative-language writing is a lifelong struggle, so both students and their teachers must expect language errors in student writing.

Finally, because most international ("eye" learner) students have had many opportunities to practice written English at the single-sentence level but only limited practice with writing English in extended discourse, they will discover that they make grammatical and sentence structure errors even while they are following their "eye"-learned rules. For example, recent work in genre studies has shown that narrative writing, which occurs history textbooks, research reports, newspaper articles, and in background sections of textbooks in many fields, is usually taught as occurring in the past tense. Yet work by Doug Biber [2], and expanded on by Pat Byrd [3] and Katherine Bardovi-Harling [1], demonstrates that the "backgrounding" in narrative (seen, for instance, in backgrounding and interpretation of the narrative) uses other verb forms, including past perfect and present perfect tenses.

In light of this discussion, teachers should consider the following points:

- Although ESL writing errors rarely approximate those of NESs either in number or in kind, their visibility should not immediately trigger negative responses.

- Looking beyond the irritating errors to rhetorical and contextual successes or problems, as teachers commonly do with NES writing, is essential.

- Habituated errors are difficult for students to see and even more difficult to supplant with habituated correct forms.

- Even ESL student writers who both comprehend and are able to produce correct English grammar and sentence structures in discrete exercises often cannot manage the complexities of language use in extended English discourse.

- Most ESL errors are a normal, natural, and necessary part of the learning process.

Teachers of ESL students who are interested in their students' errors may fruitfully investigate contrastive analysis studies that examine features of a native language (e.g., English) that contrast with features of another language (e.g., Spanish, Japanese) to determine what areas of second-language learning are most likely to cause difficulty for their students [25, 26]. In such an investigation, teachers may well discover that the students themselves are the best sources of contrastive analysis information and, more important, that asking students to analyze (and perhaps to log) their errors may prove beneficial to their learning processes.

Another interesting area for examination is "error gravity" studies, in which researchers investigate the "irritation" or "acceptance" levels of NESs—usually university non-ESL faculty—to specific second-language errors. To help teachers and students prioritize language errors and edit more successfully, error gravity studies focus on what second-language errors either interfere most with NES comprehension or irritate the NES academic reader. For example, Roberta Vann and her colleagues investigated the responses of 164 faculty members to twelve typical ESL errors [27]. They found that most respondents did not judge all errors as equally severe; incorrect word order (as in the direct translation of our sample Korean sentence) and incorrect word use were considered the most serious, and spelling errors the least severe.

Evaluation

Given the problems any second-language learner can have with accuracy in writing the problem of evaluation facing the composition teacher with ESL students is substantial. "Lowering standards" or asking less of ESL student writers is not a viable solution, yet language errors must be seen in perspective: ESL students (and any writers in a second or foreign language) may have adequate knowledge of correct usage but find it difficult to produce accurate prose consistently. There is more, much more, to successful written communication than the use of articles. Liz Hamp-Lyons notes that evaluation works best and is most fair to learners when it takes into account who the learner is, the situation in which the writers produce writing, and the overall context in which educational success is to be measured for the student writer [13].

Therefore, as teachers carefully develop evaluative criteria—as they develop the writing assignment and before they assign the writing—the criteria should be realistically grounded in the discourse communities the students will face outside the classroom. The composition teacher might then consider giving a separate grade for language or perhaps three grades for each assignment: organization, content, and mechanics. Or teachers might even give several grades for each paper in areas of focus for that paper: coherence, use of detail, audience awareness, and so on. Such a grading scheme would allow students to identify their writing strengths and weaknesses more easily. An average of those grades, some of which might be weighted differently, might be the overall grade for the paper. Finally, the evaluative criteria must be explicitly articulated: Students have the right to know the bases on which they are being evaluated.

Moreover, students learn to do best what teachers can demonstrate. Dana Ferris's seminal large-scale study with ESL students and revision indicates that because "a significant proportion of the comments appeared to lead to substantive student revisions" [9], teachers should be careful in develop-

ing their responding strategies, explaining their responding strategies to their students, helping students learn to revise, and holding students accountable for considering feedback they receive. In short, feedback without follow-up (in the form of discussion, practice, and graded revisions) will be less than effective. Researchers Ann Fathman and Elizabeth Whalley [8], as well as Ferris [10], found that students can become independent editors of their own written work when teacher response and intervention during the writing process and teacher correction of error are clear. In other words, the response or correction must adequately describe the problem and then suggest a means of correction. And of course, early intervention and explanation feedback can help students identify and solve language problems before evaluation occurs.

In contrast, in any teacher intervention, marking local (discrete) errors or commenting on global alternatives must occur with consideration of the student and the writing context. For example, marks that do not identify errors are ineffectual; after all, virtually no student intentionally turns in an error-ridden paper for evaluation. For the same reason, comments asking students to "organize" when they think they already have done so are at best confusing for the students. Instead, teachers might begin by marking, but not correcting, language errors and then asking students to distinguish between errors that they immediately recognize (and can therefore monitor) and errorss that they do not recognize (and so need intervention and explanation). Identifying and then prioritizing language errors ("Work on X first because those errors interfere with reader comprehension") can make monitoring for error easier for ESL students.

Next, careful planning of peer response groups and teacher intervention throughout the writing process can help ESL students identify problems and solutions. Conferencing, individually or in small groups, is another intervention technique that can prove useful for ESL students. Lynn Goldstein and Susan Conrad discuss the problems and the benefits of conferencing with ESL students about specific language and rhetorical problems during the drafting process; they advise prior training of students to prepare them for the different role of a conferee, and they agree that successful conferencing can strengthen writing skills and develop independent decision making, so vital in successful writing [11].

Finally, as Rebecca Oxford points out, ESL students (and NESs as well) must be trained in necessary strategies to deal with peer and teacher feedback and to correct their errors and must be given the time to digest appropriately and then to practice corrections [21]. Students must also acquire effective strategies in the processes of composing, drafting, and editing that facilitate student learning. Knowledge of resources other than the teacher (reference books, World Wide Web, interviews and surveys, textbooks, peers, the campus writing center) will enable students to seek help with their academic writing outside of class, even after the course has ended.

Conclusion

Identifying and studying, the differences in communication styles and strategies between cultures is worthwhile, even necessary, for both ESL students and their teachers. The more understanding that exists, the better prepared teachers will be to communicate effectively with their students; the more students understand about those differences, the more easily they will fulfill their academic readers' expectations. Building background knowledge about academic writing can facilitate student success by enabling students to learn the social processes, the appropriate use of language, and the rhetorical conventions for written communication within academic discourse communities.

How teachers focus on ESL students in their classrooms depends, at least in part, on their goals for all students, on how and for whom they want to empower those students. If, as Robert Land and Catherine Whitley suggest, the objective of a composition class, particularly a class with ESL students, is "to acquire enough facility with Standard Written English (SWE) to succeed in school and in the workplace," an effective pedagogy would include teaching composition not only as a skills course but also as a content course [19]. Grabe and Kaplan have indicated that for ESL students, the content of a composition course must include such areas as composing and revision strategies, coherence systems and mechanisms, language features, rhetorical patterns, audience characteristics and expectations, and genre conventions [12].

Annotated Bibliography: Suggested Reading

1. Bardovi-Harling, Katherine. "Tense and Aspect in (Con)Text." *Grammar and Discourse* 3 (1996): 19–33.
2. Biber, Douglas. *Variation across Speech and Writing*. Cambridge: Cambridge UP, 1988.
   For this original research, Biber wrote a computer text analysis program, then gathered a large corpus of spoken and written English. His computer text analysis of this corpus revealed that the grammar of spoken and of written English differs in several ways and that the grammar in each is used in "clusters." For teachers interested in language and genre, an essential book.
3. Brislin, R. W., K. Cushner, C. Cherrie, and M. Yong, *Intercultural Interactions: A Practical Guide*. Newbury Park, CA: Sage, 1986.
   The most practical book in the Sage Series on Cross-Cultural Research and Methodology, this book contains "100 Critical Incidents." Each situation focuses on some common (and perhaps universal) characteristic of interpersonal interaction. Following are essays that integrate and interpret the points made in the critical incidents. Accessible, discussible, and eminently educational.
4. Byrd, Pat, ed. *Teaching across Cultures in the University ESL Program*. Washington, DC: NAFSA, 1986.
   An excellent collection of articles that provides background discussions of relevant issues in cross-cultural communication, useful descriptions of cultural programs developed at several institutions, and explanations of materials and methods developed by individual teachers for use in cross-cultural classrooms.
5. Byrd, Pat, and Joy Reid. *Grammar in the Composition Classroom*. Boston: Heinle and Heinle, 1998.
   Insights into the paradigm that demonstrates grammar *from* context and grammar "clusters," as well as additional information about responding to and evaluating ESL writing, offer teachers both theoretical and practical ideas.
6. Connor, Ulla. *Contrastive Rhetoric: Cross-Cultural Aspects of Second Language Writing*. Cambridge: Cambridge UP, 1996.
   Draws on a wide body of interdisciplinary literature to define and explain contrastive rhetoric. Using a variety of languages, she demonstrates how ESL writers draw on a range of cross-linguistic and cross-cultural influences. Of special interest to teachers of ESL writers are Chapter 2, "Contrastive Rhetoric in Applied Linguistics," and Chapter 8, "Genre-Specific Studies in Contrastive Rhetoric."
7. ———, and Robert B. Kaplan, eds. *Writing across Languages: Analysis of L2 Text*. Reading, MA: Addison-Wesley, 1987.
   Describes the concept of contrastive rhetoric, discusses empirical research in the contrastive rhetoric of many languages with English, and suggests applications of such research in the teaching of ESL writing.
8. Fathman, Ann, and Elizabeth Whalley. "Teacher Response to Student Writing: Focus on Form vs. Content." *Second Language Writing: Research Insights for the Classroom*. Ed. Barbara Kroll. New York: Cambridge UP, 1990. 178–190.
9. Ferris, Dana R. "The Influence of Teacher Commentary on Student Revisions." *TESOL Quarterly* 31 (1997): 315–339.

10. ———. "Student Reactions to Teacher Response in Multiple-Draft Composition Classrooms." *TESOL Quarterly* 29 (1995): 33–53.

11. Goldstein, Lynn M., and Susan M. Conrad. "Student Input and Negotiation of Meaning in ESL Writing Conferences." *TESOL Quarterly* 24 (1990): 441–460.
    A detailed description of an ethnographic study that demonstrated the problems of group work and, particularly, student teacher conferences with ESL students. The authors provide advice and activities for training ESL students to assume appropriate roles in conferences and small group settings.

12. Grabe, William, and Robert B. Kaplan. "Writing in a Second Language: Contrastive Rhetoric." *Richness in Writing: Empowering ESL Students*. Ed. D. Johnson and D. Roen. New York: Longman. 263–283.
    In this article (in a book that contains many valuable articles about teaching ESL writing), the authors summarize and synthesize prior and current research in contrastive rhetoric, then detail suggestions for raising awareness and informing teachers about the fundamentals of contrastive rhetoric. In addition, they offer specific pedagogical advice for teaching writing to ESL students from different language and cultural backgrounds.

13. Hamp-Lyons, Liz, ed. *Assessing ESL Writing in Academic Contexts*. Norwood, NJ: Ablex, 1992.
    This collection of articles written by the growing number of researchers in ESL testing, focuses on the testing of ESL writing. It follows a clear, carefully written explanation of the issues in this research area; the assessment issues discussed range from validity questions concerning commercial writing tests to practical questions concerning classroom testing. Other issues discussed include cross cultural assessment, academic literacy, criteria and scoring models, needs assessment, and models of feedback.

14. Johnson, K. *Understanding Communication in Second Language Classrooms*. Cambridge: Cambridge UP, 1995.
    Using data from authentic classroom discourse, Johnson examines teacher-student interaction from both teacher and learner perspectives. By investigating classroom dynamics, teachers can recognize the patterns of culturally based classroom communication and the effect these patterns have on second-language learning.

15. Kaplan, Robert B., ed. *Annual Review of Applied Linguistics, 1982*. Rowley, MA: Newbury House, 1983.
    The third volume of the series is directed toward studies related to written text, more specifically to rhetorical differences between English and such languages as German, Hindi, Korean, Mandarin, and Marathi. Kaplan introduces the collection and provides an integrative essay in conclusion.

16. ———. "Cultural Thought Patterns in Intercultural Education." *Language Learning* 16 (1966): 1–20.
    Kaplan's seminal article on contrastive rhetoric has influenced a generation of researchers. Though not empirically based, it provided the basis for understanding the principles of the body of research that followed.

17. Kroll, Barbara. "The Rhetoric-Syntax Split: Designing a Curriculum for ESL Students." *Journal of Basic Writing* 9 (1990): 40–55.

18. ———, ed. *Second Language Writing: Research Insights for the Classroom*. New York: Cambridge UP, 1990.
    This seminal collection of thirteen articles is addressed to teachers in training and to experienced teachers in the field of ESL teaching as well. The first of two sections presents "the current state of thinking on what the teaching of writing to normative speakers entails"; the second presents a "variety of specific studies, each focused on a different aspect of writing and/or the writing classroom."

19. Land, Robert, and Catherine Whitley. "Evaluating Second Language Essays in Regular Composition Classes: Toward a Pluralistic Society." *Richness in Writing: Empowering ESL Students*. Ed. D. Johnson and D. Roen. New York: Longman, 1989. 284–293.

20. Leki, Ilona. *Understanding ESL Writers: A Guide for Teachers*. New York: St. Martin's, 1992.
    Written particularly for NES teachers of NES freshman English classes in which there are ESL students, the focus of this book is on immigrant students rather than international students. Their problems with reading and writing, and the problems faced by their teachers, are discussed in clear and cogent detail, with practical suggestions offered that are based on second-language acquisition research and composition theory.

21. Oxford, Rebecca L. *Language Learning Strategies: What Every Teacher Should Know*. Boston: Newbury House, 1990.
    Oxford bases her practical suggestions in this volume on theory and fieldwork that she explains with clarity and simplicity. Her objective is to train teachers to train students to be more successful language learners by learning about, experimenting with, and practicing learning strategies. Especially useful for composition teachers of ESL students.

22. Purves, Alan, ed. *Writing across Languages and Cultures: Issues in Contrastive Rhetoric*. Newbury Park, CA: Sage, 1988.
    The collection of research articles from scholars of several countries addresses the issue of cultural expectations in the assessment of ESL writing. How these writers deviate from the norms of the foreign culture in the kinds of material they choose, the style, and the organization of their prose is examined.

23. Samovar, Richard, and Larry Porter, eds. *Intercultural Communication: A Reader*. 6th ed. Belmont, CA: Wadsworth, 1991.
Interesting and informative articles by a large number of international educators in the field of cross-cultural communication. Each chapter examines current issues in the field, on such wide-ranging topics as the sociocultural necessity of effective communication, the impact of Confucianism in East Asia, Arabic concepts of effective persuasion, and the cultural patterns of the Masai.

24. Swales, John. *Genre Analysis: English in Academic and Research Settings*. Cambridge: Cambridge UP, 1990.
Focuses on rhetorical conventions and discourse styles employed in various academic settings and how such norms are effectively taught to NES and ESL writers. Swales analyzes specific text types, specifically research-related genres, and addresses the pedagogic issues involved in preparing students to achieve the purposes of each for its intended audience.

25. Swan, M., and B. Smith, eds. *Learner English: A Teacher's Guide to Interference and Other Problems*. Cambridge: Cambridge UP, 1987.

26. *Thirteen Language Profiles: Practical Application of Contrastive Analysis for Teachers of English as a Second Language*. Vancouver, BC: Vancouver Community College English Language Training Night School, 1983.
Presents the basics of thirteen languages in sections that range from borrowed vocabulary and potential phonology problems for speakers of that language who are learning English to the written script and writing problems that those students might have. Very easy to understand and very worthwhile reading for teachers of ESL writers.

27. Vann, Roberta, D. E. Meyer, and F. D. Lorenz. "Error Gravity: A Study of Faculty Opinion of ESL Errors." *TESOL Quarterly* 18 (1984): 427–440.
One of the first empirical studies to examine the response of university faculty to ESL essay errors. The authors clearly describe the research methods, and the results have been widely used to prioritize error monitoring in ESL writing.

FIFTH EDITION

SIMON & SCHUSTER HANDBOOK FOR WRITERS

Lynn Quitman Troyka

PRENTICE HALL
Upper Saddle River, New Jersey 07458

Library of Congress Cataloging-in-Publication Data

Troyka, Lynn Quitman
    Simon and Schuster handbook for writers/Lynn Quitman Troyka.—5th ed.
      p. cm.
    Includes indexes
    ISBN 0–13–079783–9 (case)
      1. English language—Rhetoric—Handbooks, manuals, etc.
      2. English language—Grammar—Handbooks, manuals, etc.   I. Title.
PE1408.T696   1999
808'.042—dc21   98-24398
                                                          CIP

Editorial Director: Charlyce Jones Owen
Editor in Chief: Leah Jewell
Senior Development Editor: Joyce Perkins
Assistant Vice President of Humanities and Social Science: Barbara Kittle
Senior Managing Editor: Bonnie Biller
Senior Project Manager: Shelly Kupperman
Manufacturing Manager: Nick Sklitsis
Prepress and Manufacturing Buyer: Mary Ann Gloriande
Creative Design Director: Leslie Osher
Interior and Cover Designer: Ximena P. Tamvakopoulos
Manager, Production Services: John J. Jordan
Electronic Page Layout: Lori Clinton
Art: Mirella Signoretto, Michael D'Angelo
Marketing Director: Gina Sluss
Editorial Assistant: Patricia Castiglione

For permission to use copyrighted material, grateful acknowledgment is made to the copyright holders on pages xxvii-xxviii, which is considered an extension of this copyright page.

This book was set in 10/11 New Caledonia by Prentice Hall Production Services and printed and bound by World Color. The cover was printed by The Lehigh Press, Inc.

10   9   8   7   6   5   4   3   2   1

ISBN 0-13-079783-9 (student version)
ISBN 0-13-095512-4 (professional version)

Prentice-Hall International (UK) Limited, *London*
Prentice-Hall of Australia Pty. Limited, *Sydney*
Prentice-Hall Canada Inc., *Toronto*
Prentice-Hall Hispanoamericana, S.A., *Mexico*
Prentice-Hall of India Private Limited, *New Delhi*
Prentice-Hall of Japan, Inc., *Tokyo*
Simon & Schuster Asian Pte. Ltd., *Singapore*
Editora Prentice-Hall do Brasil, Ltda., *Rio de Janeiro*

CONTENTS

Contents

PART TWO: UNDERSTANDING GRAMMAR AND WRITING CORRECT SENTENCES   157

7   Parts of Speech and Sentence Structures   158

PARTS OF SPEECH   158

SENTENCE STRUCTURES   167

8   Verbs   183

Contents

Contents

Contents

Contents

PART SEVEN: WRITING WHEN ENGLISH IS A SECOND LANGUAGE 717

Contents

PREFACE

TO INSTRUCTORS

In the *Simon & Schuster Handbook for Writers*, Fifth Edition, my stance toward students remains as it has been always. I consider students emerging writers who deserve clarity of information, unwavering support from teachers, and enduring respect as they practice writing. Central to this stance is my belief that knowledge empowers. I disagree with those who claim that students today are easily intimidated by the challenge of learning. In my experience with successive editions of the *Simon & Schuster Handbook for Writers*, as long as content is carefully crafted to be clear, direct, and reasonable in pace, students heartily enjoy diving in.

My vision for the *Simon & Schuster Handbook for Writers* is that it serve simultaneously as classroom text, as a source for self-instruction, and as a comprehensive reference volume. I have composed it with students in mind to help them succeed in college, in their careers, and during their personal pursuits. Students can use it to remind themselves of what they already know. They can use it to teach themselves new information they need. And they can use it to immerse themselves in the habits of mind that develop dramatically when people write, read, and reflect critically. Such habits greatly increase all people's chances to fulfill their academic, business, and personal potentials.

Scholarship and theory-based practice for teachers of writing and rhetoric are quite advanced today compared to fifty years ago when handbooks for writers began to gain popularity. In the *Simon & Schuster Handbook for Writers*, Fifth Edition, I frankly ignore fads and include only major contributions that have emerged time-proven in rhetoric, composing processes, and language.

I now list here the core elements that I have retained from earlier versions of the *Simon & Schuster Handbook for Writers* that teachers and students have told me they find especially helpful, along with material that is newly central to the enterprise of teaching and learning writing.

- The *Handbook* starts with six chapters about the whole essay, thus establishing contexts for writing. The ensuing chapters build upon these contexts.

- It sets the scene with a short first chapter about purposes and audiences for writing. *NEW* for this edition are expanded discussions of tone and of using outside sources for writing (linked explicitly to detailed discussion of source-based writing throughout the book). Also, *NEW* for this edition, peer response groups are discussed in detail as audience for writing. And also *NEW* for this edition are explicit directions for engaging in collaborative writing activities.

- It explains that the writing process is rarely linear and varies always with the writer, the topic, and the writing situation.

- It illustrates the variety of writing processes and purposes with four complete student essays. The essay with an informative purpose, on women pumping iron, is shown in three drafts, complete with the student's and the instructor's comments on interim drafts.

- It engages in an extensive discussion of critical thinking related to writing (Chapter 5). It includes a specific sequence for critical thinking; it differentiates the separate processes of summary and synthesis, offers concrete advice on reading closely, and is linked to guidance on writing critically in response to a source. (This last process is illustrated with a student's critical response essay based on an outside source synthesized with her own thinking.)

- It devotes an entire chapter to writing argument, with two student essays, each taking a different position on the same topic. Both the classical model and the Toulmin model for argument are explained and linked to the student essays.

- It covers all topics of grammar, style, language, punctuation, and mechanics, with explanations and examples to facilitate visual as well as verbal learning. Focus on Revising sections apply concepts of revision to selected matters of grammar and style.

- It explains research writing as three processes: conducting research, understanding the results of that research, and writing a paper based on that understanding. Critical thinking and reading are consistently and explicitly integrated into the research process. *NEW* for this edition is extensive information on using and documenting online sources, on evaluating the relative value (or lack thereof) of different types of online offerings, and on using search engines for the World Wide Web.

- It presents three different "search strategies" for planning and executing a research project.

- It includes, *NEW* for this edition, an all-new student research paper in MLA style (in Chapter 34) on "multiple intelligences" that draws not only on print sources but also on electronic and online sources. Commentary accompanies the paper the student's "process notes" on pivotal points in her decision making along the way.

- It contains an MLA-style research paper (in Chapter 37) in literary analysis.

- It presents an APA-style research paper, with a narrative of the student's research and writing processes.

- It offers, *NEW* for this edition, vastly expanded coverage of online documentation in MLA style and in APA style in line with the latest 1998 MLA and APA guidelines.

- It covers four major documentation styles comprehensively: MLA, APA, CM (*Chicago Manual*), and CBE.

- It includes five chapters on writing across the curriculum. Writing about literature is illustrated with three complete student essays, one each on fiction, drama, and poetry. The last is a literary research paper.

- It addresses students for whom English is a second language, offering ESL Notes throughout the text to augment six chapters on matters that deserve longer discussion.

In writing the *Simon & Schuster Handbook for Writers*, Fifth Edition, I have sought to be inclusive of all people. Role stereotyping and sexist language are avoided; *man* is never used generically for the human race (the few exceptions are in quotations from published writers); male and female writers are represented equally in examples; and many ethnic groups are represented in the mix of student and professional writing examples.

To unify this *Handbook* and to avoid its being a grab bag of isolated components, the function of context in writing situations is emphasized. With a very few exceptions, the exercises contain connected discourse rather than random sentences. This helps when students work the exercises because they can experience what writers face when they revise and edit. The content of the exercises, drawn from subjects across the curriculum, is chosen for its intrinsic interest. Similarly, most clusters of examples have related contents so that students can focus on the instruction instead of being distracted by a new topic with each new example.

Also, because students today are strongly visual, this Fifth Edition of the *Handbook* has new features to help students find the information they need more easily than ever before. First among these new features is color coding. Each part of the *Handbook* has a distinctive color bar on the top of its pages. A key to these colors appears on the back cover, and both the Overview of Contents inside the front cover and the longer Contents that starts on page iii reinforce this intuitive location aid. Colors help memory work efficiently: For example, green is the color of the writing process section and red is the color of the research section. Another application of color to help you occurs in Chapter 33, on documentation: Each documentation style has its own special color running along the outside edges of the pages.

Charts and other visual displays have been an important feature of my *Handbook* since the First Edition, and in this Fifth Edition, the charts have a new look. Icons help students identify chart types: for summaries of information, for checklists, and for grammatical and other language patterns.

In addition, the *Simon & Schuster Handbook for Writers*, Fifth Edition, draws on research findings concerning cognition and learning by employing these aids:

- An ALERT system makes students aware of small matters in larger contexts. For example, a brief Punctuation Alert in an explanation of coordination puts into context a particular function of a comma. Full coverage of topics distilled in Alerts completes this dual-entry system, to help students handle the interplay of variables during writing.

- Small capital letters are used for all terms that are defined in the Terms Glossary. This identification feature allows students to concentrate on the material at hand, with the assurance that they can easily locate a definition they might need.

- Inside the back cover, a guide on how to use the *Handbook* leads students through four steps for locating information, as well as visually displaying *Handbook* page elements.

- Response symbols, at the back of the *Handbook*, include symbols to praise good students writing in addition to the traditional correction symbols.

In closing, a memory: As an undergraduate, I never encountered a handbook for writers. Questions about writing (yes, including grammar, punctuation, and usage) nagged at me, but I limped along relying on my less-than-precise ear, not daring to reveal my ignorance of—or worse, my interest in—such matters. When one day in the library at my graduate school, I discovered a dusty volume that could begin to answer my questions, I treasured it. Then, a few years later, I began to see new handbooks in bookstores. I'd browse through them happily, sometimes to locate specific information and sometimes to enjoy simply rooting around their pages. I could not have imagined than that I might someday set my hand to composing such a book. Now that I have completed the *Simon & Schuster Handbook for Writers*, Fifth Edition, I am amazed that I ever had the audacity to start. This proves, it seems to me, that anyone can write. The trick is to begin. In that spirit, I hope that students and colleagues alike will consider this *Handbook* an evolving text. All are welcome to join in the conversation its pages seek to invite.

TO STUDENTS

You, along with each student I have ever taught in my writing classes, were in my mind's eye as I wrote this *Simon & Schuster Handbook for Writers*, Fifth Edition. I want you to have uncomplicated, yet complete, explanations; contexts to enjoy (sometimes even smile at) the examples and exercises; and a format for easy access to the information you want each time you consult the book's pages. If I have succeeded, I hope you will keep your copy of my *Handbook* as a reference source throughout your college years and the rest of your life.

This is a thick book. Few people read it straight through from beginning to end. They browse. To help you dive into my pages, I suggest you become familiar with the contents by scanning the Overview of Contents on the inside front cover or the Contents list before this Preface or the detailed Index. Practice with different topics until the process is easy for you.

Also, browse through the section of this Preface that I wrote for your instructors. Note especially the explanation of the *Handbook*'s color coding. As you begin to identify the contents of the book with the color of the part, I believe you will discover that you have an easy-to-remember system for navigating through the book.

Also note the explanation of the small capital letters. When a term is used but not defined, it is printed in small capital letters to signal that you can find its definition in the Terms Glossary. (The Terms Glossary begins on page 778.) This feature helps you move through material with the confidence that you have easy access to the meaning of unfamiliar terms.

For more guidance on how to use this *Handbook* and its other features, turn to the inside back cover.

I am aware, my friends, that the course for which you have bought this book can greatly influence your future. Keep the book close at hand in your permanent library, along with a dictionary. Writing is a skill you need for whatever career path and life journey you pursue. I hope these pages prove to be your trusted companions and friendly resources for many years. If you would like to be in touch with me through e-mail, please write me at this address:

LQTBOOK@aol.com

Lynn Quitman Troyka

ACKNOWLEDGMENTS

Among my greatest pleasures in acknowledging others is to thank all the students who gave me permission to show their writing as exemplary models in the *Simon &Schuster Handbook for Writers*, Fifth Edition. Each is now officially a "published writer." My congratulations. I also thank the hundreds of students who have met with me in groups or who have written me to share their experiences with, and suggestions for, my handbooks. I take their words very seriously, and whatever flaws remain on these pages are my doing, not theirs.

During my composing of some specific sections of this edition of the *Handbook*, I was privileged to draw on the expertise of stellar people. Paulette Smith, Reference Librarian, Valencia Community College, tutored me in literate use of electronic databases, including those online; and then with wisdom and a finely tuned sense of what helps students find, evaluate, and use online sources, she oversaw the update of my chapters on research processes. Lisa Lavery, a journalism major in college and currently a law student, used her special flair for writing and her eye for topics that appeal to students to draft new content for some of the "connected discourse" exercises in this edition. Cy Strom, Colborne Communications Center, also wrote first-rate exercises for this edition, and Andrew Roney skillfully put the finishing touches on the collection. Bradley Bleck at the University of Nevada helped with computer tips.

Other valued colleagues whose excellent contributions are carried over from previous editions are Don Jay Coppersmith, Internet Consultant; Jo Ellen Coppersmith, Utah Valley State College, who offered outstanding material on critical thinking and research writing; Michael J. Freeman, Director of the Utah Valley State College Library; Scott Leonard, Youngstown State University, adviser on drafting and revision; Darlene Malaska, Youngstown Christian University, adviser on the critical response essay; Mary Ruetten and Barbara Gaffney, University of New Orleans, advisers on ESL; and Matilda Delgado Saenz, adviser on the Toulmin model for argument. To these major advisers to the prior editions, I renew my gratitude: Ann B. Dobie, University of Southwestern Louisiana; Dorothy V. Lindman, Brookhaven College; Alice Maclin, DeKalb College; and Patricia Morgan, Louisiana State University.

Behind the pages of this edition reside many voices of wise colleagues. I am particularly grateful to members of the Regional Advisory Boards for Prentice Hall and Lynn Troyka, who set aside precious days in their busy lives to discuss key issues with me. In the Southeast, they are Peggy Jolly, University of Alabama at Birmingham; Stephen Prewitt, David Lipscomb University; Mary Anne Reiss, Elizabethtown Community College; Michael Thro, Tidewater Community College at Virginia Beach; and Sally Young, University of Tennessee at Chattanooga. In the Southwest, they are Jon Bentley, Albuquerque Technical-Vocational Institute; Kathryn Fitzgerald, University of Utah; Maggy Smith, University of Texas at El Paso; Martha Smith, Brookhaven College; Donnie Yeilding, Central Texas College. In Florida they are Kathleen Bell, University of Central Florida; David Fear, Valencia Community College; D. J. Henry, Daytona Beach Community College; Marilyn Middendorf, Embry Riddle University; Phillip Sipiora, University of South Florida; and Valerie Zimbaro, Valencia Community College.

My thanks to reviewers for the current edition, whose thoughtful comments are of immeasurable value: Judith A. Burnham, Tulsa Community College; Marilyn M. Cleland, Purdue University, Calumet; Carol L. Gabel, William Paterson College; Julie Hagemann, Purdue University, Calumet; Michael J. Martin, Illinois State University; Rosemary G. Moffett, Elizabethtown Community College; Nancy B. Porter, West Virginia Wesleyan College; Eileen B. Seifert, DePaul University; William P. Weiershauser, Iowa Wesleyan College; and Joe Wenig, Purdue University.

My special thanks go to an eminent group of colleagues who contributed to the *Annotated Instructor's Edition of the Simon & Schuster Handbook for Writers*, Fifth Edition: Valerie P. Zimbaro, Valencia Community College; Catherine L. Hobbs, University of Oklahoma; Irwin Weiser, Purdue University; Margot I. Soven, La Salle University; Joy Reid, University of Wyoming; and D. J. Henry, Daytona Beach Community College.

Over the course of my writing the prior edition of the *Handbook*, the reviews of many colleagues helped me draft and revise. I renew my thanks to all of them, including Nancy Westrich Baker, Southeast Missouri State University; Norman Bosley, Ocean Community College; Phyllis Brown, Santa Clara University; Robert S. Caim, West Virginia University at Parkersburg; Joe R. Christopher, Tarleton State University; Thomas Copeland, Youngstown State University; Joanne Ferreira, State University of New York at New Paltz and Fordham University; Michael Goodman, Fairleigh Dickinson University; Mary Multer Greene, Tidewater Community College at Virginia Beach; John L. Hare, Montgomery College; Lory Hawkes, DeVry Institute of Technology, Irving; Janet H. Hobbs, Wake Technical Community College; Frank Hubbard, Marquette University; Rebecca Innocent, Southern Methodist University; Ursula Irwin, Mount Hood Community College; Denise Jackson, Southeast Missouri State University; Margo K. Jang, Northern Kentucky University; Myra Jones, Manatee Community College; Judith C. Kohl, Dutchess Community College; James C. McDonald, University of Southwestern Louisiana; Susan J. Miller, Santa Fe Community College; Jon F. Patton, University of Toledo; Pamela T. Pittman, University of Central Oklahoma; Kirk Rasmussen, Utah Valley State College; Edward J. Reilly, St. Joseph's College; Peter Burton Ross, University of the District of Columbia; Eileen Schwartz, Purdue University at Calumet; Lisa Sebti, Central Texas College; John S. Shea, Loyola University at Chicago; Tony Silva, Purdue University; Bill M. Stiffler, Harford Community College; Jack Summers, Central Piedmont Community College; Vivian A. Thomlinson, Cameron University; Carolyn West, Daytona Beach Community College; and Roseanna B. Whitlow, Southeast Missouri State University.

At Prentice Hall/Simon & Schuster, many people contribute their outstanding talents to the *Simon & Schuster Handbook for Writers*. Joyce Perkins, Senior Development Editor, who oversaw book development and project coordination, once again has provided a smart eye for detail. Leah Jewell, Editor in Chief for English, joined our team for the Fifth Edition as a major force for lively ideas and rigorous thinking. Shelly Kupperman, Senior Project Manager, attended to myriad details with quiet, relentless dedication, skill, and warmth. Shelly and Bonnie Biller, Senior Managing Editor, in addition to their intelligent and painstaking production work, provided matchless copyediting and proofreading professionals, Bruce Emmer and Diane Garvey Nesin. Lori Clinton, Production Services, worked tirelessly as expert compositor, formatter, and problem solver. Creative Design Director Leslie Osher used her usual fine aesthetic to supervise all aspects of cover and page design. Designer Ximena P. Tamvakopoulos managed with great intelligence to translate onto paper the vision that I and others at Prentice Hall had for the Fifth Edition. A topnotch person officially located in the Marketing Department served as an important de facto member of our editorial team: Gina Sluss, Director of Marketing. Others at Prentice Hall who inspired me and gave generously of their time include J. Phillip Miller, President of Humanities and Social Sciences; Charlyce Jones Owen, Editorial Director; Bud Therien, Publisher for Art and Music; and Patricia Castiglione, Editorial Assistant.

In my personal life, I am blessed with dear friends and wonderful family. Ida Morea, my Administrative Assistant and friend, daily enhances my work with her lovely warmth, conscientiousness, and excellence. Family members whose love I treasure always include my late parents, Belle and Sidney Quitman; my sister, Edith Klausner; my sister-in-law and brother-in-law Rita and Hy Cohen; my niece, Randi Klausner Friedman, and nephews, Michael and Steven Klausner; and my first cousins, Alan and Lynne Furman and Elaine Gilden Dushoff; Martha and Chuck Schliefer; Zina Rosenthal; and Tzila and Gideon Zwas. Indispensable to my well-being are my great pals Susan Bartlestone; Kristen Black; Dan, Lindsey, and Ryan Black; Elliot Goldhush; Myra Kogen; Lisa Lavery; Jo Ann Lavery; Betty Renshaw; Magdalena Rogalskaja; Shirley and Don Stearns; Marilyn and Ernest Sternglass; Elsie Tischler; and Muriel Wolfe. Above all, I thank my husband David Troyka, my heart's home, my discerning reader, and my dearest friend.

CREDITS

ABOUT THE AUTHOR

Lynn Quitman Troyka earned her Ph.D. at New York University and has taught for many years at the City University of New York (CUNY), including Queensborough Community College, the Center for Advanced Studies in Education at the Graduate School, and the graduate program in Language and Literacy at City College. She also served as Senior Research Associate in the Office of Academic Affairs, CUNY.

Dr. Troyka is an author in composition/rhetoric for the *Encyclopedia of English Studies and Language Arts, Scholastic*, 1993; and in basic writing for the *Encyclopedia of Rhetoric*, 1994. Former editor of the *Journal of Basic Writing*, she publishes in journals such as *College Composition and Communication, College English*, and *Writing Program Administration* and in books from Southern Illinois Press, Random House, and Heinemann/Boynton/Cook. She has conducted seminars at numerous colleges, universities, and national and international meetings.

Dr. Troyka is the author of the *Simon & Schuster Handbook for Writers*, Fifth Edition, Prentice Hall, 1999; *Simon & Schuster Handbook for Writers*, Second Canadian Edition (with Joanne Buckley and David Gates), Prentice Hall Canada, 1999; *Simon & Schuster Quick Access Reference for Writers*, Prentice Hall, 1998; *Simon & Schuster Concise Handbook*, Prentice Hall, 1992; *Structured Reading*, Fifth Edition (coauthored with Joseph Wayne Thweatt), Prentice Hall, 1999; *Steps in Composition*, Seventh Edition (with Jerrold Nudelman),

Prentice Hall, 1999; and the *Simon & Schuster Workbook for Writers*, Fifth Edition, Prentice Hall, 1999. She is coauthor (with John Gerber, Richard Lloyd-Jones et al.) of *A Checklist and Guide for Reviewing Departments of English*, ADE of the Modern Language Association, 1985.

The first elected chair of the Two-Year College English Association (TYCA) of the National Council of Teachers of English (NCTE), Dr. Troyka is also past chair of the Conference on College Composition and Communication (CCCC), of the College Section of NCTE, and of the Writing Division of the Modern Language Association.

Dr. Troyka's personal passions are preserving wildlife, protecting endangered species, and expedition travel. The photograph on page xxix shows Dr. Troyka sitting among penguins on the shores of Antarctica.

"All this information," says Dr. Troyka, "tells what I've done, not who I am. I am a teacher. Teaching is my life's work, and I love it."

For David,
who makes it all incredibly special

PART ONE

WRITING AN ESSAY

When you write an essay, you engage in a process. The parts of that process vary with the writer and the demands of the subject. Part One explains all aspects of the act of writing, and of thinking and reading in relation to writing, so that you can evolve your personal style of composing and thereby become an effective writer.

WEB SITE

English Central is Prentice Hall's Web site for English instructors and their students. English Central offers much general information about English, hyperlinks to interesting and important sites for students and instructors of English composition and literature, and sites for Prentice Hall's major English textbooks. At the Troyka Web site, you will find supplementary resources and activities. These include quotations (twenty-five, with suggestions to students for using them to stimulate writing), practice exercises on key topics, other sample student essays, e-mail contact with the author, and an invitation to students to submit model essays (for Chapters 3 or 6), model paragraphs (for Chapter 4), model research papers (for Chapter 34), and model literature papers (for Chapter 37).

WHAT ELSE?

Strategies and Resources for Teaching Writing with the Simon & Schuster Handbook for Writers, a free 400-page book for faculty who use this handbook, offers specific, practical ways to apply this statement: "But we all know that it is totally unrealistic simply to plunk copies of the handbook down on students' desks and instruct the students to use the handbooks as tools. Few students know how to use a handbook."

WHAT ELSE?

Strategies and Resources, a free 400-page book for faculty who use this handbook, offers specific, practical ways to apply this statement: "You may wish to have students do exercises [provided here] that show them how to locate kinds of information in the handbook."

1

THINKING ABOUT PURPOSES AND AUDIENCES

Why bother to write? In this age of telephones, e-mail, the Internet, computers, and communication satellites, does your ability to write effectively matter? "Yes!" I say—which you probably predicted since you are holding the book I wrote specifically to help student writers become the best they can be. Permit me to explain the reasons that support my resounding yes.

Writing is a way of discovering and learning. Writing gives you unique ways to think through ideas deeply, come to know subjects well, and absorb those subjects into your lifelong store of knowledge. Even thirty years later, many people can recall details about the topics and content of essays they wrote in college, but far fewer people can recall specifics of a classroom lecture or a textbook chapter. By writing, you activate brain processes that help you make connections among your thoughts. Such connecting gives you potential access to the pleasures of "shocks of recognition," moments when suddenly your mind leaps from what you know to what you did not "see" before. This access to new insights and increased knowledge are usually unavailable until the physical act of writing begins.

Writing is a way of thinking and reflecting. Writing helps you clarify your ideas by having to think about them and put them into words. The ability to "think about thinking" belongs uniquely to humans beings. Such reflective thinking permits you to look back at your ideas, reconsider and perhaps rearrange them, and then perhaps revise them in writing—each time getting closer to what you want to say. The writer E. M. Forster said this about writing, thinking, and reflecting: "How can I know what I mean until I've seen what I said?"

Writing is a way of teaching by creating reading for others. Your writing teaches others about your subject. Through writing, you create a permanent record of your ideas for others to read and think about. Reading informs and shapes human thought. In an open, free, democratic society, every person is welcome to write and thereby create reading for others. For such freedom of idea exchange to thrive, writing and reading skills cannot be concentrated in only a select group of people.

All of us need access to the power of the written word. In college, you can exercise that power by writing many different types of assignments. Doing so prepares you for today's highly technological workplace, in which jobs demand reading with understanding and writing with skill when creating documents that range from letters to formal reports. Also, the ability to write well identifies you as an educated person, someone who is well-informed and up-to-date and can be depended on to use language clearly and effectively.

1a Understanding the elements of writing

Four elements define writing: Writing is a way of *communicating* a *message* for a *purpose* to *readers*. **Communicating** in writing means sending a message that has a destination. The **message** of the writing is its content, which originates in your engaging in one or more of the processes of *observing, remembering, reporting, explaining, exploring, interpreting, speculating*, and *evaluating*. **Purposes** for writing can be many, as discussed in section 1b. **Readers,** also called your *audience,* are the destination your writing must reach. Taking readers into account as you write is crucial to your success as a communicator, as explained in section 1c.

1b Understanding purposes for writing

Purposes for writing concern a writer's goals, sometimes called *aims of writing* or *writing intentions.* Purposes for writing originate from the motivating forces behind what is being written. As a student, you might assume that your only purpose for writing is to fulfill a class assignment. The reality is much more complex, however. As a writer in college, you need to consider how the message you seek to communicate meshes not only with the content of your material but also with your underlying purpose for writing it. Four useful categories of purposes, listed in Chart 1, emerge from the analysis of respected writing scholar James Kinneavy.

◉ **Purposes for writing***   **1**

- ■ to express yourself
- ■ to inform a reader
- ■ to persuade a reader
- ■ to create a literary work

*Adapted from ideas that James L. Kinneavy, a modern rhetorician, discusses in *A Theory of Discourse.* 1971. New York: Norton, 1980.

QUOTATION: ON WRITING

The role of writers is not to say what we can all say, but what we are unable to say.

—Anaïs Nin

TEACHING TIP

As a collaborative project, choose a single subject about which your students are likely to have some knowledge (for example, their first experiences at college). Assign to each group an audience to which they will write a letter describing the situation: a parent, a grandparent, a good friend, a sibling, a former teacher, their former high school principal. To get them to think about the different language choices they must use to make a favorable impression on different audiences, it is often very effective to assign groups a comparatively informal, friendly audience first. After they have finished writing to a friend or sibling, have them describe the same event to someone with whom they have a more formal, yet still friendly, relationship—a grandparent, a member of the clergy, a favorite high school teacher. Even without being coached, students will notice the difference that audience makes to word choice, information selection, and tone.

BACKGROUND

A Theory of Discourse by James L. Kinneavy is a classic citation in composition and rhetoric. To this day, many theorists, researchers, and practioners rely on Kinneavy's work. Kinneavy explores the fundamental purposes for which people use language. He explains the centrality of the concept of *purpose* in writing:

> Purpose in discourse is all important. The aim of a discourse determines everything else in the process of discourse. "What" is talked about, the oral or written medium which is chosen, the words and grammatical patterns used—all of these are largely determined by the purpose of the discourse. (48)

Kinneavy is enthusiastic about the potential for composition as a field of scholarship:

The purposes of writing *to express yourself* (see 1b.1) and *to create a literary work* contribute importantly to human thought and culture. These purposes offer you the pleasures of writing for yourself as audience and of creatively composing a work of literature for others to read. In this handbook, I concentrate on the two purposes most prominent and practical in your academic life: *to inform a reader* (see 1b.2) and *to persuade a reader* (see 1b.3). In the service of these purposes, writers can choose among—and even combine—many effective writing strategies. These strategies, discussed in detail in Chapter 4 (especially section 4f), including narrating, describing, illustrating, defining, analyzing and classifying, comparing and contrasting, drawing an analogy, and considering cause and effect.

1b.1 Writing to express yourself

Expressive writing allows you to express your thoughts and feelings. (When expressive writing is intended for public reading, it becomes more like literary writing.) Consider this personal journal entry written by one of the students whose essays appear in Chapter 6. Though this is his private writing, I publish it here with his permission.

> When we lived in Maine, the fall and winter holidays were my touchstones—the calendar moved along in comforting sequence. I wrapped the snow and foods and celebrations around me like a soft blanket. I burrowed in. Now that we live in New Mexico, I don't need that blanket. But I surely do miss it.
>
> —Daniel Casey, student

1b.2 Writing to inform a reader

Informative writing seeks to give information and, often, to explain it. Informative writing can also be called **expository writing** because it expounds on, or sets forth, ideas and facts. Informative writing includes reports of observations, ideas, scientific data, facts, and statistics. It can be found in textbooks, encyclopedias, technical and business reports, nonfiction, newspapers, and magazines.

When writing to inform a reader, you are expected to offer information with a minimum of bias. Your aim is to relay material that can educate. Your goal here is not to persuade your reader. Like all effective teachers, you need to present the information completely, clearly, and accurately. Readers should be able to verify your material by additional reading, talking with others, or personal experiences. Consider this passage that was written to inform readers:

> In 1914 in what is now Addo Park in South Africa, a hunter by the name of Pretorius was asked to exterminate a herd of 140 elephants. He killed all but 20, and those survivors became so cunning at evading him that he was forced to abandon the hunt. The area became a preserve in 1930, and the elephants have been protected ever since. Nevertheless,

elephants now four generations removed from those Pretorius hunted remain shy and strangely nocturnal. Young elephants evidently learn from the adults' trumpeting alarm calls to avoid humans.

—Carol Grant Gould, "Out of the Mouths of Beasts"

This passage is successful because it *communicates* (transmits) a *message* (about young elephants learning to avoid humans) to a *reader* (a person who might become or already is interested in the subject) for a *purpose* (to inform). In this passage, the writer's last sentence states the main idea. The other sentences offer support for the main idea. Chart 2 lists the major features of informative writing.

Checklist for informative writing   2

- Is its major focus the subject being discussed?
- Is its primary purpose to inform rather than persuade?
- Is its information complete and accurate?
- Can its information be verified?
- Is its information arranged for clarity?

1b.3 Writing to persuade a reader

Persuasive writing seeks to convince readers about a matter of opinion. This writing is sometimes called **argumentation** because some forms of it argue a position. (Because the techniques of written argument can be especially demanding on a writer, I devote all of Chapter 6 in this handbook to them.)

When you write to persuade, you deal with the debatable, that which has other sides to it. Persuasive writing seeks to change your reader's mind or at least to bring your reader's point of view closer to yours. Even if you feel quite certain that your reader's position on the subject will never change, you are expected to present your position as convincingly as possible.

How do you persuade convincingly? You go beyond merely stating an opinion. You offer convincing support for that opinion. Such support relies on clear presentation of whatever information (see 1b.2) your reader needs to understand your topic, your position on that topic, and your evidence—such as examples and reasons—that backs up your point of view. Only with support can you hope to convince readers. Examples of persuasive writing include newspaper editorials, letters to the editor, business and research proposals that advocate certain approaches over others, essays of opinion in newspapers and magazines, reviews, sermons, and books that argue a point of view. Consider the following passage, which aims to persuade the reader:

Background (continued)

It is the thesis of this work that the field of composition—or discourse as it will presently be termed—is a rich and fertile discipline with a worthy past which should be consulted before being consigned to oblivion, an exciting present, and a future that seems as limitless as either linguistics or literature. (2)

Other modern influential theorists who concentrate on writers' purposes include the highly respected James Britton, who classifies purposes as *poetic, expressive,* and *transactional.*

More recently, scholars of rhetoric and composition have discussed the problems caused when teachers expect writers always to have a clear purpose in mind before writing. Writers often discover their purpose as they write, and their purpose may change from draft to draft.

BACKGROUND

Writing is sometimes classified according to four modes of discourse: *narration, description, exposition,* and *argumentation.* These modes describe the *what* of writing. They describe characteristics that written products seem to feature, although much overlap exists. A writer can narrate an incident in the service of arguing an opinion; a writer can describe a scene in the service of offering information.

This handbook starts with the *why* of writing. Thus it begins with *purposes* for writing. Purposes are familiar territory for instructors used to modes, because two of the modes are purposes: People write for the purpose of informing (expositing) and for the purpose of persuading (arguing). Purposes are based on the notion that people write for a reason; most college writing is done either to inform or to persuade. Research shows that few writers sit down and say to themselves, "I am going to write a comparison-and-contrast essay"; instead they say to themselves, "I want to give my readers some information" or "I want to convince my readers to change

The search for some biological basis for math ability or disability is fraught with logical and experimental difficulties. Since not all math underachievers are women, and not all women are mathematics-avoidant, poor performance in math is unlikely to be due to some genetic or hormonal difference between the sexes. Moreover, no amount of research so far has unearthed a "mathematical competency" in some tangible, measurable substance in the body. Since "masculinity" cannot be injected into women to test whether or not it improves their mathematics, the theories that attribute such ability to genes or hormones must depend for their proof on circumstantial evidence. So long as about 7 percent of the PhD's in mathematics are earned by women, we have to conclude either that these women have genes, hormones, and brain organization different from those of the rest of us, or that certain positive experiences in their lives have largely undone the negative fact that they are female, or both.

—Sheila Tobias, *Overcoming Math Anxiety*

This passage is successful because it sends a *message* (about math ability and disability) to a *reader* (a person who might become or already is interested in the subject) for a *purpose* (to persuade the reader that math ability or disability is not related to gender). The writer's first sentence summarizes the point of view that she argues in the rest of the paragraph. The other sentences support the writer's assertion. Chart 3 lists the major features of persuasive writing.

 Checklist for persuasive writing 3

- Is its major focus the reader?
- Is its primary purpose to convince rather than inform?
- Does it offer information or reasons to support its point of view?
- Is its point of view based on sound reasoning and logic?
- Are the points of its argument arranged for clarity?
- Does it evoke an intended reaction from the reader?

Background (continued)

BACKGROUND

WHAT ELSE?

ANSWERS: EXERCISE 1-1

A. Dominant purpose is persuasive. It meets the criteria.

B. Dominant purpose is informative. It meets the criteria.

C. Dominant purpose is informative. It meets the criteria.

EXERCISE 1-1

For each paragraph, decide if the dominant purpose is informative or persuasive. Then, answer the questions in Chart 2 or Chart 3 in relation to the paragraph, and explain your answers.

A.   We know very little about pain, and what we don't know makes it hurt all the more. Indeed, no form of illiteracy in the United States is so widespread or costly as ignorance about pain—what it is, what causes it, and how to deal with it without panic. Almost everyone can rattle off the names of at least a dozen drugs that can deaden pain from every conceivable cause—all the way from headaches to hemorrhoids. There is far less knowledge about the fact that about ninety percent of pain is self-limiting, that it is not always an indication of poor health, and that, most frequently, it is the result of tension, stress, idleness, boredom, frustration, suppressed rage, insufficient sleep, overeating, poorly balanced diet, smoking, excessive drinking, inadequate exercise, stale air, or any of the other abuses encountered by the human body in modern society.

—Norman Cousins, Anatomy of an Illness

B.   Efforts to involve the father in the birth process, to enhance his sense of paternity and empowerment as he adjusts to his new role, should be increased. Having the father involved in labor and delivery can significantly increase his sense of himself as a person who is important to his child and to his mate. Several investigators have shown that increased participation of fathers in the care of their babies, increased sensitivity to their baby's cues at one month, and significantly increased support of their wives can result from the rather simple maneuver of sharing the newborn baby's behavior with the new father at three days, using the Neonatal Behavioral Assessment Scale (NBAS). In light of these apparent gains, we would do well to consider a period of paid paternity leave, which might serve both symbolically and in reality as a means of stamping the father's role as critical to his family. Ensuring the father's active participation is likely to enhance his image of himself as a nurturing person and to assist him toward a more mature adjustment in his life as a whole.

—T. Berry Brazelton, "Issues for Working Parents"

C.   After proposing marriage to a neighbor girl, my grandfather used this hammer to build a house for his bride on a stretch of river bottom in northern Mississippi. The lumber for the place, like the hickory for the handle, was cut on his own land. By the day of the wedding he had not quite finished the house, and so right after the ceremony he took his wife home and put her to work. My grandmother had worn her Sunday dress for the wedding, with a fringe of lace tacked on around the hem in honor of the occasion. She removed this lace and folded it away before going out to help my grandfather nail siding on the house. "There she was in her good dress," he told me some fifty-odd years after that wedding day, "holding up them long pieces of clapboard while I hammered, and together we got the place covered up before dark." As the family grew to four, six, eight, and eventually thirteen, my grandfather used this hammer to enlarge his house room by room, like a chambered nautilus expanding its shell.

—Scott Russell Sanders, "The Inheritance of Tools"

ANSWERS: EXERCISE 1-2

For each topic, the student should write one paragraph (or more, according to how you have assigned the exercise) with an informative purpose and one paragraph with a persuasive purpose. The student should also be prepared to discuss (orally or in writing, according to your assignment) the differences in the two treatments of the same topic.

TEACHING TIP

The concept of *audience* is meant to help writers get their message across. The concept is supposed to facilitate, not block. A writer is not expected to tell readers what they want to hear even if the writer disagrees with the readers. A writer is, however, expected to choose words the readers know and to use a tone suitable to the occasion.

You might find that some students feel inhibited when they have to think about an audience for their writing. Studies show that some students misunderstand the concept of *audience*. They think it means that writers should act as if someone is constantly looking over their shoulders. Other students have trouble with the concept of *audience* because they think that they can never say something that would be unpopular with their audience. Some students might not want to admit these or other misunderstandings of the concept, so you might want to clear the matter up without asking anyone to give you their negative impressions. Once you start talking about the subject, you will often find that the students start chiming in to help you get at their concerns.

BACKGROUND

In "What Works for Me: Letters to the Editor" (*Teaching English in the Two-Year College*, February 1994: 45), Keflyn X. Reed describes his requirements that students write letters to the editors of popular magazines and are graded for form and content. (Some letters even get published!)

EXERCISE 1-2

Consulting section 1b, assume that you have to write on each of these topics twice, once to inform and once to persuade your reader: diets, music, modern ways to dress, tourists, good manners. Be prepared to discuss how your two treatments of each topic would differ.

1c Understanding audiences for writing

Readers are the **audience** for your writing. Your ability to reach your intended audience determines how good your writing is. Your writing must show that you are aware of your readers and are trying to reach them. If you write without considering your readers, you risk communicating only with yourself.

To orient yourself to remaining aware of your readers as you write, think about the various reader characteristics listed in Chart 4. In considering who your readers are, think about their backgrounds. A sales report filled with technical language assumes that its readers know the specialized vocabulary. General readers would have trouble understanding such a report. If, however, you rewrote the material without technical terms, general readers could understand it. Similarly, if you want to persuade homemakers to vote for a particular candidate, you would offend your audience if you implied disrespect for people who stay home to raise children.

  Checklist of basic audience characteristics   **4**

Who Are They?

- age, gender
- ethnic backgrounds, political philosophies, religious beliefs
- roles (student, parent, voter, wage earner, property owner, veteran, other)
- interests, hobbies

What Do They Know?

- level of education
- amount of general or specialized knowledge about the topic
- preconceptions brought to the material

If you know or can reasonably assume even a few of the characteristics listed in Chart 4, your chances of reaching your audience improve. And the more explicit your knowledge about your audience, the better your chances to reach it.

1c.1 Understanding the general reading public

The **general reading public** is composed of educated, experienced readers, people who regularly read newspapers, magazines, and books. These readers often have some general information about your subject, but they expect to learn something new or to see the subject from a different perspective during their reading. Advanced technical information, unless you create a firm foundation for presenting it, should be avoided for the general reading public as such readers are not likely to possess specialized knowledge on every subject.

1c.2 Understanding specialists as readers

Specialists are members of the general reading public who have expert knowledge on specific subjects. In writing for specialists, you are expected to realize that your readers have advanced expertise. For example, they may be members of a club devoted to a hobby, such as amateur astronomy or orchid raising. Specialized readers often share more than knowledge: They share assumptions and beliefs. For example, perhaps your readers recently emigrated to the United States from another country and want never to lose their cultural traditions. As a writer for such an audience, you can assume that everyone knows those traditions and cares deeply about them. You do not, therefore, have to give extensive background information. When you write for readers who share specialized knowledge, you need to balance the need to be thorough with the demand to avoid going into too much detail to explain technical terms and special references.

1c.3 Understanding your peers as readers

In some writing classes, instructors divide students into "peer response groups." Such groups usually mean that your fellow students give you feedback on your writing drafts. This arrangement can prove very useful to you, because responses from **peers** allow you to benefit from others' ways of reading your writing—with the added advantage of seeing or hearing other students' writing for the same assignment. (If your instructor does not use peer response groups, check whether you are permitted to ask other students to help you. A fine line exists between giving opinions and doing others' work for them.)

By responding in a peer group, you participate in a respected tradition of colleagues helping colleagues. Professional writers often seek to improve their rough drafts by asking other writers for comments. When you respond as a fellow student writer, you are not expected to be an expert. Rather, you can offer valuable responses as a practiced reader and as a fellow writer who understands what other writers in your group are going through.

Specific setups for peer response groups can vary greatly among instructors, so be clear about exactly what is expected of you as both peer responder and writer in each situation. If your instructors give out

USING COLLABORATION

Although students may understand the concept of audience in a general way, many find that consciously writing for others can be intimidating. The following group exercise can help students overcome this anxiety and simultaneously explore the concrete characteristics of an audience.

Assign students to work in groups of three to four. Ask the class to envision a group of people who are time travelers from an earlier era. They now take refuge in a modern American city. Even after being shown how to operate the lights and faucets in their apartments, these people remain innocent of technologies we take for granted. For example, they have no idea how to use modern appliances and so they wash their clothes by soaking them in the sink and then pounding them with heavy objects.

Ask each group to craft a set of instructions that would tell the time travelers how to wash and dry their clothes using a modern washer and dryer. Students will have to bear in mind that they cannot take what they would consider "common knowledge" for granted. Even simple commands like "open the lid" or "check the lint filter" will require careful explanation—perhaps even illustration.

Because this exercise requires intense focus on audience, it encourages students to *articulate and practice* what they know about the needs of readers. By your visiting each of the groups as they work, you can help keep students on track, ask focusing questions, and encourage peer interaction.

TEACHING TIP

To help students understand the importance of audience, you may want to ask them to collect articles from various magazines and newspapers that are addressed to different types of readers. The articles and the diverse audiences they assume can lead to lively conversations, especially if the class is divided into groups for early discussion and later reconvenes as a whole class. Giving students a list of publications popular with varied groups of people will ensure effective contrasts in the articles they find. (*Writer's Digest* can be helpful in composing such a list, because in its listing of publication sources, it provides a brief description of audiences for numerous magazines.)

WHAT ELSE?

Strategies and Resources, a free 400-page book for faculty who use this handbook, offers specific, practical ways to apply this statement: "Newspaper editorial boards, for example, routinely engage in 'peer response' critique and in group brainstorming when determining the position their paper will take on a given issue. Such technical fields as computer science, engineering, or pharmaceuticals consider the planning and writing and editing of multiauthor documents standard procedure. Small groups of workers in such nontechnical fields as insurance, psychology, and social work also share the work of creating a wide variety of written products."

BACKGROUND

In "The Effect of Teacher Conferences on Peer Response Discourse" (*Teaching English in the Two-Year College*, May 1996: 112–126), Tim Hacker explains how teacher responses to student writing, especially during student-teacher conferences, model for students how to participate in peer response groups.

guidelines or directions for working in a peer response group, follow them carefully. One arrangement might call for students to pass around and read each others' drafts silently and then to jot helpful reactions or questions in the margins or on instructor-designed response forms. Another arrangement might have students reading their drafts aloud, after which each person in the peer response group responds either orally or on instructor-designed forms. Yet another arrangement might require response to only one feature of a draft.

If you have no experience working as a member of a peer response group or in the particular system for peer response required by your instructor, you can confidently assume you are not alone in feeling a bit lost. Consult the guidelines in Chart 5, watch what experienced people do (though some people can seem experienced when they are not), ask questions of your instructor (your interest demonstrates a positive, cooperative attitude), or dive in knowing you will learn as you go along.

Now to the sometimes sticky issue of how to take criticism of your writing: Here is my personal advice for being able (or at least appearing able) to take constructive criticism gracefully. First, know that if criticism tends to jar your nerves, even when intended as constructive, you are not alone in your reaction. You have much company among professional writers if your initial reaction to criticism is defensive. Of course, if a response is purposely destructive or cruel, you and all others in your peer response group have every right to say so and ask that it be withdrawn or rephrased. Second, if a response is not clear to you, ask for clarification. You cannot learn what you do not understand. Third, realize that most students dislike having to criticize their peers. They fear they will lose friendships. They worry about being impolite, inaccurate, or plain wrong. If you want to set an atmosphere that encourages your peers to respond freely to you and therefore to be as helpful as possible, show that you can listen without anger or feeling intruded on. Finally, remember that whatever you have written is yours alone. You retain "ownership" of your writing always. Your revisions reflect your sense of what is needed to help it move closer to reaching your intended audience.

⊙ **Guidelines for participating in peer response groups** 5

One basic principle guides your work in a peer response group: Approach it with an upbeat, constructive attitude, whether you are responding to someone else's writing or you are being responded to by others.

→

Guidelines for participating in peer response groups *(continued)*   5

As a Responder

- Think of yourself in the role of a coach, not a judge.

- Consider your peers' writing as "works in progress."

- After hearing or reading your peer's writing, briefly summarize it as a check to determine that what you understand is what the writer intended.

- Start with what you think is well done. No one likes to hear only negative comments.

- Be honest in your suggestions for improvements.

- Ground your responses in an understanding of the writing process, remembering that you are dealing with drafts, not finished products. All writing can be revised (see 3c). Then the editing (see 3d) of surface features, such as spelling, can follow.

- Give concrete and specific responses. General comments such as "this is good" or "that is weak" say little. What, specifically, is good or bad? Ideas? Patterns of organization? Sentence styles? Word choice?

- Follow your instructor's system for getting your comments into writing so that your fellow writer can recall what you said. If one member of your group is supposed to take notes, speak clearly so that the person can be accurate.

As a Writer

- Adopt an attitude that encourages your peers to respond freely. Try to avoid overly defending your writing.

- Remain open-minded when you hear responses. Your peers' comments can help you reread your writing in a fresh way that results in your writing a better revised draft.

- Ask for clarification if a comment is not clear to you. Ask for specifics, not generalities.

- As much as you encourage your peers to be honest, remember that the writing is yours. You are its owner. You decide what comments to use or not use.

BACKGROUND

In "Publication Project in Alaska Offers Ways to Open New Worlds to Basic Writing Students" (*Journal of Basic Writing*, Spring 1994: 3–13), John Creed and Susan B. Andrews explain how a publication project—in the form of a public newspaper published Kotzebue, Alaska—encourages "real world" writing with attention to audience, accuracy, and multiple revisions.

WHAT ELSE?

Strategies and Resources, a free 400-page book for faculty who use this handbook, offers specific, practical ways to apply this statement: "The teacher's control of peer evaluation and careful direction to students about the goals of it are critical."

QUOTATION: ON WRITING

[Writing is] the sense of being in contact with people who are part of a particular audience that really makes a difference to me.

—Sherley Anne Williams

BACKGROUND

In "Voices from the Computer Classroom: Novice Writers and Peer Response to Writing" (*Teaching English in the Two-Year College*, October 1996: 213–218), Sandy Varone explains how a "computer-integrated class" can help build a classroom as a community and enhance the peer response process.

EXTRA EXERCISE

Ask students to write three letters: one to a close friend, a second to their parents, and a third to the class. In each, they are to recount an experience they had at an imaginary party when someone they knew (perhaps the person they went to the party with) embarrassed them in some way. In writing groups, they can read the letters, discussing the differences in them that result from the different readers to whom they were written.

TEACHING TIP

To start a course in composition, you might ask students to think of personal experiences that support the claims about writing that open this chapter. To get things started, you might talk about a few of your own experiences that support the claims. Do you recall a college paper you wrote? What do you remember about its content and the experience of writing it? Have you found that writing about something makes you better able to teach it? Have you ever discovered what you wanted to say—or a connection among the ideas you already had in mind—as the words were formed "at the point of utterance"?

To encourage students to share their experiences, you might ask them first to jot down some notes and then participate in a discussion. If the group is large, you might divide it into small groups and give each group specific directions (written are more effective than oral) about what to discuss. The directions can have students discuss in turn each question listed in the preceding paragraph. After a suitable amount of time, you might ask each group to report to the whole class.

1c.4 Understanding your instructor as a reader

Eventually, of course, your audience for a college writing assignment is your **instructor.** Your instructor is a member of the general reading public, with a commitment to helping you improve your writing. Your instructor knows that few students are experienced writers or complete experts on their subjects. Still, your instructor expects always that your writing reflect your having taken the time to learn the material thoroughly and to write about it well. Instructors are very experienced readers who can recognize a minimal effort. In part, therefore, your instructor is a judge, someone who expects you to demonstrate that you tried your best.

When writing for college, be aware that all instructors are members of a group whose professional lives center on intellectual endeavors. You must therefore write within the constraints of academic writing. Even if you are told to choose your writing topic, you do not have total freedom to select one. Your topic must have some intrinsic intellectual interest.

Inexperienced writers sometimes wrongly assume that instructors will fill in mentally what is missing on the page. Do not fall into this trap. Instructors—indeed, all readers—expect your writing to include everything you want to say or imply. Do not leave out material. Even if you write immediately after your instructor has heard you give an oral report on the same subject, write as if no one is aware of what you know.

1d Understanding the effect of tone

Tone relates not so much to *what* you say as to *how* you say it. The tone of your writing has a major impact on what you are trying to communicate to your audience (see 1c). Tone involves your choice of words interacting with your message. Have you ever reacted to someone's understanding of what you wrote with "That's not what I meant to say"? Your tone can be what has thrown your readers off track, although you can also be misunderstood if your writing is unclear or imprecise.

Words are not just words. They must fit your message and the audience you want to reach. As you combine words into sentences and paragraphs, the words work together to convey your attitude toward your subject and toward your readers. For example, if you write a chatty, informal message to your superiors about safety hazards in your workplace, you communicate that you do not take the hazards seriously and that you likely disrespect your peers and your superiors. Similarly, if you report bad news, jokes are in bad taste. And if you report good news, choose more formal language for officials and more informal language for your friends. Equally important, if your tone shows you are uninformed or unsure about your topic, readers quickly lose confidence in what you are saying.

In academic writing, you want to convey a reasonable tone in both the content of your material and your choice of words. For example, readers might think a writer unreasonable if the writing is trying to manipulate emotions by using slanted language (see 21a.4). Always reject loaded, biased words (*the corrupt, deceitful politician*) in favor of even-handed, neutral ones (*the politician being investigated for taking bribes*). Also, language with sexist overtones (see 21b) tells your readers that you are insensitive to gender issues or simply crude. Choose gender-neutral language that represents both men and women fairly (replace *policeman* with *police officer;* replace *doctors' wives* with *doctors' spouses*). Similarly, using pretentious language (see 21e.1) reflects negatively on you because your readers assume you are showing off or are trying to obscure a message. Choose straightforward rather than overblown words (*concert,* not *orchestral event*) and tactfully honest words rather than the "double-speak" discussed in 21c.4 (*cutting jobs,* not *downsizing*). The level of formality (see 21a.1) in your writing should vary according to the setting in which it will be read. When you move from writing privately for yourself to writing for an audience, the level of formality necessarily changes. Although many readers enjoy lively language, they can be jarred by an overly informal tone in a serious discussion. A medium level of formality is best. For example, in a newspaper report about election results, do not refer to a candidate as a *guy* or a *gal,* no matter how relaxed and friendly the behavior of the candidate. To control the tone in your writing, follow the guidelines in Chart 6.

⊙ **Guidelines for handling tone in your writing**   **6**

- Choose words appropriate to your subject and your readers.
- Control your choice of words so that they work with your message, not against it.
- Use an highly informal tone only when you want to sound as if you are speaking conversationally.
- Use a formal or medium level of formality in your academic writing and when you write for supervisors, professionals, and other people you know from a distance.
- Whatever tone you choose, be consistent in each piece of writing.

EXERCISE 1-3

Consulting sections 1c and 1d, read each paragraph, and decide what audiences the writing seems appropriate for as revealed by its tone. Explain your answers.

A.   Pernicious anemia, a uniformly fatal disease, was spectacularly reversed by liver extract (much later found to be due to the presence

ANSWERS: EXERCISE 1-3

A. The tone is appropriate for academic writing. The material assumes a specialized reader who would be familiar with words such as *diabetes mellitus*, *acidosis*, and *bacilli*.

B. The tone is informal and may be inappropriate for academic writing in some courses. The material does not assume a specialized reader.

C. The tone is appropriate for academic writing. The material does not assume a specialized reader.

of vitamin B_{12} in the extract). Diabetes mellitus could be treated—at least to the extent of reducing the elevated blood sugar and correcting the acidosis that otherwise led to diabetic coma and death—by the insulin preparation isolated by Banting and Best. Pellagra, a common cause of death among the impoverished rural populations in the South, had become curable with Goldberger's discovery of the vitamin B complex and the subsequent identification of nicotinic acid. Diphtheria could be prevented by immunization against the toxin of diphtheria bacilli and, when it occurred, treated more or less effectively with diphtheria antitoxin.

—Lewis Thomas, "1933 Medicine"

B.   Joey played a great game yesterday, but we got pretty steamed up when he started with an "I'm better than you are" attitude. Who needs that?

—Claire Newborne, student

C.   My husband and I constantly marvel at the fact that our two sons, born of the same parents and only two years apart in age, are such completely opposite human beings. The most obvious differences became apparent at their births. Our firstborn, Mark, was big and bold—his intense, already wise eyes, broad shoulders, huge and heavy hands, and powerful, chunky legs gave us the impression that he could have walked out of the delivery room on his own. Our second son, Wayne, was delightfully different. Rather than have the football physique that Mark was born with, Wayne came into the world with a long, slim, wiry body more suited to running, jumping, and contorting. Wayne's eyes, rather than being intense like Mark's, were impish and innocent. When Mark was delivered, he cried only momentarily, then seemed to settle into a state of intense concentration, as if trying to absorb everything he could about the strange, new environment he found himself in. Conversely, Wayne screamed from the moment he first appeared until the nurse took him to the nursery. There was nothing helpless or pathetic about his cry either—he was damned angry!

—Roseanne Labonte, student

1e Using outside sources for writing

An **outside source** presents someone else's ideas, not yours. Outside sources include practically everything contained in libraries, credible material on the Internet (beware of using anything that you cannot absolutely verify as credible; see Charts 146 and 147 in Chapter 32), and the spoken words of experts on your topic. When you can bolster the validity of your information or of your point of view on a debatable topic with support from outside sources, you bring more authority to what you are writing. But be careful: Instructors have differing policies on whether or not students may draw on outside sources to support what they are writing. Some instructors forbid students to consult and use outside sources except in connection with a research paper (see Part Five). Other instructors encourage students to do "source-based writing" for most assignments. Still other instructors never want you to use outside sources for your writing. Whenever you are in doubt about an instructor's policy, ask for clarification, and make sure you understand the answers you get.

One huge issue in students' using outside sources in their writing concerns the offense of *plagiarism*. Plagiarism occurs when a writer takes ideas or words from an outside source without specifically giving credit to that source. Giving credit means using the practice of documentation (see especially Chapter 31) in line with the accepted documentation style of each academic discipline (see Chapter 33). Plagiarism is such a major offense that it can lead to a student's instantly failing a course or being asked to leave a college.

Still, do not let this warning about plagiarism stop you from consulting outside sources. You can do so freely (within the limits of your instructor's policy) as long as you accurately and completely document the ideas or words you are using. Refer to Chart 7 for guidelines for using outside sources.

Guidelines for using outside sources in writing 7

- Evaluate sources critically, as explained in section 5h.2, Chart 36.
- Be sure to represent the material in each source accurately. For guidance in quoting, paraphrasing, or summarizing source material, see Chapter 31.
- Synthesize source material; do not merely report it. Make connections for your reader between the ideas and details in the source and your own ideas as stimulated by the source. For guidance in how to synthesize, as part of critical thinking, see sections 5b and 5f.
- Credit your source by naming it clearly and completely. Ask your instructor what method to use to give credit to the sources you use. Four widely used systems for documenting sources are described in Chapter 33.
- Remember that using a source without informing readers of that use is plagiarism. For help in avoiding plagiarism, see Chapter 31.

Many students wonder whether referring in their writing to outside sources carries the message that students cannot think or come up with

QUOTATION: ON WRITING

Writing is the hardest work in the world not involving heavy lifting.
—Pete Hamill

QUOTATION: ON WRITING

I can say now that one of the big reasons [for writing] was this: I instinctively recognized an opportunity to transcend some of my personal failings—things about myself I didn't particularly like and wanted to change but didn't know how.
—John Steinbeck

ideas and words on their own. Only the opposite is true when outside sources are used well. Using outside sources well tests your ability to find relevant sources, to assess whether the sources are credible and therefore worth using, and to blend outside sources smoothly into the language you are using to make your point.

No matter how many outside sources you use, always know that *you* are your first source for writing. To plan and develop a point, first draw on your own prior knowledge on the subject. You have been adding to your fund of prior knowledge throughout your life: reading, studying, listening to lectures and speeches, watching television. And you have been drawing on your prior knowledge ever since you started putting pencil (or crayon) to paper. Realize that *you* are the source of your thoughts, reactions, and opinions. They form the basis for all your writing; outside sources merely support and lend authority to what *you* are writing.

2

PLANNING AND SHAPING

2a Understanding the writing process

Many people assume that a real writer can pick up a pen (or sit at a computer) and magically write a finished product, word by perfect word. Experienced writers know better. They know that **writing is a process,** a series of activities that start the moment they begin thinking about a subject and end when they complete a final draft. Experienced writers know, also, that good writing is rewriting. Their drafts are filled with additions, deletions, rearrangements, and rewordings.

> ~~Chapter One discusses what writing ℞.~~ ~~This chapter~~
> ~~explains how writing happens~~. Many people assume that a real
> *pick up a pen*
> writer can ∧~~put pen to paper~~ (or sit at ~~the keyboard of~~ a
> *magically* ∧*a* *word by perfect word.*
> computer) and ∧write ∧finished product, ∧Experienced writers
> ~~all~~ know better. They know that writing is a process,
> ~~Writing is~~ a series of activities that start the moment *they begin*
> thinking about a subject ~~begins~~ and end when they ∧final *complete. ∧∞ a.*
> draft. ~~is complete℞~~ Experienced writers know, also, that good
> writing is rewriting. Their drafts are filled with additions,
> deletions, rearrangements, and rewordings.

Draft and revision of the opening paragraph of Chapter 2 by Lynn Troyka

For example, here you can see how I revised the paragraph you just read into final form. Notice that two sentences were dropped, two sentences were combined, one sentence was added, and various words were dropped, changed, or added. Such activities are typical of writing.

Writing is an ongoing process of considering alternatives and making choices. The better you understand the writing process, the better you will write and the more you can enjoy writing. I discuss the parts of the

WHAT ELSE?

In the *Prentice Hall/Simon & Schuster Transparencies for Writers* by Duncan Carter, you will find color transparencies to illustrate and reinforce concepts in this chapter.

QUOTATION: ON WRITING

At the time of writing, I don't write for my friends or myself, either; I write for *it*, for the pleasure of *it*.
—Eudora Welty

TEACHING TIP

The facsimile of my writing and revising at the opening of this chapter is completely authentic (though the handwriting is not mine because I tend to scrawl illegibly). I have included this draft to show students that most teachers and professional writers *evolve* a text rather than produce it in one swoop. When I do this in my writing classes, the students never fail to be surprised that their instructor's first draft could be so rough. You might also call attention to the clumsy opening sentences that I deleted and to other revisions that I made in my first draft.

You might also bring in a few examples of your own drafts. A paragraph or two can suffice. And if you write at a computer, as I do, plan ahead and keep those sentences you love to delete with the press of a key. Interestingly, I have found that a few students sometimes think that my rough drafts are better than their final drafts, which can be discouraging. I try to emphasize that I am not as much of an apprentice writer as the students are. And I am writing from a base of where I am after decades of writing, not from the base where I started back in college.

QUOTATION: ON WRITING

Writers are notorious for using any reason to keep from working: overresearching, retyping, going to meetings, waxing the floors—anything.

—Gloria Steinem

WHAT ELSE?

Strategies and Resources is a free 400-page book written especially for instructors who adopt this handbook. Its Part Two addresses many aspects of using collaborative writing in the classroom: the rationales for using collaboration, the specifics of training students to work productively in collaborative groups, the details of troubleshooting, and the ways to design successful writing assignments.

BACKGROUND

Donald Graves was the first to use the term *rehearsing* to describe the activities that precede a completed draft. His pioneering work, still a central force in composition and rhetoric, began with *Balance the Basics: Let Them Write* (Ford Foundation Papers on Research About Learning, 1978). He discusses the stage of the writing process in which the writer (mentally and on paper) prepares to write, without yet knowing what that writing will be. Drawing conclusions for all writers based on his observations of children writing, Graves points out the importance of experimenting with meaning, form, and voices, an attitude of play that is important in making meaning.

writing process separately in this chapter for the sake of explanation. In real life, the steps overlap. The steps loop back and forth as each piece of writing evolves. Understanding writing as a multistage process allows you to work efficiently, concentrating on one activity at a time rather than trying to juggle all of the facets of a writing project simultaneously. Chart 8 summarizes the steps in the writing process.

> ⊙ **The writing process**   8
>
> - **Planning** calls for you to gather ideas and think about a focus.
> - **Shaping** calls for you to consider ways to organize your material.
> - **Drafting** calls for you to write your ideas in sentences and paragraphs.
> - **Revising** calls for you to evaluate your draft and, based on your decisions, rewrite it by adding, cutting, replacing, moving—and often totally recasting material.
> - **Editing** calls for you to check the technical correctness of your grammar, spelling, punctuation, and mechanics.
> - **Proofreading** calls for you to read your final copy for typing errors or handwriting legibility.

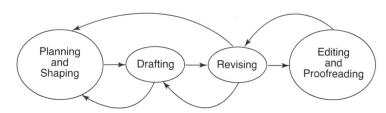

Visualizing the writing process

If you like to visualize a process, the diagram above might help. A straight line would not be adequate because it would exclude the recursive nature of writing. The arrows on the diagram imply movement. Planning is not over when drafting begins, drafting is not necessarily over merely because the major activity shifts to revision, and editing sometimes inspires writers to see the need for additional revising—and perhaps some new planning.

As you work with the writing process, rest assured that there is no one way to write. When you start, allow yourself to move through each stage of the writing process and see what is involved. Then as you gain experience, begin to observe what works best for you. Once you have a general sense of the pattern of your writing process, you can adapt the process to suit each new situation that you encounter as a writer.

Most writers struggle some of the time with ideas that are difficult to express, sentences that will not take shape, and words that are not precise. Do not be impatient with yourself, and do not get discouraged. Writing takes time. The more you write, the easier it will be, but remember that experienced writers know that writing never happens magically.

An aside about the words used to discuss writing: Instructors refer to written products in different ways. Often the words are used interchangeably, but sometimes they have specific meanings for specific instructors. Listen closely, and ask if you are unsure of what you hear. For example, the words *essay, theme,* and *composition* usually—but not always—refer to writing that runs from about 500 to 1,000 words. I use *essay* in this handbook. The word *paper* can mean anything from a few paragraphs to a long and detailed report or a complex research project. I use *paper* in this handbook to refer to longer writing projects, such as research papers.

2b Adjusting for each writing situation

Writing begins with thinking about each **writing situation.** Your thinking involves answering the questions in Chart 9. Then you adjust your writing process (see 2a) to accommodate each particular writing situation.

⊙ **Guidelines for analyzing each writing situation   9**

- **Topic:** What will you be writing about in this situation?
- **Purpose:** What will be your writing purpose in this situation?
- **Audience:** Who will be your audience in this situation?
- **Special requirements:** How much time were you given, and how long should the paper be?

The **topic** is the foundation of each writing situation. If you choose your own topic or narrow an assigned topic, keep in mind the constraints of academic writing (see 2c). If the topic is assigned, stick to it so you don't risk going "off the topic." Whatever the topic, you are the starting place for your writing. Draw on yourself as a source. Whatever you have seen, heard, read, and even dreamed contributes to your fund of ideas and prior knowledge. As you think about your topic, remember that in your writing, you will need to include specific support for the points you intend to make.

The **purpose** of your college writing is usually to inform or to persuade (see 1b). Effective writing reflects a sense of its purpose. Some

TEACHING TIP

The concept of a *writing situation* may be new to many students. It is an inclusive term for the combination of topic, purpose, audience, and special requirements such as word or time limits. Each of these variables influences every decision a writer makes. You might want to ask your students to memorize that short list of key variables: TOPAS (**TO** for *topic*, **P** for *purpose*, **A** for *audience*, and **S** for *special requirements*) can be an easy memory device for students. These variables are especially important in narrowing a topic, as demonstrated by the inclusion of "writing situation" in the examples for narrowing a topic I give here.

STATEWIDE TESTING

If you teach in a state that requires students to pass basic competency tests in English, see the free publications coordinated with this handbook: One is for the CLAST (Florida), and another is for the TASP Exam (Texas).

BACKGROUND

Much of what we believe about the composing processes of students comes from the work of three researchers and their colleagues. Although their work was done years ago, the influence of their ideas remains strong. James Britton, in Britain's School Council Project *The Development of Writing Abilities, 11–18* (London: Macmillan Education, 1975), observed that "writing is a deliberate act; one has to make up one's mind to do it." Once we decide to write, he points out, we begin the process by prewriting, which involves trying to understand and solve a particular writing problem. Also fundamental to our current understanding of the writing process is the work of Janet Emig, reported in *The Composing Processes of Twelfth Graders* (NCTE Research Report No. 13, Urbana: NCTE, 1971). As the title suggests, she followed in detail the methods of high school seniors as they made their way through writing tasks. Finally, John R. Hayes and Linda S. Flower provided a model for other researchers with their "thinking aloud" protocols, verbal descriptions of what writers report they think and do while they compose ("Identifying the Organization of Writing Processes" and "The Dynamics of Composing: Making Plans and Juggling Constraints," *Cognitive Processes in Writing*, ed. Lee W. Gregg and Erwin R. Steinberg, Hillsdale, NJ: Erlbaum, 1980, 3–50). Although the methods and terminology of these investigators vary, they arrived at fundamental agreement about the writing process.

writing assignments include or clearly imply a statement of purpose. For example, your purpose is *informative* if you are writing about the dangers of smoking. Conversely, your purpose is *persuasive* if you are writing an argument against smoking. When an assignment does not stipulate the writing purpose, you must choose either an informative or a persuasive purpose, based on the topic, what you want to say about it (often referred to as the *focus*), and how you intend to develop the topic.

The **audience** for your college writing consists of everyone who will read it. To reach your audience effectively, you need to analyze who might be in it. To do this, see the longer discussion in 1c.

Special requirements—the time allotted for the assignment, the expected length of the writing, and other practical constraints—influence every writing situation. If an assignment is due in one week, expect that your instructor wants writing that shows more than one day's work. If the paper is due overnight, you might have to write it hastily, though never carelessly. If reading or other research is required, you have to build time for it in to your schedule.

Your assignment is a major resource for you as you write. Refer to it often. Ideally, your instructor writes the assignment on the board or distributes it on paper. Some instructors, however, only announce an assignment, in which case you are expected to write it down. Try to record every word spoken, always ask questions if you need clarifications, and write down the answers you get or any given in response to other students' questions.

To give you examples of the writing process in progress, this chapter shows you the work of two actual students, Carol Moreno and Daniel Casey, as they plan and shape their essays. In Chapter 3, Carol Moreno's essay is discussed as it evolves through three drafts (shown in section 3f). Daniel Casey's essay is developed in Chapter 6, and its final draft appears in section 6i. Here is the written statement of the assignment that each student received.

Carol Moreno was given this assignment: Write an essay of 700 to 800 words in which you discuss a challenge you faced and tried to meet. Your writing purpose can be informative or persuasive. Expect to write three drafts. Your first draft (in rough form, showing your comments to yourself and changes you made) and your second (cleanly typed) draft are due in one week. I will read your second draft as an "essay in progress" and will make comments to help you toward a third, final draft. That third, final draft (cleanly typed) is due one week after I hand back your second draft with my comments.

Daniel Casey was given this assignment: Write an essay of 500 to 700 words that argues about whether holidays have become too commercialized in the United States. Your final draft is due in one week. Bring your earlier drafts to class for possible discussion.

Moreno read her assignment with an eye toward analyzing the elements of her writing situation. The *topic* was a challenge she faced and tried to meet, a subject that Moreno realized she would have to narrow considerably (for her narrowing process, see 2c.2). Moreno tentatively chose an informative writing *purpose,* knowing that as she got further into her planning, she might change her mind. She saw that her instructor was to be her *audience* and that the *special requirements* of length and time were given in the assignment.

Casey read his assignment to analyze his writing situation. He saw immediately that most elements were stated. The *topic* was commercialization of holidays in the United States, and the *purpose* was persuasive because students were expected to adopt and argue a position about the topic. The *audience* was the instructor, though Casey realized that the class might hear or see earlier drafts once the final draft was finished. The *special requirements* of length and time were given in the assignment.

EXERCISE 2-1

Consulting section 2b, for each assignment listed here, answer these questions: (a) What is its topic? (b) Is its purpose to inform or to persuade? (c) Who are your readers likely to be? (d) What special requirements of length and time are stated or implied?

1. *English:* Write a 500- to 700-word essay arguing for or against doubling the size of your college's student body. This assignment is due in one week.
2. *Journalism:* Write a 300-word editorial for the student newspaper (to be published next week) praising or criticizing your college's policy on selling parking stickers to students and faculty. Draw on your personal experience, if any.
3. *Art:* You have twenty minutes in class to compare and contrast Greek and Roman styles of architecture.
4. *Chemistry:* Write a one-paragraph description of the process of hydration.
5. *Economics:* Write a 1,000-word essay on the broad impact of capitalism since 1989 on the former communist nations of eastern Europe. Draw on your reading. This assignment is due in two weeks.

2c Thinking a topic through for writing

As you choose a topic for writing, you need to make sound decisions. Experienced writers know that the quality of their writing depends on how they handle a topic. Always think a topic through before you rush in and get so deeply involved that you cannot switch to a more suitable topic in the time allotted.

BACKGROUND

In "Say It, Don't Write It: Oral Structures as Framework for Teaching Writing" (*Journal of Basic Writing*, Spring 1994: 41–49), Pamela D. Dykstra explains how students benefit from becoming aware that speaking and writing are "two valid but different forms of communication."

ANSWERS: EXERCISE 2-1

1. (a) Topic is doubling the size of the student body. (b) Purpose is to persuade. (c) Audience is instructor. (d) Special requirements are 500- to 700-word limit and a due date of one week.

2. (a) Topic is the college policy on parking permits. (b) Purpose is to persuade. (c) Audience is the college community. (d) Special requirements are the 300-word limit and the newspaper deadline.

3. (a) Topic is comparison of Greek and Roman architecture. (b) Purpose is to inform. (c) Audience is instructor and perhaps other students. (d) Special requirements include the 20-minute time limit and writing in class.

4. (a) Topic is the process of hydration. (b) Purpose is to inform. (c) Audience is instructor and perhaps other students. (d) Special requirement is the strict length limit of one paragraph.

5. (a) Topic is impact of capitalism on the former communist nations of eastern Europe. (b) Purpose is primarily to inform; student should ask if a persuasive purpose is acceptable. (c) Audience is instructor. (d) Special requirements are the use of outside sources, the 1,000-word limit, and the due date in two weeks.

BACKGROUND

In "The Sounding of the Sirens: Computer Contexts for Writing at the Two-Year College" (*Teaching English in the Two-Year College*, October 1996: 205–212), Paul Resnick and Kip Strasma explain the crucial role of faculty participation in decisions affecting computer uses for writing. Using three situational narratives, they sound an alarm and propose ways to avoid problems.

BACKGROUND

In his classic, often-cited essay "Writing as Process: How Writing Finds Its Own Meaning" (*Eight Approaches to Teaching Composition*, ed. Timothy Donovan and Ben McClelland, Urbana: NCTE, 1980, 3–20), Donald Murray discusses four forces that interact as the writer goes through the stages of rehearsing, drafting, and revising, moving in a recursive manner from exploration to clarification. They are the forces of collecting and connecting, writing and reading. Although writing may be ignited by any one of these forces in conjunction with any other, says Murray, once writing has begun, all of them begin to interact. The writer is often unaware of this interaction as innate curiosity leads naturally to the act of collecting information, which at some point calls for control and order that make the act of connecting necessary. Connections, in turn, make the writer see information in a new way, generating more collected data. The acts of writing and reading act in a similar fashion. The writer sets down what is heard mentally, then reads the product, checking it against what was heard, and then rewrites it. Murray asserts that although each writing act is a complex, instantaneous interaction, the scale tips rapidly from one force to the other in response to the various needs of the writer dealing with rehearsing, drafting, or revising.

Some assignments leave no room for making choices about the topic. You may be given very specific instructions, such as "Explain how oxygen is absorbed from the lungs," or you may be asked to describe the view from your classroom window. Your job with such assignments is to do precisely what is asked without wandering off the topic.

2c.1 Selecting a suitable topic on your own

Some instructors ask students to choose their own topic. In such situations, do not assume that all subjects are suitable for college writing. The topic you choose has to demonstrate your ability to think ideas through. For example, the old reliable essay about a summer vacation is rarely suitable for college writing unless you have something compelling or extraordinary to report. Similarly, you would likely reach a dead end if you tried to write a 2,500-word essay on the narrow topic of what your cat looks like. Your essay needs to dive into issues and concepts. It must also allow you to demonstrate that you can use specific, concrete details to support what you are saying.

2c.2 Narrowing an assigned topic

The real challenge in dealing with topics comes when you have a very broad subject. You have to narrow the subject. *Narrowing* means thinking of subdivisions of the subject, of different areas within the subject. Most very broad subjects can be broken down in hundreds of ways, but you need not think of all of them. When one seems possible, think it through at the start so that you can decide whether you can develop it well in writing. **What separates most good writing from bad is the writer's ability to move back and forth between general statements and specific details.**

For example, if the subject is marriage, you might narrow it to what makes marriages successful. But you cannot depend merely on generalizations such as "In successful marriages, husbands and wives learn to accept each other's faults." You need to explain why accepting faults is important, and you need to give concrete illustrations of what you are talking about. Also, at all times as you narrow a broad subject to a writing topic, keep the writing situation (see 2b) of the assignment in mind.

SUBJECT	*music*
WRITING SITUATION	freshman composition class
	informative purpose
	instructor as audience
	500 words, one week
POSSIBLE TOPICS	the moods music creates
	classical music of the Renaissance
	country music as big business

SUBJECT	*cities*
WRITING SITUATION	sociology course
	persuasive purpose
	students and then instructor as audience
	500 to 700 words, one week
POSSIBLE TOPICS	comforts of city living
	discomforts of city living
	why city planning is important
SUBJECT	*mythology*
WRITING SITUATION	humanities course
	informative purpose
	instructor, a specialist in mythology, as audience
	1,000 words, two weeks
POSSIBLE TOPICS	*the purpose of myths*
	comparison of Navajo and Roman myths explaining why seasons change

Carol Moreno narrowed the topic of her assignment (shown on page 20) because "a challenge you faced and tried to meet" was too vague and general. To stimulate her thinking, Moreno used some of the techniques for gathering ideas presented in the rest of this chapter. She used an entry from her journal (shown in 2e), freewriting (in 2f), and mapping (in 2i). After that, Moreno decided to write about her need to build up her strength and stamina. Her essay is discussed in Chapter 3 as it evolves through three drafts, all of which are shown in section 3f.

Daniel Casey did not have to narrow his topic because it was stated in his assignment (see page 20): the commercialization of holidays in the United States. He did, however, have to choose a position to argue on the topic. What helped him the most were brainstorming (see his work in 2g), asking the "journalist's questions" (see his work in 2h), and using a subject tree (see his work in 2l). The development of Casey's essay is discussed in Chapter 6, and his final draft appears in section 6i.

2d Gathering ideas for writing

Techniques for gathering ideas, sometimes called *prewriting strategies* or *invention techniques,* can help you discover how much you know about a topic before you decide to write about it. Chart 10 lists various ways to gather ideas and indicates where in this handbook you can find others.

BACKGROUND

Many instructors today accept the system defined by Richard Young that classifies the theoretical bases for teaching invention (planning) into four main categories: classical invention, romantic invention, dramatism, and tagmemic invention. *Classical invention* refers to various systems based on the theories of ancient Greek and Roman rhetoricians such as Aristotle and Cicero. *Romantic invention,* associated with D. Gordon Rohman, tries to tap into the mysterious nonconscious and nonrational creative powers of the mind and often eschews formal methods of invention. *Dramatistic invention* is based on Kenneth Burke's pentad of agent, scene, act, agency, and purpose, first described in *A Grammar of Motives* (1945). *Tagmemic invention* is derived from Kenneth Pike's tagmemic linguistic theory, but it has its fullest realization in Richard Young, Alton Becker, and Kenneth Pike's *Rhetoric: Discovery and Change* (1950).

Ways to gather ideas for writing **10**

- Keep an idea book (see 2e).
- Write in a journal (see 2e).
- Freewrite (see 2f).
- Brainstorm (see 2g).
- Use the journalist's questions (see 2h).
- Map (see 2i).
- Read (see 1e and Chapter 5).
- Incubate (see 2j).

Students sometimes worry that they have nothing to write about. Often, however, students know far more than they give themselves credit for. The challenge is to uncover what is there. As you use these various techniques for gathering ideas, find out which work best for *you* and *your* style of thinking in each writing situation.

No one technique of generating ideas always works for all topics. Experiment. If one method does not provide enough useful material, try another. Also, even if one strategy produces some good material, try another to turn up additional possibilities.

COMPUTER TIPS: (1) When freewriting (2f) or brainstorming (2g) on the computer, consider turning off the monitor. Then, you can focus on getting the words out without the temptation to stop, read, and revise what you are writing. When you can write no more, turn on the monitor to see what you have.

(2) As you use idea-gathering techniques, do not delete material. You never know what you might want later. A computer can save everything for you in one file and then retrieve it when you are ready to decide which material you might use and in what order. ◘

2e Keeping an idea book and writing in a journal

Your ease with writing will grow as you develop the habits of mind and behavior of writers. Professional writers are always on the lookout for ideas to write about and for details to develop their ideas. They listen, watch, talk with people, and generally keep their minds open. Many writers carry an **idea book**—a pocket-size notepad—to jot down ideas that spring to mind. Good ideas can melt away like snowflakes. Use an idea book throughout your college years, and you will see your powers of observation increase dramatically.

Many writers write in a **journal.** Keeping a journal allows you to have a "conversation on paper" with yourself. Fifteen minutes a day can be enough—jot down thoughts before going to bed, between classes, on a bus. Your audience is *you*, so the content and tone can be as personal and informal as you wish.

Unlike a diary, a journal is not merely for recording what you do each day. A journal is for your *thoughts*. You can draw on your reading, your observations, even your dreams. You can respond to quotations, react to movies or plays, or reflect on your opinions, beliefs, and tastes.

Keeping a journal can help you in three ways. First, writing every day gives you the habit of productivity. The more you write, the more you get used to the feeling of words pouring out of you onto paper, and the easier it will become for you to write in all situations. Second, a journal instills the habit of close observation and discovery. Third, a journal serves as an excellent source of ideas for assignments.

Here is an excerpt of a journal entry Carol Moreno had written before she got the assignment to write an essay about facing a challenge (see page 20). When reading through her journal for ideas for her essay, Moreno realized that she had faced the challenge of needing to develop more strength and stamina.

> September 30. I got to add 5 more reps today and it's only the sixth weight lifting class. I wasn't really surprised—I can tell I'm stronger. I wonder if I'm strong enough yet to lift Gran into the wheelchair alone. I was so scared last summer when I almost dropped her. Besides being terrified of hurting her, I thought that somehow the admissions committee would find out and tell me I was too weak to be accepted into nursing school. What if I hadn't noticed the weight lifting course for P.E. credit!?! Weight lifting is the best exercise I've ever done and I'm not getting beefy looking either.

Excerpt from Carol Moreno's journal

TEACHING TIP: ESL

An activity that both ESL students and native speakers enjoy is the exchange journal. ESL students exchange entries on cultural matters with native speakers in a different class. In the first entry, students introduce themselves to their partners, perhaps including information like age, sex, marital status, place of birth, college major, and hobbies or interests. They then list some topics they are interested in learning about. In each subsequent weekly or biweekly entry, students explain an aspect of their culture: dating, courtship, family structure, food, school, manners, holidays, language, sports, entertainment, and so on. Entries are as long as students want to make them. Instructors do not necessarily read the journals—and certainly do not correct them—but the teachers may require a report about the experience at the end of the term (and perhaps interim reports). The two instructors pass the journals back and forth to each other to distribute in classes; they should also arrange for the students to meet and interview each other near the end of the term, if possible. The assignment helps break down stereotypes and develops students' fluency in writing; indeed, some students write considerably better in journals than in compositions.

Note: Using two journals—one from ESL student to native speaker and one from native speaker to ESL student—makes it more convenient for students to write their reports. Blue books may be used for easy portability; when one is filled, the student can staple another to the back of the previous one.

TEACHING TIP

In his classic work *Writing with Power* (New York: Oxford UP, 1981), Peter Elbow suggests that keeping a freewriting diary can help an aspiring writer. Writing for only ten minutes a day can provide "a brief mind sample" of that day. He also discusses a variance of freewriting called looping, which allows the reader a degree of control over the material that the mind produces. Looping involves a series of freewritings about a subject. After writing nonstop for several minutes for the first loop, the writer composes a "center of gravity" sentence that summarizes the main idea in the first loop as precisely as possible. The freewriting of the second loop responds to the center-of-gravity sentence. For each new loop, the writer composes a new center-of-gravity sentence, each loop further refining and elaborating on the main idea. You may want to ask students to try looping as an in-class prewriting activity for a paper, to help choose a topic, or to discover a tentative thesis statement.

TEACHING TIP

Journal writing and freewriting are sometimes unpopular with students at first, but on their end-of-the-semester evaluations of my classes, students consistently mention these activities as being among the most helpful in my course. Perhaps one of the reasons students resist at first is that they think journal writing and freewriting will be corrected or graded. Few teachers do that. It is important, however, to respond to students' journals, although teachers should not feel obliged to read and respond to every entry of every journal. Responses should not be directive or critical but should create an informal dialogue with students that encourages them to discuss their ideas and experiences in greater depth and detail.

2f Freewriting

Freewriting is writing nonstop. You write down whatever comes into your mind without stopping to worry about whether the ideas are good or the spelling is correct. When you freewrite, do nothing to interrupt the flow. Do not censor any thoughts or flashes of insight. Do not go back and review. Do not cross out.

Freewriting helps get you used to the "feel" of your pen moving across paper or of your fingers in constant motion at a computer. Freewriting works best if you set a goal—perhaps writing for fifteen minutes or filling one or two pages. Keep going until you reach that goal, even if you have to write one word over and over until a new word comes to mind. Some days your freewriting might seem mindless when you reread it, but other days interesting ideas can pop up.

If you write at a computer, you can avoid the temptation to stop and criticize your writing by doing "invisible writing." Dim the screen so that you cannot see your writing. The computer will still be recording your ideas, but you will not be able to see them until you brighten the screen again. To create the same effect writing by hand, use a worn-out ballpoint pen and a piece of carbon paper between two sheets of paper.

Focused freewriting involves starting with a set topic, a quotation you like, or a sentence you take from your looser, more general freewriting. Using the focus as a starting point, write until you meet the time or page limit you have set as a goal. Again, do not censor what you say. Keep moving forward.

Like a journal, freewriting can be a source for ideas and details to write about. Carol Moreno wanted to explore the topic of her having learned to

Pumping iron—what the steroid jocks call it and exactly what I DO NOT want to be—a muscle cube. Great that Prof. Moore told us women's muscles don't bulk up much unless a weight lifting program is really intense—they just get longer. No bulk for me PLEASE. Just want upper body strength—oh and the aerobic stuff from swimming, which makes me feel great. Lift sweat swim, lift sweat swim, lift sweat swim.

Excerpt from Carol Moreno's freewriting

lift weights. She felt it had potential for her essay assignment (on page 20). On page 26, see an excerpt from Moreno's focused freewriting on "pumping iron."

2g Brainstorming

Brainstorming means listing all the ideas that come to mind associated with a topic. The ideas can be listed as words, phrases, or even random sentences. Let your mind range freely, generating quantities of ideas before eliminating some. You can brainstorm in one concentrated session or over several days, depending on how much time is available for the assignment. In a class where peer response groups or collaborative work is permitted, brainstorming in groups can work especially well: One person's ideas bounce off the next person's, and collectively more ideas get listed.

Brainstorming has two steps: First, you make a list, and then you try to find patterns in the list and ways to group the ideas into categories. Set aside any items that do not fit into groups. If an area interests you but its list is short, brainstorm on that area alone. If you run out of ideas, ask yourself questions to stimulate your thinking. You might try exploratory questions about the topic, such as *What is it? What is it the same as? How is it different? Why or how does it happen? How is it done? What caused it or results from it? What does it look, smell, sound, feel, or taste like?*

Daniel Casey's essay, discussed in Chapter 6, develops an argument concerning the benefits of the commercialization of holidays. (For Casey's final draft, see section 6i.) Realizing that his position was open to debate, Casey used the technique of brainstorming to help himself think his opinion through. Here is an excerpt from the ideas as they came to Casey at random. The items followed by an asterisk (*) are those that Casey chose for the fourth paragraph—about the spirit of the holidays—of his essay, shown in section 6i.

PART OF DANIEL CASEY'S BRAINSTORMED LIST

people feel cheerful*
the economy is stimulated
people give to charities
strangers exchange friendly greetings*
everyone gives and gets gifts
children love visiting Santa (and the Easter Bunny)*
festive atmosphere in stores*
sending greeting cards helps friends stay in touch*
arouses positive sentimental feelings
stimulates goodwill

BACKGROUND
Peter Elbow, among the first theorists to discuss why freewriting is fundamental, explains that freewriting helps him as a writer and as a teacher because it allows him to move "more easily and fully" into writing and thinking.

ANSWERS: EXERCISE 2-2

Class discussion will likely reveal disagreement about the main categories and the distribution of items. You can emphasize the role of the individual writer as decision maker. The list might be arranged in this way:

Advertising appeals: coming attractions, TV ads, sneak previews, newspaper ads

Other publicity: movie reviews, word of mouth, personal interviews

People: director, stars

Aspects to feature: topical subject, special effects, book, locations, dialogue, photography, how movie was made

Characteristics: provocative, suspense, adventure, excitement

EXERCISE 2-2

Here is a brainstormed list for an assignment in a business class on ways to entice people to see a new movie. Consulting section 2g, look over the list, and then group ideas. Some ideas may not fit into any group. You are welcome to add ideas to the list.

coming attractions	suspense
TV ads	book the movie was based on
provocative	locations
movie reviews	rating
how movie was made	adventure
sneak previews	newspaper ads
word of mouth	stars
director	dialogue
topical subject	excitement
special effects	photography
personal interviews	

2h Using the journalist's questions

Journalist's questions ask *Who? What? When? Why? Where?* and *How?* Asking these questions forces you to approach a topic from several different perspectives.

Daniel Casey used the journalist's questions to explore and expand his thinking about specific benefits of the commercialization of holidays in the United States. His answers to the questions helped him decide that he had enough details to write an effective essay (for his final draft, see section 6i).

WHO Who specifically benefits from the commercial aspects of holidays?

WHAT What specific benefits result from commercialization of holidays?

WHEN When specifically do beneficial holidays fall?

WHY Why specifically do some people object to the commercial aspects of holidays?

WHERE Where specifically can evidence of benefits be seen or felt?

HOW How do specific commercial aspects of holidays create benefits?

2i Mapping

Mapping, also called *clustering* or *webbing,* is similar to brainstorming (see 2g). It is more visual, so it helps writers who are more comfortable with such an approach. Many writers find that mapping frees them to think more creatively as they associate ideas more easily.

To map, start with your topic circled in the middle of a sheet of unlined paper. Next, draw a line radiating out from the center, and label it with the name of a major subdivision of your topic. Circle the label, and radiate out from that circle to more specific subdivisions. When you finish with one major subdivision of your subject, go back to the center and start again with another major division. As you go along, add anything that occurs to you for any section of the map. Continue the process until you run out of ideas. You can also be used mapping like a subject tree (see 2l) to lay out the logical relationships of ideas to each other. But many writers seem to prefer to use mapping for discovering ideas already known but not remembered. You use the techniques as they suit you best.

Here is Carol Moreno's mapping for ideas to use in her essay about women lifting weights (for the three drafts of her essay, see section 3f). After Moreno finished mapping, she was satisfied that she had enough information to use in her essay.

Carol Moreno's mapping

2j Using incubation

When you allow your ideas to *incubate,* you give them time to grow and develop. **Incubation** works especially well when you need to solve a problem in your writing (for example, if your material is skimpy, the material tries to covers too much, or connections among your ideas are not stated clearly enough). Time is a key element for successful incubation. Arrange your time to make sure that you will not be interrupted. You need time to think, to allow your mind to wander, and then to come back and focus on the writing. Sometimes incubating an idea overnight can help you discover or clarify an idea.

One strategy to stimulate useful incubation is to turn your attention to something entirely unrelated to your writing problem. Concentrate very hard on that other matter so that your conscious mind is totally distracted from the writing problem. After a while, relax and guide your mind back to the writing problem you want to solve.

Another strategy is to allow your mind to relax and wander, without concentrating on anything in particular. Open your mind to random thoughts, but do not dwell on any one thought very long. After a while, guide your mind back to the writing problem you are trying to solve. When you come back to the writing problem, you might see solutions that did not occur to you before.

EXERCISE 2-3

Consulting sections 2d through 2j, practice each method for gathering ideas at least once. Use your own topics, or select from these: pizza, procrastinating, a dream vacation, meeting deadlines, playing a sport, telling jokes, libraries, chocolate, falling in love, world peace.

2k Shaping ideas

Shaping activities relate to the concept that writing is often called *composing.* Composing allows you to put together ideas to create a *composition,* a synonym for *essay.* To shape the ideas that you have gathered about your topic, you need to group them (see 2l) and sequence them (see 2m).

As you shape ideas, keep in mind that the form of an essay is related to the classical notion of a story's having a beginning, a middle, and an end. An academic essay always has an introduction, a body, and a conclusion. The length of each paragraph is in proportion to the overall length of the essay. Introductory and concluding paragraphs are generally shorter than body paragraphs, and no body paragraph should overpower the others by its length. (Different types of paragraphs useful for academic writing are discussed in Chapter 4.)

21 Grouping ideas

When you group ideas, you divide them into groups by making connections and finding patterns. As you create groups, use the concept of **levels of generality** to help you make decisions: One idea is more general than another if it falls into a larger, less specific category than the other. Generality is relative, of course. Each idea exists in context—in a relationship with other ideas. One idea may be general in relation to one set of ideas but specific in relation to another set. For example, "bank account" is more general than "checking account." "Checking account" is more general than "business checking account" or "regular checking account," in turn, And those terms are more general than "account 221222 at the EZ-Come EZ-Go Bank."

To identify groups of ideas, review the material you have accumulated while gathering ideas (see 2e through 2j). Look for general ideas. Then, group less general ideas under them. If your notes contain only general ideas, or only very specific details, return to techniques for gathering ideas (see 2d) to supply what you need. One popular tool for grouping ideas is a "subject tree." It usually reveals whether you have enough content to write about. A subject tree resembles a map (see 2i): It shows ideas and details in order from most general at the top to most specific at the bottom.

Daniel Casey, while shaping his essay, used a subject tree. The essay takes the position that benefits result from the commercialization of holidays in the United States (for his final draft, see section 6i). He used the subject tree to lay out the ideas in his third paragraph according to their relative levels of generality. You can write out a subject tree for single paragraphs and for checking the interrelationships of the ideas in a whole essay. Use whatever techniques suit you best.

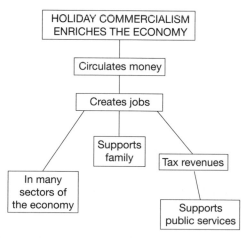

Daniel Casey's subject tree

BACKGROUND

Writers, both amateurs and professionals, tend to devise rituals that help them begin and carry out a piece of writing. Some of them are elaborate; some are relatively simple. They are identifiable by the fact that they are repeated actions that seem to be irrelevant to the task at hand but that are in some way helpful to the writer looking for ideas and ways to express them. Some are silly, such as using the same coffee mug each time one writes, or illogical, such as sweeping the front walk before getting started, but the fact is that they are effective in helping a writer make the transition from some other activity to that of composition.

Writers who are in the process of devising writing rituals can make their individual habits more productive by being aware of which steps are helpful and which are not. They can begin by asking themselves questions about where, when, and with what they write. Where do they get the most work done? Does it afford them access to materials they need? Is it free from interruptions? Does it make them comfortable but not too relaxed? Can they see well? Do they have room to spread out notes and books? What time of day or night do they usually do their writing? Are they alert and energetic at that time? Does it give them a block of time in which to work? Do they use a typewriter? A legal pad? A word processor? A spiral notebook? What objects, environments, or activities that are not directly connected with writing provide a sense of well-being during the process? The answers will vary from one writer to another, but for best results, the process should remain fairly constant with the individual.

Rituals are habits that provide structure—reassurance that the writer has done a task this way once before. With each repetition, they become more comfortable, making the writer feel more competent, more at home with the act of writing.

2m Sequencing ideas for writing

When you sequence ideas for writing, you need to decide what you want your readers to encounter first, second, and so on. The more easily readers can follow your line of reasoning, more likely they are to understand the message that you want your material to deliver.

Within paragraphs, you have many choices of ways to present ideas, as explained in Chapter 4. Within an essay, the sequence of those paragraphs gradually reveals your material to your audience. No one sequence or structure fits all college essays, but certain elements are usually present. For the major elements in essays with a persuasive purpose, see Chart 43 in section 6d. For the major elements in essays with an informative purpose, see Chart 11. (These elements are labeled in the final draft of Carol Moreno's essay in section 3f.3.)

⊙ Elements in an essay with an informative purpose   **11**

1. **Introductory paragraph:** leads in to the topic of the essay, trying to capture the reader's interest. (For a discussion of introductory paragraphs, see 4g.)

2. **Thesis statement:** states the central message of the essay, accurately reflecting the essay's content. In an academic essay, the thesis statement usually appears at the end of the introductory paragraph. (For a discussion of thesis statements, see 2n.)

3. **Background information:** gives basic material, providing a context for the points being made in the essay. Depending on its complexity, this information appears in its own paragraph or is integrated into the introductory paragraph. (For an example of integrating background information into the introductory paragraph, see Daniel Casey's essay in 6i. For an example of a separate paragraph for background information, see Carol Moreno's essay in 3f.)

4. **Points of discussion:** support the essay's thesis, each consisting of a general statement backed up by specific details. This material forms the core of the essay, with each point occupying one or two paragraphs, depending on the overall length of the essay. The general statements, seen as a group, comprise a "mini-outline" of the essay. The specific details bring the generalizations to life by using RENNS. (For a discussion of RENNS, see 4c.)

5. **Concluding paragraph:** ends the essay smoothly, not abruptly, flowing logically from the rest of the essay. (For a discussion of concluding paragraphs, see 4g.)

2n Shaping writing by drafting a thesis statement

A **thesis statement** is the central message of an essay. It is evidence that you have something definite to say about the topic. An effective thesis statement prepares your readers for the essence of what you discuss in an essay. As the writer, you want to compose a thesis statement with care so that it accurately reflects the content of your essay. If you discern a mismatch between your thesis statement and the rest of your essay, revise to coordinate them better. The basic requirements for a thesis statement are presented in Chart 12.

◉ Basic requirements for a thesis statement   12

- It states the essay's **subject**—the topic that you are discussing.
- It reflects the essay's **purpose**—either to give your readers information or to persuade your readers to agree with you.
- It includes a **focus**—your assertion that conveys your point of view.
- It uses **specific language**—vague words are avoided
- It may briefly state the major **subdivisions** of the essay's topic.

Some instructors ask for more than the basic requirements. For example, you might be required to put your thesis statement at the end of your introductory paragraph. (See the final draft of Carol Moreno's essay in section 3f.3.) Also, many instructors require that the thesis statement be contained in one sentence. Other instructors permit two sentences if the material to be covered warrants such length. All requirements, basic and additional, are designed to help you think in structured patterns that communicate clearly with readers. Be sure not to confuse a *title* (see 3c.2) with a thesis statement.

🌐 **ESL NOTE:** The use of a thesis statement in the introductory paragraph of an essay is typical of English-speaking and certain other cultures. Even if you are not accustomed to writing such a straightforward statement of your point, you need to master the skill for writing in North America. 🌐

Until you have written one or more drafts, your thesis statement may not yet reflect what you say in the essay. Still, you can begin. At the start, make an **assertion**—a sentence stating your topic and the point you want to make about it. The exact wording of this assertion will probably not appear in your final draft, but it serves to focus your thinking as you progress through a preliminary thesis statement toward a fully developed one.

TEACHING TIP

You may want to ask your students to test their thesis statements by exchanging them with one another. By asking the readers to answer questions about the thesis statements, the writers may discover weaknesses (and strengths) that were not apparent to them. Some questions they can ask are the following:

 1. Is the main idea, the central point, clearly stated?

 2. Is the purpose of the essay clear?

 3. What is the purpose: to inform or persuade?

 4. What is the focus of the essay?

 5. Does the thesis statement identify the major subdivisions of the essay's topic?

 6. Does the thesis statement make the topic seem interesting?

 7. Can this thesis be developed in the time available?

 8. Can this thesis be developed in an essay of the length planned?

 9. Is the thesis limited enough for development but general enough to be worth the effort?

 10. Is the thesis stated in specific terms? Does it avoid overly general, vague ones?

QUOTATION: ON WRITING

Writing is just having a sheet of paper, a pen and not a shadow of an idea of what you're going to say.

—Françoise Sagan

To write her essay about women lifting weights, Carol Moreno used this progression from basic assertion to final thesis statement. The final version fulfills the requirements for a thesis statement described in Chart 12.

> **NO**   I think women can "pump iron" like men. [This assertion is a start.]
>
> **NO**   If she is trained well, any woman can "pump iron" well, just like a man. [This preliminary thesis is more developed because it mentions training, but the word *well* is used twice and is vague, and the word *any* is inaccurate.]
>
> **NO**   In spite of most people thinking only men can "pump iron," women can also do it successfully with the right training. [This draft is better because it is becoming more specific, but "most people thinking only men" is not an aspect of the topic Moreno intends to explore. Also, the concept of building strength, a major aspect of Moreno's final draft, is missing.]
>
> **YES**   With the right training, women can also "pump iron" successfully to build strength. [This is the final version of Moreno's thesis statement. *Also* is a transitional word connecting the thesis statement to the sentence that comes before it in Moreno's introductory paragraph.]

Here are more examples of thesis statements, written for 500- to 700-word essays with an informative purpose (see section 1b.2). The ineffective versions resemble assertions or preliminary thesis statements. The effective versions are final thesis statements written by students after they had gathered and grouped ideas. The good versions fulfill the requirements in Chart 12.

TEACHING TIP

The notion of *focus* in a thesis statement might be new to some students. A useful analogy can be that the topic is the subject but the focus is the predicate. Without predication, sentences make no assertion. As Josephine Miles said in her classic monograph "Working Out Ideas: Predication and Other Uses of Language": "Sentence making is predication, and to predicate is to assert an idea, selecting and treating facts from a point of view." Predication says something, asserts something, answers a question, or takes a position about the topic. It may, for example, define the topic, describe it, evaluate it, compare it to something, explain its purpose, or identify its causes.

> **TOPIC**   *classical music*
> **NO**   Classical music combines many different sounds.
> **YES**   Classical music can be played by groups of various sizes, ranging from chamber ensembles to full symphony orchestras.

> **TOPIC**   *malpractice suits*
> **NO**   There are many kinds of malpractice suits.
> **YES**   Most people are familiar with malpractice suits against physicians, but an increasing number of suits are being filed against lawyers, teachers, and even parents.

> **TOPIC**   *woman artists*
> **NO**   The paintings of women are getting more attention.
> **YES**   During the past ten years, the works of artists Mary Cassatt and Rosa Bonheur have finally gained widespread critical acclaim.

For a persuasive purpose, Daniel Casey wrote this thesis statement for his essay about the commercialization of holidays:

> After all, commercial uses of holidays benefit the economy and lift people's spirits.

Casey's thesis statement reveals that the topic is commercialization of holidays, the purpose is to persuade, and the focus is the benefits of holidays' commercial uses. For a discussion about how Casey moved from assertion to this final version, see section 6i.

Here are more examples of thesis statements, this time written for 500- to 700-word essays with a persuasive purpose (see 1b.3). The ineffective versions resemble assertions or preliminary thesis statements. The effective versions are final thesis statements written by students after they had gathered and grouped ideas. (Note that the examples on city living are built on one of the "possible topics" evolved when narrowing the subject of *cities* in section 2c.2.) The good versions fulfill the requirements in Chart 12.

TOPIC *discomforts of city living*

NO The discomforts of living in a modern city are many.

YES Rising crime rates, increasingly overcrowded conditions, and growing expenses make living comfortably in a modern city difficult.

TOPIC *government loans for higher education*

NO The federal government has inadequate loan programs for people seeking higher education.

YES Congress should enact a law setting up an education loan account for each U.S. citizen for college or for retraining.

TOPIC *deceptive advertising*

NO Deceptive advertising can cause many problems for consumers.

YES Deceptive advertising can cost consumers not only money but also their health.

The *no* examples of thesis statements suffer from being too broad. They are so general that they offer no focus, and readers cannot predict the essay's thrust. Another type of ineffective thesis statement results from an overly narrow focus. In such cases, the thesis statement is closer in scope to a topic sentence that begins a paragraph.

NO Car thefts on Silver Avenue between First and Second Streets are intolerable.

YES Neighbors have overcome language obstacles and differences in customs to combat increasing car thefts on Silver Avenue.

QUOTATION: ON WRITING

Looking back, I imagine I was always writing. Twaddle it was too. But better far write twaddle or anything, anything, than nothing at all.

—Katherine Mansfield

EXTRA EXERCISE

Write thesis statements for persuasive papers on the following topics, making sure that they have the five characteristics of a good thesis statement listed in the basic requirements chart (Chart 12).

1. Rap music
2. Athletic scholarships
3. Ethnic foods
4. A holiday ritual
5. Mothers and daughters

ANSWERS: EXERCISE 2-4

A. The fourth thesis statement succeeds because it states a main idea (about magazine advertisements' appeal to readers); it reflects a purpose (to persuade); it has a focus (that magazine advertisements must be skillfully done); and it briefly presents subdivisions (language, color, and design). The first and second thesis statements are too general, showing neither a purpose nor a focus. The third thesis statement shows a persuasive purpose but is still too general and has no focus ("must" is not explained).

B. The fourth thesis statement succeeds because it states a main idea (about playing tennis for fun and exercise); it reflects a purpose (to inform); it has a focus (what is required for playing tennis for fun and exercise); and it briefly presents subdivisions (agility, stamina, and strategy). The first statement is too general ("excellent" is a very broad term) and shows no purpose or focus. The second statement is also too vague ("fun" is a very broad term when used without a context) and shows no purpose or focus. The third statement reflects an informative purpose but lacks a focus ("various skills" is too vague).

C. The fourth statement succeeds because it states a main idea (characters in *Hamlet* seek revenge); it reflects a purpose (to inform); it has a focus (all three characters seek revenge); and it briefly states the major subdivisions (Hamlet, Fortinbras, and Laertes). The first statement is much too general, and though it suggests an informative intent, the statement lacks a focus. The second and third statements reflect an informative purpose but lack a focus ("must" and "want" are vague words here).

D. The fourth statement succeeds because it states a main idea (strong friendships); it reflects a purpose (to persuade); it has a focus (what builds strong friendships); and it briefly states the major subdivisions (sensitivity and communication). The first statement uses vague language ("maintaining" and "work"), and it suggests neither a persuasive nor informa-

EXERCISE 2-4

Each of the following sets of sentences offers several versions of a thesis statement. Within each set, the thesis statements progress from weak to strong. The fourth thesis statement in each set is the best. Based on the basic requirements listed in Chart 12, identify the characteristics of the fourth thesis statement in each set. Then explain why the other choices in each set are weak. (The first set relates to the material in Exercise 2-2.)

A. 1. Advertising is complex.
   2. Magazine advertisements appeal to readers.
   3. Magazine advertisements must be creative.
   4. To appeal to readers, magazine advertisements must skillfully use language, color, and design.
B. 1. Tennis is excellent exercise.
   2. Playing tennis is fun.
   3. Tennis requires various skills.
   4. Playing tennis for fun and exercise requires agility, stamina, and strategy.
C. 1. *Hamlet* is a play about revenge.
   2. Hamlet must avenge his father's murder.
   3. Some characters in *Hamlet* want revenge.
   4. In *Hamlet,* Hamlet, Fortinbras, and Laertes all seek revenge.
D. 1. Maintaining friendships requires work.
   2. To have good friends, a person must learn how to be a good friend.
   3. To be a good friend, a person must value the meaning of friendship.
   4. Unless a person is sensitive to others and communicates with them honestly, that person will not be able to build strong friendships.
E. 1. Many people are uninterested in politics.
   2. Adults have become increasingly dissatisfied with the political process.
   3. Fewer adults than ever vote in local elections.
   4. Fewer college students participated in state primaries and voted in state elections this year than in either of the last two elections.

EXERCISE 2-5

Here are writing assignments, narrowed topics, and tentative thesis statements. Evaluate each thesis statement according to the basic requirements in Chart 12.

1. *Marketing assignment:* 700- to 800-word persuasive report on the college's cafeteria. *Audience:* the instructor and the cafeteria's manager. *Topic:* cafeteria conditions. *Thesis:* The college cafeteria could attract more students if it improved the quality of its food, its appearance, and the friendliness of its staff.

2. *Music assignment:* 300- to 500-word review of a performance. *Audience:* the instructor and other students in the class. *Topic:* the local symphony's final spring concert. *Thesis:* The "Basically Beethoven" program that ended the local symphony's spring season was pleasing.

3. *Chemistry assignment:* 800- to 1,000-word informative report about the ozone layer. *Audience:* the instructor and visiting students and instructors attending a seminar at the state college. *Topic:* recent research on the ozone layer. *Thesis:* The United States should increase efforts to slow the destruction of the ozone layer.

4. *Journalism assignment:* 200- to 300-word article about campus crime. *Audience:* the instructor, the student body, and the college administration. *Topic:* recent robberies. *Thesis:* During the fall term, campus robberies at the college equaled the number of robberies that took place in the prior five years combined.

5. *Business writing assignment:* 400- to 500-word persuasive report about the career-counseling services of the college. *Audience:* college seniors, career counselors, and the instructor. *Topic:* job placement for seniors. *Thesis:* The college's liberal arts graduates are hired mainly by business and industry.

2o Knowing how to outline

Many writers find **outlining** a useful planning strategy; others do not, preferring to outline after a first draft as a check on the flow and completeness of the essay. Often, instructors require outlines because they want students to practice planning the arrangement and organization of a piece of writing. If outlines are required, be sure to write them.

If you are expected to work from an outline and make changes in the essay's organization as you write, be sure to revise your outline if you must submit it as part of an assignment. An outline helps pull together the results of gathering and ordering ideas and preparing a thesis statement. It also provides a visual guide and checklist. Some writers employ outlines at various points in the writing process: before drafting, to arrange material; during drafting, to keep track of evolving material; or while revising, to check the logic of an early draft's organization. Especially for academic writing, outlines can reveal flaws: missing information, undesirable repetitions, digressions from the thesis.

Answers: Exercise 2-4 (continued)

tive intent. The second statement reflects a persuasive purpose but depends on "good" used in a vague sense. The third statement reflects a persuasive purpose but "value" is too vague to provide a focus.

E. The fourth statement succeeds because it states a main idea (college students' voting); it reflects a purpose (to inform); and it has a focus (how these students voted in state primaries and state elections this year compared with the last two years). The first statement relies on too much vague language ("many," "people," "uninterested") and lacks a purpose or focus. The second statement suggests an informative purpose, but it relies on vague language ("dissatisfied" and "political process") and lacks a focus. The third statement suggests an informative purpose but lacks a focus.

ANSWERS: EXERCISE 2-5

1. The thesis is good because it reflects the purpose (to persuade), states a main idea, and focuses specifically on logical subdivisions of the topic.

2. The thesis suggests that the concert review will do what such reviews should do: evaluate in an attempt to persuade a reader. The words "was pleasing," however, are too vague; they need to be revised to be more specific. A brief indication of subdivisions might help the thesis communicate its message.

3. The thesis, though specific and focused, does not reflect a careful response to the assignment: the assignment requires an informative report, but this thesis reflects a persuasive purpose.

4. This thesis is good because it states a main idea, reflects a purpose (to inform), and includes a focus.

5. This thesis does not address the assignment adequately because it deals only with liberal arts majors (not all of the seniors) and reflects an informative rather than a persuasive purpose, as was required by the assignment.

An **informal outline** does not have to follow all the formal conventions of outlining. An informal outline is particularly useful for planning when the order within main ideas is still evolving in your mind or when topics imply their own arrangement, such as spatial arrangement for describing a room. An informal outline can also be considered a *working plan,* a layout of the major parts of the material intended for an essay. Here is part of an informal outline that served as a working plan for Carol Moreno when she was writing her essay on weight lifting for women. (For Moreno's techniques of gathering ideas for writing, see sections 2e, 2f, and 2i; for the three drafts of her essay, see 3f.) This excerpt includes the essay's thesis statement and third paragraph.

SAMPLE INFORMAL OUTLINE

Thesis statement: With the right training, women can also "pump iron" for increased strength and stamina.

> using weights
>> safety is vital
>> free weights
>>> don't bend at waist
>>> do align neck and back
>>> do look straight ahead
>> weight machines—safety is easier

💻 **COMPUTER TIP:** You can informally outline an essay on a computer, especially after one draft. Read what you have written, and put a symbol near what seems most important. Then, look over the marked parts, and copy them to the bottom of your text so that you can see them grouped together. Shuffle them into several different orders. Does it matter which part comes first, second, and so on? Are the parts equally important, or do some seem subordinate to others? Try indenting the subordinate parts to make a rough outline. ◙

A **formal outline** follows conventions concerning content and format. The conventions are designed to display material so that relationships among ideas are clear and so that the content is orderly. A formal outline can be either a topic outline or a sentence outline. Each item in a topic outline is a word or phrase; each item in a sentence outline is a complete sentence. Formal outlines never mix the two.

Many writers who use formal outlines find that a sentence outline brings them closer to drafting than a topic outline does. For example, a topic outline carries less information with the item "Gathering information" than a sentence outline with the corresponding item "Gathering information is the first step to being well-prepared to write does."

See Chart 13 for a summary of the conventions of formal outlining.

Guidelines for a formal outline 13

Formal Outline Pattern

Thesis statement

I. First main idea

    A. First subdivision of the main idea

        1. First reason or example

        2. Second reason or example

           a. First supporting detail

           b. Second supporting detail

    B. Second subdivision of the main idea

II. Second main idea

Formal Outline Guidelines

- Numbers, letters, and indentations signal groupings and levels of importance.
- Each level has more than one entry.
- All subdivisions are at the same level of generality.
- Headings do not overlap.
- Entries are grammatically parallel (see Chapter 18).
- Only the first word of each entry is capitalized. (All proper nouns are also capitalized, of course.)
- Periods end each sentence in a sentence outline but not the items in a topic outline.
- The introductory and concluding paragraphs are omitted, but the thesis statement is usually given above the outline itself (see examples at end of this chapter).

- **Numbers, letters, and indentations.** All parts of a formal outline are systematically indented and numbered or lettered. Capital roman numerals (I, II, III) signal major subdivisions of the topic. Indented capital letters (A, B) signal the next level of generality. Further indented arabic numbers (1, 2, 3) show the third level of generality. Indented lowercase letters (a, b) show the fourth level, if there is one. The principle here is that within each major subdivision, each succeeding level of the outline shows more specific detail than the one before it. If an outline entry is longer than one line, the second line is indented as far as the first word of the preceding line.

- **More than one entry at each level.** At all points on an outline, there is no I without a II, no A without a B, and so on. Unless a category has at least two parts, it cannot be divided. If a category has only one subdivision, you need either to eliminate that subdivision or to expand the material to at least two subdivisions.

  NO A. Free weights
          1. Safe lifting technique
      B. Weight machines

  YES A. Free weights
      B. Weight machines

  YES A. Free weights
          1. Unsafe lifting techniques
          2. Safe lifting techniques
      B. Weight machines

- **Levels of generality.** All subdivisions are at the same level of generality. A main idea cannot be paired with a supporting detail.

  NO A. Free weights
          1. Safe lifting techniques
      B. Weight machines

  YES A. Free weights
      B. Weight machines

- **Overlap.** Headings do not overlap. What is covered in subdivision 1, for example, must be quite distinct from what is covered in subdivision 2.

  NO A. Free weights
          1. Unsafe lifting techniques
          2. Not aligning head and neck

  YES A. Free weights
          1. Unsafe lifting techniques
          2. Safe lifting techniques

- **Parallelism.** All entries within a level are parallel. For example, all might start with the -*ing* forms of VERBS.* (For more about parallelism in outlines, see section 18h).

  NO A. Free weights
      B. Using weight machines

*You can find the definition of a word printed in small capital letters (such as VERBS) in the Terms Glossary toward the end of this handbook.

YES   A. Free weights
         B. Weight machines

YES   A. Using free weights
         B. Using weight machines

- **Capitalization and punctuation.** Except for PROPER NOUNS, only the first word of each entry is capitalized. In a sentence outline, end each sentence with a period. Do not punctuate the ends of entries in a topic outline.

- **Introductory and concluding paragraphs.** The content of the introductory and concluding paragraphs is not part of a formal outline. The thesis statement comes before (above) the roman numeral I entry.

Here is a topic outline of the final draft of Carol Moreno's essay on weight lifting for women (see 3f). A sentence outline follows it so that you can compare the two types of outlines.

TOPIC OUTLINE

Thesis statement: With the right training, women can also "pump iron" successfully for increased strength and stamina.

    I. Avoiding massive muscle development
        A Role of women's biology
           1. Not much muscle-bulking hormone
           2. Muscles get longer, not bulkier
        B. Role of combining exercise types
           1. Anaerobic (weight lifting)
           2. Aerobic (swimming)
   II. Using weights safely
        A. Free weights
           1. Unsafe lifting technique
           2. Safe lifting technique
              a. Head alignment
              b. Neck and back alignment
        B. Weight machines (built-in safeguards)
  III. Individualizing the program based on physical condition
        A. Role of resistance and reps
        B. Characteristics considered for personalizing the program
           1. Weight
           2. Age
           3. Physical condition

QUOTATION: ON WRITING

A work has form insofar as one part of it leads a reader to anticipate another part, to be gratified by the sequence.

—Kenneth Burke

QUOTATION: ON WRITING

My writing is a conscious letter to myself. It's a way for me to hold on to pieces as I grow and change and get on with my life.
—Joan Stein

IV. Individualizing the program for other reasons
    A. Upper body strength
    B. Individual objectives
        1. Mine
        2. Car crash victim's
        3. Physical therapist's

SENTENCE OUTLINE

Thesis statement: With the right training, women can also "pump iron" successfully for increased strength and stamina.

  I. The right training lets women who lift weights avoid developing massive muscles.
    A. Women's biology plays a role.
        1. Women don't produce much of a specific muscle-bulking hormone.
        2. Women's muscles tend to grow longer rather than bulkier.
    B. Combining exercise types plays a role.
        1. Anaerobic exercise, like weight lifting, builds muscle.
        2. Aerobic exercise, like swimming, builds endurance and stamina.
 II. The right training shows women how to use weights safely to prevent injury.
    A. Free weights require special precautions.
        1. Bending at the waist and jerking a barbell up is unsafe.
        2. Squatting and using leg and back muscles to straighten up is safe.
           a. The head is held erect and faces forward.
           b. The neck and back are aligned and held straight.
    B. Weight machines make it easier to lift safely because they force proper body alignment.
III. The right training includes individualized programs based on a woman's physical condition.
    A. Progress comes from resistance and from repetitions tailored to individual capabilities.
    B. Programs consider a woman's physical characteristics.
        1. Her weight is considered.
        2. Her age is considered.
        3. Her physical conditioning is considered.
IV. The right training includes individualized programs based on a woman's personal goals.
    A. Certain muscle groups are targeted to increase women's upper body strength.

WHAT ELSE?

Strategies and Resources, a free 400-page book for faculty who use this handbook, offers specific, practical ways to apply this statement: "It is the conversation of students working together that disseminates information more surely and erects conceptual scaffolding more efficiently."

B. Other muscle groups are targeted based on individual objectives.
   1. I wanted to strengthen muscles needed for lifting patients.
   2. An accident victim wanted to strengthen her neck muscles.
   3. A physical therapist wanted to strengthen her fingers and hands.

COMPUTER TIP: Do not rely on a word processor's outlining function. It simply places a bullet at the beginning of each paragraph. It cannot determine where material belongs in your essay. ◼

EXERCISE 2-6

Here is a sentence outline. Consulting section 2o, revise it into a topic outline. Then, decide which form you would prefer as a guide to writing, and explain your decision.

Thesis statement: Common noise pollution, although it causes many problems in our society, can be reduced.

I. Noise pollution comes from many sources.
   A. Noise pollution occurs in many large cities.
      1. Traffic rumbles and screeches.
      2. Construction work blasts.
      3. Airplanes roar overhead.
   B. Noise pollution occurs in the workplace.
      1. Machines in factories boom.
      2. Machines used for outdoor construction thunder.
   C. Noise pollution occurs during leisure-time activities.
      1. Stereo headphones blare directly into eardrums.
      2. Film soundtracks bombard the ears.
      3. Music in discos assaults the ears.
II. Noise pollution causes many problems.
   A. Excessive noise damages hearing.
   B. Excessive noise alters moods.
   C. Constant exposure to noise limits learning ability.
III. Reduction in noise pollution is possible.
   A. Pressure from community groups can support efforts to control excessive noise.
   B. Traffic regulations can help alleviate congestion and noise.
   C. Pressure from workers can force management to reduce noise.
   D. People can wear earplugs to avoid excessive noise.
   E. Reasonable sound levels for headphones, soundtracks, and discos can be required.

QUOTATION: ON WRITING

All you need is a room without any particular interruptions.

—John Dos Passos

ANSWERS: EXERCISE 2-6

Answers may vary.

I. Sources of noise pollution
   A. Large cities
      1. Traffic
      2. Construction work
      3. Airplanes
   B. Workplace
      1. Factory machines
      2. Outdoor construction machines
   C. Leisure-time activities
      1. Stereo headphones
      2. Film soundtracks
      3. Disco music
II. Problems from noise pollution
   A. Damages hearing
   B. Alters moods
   C. Limits learning ability
III. How to reduce noise pollution
   A. Pressure from community groups
   B. Traffic regulations
   C. Pressure on management by workers
   D. Earplugs
   E. Reasonable sound levels

USING COLLABORATION

Starting a course with a collaborative component

The concept underlying collaboration is that the whole is greater than the sum of its parts. Providing opportunities for students to work together allows them to see other points of view, to capitalize on each other's strengths, to develop concepts more extensively than they could on their own, and to learn from each other. When you assign groups, allow students a little time to introduce themselves and get to know one another. Personalizing learning can be an important part of collaboration.

Collaborative groups work best when they comprise two or three students whose schedules allow them to work together outside class, if practical. When groups meet in class only, students can work toward the group's goals by completing individual responsibilities outside class and then merging their work during class time. Collaborative papers, like single-authored texts, go through a series of drafts. But unlike single-authored texts, collaborative papers will actively integrate concepts of audience, tone, planning, and purpose into the writing process because at every step students must articulate to one another what they think the paper needs and why.

BACKGROUND

In "Preparing Students for Teamwork Through Collaborative Writing and Peer Review Techniques" (*Teaching English in the Two-Year College*, May 1996: 127–136), Vidya Singh-Gutpa and Eileen Troutt-Ervin argue that students who learn the techniques of effective collaboration are far better prepared for today's workplace.

2p Understanding collaborative writing

In some classes, instructors require students to collaborate in groups on a writing project. Why write collaboratively? Working in a group can stimulate people to think of ideas and to support each other during the writing process (see 2g). Also, working collaboratively allows students to discuss their ideas and bounce them off each other, an activity that often inspires greater creativity and shared confidence. The idea behind collaborative writing is that two (or more) heads are better than one. Chart 14 gives guidelines for collaborative writing.

The benefits of getting experience in writing collaboratively extend far beyond your college years. Many professions require people to serve on writing committees, to reach general agreement on how to proceed, and to contribute equally to a written report. For example, marketing executives might be told to develop a new product that fits the company's existing product line, to conduct marketing research to predict the product's success, and then to write up the results of their research in a final document that includes a plan for further action.

⊙ Guidelines for collaborative writing   14

Getting Under Way

1. Get to know each other's names. If you exchange phone numbers, you can be in touch outside of class.
2. Participate in the group process. During discussions, help set a tone that encourages everyone to participate, including people who do not like to interrupt, who want time to think before they talk, or who are shy. If you are not used to contributing in a group setting, plan ways to take a more active role.
3. Facilitate the collaboration. As a group, assign work to be done between meetings. Distribute the responsibilities as fairly as possible. Also, decide whether to choose one discussion leader or to rotate leadership.

Planning the Writing

4. After discussing the project, brainstorm (see 2g) or use other techniques to think of ideas (see 2d through 2j).
5. As a group, choose the ideas that seem best. Incubate (see 2j), if time permits, and discuss the choices again.

→

Guidelines for collaborative writing *(continued)* 14

6. As a group, divide the project into parts, and distribute assignments as fairly as possible.
7. As you work on your part of the project, take notes so that you can be ready to report to the group.
8. As a group, sketch an overview (if you choose to outline, see 2o) of the paper to get a preliminary idea of how best to use the material contributed by individuals.

Drafting the Writing

9. DRAFT a first paragraph or two. This material sets the direction for the rest of the paper. Each member of the group can draft a version, but agree on one draft for these paragraphs before getting too far into the rest of the draft. Your group might rewrite once the whole paper has been drafted, but a preliminary version helps everyone focus.
10. Work on the rest of the paper. Decide whether each member of the group should write a complete draft or a different part of the whole. Use photocopies to share work.

Revising the Writing

11. Read over the drafts. Check that everything useful has been incorporated into the draft.
12. Use the revision checklists in section 3c.3 to decide on revisions. Work as a group, or assign sections to subgroups. Use photocopies to share work.
13. Agree on a final version. Assign someone to prepare it in final form and make photocopies.

Editing the Writing

14. As a group, review photocopies of the final version. Do not leave the last stages to a subgroup. Draw on everyone's knowledge of grammar, spelling, and punctuation. Use everyone's eyes proofreading.
15. Use the editing checklist in section 3d to make sure that the final version has no errors. If necessary, retype. No matter how well the group has worked collaboratively or how well the group has written the paper, a sloppy final version reflects negatively on the entire group.

USING COLLABORATION

In both workplace and college settings, writers may team up to develop a single document. When two or three students write a paper together, they usually see the need to articulate the *how* and *why* of every dimension of the writing task from topic selection to word choice. This ongoing discussion within collaborative groups about their writing encourages them to view effective writing as a process under each individual's conscious control.

USING COLLABORATION

Recent research on small group dynamics suggests that the quality and number of ideas generated by invention can be enhanced by having group members first engage individually in such planning activities as mapping, clustering, and focused freewriting before coming together for group brainstorming.

Sometimes, the group will decide to narrow its focus to one of the ideas suggested during a brainstorming session. Before the group pursues its topic any further, you might repeat the individual-first, group-second planning process on the new, narrower idea.

QUOTATION: ON WRITING

Writing is a deliberate act; one has to make up one's mind to do it.

—James Britton

WHAT ELSE?

Strategies and Resources, a free 400-page book written especially for instructors who adopt this handbook. Its Part Three gives detailed help to writing instructors who want to use portfolios to enhance learning as well as to assess student writing.

For a discussion of portfolios in this *Annotated Instructor's Edition*, see the annotations in Part Five.

TEACHING TIP

Getting started seems hardest for writers at the point when they have to move from planning and shaping to actual writing. Dealing with writer's block is no small matter for writers, instructors of writing, and students. You might take some class time to discuss myths about writing. I am interested in gathering more myths. If you or your students know any, please send me the MYTH/TRUTH information for publication—with a byline—in the next edition of this *Annotated Instructor's Edition*. Send the material to me c/o English Editor, Prentice Hall, One Lake Street, Upper Saddle River, NJ 07458.

3

DRAFTING AND REVISING

In the writing process, drafting and revising follow from the activities of planning and shaping, as discussed in detail in Chapter 2. **Drafting** means getting ideas onto paper in sentences and paragraphs. In everyday conversation, people usually use the word *writing* when they talk about the activities involved in drafting. In discussing the writing process, however, the word *drafting* is more descriptive. It conveys the idea that the final product of the writing process is the result of a number of versions, each successively closer to what the writer intends and to what will communicate clearly to readers. **Revising** means taking a draft from its preliminary to its final version by evaluating, adding, cutting, moving material, editing, and proofreading.

3a Getting started

If ever you have trouble getting started when the time arrives for drafting (or any other part of the writing process), you are not alone. When experienced writers get stalled, they recognize what is happening and deal with it. If you run into a writing block, it may be the result of one of these common myths about writing.

MYTH	Writers are born, not made.
TRUTH	Everyone can write. Writers do not expect to "get it right" the first time. Being a good writer means being a patient rewriter.
MYTH	Writers have to be "in the mood" to write.
TRUTH	If writers always waited for "the mood" to descend, few would write at all. After all, news reporters and other professional writers often have to meet deadlines.
MYTH	Writers have to know how to spell every word and to recite the rules of grammar perfectly.
TRUTH	Writers do not let spelling and grammar block them. They write and then check themselves. A good speller is someone who does not ignore the quiet inner voice that urges

checking a dictionary. Similarly, writers use a handbook to check grammar rules.

MYTH Writers do not have to revise.

TRUTH Writers expect to revise. Once words are on paper, writers can see what readers see. This "re-vision" helps writers revise so that their writing delivers its intended message.

MYTH Writing can be done at the last minute.

TRUTH Drafting and revising take time. Ideas do not leap onto paper in final, polished form.

⊙ Ways to overcome writer's block 15

- **Avoid staring at a blank page.** Relax and move your hand across the page or keyboard. Write words, scribble, or draw while you think about your topic. The movement of filling the paper can help stimulate your mind to turn to actual drafting.
- **Visualize yourself writing.** Many professional writers say that they write more easily if they first picture themselves doing it. Before getting up in the morning, or while waiting for a bus or walking to classes, summon a full visual image of yourself in the place where you usually write, with the materials you need, busy at work.
- **Picture an image or a scene, or imagine a sound that relates to your topic.** Start writing by describing what you see or hear.
- **Write about your topic in a letter to a friend.** Relax and chat on paper to someone you feel comfortable with.
- **Try writing your material as if you were someone else.** Once you take on a role, you might feel less inhibited about writing.
- **Start in the middle.** Begin with a body paragraph. Write from the center of your essay out, instead of from beginning to end.
- **Use focused freewriting** (see 2f).
- **Switch your method of writing.** If you usually typewrite or use a computer, try writing by hand. If you usually use a pen, switch to a pencil. When you write by hand, try to treat yourself to good-quality paper. The pleasure of writing on smooth, strong paper helps many experienced writers want to keep going.

Once you realize the truths behind myths about writing, you can try the proven ways that experienced writers use when they are blocked (see Chart 15). As you apply these strategies, suspend judgment; do not

Students may be skeptical of the value of picturing themselves working. Share with them these examples of successful people who use visualization.

John Ueless, a champion pole-vaulter, used visualization before each meet. He would see himself winning by clearing the bar at a particular height. In his mind, he rehearsed every movement, as well as seeing the crowd and even smelling the grass when pole-vaulting out of doors.

Jack Nicklaus says that visualization gives him a "winning feeling": "This gives me a line to the cup just as clearly as if it's been tattooed on my brain. With that feeling, all I have to do is swing the club and let nature take its course."

You might want to give students time to visualize in class prior to writing. Tell them to close their eyes and sit comfortably. Tell them to imagine themselves reading a question and realizing they know how they want to respond. Tell them to imagine themselves making a list of notes, rearranging their material, or writing. At each stage, remind them to imagine themselves feeling confident and successful. Then have them write. Later, discuss how they felt when writing this time in contrast to their past experiences. This technique often does little for people at first, so try to give your students frequent opportunities to employ visualization techniques.

BACKGROUND

Erica E. Goode cites tips for people who tend to procrastinate. They include the following helpful suggestions.

- Break your work into small, clearly defined steps. Instead of vowing vaguely to "catch up on paperwork," resolve to spend one hour sorting out the papers on your desk.
- Reward yourself for progress toward your goal. Ice cream is nice; so is a walk in the park.

→

Background (continued)
- The hardest step to take is the first, so pick something easy. A task that can be polished off in fifteen minutes is a good one for a starter.
- Set a series of small but realistic interim deadlines rather than a final date.
- Enlist support. Other people may be able to tell you if you're setting up expectations that are impossible to meet.

WHAT ELSE?

See transparency 3-1 for drafting techniques in the *Prentice Hall/Simon & Schuster Transparencies for Writers* by Duncan Carter.

TEACHING TIP

Your students may find it helpful to keep a writing log. At the top of each piece of writing, they can note where, when, and how they are working. The more detailed the notations, the more they will help students draw conclusions about the manner in which their best writing takes place. After making a number of such notations, the students can write a paragraph evaluating the approaches used, trying to assess their effectiveness.

---

criticize yourself when trying to get under way. The time for evaluation comes during revision, but revising too soon can stall some writers. Although the writing is certainly not a final draft, having something on paper is a comfort—and can serve as a springboard to further drafting.

As you write, seek out places and times of the day that encourage you to write. You might write best in a quiet corner of the library, at 4:30 a.m. at the kitchen table before anyone else is awake, or outside when people are walking by. Most experienced writers find that they concentrate best when they are alone, working without the risk of interruption. But occasionally background noise—in a crowded cafeteria, for example—might be comforting. Be sure, however, not to mislead yourself: You will not write well or efficiently while you are talking to other people, stopping now and then to jot down a sentence or two. Also, do not mistake delaying tactics for preparation: You do need pencil and paper (or their equivalent) to write, but you do not need fifteen perfectly sharpened pencils sitting in a neat row.

💻 **COMPUTER TIP:** Tailor your use of the computer to your personal needs. Some experienced writers prefer to use a computer only for preparing the final copy. Others like to plan and shape by hand and to write all drafts on a computer. Still others like to use a computer throughout the writing process. Consider these facts, however. If you learn to compose your essays on the computer from the start, you will save yourself having to retype them. Also, you will be developing a skill you may be expected to have when you enter the workplace. ◙

3b Knowing how to draft

Dive in. You have planned and shaped your ideas (see Chapter 2), and now you are ready to compose them into an essay. When you compose, you combine paragraphs, sentences, and words into a unified whole. The direction of drafting is forward: Keep pressing ahead. If you are worried about the spelling of a word or a point in grammar, underline the material to check it later—and keep moving ahead. If you cannot think of an exact word, write an easy synonym, circle it to change later—and move on. If you are worried about your sentence style or the order in which you present the supporting details within a paragraph, write *Style?* or *Order?* in the margin so you can return to it later—and press forward. If you begin to run dry, reread what you have written—but only to propel yourself to further writing, not to distract you into rewriting.

💻 **COMPUTER TIP:** Save or back up your work every two pages or every ten to fifteen minutes. Also, consider printing it out regularly. This gives you a physical record of your work, in case disk or computer problems develop. You may also find that editing is easier on the printout (or hard copy) than on the computer. ◙

A first draft is a preliminary draft. Its purpose is to get your ideas onto paper or disk or into computer memory. In your first draft, you do not refine grammar and style (that comes later, during revising). First drafts are not meant to be perfect; they are meant to give you something to revise. According to your personal preferences and each writing situation, try the following ways (or your own ways) of writing a first draft:

- **Put aside all your notes from planning and shaping.** Write a "discovery draft." As you write, be open to discovering ideas and making connections that spring to mind during the physical act of writing. When you finish a discovery draft, you can decide to use it either as a first draft or as part of your notes when you write a structured first draft.

- **Keep your notes from planning and shaping in front of you and use them as you write.** Write a structured first draft by arranging your notes in a preliminary sequence and working through them. Draft either the entire essay or blocks of a few paragraphs at one time.

- **Use a combination of approaches.** When you know the shape of your material, write according to that structure. When you feel "stuck" about what to say next, switch to writing as you would for a discovery draft.

💻 **COMPUTER TIP:** Try to write a whole draft at one session, limiting your second-guessing and rewriting as much as possible. If you have questions or want to elaborate on something, insert a symbol that will alert you when you finish the draft and begin revising. You can search for the symbols to find those places that need special attention. Or write yourself brief notes in all capital letters, which are easy to spot. ◼

As you draft, use your essay's thesis statement (see 2n) as a springboard. A thesis statement has great organizing power, for it controls and limits what the essay will cover. Also, use your thesis statement as a connecting thread that unifies the essay. **Unity** is important for communicating clearly to an audience. You achieve unity when all parts of your essay relate to your thesis statement and to each other. Specifically, you can consider an essay unified when it meets two criteria: The thesis statement clearly ties in to all topic sentences (see 4b), and support for each topic sentence—its paragraph development—contains examples, reasons, facts, and details directly related to the topic and, in turn, to the thesis statement (see 4c).

Coherence is also central for communicating clearly to an audience. Your essay is coherent when it supplies guideposts that help your readers understand relations among your ideas. Coherence is achieved with word choice, transitional expressions, pronouns, repetition, and parallel structures. These techniques operate within paragraphs and to connect paragraphs within essays (see 4d).

WEB SITE

English Central is Prentice Hall's Web site for English instructors and their students. English Central offers much general information about English, hyperlinks to interesting and important sites for students and instructors of English composition and literature, and sites for Prentice Hall's major English textbooks. At the Troyka Web site, you will find supplementary resources and activities. These include quotations (twenty-five, with suggestions to students for using them to stimulate writing), practice exercises on key topics, other sample student essays, e-mail contact with the author, and an invitation to students to submit model essays (for Chapters 3 or 6), model paragraphs (for Chapter 4), model research papers (for Chapter 34), and model literature papers (for Chapter 37).

BACKGROUND

In a still-cited classic article, Janet Emig suggests that the reason many experienced writers prefer to write in longhand is that it gives them more time to think. The slower pace of handwriting, as opposed to the computer, allows ideas to develop and surface ("Hand, Eye, Brain: Some 'Basics' in the Writing Process," *Research on Composing: Points of Departure*, ed. Charles Cooper and Lee Odell, Urbana: NCTE, 1978, 61).

BACKGROUND

In "Correctness and Its Conceptions: The Meaning of Language Form for Basic Writers" (*Journal of Basic Writing*, Summer 1996: 23–38), Michael Newman suggests that error taught from a sociolinguistic perspective gives students a context for making choices about the identity they choose for each text.

QUOTATION: ON WRITING

To write is to write is to write is to write is to write is to write is to write.

—Gertrude Stein

BACKGROUND

In "Emphasizing the 'What If' of Revision: Serial Collaboration and Quasi-Hypertext" (*Teaching English in the Two-Year College*, February 1997: 34–41), Jane Lightcap Brown describes the concepts and classroom use of "serial collaboration." She sees many benefits in this approach, particularly students taking a more active "what if?" stance toward revision.

WHAT ELSE?

Strategies and Resources, a free 400-page book for faculty who use this handbook, offers specific, practical ways to apply this statement: "But even experienced teachers fret over obvious inconsistencies among philosophies of grading and inconsistencies between theory and application. Evaluation of writing is possibly the single most difficult task required of us, yet it may well be the most important part of our job insofar as helping individual students."

When you write, plan your practical arrangements. For example, try to work in a place where you are comfortable and will not be disturbed. If someone interrupts, you might lose a train of thought or an idea that has flashed into your mind. Also, keep enough paper at hand so that you use only one side of each sheet of paper. Later, you will need to spread your full draft in front of you so that you can physically check your organization and rearrange parts that do not seem to relate to one another. As you write, leave large margins and plenty of room between lines to give yourself space to enter revisions or your notes to yourself about your revision plans.

To give you examples of the writing process used by college students, this chapter discusses the drafting and revising of two students, Carol Moreno and Daniel Casey, who wrote in response to the assignments shown on page 20. You can see three complete drafts of Moreno's essay in section 3f and the final draft of Daniel Casey's essay in section 6i. For examples of Moreno's and Casey's uses of the techniques of planning and shaping before they began drafting, see sections 2b through 2o.

3c Knowing how to revise

To **revise,** you must evaluate. Academic writing, especially through the vehicle of revision, can be an engaging intellectual endeavor that pushes your thinking to the maximum. You assess each draft to determine where improvements are needed. Then, you make the improvements and evaluate each on its own and in the context of the surrounding material. This process continues until you are satisfied that the essay is the best that you can make it in the time available.

To revise successfully, you need first to *expect* to revise. Some people think that if you need to revise, you are not a good writer. In reality, the opposite is true. Writing is largely revising. Experienced writers know that the final draft of any writing project shows on paper only a fraction of the decisions made from draft to draft. As mentioned earlier, *revise* means "see again," to look with fresh eyes. Good writers view their drafts honestly. This lets them see ways to improve their work and help it evolve.

To revise successfully, you need also to distance yourself from each draft, to read your writing with objective eyes. A natural reaction of student writers is to want to hold on to their every word, especially if they had trouble getting started with a draft. Resist such feelings. Practice distancing yourself from the material and developing an objective sense of your work. Before revising, give yourself some time to allow the rosy glow of authorial pride to dim a bit. The classical writer Horace recommended waiting nine years. That is impossible, but do try to wait a few hours before going back to look anew at your work.

If an objective perspective still eludes you, try reading your draft aloud. Hearing your writing can give you a fresh new sense of content and organization. Another useful method of achieving distance is to read your paragraphs in reverse order, starting with the conclusion.

3c.1 Knowing the steps and activities of revision

Once you understand the attitudes that underlie the revision process, you are ready to move into actual revising. To revise, you work to improve your draft at all levels: whole essay, paragraph, sentence, and word. A revised draft usually looks quite different from its preceding draft. To revise effectively, you likely need to engage in all the activities in Charts 16 and 17.

◉ Steps for revising 16

1. Shift mentally from suspending judgment (during idea gathering and drafting) to making judgments.
2. Read your draft critically to evaluate it. Be guided by the questions on the revision checklists (Charts 19 and 20) in this chapter or by material supplied by your instructor.
3. Decide whether to write an entirely new draft or to revise the one you have. Do not be overly harsh. While some early drafts serve best as "discovery drafts" rather than first drafts, many early drafts provide sufficient raw material for the revision process to get under way.
4. Be systematic. Do not evaluate at random. You need to pay attention to many different elements of a draft, from overall organization to choice of words. Some writers prefer to consider all elements concurrently, but most writers work better when they concentrate on different elements sequentially during separate rounds of revision.

◉ Major activities during revision 17

- **Add.** Insert needed words, sentences, and paragraphs. If your additions require new content, return to idea-gathering techniques (see 2d through 2j).
- **Cut.** Get rid of whatever goes off the topic or repeats what has already been said.
- **Replace.** As needed, substitute new words, sentences, and paragraphs for what you have cut.
- **Move material around.** Change the sequence of paragraphs if the material is not presented in logical order (see 2k through 2m). Move sentences within paragraphs or to other paragraphs if any paragraph arrangement seems illogical (see 4e).

TEACHING TIP

Revising is a process just as composing is a process. Students may find it helpful to examine the steps they go through when revising, editing, and proofreading. Here are some questions they can use to look carefully at how they approach these final stages of writing a paper.

1. How did you make the mental shift from suspending judgment to making judgment?

2. Did you use the questions in the revision checklists in Charts 19 and 20 or material supplied by your instructor?

3. How did you decide whether to write an entirely new draft or to revise the one you had?

4. If you had readers other than the teacher, how did you use their suggestions? Did you use all of them? None of them?

5. Did you reconsider your original purpose and audience?

6. Did you need to make any changes in your introduction or conclusion because of other changes in your text?

7. Was your original title still appropriate?

8. Did you consider different elements of your writing during separate rounds of revision?

9. How much new material did you add? In how many places did you add new words, sentences, or paragraphs?

10. How much material did you delete? In how many places did you cut out words, sentences, or paragraphs?

11. How many changes in the sequence of paragraphs did you make?

12. Did you use a checklist, either one in this chapter, your own, or one supplied by your instructor, to examine your writing for grammar, spelling, punctuation, or capitalization problems?

13. Did you edit your paper in a single reading or look for possible errors in a series of readings?

→

Teaching Tip (continued)

14. Did you read your paper aloud to find errors? Did you start at the end? Did you read it line by line?

15. Did you reconsider the format of your paper?

TEACHING TIP

You might want to emphasize to your students that a change in attitude is quite noticeable when writers switch from generating prose to revising it. Making students aware of this fact often helps them understand and feel comfortable with the notion of writing as a process.

TEACHING TIP

Students may find it helpful to know that the strengths and weaknesses in a piece of writing are often easier for the writer to recognize if a "cooling off" period intervenes between the time of writing and the time of revision. If there is an opportunity to put the piece away for a day or so, the writer returns to it not as the composer but as a reader, thus finding it easier to spot confusing passages or awkward statements. Since students are not famous for working far ahead of schedule, they should be encouraged to provide at least a few hours to distance themselves from the writing before trying to revise it. However, if too much time elapses between the draft and the rereading, the writer is likely to lose the sense of purpose and meaning that accompanied the original effort.

As you engage in each revision activity, keep the whole picture in mind. Changes affect more than the place revised. Check that your separate changes work well in the context of a particular paragraph or the whole essay.

Revising is usually separate from *editing* (see 3d). Editing involves concentrating on important surface features such as spelling and punctuation. During revising, however, you concentrate on the content, the meaning that you want your material to deliver effectively.

▣ COMPUTER TIP: Relieved of the sometimes tedious work of copying and recopying material, many writers feel more creative when they use a computer. Their ideas seem to flow more freely when each new thought does not lead to a recopying job. Nevertheless, do not let yourself be seduced by the wonders of computers. They are only machines. A neatly printed page might look like a final draft, but resist the urge to believe that because your paper looks neat, it is finished. ▣

3c.2 Using the organizing power of your thesis statement and essay title during revision

As you revise, pay special attention to your essay's thesis statement and title. Both features can help you stay on track. Also, both tell your readers what to expect, which helps you communicate your message as clearly as possible.

If your **thesis statement** (see 2n, especially Chart 12) does not match what you say in your essay, you need to revise either the thesis statement or the essay—and sometimes both. Your thesis statement must present the topic of the essay, your particular focus on that topic, and your purpose for writing the essay. The first draft of a thesis statement is often merely an estimate of what will be covered in the essay. Early in the revision process, check the accuracy of your estimate. Then use the thesis statement's controlling power to bring it and your essay in line with each other.

Each writer's experience with revising a thesis statement varies from essay to essay. Carol Moreno wrote a number of versions of her thesis statement (as shown in section 2n) before she started to draft. After writing her first draft, she checked the thesis statement and satisfied herself that it communicated what she wanted to say. But then she decided to change parts of her essay to conform more closely to her thesis statement. (For an example of a thesis statement for a research paper being revised from the first through the final draft, see section 32r.)

The **title** of an essay also plays an important organizing role during revision. An effective title sets you on your course and tells your reader what to expect. (Some writers like to start a first draft with a title at the top of the page to focus their thinking. As they revise drafts, they revise the title as needed.) An effective title might not come to mind until you have drafted, revised, and edited your essay, by which time your thinking about your topic has crystallized. Remember that a title is never the same as a thesis statement.

PUNCTUATION ALERT: When you put your paper's title at the top of the page or on a title page, do not enclose it in quotation marks or underline it. For the only exception, see 28d. ❗

Titles can be *direct* or *indirect*. A *direct title* tells exactly what the essay will be about. A direct title contains key words under which the essay would be cataloged in a library or other database system. The title of Carol Moreno's essay shown in section 3f.3 is direct: "Women Can Pump Iron, Too." Similarly, the title of Daniel Casey's essay in section 6i is direct: "Commercialism at Holiday Time Benefits the Nation."

A direct title should not be too broad. An overly broad title implies that the writer has not given sufficient thought to the essay's content. Carol Moreno's earlier title, "Pumping Iron," would be too broad for her final essay. Conversely, a direct title should not be too narrow. Equally unsatisfactory would be an overly long title—for example, listing the topics of most of the essay's body paragraphs: "Women Pump Iron to Meet a Wide Range of Physical and Personal Objectives."

An *indirect title* is also acceptable for some academic writing. Be guided by your taste and each instructor's requirements. An indirect title hints at the essay's topic. It presents a puzzle that can be solved by reading the essay. This approach can be intriguing for the reader, but the writer has to make sure that the title is not too obscure. For example, for Carol Moreno's essay, a satisfactory indirect title would be "The Meaning of Muscles." "Equal Play" would be an unsatisfactory indirect title because it is too obscure.

Whether direct or indirect, a title stands alone. Do not construe it as the opening sentence of an essay. For example, Carol Moreno, whose essay's good title is "Women Can Pump Iron, Too," would have been wrong had she written as her essay's first sentence "They certainly can" or "I am proof of that." Chart 18 gives guidelines for titles.

⊙ Guidelines for essay titles 18

- Do not wait until the last minute to tack on a title. You might write a title before you start to draft or while you are revising, but always check as you review your essay, to make sure that the title clearly relates to the content of the evolving essay.
- For a direct title, use key words relating to your topic, but do not reveal your entire essay.
- For an indirect title, be sure that it hints accurately and that its meaning will be clear once a reader finishes your essay.
- Do not use quotation marks or underlining with the title (unless your title includes another title; see 30f).
- Do not treat your essay title as the first sentence of the essay.

Many of us have had the experience of reading what is supposedly a student's revision of an essay we have already read and responded to, only to find that most of our comments have been ignored; the revision turns out to be the original essay with a few spelling errors corrected. Sometimes, students do not know how to respond fully to an instructor's comments.

One step in demystifying comments is to have the class collectively respond to the instructor's comments on Carol Moreno's second draft. Ask the students to read the instructor's comments on Moreno's essay and decide what Moreno might do in response to each one. You might lead a discussion of the options for fixing each problem. As you come to each comment, allow sufficient time for students to think about and draft revisions or to look up the needed information in their handbook. Invite students to offer their revisions at each comment, and keep students alert to the many good alternatives that can emerge in response to the instructor's questions. You might also point out that responses are more likely to be identical to the coded comments of the instructor because most of them call for corrections of grammar or punctuation.

An alternative to comment-by-comment class discussion is to assign the entire revision as a home or class exercise. Then, students can discuss their thought-through answers and compare their results.

As much as possible, try to use copies of the material or overhead transparencies for the discussion of alternate complete third drafts. Students often cannot follow the discussion if too much relies on memory of various similar versions.

BACKGROUND

In "Finding Grand's Works: A Case Study in the Art of Revising" (*Journal of Basic Writing*, Summer 1996: 3–22), Rebecca Williams Mlynarczyk suggests how teacher responses can help students become revisers who move beyond surface-level features to content-based analysis.

3c.3 Using revision checklists

Revision checklists can help you focus your attention as you evaluate your writing to revise it. Use a checklist provided by your instructor, or compile your own based on the revision checklists in Charts 19 and 20. The checklists here are comprehensive and detailed; do not let them overwhelm you. Feel free to adapt them to your writing assignments as well as to your personal weaknesses and strengths. Also, the checklists here move from the larger elements of the whole essay and paragraphs to the smaller elements of sentences and words. This progression for the sake of self-evaluation works well for many writers. (To see how Carol Moreno used these revision checklists, see section 3f.)

 Revision checklist: Whole essay and paragraphs   **19**

The answer to each question should be yes. If it is not, you need to revise. The reference numbers in parentheses tell you what section of this handbook to consult.

1. Is your essay topic suitable and sufficiently narrow (2c)?
2. Does your thesis statement communicate your topic and focus (2n) and your purpose (1b)?
3. Does your essay reflect awareness of your audience (1c)?
4. Is your tone appropriate (1d)?
5. Is your essay logically organized (2m) and are your paragraphs logically arranged (4e)?
6. Have you cut material that goes off the topic?
7. Is your reasoning sound (5h through 5j), and do you avoid logical fallacies (5k)?
8. Is your introduction related to the rest of your essay (4g)?
9. Does each body paragraph express its main idea in a topic sentence as needed (4b)? Are the main ideas clearly related to the thesis statement, and have you covered all that your thesis statement "promises" (2n)?
10. Are your body paragraphs sufficiently developed with concrete support for their main idea (4c)?
11. Have you used necessary transitions (4d.1, 4d.5)?
12. Do your paragraphs maintain coherence (4d)?
13. Does your conclusion provide a sense of completion (4g)?
14. Does your title reflect the content of the essay (3c.2)?

Revision checklist: Sentences and words   **20**

The answer to each question should be yes. If it is not, you need to revise. The reference numbers in parentheses tell you what chapter or section of this handbook to consult.

1. Have you eliminated sentence fragments (13)?
2. Have you eliminated comma splices and run-together sentences (14)?
3. Have you eliminated confusing shifts (15a)?
4. Have you eliminated misplaced and dangling modifiers (15b and 15c)?
5. Have you eliminated mixed and incomplete sentences (15d and 15e)?
6. Are your sentences concise (16)?
7. Do your sentences show clear relationships among ideas (17)?
8. Do you use parallelism to help your sentences deliver their meaning gracefully, and do you avoid faulty parallelism (18)?
9. Does your writing reflect variety and emphasis (19)?
10. Have you used exact words (20b)?
11. Is your usage correct (Usage Glossary)?
12. Do your words reflect an appropriate level of formality (21a.1)?
13. Do you avoid sexist language (21b), slang and colloquial language (21a.3), slanted language (21a.4), clichés (21d), and artificial language (21e)?

ESL NOTE: If English is not your first language, you may want to consult Part Seven to check your use of VERB-PREPOSITION combinations, ARTICLES, word order, VERBALS, and MODAL AUXILIARIES in addition to using the revision checklists.

COMPUTER TIP: The computer makes rearranging relatively painless. You can make endless versions of your draft until you are satisfied with the order. Try reordering your body paragraphs, splitting or joining some existing paragraphs, and moving your last paragraph to the first position. You may be surprised. Save the most promising versions, and perhaps ask your peers to react to them. Do not, however, be tempted to rearrange endlessly. Set limits, or you will never finish.

3d Knowing how to edit

When you **edit,** you check the technical correctness of your writing. Your job during editing is not to generate a new draft but to fine-tune the surface features of the draft you have. You pay attention to surface features of your writing, such as grammar, spelling, and punctuation, and the correct use of capitals, numbers, italics, and abbreviations. Writers sometimes refer to editing as *revising* (see 3c). In this handbook, I discuss editing separately to emphasize that editing focuses more on presentation than on meaning.

If you edit too soon in the writing process, you might distract yourself from checking to see if your material delivers its meaning effectively. You are ready to edit when you have a final draft that contains suitable content, organization, development, and sentence structure. Once you have polished your work, you are ready to transcribe it into a final copy and proofread it (see 3e).

Editing is crucial in writing. Slapdash editing will distract your readers and, in writing for assignments, lower your grade. No matter how much attention you have paid to planning, shaping, drafting, and revising, you must edit carefully.

Editing takes patience. Inexperienced writers sometimes rush editing, especially if they feel that they have revised well. When you edit, resist any impulse to hurry. Matters of grammar and punctuation take concentration—and, frequently, the time to check yourself by looking up rules and conventions in this handbook. As you edit, be systematic. Use a checklist supplied by your instructor or one that you compile from the editing checklist in Chart 21.

 Editing checklist 21

The answer to each question should be yes. If it is not, you need to edit. The reference numbers in parentheses tell you what chapter of this handbook to consult.

1. Is your grammar correct (7 through 15)?
2. Is your spelling correct, and are your hyphens correct (22)?
3. Have you used commas correctly (24)?
4. Have you used all other punctuation correctly (23, 25 through 29)?
5. Have you used capital letters, italics, abbreviations, and numbers correctly (30)?

3e Knowing how to proofread

When you **proofread,** you check your final version carefully before handing it in. Make sure that your work is an accurate, clean transcription of your final draft. Resist trying to proofread while you edit; one process can distract you from the other.

Proofreading involves a careful, line-by-line reading of your writing. You may want to proofread with a ruler so that you cannot look beyond the line you are reading at any given time. Proofreading backward, starting at the end, helps some writers avoid becoming distracted by the content of the paper. Another useful proofreading technique is to read your final draft aloud, to yourself or to a friend. This can help you hear errors that have slipped past your notice.

COMPUTER TIP: You can use the screen to help you proofread and edit. Highlight a five- or six-line section, and read each section slowly and carefully. This strategy allows you to work in small segments, reducing any tendency to read too quickly and ignore errors.

You might try compiling a list of the mistakes you caught when proofreading before. If the difference between *its* and *it's* always escapes you or if you know that you tend to misuse the colon, access your personal mistake file, to remind you to search your draft for those items. ◙

In proofreading, look for letters or words inadvertently left out. If you handwrite your material, be legible. If you type, neatly correct any typing errors. If a page has numerous errors, retype the page. Do not expect your instructor to make allowances for crude typing; if you cannot type well, arrange to have your paper typed properly. No matter how hard you have worked on other parts of the writing process, if your final copy is inaccurate or messy, you will not reach your audience successfully.

COMPUTER TIP: Get to know any special tools for writers that are included in the software programs for your computer; for example:

- *Spell-check programs* call attention to words that do not match their dictionaries. The programs are a big help for spotting typos, but they have limits. Suppose you intended to type *west* but instead typed *rest*. Because *rest* is a correctly spelled word in the program's dictionary, the program will not call *west* to your attention. Always read your work carefully yourself.

- *Thesaurus programs* are no different from printed thesauruses (see 20b.1). You must evaluate each suggested substitution for sense within the context and purpose of what you are writing.

- *Style-check programs* examine your file against strict interpretations of grammar, usage, mechanics, and punctuation rules, alerting you to writing that differs from the program's standards. Grammar and style checkers cannot substitute for understanding grammar and mechanics. These programs may give ineffective or wrong advice, so consult this handbook if you are unsure what the program is suggesting and how to fix the problem. ◙

3f Case study: A student writing an essay

This section is a case study of a student, Carol Moreno, going through the process of writing an essay. As you examine her three drafts, refer back to her writing assignment on page 20. In addition, look at the discussion of how she mapped her ideas (see 2i) and wrote her thesis statement (see 2n). See section 2o for sample outlines.

3f.1 Writing and revising a first draft

Carol Moreno wrote about a challenge she faced and met. As a result of using planning techniques (see 2e, 2f, and 2i), she chose the topic of weight lifting for women who want to build up their strength. She decided that her writing purpose would be *to inform* (see 1b.2). She then wrote the first draft, expecting to revise it later.

As Moreno revised her first draft, she worked systematically through the larger elements of the whole essay and paragraphs, and then she turned to her sentences and words. As she did this, she referred to the revision checklists in Charts 19 and 20. Here is Moreno's first draft, along with her notes to herself about revisions she wanted to make when she wrote her second draft.

First Draft, Revised by Student

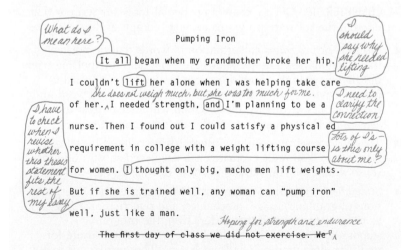

QUOTATION: ON WRITING

I love spending an hour or two with a dictionary and a thesaurus looking for a more nearly perfect word. Or taking my pen and ruthlessly pruning all the unnecessary adjectives, or fooling around with the rhythm of a sentence or a paragraph by changing a verb into a participle or making any number of little changes that a magazine editor I work with calls "mouse milking."

—Marie Winn

MOVE:
[This should be my third ¶. My second ¶ should give background]

~~talked about who we are and why we wanted to take the~~ *¶*
~~course. We heard about how to avoid~~ *can lead to* *unless lifters* injury *by learning*
and weight machines. *Free weights are barbells.*
the safe use of free weights ∧(barbells)∧ To be safe,
no matter how little the weight, lifters must never
raise a barbell by bending at the waist. Instead, they
should squat, *grasp* ~~grab~~ the barbell, and then straighten up
To avoid a *that* *serious*
into a standing position. ∧Twists∧ can lead to ∧injury, ~~so~~

[I need to go into more detail here]

lifters must keep head erect, facing forward, back and
neck aligned. [Lifters use weight machines sitting
down, which is a big advantage of the Nautilus and
Universal.

[I have to bring in more than myself to say who we are]

happy
(I) was {relieved} that (I) won't develop overly

[move up to be #2 (background)]

masculine muscle mass. (We) learned that we can rely on
women's biology. Our bodies produce only very small
amounts of the hormones that enlarge muscles in men.

[I need to tie these together (check 4d)]

With normal training, *muscles*
~~Normally,~~ ∧women's ∧grow longer rather than bulkier.
Weight lifting is a form of (anareobic) exercise. It
(SP)
does not make people breathe harder or their hearts
(SP)
running, walking, and
beat faster. (Arobic) exercise like ∧swimming build

[am I too informal here?]

endurance, so I (took up) swimming.

[My topic sentence needs work]

    After safety comes our needs for physical
strength. A well-planned, progressive weight training
It *a person*
program. ~~You~~ ∧begins∧with whatever weight ∧~~you~~ can lift
to the base weight as she gets stronger.
comfortably and ~~then~~ gradually add∧What builds
the lifter does,
muscle strength is the number of "reps", ∧~~we do,~~ not
resistance from adding
necessarily an increase in the amount of ~~added~~∧
weight. In my class, we ranged from 18 to 43, scrawny
pudgy *couch potato*
to ∧fat, and ∧~~lazy~~ to superstar, and we each developed

→

[handwritten: I'm not trying here] a program that was (OK) for us. Some women didn't listen to our instructor who urged us not to ~~do~~ more *[handwritten: try]* *[handwritten: Start sentence here? not sure]* reps or weight than our programs called for, even if ~~it~~ *[handwritten: our first workouts]* seemed too easy. This turned out to be good

advice because those of us who didn't listen woke up *[handwritten: the next morning]* feeling as though our bodies had been twisted by evil forces.

[handwritten: In addition to fitting to] ~~After meeting~~ her physical capabilities, a weight lifter needs to design her personal goals. Most students in my group wanted to improve their *[handwritten: I need specific examples of students]* upper body strength. (Each) student learned to use specific exercises to isolate certain muscle groups, for example we might work on our arms and (abdomen) *[handwritten: sp?]* one day and our shoulders and chest the next day. My goal is nursing, which I want to pursue. I want *[handwritten: I'm off the topic]* to help others, but I'm also very interested in the science I'll learn. I hear there is a lot of memorization, which I'm pretty good at. I also will have "clinical" assignments to give us hands ~~on~~ ~~experience in hospitals.~~ Because I had had such trouble lifting my grandmother, I added exercises to strengthen my legs and back. Another student added neck strengthening exercises. Someone else added finger and hand exercises.

At the end of the course, we had to evaluate our progress. When I started, I could lift 10 pounds, *[handwritten: over my head for 3 reps.]*

→

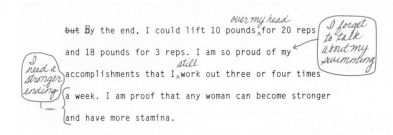

but ~~B~~y the end, I could lift 10 pounds *over my head* for 20 reps *[I forget to talk about my swimming]* and 18 pounds for 3 reps. I am so proud of my *[I need a stronger ending]* accomplishments that I *still* work out three or four times a week. I am proof that any woman can become stronger and have more stamina.

3f.2 Revising a second draft

After Carol Moreno finished writing and entering notes to herself on her first draft (see 3f.1), she revised her work into a second draft and typed a clean copy to give to her instructor. As stated in the assignment (see page 20), Moreno's instructor considered the second draft an "essay in progress," so that all comments by the instructor were aimed at helping Moreno write an effective third, final draft.

Here is Moreno's second draft with two types of comments from the instructor: **questions** to stimulate Moreno to clarify and expand on ideas in the draft and **section codes**—number-letter combinations—for Moreno to consult in this handbook.

Second Draft with Instructor's Comments

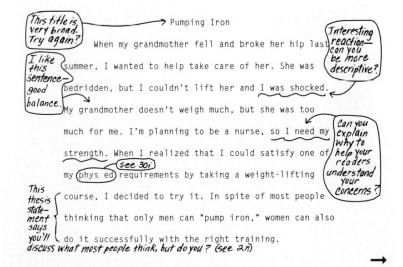

QUOTATION: ON WRITING

What makes me happy is rewriting. . . . It's like cleaning house, getting rid of all the junk, getting things in the right order, tightening things up.

—Ellen Goodman

TEACHING TIP

Certainly, all of us sometimes feel that we are drowning in student writing. The battle rages constantly: Do I spend twenty minutes on each short essay, or do I spend five minutes and get to respond to more of what my students write?

Given the few minutes that we have for each essay, decisions about what and how to write are important. Codes (abbreviations such *sp* and *agr;* references to the text, such as *15a*) are a clear, fast way to refer to unambiguous matters in grammar, punctuation, and mechanics. Make sure students know what the symbols mean—you might review the symbols you ordinarily use as part of the follow-up to their receiving their first piece of writing back from you. Along with citing errors, many symbols send a secondary message: "This matter is important but relatively uninspiring. Fix it quickly (and learn the information) and move on to the more interesting aspects of your essay."

Many issues of substance are difficult to discuss exclusively by code. Besides, students like to feel that a real human being is reading their work—and real people ask questions when they are puzzled. Therefore, whenever possible, phrase your reactions as questions. Instead of writing "unclear," ask "How does this relate to your thesis?" If you do not have time to write many questions, try to get at least one in per paper. Psychologically, people can't help but answer questions—at least in their own minds. So to ask a question is to guarantee an answer. And with the answer in mind, a student can revise.

Whenever time permits, a good description deserves more than "nice" scribbled in the margin; you might say, "You really made me see the lake at sundown." If a student tells you about a cooking disaster, you might say, "You had me laughing in sympathy. The same thing happened to me." Such comments validate students' experiences and also demonstrate compassionate reading.

→

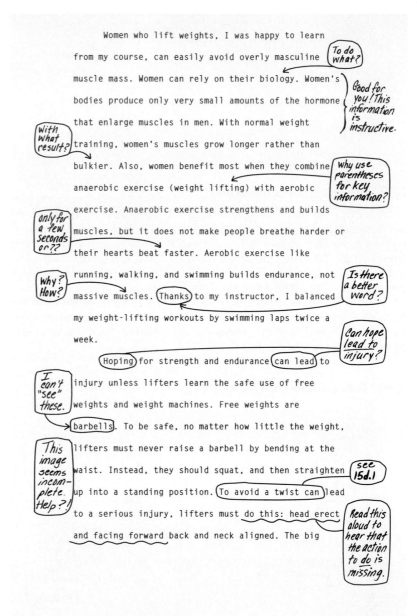

→

see 19b

{ advantage of weight machines is that lifters must use them sitting down, so machines like the Nautilus and Universal pretty much force lifters to sit straight, which really does reduce the chance of injury.

Do you want to use one word so much?

Once a weight lifter understands how to lift safely, she (needs) to meet her personal (needs). No one (needs) to be strong to get started. A well-planned progressive weight training program It begins with *See 13a* whatever weight a person can lift comfortably and gradually adds to the base weight as she gets stronger. What builds strength is the number of ("reps") the lifter does, not necessarily an increase in the amount of (resistance) from adding weight. Our *meaning?* instructor helped the women in our class, who ranged

These adjectives are fun.

{ from 18 to 43, scrawny to pudgy, couch potato to superstar, to develop a program that suited us. Our instructor urged us not to try more reps or weight than our programs called for, even if our first workouts seemed too easy. This turned out to be good ⎤ *Fun again.* advice because those of us who did not listen woke up ⎬ *Your voice (personality) comes through.* the next morning feeling as though our bodies had ⎦ been twisted by evil forces.

In addition to fitting a program to her physical ⎤ *Does one design a goal?* capabilities, a weight lifter needs to design her ← personal goals. Most students in my group wanted to improve their upper body strength, so we focused on

good details

{ exercises to strengthen our arms, shoulders, abdomens, and chests. Each student learned to use specific

---

Teaching Tip (continued)

In many cases, reaction comments are most useful in the final response to an essay. Many students turn to the end of the essay before reading marginal comments. After the grade, this is the part of our response that is most crucial to students. The final comment is our total impression; the margins are a kind of running commentary. To be useful, a closing comment needs to clarify our response, not duplicate the grade: A student whose grade has jumped from D to B knows his or her work is "better," so try to be specific.

A useful end comment consists of at least several sentences. A serviceable pattern consists of a personal response, a sentence about the content and organization of the piece (positive as well as negative observations—see the end comment to Foster), and, where pertinent, a few sentences about a recurring mechanical or grammatical issue (for example, "Try to hear and pronounce the ends of words. You frequently omit *-s* and *-ed* endings, resulting in tense and number errors that can confuse a reader").

→

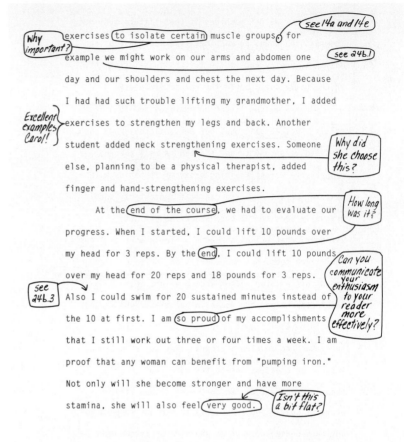

Dear Carol,
   You have truly earned the right to feel proud of yourself. You've also inspired me to consider weight training myself!
   As you revise for your final draft, I'd urge you to get more _voice_ (your personality) into the essay. To do this, you don't have to become too informal; instead, find how you _felt_ about what you were doing and try to put that into words. Also, think about my questions and the codes that refer you to sections of the Troyka handbook. I will enjoy reading your final draft, I'm sure.
                                        K.N.

3f.3 Revising, editing, and proofreading a final draft

Moreno revised her essay in a third, final draft by working with the instructor's comments. Moreno started with the larger elements of the essay by thinking about the instructor's questions and suggestions. Next, Moreno used the codes—the number-letter combinations—that referred her to specific sections in this handbook concerning matters of word choice, style, grammar, and punctuation. She also referred to the revision checklists in Charts 19 and 20. Before typing a clean copy of her third, final draft, Moreno edited her writing by referring to the editing checklist in Chart 21. Here is the third, final draft of Moreno's essay. The labels in the margins are guideposts for you only in this handbook; do not use them on your final drafts.

Third, Final Draft by Student

Moreno 1

title
Women Can Pump Iron, Too

introduction
When my grandmother fell and broke her hip last summer, I wanted to help take care of her. Because she was bedridden, she needed to be lifted at times, but I was shocked to discover that I could not lift her without my mother's or brother's help. My grandmother does not weigh much, but she was too much for me. My pride was hurt, and even more important, I began to worry about my plans to be a nurse specializing in the care of elderly people. What if I were too weak to help my patients get around? When I realized that I could satisfy one of my Physical Education requirements by taking a weight-lifting course for women, I decided to try it. Many people picture only big, macho men wanting

thesis statement
to lift weights, but times have changed. With the right training, women can also "pump iron" successfully to build strength.

background information
Women who lift weights, I was happy to learn from my course, can easily avoid developing overly masculine muscle mass. Women can rely on their

QUOTATION: ON WRITING

I am convinced that all writers are optimists whether they concede the point or not. . . . How otherwise could any human being sit down to a pile of blank sheets and decide to write . . . ?

—Thomas Costain

QUOTATION: ON WRITING

Let your literary compositions be kept from the public eye for nine years at least.
—Horace

biology to protect them. Women's bodies produce only very small amounts of the hormones that enlarge muscles in men. With normal weight training, women's muscles grow longer rather than bulkier. The result is smoother, firmer muscles, not massive bulges. Also, women benefit most when they combine weight lifting, which is a form of anaerobic exercise, with aerobic exercise. Anaerobic exercise strengthens and builds muscles, but it does not make people breathe harder or their hearts beat faster for sustained periods. In contrast, aerobic exercises like running, walking, and swimming build endurance, but not massive muscles, because they force a person to take in more oxygen, which increases lung capacity, improves circulatory health, and tones the entire body. Encouraged by my instructor, I balanced my weight-lifting workouts by swimming laps twice a week.

support:
first
aspect of
training

Striving for strength can end in injury unless weight lifters learn the safe use of free weights and weight machines. Free weights are barbells, the metal bars that round metal weights can be attached to at each end. To be safe, no matter how little the weight, lifters must never raise a barbell by bending at the waist, grabbing the barbell, and then straightening up. Instead, they should squat, grasp the barbell, and then use their leg muscles to straighten into a standing position. To avoid a twist that can lead to serious injury, lifters must use this posture: head erect and facing forward, back and neck aligned. The big advantage of weight machines, which use weighted handles and bars hooked to wires and pulleys, is that lifters must use them sitting down. Therefore, machines like the Nautilus and Universal actually force lifters to keep their bodies properly aligned, which drastically reduces the chance of injury.

support:
second
aspect of
training

    Once a weight lifter understands how to lift safely, she needs a weight-lifting regimen personalized to her specific physical needs. Because benefits come from "resistance," which is the stress that lifting any amount of weight puts on a muscle, no one has to be strong to get started. A well-planned, progressive weight-training program begins with whatever weight a person can lift comfortably and gradually adds to the base weight as she gets stronger. What builds muscle strength is the number of repetitions, or "reps," the lifter does, not necessarily an increase in the amount of resistance from adding weight. Our instructor helped the women in the class, who ranged from 18 to 43, scrawny to pudgy, and couch potato to superstar, develop a program that was right for our individual weight, age, and overall level of conditioning. Everyone's program differed in how much weight to start out with and how many reps to do for each exercise. Our instructor urged us not to try more weight or reps than our programs called for, even if our first workouts seemed too easy. This turned out to be good advice because those of us who did not listen woke up the next day feeling as though our bodies had been twisted by evil forces.

support:
third
aspect of
training

    In addition to fitting a program to her physical capabilities, a weight lifter needs to design an individual routine to fit her personal goals. Most students in my group wanted to improved their upper body strength, so we focused on exercises to strengthen arms, shoulders, abdomens,

QUOTATION: ON WRITING

When you say something, make sure you have said it. The chances of your having said it are only fair.

—E. B. White

➡

Moreno 4

and chests. Each student learned to use specific exercises to isolate certain muscle groups. Because muscles strengthen and grow when they are rested after a workout, our instructor taught us to work alternate muscle groups on different days. For example, a woman might work on her arms and abdomen one day and then her shoulders and chest the next day. Because I had had such trouble lifting my grandmother, I added exercises to strengthen my legs and back. Another student, who had hurt her neck in a car crash, added neck-strengthening exercises. Someone else, planning to be a physical therapist, added finger- and hand-strengthening exercises.

conclusion: outcome with call to action

At the end of our 10 weeks of weight training, we had to evaluate our progress. Was I impressed! I felt ready to lift the world. When I started, I could lift only 10 pounds over my head for 3 reps. By the end of the course, I could lift 10 pounds over my head for 20 reps, and I could lift 18 pounds for 3 reps. Also, I could swim laps for 20 sustained minutes instead of the 10 I had barely managed at first. I am so proud of my weight-training accomplishments that I still work out three or four times a week. I am proof that any woman can benefit from "pumping iron." Not only will she become stronger and have more stamina, but she will also feel energetic and confident. After all, there is nothing to lose--except maybe some flab.

4

RHETORICAL STRATEGIES
IN PARAGRAPHS

BACKGROUND

u·ni·ty (yoo′ nə tē) n. *pl.* -ties (1) The state, property, or product of being united physically, socially, or morally; oneness; opposed to *division, plurality.*
—*Britannica World Language Dictionary*

Rhetorical strategies in writing are techniques for presenting ideas so that a writer's intended message is delivered with clarity and impact. The rhetorical strategies available to you as a writer are sufficiently varied to give you many choices of ways to make your writing effective. As you can see from the explanations and examples in this chapter, all rhetorical strategies reflect the typical patterns of thought that humans use quite naturally. As you try out these strategies, especially as they keep you aware of sequencing and arranging sentences, you can apply them to composing your paragraphs and, in some situations, whole essays.

4a Understanding paragraphs

A **paragraph** is a group of sentences that work in concert to develop a unit of thought. Paragraphing permits you to subdivide material into manageable parts and, at the same time, to arrange those parts into a unified whole that effectively communicates its message.

Paragraphing is signaled by indentation. The first line is indented five spaces in a typewritten paper and one inch in a handwritten paper. (Business letters are sometimes typed in "block format," with paragraphs separated by a double space but no paragraph indentations. Generally, block format is not appropriate for essays.)

The purpose of a paragraph helps you determine its structure. In college, the most common purposes for academic writing are to inform and to persuade (see 1b). Some paragraphs introduce, conclude, or provide transitions. Most paragraphs, however, are **topical paragraphs,** also called *developmental paragraphs* or *body paragraphs.* They consist of a statement of a main idea and specific, logical support for that main idea. Consider paragraph 1, a topical paragraph that seeks to inform. (To help discussion and reference in this chapter, a red number appears at the left side of each sample paragraph.)

The cockroach lore that has been daunting us for years is mostly true. Roaches can live for twenty days without food, fourteen days without

TEACHING TIP

Essay paragraphing differs considerably from newspaper-article paragraphing. Anyone can see at a glance that newspapers frequently have paragraphs of only a sentence or two. Such short paragraphs are rare in essays, except perhaps as transitions. The reason for the difference in the look of essays and articles is the rationale behind each. Essays attempt to present material in a simultaneously logical and dramatic way. They begin with a hook to grab the reader's interest and then usually proceed from point to point until the end (of the narrative or of the list of causes) is reached. Rarely is the first paragraph used to reveal key information. Essays are written on the assumption that they will be read from beginning to end.

In contrast, newspaper articles (not to be confused with essays in newspapers) use few such dramatic devices for suspense purposes. Usually, the only hook is the headline. Then, in paragraph 1, the reader gets the *who, what, where, when, why,* and *how.* Subsequent paragraphs reveal additional details, but all the key facts are given in paragraph 1—the opposite of the procedure in the essay's first paragraph. The further one gets into most newspaper articles, the less important the content. In some cases, a reader can get the idea that the piece doesn't conclude so much as trail off. This is because newspaper articles are written on the assumption that they will *not* be read from beginning to end. Editors may cut off the last few inches of a story to make it fit on a page; readers may go only as far as the first paragraph.

These differences have several implications in the writing classroom. First, most newspaper articles and many magazine arti-

→

1 water; they can flatten their bodies and crawl through a crack thinner than a dime; they can eat huge doses of carcinogens and still die of old age. They can even survive "as much radiation as an oak tree can," says William Bell, the University of Kansas entomologist whose cockroaches appeared in the movie *The Day After*. They'll eat almost anything—regular food, leather, glue, hair, paper, even the starch in book bindings. (The New York Public Library has quite a cockroach problem.) They sense the slightest breeze, and they can react and start running in .05 second; they can also remain motionless for days. And if all this isn't creepy enough, they can fly too.

—Jane Goldman, "What's Bugging You"

Goldman states her main idea in the first sentence. She then gives concrete examples supporting her claim that there is much truth to the lore about cockroaches. This paragraph relates to the thesis of the whole essay: "Roaches cannot be banished from the world, but they can be controlled in people's homes and apartments."

Consider this topical paragraph, which seeks to persuade. It, too, consists of a main idea and support.

2 The public library is the best, most democratic, most economical mechanism ever devised to provide access to information and enlightenment on issues that range from the intensely personal to those that are global in nature. Individuals of all ages and from all walks of life, community groups, agencies, businesses, unions, and government institutions of every kind increasingly turn to the public library for assistance. It is the only library that is available to everyone in the community. Typically, it receives half of 1 percent of the government's budget yet serves 30 to 50 percent of the people. No other community service is more cost effective.

—Clara Bennett, president of the board of trustees, Nassau County Library System

Bennett states her main idea in the first two sentences. The second sentence narrows the focus of the first and sets the stage for the supporting statements that follow.

Goldman's and Bennett's paragraphs demonstrate the three major characteristics of an effective paragraph. (See Chart 22.)

⊙ Major characteristics of an effective paragraph 22

- **Unity:** clear, logical relationship between the main idea of a paragraph (see 4b) and supporting evidence for that main idea (see 4c)
- **Coherence:** smooth progression from one sentence to the next within a paragraph (see 4d)
- **Development:** logical arrangement of paragraphs (see 4e) and specific, concrete support for the main idea of each paragraph (see 4f)

4b Writing unified paragraphs

A paragraph is **unified** when all its sentences clarify or help support the main idea. Unity is lost if a paragraph goes off the topic by including sentences unrelated to the main idea. Here is a paragraph about databases that lacks unity because two deliberately added sentences go off the topic.

> **NO**
>
> 3
>
> We have all used physical databases since our grammar school days. Grammar school is known today as grade school or elementary school. Our class yearbooks, the telephone book, the shoebox full of receipts documenting our deductions for the IRS—these are all databases in one form or another, for a database is nothing more than an assemblage of information organized to allow the retrieval of that information in certain ways. Anyone who is well organized has a better chance of succeeding in college or in the business world.

In paragraph 3, the second and last sentences wander away from the topic of databases. As a result, unity is lost. A reader quickly loses patience with material that rambles and consequently fails to communicate a clear message. Paragraph 4 is the original version. It is unified because all its sentences, including the ones adding interesting details, relate to the subject of databases.

> **YES**
>
> 4
>
> We have all used physical databases since our grammar school days. Our class yearbooks, the telephone book, the shoebox full of receipts documenting our deductions for the IRS—these are all databases in one form or another, for a database is nothing more than an assemblage of information to allow the retrieval of that information in certain ways. A telephone book, for example, assuming that you have the right one for the right city, will enable you to find the telephone number for, say, Alan Smith. Coincidentally it will also give you his address, provided there is only one Alan Smith listed. Where there are several Alan Smiths, you would have to know the address, or at least part of it, to find the number of the particular Alan Smith you had in mind. Even without the address, however, you would still save considerable time by the telephone database. The book might list 50,000 names but only 12 Alan Smiths, so at the outset you could eliminate 49,988 telephone calls when trying to contact the elusive Mr. Smith.
>
> —Erik Sanberg-Diment, "Personal Computers"

The sentence that contains the main idea of a paragraph, called the **topic sentence,** shapes and controls the content of the rest of the paragraph. Some paragraphs use two sentences to present a main idea. In such cases, the topic sentence is followed by a **limiting** or **clarifying sentence,** which serves to narrow the paragraph's focus. In paragraph 4, the second sentence is its topic sentence, and the third sentence is its limiting sentence.

BACKGROUND

The use of topic sentences by published writers has been the subject of a great deal of research and study over the past two decades. Richard Braddock's groundbreaking research in the 1970s revealed that in the essays he examined, he found topic sentences in paragraphs only 13 percent of the time. The percentage has varied in other studies, but most have found that under half of the paragraphs in published writing begin with topic sentences.

Braddock felt that the essays he studied would have been improved if the paragraphs had used more explicit topic sentences. Recent research shows that people are able to read faster and remember and comprehend more when a paragraph begins with a sentence that states the main idea and indicates the organization of the material to follow.

TEACHING TIP

You may want to encourage students to look for topic sentences in the newspapers and magazines they read. They may be surprised to discover that in materials published for a nonacademic setting, topic sentences occur at beginnings and endings of paragraphs, just as they do in textbook examples. In some cases, they will probably find that paragraphs manage to make a unified statement without the presence of a stated topic sentence. The examples they find can provide a basis for class discussion.

QUOTATION: ON WRITING

I have everything I need. A square of sky, a piece of stone, a page, a pen, and memory raining down on me in sleeves.

—Harriet Doerr

BACKGROUND

The concept of the paragraph as a self-contained or organic unit of language first appeared in *English Composition and Rhetoric* (1866), a textbook by Alexander Bain, professor of rhetoric at the University of Aberdeen in Scotland. Bain defined the paragraph as "a collection of sentences with unity of purpose" and declared unity, coherence, and emphasis to be the characteristics of an effective paragraph, a proclamation that has had a vast influence on textbooks ever since. He gave students seven guidelines for achieving these effects:

1. Distribution into sentences: The paragraph is composed of individual sentences, each with its own unity, working together to form the whole.

2. Explicit reference: The connection of each sentence to the ones preceding it must be clear.

3. Parallel construction: Consecutive sentences that carry the same meaning or idea should be formed alike.

4. Indication of the theme: The first sentence should indicate the scope of the paragraph.

5. Unity: Unity derives from a sustained purpose and admits neither digressions nor irrelevancies.

6. Consecutive arrangement: Related topics should be placed close together.

7. Marking of subordination: The principal and subordinate statements should have their relative importance clearly indicated, as such elements in a sentence do.

Later textbooks influenced by Bain, notably Fred Newton Scott and Joseph Villiers Denney's *Paragraph-Writing* (1891), treated the paragraph as an "essay in miniature" and encouraged a meristic or parts-to-whole approach to teaching the essay, first teaching students how to write sentences and paragraphs and then teaching them to put these parts together to build essays.

Professional essay writers do not always use topic sentences, because these writers have the skill to carry the reader along without explicit signposts. Student writers are often advised to use topic sentences so that their essays will be clearly organized and their paragraphs will not stray from the main idea.

Topic sentence at the beginning of a paragraph

Most paragraphs place the topic sentence (shown in italics) first so that a reader knows immediately what to expect.

5 *To travel the streets of Los Angeles is to glimpse America's ethnic future.* At the bustling playground at McDonald's in Koreatown, a dozen shades of kids squirt down the slides and burrow through tunnels and race down the catwalks, not much minding that no two of them speak the same language. Parents of grade-school children say they rarely know the color of their youngsters' best friends until they meet them; it never seems to occur to the children to say, since they have not yet been taught to care.

—Nancy Gibbs, "Shades of Difference"

Sometimes the main idea in the topic sentence starts a paragraph and is then restated at the end of the paragraph.

6 *Every dream is a portrait of the dreamer.* You may think of your dream as a mirror that reflects your inner character—the aspects of your personality of which you are not fully aware. Once we understand this, we can also see that every trait portrayed in our dreams has to exist in us, somewhere, regardless of whether we are aware of it or admit it. *Whatever characteristics the dream figures have, whatever behavior they engage in, is also true of the dreamer in some way.*

—Robert A. Johnson, *Inner Work*

Topic sentence at the end of a paragraph

Some paragraphs reveal their supporting details before the main idea. In such cases, the topic sentence comes at the end of a paragraph. This approach is particularly effective for building suspense and for dramatic effect.

Paragraphs 7 and 8 end with a topic sentence. In paragraph 7, the main idea is fairly easy to predict as the specific suggestions accumulate. In paragraph 8, the main idea is less predictable, which makes it more satisfying for some readers but more difficult for others.

7 Burnout is a potential problem for any hardworking and persevering student. A preliminary step for preventing student burnout is for students to work in moderation. Students can concentrate on school every day, provided that they do not overtax themselves. One method students can use is to avoid concentrating on a single project for an extended period of time. For example, if students have to read two books for a midterm history test, they should do other assignments at intervals so that the two

books will not get boring. Another means to moderate a workload is to regulate how many extracurricular projects to take on. *When a workload is manageable, a student's immunity to burnout is strengthened.*

—Bradley Howard, student

8   Most people do not lose ten dollars or one hundred dollars when they trade cars. They lose many hundreds or even a thousand. They buy used cars that will not provide them service through the first payment. They overbuy new cars and jeopardize their credit, only to find themselves "hung," unable even to sell their shiny new toys. *The car business is one of the last roundups in America, the great slaughterhouse of wheeling and dealing, where millions of people each year willingly submit to being taken.*

—Remar Sutton, *Don't Get Taken Every Time*

Topic sentence implied

Some paragraphs are a unified whole even without the use of a topic sentence. Writers must construct such paragraphs carefully so that a reader can easily discern the main idea.

9   The Romans were entertained by puppets, as were the rulers of the Ottoman Empire with their favorite shadow puppet, Karaghoiz, teller of a thousand tales. In the Middle Ages, puppets were cast as devil and angel in religious mystery and morality plays until cast out entirely by the church. For centuries, there has been a rich puppetry heritage in India that matches that country's multilayered culture. The grace of Bali is reflected in its stylized, ceremonial rod and shadow puppets. The Bunraku puppets of Japan, unequaled for technique anywhere in the world, require a puppet master and two assistants to create one dramatic character on stage.

—Dan Cody, "Puppet Poetry"

EXERCISE 4-1

Consulting sections 4a and 4b, identify all topic sentences, limiting sentences, and topic sentences repeated at the ends of paragraphs. If there is no topic sentence, compose an implied one.

10   A.   A good college program should stress the development of high-level reading, writing, and mathematical skills and should provide you with a broad historical, social, and cultural perspective, no matter what subject you choose as your major. The program should teach you not only the most current knowledge in your field but also—just as important—prepare you to keep learning throughout your life. After all, you will probably change jobs, and possibly even careers, at least six times, and you'll have other responsibilities, too—perhaps as a spouse and as a parent and certainly as a member of a community whose bounds extend beyond the workplace.

—Frank T. Rhodes, "Let the Student Decide"

QUOTATION: ON WRITING

I have two methods of working. One of them involves tapping the sources of creativity. . . . I might be anywhere when it comes and I could end up writing all over the floor or up the walls and not knowing what is going on. It is like having a fit. . . .

The second method is following a trail made by my words themselves—by sitting down and writing . . . writing anything, fast. The words include the vision. That rush—that vision or high or whatever it is—doesn't last very long. A lot of writing gets done in a very short time, but it's not very good writing. Often it turns out to be just a reminder about how something felt. It has to be reworked.

—Maxine Hong Kingston

ANSWERS: EXERCISE 4-1

A. The topic sentence is the first sentence.

B. The topic sentence is the last sentence.

C. The topic sentence is the first sentence, and the second sentence is a limiting sentence.

B.   The once majestic oak tree crashes to the ground amid the destructive flames, as its panic-stricken inhabitants attempt to flee the fiery tomb. Undergrowth that formerly flourished smolders in ashes. A family of deer darts furiously from one wall of flame to the
11 other, without an emergency exit. On the outskirts of the inferno, firefighters try desperately to stop the destruction. Somewhere at the source of this chaos lies a former campsite containing the cause of this destruction—an untended campfire. This scene is one of many which illustrate how human apathy and carelessness destroy nature.

—Anne Bryson, student

C.   Rudeness is not a distinctive quality of our own time. People today would be shocked by how rudely our ancestors behaved. In the colonial period, a French traveler marveled that "Virginians do not use napkins, but they wear silk cravats, and instead of carrying white handkerchiefs they blow their noses either with their fingers or with a
12 silk handkerchief that also serves as a cravat, a napkin, and so on." In the 19th century, up to about the 1830s, even very distinguished people routinely put their knives in their mouths. And when people went to the theater, they would not just applaud politely—they would chant, jeer, and shout. So, the notion that there has been a downhill slide in manners ever since time began is just not so.

—"Horizons," *U.S. News & World Report*

4c Supporting the main idea of a paragraph

When you use effective **paragraph development** in your writing, your material is far more likely to deliver its message to the audience you want it to reach. Most successful topical paragraphs contain a generalization, which is communicated in the topic sentence of the paragraph (see 4b). But more is needed. In writing most topical paragraphs, you must be sure to *develop* the paragraph. Paragraph development comes from specific, concrete details that support the generalization. Without development, a topical paragraph contains only the broad claim of the generalization. It goes around in circles by merely repeating the generalization over and over.

Here is a paragraph that is unsuccessful because it contains one generalization restated three times in different words. It is stalled. It goes nowhere. Compare it with paragraph 1, an example of a successful paragraph about cockroaches, early in this chapter.

NO   The cockroach lore that has been daunting us for years is mostly true. Almost every tale we have heard about cockroaches
13   is true. These tales have been disheartening people for generations. No one seems to believe that it is possible to control roaches.

When you write a topical paragraph, remember that **what separates most good writing from bad is the writer's ability to move back and forth between generalizations and specific details.** A successful topical paragraph includes a generalization and specific, concrete supporting details.

Using detail is one of the keys to effective, successful development in topical paragraphs. Details bring generalizations to life by providing concrete, specific illustrations. **RENNS** is a memory device you can use to check whether you have included sufficient detail in a topical paragraph. Chart 23 explains RENNS.

 Checklist for using RENNS to test 　　　　　**23**
for specific, concrete details

- Give **r**easons.
- Use **e**xamples.
- Give **n**ames.
- Use **n**umbers.
- Appeal to the **s**enses (sight, sound, smell, taste, touch).

A well-supported paragraph usually has only a selection of RENNS, so do not expect your paragraphs to have all categories in the list. Also, RENNS does not mean that the supporting details must occur in the order of the letters in RENNS. To see RENNS in action, read the many sample paragraphs in this chapter with an eye for the details. Also, consider paragraphs 14, 15, and 16 especially. Paragraph 14 has three of the five types of RENNS. Locate as many RENNS as you can before you read the analysis that follows the paragraph.

14　U.S. shores are also being inundated by waves of plastic debris. On the sands of the Texas Gulf Coast one day last September, volunteers collected 307 tons of litter, two-thirds of which was plastic, including 31,733 bags, 30,295 bottles, and 15,631 six-pack yokes. Plastic trash is being found far out to sea. On a four-day trip from Maryland to Florida that ranged 100 miles offshore, John Hardy, an Oregon State University marine biologist, spotted "Styrofoam and other plastic on the surface, most of the whole cruise."

　　　　　　　　　　　　　　　—"The Dirty Seas," *Time*, August 1, 1988

Paragraph 14 succeeds because it does more than merely repeat its topic sentence, which is its first sentence. The paragraph develops the topic sentence by offering concrete, specific illustrations to support the

QUOTATION: ON WRITING

I just write, and things come to a crest, and that's how it is. My mind works in this way—it's sort of like a puzzle. I know where the pieces are, but I don't want to fit them for myself or for the reader. I just write.

　　　　　　　　　　　—Jamaica Kincaid

BACKGROUND

In "What Works for Me: Letting Students Critique Textbooks" (*Teaching English in the Two-Year College*, December 1996: 313), Charles Kovach reports that when students challenge the rhetorical categories in their readers (textbooks), they improve their skills in critical reading and analysis.

QUOTATION: ON WRITING

When I sit down to write I feel extraordinarily at ease, and I move in an element which, it seems to me, I know extraordinarily well; I use tools that are familiar to me and they fit snugly in my hands.

—Natalia Ginzburg

USING COLLABORATION

With full class participation, establish a shared text by having students retell a traditional children's story such as *Jack in the Beanstalk* or *Little Red Riding Hood*. Divide the class into groups, assigning each group one pattern for developing a paragraph. Ask each group to choose any element in the story and write a paragraph according to the assigned pattern of development. One group might write a detailed *description* of the hen that lays golden eggs. Another might explain the *process* by which Jack climbs the beanstalk. Another might *analyze* the root cause of Jack and his mother's poverty. Have one member of each group read its paragraph aloud, providing you and the class with an opportunity for comment and response. Such entertaining activities can also make the writing process seem less onerous to resistant students.

generalization that waves of plastic debris are inundating U.S. shores. It has *examples,* including the kinds of litter found washed up on the beach and seen offshore. It has *names*—Texas Gulf Coast; bags, bottles, six-pack yokes, which describe more specifically the general idea of 307 tons of litter; Maryland; Florida; John Hardy; Oregon State University; marine biologist; Styrofoam. It has *numbers* that describe the volume of litter collected (307 tons), counts of specific items (such as 31,733 bags and 30,295 plastic bottles), and the 100-mile distance from shore where John Hardy found floating plastic litter.

Paragraph 15 has four of the five types of RENNS. Identify as many RENNS as you can before you read the analysis of RENNS that follows the paragraph.

15   We live in a changed world from that of 1888, and we are a changed nation. Our founders knew an America with rising expectations, while we see a superpower riddled with self-doubt. Tropical rain forests were a mysterious challenge in 1888. The challenge in 1988 is saving them from disappearance. Automobiles had just been invented, and airplanes were unknown. Would our founders be impressed by rush-hour traffic, a brown cloud over Denver, or aerial gridlock at Chicago's O'Hare Airport? Could they have conceived of a Mexico City with 20 million people in an atmosphere so murky that the sun is obscured, so poisonous that school is sometimes delayed until late morning, when the air clears?

—Gilbert M. Grosvenor, "Will We Mend Our Earth?"

Paragraph 15 succeeds because it does more than repeat its topic sentence, which is the first sentence. The paragraph develops its topic sentence with specific, concrete illustrations of the changed world that makes the United States a changed nation. It has *examples,* including rain forests disappearing, automobiles and the rush-hour traffic they cause, airplanes and the aerial gridlock they cause, and air pollution that cars and planes cause. It has *names:* America, Denver, Chicago's O'Hare Airport, and Mexico City. It has *numbers:* the years 1888 and 1988, 20 million people. And it elicits one of the five *senses:* the sight of a "brown cloud" over Denver and of a murky atmosphere that obscures the sun.

Some well-developed paragraphs have a single extended example to support the topic sentence, as illustrated by paragraph 16.

16   He was one of the greatest scientists the world has ever known, yet if I had to convey the essence of Albert Einstein in a single word, I would choose *simplicity.* Perhaps an anecdote will help. Once, caught in a downpour, he took off his hat and held it under his coat. Asked why, he explained, with admirable logic, that the rain would damage the hat, but his hair would be none the worse for its wetting. This knack of going instinctively to the heart of the matter was the secret of his major scientific discoveries—this and his extraordinary feeling for beauty.

—Banesh Hoffman, "My Friend, Albert Einstein"

EXERCISE 4-2

Reread the paragraphs in Exercise 4-1, and identify the RENNS (see 4c) in each paragraph.

4d Writing coherent paragraphs

A paragraph is **coherent** when its sentences are related to each other, not only in content but also in grammatical structures and choice of words. A coherent paragraph gives a reader a sense of continuity. To achieve coherence in your writing, write each sentence of a paragraph so that it flows sensibly from the one before. Note in paragraphs 17 through 20 that each sentence continues from the previous sentence, by the writer having used the techniques of coherence listed in Chart 24.

◉ Techniques of coherence   24

- Use **transitional expressions** effectively (see 4d.1).
- Use **pronouns** effectively (see 4d.2).
- Use **repetition** effectively (see 4d.3).
- Use **parallel structures** effectively (see 4d.4).

4d.1 Using transitional expressions

Transitional expressions are words and phrases that signal connections among ideas. By signaling how ideas relate to each other, you achieve coherence in your writing. Commonly used transitional expressions are listed in Chart 25. When you use them, be sure to vary your choices within each list to achieve variety in your writing.

◉ Common transitional expressions and the relationships they signal   25

Relationship	Words
ADDITION	also, in addition, too, moreover, and, besides, furthermore, equally important, then, finally
EXAMPLE	for example, for instance, thus, as an illustration, namely, specifically

➡

ANSWERS: EXERCISE 4-2

A (paragraph 10). Reasons include learning current knowledge, keeping you learning through life, having a job, and being a spouse, a parent, and a member of the community. Examples include job, spouse, parent, and member of the community. Number named is six.

B (paragraph 11). Names include oak, deer, firefighters. Senses are invoked by sound of crashing oak, sight of flames, "fiery tomb," smoldering in ashes, deer family darting furiously, and the smell (implied) of burning trees.

C (paragraph 12). Examples include colonial Virginians using their cravats as handkerchiefs and people putting their knives in their mouths. Names include the French traveler, distinguished people, people in the theater. Numbers include the dates the 1830s and the 19th century. Senses include the noise—chants, jeers, and shouts—made by the audience in the theater.

EXTRA EXERCISE A

Mark all of the transitional expressions used in the following paragraph.

Edith Newbold Jones was the descendant of wealthy, socially prominent New York families. As a result, she made her formal debut before she married Edward Wharton of Boston in 1885. Soon after her marriage, she began writing as a therapeutic measure. She also used her writing as a means of occupying her free time when her husband was suffering from a mental illness. Naturally, much of her writing was concerned with the closed, wealthy New York society she had known as a child. In the 1890s, as a result of her "hobby," she published her first short stories in *Scribner's* magazine, using her married name, Edith Wharton. Subsequently, she was recognized as one of America's best popular writers. For example, in 1924 she became the first

➡

woman ever to receive an honorary degree   from

Extra Exercise A (continued)

Yale University. Equally important, she was awarded the Pulitzer Prize in 1921 for *The Age of Innocence*, a novel about the unbreakable moral code of Victorian society. Her most famous work, however, is *Ethan Frome*, a tragic love story. Although she continued to write about American subjects and characters, she spent much of her later life in France, where she had a home. She died there in 1937.

EXTRA EXERCISE B

Rewrite the following paragraph, using transitional words and phrases to make it more coherent. Combine and rearrange the sentences as you think necessary.

Americans are beginning to recognize the importance of regular exercise. Jogging gives the heart a good workout. It can damage the runner's ankles and calves. Jogging by itself does little to exercise the upper body. Some people prefer to walk. Bicycling is popular. In a pleasant setting, it provides visual pleasures as well as a way to burn up calories. Some people ride a stationary bicycle at home. They can watch television while they rotate the pedals. Swimming involves the upper body as well as the legs. It allows a person to exert as much energy as possible without straining muscles. On a hot summer day, swimming seems more like fun than like exercise.

QUOTATION: ON WRITING

I don't wait for moods. You accomplish nothing if you do that. Your mind must know it has got to get down to work.
—Pearl Buck

Common transitional expressions and the relationships they signal *(continued)*   **25**

Relationship	Words
CONTRAST	but, yet, however, on the one hand/on the other hand, nevertheless, nonetheless, conversely, in contrast, still, at the same time
COMPARISON	similarly, likewise, in the same way
CONCESSION	of course, to be sure, certainly, granted
RESULT	therefore, thus, as a result, so, accordingly
SUMMARY	hence, in short, in brief, in summary, in conclusion, finally
TIME SEQUENCE	first, second, third, next, then, finally, afterwards, before, soon, later, meanwhile, subsequently, immediately, eventually, currently
PLACE	in the front, in the foreground, in the back, in the background, at the side, adjacent, nearby, in the distance, here, there

🛑 **COMMA ALERT:** Transitional expressions are usually set off with commas; see section 24b.3. Here are some illustrations:

CONTINUITY BY ADDITION

Woodpeckers use their beaks to find food and to chisel out nests. **In addition,** they claim their territory and signal their desire to mate by drumming their beaks on trees.

CONTINUITY BY CONTRAST

Most birds communicate by singing. Woodpeckers, **however,** communicate by the duration and rhythm of the drumming of their beaks.

CONTINUITY BY RESULT

Woodpeckers communicate by drumming their beaks on dry branches or tree trunks. **As a result,** they can communicate across greater distances than songbirds can. ❗

Consider how the transitional expressions (shown in boldface) help make paragraph 17 coherent.

In addition to causing viewers to lose touch with society, television has had negative effects on viewers' imagination. Before the days of television, people were entertained by exciting radio shows such as *Superman, Batman,* and "War of the Worlds." Of course, the listener was required to pay careful attention to the story if all details were to be comprehended. **Better yet,** while listening to the stories, listeners would form their own images of the actions taking place. When the broadcaster would give brief descriptions of the Martian space ships invading earth, **for example,** every member of the audience would imagine a different 17 space ship. **In contrast,** television's version of "War of the Worlds" will not stir the imagination at all, **for** everyone can clearly see the actions taking place. All viewers see the same space ship with the same features. Each aspect is clearly defined, and **therefore,** no one will imagine anything different from what is seen. **Thus,** television cannot be considered an effective tool for stimulating the imagination.

Tom Paradis, "A Child's Other World"

4d.2 Using pronouns

PRONOUNS that clearly refer to NOUNS or other pronouns (see Chapter 10) can help your reader follow the bridges you build from one sentence to the next. Consider how the pronouns shown in boldface help make paragraph 18 coherent.

18 The funniest people I know are often unaware of just how ticked off **they** are about things until **they** start to kid around about **them**. Nature did not build **these** people to sputter or preach; instead, in response to the world's irritations, **they** create little plays in their minds—parodies, cartoons, fantasies. When **they** see how funny **their** creations are, **they** also understand how really sore **they** were at **their** sources. **Their** anger is a revelation, one that works backward in the minds of an audience: the audience starts out laughing and winds up fuming.

—Roger Rosenblatt, "What Brand of Laughter Do You Use?"

4d.3 Using deliberate, selective repetition

Another way to achieve coherence is by repeating key words in a paragraph. A **key word** is usually related to the main idea in the topic sentence or to a major detail in one of the supporting sentences. Repeating a key word now and then helps your reader follow your material. This technique must be used sparingly, however, to avoid being monotonous. The shorter a paragraph, the less likely that repeated words will be effective. Consider how the careful reuse of key words (shown in boldface) helps make paragraph 19 coherent.

19 Anthropologist Elena Padilla, author of *Up from Puerto Rico*, describing Puerto Rican **life** in a poor and squalid district of New York, tells **how** much people know about each other—**who** is to be trusted and **who** not, **who** is defiant of the law and **who** upholds it, **who** is competent and well informed and **who** is inept and ignorant—and **how** these things are known from the **public life** of the sidewalk and its associated enterprises. These are matters of **public** character. But she also tells **how**

QUOTATION: ON WRITING

There is no pleasure in the world like writing well and going fast. It's like nothing else. It's like a love affair, it goes on and on, and doesn't end in marriage. It's all courtship.

—Tennessee Williams

ANOTHER EXAMPLE OF PARALLEL STRUCTURES

I am not complaining that the brewing and baking were taken over by the men. If they can brew and bake as well as women or better, then by all means let them do it. But they cannot have it both ways. If they are going to adopt the very sound principle that the job should be done by the person who does it best, then that rule must be applied universally. If the women make better office-workers than men, then they must have the office work. If any individual woman is able to make a first-class lawyer, doctor, architect or engineer, then she must be allowed to try her hand at it. Once lay down the rule that the job comes first and you throw that job open to every individual, man or woman, fat or thin, tall or short, ugly or beautiful, who is able to do that job better than the rest of the world.

—Dorothy L. Sayers, "Are Women Human?"

select are those permitted to drop into the kitchen for a cup of coffee, **how** strong are the ties, and **how** limited the number of a person's genuine confidants, those **who** share in a person's **private life** and **private affairs.** She tells **how** it is not considered **dignified** for everyone to know one's **affairs.** Nor is it considered **dignified** to snoop on others beyond the face presented in **public.** It does violence to a person's **privacy** and rights. In this, the people she describes are essentially the same as the people of the mixed, Americanized city street on which I **live,** and essentially the same as the people **who live** in high-income apartments or fine town houses, too.

—Jane Jacobs, *The Economy of Cities*

4d.4 Using parallel structures

Using **parallel structures** is yet another useful way to achieve coherence in a paragraph. Parallelism is created when grammatically equivalent forms appear in a set of two or a series of three or more. The repeated tempos and sounds of parallel structures reinforce connections among ideas and create a dramatic effect.

In paragraph 20, the authors use many parallel structures (shown in boldface): a parallel series of words (*the sacred, the secular, the scientific*), parallel PHRASES (*sometimes smiled at, sometimes frowned upon*), and a group of six parallel CLAUSES (starting with *banish danger with a gesture*).

20 Superstitions are **sometimes smiled at** and **sometimes frowned upon** as observances characteristic of **the old-fashioned, the unenlightened,** children, peasants, servants, immigrants, foreigners or backwoods people. Nevertheless, they give all of us ways of moving back and forth among the different worlds in which we live—**the sacred, the secular,** and **the scientific.** They allow us to keep a private world also, where, smiling a little, we can **banish danger with a gesture** and **summon luck with a rhyme, make the sun shine in spite of storm clouds, force the stranger to do our bidding, keep an enemy at bay,** and **straighten the paths of those we love.**

—Margaret Mead and Rhoda Metraux, "New Superstitions for Old"

4d.5 Showing relationships among paragraphs

Paragraphs in an essay do not stand in isolation. The techniques of coherence discussed here in section 4d can also communicate relationships among paragraphs in an essay. Transitional expressions, pronouns, deliberate repetition, and parallel structures can all help you link ideas from paragraph to paragraph throughout an essay.

One excellent way to connect paragraphs is to start a new paragraph with a pronoun that refers to the previous paragraph. Passage 21 uses this technique. Other ways to connect paragraphs are to pick up a key word from the previous paragraph or from the essay's thesis statement. Examine the student essays and research paper in this handbook to see how they make connections among paragraphs that help maintain coherence in longer pieces of writing.

Passage 21 shows two full paragraphs and the start of a third paragraph from an essay on the costs of health care that appeared in the journal *Science*. Repeated words connecting these paragraphs include *commission, commissioners, list,* and *Oregon*. The first sentence of the second paragraph—"It sounds great"—tightly links the paragraphs: Only by reflecting on the information about cost-benefit ratios in the first paragraph can a reader know what "sounds great." Similarly, the opening sentence of the third paragraph, "While commission members dismiss the first draft's failure . . . ," creates another strong link to the paragraphs that preceded it. Only by recalling the content of those paragraphs can the reader understand what is meant by "the first draft's failure."

> Oregon's commission thought it had the solution. And so did all the newspapers, magazines, and television stations that covered the commission's announcement last May. A means had been found, the stories went, to assign a cost-benefit rating to nearly 2,000 medical procedures. The basis of the list was a mathematical formula. All that had to be done was to feed piles of data into a computer, and the machine would respond with a list of procedures, carefully ordered according to their cost-benefit ratios.
>
> 21   It sounds great. But the list the computer actually spit out last May left the 11 commissioners reeling. Take thumb-sucking and acute headaches: treatments for these problems ranked higher than those for cystic fibrosis and AIDS. Immunizations for childhood diseases did not appear. Deeply embarrassed, the commissioners hastily withdrew the list, and three months later Oregon appears to be no closer to a second version. The current prognosis: a revised list is not expected until some time in the fall.
>
> While commission members dismiss the first draft's failure as unimportant, it does indicate the complexity of the problem they face. . . . [The paragraph goes on to discuss specific details of the problem's complexity.]
>
> —Virginia Morell, "Oregon Puts Bold Health Plan on Ice"

EXERCISE 4-3

Consulting section 4d, identify the techniques of coherence—words of transition, pronouns, deliberate repetition, and parallel structures—in each paragraph.

A.   Kathy sat with her legs dangling over the edge of the side of the hood. The band of her earphones held back strands of straight copper hair which had come loose from two thick braids that hung down her back. She swayed with the music that only she could hear. Her shoulders raised, making circles in the warm air. Her arms reached out to her side; her opened hands reached for the air; her closed hands

  22

ANSWERS: EXERCISE 4-3

A (paragraph 22). *Pronouns*: her, she. *Deliberate repetition*: Kathy, arms, hands opened, closed. *Parallel structures*: Many parallel clauses, starting with "Her shoulders raised"; open hands reaching out and closed hands bringing back.

B (paragraph 23). *Pronouns*: we, whom, this. *Deliberate repetition*: we, world. *Parallel structures*: Once set in motion, must remain in motion; we must.   ➡

brought the air back to her. Her arms reached over her head;
her opened hands reached for a cloud; her closed hands brought
the cloud back to her. Her head moved from side to side;
her eyes opened and closed to the tempo of the tunes. Kathy
was motion.

—Claire Burke, student

B.   Newton's law may have wider application than just the physical
world. In the social world, racism, once set into motion, will remain
in motion unless acted upon by an outside force. The collective
"we" must be the outside force. We must fight racism through
23 education. We must make sure every school has the resources
to do its job. We must present to our children a culturally diverse
curriculum that reflects our pluralistic society. This can help students
understand that prejudice is learned through contact with prejudiced
people, rather than with the people toward whom the prejudice is
directed.

—Randolph H. Manning, "Fighting Racism with Inclusion"

C.   The snow geese are first, rising off the ponds to breakfast
in the sorghum fields up the river. Twenty thousand of them,
perhaps more, great white birds with black wing tips rising out
of the darkness into the rosy reflected light of dawn. They make
a sweeping turn, a cloud of wings rising above the cottonwoods.
24 But *cloud* is the wrong word. They do not form a disorderly blackbird
rabble but a kaleidoscope of goose formations, always shifting,
but always orderly. The light catches them—white against the tan
velvet of the hills. Then they are overhead, line after line, layer
above layer of formations, and the sky is filled with the clamor of an
infinity of geese.

—Tony Hillerman, *Hillerman Country*

ANSWERS: EXERCISE 4-4

Each paragraph will obviously differ in content, but this exercise should help students
see that they need to support general statements with graphic details (developed
through RENNS) that are smoothly linked
by the techniques of coherence discussed
in 4b: transitional expressions, pronouns,
repetition, and parallelism.

EXERCISE 4-4

Consulting sections 4c and 4d, develop three of the following topic
sentences into paragraphs that are unified with RENNS and techniques of
coherence. After you finish, list the RENNS and the techniques of
coherence you have built in to each paragraph.

1. Newspaper comic strips reflect many current problems.
2. What constitutes garbage in the United States says a great deal
   about American culture.
3. Children are taught to compete with each other at too early an age.
4. Learning to do laundry can be dangerous to one's clothes.
5. College athletics is big business.

4e Arranging a paragraph

Arranging a paragraph means you put its sentences into an order logical for communicating the message of the paragraph clearly and effectively. Choices for arranging a paragraph include sequencing according to time and to location; moving from general to specific, from specific to general, and from least to most important; and progressing from problem to solution.

As you write, you might prefer to postpone your final decisions about the arrangement of your paragraphs until after you have written a first draft. As you revise, you can experiment to see how your sentences can be arranged for greatest impact.

According to time

A paragraph arranged according to time is put into a chronological sequence. It tells what happened in the order in which the events actually occurred.

> Other visitors include schools of dolphin swimming with synchronized precision and the occasional humpback whale. Before 1950, these 14-meter marine mammals were a common sight in the waters of the Great Barrier Reef as they passed on their annual migration between Antarctic waters and the tropics, where their calves were born. Then in the 1950s, 25 whaling stations were set up on the New South Wales and Queensland coasts, and together with the long-established Antarctic hunts by the Soviet Union and America, whales were slaughtered in the thousands. By the time the whaling stations on the eastern Australian coast closed in the early 1960s, it was estimated that only two hundred remained in these waters. Today, their numbers are slowly increasing, but sightings are still rare.
> —Allan Moult, "Volcanic Peaks, Tropical Rainforest, and Mangrove Swamps"

According to location

A paragraph arranged according to location is put into a spatial sequence. For example, paragraph 26 cites specific U.S. geographical areas and the most common natural disasters they can experience. The list moves across the United States from west to east.

> In the United States, most natural disasters are confined to specific geographical areas. For example, the West Coast can be hit by damaging earthquakes at any time. Most Southern and Midwestern states can 26 be swept by devastating tornadoes, especially in the spring, summer, and early fall. The Gulf of Mexico and the Atlantic Ocean can experience violent hurricanes in late summer and fall. These different natural disasters, and others as dangerous, teach people one common lesson—advance preparation can mean survival.
> —Dawn Seaford, student

ANOTHER EXAMPLE OF SPATIAL SEQUENCE

The wash [low land that is sometimes flooded and at other times nearly dry] looked perfectly dry in my headlights. I drove down, across, up the other side and on into the night. Glimpses of weird humps of pale rock on either side, like petrified elephants, dinosaurs, stone-age hobgoblins. Now and then something alive scurried across the road: kangaroo mice, a jackrabbit, an animal that looked like a cross between a raccoon and a squirrel—the ringtail cat. Farther on a pair of mule deer started from the brush and bounded obliquely through the beams of my lights, raising puffs of dust which the wind, moving faster than my pickup truck, caught and carried ahead of me out of sight into the dark. The road, narrow and rocky, twisted sharply left and right, dipped in and out of tight ravines, climbing by degrees toward a summit which I would see only in the light of the coming day.
—Edward Abbey, "The Most Beautiful Place on Earth"

BACKGROUND

A. L. Becker, working in the mid-1960s, wrote a now classic article on paragraph structures: "A Tagamemic Approach to Paragraph Analysis" (*College Composition and Communication*, December 1965: 237–242). He noted that paragraphs for exposition often follow two basic patterns: topic-restriction-illustration (TRI) and problem-solution (PS).

The TRI pattern has three "slots"—topic, restriction, and illustration. It begins with a topic sentence or proposition in the **T** slot. The **R** slot defines, restates, or explains the proposition at a lower level of generality. The **I** slot often provides one or more examples, an extended analogy, or a series of comparisons that describe or exemplify the topic at a still lower level of generality.

From general to specific

An arrangement of sentences from the general to the specific is the most common organization for a paragraph. Seen in many of the examples earlier in this chapter, a general-to-specific arrangement begins with a topic sentence (perhaps followed by a limiting or clarifying sentence) and ends with specific details.

27 Unwanted music is privacy's constant enemy. There is hardly an American restaurant, store, railroad station or bus terminal that doesn't gurgle with melody from morning to night, nor is it possible any longer to flee by boarding the train or bus itself, or even by taking a walk in the park. Transistor radios have changed all that. Men, women and children carry them everywhere, hugging them with the desperate attachment that a baby has for its blanket, fearful that they might have to generate an idea of their own or contemplate a blade of grass. Thoughtless themselves, they have no thought for the sufferers within earshot of their portentous news broadcasts and raucous jazz. It is hardly surprising that RCA announced a plan that would pipe canned music and pharmaceutical commercials to 25,000 doctors' offices in eighteen big cities—one place where a decent quietude might be expected. This raises a whole new criterion for choosing a family physician. Better to have a second-rate healer content with the sounds of his stethoscope than an eminent specialist poking to the rhythms of Gershwin.

—William Zinsser, *The Haircurl Papers*

From specific to general

A less common arrangement moves from the specific to the general. Like paragraphs 7 and 8 earlier in this chapter, a paragraph with a specific-to-general arrangement ends with a topic sentence and begins with the details that support the topic sentence.

28 Replacing the spark plugs probably ranks number one on the troubleshooting list of most home auto mechanics. Too often this effort produces little or no improvement, as the problem lies elsewhere. Within the ignition system, the plug wires, distributor unit, coil, and ignition control unit play just as vital a role as the spark plugs. However, performance problems are by no means limited to the ignition system. The fuel system and emissions control system also help determine engine performance, and each of these systems contains several components which equal the spark plug in importance. The do-it-yourself mechanic who wants to provide basic care for a car should be able to do more than change the spark plugs.

—Danny Witt, student

From least to most important

A sentence arrangement that moves from least to most important is known as *climactic order* because it saves the climax for the end. This arrangement can be effective in holding the reader's interest because the best part comes last. Climactic order usually calls for the topic sentence at the beginning of the paragraph, as in paragraph 29, although sometimes the topic sentence works well at the end.

> 29   But probably the most dumbfounding of nature's extraordinary creations is the horned toad of our Southwest. A herpetologist once invited me to observe one of these lizards right after it had molted. In a sand-filled glass cage I saw a large male. Beside him lay his old skin. The herpetologist began to annoy the beast with mock attacks, and the old man of the desert with his vulnerable new suit became frightened. Suddenly his eyeballs reddened. A final fast lunge from my friend at the beast and I froze in astonishment—a fine spray of blood shot from the lizard's eye, like fire from a dragon! The beast struck back with a weapon so shocking that it terrifies even the fiercest enemy.
>
> —Jean George, "That Astounding Creator—Nature"

From problem to solution

Another effective arrangement presents a problem and moves quickly to a solution. Usually, the topic sentence presents the problem. The very next sentence (the limiting or clarifying sentence; see 4b) presents the main idea of the solution, and the rest of the sentences cover the specifics of the solution.

> 30   When I first met them, Sara and Michael were a two-career couple with a home of their own, and a large boat bought with a large loan. What interested them in a concept called voluntary simplicity was the birth of their daughter and a powerful desire to raise her themselves. Neither one of them, it turned out, was willing to restrict what they considered their "real life" into the brief time before work and the tired hours afterward. "A lot of people think that as they have children and things get more expensive, the only answer is to work harder in order to earn more money. It's not the only answer," insists Michael. The couple's decision was to trade two full-time careers for two half-time careers, and to curtail consumption. They decided to spend their money only on things that contributed to their major goal, the construction of a world where family and friendship, work and play, were all of a piece, a world, moreover, which did not make wasteful use of the earth's resources.
>
> —Linda Weltner, "Stripping Down to Bare Happiness"

EXERCISE 4-5

For each paragraph, arrange the sentences into a logical sequence. Begin by identifying the topic sentence and placing it at the beginning of the paragraph. As you work, consult sections 4b and 4e.

PARAGRAPH A

1. Remember, many people who worry about offending others wind up living according to other people's priorities.

Background (continued)

The problem-solution (PS) pattern states a problem or effect in the opening **P** slot, sometimes in question form, and follows by stating the solution or cause in the **S** slot. If the explanation of the solution or cause is extended, it may follow the TRI pattern.

Becker illustrates both the TRI and PS patterns with a paragraph from Frank Gibney's *Five Gentlemen of Japan*:

(**P**) How obsolete is Hearn's judgment? (**S1**) (**T**) On the surface the five gentlemen of Japan do not themselves seem to be throttled by this rigid society of their ancestors. (**R**) Their world is in fact far looser in its demands upon them than it once was. (**I**) Industrialization and the influence of the West have progressively softened the texture of the web. Defeat in war badly strained it. A military occupation, committed to producing a democratic Japan, pulled and tore at it. (**S2**) (**T**) But it has not disappeared. (**R**) It is still the invisible adhesive that seals the nationhood of the Japanese. (**I**) Shimizu, Sanada, Yamazaki, Kisfi and Hirohito were all born within its bonds. Despite their individual work, surroundings and opinions, they have lived most of their lives as cogs geared into a group society. Literally as well as figuratively speaking, none of them has a lock on his house door.

ANSWERS: EXERCISE 4-5

Answers may vary; alternate versions that can be defended are acceptable.

A. In the original paragraph, the sentences appeared in this order: 3, 2, 4, 1.
B. In the original paragraph, the sentences appeared in this order: 3, 7, 6, 1, 5, 2, 4.
C. In the original paragraph, the sentences appeared in this order: 4, 3, 1, 2.

QUOTATION: ON WRITING

Writing is a lot like sewing. You bring pieces together and make a quilt.

—Rosario Ferre

2. Learn to decline, tactfully but firmly, every request that does not contribute to your goals.
3. Of all the time-saving techniques ever developed, perhaps the most effective is the frequent use of the word *no*.
4. If you point out that your motivation is not to get out of work but to save your time to do a better job on the really important things, you'll have a good chance of avoiding unproductive tasks.

—Edwin Bliss, "Getting Things Done: The ABC's of Time Management"

PARAGRAPH B

1. After a busy day, lens wearers often do not feel like taking time out to clean and disinfect their lenses, and many wearers skip the chore.
2. When buying a pair of glasses, a person deals with just the expense of the glasses themselves.
3. Although contact lenses make the wearer more attractive, glasses are easier and less expensive to care for.
4. However, in addition to the cost of the lenses themselves, contact lens wearers must shoulder the extra expense of cleaning supplies.
5. This inattention creates a danger of infection.
6. In contrast, contact lenses require daily cleaning and weekly enzyming that inconvenience lens wearers.
7. Glasses can be cleaned quickly with water and tissue at the wearer's convenience.

—Heather Martin, student

PARAGRAPH C

1. The researchers found that the participation of women in sport was a significant indicator of the health and living standards of a country.
2. Today, gradually, women have begun to enter sport with more social acceptance and individual pride.
3. In 1952, researchers from the Finnish Institute of Occupational Health who conducted an intensive study of the athletes participating in the Olympics in Helsinki predicted that "women are able to shake off civil disabilities which millennia of prejudice and ignorance have imposed upon them."
4. Myths die hard, but they do die.

—Marie Hart, "Sport: Women Sit in the Back of the Bus"

EXERCISE 4-6

Consulting section 4e, identify the arrangement or arrangements that organize the sentences in each paragraph. Choose from time, location, general to specific, specific to general, least to most important, and problem to solution.

A.   A combination of cries from exotic animals and laughter and gasps from children fills the air along with the aroma of popcorn and peanuts. A hungry lion bellows for dinner, his roar breaking through the confusing chatter of other animals. Birds of all kinds chirp endlessly at curious children. Monkeys swing from limb to limb perform-
31   ing gymnastics for gawking onlookers. A comedy routine by orangutans employing old shoes and garments incites squeals of amusement. Reptiles sleep peacefully behind glass windows, yet they send shivers down the spines of those who remember the quick death many of these reptiles can induce. The sights and sounds and smells of the zoo inform and entertain children of all ages.

—Deborah Harris, student

B.   No one even agrees anymore on what "old" is. Not long ago, 30 was middle-aged and 60 was old. Now, more and more people are living into their 70s, 80s and beyond—and many of them are living
32   well, without any incapacitating mental or physical decline. Today, old age is defined not simply by chronological years, but by degree of health and well-being.

—Carol Tavris, "Old Age Is Not What It Used to Be"

C.   Lately, bee researchers have been distracted by a new challenge from abroad. It is, of course, the so-called "killer bee" that was imported into Brazil from Africa in the mid-1950s and has been heading our way ever since. The Africanized bee looks like the Italian bee
33   but is more defensive and more inclined to attack in force. It consumes much of the honey that it produces, leaving relatively little for anyone who attempts to work with it. It travels fast, competes with local bees and, worse, mates with them. It has ruined the honey industry in Venezuela and now the big question is: Will the same thing happen here?

—Jim Doherty, "The Hobby That Challenges You to Think like a Bee"

EXERCISE 4-7

Often more than one arrangement can be effective for writing on a subject. Using the topics listed here, consider what arrangement (one or more) might be effective for discussing the subject. Consulting section 4e, choose from general to specific, specific to general, least to most important, problem to solution, location, and time. Be ready to explain your choices, remembering that other arrangements could also work.

1. ways to make friends
2. automobile accidents
3. how to combine work and college
4. the problems with junk food
5. music favorites today

ANSWERS: EXERCISE 4-6

Students will likely see more than one arrangement in some of these paragraphs.

Note: You might also ask students to analyze these paragraphs in light of what was previously discussed in this chapter: the topic sentence, words in topic sentences that create focus and control (4a), development with RENNS (4c), and techniques of coherence (4d).

A (paragraph 31). Topic sentence last; specific to general

B (paragraph 32). Topic sentence last; problem to solution (and perhaps time)

C (paragraph 33). Topic sentence first; least to most important

ANSWERS: EXERCISE 4-7

Answers will vary according to how each student conceives of each subject. Comparisons of the methods of arrangement can reveal the multiplicity of available choices.

4f Knowing patterns for paragraphs

Patterns for paragraph development have evolved as writers created better methods to express their ideas. If you get to know a variety of patterns for paragraph development, you will always have more choices as a writer to help your paragraphs deliver their meanings most effectively.

For the purpose of illustration, the patterns in this section (see Chart 26) are discussed separately. In essay writing, however, paragraph patterns often overlap. For example, narrative writing often contains descriptions, and explanations of processes often include comparisons and contrasts. Your goal is to use paragraph patterns in the service of communicating meaning, not for their own sake.

Common patterns for paragraph development 26

- narration
- description
- process
- example
- definition

- analysis and classification
- comparison and contrast
- analogy
- cause-and-effect analysis

4f.1 Using narration

Narrative writing tells about what is happening or what has happened. In informative and persuasive writing, narration is usually written in chronological sequence. Narrative paragraphs that illustrate other aspects of informative and persuasive writing include paragraphs 16 and 29 and passage 21. Another example of a narrative paragraph is paragraph 34. Its main idea appears in the next-to-last sentence, when Gordon Parks explains what kind of "weapon" cameras have been for him.

34   Gordon Parks speculates that he might have spent his life as a waiter on the North Coast Limited train if he hadn't strolled into one particular movie house during a stopover in Chicago. It was shortly before World War II began, and on the screen was a hair-raising newsreel of Japanese planes attacking a gunboat. When it was over the cameraman came out on stage and the audience cheered. From that moment on Parks was determined to become a photographer. During his next stopover, in Seattle, he went into a pawnshop and purchased his first camera for $7.50. With that small sum, Parks later proclaimed, "I had bought what was to become my weapon against poverty and racism." Eleven years later, he became the first black photographer at *Life* magazine.

—Susan Howard, "Depth of Field"

4f.2 Using description

Descriptive writing appeals to a reader's senses—sight, sound, smell, taste, and touch. Descriptive writing permits you to share your sensual impressions of a person, a place, or an object. Descriptive paragraphs that illustrate other aspects of informative and persuasive writing include paragraphs 1, 14, 18, 19, and 26. Here is another example of a descriptive paragraph.

> Walking to the ranch house from the shed, we saw the Northern Lights. They looked like talcum powder fallen from a woman's face. Rouge and blue eyeshadow streaked the spires of a white light which exploded, then pulsated, shaking the colors down—like lives—until they faded from sight.
>
> 35
>
> —Gretel Ehrlich, "Other Lives"

4f.3 Using process

Process is a term used for writing that describes a sequence of actions by which something is done or made. Usually, a process description is developed in chronological order. To be effective, process writing must include all steps. The amount of detail depends on whether you want to instruct the reader about how to do something (as in paragraph 36) or you want to offer a general overview of the process (as in paragraph 37).

> Making chocolate is not as simple as grinding a bag of beans. The machinery in a chocolate factory towers over you, rumbling and whirring. A huge cleaner first blows the beans away from their accompanying debris—sticks and stones, coins and even bullets can fall among cocoa beans being bagged. Then they go into another machine for roasting. Next comes separation in a winnower, shells sliding out one side, beans falling from the other. Grinding follows, resulting in chocolate liquor. Fermentation, roasting, and "conching" all influence the flavor of chocolate. Chocolate is "conched"—rolled over and over against itself like pebbles in the sea—in enormous circular machines named conches for the shells they once resembled. Climbing a flight of steps to peer into this huge, slow-moving glacier, I was expecting something like molten mud but found myself forced to conclude it resembled nothing so much as chocolate.
>
> 36
>
> —Ruth Mehrtens Galvin, "Sybaritic to Some, Sinful to Others"

Contrast the general process description in paragraph 36 with the following one, which gives specific, step-by-step instructions.

> Carrying loads of equal weight like paint cans and toolboxes is easier if you carry one in each hand. Keep your shoulders back and down so that the weight is balanced on each side of your body, not suspended in front. With this method, you will be able to lift heavier loads and also to walk and stand erect. Your back will not be strained by being pulled to one side.
>
> 37
>
> —John Warde, "Safe Lifting Techniques"

Background (continued)

Christensen proposes nine principles that can be applied and taught. Your students need not regard these principles as laws but should regard them rather as rules of thumb that can help them generate certain kinds of paragraphs.

1. The paragraph may be defined as a sequence of sentences that are related by coordination and subordination.

2. The most general sentence of the sequence is often the topic sentence, the sentence on which the others depend.

3. The topic sentence is typically the first sentence of the sequence. Topics may be established explicitly or may be only suggested.

4. Simple sequences are of two sorts—coordinate and subordinate. In a coordinate sequence, repetition of structure—parallelism—is necessary; in a subordinate sequence, repetition must be avoided, each added sentence taking a different form.

5. The two sorts of sequence combine to produce the commonest sort—the mixed sequence. The opportunity to generate the paragraph lies here with the addition of subordinate sentences to clarify and of coordinate sentences to emphasize or to enumerate.

6. Some paragraphs have no topic sentence; in these cases, the topic can usually be inferred from the preceding paragraph, where it may be implied or stated.

7. Some paragraphs have sentences at the beginning or at the end that do not belong to the sequence. They furnish a transition either to the new paragraph (at the beginning) or from the current paragraph (at the end), or they may provide a conclusion or coda at the end.

8. Some paragraphing is illogical.

9. Punctuation should be by the paragraph, not by the sentence. Paragraph punctuation involves choosing whether to make compound sentences or not.

BACKGROUND

Description, for example, is related to definition. Describing something provides a means of analyzing and identifying it. Defining is a kind of abstract description. Definition, division into parts, and classification share fundamental relationships: to define is to limit or set boundaries to a thing by separating it from other things (division); to define is to put the thing to be defined into a class (classification); to classify is to divide into categories, so classification and division are related categories. Exemplification is related to definition (giving examples is one way of defining), to division in parts (examples are parts of wholes), and to classification (each example is a member of a group or class of persons and things).

—Frank D'Angelo

EXTRA EXERCISE C

Write a paragraph defining one of the terms listed below. You may find it helpful to begin by determining the class (genus) of the term and the characteristics that distinguish it from other members of the class. In a paragraph of definition, you might find using synonyms, etymological information, and contrasting examples helpful.

1. chemistry
2. extrasensory perception
3. movies
4. weather
5. physical fitness

EXTRA EXERCISE D

The sentences in the following paragraph have been jumbled. It is intended as a paragraph of definition. Indicate which is the topic sentence; then, record the order of the remaining sentences by numbering them.

_____ **1.** It is the total of all substantive things called economic goods.

_____ **2.** In other words, wealth is a stock, while income is a flow of economic goods.

→ 90

4f.4 Using examples

A paragraph developed by example uses illustrations to provide evidence in support of the main idea. Examples are highly effective for developing topical paragraphs. They supply a reader with concrete, specific information. Many of the sample paragraphs in this chapter are developed with examples, among them paragraphs 1, 4, 6, 7, 14, and 27. Here is another paragraph with examples used to develop the topic sentence.

38 One major value of rain forests is biomedical. The plants and animals of rain forests are the source of many compounds used in today's medicines. A drug that helps treat Parkinson's disease is manufactured from a plant that grows only in South American rain forests. Some plants and insects found in rain forests contain rare chemicals that relieve certain mental disorders. Discoveries, however, have only begun. Scientists say that rain forests contain over a thousand plants that have great anticancer potential. To destroy life forms in these forests is to deprive the human race of further medical advances.

—Gary Lee Houseman, student

4f.5 Using definition

A paragraph of definition develops a topic by explaining the meaning of a word or a concept. A paragraph of definition is an *extended definition*—it is more extensive than a dictionary entry (although the paragraph may include a dictionary definition). An effective paragraph of definition does not use abstractions to explain abstractions. Here is a paragraph that offers an extended definition of tolerance.

39 The Latin root of the word "tolerance" refers to things that can be borne, endured, are supportable. The intrinsic meaning of "tolerance" is the capacity to sustain and endure, as of hardship. From this comes the inferential meaning of patience with the opinions and practices of those who differ. It is interesting that the word is used in connection with the coining of money and with machinery, to indicate the margin within which coins may deviate from the fixed standard, or dimensions or parts of machine from the norm.

—Dorothy Thompson, "Concerning Tolerance"

4f.6 Using analysis and classification

Analysis (sometimes called *division*) divides things up; *classification* groups things together. A paragraph developed by analysis divides one subject into its component parts. Paragraphs of analysis written in this pattern usually start by identifying the one subject and continue by explaining that subject's distinct parts. For example, here is a paragraph that identifies a new type of zoo design and then analyzes changes in our world that have brought about that design.

> The current revolution in zoo design—the landscape revolution—is driven by three kinds of change that have occurred during this century. First are great leaps in animal ecology, veterinary medicine, landscape design, and exhibit technology, making possible unprecedented realism in zoo exhibits. Second, and perhaps most important, is the progressive disappearance of wilderness—the very subject of zoos—from the earth. Third is knowledge derived from market research and from environmental psychology, making possible a sophisticated focus on the zoo-goer.
>
> —Melissa Greene, "No Rms, Jungle Vu"

A paragraph developed by classification groups information according to some scheme. The separate groups must be from the same class—they must have some underlying characteristics in common. For example, different types of building violations can be classified into two large, general groups: inside violations and outside violations. Here is a paragraph that discusses many violations grouped into these two main categories.

> A public health student, Marian Glaser, did a detailed analysis of 180 cases of building code violation. Each case represented a single building, almost all of which were multiple-unit dwellings. In these 180 buildings, there were an incredible total of 1,244 different recorded violations—about seven per building. What did the violations consist of? First of all, over one-third of the violations were exterior defects: broken doors and stairways, holes in the walls, sagging roofs, broken chimneys, damaged porches, and so on. Another one-third were interior violations that could scarcely be attributed to the most ingeniously destructive rural southern migrant in America. There were, for example, a total of 160 instances of defective wiring or other electrical hazards, a very common cause of the excessive number of fires and needless tragic deaths in the slums. There were 125 instances of inadequate, defective, or inoperable plumbing or heating. There were 34 instances of serious infestation by rats and roaches.
>
> —William Ryan, "Blaming the Victim"

4f.7 Using comparison and contrast

Comparison deals with similarities, and *contrast* deals with differences. Paragraphs using comparison and contrast can be structured in two ways (see Chart 27). A *point-by-point structure* allows you to move back and forth between the two items being compared. A *block structure* allows you to discuss one item completely before discussing the other.

Extra Exercise D (continued)

_____ **3.** The wealth of a nation is the stock of economic goods owned by its inhabitants as individuals or as members of the national group.

_____ **4.** Economists use the term *economic goods* to refer to sources of satisfaction that are scarce enough to command a price.

_____ **5.** Wealth differs from income in that wealth is the sum of the goods owned at a particular time, whereas income is derived from the quantity of goods consumed during a specific period.

Answer to Extra Exercise D
The order of sentences should be 3, 1, 4, 5, 2.

EXTRA EXERCISE E
To practice the principles of classification, arrange the following terms into three groups based on their similarities. Give each group a heading.

1. violin
2. helmet
3. bulb
4. conductor
5. perennial
6. referee
7. concerto
8. touchdown
9. blossom
10. baton
11. Mozart
12. quarterback
13. leaves and stems
14. spectators
15. nursery

Answers to Extra Exercise E
Symphony Orchestra: violin, conductor, concerto, baton, Mozart
Football: helmet, referee, touchdown, quarterback, spectators
Flowers: bulb, perennial, blossom, leaves and stems, nursery

EXTRA EXERCISE F

To practice the skills of comparing and contrasting, list the most important aspects of the following pairs of words. Using that information, write a topic sentence about their relative value or about their similarities and differences.

1. baseball and football
2. Halloween and the Fourth of July
3. small towns and large cities
4. apartments and houses
5. books and television

Answers to Extra Exercise F

Answers will vary, but the information listed should lead to a topic sentence.

BACKGROUND

Many of the patterns of development for informative and persuasive paragraphs were first developed by Fred Newton Scott and Joseph Villiers Denney in their influential 1891 textbook, *Paragraph-Writing*. Scott and Denney's textbook was the first devoted entirely to teaching the paragraph, and it instructed students in such now familiar patterns as definition, comparison and contrast, example, and cause and effect. This list of patterns appeared earlier in classical rhetoric as *topoi*, or lines of reasoning for invention that speakers and writers used to generate ideas about a subject.

Patterns for comparison and contrast	**27**

Point-by-Point Structure

> *Student body:* college A, college B
> *Curriculum:* college A, college B
> *Location:* college A, college B

Block Structure

> *College A:* student body, curriculum, location
> *College B:* student body, curriculum, location

Here is a paragraph structured point by point for comparison and contrast.

42 In the business environment, tone is especially important. Business writing is not literary writing. Literary artists use unique styles to "express" themselves to a general audience. Business people write to particular persons in particular situations, not so much to express themselves as to accomplish particular purposes, "to get a job done." If a reader does not like a novelist's tone, nothing much can happen to the writer short of failing to sell some books. In the business situation, however, an offensive style may not only prevent a sale but may also turn away a customer, work against a promotion, or even cost you a job.

—John S. Fielden, "What Do You Mean, You Don't Like My Style!"

Here is a block-form comparison of games and business.

43 Games are of limited duration, take place on or in fixed and finite sites and are governed by openly promulgated rules that are enforced on the spot by neutral professionals. Moreover, they are performed by relatively evenly matched teams that are counseled and led through every move by seasoned hands. Scores are kept, and at the end of the game, a winner is declared. Business is usually a little different. In fact, if there is anyone out there who can say that the business is of limited duration, takes place on a fixed site, is governed by openly promulgated rules that are enforced on the spot by neutral professionals, competes only on relatively even terms, and performs in a way that can be measured in runs or points, then that person is either extraordinarily lucky or seriously deluded.

—Warren Bennis, "Time to Hang Up the Old Sports Clichés"

4f.8 Using analogy

Analogy is a type of comparison. It compares objects or ideas from different classes—things not normally associated. For example, a fatal disease has certain points in common with war. Analogy is particularly effective when you want to explain the unfamiliar in terms of the familiar. Often, a paragraph developed with analogy starts with a simile or metaphor (see 21c) to introduce the comparison. Here is a paragraph developed by analogy that starts with a simile and then explains the effect of casual speech by comparing it to casual dress.

44

Casual dress, like casual speech, tends to be loose, relaxed and colorful. It often contains what might be called "slang words": blue jeans, sneakers, baseball caps, aprons, flowered cotton housedresses, and the like. These garments could not be worn on a formal occasion without causing disapproval, but in ordinary circumstances they pass without remark. "Vulgar words" in dress, on the other hand, give emphasis and get immediate attention in almost any circumstances, just as they do in speech. Only the skillful can employ them without some loss of face, and even then they must be used in the right way. A torn, unbuttoned shirt or wildly uncombed hair can signify strong emotions: passion, grief, rage, despair. They are most effective if people already think of you as being neatly dressed, just as the curses of well-spoken persons count for more than those of the customarily foul-mouthed.

—Alison Lurie, *The Language of Clothes*

4f.9 Using cause-and-effect analysis

Cause-and-effect analysis involves examining outcomes and the reasons for those outcomes. Causes lead to an event or an effect, and effects result from causes. (Section 5i describes making reasonable connections between causes and effects.) Here is a paragraph developed through a discussion of how television (the cause) becomes indispensable (the effect) to parents of young children.

45

Because television is so wonderfully available as child amuser and child defuser, capable of rendering a volatile three-year-old harmless at the flick of a switch, parents grow to depend upon it in the course of their daily lives. And as they continue to utilize television day after day, its importance in their children's lives increases. From a simple source of entertainment provided by parents when they need a break from child care, television gradually changes into a powerful and disruptive presence in family life. But despite their increasing resentment of television's intrusions into their family life, and despite their considerable guilt at not being able to control their children's viewing, parents do not take steps to extricate themselves from television's domination. They can no longer cope without it.

—Marie Winn, *The Plug-In Drug*

ANOTHER EXAMPLE OF ANALOGY

Consider the analogies developed by George Herbert in this poem.

The Coming of Good Luck
So Good Luck came, and on my roof
   did light,
Like noiseless snow, or as the dew of
   night:
Not all at once, but gently, as the trees
Are, by the sun beams, tickled by
   degrees.

ANSWERS: EXERCISE 4-8

Some paragraphs can be interpreted to illustrate more than one pattern. This is a basic list only. *Note:* Exercise 4-10 asks students to analyze these paragraphs for many other features.

A (paragraph 46). comparison and contrast—point by point, example

B (paragraph 47). description, narration, analysis, example

C (paragraph 48). cause and effect, definition, analogy

D (paragraph 49). narration, description

E (paragraph 50). classification, example

QUOTATION: ON WRITING

Philosophers sometimes talk about cause-and-effect thinking as "the billiard ball model of the universe." In cause-and-effect reasoning, events are explained in much the same way as a motion on the billiard table.... One billiard ball ("the cause") strikes another, which moves ("the effect"). But if the second ball also strikes something, it becomes a cause and the reaction of that something becomes an effect.

—Richard M. Coe

EXERCISE 4-8

Consulting section 4f, identify the pattern or patterns each paragraph illustrates. Choose from narration, description, process, example, definition, analysis, classification, comparison and contrast, analogy, and cause and effect.

A. What was South Vietnam still seems like a different country from the North—more commercial, more casual, seemingly less wrapped up in political correctness. The main market in Hanoi had little to offer except local vegetables, a few plastic tools, and the incongruously colonial-looking green pith helmets that most northern men wear. (Hanoi's market also featured several tubs of live bullfrogs while we were there. Two market ladies chatted with each other while lopping the frogs' legs off with strokes of their cleavers.) In Saigon,

46   there are rows of "shop-houses," the tan-colored buildings with red-tile roofs and open storefronts that are found throughout Southeast Asia, and stores selling paintings, lacquerware, and a few cheap imported calculators and digital watches. In Hanoi, there are virtually no private cars—the streets look the way China's must have looked fifteen or twenty years ago, dense with bicycle traffic but very quiet. In Saigon, there are lots of motorcycles and a few private cars, including original Mustangs and other veteran American models. Still, no place in Vietnam has anything like the bustle of a typical Southeast Asian trading center.

—James Fallows, "No Hard Feelings?"

B. I retain only one confused impression from my earliest years: it is all red, and black, and warm. Our apartment was red: the upholstery was of red moquette, the Renaissance dining-room was red, the figured silk hangings over the stained-glass doors were red, and the velvet curtains in Papa's study were red too. The

47 furniture in this awful sanctum was made of black pear wood; I used to creep into the knee-hole under the desk and envelop myself in its dusty glooms; it was dark and warm, and the red of the carpet rejoiced my eyes. That is how I seem to have passed the early days of infancy. Safely ensconced, I watched, I touched, I took stock of the world.

—Simone de Beauvoir, *Memoirs of a Dutiful Daughter*

C. In the case of wool, very hot water can actually cause some structural changes within the fiber, but the resulting shrinkage is minor. The fundamental cause of shrinkage in wool is felting,

48 in which the fibers scrunch together in a tighter bunch, and the yarn, fabric, and garment follow suit. Wool fibers are curly and rough-surfaced, and when squished together under the lubricating influence of water, the fibers wind around each other, like two

springs interlocking. Because of their rough surfaces, they stick together and cannot be pulled apart.

—James Gorman, "Gadgets"

D.   After our lunch, we drove to the Liverpool public library, where I was scheduled to read. By then, we were forty-five minutes late, and on arrival we saw five middle-aged white women heading away toward an old car across the street. When they recognized me, the women came over and apologized: They were really sorry, they said, but they had to leave or they'd get in trouble on the job. I looked at them.
49 Every one of them was wearing an inexpensive, faded housedress and, over that, a cheap and shapeless cardigan sweater. I felt honored by their open-mindedness in having wanted to come and listen to my poetry. I thought and I said that it was I who should apologize: I was late. It was I who felt, moreover, unprepared: What in my work, to date, deserves the open-minded attention of blue-collar white women terrified by the prospect of overstaying a union-guaranteed hour for lunch?

—June Jordan, "Waiting for a Taxi"

E.   Lacking access to a year-round supermarket, the many species—from ants to wolves—that in the course of evolution have learned the advantages of hoarding must devote a lot of energy and ingenuity to protecting their stashes from marauders. Creatures like beavers and honeybees, for example, hoard food to get them through cold winters. Others, like desert rodents that face food scarcities throughout the
50 year, must take advantage of the short-lived harvests that follow occasional rains. For animals like burying beetles that dine on mice hundreds of times their size, a habit of biting off more than they can chew at the moment forces them to store their leftovers. Still others, like the male MacGregor's bowerbird, stockpile goodies during mating season so they can concentrate on wooing females and defending their arena d'amour.

Jane Brody, "A Hoarder's Life: Filling the Cache—and Finding It"

4g Writing introductory, transitional, and concluding paragraphs

Introductory, transitional, and concluding paragraphs are generally shorter than the topical paragraphs with which they appear in an essay.

Introductory paragraphs

The introductory paragraph sets the stage and prepares readers for what lies ahead. Introductions provide a bridge for readers to begin entering your mind, to arouse the interest of your readers in your subject. An introductory paragraph must relate clearly to the rest of the essay: If your introduction points in one direction and your essay goes off in another, your reader will be confused, lose confidence in your thinking, and perhaps stop reading.

For college writing, many instructors require an introductory paragraph to include a statement of the essay's thesis (see 2n). These instructors want students to demonstrate from the start that they are in control of both their ideas and the way those ideas are presented. Professional writers do not necessarily include a thesis statement in their introductory paragraphs; with experience comes skill at maintaining a line of thought without overtly stating a central idea. Student writers, however, need to give clear external clues to essay organization. As you revise drafts of your essays, keep a sharp eye on your introductions, taking care that they work well in concert with your other paragraphs.

When instructors require a thesis statement, they often want it to be in the last sentence or two of the introductory paragraph. Here is an example of an introductory paragraph with a thesis statement (shown in italics). You can find additional examples in the student essays in sections 3f and 6i.

> 51   Most sprinters live in a narrow corridor of space and time. Life rushes at them quickly, and success and failure are measured by frustrating, tiny increments. Florence Griffith Joyner paints her running world in bold, colorful strokes. *For her, there's a lot of romance to running fast.*
> —Craig A. Masback, "Siren of Speed"

An introductory paragraph usually includes one or more **introductory devices** that serve to stimulate a reader's interest in the subject of the essay. Usually, the introductory device comes before the thesis statement. Consult Chart 28 for devices and for strategies to avoid.

⦿ **Introductory paragraphs**   28

Devices to Try

- Providing relevant background information
- Relating a brief, interesting story or anecdote
- Giving a pertinent statistic or statistics
- Asking a provocative question or questions
- Using an appropriate quotation
- Making an analogy
- Defining a term used throughout the essay
- Identifying the situation

→

Introductory paragraphs (*continued*)   28

Strategies to Avoid

- Obvious statements that refer to what the essay is about or will accomplish, such as "I am going to discuss the causes of falling oil prices."
- Apologies, such as "I am not sure this is right, but this is my opinion."
- Overworked expressions, such as "Haste really does make waste, as I recently discovered" or "Love is grand."

> Like narration, process suggests ongoing movement and continuous action. The emphasis in a process theme, however, is on the *how*, rather than on the *what*.
> —Frank D'Angelo

Here is an introduction that uses two anecdotes before its thesis statement (shown in italics).

> On seeing another child fall and hurt himself, Hope, just nine months old, stared, tears welling up in her eyes, and crawled to her mother to be comforted—as though she had been hurt, not her friend. When 15-month-old Michael saw his friend Paul crying, Michael fetched his own teddy bear and offered it to Paul; when that didn't stop Paul's tears, Michael brought Paul's security blanket from another room. *Such small acts of sympathy and caring, observed in scientific studies, are leading researchers to trace the roots of empathy—the ability to share another's emotions—to infancy, contradicting a longstanding assumption that infants and toddlers were incapable of these feelings.*
> —Daniel Goleman, "Researchers Trace Empathy's Roots to Infancy"

An introductory device must be well integrated into the paragraph, not mechanically slotted in for its own sake. Note how smoothly the message of the quotation in the following introduction becomes a dramatic contrast that leads into the thesis statement (shown in italics).

> "Alone one is never lonely," says May Sarton in her essay "The Rewards of Living a Solitary Life." Most people, however, do not share Sarton's opinion: They are terrified of living alone. They are used to living with others—children with parents, roommates with roommates, friends with friends, husbands with wives. When the statistics catch up with them, therefore, they are rarely prepared. *Chances are high that most adult men and women will need to know how to live alone, briefly or longer, at some time in their lives.*
> —Tara Foster, student

In the following paragraph, the author uses a question and some dramatic description to arouse interest and to set the stage for his thesis statement (shown in italics).

> You must *write*, not just think you're going to. . . . And you must widen your vocabulary, enjoy words. You just read widely, not in order to copy, but to find your own voice. It's a matter of going through life with all one's senses alive, to be responsive to experience, to other people.
> —P. D. James

QUOTATION: ON WRITING

The perfect ending should take the reader slightly by surprise and yet seem exactly right.

—William Zinsser

BACKGROUND

Many of the conventions followed by contemporary writers did not exist in the ancient world. For example, words were not divided from each other until sometime in the seventh century A.D., and word division was not systematically practiced until the eleventh. Some marks of punctuation, such as the question mark and the exclamation point, evolved during the Middle Ages. Paragraphs had been indicated since pre-Christian days, first by short horizontal strokes or wedge-shaped signs. Later, they were noted in Latin manuscripts by a new line. At the same time, it became the practice to indicate the beginning of a new paragraph with enlarged letters, sometimes extending the length of the page. Such elaborate figures became the ancestors of our capital letters. The paragraph as it is known today took shape late in the seventeenth century but was not systematically described until the nineteenth century, when Alexander Bain published his *English Composition and Rhetoric* (1866).

54   What should you do? You are out riding your bike, playing golf, or in the middle of a long run when you look up and suddenly see a jagged streak of light shoot across the sky, followed by a deafening clap of thunder. *Unfortunately, most outdoor exercisers do not know whether to stay put or make a dash for shelter when a thunderstorm approaches, and sometimes the consequences are tragic.*

—Gerald Secor Couzens, "If Lightning Strikes"

Transitional paragraphs

Transitional paragraphs are found in long essays. Such a paragraph usually consists of one or two sentences that help readers move from a few pages on one subtopic to the next sequence of paragraphs on a second subtopic. In longer essays, transitional paragraphs sometimes sum up the essay's thesis in the specific context of what has been discussed and what will follow. Here is a two-sentence transitional paragraph written as a bridge between a lengthy discussion of people's gestures and a long discussion of people's eating habits.

55   Like gestures, eating habits are personality indicators, and even food preferences and attitudes toward food reveal the inner self. Food plays an important role in the lives of most people beyond its obvious one as a necessity.

—Jean Rosenbaum, M.D., *Is Your Volkswagen a Sex Symbol?*

Concluding paragraphs

The concluding paragraph serves to bring your discussion to an end, one that follows logically from your essay's thesis and your topical paragraphs. A conclusion that is hurriedly and carelessly tacked onto an essay robs the reader of the pleasure of completion. An ending that flows gracefully and sensibly from what has come before it reinforces your ideas and enhances your essay. A concluding paragraph often includes one or more **concluding devices.** Consult Chart 29 for devices and for strategies to avoid in conclusions.

⊙   **Concluding paragraphs**   **29**

Devices to Try

- Using any device appropriate for introductory paragraphs (see Chart 28)—but avoid using the same one in both the introduction and the conclusion
- Summarizing the main points of the essay—but avoid a summary if the essay is less than three pages long

                                                      ➞

Concluding paragraphs *(continued)* 29

- Asking for awareness, action, or a similar resolution from readers
- Looking ahead to the future

Strategies to Avoid

- Introducing new ideas or facts that belong in the body of the essay
- Rewording your introduction
- Announcing what you have done, as in "In this paper, I have explained the drop in oil prices."
- Making absolute claims, as in "I have proved that oil prices do not affect gasoline prices."
- Apologizing, as in "Even though I am not an expert, I feel my position is correct" or "I may not have convinced you, but there is good evidence for my position."

Here is a concluding paragraph summarizing an essay that discusses the many versions of pizza various cultures have enjoyed throughout time.

> For a food that is traced to Neolithic beginnings, like Mexico's tortillas, Armenia's lahmejoun, Scottish oatcakes, and even matzohs, pizza has remained fresh and vibrant. Whether it is galettes, the latest thin-crusted invasion from France with bacon and onion toppings, or a plain slice of a cheese pie, the varieties of pizza are clearly limited only by one's imagination.
>
> —Lisa Pratt, "A Slice of History"

56

The following conclusion ends an essay that discusses the risks of genetic engineering. The author points to the future and calls for action.

> I am not advocating that we stop the development of the new biology. I believe that we can achieve wonderful and important results with it. But we do need to ensure that its application is both peaceful and safe. We have to learn from the history of nuclear physics and organic chemistry. Indeed, I believe we have no real choice. We cannot afford to develop the new biological technologies without controlling them.
>
> —Susan Wright, "Genetic Engineering: The Risks"

57

TEACHING TIP

One way to help students succeed with Exercise 4-9 is to talk them through these imaginary essays before they think about the beginnings and endings. A class discussion about what details might support the topics of each paragraph can strengthen students' understanding of the importance of evidence. At the same time, it can give students a fuller concept of the essay on which to base their introductory and concluding paragraphs. When the students write the introductions and conclusions, you can alert them to the lists of useful devices and of what to avoid, explained in Charts 28 and 29 in section 4g.

ANSWERS: EXERCISE 4-9 (on page 100)

Answers will vary.

ANSWERS: EXERCISE 4-10 (on page 100)

1. **Topic sentences**
   A **(paragraph 46).** first sentence
   B **(paragraph 47).** first sentence
   C **(paragraph 48).** second sentence
   D **(paragraph 49).** last sentence
   E **(paragraph 50).** first sentence
2. **RENNS**
   A **(paragraph 46).** *Reasons:* Hanoi's main market has little to offer. Saigon has rows of "shop-houses." Hanoi has bicycles, while Saigon has motorcycles and a few private cars. *Examples:* The specific products in each market. *Names:* South Vietnam, Hanoi, Saigon, China, Mustangs. *Senses:* The sight of the frogs' legs being chopped off, the sight of dense bicycle traffic.
   B **(paragraph 47).** *Examples:* upholstery, Renaissance dining room, figured silk hangings over stained-glass doors, velvet curtains, black pear wood. *Names:* Renaissance dining room, Papa's study, black pear wood. *Senses:* sight of red and black, sight of "dusty glooms," darkness, watching, touching.

Answers: Exercise 4-10 (continued)

    C (paragraph 48). *Reasons:* felting causes wool to shrink, wool fibers stick together and cannot be pulled apart. *Names:* wool, fiber, yarn, fabric, garment. *Senses:* curly, rough surfaces

    D (paragraph 49). *Names:* Liverpool public library, middle-aged white women, old car, faded housedress, shapeless cardigan sweater. *Numbers:* forty-five, five.

    E (paragraph 50). *Reasons:* animals hoard because food is not available to them all year around. *Examples:* beavers, honeybees, desert rodents, burying beetles, etc. *Names:* ants, wolves, creatures, goodies, rains, MacGregor's bowerbird, etc.

3. Techniques of coherence. In this order, if they appear: transitional expressions (*te*), pronouns (*p*), deliberate repetition (*dr*), and parallel structures (*ps*).

    A (paragraph 46). *te:* still; *dr:* Hanoi, Saigon; *ps:* In Saigon, there are / in Hanoi, there are.

    B (paragraph 47). *p:* I, it; *dr:* red, black; *ps:* red, and black, and warm / I watched, I touched, I took stock.

    C (paragraph 48). *te:* but; *p:* their, they.

    D (paragraph 49). *te:* by then, moreover. *p:* our, I, we, they, them, their, it; *ps:* I thought and I said / it was I.

    E (paragraph 50). *te:* for example, still, so; *p:* their, they; *dr:* others; *ps:* creatures / others / still others.

4. Paragraph arrangement

    A (paragraph 46). general to specific

    B (paragraph 47). least to most important

    C (paragraph 48). general to specific

    D (paragraph 49). time, least to most important

    E (paragraph 50). general to specific

EXERCISE 4-9

Consulting section 4g, write an introduction and conclusion for each essay informally outlined here. To gain additional experience, write an alternate introductory and concluding paragraph for one of the essays.

    A.   Reading for fun

        Thesis: People read many kinds of books for pleasure.

        Topical paragraph 1: murder mysteries and thrillers

        Topical paragraph 2: romances and westerns

        Topical paragraph 3: science fiction

    B.   Computer games

        Thesis: Interactive video games require players to exercise their skills of dexterity, intelligence, and imagination.

        Topical paragraph 1: manual dexterity

        Topical paragraph 2: intelligence

        Topical paragraph 3: imagination

    C.   Using credit cards

        Thesis: Although credit cards can help people manage their finances wisely, they can also offer too much temptation.

        Topical paragraph 1: convenience and safety

        Topical paragraph 2: tracking purchases

        Topical paragraph 3: overspending dangers

EXERCISE 4-10

Reread the paragraphs in Exercise 4-8 and do the following:

1. Consulting section 4b, identify all topic sentences, limiting sentences, and implied topic sentences.
2. Consulting section 4c, identify all RENNS.
3. Consulting section 4d, identify all techniques of coherence.
4. Consulting section 4e, identify paragraph arrangements.

5

CRITICAL THINKING, READING, AND WRITING

This chapter shows you how to participate actively in the ongoing exchanges of ideas and opinions that you encounter in college and beyond. To participate, you need to understand **critical thinking** as a concept (see 5a) and as an activity (see 5b), **critical reading** as a concept (see 5c) and as an activity (see 5d through 5f), **writing critically** (see 5g), and **reasoning critically** (see 5h through 5k).

5a Understanding critical thinking

Thinking is not something you choose to do, any more than a fish chooses to live in water. To be human is to think. But while thinking may come naturally, awareness of how you think does not. Thinking about thinking is the key to **critical thinking.** When you think critically, you take control of your conscious thought processes. Without such control, you risk being controlled by the ideas of others. Indeed, critical thinking is at the heart of a liberal (from the Latin word for *free*) education.

The word *critical* here has a neutral meaning. It does not mean taking a negative view or finding fault, as when someone criticizes another person for doing something wrong. The essence of critical thinking is thinking beyond the obvious—beyond the flash of visual images on a television screen, the alluring promises of glossy advertisements, the evasive statements by some people in the news, the half-truths of some propaganda, the manipulations of slanted language and faulty reasoning.

Critical thinking is an attitude as much as an activity. If you face life with curiosity and a desire to dig beneath the surface, you are a critical thinker. If you do not believe everything you read or hear, you are a critical thinker. If you find pleasure in contemplating the puzzle of conflicting ideologies, theories, personalities, and facts, you are a critical thinker.

Activities of the mind and higher-order reasoning—the core of a college education—are processes of contemplation and deliberation. These

QUOTATION: ON THINKING

Man is but a reed, the weakest in nature,
but he is a thinking reed.

—Blaise Pascal

processes take time. They contrast with the glorification of speed in today's culture: fast foods, instant mixes, self-developing film, short-spurt images in movies and videos. If you are among the people who assume that speed is a measure of intelligence, consider this true anecdote about Albert Einstein. The first time that Banesh Hoffman, a scientist, was to discuss his work with Albert Einstein, Hoffman was speechless and over-awed. But Einstein instantly put Hoffman at ease by saying, "Please go slowly. I don't understand things quickly."

5b   Engaging in critical thinking

Critical thinking is a process that progresses from becoming fully aware of something to reflecting on it to reacting to it. You use this sequence often in your life, even if you have never called the process critical thinking. You engage in it when you meet someone new and decide whether you like the person, when you read a book and form an opinion of it, or when you learn a new job and then evaluate the job and your ability to do the work.

Applied in academic settings, the general process of critical thinking is described in Chart 30. That process holds not only for thinking critically but also for reading critically (see 5c and 5e) and writing critically (see 5g).

QUOTATION: ON READING

A reflection on having once read eight hundred pages of *War and Peace* in one day:

It took me a long time to forget the way I read that book. For a long time it seemed to me I had betrayed reading itself. Coming back to it now, I still find it disturbing. Something had been sacrificed in my quick dash through the book—another reading altogether. I had limited myself to the story at the expense of a deep, receptive, non-narrative reading of Tolstoy's writing itself. It was as though I had realized that day, once and for all, that a book consists of two layers: on top, the readable layer I had read that day on the train, and underneath, a layer that was inaccessible. You only sense its existence in a moment of distraction from the literal reading, the way you see childhood through a child. It would take forever to tell what you see, and it would be pointless.

—Marguerite Duras

⊙ **Steps in the critical thinking process**   30

1. **Analyze:** Consider the whole, and then break it into its component parts so that you can examine them separately. By seeing them as distinct units, you can come to understand how they interrelate.

2. **Summarize:** Extract and restate the material's main message or central point at the literal level (see 5d.1). (For a discussion of the differences between summary and synthesis, see 5f; for guidelines on writing a summary, see 31e.)

3. **Interpret:** Read "between the lines" to make inferences (see 5d.2) about the unstated assumptions implied by the material. Also, evaluate the material for its underlying currents as conveyed by tone, slant, and clarity of distinctions between fact and opinion (see 5d.3); by the quality of evidence (see 5h); and by the rigor of its reasoning (see 5i and 5j) and logic (see 5k).

→

Steps in the critical thinking process *(continued)*　　**30**

4. **Synthesize:** Pull together what you have summarized, analyzed, and interpreted to connect it to what you already know (your prior knowledge) or what you are currently learning. Find links that help you grasp the new material to create a new whole, one that reflects your ability to see and explain relationships among ideas (see also 5f).

5. **Assess critically:** Judge the quality of the material on its own and as it holds up in your synthesis of it with related material.

As with the writing process (see 2a), the steps of the critical thinking process are not rigidly in place. I describe each element separately in this handbook to help you understand the separate operations, but in reality the elements are intertwined. Expect sometimes to combine steps, reverse their order, and return to parts of the process needed anew. Synthesis and assessment, in particular, tend to operate concurrently. Still, stay aware that they are two different mental activities: Synthesis is making connections, and assessment is making judgments.

❶ **ALERT:** Summarizing (step 2 in Chart 30) and synthesizing (step 4) are two different processes. Be careful not to think that your summary is a synthesis. For fuller discussion of the differences, see section 5f. ❗

5c Understanding the reading process

If you understand the **reading process,** you can effectively compose meaning. Reading is not a passive activity. It involves more than looking at words. Reading is an active process—a dynamic, meaning-making encounter involving the interaction of page, eye, and brain. When you read, your mind actively makes connections between what you already know and what is new to you. By this process, you comprehend and absorb new material and refine previously acquired knowledge.

Reading calls for **making predictions.** As you read, your mind is always involved in guessing what is coming next. Once it discovers what comes next, it either confirms or revises its prediction and moves on. For example, if you encountered a chapter titled "The Heartbeat," your predictions of its topic might range from romance to how the heart pumps blood. As you read on, you would confirm or revise your prediction according to what you found—you would be in the realm of romance if you encountered a paragraph about lovers and roses, and you would be in the realm of biology if you encountered material that included diagrams of the physiology of the heart.

QUOTATION: ON WRITING

If any man wishes to write in a clear style, let him first be clear in his thoughts.
　　　　　　　　　　—Goethe

BACKGROUND

In "Computers, Reading, and Basic Writers: Online Strategies for Helping Students with Academic Texts" (*Teaching English in the Two-Year College*, October 1996: 170–178), Linda Adler-Kassner and Thomas Reynolds explain how students can improve their reading skills by using computers. Most of all, students' use of online databases seems to encourage close, careful reading.

BACKGROUND

Two pioneers in research about reading as a process are Robert J. Tierney and P. David Pearson. They have drawn many parallels between the processes of writing and reading. They have found that like writers, readers plan by determining their purposes for reading a text, assessing what they know about the topic, focusing their goals and topics, and questioning themselves. Each reader's goals and knowledge influence how he or she reads and understands the text. Like writers, when they begin, readers approach the text with particular goals and review what they know about a subject and then discover, revise, and delete goals and call up other knowledge as they read.

Like writers, readers draft, at first trying to discover a lead or hypothesis that will help them make sense of the rest of the →

Background (continued)
text, refining and developing that lead as they read, making connections and filling in gaps in the text with their own inferences and knowledge, and trying to fit all the pieces of the text together into a coherent whole. Readers and writers also both engage in aligning. Readers take a stance (passive, critical, sympathetic, challenging) in relation to the author to help them construct meaning from the text, just as writers take a stance toward their audiences.

Readers and writers both need to revise. Readers need to reflect on and evaluate the meanings they have constructed from the text, rereading the text and questioning and revising their interpretations. Finally, readers and writers need to monitor themselves as they compose, distancing themselves from the meaning they compose and examining their composing activities. Readers and writers should both be in dialogue with their "other self," to determine how well they are accomplishing their purposes.

QUOTATION: ON READING

Books: The most effective weapon against intolerance and ignorance.
—Lyndon Baines Johnson

TEACHING TIP

You might want to discuss with your students the research finding that most students believe the mark of a competent reader is the ability to read a text once quickly and remember much of what was read. Students seldom see a need to reread a text, to reflect on what they read, or to question their interpretation. To get used to critical reading practices, students need support and encouragement from teachers, in the same way they do learn and use planning and revising strategies when they write.

Predicting during reading happens at split-second speed without your being aware of it. Without predictions, the mind would have to consider infinite possibilities for assimilating every new piece of information; with predictions, the mind can narrow its expectations to reasonable proportions.

Deciding on your **purpose for reading** before you begin can help your prediction process. Purposes for reading vary. Most reading in college is for the purpose of learning new information, appreciating literary works, or reviewing notes on classes or course materials. Such reading involves much *rereading;* one encounter with the material rarely suffices. As Vladimir Nabokov, a respected novelist and teacher, once observed: "One cannot read a book: one can only reread it. A good reader, a major reader, an active and creative reader, is a rereader."

Your purpose for reading determines the speed at which you can expect to read. When you are hunting for a particular fact in an almanac, you can skim the material until you come to what you want. When you read about a subject you know well, your mind is already familiar with the material, so you can move somewhat rapidly, slowing down when you come to new material. When you are unfamiliar with the subject, your mind needs time to absorb the new material, so you have to proceed slowly.

5d Engaging in the reading process

During the reading process, full meaning emerges on the three levels described in Chart 31. To avoid the trap some readers fall into, do not stop at the literal level. Keep moving to the next two levels so that you can understand what you are reading as deeply as possible.

⊙ Steps in the reading process   31

1. **Read for literal meaning:** Read "on the lines" to see what is stated (see 5d.1).
2. **Read to make inferences:** Read "between the lines" to see what is not stated but implied (see 5d.2).
3. **Read to evaluate:** Read "beyond the lines" to assess the soundness of the writer's reasoning, the accuracy of the writer's choice of words, and the fairness of the writer's treatment of the reader (see 5d.3).

5d.1 Reading for literal meaning

Reading for literal meaning, sometimes called *reading on the line,* calls for you to understand what is said. It does not include impressions or opinions about the material. The literal level concerns the key facts, the line of reasoning in an argument, or the central details of plot and character, as well as the minor details that lend texture to the picture.

When you find a concept that you need to think through, take the time to come to know the new idea. Although no student has unlimited time for reading and thinking, rushing through material to "cover" it rather than understand it costs more time in the long run. Chart 32 offers suggestions that can help you comprehend most efficiently what you are reading.

◉ **Ways to help your reading comprehension**   **32**

- **Make associations.** When reading about an unfamiliar subject, associate the new material with what you already know. If necessary, build your store of prior knowledge by reading easier material on the subject in other sources. Then, return to the more difficult material; your way will be eased by having established a knowledge base.

- **Make it easy for you to focus.** If your mind wanders, comprehension can elude you because your mind is occupied with extraneous material. Be fiercely determined to concentrate, and resist the appeal of other thoughts. Do whatever it takes: Arrange for silence or music, for being alone or in a crowded library's reading room, for reading at your best time of day (some people concentrate better in the morning, others in the evening).

- **Allot the time you need.** Unless you have devoted sufficient time to working with new material, you cannot comprehend it. College students can be pulled in many different directions, so be sure to discipline yourself to balance classes, working, socializing, and participating in family activities with the unavoidable, time-consuming, and totally engaging demands of reading, learning, and studying. Nothing sabotages your success as much as failing to budget your time appropriately.

- **Master the vocabulary.** If you are unfamiliar with any key terms in your reading, you cannot fully understand the material. Take time to list them and their meanings. Try to figure meanings out by using context clues (see 20c.2). Also, many textbooks have a list of important terms and their definitions (a glossary) at the end of each chapter or at the back of the book. Always have a good dictionary at hand (see 20a). As you accumulate new words, keep your list taped inside your book so that you can consult the information easily.

QUOTATION: ON READING

When I am not walking, I am reading; I cannot sit and think. Books think for me.
—Charles Lamb

BACKGROUND

In the highly respected *Elements of Critical Reading* (New York: Macmillan, 1991), John Peters explains several useful reading habits.

1. Examine organizational features. "When you first encounter a text of any kind, you should pause to examine its outward features. Depending on the kind of text, those may include cover, title page, table of contents, chapter or section divisions, glossary, notes, bibliography, and other accessories" (13). They will provide a useful first impression of the text.

2. Know when the text was written.

3. Determine apparent aims. "Spot-reading" selected passages (also known as "pre-reading" and "X-raying") "allows you to inspect parts which can give you an idea of the text's aims and audience level" (15). Generally, begin with the preface or the opening paragraphs and, with nonfiction texts, then skip to the conclusion because it often summarizes the main points and purposes of the text. You should also drift a little back and forth through the center of the text, "eyeing those spots where expository writing often focuses its aims" (15–16), such as the first and last paragraphs of a section, the first sentence of each body paragraph, and any visual aids and illustrations.

4. Adapt to the genre. "From nonfiction you should usually expect an orderly discussion such as you might hear at a lecture or business meeting. In general, your relation to nonfiction is that of a student, colleague, or general reader who wants information upon which to base opinions, decisions, or future activity related to the subject—but it's a good idea to be slightly skeptical, aware that a text may have misinformation or raise more questions than it answers" (16–17).

Whenever you encounter a complex writing style, take time to "unpack" the sentences. Try to break them down into shorter units or reword them into a simpler style. Do not assume that all writing is clear merely because it is in print. Authors write with a rich variety of styles, and all are not equally accessible on a first reading.

5d.2 Reading to make inferences

Reading to make inferences, sometimes called *reading between the lines*, means understanding what is implied but not stated. Often, you have to infer information, background, or the author's purpose. Consider this passage:

> How to tell the difference between modern art and junk puzzles many people, although few are willing to admit it. The owner of an art gallery in Chicago had a prospective buyer for two sculptures made of discarded metal and put them outside his warehouse to clean them up. Unfortunately, some junk dealers, who apparently didn't recognize abstract expressionism when they saw it, hauled the two 300-pound pieces away.
>
> —Ora Gygi, "Things Are Seldom What They Seem"

The literal meaning is that many people cannot tell the difference between art and junk. A summary of the passage would say that two abstract metal sculptures were carted away as junk when an art dealer set them outside a warehouse to clean them.

Now reread the material for its inferential meaning. You might begin with the unexplained statement that few people are willing to admit that they do not know the difference between art and junk. Reading between the lines, you realize that the author might be implying that people feel embarrassed not to know; they feel uneducated, lacking in good taste, or perhaps left out. With this inference in mind, you can move to the last two sentences, in which the author offers not only the literal irony (see 21c) of the art's being carted away as junk but also the implied irony that the people who carted it away are not among those who might feel embarrassed. This implied irony suggests either that the people do not care if they know the difference between art and junk (after all, they assumed it was junk and went on their way) or that they "apparently" (a good word for inference making) want to give the impression that they do not know the difference. Thus, it is the art dealer who ends up being embarrassed, for it is he who created the problem by leaving the sculptures outdoors unattended.

The process of inferring adds texture and background to facilitate your interpretation of a passage. As you read to make inferences, consult Chart 33.

→

> ### Checklist for making inferences during reading   33
>
> - What is being said beyond the literal level?
> - What is implied rather than stated?
> - What words need to be read for their implied meanings (connotations) as well as for their stated meanings (denotations)? (For more about word meanings, see 20b.1.)
> - What information does the author expect me to have before I start to read the material?
> - What information does the author expect me to have about his or her background, philosophy, and the like?
> - What does the author seem to assume are my biases?
> - What do I need to be aware of concerning author bias?

5d.3 Reading to evaluate

Evaluative reading, sometimes called *reading beyond the lines,* calls for many skills, including recognizing the impact of the author's tone, detecting prejudice, and differentiating fact from opinion.

Recognizing whether an author's tone is appropriate

Tone (see 1d) is communicated by all aspects of a piece of writing, from the writer's choice of words to the content of the message. In academic writing, most authors use a serious tone. Sometimes, however, they use humor to get their point across. If you read humorous material exclusively for its literal meaning, you will likely miss the point. Here is a passage from an argument against the destruction of buildings that house small, friendly neighborhood stores and their replacement by large, impersonal buildings.

> Every time an old building is torn down in this country, and a new building goes up, the ground floor becomes a bank. The reason for this is that banks are the only ones who can afford the rent for the ground floor of the new buildings going up. . . . Most people don't think there is anything wrong with this, and they accept it as part of the American free-enterprise system. But there is a small group of people in this country who are fighting for Bank Birth Control.
>
> —Art Buchwald, "Birth Control for Banks"

Art Buchwald clearly expects that his readers will realize that (1) even though he is talking only of banks, the banks stand for many aspects of

---

Background (continued)

5. Listen to the language. Reading only for the message of the text, ignoring its emotions, tone, and rhythms, can cause a reader to miss much of what the text offers as well as much of the pleasure in reading.

6. Become aware of contrasts. "It is said that there are two sides to everything. As a reader you should become aware of the contrasts within a text. The inner structure is bound to reveal a play of opposites that close reading uncovers" (21).

7. Get to the heart of the matter. "For some readers, the heart of a text may be a passage or series of passages that seem to tie everything together and coordinate the flow of ideas throughout the entire work" (23). "The 'heart' can also be viewed as a sort of overall personality that characterizes the text. . . . But on the best occasions and as a result of our patient attentiveness, the heart of a text may reveal itself in the fullness of its meaning, both logical and emotional, and make us feel that we truly *know* what we've read" (25).

8. Sense what may be missing. "Of the many responses that reading can inspire, a few may be strong while plenty of others remain inactive. The intensity of your feelings is important, but so is the absence of those emotions which a text might have brought you but did not. . . . Knowing what a text means to you depends on your sense of what is present or missing in the relationship you've just concluded" (26).

QUOTATION: ON WRITING AND READING

Read, read, read. Read everything—trash, classics, good and bad, and see how they do it. Just like a carpenter who works as an apprentice and studies the master. Read! You'll absorb it. Then write. If it is good, you'll find out. If it's not, throw it out the window.

—William Faulkner

BACKGROUND

In "Remembering Writing, Remembering Reading" (*College Composition and Communication*, December 1994: 459–479), Deborah Brandt discusses reading-writing relationships from a cultural perspective. She focuses mainly on literacy practices within families.

BACKGROUND

In *Society and Solitude*, Ralph Waldo Emerson suggests three practical rules for reading.

1. Never read any book that is not a year old.
2. Never read any but the famed books.
3. Never read any but what you like.

urban renewal; (2) the first sentence is an exaggeration intended to elicit a smile—Buchwald is being slightly ridiculous to get across his point; and (3) the group "Bank Birth Control" does not exist—it is Buchwald's creation to advance his argument.

As a writer and a reader, be wary of a highly emotional tone. Chances are good that the author's goal is to upset readers, not to teach them. Writers of such material lack respect for their readers, for such writers assume that readers do not recognize screaming in print when they see it. Discerning readers instantly know when the tone is emotional and unreasonable. The exaggerations in the following example (*robbing treasures, politicians are murderers*) hint at the truth of some cases, but they are generalizations too extreme to be taken seriously.

> **NO** Urban renewal must be stopped! Urban redevelopment is ruining this country. Money-hungry capitalists are robbing treasures from law-abiding citizens! Corrupt politicians are murderers, caring nothing about people being thrown out of their homes into the streets.

If a writer's tone sounds moderate and reasonable, readers are more likely to pay attention.

> **YES** Urban renewal is revitalizing our cities, but it has caused some serious problems. While investors are trying to replace slums with decent housing, they must also remember that they are displacing people who do not want to leave their familiar neighborhoods. Surely a cooperative effort between government and the private sector can lead to creative solutions.

Detecting prejudice

Prejudice is revealed in negative opinions based on beliefs and indoctrination rather than on facts or evidence. Negative opinions can be expressed in positive language—which is a strategy that tries to distract readers from the truth—but the underlying assumptions are definitely negative.

Writers may imply their prejudices rather than state them outright: Poor people like living in crowded conditions because they are used to the surroundings; women are not aggressive enough to succeed in business; men make good soldiers because they enjoy killing. As a reader, you need to detect underlying negative opinions that distort information so that you can call into question any argument that rests on a weak foundation. (See also "Hasty Generalization" in section 5k.)

Differentiating fact from opinion

Facts are statements that can be verified. A person may use experiment, research, or observation to verify facts. *Opinions* are statements of personal beliefs. Because they contain ideas that cannot be verified, opinions are open to debate.

A writer sometimes intentionally blurs the distinction between fact and opinion. A critical reader needs to know the difference. Sometimes that difference is quite obvious. Consider these statements:

A. A woman can never make a good mathematician.
B. Although fear of math is not purely a female phenomenon, girls tend to drop out of math sooner than boys, and some adult women experience an aversion to math and math-related activity that is akin to anxiety.

Because of the word *never*, statement A is clearly an opinion. Statement B seems to be factual but might not be. The reader has to go further. Finding out who made a statement can sometimes help a reader distinguish between fact and opinion. Statement A is by a male Soviet mathematician living in Russia, as reported by David K. Shipler, a well-respected veteran reporter on Russian affairs for the *New York Times*. Statement B is from a book called *Overcoming Math Anxiety* by Sheila Tobias, a university professor who has undertaken research studies to find out why many people dislike math. Her credentials help us accept statement B as fact. (If, however, the same statement B had been made by a nonresearcher who is known for belittling women, we would be wise to be a bit more skeptical.)

One aid for differentiating between fact and opinion is to *think beyond the obvious*. For example, is this a fact: "Strenuous exercise is good for your health"? The statement has the ring of truth, but it is not a fact. The statement is untrue because people with severe arthritis or heart trouble could be harmed by some forms of exercise. Also, what does *strenuous* mean—a dozen pushups, jogging, aerobics, or playing tennis?

A second aid in differentiating between fact and opinion is *be skeptical*, keeping in mind that facts sometimes masquerade as opinions and opinions sometimes try to pass for facts. Evaluative reading demands concentration and a willingness to deal with matters that are relative and sometimes ambiguous. For example, in an essay for or against capital punishment, you would likely evaluate the argument differently if you knew that the writer is currently on death row or the writer is a disinterested party with a philosophy to discuss.

At times, the stance (the author's relationship to the material) calls for closer examination. Consider these statements:

C. Common warts usually occur on the hands, especially on the backs of the fingers, but they may occur on any part of the skin. These dry, elevated lesions have numerous projections on their surface.
D. Warts are wonderful structures. They can appear overnight on any part of the skin, like mushrooms on a damp lawn, full grown and splendid in the complexity of their architecture.

QUOTATION: ON READING

I took a course in speed reading and was able to read *War and Peace* in twenty minutes. It's about Russia.
—Woody Allen

EXTRA EXERCISE A

Determine which sentences state facts and which state opinions.

1. Nuclear fusion releases energy.
2. Nuclear fusion is a possible solution of our energy problems.
3. Solar energy has attracted a great deal of public attention over the past decade.
4. Many people hope that it will produce a clean, nonpolluting means of heating our homes and offices.
5. Oil and gas production in the United States has been falling for over a decade.
6. The petroleum industry is shrinking yearly.
7. In the interest of national security, the petroleum industry should be encouraged by government legislation.
8. The early pioneers generated energy from the wind on the frontier.
9. Such nonpolluting means of creating energy should replace those produced by fossil fuels immediately.
10. Because natural gas, methane, is a clean fuel, the government should encourage its use.

Answers to Extra Exercise A

1. fact
2. opinion
3. fact
4. fact
5. fact
6. fact
7. opinion
8. fact
9. opinion
10. opinion

ANSWERS: EXERCISE 5-1

1. opinion	**6.** fact
2. fact	**7.** fact
3. opinion	**8.** opinion
4. opinion	**9.** opinion
5. fact	**10.** fact

ANSWERS: EXERCISE 5-2

Answers may vary somewhat, but here is a fairly complete list of possibilities.

A. *Literal information*
1. It is the first of February.
2. "Everyone" (see "implied information") is talking about starlings.
3. Starlings came to this country on a passenger liner from Europe.
4. "This country" is the United States. (Central Park and New York are mentioned.)
5. One hundred starlings were deliberately released in Central Park.
6. From these hundred are descended the countless millions of starlings today.
7. Edwin Way Teale said, "Their . . . Shakespeare."
8. Eugene Schieffelin was a wealthy New York drug manufacturer.
9. Schieffelin's hobby was introducing into America all the birds mentioned in Shakespeare.
10. The starlings adapted to their new country.

Implied information
1. "Everyone" is used for effect; the author does not mean each and every person.
2. By saying that the birds came "on a passenger liner" (rather than, for example, "in the cargo hold of a ship"), the author begins to alert the reader to expect the unexpected (in this case, that someone wanted to introduce to America all the birds in Shakespeare).

Both statements are about warts. Judging only from the words—often all the evidence available—and without knowing who the writers are, we might say that C is fact and D is opinion. With information about the authors, your judgments can be more subtle and therefore more reliable. Statement C is from a respected medical encyclopedia; thus it can be confirmed as fact. Statement D is by Lewis Thomas, a distinguished physician, hospital administrator, researcher, and writer, as well as a winner of the National Book Award for his popular essays revealing the intricacies of biology to laypeople. Armed with this information, you would be justified in judging Thomas's statement D to be factual—facts brought to life by metaphor (see 21c).

EXERCISE 5-1

Consulting section 5d, decide if each statement is a fact or an opinion. When the author and source are provided, explain how that information influences your judgment.

1. The life of people on earth is better now than it has ever been— certainly much better than it was 500 years ago.
   —Peggy Noonan, "Why Are We So Unhappy When We Have It So Good?"
2. Every three minutes a woman in the United States learns she has breast cancer.
3. Every journey into the past is complicated by delusions, false memories, false namings of real events.
   —Adrienne Rich, poet, *Of Woman Born*
4. A mind is a terrible thing to waste.
   —United Negro College Fund
5. History is the branch of knowledge that deals systematically with the past.
   —*Webster's New World College Dictionary,* Third Edition
6. In 1927, F. E. Tylcote, an English physician, reported in the medical journal *Lancet* that in almost every case of lung cancer he had seen or known about, the patient smoked.
   —William Ecenbarger, "The Strange History of Tobacco"
7. The earth's temperature is gradually rising.
8. You can, Honest Abe notwithstanding, fool most of the people all of the time.
   —Stephen Jay Gould, "The Creation Myths of Cooperstown"
9. You change laws by changing lawmakers.
   —Sissy Farenthold, political activist, *Bakersfield Californian*
10. Since it opened to the public in 1982, Elvis's place in suburban Whitehaven, a 30-minute drive from downtown Memphis, has attracted more than 3 million visitors. That figure makes it one of the top house attractions in the U.S. This year alone, some 640,000

people will visit Graceland, and in the process they will spend more than $10 million on tickets, food, and souvenirs.

—J. D. Reed, "The Mansion Music Made," *Time*

EXERCISE 5-2

Consulting section 5d, after you read this passage, (1) list all literal information, (2) list all implied information, and (3) list the opinions stated.

EXAMPLE   The study found many complaints against the lawyers were not investigated, seemingly out of a "desire to avoid difficult cases."

—Norman F. Dacey

Literal information: Few complaints against lawyers are investigated.

Implied information: The words *difficult cases* imply a coverup: Lawyers, or others in power, hesitate to criticize lawyers for fear of being sued or for fear of a public outcry if the truth about abuses and errors were revealed.

Opinions: None—all is factual because it refers to, and contains a quote from, a study.

A.   It is the first of February, and everyone is talking about starlings. Starlings came to this country on a passenger liner from Europe. One hundred of them were deliberately released in Central Park, and from those hundred descended all of our countless millions of starlings today. According to Edwin Way Teale, "Their coming was the result of one man's fancy. That man was Eugene Schieffelin, a wealthy New York drug manufacturer. His curious hobby was the introduction into America of all the birds mentioned in William Shakespeare." The birds adapted to their new country splendidly.

—Annie Dillard, *Terror at Tinker Creek*

B.   The kind of constitution and government Gandhi envisaged for an independent India was spelled out at the forty-fifth convention of the All-India Congress, which began at Karachi on March 27, 1931. It was a party political convention the like of which I had not seen before—nor seen since—with its ringing revolutionary proclamations acclaimed by some 350 leaders, men and women, just out of jail, squatting in the heat under a tent in a semicircle at Gandhi's feet, all of them, like Gandhi, spinning away like children playing with toys as they talked. They made up the so-called Subjects Committee, selected from the five thousand delegates to do the real work of the convention, though in reality, it was Gandhi alone who dominated the proceedings, writing most of the resolutions and moving their adoption with his customary eloquence and surprising firmness.

—William L. Shirer, *Gandhi: A Memoir*

Answers: Exercise 5-2 (continued)

3. Central Park is in New York City. (This is information the author assumes the reader has.)
4. "One man's fancy" are words that suggest that the man had somewhat unusual tastes.
5. The drugs that Schieffelin manufactured were legitimate, not illegal.
6. See item 2 in "Opinions."

Opinions

1. (In Teale's opinion) Schieffelin's hobby was somewhat strange ("curious").
2. (In Dillard's opinion) the starlings adapted too well ("splendidly"); here Dillard assumes that the reader knows that flocks of starlings can be a nuisance and even a danger (if they get into airplane engines).

B. *Literal information*

1. Gandhi envisaged a constitution and government for an independent India.
2. The constitution was spelled out at the forty-fifth convention of the All-India Congress.
3. The Congress began at Karachi on March 27, 1931.
4. The Congress was a political convention.
5. The Congress was attended by some 350 leaders.
6. The leaders were both men and women.
7. The leaders were just out of jail.
8. The leaders squatted in the heat under a tent in a semicircle at Gandhi's feet.
9. They all worked at spinning wheels.
10. They made up the so-called Subjects Committee, which was selected from the five thousand delegates.
11. Gandhi wrote most of the resolutions and moved their adoption.

→

Answers: Exercise 5-2 (continued)

Implied information

1. India was not independent before March 27, 1931.
2. Even though the Congress had met forty-five times, India was still not independent.
3. The Congress took more than one day—it only "began" on March 27, 1931.
4. Most of the leaders likely were revolutionaries who had been political prisoners—because all were "just out of jail."
5. The leaders were very dedicated—they were willing to squat in the heat under a tent.
6. The ruling government did not provide the basic amenities for a convention: room in a building, decent ventilation, chairs, tables, and so forth.
7. The leaders' sitting at Gandhi's feet implies how they respected him.
8. Gandhi often worked at a spinning wheel as he spoke.
9. Everyone's spinning implies that they wanted to imitate Gandhi.
10. Five thousand people is too large a group to get policy matters decided.
11. Gandhi dominated the proceedings because everyone respected him so much.

Opinions

1. The author had not seen before—or since—a political convention like this one in achievement and tone.
2. The revolutionary proclamations were "ringing."
3. The leaders were spinning away like children playing with toys as they talked.
4. Gandhi dominated the proceedings.
5. Gandhi wrote and spoke with his customary eloquence and surprising firmness.

5e Engaging in critical reading

The concept of **critical reading** parallels that of critical thinking (see 5a and 5b). To read critically is to think about what you are reading while you are reading it. As a critical reader, you cannot let words merely drift by as your eyes scan the lines. Remain conscious of how the reading process operates, especially the roles of prior knowledge and prediction (see 5c). Also, probe the material on all three levels of meaning—the literal, the inferential, and the evaluative (see 5d). To help yourself along, use specific approaches such as reading systematically (see 5e.1) and reading closely and actively (see 5e.2). As you use them, adapt these approaches to your personal style of getting the most out of your reading.

5e.1 Reading systematically

To **read systematically** is to use a structured plan for delving into the material. Your goal is to come to know and truly understand the material and—equally important—to be able to discuss it and even write about it. Here are some guidelines for reading systematically.

1. **Preview:** Before you start reading, look ahead. Glance over the pages you intend to read so that your mind can start making predictions (see 5c). Looking ahead prepares your mind for the material. As you look over the pages, ask yourself questions that the material stimulates. Do not expect to answer all the questions at this point; their purpose is to focus your thoughts.

   ■ To preview a textbook, first survey the whole book by reading chapter titles for an overview (book titles can be misleading). Next, survey the chapter you are assigned by reading all headings, large and small; all boldfaced words (in darker print); and all visuals and their captions, including photographs, drawings, tables, figures, and charts. If a glossary is at the end of the chapter, scan it for words you do and do not know.

   ■ To preview material that has few or no headings, read and ask questions of the book and (if any) chapter titles; of the author's name and any introductory notes about the author, such as those that precede the essays in many books of collected essays; and of pivotal paragraphs, such as the first few paragraphs and (unless you are reading for suspense) the last pages or paragraphs. If the book has a preface or introduction, skim it.

2. **Read:** Read the material closely and actively, as explained in section 5e.2. Seek the full meaning at all levels explained in 5d. Most of all, expect to reread. College-level material can rarely be fully understood and absorbed in one reading. Budget your time so that you can make many passes through the material.

3. **Review:** Go back to the spots you looked at when you previewed the material. Look, too, at other pivotal places that you discovered. Ask yourself the same sort of questions, this time answering them as fully as possible. If you cannot, reread for the answers. For best success, review in *chunks*—small sections that you can capture comfortably. Do not try to cover too much at once.

   - To stimulate your concentration during reading, keep in mind that you intend to review. This awareness will help you stay alert. Also, the next day, and again about a week later, repeat your review, always adding new material that you have learned since the previous review. As much as time permits, review at intervals during a course. The more reinforcement, the better.

   - Collaborative learning can help you reinforce what you learn from reading. Ask a friend or classmate who knows the material to discuss it with you and even test you. Conversely, offer to teach the material to someone; you will quickly discover whether or not you have mastered it well enough to communicate it.

The steps for reading systematically closely parallel those in the **writing process** (see Chapters 2 and 3). Like *planning* in writing, *previewing* gets you ready and keeps you from plunging ahead inefficiently. Like *drafting* in writing, *reading* means moving through the material so that you come to know it and gain authority over it. Like *revising* in writing, *reviewing* involves going back over the material to clarify, fine-tune, and make it thoroughly your own.

5e.2 Reading closely and actively

The secret to **reading closely** and **actively** is to annotate as you read. *Annotating* means writing notes to yourself in a book's margins, underlining or highlighting key passages, or using asterisks and other codes to alert you to special material. A well-annotated book is usually a well-read book. Most readers annotate only after they have previewed the material and read it once, as explained in section 5e.1. You might find, however, that you like to have a pencil in your hand from the moment you start to read. Experiment to find what works best for you.

Close reading calls for making annotations that relate to the content and meaning of the material. Restate major points "in a nutshell" in the margin. When you review, they will stand out. If you underline or highlight, be sure to jot in the margin key words or phrases that will jog your memory when you need to recall what is important. Extract meaning on the literal, inferential, and evaluative levels (see 5d). The excerpt illustrated on this page shows close-reading annotations in blue ink.

Active reading calls for making annotations that record the connections you make between the material and your prior knowledge and experience. Active reading can also elicit questions and opinions about the material. This is your chance to think on paper. It opens a conversation between you and the author. If this is a relatively new practice for you, do not lose your nerve or get discouraged. Let your mind range

Annotations of an excerpt from the essay shown in Exercise 5-3 using blue for content (close reading) and black for synthesis (active reading).

across ideas that you associate with what you are reading. Consider yourself a partner in the making of meaning, a full participant in the exchange of ideas, opinions, and experiences that typify a college education. The excerpt on page 114 shows active-reading annotations in black ink.

If you feel uncomfortable writing in a book—even though the practice of annotating texts dates back to the Middle Ages—try keeping a *double-entry notebook*. On one side of each sheet of paper write close-reading notes on the content; on the other side, enter active-reading notes detailing the connections you make. Be sure to include information that identifies the passages referred to so that you can easily relocate them. Below is a short example from a double-entry notebook (the symbol ¶ stands for "paragraph").

S. Harris essay. "Sports Only"

content	connections I make
¶1 H. likes sports and exercise. He even built a tennis court for his summer home.	H. isn't "everyman." It takes big bucks to build one's own tennis court.
¶2 H. thinks the average American male is obsessed with sports.	That "average" (if there is such a thing) male sounds a lot like my husband.
¶3 Athletics/Sports are one strand, not the web, of society.	It's worth thinking why sports have such a major hold on men. And why not women, on "average"? (This might be a topic for a a paper someday.)

Double-entry notebook excerpt, based on the first three paragraphs of the essay in Exercise 5-3. The left column deals with content (close reading), and the right covers synthesis (active reading).

115

ANSWERS: EXERCISE 5-3

Answers will vary.

EXERCISE 5-3

The following essay was published as an informal opinion in a newspaper column. Annotate the entire essay, making notes about content in blue and notes that synthesize the material in black, as shown in the annotated excerpt on page 114.

Sports Only Exercise Our Eyes

Sydney J. Harris

Before I proceed a line further, let me make it clear that I enjoy physical exercise and sport as much as any man. I like to bat a baseball, dribble a basketball, kick a soccer ball and, most of all, swat a tennis ball. A man who scorned physical activity would hardly build a tennis court on his summerhouse grounds, or use it every day.

Having made this obeisance, let me now confess that I am puzzled and upset—and have been for many years—by the almost obsessive interest in sports taken by the average American male.

Athletics is one strand in life, and even the ancient Greek philosophers recognized its importance. But it is by no means the whole web, as it seems to be in our society. If American men are not talking business, they are talking sports, or they are not talking at all.

This strikes me as an enormously adolescent, not to say retarded, attitude on the part of presumed adults. Especially when most of the passion and enthusiasm center around professional teams which bear no indigenous relation to the city they play for, and consist of mercenaries who will wear any town's insignia if the price is right.

Although I like to play, and sometimes like to watch, I cannot see what possible difference it makes which team beats which. The tactics are sometimes interesting, and certainly the prowess of the players deserves applause—but most men seem to use commercial sports as a kind of narcotic, shutting out reality, rather than heightening it.

QUOTATION: ON READING

The best effect of any book is that it excites the reader to self-activity.
—Thomas Carlyle

There is nothing more boring, in my view, than a prolonged discussion by laymen of yesterday's game. These dreary conversations are a form of social alcoholism, enabling them to achieve a dubious rapport without ever once having to come to grips with a subject worthy of a grown man's concern.

It is easy to see the opiate quality of sports in our society when tens of millions of men will spend a splendid Saturday or Sunday fall afternoon sitting stupefied in front of the TV, watching a "big game," when they might be out exercising their own flaccid muscles and stimulating their lethargic corpuscles.

Ironically, our obsession with professional athletics not only makes us mentally limited and conversationally dull, it also keeps us physically inert—thus violating the very reason men began engaging in athletic competitions. It is tempting to call this national malaise of "spectatoritis" childish—except that children have more sense, and would rather run out and play themselves.

5f Distinguishing between summary and synthesis

A crucial distinction in critical thinking, critical reading, and critical writing resides in the differences between *summary* and *synthesis*.

Summary comes before synthesis (see Chart 30 in section 5b) in the critical thinking process. To summarize is to extract the main message or central point of a passage. A summary does not include supporting evidence or details. It is the gist, the hub, the seed of what the author is saying; it is not your reaction to it. Most people summarize informally during conversation. When you write a summary, use the guidelines in Chart 139 in section 31e. They apply generally to the kind of summarizing you do in content annotations (see 5e.2), in writing an essay that draws on only one source (see 5g), and in a research paper based on multiple sources (see Chapters 32, 34, and 35).

Synthesis comes after summary (see Chart 30 in section 5b). To synthesize is to weave together ideas from more than one source. You connect ideas from one source to your prior knowledge gained by many years of having read, listened, and experienced life. Synthesis allows you to create a new whole, one that is your own as a result of your thinking about diverse yet related ideas. Unsynthesized ideas and information are like separate spools of thread, neatly lined up, possibly coordinated but not integrated. Synthesized ideas and information become threads woven into a tapestry that creates a new whole. Synthesis is the evidence of your ability to tie ideas together in the tapestry of what you learn, know, and experience.

When you synthesize unconsciously, your mind connects ideas by thought processes mirrored in the rhetorical strategies discussed in section 4f. To synthesize, consciously apply those strategies. For example, compare ideas in sources, contrast ideas in sources, create definitions that combine and extend definitions in individual sources, apply examples or descriptions from one source to illustrate ideas in another, find causes and effects described in one source that explain another.

❶ **ALERT:** "Synthesis by summary"—a mere listing of who said what about a topic—is not synthesis. To synthesize is to create *new* connections among ideas. ❗

Let us examine two examples of synthesis. They connect the essay in Exercise 5-3 to the following excerpt by Robert Lipsyte. (Lipsyte, a sports columnist for the *New York Times,* published his long essay in the spring of 1995 at the end of a nine-month U.S. baseball strike. Lipsyte asserts that sports have become too commercialized and therefore no longer inspire loyalty, teach good sportsmanship, or provide young people with admirable role models.)

> Baseball has done us a favor. It's about time we understood that staged competitive sports events—and baseball can stand for all the games—are no longer the testing ground of our country's manhood and the theater of its once seemingly limitless energy and power.
> As a mirror of our culture, sports now show us spoiled fools as role models, cities and colleges held hostage and games that exist only to hawk products.
> The pathetic posturing of in-your-face macho has replaced a once self-confident masculinity.
>
> —Robert Lipsyte, "The Emasculation of Sports"

SYNTHESIS BY COMPARISON AND CONTRAST

Both Harris and Lipsyte criticize professional sports, but their reasons differ. In part, Harris thinks that people who passively watch sports on TV and rarely exercise are destroying their physical health. Lipsyte sees something less obvious but potentially more sinister: the destruction of traditional values in sports. No longer are athletes heroes who inspire; they are puppets of sports as "big business."

SYNTHESIS BY DEFINITION

The omission of women from each writer's discussion seems a very loud silence. Considered together, these essays define sports as a male preoccupation and undertaking. Harris condemns only men for their inability to think and talk beyond sports and business, an insulting and exaggerated description made even less valid by the absence of women. Lipsyte, even in the 1995 atmosphere of women excelling in many team and individual sports, claims that we have lost a "once self-confident masculinity." An extended definition would include women, even though they might prefer to avoid the negative portraits of Harris and Lipsyte.

Each synthesis belongs to the person who made the connections. Someone else might make entirely different connections. Still, any synthesis needs to be sensibly reasoned and informed by an individual intelligence.

Here is a list of techniques for stimulating your mind to recall prior knowledge and work toward creating a synthesis. (The critical response essay by a student, Anna Lozanov, in section 5g, is an excellent example of making connections between reading and one's personal experience.)

- Use the technique of mapping (see 2i) to lay out and discover relationships between elements in the material and between the material and other ideas.

- Use your powers of play. Mentally toss ideas around, even if you make connections that seem outrageous. Try opposites (for example, read about athletes and think about the most unathletic person you know). Try turning an idea upside down (for example, read about the value of being a good sport and list the benefits of being a bad sport). Try visualizing what you are reading about, and then tinker with the mental picture (for example, picture two people playing tennis and substitute dogs playing Frisbee or seals playing table tennis). The possibilities are endless—make word associations, think up song lyrics, draft a TV advertisement. The goal is always to jump-start your thinking so that you can see ideas in new ways.

- Discuss your reading with someone else. Summarize its content, and elicit the other person's opinion or ideas. Deliberately debate that opinion or challenge those ideas. Discussions and debates can get your mind moving.

EXERCISE 5-4

Here is another excerpt from the essay by Robert Lipsyte. The words in brackets are added in this exercise to supply background information some readers might need.

> We have come to see that [basketball star Michael] Jordan, [football star] Troy Aikman and [baseball star] Ken Griffey have nothing to offer us beyond the gorgeous, breathtaking mechanics of what they do. And it's not enough, now that there is no longer a dependable emotional return beyond the sensation of the moment itself. The

QUOTATION: ON WRITING

I think the writer ought to help the reader as much as he can without damaging what he wants to say; and I don't think it ever hurts the writer to sort of stand back now and then and look at his stuff as if he were reading it instead of writing it.

—James Jones

ANSWERS: EXERCISE 5-4

Answers will vary.

119

changes in sports—the moving of franchises, free agency—have made it impossible to count on a player, a team, an entire league still being around for next year's comeback. The connection between player and fan has been irrevocably destabilized, for love and loyalty demand a future. Along the way, those many virtues of self-discipline, responsibility, altruism and dedication seem to have been deleted from the athletic contract with America.

—Robert Lipsyte, "The Emasculation of Sports"

Consulting sections 5e.2 and 5f, do this:

1. Summarize the excerpt here.
2. Annotate it for its content and for the connections you make to its content.
3. Draft a synthesis connecting this excerpt and the essay by Sydney J. Harris reprinted in Exercise 5-3.

5g Writing a critical response

A **critical response** essay has two missions: to summarize a source's central point or main idea and to respond to the source's main idea with your reactions based on your synthesis (see 5b and 5f).

A well-written critical response accomplishes these two missions with grace and style. That is, it does not say "My summary is . . ." and "Now, here's what I think. . . ." Your goal is to write a well-integrated essay. Its length and whether you respond to a single passage or to an entire work vary with the assignment. Chart 34 gives general guidelines for writing a critical response.

> ⊙ **Guidelines for writing a critical response** 34
>
> 1. Write a summary of the main idea or central point of what you are responding to (whether you are responding to part or all of a source).
> 2. Write a smooth transition between that summary and your response. Although a statement bridging the two parts of a critical response paper need not observe all the formal requirements of a thesis statement (see 2n), it should at least subtly signal the beginning of your response.
> 3. Respond to the source, basing your reaction on the influences of your own experience, your prior knowledge, and your opinions.
> 4. Fulfill all documentation requirements. See Chapter 33 for coverage of four widely used documentation systems (MLA, APA, CM, and CBE), and ask your instructor which to use.

Here is a critical response essay written by Anna Lozanov, a student at a state university. The assignment was to read and respond to the brief essay "Sports Only Exercise Our Eyes" by Sydney J. Harris shown in Exercise 5-3. Lozanov's bridge statement comes at the beginning of the third paragraph: "Just this weekend, however, I had an occasion to reconsider the value of sports." The essay uses MLA documentation style (see 33c). The numbers in parentheses in the essay indicate the pages in the cited work where the quoted words can be found. The work itself is cited at the end of the student essay.

```
                Critical Response by Anna Lozanov
        to "Sports Only Exercise Our Eyes" by Sydney J. Harris
          Except for a brief period in high school when I was
wild about a certain basketball player, I never gave sports
much thought. I went to games because my friends went, not
because I cared about football or baseball or track. I
certainly never expected to defend sports, and when I first
read Sydney Harris's essay "Sports Only Exercise Our Eyes,"
I thoroughly agreed with him. Like Harris, I believed that
men who live and breathe sports are "mentally limited and
conversationally dull" (111).
          For the entire thirteen years of my marriage, I have
complained about the amount of time my husband, John, spends
watching televised sports. Of course, I've tried to get him
to take an interest in something else. There was the time
as a newlywed when I flamboyantly interrupted the sixth game
of the World Series--wearing only a transparent nightie.
Then, in 1978, I had the further audacity to go into labor
with our first child--right in the middle of the Super Bowl.
Even the child tried to help me cure my husband of what
Harris calls an "obsession" (111). Some months after the
fateful Super Bowl, the kid thoroughly soaked his father,
who was concentrating so intently on the Tigers' struggle
for the American League pennant that he didn't even notice!
Only a commercial brought the dazed sports fan back into the
living room from Tiger Stadium.
          Just this weekend, however, I had an occasion to
reconsider the value of sports. Having just read the Harris
essay, I found myself paying closer attention to my husband
```

121

and sons' Saturday afternoon television routine. I was surprised to discover that they didn't just "vegetate" in front of the TV; during the course of the afternoon, they actually discussed ethics, priorities, commitments, and the consequences of abusing one's body. When one of the commentators raised issues like point shaving and using steroids, John and the kids talked about cheating and using drugs. When another commentator brought up the issue of skipping one's senior year to go straight to the pros, John explained the importance of a college education and discussed the short career of most professional football players.

Then, I started to think about all the times I've gone to the basement and found my husband and sons performing exercise routines as they watched a game on TV. Even our seven-year-old, who loathes exercise, pedals vigorously on the exercise bike while the others do sit-ups and curls. Believe it or not, there are times when they're all exercising more than just their eyes.

I still agree with Harris that many people spend too much time watching televised sports, but after this weekend, I certainly can't say that all of that time is wasted--at least not at my house. Anything that can turn my couch potatoes into thinking, talking, active human beings can't be all bad. Next weekend, instead of putting on a nightie, I think I'll join my family on the couch.

Work Cited
Harris, Sydney J. "Sports Only Exercise Our Eyes." _The Best of Sydney J. Harris_. Boston: Houghton, 1975. 111-12.

5h Assessing evidence critically

The cornerstone of all reasoning is evidence. As a reader, you expect writers to provide solid evidence for any claim made or conclusion reached. As a writer, you want to use evidence well to support your claims or conclusions. Evidence consists of facts, statistical information, examples, and opinions of experts.

5h.1 Evaluating evidence

Chart 35 lists guidelines for evaluating evidence that you read and for deciding what evidence to include in your writing. Each guideline is discussed after the chart.

 Checklist for evaluating evidence   **35**

- Is the evidence sufficient?
- Is the evidence representative?
- Is the evidence relevant?
- Is the evidence accurate, whether from primary or secondary sources?
- Are the claims qualified fairly, based on the evidence?

- **Is the evidence sufficient?** A general rule for both readers and writers is the more evidence, the better. As a reader, you would tend to have more confidence in the results of a survey that draws on a hundred respondents than in one that draws on ten. As a writer, you may convince your reader that violence is a serious problem in high schools on the basis of two specific examples, but you will be more convincing if you can give five examples—or, better still, statistics for a school district, a city, or a nation.

- **Is the evidence representative?** As a reader, assess objectivity and fairness; do not assume them because words are in print. Do not trust a claim or conclusion about the group based on only a few members rather than on a truly representative or typical sample. A pollster surveying national political views would not get representative evidence by asking questions of the first fifteen hundred people to walk by a street corner in Austin, Texas, because that group would not truly represent the actual regional, racial, political, and ethnic makeup of the U.S. electorate. As a writer, make sure the evidence you offer represents your claim fairly; do not base your point on exceptions.

- **Is the evidence relevant?** Determining relevance can demand subtle thinking. Suppose you read evidence that one hundred students who had watched television for more than two hours a day throughout high school earned significantly lower scores on a college entrance exam than one hundred students who had not. Would you conclude that students who watch less television perform better on college entrance exams? Perhaps, but closer examination of the evidence might reveal other differences between the two groups—differences in geographical region, family background, socioeconomic group, quality of schools attended. Therefore, the evidence would not be relevant to the conclusion about TV watching and college entrance exams.

■ **Is the evidence accurate?** Inaccurate evidence is useless. Evidence must come from reliable sources, whether they are primary sources or secondary sources (see 5h.2). Equally important, reliable evidence must be carefully presented so that it does not misrepresent or distort information.

■ **Is the evidence qualified?** Evidence rarely justifies claims that use words such as *all, certainly, always,* or *never.* Conclusions are more reasonable when qualified with words such as *some, many, a few, probably, possibly, perhaps, may, usually,* and *often.* Remember that today's "facts" may be revised as time passes, information changes, and knowledge grows.

5h.2 Understanding differences between primary and secondary sources as evidence

Primary sources present firsthand evidence based on your own or someone else's original work or direct observation. Firsthand evidence has the greatest impact on a reader. Consider this eyewitness account:

> Poverty is dirt. . . . Let me explain about housekeeping with no money. For breakfast I give my children grits with no oleo or cornbread without eggs and oleo. This does not use up many dishes. What dishes there are, I wash in cold water and with no soap. Even the cheapest soap has to be saved for the baby's diapers. Look at my hands, so cracked and red. Once I saved for two months to buy a jar of Vaseline for my hands and the baby's diaper rash. When I had saved enough, I went to buy it and the price had gone up two cents. The baby and I suffered on. I have to decide every day if I can bear to put my cracked sore hands into the cold water and strong soap. But you ask, why not hot water? Fuel costs money. If you have a wood fire, it costs money. If you burn electricity, it costs money. Hot water is a luxury. I do not have luxuries. . . .
>
> —Jo Goodwin Parker, "What Is Poverty?"

As a reader and as a writer, remember that not all eyewitness accounts are equally reliable. What is it about Parker's account that makes you trust what she says? She is specific. She is also authoritative. It is doubtful that anyone would have invented the story about being two cents short of the price of a jar of Vaseline. As a writer of personal observations, you need to be as specific as possible—to prove that you truly saw what you say you saw. Use language that appeals to all five senses: describe sights, sounds, and experiences that could have been seen, heard, or experienced only by someone who was there. Show your readers *your* cracked, red hands.

As evidence, primary sources that meet the guidelines in Chart 35 can provide valuable reports of observations. Few of us will ever see the surface of the moon or the top of Mount Everest. People rely, therefore, on the firsthand reports of the astronauts and mountain climbers who have been there. Indeed, much of history depends heavily on letters, diaries, and journals—the reports of eyewitnesses who saw events unfold.

Surveys, polls, and experiments are some of the means by which people extend their powers of observation beyond what can be seen in the everyday sense of the word. Jo Parker could look at her hands. Who can see, however, the attitude of the American public toward marriage, toward a presidential candidate, toward inflation? For evidence on such matters, polls or surveys are necessary. They constitute primary evidence and must be carefully controlled—through weighing, measuring, or quantifying information that would otherwise not be available.

Secondary sources report, describe, comment on, or analyze the experiences or the work of others. As evidence, a secondary source is at least once removed from the primary source. It reports *about* the original work, the direct observation, or the firsthand experience. Still, such evidence can have great value and enormous impact. Consider this secondhand reported observation.

> The immediate causes of death from nuclear attack are the blast wave, which can flatten heavily reinforced buildings many kilometers away, the firestorm, the gamma rays and the neutrons, which effectively fry the insides of passersby. A schoolgirl who survived the American nuclear attack on Hiroshima, the event that ended the Second World War, wrote this firsthand account:
>
> > Through a darkness like the bottom of hell, I could hear the voices of the other students calling for their mothers. And at the base of the bridge, inside a big cistern that had been dug out there, was a mother weeping, holding above her head a naked baby that was burned bright red all over its body. . . . But every single person who passed was wounded, all of them, and there was no one, there was no one to turn to for help. And the singed hair on the heads of the people was frizzled and whitish and covered with dust. They did not appear to be human, not creatures of this world.
>
> —Carl Sagan, *Cosmos*

As with Parker's eyewitness account, the strength or value of a secondhand account hinges on the reliability of the reporter. That reliability is a function of how specific, accurate, and authoritative the observations are. Here the standard maxim "consider the source" becomes crucial. An expert's reputation must stem from some special experience (as the parents of many children could be "experts" on child rearing) or training (as

The main suggestion from me is *read*. It is impossible for a writer to be able to write honestly and eloquently without having at one time or another acquainted himself with such writers as Sir Thomas Browne.
—William Styron

an accountant could be an expert on taxes). Because the author of the example paragraph, Carl Sagan, is a respected scientist, scholar, and writer, his report of the schoolgirl's eyewitness account is likely to be reliable, authoritative, worthwhile secondary evidence.

Sagan is a secondary source because although readers can feel quite confident that Sagan is fully and fairly representing what the schoolgirl said, no one can be sure of that without seeing her original account. If you were to use Sagan's version of her account as evidence, it would be thirdhand evidence: one person (you) further removed from another (Sagan) and yet further from the original source (the schoolgirl). In college, you must often depend on secondary sources (for example, most textbooks), but sometimes you are expected to use primary sources (for example, a published diary, scientists' journal articles reporting their research, works of literature). Chart 36 gives guidelines for evaluating a secondary source.

 Checklist for evaluating a secondary source   36

- **Is the source authoritative?** Was it written by an expert or a person whom you can expect to write credibly on the subject?
- **Is the source reliable?** Does the material appear in a reputable publication—in a book published by an established publisher, in a respected journal or magazine, or on a reliable Internet site?
- **Is the source well known?** Is the source cited elsewhere as you read about the subject? (If so, the authority of the source is probably widely accepted.)
- **Is the information well supported?** Is the source based on primary evidence? If secondary evidence, is it authoritative and reliable?
- **Is the tone balanced?** Is the language relatively objective (and therefore more likely reliable) or slanted (probably not reliable)?
- **Is the source current?** Is the material up-to-date (and therefore more likely reliable), or has later authoritative and reliable research made it outdated? ("Old" is not necessarily unreliable. In many fields, classic works of research remain authoritative for decades or even centuries.)

---

❶ ALERT: You can use the guidelines in Chart 36 to evaluate electronic sources as well as conventional print sources. Be skeptical about any electronically accessed source that cannot be verified according to these guidelines. ❗

EXERCISE 5-5

Consulting section 5h, decide the following: (1) Would each passage constitute primary or secondary evidence? (2) Is the evidence acceptable? Why or why not?

A.   I went one morning to a place along the banks of the Madeira River where the railroad ran, alongside rapids impassable to river traffic, and I searched for any marks it may have left on the land. But there was nothing except a clearing where swarms of insects hovered over the dead black hen and other items spread out on a red cloth as an offering to the gods of macumba, or black magic. This strain of African origins in Brazil's ethnic character is strong in the Northwest Region.

—William S. Ellis, "Brazil's Imperiled Rain Forest"

B.   Most climatologists believe that the world will eventually slip back into an ice age in 10,000 to 20,000 years. The Earth has been unusually cold for the last two to three million years, and we are just lucky to be living during one of the warm spells. But the concern of most weather watchers looking at the next century is with fire rather than ice. By burning fossil fuels and chopping down forests, humans have measurably increased the amount of carbon dioxide in the atmosphere. From somewhere around 300 parts per million at the turn of the century, this level has risen to 340 parts per million today. If the use of fossil fuels continues to increase, carbon dioxide could reach 600 parts per million during the next century.

—Steve Olson, "Computing Climate"

C.   Marriages on the frontier were often made before a girl was half through her adolescent years, and some diaries record a casualness in the manner in which such decisions were reached. Mrs. John Kirkwood recounts:

> The night before Christmas, John Kirkwood . . . the path finder, stayed at our house over night. I had met him before and when he heard the discussion about my brother Jasper's wedding, he suggested that he and I also get married. I was nearly fifteen years old and I thought it was high time that I got married so I consented.

—Lillian Schlissel, *Women's Diaries of the Westward Journey*

5i Assessing cause and effect critically

Cause and effect is a mode of thinking that seeks to establish some relationship, or link, between two or more specific pieces of evidence.

127

ANSWERS: EXERCISE 5-5

A. (1) Primary evidence. The author is describing his own experiences in a first-person narrative. (2) It seems to be balanced and objective, but a reader cannot know whether the information is reliable from the paragraph.

B. (1) Secondary evidence. (2) The assertions are carefully qualified and seem well substantiated by evidence. Students cannot know whether the information is reliable from this paragraph.

C. (1) Both secondary and primary evidence. The opening paragraph presents secondary evidence, but the second paragraph presents primary evidence—a first-hand account from a diary by Mrs. John Kirkwood. (2) The quoted material makes Schlissel's observations reliable.

TEACHING TIP

You may want to ask your students to think about their own experiences, analyzing them for their causes and effects. You might ask your students to diagram these causes and effects and to write some of these diagrams on the board for discussion. The questions that follow can help stimulate students' thinking.

1. How did you get your first job?
2. What did you learn from that job?

→

Teaching Tip (continued)

3. Whose advice is particularly important to you?

4. How do you reach a decision?

5. What difference do you expect college to make in your life?

6. Why do you have a particular way of doing something?

7. How do you make friends?

8. Who is the most important person in your life? Why?

9. When did you learn to drive a car?

10. What will you be doing in ten years?

EXTRA EXERCISE B

Supply answers for the blanks in the sentences that follow, checking each choice by the guidelines for evaluating cause and effect to be sure that it is accurate.

1. Frequently eating food with high sodium content can cause _____.

2. _____ can lead to a traffic violation.

3. Regular exercise produces _____.

4. _____ is a leading cause of _____.

5. Because she _____, she is expected to be named Gourmet of the Year.

6. Her mother refuses to intervene so that _____.

7. If you don't quit _____, you are likely to end up in a lawsuit.

8. She decided to stay in college when she learned that _____.

9. Additional funding for preschool education is needed in order to _____.

10. _____ has resulted in increased numbers of homeless people in our major cities.

→

Regardless of whether you begin with a cause or an effect, you are working with this basic pattern:

BASIC PATTERN FOR CAUSE AND EFFECT

Cause A ⟶ produces ⟶ effect B

You may seek to understand the effects of a known cause (for example, studying two more hours each night):

More studying ⟶ produces ⟶ ?

Or you may attempt to determine the cause or causes of a known effect (for example, recurrent headaches):

? ⟶ produces ⟶ recurrent headaches

If you want to use reasoning based on a relationship of cause and effect, evaluate the connections carefully. As you evaluate cause-and-effect relationships, keep in mind the guidelines in Chart 37. Each guideline is discussed after the chart.

Checklist for assessing cause and effect　　**37**

■　Is there a clear relationship between events?

■　If the events recur, are they always in the same sequence?

■　Are there multiple causes and/or effects?

■ **Is there a clear relationship between events?** When you read or write about causes and effects, carefully think the reasoning through. Related causes and effects happen in sequence: A cause exists or occurs before an effect. First the wind blows; then a door slams; then a pane of glass in the door breaks. But just because the order of events implies a cause-and-effect relationship, that relationship does not necessarily exist. Perhaps someone slammed the door shut. Perhaps someone threw a baseball through the glass pane. A cause-and-effect relationship must be linked by more than chronological sequence. The fact that B happens after A does not prove that A causes B.

■ **Is there a pattern of repetition?** To establish that A causes B, there must be proof that every time A is present, B occurs—or that B never occurs unless A is present. The need for a pattern of repetition explains why the Food and Drug Administration performs thousands of tests before declaring a new food or medicine safe for human consumption.

- **Are there multiple causes and/or effects?** Avoid oversimplification. The basic pattern of cause and effect—single cause, single effect (A causes B)—rarely represents the full picture. It was oversimplification when some people assumed that high schools were the only cause of a dramatic nationwide decline in SAT scores between 1964 and 1984. Not only was that unfair to high schools, but it also ignored a variety of other causes, including such factors as television viewing habits, family life, and level of textbooks. Similarly, one cause can produce multiple effects: Oversimplification of effects usually involves focusing on one effect and ignoring others. For example, advertisements about a liquid diet drink focus on its most appealing effect, rapid weight loss. But they ignore other, less desirable effects such as loss of nutrients and vulnerability to regaining the weight.

5j Assessing reasoning processes critically

To think critically, you need to understand reasoning processes so that you can recognize and evaluate them in your reading and use them correctly in your writing. **Induction** and **deduction** are reasoning processes. They are natural thought patterns that people use every day to think through ideas and make decisions. The differences between the two processes are summarized in Chart 38.

⊙ **Comparison of inductive and deductive reasoning**   **38**

	Inductive Reasoning	Deductive Reasoning
Argument begins . . .	with specific evidence	with a general claim
Argument concludes . . .	with a general claim	with a specific statement
Conclusion is . . .	reliable or unreliable	true or false
Reasoning is used . . .	to discover new something	to apply what is known

5j.1 Recognizing and using inductive reasoning

Induction is the process of arriving at general principles from particular facts or instances, as summarized in Chart 39. Suppose that you go to the Registry of Motor Vehicles to renew your driver's license, and you have to stand in line for two hours until you get the document. Then a few months later, when you return to the registry for new license plates,

TEACHING TIP

Using analogy is a way to think inductively. An analogy compares two dissimilar objects, ideas, or experiences by focusing on what they have in common. For example, some people make an analogy between the role of a teacher and that of a coach. Like coaches, teachers train people in fundamentals through repetition and practice, recommend changes in technique, and try to inspire excellence. However, despite points of similarity, two dissimilar items remain dissimilar.

First, coaches work primarily with the body rather than the mind, developing physical rather than mental skills. Second, team coaches praise the team player, whereas good teachers reward independence and originality. Thus the analogy between teachers and coaches breaks down at some point.

In the absence of other evidence, an analogy will not *prove* anything. Nevertheless, although an analogy can always be shown as flawed under close scrutiny, it can still help explain a point and thus help persuade an audience.

a clerk gives you the wrong advice, and you have to stand in two different lines for three hours. Another time you go there in response to a letter asking for information, and you discover that you should have brought your car registration form, although the letter failed to mention that fact. You conclude that the registry is inefficient and seems not to care about the convenience of its patrons. You have arrived at this conclusion by means of induction.

◎ **Summary of inductive reasoning**   39

■ **Inductive reasoning moves from the specific to the general.** It begins with the evidence of specific facts, observations, or experiences and moves to a general conclusion.

■ Inductive conclusions are considered reliable or unreliable, not true or false. An inductive conclusion indicates probability, the degree to which the conclusion is likely to be true. Frustrating though it may be for those who seek certainty, inductive thinking is, of necessity, based only on a sampling of the facts.

■ An inductive conclusion is held to be reliable or unreliable in relation to the quantity and quality of the evidence (see 5e) supporting it.

■ Induction leads to new "truths." Induction can support statements about the unknown on the basis of what is known.

5j.2 Recognizing and using deductive reasoning

Deduction is the process of reasoning from general claims to a specific instance. If several unproductive visits to the Registry of Motor Vehicles have convinced you that the registry cares little about the convenience of its patrons (as the experiences described in 5j.1 suggest), you will not be happy the next time you must return. Your reasoning might go something like this:

The registry wastes people's time.
I have to go to the registry tomorrow.
Therefore, tomorrow my time will be wasted.

You reached the conclusion—"therefore, tomorrow my time will be wasted"—by means of deduction.

Deductive arguments have three parts: two **premises** and a **conclusion.** This three-part structure is known as a **syllogism.** The first premise of a deductive argument may be a fact or an assumption. The second premise may also be a fact or an assumption.

Whether or not an argument is **valid** has to do with the argument's form or structure. Here the word *valid* is not the general term people use in conversation to mean "acceptable" or "well grounded." In the context of reading and writing logical arguments, the word *valid* has a very specific meaning. A deductive argument is *valid* when the conclusion logically follows from the premises. The following argument is valid.

VALID

PREMISE 1	When it snows, the streets get wet. [fact]
PREMISE 2	It is snowing. [fact]
CONCLUSION	Therefore, the streets are getting wet.

The following argument is invalid.

INVALID

PREMISE 1	When it snows, the streets get wet. [fact]
PREMISE 2	The streets are getting wet. [fact]
CONCLUSION	Therefore, it is snowing.

The invalid argument has acceptable premises because the premises are facts. The argument's conclusion, however, is wrong. It ignores other reasons why the streets may be wet. The street could be wet from rain, from street-cleaning trucks that spray water, or from people washing their cars. Because the conclusion does not follow logically from the premises, the argument is invalid.

The following argument is also invalid. The conclusion does not follow from the premises (the car may not start for many reasons other than a dead battery).

INVALID

PREMISE 1	When the battery is dead, a car will not start. [fact]
PREMISE 2	My car will not start. [fact]
CONCLUSION	My battery is dead.

When a premise is an assumption, the premise must be able to be defended with evidence. The next argument about the unemployment rate and recession is valid. Its conclusion follows logically from the premises. An argument's validity, however, is independent of its truth. Is premise 1 true? Different economists will offer different opinions. Only if both premises are true is an argument true. This argument may be true or false, depending on whether the first premise is true or false. The writer must support the claim that is the first premise.

VALID (AND POSSIBLY TRUE)

PREMISE 1	When the unemployment rate rises, an economic recession occurs. [assumption: the writer must present evidence in support of this statement]
PREMISE 2	The unemployment rate has risen. [fact]
CONCLUSION	An economic recession will occur.

OTHER EXAMPLES

INVALID

Some round things are bubbles.
Some human heads are round things.
Therefore, some human heads are bubbles.

VALID

All mammals are animals.
All whales are mammals.
Therefore, all whales are animals.

QUOTATION: ON READING

Do not dictate to your author; try to become him. Be his fellow-worker and accomplice. If you hang back, and reserve and criticize at first, you are preventing yourself from getting the fullest possible value from what you read. But if you open your mind as widely as possible, then signs and hints of almost imperceptible fineness, from the twist and turn of the first sentences, will bring you in the presence of a human being unlike any other. Steep yourself in this, acquaint yourself with this, and soon you will find that your author is giving you, or attempting to give you, something far more definite.

—Virginia Woolf

The following argument is valid. Its conclusion follows from its premises. Is the argument, however, true? Because the argument contains an assumption in its first premise, the argument can be true only if the premise is proved true. Such proof is not possible. Therefore, although the argument is valid, it is not true.

VALID (BUT NOT TRUE)

PREMISE 1	If you buy a Supermacho 357 sports car, you will achieve instant popularity. [assumption]
PREMISE 2	Kim just bought a Supermacho 357 sports car. [fact]
CONCLUSION	Kim will achieve instant popularity.

In any deductive argument, beware of premises that are implied but not stated—called **unstated assumptions.** Remember that an argument can be logically valid even though it is based on wrong assumptions. The response to such an argument is to attack the assumptions, not the conclusion. Often, the assumptions are wrong. For example, suppose a corporation argued that it should not be required to install pollution control devices because the cost would cut into its profits. This argument rests on the unstated assumption that no corporation should do something that would lower its profits. That assumption is wrong, and so is the argument. But it can be shown to be wrong only when the assumptions are challenged. Similarly, if someone says that certain information has to be correct because it was printed in a newspaper, the person's deductive reasoning is flawed. Here the unstated assumption is that everything in a newspaper is correct—which is not true. Whenever there is an unstated assumption, supply it and then check to make sure it is true. Deductive reasoning is summarized in Chart 40.

⊙ **Summary of deductive reasoning** 40

- **Deductive reasoning moves from the general to the specific.** The three-part structure that makes up a deductive argument includes two premises and a conclusion drawn from them.

- A deductive argument is valid if the conclusion logically follows from the premises.

- A deductive conclusion may be judged true or false. If both premises are true, the conclusion is true. If the argument contains an assumption, the writer must prove the truth of the assumption to establish the truth of the argument.

- Deductive reasoning applies what the writer already knows. Though it does not yield anything new, it builds stronger arguments than inductive reasoning does because it offers the certainty of a conclusion's being true or false.

EXERCISE 5-6

Consulting section 5j.2, ignore for the moment whether the premises seem to you to be true, but determine if each conclusion is valid. Explain your answer.

1. Faddish clothes are expensive.
   This shirt is expensive.
   This shirt must be part of a fad.

2. When a storm is threatening, small-craft warnings are issued.
   A storm is threatening.
   Small-craft warnings will be issued.

3. The Pulitzer Prize is awarded to outstanding literary works.
   The Great Gatsby never won a Pulitzer Prize.
   The Great Gatsby is not an outstanding literary work.

4. All states send representatives to the United States Congress.
   Puerto Rico sends a representative to the United States Congress.
   Puerto Rico is a state.

5. All risks are frightening.
   Changing to a new job is a risk.
   The change to a new job is frightening.

6. Before an occupancy permit can be issued, a new home must be inspected.
   Our new home has been issued an occupancy permit.
   Our new home has been inspected.

7. Most weekly newsmagazines give only superficial coverage of world affairs.
   This is a weekly newsmagazine.
   This newsmagazine will give only superficial coverage of world affairs.

8. Science fiction novels are usually violent.
   This is a science fiction novel.
   This novel is obviously violent.

9. All veterans are entitled to education benefits.
   Elaine is a veteran.
   Elaine is entitled to education benefits.

10. Midwestern universities produce great college basketball teams.
    Georgetown has a great college basketball team.
    Georgetown is a Midwestern university.

5k Recognizing and avoiding logical fallacies

Logical fallacies are flaws in reasoning that lead to illogical statements. They tend to occur most often when ideas are being argued, although they can be found in all types of writing. Most logical fallacies

ANSWERS: EXERCISE 5-6

1. Invalid. The shirt's being expensive does not mean that it shares other characteristics of faddish clothing.

2. Valid. The conclusion follows logically from the premises.

3. Invalid. Some outstanding literary works have not received a Pulitzer Prize.

4. Invalid. All states do send representatives, but that does not mean that all representatives come from a state.

5. Valid. The argument is valid, although some people may not agree that all risks are frightening.

6. Valid. The conclusion flows logically from the premises.

7. Invalid. The premises do not contain the conclusion. It is impossible to know whether this magazine is part of "most."

8. Invalid. The qualifying word "usually" in the first premise leaves open the possibility that there are science fiction novels that are not violent.

9. Valid. The conclusion is contained in the premises.

10. Invalid. The first premise does not stipulate that all great college basketball teams come from the Midwest (and Georgetown is among universities not in the Midwest that produce great basketball teams).

TEACHING TIP

Many students enjoy finding and correcting logical fallacies in newspaper editorials and opinion columns, as well as in the work of their peers. You might distribute copies of works containing fallacies, as a spur to class discussion or for revision. A less adept class might benefit from a preliminary lesson based on a list of logical fallacies you can cull from assorted sources (newspapers, political literature, advertisements, student papers); tell the students all the passages are illogical and have them explain why, as a prelude to revision (oral or written, as time allows).

Teaching Tip *(continued)*

Your analytically minded students may be interested in additional logical fallacies:

A *question-begging phrase* (sometimes called *alleged certainty*) presents something as certain that is open to debate: "Everyone knows" and "It is obvious that" are typical phrases that beg the question. This statement is flawed: "It is common knowledge that jobs in Texas pay more than jobs in Idaho"; this statement is logical: "A recent government survey revealed that, on the average, workers in the oil fields of Texas are paid more than loggers in the timber industries of Idaho." *To correct*: Drop the phrase and substitute evidence that supports your claim.

A *complex question* (also known as a *loaded question*) contains one or more unproven assumptions: "Are you still spending time with known drug addicts?" Notice what happens when you try to answer such a question. If you say "yes," you are guilty. If you say "no," you are still guilty, because you are admitting that you used to spend time with drug addicts. *To correct*: Split the question into its parts ("Are you still spending time with those people?" "Are those people drug addicts?") and deal with each separately.

Appeal to fear uses scare tactics instead of legitimate evidence. Such an argument implies danger: "Anyone who stages a protest against the government is a communist, so we must outlaw all protests."

Appeal to the people (also known as an *ad populum appeal*) draws on whatever the people hold dear—for example, country, religion, or family. This approach tries to sway people by using a favorable label instead of providing reasons: "A vote for Joe Smith is a vote for the flag."

Name-calling attaches an unpleasant label to something or someone. Consider how a label can stop people from thinking: "Jane Jones was once an alcoholic, so she cannot possibly say anything of value about politics."

Appeal to pity attempts to arouse sympathy: "He embezzled $1,500 of company

masquerade as reasonable statements, but they are in fact attempts to manipulate readers by reaching their emotions instead of their intellects, their hearts rather than their heads. Most logical fallacies are known by labels; each indicates a way that thinking has gone wrong during the reasoning process. They are summarized in Chart 41.

◉ Summary of logical fallacies   41

- **Hasty generalization:** generalizing from inadequate evidence; stereotyping is hasty generalization using prejudiced claims about a group of people
- **False analogy:** using a comparison in which the differences outweigh the similarities or in which the similarities are irrelevant to the claim the analogy is intended to support
- **Begging the question:** using a kind of circular reasoning that offers as proof of an argument a version of the argument itself or using a (presumably) shared assumption to stand for proof
- **Irrelevant argument:** reaching a conclusion that does not follow from the premises
- **False cause:** assuming that because two events are related in time, the first caused the second
- **Self-contradiction:** using two premises that cannot both be true
- **Red herring:** sidetracking the issue by raising a second, unrelated issue
- **Argument to the person:** attacking the person making the argument rather than the argument itself
- **Guilt by association:** attacking a person's ideas because of that person's interests or associates
- **Jumping on the bandwagon:** implying that something is right or is permissible because "everyone does it"
- **False or irrelevant authority:** citing the opinion of a person who has no expertise about the subject
- **Card-stacking:** ignoring evidence on the other side of a question
- **Either-or fallacy:** offering only two alternatives when more exist
- **Taking something out of context:** distorting an idea or a fact by separating it from the material surrounding it
- **Appeal to ignorance:** assuming that an argument is valid simply because there is no evidence on the other side of the issue
- **Ambiguity and equivocation:** using expressions that are not clear because they have more than one meaning

Hasty generalization

A **hasty generalization** occurs when someone generalizes from inadequate evidence. If the statement "My hometown is the best place in the state to live" is supported with only two examples of why it is pleasant, the generalization is hasty. **Stereotyping** is a type of hasty generalization that occurs when someone makes prejudiced, sweeping claims about all of the members of a particular religious, ethnic, racial, or political group: "Everyone from country X is dishonest." **Sexism** occurs when someone discriminates against people on the basis of sex. (See sections 11q and 21b for advice on how to avoid sexist language in your writing.) An observer at the scene of a minor traffic accident who makes comments about "women drivers" would be guilty of a combination of stereotyping and sexism.

False analogy

A **false analogy** is a comparison in which the differences outweigh the similarities or the similarities are irrelevant to the claim the analogy is intended to support. "Old Joe Smith would never make a good president because an old dog cannot learn new tricks." Homespun analogies like this often seem to have an air of wisdom about them, but just as often they fall apart when examined closely. Humans are not dogs, and learning the role of president is hardly comparable to learning animal tricks.

Begging the question

An argument that **begs the question** states a claim, but the support is based on the claim, so the reasoning is circular. Sometimes, the support simply restates the claim: "Wrestling is a dangerous sport because it is unsafe." *Unsafe* conveys the same idea as *dangerous;* it does not provide evidence to support the claim that wrestling is dangerous. Another question-begging argument offers a second statement as support, but the support for the second statement is the argument in the first statement: "Wrestling is a dangerous sport because wrestlers get injured. Anyone as big and strong as a wrestler would not get injured if the sport were safe." Begging the question also occurs in statements such as "Wrestlers love danger." There is an unstated assumption that wrestling is dangerous as well as an assumption that no proof is called for because the audience shares the opinion that wrestling is dangerous.

Irrelevant argument

An **irrelevant argument** is a *non sequitur* (Latin for "it does not follow"). It occurs when a conclusion does not follow from the premises: "Jane Jones is a forceful speaker, so she will make a good mayor." It does not follow that speaking ability is an indicator that a person would be a good mayor.

135

EXTRA EXERCISE C

Each analogy here can be defended. Like all analogies, each can also be attacked. First, defend each one—give one or more arguments to show that the two parts of the analogy are similar and are relevant to the claim being made. Second, attack each one by pointing out how they are not similar. Finally, offer other types of evidence that would help make the claim ultimately more convincing.

1. Like warfare, the aim of football is to destroy.

2. Don't bother to take your books home over vacation. Vacation is like a "study date"—no studying ever takes place.

3. Taking care of a group of young children is like trying to string beads without a knot on the end of the string.

4. The atom is like a small solar system, with its own "sun" and its own satellites.

Answers to Extra Exercise C

Answers will vary. Answers here are intended to be suggestive.

1. *Pro:* Both involve uniformed "teams" inflicting injury on each other in pursuit of territorial gain. *Con:* Football is played according to rules, with clear time limits, for entertainment. *To revise:* Add statistics on actual injuries inflicted on high school, college, and professional football players, as well as evidence of asocial attitudes (if any) developed by players.

→

***Answers to Extra Exercise C
(continued)***

2. *Pro:* In both cases, serious intentions readily give way to the pursuit of pleasure. *Con:* A study date ostensibly has a serious purpose, whereas vacation, by definition, is unstructured free time. *To revise:* Add eyewitness accounts or reported observations about how time was spent on actual study dates, actual vacations.

3. *Pro:* Both are nearly impossible to control. The moment you get one "on the string," the others fall off. *Con:* Beads are much easier to control. *To revise:* Provide eyewitness accounts of baby-sitting experiences.

4. *Pro:* Both have large centers with smaller objects orbiting them. *Con:* The sun is chemically more complex than the nuclei of atoms; planets orbit the sun because of gravity rather than electrical charge. *To revise:* Other than listing additional similarities, the analogy cannot be made stronger—the properties of the solar system and of the atom are what they are.

False cause

The fallacy of **false cause** is called in Latin ***post hoc, ergo propter hoc***—which means "after this, therefore because of this." This fallacy results when someone assumes that because two events are related in time, the first one causes the second one. This cause-and-effect fallacy is very common. "A new weather satellite was launched last week, and it has been raining ever since" implies—illogically—that the rain (the second event) is a result of the satellite launch (the first event).

Self-contradiction

Self-contradiction occurs when two premises are used that cannot simultaneously be true: "Only when nuclear weapons have finally destroyed us will we be convinced of the need to control them." This statement is self-contradictory in that no one would be around to be convinced if everyone had been destroyed.

Red herring

A **red herring,** sometimes referred to as **ignoring the question,** sidetracks an issue by bringing up a totally unrelated issue: "Why worry about pandas becoming extinct when we should be concerned about the plight of the homeless?" Someone who introduces an irrelevant issue hopes to distract the audience as a red herring might distract bloodhounds from a scent.

Argument to the person

An **argument to the person,** also known as an **ad hominem attack,** criticizes a person's appearance, personal habits, or character instead of dealing with the merits of the individual's arguments, ideas, or opinions. "We could take her position on child abuse seriously if she were not so nasty to the children who live next door to her" is an example of an ad hominem attack. It may seem reasonable to belittle suggestions from someone who may (or may not) be nasty to children; in truth, however, the suggestions, not the person who makes them, must be dealt with. The arguer is not the argument.

Guilt by association

Guilt by association is a kind of ad hominem attack implying that an individual's arguments, ideas, or opinions lack merit because of that person's activities, interests, or associates. The claim that because Jack belongs to the International Hill Climbers Association, which declared bankruptcy last month, he is unfit to be mayor uses guilt by association.

Jumping on the bandwagon

Jumping on the bandwagon, also known as **going along with the crowd** or ***ad populum,*** implies that something is right because everyone is doing it, that truth is determined by majority vote: "Smoking is not bad for people because millions of people smoke."

False or irrelevant authority

Using **false or irrelevant authority,** sometimes called *ad verecundiam,* means citing the opinion of an "expert" who has no claim to expertise about the subject at hand. This fallacy attempts to transfer prestige from one area to another. Many television commercials rely on this tactic—a famous tennis player praising a brand of motor oil or a popular movie star lauding a brand of cheese.

Card-stacking

Card-stacking, also known as **special pleading,** ignores evidence on the other side of a question. From all the available facts, the person arguing selects only those that will build the best (or worst) possible case. Many television commercials use this strategy. When three slim, happy consumers rave about a new diet plan, they do not mention that the plan does not work for everyone and that other plans work better for some people. The makers of the commercial select evidence that helps their cause and ignore any that does not.

The either-or fallacy

The **either-or fallacy,** also known as a **false dilemma,** offers only two alternatives when more exist. Such fallacies often touch on emotional issues and can therefore seem accurate at first. When people reflect, however, they quickly come to realize that more alternatives are available. "Either go to college or forget about getting a job" is a typical example of an either-or fallacy. This statement implies that a college education is a prerequisite for all jobs, which is not true.

Taking something out of context

Taking something out of context separates an idea or a fact from the material surrounding it, thus distorting it for special purposes. Suppose a critic for the *Sun* writes about a movie saying, "The plot was predictable and boring but the music was sparkling." Then an advertisement for the movie says, "*Sun* calls it 'sparkling'!" The critic's words have been taken out of context—and distorted.

Appeal to ignorance

An **appeal to ignorance** assumes that an argument is valid simply because it has not been shown to be false or that something is not false simply because it has not been shown to be true. Appeals to ignorance can be very persuasive because they prey on people's superstitions or lack of knowledge. Here is a typical example of such flawed reasoning:

QUOTATION: ON READING

Rereading books is an antisocial habit. If I keep it up, I'm not going to be invited out anymore. It's a pity, because rereading books has become a sort of addiction. If a book is really good, it deserves to be read again, and if it's great, it should be read at least three times.

It's not a question of paying homage to the book, but of doing it justice. In a first reading, you're distracted by pleasure, excitement, curiosity. The book may so seize you that you rush through it in a kind of delirium. In my own case, the more I like a book, the more slowly I read, and this has its distractions too. When you read slowly, as the speed-reading courses point out, you have time to free-associate to the material, and this blurs your recollection of it, confusing stimulus and response. Yet I wouldn't want to give up these associations, this spontaneous talking back to a book, because it's one of the things that makes reading so valuable. In mingling your ideas and feelings with the author's, you raise and complicate the level of your own imagining.

—Anatole Broyard

"Since no one has proved that depression does not cause cancer, we can assume that it does." The absence of opposing evidence proves nothing.

Ambiguity and equivocation

Ambiguity and **equivocation** rely on expressions that are not clear because they can be interpreted in more than one way. In answer to the question "Is she doing a good job?" the statement "She is performing as anticipated" is ambiguous. The answer can be interpreted positively or negatively. An equivocation also appears to provide information, but it does not really answer the question. For example, if the question is "Is progress being made?" the answer "Meetings have been held" equivocates.

EXERCISE 5-7

Consulting section 5k, identify and explain the fallacy in each item. If the item does not contain a logical flaw, circle its number.

EXAMPLE Seat belts are the only hope for reducing the death rate from automobile accidents. [This is an either-or fallacy because it assumes that nothing but seat belts can reduce the number of fatalities from car accidents.]

1. Joanna Hayes should write a book about the Central Intelligence Agency. She has starred in three films that show the inner workings of the agency.
2. It is ridiculous to have spent thousands of dollars to rescue those two whales from being trapped in the Arctic ice. Why, look at all of the people trapped in jobs that they don't like.
3. Every time my roommate has a math test, she becomes extremely nervous. Clearly, she is not good at math.
4. Plagiarism is deceitful because it is dishonest.
5. The local political coalition to protect the environment would get my support and that of many other people if its leaders did not drive cars that get poor gasoline mileage.
6. UFOs must exist because no reputable studies have proved conclusively that they do not.
7. Water fluoridation affects the brain. Citywide, students' test scores began to drop five months after fluoridation began.
8. Learning to manage a corporation is exactly like learning to ride a bicycle: Once you learn the skills, you never forget how, and you never fall.
9. Medicare is free; the government pays for it from taxes.
10. Reading good literature is the one way to appreciate culture.

ANSWERS: EXERCISE 5-7

1. *False authority.* An actor is not an authority on the CIA.

2. *Red herring.* The social issue is introduced to divert attention from the real issue—whether or not money should have been spent to rescue the whales.

3. *Irrelevant argument*, or *non sequitur.* A person can be nervous about something and still be good at it.

4. *Begging the question* or *circular argument.* "Dishonest" is merely a slightly different term for "deceitful."

5. *Argument to the person*, or *ad hominem.* These people are being attacked for materialism, but they are perhaps excellent environmentalists, whose cars and shoes are irrelevant to their environmental stance.

6. *Appeal to ignorance.* Just because no evidence exists for one side of the argument does not mean that the other side of the argument is valid.

7. *False cause*, or *post hoc ergo propter hoc.* The sequence of events does not prove any connection between them.

8. *False analogy.* Analogies are dangerous in argument because they equate things that are not the same. Riding a bicycle is much different from learning to run a company, and although the skills for riding a bicycle remain the same, those of running a company may change with the economy and other pressures so that one could "fall" if he or she did not adopt those skills.

9. *Self-contradiction.* Medicare cannot be free if it is paid for.

10. *Either-or.* Reading good literature is not the only way to appreciate culture.

6

WRITING ARGUMENT

When writing **argument** for your college courses, you seek to convince a reader to agree with you concerning a topic open to debate. The terms *persuasive writing* (see 1b.3) and *argumentative writing* are often used interchangeably. When a distinction is made between them, *persuasive writing* is the broader term. It includes advertisements, letters to editors, emotional pleas in speeches or writing, and formal written arguments. The focus of this chapter is formal written argument as usually assigned in college courses.

A written argument states and supports one position about the debatable topic. Support for that position depends on evidence, reasons, and examples chosen for their direct relation to the point being argued. One section of the written argument might present and attempt to refute other positions on the topic, but the central thrust of the essay is to argue convincingly for one point of view.

Taking and defending a position in a written argument is an engaging intellectual process, especially when it involves a topic of substance about which universal agreement is unlikely. The ability to think critically (see Chart 30 in section 5b) is central to planning an essay of argument. Also, you must examine all sides of a topic, choosing one side to defend and marshaling convincing support for that one side.

If you are among the people who find any type of arguing distasteful, you are not alone. But rest assured that written argument differs drastically from everyday, informal arguing. Informal arguing sometimes originates in anger and might involve bursts of temper or unpleasant emotional confrontations. Written argument, in contrast, can always be a constructive activity. When you write an argument, you can disagree without being disagreeable. An effective written argument sets forth its position calmly, respectfully, and logically. Any passion that underlies a writer's position is evident not from angry words but from the force of a balanced, well-developed, clearly written discussion.

The ability to argue reasonably and effectively is an important skill that people need not only in college but throughout their lives—in family relationships, with friends, and in the business world. People engage in debates (perhaps more often in speaking than in writing) that call for an exchange

REFERENCE TO SUPPLEMENTS

For more on the fact that ESL students sometimes need help adapting to argumentation style in the U.S. classroom, see C. Myers, "ESL Writers in the Composition Class," in *Strategies and Resources*.

BACKGROUND

In "Moments of Argument: Agonistic Inquiry and Confrontational Cooperation" (*College Composition and Communication*, February 1997: 61–85), Dennis A. Lynch, Diana George, and Marilyn M. Cooper argue that we need to stimulate students to debate, challenge, and oppose in writing arguments. They explain that the approach of cooperation and collaboration in finding common ground does not prepare students for a "bureaucratic world that resists change."

BACKGROUND

Chapter Two of this handbook lists four aspects of writing situations that affect the decisions that the writer makes. They are (1) the topic, (2) the purpose, (3) the audience that will read or hear it, and (4) the special requirements that influence every writing situation, such as deadlines and length. For explanations of each aspect, see section 2b.

---

of solidly supported views. Once you become adept at the techniques of written argument, you can use them equally effectively for oral argument.

Much material in the earlier chapters of this handbook can help you compose a written argument; they are listed in Chart 42. Also, to demonstrate the application of this chapter to student writing two student essays are discussed in this chapter, and the final draft of each appears in section 6i.

⊙ **Sections of this handbook to use when writing argument**   **42**

- Checklist for persuasive writing (1b.2)
- Audiences for writing (1c)
- Establishing a suitable tone (1d)
- Choosing a topic (2c)
- The writing process: planning and shaping (Chapter 2)
- The writing process: drafting and revising (Chapter 3)
- Writing paragraphs (Chapter 4)
- Thinking, reading, and writing critically (Chapter 5)
- Using evidence to think critically (5h)
- Analyzing cause and effect (5i)
- Using inductive and deductive reasoning (5j)
- Avoiding logical fallacies (5k)

6a Choosing a topic for a written argument

When you choose a topic for written argument, be sure that it is open to debate. Be careful not to confuse matters of information (facts) with matters of debate. An essay becomes an argument when it takes a position concerning a fact or other piece of information.

FACT	Students at Deitmer College **are required** to take physical education.
POSITION OPEN TO DEBATE	Students at Deitmer College **should not be required** to take physical education.
OPPOSITE POSITION OPEN TO DEBATE	Students at Deitmer College **should be required** to take physical education.

A written argument could take one of these opposing positions and defend it. The essay could not argue for two or more sides, though it might mention other points of view and attempt to refute them.

When you are assigned a written argument, be sure to read the assignment carefully and think it through. Instructors construct assignments for written argument in a number of ways. You might be given both the topic and the position to take on that topic. In such cases, you are expected to fulfill the assignment whether or not you agree personally with the given point of view. You are judged on your ability to marshal a defense of the assigned position and to reason logically about it. Another type of assignment is unstructured, requiring you to choose the debatable topic and the position to defend. In such cases, the topic that you choose should be **suitable for college writing** (see 2c.1), not trivial (for example, not the best way to chew gum). The topic should be **narrowed sufficiently** (see 2c.2) to fit the writing situation. You are judged on your ability to think of a debatable topic of substance, to narrow the topic so that your essay can include general statements and specific details, to choose a defensible position about that topic, and to present and support your position convincingly. If you cannot decide what position you agree with personally because all sides of a debatable topic have merit, do not get blocked. You need not make a lifetime commitment to your position. Rather, concentrate on the merits of one position, and present that position as effectively as possible.

The two sample essays at the end of this chapter were written in response to the assignment shown in the box. This assignment states the topic but asks students to take a position about it.

Lindsey Black and Daniel Casey were given this assignment: Write an essay of 500 to 700 words that argues about whether holidays have become too commercialized in the United States. Your final draft is due in one week. Bring your earlier drafts to class for possible sharing and discussion.

Black and Casey analyzed the four aspects of the **writing situation** (see 2b) reflected in the assignment. The essay *topic* is stated (whether holidays have become too commercialized in the United States). The essay's *purpose* is persuasive, but students are free to choose the position to argue for (the student can choose to argue that the holidays have become too commercialized or that they have not become too commercialized). The *audience* for the essay is not specified and is therefore assumed to be the instructor and, perhaps, other members of the class. The *special requirements* include the essay's length (between 500 and 700 words) and the time for getting the essay into final draft (one week).

EXTRA EXERCISE A

Which of the following topics are concerned with fact, and which state a position open to debate?

1. The term *journalism* refers to the business of publishing a regularly recurring text.

2. Television news programs are more influential than they should be.

3. Journalists in the United States operate under the protection of the First Amendment to the Constitution.

4. Most reporters are biased in their descriptions of political figures.

5. The government should not let journalists have access to information dealing with national security.

6. Journalism involves both reporting the news and forming public opinion.

7. Reporters should verify a controversial story with two sources before running it.

8. Weekly newspapers are becoming increasingly popular in large cities.

9. Cartoons are one of the most entertaining features of newspapers.

10. Television commentators should not give their own opinions about political and social matters.

Answers to Extra Exercise A

1. fact
2. opinion
3. fact
4. opinion
5. opinion
6. fact
7. opinion
8. fact
9. opinion
10. opinion

QUOTATION: ON WRITING

Rhetoric may be defined as the faculty of observing in any given case the available means of persuasion.

—Aristotle

BACKGROUND

Many techniques for discovering means of developing a subject have been devised in recent years. It is helpful to be reminded, however, that the ancient Greeks devised a set of topics—*topoi*, meaning "places or regions"—that can be used to generate "arguments" to persuade an audience. They suggest material for the writer who does not have a ready opinion on a subject or an effective way to present it. They include the topics of definition (including genus and division), comparison (similarity, difference, and degree), relationship (cause and effect, antecedent and consequence, contraries, and contradictions), circumstance (the possible and impossible, past and future fact), and testimony (authority, testimonial, statistics, maxims, law, and examples). They remain the basis for many arguments of a general nature presented today. Particular kinds of argument were (and are) drawn from special topics devised to suit the type of discourse chosen by the writer. For example, the writer, or speaker, engaged in judicial discourse is concerned with justice and injustice, making it necessary to establish whether something happened (evidence), what it is (definition), and what kind of thing it is (cause and effect).

6b   Developing an assertion and a thesis statement for written argument

An **assertion** is a statement that gives a position about a debatable topic and that can be supported by evidence, reasons, and examples (including facts, statistics, names, experiences, and experts). The thinking process that moves you from a topic to a defensible position calls, first, for you to make an assertion about the topic. The exact wording of the assertion often does not find its way into the essay, but the assertion serves as a focus for your thinking and your writing.

TOPIC	The commercialization of holidays.
ASSERTION	Holidays have become too commercialized.
ASSERTION	Holidays have not become too commercialized.

Before you decide on an assertion—the position that you want to argue—you need to explore the topic. Do not rush into deciding on your assertion. Try to wait until you have as full a picture as possible. Consider all sides. Remember that **what mainly separates most good writing from bad is the writer's ability to move back and forth between general statements and specific details.** Try to avoid a position that limits you to only general statements or to only specific details. In deciding on your assertion, apply the memory device of RENNS (see 4c) to see whether you can marshal sufficient details to support your generalizations.

Even if you know immediately what assertion you want to argue for, do not stop there. The more thoroughly you think about all sides of the topic, the broader will be the perspective that you bring to your writing. Also, as you think your position through and consider alternative points of view, be open to changing your mind and taking an opposite position. Before too long, however, do settle on a position; switching positions at the last minute lessens your chances of writing an effective essay.

To stimulate your thinking about the topic and your assertion about it, use the techniques for gathering ideas explained and illustrated in sections 2d through 2l. Jot down your thoughts as they develop. Do not lose the unique opportunity that the act of writing gives you to discover new ideas and fresh insights. Writers of effective arguments often list for themselves the various points that come to mind, using two columns to represent visually two contrasting points of view. (Head the columns with labels that emphasize contrast: for example, *agree* and *disagree* or *for* and *against*.) The lists can then supply ideas during drafting and revising.

Whenever possible, use outside resources for developing an assertion. These include talking with other people and conducting research. Getting points of view from other people helps you explore a debatable topic. As you talk with people, interview them rather than argue with them. Your goal is to come to know opposing points of view, so resist any temptation to "win" a verbal argument; people will hesitate to offer their ideas fully and openly to a hostile listener. If your assignment permits you to use the library, do so. Written argument can be particularly enhanced when your position is supported with facts and reference to experts. (See 1e, 5h, and Part Five.)

Next, using your assertion as a base, compose a thesis statement (see 2n). It states the position that you present and support in the essay. For his essay about holiday commercialism (see 6i), Daniel Casey used this progression from basic assertion to final thesis statement.

I think holiday commercialism is a good thing. [This assertion is a start.]

All commercial uses of holidays are very good for our economy and people's spirits. [This preliminary thesis is more developed because it gives reason—economic and emotional benefits—but the word *all* is misleading, and the vocabulary level of *very good* needs work.]

In spite of what some people think, commercial uses of holidays benefit the nation's economy and people's spirits. [This draft is better, but "what some people think" was not an aspect of the topic Casey intended to explore. Also, *benefit . . . spirits* needs revision.]

Such commercial uses of holidays benefit the nation's economy and lift people's spirits. [This is the final version of Casey's thesis statement. *Such* is a transitional word connecting the thesis statement to sentences in the introductory paragraph that describe several holiday activities. The final version meets the requirements listed in Chart 12 in section 2n.]

EXERCISE 6-1

Develop an assertion and a thesis statement for a written argument on each of the listed topics. You may choose any defensible position.

EXAMPLE   *Topic:* Book censorship in high school
Assertion: Books should not be censored in high school.
Thesis statement: When books are taken off high school library shelves and are dropped from high school curricula, students are denied exposure to an open exchange of ideas.

1. television
2. prisons
3. drugs and athletics
4. diets for weight loss
5. grades

6c Considering the audience for written argument

The purpose of written argument is to convince a reader—the audience—about a matter of opinion. Key factors in considering audience are

Background (continued)

Fair statement of the writer's position. The goal of this section is to get readers to understand the writer's position as fairly and thoroughly as the writer has understood theirs.

Statement of contexts in which the writer's position is valid. The writer tries to get readers to look at the problem from new perspectives and in new contexts.

Statement of how readers would benefit by adopting at least some elements of the writer's position. The writer appeals to readers' self-interest. In this section, the writer's position turns from a threat to a promise.

BACKGROUND

Although rhetoric, as defined by Aristotle, appears in the speeches and debates of the epics and plays of ancient Greece, its principles were not systematically formulated until the fifth century B.C. Corax of Syracuse, recognizing the need for a system by which citizens of Sicily could argue in the courts to recover property that they had lost during the reign of Thrasybulus, began to set down the principles of argumentation. Lacking documents to prove their claims, ordinary citizens had to argue their cases by relying on inferential reasoning and probability. Tisias, the student of Corax, extended the study of rhetoric from the courtroom and wrote speeches for other people to deliver. Others who quickly followed to develop the art of rhetoric, or persuasion, include Gorgias of Leotini (fl. 420 B.C.), known principally for his ornate style characterized by extensive use of figures of speech, and Isocrates (436–338 B.C.), one of the leading Athenian teachers of rhetoric and an author of influential books on rhetorical theory.

discussed in section 1c. When you write argument, consider one additional factor about audience: the degree of agreement expected from the reader.

When a topic is emotionally charged, chances are high that any position being argued will elicit either strong agreement or strong disagreement. For example, topics such as abortion, capital punishment, and gun control arouse very strong emotions in many people. Such topics are emotionally loaded because they touch on matters of personal beliefs, including religion and individual rights. A topic such as the commercialization of holidays (see the two essays in section 6i) is somewhat less emotionally loaded. Even less emotionally loaded, yet still open to debate, are topics such as whether everyone needs a college education or whether computer X is better than computer Y.

The degree to which a reader might be friendly or hostile can influence what strategies you use to try to convince that reader. For example, when you anticipate that many readers will not agree with you, consider using techniques of **Rogerian argument.** Rogerian argument has been adapted from the principles of communication developed by psychologist Carl Rogers. Communication, according to Rogers, is eased when people find common ground in their points of view. The common ground in a debate over capital punishment might be that both sides find crime to be a growing problem today. Once both sides agree about the problem, they might have more tolerance for the divergence of opinion concerning whether capital punishment is a deterrent to crime.

6d Using the classical pattern for written argument

No one structure fits all written argument. For college courses, most written arguments include certain elements. Lindsey Black's essay in section 6i uses a structure based on the **classical pattern of argument** developed by the ancient Greeks and Romans and still highly respected today. Daniel Casey's essay in section 6i uses a modified form of that structure. Chart 43 will help you recognize the elements in a written argument.

⊙ **Elements in the classical pattern for written argument** **43**

1. **Introductory paragraph:** sets the context for the position that is argued in the essay. (For a discussion of introductory paragraphs, see 4g.) ⟶

Elements in the classical pattern for written argument *(continued)* — 43

2. **Thesis statement:** states the position being argued. In a short essay, the thesis statement often appears at the end of the introductory paragraph. (For a discussion of thesis statements, see 2n.)

3. **Background information:** gives the reader basic information needed for understanding the position being argued. This information can be part of the introductory paragraph (as in Daniel Casey's essay in 6i) or can appear in its own paragraph (as in Lindsey Black's essay in 6i).

4. **Reasons or evidence:** support the position being argued. This material is the core of the essay. If the support consists of evidence, consult the discussion in section 5h. Also, be sure that your reasoning is logical (see 5k). Each type of reason or evidence usually consists of a general statement backed up with specific details or examples. Depending on the length of the essay, one or two paragraphs are devoted to each reason or type of evidence.

   The best sequence for presenting the complete set of reasons and evidence depends on the impact you want to achieve. Moving from evidence most familiar to the reader to evidence least familiar helps the reader move from the known to the unknown. This order might catch the reader's interest early on. Moving from the least important to the most important evidence might build the reader's suspense. (For more about various types of paragraph arrangement, see 4e.)

5. **Anticipation of objections and responses to them:** mentions positions opposed to the one being argued and rebuts them briefly. In classical argument, this "refutation" appears in its own paragraph, immediately before the concluding paragraph (as in Lindsey Black's essay). An alternative placement is immediately after the introductory paragraph, as a bridge to the rest of the essay; in such arrangements, the essay's thesis statement falls either at the end of the introductory paragraph or at the end of the refutation paragraph (as in Daniel Casey's essay). In still another arrangement, each paragraph that presents a type of evidence or reason (item 4 on this list) also mentions and responds to the opposing position.

6. **Concluding paragraph:** brings the essay to an end that flows logically and gracefully from the rest of the essay. It does not cut off the reader abruptly. (For a discussion of concluding paragraphs, see 4g.)

BACKGROUND

Classical persuasion consisted of six parts that represented six basic functions. Although the writer or orator was granted some flexibility in how and in what order the parts were presented, they provided effective guidelines for presenting an argument. Often used today, the six parts of an argument, according to the classical precept, are as follows:

1. *Exordium*, meaning "beginning a web." As an introduction, the purpose of the exordium is to attract the attention of the audience, indicate the subject, and favorably dispose the audience to what will follow.

2. *Narratio.* In this section, now usually referred to as "statement of fact," the issue is defined by stating pertinent facts about the subject. It is, therefore, basically expository.

3. *Partitio.* If the thesis has not yet been identified, it will be presented here, along with an indication of how the rest of the argument will be organized. The purpose of partitio is to prepare the reader or listener for what will follow.

4. *Confirmatio.* Arguments to support the thesis, forming the bulk of the piece, are developed at this point. The question of the order of presentation of arguments is critical to the effectiveness of the confirmation.

5. *Refutatio.* Opposing arguments are considered and rendered ineffective in the refutation section. To ignore them is to risk letting them appear to be more attractive than one's own thesis. The refutation may be placed at various points in the piece, depending on where it will be most effective.

6. *Peroratio.* The classical rhetoricians used a number of terms to indicate the conclusion of a piece; it usually furnished a summary of proofs and refutations, a restatement of the major points, and a recreation of emotional and ethical appeals.

BACKGROUND

BACKGROUND

According to Aristotle's *Rhetoric*, the conclusion of an argument can have as many as four functions. It should create a favorable impression toward the speaker and an unfavorable impression toward the speaker's opponents. It should emphasize the points of the speaker while minimizing the points of the opposition. It should appeal strongly to the audience's emotions. And it should summarize the chief points of the argument.

TEACHING TIP

Persuasive writing has much in common with argumentation. Both aim to lead the audience to agreement with the opinions of the writer. Persuasion additionally attempts to induce the reader to commit to a particular action. Advertising is probably the form of persuasive writing we encounter most often in the course of our daily lives. Because students enjoy looking at familiar advertisements in an analytical way, you may want to ask them to bring their favorites to class, or perhaps you will prefer to provide some. Helpful background information is available in such publications as *Advertising Age*.

STATEWIDE TESTING

If you teach in a state that requires students to pass basic competency tests in English, see the free publications coordinated with this handbook: One is for the CLAST (Florida), and another is for the TASP Exam (Texas).

6e Using the Toulmin model for argument

The **Toulmin model** for argument has recently gained popularity among teachers and students because it clarifies the major elements in an effective argument. The terms used in the Toulmin model may seem unfamiliar, even intimidating, at first. But worry not. The concepts that the terms describe are ones you have encountered before. What is new is placing those concepts into the vocabulary and structure of the Toulmin model.

The essential elements of the Toulmin model are presented in Chart 44.

⊙ Elements in the Toulmin model of argument   44

Toulmin's Term	More Familiar Terms
claim	the main point or central message, usually disclosed in the thesis statement
support	data or other evidence, from broad reasons to specific details
warrant	underlying assumptions, usually not stated but clearly implied; readers infer assumptions

---

The elements in Chart 44 can be identified in Daniel Casey's written argument, shown in section 6i:

- **Casey's claim:** Commercial uses of holidays benefit the nation's economy and lift people's spirits.

- **Casey's support:** (1) Economic prosperity creates circulation of money, which in turn creates jobs. (2) Holidays are festive times that cheer people up with decorations, costumes, gift-giving, and a friendly atmosphere. (3) Successful businesses improve everyone's quality of life by sponsoring charitable causes, parades, fireworks displays, and cultural events.

- **Casey's warrants:** (1) Benefiting the nation's economy is an important objective from which everyone gains. (2) Even the spiritual aspects of the holidays are not paramount.

The concept of a *warrant* may seem difficult to understand. It can help to think of warrants as related to the concept of reading to make inferences, a key part of reading critically (see 5d). Like inferences, which are implications you must find "between the lines," warrants are implied assumptions you must infer from the stated argument.

To help you figure out the warrant that underlies an argument you are writing or reading, try placing it into one of Toulmin's three broad categories for warrants: (1) A warrant based on **authority** rests on respect for the credibility and trustworthiness of the person; (2) a warrant based on **substance** rests on the reliability of factual evidence; (3) a warrant based on **motivation** rests on the values and beliefs of the audience and the writer. Daniel Casey's second warrant is a motivational warrant because it is not based on authority or factual evidence—it is based on the writer's valuing of economic prosperity over spiritual considerations.

The concepts in the Toulmin model can help you read arguments with a critical eye. The concepts are equally useful for you as a writer. As you draft and revise your written argument, evaluate what you are saying by checking whether you can analyze it for the elements in the Toulmin model. If you can't, your argument needs work.

6f Defining terms in written argument

When you **define terms,** you explain what you mean by key words that you use. Words are key words when they are central to the message that you want to communicate. The meaning of some key words is readily evident. Key words open to interpretation, however, should be made specific enough to be clear.

NO   Commercialism at holiday time is **bad.**

YES   Commercialism at holiday time is **ruining the spirit of the holidays.**

YES   Commercialism at holiday time **tempts too many people to spend more money than they can afford.**

Some key words might vary with the context of a discussion and should be explained in an essay. Abstract words such as *love, freedom,* and *democracy* have to be explained because they have different meanings in different contexts. Daniel Casey uses *economy,* a word with many meanings, in the topic sentence of the third paragraph of his essay (see 6i). He relates *economy* to the "ongoing circulation of money," and he uses the rest of the paragraph to explain how that circulation operates. In this way, Casey makes clear that he is not referring to any of the other meanings of *economy:* the management of finances, the avoidance of waste, or the efficient use of resources.

Other key terms might be unfamiliar to the reader even though they are known words. For example, Casey opens his essay with the words *signs of commercialism.* Although each word by itself is familiar, the expression as a whole is not. Casey therefore gives examples to illustrate the concept. In so doing, he creates an effective introduction to his essay by bringing the reader to a quick understanding of his topic.

Many students ask whether they should use actual dictionary definitions in an essay. Looking words up in a dictionary to understand precise meanings is a very important activity for writers. Quoting a dictionary definition, however, is not always wise. Dictionary definitions tend to be

QUOTATION: ON WRITING

The art of writing has for backbone some fierce attachment to an idea.

—Virginia Woolf

EXTRA EXERCISE C

Rewrite the following paragraph, improving its persuasiveness by defining key words that may be vague to the reader.

> Some Americans react strongly to actions that show disrespect for our flag. They revere it as a symbol of the values for which the United States is known around the world. They are quick to rise up against those who would use their freedom to desecrate Old Glory, calling them traitors to the Constitution and all it upholds: our rights and our democratic form of government. Calling for a Constitutional amendment, they even want to restrict our freedoms by making it illegal to misuse the flag. Wouldn't such an amendment show disrespect for the freedom the flag represents?

Sample Answer to Extra Exercise C

Some Americans react strongly to acts that they construe to be insulting to our flag. Television news footage showing the flag being burned or torn apart makes them violently angry because they revere it as a symbol of the freedom and liberty for which this country is known around the world. They are quick to rise up against fellow citizens who use their freedom to desecrate Old Glory, calling them traitors to the Constitution and its guarantees of legislative representation and civil rights, such as the right of free speech. Calling for a Constitutional amendment, they even want to restrict citizens' freedoms by making it illegal to misuse the flag. But what constitutes misuse: wearing it? letting it fly outside on a rainy day? displaying it on a banquet table? A more important question is, Wouldn't such an amendment show disrespect for the freedom the flag represents?

OTHER EXAMPLES

Emotional Appeal

A child's world is fresh and new and beautiful, full of wonder and excitement. It is our misfortune that for most of us that clear-eyed vision, that true instinct for what is beautiful and awe-inspiring, is dimmed and even lost before we reach adulthood. If I had influence with the good fairy who is supposed to preside over the christening of all children I should ask that her gift to each child in the world be a sense of wonder so indestructible that it would last throughout life, as an unfailing antidote against the boredom and disenchantments of later years, the sterile preoccupation with things that are artificial, the alienation from the sources of our strength.

I sincerely believe that . . . it is not half so important to *know* as to *feel*. If facts are the seeds that later produce knowledge and wisdom, then the emotions and the impressions of the senses are the fertile soil in which the seeds must grow. The years of early childhood are the time to prepare the soil. Once the emotions have been aroused—a sense of the beautiful, the excitement of the new and the unknown, a feeling of sympathy, pity, admiration or love—then we wish for knowledge about the object of our emotional response.

—Rachel Carson,
The Sense of Wonder

Ethical Appeal

Our tragedy today is a general and universal physical fear so long sustained by now that we can even bear it. There are no longer problems of the spirit. There is only the question: When will I be blown up? Because of this, the young man or woman writing today has forgotten the problems of the human heart in conflict with itself which alone can make good writing because only this is worth writing about, worth the agony and the sweat.

He must learn them again. He must teach himself that the basest of all things is to be afraid; and, teaching himself that, forget it forever, leaving no room in his

overused in student writing, and they are often seen as an "easy way out." Using an **extended definition** is usually a more effective approach, which is what Casey did for *economy* in the third paragraph of his essay. (For another example of extended definition, of *tolerance,* see paragraph 39 in section 4f.5.) If you do use a dictionary definition in your writing, be sure to work it into your material gracefully. Do not simply tack it on abruptly to what you are saying. In general, do not rely on it for your opening sentence. Also, be aware that references to a dictionary must be complete. Do not simply refer to "Webster's," for many dictionaries feature that name in the title. Give the complete title of the dictionary you are citing— for example, *Webster's New World College Dictionary,* Third Edition.

6g Reasoning effectively in written argument

When you reason effectively, you increase your chances of convincing your reader to agree with you. In many instances, of course, you cannot expect actually to change your reader's mind. The basis for a debatable position is often personal opinion or belief, neither of which can be expected to change as the result of one written argument. Nevertheless, you still have an important goal: to convince your reader that your point of view has merit. People often "agree to disagree," in the best spirit of intellectual exchange. Round-table discussions among various experts heard on National Public Radio (NPR) or television's Public Broadcasting System (PBS) are conducted in such a spirit.

The opposite positions taken by Lindsey Black and Daniel Casey (see 6i) concerning commercialism at holiday time stem from their personal beliefs and perceptions of the world. Black feels that commercialism is ruining the holidays. Casey recognizes the existence of commercialism, but he sees it as beneficial. The chance of either person convincing the other is slight. What can happen, however, is that each person can respect the quality of the other's argument.

An argument of good quality relies on three types of appeals to reason: the logical, the emotional, and the ethical. Chart 45 gives a summary of how to use the three appeals.

> **Guidelines for reasoning effectively in written argument** 45
>
> - **Be logical:** Use sound reasoning.
> - **Enlist the emotions of the reader:** Appeal to the values and beliefs of the reader, usually by arousing the reader's "better self."
> - **Establish credibility:** Show that you as the writer can be relied on as a knowledgeable person with good sense.

The most widely used appeal in written argument is the **logical appeal,** called *logos* by the ancient Greeks. Logical reasoning is sound reasoning. This type of reasoning is important in all thinking and writing. Chapter 5 of this handbook, therefore, is a close companion to this chapter. Logical reasoning calls for using evidence well, as explained in section 5h. Logical reasoning also means analyzing cause and effect correctly, as explained in 5i. A sound argument uses patterns of inductive reasoning and deductive reasoning, as explained in 5j. A sound argument also clearly distinguishes between fact and opinion, as explained in 5d.3. Finally, sound reasoning means avoiding logical fallacies, as explained in 5k.

Written argument for college courses relies heavily on logic. Both Lindsey Black and Daniel Casey (see 6i) used logical reasoning throughout their essays. Though the reader might not agree with the reasons or types of evidence presented, the reader can respect the logic of each writer's arguments.

The **emotional appeal,** called *pathos* by the ancient Greeks, can be effective when used in conjunction with logical appeals. The word *emotional* has a specific meaning in this context. It means arousing and enlisting the emotions of the reader. Often, it arouses the "better self" of the reader by eliciting sympathy, civic pride, or other feelings based on values and beliefs. Effective emotional appeals use description and examples to stir emotions, but they leave the actual stirring to the reader. Restraint is more effective than excessive sentimentality.

Both Casey and Black (see 6i) use emotional appeals in their essays, but always in conjunction with a logical presentation of material. Casey appeals to the emotions when in his fifth paragraph he mentions stores giving toys to children in hospitals. But he does not overdo it. He does not say that anyone who disagrees with him hates children and feels no pity for their suffering from dreadful illnesses that ravage their tiny bodies. If he had indulged in such excesses, the reader would resent being manipulated and might reject his argument. Black appeals to the emotions when she writes in her second paragraph about the origins of the holiday spirit. With restraint, she mentions the meaning of each holiday. She does not attempt to tell the reader how to feel; she simply points out facts that support the logic of her argument and that might also stir the reader's pride in country and heritage.

The **ethical appeal,** called *ethos* by the ancient Greeks, means establishing the ethics and credibility of the writer. Credibility is gained if the writer uses correct facts, undistorted evidence, and accurate interpretations of events. Readers do not trust a writer who states opinions as fact or who makes a claim that cannot possibly be supported. The statement "A child who does not get gifts for Christmas suffers a trauma from which recovery is impossible" is an opinion as well as an exaggeration. It has no place in written argument. Ethical appeals cannot take the place of logical appeals, but the two types of appeals work well together. One effective way to make an ethical appeal is to draw on personal experience.

Other Examples (continued)

workshop for anything but the old verities and truths of the heart, the old universal truths lacking which any story is ephemeral and doomed—love and honor and pity and pride and compassion and sacrifice. Until he does so, he labors under a curse. He writes not of love but of lust, of defeats in which nobody loses anything of value, of victories without hope and, worst of all, without pity or compassion. His griefs grieve on no universal bones, leaving no scars. He writes not of the heart but of the glands.

—William Faulkner,
Nobel Prize acceptance speech

EXTRA EXERCISE D

Analyze the following paragraphs to discover the dominant appeal of each.

1. We observe today not a victory of party but a celebration of freedom—symbolizing an end as well as a beginning—signifying renewal as well as change. For I have sworn before you and Almighty God the same solemn oath our forebears prescribed nearly a century and three quarters ago.

The world is very different now. For man holds in his mortal hands the power to abolish all forms of human poverty and all forms of human life. And yet the same revolutionary beliefs for which our forebears fought are still at issue around the globe—the belief that the rights of man come not from the generosity of the state but from the hand of God.

We dare not forget today that we are the heirs of that first revolution. Let the word go forth from this time and place, to friend and foe alike, that the torch has been passed to a new generation of Americans—born in this century, tempered by war; disciplined by a hard and bitter peace, proud of our ancient heritage—and unwilling to witness or permit the slow undoing of those human rights to which this nation has always been committed, and to which we are committed today at home and around the world.

—John F. Kennedy,
inaugural address

Extra Exercise D (continued)

2. Harlem got its first private project, Riverton—which is now, naturally, a slum—about twelve years ago because at that time Negroes were not allowed to live in Stuyvesant Town. Harlem watched Riverton go up, therefore, in the most violent bitterness of spirit, and hated it long before the builders arrived. They began hating it at about the time people began moving out of their condemned houses to make room for this additional proof of how thoroughly the white world despised them. And they had scarcely moved in, naturally, before they began smashing windows, defacing walls, urinating in the elevators, and fornicating in the playgrounds. Liberals, both white and black, were appalled at the spectacle. I was appalled by the liberal innocence—or cynicism, which comes out in practice as much the same thing. Other people were delighted to be able to point to proof positive that nothing could be done to better the lot of the colored people. They were, and are, right in one respect: that nothing can be done as long as they are treated like colored people. The people in Harlem know they are living there because white people do not think they are good enough to live anywhere else. No amount of "improvement" can sweeten this fact. Whatever money is now being earmarked to improve this, or any other ghetto, might as well be burnt. A ghetto can be improved in one way only: out of existence.

> —James Baldwin,
> "Fifth Avenue Uptown:
> A Letter from Harlem"

Sample Answers to Extra Exercise D

1. In his Inaugural Address, John F. Kennedy makes extensive use of ethical appeal. By referring to the "solemn oath" he had just taken before God and the American people, he calls attention to his commitment to work for what is good and right. When, in reference to the complexity of the modern world, he again invokes the name of God as the source of "the rights of man," he underscores the high

(Some college instructors do not want students to write in the first person, so ask your instructor before you use it.) If you use personal experience, always be sure that it relates directly to a generalization that you are supporting. Also, be aware that a personal experience can say as much about the writer as about the experience. For example, if Casey had been a volunteer at a hospital when gifts from a local business were distributed, the story of the experience not only would have supported his claim in his fifth paragraph but also would have illustrated his good character.

6h Establishing a reasonable tone in written argument

To be reasonable, you have to be fair. By anticipating opposing positions and responding to them (see 6c), you have a particularly good chance to show that you are fair. When you alert your reader to other ways of thinking about the issue, you demonstrate that you have not ignored other positions. Doing this implies respect for the other side, which in turn makes the tone (see 1d) of the essay more reasonable.

To achieve a reasonable tone, choose your words carefully. Avoid words that exaggerate. Use figurative language, such as similes and metaphors (see 21c), to enhance your point rather than distort it. No matter how strongly you disagree with opposing arguments, never insult the other side. Name-calling is impolite and reflects poor judgment and a lack of self-control. The more emotionally loaded a topic (for example, abortion, capital punishment, or gun control), the more might be the temptation to use angry words. Words such as *stupid* or *pigheaded,* however, say more about the writer than about the issue.

Artificial language (see 21e) also ruins a reasonable tone. The *yes* example that follows is used by Daniel Casey as the first sentence in his essay in section 6i. Compare its impact with what would happen if Casey had used the *no* example.

> **NO** Emblems of commercial enterprise are ubiquitously visible as the populace prepares for the celebration of festivals and commemorations throughout the venerable United States of America.
>
> **YES** Signs of commercialism at holiday time are easy to see in the United States.

6i Writing and revising a written argument

Lindsey Black chose the position that holidays have become too commercialized. Daniel Casey, by contrast, chose the position that the commercialization of holidays has advantages. The final draft of each essay appears at the end of this chapter. The labels identify the structural elements of written argument discussed in section 6d.

In an early draft of her essay, Black wrote an introduction that included the background information on the holidays, now in her second paragraph. When she revised, she moved the information to a separate paragraph because she saw that the introductory paragraph was too long and the thesis statement was being overshadowed. Also, she felt that a separate paragraph giving background information had the additional advantage of giving her enough space to use an emotional appeal (see 6g). An early draft of Black's third paragraph consisted only of the topic sentence and the last three sentences of the final draft. When she revised, Black saw that she needed more examples to support the generalization in her topic sentence. She added the material about greeting cards and about time and stress.

Daniel Casey wrote a discovery draft (see 3b) to explore the ideas that he evolved while planning his essay (for his brainstorming, see section 2g; for his use of the journalist's questions, see section 2h; for the grouping of his ideas, see section 2l). As he wrote his draft, he discovered, for example, that he needed to define the expression *signs of commercialism* by giving specific examples. He also found that he had two reasons he could develop in support of his thesis: an enriched economy and an enhanced spirit. He wanted a third reason, so he interviewed some friends who worked in a shopping mall, and they mentioned what some of the stores do for the community at holiday time. The second paragraph of Casey's essay was the next-to-last paragraph in an early draft. He moved it when he revised because he decided that it built an effective bridge to his thesis statement.

As both Black and Casey revised, they consulted the revision checklists in section 3c to remind them of general principles of writing, and they referred to the checklist in Chart 46.

✓	**Checklist for revising written argument**	**46**

- Does the thesis statement concern a debatable topic (see 6b)?
- Is the material structured well for a written argument (see 6d)?
- Do the reasons or evidence support the thesis statement? Are the generalizations supported by specific details? (See 6d.)
- Are opposing positions mentioned and responded to (see 6d)?
- Are terms defined (see 6f)?
- Are the appeals to reason used correctly and well (see 6g)?
- Is the tone reasonable (see 6h)?

Sample Answers to Extra Exercise D (continued)

moral calling of his office. In the final paragraph, he appeals to the ethical sense of the audience by exhorting citizens to join him in the struggle to make a better world. By using the pronoun *we*, he repledges himself to work with all Americans for the spread and preservation of the beliefs on which this country was founded.

2. James Baldwin's comments about Riverton seethe with anger, bitterness, and even hatred. The strong emotions that the reader hears and feels emanate not only from words such as "violent bitterness of spirit," "hated it," "hating it," and "despised them" but also from the images of destruction that he provides: "smashing windows, defacing walls, urinating in the elevators, and fornicating in the playgrounds." Any positive term that Baldwin uses, such as "improvement," he puts in quotation marks, suggesting its unreality.

BACKGROUND

In "Using Role Playing in Argument Papers to Deconstruct Stereotypes" (*Teaching English in the Two-Year College*, October 1995: 190–196), Vincent Moore describes how role playing can expand student awareness of multiple points of view on a topic.

ANSWERS: EXERCISE 6-2

Answers will vary.

TEACHING TIP

Most newspapers, including campus newspapers, carry numerous pieces of persuasive discourse in the letters to the editor, daily columns, and editorials. You may want to ask students to bring examples to class that can be analyzed in terms of assertions and thesis, as well as the order and means of development.

A different kind of experience, but an equally interesting one, can come from analysis of a longer, more sustained argument, such as Thoreau's essay "Civil Disobedience" or Martin Luther King Jr.'s "Letter from Birmingham Jail."

EXERCISE 6-2

Choose a topic from this list, and write an essay that argues for a debatable position about the topic. Apply all the principles you have learned in this chapter.

1. animal experimentation
2. nuclear power
3. value of the space program
4. celebrity endorsements
5. day-care centers

6. surrogate mothers
7. gun control
8. school prayer
9. optimism
10. highway speed limits

Black 1

Lindsey Black
Professor Gregory
English 101
April 10, 2000

Commercialism Is Ruining the Holidays

introduction: identification of the situation
Holidays should be special occasions that have religious, historical, and cultural significance. Increasingly, however, holidays in the United States are turning into little more than business opportunities. From coast to coast, the jingles and beeps of cash registers drown out the traditional sounds of holiday observance. The spirit of the

thesis statement
holidays is being destroyed by commercialism.

background: origins and significance
The origins of the holiday spirit are varied in the United States. Thanksgiving reminds Americans to be grateful for their blessings, and the Fourth of July stimulates pride in the founding of the nation. Labor Day is a tribute to workers. Memorial Day honors soldiers who died in defense of the country, and Veterans Day honors all veterans of the armed forces. Christmas and Easter have great religious significance to Christians. Holidays used to be occasions for people to come together and celebrate their heritages. Today, however, the overriding message of the holidays is "spend money."

Black 2

evidence: one type

The most visible evidence that commercialism now dominates holidays is the unfortunate emphasis on spending money in preparation for religious holidays. For example, buying and mailing Christmas cards has become standard practice for individuals, families, and industry. How many people can ignore the social and business pressures to mail cards? The commitment of money and time for this activity is not small. The gift situation is equally stressful. Although exchanging gifts on Christmas or Hanukkah was always part of the celebration, the thought behind the present used to be the point. Today, however, advertising--particularly on television--sets a high standard of expectations. Can home-baked cookies compare to a microwave oven? Can hand-drawn, handwritten cards be as impressive as elaborate greeting cards that play music?

evidence: another type

Other evidence that commercialism is ruining holidays is the emphasis on shopping for bargains rather than on activities related to cultural history. Huge sales held before holidays, and often on the holiday itself, are advertised heavily in newspapers, on television, and on radio. Veterans Day has become the day to buy fall and winter clothing at reduced prices, and Memorial Day means specially lowered prices on products for the coming summer. Parades and ceremonies on Labor Day honoring the workers of America get less attention than back-to-school sales. The image of the family gathering on Thanksgiving Day is being replaced with the image of the family shopping the day after Thanksgiving, when stores are more crowded than any other day except the day before Christmas.

possible objections and responses

In spite of all this, not all people are troubled by the spirit of commercialism on holidays.

→

QUOTATION: ON WRITING

I work four hours a day and then usually early in the evening I read over what I've written during the day and I do a lot of changing and shifting around. See, I write in longhand and I do two versions of whatever I'm doing. I write first on yellow paper and then I write on white paper and then when I finally have it more or less settled the way I want, then I type it. When I'm typing it, that's when I do my final rewrite. I almost never change a word after that.

—Truman Capote

BACKGROUND

In "Catching the Ephemeral: A Teacher Studies Classroom Talk" (*Teaching English in the Two-Year College*, May 1995: 89–101), Lois Rubin explores differing perceptions about what is said in a discussion. Among other topics, she talks of what students versus what teachers want or expect from a conclusion to a debate or discussion.

QUOTATION: ON WRITING

I write double-spaced to leave plenty of room for the inevitable revisions and I never write on both sides of the paper. I write on a right hand page, leaving the facing page blank for insertions and revisions. Then I leave the following double-page blank.

—Len Deighton

Black 3

Many people enjoy the festivity of exchanging cards and gifts. Some people feel that the chance to buy at sales helps them stay within their budgets and therefore enjoy life more. What these people do not realize is that the festive spirit of giving can quickly turn sour when large amounts of money are suddenly not available for necessities. Also, these people do not realize that holiday sales tend to lure shoppers into spending more money than they had planned, often for things that they did not think they needed until they saw them "on sale."

conclusion:
call for
awareness

Holiday celebrations in the United States today have more to do with the wallet than the spirit. Some people refuse to participate in the frenzy of a commercial interpretation of holidays, of course. But for too many people, holidays are becoming stressful rather than joyful, upsetting rather than uplifting.

Casey 1

Daniel Casey

Professor Gregory

English 101

April 10, 2000

Commercialism at Holiday Time Benefits the Nation

introduction:
gives
background

Signs of commercialism at holiday time are easy to see in the United States. Christmas decorations begin their call to consumers in October. Memorial Day and Labor Day remind shoppers to prepare for the seasonal change in clothing fashions. Halloween and Easter mean children can make toll calls to the Great Pumpkin or the Easter Bunny.

→

Casey 2

presentation and refutation of opposite view

Some people disapprove of these commercial uses of holidays in the United States. These people feel that the meaning of a holiday gets lost when television is blaring news of the latest holiday sale or expensive gift item. Many people also feel that the proliferation of gifts and greeting cards creates stressful pressure on budgets and ruins any pleasure derived from giving and receiving. No one, however, has to forget the meaning of a holiday simply because commerce is involved. In fact, commercialism can increase people's enjoyment of the holidays. After all, commercial uses of holidays benefit the nation's economy and lift people's spirits.

thesis statement

reason: one effect

Commerce at holiday time in the United States enriches the economy. Prosperity in the United States is based on the ongoing circulation of money, which holidays encourage. When people spend money on gifts and holiday products, jobs are created. The jobs are in many sectors of the economy: manufacturing, distribution, advertising, and retailing. Jobs help people support their families. Profits help business and industry grow. Salaries and profits bring about tax revenues that support schools, police, hospitals, and other government services.

reason: second effect

In addition to economic benefits, commercial activity enhances the spirit of holidays. Most people feel more cheerful at holiday time. Everyone takes part in one big party. Advertising related to holidays, along with stores filled with holiday products, creates an atmosphere of festivity across the nation. Being able to say "Happy Thanksgiving" or "Merry Christmas" to strangers while shopping breaks down barriers and helps everyone feel part

→

QUOTATION: ON WRITING

You must now draw up a timetable and stick to it. When you'll write and what rate you'll write at are a matter of individual capacity and circumstance, but I suggest that three two-hourly sessions a week are quite enough. It is essential that you record the number of words written each session. This has a valuable psychological effect. Whether you're pleased with what you've written or not, you have before you the proof that you're achieving something, that you actually are working.

—John Braine

QUOTATION: ON WRITING

To persuade, there are two things which must be carefully studied by the orator. The first is to excite some desire or passion in the hearers; the second is to satisfy their judgment that there is a connection between the action to which he would persuade them and the gratification of the desire or passion he excites.

—George Campbell

Casey 3

of one big family. The festivity on the streets, in malls, and in stores is infectious. Giving and getting gifts and greeting cards helps people stay in touch with each other and express their feelings. Children look forward all year to wearing a store-bought costume for Halloween, sitting on Santa's lap in a department store, and talking to the Easter Bunny at the local shopping mall.

reason:
third effect

The holiday activities that help businesses prosper also inspire many businesses to improve everyone's quality of life. Many companies, for example, organize collections of clothing and preparation of hot meals for needy people at holiday time. Toy stores often give away toys for Christmas and Hanukkah to children in hospitals and in caretaking homes. Macy's department store annually delights people of all ages with its Thanksgiving Day Parade in New York City. The entire nation is invited to enjoy the parade in person or on television. In small towns and large cities, many businesses sponsor fireworks, mounted and displayed safely by professionals, to celebrate the Fourth of July. Goodwill and good business go together to everyone's benefit at holiday time.

conclusion:
summary of
main points

The United States is a nation blessed with economic strength and resourceful people. Although commercialism can detract from the true meaning of a holiday, it does not have to. People can discipline themselves to balance the spiritual with the commercial. Americans recognize that the advantages of a stimulated economy and a collective festive spirit are worth the effort of such self-discipline.

PART TWO

UNDERSTANDING GRAMMAR AND WRITING CORRECT SENTENCES

The descriptions of grammar in Chapters 7 through 12 give you one tool for discussing language. The explanations of correct sentences in Chapters 13 through 15 give you the foundation for building an effective writing style.

7

PARTS OF SPEECH AND SENTENCE STRUCTURES

PARTS OF SPEECH

Knowing about **parts of speech** gives you a basic vocabulary for understanding how language works to create meaning. As you learn to identify a word's part of speech, check how the word is functioning because sometimes the same word functions differently in different sentences.

We ate **fish.** [*Fish* is a noun. It names a thing.]

We **fish** on weekends. [*Fish* is a verb. It names an action.]

7a Recognizing nouns

A **noun** names a person, place, thing, or idea: *student, college, textbook, education.* Different types of nouns are shown in Chart 47.

◉ Nouns		47
PROPER	names specific people, places, or things (first letter is always capitalized)	*John Lennon, Paris, Buick*
COMMON	names general groups, places, people, or things	*singer, city, automobile*
CONCRETE	names things experienced through the senses: sight, hearing, taste, smell, and touch	*landscape, pizza, thunder*
ABSTRACT	names things not knowable through the senses	*freedom, shyness*
COLLECTIVE	names groups	*family, team* →

Nouns *(continued)*		47
NONCOUNT OR MASS	names "uncountable" things	*water, time*
COUNT	names countable items	*lake, minute*

⊕ **ESL NOTES:** (1) Words that appear with nouns often tell how much or how many, whose, which one, and similar information. These words include **articles** *(a, an, the)* and other **determiners** or **limiting adjectives,** as explained in section 7e and Chapter 42. (2) Sometimes a suffix (a word ending) can help you identify the part of speech. Usually, words with the suffixes *-ness, -ence, -ance, -ty,* and *-ment* are nouns. For more on suffixes, see sections 20c.1 and 22d.2. ⊕

7b Recognizing pronouns

A **pronoun** takes the place of a NOUN.* For information about using pronouns, see Chapters 9, 10, and 11. Different types of pronouns are explained in Chart 48.

David is an accountant. [noun]

He is an accountant. [pronoun]

The finance committee needs to consult **him**. [The pronoun *him* refers to the noun *David.*]

◉ **Pronouns**		48
PERSONAL *I, you, they, her, its, ours,* and others	refers to people or things	**I** saw **her** take a book to **them.**
RELATIVE *who, which, that*	introduces certain NOUN CLAUSES and ADJECTIVE CLAUSES	The book **that** I lost was valuable.
INTERROGATIVE *who, whose, what, which,* and others	introduces a question	**Who** called?
		→

*You can find the definition of a word printed in small capital letters (such as NOUN) in the Terms Glossary toward the back of this handbook.

TEACHING TIP: ESL

ESL students may have questions about the difference in usage between indefinite *a* or *an* and definite *the*. In sentence 3 in Exercise 7-1, the article *a* is used because the nouns *lobster* and *mask* are mentioned for the first time. (The "first mention" rule applies only to singular countable nouns, not to plurals like *humans, scientists, experiments,* or *treadmills*.) In sentence 4, *a* and *an* mean "one," reflecting their historical origin; the indefinite articles developed from the Anglo-Saxon word for *one*.

The refers to a noun that is definite, often because it has already been mentioned ("the lobster," "the mask," "the crustacean," which is a synonym for *lobster*) or because the context makes it specific, usually with a phrase ("of the crustacean") or clause ("that they are studying") following the noun. See Chapter 42.

QUOTATION: ON WRITING

If you want to write, and I hope you do, the sentence is your point of departure. Part of the art of creating a sentence is knowing the substance and elements of which it is composed. We all know, or let us assume, that sentences are made of words. But words come in various guises, whatever they are intended to hide or reveal, and so we must begin with them—seeing just what they think they are, as grammarians have defined them, and bringing them together into the realm of sense.

—Karen Elizabeth Gordon

Pronouns *(continued)*		48
DEMONSTRATIVE *this, these, that, those*	points out the ANTECEDENT	Whose books are **these?**
REFLEXIVE OR INTENSIVE *myself, themselves,* and other *-self* or *-selves* words	reflects back to the antecedent; intensifies the antecedent	They claim to support **themselves. I myself** doubt it.
RECIPROCAL *each other, one another*	refers to individual parts of a plural antecedent	We respect **each other.**
INDEFINITE *all, anyone, each,* and others	refers to nonspecific persons or things	**Everyone** is welcome here.

ANSWERS: EXERCISE 7-1

1. Not only <u>humans</u>^{N} use <u>them</u>.^{P}

2. <u>Scientists</u>^{N} conduct <u>experiments</u>^{N} by placing <u>lobsters</u>^{N} on <u>treadmills</u>.^{N}

3. <u>Scientists</u>^{N} can study ⓐ<u>lobster</u>^{N} when <u>it</u>^{P} is fitted with ⓐ small <u>mask</u>.^{N}

4. The <u>lobster</u>^{N} may reach <u>speeds</u>^{N} up to ⓐ<u>kilometer</u>^{N} ⓐn <u>hour</u>.^{N}

5. Through ⓣⓗⓔ <u>mask</u>,^{N} <u>researchers</u>^{N} can monitor ⓣⓗⓔ <u>heartbeat</u>^{N} of the <u>crustacean</u>^{N} <u>that</u>^{P} <u>they</u>^{P} are studying.

TEACHING TIP

Using the most appropriate verb can make the difference between a vague sentence and a meaningful one. You might stimulate a lively discussion if you ask students to explain the differences in meanings (and to compose a sentence for each meaning) of these verbs that deal with the same subjects.

1. stride, march, glide, strut

2. gobble, nibble, devour, eat

3. giggle, guffaw, chuckle, snicker

EXERCISE 7-1

Consulting sections 7a and 7b, underline and label all nouns (N) and pronouns (P). Circle all articles.

EXAMPLE   <u>Treadmills</u>^{N} can be ⓐ <u>way</u>^{N} to <u>fitness</u>^{N} and <u>rehabilitation</u>.^{N}

1. Not only humans use them.
2. Scientists conduct experiments by placing lobsters on treadmills.
3. Scientists can study a lobster when it is fitted with a small mask.
4. The lobster may reach speeds up to a kilometer an hour.
5. Through the mask, researchers can monitor the heartbeat of the crustacean that they are studying.

7c Recognizing verbs

Main verbs express action, occurrence, or state of being. (For a detailed discussion of verbs, see Chapter 8.)

I **dance.** [action]

The audience **became** silent. [occurrence]

Your dancing **was** excellent. [state of being]

❶ ALERT: If you are not sure whether a word is a verb, try putting the word into a different TENSE. If the sentence still makes sense, the word is a verb. (For an explanation of verb tense, see 8g.)

NO   He is a **changed** man. He is a **will change** man. [*Change* is not a verb because the sentence does not make sense with *will change*.]

YES   The store **changed** owners. The store **will change** owners. [*Change* is a verb because the sentence makes sense when the verb *will change* is substituted.]**!**

EXERCISE 7-2

Consulting section 7c, underline all verbs.

EXAMPLE   Homeless pigs <u>are pampered</u> at a resort in West Virginia.

1. Hundreds of Americans bought tiny Vietnamese potbellied pigs as house pets in the 1980s.
2. These intelligent animals were taught many of the same tricks as dogs.
3. Some people even walked their pet pigs on a leash.
4. But many owners soon abandoned these hungry, messy pets.
5. Now, a shelter in West Virginia treats 180 of the pigs to swimming pools, belly rubs, classical music, and plenty of mud.

7d Recognizing verbals

Verbals are verb parts. Verbals function as NOUNS, ADJECTIVES, or ADVERBS. Different types of verbals are explained in Chart 49.

◉ **Verbals and their functions**		49
INFINITIVE *to* + verb	1. noun	**To eat** now is inconvenient.
	2. adjective or adverb	Still, we have far **to go.**
PAST PARTICIPLE *-ed* form of REGULAR VERB or equivalent in IRREGULAR VERB	adjective	**Boiled, filtered** water is usually safe to drink.
		➡

QUOTATION: ON WRITING

I work on each sentence until I'm satisfied with it and go on. I may rewrite one sentence nineteen times, and the next sentence eight times, and the next sentence three times. When I'm lucky, one sentence just once.

—Larry L. King

ANSWERS: EXERCISE 7-2

1. Hundreds of Americans <u>bought</u> tiny Vietnamese potbellied pigs as house pets in the 1980s.

2. These intelligent animals <u>were taught</u> many of the same tricks as dogs.

3. Some people even <u>walked</u> their pet pigs on a leash.

4. But many owners soon <u>abandoned</u> these hungry, messy pets.

5. Now, a shelter in West Virginia <u>treats</u> 180 of the pigs to swimming pools, belly rubs, classical music, and plenty of mud.

TEACHING TIP

To give students a sense of the range of uses for -*ing* words, you might hand out a list of -*ing* words and ask your students to use each word in three different sentences: in one as a noun, in another as an adjective, and in a third as part of a verb phrase. Then you can collect the sentences and select twenty-five to thirty to reproduce and distribute. As an exercise or quiz, you can ask the students to identify each -*ing* word as a noun, an adjective, or part of a verb phrase. Often, the author of a sentence is eager for others to get the identification correct and is therefore quite willing to explain the answer.

Verbals and their functions *(continued)*		49
PRESENT PARTICIPLE		
-ing form of verb	1. adjective	**Running** water may not be safe.
	2. noun (called a GERUND)	**Eating** in roadside restaurants can be an adventure.

TEACHING TIP: ESL

An inductive way to help students discover and thus remember the differences among *-ing* forms is to have them circle the forms in a piece of writing and discuss which type is used: participles (adjectives), gerunds (nouns), or parts of verb phrases. For example, they could exchange papers with other students and then analyze and discuss all the *-ing* forms. See Chapter 45.

TEACHING TIP

The following passage provides important sensory details through the use of well-chosen adjectives. To heighten student awareness of strong adjectives, you may want to read the excerpt aloud, asking students afterward how many of those details they can recall.

> Perhaps it was the middle of January in the present year that I first looked up and saw the mark on the wall. In order to fix a date it is necessary to remember what one saw. So now I think of the fire; the steady film of yellow light upon the page of my book; the three chrysanthemums in the round glass bowl on the mantelpiece. Yes, it must have been the wintertime, and we had just finished our tea, for I remember that I was smoking a cigarette when I looked up and saw the mark on the wall for the first time. I looked up through the smoke of my cigarette and my eye lodged for a moment upon the

⊕ **ESL NOTE:** For information about using the verbals called GERUNDS and INFINITIVES as objects, see Chapter 45. ⊕

7e Recognizing adjectives

Adjectives modify—that is, they describe or limit—NOUNS and PRONOUNS. For a detailed discussion of adjectives, see Chapter 12.

I saw a **green** tree. [*Green* modifies the noun *tree*.]

It was **leafy.** [*Leafy* modifies the pronoun *it*.]

The flowering trees were **beautiful.** [*Beautiful* modifies the noun phrase *the flowering trees*.]

⊕ **ESL NOTE:** Usually, words with the suffixes *-ful*, *-ish*, *-less*, and *-like* are adjectives. For more about suffixes, see sections 20c.1 and 22d.2. ⊕

Limiting adjectives are usually called *determiners*. **Determiners** tell whether a noun is general (*a tree*) or specific (*the tree*). Determiners also tell which one (*this tree*), how many (*twelve trees*), whose (*our tree*), and similar information.

The determiners *a, an,* and *the* are also called **articles.** *The* is a **definite article.** Before a noun, *the* conveys that the noun refers to a specific item (*the plan*). *A* and *an* are **indefinite articles.** They convey that a noun refers to an item in a nonspecific or general way (*a plan*).

❶ **ALERT:** Use *a* when the word following it starts with a consonant sound: *a carrot, a broken egg, a hip.* Use *an* when the word following it starts with a vowel sound: *an egg, an old carrot, an honor.* ❗

For more on articles, see Chapter 42. Types of determiners are explained in Chart 50. Please note that some words in Chart 50 also function as pronouns. When you want to identify a word's part of speech, see how it functions in each particular sentence.

That car belongs to Harold. [*that* = demonstrative adjective]

That is Harold's car. [*that* = demonstrative pronoun]

🎯 Determiners (limiting adjectives)　　50

ARTICLES
a, an, the

A reporter working on **an** assignment is using **the** telephone.

DEMONSTRATIVE
this, these, that, those

Those students rent **that** house.

INDEFINITE
any, each, few, other, some, and others

Few films today have complex plots.

INTERROGATIVE
what, which, whose

What answer did you give?

NUMERICAL
one, first, two, second, and others

The **fifth** question was tricky.

POSSESSIVE
my, your, their, and others

My violin is older than **your** cello.

RELATIVE
what, which, whose, whatever, and others

We do not know **which** road to take.

7f　Recognizing adverbs

Adverbs modify—describe or limit—VERBS, ADJECTIVES, other adverbs, and entire sentences. For a detailed discussion of adverbs, see Chapter 12.

Chefs plan meals **carefully.** [*Carefully* modifies the verb *plan*.]

Vegetables provide **very** important vitamins. [*Very* modifies the adjective *important*.]

Those potato chips are **too** heavily salted. [*Too* modifies the adverb *heavily*.]

Fortunately, people are learning that salt can be harmful. [*Fortunately* modifies rest of the sentence.]

Descriptive adverbs can show levels of intensity, usually by adding *more* (or *less*) and *most* (or *least*): *more happily, least clearly* (see 12e).

TEACHING TIP

To help students become aware of adverbs and how they function, you may want to provide a series of sentences that have blanks to be filled in with appropriate adverbs. Here is an example:

> The cat sat _____ under the kitchen table, _____ watching the mouse scampering _____ly, _____ly, almost _____ly.

BACKGROUND

R. Baird Shuman addresses the ongoing debate about the value of grammar instruction and provides exercises designed to help students both understand the vocabulary of grammar and develop a repetoire of strategies related to recognizing options of style. ("Grammar for Writers: How Much Is Enough?" in *The Place of Grammar in Writing Instruction: Past, Present, Future,* ed. Susan Hunter and Ray Wallace, Portsmouth, NH: Boynton-Cook, 1995).

ANSWERS: EXERCISE 7-3

Some students may also underline *a, an,* and *the* as limiting adjectives.

1. determined (ADJ); successfully (ADV); three (ADJ); very (ADV); old (ADJ)
2. Eventually (ADV); civic (ADJ); closely (ADV); local (ADJ); only (ADV); native (ADJ); open (ADJ)

→

Conjunctive adverbs modify by creating logical connections in meaning, as listed in Chart 51. Conjunctive adverbs can appear anywhere: at the start, in the middle, or at the end of a sentence.

> **However,** we consider Isaac Newton an even more important scientist.

> We consider Isaac Newton, **however,** an even more important scientist.

> We consider Isaac Newton an even more important scientist, **however.**

◉ Conjunctive adverbs and the relationships they express   51

Relationship	Words
ADDITION	*also, furthermore, moreover, besides*
CONTRAST	*however, still, nevertheless, conversely, nonetheless, instead, otherwise*
COMPARISON	*similarly, likewise*
RESULT OR SUMMARY	*therefore, thus, consequently, accordingly, hence, then*
TIME	*next, then, meanwhile, finally, subsequently*
EMPHASIS	*indeed, certainly*

EXERCISE 7-3

Consulting sections 7d, 7e, and 7f, underline and label all adjectives (ADJ) and adverbs (ADV).

EXAMPLE   Do you believe the <u>common</u> claim that <u>one</u> person
              (ADJ)   (ADJ)

              can <u>really</u> make a <u>big</u> difference?
                   (ADV)   (ADJ)

1. A determined woman in Atlanta fought successfully to save three very old oaks from being cut down.
2. Eventually, she founded a civic group, which works closely with local businesspeople, to plant only native trees in the open places in Atlanta.

3. A second individual carefully mapped the recycling sites in his town and then widely distributed the unusual map.

4. New residents gratefully consult this map to learn where to take discarded newspapers, glass bottles, and aluminum cans for mandatory recycling.

5. A third person spoke so passionately about the beautiful tall grass of her Texas homeland that the city turned those grassy plains into a popular park.

7g Recognizing prepositions

Prepositions include common words such as *in, under, by, after, to, on, over,* and *since.* **Prepositional phrases** consist of a preposition and one or more other words, often used to set out relationships in time or space: *in April, under the orange umbrella.*

In the fall, we will hear a concert **by our favorite tenor.**

After the concert, he will fly **to Paris.**

🌐 **ESL NOTE:** For a list of prepositions and the idioms they involve, see Chapter 44. 🌐

7h Recognizing conjunctions

A **conjunction** connects words, PHRASES, or CLAUSES. **Coordinating conjunctions,** listed in Chart 52, join two or more grammatically equivalent structures.

◎ **Coordinating conjunctions and the relationships they express**   **52**

Relationship	Words
ADDITION	*and*
CONTRAST	*but, yet*
RESULT OR EFFECT	*so*
REASON OR CAUSE	*for*
CHOICE	*or*
NEGATIVE CHOICE	*nor*

Answers: Exercise 7-3 (continued)

3. second (ADJ); carefully (ADV); recycling (ADJ); his (ADJ); widely (ADV); unusual (ADJ)

4. New (ADJ); gratefully (ADV); this (ADJ); discarded (ADJ); glass (ADJ); aluminum (ADJ); mandatory (ADJ)

5. third (ADJ); so (ADV); passionately (ADV); beautiful (ADJ); tall (ADJ); her (ADJ); Texas (ADJ); those (ADJ); grassy (ADJ); popular (ADJ)

A HUMOROUS NOTE

Misplaced prepositions and prepositional phrases can sometimes turn the serious into the comical, as Richard Lederer demonstrates in sentences he has collected and published in *Anguished English.*

- The patient was referred to a psychiatrist with a severe emotional problem.
- The judge sentenced the killer to die in the electric chair for the second time.
- Two cars were reported stolen by the Groveton police yesterday.
- Please take time to look over the brochure that is enclosed with your family.
- Berra had driven over with his wife, Carmen, from their home in a Mercedes for the softball game.

TEACHING TIP

Grammar is more a way of thinking, a style of inquiry, than a way of being right.
—Mina P. Shaughnessy,
Errors and Expectations

TEACHING TIP

To help students become aware of what conjunctions do, you might want to distribute the following passage by Langston Hughes. Omit all conjunctions and ask students to supply them. When the passage is complete, ask students to discuss the function and the effect of each word they supplied. Then distribute the original, complete passage.

I was saved from sin *when* I was going on thirteen. *But* not really saved. It happened like this. There was a big revival at my Auntie Reed's church. Every night for weeks there had been much preaching, singing, praying *and* shouting, *and* some very hardened sinners had been brought to Christ, *and* the membership of the church had grown by leaps *and* bounds. Then just *before* the revival ended, they held a special meeting for children, "to bring the young lambs to the fold." My aunt spoke of it for days ahead. That night I was escorted to the front *and* placed on the mourners' bench with the other young sinners, who had not yet been brought to Jesus. . . . Then I was left all alone on the mourners' bench. My aunt came *and* knelt at my knees *and* cried, *while* prayers *and* songs swirled all around me in the little church. The whole congregation prayed for me alone, in a mighty wail of moans *and* vices. *And* I kept waiting serenely for Jesus, waiting, waiting—*but* he didn't come. I wanted to see him, *but* nothing happened to me. Nothing! I wanted something to happen to me, *but* nothing happened.
—Langston Hughes, "Salvation"

We hike **and** camp every summer. [*And* joins two words.]

I love the outdoors, **but** my family does not. [*But* joins two INDEPENDENT CLAUSES.]

Correlative conjunctions work in pairs. They include *both . . . and, either . . . or, neither . . . nor, not only . . . but (also), whether . . . or,* and *not . . . so much as.*

Both English **and** Spanish are spoken in many homes in the United States.

Not only students **but also** businesspeople should study a second language.

Subordinating conjunctions, listed in Chart 53, introduce DEPENDENT CLAUSES.

Many people were happy **after** they heard the news.

Because it snowed, school was canceled.

⊙ **Subordinating conjunctions and the relationships they express**   **53**

Relationship	Words
TIME	*after, before, once, since, until, when, whenever, while*
REASON OR CAUSE	*as, because, since*
RESULT OR EFFECT	*in order that, so, so that, that*
CONDITION	*if, even if, provided that, unless*
CONTRAST	*although, even though, though, whereas*
LOCATION	*where, wherever*
CHOICE	*rather than, than, whether*

7i Recognizing interjections

An **interjection** is a word or expression that conveys surprise or another strong emotion. Alone, an interjection is usually punctuated with an exclamation point (!). As part of a sentence, an interjection is set off by a comma (or commas).

Hooray! I bowled a strike!

Oh, they are late.

EXERCISE 7-4

Consulting sections 7a through 7i, identify the part of speech of each numbered and underlined word. Choose from *noun, pronoun, verb, adjective, adverb, preposition, coordinating conjunction, correlative conjunction*, and *subordinating conjunction*.

      1   2   3
<u>Although</u> <u>few</u> people realize that coffee is drunk <u>by</u> more people

                     4   5   6
than any other <u>beverage</u>, <u>it</u> is actually the second <u>best-selling</u> item of

   7   8   9
<u>international</u> commerce. Petroleum is the <u>first</u> item. <u>People</u> in the

                           10
United States consume 1.5 million tons <u>of</u> coffee beans per year.

                         11
That is more coffee than the entire world <u>drank</u> only fifty years ago.

     12   13   14
<u>Nevertheless</u>, the Swedish <u>are</u> the world's <u>heaviest</u> coffee consumers.

15   16
<u>In</u> an average year, <u>each</u> Swede consumes nearly 30 pounds of coffee,

17   18   19   20   21
<u>and</u> this <u>consumption</u> is <u>slowly</u> rising. Therefore, if both Americans and

Swedes continue to consume coffee at this rate, coffee may

   22   23 24   25
<u>eventually</u> equal <u>or</u> <u>surpass</u> <u>petroleum</u> as the largest item of

international commerce.

SENTENCE STRUCTURES

Knowing how sentences are formed gives you an important tool for understanding the art of writing.

7j   Defining the sentence

The sentence has several definitions, each of which views it from a different perspective. On its most mechanical level, a sentence starts with a capital letter and finishes with a period, question mark, or exclamation point.

ANSWERS AND COVERAGE: EXERCISE 7-4

Instructors can require students to identify the part of speech of any word in this paragraph, in addition to those with superscript numbers.

1. subordinating conjunction [7h]
2. adjective (determiner) [7c]
3. preposition [7g]
4. noun [7a]
5. pronoun [7b]
6. adjective [7e]
7. adjective [7e]
8. adjective [7c]
9. noun [7a]
10. preposition [7g]
11. verb [7c]
12. conjunctive adverb [7f]
13. verb [7c]
14. adjective [7e]
15. preposition [7g]
16. adjective (determiner) [7e]
17. coordinating conjunction [7h]
18. noun [7a]
19. adverb [7f]
20. conjunctive adverb [7f]
21. correlative conjunctions [7h]
22. adverb [7f]
23. coordinating conjunction [7h]
24. verb [7c]
25. noun [7a]

QUOTATION: ON WRITING

Language, like the body, is so comfortable and familiar that we hardly notice its presence or complexity. Yet once examined closely, the accomplishment of any ordinary speaker is rather astonishing. He can produce and understand an indefinite number of new sentences—sentences he has never encountered previously.

—Richard Ohmann

A sentence can be defined according to its purpose. A **declarative sentence** makes a statement: *Sky diving is dangerous.* An **interrogative sentence** asks a question: *Is sky diving dangerous?* An **imperative sentence** gives a command: *Be careful when you sky-dive.* An **exclamatory sentence** begins with *What* or *How* and expresses strong feeling: *How I love sky diving!*

Grammatically, a sentence consists of an INDEPENDENT CLAUSE: *Sky diving is dangerous.* Sometimes a sentence is described as a "complete thought," but that definition is too vague to be reliable.

Sections 7k through 7p present the basic structures of sentences.

7k Recognizing subjects and predicates

A sentence consists of two basic parts: a **subject** and a **predicate,** as shown in Chart 54.

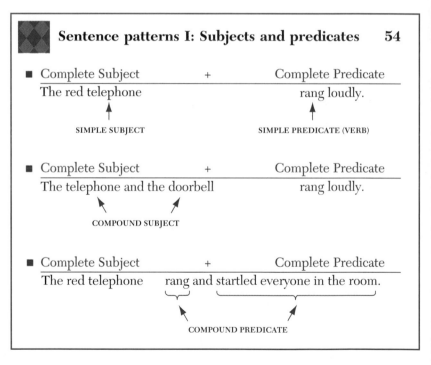

Sentence patterns I: Subjects and predicates 54

- Complete Subject + Complete Predicate
  The red telephone rang loudly.
  SIMPLE SUBJECT / SIMPLE PREDICATE (VERB)

- Complete Subject + Complete Predicate
  The telephone and the doorbell rang loudly.
  COMPOUND SUBJECT

- Complete Subject + Complete Predicate
  The red telephone rang and startled everyone in the room.
  COMPOUND PREDICATE

The **simple subject** is the word or group of words that acts, is described, or is acted upon.

The **telephone** rang. [Simple subject, *telephone,* acts.]

The **telephone** is red. [Simple subject, *telephone,* is described.]

The **telephone** was being connected. [Simple subject, *telephone*, is acted upon.]

The **complete subject** is the simple subject and its MODIFIERS: ***The red telephone*** rang.

A **compound subject** consists of two or more NOUNS or PRONOUNS and their modifiers: ***The telephone and the doorbell*** rang.

The **predicate** is the part of the sentence that contains the VERB. The predicate tells what the subject is doing or experiencing or what is being done to the subject.

The telephone **rang**. [*Rang* tells what the subject, *telephone*, did.]

The telephone **is** red. [*Is* tells what the subject, *telephone*, experiences.]

The telephone **was being connected**. [*Was being connected* tells what was being done to the subject, *telephone*.]

A **simple predicate** contains only the verb: *The lawyer **listened**.* A **complete predicate** contains the verb and its modifiers: *The lawyer **listened carefully**.* A **compound predicate** contains two or more verbs: *The lawyer **listened and waited**.*

⊕ ESL NOTES: (1) In sentences that make a statement, the subject usually comes before the predicate. (To learn about INVERTED WORD ORDER, see 10f.) In sentences that ask a question, part of the predicate usually comes before the subject. For more about word order, see Chapter 43. (2) Avoid repeating a subject with a personal pronoun in the same clause.

NO My grandfather **he** lived to be eighty-seven.

YES My grandfather lived to be eighty-seven.

NO Winter storms that bring ice, sleet, and snow **they** can cause traffic problems.

YES Winter storms that bring ice, sleet, and snow can cause traffic problems. ⊕

EXERCISE 7-5

Consulting section 7k, separate the complete subject from the complete predicate with a slash.

EXAMPLE   One of the most devastating natural disasters of recorded history / began on April 5, 1815.

1. Mount Tambora, located in present-day Indonesia, erupted.
2. The eruption exploded the top 4,000 feet of the mountain.
3. The blast was heard over 900 miles away.
4. A thick cloud of volcanic ash circled the globe and reached North America the following summer.
5. Sunlight could not penetrate the cloud throughout the entire summer.

QUOTATION: ON WRITING

Just as verbs and actions go together, so do subjects and characters. There are different kinds of characters. Usually—but not always—the most important characters are the agents of actions, the source of action or the condition that the writer is describing.
—Joseph M. Williams

ANSWERS: EXERCISE 7-5

1. Mount Tambora, located in present-day Indonesia, / erupted.
2. The eruption / exploded the top 4,000 feet of the mountain.
3. The blast / was heard over 900 miles away.
4. A thick cloud of volcanic ash / circled the globe and reached North America the following summer.
5. Sunlight / could not penetrate the cloud throughout the entire summer.

71 Recognizing direct and indirect objects

Direct objects and **indirect objects** are always found in the PREDICATE of a sentence. Chart 55 shows the relationships of direct and indirect objects in sentences.

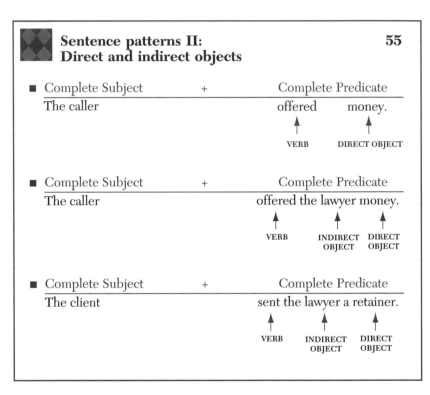

Sentence patterns II: 55
Direct and indirect objects

A **direct object** completes the meaning of a TRANSITIVE VERB. To check for a direct object, make up a *whom?* or *what?* question about the verb.

To check for an **indirect object,** make up a *to whom? for whom? to what?* or *for what?* question about the verb.

ESL NOTES: (1) In sentences with indirect objects followed by the word *to* or *for,* put the direct object before the indirect object.

    NO   Please give **to John** this letter.

    YES   Please give this letter **to John.**

(2) When a pronoun is used as an indirect object, some verbs require *to* or *for* before the pronoun, and others do not.

NO   Please explain **me** the rule.

YES   Please explain the rule **to me.** [Explain requires <u>to</u> before an indirect object.]

NO   Please **give to me** the letter.

YES   Please **give me** the letter. [Give does not require <u>to</u> before an indirect object.]

Even though a verb does not require *to* before an indirect object, you may use *to* if you prefer. If you do, be sure to put the direct object before the indirect object.

YES   Please give the letter **to me.** ✥

EXERCISE 7-6

Consulting section 7l, draw a single line under all direct objects and a double line under all indirect objects.

EXAMPLE   Maya Angelou's poems and books bring many people an inspirational message.

           Maya Angelou's poems and books bring many <u>people</u> an inspirational <u>message</u>.

1. Maya Angelou read President Clinton her poem "On the Pulse of Morning" on the day of his first presidential inauguration in 1993.
2. Her widely acclaimed autobiography, *I Know Why the Caged Bird Sings*, won her national recognition.
3. *I Know Why the Caged Bird Sings* offers a moving account of her childhood in segregated Arkansas.
4. Her later book, *Wouldn't Take Nothing for My Journey Now*, contains the wisdom of a woman who gained strength from hardships.
5. Angelou currently teaches college students poetry.

7m Recognizing complements, modifiers, and appositives

7m.1 Recognizing complements

A **complement** occurs in the PREDICATE of a sentence. It renames or describes a SUBJECT or an OBJECT.

A **subject complement** is a NOUN, PRONOUN, or ADJECTIVE that follows a LINKING VERB (see 8a, especially Chart 60). **Predicate nominative** is another term for a noun used as a subject complement, and **predicate adjective** is another term for an adjective used as a subject complement.

QUOTATION: ON WRITING

The grammar is an attempt to make explicit and conscious what the speaker of English does intuitively and unconsciously.
—Mark Lester

ANSWERS: EXERCISE 7-6

1. Maya Angelou read <u>President Clinton</u> <u>her poem</u> "On the Pulse of Morning" on the day of his first presidential inauguration in 1993.

2. Her widely acclaimed autobiography, *I Know Why the Caged Bird Sings*, won <u>her</u> national <u>recognition</u>.

3. *I Know Why the Caged Bird Sings* offers a moving <u>account</u> of her childhood in segregated Arkansas.

4. Her latest book, *Wouldn't Take Nothing for My Journey Now*, contains the <u>wisdom</u> of a woman who gained <u>strength</u> from hardships.

5. Angelou currently teaches <u>college students</u> <u>poetry</u>.

An **object complement** follows a DIRECT OBJECT and either describes or renames the direct object. Chart 56 shows the relationships of subject complements and object complements in sentences.

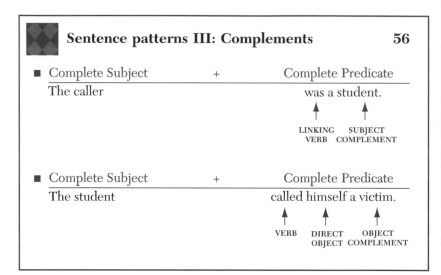

Sentence patterns III: Complements 56

- Complete Subject + Complete Predicate

  The caller was a student.

  LINKING SUBJECT
  VERB COMPLEMENT

- Complete Subject + Complete Predicate

  The student called himself a victim.

  VERB DIRECT OBJECT
  OBJECT COMPLEMENT

EXERCISE 7-7

Consulting section 7m.1, underline all complements and identify each as a subject complement (SUB) or an object complement (OB).

EXAMPLE   The Native American Shawnee of Tennessee called

OB
their main food <u>rockahominie</u>.

1. Many people know this food today as hominy.
2. Hominy is whole dried corn kernels cooked until the skins come off.
3. The process of turning dried corn into hominy is inexpensive but time-consuming.
4. In the southern United States, many people consider hominy a breakfast treat.
5. Fried patties of hominy grits, which are ground kernels rather than whole ones, taste delicious.

7m.2 Recognizing modifiers

A **modifier** is a word or group of words that describe or limit other words. Modifiers appear in the SUBJECT or the PREDICATE of a sentence.

The **large red** telephone rang. [The adjectives *large* and *red* modify the noun *telephone*.]

The lawyer answered **quickly.** [The adverb *quickly* modifies the verb *answered*.]

The person **on the telephone** was **extremely** upset. [The prepositional phrase *on the telephone* modifies the noun *person;* the adverb *extremely* modifies the adjective *upset*.]

Therefore, the lawyer spoke **gently.** [The adverb *therefore* modifies the independent clause *the lawyer spoke gently;* the adverb *gently* modifies the verb *spoke*.]

Because the lawyer's voice was calm, the caller felt reassured. [The ADVERB CLAUSE *because the lawyer's voice was calm* modifies the independent clause *the caller felt reassured*.]

7m.3 Recognizing appositives

An **appositive** is a word or group of words that renames the NOUN or PRONOUN preceding it.

The student's story, **a tale of broken promises,** was complicated. [The appositive *a tale of broken promises* renames the noun *story*.]

The lawyer consulted an expert, **her law professor,** [The appositive *her law professor* renames the noun *expert*.]

The student, **Joe Jones,** asked to speak to his lawyer. [The appositive *Joe Jones* renames the noun *student*.]

⓿ **PUNCTUATION ALERT:** When an appositive is not essential for identifying what it renames (that is, when it is *nonrestrictive*), use a comma or commas to set off the appositive from whatever it renames and any words following it (see 24e). ❗

7n Recognizing phrases

A **phrase** is a word group that contains a SUBJECT or a PREDICATE but not both. A phrase cannot stand alone as an independent unit.

A **noun phrase** functions as a NOUN in a sentence.

The modern census dates back to the **seventeenth century.**

A **verb phrase** functions as a VERB in a sentence.

Two military censuses **are mentioned** in the Bible.

A **prepositional phrase** always starts with a PREPOSITION and functions as a MODIFIER.

William the Conqueror conducted a census **of landowners in newly conquered England in 1086.** [three prepositional phrases in a row, beginning with *of, in, in*]

TEACHING TIP

Combining sentences by using modifiers and appositives can not only reduce repetition but also create more graceful statements. Students are sometimes surprised by what they produce when they are asked to combine several choppy sentences into a single effective one.

A HUMOROUS NOTE

Dangling participial phrases can produce some unintended meanings, such as these:

- Plunging 1,000 feet into the gorge, we saw Yosemite Falls.
- He rode his horse across Highway 12 and up and down the sidewalk in front of the saloon a good half hour before deputies arrived, shouting obscenities and being obnoxious.
- Locked in a vault for 50 years, the owner of the jewels has decided to sell them.
  —Richard Lederer,
  Anguished English

TEACHING TIP

Because students sometimes feel that phrases are peculiar constructions of grammar books, you might find it useful to reproduce and distribute copies of a newspaper article on a popular subject. Ask students to identify noun phrases, verb phrases, and prepositional phrases. Students will be amazed at how often phrases appear in "real" writing. Class discussion might next cover the functions of the noun phrases and prepositional phrases (subject, object, complement, adjective, adverb).

ANSWERS AND COVERAGE: EXERCISE 7-8

Answers will vary. Here is one set of possibilities.

1. *Cutting their expenses by downsizing,* companies cause stress levels among businesspeople to increase. [verbal (participial) phrase]

2. Researchers have spent years studying stress in the workplace *and have devised* sophisticated treatment and prevention techniques to help businesspeople reduce stress. [verb phrase]

3. *Compiling a list of symptoms of stress and the common reasons for it* was one of the objectives of management psychologist John H. Howard when he began studying stress in 1971. [gerund phrase as subject]

An **absolute phrase** usually contains a noun or PRONOUN and a PRESENT or PAST PARTICIPLE. An absolute phrase modifies the entire sentence that it is part of.

> **Censuses being the fashion,** Quebec and Nova Scotia took sixteen counts between 1665 and 1754.

> Eighteenth-century Sweden and Denmark had complete records of their populations, **each adult and child having been accounted for.**

A **verbal phrase** contains a verb part that functions not as a verb but as a noun or an ADJECTIVE. Verbs are INFINITIVES, present participles, and past participles.

> In 1624, Virginia began **to count its citizens** in a census. [*To count* is an INFINITIVE PHRASE.]

> **Going from door to door,** census takers interview millions of people. [*Going from door to door* is a present PARTICIPIAL PHRASE.]

> **Amazed by some people's answers,** census takers always listen carefully. [*Amazed by some people's answers* is a past participial phrase.]

A **gerund phrase** functions as a noun. Telling the difference between a gerund phrase and a present participial phrase can be tricky because both use the *-ing* verb form. The key is to determine how the verbal phrase is functioning: A gerund phrase functions *only* as a noun, and a participial phrase functions *only* as a modifier.

> **Including each person in the census** was important. [gerund phrase because noun used as the subject]

> **Including each person in the census,** Abby spent many hours on the crowded city block. [present participial phrase because modifier used as an adjective describing Abby]

EXERCISE 7-8

Consulting section 7n, combine each set of sentences into a single sentence, converting one sentence into a phrase. Choose from among *absolute phrases, noun phrases, verb phrases, prepositional phrases, participial phrases,* and *gerund phrases.* You can omit, add, or change words. Most sets can be combined in several equally correct ways, but be sure to check that your combined sentence makes sense.

EXAMPLE Stress has become an increasingly terrible burden to businesspeople. Because of this, there is a need to lessen the pressures of work.

With stress becoming an increasingly terrible burden to businesspeople, there is a need to lessen the pressures of work. *(prepositional phrase)*

1. Stress levels among businesspeople are increasing. This increase is caused by companies that are cutting their expenses by downsizing.
2. Researchers have spent years studying stress in the workplace. They have devised sophisticated treatment and prevention techniques to help businesspeople reduce stress.
3. Management psychologist John H. Howard began studying stress in 1971. As one of his objectives, he compiled a list of symptoms of stress and the common reasons for it.
4. According to Dr. Howard, uncertainty and feeling overworked are the most common reasons for work-related stress. These feelings are a result of increasingly harsh competition.
5. Dr. Howard discovered simple ways to combat stress. His techniques include exercising, deep breathing, and visualizing.
6. Dr. Salvatore R. Maddi believes stress levels fall when business-people deal properly with change. Successful businesspeople see the change as a challenge, not a threat.
7. According to Dr. Maddi, businesspeople with a strong sense of commitment and control cope best with change. They do this by examining the reasons for change and focusing on self-improvement.
8. This technique is called compensatory self-improvement. It can result in a renewed sense of accomplishment and self-esteem.
9. These techniques for reducing stress are valuable. They enable businesspeople to overcome anxieties and provide them with more time to escape the pressures of work.
10. More time enables businesspeople to discover new personal interests. New interests can sometimes lead to more enjoyable jobs.

7o Recognizing clauses

A **clause** is a word group with both a SUBJECT and a PREDICATE. Clauses are divided into two categories: **independent clauses** (also known as **main clauses**) and **dependent clauses** (also known as **subordinate clauses**).

7o.1 Recognizing independent clauses

An **independent clause** contains a subject and a predicate. It can stand alone as a sentence. Chart 57 shows the basic pattern.

Answers and Coverage: Exercise 7-8 (continued)

4. *Competition being increasingly harsh,* uncertainty and feeling overworked are the most common reasons for work-related stress, according to Dr. Howard. [absolute phrase]

5. *To combat stress in simple ways,* Dr. Howard suggests exercising, deep breathing, and visualizing. [infinitive phrase, modifier]

6. Dr. Salvatore R. Maddi believes stress levels fall when businesspeople deal properly with change, *seeing the change as a challenge, not a threat.* [participial phrase]

7. According to Dr. Maddi, those businesspeople with a strong sense of commitment and control cope best with change *by examining the reasons for change and focusing on self-improvement.* [prepositional phrase]

8. *Called compensatory self-improvement,* this technique can result in a renewed sense of accomplishment and self-esteem. [verbal (participial) phrase]

9. *These valuable stress-reducing techniques* enable businesspeople to overcome anxieties, thus providing them with more time to escape the pressures of work. [noun phrase]

10. *With more time to escape the pressures of work,* businesspeople can discover new personal interests that can sometimes lead to more enjoyable jobs. [prepositional phrase]

TEACHING TIP

To determine whether a clause is independent or dependent, students can make up a yes/no question about the clause's statement. An independent clause leads to a sensible question; a dependent clause does not.

The knave stole the tarts.
Did the knave steal the tarts?
[a sensible question]
Because he was very hungry.
Because was he very hungry?
[not a sensible question]

To improve students' recognition of adjective and adverb clauses, as well as to increase their powers of concentration, you may want to read aloud the following passage by Katherine Anne Porter. Ask students to note every use of an adverb or adjective clause by listening for key words such as relative pronouns and subordinating conjunctions. After you read the passage, you may want to distribute and discuss it.

In my grandmother's day, in Texas, everybody seemed to remember that man *who* had a way of showing up with a dozen grains of real coffee in his hand, *which* he exchanged for a month's supply of corn meal. My grandmother parched a mixture of sweet potato and dried corn *until* it was black, ground it up and boiled it, *because* her family couldn't get over its yearning for a dark hot drink in the mornings, but she would never allow them to call it coffee. It was known as That Brew. ... The woman *who* made That Brew and the soldier *who* ate the bacon rind had been bride and groom in a Kentucky wedding somewhere around 1850. Only a few years ago a cousin of mine showed me a letter from a lady then rising ninety-five *who* remembered that wedding *as if* it had been only yesterday.

—Katherine Anne Porter, "Memories of the Old South"

QUOTATION: ON WRITING

When you write, you lay out a line of words. The line of words is a miner's pick, a woodcarver's gouge, a surgeon's probe. You wield it, and it digs a path you follow. Soon you find yourself deep in new territory. Is it a dead end, or have you located the real subject? You will know tomorrow, or this time next year.

—Annie Dillard

> **◈ Sentence patterns IV: Independent clauses   57**
>
> Independent Clause
>
> ■ Complete Subject   +   Complete Predicate
> The telephone   rang.

7o.2   Recognizing dependent clauses

A **dependent clause** contains a subject and a predicate but cannot stand alone as a sentence. A dependent clause must be joined to an independent clause (see 7o.1).

Some dependent clauses start with subordinating conjunctions such as *although, because, when,* or *until.* A SUBORDINATING CONJUNCTION expresses a relationship between the meaning in the dependent clause and the meaning in the independent clause (see Chart 53).

Clauses that start with subordinating conjunctions function as ADVERBS and so are called **adverb clauses** (or sometimes **subordinate clauses**). Adverb clauses usually answer some question about the independent clause: *How? Why? When? Under what circumstances?*

> **If the bond issue passes,** the city will install sewers. [The adverb clause modifies the verb *install;* it explain under what circumstances.]
>
> They are drawing up plans **as quickly as they can.** [The adverb clause modifies the verb *drawing up;* it explains how.]
>
> The homeowners feel happier **because they know the flooding will soon be better controlled.** [The adverb clause modifies the entire independent clause; it explains why.]

❶ PUNCTUATION ALERT: When an adverb clause comes before its independent clause, the clauses are usually separated by a comma (see 24b.1). **!**

Adjective clauses (also called **relative clauses**) start with RELATIVE PRONOUNS, such as *who, which,* and *that,* or with RELATIVE ADVERBS, such as *when* or *where.* An adjective clause modifies the NOUN or PRONOUN that it follows.

> The car **that Jack bought** is practical. [The adjective clause describes the noun *car; that* is a relative pronoun referring to *car.*]
>
> The day **when I can buy my own car** is getting closer. [The adjective clause modifies the noun *day; when* is a relative adverb referring to *day.*]

Chart 58 shows common sentence patterns for adverb and adjective clauses.

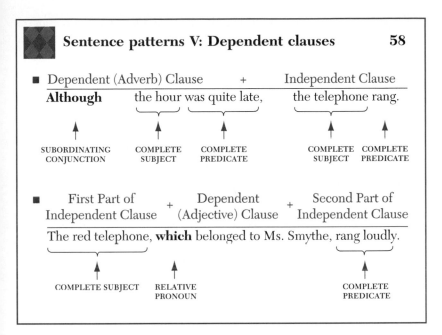

Sentence patterns V: Dependent clauses 58

■ Dependent (Adverb) Clause + Independent Clause

Although the hour was quite late, the telephone rang.

| SUBORDINATING CONJUNCTION | COMPLETE SUBJECT | COMPLETE PREDICATE | COMPLETE SUBJECT | COMPLETE PREDICATE |

■ First Part of Independent Clause + Dependent (Adjective) Clause + Second Part of Independent Clause

The red telephone, **which** belonged to Ms. Smythe, rang loudly.

| COMPLETE SUBJECT | RELATIVE PRONOUN | COMPLETE PREDICATE |

Use *who, whom, whoever, whomever,* and *whose* when your adjective clause refers to a person or an animal with a name.

The Smythes, **who collect cars,** are wealthy.

Their dog Bowser, **who is quite large,** is spoiled.

Use *which* or *that* when your adjective clause refers to a thing or an animal that is not a pet.

❶ PUNCTUATION ALERT: When an adjective clause is nonrestrictive, use commas to separate it from the independent clause. (A restrictive clause is essential to limit meaning; a nonrestrictive clause is nonessential; see 24e.)

The car **that** [or **which**] **I want to buy** has a cassette player. [The adjective clause is restrictive, so either *that* or *which* is correct.]

My current car, **which I bought used,** needs major repairs. [The adjective clause is nonrestrictive, so it begins with *which* and is set off with commas.]❗

Sometimes, *that* is omitted from an adjective clause. For purposes of grammatical analysis, however, the omitted *that* is implied and, therefore, present.

The car [that] I buy will have to get good mileage.

QUOTATION: ON WRITING

In all speech, words and sense are as the body and the soul.

—Ben Jonson

ANSWERS: EXERCISE 7-9

1. *Although Sao Miguel's Furnas volcano erupted thousands of years ago* (ADV), the collapsed mountaintop formed a lake bed *that is still hot* (ADJ).

2. The ground around Lake Furnas acts as a natural oven *because its temperature is more than 200 degrees Fahrenheit* (ADV).

3. To prepare the famous stew, *which is called* cozido (ADJ), cooks assemble chicken, beef, sausage, and vegetables in a pan.

4. *After the pan is tied in a cloth bag* (ADV), it is buried in the hole.

5. The *cozido* simmers for about six hours, a cooking time *that brings it to tasty perfection* (ADJ).

TEACHING TIP

Elliptical clauses: To enhance students' appreciation of their options, you might ask them whether they prefer the elliptical or full forms of the text's sentences—and why. Here are alternate examples to use.

!) ALERT: Omitting the word *that* can make a sentence harder to understand. Be sure to use *that* when it makes your writing clearer.

NO I talked to the instructor Miranda Jones recommended.

YES I talked to the instructor **that** Miranda Jones recommended. **!**

EXERCISE 7-9

Consulting section 7o.2, underline the dependent clauses. Write ADJ at the end of adjective clauses and ADV at the end of adverb clauses.

EXAMPLE   When cooks on São Miguel Island in the Azores decide to

ADV

prepare their favorite stew, they dig a hole on the shores of Lake Furnas.

1. Although São Miguel's Furnas volcano erupted thousands of years ago, the collapsed mountaintop formed a lake bed that is still hot.
2. The ground around Lake Furnas acts as a natural oven because its temperature is more than 200 degrees Fahrenheit.
3. To prepare the famous stew, which is called *cozido,* cooks assemble chicken, beef, sausages, and vegetables in a pan.
4. After the pan is tied in a cloth bag, it is buried in the hole.
5. The *cozido* simmers for about six hours, a cooking time that brings it to tasty perfection.

Noun clauses function as nouns. Noun clauses often begin with many of the same words as adjective clauses: *that, who, which,* and their derivatives, as well as *when, where, whether, why,* or *how.*

Promises are not always dependable. [noun]

What politicians promise is not always dependable. [noun clause]

The electorate often cannot figure out the **truth.** [noun]

The electorate often cannot know **that the truth is being manipulated.** [noun clause]

Because they start with similar words, noun clauses and adjective clauses are sometimes confused with each other. The word starting an adjective clause has an ANTECEDENT in the sentence. The word starting a noun clause does not.

Good politicians understand **whom they must please.** [Noun clause; *whom* does not have an antecedent.]

Good politicians **who make promises** know all cannot be kept. [Adjective clause modifies *politicians,* which is the antecedent of *who.*]

🌐 **ESL NOTE:** Noun clauses in indirect questions are phrased as statements, not questions: *Kara asked why we needed the purple dye.* Avoid such sentences as *Kara asked why did* [or *do*] *we need the purple dye?* Tense, pronoun, and other changes may be necessary when a direct question is rephrased as an indirect question (see 15a.4). 🌐

Elliptical clauses have words deliberately left out to make them concise (see Chapter 16). The term *elliptical* comes from the word *ellipsis*, meaning "omission." An elliptical clause delivers its meaning only if the context makes clear what the missing elements are.

> Engineering is one of the majors **[that] she considered.** [*that* functioning as relative pronoun omitted from adjective clause]

> She decided **[that] she would prefer to major in management.** [*that* functioning as a conjunction omitted between clauses]

> **After [he takes] a refresher course,** he will be eligible for a raise. [subject and verb omitted from adverb clause]

> Broiled fish tastes better **than boiled fish [tastes].** [second half of the comparison omitted]

EXERCISE 7-10

Consulting section 7o, use some of the subordinating conjunctions and relative pronouns from the list to combine each pair of sentences. The words may be used more than once, but try to use as many different ones as possible. Some pairs may be combined in a variety of ways. Create at least one elliptical construction.

EXAMPLE   The Pacific fighting was reaching its peak during World War II. U.S. and Japanese forces began to pick up strange radio messages.

As the Pacific fighting was reaching its peak during World War II, U.S. and Japanese forces began to pick up strange radio messages.

who	that	although	because	if	when
which	after	as	even though	since	unless

1. Most U.S. military personnel thought that the unintelligible messages were some strange Japanese code. The U.S. military personnel overheard the messages.
2. The Japanese were listening in. They could not understand the messages either.
3. A few members of the U.S. forces understood what the messages said. Those members of the U.S. forces were Navajo speakers.
4. The overheard messages were in a code. This code was based on the Navajo language.

Teaching Tip (continued)

- Living in Spain was one of the best experiences [that] Carol had during college. When [she was] living with a family in Spain, Carol started to feel like a native. Air travel is faster than sea [travel].

- James Naismith, [who was] a Presbyterian minister, believed that through athletics he could teach lessons in Christian ideals. After [he had graduated from] divinity school, Naismith enrolled in the School for Christian Workers, [which] later [became] known as the International YMCA Training School. Naismith, [who was] a young man full of ideas, was given the job of devising a game that had less running and tackling than other ball games [had]. Limited indoor space and the hard surface of a wooden floor were two of the biggest problems [that] he faced. The game [that] he devised is known today as basketball.

ANSWERS: EXERCISE 7-10

1. Most U.S. military personnel who overheard the unintelligible messages thought that they were some strange Japanese code. (One elliptical possibility is *Most U.S. military personnel who overheard the unintelligible messages thought them some strange Japanese code*, with *thought them* replacing *thought that they were*.)

2. When the Japanese were listening in, they could not understand the messages either. (One elliptical possibility is *The Japanese listening in could not understand the messages either*.)

3. A few members of the U.S. forces, Navajo speakers, understood what the messages said. (The elliptical phrase *Navajo speakers* omits *who were*.)

4. The overheard messages were in a code based on the Navajo language.

5. After Navajo Marines were specially recruited for this assignment, only they sent and received these messages. (One elliptical version is *Only Navajo Marines specially recruited for this assignment sent and received these messages*.) ➡

Answers: Exercise 7-10 (continued)

6. Since the messages conveyed meaning by tone of voice as well as vocabulary, decoding techniques using only written words could not break the code.

7. If any Navajos were living in Japan, they never explained the mystery of the messages.

8. Because Navajo is an extraordinarily complex language, the Japanese were never able to break the code.

9. The Navajo code talkers conveyed important messages that affected the key battles of Saipan, Guadalcanal, and Iwo Jima.

10. Even though the Navajos were asked to avoid publicity after the war in case the code was needed again, ultimately, their achievement was widely recognized.

TEACHING TIP

Imitation can be an effective means of expanding students' sentence-writing strategies. You can provide some samples, asking students to write a sentence on another topic, following the pattern of clauses and phrases in the model. Here are some varied possibilities for imitation, though you may want to choose your own.

A. The sea, which looks so near and so tempting, is often difficult to reach.
    —Henry Miller,
    "The Big Sur"

B. Hearing the rising tide, I think how it is pressing also against other shores I know—rising on a southern beach where there is no fog, but a moon edging all the waves with silver and touching the wet sands with lambent sheen, and on a still more distant shore sending its streaming currents against the moonlit pinnacles and the dark caves of the coral rock.
    —Rachel Carson,
    "The Enduring Sea"

5. Only Navajo Marines sent and received these messages. The Navajo Marines were specially recruited for this assignment.

6. The messages conveyed meaning by tone of voice as well as vocabulary. Decoding techniques using only written words could not break the code.

7. Were any Navajos living in Japan? The mystery of the messages was never explained.

8. Navajo is an extraordinarily complex language. The Japanese were never able to break the code.

9. The Navajo code talkers conveyed important messages. The messages affected the key battles of Saipan, Guadalcanal, and Iwo Jima.

10. The Navajos were asked to avoid publicity after the war in case the code was needed again. Ultimately, their achievement was widely recognized.

7p Recognizing sentence types

Sentences can be **simple, compound, complex,** and **compound-complex.**

A **simple sentence** is composed of a single INDEPENDENT CLAUSE and no DEPENDENT CLAUSES.

Charlie Chaplin was born in London on April 16, 1889.

A **compound sentence** is composed of two or more independent clauses. These clauses may be connected by a coordinating conjunction (*and, but, for, or, nor, yet,* or *so*), a semicolon alone, or a CONJUNCTIVE ADVERB.

His father died early, **and** his mother spent time in mental hospitals.

A mime, Chaplin became famous for creating the Little Tramp, a character whose misfortunes were many and whose pleasures were few; **and** ultimately, everyone wanted to protect him.

Many people enjoy Chaplin films; others do not.

Many people enjoy Chaplin films; **however,** others do not.

❶ **PUNCTUATION ALERT:** Use a comma before a coordinating conjunction connecting two independent clauses (see 24a). When the independent clauses are long or contain commas, use a subordinating conjunction, or you can choose to use a semicolon to connect them (see 25c and 25d). ❗

A **complex sentence** is composed of one independent clause and one or more dependent clauses.

When times were bad, Chaplin lived in the streets. [dependent clause starting *When*; independent clause starting *Chaplin*]

When Chaplin was performing with a troupe that was touring the United States, he was hired by Mack Sennett, **who owned the Keystone Company.** [dependent clause starting *When*; dependent clause starting *that*; independent clause starting *he*; dependent clause starting *who*]

🛑 PUNCTUATION ALERT: When a dependent clause comes before its independent clause, the clauses are usually separated by a comma (see 24b.1). ❗

A **compound-complex sentence** joins a compound sentence and a complex sentence. It contains two or more independent clauses and one or more dependent clauses.

Chaplin's comedies were immediately successful, **and** his salaries were huge **because of the enormous popularity of his tramp character, who was famous for his tiny mustache, baggy trousers, big shoes, and trick derby.** [independent clause starting *Chaplin's*; independent clause starting *his salaries*; dependent clause starting *because*; dependent clause starting *who*]

Once studios could no longer afford him, Chaplin cofounded United Artists, **and** then he was able to produce and distribute his own films. [dependent clause starting *Once*; independent clause starting *Chaplin*; independent clause starting *then he was able*]

EXERCISE 7-11

Consulting section 7p, identify each sentence as simple, compound, complex, or compound-complex.

EXAMPLE   Medical doctors are constantly fighting a battle against harmful bacteria. *(simple)*

1. When bacteria develop resistance to an antibiotic drug, that drug can no longer fight those bacteria.
2. A simple experiment shows this resistance in action.
3. In the morning, a researcher puts a single bacterial cell into a glass dish that is known as a Petri dish.
4. Bacteria multiply rapidly, and this one cell will increase to 10 million bacterial cells by midafternoon.
5. In the Petri dish, these 10 million bacteria look like a heap of salt to the naked eye.
6. Then the researcher puts an antibiotic drug into the Petri dish, and the drug begins killing off the bacteria.

TEACHING TIP

The class discussion of compound sentences may be a good time to review compounding of all sorts. A series of examples to show compound subjects, objects, verbs, adjectives, adverbs, phrases, and clauses may help your students see the compound sentence as the final step in a logical progression.

John F. Kennedy and Richard M. Nixon were the candidates in the 1960 presidential election. [compound subject] Kennedy won the election because of his popularity in *the South and the East.* [compound object of preposition] Many people admired *his energy and his wholesomeness.* [compound object] He *made* respected cabinet appointments *and sponsored* farsighted legislation. [compound verb] The first months of his administration were *smooth-running and successful.* [compound adjectives] However, the period *quickly and unexpectedly* came to an end. [compound adverbs] There were many successes: *establishment of the Alliance for Progress to aid Latin America, increased foreign aid to underdeveloped nations, the development of the Peace Corps, and reduced tariffs to encourage foreign trade.* [compound noun phrases] *Yet within a few months, an attempt by Cuban exiles to invade Cuba failed, communist forces expanded their operations in Laos and Vietnam, and the East Germans built the Berlin Wall.* [compound independent clauses, which form a compound sentence]

ANSWERS: EXERCISE 7-11

1. complex
2. simple
3. complex
4. compound
5. simple
6. compound

➡

Answers: Exercise 7-11 (continued)
  7. compound
  8. compound-complex
  9. compound-complex
 10. complex

7. The heap of bacteria disappears quickly, but a few bacteria always survive contact with the antibiotic.

8. These surviving bacteria are immune to that antibiotic, and they are very dangerous because they pass on this immunity to all their descendants.

9. The bacteria once again multiply, and in a few hours, they build up another heap that looks just like the first one.

10. This time, however, the researcher finds that the antibiotic will not kill the growing pile of bacteria in the Petri dish.

8

VERBS

8a Understanding verbs

In English, a **verb** tells of an action, an occurrence, or a state of being. Verbs also tell when something occurs: in the present, in the past, or in the future.

Many people **will overeat** on Thanksgiving. [action]

Mother's Day **fell** early this year. [occurrence]

Memorial Day **is** tomorrow. [state of being]

To learn more about the information verbs convey, see Chart 59. For types of verbs, see Chart 60.

⊙ **Information that verbs convey**   **59**

PERSON	Who or what acts or experiences an action—*first person* (the one speaking), *second person* (the one being spoken to), or *third person* (the person or thing being spoken about)
NUMBER	How many SUBJECTS act or experience an action—*singular* (one) or *plural* (more than one)
TENSE	When an action occurs—*past, present,* or *future* (see 8g–8k)
MOOD	What attitude is expressed toward the action—*indicative, imperative,* or *subjunctive* (see 8l and 8m)
VOICE	Whether the subject acts or is acted upon—*active voice* or *passive voice* (see 8n and 8o)

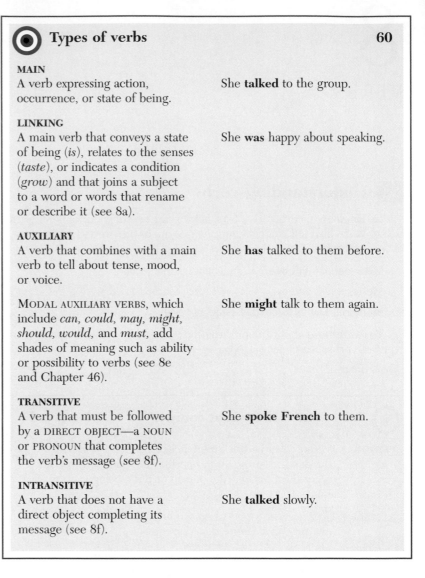

Types of verbs   **60**

MAIN
A verb expressing action, occurrence, or state of being.

She **talked** to the group.

LINKING
A main verb that conveys a state of being (*is*), relates to the senses (*taste*), or indicates a condition (*grow*) and that joins a subject to a word or words that rename or describe it (see 8a).

She **was** happy about speaking.

AUXILIARY
A verb that combines with a main verb to tell about tense, mood, or voice.

She **has** talked to them before.

MODAL AUXILIARY VERBS, which include *can, could, may, might, should, would,* and *must,* add shades of meaning such as ability or possibility to verbs (see 8e and Chapter 46).

She **might** talk to them again.

TRANSITIVE
A verb that must be followed by a DIRECT OBJECT—a NOUN or PRONOUN that completes the verb's message (see 8f).

She **spoke French** to them.

INTRANSITIVE
A verb that does not have a direct object completing its message (see 8f).

She **talked** slowly.

Linking verbs are main verbs that indicate a state of being or a condition. They link a SUBJECT with a word (or words) that renames or describes the subject, a **subject complement.** Some people think of a linking verb as an equal sign between a subject and its complement. Chart 61 presents an overview of linking verbs.

◎ Linking verbs 61

■ Linking verbs may be forms of the verb *be* (*am, is, was, were;* see section 8e for a complete list).

George Washington **was** president.

SUBJECT — LINKING VERB — COMPLEMENT (PREDICATE NOMINATIVE: RENAMES SUBJECT)

■ Linking verbs may deal with the senses (*look, smell, taste, sound, feel*).

George Washington **sounded** confident.

SUBJECT — LINKING VERB — COMPLEMENT (PREDICATE ADJECTIVE: DESCRIBES SUBJECT)

■ Certain other verbs that convey a sense of existing or becoming—*appear, seem, become, get, grow, turn, remain, stay,* and *prove,* for example—can be linking verbs.

George Washington **grew** old.

SUBJECT — LINKING VERB — COMPLEMENT (PREDICATE ADJECTIVE: DESCRIBES SUBJECT)

■ To test whether a verb other than a form of *be* is functioning as a linking verb, substitute *was* (for a singular subject) or *were* (for a plural subject) for the original verb. If the sentence makes sense, the original verb is functioning as a linking verb.

NO George Washington **grew** a beard → George Washington **was** a beard. [*Grew* is not functioning as a linking verb.]

YES George Washington grew old → George Washington **was** old. [*Grew* is functioning as a linking verb.]

Some grammar systems call a NOUN or PRONOUN following a linking verb a **predicate nominative** and an ADJECTIVE following a linking verb a **predicate adjective**.

QUOTATION: ON WRITING

Writers have two main problems. One is writer's block, when the words won't come at all, and the other is "logorrhea," when the words come so fast that they can hardly get to the wastebasket in time.
—Cecilia Bartholomew

TEACHING TIP

Although *be* is always a linking verb, other verbs may or may not be, depending on how they are used in a given sentence. When in doubt, try substituting a form of *be:* If the sentence makes sense, it contains a linking verb; if it no longer makes sense, it does not contain a linking verb.

He *seems* ill. / He *is* ill. [The verb *be* makes sense, so *seems* is a linking verb.]

Daisies *grow* in the park. / Daisies *are* in the park. [The verb *be* makes sense, so *grow* is a linking verb.]

Joyce *grows* orchids. / Joyce *is* orchids. [The verb *be* does not make sense, so *grows* is not a linking verb.]

WORD HISTORY

Infinitive comes from the Latin *infinitivus*, meaning "unlimited" or "indefinite." This is appropriate, since the infinitive shows no person or number. Coming from the same Latin verb, *finire* ("to limit"), the term *finite verb* refers to a verb that is limited by person and number. In contrast, a *nonfinite verb* (also known as a *verbal*) is not limited in these ways.

TEACHING TIP

Leaving the *-s* off verbs is a common error, even among students who can quote the rule for its use. Many of these students speak or have studied second languages that have more complex systems of verb endings than English does. A discussion of the English *-s* in the context of other languages the students know may reduce the number of carelessly omitted *-s*'s.

Here is a comparison of the verb *speak* (present tense) in four languages, with endings shown in boldface. When no pronouns appear, the pronoun is communicated by the verb's ending.

Singular	*Plural*
ENGLISH	
I speak	we speak
you speak	you speak
he, she, it speaks	they speak
SPANISH	
habl**o**	habl**amos**
habl**as**	habl**áis**
habl**a**	habl**an**
ITALIAN	
parl**o**	parl**iamo**
parl**i**	parl**ate**
parl**a**	parl**ano**
FRENCH	
je parl**e**	nous parl**ons**
tu parl**es**	vous parl**ez**
il, elle, on parl**e**	ils, elles parl**ent**

VERB FORMS

8b Recognizing the forms of main verbs

A **main verb** names an action (*People **dance***), an occurrence (*Mother's Day **fell** early this year*), or a state of being (*It **will be** warm tomorrow*). Every main verb has five forms.

■ The **simple form** conveys an action, occurrence, or state of being taking place in the present (*I **laugh***) or, with an AUXILIARY VERB, in the future (*I **will laugh***).

■ The **past-tense form** is the basis for conveying an action, occurrence, or state completed in the past (*I **laughed***). REGULAR VERBS add *-ed* or *-d* to the simple form. IRREGULAR VERBS vary (see Chart 62).

■ The **past-participle form** in regular verbs uses the same form as the past tense. Irregular verbs vary; see Chart 62. To function as a verb, a past participle must combine with a SUBJECT and one or more auxiliary verbs (*I **have laughed***). Otherwise, past participles function as ADJECTIVES (***crumbled** cookies*).

■ The **present-participle form** adds *-ing* to the simple form (*laughing*). To function as a verb, a present participle combines with a subject and one or more auxiliary verbs (*I **was laughing***). Otherwise, present participles function as adjectives (*my **laughing** friends*) or as NOUNS (***Laughing** is healthy*).

■ The **infinitive** uses the simple form, usually but not always following *to* (*I started **to laugh***). The infinitive functions as a noun or an adjective, not a verb.

⊕ **ESL NOTE:** When they function as parts of speech other than verbs, verb forms are called **verbals** (see 7d). Present participles functioning as nouns are called **gerunds.** For information about using gerunds and infinitives as objects after certain verbs, see Chapter 45. ⊕

8c Using the -s form of verbs

The *-s* form of a verb is the third-person singular in the PRESENT TENSE. The ending *-s* (or *-es*) is added to the verb's simple form (for example, *smell* becomes *smells*: *The bread **smells** delicious*).

Be and *have* are irregular verbs. For the third-person singular, present tense, *be* uses *is* and *have* uses *has*.

The cheesecake **is** popular.

The eclair **has** chocolate on top.

Even if you tend to drop the *-s* or *-es* ending when you speak, use it when you write. Proofread carefully for the correct use of the *-s* form.

❶ **USAGE ALERT:** Academic writing requires standard third-person singular forms in the present tense: for example, **he is** (not *he be*) *hungry*; *the* **bakery has** (not *the bakery have*) *fresh bread*. ❗

EXERCISE 8-1

Consulting sections 8b and 8c, rewrite each sentence, changing the subject to the word or words given in parentheses. Change the form of the verb shown in italics to match this new subject. Keep all sentences in the present tense.

EXAMPLE   The song of a bird *represents* different things to different
listeners. (The songs of birds)

The songs of birds represent different things to different
listeners.

1. A poet *imagines* a songbird as a fellow poet creating beautiful art. (Poets)
2. To a biologist, however, singing birds *communicate* practical information. (a singing bird)
3. A male sparrow that *whistles* one melody to attract a mate *sings* a different tune to warn off other male sparrows. (Male sparrows)
4. Female redwing blackbirds usually *distinguish* a male redwing's song from a mockingbird's imitation, but a male redwing almost never *hears* the difference. (A female redwing blackbird) (male redwings)
5. Nevertheless, in experiments, female birds *are* sometimes fooled by a carved wooden male and a recorded mating song. (a female bird)

8d   Using regular and irregular verbs

Most verbs in English are *regular*. A **regular verb** forms its past tense and past participle by adding *-ed* or *-d* to the simple form.

Speakers sometimes skip over the *-ed* sound, pronouncing it softly or not at all. If you are not used to hearing or pronouncing this sound, proofread carefully for *-ed* endings in your writing.

NO   The cake was **suppose** to be tasty.

YES   The cake was **supposed** to be tasty.

About two hundred verbs in English are *irregular*. Unfortunately, a verb's simple form does not provide a clue about whether the verb is irregular or regular. **Irregular verbs** do not consistently add *-ed* or *-d* to form the past tense and past participle. Some irregular verbs change an internal vowel to make past tense and past participle: *sing, sang, sung*. Some change an internal vowel and add an ending other than *-ed*

ANSWERS: EXERCISE 8-1

1. Poets imagine
2. a singing bird communicates
3. Male sparrows that whistle . . . sing
4. A female redwing blackbird usually distinguishes; male redwings almost never hear
5. a female bird is

QUOTATION: ON WRITING

I set myself 600 words a day as a minimum output, regardless of the weather, my state of mind or if I'm sick or well. There must be 600 finished words—not almost right words. Before you ask, I'll tell you that yes, I do write 600 at the top of my pad every day, and I keep track of the word count to insure I reach my quota daily—without fail.

—Arthur Hailey

WORD HISTORY

The word *conjugation* has been used since the early sixteenth century to refer to all the forms of a particular verb. *Conjugation* and *conjugate* both come from the Latin *conjugāre*, basically meaning "to join together." In Latin, a list of the forms of a verb was called a *conjugatio*, and *conjugata verba* (literally "joined words") referred to words that were etymologically related.

True ease in writing comes from art, not chance,
As those move easiest who have learned to dance.
'Tis not enough no harshness gives offense,
The sound must seem an echo to the sense.

—Alexander Pope

BACKGROUND

Old English, ancestor of our language as we know it today, used only two tenses, present and past. All other information, such as number, person, mood, and voice, was indicated by inflectional endings. All that remains of the personal endings is the -*es* or -*s* of the third-person singular, which comes from the Middle English and Early Modern English -*eth* used by Chaucer, translators of the King James Bible, and Shakespeare. English verbs, like all their Germanic cognates, are distinguished by their division into weak and strong classes. In Old English, the strong classes indicated tense by changing the medial vowels; the weak ones did so by their endings. After the Norman Invasion, when French and Latin became the languages of power (the court and the church), many strong English verbs became weak, adopting the -*ed* ending to indicate tense changes. New verbs admitted to the language were all placed in the weak category. Today, the mixture of strong and weak forms makes it necessary for English speakers to memorize the principal parts of irregular verbs.

or -*d*: *grow, grew, grown.* Some use the simple form throughout: *cost, cost, cost.*

Although you can always look up the principal parts of any verb, memorizing any you do not know is much more efficient in the long run. The most frequently used irregular verbs are listed in Chart 62.

⊙ **Common irregular verbs** **62**

SIMPLE FORM	PAST TENSE	PAST PARTICIPLE
arise	arose	arisen
awake	awoke *or* awaked	awaked *or* awoken
be (is, am, are)	was, were	been
bear	bore	borne *or* born
beat	beat	beaten
become	became	become
begin	began	begun
bend	bent	bent
bet	bet	bet
bid ("to offer")	bid	bid
bid ("to command")	bade	bidden
bind	bound	bound
bite	bit	bitten *or* bit
blow	blew	blown
break	broke	broken
bring	brought	brought
build	built	built
burst	burst	burst
buy	bought	bought
cast	cast	cast
catch	caught	caught
choose	chose	chosen
cling	clung	clung
come	came	come
cost	cost	cost
creep	crept	crept
cut	cut	cut
deal	dealt	dealt
dig	dug	dug
dive	dived *or* dove	dived
do	did	done
draw	drew	drawn
drink	drank	drunk

→

Common irregular verbs (*continued*) 62

SIMPLE FORM	PAST TENSE	PAST PARTICIPLE
drive	drove	driven
eat	ate	eaten
fall	fell	fallen
feed	fed	fed
feel	felt	felt
fight	fought	fought
find	found	found
flee	fled	fled
fling	flung	flung
fly	flew	flown
forbid	forbade *or* forbad	forbidden
forget	forgot	forgotten *or* forgot
forgive	forgave	forgiven
forsake	forsook	forsaken
freeze	froze	frozen
get	got	got *or* gotten
give	gave	given
go	went	gone
grow	grew	grown
hang ("to suspend")*	hung	hung
have	had	had
hear	heard	heard
hide	hid	hidden
hit	hit	hit
hurt	hurt	hurt
keep	kept	kept
know	knew	known
lay	laid	laid
lead	led	led
leave	left	left
lend	lent	lent
let	let	let
lie	lay	lain
light	lighted *or* lit	lighted *or* lit
lose	lost	lost
make	made	made
mean	meant	meant

*When it means "to execute by hanging," *hang* is a regular verb: *In wartime, some armies routinely **hanged** deserters.*

→

QUOTATION: ON WRITING

I started off with the desire to use language experimentally. Then I saw that the right way was the way of simplicity. Straight sentences, no involutions, no ambiguities. Not much description, description isn't my line. Get on with the story. Present the outside world economically and exactly.

—Graham Greene

BACKGROUND

In late antiquity and the Middle Ages, grammar, rhetoric, and logic were organized into the *trivium*, the three language arts of education. The trivium and *quadrivium* (geometry, arithmetic, astronomy, and music) together formed the seven liberal arts. Grammar meant the study of Latin until the eighteenth and nineteenth centuries, when English and other vernacular languages began to displace Latin as the language of education.

Common irregular verbs (*continued*)   62

SIMPLE FORM	PAST TENSE	PAST PARTICIPLE
pay	paid	paid
prove	proved	proved *or* proven
quit	quit	quit
read	read	read
rid	rid	rid
ride	rode	ridden
ring	rang	rung
rise	rose	risen
run	ran	run
say	said	said
see	saw	seen
seek	sought	sought
send	sent	sent
set	set	set
shake	shook	shaken
shine ("to glow")*	shone	shone
shoot	shot	shot
show	showed	shown *or* showed
shrink	shrank	shrunk
sing	sang	sung
sink	sank *or* sunk	sunk
sit	sat	sat
slay	slew	slain
sleep	slept	slept
sling	slung	slung
speak	spoke	spoken
spend	spent	spent
spin	spun	spun
spring	sprang *or* sprung	sprung
stand	stood	stood
steal	stole	stolen
sting	stung	stung
stink	stank *or* stunk	stunk
stride	strode	stridden
strike	struck	struck
strive	strove	striven
swear	swore	sworn

*When it means "to polish," *shine* is a regular verb: We **shined** our shoes.

→

SIMPLE FORM	PAST TENSE	PAST PARTICIPLE

Common irregular verbs (continued)   62

SIMPLE FORM	PAST TENSE	PAST PARTICIPLE
sweep	swept	swept
swim	swam	swum
swing	swung	swung
take	took	taken
teach	taught	taught
tear	tore	torn
tell	told	told
think	thought	thought
throw	threw	thrown
understand	understood	understood
wake	woke *or* waked	waked *or* woken
wear	wore	worn
wring	wrung	wrung
write	wrote	written

🛈 **SPELLING ALERT:** For information about when to change a *y* to an *i* or double a final consonant before adding the *-ed* ending, see Chart 108 in section 22c. ❗

EXERCISE 8-2

Consulting section 8d, write the correct past-tense form of the regular verb (simple form) in parentheses.

EXAMPLE   Psychologists often (wonder) **wondered** about the saying that people's emotions are contagious.

(1) Researchers (report) _____ that people looking at pictures of smiling or angry faces unconsciously (imitate) _____ the same expressions. (2) The subjects who (display) _____ these facial expressions (experience) _____ the feelings that go with them. (3) People who (copy) _____ each other's gestures when talking also (transmit) _____ emotions to one another. (4) The researchers (describe) _____ the entire process in medical terms. (5) According to the researchers, the people in the study ("catch") _____ an "emotional virus," which (seem) _____ to make it easier for them to get along.

ANSWERS: EXERCISE 8-2
1. reported; imitated
2. displayed; experienced
3. copied; transmitted
4. described
5. "caught"; seemed

ANSWERS: EXERCISE 8-3

1. rose; saw; crept
2. sprang; caught; ate
3. stole; stood
4. bent; drank
5. drew; froze; fled
6. laid: swam; lay
7. wore; grew; left; flew
8. saw; came; sat; took; did
9. found; caught; brought; fed
10. shrank; led; sought
11. broke; burst; fell; swept

EXERCISE 8-3

Consulting section 8d, in each blank write the correct past-tense form of the irregular verb for which the simple form is given in parentheses. Use the list of irregular verbs in Chart 62.

EXAMPLE   In a small hole at the top of a tall saguaro cactus, two elf owls (sit) **sat** watching the desert.

(1) As the sun (rise) _____, the elf owls (see) _____ a roadrunner stalking a kingsnake as it (creep) _____ toward their nest. (2) The roadrunner (spring) _____ onto the snake, (catch) _____ it by the head, and then (eat) _____ it slowly. (3) At night, the coyotes, foxes, skunks, and rabbits of the desert (steal) _____ to the waterhole at the foot of the saguaro and (stand) _____ there drinking thirstily. (4) A shaggy mountain sheep, with huge corkscrew horns, (bend) _____ its head and (drink) _____ at the pool. (5) When a mountain lion (draw) _____ near, the terrified sheep (freeze) _____ and then (flee) _____. (6) The mountain lion (lay) _____ down its catch, (swim) _____ in the waterhole, and then (lie) _____ in the sand to eat the rabbit it had caught. (7) As the night (wear) _____ on, the female elf owl (grow) _____ tired of tending her eggs, so she (leave) _____ the nest in the saguaro and (fly) _____ off. (8) When the male elf owl (see) _____ her leave, he (come) _____ to the nest and (sit) _____ on the eggs for the female while she (take) _____ a break and (do) _____ the hunting. (9) While hunting, the female (find) _____ a wood spider, (catch) _____ it, (bring) _____ it to the nest, and (feed) _____ it to her mate. (10) In time, the waterhole (shrink) _____ to a puddle, and the desert animals, (lead) _____ by the elf owls, desperately (seek) _____ new sources of water. (11) The drought (break) _____ in late July, when storm clouds (burst) _____ overhead, rain (fall) _____ in torrents, and flash floods (sweep) _____ through, restoring the desert to life.

8e Using auxiliary verbs

Auxiliary verbs, also called **helping verbs,** combine with MAIN VERBS to make VERB PHRASES.

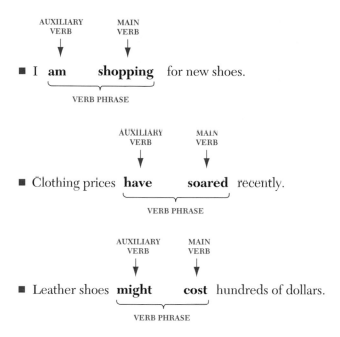

■ I **am** **shopping** for new shoes.

AUXILIARY VERB | MAIN VERB
VERB PHRASE

■ Clothing prices **have** **soared** recently.

AUXILIARY VERB | MAIN VERB
VERB PHRASE

■ Leather shoes **might** **cost** hundreds of dollars.

AUXILIARY VERB | MAIN VERB
VERB PHRASE

WORD HISTORY

An auxiliary verb is also called a helping verb, and, not surprisingly, auxiliary comes from *auxiliarius*, a Latin word for "help." Linking verbs were, until recently, often called *copulative verbs*. This usage dates back to the seventeenth century and comes from the Latin *copulativus*, meaning "connective."

The three most common auxiliary verbs—*be*, *do*, and *have*—can also be main verbs. Their forms vary more than usual; see Charts 63 and 64.

◉ **The forms of the verb** *be*   **63**

SIMPLE FORM	be
-s FORM	is
PAST TENSE	was, were
PRESENT PARTICIPLE	being
PAST PARTICIPLE	been

Person	Present Tense	Past Tense
I	am	was
you (singular)	are	were
he, she, it	is	was
we	are	were
you (plural)	are	were
they	are	were

EXTRA EXERCISE A

Identify all modal auxiliaries in the following passage. (Answers appear in italics.)

Most professionals in the field of medicine agree that the public *ought to* be better informed about recent developments in medical science. One of the tools that patients frequently experience but *may* know little about is the X-ray. Its discoverer, Professor Wilhelm Roentgen, thought he *might* have a powerful new means of examining the body when, in 1895, he saw the glimmer of a fluorescent screen. His discovery meant that medical professionals *could* peer into the innermost recesses of the body without surgery. For example, Dr. William B. Cannon realized that fluoroscopy *could* be used to examine the alimentary canal or digestive system. Today X-ray means that doctors *can* carry diagnostic methods to previously inaccessible areas of the human body by painless techniques. A list of all of the diagnostic uses of X-ray films *would* be too lengthy to include here, but it is safe to say that they *can* be used on all parts of the body. Of course, because improper use of X-rays *may* be harmful, technologists *should* have adequate training. They *must* complete a rigorous course of study before being allowed to operate X-ray machines.

—Emily Gordon

ANSWERS: EXERCISE 8-4

The following answers create the only possible set. Although *can* is not grammatically incorrect in item 3, it makes no sense in this context, and only *can* is correct in item 5. Some varieties of English would →

⊙ The forms of the verbs *do* and *have*   64

SIMPLE FORM	do	have
PAST TENSE	did	had
PAST PARTICIPLE	done	had
-s FORM	does	has
PRESENT PARTICIPLE	doing	having

🔴 **ALERT:** Academic writing requires standard forms and uses of the verb *be* as a main verb and as an auxiliary verb.

The gym **is** [not *be*] a busy place. [*is* = linking verb, which acts as a main verb; *busy place* is the subject complement.]

The gym **is** [not *be*] filling with spectators. [*is* = auxiliary verb] ❗

Be, do, and *have* are also the only auxiliary verbs that change form. For more about verb forms, see sections 8b and 8c.

🌐 **ESL NOTE:** When used as auxiliary verbs, *be, do,* and *have* change form to agree with a third-person singular subject, and the main verb does not add *-s*.

NO **Does** the library **closes** at 6:00?

YES **Does** the library **close** at 6:00? 🌐

Can, could, may, might, must, shall, should, will, and *would,* among others, are **modal auxiliary verbs.** Modals never change form. They communicate attitudes of ability, permission, obligation, advisability, necessity, or possibility.

Exercise **can lengthen** lives. [possibility]

The exercise **must occur** regularly. [necessity, obligation]

People **should protect** their bodies. [advisability]

May I exercise? [permission]

She **can jog** for five miles. [ability]

🌐 **ESL NOTE:** For more about modal auxiliary verbs and the meanings they communicate, see Chapter 46. 🌐

EXERCISE 8-4

Consulting section 8e, use the auxiliary verbs from the following list to fill in the blanks. Although more than one correct answer is possible for some sentences, you should use each auxiliary verb only once.

are   ~~may~~   should   can   has   do

EXAMPLE   It **may** come as a surprise to discover that perfumes, hair sprays, and smelly soaps attract bears.

(1) Many people who camp in the wild know that the smell of food _____ often brought a hungry bear to a campsite. (2) Fewer people realize that curious bears _____ sometimes attracted to campsites that smell of perfume, hair spray, or soap. (3) Therefore, if you go camping in the woods or the mountains, you _____ avoid smelly cosmetics and put away all your food and garbage. (4) If you ever _____ meet a bear in the wild, stay calm and do not try to protect your food. (5) Talking to the animal in a quiet voice while backing off slowly is a better strategy than running away, because an excited bear _____ run as fast as a racehorse.

EXERCISE 8-5

Consulting section 8e, use each of the auxiliary verbs listed here to fill in the blanks. Although more than one correct answer is possible for some sentences, you should use each auxiliary verb only once.

could   have   ~~may~~   was   can   will

EXAMPLE   If you have saved your old comic books, you **may** be able to sell them to a collector.

(1) Collectors _____ paid huge sums for old toys and many other mass-produced items, even ones that are not antiques.
(2) A Superman ring that was given away as a free promotion in 1940 _____ recently sold for $125,000. (3) An original 1959 Barbie doll _____ bring its seller well over $1,000.
(4) Unfortunately, a damaged Barbie doll or other toy _____ nearly always sell for much less than one in perfect condition.
(5) Some young people who threw out their old baseball card collections years ago _____ be wealthy adults now if only they had saved those cards!

8f Using intransitive and transitive verbs

A verb is **intransitive** when an object is not required to complete its meaning: *I sing*. A verb is **transitive** when an object is necessary to complete its meaning: *I need a guitar*. Some verbs are transitive only (for

Answers: Exercise 8-4 (continued)
allow *should* in item 4 (expressing a somewhat remote possibility), but this usage is not normally found in contemporary American English, and only *should* is correct in item 3.

1. has
2. are
3. should
4. do
5. can

ANSWERS AND COVERAGE: EXERCISE 8-5

Item 3 in this exercise has three possible answers, but in the context of the other items, its answer must be *can*. *Will* must be reserved for item 4, where it is the only possible choice, and *could* must be saved for item 5, for which no other choice is appropriate.

1. have
2. was
3. can [*will* is acceptable, suggesting certainty; *could* is an acceptable choice for expressing a remote possibility or speculation]
4. will
5. could

A HUMOROUS NOTE

The English major was working for the summer as morning shift manager at a fast-food restaurant. One day, her least reliable worker was missing again. She called over a friend of the boy and asked, "Where's Bill?"

"He decided to lay on the beach," replied the friend.

Not wishing to embarrass the worker but unable to overcome the urge to correct him, the manager whispered, "Lie."

"All right," he said with a shrug. "Bill had to take his cat to the vet for an emergency appendectomy."

EXTRA EXERCISE B

Circle all transitive verbs and underline all intransitive verbs in the following paragraph.

1. Yellowstone National Park is the oldest and largest park in the national system.
2. It lies in the northwestern corner of Wyoming, slightly overlapping the boundaries of Montana on the north and Idaho on the west and south.
3. The planners originally designed the park to run 62 miles from east to west and 54 miles from north to south.
4. Yellowstone has several lofty plateaus, and the Continental Divide crosses it.
5. The Yellowstone River flows north into Yellowstone Lake and then through its canyon across Montana to join the Missouri.
6. The most famous sights in Yellowstone Park are the geysers.
7. The park has more than three thousand springs, pools, and geysers.
8. Old Faithful is the most famous of the geysers, but in the same basin with it are a number of other impressive water jets.
9. Wildlife in the park, which includes bear, deer, elk, antelope, and mountain sheep, is protected.

example, *need, have, like, owe, remember*). Many verbs have both transitive and intransitive meanings. Other verbs are intransitive only. Dictionaries usually label verbs as transitive (*vt*) or intransitive (*vi*). Chart 65 shows how transitive and intransitive verbs function.

◎ Comparison of intransitive and transitive verbs · 65

INTRANSITIVE (OBJECT NOT NEEDED)

They **sat** together quietly. [*Together* and *quietly* are not DIRECT OBJECTS; they are MODIFIERS.]

The cat **sees** in the dark. [*In the dark* is not a direct object; it is a modifier.]

I can **hear** well. [*Well* is not a direct object; it is a modifier.]

TRANSITIVE (OBJECT NEEDED)

They **sent** a birthday card to me. [*birthday card* = direct object]

The cat **sees** the dog. [*dog* = direct object]

I can **hear** you. [*you* = direct object]

The verbs *lie* and *lay* are particularly confusing. *Lie* is intransitive (it cannot be followed by an object). *Lay* is transitive (it must be followed by an object). Some of their forms, however, are similar. Get to know these forms so that you can use them with ease.

	LIE	LAY
SIMPLE FORM	lie	lay
PAST TENSE	lay	laid
PAST PARTICIPLE	lain	laid
-s FORM	lies	lays
PRESENT PARTICIPLE	lying	laying

Lie means "to recline, to place oneself down, or to remain"; *lay* means "to place something down." Note from the examples that the word *lay* is both the past tense of *lie* and the present-tense simple form of *lay*.

	INTRANSITIVE
PRESENT TENSE	The hikers **lie** down to rest.
PAST TENSE	The hikers **lay** down to rest.
	TRANSITIVE
PRESENT TENSE	The hikers **lay** their backpacks on a rock. [*Backpacks* is an object.]
PAST TENSE	The hikers **laid** their backpacks on a rock. [*Backpacks* is an object.]

196 →

Two other verb pairs may also be confusing: *raise* and *rise* and *set* and *sit*.

Raise and *set* are transitive (they must be followed by an object). *Rise* and *sit* are intransitive (they cannot be followed by an object). These two pairs do not cause as much confusion as *lay* and *lie*, however, because, unlike *lay* and *lie*, they do not share any forms: *raise, raised, raised; rise, rose, risen; set, set, set; sit, sat, sat.*

EXERCISE 8-6

Consulting section 8f, circle the correct word of each pair in parentheses.

EXAMPLE   Whenever I come home, I always check to see where my cat is (laying, (lying)).

(1) Coming home from jogging one morning, I (laid, lay) my keys on the counter and saw my cat, Andy, (laying, lying) in a patch of sunlight on the living room floor. (2) When I (sat, set) down beside him, he (raised, rose) up on his toes, stretched, and then (laid, lay) down a few feet away. (3) (Sitting, Setting) there, I reached out to Andy, and my contrary cat jumped up onto the couch. As he landed, I heard a clinking noise. (4) I (raised, rose) the bottom of the slip-cover, and there (laid, lay) my favorite earrings, the ones I thought I had lost last week. Deciding he had earned a special privilege, Andy curled up on a red silk pillow in the corner of the couch. (5) Since the earrings now (laid, lay) safely in my pocket, I let him (lay, lie) there undisturbed.

VERB TENSE

8g   Understanding verb tense

Verb **tense** conveys time. Verbs show tense (time) by changing form. English has six verb tenses, divided into *simple* and *perfect* groups. The three **simple tenses** divide time into *present, past,* and *future.* The **present tense** describes what happens regularly, what takes place in the present, and what is consistently or generally true: *Rick **wants** to speak Spanish fluently.* The **past tense** tells of an action completed or a condition ended: *Rick **wanted** to improve rapidly.* The **future tense** indicates action yet to be taken or a condition not yet experienced: *Rick **will want** to progress even further next year.*

The three **perfect tenses** also divide time into *present, past,* and *future.* They show more complex time relationships than the simple tenses do, as explained in section 8i.

Answers to Extra Exercise B

1. is (intransitive)
2. lies (intransitive)
3. designed (transitive)
4. has (transitive); crosses (transitive)
5. flows (intransitive)
6. are (intransitive)
7. has (transitive)
8. is (intransitive); are (intransitive)
9. includes (transitive); is (intransitive)

ANSWERS AND COVERAGE: EXERCISE 8-6

1. laid [first-person singular past of *lay*]; lying [third-person singular present progressive form of *lie*]
2. sat; rose; lay [third person singular past of *lie*]
3. Sitting [past participle of *sit*]
4. raised; lay [third-person plural present of *lay*]
5. lay [third-person plural past of *lie*]; lie [third-person singular present of *lie*]

For practice identifying verbs and forming past-tense verbs, rewrite the following paragraph by Gretel Ehrlich, changing the present-tense verbs to past tense. (Answers appear in italics.)

Recuperation is (*was*) like spring: dormancy and vitality collide (*collided*). In any year I'm (*I was*) like a bear, a partial hibernator. During January thaws I stick (*stuck*) my nose out and peruse (*perused*) the frozen desolation as if reading a book whose language I don't (*didn't*) know. In March I'm (*I was*) ramshackle, weak in the knees, giddy, dazzled by broken-backed clouds, the passing of Halley's comet, the on-and-off strobe of sun. Like a sheepherder I X (*Xed*) out each calendar day as if time were (*no change, subjunctive voice*) a forest through which I could clear-cut (*no change, subjunctive voice*) a way to the future. My physicist friend straightens (*straightened*) me out on this point too. The notion of "time passing," like a train through a landscape, is (*was*) an illusion, he says (*said.*) I hold (*held*) the Big Ben clock taken from a dead sheepherder's wagon and look (*looked*) at it. The clock measures (*measured*) intervals of time, not the speed of time, and the calendar is (*was*) a scaffolding we hang (*hung*) as if time were (*no change, subjunctive voice*) rushing water we could harness (*no change, subjunctive voice.*) Time-bound, I hinge (*hinged*) myself to a linear bias—cause and effect all laid out in a neat row—and in this we learn (*learned*) two things: blame and shame.

—Gretel Ehrlich, "Spring"

The three simple tenses and the three perfect tenses also have **progressive forms.** These forms show an ongoing or a continuing dimension to whatever the verb describes, as explained in section 8j. Chart 66 summarizes verb tenses and progressive forms.

⊙ Summary of tenses, including progressive forms   66

Simple Tenses

	REGULAR VERB	IRREGULAR VERB	PROGRESSIVE FORM
PRESENT	I talk	I eat	I am talking; I am eating
PAST	I talked	I ate	I was talking; I was eating
FUTURE	I will talk	I will eat	I will be talking; I will be eating

Perfect Tenses

	REGULAR VERB	IRREGULAR VERB	PROGRESSIVE FORM
PRESENT PERFECT	I have talked	I have eaten	I have been talking; I have been eating
PAST PERFECT	I had talked	I had eaten	I had been talking; I had been eating
FUTURE PERFECT	I will have talked	I will have eaten	I will have been talking; I will have been eating

---

🌐 **ESL NOTE:** Chart 66 shows that most verb tenses are formed by combining one or more AUXILIARY VERBS with the SIMPLE FORM, the PRESENT PARTICIPLE, or the PAST PARTICIPLE of a MAIN VERB. Auxiliary verbs are necessary in the formation of most tenses, so be sure not to omit them.

NO   I **talking** to you.

YES   I **am talking** to you. ✦

8h Using the simple present tense

The **simple present tense** uses the simple form of the verb (see 8b). It describes what happens regularly, what takes place in the present, and what is generally or consistently true. Also, it can convey a future occurrence with verbs like *start, stop, begin, end, arrive,* and *depart.*

Calculus class **meets** every morning. [regularly occurring action]

Mastering calculus **takes** time. [general truth]

The course **ends** in eight weeks. [specific future event]

🛑 **VERB ALERT:** Use the present tense to describe or discuss the action in a work of literature, no matter how old the work (see 37b.2).

In Shakespeare's *Romeo and Juliet,* Juliet's father **wants** her to marry Paris, but Juliet **loves** Romeo. ❗

For action prior to or after the action you are describing or discussing, use the correct sequence of tenses as explained in section 8k.

8i Forming and using the perfect tenses

The **perfect tenses** generally describe actions or occurrences still having an effect at the time of speaking or having an effect until a specified time. They use the AUXILIARY VERB plus the main verb's PAST PARTICIPLE (see 8b). The present perfect uses *has* for THIRD-PERSON SINGULAR SUBJECTS and *have* for all other subjects, along with the past participle.

PRESENT PERFECT	Our government **has offered** to help. [action still in effect]
PRESENT PERFECT	The drought **has created** terrible hardship. [condition still prevailing]
PRESENT PERFECT	We **have** always **believed** in freedom of speech. [condition still true]

For the past perfect, use *had* with the past participle. For the future perfect, use *will have* with the past participle.

PAST PERFECT	As soon as the tornado **had passed,** the heavy rain started. [Both events occurred in the past; the tornado occurred before the rain, so the earlier event uses *had.*]
FUTURE PERFECT	Our chickens' egg production **will have reached** five hundred per day by next year. [The event will occur before a specified time.]

TEACHING TIP: ESL

The term *present* can be confusing for ESL students because in English, the simple present tense does not describe the present moment. Rather, our simple present is "timeless" (The sun *rises* in the east and *sets* in the west) or general (*Democracy* means "rule by the people"). In English, the present moment is expressed in the present progressive. ESL students might need many examples and much practice to grasp the confusing labels. For example, I work in an office [simple present tense]. I am working on a report [present progressive].

Supply the progressive form of an appropriate verb in the blanks in the following sentences. (Answers will vary.)

1. Don't bother me now; I am _____.

2. My brother is _____ to apply for a job in France.

3. The committee is _____ at 5 p.m.

4. The professor was _____ on the topic of the European Union.

5. The doctor was _____ in the hospital.

6. My dog was _____ in the yard.

7. I can't go swimming because I am _____.

8. The garden is _____ more beautifully every day.

9. Whose car is _____ in the driveway?

10. The telephone has been _____ all day.

ANSWERS AND COVERAGE: EXERCISE 8-7

1. discovered [8g, past tense for completed action]

2. was emitting [8j, past progressive for a continuing past action in the past concurrent with the time of *were astounded*]

3. use [8h, simple present for regularly recurring action]; stands, means [8h, simple present for general truth]

4. have been found [8i, present perfect for action completed and condition still prevailing]

5. agree [8h, simple present for general truth]; contradict [8h, simple present for recurring action]

6. believes [8h, simple present for current action]; consist [8h, simple present for general truth]

7. say [8h, simple present for regularly recurring actions]; is collapsing, are generating [8j, present progressive for ongoing events]

8j Forming and using progressive forms

Progressive forms describe an ongoing action or condition. They also express habitual or recurring actions or conditions.

The **present progressive** uses the present-tense form of *be* that agrees with the subject in PERSON and NUMBER, plus the *-ing* form (present participle) of the main verb: *I am thinking, you are thinking, she is thinking.* The **past progressive** uses *was* or *were* to agree with the subject in person and number, plus the present participle of the main verb: *I was thinking, you were thinking, she was thinking.* The **future progressive** uses *will be* plus the present participle: *I will be thinking, you will be thinking, she will be thinking.* The **present perfect progressive** uses *have been* or *has been* to agree with the subject, plus the *-ing* form of the main verb. The **past perfect progressive** uses *had been* and the *-ing* form of the main verb. The **future perfect progressive** uses *will have* plus the PAST PARTICIPLE (see 8b).

PRESENT PROGRESSIVE	The smog **is stinging** everyone's eyes. [event taking place now]
PAST PROGRESSIVE	Eye drops **were selling** well last week. [event ongoing in the past within stated limits]
FUTURE PROGRESSIVE	We **will be ordering** more eye drops than usual this month. [recurring event that will take place in the future]
PRESENT PERFECT PROGRESSIVE	Scientists **have been warning** us about air pollution for years. [recurring event that took place in the past and may still take place]
PAST PERFECT PROGRESSIVE	We **had been ordering** three cases of eye drops a month until the smog worsened. [recurring past event that has now ended]
FUTURE PERFECT PROGRESSIVE	In May, we **will have owned** this pharmacy for five years. [ongoing condition to be completed at a specific time in the future]

EXERCISE 8-7

Consulting sections 8g through 8j, select the verb in parentheses that best suits the meaning. If more than one answer is possible, be prepared to explain the differences in meaning between the choices.

EXAMPLE   Before 1960, astronomers (have not spotted, had not spotted) stars that send out both light and sound waves.

Before 1960, astronomers *had not spotted* stars that send out both light and sound waves.

1. In 1960, two astronomers at Mount Palomar Observatory (had discovered, discovered) a starlike object at the edge of the universe.

2. The astronomers were astounded to discover that this object (emits, was emitting) as much light as a thousand galaxies.

3. Today, we (use, are using) the name *quasar,* which (stands, stood) for *quasistellar. Quasistellar* (meant, means) "starlike object."

4. So far, more than three hundred quasars (had been found, have been found) in space.

5. Although astronomers today generally (had agreed, agree) that quasars are powerful, fast-moving energy sources, they (will contradict, contradict) each other's theories about the origin of quasars.

6. One group currently (has been believing, believes) that quasars (consisted, consist) of giant, swirling masses of gas.

7. These astronomers (say, said) that the gas (collapsed, is collapsing) on itself all the time, which is why quasars (had generated, are generating) so much energy.

8. Other scientists (were asserting, assert) that quasars (develop, have been developing) from explosions of matter and antimatter, just as science fiction writers (predict, have been predicting) for many years.

9. When scientists (had conducted, conduct) experiments that (brought, bring) matter and antimatter together, an explosion (will occur, occurs).

10. Until we (understand, understood) more about the birth and death of galaxies, we probably (will not discover, have not discovered) the real story behind quasars.

8k Using accurate tense sequences

Sequences of verb tenses help you deliver messages about actions, occurrences, or states that occur at different times. Using **accurate tense sequences**—that is, showing time relationships correctly—is important for clear communication (see Chart 67).

◉ Summary of sequence of tenses 67

Independent-Clause Verb: Simple Present Tense

Dependent-Clause Verb:

- Use the PRESENT TENSE to show same-time action.
  The director **says** that the movie **is** a tribute to Chaplin.
  I **avoid** shellfish because I **am** allergic to it.

- Use the PAST TENSE to show earlier action.
  I **am** sure that I **deposited** the check.

  →

EXTRA EXERCISE E

Circle the verbs in the following sentences; then name their tenses and explain what meaning is expressed.

1. Dolphins, porpoises, and whales belong to the order Cetacea, which means that they are not fish but mammals.

2. They give birth to their young, nourish them with milk, and have warm blood.

3. Once whales probably lived on the land and walked on four legs, but now they are completely aquatic.

4. Once they had left the land and moved to the water, their body structure changed radically.

5. Because they are land mammals that have become adapted to an aquatic existence, if water enters their lungs, they will die.

6. Consequently, when a whale is diving beneath the surface, it literally holds its breath by closing its nostrils.

7. Whales dive for different periods of time to various depths.

8. The humpback whale has been known to remain submerged for twenty minutes and the blue whale for fifty, though both could probably remain longer if necessary.

9. For years, scientists have been researching the depths to which the various types of whale can dive.

10. The sperm whale has been known to dive to a depth of over 3,000 feet, subjecting it to a pressure of around 1,400 pounds per square inch.

→

Answers to Extra Exercise E

1. belong; means; are [all present tense; express general truths]

2. give; nourish; have [all present tense; express general truths]

3. lived; walked [both past tense; express past events]; are [present tense; expresses current fact]

4. had left [past perfect tense; expresses an act completed in the past before another one took place]; moved, changed [past tense; both express an act completed in the past]

5. are [present tense; expresses current truth]; have become adapted [present perfect tense; act begun and completed in the past but continuing into the present]; enters [present tense; expresses general truth]; will die [future tense; expresses future action]

6. is diving [present progressive tense; expresses an action taking place at the moment]; holds [present tense; expresses regularly occurring action]

7. dive [present tense; expresses habitual action]

8. has been known [present perfect tense; expresses action in the past that continues into the present]; could remain [present tense with modal auxiliary; expresses possible action]

9. have been researching [present perfect progressive; expresses action ongoing in the past and likely to continue into the future]; can dive [present tense with modal auxiliary; expresses possible action]

10. has been known [present perfect tense; expresses action in the past that continues into the present]

Summary of sequence of tenses *(continued)*   67

■ Use the PRESENT PERFECT TENSE to show (1) a period of time extending from some point in the past to the present— often accompanied by *for* or *since*—or (2) an indefinite past time.

They **say** that they **have lived** in Canada since 1979.
I **believe** that I **have seen** that movie before.

■ Use the FUTURE TENSE for action to come.
The book **is** open because I **will be reading** it later.

Independent-Clause Verb: Past Tense
Dependent-Clause Verb:

■ Use the PAST PERFECT TENSE to show earlier action.
The sprinter **knew** that she **had broken** the record.

■ Use the present tense to state a general truth.
Christopher Columbus **discovered** that the world **is** round.

Independent-Clause Verb: Present Perfect or Past Perfect Tense
Dependent-Clause Verb:

■ Use the past tense.
The agar plate **has become** moldy since I **poured** it last week.
Sugar prices **had** already **declined** when artificial sweeteners first **appeared**.

Independent-Clause Verb: Future Tense
Dependent-Clause Verb:

■ Use the present tense to show action happening at the same time.
You **will be** rich if you **win** the prize.

■ Use the past tense to show earlier action.
You **will** surely **win** the prize if you **remembered** to mail the entry form.

■ Use the present perfect tense to show future action earlier than the action of the independent-clause verb.
The river **will flood** again next year unless we **have built** a better dam by then.

→

Summary of sequence of tenses *(continued)*   67

Independent-Clause Verb: Future Perfect Tense
Dependent-Clause Verb:

■ Use either the present tense or the present perfect tense.

Dr. Chang **will have delivered** five thousand babies by the time she **retires.**

Dr. Chang **will have delivered** five thousand babies by the time she **has retired.**

---

❶ **ALERT:** When an independent-clause verb is in the future tense, do not use a future-tense verb in the dependent clause.

NO   The river **will flood** again next year unless we **will build** a better dam.

YES   The river **will flood** again next year unless we **build** a better dam. [Dependent-clause verb *build* is in the present tense.]

YES   The river **will flood** again next year unless we **have built** a better dam by then. [Dependent-clause verb *have built* is in the present perfect tense.] ❗

Tense sequences may include INFINITIVES or PARTICIPLES. To name or describe an activity or occurrence coming either at the same time or after the time expressed in the MAIN VERB, use the **present infinitive.**

I **hope to buy** a used car. [*To buy* comes at a future time. *Hope* is the main verb, and its action is now.]

I **hoped to buy** a used car. [*Hoped* is the main verb, and its action is over.]

I **had hoped to buy** a used car. [*Had hoped* is the main verb, and its action is over.]

The **present participle** (a verb's *-ing* form) can describe action happening at the same time.

Driving his new car, the man **smiled.** [The driving and the smiling happened at the same time.]

To describe an action that occurs before the action in the main verb, use the **perfect infinitive** (*to have gone, to have smiled*), the past participle, or the **present perfect participle** (*having gone, having smiled*).

QUOTATION: ON WRITING

Grammar is the prism through which all writing is refracted.

—Patricia Robertson

ANSWERS AND COVERAGE: EXERCISE 8-8

1. was born [dependent clause in past tense for completed action]; lives [independent clause in present tense for current action]; tours [present tense for regularly occurring action]

2. will treasure [independent clause in future tense for situation continuing beyond action of dependent clause]

3. began [dependent clause in past tense]

4. became [dependent clause in simple past for a completed action]; plays [independent clause in simple present for regularly occurring action]

5. continues [independent clause in simple present]; take [dependent clause in simple present for same-time action]

6. know [dependent clause in simple present for general truth]; has made [independent clause in present perfect for action completed but condition still in effect]

7. was traveling [dependent clause in past progressive for ongoing action completed in the past]; filmed [independent clause in simple past for action completed in the past]

8. became; studied [independent and dependent clauses in simple past for actions completed in the past]

9. fell asleep; was [dependent clauses in simple past for completed past action]

10. failed [dependent clause in simple past for completed past action]

Candida **claimed to have written** fifty short stories in college. [*Claimed* is the main verb, and *to have written* happened first.]

Pleased with the short story, Candida **mailed** it to several magazines. [*Mailed* is the main verb, and *pleased* happened first.]

Having sold one short story, Candida **invested** in a word processor. [*Invested* is the main verb, and *having sold* happened first.]

EXERCISE 8-8

Consulting section 8k, select the verb form in parentheses that best suits the sequence of tenses. Be ready to explain your choices.

EXAMPLE   When he (is, was) seven years old, Yo Yo Ma, possibly the world's greatest living cellist, (moves, moved) to the United States with his family.

When he *was* seven years old, Yo Yo Ma, possibly the world's greatest living cellist, *moved* to the United States with his family.

1. Yo Yo Ma, who (had been born, was born) in France to Chinese parents, (lived, lives) in Boston, Massachusetts, today and (toured, tours) as one of the world's greatest cellists.
2. Years from now, after Mr. Ma has given his last concert, music lovers still (treasure, will treasure) his many fine recordings.
3. Mr. Ma's older sister, Dr. Yeou-Cheng Ma, was nearly the person with the concert career. She had been training to become a concert violinist until her brother's musical genius (began, had begun) to be noticed.
4. Even though Dr. Ma eventually (becomes, became) a physician, she still (had been playing, plays) the violin.
5. The family interest in music (continues, was continuing), for Mr. Ma's children (take, had taken) piano lessons.
6. Although most people today (knew, know) Mr. Ma as a brilliant cellist, he (was making, has made) films as well.
7. One year, while he (had been traveling, was traveling) in the Kalahari Desert, he (films, filmed) dances of southern Africa's Bush people.
8. Mr. Ma first (becomes, became) interested in the Kalahari people when he (had studied, studied) anthropology as an undergraduate at Harvard University.
9. When he shows visitors around Boston now, Mr. Ma has been known to point out the Harvard University library where, he claims, he (fell asleep, was falling asleep) in the stacks when he (had been, was) a student.
10. Indicating another building, Mr. Ma admits that in one of its classrooms he almost (failed, had failed) German.

EXERCISE 8-9

The verbs in each of the following sentences are in correct sequence. For each sentence, change the main verb as directed in the parentheses. Then, consulting section 8k, adjust dependent-clause verbs, infinitives, or participles if necessary to maintain correct verb sequence. Some sentences may have several correct answers.

EXAMPLE   Swimmers who prepare to swim the 21.4-mile English Channel that separates England from France face a difficult challenge. (Change *prepare* to *prepared*.)

Swimmers who *prepared* to swim the 21.4-mile English Channel that separates England from France *faced* a difficult challenge.

1. The swimmers depart from either shore and arrive on a French beach or at the English cliffs equipped with only noninsulated swimsuits, bathing caps, goggles, noseclips, earplugs, grease, and light sticks for night swimming. (Change *depart* to *departed*.)

2. They prepare for the swim by greasing themselves with lanolin and special oils, which make them glide more easily through the cold water. (Change *prepare* to *had prepared*.)

3. Throughout the journey, the swimmers faced obstacles like sewage and oil slicks that sometimes made their tongues and throats swell and caused breathing problems. (Change *faced* to *face*.)

4. Confronting water temperatures as low as 55 degrees Fahrenheit also threatened the swimmers, and many of them fell victim to hypothermia, a below-normal body temperature that can cause death. (Change *threatened* to *threatens*.)

5. Often, after a few miles, even the best swimmers had blue lips and shivering bodies, and they became confused. (Change *had* to *will have*.)

ANSWERS: EXERCISE 8-9

1. The swimmer *departed* from either shore and *arrived* on a French beach or at the English cliffs equipped with only non-insulated swimsuits, bathing caps, goggles, noseclips, earplugs, grease, and light sticks for night swimming.

2. They *had prepared* for the swim by greasing themselves with lanolin and special oils, which *made* them glide more easily through the cold water.

3. Throughout the journey, the swimmers *face* obstacles like sewage and oil slicks that sometimes *make* their tongues and throats swell and *cause* breathing problems.

4. Confronting water temperatures as low as 55 degrees Fahrenheit also *threatens* the swimmers, and many of them *fall* victim to hypothermia, a below-normal body temperature that can cause death.

5. Often, after a few miles, even the best swimmers *will have* blue lips and shivering bodies, and they *will become* confused.

MOOD

81 Understanding mood

Mood refers to a verb's ability to convey an attitude in a sentence. The most common mood in English is the **indicative mood.** It is used for statements about real things, or highly likely ones, and for questions about fact.

INDICATIVE   The door to the tutoring center opened.

She seemed to be looking for someone.

Do you want to see a tutor?

The **imperative mood** expresses commands and direct requests. When the subject is omitted in an imperative sentence—and it often

QUOTATION: ON WRITING

If it were not for the subjunctive, we would be less able to express desire, supposition, doubt; more important, we would find it hard to set up a situation contrary to fact—a shocker, something ridiculous—to see how we would deal with it.

—William Safire

OTHER EXAMPLES OF SUBJUNCTIVE MOOD

People find it interesting to speculate about how the future *could be* affected if a single aspect of our world *were* different today. For example, if the average yearly temperature *were* only a few degrees higher, the oceans *would* rise due to the melting of the polar icecaps. If serious worldwide droughts *were* to occur in several successive summers, the food supply *would* dwindle. Unless science *were* able to divert the swelling oceans or grow crops without the use of water, civilization as we know it *would be* radically changed. It is, consequently, important that everyone *recognize* the importance of environmental decisions. The world *should* not act as though the future *were* inevitably bad. If, in the early part of this century, the industrialized world *had considered* the effects of water and air pollution, our world *would* be a healthier one today.

is—the subject is implied to be either *you* or the indefinite pronoun *anybody, somebody,* or *everybody.*

⊘ **PUNCTUATION ALERT:** Use an exclamation point after a strong command. Use a period after a mild command or a request (see 23a and 23e).

> **IMPERATIVE**   Please shut the door.
> Watch out! That hinge is broken. **!**

The **subjunctive mood** can express speculations and other unreal conditions, conjectures, wishes, recommendations, indirect requests, and demands. Subjunctive verb forms are used much less often in English than they once were. Still, they are common for expressing unreal conditions or conjectures in *if* CLAUSES and in such PHRASES as *far be it from me* and *suffice it to say.*

> **SUBJUNCTIVE**   If **I were** you, I would ask for a tutor.

8m   Using correct subjunctive forms

For the **present subjunctive,** always use the simple form of the verb (see 8b) for all PERSONS and NUMBERS.

> The prosecutor asks that **she testify** [not *testifies*] again.

> It is important that **they be** [not *are*] allowed to testify.

For the **past subjunctive,** use the same form as the simple past tense: *I wish that **I had** a car.* The one exception is for the past subjunctive of *be:* Use *were* for all persons and numbers.

> I wish that **I were** [not *was*] leaving on vacation today.

> They asked if **she were** [not *was*] leaving on vacation today.

8m.1   Using the subjunctive in *if, as if, as though,* and *unless* clauses

In dependent clauses introduced by *if* and sometimes by *unless,* the subjunctive is often used to describe speculations or conditions contrary to fact.

> If **it were** [not *was*] to rain, attendance at the race would be disappointing. [speculation]

> The runner looked as if **he were** [not *was*] winded.

In an *unless* clause, the subjunctive signals that what the clause says is highly unlikely.

> Unless **rain were** [not *was*] to create floods, the race will be held this Sunday. [Floods are highly unlikely.]

❶ **ALERT:** Not every clause introduced by *if, unless, as if,* or *as though* requires the subjunctive. Use the subjunctive only when the dependent clause describes a speculation or condition contrary to fact.

INDICATIVE	If **she is** going to leave late, **I will** drive her to the race. [Her leaving late is highly likely.]
SUBJUNCTIVE	If **she were** going to leave late, **I would** drive her to the race. [Her leaving late is speculative.] ❗

8m.2 Using the subjunctive in *that* clauses for wishes, indirect requests, demands, and recommendations

When *that* clauses describe wishes, requests, demands, or recommendations, the subjunctive can convey the message.

I wish that this **race were** [not *was*] over. [wish about something happening now]

He wishes that **he had seen** [not *saw*] the race. [wish about something that is past]

The judges are demanding that the **doctor examine** [not *examines*] the runners. [demand for something to happen in the future]

❶ **ALERT:** MODAL AUXILIARY VERBS like *would, could, might,* and *should* can convey speculations and conditions contrary to fact: *If the **runner** were* [not *was*] *faster, **we would** see a better race.* When the independent clause expresses a conditional statement with a modal auxiliary verb, be sure to use, in the dependent clause, the appropriate subjunctive form, not another modal auxiliary.

NO	If **I would have** trained for the race, **I might have** won.
YES	If **I had** trained for the race, **I might** have won. ❗

EXERCISE 8-10

Consulting sections 8l and 8m, fill in the blanks with the appropriate subjunctive form of the verb in parentheses.

EXAMPLE Imagining the possibility of brain transplants requires that we (to be) **be** open-minded, as it (to be) **were**.

(1) If almost any organ other than the brain (to be) _____ the candidate for a swap, we would probably give our consent. (2) If the brain (to be) _____ to hold whatever impulses form our personalities, few people would want to risk a transplant. (3) Many popular movies have asked that we (to suspend) _____ disbelief and imagine the consequences should a personality actually (to be) _____ transferred to another body. (4) In real life, however, the

complexities of a successful brain transplant require that not-yet-developed surgical techniques (to be) _____ used. (5) For example, it would be essential that during the actual transplant each one of the 500 trillion nerve connections within the brain (to continue) _____ to function as though the brain (to be) _____ lying undisturbed in a living human body.

VOICE

8n Understanding voice

Voice refers to a verb's ability to show whether a SUBJECT acts or receives the action named by the verb. English has two voices: *active* and *passive.* In the **active voice,** the subject performs the action.

> Most clams **live** in salt water. [The subject *clams* does the acting; clams *live.*]

> They **burrow** into the sandy bottoms of shallow waters. [The subject *they* does the acting; they *burrow.*]

In the **passive voice,** the subject is acted upon, and the person or thing doing the acting often appears in a *by* PHRASE. Verbs in the passive voice add forms of *be* and *have,* as well as *will,* as auxiliaries to the PAST PARTICIPLE of the MAIN VERB.

> Clams **are considered** a delicacy by many people. [The subject *clams* is acted upon *by many people.*]

> They **are** also **admired** by crabs and starfish. [The subject *they* is acted upon *by crabs and starfish.*]

8o Writing in the active voice, not the passive voice, except to convey special types of emphasis

Because the active voice emphasizes the doer of an action, active constructions are more direct and dramatic. Active constructions often use fewer words than passive constructions and are therefore more concise (see 16a.2). Most sentences in the passive voice that indicate the doer of the action can easily be converted to the active voice.

PASSIVE   African tribal masks are often imitated by Western sculptors.

ACTIVE   Western sculptors often imitate African tribal masks.

The passive voice, however, does have some uses. If you learn what they are, you can use the passive to advantage (see 80.1 and 80.2).

80.1 Using the passive voice when the doer of the action is unknown or unimportant

When no one knows who or what did something, the passive voice is useful.

> The lock **was broken** sometime after four o'clock. [Who broke the lock is unknown.]

When the doer of an action is unimportant, writers often use the passive voice.

> In 1899, the year I was born, a peace conference **was held** at The Hague. [The doers of the action—holders of the conference—are unimportant to White's point.]
>
> —E. B. White, "Unity"

80.2 Using the passive voice to focus attention on the action rather than on the doer of the action

The passive voice emphasizes the action, whereas the active voice focuses on the doer of the action. In a passage about important contributions to the history of science, you might want to emphasize a doer by using the active voice.

> **ACTIVE**   **Joseph Priestley discovered** oxygen in 1774.

But in a passage summarizing what is known about oxygen, you may want to make oxygen, rather than Priestley, the sentence subject. Doing so requires a passive-voice verb.

> **PASSIVE**   **Oxygen was discovered** in 1774 by Joseph Priestley.
>
> **PASSIVE**   The unsigned letter **was sent** before it **could be retrieved** from the mailroom. [emphasis on events, not on the doers of the action]
>
> **ACTIVE**   The **postal clerk sent** the unsigned letter before **I could retrieve** it from the mailroom. [emphasis on the people rather than the actions]

80.3 Using active or passive voice in the social and natural sciences

Many writers in scientific disciplines (see Chapter 38) use the passive voice. Yet style manuals for scientific disciplines agree with the advice in this handbook: Prefer the active voice. "Verbs are vigorous, direct communicators," point out the editors of the *Publication Manual*

EXTRA EXERCISE G

Identify the verbs in the following sentences; then decide if they are in the active or the passive voice.

1. Windsor Castle is an official residence of the monarchs of Great Britain.

2. In the year 1070, William the Conqueror built a fortress on the site it now occupies.

3. It was improved by succeeding rulers until the reign of Edward III (1327–1377).

4. Edward III demolished the old castle and built a new one.

5. Additions were made by later kings of England.

6. Sir Christopher Wren was asked by Charles II to design several important additions.

7. The state apartments are open to the public when the royal family is not in residence.

8. The state apartments include the grand staircase, state bedrooms, and reception rooms.

9. Many rulers were buried at Windsor Castle, including Henry VIII.

Answers to Extra Exercise G

1. is (active)

2. built (active); occupies (active)

3. was improved (passive)

4. demolished (active); built (active)

5. were made (passive)

6. was asked (passive)

7. are (active); is (active)

8. include (active)

9. were buried (passive)

of the American Psychological Association. "Use the active rather than the passive voice. . . ."*

ANSWERS AND COVERAGE: EXERCISE 8-11

Rewrites may vary somewhat from the possibilities shown here. Coverage is three passive to active sentences; two active to passive sentences.

1. *Passive, change to active*: A farmer chose a coffin in the shape of a green onion.

2. *Active, change to passive*: A hunter was buried by his family in a wooden coffin shaped like a leopard.

3. *Passive, change to active*: The friends and relatives of a dead chief carried his body through his fishing village in a large, pink, wooden replica of a fish.

4. *Active, change to passive*: About ten coffins a year can be turned out by wood-carver Paa Joe.

5. *Passive, change to active*: Museums have displayed a few of these fantasy coffins, although most of the coffins end up buried in the ground.

EXERCISE 8-11

Consulting sections 8n and 8o, determine first whether each of these sentences is in the active voice or the passive voice. Second, rewrite the sentence in the other voice. Then decide which voice better suits the meaning, and be ready to explain your choice.

EXAMPLE   In the West African country of Ghana, a few woodcarvers are creating coffins that reflect their occupants' special interests. *(Active; change to passive.)*

In the West African country of Ghana, coffins that reflect their occupants' special interests are being created by a few woodcarvers.

1. A coffin in the shape of a green onion was chosen by a farmer.
2. A hunter's family buried him in a wooden coffin shaped like a leopard.
3. A dead chief was carried through his fishing village by friends and relatives bearing his body in a large, pink, wooden replica of a fish.
4. Woodcarver Paa Joe can turn out about ten coffins a year.
5. Although a few of these fantasy coffins have been displayed in museums, most of them end up buried in the ground.

*American Psychological Association, *Publication Manual of the American Psychological Association*, 4th ed. (Washington: APA, 1994) 32.

Focus on Revising

Revising Your Writing

If you have trouble with your verbs when you write, including unnecessary use of the passive voice, go back to your writing and locate the problems. Using this chapter as a resource, revise your writing to correct these kinds of problems: -s endings (see 8c); -ed endings (see 8d); auxiliary verbs (see 8e); transitive and intransitive verbs, including *lie* and *lay* (see 8f); tenses (see 8g–8j); tense sequences (see 8k); the subjunctive mood (see 8l–8m); active versus passive voice (see 8n–8o).

Case Studies: Revising to Eliminate Verb Errors

In these case studies, you can observe a student writer revising. Then, you have the chance to revise other student writing on your own.

Observation

A student wrote the following draft for a course called Popular Culture. The assignment called for choosing one year in which important contributions were made to popular culture in the United States and then writing about it. Although this paragraph is well organized and offers good examples to support its topic, the draft's effectiveness is diminished by the presence of errors in verb forms and verb tense and by the unnecessary use of the passive voice.

Read through the draft. The verb errors are highlighted and explained. Before you look at the student's revision, revise the material yourself. Then, compare your revision to the student's.

unneeded passive voice: 8n

past perfect tense used; need simple past: 8i

subjunctive needed for *if* clause: 8m.1

subjunctive needed for *if* clause: 8m.1

A number of important contributions in the year 1925 likely will be agreed upon by anyone who has studied popular culture in the United States. The Charleston, a dance most often associate with the 1920s, had become popular in 1925. Along with the new dance comes a new fashion trend. If a woman of today was to find herself transported to 1925, she would be in style if she was to appear in a straight, long-waisted dress with a hemline above

-ed missing: 8d

present tense used; need simple past: 8h

→

PARTICIPATION ESSAY

Coverage

At election time, government leaders and the media always *encouraged* [8h, simple present needed] citizens to exercise one of their most basic rights: the right to vote. How many young women today realize that until the Nineteenth Amendment to the United States Constitution *was being approved* [8d, past progressive used; simple past needed] in 1920, women in the United States were *deny* [8d, present used; past needed] the right to vote?

In the 1830s, almost a century before the Nineteenth Amendment *had been approved* [8d, past perfect used; simple past needed], *the battle for women's rights was being waged by Elizabeth Cady Stanton and other leading women*. [8o, unneeded passive voice] In 1848, the first women's rights convention *take* [8h, present tense used; need simple past of irregular verb] place in Seneca Falls, New York. Stanton *rises* [8f, present tense of intransitive verb used; simple past needed] to the occasion and produced what was *call* [8d, -ed needed] "A Declaration of Sentiments." Its inspiration *lays* [8f, -s form of transitive verb used; past tense of intransitive verb needed] in the Declaration of Independence, but it revealed one shortcoming in Thomas Jefferson's language. Instead of the words "all men are created equal," Stanton's document *proclaim* [8d, -ed needed] that "all men and women are created equal."

Later, Stanton *was working* [8d, past progressive used; simple past needed] to convince California Senator Aaron Sargeant to propose a constitutional amendment that would give women the vote. *It was introduced to the U.S. Congress by him* in 1878. [8o, unneeded passive voice] Forty years later, the amendment was approved, but Stanton never *seen* [8d, past participle of irregular verb used; simple past needed] the victory because she died eighteen years before the amendment became law. Her legacy lives and should be remembered by all

➡

unneeded passive voice: 8o ——— the knee. This revealing look was found to be shocking by some people of that era. A less controversial development was the opening of Madison Square Garden in New York City.

unneeded passive voice: 8o ——— Boxing and other events were now able to be seen by thousands of people. While sports fans were enjoying the new facility, movie

-ed missing: 8d ——— audiences laugh at Charlie Chaplin in his popular film *The Gold Rush*. Clearly, popular culture in the year 1925 had been thriving. ———

past perfect progressive tense used; need simple past: 8j

Here is how the student revised the material to eliminate the verb errors. In revising from the unneeded passive voice to the active voice, the student had alternatives in word choice. Your revisions into the active voice might differ in wording from the student's.

> Anyone who has studied popular culture in the United States likely will agree upon a number of important contributions in the year 1925. The Charleston, a dance most often associated with the 1920s, became popular in 1925. Along with the new dance came a new fashion trend. If a woman of today were to find herself transported to 1925, she would be in style if she were to appear in a straight, long-waisted dress with a hemline above the knee. Some people of that era found this revealing look shocking. A less controversial development was the opening of Madison Square Garden in New York City. Thousands of people could now see boxing and other events. While sports fans were enjoying this new facility, movie audiences laughed at Charlie Chaplin in his popular film *The Gold Rush*. Clearly, popular culture in the year 1925 was thriving.

Participation

A student wrote the following draft for a course called Introduction to Women's Studies. The assignment was to write a brief report about a significant contribution to society in the United States. The material is concise and logical, but the draft's effectiveness is diminished by errors in verb forms and verb tense and by the unnecessary use of the passive voice.

Read through the draft. Then, revise it to eliminate the errors. Also, make any additional revisions you think would improve the content, organization, and style of the material.

At election time, government leaders and the media always encouraged citizens to exercise one of their most basic rights: the right to vote. How many young women today realize that until the Nineteenth Amendment to the United States Constitution was being approved in 1920, women in the United States were deny the right to vote?

In the 1830s, almost a century before the Nineteenth Amendment had been approved, the battle for women's rights was being waged by Elizabeth Cady Stanton and other leading women. In 1848, the first women's rights convention take place in Seneca Falls, New York. Stanton rises to the occasion and produced what was call "A Declaration of Sentiments." Its inspiration lays in the Declaration of Independence, but it revealed one shortcoming in Thomas Jefferson's language. Instead of the words "all men are created equal," Stanton's document proclaim that "all men and women are created equal."

Later, Stanton was working to convince California Senator Aaron Sargeant to propose a constitutional amendment that would give women the vote. It was introduced to the U.S. Congress by him in 1878. Forty years later, the amendment was approved, but Stanton never seen the victory because she died eighteen years before the amendment became law. Her legacy lives and should be remembered by all women when the time come to vote.

Coverage (continued)
women when the time *come* [8c, simple present used; *-s* form needed] to vote.

Answer to Participation Essay
This version revises the errors in verb forms and verb tense and the unnecessary use of the passive voice. Answers may vary slightly, especially in the revisions of the passives. Also, answers will vary if students have revised for content, organization, or style.

At election time, government leaders and the media always encourage citizens to exercise one of their most basic rights: the right to vote. How many young women today realize that until the Nineteenth Amendment to the United States Constitution was approved in 1920, women in the United States were denied the right to vote?

In the 1830s, almost a century before the Nineteenth Amendment was approved, Elizabeth Cady Stanton and other leading women waged the battle for women's rights. In 1848, the first women's rights convention took place in Seneca Falls, New York. Stanton rose to the occasion and produced what was called "A Declaration of Sentiments." Its inspiration lay in the Declaration of Independence, but it revealed one shortcoming in Thomas Jefferson's language. Instead of the words "all men are created equal," Stanton's document proclaimed that "all men and women are created equal."

Later, Stanton convinced California Senator Aaron Sargeant to propose a constitutional amendment that would give women the vote. He introduced it to the U.S. Congress in 1878. Forty years later the amendment was approved, but Stanton never saw the victory because she died eighteen years before the amendment became law. Her legacy lives and should be remembered by all women when the time comes to vote.

9

CASE OF NOUNS AND PRONOUNS

9a Understanding case

Case is a term used to describe the different forms that NOUNS and PRONOUNS take to deliver information. Case communicates how the noun or pronoun relates to other words in a sentence.

Nouns "show" case only in the possessive, by the use of the apostrophe: for example, *Nobu's hat* (see Chapter 27). Pronouns have three cases: subjective, objective, and possessive.

Personal pronouns, the most common type of pronouns, have SINGULAR and PLURAL forms for all three cases (see Chart 68).

⊙ **Cases of personal pronouns** 68

	Subjective		Objective		Possessive	
Person*	SING.	PLUR.	SING.	PLUR.	SING.	PLUR.
FIRST	I	we	me	us	my/mine	our/ours
SECOND	you	you	you	you	your/yours	your/yours
THIRD	he	they	him	them	his	their/theirs
	she		her		her/hers	
	it		it		its	

*For more about the concepts of person and number (singular and plural), see Chart 75 in section 11a.

A pronoun in the **subjective case** functions as a SUBJECT.

We were going to get married. [*We* is the subject.]

John and **I** wanted an inexpensive band to play at our wedding. [*I* is part of the compound subject *John and I.*]

He and **I** found an affordable one-person band. [*He* and *I* are part of the compound subject.]

214

A pronoun in the **objective case** functions as an OBJECT.

We saw **him** perform in a public park. [*Him* is the direct object.]

We showed **him** our budget. [*Him* is the indirect object.]

He wrote down what we wanted and shook hands with **us**. [*Us* is the object of the preposition *with*.]

A noun or pronoun in the **possessive case** indicates ownership. (Special rules apply to use of the possessive case before GERUNDS; see 9h.)

The **musician's** contract was in the mail the next day. [*Musician's*, a noun in the possessive case, indicates ownership.]

The first signature on the contract was **mine**. [*Mine*, a pronoun in the possessive case, indicates ownership and refers to the noun *signature*.]

My fiancé signed **his** name next to **mine**. [*His* and *mine*, pronouns in the possessive case, indicate ownership and refer to the noun *name*.]

🛇 **PUNCTUATION ALERT:** Do not use an apostrophe in a personal pronoun (see 27b). ❗

The pronouns *who* and *whoever* also have different forms for each case (see 9e).

9b Using pronouns in compound constructions

A compound construction contains more than one SUBJECT or OBJECT.

He saw the eclipse of the sun. [single subject]

He and I saw the eclipse of the sun. [compound subject]

That eclipse astonished **us**. [single object]

That eclipse astonished **him and me**. [compound object]

A compound construction does not affect pronoun case. A compound subject uses the subjective case, and a compound object uses the objective case. Sometimes, however, people make the mistake of switching cases for compounds. If you are unsure which case to use, try the "drop test." Temporarily drop all words of the compound element except the pronoun in question, as explained in Chart 69.

TEACHING TIP

English once distinguished between the personal and impersonal relationships in the second-person pronoun *you*. Some modern languages continue to do so. French, for example, makes a distinction between *tu* and *vous*; Spanish does so between *tu* (singular), *vosotros* (plural), informally, and *usted* (singular), *ustedes* (plural), formally. You might wish to have your bilingual students explain the difference in such forms.

STATEWIDE TESTING

If you teach in a state that requires students to pass basic competency tests in English, see the free publications coordinated with this handbook: One is for the CLAST (Florida), and another is for the TASP Exam (Texas).

LANGUAGE HISTORY

Changes in the second-person singular pronouns (subjective and objective cases) are rooted in the Roman Empire of the fourth century A.D. At that time, there were two emperors, one in Rome and one in Constantinople. People speaking to either emperor were required to use the plural form of address. The practice of using the plural as a sign of respect slowly spread to France, where *tu* is the second-person singular pronoun (*toi* in the objective case) and *vous* the plural. During the thirteenth century, in imitation of the French nobles who occupied their country, the English began using *thou* (*thee* in the objective case) and *you* the same way. *You* became a mark of mutual respect in conversations among the elite and a sign of deference when a person spoke to a social superior. In contrast, *thou* became a sign of intimacy among members of the same family or among those who believed in the same things.

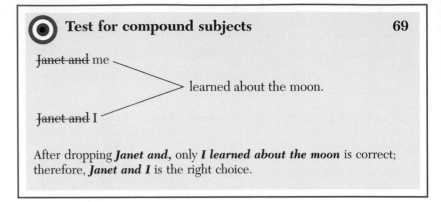

⊙ **Test for compound subjects**   69

~~Janet and~~ me ⟶

~~Janet and~~ I ⟶ learned about the moon.

After dropping ***Janet and,*** only ***I learned about the moon*** is correct; therefore, ***Janet and I*** is the right choice.

This "drop test" also works when a compound subject contains only pronouns: ***She and I*** [not *Her and me, She and me,* or *Her and I*] *learned about the moon.*

The "drop test" in Chart 70 works for compound objects. This test also works when a compound object contains only pronouns: *The instructor told **her and me*** [not *she and I, her and I,* or *she and me*] *about the moon's phases.*

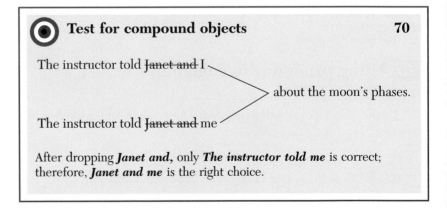

⊙ **Test for compound objects**   70

The instructor told ~~Janet and~~ I ⟶

The instructor told ~~Janet and~~ me ⟶ about the moon's phases.

After dropping ***Janet and,*** only ***The instructor told me*** is correct; therefore, ***Janet and me*** is the right choice.

These principles apply to all sequences of pronouns (for example, the rules that govern *her and me* apply also to *me and her*). Also, when you write compound constructions that contain pronouns, do not mix pronouns in the subjective case with pronouns in the objective case: For example, do not use the combinations *him and I* (objective and subjective) or *she and me* (subjective and objective).

When pronouns in a PREPOSITIONAL PHRASE are compound, they must be in the objective case.

NO The instructor gave an assignment **to Sam and I.** [*To* is a preposition; *I* is in the subjective case and cannot follow a preposition.]

YES The instructor gave an assignment **to Sam and me.** [*To* is a preposition; *me* is in the objective case, so *me* is correct.]

NO The instructor spoke **with he and I.** [*With* is a preposition; both *he* and *I* are in the subjective case and cannot follow a preposition.]

NO The instructor spoke **with him and I.** [*With* is a preposition; *him* is in the objective case, so *him* is correct, but *I* is in the subjective case and cannot follow a preposition.]

YES The instructor spoke **with him and me.** [*With* is a preposition; *him* and *me* are both in the objective case, so this construction is correct.]

Between is a preposition that frequently leads people to pronoun error. Pronouns after *between*, like those after other prepositions, must always be in the objective case.

NO The instructor divided the work **between Sam and I.** [*Between* is a preposition; *I* is in the subjective case and cannot follow a preposition.]

YES The instructor divided the work **between Sam and me.** [*Between* is a preposition; *me* is in the objective case, so *me* is correct.]

When you are in doubt about pronoun case in prepositional phrases, use the "drop test" for compound objects in Chart 70.

EXERCISE 9-1

Consulting section 9b, circle the correct pronoun from each pair in parentheses.

EXAMPLE   "Just between you and (I, (me,))" said my workout partner, "I could stand to lose a few pounds."

(1) I suggested that (us, we) both consider going on a low-fat diet. (2) Consulting a doctor first seemed like the right plan

---

QUOTATION: ON LANGUAGE

A writer lives in awe of words for they can be cruel or kind, and they can change their meanings right in front of you. They pick up flavors and odors like butter in a refrigerator.

—John Steinbeck

ANSWERS AND COVERAGE: EXERCISE 9-1

1. we [subjective case]

2. Al and me [objective case after preposition *for*]; him and me [objective case after preposition *for*]

➞

217

Answers and Coverage: Exercise 9-1 (continued)

3. We [subjective case]

4. me [objective case, compound direct object]; him and me [objective case after preposition *between*]; we [subjective case]

5. us [objective case after preposition *to*]

6. I [subjective case, inverted word order]

8. him and me [objective case after preposition *for*]; us [objective case after *between*]

10. me [objective case following preposition *versus*]

for Al and (I, me), and so I made appointments for (he and I, him and me) with Mary Standish, my own physician. (3) (We, Us) both were seen the next evening. (4) After examining us separately, Dr. Standish told Al and (I, me) that between (he and I, him and me), (we, us) should lose 25 pounds. (5) Dr. Standish gave a list of desirable and undesirable foods to (we, us) two. (6) Naturally, the desirable list seemed undesirable and the undesirable delicious, agreed Al and (I, me). (7) Al had a different problem. (8) Because the diet was now the same goal for both (he and I, him and me), he dreaded the competition between (we, us) two. (9) "Don't worry," I told Al. (10) "It's not a matter of you versus (me, I) because the big loser is the real winner!"

9c Matching noun and pronoun cases in appositives

The rule that pronouns and nouns must be in the same case holds when pronouns are renamed by APPOSITIVES and when pronouns are appositives themselves. To check, temporarily drop the noun to see whether subjective or objective pronouns read correctly.

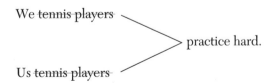

We ~~tennis players~~

Us ~~tennis players~~

practice hard.

After dropping *tennis players*, only *we* is correct; therefore, *We practice hard* is the right choice.

This test also works when the pronouns function as the appositive, coming after the noun: *The winners, **she and I** [not *her and me*], advanced to the finals.* Because they rename *winners*, which is the subject, the pronouns must be in the subjective case.

This test also works when the nouns and pronouns are in the objective case: *The coach tells **us** [not *we*] tennis players to practice hard. The crowd cheered the winners, **her and me** [not *she and I*].*

9d Avoiding the objective case after linking verbs

A **linking verb** connects a SUBJECT to a word that renames it (see Chart 61 in 8a). Linking verbs indicate a state of being (*am, is, are, was, were,* and so on), relate to the senses (*look, smell, taste, sound, feel*), or indicate a condition (*appear, seem, become, grow, turn, remain, prove*).

Because a pronoun following a linking verb renames the subject, the pronoun must be in the subjective case.

> The contest winner was **I.** [*I* renames *the contest winner,* the subject, so the subjective case is correct.]

> The ones who will benefit are **they and I.** [*They and I* rename *the ones who will benefit,* the subject, so the subjective case is correct.]

> Who is there? It is **I.** [*I* renames *it,* the subject, so the subjective case is correct.]

Although in speech and informal writing, the objective case is sometimes substituted in the constructions shown in the last two examples, always use the subjective case in academic writing.

EXERCISE 9-2

Consulting sections 9a through 9d, circle the correct pronoun of each pair in parentheses.

EXAMPLE Dad, because your wedding anniversary is next week, ((we), us) sisters decided to get you and Mother a gift you will never forget.

(1) Anne and (me, I) have given this a great deal of thought, especially in light of the conversations you and Mom have had with us about stress at work. (2) You and Mom have always insisted that (we, us) children save money for special occasions, and Anne asked (me, I) if she and I could use our savings for a weekend getaway for you as the perfect anniversary gift. (3) It is (she and I, she and me) who most worry about how (you and her, you and she) are doing, so Anne and (I, me) think this trip will be beneficial for everyone. (4) In fact, Dad, Mom mentioned to Anne just last week how much she would love it if you and (she, her) could spend some more time together. (5) It will really make Anne and (me, I) feel great to do

Our mother tongue is bettered or worsened by the way each generation uses it. Languages evolve like species. They can degenerate; just as oysters and barnacles have lost their head.

—F. S. Lucas

ANSWERS AND COVERAGE: EXERCISE 9-2

1. I [9b, subjective case]

2. we [9a, appositive: subjective case], me [9a, objective case]

3. she and I [9a, subjective case after linking verb]; you and she [9b, subjective case]; I [9b, subjective case]

4. she [9b, subjective case]

5. me [9b, objective case]

6. she [9b, subjective case]

7. I [9b, subjective case]

something nice for you and Mom. (6) So, Dad, you and Mom start packing for a weekend at your favorite bed and breakfast, a weekend you and (her, she) desperately need and deserve. (7) Anne and (I, me) will be waiting when you and Mom come home rested and free of stress.

Using *who, whoever, whom,* and *whomever*

The pronouns *who* and *whoever* are in the subjective case. The pronouns *whom* and *whomever* are in the objective case (see Chart 71).

⊙ **Cases of relative and interrogative pronouns**   **71**

SUBJECTIVE	OBJECTIVE	POSSESSIVE
who	whom	whose
whoever	whomever	—

9e.1 Using *who, whoever, whom,* and *whomever* in dependent clauses

The pronouns *who, whoever, whom,* and *whomever* start many DEPENDENT CLAUSES. To find the correct pronoun case in a dependent clause, find out whether the pronoun is functioning as a SUBJECT or an OBJECT. Informal spoken English tends to blur distinctions between *who* and *whom,* so you might not want to rely entirely on what sounds right.

To check your use of *who* and *whom,* adapt the "drop test" introduced in section 9b. As Chart 72 shows, temporarily drop everything in the sentence up to the pronoun in question, and then make substitutions. Remember that *he, she, they, who,* and *whoever* are subjects and *him, her, them, whom,* and *whomever* (the -*m* forms and *her*) are objects.

⊙ **Test for *who* or *whom* in the subjective case**   **72**

EXAMPLE	I wondered **(who, whom)** would vote.
1. DROP	I wondered

→

**Test for *who* or *whom*   72
in the subjective case** *(continued)*

2. TEST   Temporarily substitute *he* and *him* (or *she* and *her*): "**He** would vote" or "**Him** would vote."

3. ANSWER   **He.** Therefore, because *he* is subjective, *who*, which is also subjective, is correct: "I wondered **who** would vote."

The subjective case is used even if words such as *I think* or *he says* come between the subject and verb. Ignore these expressions to determine the correct pronoun: *She is the candidate **who** [I think] will get my vote.* The "drop test" in Chart 73 also works for *whoever:*

Voter registration drives attempt to enroll **whoever** is eligible to vote. [***He*** (not *him*) *is eligible to vote* proves that the subjective case, *whoever,* is needed.]

◉ **Test for *who* or *whom* in the objective case   73**

EXAMPLE   Volunteers go to senior citizen centers hoping to enroll people (**who, whom**) others have ignored.

1. DROP   Volunteers go to senior citizen centers hoping to enroll people

2. TEST   Try *they* and *them* at the end of the sentence: "Others have ignored **they**" or "Others have ignored **them.**"

3. ANSWER   **Them.** Therefore, because *them* is objective, *whom*, which is also objective, is correct: "Volunteers go to senior citizen centers hoping to enroll people **whom** others have ignored."

The "drop test" in Chart 73 also works for *whomever:*

The senior citizens can vote for **whomever** they wish. [*The senior citizens can vote for **him** (not he) proves that the objective case, whomever, is needed.*]

If your students have trouble choosing the appropriate pronoun in questions, you might offer them practice with these questions:

1. (Who, whom) was initially responsible for the making of silk? [*Who*]

2. (Who, whom) developed the first method of weaving silk? [*Who*]

3. In the nineteenth century, (who, whom) claimed to produce the best silk? [*who*]

4. Theories about early fabrics come from (who, whom)? [*whom*]

5. Silkworm eggs were carried out of China by (who, whom)? [*whom*]

6. The French silk industry was developed for (who, whom)? [*whom*]

ANSWERS AND COVERAGE: EXERCISE 9-3

1. who [subjective case]

2. whoever [subjective case]

3. whom [objective case]

4. whom [objective case]

5. who [subjective case]

6. who [subjective case]

7. whomever [objective case]

9e.2   Using *who* and *whom* in questions

At the beginning of questions, use *who* if the question is about the subject and *whom* if the question is about the object. If you want to test for case, recast the question into a statement, temporarily substituting *he* or *she* (subject-case pronouns) or *him* or *her* (objective-case pronouns).

> **Who** watched the space shuttle lift off? [**He** (not *Him*) *watched the space shuttle lift off* uses the subjective case, so *who* is correct.]

> Ann admires **whom**? [*Ann admires* **him** (not *he*) uses the objective case, so *whom* is correct.]

> **Whom** does Ann admire? [*Ann admires* **him** (not *he*) uses the objective case, so *whom* is correct.]

> To **whom** does Ann speak about becoming an astronaut? [*Ann speaks to* **her** (not *she*) *about becoming an astronaut* uses the objective pronoun *her. Whom* is, therefore, correct.]

EXERCISE 9-3

Consulting section 9e, circle the correct pronoun of each pair in parentheses.

EXAMPLE   ((Whoever), Whomever) has been dragged out of bed by the urge for a peanut butter sandwich can join millions of other people with similar cravings.

(1) There is nothing strange about a person (who, whom) experiences late-night cravings for favorite snacks. (2) (Whoever, Whomever) has worried about such habits can take comfort from a Canadian researcher. (3) Among the one thousand college students (who, whom) he studied, a large majority admitted that they craved specific foods. (4) Women (who, whom) these cravings strike tend to desire chocolate and sweets; men usually crave high-protein foods like meat. (5) Few people (who, whom) are told about this difference are very surprised. (6) What may be surprising is that researchers have not found many pregnant women (who, whom) crave dill pickles. (7) Nevertheless, (whoever, whomever) researchers ask about cravings, the pickle myth is bound to come up.

9f Using the appropriate pronoun case after *than* or *as*

A sentence of comparison using *than* or *as* often implies the comparison rather than stating it in words. For example, *are* need not be expressed at the end of this sentence: *My two-month-old Saint Bernard is larger **than** most full-grown dogs [are].*

When a pronoun follows *than* or *as*, the pronoun case carries essential information about what is being said. For example, these two sentences convey two very different messages, simply because of the choice between the words *me* and *I* after *than.*

1. My sister loved that dog more **than me.**
2. My sister loved that dog more **than I.**

Because *me* is an objective-case pronoun, sentence 1 means "My sister loved that dog more *than she loved me.*" Because *I* is a subjective-case pronoun, sentence 2 means "My sister loved that dog *more than I loved it.*" To make sure that any sentence of comparison delivers its message clearly, either mentally fill in the words to check that you have chosen the correct pronoun case or write in all words after *than* or *as.*

9g Using pronouns with infinitives

An **infinitive** is the SIMPLE FORM of a verb usually, but not always, following *to: to laugh.* Objective-case pronouns serve as both SUBJECTS of infinitives and OBJECTS of infinitives.

Our tennis coach expects **me to serve.** [The word *me* is the subject of the infinitive *to serve,* and so it is in the objective case.]

Our tennis coach expects **him to beat me.** [The word *him* is the subject of the infinitive *to beat,* and *me* is the object of the infinitive, so both are in the objective case.]

9h Using pronouns with *-ing* words

A **gerund** is a verb's *-ing* form functioning as a NOUN: *Brisk **walking** is excellent exercise.* When a noun or PRONOUN precedes a gerund, the possessive case is called for: *Kim's* brisk **walking** built up his stamina. **His** brisk **walking** built up his stamina.* In contrast, a PRESENT PARTICIPLE—a form that also ends in *-ing*—functions as a MODIFIER. It does not take the possessive case: *Kim, **walking** briskly, caught up to me.*

The possessive case, therefore, communicates important information. Consider these two sentences, which convey two different messages, entirely as a result of the possessive:

1. The detective noticed the **man staggering.**
2. The detective noticed the **man's staggering.**

Sentence 1 means that the detective noticed the *man;* sentence 2 means that the detective noticed the *staggering.*

TEACHING TIP

If your students have trouble choosing the appropriate pronoun after *than* or *as,* you might try expanding elliptical comparisons with them to verify the best choice. Here are a few practice sentences.

1. You are taller than (I, me). [*I*]
2. Your parents are taller than (me, mine). [*mine*]
3. My brother is as thin as (I, me). [*I*]
4. Your sisters are as smart as (me, mine). [*mine*]

EXTRA EXERCISE B

Circle the correct pronoun in each pair in parentheses.

1. Carl's resolution to study more is a result of (him, his) getting poor grades last semester. [*his*]
2. The dean almost required (he, him) to take a semester off. [*him*]
3. His parents complained about (him, his) partying too much. [*his*]
4. Carl thought that nobody cared more about his grades than (him, he). [*he*]
5. So he was surprised when his parents told (he, him) they were disappointed with his schoolwork. [*him*]
6. (Them, Their) expressing their concern showed how much they cared about (he, him). [*Their, him*]
7. After that, whenever his parents looked for (he, him), they found (his, him) studying. [*him, him*]

223

EXTRA EXERCISE C

From each group of pronouns in parentheses, select the correct word.

EXAMPLE

My softball teammates and (myself, me, I) are confident we will make the finals this year. [*I*]

1. I am so certain that I have already bought (me, myself) a new glove to celebrate. [*myself*]

2. Every practice session, the coach tells the others and (me, myself) that we are getting better and better. [*me*]

3. The sponsor (himself, hisself), Big Al of Big Al's Used Cars, even comes to games now. [*himself*]

4. The other women and (I, myself) are glad that our hard work has paid off. [*I*]

5. We had an exhibition game against our husbands, who tired (theirselves, themselves) out and lost by four runs. [*themselves*]

ANSWERS AND COVERAGE: EXERCISE 9-4

1. he [9f, subjective case in elliptical *as the careers that he and his friend Steve Jobs have had*]

2. their [9h, possessive case before gerund]; them [9g, objective case for object of infinitive *to get*]

3. they [9f, subjective case as subject of elliptical clause *than they are*]

4. its [9h, possessive case before gerund *creating*]

5. their [9h, possessive case before gerund *leaving*]; them [9g, objective case for object of infinitive *to interest*]

6. him [9g, objective case for object of infinitive *to want*]

The same distinction applies to pronouns:

1. The detective noticed **him staggering.**
2. The detective noticed **his staggering.**

In conversation, such distinctions are often ignored, but readers of academic writing expect information to be precise. Consider the difference in the following two examples:

GERUND (AS SUBJECT)	The **governor's calling for a tax increase** surprised her supporters.
PARTICIPLE (AS MODIFIER)	The **governor, calling for a tax increase,** surprised her supporters.

EXERCISE 9-4

Consulting sections 9f through 9h, circle the correct pronoun of each pair in parentheses.

EXAMPLE   When executives at the Hewlett-Packard Company decided not to manufacture a personal computer brought to them by its designer, young Steve Wozniak, the rejection motivated (him, his) founding the Apple Computer Company.

(1) Few people in Steve Wozniak's world of personal computers have had careers as rewarding as (he, him) and his friend Steve Jobs. (2) Their story begins with (them, their) selling a van and a calculator to get (they, them) enough cash to make a prototype computer. (3) Many people with an idea like Wozniak and Jobs's are less willing than (them, they) to take risks. (4) Apple's early spectacular success as a company came from (it, its) creating computers easy for individuals to own and use. (5) Because their idea made both Wozniak and Jobs multimillionaires before age thirty, the notion of (them, their) leaving the business world seemed to interest (they, them). (6) Wozniak went back to college but eventually returned to Apple, which continued to want (his, him) inventing and engineering computers for it. Meanwhile, Jobs's decision to start a new computer company led him to gamble once again on his talent and business skill, which eventually took him back to Apple.

9i Using -*self* pronouns

Reflexive pronouns reflect back on the SUBJECT or OBJECT: *The detective disguised* **himself**. *He relied on* **himself** *to solve the mystery.*

Do not use reflexive pronouns to substitute for PERSONAL PRONOUNS: *The detective and* **I** [not *myself*] *had a long talk. He wanted my partner and* **me** [not *myself*] *to help him.*

Intensive pronouns provide emphasis by making another word more intense in meaning: *The detective felt that his career* **itself** *was at stake.*

❶ **USAGE ALERT:** Avoid nonstandard forms of reflexive and intensive pronouns. Use *himself,* never *hisself;* use *themselves,* never *theirselves.* ❗

From the pronouns in parentheses, select the correct one and circle it.

1. My girlfriend and (I, me) agreed long ago that we would someday take a romantic ocean cruise together. [*I*]

2. (We, Us) and a few friends would sail the legendary seas and dock at exotic ports. [*We*]

3. Together, (we, us) and (they, them) would shop in the mysterious bazaars of ancient cultures and eat the spicy foods of distant lands. [*we, they*]

4. Unfortunately, an unexpected misfortune was visited on (she, her) and (I, me). [*her, me*]

5. The day we were to leave, (she, her) and (I, me) both discovered that we had chicken pox! [*she, I*]

6. Instead of visiting romantic places, the romantic places visited (she, her) and (I, me). [*her, me*]

7. Our friend Tom gave (we, us) travel books with pictures of the many places we longed to see. [*us*]

8. They were the same books someone had given (he, him) when he missed a trip to Mexico. [*him*]

9. I guess (we, us) will have to give them to (whoever, whomever) can't make the next scheduled vacation trip. [*we, whoever*]

10

PRONOUN REFERENCE

Pronoun reference concerns the relationship of a PRONOUN to its **antecedent,** which is always a NOUN or another pronoun. For writing to communicate a clear message, each pronoun must relate directly to an antecedent.

Consider these sentences and lines of poetry in which each pronoun has a clear referent.

> **Facts** do not cease to exist just because **they** are ignored.
>
> —Aldous Huxley

> I have found that the best way to give advice to **children** is to find out what **they** want and then advise **them** to do it.
>
> —Harry S Truman

> I knew a **woman,** lovely in **her** bones,
> When small **birds** sighed, **she** would sigh back at **them.**
>
> —Theodore Roethke, "I Knew a Woman"

Chart 74 shows how to keep pronoun references clear.

◉ **How to correct faulty pronoun reference** **74**

- Make a pronoun refer clearly to a single nearby antecedent (see 10a).
- Place pronouns close to their antecedents (see 10b).
- Make a pronoun refer to a definite antecedent (see 10c).
- Do not overuse *it* (see 10d), and reserve *you* only for DIRECT ADDRESS (see 10e).
- Use *who, which,* and *that* correctly (see 10f).

10a Making a pronoun refer clearly to a single antecedent

Be sure that each pronoun you use refers clearly to a single, nearby antecedent. If you find that you need the same pronoun to refer to more than one antecedent, revise the passage by replacing some pronouns with nouns so that all the remaining pronouns clearly refer to a single antecedent.

NO In 1911, **Roald Amundsen** reached the South Pole just thirty-five days before **Robert F. Scott** arrived. **He** [who? Amundsen or Scott?] had told people that **he** [who? Amundsen or Scott?] was going to sail for the Arctic, but **he** [who? Amundsen or Scott?] was concealing **his** [whose? Amundsen's or Scott's?] plan. Soon, **he** [who? Amundsen or Scott?] turned south for the Antarctic. On the journey home, **he** [who? Amundsen or Scott?] and **his** [whose? Amundsen's or Scott's?] party froze to death just a few miles from safety.

YES In 1911, **Roald Amundsen** reached the South Pole just thirty-five days before **Robert F. Scott** arrived. **Amundsen** had told people that **he** was going to sail for the Arctic, but **he** was concealing **his** plan. Soon, **Amundsen** turned south for the Antarctic. On the journey home, **Scott** and **his** party froze to death just a few miles from safety.

When you use more than one pronoun in a sentence, be sure that each has a clear antecedent.

Robert F. Scott used **horses** for **his** trip to the pole, but **they** perished quickly because **they** were not suited for travel over ice and snow.

Said and *told,* when used with pronouns that refer to more than one person, are particularly likely to create confusion for readers. Quotation marks and slight rewording can clarify meaning.

NO Her mother told her she was going to visit Alaska.

YES Her mother told her, "You are going to visit Alaska."

YES Her mother told her, "I am going to visit Alaska."

10b Placing pronouns close to their antecedents for clarity

If too much material comes between a pronoun and its antecedent, even though they are logically related, pronoun reference may be unclear.

STATEWISE TESTING

If you teach in a state that requires students to pass basic competency tests in English, see the free publications coordinated with this handbook: One is for the CLAST (Florida), and another is for the TASP Exam (Texas).

QUOTATION: ON WRITING

We are all apprentices in a craft where no one ever becomes a master.
                              —Ernest Hemingway

TEACHING TIP

To help students become more aware of the connections between pronouns and their antecedents, you might want to use this excerpt by Jim Bouton. You might ask students to draw connecting lines between the pronoun and the antecedent in each pair. (The pronouns are italicized here.) Do they find any misleading or vague references?

→

Teaching Tip (continued)

Another thing to watch during one of the little delays *that* make up such a big part of the [baseball] game is *what* the pitcher is up to. *I* don't mean when *he's* looking in to get the sign, winding up, throwing the ball. *I* mean during the time *he* steps off the mound and seems to be looking out at *his* outfielders or into the stands at girls. What *he's* really doing is rubbing up the ball and under the latest rules *he* has to walk off the mound to do so.

This gives him some marvelous opportunities. *He* can, for one thing, stick a finger between *his* belt and trousers and come up with a gob of previously concealed vaseline. *This* while *he* has *his* back to the plate umpire. And what good is vaseline? Well, *it's* slippery like spit. *This* means *you* can throw the ball exactly as hard as *you* would a fastball and have *it* come off *your* hand behaving like a curve. *This* is very confusing for the hitter.

—Jim Bouton,
"A Few World Series Sinkers"

ANSWERS: EXERCISE 10-1

Answers may vary somewhat. Some students may think that some of the pronouns replaced here are acceptable, but clarity is the issue—avoiding intervening information that distracts the reader, ambiguous references, and so on. Here is one possible answer.

Most companies used to frown on employees who became involved in office romances. Companies often considered these employees to be using company time for their own enjoyment. Now, however, managers realize that happy employees are productive employees. With more women than ever before in the workforce and with people working longer hours, managers have begun to see that male and female employees want and need to socialize. Managers are also dropping their opposition to having married couples on the payroll, because they no longer automatically believe that such couples will bring family matters into the

NO   **Alfred Wegener,** a highly trained German meteorologist and professor of geophysics and meteorology at the University of Graz in Austria, was the first person to suggest that all the continents on earth were originally part of one large landmass. According to his theory, the supercontinent broke up long ago, and the fragments drifted apart. **He** named this supercontinent Pangaea. [Although *he* can refer only to *Wegener,* too much material intervenes between the pronoun and its antecedent.]

YES   **Alfred Wegener,** a highly trained German meteorologist and professor of geophysics and meteorology at the University of Graz in Austria, was the first person to suggest that all the continents on earth were originally part of one large landmass. According to his theory, the supercontinent broke up long ago, and the fragments drifted apart. **Wegener** named this supercontinent Pangaea.

Be cautious about beginning a new paragraph with a pronoun referring to a name in a prior paragraph. Repeating the name instead of using a pronoun for it can help your reader more easily follow your message.

ESL NOTE: Many languages omit a pronoun as a subject because the verb delivers the needed information. English, however, requires the use of the pronoun as a subject.

NO   Political science is an important academic subject; **is** studied all over the world.

YES   Political science is an important academic subject; **it is** studied all over the world. ✦

EXERCISE 10-1

Consulting sections 10a and 10b, revise so that each pronoun refers clearly to its antecedent. Either replace pronouns with nouns or restructure the material to clarify pronoun reference.

EXAMPLE   People who return to work after years away from the corporate world often discover that business practices have changed. They may find fiercer competition in the workplace, but they may also discover that they are more flexible than before.

Here is one acceptable revision: *People who return to work after years away from the corporate world often discover that business practices have changed. Those people may find fiercer competition in the workplace, but they may also discover that business practices are more flexible than before.*

Most companies used to frown on employees who became involved in office romances. They often considered them to be using company time for their own enjoyment. Now, however, managers realize that happy employees are productive employees. With more women than ever before in the workforce and with people working longer hours, they have begun to see that male and female employees want and need to socialize. They are also dropping their opposition to having married couples on the payroll. They no longer automatically believe that they will bring family matters into the workplace or stick up for one another at the company's expense.

One departmental manager had doubts when a systems analyst for research named Laura announced that she had become engaged to Peter, who worked as a technician in the same department. She told her that either one or the other might have to transfer out of the research department. After listening to her plea that they be allowed to work together on a trial basis, the manager reconsidered. She decided to give Laura and Peter a chance to prove that their relationship would not affect their work. The decision paid off. They demonstrated that they could work as an effective research team, right through their engagement and subsequent marriage. Two years later, when Laura was promoted to assistant manager of a different department and after he asked to move also, she enthusiastically recommended that Peter follow Laura to her new department.

10c | Making a pronoun refer to a definite antecedent

10c.1 Using a pronoun to refer to a noun's possessive form

Careful writers make sure that a noun's possessive form serves as the ANTECEDENT for only a possessive pronoun. They would avoid a construction such as *The geologist's discovery brought him fame* because the pronoun *him* is not possessive and therefore should not refer to the possessive *geologist's*. However, many experts now agree that sentences with this usage are common and acceptable as long as the intended meaning is clear.

10c.2 Not using a pronoun to refer to an adjective

An ADJECTIVE cannot be an antecedent. A pronoun, therefore, cannot refer to an adjective.

NO Avery likes to study **geological** records. **That** will be her major. [*That* cannot refer to the adjective *geological*.]

YES Avery likes to study **geological** records. **Geology** will be her major.

229

10c.3 Making *it, that, this,* and *which* refer to only one antecedent

When you use *it, that, this,* and *which,* check to see that the referent of these pronouns can be determined easily by your readers.

NO   Comets usually fly by the earth at 100,000 mph, whereas asteroids sometimes collide with the earth. **This** interests scientists. [Does *this* refer to the speed of the comets, comets flying by the earth, or asteroids colliding with the earth?]

YES   Comets usually fly by the earth at 100,000 mph, whereas asteroids sometimes collide with the earth. **This difference** interests scientists. [Adding a noun after *this* or *that* is an effective way to make your meaning clear.]

NO   I told my friends that I was going to major in geology, **which** annoyed my parents. [What does *which* refer to?]

YES   My parents were annoyed **because I discussed my major with my friends.**

YES   My parents were annoyed **because I chose to major in geology.**

10c.4 Using *they* and *it* precisely

The expression *they say* cannot take the place of stating precisely who is doing the saying. Your reader is entitled to more than a *they* to provide authority for a statement.

NO   **They** say that earthquakes are becoming more frequent.

YES   **Seismologists** say that earthquakes are becoming more frequent.

In speech, common statement openings are *It said in the newspaper* or *In Washington, they say.* Avoid these inexact and wordy expressions in academic writing: **The newspaper reports** [not *It said in the newspaper*] *that minor earthquakes occur almost daily in California.*

10c.5 Not using a pronoun in the first sentence of a work to refer to the work's title

When referring to a title, repeat or reword whatever part of the title you want to use.

TITLE Geophysics as a Major

FIRST SENTENCE

NO   **This subject** unites the sciences of physics, biology, and ancient life.

YES   **Geophysics** unites the sciences of physics, biology, and ancient life.

10d Not overusing *it*

It has three different uses in English.

1. *It* is a **personal pronoun:** *Doug wants to visit the 18-inch Schmidt telescope, but **it** is on Mount Palomar.*
2. *It* is an **expletive,** a word that postpones the subject: ***It** is interesting to observe the stars.*
3. *It* is part of **idiomatic expressions** of weather, time, or distance: ***It** is sunny. **It** is midnight. **It** is not far to the hotel.*

All three uses are acceptable, but combining them in the same sentence can create confusion.

> **NO** Because our car was overheating, **it** came as no surprise that **it** broke down just as **it** began to rain. [*It* is overused here, even though all three uses—2, 1, and 3 on the list, respectively—are acceptable.]

> **YES** **It** came as no surprise that our overheating car broke down just as the rain began to fall.

See section 16a.1 for advice about revising wordy sentences that use expletive structures, and see section 11f for advice about using singular verbs with *it* expletives.

🌐 **ESL NOTE:** Be careful not to omit *it* from an expletive (also called a *subject filler*).

> **NO** **Is** a lovely day.

> **YES** **It is** a lovely day. 🌐

10e Using *you* only for direct address

In academic writing, *you* is not a suitable substitute for specific words that refer to people, situations, and occurrences. Choose exact language. This handbook uses *you* to address *you* directly as the reader but never to refer to people in general.

> **NO** In many states, **you** have **your** prisons with few rehabilitation programs. [Do *you,* the reader of this handbook, have few programs? Are the prisons *yours*?]

> **YES** In many states, **prisons** have few rehabilitation programs.

> **NO** In Russia, **you** usually have to stand in long lines to buy groceries. [Are *you,* the reader, planning to do your grocery shopping in Russia?]

> **YES** **Russian consumers** usually have to stand in long lines to buy groceries.

ANOTHER EXAMPLE

You might want to ask your students to work in groups to identify the missing antecedents of the pronouns underlined in the following sentences and then to discuss how changes could give the paragraph greater clarity and more formal style.

In India, they have cultivated cotton for centuries. You could wear cotton garments there as far back as 1500 B.C. It was logical that it should become an important crop because you have few winter frosts there. They are also free of excessive humidity. In eighteenth-century England the invention of machines that could make cotton cloth brought them a worldwide market. It was a time of great prosperity. Today you can buy cotton products from many countries.
    —Emily Gordon

QUOTATION: ON WRITING

If there is a special hell for writers, it would be in the forced contemplation of their own works.
    —John Dos Passos

QUOTATION: ON WRITING

I do not choose the right word. I get rid of the wrong one.
    —A. E. Housman

ANSWERS: EXERCISE 10-2

Answers will vary somewhat. Here is one set of possibilities.

1. Scientific evidence supports lovers who claim that they feel swept away. [10c.1, revision changes referent for *they* from the possessive case, *lovers'*, to *lovers*, a noun in the objective case] [Could also be considered correct as originally written]

2. A person who falls in love is flooded with substances that the body manufactures. *Or:* When people fall in love, they are flooded with substances that their body manufactures. [10e, revision changes person from *you* not used for direct address to third person]

3. Surprisingly, love owes its "natural high" to phenylethylamine (PEA), a chemical cousin of the amphetamines, as well as to emotion. [10c.4, 10d, revision eliminates overuse and imprecise use of *it* and *its*]

4. As the body builds up a tolerance for PEA, more and more must be produced to create the euphoria of romantic love. [10c.3, revision eliminates two *its* with different referents]

5. Although chocolate is high in PEA, gobbling it will not revive a wilting love affair. [10e, revision eliminates *your* not used for direct address]

6. Infatuation based on PEA lasts no longer than four years. Most divorces take place after four years of marriage. [10c.3, revision eliminates imprecise use of *this*]

7. Chemicals called endorphins are good news for romantics. Endorphins promote long-term intimate attachments. [10c.4, revision removes *they*, which could have referred to either *endorphins* and *romantics*]

8. Endorphins' special effects on lovers allow these drugs to exert a soothing, not an exciting, influence. [10c.1, revision eliminates *they*, which could have referred to either a possessive noun, *endorphins'*, or *lovers*]

9. Oxytocin is called the "cuddle chemical" because it seems to encourage moth-

EXERCISE 10-2

Consulting sections 10a through 10e, revise each sentence so that all pronoun references are clear. If you consider a passage correct as written, circle its number.

EXAMPLE   In a research study, it says that romantic love is a chemical process.

A research study claims that romantic love is a chemical process. [Revision avoids imprecise *it says*.]

1. Scientific evidence supports lovers' claims that they feel swept away.
2. When you fall in love, you are flooded with substances that your body manufactures.
3. It is surprising that love owes its "natural high" to phenylethylamine (PEA), a chemical cousin of the amphetamines, as well as to emotion.
4. As the body builds up a tolerance for PEA, it is necessary to produce more and more of it to create the euphoria of romantic love.
5. Although chocolate is high in PEA, gobbling it will not revive your wilting love affair.
6. Infatuation based on PEA lasts no longer than four years. This is when most divorces take place.
7. Chemicals called endorphins are good news for romantics. They promote long-term intimate attachments.
8. Endorphins' special effects on lovers allow them to exert a soothing, not an exciting, influence.
9. Oxytocin is called the "cuddle chemical" because it seems that it encourages mothers to nuzzle their babies.
10. Romantic love also owes a debt to this, for it promotes similar feelings in adult lovers.

10f Using *who*, *which*, and *that* correctly

Who refers to people or to animals with names or special talents.

Theodore Roosevelt, who served as the twenty-sixth president of the United States, inspired the creation of the stuffed animal known as the teddy bear.

Lassie, who was known for her intelligence and courage, was actually played by a series of male collies.

Which and *that* refer to animals, things, and sometimes anonymous or collective groups of people. Some writers use *which* both for **restrictive clauses** (clauses that add essential information to a sentence) and for nonrestrictive clauses (clauses that could be omitted from a sentence without changing the essential meaning). Other writers reserve *which* for nonrestrictive clauses and *that* for restrictive clauses. You can follow either practice as long as you are consistent in each piece of writing. For help in distinguishing between restrictive and nonrestrictive clauses, see section 24e.

> The zoos **that most delight children** display newborn animals as well as animals that can be touched safely. [*That* introduces information essential for understanding which zoos are being referred to.]

> Zoos, **which delight most children,** have been attracting fewer visitors each year. [*Which* introduces information that could be dropped from the sentence without changing the essential message.]

> *Who* can be used for restrictive and nonrestrictive clauses alike.

❶ **COMMA ALERT:** Set off nonrestrictive clauses with commas. Do not set off restrictive clauses with commas (see 24e). **!**

EXERCISE 10-3

Consulting section 10f, fill in the blanks with *who, which,* or *that.*

EXAMPLE   People **who** find their long-hidden cache of U.S. dollar bills eaten by mice, charred by fire, or rotting in a puddle of water can usually rescue the money.

1. As a free public service, the U.S. Department of the Treasury redeems U.S. paper money _____ has been badly damaged.

2. "Mutilated currency," _____ the Treasury defines as paper money _____ is less than 50 percent intact or of doubtful value, can be turned in at an office in Washington.

3. A "mutilated currency examiner," _____ inspects the damaged bills to determine their value, authorizes the payment _____ is to be made to their owners.

4. People _____ prefer to save their old, damaged money would never think of using this service.

5. This group of people, _____ includes many collectors of various odds and ends, values nostalgic objects more than a check from the Treasury Department.

QUOTATION: ON WRITING

I'm just going to write because I cannot help it.

—Charlotte Brontë

ANOTHER EXAMPLE

Notice how many subject-verb pairs are in the following passage.

It is common to refer to the sky as blue. Actually, the *sky is* black and our *atmosphere is* blue. *That is* because the tiny particles of *dust* and little moisture *droplets* in the air *are* small enough to interfere with and scatter the shorter wavelengths of the sun's light, the blue and violet colors, to produce an illusion of a blue sky. *Astronauts,* circling our planet at heights of hundreds of miles, *report* that the *sky is* black and that the *sun, moon, stars,* and *planets can be seen* in the daytime hours.

—Phillip D. Stern, *Our Space Environment*

11
AGREEMENT

Agreement implies that people hold the same ideas. Grammatical agreement is also based on sameness—specifically, matching. Applying the rules governing grammatical agreement can be tricky, so feel free to do what most people do: Consult a handbook to check the rules. Sections 11a through 11l discuss agreement between subjects and verbs. Sections 11m through 11r discuss agreement between pronouns and antecedents.

SUBJECT-VERB AGREEMENT

11a Understanding subject-verb agreement

Subject-verb agreement means that a SUBJECT and its VERB match in form. To agree grammatically, subjects and verbs must match in NUMBER (singular or plural) and in PERSON (first, second, or third person). The major concepts in grammatical agreement are explained in Chart 75.

> The **firefly glows.** [*firefly* is a singular subject in the third person; *glows* is a singular verb in the third person]

> **Fireflies glow.** [*fireflies* is a plural subject in the third person; *glow* is a plural verb in the third person]

◉ **Major concepts in grammatical agreement**   **75**

■ **Number,** as a concept in grammar, refers to *singular* (one) and *plural* (more than one).

■ The **first person** is the speaker or writer. *I* (singular) and *we* (plural) are the only subjects that occur in the first person.

SINGULAR	**I see** a field of fireflies.
PLURAL	**We see** a field of fireflies.

→

Major concepts in grammatical agreement   75
(continued)

- The **second person** is the person spoken or written to. *You* (for both singular and plural) is the only subject that occurs in the second person.

  SINGULAR   **You see** a shower of sparks.

  PLURAL   **You see** a shower of sparks.

- The **third person** is the person or thing being spoken or written about. Most rules for subject-verb agreement involve the third person.

  SINGULAR   The **scientist sees** a cloud of cosmic dust.

  PLURAL   The **scientists see** a cloud of cosmic dust.

11b   Using the final -*s* or -*es* either for plural subjects or for singular verbs

Subject-verb agreement often involves one letter: *s*. The basic pattern for agreement is shown in Chart 76. Keep in mind that the -*s* added to subjects and the -*s* added to verbs serve very different functions.

Pattern for basic subject-verb agreement   76

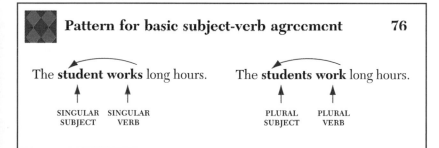

Most **plural subjects** are formed by adding -*s* or -*es*: *lip* becomes *lips; princess* becomes *princesses*. Exceptions include most pronouns (*they, it*) and a few nouns that for singular and plural either do not change (*deer, deer*) or change internally (*mouse, mice; child, children*).

In the present tense, third-person **singular verbs** are formed by adding -*s* or -*es* to the SIMPLE FORM: *laugh, laughs; kiss, kisses*. Even the exceptions—the verbs *be* (*is*) and *have* (*has*)—end in *s*.

BACKGROUND

Although English requires agreement between subject and verb, it is unlike some other modern languages in that it does not extend agreement to the gender and number of adjectives. Mario Pei, in *The Story of English* (New York: Fawcett, 1952), says that although the diminished number of endings used to indicate number and gender is thought to represent a great economy of time, space, and thought, it is probably as natural for a Spanish speaker to indicate that information by the article, adjective, and noun— for example, *las muchachas bonitas*—as it is for the English speaker not to do so. Another situation is found in the Chinese languages, which use word order instead of agreement to establish relationships among words.

EXTRA EXERCISE A

Fill in the blank with the correct present-tense form of the verb in parentheses.

EXAMPLE

Psychologists often (to use) _____ projective tests to investigate clients' unconscious memories and drives. [*use*]

1. Psychologists sometimes (to present) _____ their clients with questions to which there are no correct answers.
2. The client then (to tell) _____ what he (to see) _____ , thus showing the psychologist some of his inner self.
3. The popular *Rorschach Psychodiagnostic Inkblot Test* (to require) _____ that the client examine ten cards containing symmetrical inkblots and say what he or she (to think) _____ each means.
4. Next, the client (to point) _____ out where in the blot he or she (to find) _____ each image or idea.
5. Several scoring systems (to exist) _____ to help psychologists interpret clients' responses.

Answers to Extra Exercise A

1. present
2. tells; sees
3. requires; thinks
4. points; finds
5. exist

ANSWERS: EXERCISE 11-1

Answers will vary. Each set of sentences must use the subject once as a singular and once as a plural, and the verbs must agree accordingly.

One **student disagrees** that **students watch** too much television.
Most part-time **jobs involve** ten or twenty hours a week; **studying requires** all the remaining time.

Here is a memory device to help you visualize how the *-s* ending works in most cases of agreement. The *-s* (or *-es*) can take only one path at a time, going either to the top or to the bottom.

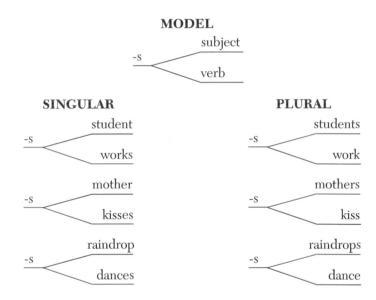

The principle of the memory device holds, even for the exceptions mentioned earlier in this section: ***It*** (singular pronoun) ***is*** *late; the* ***mice*** (plural with internal change) ***are*** *asleep.*

❶ USAGE ALERT: Do not add *-s* to a main verb used with an auxiliary verb (a helping verb such as *be, do, can, might, must,* or *would;* see 8e): *The coach* ***can walk*** [not *can walks*] *to campus.* **!**

EXERCISE 11-1

Consulting sections 11a and 11b, use the subject and verb in each set to write two complete sentences—one with the subject as a singular and one with the subject as a plural. Keep all verbs in the present tense.

1. child, laugh
2. theory, state
3. match, might light
4. committee, vote
5. man, smile
6. it, change
7. bus, speed
8. parade, celebrate

11c For agreement, ignoring words between a subject and its verb

Words that separate a SUBJECT from its VERB do not affect what the verb should agree with. The pattern is shown in Chart 77. If words modifying a subject come between subject and verb, ignore them; focus on the subject and verb.

NO **Winners** of the state contest **goes** to the national finals.
[*Winners* is the subject; the verb must agree with it. Ignore *of the state contest.*]

YES **Winners** of the state contest **go** to the national finals.

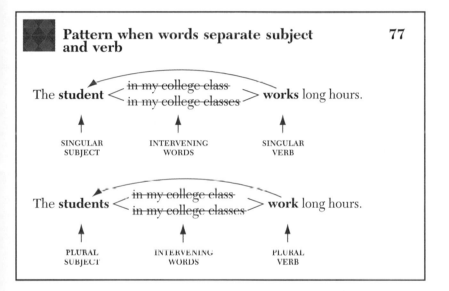

Pattern when words separate subject and verb 77

The **student** ⟨in my college class / in my college classes⟩ **works** long hours.

SINGULAR SUBJECT → INTERVENING WORDS → SINGULAR VERB

The **students** ⟨in my college class / in my college classes⟩ **work** long hours.

PLURAL SUBJECT → INTERVENING WORDS → PLURAL VERB

Be especially careful when you see the words *one of the.* This phrase takes a singular verb to agree with the word *one.* Do not be distracted by the plural noun that comes after *of the.* For the phrase *one of the . . . who,* see 11j.

NO **One** of the problems **are** broken equipment.

NO One of the problem **is** broken equipment.

YES **One** of the problems **is** broken equipment.

Similarly, eliminate word groups that start with *including, together with, along with, accompanied by, in addition to, except,* and *as well as* that separate a subject from its verb. Be sure that the verb agrees with the subject, not with the intervening words.

237

EXTRA EXERCISE B

Fill in the blank with the correct present-tense form of the verb in parentheses.

EXAMPLE

In the eyes of many people, the Rorschach inkblots (to be) _____ the psychologists' standard tool for getting at clients' hidden thoughts and feelings. [*are*]

1. Yet either the Holtzman Inkblot Technique or the Thematic Apperception Test (TAT) (to be) _____ given by psychologists who feel the Rorschach is unreliable.

2. Not only does the Holtzman series have more inkblots (forty-five) than the Rorschach (ten), but it also (to have) _____ a more standardized system of administration.

3. The TAT (to use) _____ a series of pictures showing people engaged in a wide range of activities.

4. Although the pictures show people in realistic situations, there (to be) _____ many possible acceptable answers.

5. It (to be) _____ the task of the person interpreting the picture to make up a story, deciding what has occurred and what the characters are thinking and feeling.

Answers to Extra Exercise B

1. is
2. has
3. uses
4. are
5. is

EXTRA EXERCISE C

Rewrite the following passages making the following changes: For *children,* substitute *a child.* For *adults,* substitute *an adult.* For *unicorns* substitute *a unicorn.* For *books,* substitute *a book.* For *a dragon,* substitute *dragons.* For *they,* substitute *he, she,* or *it,* considering the antecedent. Make sure that the verbs agree with the new subjects. →

Extra Exercise C (continued)

So I believe that we should trust our children. Normal children do not confuse reality and fantasy—they confuse them much less often than we adults do (as a great fantasist pointed out in a story called "The Emperor's New Clothes"). Children know perfectly well that unicorns aren't real, but they also know that books about unicorns, if they are good books, are true books. All too often, that's more than Mummy and Daddy know; for, in denying . . . childhood, the adults have denied half their knowledge, and are left with the sad, sterile little fact: "Unicorns aren't real." And that fact is one that never got anybody anywhere (except in the story "The Unicorn in the Garden," by another great fantasist, in which it is shown that a devotion to the unreality of unicorns may get you straight into the loony bin). It is by such statements as, "Once upon a time there was a dragon," or "In a hole in the ground there lived a hobbit"—it is by such beautiful non-facts that we fantastic human beings may arrive, in our peculiar fashion, at the truth.

—Ursula K. Le Guin,
"Why Are Americans Afraid
of Dragons?"

Answers to Extra Exercise C

So I believe that we should trust a child. A normal child does not confuse reality and fantasy—he or she confuses them much less often than an adult does (as a great fantasist pointed out in a story called "The Emperor's New Clothes"). A child knows perfectly well that a unicorn isn't real, but he or she also knows that a book about a unicorn, if it is a good book, is a true book. All too often, that's more than Mummy and Daddy know; for, in denying . . . childhood, an adult has denied half his or her knowledge, and is left with the sad, sterile little fact: "A unicorn isn't real." And that fact is one that never got anybody anywhere (except in the story "The Unicorn in the Garden," by another great fantasist, in

→

NO	The **moon,** along with Venus, **are** visible in the night sky. [*Moon* is the subject. The verb must agree with it. Ignore *as well as Venus*.]
YES	The **moon,** along with Venus, **is** visible in the night sky.
NO	The **Big Dipper,** as well as many other constellations, **are** easy to learn to find. [*Big Dipper* is the subject. The verb must agree with it. Ignore *along with many other constellations*.]
YES	The **Big Dipper,** as well as many other constellations, **is** easy to learn to find.

11d   Using verbs with subjects connected by *and*

Two subjects connected with *and* create a COMPOUND SUBJECT (see 7k) and require a plural verb. Chart 78 shows this pattern.

The Cascade Diner *and* the Wayside Diner *have* [not *has*] fried catfish today. [two separate diners]

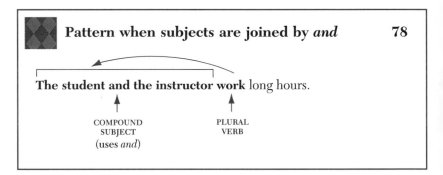

Pattern when subjects are joined by *and*   **78**

The student and the instructor work long hours.

COMPOUND SUBJECT (uses *and*)   PLURAL VERB

An exception occurs when *and* joins parts that combine to form a single thing or person.

My **friend *and* neighbor *makes*** [not *make*] excellent chili. [The friend is the same person as the neighbor. If two different people were involved, *makes* would become *make*.]

Macaroni *and* cheese *contains* [not *contain*] pasta, protein, and many calories.

each, every

The words *each* and *every* are singular even if they refer to a compound subject. Therefore, when *each* or *every* is used with a compound subject, the verb is singular. (For more information about agreement with *each* and *every*, see 11g.)

Each human hand and foot *makes* [not *make*] a distinctive print.

To identify lawbreakers, *every* police chief, sheriff, and federal marshal *depends* [not *depend*] on such prints.

🔴 **USAGE ALERT:** Use either *each* or *every*, not both together: *Each* [not *Each and every*] *robber has been caught.* ❗

11e Making the verb agree with the nearest subject

When subjects are joined by *or, either . . . or, neither . . . nor,* or *not only . . . but (also),* make the verb agree with the subject closest to it. For subject-verb agreement, ignore everything before the final subject. Chart 79 shows this pattern with *or.*

~~Not only the spider but also all other~~ **arachnids have** four pairs of legs.

~~Neither spiders nor~~ **flies appeal** to me.

~~Six clam fritters, four blue crabs, or one steamed~~ **lobster appeals** to me. [For less awkward wording, rearrange the items to place the plural subject next to the verb: *One steamed lobster, four blue crabs, or six clam fritters appeal to me.*]

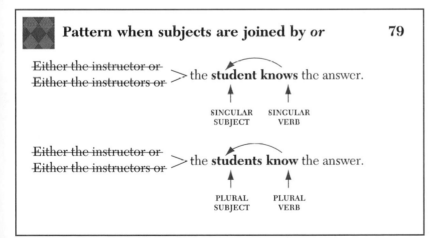

Pattern when subjects are joined by *or*   79

~~Either the instructor or~~
~~Either the instructors or~~ > the **student knows** the answer.

SINGULAR SUBJECT   SINGULAR VERB

~~Either the instructor or~~
~~Either the instructors or~~ > the **students know** the answer.

PLURAL SUBJECT   PLURAL VERB

11f Using verbs in inverted word order

In English, a SUBJECT normally comes before its VERB: *Astronomy is interesting.* **Inverted word order** changes that pattern. Most questions use inverted word order. *Is astronomy interesting?* Be sure to look after the verb, not before it, to check that the subject and verb agree.

Answers to Extra Exercise C (continued)

which it is shown that a devotion to the unreality of unicorns may get you straight into the loony bin). It is by such statements as, "Once upon a time there were dragons," or "In a hole in the ground there lived a hobbit"—it is by such beautiful non-facts that we fantastic human beings may arrive, in our peculiar fashion, at the truth.

QUOTATION: ON WRITING

After college, I sat all day in a captain's chair up on 84th Street trying to write plays for live television. Each morning I would thread my bathrobe sash through the spokes of the chair and tie myself in.
—John McPhee

Is astronomy interesting?

What **are** the **requirements** for the major?

Do John and Mary study astronomy?

If you occasionally choose to write a sentence in inverted word order to convey emphasis (see 19f), be sure to locate the subject and then make the verb agree with it.

Into deep space **shoot** probing **satellites.** [The plural verb *shoot* agrees with the inverted plural subject *satellites*.]

On the television screen **appears** an **image** of Saturn. [The singular verb *appears* agrees with the inverted singular subject *image*.]

Expletive constructions invert word order. Using *there* or *it* plus a form of the verb *be*, these phrases postpone the subject. In sentences with *there*, check ahead to identify the subject, and then choose the right form of *be* to agree with the subject.

There are nine **planets** in our solar system. [The verb *are* agrees with the subject *planets*.]

There is probably no **life** on eight of them. [The verb *is* agrees with the subject *life*.]

In sentences with *it*, the form of *be* is always singular, to agree with *it*.

It is property owners who are seeking changes in the tax laws.

For advice on eliminating some expletives for conciseness, see section 16a.1.

EXERCISE 11-2

Consulting sections 11c through 11f, supply the correct present-tense form of the verb in parentheses.

EXAMPLE   One of the many new programs taking hold in U.S. school systems (to be) **is** the self-esteem movement.

1. Of course, there (to be) _____ some skeptics who doubt the self-esteem movement's claim to address widespread social problems.

2. California schoolteacher Jack Canfield and many of his colleagues (to believe) _____ that motivational training in self-esteem can help reduce drug abuse, teenage pregnancy, and welfare dependency.

3. In Canfield's seminars, either his team leaders or Canfield himself (to ask) _____ participants to make up events, act out their responses, and explain the outcomes.

4. From such role-playing techniques (to come) _____ awareness that actions have consequences.

5. There (to be) _____ also great security in being able to act out a risky situation in a safe environment.

11g Using verbs with indefinite pronouns

Many **indefinite pronouns** refer to unknown persons, things, quantities, or ideas—hence the label "indefinite." In context in a sentence, even indefinite pronouns that do not have a specific ANTECEDENT can take on clear meaning. Most indefinite pronouns are singular and require a singular verb for agreement. Two indefinite pronouns, *both* and *many,* are always plural and require a plural verb. A few indefinite pronouns can be singular or plural. See Chart 80 for a list of indefinite pronouns and their numbers. (For advice on avoiding sexist language with indefinite pronouns, see sections 11q and 21b.)

◉ **Common indefinite pronouns** **80**

Always Plural

both	many

Always Singular

another	every	no one
anybody	everybody	nothing
anyone	everyone	one
anything	everything	somebody
each	neither	someone
either	nobody	something

Singular or Plural, Depending on Context

all	more	none
any	most	some

SINGULAR INDEFINITE PRONOUNS

Everything about that intersection **is** dangerous.

But whenever **anyone says** anything, **nothing is** done.

BACKGROUND ON LANGUAGE

According to Martha Kolln of Pennsylvania State University, a major theorist in language studies, we shouldn't be too concerned about the usage *everyone . . . their* or *anybody . . . their.* She notes in "Everyone's Right to Their Own Language" (*College Composition and Communication* 37, 1986. 100–102), that *everybody* has been treated as a plural for over four hundred years and *everyone* for over two hundred, appearing this way in the works of Cardinal Newman, Shakespeare, and Swift. Despite this evidence (available since 1957), the rule stands—at least on the record.

Kolln argues for treating indefinite pronouns as we treat collective nouns. A collective noun such as *crowd* takes a singular verb but takes a plural pronoun when it clearly refers to more than one person. She gives as an example:

> At first *the crowd* was singing; then *they* began to laugh.

Kolln gives this example for indefinite pronouns:

> At first *everyone* in the room was singing; then *they* began to laugh.

In fact, any singular pronoun other than *everyone* or *someone* would be out of place in the second clause. She demonstrates that the same applies when the indefinite pronoun appears as the direct object or as the subject of a tag question.

Kolln ends by calling for the acceptance of the plural possessive pronoun (*their*) after collective indefinite pronouns:

> These dicta that designate all indefinite pronouns as singular have no basis either in actual usage or in the rules of logic. Yet the current handbooks apply the same rule to all of the indefinite pronouns, whether they are collective or not, whether singular or not. (102)

Whether you agree or disagree with Kolln, the issue is certainly worth discussion.

Each of us **has** [not *have*] to shovel snow; **each is** [not *are*] expected to help.

Every snowstorm of the past two years **has** [not *have*] been severe. **Every** one of them **has** [not *have*] caused massive traffic jams.

SINGULAR OR PLURAL INDEFINITE PRONOUNS

Some of our streams **are** polluted. [*Some* refers to the plural noun *streams,* so the plural verb *are* is correct.]

Some pollution **is** reversible, but **all** pollution **threatens** the balance of nature. [*Some* and *all* refer to the singular noun *pollution,* so the singular verbs *is* and *threatens* are correct.]

All that environmentalists ask **is** to give nature a chance. [*All* has the meaning here of "everything" or "the only thing," so the singular verb *is* is correct.]

Winter has driven the birds south; **all have** left. [*All* refers to the plural noun *birds,* so the plural verb *have* is correct.]

🛑 **USAGE ALERT:** Do not mix singular and plural with *this, that, these,* and *those,* as in *this kind, this type, these kinds,* and *these types. This* and *that* are singular, as are *kind* and *type; these* and *those* are plural, as are *kinds* and *types: **This** [or *That*] **kind** of weather makes me shiver. **These** [or *Those*] **kinds** of sweaters keep me warm.* ❗

11h Using verbs in context for collective nouns

A **collective noun** names a group of people or things: *family, group, audience, class, number, committee, team,* and the like. To show that the group acts as one unit, use a singular verb. When the members of the group act individually, thus creating more than one action, you can use a plural verb with the collective noun, as long as you do not shift back and forth between singular and plural for the same noun. Note that for the plural sense, changing to a plural noun usually sounds better in American English.

The senior **class** nervously **awaits** final exams. [The class is acting as a single unit, so the verb is singular.]

The senior **class were** fitted for their graduation robes today. [Each member was fitted individually, so because more than one fitting was involved, the verb is plural.]

The **seniors were** fitted for their graduation robes today.

The **members of the senior class were** fitted for their graduation robes today.

11i Making a linking verb agree with the subject, not the subject complement

LINKING VERBS connect the SUBJECT to a **subject complement,** a word that renames or describes the subject. You can think of a linking verb as an equal sign between a subject and its complement.

The car **looks** new. [*Car* is the subject, *looks* is the linking verb, and *new* is the subject complement.]

When you write a sentence that contains a subject complement, remember that the verb always agrees with the subject. For the purposes of agreement, ignore the subject complement.

NO   The worst **part** of owning a car **are** the bills. [The subject is the singular word *part,* so the plural verb *are* is wrong. That the subject complement is a plural word, *bills,* does not affect subject-verb agreement.]

YES   The worst **part** of owning a car **is** the bills. [The singular subject *part* agrees with the singular verb *is.*]

NO   **Bills is** the worst part of owning a car. [The plural word *bills* is the subject; it needs a plural verb.]

YES   **Bills are** the worst part of owning a car. [The plural subject *bills* agrees with the plural verb *are.*]

11j Using verbs that agree with the antecedents of *who, which,* and *that*

The pronouns *who, which,* and *that* have the same form in singular and plural. Before deciding whether the verb should be singular or plural, find the pronoun's ANTECEDENT.

The scientist will share the income from her new patent with the graduate **students who work** with her. [*Who* refers to *students,* so the plural verb *work* is used.]

George Jones is the **student who works** in the science lab. [*Who* refers to *student,* so the singular verb *works* is used.]

Be especially careful when you use *one of the* or *the only one of the* in a sentence before *who, which,* or *that.* With *one of the,* the pronoun refers to the plural word after *one of the,* requiring a plural verb. With *the only one of the, who* (or *which* or *that*) refers to the singular *one,* requiring a singular verb.

243

ANSWERS: EXERCISE 11-3

1. works
2. is
3. encourages
4. says; have
5. listens; makes

EXTRA EXERCISE D

In writing groups, students can work together to edit the following sentences for subject-verb agreement.

1. When a couple move into a new apartment, they face many decisions.

2. One of the biggest choices have to do with how to decorate it.

3. Probably the most important decision of all are the color choices.

4. Green is one of the colors that looks good in any room.

Answers to Extra Exercise D

1. When a couple *moves* into a new apartment, *it faces* many decisions.

2. One of the biggest choices *has* to do with how to decorate it.

3. Probably the most important decision of all *is* the color choices.

4. Green is one of the colors that *look* good in any room.

Tracy is one of the students **who talk** in class. [*Who* refers to *students*, so *talk* is plural.]

Jim is the only one of the students **who talks** in class. [*Who* refers to *one*, so *talks* is singular.]

EXERCISE 11-3

Consulting sections 11g through 11j, supply the correct present-tense form of the verb in parentheses.

EXAMPLE   Everyone (to know) **knows** that a good laugh (to make) **makes** most people feel better.

1. Daily, a group of humor consultants (to work) _____ to introduce laughter into American businesses.
2. The humorists believe that the best introduction for a speech (to be) _____ jokes and humorous observations.
3. C. W. Metcalf has developed one of the programs that (to encourage) _____ people to laugh at their own problems.
4. A large number of personnel officers (to say) _____ they prefer to hire workers who (to have) _____ a sense of humor.
5. Sales representatives find that almost anyone (to listen) _____ more attentively to a person who (to make) _____ an amusing comment.

11k Using singular verbs with subjects that specify amounts and with singular subjects in plural form

Subjects that refer to times, sums of money, distance, or measurement are considered singular and take singular verbs.

Two hours is not enough time to finish. [time]

Three hundred dollars is what we must pay. [sum of money]

Two miles is a short sprint for some serious joggers. [distance]

Three-quarters of an inch is needed for a perfect fit. [measurement]

Many NOUNS that end in -s or -ics are singular in meaning and so need singular verbs, despite their plural appearance. These words include *news*, *ethics*, and *measles*. They also include *economics*, *mathematics*, *physics*, and *statistics* when these words refer to courses of study. Also, *United States of America* is singular (see also 41c).

The **news gets** better each day. [*News* is singular, so the singular verb *gets* is correct.]

Statistics is required of science majors. [*Statistics* is a course of study, so the singular verb *is* is correct.]

Statistics show that a teacher shortage is coming. [*Statistics* refers to separate pieces of information, so the plural verb *show* is correct.]

Some nouns, such as *politics* and *sports,* agree with singular or plural verbs, depending on the meaning of the sentence.

Sports is a good way to build physical stamina. [Here, *sports* is one general activity, so it agrees with the singular verb *is*.]

Three **sports are** offered at the recreation center. [Here, separate activities are being considered, so the plural verb *are* is correct.]

Some words require a plural verb even though they refer to one thing: *jeans, pants, scissors, clippers, tweezers, eyeglasses, thanks, riches.* However, if the word *pair* is used in conjunction with *jeans, pants, scissors, clippers, tweezers,* or *eyeglasses,* a singular verb is required to agree with *pair.*

Those **slacks need** pressing. [plural]

That **pair of slacks needs** pressing. [singular]

Series and *means* have the same form in singular and plural, so the meaning determines whether the verb is singular or plural.

Six new television **series are** beginning this week.

A **series of disasters is** plaguing our production.

111 Using singular verbs for titles of written works, companies, and words as terms

Even when PLURAL and COMPOUND NOUNS are in a title, the title itself refers to one work or entity. Therefore, titles of written works are singular and require singular verbs.

Breathing Lessons by Anne Tyler **is** a prize-winning novel.

If a plural word is referred to as a term, it requires a singular verb.

We implies that everyone is included.

During the Vietnam War, ***protective reaction strikes*** **was** a euphemism the U.S. government used to refer to bombing.

EXTRA EXERCISE E
Complete the following sentences by supplying an appropriate verb.

1. Physics _____ a demanding subject.
2. Do you think physics or economics _____ harder?
3. Sports _____ the popular favorite.
4. Three-quarters of an hour of exercise several times a week _____ enough to keep a person in reasonably good shape.
5. Statistics _____ that exercise of the body as well as the mind _____ important for good health.

Answers to Extra Exercise E
1. is
2. is
3. is
4. is
5. show (indicate); is

ANSWERS AND COVERAGE: EXERCISE 11-4

1. realizes [11g, *anyone* is always singular]

2. are [11i, linking verb agrees with subject *explanations*]

3. agrees [11h, subject is *assortment*, a collective noun meant as a unit]

4. is [11g, *one* is always singular]

5. knows [11j, *who* refers to the singular noun *individual*]

ANSWERS AND COVERAGE: EXERCISE 11-5

1. invites [11g, singular verb with subject modified by *each*]

2. are [11f, words in inverted order]; remain [11b, plural subject *roses*]

3. symbolizes [11g, singular verb with *each*]

4. are [11f, words in inverted order]; flourish [11b, plural subject, *thirty-five*]

5. was [11a, singular subject, *rose*]

6. suggests [11c, singular verb with *one*]

7. says [11c, ignoring intervening words]

8. explain [11b, plural subject, *theories*]

9. demonstrates [11h, singular-context collective noun]

10. remains [11i, agreeing with subject *best-seller*]

EXERCISE 11-4

Consulting sections 11k and 11l, supply the correct present-tense form of the verb in parentheses.

EXAMPLE   Everyone (to use) **uses** phrases involving color in daily conversations, as when they say that someone "has the blues" or was "caught red-handed."

1. Hardly anyone (to realize) _____ that in such phrases, *red-handed* or *the blues* has a significant and generally unknown meaning.
2. Explanations about the origins of phrases like *red-letter day* (to be) _____ often a surprise.
3. An assortment of language experts (to agree) _____ that because special dates, such as national holidays, were often printed in red on calendars, people started to use *red letter* to refer to any special day.
4. There are many other curious uses of such color words; one (to be) _____ *greenroom*, a waiting room for guests who are going to appear on a TV talk show.
5. People rarely meet an individual who (to know) _____ that the term *greenroom* originated in the nineteenth century, when theaters always used green paint for an actor's dressing room.

EXERCISE 11-5

Consulting sections 11a through 11l, supply the correct form of the verb in parentheses.

EXAMPLE   Of the thirty thousand plant species on earth, the rose (to be) **is** the most universally known.

1. Each plant species (to invite) _____ much discussion about origins and meanings, and when talk turns to flowers, the rose is usually the first mentioned.
2. More fragrant and colorful (to be) _____ other types of flowers, yet roses (to remain) _____ the most popular worldwide.
3. Each of the types of roses (to symbolize) _____ beauty, love, romance, and secrecy.
4. There (to be) _____ over two hundred pure species of roses and thousands of mixed species, thirty-five of which (to flourish) _____ in the soil of North America.
5. It is impossible to determine exactly where or when the first rose (to be) _____ domesticated, because roses have existed for so many centuries; one of the earliest references dates back to 3000 B.C.
6. One such myth from Greek mythology (to suggest) _____ that the rose first appeared with the birth of the goddess Aphrodite.

7. Another myth, which focuses on the rose's thorns, (to say) _____ than an angry god shot arrows into the stem to curse the rose forever with arrow-shaped thorns.

8. While theories of this kind (to explain) _____ the significance and evolution of the rose, few people can explain the flower's enduring popularity.

9. Even today, a couple (to demonstrate) _____ love by exchanging red roses.

10. Of all flowers, the best-seller (to remain) _____ the rose.

PRONOUN-ANTECEDENT AGREEMENT

11m Understanding pronoun-antecedent agreement

Pronoun-antecedent agreement means that PRONOUNS (see 7b) must match the form of their **antecedents**, the words they are replacing. To agree grammatically, pronouns must match in NUMBER (singular or plural) and in PERSON (first, second, or third person); Chart 81 shows these relationships. For explanations and examples of the concepts of number and person, see Chart 75 in section 11a, where you can find related material on agreement between SUBJECTS and VERBS. For advice about staying consistent in person and number, see section 15a.1.

The **firefly** glows when **it** emerges from **its** nest at night. [The singular pronouns *it* and *its* match their singular antecedent, *firefly*.]

Fireflies glow when **they** emerge from **their** nests at night. [The plural pronouns *they* and *their* match their plural antecedent, *fireflies*.]

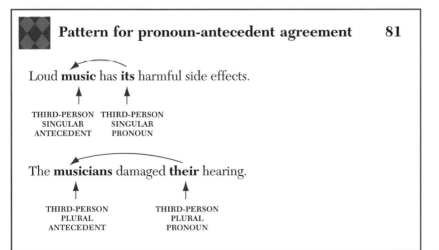

Pattern for pronoun-antecedent agreement 81

Loud **music** has **its** harmful side effects.

THIRD-PERSON SINGULAR ANTECEDENT — THIRD-PERSON SINGULAR PRONOUN

The **musicians** damaged **their** hearing.

THIRD-PERSON PLURAL ANTECEDENT — THIRD-PERSON PLURAL PRONOUN

Plaids have been a favorite fabric design for many centuries. It consists of bars of color crossing each other at right angles. Scotland is the home of the plaid, where they are called a tartan, or, in song, story, and legend, *plaidies*. The tartan, which distinguish the clan of their wearers, is ancient, but their origin is unknown. In its earliest forms they were pieces of cloth about two yards broad and four yards long, which was drawn round the waist in folds that was tightly buckled with a belt. The lower part came down to the knees, and the upper part fell over the left shoulder so that they left the right arm free. Early in the eighteenth century, the "belted plaid" disappeared. They were replaced by the kilt. The particular pattern of tartans which distinguish each clan must have been fixed before 1645, probably before 1600. Later, in 1746, trying to end the clan system, the British Parliament prohibited the Scots from wearing tartans. The action against it was taken following the Battle of Culloden where Prince Charles Edward Stuart, grandson of James II, was defeated by the Duke of Cumberland. To be caught wearing them carried a penalty of six months' imprisonment. The kilt is worn today so that when the wearer is standing erect, their edges should reach the center of the kneecap. They should be made of a tartan associated with the name of the wearer. In the absence of a family claim to wear them, the Scots allow the wearing of the Royal Stuart tartan.

—Emily Gordon

Answers to Extra Exercise F

Plaids have been favorite fabric *designs* for many centuries. *They consist* of bars of color crossing each other at right angles. Scotland is the home of the plaid, where *it*

→

is called a tartan, or, in song, story, and legend, *a plaidie*. The tartan, *which distinguishes* the clan of *its wearer*, is ancient, but *its* origin is unknown. In its earliest *form, it was a piece* of cloth about two yards broad and four yards long, which was drawn round the waist in folds that *were* tightly buckled with a belt. The lower part came down to the knees, and the upper part fell over the left shoulder so that *it* left the right arm free. Early in the eighteenth century, the "belted plaid" disappeared. *It was* replaced by the kilt. The particular pattern of *tartan which distinguishes* each clan must have been fixed before 1645, probably before 1600. Later, in 1746, trying to end the clan system, the British Parliament prohibited the Scots from wearing *the tartan*. The action against it was taken following the Battle of Culloden where Prince Charles Edward Stuart, grandson of James II, was defeated by the Duke of Cumberland. To be caught wearing *it* carried a penalty of six months' imprisonment. The kilt is worn today so that when the wearer is standing erect, *its* edges should reach the center of the kneecap. *It* should be made of a tartan associated with the name of the wearer. In the absence of a family claim to wear *one*, the Scots allow the wearing of the Royal Stuart tartan.

EXTRA EXERCISE G

Rewrite this paragraph so that pronoun-antecedent agreement in person and number is maintained. It may also be necessary to change verbs or other words.

Buying stock involves many steps. Once a stockbroker receives an order, they call their firm's telephone clerk, who is located near the edge of the trading area. The telephone clerk summons his firm's floor broker by flashing their code number on a large electronic board posted in the trading area. Seeing their number, the floor broker goes to the tele-

→

11n Using pronouns with antecedents connected by *and*

When *and* is used to connect two or more antecedents, they require a plural pronoun, even if the separate antecedents are singular. (For related material on subjects and verbs, see 11d.)

The Cascade Diner *and* the Wayside Diner closed for New Year's Eve to give **their** [not *its*] employees the night off. [separate diners]

When *and* joins singular nouns that combine to form a single thing or person, they require a singular pronoun.

My **friend *and* neighbor** makes **his** [not *their*] excellent chili every Saturday. [The friend is the same person as the neighbor. If two different people were involved, *his* should be *their,* and *makes* should be *make*.]

each, every

The words *each* and *every* are always singular. Even if *each* or *every* precedes antecedents joined by *and*, the pronoun must be singular. (For related material on subjects and verbs, see 11d. Also, for advice about pronoun agreement for *each* or *every* used alone, see 11p.)

***Each* human hand and foot** leaves **its** [not *their*] distinctive print.

The same rule holds when the construction *one of the* follows *each* or *every:* ***Each one of the robbers*** *left* **his** [not *their*] *fingerprints at the scene.*

11o Making the pronoun agree with the nearest antecedent

Antecedents joined by *or* or correlative conjunctions such as *neither . . . nor* or *not only . . . but (also)* (see 7h) often mix singular and plural. For the purposes of agreement, ignore everything before the final antecedent. (For related material on subject-verb agreement, see 11e.) The pattern in Chart 82 illustrates this principle.

Each night after the restaurant closes, either the resident mice or **the owner's cat** manages to get **itself** a good meal of leftovers.

Each night after the restaurant closes, either the owner's cat or **the resident mice** manage to get **themselves** a good meal of leftovers.

Pattern when antecedents are joined by *or* 82

~~Either the loudspeakers or~~ **the microphone** needs **its** electric cord repaired.

SINGULAR ANTECEDENT   SINGULAR PRONOUN

~~Either the microphone or~~ **the loudspeakers** need **their** electric cords repaired.

PLURAL ANTECEDENT   PLURAL PRONOUN

11p Using pronouns with indefinite-pronoun antecedents

Many indefinite pronouns refer to unknown persons, things, quantities, or ideas. In context within a sentence, an indefinite pronoun can have clear meaning even if it does not have a specific antecedent. Most indefinite pronouns are singular. Two indefinite pronouns, *both* and *many,* are plural. A few indefinite pronouns can be singular or plural, depending on the meaning of the sentence. (For a list of indefinite pronouns, grouped as singular or plural, see Chart 80 in section 11g. For advice on avoiding sexist language with indefinite pronouns, see sections 11q and 21b.)

SINGULAR INDEFINITE PRONOUNS

Everyone taking this course hopes to get **his or her** [not *their*] college degree within a year.

Anybody wanting to wear a cap and gown at graduation must have **his or her** [not *their*] measurements taken.

Each student **is** [not *are*] hoping for a passing grade.

Each of the students handed in **his or her** [not *their*] final term paper.

Every student **needs** [not *need*] encouragement now and then.

Every student in my classes **is** [not *are*] studying hard.

SINGULAR OR PLURAL INDEFINITE PRONOUNS

When winter break arrives for students, **most** leave **their** dormitories for home. [*Most* refers to *students,* so the plural pronoun *their* is correct.]

As for the luggage, **most is** already on its way to the airport. [*Most* refers to *luggage,* so the singular pronoun *its* is correct.]

None fear that **they** will get to the airport late. [The entire group does not expect to get to the airport late, so a plural pronoun is correct.]

None fears that **he or she** will get to the airport late. [No one individual expects to get to the airport late, so a singular pronoun is correct; note that *he or she* always functions as a singular pronoun (see Chart 83).]

11q Avoiding sexist pronoun use

In the past, grammatical convention specified using masculine pronouns to refer to indefinite pronouns: "***Everyone** open **his** book.*" Today, people are more conscious that the pronouns *he, his, him,* and *himself* exclude women, who comprise over half the population. Many experienced writers try to avoid using masculine pronouns to refer to the entire population. Chart 83 shows three ways to avoid using masculine pronouns when referring to males and females together. (For advice on how to avoid other types of sexist language, see section 21b.)

◎ **Ways to avoid using only the masculine**   **83**
pronoun to refer to males and females together

- **Solution 1:** Use a pair of pronouns—but try to avoid a pair more than once in a sentence or in many sentences in a row. When you use a *he or she* construction, remember that it acts as a singular pronoun.
  Everyone hopes that **he or she** will win a scholarship.
  With the explosion of information, a **doctor** usually has time to read only in **his or her** specialty.

- **Solution 2:** Revise into the plural.
  Many people hope that **they** will win a scholarship.
  With the explosion of information, few **doctors** have time to read outside **their** specialties.

- **Solution 3:** Recast the sentence.
  Everyone hopes to win a scholarship.
  With the explosion of medical information, few specialists have time for general reading.

11r Using pronouns with collective-noun antecedents

A **collective noun** names a group of people or things, such as *family, group, audience, class, number, committee,* and *team.* When the group acts as one unit, use a singular pronoun to refer to it. When the members of the group act individually, thus creating more than one action, use a plural pronoun. (In the latter situation, it is often advisable to substitute a plural noun for the collective noun; see 11h.)

The **audience** was cheering as **it** stood to applaud the performers. [The audience was acting as one unit, so the singular pronoun *it* is correct.]

The **audience** put on **their** coats and walked out. [The members of the audience were acting as individuals, so all actions collect to become plural; therefore, the plural pronoun *their* is correct.]

The **family** is spending **its** vacation in Rockport, Maine. [All the family members went to one place together.]

The **family** are spending **their** vacations in Maine, Hawaii, and Rome. [Each family member went to a different place.]

The **family members** are spending **their** vacations in Maine, Hawaii, and Rome. [Plural noun makes the sense of the plural pronoun even clearer.]

EXERCISE 11-6

Consulting section 11m through 11r, circle the correct pronoun of the choices in parentheses.

EXAMPLE   Many people wonder what gives certain leaders (his or her, (their)) spark and magnetic personal appeal.

1. The cluster of personal traits that produces star quality is called *charisma,* a state that bestows special power on (its, their) bearers.

2. Charisma is the quality that allows an individual to empower (himself, herself, himself or herself, themselves) and others.

3. Power and authority alone do not guarantee charisma; to produce it, (it, they) must be combined with passion and strong purpose.

4. A charismatic leader has the ability to draw other people into (his, her, his or her, their) dream or vision.

5. (He, She, He or she, They) can inspire followers to believe that the leader's goals are the same as (his, her, his or her, their) own.

6. Not all leaders who possess charisma enjoy having this ability to attract and influence (his, his or her, their) followers.

7. Charismatic leaders are often creative, especially in (his, his or her, their) capacity for solving problems in original ways.

ANSWERS AND COVERAGE: EXERCISE 11-6

1. its [11m]
2. himself or herself [11q]
3. they [11n]
4. his or her [11q]
5. He or she [11q]; their [11m]
6. their [11m]
7. their [11m]

Answers and Coverage: Exercise 11-6 (continued)

8. their [11m]

9. their [11m]; he or she [11q]

10. their [11m]; his or her [11p and 11q]; their [11m]

QUOTATION: ON WRITING

They ask me if I were on a desert island and knew nobody would ever see what I wrote, would I go on writing. My answer is most emphatically yes, I would go on writing for company. Because I'm creating an imaginary—it's always imaginary—world in which I would like to live.

—William Burroughs

8. Today, a number of major corporations offer (its, their) employees charisma-training courses to enhance leadership qualities.

9. Usually, it is not the quiet, low-profile manager but rather the charismatic manager with strong leadership qualities who convinces others that (his, her, his or her, their) best interests are served by the course of action (he, she, he or she, they) will be proposing.

10. Charisma trainers advise would-be leaders to start by bringing order to (his, her, his or her, their) activities; in stressful times, anyone who appears to have some part of (his, her, his or her, their) life under control makes others relax and perform (his, her, his or her, their) responsibilities better.

12

USING ADJECTIVES AND ADVERBS

12a Distinguishing between adjectives and adverbs

Both **adjectives** and **adverbs** are **modifiers**—words or groups of words that describe other words.

ADJECTIVE	The **brisk** *wind* blew. [Adjective *brisk* modifies noun *wind*.]
ADVERB	The wind *blew* **briskly**. [Adverb *briskly* modifies verb *blew*.]

The key to distinguishing between adjectives and adverbs is understanding that they modify different word groups. As Chart 84 shows, to modify a NOUN or a PRONOUN, use an *adjective*. To modify a VERB, an adjective, or another adverb, use an *adverb*.

⊙ Differences between adjectives and adverbs 84

WHAT ADJECTIVES MODIFY	EXAMPLES
nouns	The **busy** *lawyer* took a **quick** *look* at the members of the jury.
pronouns	*She* felt **triumphant**, for *they* were **attentive**.

WHAT ADVERBS MODIFY	EXAMPLES
verbs	The lawyer *spoke* **quickly** and **well**.
adverbs	The lawyer spoke **very** *quickly*.
adjectives	The lawyer was **extremely** *busy*.
independent clauses	**Therefore,** *the lawyer rested*.

WORD DERIVATION

Adjective comes from the Latin *adjectivus*, meaning "that is added," and *adverb* comes from the Latin *adverbum*, meaning "to a word." Both etymologies reflect the use of adjectives and adverbs as enhancers of other words' meanings.

QUOTATION: ON WRITING

The adjective is the enemy of the noun.
—Voltaire

QUOTATION: ON WRITING

What you say is found not in the noun but in what you add to qualify the noun. . . . The noun, the verb, and the main clause serve merely as the base on which meaning will rise. . . . The modifier is the essential part of any sentence.
—John Erskine

QUOTATION: ON WRITING

I don't think in any language. I think in images. I don't believe that people think in languages.
—Vladimir Nabokov

STATEWIDE TESTING

If you teach in a state that requires students to pass basic competency tests in English, see the free publications coordinated with this handbook: One is for the CLAST (Florida), and another is for the TASP Exam (Texas).

QUOTATION: ON WRITING

I don't like too many adjectives or adverbs—I say if a noun or a verb is worth describing, do it properly, take a sentence to do it.
—Fay Weldon

Some people assume that all adverbs end in *-ly*. But this not true. Many adverbs do end in *-ly* (eat *swiftly*, eat *frequently*, eat *hungrily*), but some do not (eat *fast*, eat *often*, eat *seldom*). To complicate matters further, some adjectives end in *-ly* (*lovely* flower, *friendly* dog). Use meaning, not an *-ly* ending, to identify adverbs.

EXERCISE 12-1

Consulting section 12a, first underline and label all adjectives (ADJ) and adverbs (ADV). Then, draw an arrow from each adjective and adverb to the word or words they modify.

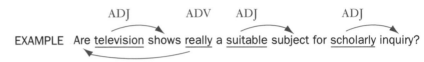

EXAMPLE   Are television shows really a suitable subject for scholarly inquiry?

1. A rapidly growing group of investigators now takes television programming seriously.
2. These investigators say that television dramatically influences everything in our lives from political campaigns to breakfast foods.
3. Most Americans usually spend many years learning to read and understand printed language but practically no time learning to understand the messages that television delivers.
4. Now, college students can take newly created courses in television studies, in which they analyze the situation comedy as intensely as the classic novel.
5. Are there better ways to observe the changes in families in the United States than to study *Father Knows Best, All in the Family,* and *Home Improvement?*

12b Using adverbs—not adjectives—to modify verbs, adjectives, and other adverbs

Do not use adjectives as adverbs. Always use adverbs to modify verbs, adjectives, and other adverbs.

> **NO** The candidate inspired us **great.** [Adjective *great* cannot modify verb *inspired.*]
>
> **YES** The candidate inspired us **greatly.** [Adverb *greatly* can modify verb *inspired.*]
>
> **NO** The candidate felt **unusual** energetic. [Adjective *unusual* cannot modify adjective *energetic.*]
>
> **YES** The candidate felt **unusually** energetic. [Adverb *unusually* can modify adjective *energetic.*]

ANSWERS: EXERCISE 12-1

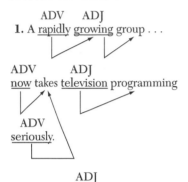

ADV   ADJ
1. A rapidly growing group . . .

ADV   ADJ
now takes television programming

ADV
seriously.

ADJ
2. These investigators . . .

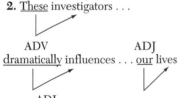

ADV   ADJ
dramatically influences . . . our lives

ADJ
from political campaigns

ADJ
to breakfast foods.

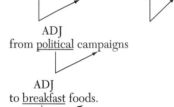

ADJ   ADV
3. Most Americans usually spend

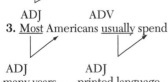

ADJ   ADJ
many years . . . printed language . . .

ADV ADJ
practically no time . . .

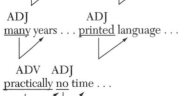

254

| NO | The candidate spoke **exceptional** forcefully. [Adjective *exceptional* cannot modify adverb *forcefully*.] |
| YES | The candidate spoke **exceptionally** forcefully. [Adverb *exceptionally* modifies adverb *forcefully*.] |

12c Not using double negatives

A **double negative** is a statement with two negative modifiers, the second of which repeats the message of the first. Negative modifiers include *no, never, not, none, nothing, hardly, scarcely,* and *barely.*

| NO | The factory workers will **never** vote for **no** strike. |
| YES | The factory workers will **never** vote for **a** strike. |

The words *not, no,* and *nothing* are particularly common in double negatives.

NO	The union members did **not** have **no** money in reserve.
YES	The union members did **not** have **any** money in reserve.
YES	The union members had **no** money in reserve.

Take special care to avoid double negatives with contractions of the word *not* (such as *isn't, don't, didn't,* or *haven't*). The negative message is conveyed by the contraction; do not add a second negative. (For advice about when contractions are appropriate, see 27c.)

NO	He did**n't** hear **nothing.**
YES	He did**n't** hear **anything.**
NO	They have**n't** had **no** meetings.
YES	They have**n't** had **any** meetings.

Also be careful when using the conjunction *nor. Nor* is correct only after *neither* (see 7h); after any other negative, use *or.*

NO	Stewart did**n't** eat dinner **nor** watch television last night.
YES	Stewart did**n't** eat dinner **or** watch television last night.
YES	Stewart **neither** ate dinner **nor** watched television last night.

12d Using adjectives—not adverbs— as complements after linking verbs

Linking verbs connect a SUBJECT to a **complement**—a word that renames or describes the subject (see 7m.1). You can think of a linking verb as an equal sign between a subject and its complement.

The *guests* **looked** *happy*. [Verb *looked* links subject *guests* to adjective *happy*.]

Answers: Exercise 12-1 (continued)

ADV ADJ
4. Now, college students can take

ADV ADJ
newly created courses

ADJ
in television studies, . . .

ADJ
analyze the situation comedy as

ADV   ADJ
intensely as the classic novel.

ADJ
5. better ways

LANGUAGE HISTORY

The rule banning double negatives in English is a relatively new one. Double, triple, and even quadruple negatives were acceptable in Old English and Middle English. They are also acceptable in many modern languages. The first attempts to regularize English were made in the eighteenth century. It was then that the first English dictionaries and usage books were written. One of these was Robert Lowth's *Short Introduction to English Grammar,* in which he stated that "two Negatives in English destroy one another, or are equivalent to an affirmative." The new rich of the merchant class, eager to fit in by speaking and writing correctly, accepted Lowth's rule, and it became the standard despite the thousand-year history of acceptable double negatives in English.

LANGUAGE HISTORY

Adverbs in Old English and Middle English were formed differently than they are today. To make an adverb, an *-e* was simply added to an adjective. The modern *-ly* ending for adverbs comes from an adjective ending, *-lice* (meaning "like"), which became softened to *-ly* and was reinterpreted as an adverb signal. Some modern adjectives ending in *-ly* (such as *friendly* and *heavenly*) are descendants of those old *-lice* adjectives.

Problems can arise with "sense verbs" (*look*, *feel*, *smell*, *taste*, *sound*, *grow*, and others) that are sometimes linking verbs and sometimes action verbs, depending on the sentence. As linking verbs, these verbs use adjectives in complements. As action verbs, these verbs use adverbs in complements.

> Zora *looks* **happy.** [*looks* = linking verb; *happy* = adjective]

> Zora *looks* **happily** at the sunset. [*looks* = action verb; *happily* = adverb]

bad, badly

The words *bad* (adjective) and *badly* (adverb) are particularly prone to misuse with linking verbs such as *feel, grow, smell, sound,* and *taste.* Only the adjective *bad* is correct when a verb is functioning as a linking verb. (When a verb functions as an action verb, *badly* is fine: *Zora played the piano* **badly***.*)

FOR DESCRIBING A FEELING

NO   The student felt **badly.**

YES   The student felt **bad.**

FOR DESCRIBING A SMELL

NO   The food smelled **badly.**

YES   The food smelled **bad.**

good, well

Well functions both as an adverb and as an adjective. As a MODIFIER, *good* is always an adjective: *He wore his* **good** *suit. Well* is an adjective referring to good health, but it is an adverb in all other contexts.

> You look **well** = You look to be in good health. [*well* = adjective]
> You write **well** = You write skillfully. [*well* = adverb]

Except when *well* is an adjective referring to health, use *good* only as an adjective and *well* only as an adverb.

NO   She sings **good.** [*sings* = action verb; adverb, not adjective, required; *good* is adjective]

YES   She sings **well.** [*well* = adverb]

EXERCISE 12-2

Consulting sections 12a through 12d, circle the correct uses of negatives and of adjectives and adverbs of the choices in parentheses.

EXAMPLE   Because she was only five when her father died, Bernice King, Martin Luther King's youngest child, ((barely), bare) remembers the details of his (solemnly, (solemn)) funeral, yet the image of her father remains strong within her.

1. Although she did feel (badly, bad) about her father's death when she was younger, King's daughter has managed to put his influence on her to good use by speaking (passionately, passionate) about issues her father first introduced.

2. In her (widely, wide) acclaimed book of sermons and speeches, titled *Hard Questions, Hard Answers,* Bernice King strives to deal with the (intensely, intense) topic of race relations.

3. Bernice King believes, as did her father, that all people must connect (genuinely, genuine), or they won't (never, ever) manage to coexist.

4. Bernice King decided to enter the ministry after she heard a (deeply, deep) voice within her directing her to this (extremely, extreme) (spiritually, spiritual) profession.

5. Bernice King entered the public eye in 1993, when she gave a (locally, local) televised Martin Luther King Day sermon at her father's church, and since then she has lived (happily, happy) in her home in Atlanta with memories of her father that are (peacefully, peaceful) recollections.

12e Using comparative and superlative forms of adjectives and adverbs

When comparisons are made, descriptive adjectives and adverbs often carry the message. Adjectives and adverbs, therefore, have forms that communicate relative degrees of intensity.

12e.1 Using correct forms of comparison for regular adjectives and adverbs

Most adjectives and adverbs show degrees of intensity by adding *-er* and *-est* endings or by combining with the words *more, most, less,* and *least* (see Chart 85). A few adjectives and adverbs are irregular, as explained in section 12e.2.

◉ **Forms of comparison for regular adjectives   85
and adverbs**

POSITIVE	used when nothing is being compared
COMPARATIVE	used when two things are being compared, with *-er* ending or *more* or *less*
SUPERLATIVE	used when three or more things are being compared, with *-est* ending or *most* or *least*

BACKGROUND

Adjectives can be made from nouns by adding different endings that can color the meaning of the word. For example, the *-ish* ending and the *-y* ending mean "similar to" or "characteristic of." A *yellowish substance* suggests a substance that is not exactly yellow, but close, and a *flowery paragraph* is so ornate and beautiful that it is reminiscent of a flower. Materials often take an *-en* ending when they turn from nouns into adjectives (as in *wooden* and *silken*), and adjectives that had a Latin origin frequently end in *-al*, *-ar*, or *-ory* (as in *beneficial*, *oracular*, and *promissory*).

EXTRA EXERCISE

Underline the adjectives and adverbs. If any adjective or adverb is in an incorrect form, write the correct form above it.

EXAMPLE

more loudly
The music played <u>loud</u> in the disco than in the restaurant.

1. The Joneses have the bigger tree on the block.

2. Colorado has some of the most prettiest scenery in the country.

3. Which of the sick twins has the highest fever?

4. Juan is friendlier than his cousin.

5. The more faster runner of the two received a ribbon.

6. The red blouse is the most attractive in the store.

7. Leontyne Price sings good.

8. That is the worse coffee shop in town.

9. Spain is near to Africa than most people realize.

10. Marc Chagall is the more famous modern artist from Russia.

Answers to Extra Exercise
1. biggest
2. prettiest (drop *most*)
3. higher
4. Correct
5. faster (drop *more*)
6. Correct
7. well
8. worst
9. nearer
10. most famous

POSITIVE	COMPARATIVE	SUPERLATIVE
green	greener	greenest
happy	happier	happiest
selfish	less selfish	least selfish
beautiful	more beautiful	most beautiful

That tree is **green.**

That tree is **greener** than this tree.

That tree is the **greenest** tree on the block.

The choice of whether to use *-er, -est* or *more, most* and *less, least* depends largely on the number of syllables in the adjective or adverb.

- With **one-syllable words,** the *-er* and *-est* endings are most common: *large, larger, largest* (adjective); *far, farther, farthest* (adverb).

- With **adjectives of two syllables,** practice varies: Some take the *-er, -est* endings, and others use *more, most* and *less, least.*

- With **adverbs of two syllables,** *more, most* and *less, least* are used: *easily, more easily, most easily.*

- With **three-syllable words,** *more, most* and *less, least* are used.

One general rule covers two-syllable adjectives ending in *-y:* Use the *-er, -est* endings after changing the *-y* to *i: pretty, prettier, prettiest.* For other two-syllable adjectives, form comparatives and superlatives intuitively, based on what you have heard or read for a particular adjective.

USAGE ALERT: Be careful not to use a double comparative or double superlative. The words *more, most, less,* and *least* cannot be used if the *-er* or *-est* ending has been used. **!**

He was **younger** [not *more younger*] than his brother.

Her music was the **loudest** [not *most loudest*] on the radio.

Children are **more easily** [not *more easier*] influenced than adults.

12e.2 Using correct forms of comparison for irregular adjectives and adverbs

A few comparative and superlative forms are irregular. They are listed in Chart 86. Memorize them so that they always spring to mind easily.

⊙ Irregular comparatives and superlatives 86

POSITIVE [1]	COMPARATIVE [2]	SUPERLATIVE [3+]
good (*adjective*)	better	best
well (*adjective* and *adverb*)	better	best
bad (*adjective*)	worse	worst
badly (*adverb*)	worse	worst
many	more	most
much	more	most
some	more	most
little	less	least

The Kogens saw a **good** movie.

The Kogens saw a **better** movie than the Smiths did.

The Kogens saw the **best** movie that they had ever seen.

The Millers had **little** trouble finding jobs.

The Millers had **less** trouble finding jobs than the Smiths did.

The Millers had the **least** trouble finding jobs of everyone.

🔴 **USAGE ALERT:** Do not use *less* and *fewer* interchangeably. Use *less* with uncountable items or values that form one whole: *The sugar substitute now has **less aftertaste**.* Use *fewer* with numbers or anything that can be counted: *The sugar substitute now has **fewer calories**.* ❗

EXERCISE 12-3

Consulting section 12e, do two things: First, complete this chart. Next, write a sentence to set a context for each word in the completed chart.

EXAMPLE   *little:* Towering redwoods dwarfed the little Douglas fir.

POSITIVE [1]	COMPARATIVE [2]	SUPERLATIVE [3+]
little	————	————
————	greedier	————
————	————	most complete
gladly	————	————
————	————	fewest
————	thicker	————
some	————	————

WORD HISTORIES

Common irregular adjectives (and adverbs) can be confusing to students because the comparative and superlative forms seem unconnected to the positive form. The realization that these irregularities are only accidents of history rather than the product of difficult rules can make them less intimidating.

For example, *good* comes from the Old English *god*, related to the German *gut*, both of which come from the Indo-European word meaning "to be suitable." *Better* and *best* come from Old English *betera* and *betst*, respectively, based on the Indo-European word meaning "good."

Another example is *worse* and *worst*, which come from their Old English synonyms, *wiersa* and *wyrsta*. However, *bad* does not come from *yfel*, the Old English word for "bad" or "evil," but from Old English *baeddel*, meaning "hermaphrodite."

ANSWERS: EXERCISE 12-3

Sentences called for in the second part of the instructions will vary. Here is the chart filled in.

Positive	Comparative	Superlative
little	littler	littlest
greedy	greedier	greediest
complete	more complete	most complete
gladly	more gladly	most gladly
few	fewer	fewest
thick	thicker	thickest
some	more	most

BACKGROUND

In *Errors and Expectations* (New York: Oxford UP, 1977), Mina P. Shaughnessy describes the use of modifiers by three groups of freshman writers. The few adverbs used by *basic* writers, she notes, usually come from the most overworked ones in the language, such as *too, very, quite,* and *hardly*. Similarly, basic writers modify their nouns and verbs with what she calls "the common adjectives": *a lot, many, good, easy, big, certain,* familiar words that slip into place without mental effort, thereby making it impossible for the writer to achieve the precision needed for complex consideration of the topic. *Intermediate* writers, moving closer to precise diction, use *-ly* adverbs and more specific adjectives. Although they are likely to use multiple adjectives, doing so does not usually increase the precision of the statement. *Advanced* freshman writers, working with more confidence, lean on adverbial conjunctions for paragraph cohesion—*furthermore, however, consequently*—and include figurative language in an effort to be descriptive.

ANSWERS AND COVERAGE: EXERCISE 12-4

1. most likely [12e, correct superlatives]

2. many [12e, positive form; nothing is being compared]

12f Avoiding too many nouns as modifiers

Nouns—words that name a person, place, thing, or idea—sometimes **modify** (describe or limit) other nouns: *truck driver, train track, security system*. These very familiar terms create no problems. However, when nouns pile up in a sequence of modifiers, the reader can have difficulty figuring out which nouns are being modified and which nouns are doing the modifying. As you revise such sentences, you can use any of several routes to clarify your material.

SENTENCE REWRITTEN

NO I asked my adviser to write **two college recommendation letters** for me.

YES I asked my adviser to write **letters of recommendation to two colleges** for me.

ONE NOUN CHANGED TO A POSSESSIVE AND ANOTHER TO AN ADJECTIVE

NO Some students might take the **United States Navy examination** for **navy engineer training**.

YES Some students might take the **United States Navy's examination** for **naval engineer training**.

NOUN CHANGED TO PREPOSITIONAL PHRASE

NO Our **student adviser training program** has won awards for excellence.

YES Our **training program for student advisers** has won awards for excellence. [Notice that this change requires the plural noun *advisers*.]

EXERCISE 12-4

Consulting all sections of this chapter, circle the better choice of each set of words in parentheses so that these sentences are suitable for academic writing.

EXAMPLE Stunt work is a visual art that (frequent, frequently) involves physical risk to the performer.

1. The first stunt performers were (most likely, likeliest) the Roman gladiators, trained to entertain the crowds with their great skill in chariot driving and sword play.

2. Actors in the early silent movies sustained (many, more) injuries during filming because they used no doubles for their stunts.

3. In a 1916 movie about the Civil War, no (fewer, less) than sixty-seven extras suffered injuries during the filming of one scene.

4. Today, more than two hundred (high, highly) trained stunt performers, ranging in age from ten to eighty-two, work (regular, regularly) in Hollywood movies.

5. In a single year, stunt performer Harry Madsen was beaten, knifed, shot, set on fire, and thrown out a fourth-floor window. He was paid (good, well) and had a (good, well) time, too.

Answers and Coverage Exercise 12-4 (continued)

3. fewer [12e, countable items use *fewer*, not *less*]

4. highly [12b, adverb used to modify adjective]; regularly [12b, adverb used to modify verb]

5. well [12d, adverb modifies verb *was paid*]; good [12d, adjective modifies noun *time*]

QUOTATION: ON WRITING

I love writing. I love the swirl and swing of words as they tangle with human emotions.

—James Michener

13

SENTENCE FRAGMENTS

A **sentence fragment** occurs when an incomplete sentence is punctuated as a complete sentence. This chapter shows how to distinguish between sentence fragments and complete sentences.

FRAGMENT	The telephone with redial capacity. [no VERB]
REVISED	The telephone has redial capacity.
FRAGMENT	Rang loudly for ten minutes. [no SUBJECT]
REVISED	The telephone rang loudly for ten minutes.
FRAGMENT	At midnight. [no verb or subject]
REVISED	The telephone rang at midnight.
FRAGMENT	Because the telephone rang loudly. [DEPENDENT CLAUSE with SUBORDINATING CONJUNCTION]
REVISED	Because the telephone rang loudly, the family was awakened in the middle of the night.
FRAGMENT	The telephone call that woke the family. [verb in dependent clause with RELATIVE PRONOUN but no INDEPENDENT-CLAUSE verb]
REVISED	The telephone call that woke the family was a wrong number.

Sentence fragments distort the message that you want your material to deliver. Avoid them.

NO	The lawyer was angry. When she returned from court. She found the key witness waiting in her office. [Was the lawyer angry when she returned from court or when she found the witness in her office?]
YES	The lawyer was angry when she returned from court. She found the key witness waiting in her office.
YES	The lawyer was angry. When she returned from court, she found the key witness waiting in her office.

Wait until the REVISING and EDITING stages of your writing process to check for sentence fragments. While you are DRAFTING, if you suspect you have written a sentence fragment, quickly underline or highlight it and move on. Then, you can easily find and check it later.

13a Testing for sentence completeness

If you write sentence fragments frequently, you need a system to check that your sentences are complete. Here is a test you can use (see Chart 87).

 Test for sentence completeness 87

Question 1: Is there a verb?
If not, there is a fragment. To revise, see section 13c.
NO   Thousands of whales in the Arctic Ocean because of an early winter. [a fragment]

Question 2: Is there a subject?
If not, there is a fragment. To revise, see section 13c.
NO   Raced to reach the whales. [a fragment]

Question 3: Does the word group start with a subordinating word even though it has a subject and a verb?
If so, there is a fragment. To revise, see section 13b.
NO   Because the ship intended to cut a path through the ice. [a fragment]

Question 1: Is there a verb?

If there is no verb, you are looking at a sentence fragment. Verbs convey information about what is happening, what has happened, or what will happen. In testing for sentence completeness, find a verb that can change form to communicate a change in time.

Yesterday, the telephone **rang.**
Now the telephone **rings.**

VERBALS look like verbs but do not function as verbs (see 7d).

FRAGMENT   Yesterday, the students registering for classes. [Here, *registering* is a present participle, not a verb.]

REVISED   Yesterday, the students **were** registering for classes. [Adding *were* to *registering* creates a verb.]

FRAGMENT   Now, the students registering for classes.

REVISED   Now, the students **are** registering for classes.

FRAGMENT   Informed about an excellent teacher. [Here, *informed* is a past participle, not a verb.]

REVISED   They **had been** informed about an excellent teacher. [Adding *had been* to *informed* creates a verb.]

TEACHING TIP

You might find it useful to have students work in groups to identify and correct fragments found in paragraphs taken from their own writing or those that occur in the following paragraph. Each group can present to the class a revision of a paragraph, pointing out the merits of the new version. In the paragraph shown here, fragments are often signaled by the words *just*, *only*, *for example*, *also*, *mainly*, and *such as*.

In their early history, the people of Asia followed the seasons through the valleys until they found no more land. Only the sea and sky and a sheet of ice stretching across the Bering Strait. They did not think about the past. Just the present. For example, making weapons. Such as tree limbs used for bows. Also knives made from sharpened stones. Just like their forefathers. Moving south, they eventually reached the Rio Grande. Mainly known today as the river that separates Mexico and the United States.

TEACHING TIP

Students sometimes create fragments as they attempt to write longer or more complicated sentences and experiment with their style. Without a range of syntactic structures available to them, students may try to vary the rhythm of their sentences, suggest pauses for emphasis, and establish sentence variety with the placement of periods. Fragments often appear because students begin using dependent clauses, participial phrases, elliptical constructions, and absolute phrases in their writing before they have enough knowledge and control of these structures. Students often benefit when they learn new sentence patterns as they learn to avoid fragments. Students who use periods to suggest a long pause may benefit from instruction on the dash (Chapter 29). Students creating fragments from dependent clauses, absolute phrases, and participial phrases may benefit from studying coordination and subordination (Chapter 17), parallelism (Chapter 18), and techniques for achieving sentence variety and emphasis (Chapter 19).

FRAGMENT	Now the students to register for classes. [Here, *to register* is an infinitive, not a verb.]
REVISED	Now the students **want** to register for classes. [Adding *want* provides the sentence with a verb.]

Question 2: Is there a subject?

If there is no subject, you are looking at a sentence fragment. To find a subject, ask the verb "who?" or "what?"

FRAGMENT	Studied hard for class. [Who studied? unknown]
REVISED	The students studied hard for class. [Who studied? the students]
FRAGMENT	Contained some difficult questions. [What contained? unknown]
REVISED	The test contained some difficult questions. [What contained? the test]

Every sentence must have its own subject. A sentence fragment without a subject often occurs when the missing subject is the same as the subject in the preceding sentence.

NO	A few students organized a study group to prepare for midterm exams. **Decided** to study together for the rest of the course.
YES	A few students organized a study group to prepare for midterm exams. **They decided** to study together for the rest of the course.
YES	A few students organized a study group to prepare for midterm exams, **and they decided** to study together for the rest of the course.

Imperative statements—commands and some requests—are an exception. They are not sentence fragments. Imperative statements imply the word *you, anybody, somebody,* or *everybody* as the subject.

Run! = (You) run!
Study hard. = (You) study hard.
Please return my books. = (You) please return my books.

Question 3: Does the word group start with a subordinating word even though it has a subject and a verb?

If the answer to question 3 is yes, you are looking at a sentence fragment. Subordinating words begin **dependent clauses.** A dependent clause cannot stand alone as an independent unit; it must be joined to an independent clause to be part of a complete sentence.

One type of subordinating word is a SUBORDINATING CONJUNCTION. The following are frequently used subordinating conjunctions (see also Chart 53 in section 7h):

after	because	since	when
although	before	unless	whenever
as	if	until	where

FRAGMENT **Because** she returned my books.

REVISED **Because** she returned my books, I can study.

FRAGMENT **When** I study.

REVISED I have to concentrate **when** I study.

🔵 PUNCTUATION ALERT: When a dependent clause starting with a subordinating conjunction comes before its independent clause, a comma usually separates the clauses (see 24b.1). ❗

Another type of subordinating word is a RELATIVE PRONOUN. The most common relative pronouns are *who, which,* and *that.*

FRAGMENT The test **that** we studied for.

REVISED The test **that** we studied for was canceled.

FRAGMENT The professor **who** taught the course.

REVISED The professor **who** taught the course was ill.

Questions can begin with words such as *when, where, who,* and *which* without being sentence fragments: *When do you want to study? Where is the library? Who is your professor? Which class are you taking?*

Chart 88 summarizes information on correcting a sentence fragment once you have identified its grammatical structure.

◎ **How to correct sentence fragments**   **88**

- If the sentence fragment is a DEPENDENT CLAUSE, join it to an adjacent INDEPENDENT CLAUSE (see 13b).
- If the sentence fragment is a dependent clause, revise it into an independent clause (see 13b).
- If the sentence fragment is a PHRASE, join it to an adjacent independent clause (see 13c).
- If the sentence fragment is a phrase, revise it into an independent clause (see 13c).

QUOTATION: ON WRITING

I am unlikely to trust a sentence that comes easily.

—William Gass

TEACHING TIP

To discuss fragments, you might ask students to bring in samples of public writing that contain fragments. Fruitful sources include advertisements, mail solicitations, and memos from companies where the students work. Collect, reproduce, and distribute a sampling of the passages. Ask students to identify all the fragments and to determine which, if any, are acceptable. Then have them revise the passages to eliminate the unacceptable fragments.

This lesson can be enlivened by the use of an overhead projector. Prepare transparencies of the original passages, and use a series of overlays to record and compare student revisions.

Students may ask why they must avoid unacceptable fragments when these errors can be found in published writing. You may want to discuss what impressions about the writers and their companies these errors create.

BACKGROUND

In a survey of eighty-four professionals representing sixty-three different occupations reported by Maxine Hairston ("Not All Errors Are Created Equal: Nonacademic Readers in the Profession Respond to Lapses in Usage," *College English*, 1981: 794–806), respondents ranked sentence fragments among the most serious of errors, below only "status markers" such as nonstandard verbs ("brung"), double negatives, and beginning a sentence with an objective pronoun.

ANSWERS AND COVERAGE: EXERCISE 13-1

Two pieces of information are given for each item: the reason for the sentence fragment and the number of the question in Chart 87 that explains what has caused each sentence fragment. (Exercise 13-3 asks students to correct the sentence fragments in this exercise.)

1. No verb (*unwrapping* is a verbal) [1]

2. No subject; starts with the subordinating word *which* [2 and 3]

3. No subject [2]

4. Complete sentence

5. Starts with a subordinating word and lacks an independent clause to complete the thought [3]

6. No verb [1]

7. No subject [2]

8. Complete sentence

9. Starts with a subordinating word but lacks an independent clause to complete the thought [3]

10. No subject [2]

ANOTHER EXAMPLE

If your students have trouble recognizing dependent clauses as fragments, you may want to give them practice. Ask them to identify the fragments in the following mixture of complete and incomplete sentences. You might also ask them to combine the sentences so that each one is complete, being careful to separate with a comma each opening dependent clause from the independent one that follows.

> Many elderly people have pets as companions. Because the elderly are often lonely. Nevertheless, pets make demands on their energy. For example, if a cat is sick, and when a dog must be bathed. Unless the owner has the strength and funds to care for the pet's needs. Then the pet is better off with a younger owner. Since the pet deserves a good home too. Before getting a cat or dog, people should be certain that they can provide adequate care.

EXERCISE 13-1

Using the test for sentence completeness in Chart 87, check each word group. If a word group is a sentence fragment, explain what makes it incomplete. If a word group is a complete sentence, circle its number.

EXAMPLE   In 1972, a mummy discovered in a Chinese tomb. [No verb; see question 1 in Chart 87]

1. Researchers unwrapping the mummy containing the carefully preserved body of a woman in an ancient tomb.
2. Which had been wound in twenty layers of silk.
3. Turned out to be a Chinese aristocrat named Lady Dai.
4. She was embalmed in a bath of mercury salts.
5. When she died around B.C. 168.
6. Bamboo matting and five tons of charcoal.
7. Absorbed excess water in the tomb and kept the body dry.
8. The body of another Chinese princess had been buried in a magnificent jade suit.
9. Because jade was also believed to preserve bodies.
10. Had decayed, unlike Lady Dai's.

13b Revising dependent clauses punctuated as sentences

A **dependent clause** contains both a SUBJECT and a VERB, but it starts with a SUBORDINATING WORD (see Chart 87 in 13a, question 3). It cannot stand on its own as a sentence.

To correct a dependent clause punctuated as a sentence, you may choose (1) to join the dependent clause to an independent clause that comes directly before or after or (2) to drop the subordinating word. Whichever strategy you use, if necessary, add words to create an independent clause that makes sense.

FRAGMENT   Many people over twenty-five are deciding to get college degrees. **Because they want the benefits of an advanced education.**

REVISED   Many people over twenty-five are deciding to get college degrees because they want the benefits of an advanced education. [joined into one sentence]

REVISED   Many people over twenty-five are deciding to get college degrees. They want the benefits of an advanced education. [SUBORDINATING CONJUNCTION dropped to create an independent clause]

FRAGMENT   College attracts many older students. **Who usually study hard.**

[REVISED]   College attracts many older students, who usually study hard. [joined into one sentence]

[REVISED]   College attracts many older students. They usually study hard. [RELATIVE PRONOUN dropped and *they* added to create an independent clause]

🛑 **USAGE ALERT:** When trying to identify dependent clauses, be especially careful with words that indicate time, such as *after, before, since,* and *until.* In some sentences, they function as subordinating conjunctions, but in other sentences, they function as ADVERBS or PREPOSITIONS. Do not automatically assume, when you see these words, that you are looking at a dependent clause.

Before, the class was never full. Now, it is overfilled. [These are two complete sentences. In the first sentence, *before* is an adverb modifying the independent clause *the class was never full.*]

Before this semester, the class was never full. [This is a complete sentence. *Before* is the preposition in the PREPOSITIONAL PHRASE *before this semester.*]

Before the professor arrived. [This is a sentence fragment, a dependent clause punctuated as a sentence. *Before* is a subordinating conjunction.]

Before the professor arrived, the room was empty. [This is a complete sentence. The dependent clause precedes an independent clause.] ❗

EXERCISE 13-2

Consulting sections 13a and 13b, find and correct any sentence fragments. If a sentence is correct, circle its number.

EXAMPLE   Kwanzaa is an African-American holiday. That is observed from December 25 to January 1.

Kwanzaa is an African-American **holiday that** is observed from December 25 to January 1.

1. Kwanzaa was created in 1966 by Maulana Karenga, an African-American teacher. Who wanted to teach people about their African heritage.
2. The word *Kwanzaa* comes from the Swahili phrase *ya kwanza.* Which means "first."
3. Although Kwanzaa allows African Americans to honor the history of black people.

TEACHING TIP

In *Grammar and the Teaching of Writing: Limits and Possibilities* (Urbana: NCTE, 1991), Rei R. Noguchi proposes that students can identify declarative sentences and fragments if they attempt to transform the construction into tag questions and yes-no questions. For example, "Doing math problems isn't one of Billy's favorite activities" can be transformed into the tag question "Doing math problems isn't one of Billy's favorite activities, is it?" and the yes-no question "Isn't doing math problems one of Billy's favorite activities?" With fragments such as "Enjoyed the baseball game on Saturday" or "Whatever you could do to help my sister," students will find it impossible to create such questions unless they add words to the fragment, revealing that the construction was an incomplete sentence. You might ask students to try this method with Exercise 13-1.

ANSWERS AND COVERAGE: EXERCISE 13-2

Answers will vary. Here is one set of possible responses.

1. Kwanzaa was created in 1966 by Maulana Karenga, an African-American teacher who wanted to teach people about their African heritage. [dependent (relative) clause attached to independent clause]

2. The word *Kwanzaa* comes from the Swahili phrase *ya kwanza,* which means "first." [dependent (relative) clause attached to independent clause]

3. Kwanzaa allows African Americans to honor the history of black people. [subordinating conjunction dropped from dependent (adverb) clause]

→

4. Correct complete sentence

5. Although Christmas and Hanukkah are religious holidays, Kwanzaa is a cultural holiday. [subordinating phrase linked to independent clause]

6. The festival, which lasts seven days, celebrates seven principles that are called the *nguzo saba* in Swahili. [dependent (relative) clause attached to independent clause]

7. The seven principles are unity, self-determination, collective responsibility, cooperative economics, purpose, creativity, and faith. [relative pronoun dropped from dependent (relative) clause]

8. Each evening during the seven days of Kwanzaa, observers light one of the candles in the *kinara*, which is a seven-cup candleholder. [dependent (relative) clause attached to independent clause]

9. They discuss how the principle of the day affects their lives. [subordinating conjunction dropped from dependent clause]

10. Correct complete sentence

TEACHING TIP

To demonstrate how phrases can be turned into complete sentences, you might ask two students to read the following dialogue aloud in class and then to improvise each comment as a sentence.

A: When are you coming?

B: In a minute.

A: Really?

B: Really.

A: Hurry up!

B: OK, OK. Just a second. How about Mother?

A: Who?

B: Mother.

A: Sure. Ready hours ago.

4. The holiday also gives other North Americans a chance to learn African traditions.

5. Although Christmas and Hanukkah are religious holidays. Kwanzaa is a cultural holiday.

6. The festival, which lasts seven days, celebrates seven principles. That are called the *nguzo saba* in Swahili.

7. The seven principles, which are unity, self-determination, collective responsibility, cooperative economics, purpose, creativity, and faith.

8. Each evening during the seven days of Kwanzaa, observers light one of the candles in the *kinara*. Which is a seven-cup candleholder.

9. When they discuss how the principle of the day affects their lives.

10. When family and friends gather on the final night, they celebrate the feast known as the *Karamu*.

13c   Revising phrases punctuated as sentences

A **phrase** is a group of words that lacks a SUBJECT or a VERB (or both). A phrase cannot stand on its own as a sentence. To revise a phrase punctuated as a sentence, you may choose (1) to rewrite it into an INDEPENDENT CLAUSE or (2) to join it to an independent clause that comes directly before or after the phrase.

A phrase containing only a VERBAL (an INFINITIVE, a PAST PARTICIPLE, or a PRESENT PARTICIPLE) but no verb is a fragment, not a sentence.

FRAGMENT   The mayor called a news conference last week. **To announce new programs for crime prevention and care for the homeless.** [*To announce* starts an infinitive phrase, not a sentence.]

REVISED   The mayor called a news conference last week to announce new programs for crime prevention and care for the homeless. [joined into one sentence]

REVISED   The mayor called a news conference last week. She wanted to announce new programs for crime prevention and care for the homeless. [rewritten]

FRAGMENT   **Introduced by her assistant.** The mayor began with an opening statement. [*Introduced* starts a participial phrase, not a sentence.]

REVISED   Introduced by her assistant, the mayor began with an opening statement. [joined into one sentence]

REVISED   The mayor was introduced by her assistant. She began with an opening statement. [rewritten]

FRAGMENT **Hoping for strong public support.** She gave many examples of problems everywhere in the city. [*Hoping* starts a participial phrase, not a sentence.]

REVISED Hoping for strong public support, she gave many examples of problems everywhere in the city. [joined into one sentence]

REVISED She was hoping for strong public support. She gave many examples of problems everywhere in the city. [rewritten]

A **prepositional phrase** is a group of words that starts with a PREPO-SITION. It is not a sentence.

FRAGMENT Cigarette smoke made the conference room seem airless. **During the long news conference.** [*During* starts a prepositional phrase, not a sentence.]

REVISED Cigarette smoke made the conference room seem airless during the long news conference. [joined into one sentence]

REVISED Cigarette smoke made the conference room seem airless. It was hard to breathe during the long news conference. [rewritten]

An **appositive** is one or more words that renames a NOUN. It is not a sentence.

FRAGMENT Most people respected the mayor. **A politician with fresh ideas and practical solutions.** [*A politician* starts an appositive, not a sentence.]

REVISED Most people respected the mayor, a politician with fresh ideas and practical solutions. [joined into one sentence]

REVISED Most people respected the mayor. She seemed to be a politician with fresh ideas and practical solutions. [rewritten]

A **compound predicate** contains two or more verbs. To be part of a complete sentence, a predicate must have a subject. When the second half of a compound predicate is punctuated as a separate sentence, it is not a sentence.

FRAGMENT The reporters asked the mayor many questions about the details of her program. **And then discussed her answers among themselves.** [*And then discussed* is the start of a compound predicate, not a sentence.]

REVISED The reporters asked the mayor many questions about the details of her program and then discussed her answers among themselves. [joined into one sentence]

REVISED The reporters asked the mayor many questions about the details of her program. Then, the reporters discussed her answers among themselves. [rewritten]

TEACHING TIP

Dictating a passage like the one here for students to copy and punctuate can be a helpful exercise for students in identifying sentence boundaries. Students can compare their versions and discuss any differences.

> We have a nine-acre lake on our ranch and a warm spring that feeds it all winter. By mid-March the lake ice begins to melt where the spring feeds in, and every year the same pair of mallards come ahead of the others and wait. Though there is very little open water they seem content. They glide back and forth through a thin estuary, brushing watercress with their elegant folded wings, then tip end-up to eat and, after, clamber onto the lip of ice that retreats, hardens forward, and retreats again
> —Gretel Ehrlich

ANSWERS AND COVERAGE: EXERCISE 13-3 (on page 270)

Answers will vary. Added or altered words are italicized in this set of possibilities.

1. Researchers *unwrapped* [verbal changed to verb] the mummy containing the carefully preserved body of a woman in an ancient tomb.

2. *The body* [subordinating word *which* dropped, noun supplied] had been wound in twenty layers of silk.

3. *She* [pronoun supplied] turned out to be a Chinese aristocrat named Lady Dai.

4. Correct complete sentence

5. *She* [subordinating conjunction *when* dropped] died around 168 B.C.

6 and 7. Combined to create correct complete sentence

8. Correct complete sentence

9. Jade was also believed to preserve bodies. [subordinating conjunction *because* dropped]

10. *Her body* [noun supplied] had decayed, unlike Lady Dai's.

ANSWERS: EXERCISE 13-4

Answers will vary. One set of possibilities is shown on page 270.

Answers: *Exercise 13-4 (continued)*

An English inventor has developed a portable radio that needs no batteries and plays when it is wound up by hand. This wind-up radio was designed to be sold in Africa, where many villages have no electricity. Also, batteries are expensive and hard to find in parts of Africa. The radio plays for half an hour before its owner has to spend a few seconds winding it up again. For a portable radio, it is bulky, and its sound is not of top quality. In countries with few newspapers or books, however, a radio is seen as an important tool. It provides information on health and other practical matters. Besides, where most people are poor, a radio is a much-desired luxury, so it has become a status symbol. In poor African villages, a radio ranks number three in prestige after a motorcycle and a bicycle. These three status symbols are able to make an unmarried man into an eligible bachelor—according to some people, at least.

Coverage

1. Correct complete sentence
2. predicate with coordinating conjunction
3. verbal phrase (past participle)
4. verbal phrase (present participle)
5. verbal phrase (present participle)
6. dependent clause with subordinating conjunction
7. Correct complete sentence
8. verbal phrase (past participle)
9. verbal phrase (infinitive)
10. Correct complete sentence
11. dependent clause with subordinating conjunction
12. verbal phrase (present participle)
13. predicate
14. prepositional phrase

EXERCISE 13-3

Go back to Exercise 13-1 and revise any sentence fragments into complete sentences. In some cases, you may be able to combine two fragments into one complete sentence.

13d   Recognizing intentional fragments

Professional writers sometimes intentionally use fragments for emphasis and effect.

> But in the main I feel like a brown bag of miscellany propped against a wall. Pour out the contents, and there is discovered a jumble of small things priceless and worthless. **A first-water diamond, an empty spool, bits of broken glass, lengths of string, a key to a door long since crumbled away, a rusty knife-blade, old shoes saved for a road that never was and never will be, a nail bent under the weight of things too heavy for any nail, a dried flower or two still a little fragrant.**
> —Zora Neale Hurston, *How It Feels to Be Colored Me*

The ability to judge the difference between an acceptable and unacceptable sentence fragment comes from much exposure to reading the work of skilled writers. Many instructors often do not accept sentence fragments in student writing until a student can demonstrate the consistent ability to write well-constructed complete sentences. As a general rule, it is wise to avoid using sentence fragments in all academic writing.

EXERCISE 13-4

Consulting sections 13a, 13b, and 13c, revise this paragraph to eliminate any sentence fragments. In some cases, you can combine word groups to create complete sentences; in other cases, you must supply missing elements to revise word groups. Some sentences may not require revision. In your final version, check not only the individual sentences but also the clarity of the whole paragraph.

(1) An English inventor has developed a portable radio that needs no batteries. (2) And plays when it is wound up by hand. (3) This wind-up radio designed to be sold in Africa, where many villages have no electricity. (4) Also, batteries being expensive and hard to find in parts of Africa. (5) The radio playing for half an hour or more. (6) Before its owner has to spend a few seconds winding it up again. (7) For a portable radio, it is bulky, and its sound is not of top quality. (8) In countries with few newspapers or books, however, a radio seen as an important tool. (9) To provide information on health and other

practical matters. (10) Besides, where most people are poor, a radio is a much-desired luxury. (11) So it has become a status symbol. (12) In poor African villages, a radio ranking number three in prestige after a motorcycle and a bicycle. (13) These three status symbols able to make an unmarried man into an eligible bachelor. (14) According to some people, at least.

EXERCISE 13-5

Consulting sections 13a, 13b, and 13c, revise this paragraph to eliminate any sentence fragments. In some cases, you can combine word groups to create complete sentences; in other cases, you must supply missing elements to revise word groups. Some sentences may not require revision. In your final version, check not only the individual sentences but also the clarity of the whole paragraph.

(1) Your car shuddering and jolting. (2) As a hubcap flies off one of the tires and clatters across the road. (3) Have just hit a pothole in the pavement. (4) Potholes, typically formed when water seeps into cracks in the road surface, freezes, and then melts. (5) Are usually found in northern regions. (6) However, can also be a problem in warmer climates. (7) Where heat and frequent rain may cause the pavement to collapse. (8) A research laboratory that has counted sixteen million potholes. (9) Scarring the roads in the United States. (10) Each one a source of grief to countless drivers. (11) Because potholes bring expense and even danger. (12) Cities are finding ingenious ways of dealing with them. (13) Including a scheme in San Antonio, Texas, for volunteers to adopt a pothole. (14) And pay for its repair by buying an adoption certificate. (15) In return, the city gives the adopted pothole's "parents" a promise. (16) To have the hole fixed within a few days.

ANSWERS: EXERCISE 13-5

Answers will vary. Here is one set of possibilities.

Your car shudders and jolts as a hubcap flies off one of the tires and clatters across the road. You have just hit a pothole in the pavement. Potholes are typically formed when water seeps into cracks in the road surface, freezes, and then melts, and they are usually found in northern regions. However, potholes can also be a problem in warmer climates, where heat and frequent rain may cause the pavement to collapse. A research laboratory has counted sixteen million potholes scarring the roads in the United States, each one a source of grief to countless drivers. Because potholes bring expense and even danger, cities are finding ingenious ways of dealing with them, including a scheme in San Antonio, Texas, for volunteers to adopt a pothole. The volunteers [or They] pay for the pothole's [or its] repair by buying an adoption certificate. In return, the city gives the adopted pothole's "parents" a promise. It promises to have the hole fixed within a few days.

Coverage
1. 13c, verbal phrase (present participles)
2. 13b, dependent clause with subordinating conjunction
3. 13a, no subject
4. 13c, verbal phrase (past participle)
5. 13a, no subject (fragment is a predicate)
6. 13a, no subject
7. 13b, dependent clause with subordinating conjunction
8. 13a, dependent clause with relative pronoun
9. 13c, verbal phrase (present participle)
10. 13c, appositive
11. 13b, dependent clause with subordinating conjunction
12. Correct complete sentence
13. 13c, verbal phrase (present participle)
14. 13c, predicate with coordinating conjunction
15. Correct complete sentence
16. 13c, verbal phrase (infinitive)

Focus on Revising

Revising Your Writing

If you write sentence fragments, go back to your writing and locate them. Then figure out why each is a sentence fragment by using the test for sentence completeness in section 13a. Next, revise each sentence fragment into a complete sentence, referring to 13a, 13b, and 13c.

Case Studies: Revising to Avoid Sentence Fragments

In these case studies, you can observe a student writer revising. Then, you have the chance to revise other student writing on your own.

Observation

A student wrote the following draft for a course called Introduction to the Novel. The assignment was to compose a paragraph about the childhood of a major novelist. This material is well organized as a narrative and tells an interesting story, but the draft's effectiveness is diminished by the presence of sentence fragments.

Read through the draft. The sentence fragments are highlighted. Before you look at the student's revision, revise the material yourself. Then, compare your revision with the student's.

dependent clause punctuated as a sentence: 13b

dependent clause punctuated as a sentence: 13b

dependent clause punctuated as a sentence: 13b

phrase with past participle of verb punctuated as a sentence: 13c

The creative imagination of Victorian novelist Charlotte Brontë got an early start. When she was a child. Her father brought her brother, Branwell, a set of wooden soldiers. Her father, who was a clergyman and who wrote poetry and a novel as well as sermons. After he gave Branwell the set. He told Charlotte and her sisters, Emily and Anne, each to pick one of the toy soldiers. And give it a name. Each sister then made up a history of her soldier. Soon creating tales of heroism. Inspired by the pleasure of telling stories. Charlotte, together with her brother, invented an

part of compound predicate punctuated as a sentence: 13c

phrase with -ing form of verb punctuated as a sentence: 13c →

PARTICIPATION ESSAY

Coverage

In seventeenth-century England, from the death of Elizabeth I in 1603 to William of Orange's ascension to the throne in 1689 [13c, prepositional phrase punctuated as a sentence]. The monarchy of England was the cause of unrest and uncertainty.

Queen Elizabeth I died single and childless in 1603. *Because she did not have a direct descendent* [13b, dependent clause punctuated as a sentence]. The throne passed to the queen's cousin. *Who was crowned James I* [13b, dependent clause punctuated as a sentence]. Discord over the relative power of Parliament and the crown emerged under James I. *And erupted during the reign of James's son, Charles I* [13c, second half of compound predicate punctuated as a sentence]. Incapable of resolving the conflicts, Charles I lost both the crown and his head to Oliver Cromwell's Puritan Revolution in 1649.

Holding fast to his antimonarchy sentiments and refusing a crown [13c, participial phrase punctuated as a sentence]. Oliver Cromwell did not establish a new line of English monarchs. Instead, he became Lord Protector of England. When Cromwell died, his son Richard lacked the charisma and political astuteness to hold on to power. As a result, the son of Charles I was recalled from France. *Where he had fled to live in safety.* [13b, dependent clause punctuated as a sentence]. He was crowned Charles II in 1660. *And had very limited power, according to new laws passed by Parliament* [13c, second half of compound predicate punctuated as a sentence]. Charles II sired no legitimate heirs, so the succession passed to his brother, James. *An apparently able man with one serious political handicap in seventeenth-century England* [13c, phrase punctuated as a sentence]. He was Catholic, at a time when England feared that the pope was plotting to reclaim England and rule it from Rome. *When James's second wife baptized her newborn son Catholic* [13b, dependent

→

imaginary kingdom. With Angria as its name. Because she treasured her fantasies and wanted to remember them. Charlotte began to write them in notebooks. Wanting them to look like miniature editions of books. She printed in a tiny, almost microscopically small handwriting. Those notebooks stand as a reminder of how early in life Charlotte Brontë expressed her creativity.

dependent clause punctuated as a sentence: 13b

prepositional phrase punctuated as a sentence: 13c

phrase using -ing form of verb punctuated as a sentence: 13c

Here is how the student revised the paragraph to eliminate the sentence fragments. In many places, the student could correct the error in more than one way. Your revision, therefore, might not be exactly like this one, but it should not contain any sentence fragments.

The creative imagination of Victorian novelist Charlotte Brontë got an early start. When she was a child, her father brought her brother, Branwell, a set of wooden soldiers. Her father was a clergyman who wrote poetry and a novel as well as sermons. After he gave Branwell the set, he told Charlotte and her sisters, Emily and Anne, each to pick one of the toy soldiers and give it a name. Each sister then made up a history of her soldier, and soon each was creating tales of heroism. Inspired by the pleasure of telling stories, Charlotte, together with her brother, invented an imaginary kingdom with Angria as its name. Because she treasured her fantasies and wanted to remember them, Charlotte began to write them in notebooks. Wanting her notebooks to look like miniature editions of books, she printed in a tiny, almost microscopically small handwriting. Those notebooks stand as a reminder of how early in life Charlotte Brontë expressed her creativity.

Participation

A student wrote the draft on page 274 for a course called European History. The assignment was to discuss the political atmosphere of a European nation during the seventeenth century. This material is effectively organized for chronological presentation of information, and it uses specific details well. The draft's effectiveness, however, is diminished by the presence of sentence fragments.

Read through the draft. Then revise it to eliminate the sentence fragments. Also, make any additional revisions that you think would improve the content, organization, and style of the material.

Participation Essay, (continued)

clause punctuated as a sentence]. Unease over James's rule escalated rapidly. *To ensure the safety of his wife and new son* [13c, phrase punctuated as a sentence]. James sent them to France and followed soon after. James's Protestant daughter Mary took the throne. *With her husband, William of Orange* [13c, phrase punctuated as a sentence]. A Dutchman who was a staunch supporter of Protestantism [13b, dependent clause punctuated as a sentence]. Their union was so popular with the English that William continued to rule after Mary's death in 1694. Thus, the century that saw much upheaval and instability in England ended in relative calm.

Answer to Participation Essay

This version is revised to correct the sentence fragments. Because of the many options available for corrections, answers will vary somewhat. Also, answers will vary if students have revised for content, organization, or style.

In seventeenth-century England, from the death of Elizabeth I in 1603 to William of Orange's ascension to the throne in 1689, the monarchy in England was the cause of unrest and uncertainty.

Queen Elizabeth I died single and childless in 1603. Because she did not have a direct descendent, the throne passed to the Queen's cousin, who was crowned James I. Discord over the relative power of Parliament and the crown emerged under James I and erupted during the reign of James's son, Charles I. Incapable of resolving the conflicts, Charles I lost both the crown and his head to Oliver Cromwell's Puritan Revolution in 1649.

Holding fast to his antimonarchy sentiments and refusing a crown, Oliver Cromwell did not establish a new line of English monarchs. Instead, he became Lord Protector of England. When Cromwell died, his son Richard lacked the charisma and political astuteness to hold on to power. As a result, the son of Charles I was recalled from France, where he had

→

Answer to Participation Essay (continued)

fled to live in safety. He was crowned Charles II in 1660 and had very limited power, according to new laws passed by Parliament. Charles II sired no legitimate heirs, so the succession passed to his brother, James, an apparently able man with one serious political handicap in seventeenth-century England. He was Catholic, at a time when England feared that the pope was plotting to reclaim England and rule it from Rome. When James's second wife baptized her newborn son Catholic, unease over James's rule escalated rapidly. To ensure the safety of his wife and new son, James sent them to France and followed soon after. James's Protestant daughter Mary took the throne with her husband, William of Orange, a Dutchman who was a staunch supporter of Protestantism. Their union was so popular with the English that William continued to rule after Mary's death in 1694. Thus, the century that saw much upheaval and instability in England ended in relative calm.

FOCUS ON REVISING FOCUS ON REVISING FOCUS ON REVISING FOCUS ON REVISING FOCUS ON REVISING

In seventeenth-century England, from the death of Elizabeth I in 1603 to William of Orange's ascension to the throne in 1689. The monarchy of England was the cause of unrest and uncertainty.

Queen Elizabeth I died single and childless in 1603. Because she did not have a direct descendant. The throne passed to the queen's cousin. Who was crowned James I. Discord over the relative power of Parliament and the crown emerged under James I. And erupted during the reign of James's son, Charles I. Incapable of resolving the conflicts, Charles I lost both the throne and his head to Oliver Cromwell's Puritan Revolution in 1649.

Holding fast to his antimonarchy sentiments and refusing a crown. Oliver Cromwell did not establish a new line of English monarchs. Instead, he became Lord Protector of England. When Cromwell died, his son Richard lacked the charisma and political astuteness to hold on to power. As a result, the son of Charles I was recalled from France. Where he had fled to live in safety. He was crowned Charles II in 1660. And had very limited power, according to new laws passed by Parliament. Charles II sired no legitimate heirs, so the succession passed to his brother, James. An apparently able man with one serious political handicap in seventeenth-century England. He was Catholic, at a time when the English feared that the pope was plotting to reclaim England and rule it from Rome. When James's second wife baptized her newborn son Catholic. Unease over James's rule escalated rapidly. To ensure the safety of his wife and new son. James sent them to France and followed soon after. James's Protestant daughter Mary took the throne. With her husband, William of Orange. A Dutchman who was a staunch supporter of Protestantism. Their union was so popular with the English that William continued to rule after Mary's death in 1694. Thus, the century that saw much upheaval and instability in England ended in relative calm.

14

COMMA SPLICES
AND RUN-TOGETHER SENTENCES

A **comma splice** (or **comma fault**) is an error that occurs when a comma by itself is used between INDEPENDENT CLAUSES. A comma is correct between two independent clauses only when it is followed by a coordinating conjunction (*and, but, for, or, nor, yet,* and *so*). The word *splice* means "to fasten ends together." The end of one independent clause and the beginning of another cannot be fastened together with a comma.

COMMA SPLICE   The iceberg broke off from the glacier**,** it drifted into the sea.

A **run-together sentence** is an error that occurs when two independent clauses are not joined by a comma and a coordinating conjunction or separated by other punctuation. Two independent clauses cannot be united as if melted together. A run-together sentence is also known as a *run-on sentence* or a *fused sentence*.

RUN-TOGETHER
SENTENCE   The iceberg broke off from the glacier it drifted into the sea.

Comma splices and run-together sentences are two versions of the same problem: incorrect joining of independent clauses. Both comma splices and run-together sentences distract readers from understanding the meaning you want your material to deliver. Chart 89 shows ways to find and correct these errors.

⊙ **How to find and correct comma splices   89
and run-together sentences**

Finding Comma Splices and Run-Together Sentences

■ Look for a PRONOUN starting the second independent clause.

   NO   The physicist Marie Curie discovered radium, **she** won two
         Nobel Prizes.
                                                              →

WHAT ELSE?

The *Prentice Hall/Simon & Schuster Transparencies for Writers*, written by Duncan Carter, is a set of clear transparencies that cover many topics, including comma splices and run-together sentences. It is available free of charge to adopters of this handbook. Ask your Prentice Hall representative.

TEACHING TIP

Students who write comma splices or run-together sentences have a better chance of finding and correcting their errors if they can find a pattern in them. To help students detect patterns, set aside one class or conference session to have students review all the paragraphs and essays they have written for the course. First, if they have not already done so, they should correct all comma splices and run-together sentences. Then, they should tally the *types* of sentences involved, using Chart 89 for reference. Encourage students to create additional categories, if needed, for errors that do not fit the three basic patterns. Make yourself available to answer questions, and encourage students to ask advice of their peers. At the end of the exercise, have students submit a review statement. Here is one student's response:

Of the twelve comma splices and run-together sentences I have written this semester, seven involved a second independent clause starting with a pronoun, four involved conjunctive adverbs, and one involved an explanation. I need to be careful, when I use a pronoun as the subject of an independent clause, to punctuate that clause as a sentence.

An explicit statement of results will force students to do the analysis, and the "I need to be careful . . ." sentence will force them to verbalize a plan of attack. Both steps work to overcome students' perceptions of punctuation errors as being random and uncontrollable.
                                                              →

Teaching Tip (continued)

You can then keep the statements on file (1) to help you determine who needs to work on a particular kind of comma splice or run-together sentence, and (2) as a contract between you and each student acknowledging that he or she knows what to do and will do it.

STATEWIDE TESTING

If you teach in a state that requires students to pass basic competency tests in English, see the free publications coordinated with this handbook: One is for the CLAST (Florida), and another is for the TASP Exam (Texas).

BACKGROUND

In the second chapter of *Errors and Expectations*, titled "Handwriting and Punctuation" (Oxford: Oxford, UP 1977), Mina P. Shaughnessy observes that the urge to string sentences together reflects a need on the part of the writer for other ways of making links between sentences. Comma splices, for example, reflect a writer's effort to control a sentence, to simplify it by breaking it up into smaller segments by the use of a comma as a conjunction. She argues that punctuation should not be studied apart from other aspects of writing; instead, it should be integrated with work in composition, for "the process whereby writers *mark* sentences is related to the process whereby they *make* them." She suggests that punctuation skills will improve as novice writers study first to recognize and create simple subject and predicate phrases; second, to embed sentences in sentences (using *who*, *which*, *that*, *when*, and *if*); third, to embed appositional forms; and fourth, to embed *-ing* phrases.

How to find and correct comma splices and run-together sentences *(continued)* 89

- Look for a CONJUNCTIVE ADVERB (see Chart 51 in section 7f) or a TRANSITIONAL EXPRESSION starting the second independent clause.

  NO Marie Curie and her husband, Pierre, worked together at first**, however,** he died at age forty-seven.

- Look for a second independent clause that explains, amplifies, contrasts with, or gives an example of information in the first independent clause.

  NO Radium can cause cancer **radium is used to cure cancer.**

Fixing Comma Splices and Run-Together Sentences

- Use a period or a semicolon between independent clauses (see 14b and 14e).

  YES The physicist Marie Curie discovered radium**. She** won two Nobel Prizes.

- Use a comma + COORDINATING CONJUNCTION between the clauses (see 14c).

  YES The physicist Marie Curie discovered radium**, and** she won two Nobel Prizes.

- Use a semicolon + CONJUNCTIVE ADVERB or transitional expression between the clauses (see 14e).

  YES Marie Curie and her husband, Pierre, worked together at first**; however,** he died at age forty-seven.

- Revise one independent clause into a DEPENDENT CLAUSE (see 14d).

  YES Radium, **which can cause cancer,** is also used to cure cancer.

If you tend to write comma splices and run-together sentences, you might have trouble recognizing them. Wait until the REVISING and EDITING stages of your writing process to check for commas splices and run-together sentences, when you can analyze your sentences individually. While you are DRAFTING, if you suspect that you have made one of these errors, quickly underline or highlight the material and move on. Then, you can easily find and check it later.

14a Recognizing comma splices and run-together sentences

To recognize comma splices and run-together sentences, you need to be able to recognize an **independent clause,** a clause that contains a SUBJECT and a PREDICATE and that does not begin with a SUBORDINATING WORD. An independent clause can stand alone as a sentence because it is an independent grammatical unit.

SUBJECT   PREDICATE

The physicist Marie Curie   discovered radium in 1898.

If you tend to write comma splices, here is a useful technique for proofreading your work. Cover all the words on one side of the comma, and see if the words remaining form an independent clause. If they do, cover that clause and uncover all the words on the other side of the comma. If the second side of the comma is also an independent clause, you have written a comma splice. Another way to help yourself avoid writing comma splices is to become familiar with correct uses for commas, explained in Chapter 24.

Experienced writers sometimes use a comma to join very brief independent clauses, especially if one independent clause is negative and the other is positive: *Mosquitos do not bite, they stab.* Many instructors consider this form an error in student writing; you will never be wrong if you use a semicolon or a period.

14b Using a period or a semicolon to correct comma splices and run-together sentences

You can use a period or a semicolon to correct comma splices and run-together sentences. For the sake of sentence variety and emphasis, however, do not always choose punctuation to correct this type of error. (Other methods are discussed in sections 14c and 14d.) Strings of short sentences rarely establish relationships and levels of importance among ideas.

COMMA SPLICE	A shark is all cartilage, it does not have a bone in its body.
RUN-TOGETHER SENTENCE	A shark is all cartilage it does not have a bone in its body.
CORRECTED	A shark is all cartilage. It does not have a bone in its body. [A period separates the independent clauses.]

QUOTATION: ON WRITING

If my doctor told me I had only six months to live, I wouldn't brood. I'd type a little faster.

—Isaac Asimov

TEACHING TIP

Students can use a simple test to determine whether a word is a conjunction or a conjunctive adverb. Conjunctive adverbs can be shifted from the beginning of a clause to another position in the middle of the clause; conjunctions cannot be shifted.

Comma splices and run-together sentences sometimes occur when students begin a sentence with *not only* but omit *but also* at the start of the second clause. Students should remember that *but* is functioning as a conjunction in this construction and that they need to separate the clauses with a period or semicolon when they omit *but.*

BACKGROUND

Professional writers often intentionally separate two independent clauses with just a comma. The clauses in these comma splices never have internal commas and are normally short, balanced, and closely related in meaning. The teacher, of course, should decide whether to allow students to experiment with this form in their writing.

COMMA SPLICE	Sharks can smell blood from a quarter mile away, they swim toward the source like a guided missile.
RUN-TOGETHER SENTENCE	Sharks can smell blood from a quarter mile away they swim toward the source like a guided missile.
CORRECTED	Sharks can smell blood from a quarter mile away; they swim toward the source like a guided missile. [A semicolon separates the independent clauses.]

ALERT: Choose a semicolon only when the separate sentences are closely related in meaning (see 25a).

14c Using coordinating conjunctions to correct comma splices and run-together sentences

You can connect independent clauses with a **coordinating conjunction** (*and, but, or, nor, for, so,* or *yet*). If you are correcting a comma splice, keep the comma and insert a coordinating conjunction after it. If you are correcting a run-together sentence, insert a comma followed by a coordinating conjunction.

PUNCTUATION ALERT: Use a comma before a coordinating conjunction that links independent clauses (see 24a).

USAGE ALERT: When using a coordinating conjunction, be sure that it fits the meaning of the material. *And* signals addition, *but* and *yet* signal contrast, *for* and *so* signal cause, and *or* and *nor* signal alternatives.

COMMA SPLICE	Every living creature gives off a weak electrical charge in the water, special pores on a shark's skin can detect these signals.
RUN-TOGETHER SENTENCE	Every living creature gives off a weak electrical charge in the water special pores on a shark's skin can detect these signals.
CORRECTED	Every living creature gives off a weak electrical field in the water, **and** special pores on a shark's skin can detect these signals.
COMMA SPLICE	The great white shark supposedly eats humans, however most white sharks spit them out after the first bite.
RUN-TOGETHER SENTENCE	The great white shark supposedly eats humans however most white sharks spit them out after the first bite.
CORRECTED	The great white shark supposedly eats humans, **but** most white sharks spit them out after the first bite.

EXERCISE 14-1

Consulting sections 14a, 14b, and 14c, revise any comma splices or run-together sentences by using a period, a semicolon, or a coordinating conjunction and comma.

EXAMPLE   In Los Angeles, animals contract skin cancer, in New York, they suffer from high-rise syndrome.

In Los Angeles, animals contract skin **cancer; in** New York, they suffer from high-rise syndrome.

1. Urban veterinarians report that summer in New York City can be hard on pets, however cats suffer less than other animals.

2. Many pets fall accidentally out of open twenty-story windows cats are the most common victims, along with dogs, rabbits, iguanas, and turtles.

3. A research paper reports an amazing finding, cats that fall five to nine stories are more seriously hurt than cats that fall much farther.

4. The average falling cat reaches maximum speed at five stories then after nine stories the cat manages to get into a position that cushions the impact of landing.

5. A Manhattan cat has set a new record for surviving a high-rise fall, it dropped forty-six stories from a midtown apartment balcony and landed unharmed on a café awning below.

14d Revising an independent clause into a dependent clause to correct a comma splice or run-together sentence

You can revise a comma splice or run-together sentence by changing one of two INDEPENDENT CLAUSES into a DEPENDENT CLAUSE. This method is suitable only when one idea can logically be subordinated to the other.

One way to create a dependent clause is to insert a SUBORDINATING CONJUNCTION (such as *because* or *although;* for a complete list, see Chart 53 in section 7h). When using a subordinating conjunction, be sure that it fits the meaning of the material—for example, *as* and *because* signal cause, *although* signals contrast, *if* signals condition, and *when* signals time. This type of dependent clause is called an **adverb clause.**

COMMA SPLICE	Homer and Langley Collyer had packed their house from top to bottom with junk, police could not open the front door to investigate a reported smell.
RUN-TOGETHER SENTENCE	Homer and Langley Collyer had packed their house from top to bottom with junk police could not open the front door to investigate a reported smell.
CORRECTED	**Because Homer and Langley Collyer had packed their house from top to bottom with junk,** police could not open the front door to investigate a reported smell.

ANSWERS AND COVERAGE: EXERCISE 14-1

The correction strategies will vary. Here is one set of possibilities.

1. Urban veterinarians report that summer in New York City can be hard on pets; however, [14c, comma splice corrected by using semicolon and comma] cats suffer less than other animals.

2. Many pets accidentally fall out of open twenty-story windows. [14b, run-together sentence corrected by using a period] Cats are the most common victims, along with dogs, rabbits, iguanas, and turtles.

3. A research paper reports an amazing finding. [14b, comma splice caused by explanation corrected by using a period] Cats that fall five to nine stories are more seriously hurt than cats that fall much farther.

4. The average falling cat reaches maximum speed at five stories. [14c, run-together sentence corrected by using a comma and a coordinating conjunction] Then, after nine stories, the cat manages to get into a position that cushions the impact of landing.

5. A Manhattan cat has set a new record for surviving a high-rise fall. [14b, run-together sentence corrected by using a period] It dropped forty-six stories from a midtown apartment balcony and landed unharmed in a café awning below.

QUOTATION: ON WRITING

Wearing down seven number two pencils is a good day's work.

—Ernest Hemingway

ANSWERS AND COVERAGE: EXERCISE 14-2

1. Correct complete sentence

2. The Internet connects thousands of online computer networks around the world, and [run-together sentence caused by pronoun corrected by comma and coordinating conjunction *and*] it has created a new form of personal communication that requires new rules.

3. Correct complete sentence

4. Sometimes, the faceless communication gives timid onliners confidence to speak their minds. However, at other times, some users have less pleasant experiences. [comma splice corrected by a period]

5. A "flame," for example, is an insulting message that is [run-together sentence corrected by relative pronoun *that* to make final clause dependent] the online equivalent of a poison-pen letter.

6. The quick response time of electronic mail encourages hasty people to react hastily, and [run-together sentence corrected by adding coordinating conjunction *and*] instant anger can be thoughtlessly expressed.

7. Flamers cannot always be identified because [comma splice caused by explanation corrected by adding subordinating conjunction *because*] their real names are concealed by "screen names."

COMMA SPLICE	Old newspapers and car parts filled every room to the ceiling, enough space remained for fourteen pianos.
RUN-TOGETHER SENTENCE	Old newspapers and car parts filled every room to the ceiling enough space remained for fourteen pianos.
CORRECTED	**Although old newspapers and car parts filled every room to the ceiling,** enough space remained for fourteen pianos.

❶ **PUNCTUATION ALERTS:** (1) If you put a period after a dependent clause that is not attached to an independent clause, you will create the error called a SENTENCE FRAGMENT (see Chapter 13). (2) Generally, use a comma between an introductory dependent clause that starts with a subordinating conjunction and the independent clause (see 24b.1). ❗

Another way to create a dependent clause is to use a RELATIVE PRONOUN (*that, which, who*). This type of dependent clause is called an **adjective clause.**

COMMA SPLICE	The Collyers had been crushed under a pile of newspapers, the newspapers had toppled onto the brothers.
RUN-TOGETHER SENTENCE	The Collyers had been crushed under a pile of newspapers the newspapers had toppled onto the brothers.
CORRECTED	The Collyers had been crushed under a pile of newspapers **that had toppled onto the brothers.**

❶ **PUNCTUATION ALERT:** To determine whether you need commas to set off an adjective clause, check whether it is NONRESTRICTIVE (nonessential) or RESTRICTIVE (essential), as explained in section 24e. ❗

EXERCISE 14-2

Consulting sections 14a through 14d, revise any comma splices or run-together sentences.

(1) Because millions of Americans are now cruising the information superhighway, traffic pileups and confrontations are more likely. (2) The Internet connects thousands of online computer networks around the world it has created a new form of personal communication that requires new rules. (3) Just as on a real highway, not all users of the information highway observe "netiquette," the rules governing online courtesy. (4) Sometimes, the faceless communication gives timid onliners confidence to speak their minds, however, at other times, some users have less pleasant experiences. (5) A "flame," for example, is an insulting message it is the online equivalent of a poison-pen letter. (6) The quick response time of electronic mail encourages hasty people to react hastily instant anger can be

thoughtlessly expressed. (7) Flamers cannot always be identified, their real names are concealed by "screen names." (8) Another prank is to impersonate another user by adopting his or her screen name, as a result, there is no way to identify the person sending a fake message. (9) Internet lurkers are undesirable too they read other people's messages in the public spaces but are too fearful of being flamed to send their own messages.

14e Using a semicolon or a period before a conjunctive adverb or other transitional expression between independent clauses

Conjunctive adverbs and other transitional expressions link ideas between sentences. When these words fall between sentences, a period or semicolon must immediately precede them.

Conjunctive adverbs include such words as *however, therefore, also, next, then, thus, furthermore,* and *nevertheless* (for a complete list, see Chart 51 in section 7f). Remember that these words are not COORDINATING CONJUNCTIONS, which work with commas to join independent clauses (see 14c).

COMMA SPLICE	Buying or leasing a car is a matter of individual preference, **however,** it is wise to consider several points before making a decision.
RUN-TOGETHER SENTENCE	Buying or leasing a car is a matter of individual preference **however** it is wise to consider several points before making a decision.
CORRECTED	Buying or leasing a car is a matter of individual preference; **however,** it is wise to consider several points before making a decision.

① PUNCTUATION ALERT: A conjunctive adverb at the beginning of a sentence is usually followed by a comma (see 24b.3). **!**

Transitional expressions include *for example, for instance, in addition, in fact, of course,* and *on the one hand/on the other hand* (for a complete list, see Chart 25 in section 4d.1).

COMMA SPLICE	Car leasing requires a smaller down payment, **for example,** in many cases, you need only $1,000 or $2,000 and the first monthly payment.
RUN-TOGETHER SENTENCE	Car leasing requires a smaller down payment **for example** in many cases, you need only $1,000 or $2,000 and the first monthly payment.
CORRECTED	Car leasing requires a smaller down payment. **For example,** in many cases, you need only $1,000 or $2,000 and the first monthly payment.

281

❶ **PUNCTUATION ALERT:** A transitional expression at the beginning of a sentence is usually followed by a comma (see 24b.3). ❗

A conjunctive adverb or other transitional expression can appear in more than one location within an INDEPENDENT CLAUSE. In contrast, a **coordinating conjunction** (*and, but, or, nor, for, so,* or *yet*) can appear only between independent clauses that it joins.

> Car leasing grows more popular every year. **However,** leasers have nothing to show for their money when the lease ends. [conjunctive adverb at beginning of sentence]
>
> Car leasing grows more popular every year. Leasers, **however,** have nothing to show for their money when the lease ends. [conjunctive adverb in middle of sentence]
>
> Car leasing grows more popular every year. Leasers have nothing to show for their money, **however,** when the lease ends. [conjunctive adverb in middle of sentence]
>
> Car leasing grows more popular every year. Leasers have nothing to show for their money when the lease ends, **however.** [conjunctive adverb at end of sentence]
>
> Car leasing grows more popular every year, **but** leasers have nothing to show for their money when the lease ends. [coordinating conjunction *but* between two independent clauses]

ANSWERS AND COVERAGE: EXERCISE 14-3

1. Lovecraft wrote vividly of monsters from beyond space and time; however, [run-together sentence: conjunctive adverb] he insisted that he did not believe in the supernatural.
2. "The Shadow over Innsmouth" is Lovecraft's famous tale about the strange inhabitants of a New England port; specifically, [comma splice: transitional expression] they are part fish and part human.
3. Correct complete sentence
4. Many of Lovecraft's stories mention a sinister volume of secret lore called the *Necronomicon*; however, it [comma splice: conjunctive adverb] was entirely a product of his imagination.
5. No such book exists. [run-together sentence: conjunctive adverb] Nevertheless, U.S. libraries still receive call slips for the *Necronomicon* filled out by gullible Lovecraft readers.

EXERCISE 14-3

Consulting section 14e, revise any comma splices or run-together sentences caused by a conjunctive adverb or other transitional expression. If an item is correct, circle its number.

EXAMPLE The horror stories of the New England writer H. P. Lovecraft were little known during his lifetime however they gained a following of enthusiastic readers after his death in 1937.

The horror stories of the New England writer H. P. Lovecraft were little known during his **lifetime. However,** they gained a following of enthusiastic readers after his death in 1937.

1. Lovecraft wrote vividly of monsters from beyond space and time however, he insisted that he did not believe in the supernatural.
2. "The Shadow over Innsmouth" is Lovecraft's famous tale about the strange inhabitants of a New England port, specifically, they are part fish and part human.
3. Lovecraft wanted his invented historical backgrounds to sound factual so he often cited impressive-sounding reference works; of course, he simply made most of them up.

4. Many of Lovecraft's stories mention a volume of secret lore called the *Necronomicon,* however, it was entirely a product of his imagination.

5. No such book exists nevertheless U.S. libraries still receive call slips for the *Necronomicon* filled out by gullible Lovecraft readers.

EXERCISE 14-4

Consulting all sections in this chapter, revise all comma splices, using a different method of correction for each one. If an item is correct, circle its number.

EXAMPLE   People hold strong but erroneous beliefs about animal behavior, for example, it is commonly thought that ostriches bury their heads in the sand.

People hold strong but erroneous beliefs about animal **behavior. For** example, it is commonly thought that ostriches bury their heads in the sand.

1. Ostriches are said to bury their heads in the sand so that their enemies will not notice them this, naturalists maintain, is a myth.

2. A South African naturalist examined eighty years of records from ostrich farms where more than 200,000 of the birds were reared, he found that no one reported a single case of an ostrich burying its head.

3. Ostriches do listen intently for chirps, cries, and approaching footsteps with their heads near the ground, sometimes, they even lower their heads just to rest their neck muscles.

4. They also poke their heads into bushes because they are curious animals.

5. They never bury their heads in sand, they would probably suffocate if they did.

EXERCISE 14-5

Consulting all sections in this chapter, revise any comma splices or run-together sentences, using as many different methods of correction as you can.

(1) For many years, the women of a village in northwestern India have walked five miles to do their laundry they do this once a week. (2) Their destination is the edge of a small canal, they can spread their wash and beat it rhythmically. (3) When they are done, they bind up the sheets and clothes then they walk the five miles back to their homes. (4) Foreign aid workers who came to help the villagers

ANSWERS AND COVERAGE: EXERCISE 14-4

Answers will vary. Here is one set of revisions.

1. Ostriches are said to bury their heads in the sand so that their enemies will not notice them, but this, naturalists maintain, is a myth. [14c, run-together sentence corrected with comma and coordinating conjunction]

2. A South African naturalist who examined eighty years of records from ostrich farms where more than 200,000 of the birds were reared found that no one reported a single case of an ostrich burying its head. [14d, comma splice corrected by creating dependent clause beginning with relative pronoun *who*]

3. Ostriches do listen intently for chirps, cries, and approaching footsteps with their heads near the ground; sometimes, they even lower their heads just to rest their neck muscles. [14b, run-together sentence corrected with semicolon]

4. Correct complete sentence

5. They never bury their heads in sand, and they would probably suffocate if they did. [14c, comma splice corrected with coordinating conjunction]

ANSWERS: EXERCISE 14-5

Answers will vary. Here is one possible revision.

(1) For many years, the women of a village in northwestern India have walked five miles to do their laundry. They do this once a week. (2) Their destination is the edge of a small canal, where they can spread their wash and beat it rhythmically. (3) When they are done, they bind up the sheets and clothes, and then they walk the five miles back to their homes. (4) Foreign aid workers who came to help the villagers believed that five miles was too far to walk with all that laundry, so they built a place for washing nearer the village. (5) The women praised the washing place, which was designed to let them

Answers: Exercise 14-5 (continued)

do their laundry in the traditional way; still, they refused to use it. (6) The women's refusal to use the new washing place was a mystery, so the aid workers asked an anthropologist to visit the village to study the problem. (7) When she gained the women's confidence, she learned that the village women are seldom allowed to go outside their homes. (8) Because they spend most of their lives inside their families' mud castles, they look forward to their weekly excursion to the canal five miles away. (9) Laundry day got them out of the village; therefore, it was their one opportunity to see their friends, to laugh, and to share stories.

believed that five miles was too far to walk with all that laundry they built a place for washing nearer the village. (5) The women praised the washing place, which was designed to let them do their laundry in the traditional way still, they refused to use it. (6) The women's refusal to use the new washing place was a mystery the aid workers asked an anthropologist to visit the village to study the problem. (7) She gained the women's confidence she learned that the village women are seldom allowed to go outside their homes. (8) They spend most of their lives inside their families' mud castles they look forward to their weekly excursion to the canal five miles away. (9) Laundry day got them out of the village therefore, it was their one opportunity to see their friends, to laugh, and to share stories.

Focus on Revising

Revising Your Writing

If you write comma splices or run-together sentences, go back to your writing and locate them. Then figure out why each is an error by using Chart 89 in the beginning of Chapter 14. Next, using the explanations in sections 14b through 14e, revise your writing to eliminate the errors.

Case Studies: Revising to Avoid Comma Splices and Run-Together Sentences

In these case studies, you can observe a student writer revising. Then, you have the chance to revise other student writing on your own.

Observation

A student wrote the following draft for a course called Introduction to Criminal Justice. The assignment was to discuss a current controversy in trial law. This material is well organized and presents its information clearly and fully. However, the draft's effectiveness is diminished by comma splices and run-together sentences.

Read through the draft. The errors are highlighted and explained. Before you look at the student's revision, revise the material yourself. Then, compare your revision with the student's.

comma splice with pronoun *it:* 14a

When fingerprinting was first introduced in the late nineteenth century, many judges hesitated to accept fingerprints as legal evidence. Recently, a similar controversy has arisen, it involves hypnosis. Over the past decade or two, various state and federal courts have issued contradictory rulings on the admissibility of testimony obtained under hypnosis, however, in 1987, the United States Supreme Court ruled that such evidence is admissible. This ruling was a major new development, but the public should not look to hypnosis as a miracle technique, because testimony obtained under hypnosis is no more reliable than that

comma splice with conjunctive adverb *however:* 14a

PARTICIPATION ESSAY

Coverage

As consumers, when we buy clothes, we often make choices on the basis of the *fabric of an article of clothing, therefore,* [14a, comma splice with conjunctive adverb] fashion designers always pay attention to matters of composition and design in fabrics.

Fabric is composed of natural fibers, synthetic fibers, and blends of the two. Natural fibers include cotton, linen, and *wool, they* [14a, comma splice with pronoun] offer the advantages of durability and absorbency. Synthetic fibers include rayon, polyester, acrylic, or combinations of them and other synthetic *fibers they* [14a, run-together sentence with pronoun] resist wrinkling and retain their color well. Fiber blends combine natural and synthetic fibers to create combinations such as cotton and polyester, which offer the advantages of each but have their own problems, such as retaining stains.

The design of fabric is affected by the way *that the fabric is produced, for example,* [14a, comma splice with transitional expression] a fabric can be produced on a loom to create woven fabrics such as crepe and *denim, conversely,* [14a, run-together sentence with transitional expression] a fabric can be produced on a knitting machine to create fabrics such as jersey and velour. Once the basic fabric is being produced, special patterns can be woven or knitted into it, *for instance,* [14a, comma splice with transitional expression] diagonal patterns can be woven into cotton fabrics for a geometric effect, and vertical patterns can be woven into a cable-stitched fabric for a thicker look and feel. Various finishes can further alter a fabric's *appearance stone* [14a, run-together sentence with example] washing, for example, gives denim a worn look, and brushing gives flannel a softer look. Puckers or wrinkles can be set into a *fabric, these* [14a, comma splice with pronoun] features characterize fabrics such as seersucker and crinkle gauze.

These many options, and others, in fabrics permit fashion designers to satisfy the

Participation Essay (continued)

needs of many different types of *people, some* [14a, run-together sentence with example] consumers care more about being in style than building a long-lasting wardrobe, while others place high priority on ease of care or on comfortable fit.

Answer to Participation Essay

This version revises the common splices and run-together sentences. Answers might vary because of the options in correcting the errors. Also, answers will vary if a student revised the content, organization, or style.

As consumers, when we buy clothes, we often make choices on the basis of the fabric of an article of clothing. Therefore, fashion designers always pay attention to matters of composition and design in fabrics.

Fabric is composed of natural fibers, synthetic fibers, and blends of the two. Natural fibers include cotton, linen, and wool. They offer the advantages of durability and absorbency. Synthetic fibers include rayon, polyester, acrylic, or combinations of them and other synthetic fibers; they resist wrinkling and retain their color well. Fiber blends combine natural and synthetic fibers to create combinations such as cotton and polyester, which offer the advantages of each but have their own problems, such as retaining stains.

The design of fabric is affected by the way that the fabric is produced. For example, a fabric can be produced on a loom to create woven fabrics such as crepe and denim; conversely, a fabric can be produced on a knitting machine to create fabrics such as jersey and velour. Once the basic fabric is being produced, special patterns can be woven or knitted into it. For instance, diagonal patterns can be woven into cotton fabrics for a geometric effect, and vertical patterns can be woven into a cable-stitched fabric for a thicker look and feel. Various finishes can further alter a fabric's appearance. Stone washing, for example, gives denim a worn look, and

➞

FOCUS ON REVISING   FOCUS ON REVISING   FOCUS ON REVISING   FOCUS ON REVISING   FOCUS ON REVISING

run-together sentence with pronoun *it:* 14a

run-together sentence with conjunctive adverb *furthermore:* 14a

run-together sentence with explanation in second independent clause: 14a

comma splice with explanation in second independent clause: 14a

comma splice with pronoun *they:* 14a

obtained when witnesses consciously search their memories.

There is one major advantage of hypnosis it usually allows witnesses to recall incidents in far greater detail than they would otherwise. Hypnotized people will still recall what they think they saw or what they wished they had seen. In fact, it is possible for people to lie when hypnotized furthermore, a hypnotist can unintentionally lead witnesses to give certain responses.

One thing is certain, more lively legal debates lie ahead. Hypnotists are not licensed professionals, they can be entertainers or serious practitioners. It would be up to a jury to decide on the competence of a hypnotist most people who sit on juries have no idea of what standards to apply.

Here is how the student revised the draft to correct comma splices and run-together sentences. In many places, the student could correct the errors in more than one way. Your revision, therefore, might not be exactly like this one, but it should deal with each error highlighted on the draft.

When fingerprinting was first introduced in the late nineteenth century, many judges hesitated to accept fingerprints as legal evidence. Recently, a similar controversy has arisen. It involves hypnosis. Over the past decade or two, various state and federal courts have issued contradictory rulings on the admissibility of testimony obtained under hypnosis. However, in 1987, the United States Supreme Court ruled that such evidence is admissible. This ruling was a major new development, but the public should not look to hypnosis as a miracle technique, because testimony obtained under hypnosis is no more reliable than that obtained when witnesses consciously search their memories.

There is one major advantage of hypnosis; it usually allows witnesses to recall incidents in far greater detail than they would otherwise. Hypnotized people will still recall what they think they saw or what they wished they had seen. In fact, it is possible for people to lie when hypnotized; furthermore, a hypnotist can unintentionally lead witnesses to give certain responses.

One thing is certain. More lively legal debates lie ahead. Hypnotists are not licensed professionals. They can be entertainers or serious practitioners. It would be up to a jury to decide on the competence of a hypnotist, but most people who sit on juries have no idea of what standards to apply.

Participation

A student wrote the following draft for a course called Introduction to Fashion Design. The assignment was to describe characteristics of fabric. This material is well organized and uses specific examples adeptly, but the draft's effectiveness is diminished by comma splices and run-together sentences.

Read through the draft. Then, revise it to eliminate the comma splices and run-together sentences. Also, make any additional revisions that you think would improve the content, organization, and style of the material.

As consumers, when we buy clothes, we often make choices on the basis of the fabric of an article of clothing, therefore, fashion designers always pay attention to matters of composition and design in fabrics.

Fabric is composed of natural fibers, synthetic fibers, and blends of the two. Natural fibers include cotton, linen, and wool, they offer the advantages of durability and absorbency. Synthetic fibers include rayon, polyester, acrylic, or combinations of them and other synthetic fibers they resist wrinkling and retain their color well. Fiber blends combine natural and synthetic fibers to create combinations such as cotton and polyester, which offer the advantages of each but have their own problems, such as retaining stains.

The design of fabric is affected by the way that the fabric is produced, for example, a fabric can be produced on a loom to create woven fabrics such as crepe and denim, conversely, a fabric can be produced on a knitting machine to create fabrics such as jersey and velour. Once the basic fabric is being produced, special patterns can be woven or knitted into it, for instance, diagonal patterns can be woven into cotton fabrics for a geometric effect, and vertical patterns can be woven into a cable-stitched fabric for a thicker look and feel. Various finishes can further alter a fabric's appearance stone washing, for example, gives denim a worn look, and brushing gives flannel a softer look. Puckers or wrinkles can be set into a fabric, these features characterize fabrics such as seersucker and crinkle gauze.

These many options, and others, in fabrics permit fashion designers to satisfy the needs of many different types of people, some consumers care more about being in style than building a long-lasting wardrobe, while others place a high priority on ease of care or on comfortable fit.

Answer to Participation Essay (continued)

brushing gives flannel a softer look. Puckers or wrinkles can be set into a fabric; these features characterize fabrics such as seersucker and crinkle gauze.

These many options, and others, in fabrics permit fashion designers to satisfy the needs of many different types of people. Some consumers care more about being in style than building a long-lasting wardrobe, while others place a high priority on ease of care or on comfortable fit.

15

AWKWARD SENTENCES

BACKGROUND

Clarity is one of the four virtues of style in classical rhetoric. The other three are correctness, appropriateness, and dignity or impressiveness. Theophrastus, a student of Aristotle, is credited with inventing the concept of the four virtues of style. The Stoics later added a fifth virtue—brevity.

A sentence can seem structurally correct at first glance, as if no grammatical principles of English had been violated, but can still have internal flaws that keep it from delivering a sensible message. While you are DRAFTING, if you suspect that you have made one of the errors identified in Chart 90, quickly underline or highlight the material and move on. Then, you can easily find and check it later.

TEACHING TIP: COLLABORATION

Whether students work on essays individually or collaboratively, students working together can make effective editing groups. Ask each group to divide a list of potential sentence problems (such as those identified in Chart 90) among its members, with each member becoming an "expert" in the assigned problem area. As each essay is passed around the group, each expert marks the problems in his or her area of expertise. Subsequently, the students work together to fix the problems, sharing with each other what they have learned in this handbook. Students are often open to hearing from peers what they resist hearing from instructors.

> ◉ **Ways that sentences send unclear messages**   **90**
>
> - Unnecessary shifts in person and number (see 15a.1), in subject and voice (see 15a.2), in tense and mood (see 15a.3), or in direct or indirect discourse (see 15a.4)
> - Misplaced modifiers (see 15b)
> - Dangling modifiers (see 15c)
> - Mixed constructions (see 15d.1)
> - Faulty predication (see 15d.2)
> - Incomplete sentences (see 15e)

Many flaws that make sentences awkward can be hard to spot because of the way the human brain works. When writers know what they mean to say, they sometimes misread what is on the paper for what they had intended. The mind unconsciously adjusts the error or fills in the missing material. Readers, however, see only what is on the paper. For suggestions to help you see such flaws, see Chart 91.

NO   Heated for thirty seconds, you get bubbles on the surface of the mixture. [This sentence says *you* are heated for thirty seconds.]

YES   After the mixture is heated for thirty seconds, bubbles form on the surface.

288

NO The chemical reaction taking place rapidly creates a salt. [*Rapidly* could refer to the speed of the reaction or to the speed at which the salt is created; readers cannot know.]

YES The chemical reaction takes place rapidly and creates a salt.

YES The chemical reaction rapidly creates a salt.

⊙ **Proofreading to find sentence flaws** 91

- Finish your revision in enough time so that you can put it aside and go back to it with fresh eyes that can spot flaws more easily.
- Work backward, from your last sentence to your first, so that you can see each sentence as a separate unit free of a context that might lure you to overlook flaws.
- Ask an experienced reader to check your writing for sentence flaws. If you make an error discussed in this chapter, you probably make that error repeatedly. Once you become aware of it, you will have made a major step toward eliminating that type of error.
- Proofread an extra time exclusively for any error that you tend to make more than any other.

15a Avoiding unnecessary shifts

A **shift** is any abrupt change in PERSON, NUMBER, SUBJECT, VOICE, TENSE, MOOD, or DIRECT or INDIRECT discourse. Unnecessary shifts blur meaning. Readers expect to stay on the track that you as the writer start them on. If you switch tracks, your readers become confused.

15a.1 Staying consistent in person and number

Person in English consists of the **first person** (*I, we*), words that designate the speaker or writer; the **second person** (*you*), words that designate the one being spoken or written to; and the **third person** (*he, she, it, they*), words that designate the person or thing spoken or written about. PRONOUNS indicate person. (For more about person, see Chart 75 in section 11a.)

NO **They** enjoy feeling productive, but when a job is unsatisfying, **you** usually become depressed. [*They* shifts to *you*.]

YES **They** enjoy feeling productive, but when a job is unsatisfying, **they** usually become depressed.

BACKGROUND

When using the generalized *you*, writers must guard against inappropriate shifts to third-person nouns and pronouns (*person, one, he, they*). Students who use the generalized *you* of adages like "You can fool some of the people some of the time . . ." may not sense the dissonance of a shift from *you* to *he* or from *you* to *they* in their writing.

ANOTHER EXAMPLE

To improve students' skills in recognizing person and number, you might ask them to read the following passage by Susan Allen Toth. Then, ask students to work in groups to label the subject of each clause by person and number. (The subjects here appear in italics.)

> When *Pete and I* [third, first, plural] go to the movies, *we* [first, plural] take turns driving so *no one* [third, singular] owes anyone else anything. *We* [first, plural] leave the car far from the theater so *we* [first, plural] don't have to pay for a parking space. If *it's* [third, singular] raining or snowing, *Pete* [third, singular] offers to let me off at the door, but *I* [first, singular] can tell *he'll* [third, singular] feel better if *I* [first, singular] go with him while *he* [third, singular] finds a spot, so *we* [first, plural] share the walk too. Inside the theater *Pete* [third, singular] will hold my hand when *I* [first, singular] get scared if *I* [first, singular] ask him. *He* [third, singular] puts my hand firmly on his knee and covers it completely with his own hand. His *knee* [third, singular] never twitches. After a while, when the scary *part* [third, singular] is past, *he* [third, singular] loosens his hand slightly and *I* [first, singular] know *that* [third, singular] is a signal to take mine away. *He* [third, singular] sits companionably close, letting his *jacket* [third, singular] just touch my sweater, but *he* [third, singular] does not infringe. *He* [third, singular] thinks *I* [first, singular] ought to know *he* [third, singular] is there if *I* [first, singular] need him.
>
> —Susan Allen Toth, "Cinematypes"

Number refers to *singular* (one) or *plural* (more than one). Do not start to write in one number and then shift for no reason to the other number. Such shifting gives your sentences an unstable quality.

NO   Because **people** are living longer, **an employee** in the twenty-first century will retire later. [The plural *people* shifts to the singular *employee*.]

YES   Because **people** are living longer, **employees** in the twenty-first century will retire later.

A common cause of inconsistency in person and number is a shift to *you* (second person) from *I* (first person) or from a NOUN (always third person) such as *person, the public,* or *people*. In academic writing, reserve *you* for sentences that address the reader directly; use the third person for general statements.

NO   **I** enjoy reading forecasts of the future, but **you** wonder which will turn out to be correct. [*I*, which is first person, shifts to *you*, which is second person.]

YES   **I** enjoy reading forecasts of the future, but **I** wonder which will turn out to be correct.

NO   By the year 2010, **Americans** will pay twice today's price for a car, and **you** will get twice the gas mileage. [*Americans*, which is third person, shifts to *you*, which is second person.]

YES   By the year 2010, **Americans** will pay twice today's price for a car, and **they** will get twice the gas mileage.

Another common shift in number is using *they*, the plural third-person pronoun, although its ANTECEDENT is a singular third-person noun. Only *he* or *she* (or *he or she*, which acts as a singular pronoun) or *it* can refer to a singular noun. Especially when you use words such as *employee* or *someone* in a general sense, without any specific employee or someone in mind, you might think that a *he* or *she* is not involved. Still, you have to choose a singular pronoun. Another choice is to change to the plural noun *employees*, in which case the plural pronoun *they* is correct. A third possibility is revising so that personal pronouns are unneeded.

NO   When **an employee** is treated with respect, **they** usually feel highly motivated.

YES   When **an employee** is treated with respect, **he or she** usually feels highly motivated.

YES   When **employees** are treated with respect, **they** usually feel highly motivated.

YES   **Employees** who are treated with respect usually feel highly motivated.

YES **An employee** who is treated with respect usually feels highly motivated.

Avoid sexist language when you use indefinite pronouns (such as *someone* or *everyone;* for a complete list, see Chart 80 in section 11g); see sections 11q and 21b for advice about nonsexist language.

❶ **VERB ALERT:** After you have revised person or number, check the verbs in your sentence to see whether any verb needs a change in number as well (see 8c). In the examples just shown, each *yes* choice contains at least one verb change. ❗

EXERCISE 15-1

Consulting section 15a.1, eliminate shifts in person and number. Be alert to shifts between, as well as within, sentences. Some sentences may not need revision.

(1) According to some experts, snobbery is measured by your mental attitude, not the extent of your worldly goods. (2) Because a snob is unsure of his or her social position, snobs are driven by what others think of them. (3) You tend to be too dependent on buying status symbols to define your place in the world, and snobs look down on others. (4) You can trace the origin of this word to the British Isles. (5) The term *snob*—from the same root, meaning "cut," as *snip* and *snub*—was originally applied to the local cobbler. (6) Some of these shoemakers tended to take on the airs of his or her wealthy customers. (7) Students at Cambridge University would taunt social climbers for "acting like a snob." (8) The students helped turn the word *snob* into our most common term for persons aspiring to a higher social level.

15a.2 Staying consistent in subject and voice

A shift in **subject** is rarely justified when it is accompanied by a shift in voice. The **voice** of a sentence is either *active (People expect changes)* or *passive (Changes are expected)*; see 8n and 8o. Some subject shifts, however, are justified by the meaning of a passage: *People look forward to the future, but the future holds many secrets.*

NO Most **people expect** major improvements in the future, but some **hardships are** also **anticipated.** [The subject shifts from *people* to *hardships,* and the voice shifts from active to passive.]

YES Most **people expect** major improvements in the future, but **they** also **anticipate** some hardships.

YES Most **people expect** major improvements in the future but also **anticipate** some hardships.

BACKGROUND

English emphasizes the number of every noun or pronoun in a sentence. In fact, it is impossible to talk or write about anything in English without signaling its number. English speakers take such information for granted, but the system is not universal. In Chinese, for example, the speaker decides if it is necessary to mention whether an item is singular or plural. Usually, number is considered irrelevant, and few sentences make any reference to it.

ANSWERS AND COVERAGE: EXERCISE 15-1

Answers may vary somewhat because of the various ways to eliminate shifts in person and number.

(1) According to some experts, snobbery is measured by mental attitude, not extent of worldly goods [reserve *you* for direct address]. (2) Because *they* are unsure of *their* social position, snobs are driven by what others think of them [shift in number]. (3) *Snobs* tend to be too dependent on buying status symbols to define *their* place in the world, and *they* look down on others [shift in person, shift in number]. (4) The origin of this word *can be traced* to the British Isles [reserve *you* for direct address]. (5) Correct sentence (6) Some *cobblers* [no plural antecedent for pronoun] tended to take on the airs of *their* [plural antecedent] wealthy customers. (7) Students at Cambridge University would taunt social climbers for "acting like *snobs*" [shift in number]. (8) The students helped turn the word *snob* into our most common term for *a person* [shift in number, must agree with singular *snob*] aspiring to a higher social level.

WORD HISTORY

According to the *Oxford English Dictionary (OED),* the word *voice* comes from the Latin word *vox,* meaning "voice" or "sound." The earliest recorded statement in English using *voice* as a grammatical term is from 1382 by Wyclif: "A participle of a present tens, either preterit, or actif vois, eithir passif."

WORD HISTORY

According to the *Oxford English Dictionary* (*OED*), the term *mood* has been used since the sixteenth century to refer to verb forms that indicate commands or wishes. The earliest recorded use of the word in this way dates back to 1573, when a scholar named Golding asked a question that still concerns our students: "How shall men directly fynde the Coniugation, Nomber, Person, Tence and Moode of Verbes togither in their Kynde?"

When we speak of the *mood* of a verb, we are not discussing its emotional state. *Mood* when it refers to a mental state is related to Latin *mos*, meaning "custom." In contrast, *mood* used to discuss verbs is an alteration of *mode*, which comes from the Latin *modus*, meaning "measure," "moderation," or (most relevant here) "manner." The earliest use of *mode* to refer to verbs dates back to 1520: "Sometyme of the infinytyve mode folowynge." Other early references make it clear that *mood/mode* was originally used for discussions of Greek and Latin rather than of English.

ANOTHER EXAMPLE

To improve your students' skill in identifying subject and voice, you might ask them to work in groups to locate the subject and name the voice in each of the clauses in the following passage by Jack London. (The subjects and verbs appear in italics.)

The *earthquake* [subject] *shook* [active] down in San Francisco hundreds of thousands of dollars' worth of walls and chimneys. But the conflagration [subject] *that* [subject] *followed* [active] *burned* [active] up hundreds of millions of dollars' worth of property. *There* ["dummy" subject] *is* [active] no estimating within hundreds of millions the actual damage *that* [subject] *was wrought* [passive].

Not in history *has* a modern imperial *city* [subject] *been* so completely *destroyed* [passive]. *San Francisco* [subject] *is* [active] gone. *Nothing* [subject] *remains* [active] of it but memories and a

15a.3 Staying consistent in tense and mood

Tense refers to the ability of verbs to show time. Tense changes are required to describe time changes: *We **will go** to the movies after we **finish** dinner.* If a tense shift within or between sentences is illogical, clarity suffers. (For information about correct sequences of tenses, see section 8k.)

NO A campaign to clean up movies in the United States **began** in the 1920s as civic and religious groups **try** to ban sex and violence from the screen. [The tense shifts from the past *began* to the present *try*.]

YES A campaign to clean up movies in the United States **began** in the 1920s as civic and religious groups **tried** to ban sex and violence from the screen.

NO Film producers and distributors **created** the Production Code in the 1930s. At first, violating its guidelines **carried** no penalty. Eventually, however, films that **fail** to get the board's seal of approval **do not receive** wide distribution. [This shift occurs between sentences—the past tense *created* and *carried* shift to the present tense *fail* and *do not receive*.]

YES Film producers and distributors **created** the Production Code in the 1930s. At first, violating its guidelines **carried** no penalty. Eventually, however, films that **failed** to get the board's seal of approval **did not receive** wide distribution.

Mood reflects whether a sentence is a statement or question (**indicative mood**), a command or request (**imperative mood**), or a conditional or other-than-real statement (**subjunctive mood**; see 8l). A shift between moods may blur the message of a passage.

NO The Production Code included two guidelines about violence: **Do not show** the details of brutal killings, and **movies should not be** explicit about how to commit crimes. [The verbs shift from the imperative mood *do not show* to the indicative mood *movies should not be*.]

YES The Production Code included two guidelines about violence: **Do not show** the details of brutal killings, and **do not show** explicitly how to commit crimes. [This revision uses the imperative mood for both guidelines.]

YES The Production Code included two guidelines about violence: **Movies were not to show** the details of brutal killings or explicit ways to commit crimes.

NO The code's writers worried that **if a crime were to be** accurately **depicted** in a movie, copycat **crimes will follow.** [The sentence shifts from the subjunctive mood *if a crime were to be depicted* to the indicative mood *copycat crimes will follow*.]

YES The code's writers worried that **if a crime were to be** accurately **depicted** in a movie, copycat **crimes would follow.**

15a.4 Avoiding unmarked shifts between indirect and direct discourse

Indirect discourse reports the gist of speech or conversation and is not enclosed in quotation marks. **Direct discourse** repeats speech or conversation exactly and encloses the spoken words in quotation marks (see 24g). Sentences that merge indirect and direct discourse without quotation marks and without other necessary changes that mark words as either reported or quoted distort the intended message.

NO A critic said that board members were acting as censors and **what you are doing is unconstitutional.** [The first clause is indirect discourse; the second clause shifts into unmarked direct discourse, garbling the message.]

YES A critic said that board members were acting as censors and **that what they were doing was unconstitutional.** [This revision consistently uses indirect discourse.]

YES A critic said that board members were acting as censors and added, **"What you are doing is unconstitutional."** [This revision uses indirect and direct discourse correctly, with quotation marks and other changes to distinguish reported words from spoken words.]

Changing a message from a direct discourse version to an indirect-discourse version usually requires changes of verb tense and other grammatical features. Simply removing the quotation marks is not enough.

NO He asked **did we enjoy the movie?** [This version has the verb form needed for direct discourse, but the pronoun *we* is wrong and quotation punctuation is missing.]

YES He asked **whether we enjoyed the movie.** [This version is entirely indirect discourse, and the verb has changed from *enjoy* to *enjoyed*.]

YES He asked, **"Did you enjoy the movie?"** [This version is direct discourse. It repeats the original speech exactly, with correct quotation punctuation.]

EXERCISE 15-2

Consulting section 15a, revise these sentences to eliminate all incorrect shifts. Some sentences can be revised in several ways.

EXAMPLE During the Victorian era, all gentlemen worthy of the name are obliged to raise their hats to ladies.

During the Victorian era, all gentlemen worthy of the name *were* obliged to raise their hats to ladies.

1. The Victorian male's custom of tipping his hat had serious drawbacks, though; for instance, if you were carrying parcels, you would have to set them down first.

Another Example (continued)

fringe of dwelling houses on its outskirts. Its industrial *section* [subject] *is* [active] wiped out. Its social and residential *section* [subject] *is* [active] wiped out. The *factories* [subject] and *warehouses* [subject], the great *stores* [subject] and newspaper *buildings* [subject], the *hotels* [subject] and *palaces* [subject] of the nabobs, *all* [subject] *are* [active] *gone.* *There* ["dummy" subject] *remains* [active] only the *fringe* [subject] of dwelling houses on the outskirts of *what* [subject] *was* [active] once San Francisco.
                                    —Jack London

ANOTHER EXAMPLE

To improve your students' skill in identifying direct and indirect discourse, you might ask them to work in groups to identify the types of discourse found in the following passage by Russell Baker.

In the country, I am told, the trick is to let the weather roam free through the house. [indirect] "You're spoofing me, aren't you?" [direct] I asked the real-estate man. He wasn't.

In the country, he explained, you're supposed to wear long underwear all winter. [indirect] "It can get itchy if you don't have freezing wind coming between the logs," [direct] he said.

In the summer, you're expected to hang flypaper in the kitchen. "If your logs are chinked tightly they'll keep out the varmints that give your flypaper a businesslike appearance," [direct] he explained.
                    —Russell Baker, "Country Living"

ANSWERS AND COVERAGE: EXERCISE 15-2

Answers will vary. Here is one set of possibilities.

1. The Victorian male's custom of tipping his hat had serious drawbacks, though; for instance, if he were carrying parcels, *he* would have to set them down first. [15a.1, shift in person]

→

Answers and Coverage: Exercise 15-2 (continued)

2. In 1896, an inventor named James Boyle developed a self-tipping hat that *solved* the problem. [15a.3, shift in tense]

3. If a man nodded while wearing Boyle's invention, *he* activated a lifting mechanism concealed in the hat's crown. [15a.1, shift in number]

4. Boyle claimed that since the novelty of the moving hat would attract attention, *it could* also be *used for advertising*. [15a.2, shift in subject and voice]

5. He said that companies could place signs on the hats, and *they would* be able to advertise any product innovatively and inexpensively. [15a.4, indirect-direct discourse shift]

ANSWERS AND COVERAGE: EXERCISE 15-3

(1) When people think positively, *their* chances of success really do seem to go up [15a.1 person]. (2) A psychologist in Kansas confirms that optimists hold an advantage over *less hopeful people* [15a.1, number]. (3) He finds that *optimists* often *do* better than expected in school and *can* handle stress at work more easily than other people [15a.1, number between sentences 2 and 3; 15a.3, tense]. (4) Other researchers praise the benefits of optimism in *their* study of patients who must cope with severe illnesses [15a.1, number]. (5) These psychologists designed a "hope scale" that ranks people according to their level of hopefulness and *places* them among either the optimistic crowd or the less optimistic crowd [15a.2, voice]. (6) The psychologists contend that optimists are not simply *people* who *think*, "I'm a winner," and therefore *say*, *"Things always turn out right for me in the end"* [15a.1, number; 15a.4, indirect-direct discourse]. (7) Rather, true *optimists combine* confidence in *their* problem-solving abilities with the readiness to seek advice from friends [15a.1, number between sentences 6 and 7]. (8) True optimists also *have* to be willing to motivate *themselves so that accomplish important goals* [15a.3, tense; 15a.1, person; 15a.2, voice].

2. In 1896, an inventor named James Boyle developed a self-tipping hat that solves the problem.

3. If a man nodded while wearing Boyle's invention, they activated a lifting mechanism concealed in the hat's crown.

4. Boyle claimed that since the novelty of the moving hat would attract attention, advertising also can be one of its uses.

5. He said that companies could place signs on the hats, and you will be able to advertise any product innovatively and inexpensively.

EXERCISE 15-3

Consulting section 15a, revise this paragraph to eliminate incorrect shifts between sentences and within sentences.

(1) When people think positively, your chances of success really do seem to go up. (2) A psychologist in Kansas confirms that optimists hold an advantage over a less hopeful person. (3) He finds that an optimist often does better than expected in school and could handle stress at work more easily than other people. (4) Other researchers praise the benefits of optimism in her study of patients who must cope with severe illnesses. (5) These psychologists designed a "hope scale" that ranks people according to their level of hopefulness and is used to place them among either the optimistic crowd or the less optimistic crowd. (6) The psychologists contend that optimists are not simply someone who thinks, "I'm a winner," and therefore says that things always turn out right for me in the end. (7) Rather, a true optimist combines confidence in his or her problem-solving abilities with the readiness to seek advice from friends. (8) True optimists also had to be willing to motivate yourself so that important goals can be accomplished.

15b Avoiding misplaced modifiers

A **modifier** is a word or word group that describes or limits another word or words. A **misplaced modifier** is positioned incorrectly in a sentence, therefore describing the wrong word, which distorts meaning. Always check to see that your modifiers are placed as close as possible to what they describe so that your reader will attach the meaning where you intend it to be.

15b.1 Avoiding ambiguous placements

With **ambiguous placement,** a modifier is confusing to a reader because it can refer to two or more words in a sentence.

Limiting words (such as *only, not only, just, not just, almost, hardly, nearly, even, exactly, merely, scarcely,* and *simply*) can change meaning according to where they are placed. When you use such words, position them precisely. Consider how different placements of *only* change the meaning of this sentence: *Professional coaches say that high salaries motivate players.*

Only professional coaches say that high salaries motivate players. [No one else says this.]

Professional coaches **only** say that high salaries motivate players. [The coaches probably do not mean what they say.]

Professional coaches say **only** that high salaries motivate players. [The coaches say nothing else.]

Professional coaches say that **only** high salaries motivate players. [Nothing except high salaries motivates players.]

Professional coaches say that high salaries **only** motivate players. [High salaries do nothing other than motivate players.]

Professional coaches say that high salaries motivate **only** players. [No others on the team, such as coaches and managers, are motivated by high salaries.]

Squinting modifiers are ambiguous because they describe both what precedes and what follows them. For clarity, revise the sentence, making sure that the modifier is positioned where its meaning is precise.

NO   The football player being recruited **fervently** believed each successive offer would be better. [What was fervent, the recruitment or the player's belief?]

YES   The football player being recruited believed **fervently** that each successive offer would be better.

YES   The football player being **fervently** recruited believed that each successive offer would be better.

15b.2 Avoiding interrupting placements

Interrupting placements break the flow of a message and thereby distract your reader from understanding your material. A **split infinitive** is one type of awkward interruption. An **infinitive** is a verb form that starts with *to: to convince, to create* (see 7d). When material comes between *to* and the verb, the meaning does not flow.

NO   Orson Welles's radio drama "War of the Worlds" managed **to, in October 1938, convince** listeners that they were hearing an invasion by Martians.

YES   **In October 1938,** Orson Welles's radio drama "War of the Worlds" managed **to convince** listeners that they were hearing an invasion by Martians.

TEACHING TIP

If your students feel that modifier placement is a slapdash business, you might ask them to look at some ludicrous sentences and have them try to draw what is written. Here are a few.

1. When people first saw whales, they were still wearing animal skins and had stone axes.
2. The man kissed the baby with a beard.
3. Walking down the street, the Eiffel Tower came into view.
4. The wildlife specialist said that most bears are dangerous on television.
5. Poison ivy is common in the forest, which gives many people an itchy rash.

ANSWERS AND COVERAGE: EXERCISE 15-4

Answers may vary somewhat. The final result must avoid all shifts.

1. *For many centuries*, the Ramah people of the Navajo nation had made this land their home [15b.2, interrupted verb phrase].
2. *Shortly after they arrived*, the Mormons established a small cemetery on a knoll surrounded by farms and ranchland [15b.2, awkward placement].
3. They were not the *only* ones to make use of this graveyard [15b.1, ambiguous placement].
4. *Even though their beliefs and practices differed strikingly from those of the Mormons*, the Navajo began burying their own dead there, too [15b.2, interruption of subject and verb].
5. Correct sentence
6. The Mormon graves, *grouped according to family relationships*, have headstones in a wide variety of handmade and commercially manufactured styles [15b.2, awkward placement (phrase modifies *graves*, not *headstones*)].
7. *Painstakingly engraved* Mormon headstones display floral designs and representations of Mormon temples in Salt Lake City and elsewhere [15b.1, squinting modifier]. →

Often, the intervening word that splits an infinitive is an adverb ending in *-ly*. Many such adverbs sound awkward unless they are placed either before or after the infinitive.

> **NO**   People feared that they would no longer be able **to happily live** in peace.
> **YES** People feared that they would no longer be able **to live happily** in peace.

Nevertheless, sometimes an adverb fits best between *to* and the verb. Many readers are not distracted by split infinitives like this one:

> Welles wanted to **realistically portray** a Martian invasion for the radio audience.

You can usually revise a sentence to avoid the split:

> Welles wanted his "Martian invasion" **to sound realistic** for the radio audience.

Words inserted between subject and verb or between verb and object can disturb the smooth flow of a sentence.

> **NO**   The **announcer,** because the script, which Welles himself wrote, called for perfect imitations of emergency announcements, **opened** with a warning that included a description of the "invasion." [subject–verb interrupted]
> **YES** Because the script, which Welles himself wrote, called for perfect imitations of emergency announcements, the **announcer opened** with a warning that included a description of the "invasion."
> **NO**   Many churches **held** for their frightened communities **"end of the world" prayer services.** [verb–direct object interrupted]
> **YES** Many churches **held "end of the world" prayer services** for their frightened communities.

EXERCISE 15-4

Consulting section 15b, revise these sentences to correct any ambiguous, wrong, or awkward placements. If a sentence is correct, circle its number.

EXAMPLE   In 1876, a group of Mormon settlers from Utah founded a community in Ramah, New Mexico, a time of shifting populations in the Southwest.

In 1876, *a time of shifting populations in the Southwest*, a group of Mormon settlers from Utah founded a community in Ramah, New Mexico.

1. The Ramah people of the Navajo nation had for many centuries made this land their home.
2. The Mormons established shortly after they arrived a small cemetery on a knoll surrounded by farms and ranchland.
3. Only they were not the ones to make use of this graveyard.
4. The Navajo, even though their beliefs and practices differed strikingly from the those of the Mormons, began burying their own dead there, too.
5. For over a century now, the cemetery has continued to serve families of both cultures.
6. The Mormon graves have headstones in a wide variety of handmade and commercially manufactured styles, grouped according to family relationships.
7. Mormon headstones that were engraved painstakingly display floral designs and representations of Mormon temples in Salt Lake City and elsewhere.
8. The Navajo graves have simple metal markers, in contrast, and are not arranged by family relationship.
9. The Navajo, to speed the soul on its journey, bury valuable turquoise jewelry with their dead.
10. The little cemetery now contains about 71 Navajo graves in all and 209 Mormon graves.

EXERCISE 15-5

Consulting section 15b, combine each list of word groups to create all the possible logical sentences (each list offers more than one possibility). Insert commas as needed. Use a slash to indicate where each word or group of words ends. Explain differences in meaning, if any, among the alternatives you create.

EXAMPLE runners
        than couch potatoes do
        have lower blood pressure
        for the most part

A. For the most part, / runners / have lower blood pressure / than couch potatoes do. /
B. Runners / have lower blood pressure, / for the most part, / than couch potatoes do. /
C. Runners, / for the most part, / have lower blood pressure / than couch potatoes do. /
D. Runners / have lower blood pressure / than couch potatoes do, / for the most part. /

---

8. *In contrast*, the Navajo graves have simple metal markers and are not arranged by family relationship [15b.2, awkward placement].

9. *To speed the soul on its journey*, the Navajo bury valuable turquoise jewelry with their dead [15b.2, interruption of subject and verb].

10. *In all*, the little cemetery now contains about 71 Navajo graves and 209 Mormon graves [15b.2, awkward placement].

ANSWERS: EXERCISE 15-5

1. (a) To become / an entertainment lawyer, / the student / studied / corporate and copyright law / intensively. /

(b) The student / studied / corporate and copyright law / intensively / to become / an entertainment lawyer. /

(c) To become / an entertainment lawyer, / the student / intensively / studied / corporate and copyright law. /

2. (a) The matchmaker / happily / introduced the / wrestler / to the / muscular artist. /

(b) The matchmaker / happily / introduced the / muscular artist / to the / wrestler. /

(c) Happily, / the matchmaker / introduced the / wrestler / to the / muscular artist. /

(d) Happily, / the matchmaker / introduced the / muscular artist / to the / wrestler. /

(e) The matchmaker / introduced the / wrestler / to the / muscular artist / happily. /

(f) The matchmaker / introduced the / muscular artist / to the / wrestler / happily. /

3. (a) The computer hacker used / only / one simple password / to break into / the company files. /

Answers: Exercise 15-5 (continued)

(b) Only / the computer hacker used / one simple password / to break into / the company files. /

(c) To break into / the company files, / the computer hacker used / only / one simple password. /

(d) To break into / the company files, / only / the computer hacker used / one simple password. /

4. (a) Not just / pediatricians / know / that / children / need / love. /

(b) Pediatricians / know / that / not just / children / need / love. /

(c) Pediatricians / know / that / children / need / not just / love. /

(d) Pediatricians / know / not just / that / children / need / love. /

5. (a) As a rule, / bus drivers / have more patience / than the average citizen. /

(b) Bus drivers, / as a rule, / have more patience / than the average citizen. /

(c) Bus drivers / have more patience, / as a rule, / than the average citizen. /

(d) Bus drivers / have more patience / than the average citizen, / as a rule. /

A HUMOROUS NOTE

Dangling modifiers can sometimes create statements that are unintentionally humorous. Consider the following examples collected and published by Richard Lederer in *Anguished English.*

- Locked in a vault for fifty years, the owner of the jewels has decided to sell them.
- Do not sit in a chair without being fully assembled.
- Washed from a layer of mudstone estimated to be more than three million years old, a young American paleoanthropologist has found several leg bones and a skull fragment.

1. studied
   an entertainment lawyer
   corporate and copyright law
   the student
   to become
   intensively

2. introduced the
   happily
   muscular artist
   the matchmaker
   to the
   wrestler

3. the computer hacker used
   to break into
   only
   one simple password
   the company files

4. need
   love
   that
   know
   pediatricians
   not just
   children

5. have more patience
   as a rule
   bus drivers
   than the average citizen

15c Avoiding dangling modifiers

A **dangling modifier** describes or limits a word or words that do not appear in the sentence. Because a reader will "attach" the information in the dangling modifier to a NOUN or PRONOUN that *does* appear in the sentence, the writer's intended meaning is lost.

Dangling modifiers can be hard for a writer to spot. Aware of the intended meaning, the writer unconsciously supplies the missing material, but the reader usually sees only the error and concludes that the meaning is flawed. You can correct a dangling modifier by revising the sentence so that the intended SUBJECT is stated.

NO **Reading Faulkner's short story "A Rose for Emily," the ending** surprised us. [This says that the ending was reading the story—not the intended meaning.]

YES **Having read Faulkner's short story "A Rose for Emily," we** were surprised by the ending.

YES **We read Faulkner's short story "A Rose for Emily"** and were surprised by the ending.

NO **When courting Emily, the townspeople** gossiped about her. [The townspeople were not courting Emily.]

YES **When Emily was being courted by Homer Barron,** the townspeople gossiped about her.

Dangling modifiers are sometimes caused by unnecessary use of the PASSIVE VOICE (see 8n and 8o).

NO **To earn money, china-painting lessons** were offered by Emily to wealthy young women. [China-painting lessons cannot earn money.]

YES **To earn money, Emily** offered china-painting lessons to wealthy young women.

EXERCISE 15-6

Consulting section 15c, identify and correct any dangling modifiers in these sentences. If a sentence is correct, circle its number.

EXAMPLE Starting out as a short-order cook, the work can be confusing at first to a trainee.

Starting out as a short-order cook, *a trainee can find the work confusing at first.*

1. Cooking in a busy coffee shop or diner, a quick pair of hands is a necessity for a short-order cook.
2. To do a good job, the ability to concentrate is also a must for a short-order cook.
3. Especially at lunchtime, customers expect their meals *yesterday morning.*
4. While preparing several orders at once, kitchen utensils and ingredients have to be located at a moment's notice.
5. Although often hard to keep straight, a long list of orders and recipes must be remembered by the cook.
6. When first learning the job, orders like "wreck two" and "cowboy" may be puzzling.
7. After catching on to the diner staff's slang, "wreck two" for an order of two scrambled eggs and "cowboy" for a Western omelet will make sense.
8. Crammed with food and utensils, an inexperienced cook may see a diner's small kitchen as a stressful place to work.
9. The pressures of the job can begin to become manageable, however, by learning how to plan ahead for the busy times.
10. Along with the diner's other workers, the opportunity also exists to enjoy the funny slang, joking conversations, and even the hectic pace.

TEACHING TIP

Students may realize that they have started a sentence with a dangling modifier when they move the modifier to follow the subject of the sentence. For example, "Shocked by her father's death, the family home became a refuge for Emily" becomes "The family home, shocked by her father's death, became a refuge for Emily" when the modifier follows the subject.

ANSWERS: EXERCISE 15-6

Answers may vary somewhat. Here is one set of possibilities.

1. Cooking in a busy coffee shop or diner, a short-order cook needs a quick pair of hands. [dangling participle]

2. To do a good job, a short-order cook must also have the ability to concentrate. [dangling infinitive]

3. Correct sentence

4. While preparing several orders at once, a cook has to be able to locate kitchen utensils and ingredients at a moment's notice. [unexpected subject]

5. The cook must also remember a long list of orders and recipes, although they are often hard to keep straight. [unnecessary passive]

6. When first learning the job, a short-order cook may find orders like "wreck two" and "cowboy" puzzling. [unexpressed subject]

7. Once the short-order cook catches on to the diner staff's slang, "wreck two" for an order of two scrambled eggs and "cowboy" for a Western omelet will make sense. [unexpressed subject]

8. Crammed with food and utensils, a diner's small kitchen may be a stressful place for an inexperienced cook to work. [dangling participle]

9. A short-order cook can begin to manage the pressures of the job, however, by learning how to plan ahead for the busy times. [unexpressed subject]

10. Along with the diner's other workers, the cook can also learn to enjoy the funny slang, joking conversations, and even the hectic pace. [unexpressed subject]

TEACHING TIP

Students frequently become aware of problem sentences when they hear their papers read aloud. Particularly with long sentences, students sometimes compose chunk by chunk and fail to notice how the sections are connected. Reading aloud forces students to read the entire sentence, and hearing themselves stumble may signal a poorly constructed sentence. At home, students can read their papers into a tape recorder and then play back the tape to identify problem sentences. In class, student groups can listen for sentences that need revision as students read their papers aloud. Because some students make verbal corrections in their problem sentences when they read aloud without noticing a problem on the page, it is often useful to ask students to exchange their papers with another student and listen to that student read the paper aloud.

MORE EXAMPLES

What is inconsistent in the following mixed constructions? You might want to ask students to work in groups to revise these four sentences so that the parts make sense together.

1. Because you want to visit the great art museums of the world is why you should go to the Louvre in Paris.

2. Paris, the capital of France, one of the great museums of the world is located there.

3. Tourists from all over the world, the Louvre draws them.

4. The collection is composed of works of art from many cultures is what distinguishes the Louvre.

15d Avoiding mixed sentences

A **mixed sentence** consists of parts that do not make sense together because the writer has lost track of the beginning of a sentence while writing the end. Careful proofreading, including reading aloud, can help writers find and fix these errors.

15d.1 Revising mixed constructions

A **mixed construction** starts out taking one grammatical form and then changes, derailing the meaning of the sentence.

NO Because television's first transmissions in the 1920s included news programs quickly became popular with the public. [The opening DEPENDENT CLAUSE starts off on one track, but the INDEPENDENT CLAUSE goes off in another direction. What does the writer want to emphasize, the first transmissions or the popularity of news programs?]

YES Television's first transmissions in the 1920s included news programs, which quickly became popular with the public. [Emphasis is on the first transmissions.]

YES Because television's first transmissions in the 1920s included news programs, television quickly became popular with the public. [Emphasis is on the popularity of the news programs.]

NO By increasing the time for network news to thirty minutes increased the prestige of network news programs. [A PREPOSITIONAL PHRASE, such as *by increasing,* cannot be the subject of a sentence.]

YES Increasing the time for network news to thirty minutes increased the prestige of network news programs. [Dropping the preposition *by* clears up the problem.]

YES By increasing the time for network news to thirty minutes, the network executives increased the prestige of network news programs. [Inserting a logical subject, *the network executives,* clears up the problem.]

The phrase *the fact that* is sometimes the cause of a mixed sentence.

NO The fact that quiz show scandals in the 1950s prompted the networks to produce even more news shows.

YES The fact is that quiz show scandals in the 1950s prompted the networks to produce even more news shows. [The added *is* clarifies the meaning.]

YES Quiz show scandals in the 1950s prompted the networks to produce even more news shows. [Dropping *the fact that* clarifies the meaning.]

15d.2 Revising faulty predication

Faulty predication, sometimes called *illogical predication,* occurs when a SUBJECT and its PREDICATE do not make sense together.

NO The purpose of television was invented to entertain people.
[A *purpose* cannot be *invented.*]

YES The purpose of television was to entertain people.

YES Television was invented to entertain people.

One key cause of illogical predication is a breakdown in the connection between a subject and its COMPLEMENT (see 7m.1).

In the following *no* example, the subject complement *credible* could logically describe *Walter Cronkite,* but *Walter Cronkite* is not the subject. The subject is *characteristic,* so the meaning calls for a subject complement that renames some *characteristic* of Walter Cronkite as a newscaster: *credibility* instead of *credible.*

NO Walter Cronkite's outstanding **characteristic** as a newscaster **was credible.** [The subject complement is *characteristic;* that is what needs to be renamed.]

YES Walter Cronkite's outstanding **characteristic** as a newscaster **was credibility.** [The noun *credibility* renames *characteristic.*]

YES **Walter Cronkite was credible** as a newscaster. [The adjective *credible* describes the subject, *Walter Cronkite.*]

Constructions that include *is when* or *is where* often create illogical predication. It is best to avoid them.

NO A disaster **is when** television news shows get some of their highest ratings.

YES Television news shows get some of their highest ratings during a disaster.

Use *reason . . . is that,* not *reason . . . is because. Because* means "for the reason that," so *reason . . . is because* is redundant. If you prefer to use *because,* construct your sentence without *reason . . . is.*

NO One **reason** that television news started to capture national attention in the 1960s **is because** it covered the Vietnam War thoroughly.

YES One **reason** that television news started to capture national attention in the 1960s **is that** it covered the Vietnam War thoroughly.

YES Television news started to capture national attention in the 1960s **because** it covered the Vietnam War thoroughly.

ANSWERS AND COVERAGE: EXERCISE 15-7

Answers will vary. Here is one set of possibilities.

1. The Cold War between the United States and Russia motivated some 200,000 American families to construct backyard bomb shelters stocked with canned food, bottled water, batteries, and board games. [15d.1, mixed grammatical construction]

2. A frenzy of bomb shelter building took place in the 1960s because President John F. Kennedy warned people that they might need to make individual preparations against nuclear attack during the Berlin Wall crisis in 1961. [15d.2, faulty predication with *reason is . . . because*]

3. A few enterprising souls always make money during periods of panic, and shelter peddlers hurried to cash in on fears of imminent mass destruction. [15d.2, faulty predication with *is when*]

4. Correct sentence

5. The purpose of a bomb shelter was to protect people underground for at least ninety days until, presumably, the air was free of radioactivity. [15d.2, faulty predication]

6. Spending their two-week honeymoon in a bomb shelter won nationwide publicity for a Miami couple. [15d.1, mixed construction]

7. When the couple declared they had spent the entire two weeks playing cards, suddenly the public lost interest. [15d.1, mixed construction]

8. One debate concerned whether a family safely locked in its bomb shelter could refuse to admit desperate neighbors. [15d.2, faulty predication]

9. In the late 1960s, when fear of the Cold War faded, bomb shelters were turned into wine cellars, mushroom gardens, or sites for teenage parties. [15d.2, faulty predication with *is when*]

10. A solid steel "shelter for four" was dug up in Fort Wayne, Indiana, and is now on exhibit at the Smithsonian National Museum of American History in Washington, D.C. [15d.1, mixed construction with *the fact that*]

EXERCISE 15-7

Consulting section 15d, revise the mixed sentences so that the beginning of each sentence fits logically with its end. If a sentence is correct, circle its number.

EXAMPLE   The main reason for the U.S. bomb shelter craze from 1950 into the 1960s was because people believed that global nuclear war was about to break out.

The main reason for the U.S. bomb shelter craze from 1950 into the 1960s was *that* people believed that global nuclear war was about to break out.

1. Because of the Cold War between the United States and Russia motivated some 200,000 American families to construct backyard bomb shelters stocked with canned food, bottled water, batteries, and board games.

2. The reason that a frenzy of bomb shelter building took place in the 1960s is because President John F. Kennedy warned people that they might need to make individual preparations against nuclear attack during the Berlin Wall crisis in 1961.

3. During periods of panic is always when a few enterprising souls make money, and shelter peddlers hurried to cash in on fears of imminent mass destruction.

4. In this era before shopping malls were common, model bomb shelters were set up outside supermarkets, at county fairs, and in downtown department stores.

5. The purpose of a bomb shelter was built to protect people underground for at least ninety days until, presumably, the air was free of radioactivity.

6. By spending their two-week honeymoon in a bomb shelter won nationwide publicity for a Miami couple.

7. When the couple declared they had spent the entire two weeks playing cards, and suddenly the public lost interest.

8. One debate concerned whether a family safely locked in its bomb shelter could refuse to admit desperate neighbors is controversial.

9. In the late 1960s is when fear of the Cold War faded and bomb shelters were turned into wine cellars, mushroom gardens, or sites for teenage parties.

10. The fact that a solid steel "shelter for four" was dug up in Fort Wayne, Indiana, and now on exhibit at the Smithsonian National Museum of American History in Washington, D.C.

15e Avoiding incomplete sentences

An **incomplete sentence** is missing words necessary for grammatical correctness or sense. Such omissions blur meaning, and a reader has to work too hard to understand the message.

15e.1 Using elliptical constructions carefully

An **elliptical construction** deliberately leaves out one or more words that appear elsewhere in the sentence to avoid repeating them. *I have my book and Joan's,* for example, is an acceptable way to express *I have my book and Joan's book.* An elliptical construction is correct only if the word or words omitted from the elliptical construction are identical to those appearing in the sentence. The words *I have my book and Joan's* says I have one book of mine and hence one book of Joan's; if Joan has given more than one book, the construction is wrong.

NO	During the 1920s in Chicago, the cornetist Manuel Perez **was leading** one outstanding jazz group, Tommy and Jimmy Dorsey another. [The words *was leading* cannot take the place of *were leading,* which the subject *Tommy and Jimmy Dorsey* requires.]
YES	During the 1920s in Chicago, the cornetist Manuel Perez **was leading** one outstanding jazz group, and Tommy and Jimmy Dorsey **were leading** another.
YES	During the 1920s in Chicago, the cornetist Manuel Perez **led** one outstanding jazz group, Tommy and Jimmy Dorsey another. [The verb *led* is correct both with *Manuel Perez* and with *Tommy and Jimmy Dorsey* and thus can be omitted after *Dorsey.*]
NO	The period of the big jazz dance bands **began** and **lasted through** World War II. [*Began* requires *in,* not *through,* to follow it.]
YES	The period of the big jazz band **began in** and **lasted through** World War II.

15e.2 Making comparisons complete, unambiguous, and logical

In writing a comparison, be sure to include all words needed to make the relationship between the items or ideas being compared perfectly clear.

NO	Individuals driven to achieve make **better** business executives. [*Better* implies a comparison, but none is stated.]
YES	Individuals driven to achieve make **better** business executives **than** people uninterested in personal accomplishments do.

TEACHING TIP

Because conversation frequently includes incomplete comparisons, you might want to ask students to turn the following spoken dialogue into a paragraph written in the third person.

> *A*: I'm so glad we came here. This restaurant is so much better.
>
> *B*: You're right. A place that has fresh flowers on the tables is more appealing.
>
> *A*: I always think linen napkins are nicer.
>
> *B*: This place has a fine reputation for good service, but it's a shame that it's so much less spacious.

ANSWERS AND COVERAGE: EXERCISE 15-8

Answers may vary somewhat. One set of possibilities is the following.

(1) A giant tsunami is as destructive <u>as</u> [15e.2, incomplete comparison] and even larger than a tidal wave. (2) The word *tsunami* is Japanese for "harbor wave," for this kind <u>of</u> wave appears suddenly in <u>a</u> [15e.3, small words omitted] harbor or bay. (3) It begins with <u>a</u> rapid shift in <u>the</u> [15e.3, small words omitted] ocean floor caused by an undersea earthquake or volcano. (4) The wave this produces in the open sea is less than three feet high, but it can grow to a height of a hundred feet as it rushes *toward* [15e.1, incorrect elliptical] and strikes against the shore. (5) For this reason, tsunamis are much more dangerous to seaside towns than <u>they are to</u> [15e.2, ambiguous comparison] ships on the open sea. (6) In 1960, a huge tsunami that struck <u>the</u> coasts of Chile, Hawaii, and Japan killed <u>a</u> [15e.3, small words omitted] total of 590 people.

NO	Most personnel officers value high achievers **more than risk takers.** [Unclear: more than risk takers value high achievers, or more than personnel officers value risk takers?]
YES	Most personnel officers value high achievers **more than they value risk takers.**
YES	Most personnel officers value high achievers **more than risk takers do.**
NO	Achievers value success **as much,** if not more than, a high salary. [Comparisons using *as . . . as* require the second *as*.]
YES	Achievers value success **as much as,** if not more than, a high salary.

15e.3 Proofreading for inadvertently omitted little words

Little words—ARTICLES, PRONOUNS, CONJUNCTIONS, and PREPOSITIONS—needed to make sentences complete may drop out when a writer is rushing or is distracted. If you tend to omit such words, proofread your work an extra time exclusively to search for missing words.

NO	On May 2, 1808, citizens Madrid rioted against French soldiers and were shot.
YES	On May 2, 1808, citizens **of** Madrid rioted against French soldiers and were shot.
NO	The Spanish painter Francisco Goya recorded both the riot the execution in a pair of pictures painted 1814.
YES	The Spanish painter Francisco Goya recorded both the riot **and** the execution in a pair of pictures painted **in** 1814.

EXERCISE 15-8

Consulting section 15e, revise this paragraph to create correct elliptical constructions, to complete comparisons, and to insert any missing words.

(1) A giant tsunami is as destructive and even larger than a tidal wave. (2) The word *tsunami* is Japanese for "harbor wave," for this kind wave appears suddenly in harbor or bay. (3) It begins with rapid shift in ocean floor caused by an undersea earthquake or volcano. (4) The wave this produces in the open sea is less than three feet high, but it can grow to a height of a hundred feet as it rushes and strikes against the shore. (5) For this reason, tsunamis are much more dangerous to seaside towns than ships on the open sea. (6) In 1960, a huge tsunami that struck coasts of Chile, Hawaii, and Japan killed total of 590 people.

Focus on Revising

Revising Your Writing

If you tend to write sentences that send unclear messages, review your writing closely, looking for errors. Using this chapter as a resource, revise your writing to eliminate unnecessary shifts (15a), misplaced modifiers (15b), dangling modifiers (15c), mixed sentences (15d), and incomplete sentences (15e).

Case Studies: Revising to Correct Sentences That Send Unclear Messages

In these case studies, you can observe a student writer revising. Then, you have the chance to revise other student writing on your own.

Observation

A student wrote the following draft for a course called Freshman Composition. The assignment was to compose a narrative of a personal experience with which other students in the class might sympathize. This narrative explains the experience clearly, uses specific examples well to illustrate the story, and draws on the writer's voice effectively. The draft's effectiveness is diminished, however, by the presence of sentences that send unclear messages due to unnecessary shifts, misplaced modifiers, dangling modifiers, mixed sentences, and incomplete sentences.

Read through the draft. The unclear messages are highlighted and explained. Before you look at the student's revision, revise the material yourself. Then, compare your revision with the student's.

dangling modifier: 15c

Moving to a different part of the United States was one of the most difficult experiences of my life. Looking forward to my senior year in high school, my father's company informed him that he had been transferred to Colorado Springs, and would we be ready to move in a month? I liked Boston much better than my father, so I was less than thrilled about having to leave. But after days of arguing and talking to my parents, I knew that the decision was final.

shift from direct to indirect discourse: 15a.4

ambiguous comparison: 15e.2

incorrect elliptical construction: 15e.1

→

FOCUS ON REVISING FOCUS ON REVISING FOCUS ON REVISING FOCUS ON REVISING FOCUS ON REVISING

PARTICIPATION ESSAY

Coverage

Most job hunters *enter business* [15e.3, missing word] world through a door labeled "Job Interviews." *Regardless of training and experience*, [15c, dangling modifier] the interview is the occasion when an employer gets an impression of the candidate. What can a person do so that *you* [15a.1, shift in person] perform successfully at what is likely to be a fifteen-minute interview?

By understanding the objectives of the interview will help an applicant prepare [15d.1, mixed construction]. *An applicant who knows the company's needs is better equipped* [15e.2, incomplete comparison]. Most businesses with a position to fill interview with three basic questions in mind: Is this applicant qualified to do the job? Will this applicant perform if hired? Will *you* [15a.1, shift in person] fit into the work environment?

A job applicant can use a well-prepared résumé to present information about experience and training. At the interview, *applicants* [15a.1, shift in number] should be prepared to talk about courses taken, jobs held, and capabilities demonstrated. *Probing for specific details* [15c, dangling

unnecessary shift in person and number: 15a.1

mixed construction: 15d.1

misplaced modifier: 15b

omitted word: 15e.3

misplaced modifier; awkward placement: 15b.2

omitted word: 15e.3

unnecessary shift in tense: 15a.3

dangling modifier: 15c

misplaced modifier; ambiguous placement: 15b.1

misplaced modifier; ambiguous placement: 15b.1

When our family arrived in Colorado Springs, I was depressed. Our house was comfortable, about twice the size of our Boston apartment, but you had the feeling that it was in the middle of nowhere. Living on the outskirts of the city, I couldn't go anywhere without car. In Boston, all I have to do is hop on the "T" to go anywhere in the city.

Also, by discovering that the expressions for some everyday things were different than in Boston was the place that I wanted to be. When I asked for a "submarine," a thick sandwich on a long roll, the convenience store clerk said she didn't have kits for making model ships with a confused look. When buying something in Colorado, salespeople offered me what they called a "sack" instead of a bag. As far as I knew, *sack* means that the quarterback has been tackled in football game.

Slowly, however, I began to realize that in Colorado even there are movies, fast-food restaurants, and shopping malls. Mostly, the people made the big difference for me. It didn't happily take long for me to get to know some students in my high school and to, much to my surprise, find that most were eager to make me feel at home. By now, I can't imagine a better place to live than Colorado Springs.

Here is how the student revised the draft to correct the errors. In a few places, the student could correct the errors in more than one way. Your revision, therefore, might not be exactly like this one, but it should deal with each error highlighted on the draft.

Moving to a different part of the United States was one of the most difficult experiences of my life. At the time that I was looking forward to my senior year in high school, my father's company informed him that he had been transferred to Colorado Springs, and we would need to be ready to move in a month. I liked Boston much better than my father did, so I was less than thrilled about having to leave. But after days of arguing with and talking to my parents, I knew that the decision was final.

When our family arrived in Colorado Springs, I was depressed. Our house was comfortable, about twice the size of our Boston apartment, but I had the feeling that it was in the middle of nowhere. Living on the outskirts of the city, I couldn't go anywhere without a car. In Boston, all I had to do was hop on the "T" to go anywhere in the city.

Also, when I discovered that the expressions for some everyday things were different, Boston was the place that I wanted to be. When I asked for a "submarine," a thick sandwich on a long roll, the convenience store clerk looked confused and said she didn't have kits for making model ships. When I would buy something in Colorado, salespeople offered me a "sack" instead of a bag. As far as I knew, *sack* means that the quarterback has been tackled in a football game.

Slowly, however, I began to realize that even in Colorado there are movies, fast-food restaurants, and shopping malls. Mostly, the people made the big difference for me. Happily, it didn't take long for me to get to know some students in my high school and to find, much to my surprise, that most were eager to make me feel at home. Now, I can't imagine a better place to live than Colorado Springs.

Participation

A student working in the college peer-counseling program for job hunters wrote the draft that begins below and continues on page 308 for an article in the campus newspaper. This material shows a very good awareness of audience, and it contains well-organized and useful information. The draft's effectiveness is diminished, however, by the presence of sentences that send unclear messages because of unnecessary shifts, misplaced modifiers, dangling modifiers, mixed sentences, and incomplete sentences.

Read through the draft. Then, revise it to eliminate the errors. Also, make any additional revisions that you think would improve the content, organization, and style of the material.

```
Most job hunters enter business world through a door labeled
"Job Interviews." Regardless of training and experience, the
interview is the occasion when an employer gets an impression of the
candidate. What can a person do so that you perform successfully at
what is likely to be a fifteen-minute interview?
```

Participation Essay (continued)

modifier], the applicant's abilities will be judged by the employer. *Job applicants should be aware that personal questions about marital status or plans to have children are illegal; however, such matters might be raised by some interviewers anyway* [15a.2, shift from passive to active voice]. *By preparing an answer like "Those areas of my life are personal" or "I make it a rule never to let my personal life interfere with business" will help an applicant's confidence* [15d.1, mixed construction].

A major concern of an interviewer is focused on whether the applicant would fit into the company [15d.2, faulty construction]. An applicant who plays *merely* [15b.1, ambiguous placement of modifier] a role to impress an interviewer is making a mistake, particularly if *you* [15a.1, shift in person used in rest of essay] are offered a job that *you* [15a.1, shift in person used in rest of essay] are not suited for. *Present a natural image. Use the interview to find out how the company's work environment will fit your* [15a.1, shift in person used in rest of essay] *personal style* [15a.3, shift in mood, with two imperative sentences].

Answer to Participation Essay

This version is revised to eliminate errors that cause sentences to send unclear messages. Because options are available for handling corrections, answers will vary somewhat. Also, answers will vary if students have revised for content, organization, or style.

Most job hunters enter the business world through a door labeled "Job Interviews." Regardless of training and experience, the job candidate makes an impression on an employer during an interview. What can a person do so as to perform successfully at what is likely to be a fifteen-minute interview?

Understanding the objectives of the interview will help an applicant prepare. An applicant who knows the company's needs is better equipped than someone who does not have such information. Most

Answer to Participation Essay (continued)

businesses with a position to fill interview with three basic questions in mind: Is this applicant qualified to do the job? Will this applicant perform if hired? Will this applicant fit into the work environment?

A job applicant can use a well-prepared résumé to present information about experience and training. At the interview, an applicant should be prepared to talk about courses taken, jobs held, and capabilities demonstrated. Probing for specific details, the employer will judge the applicant's abilities. Job applicants should be aware that personal questions about marital status or plans to have children are illegal; however, some interviewers might raise such matters anyway. Preparing an answer like "Those areas of my life are personal" or "I make it a rule never to let my personal life interfere with business" will help an applicant's confidence.

A major concern of an interviewer is whether the applicant would fit into the company. An applicant who merely plays a role to impress an interviewer is making a mistake, particularly if the person is offered a job that he or she is not suited for. A wise job candidate presents a natural image and finds out whether the company's work environment fits his or her personal style.

By understanding the objectives of the interview will help an applicant prepare. An applicant who knows the company's needs is better equipped. Most businesses with a position to fill interview with three basic questions in mind: Is this applicant qualified to do the job? Will this applicant perform if hired? Will you fit into the work environment?

A job applicant can use a well-prepared résumé to present information about experience and training. At the interview, applicants should be prepared to talk about courses taken, jobs held, and capabilities demonstrated. Probing for specific details, the applicant's abilities will be judged by the employer. Job applicants should be aware that personal questions about marital status or plans to have children are illegal; however, such matters might be raised by some interviewers anyway. By preparing an answer like "Those areas of my life are personal" or "I make it a rule never to let my personal life interfere with business" will help an applicant's confidence.

A major concern of an interviewer is focused on whether the applicant would fit into the company. An applicant who plays merely a role to impress an interviewer is making a mistake, particularly if you are offered a job that you are not suited for. Present a natural image. Use the interview to find out how well the company's work environment will fit your personal style.

PART THREE

WRITING EFFECTIVELY

Writing effectively means that you advance beyond correctness to create writing characterized by style and grace. Part Three shows you how various techniques of writing style and the impact of word choice can enhance the delivery of your message. As you use Chapters 16 through 22, remember that good writers work to combine form and content to create memorable prose.

16
CONCISENESS

Conciseness describes writing that is direct and to the point. Wordy writing is not concise. Wordiness irritates readers, who must clear away excess words before sentences can deliver their messages. Concise writing is achieved by eliminating wordy sentence structures (see 16a), dropping unneeded words (see 16b), and omitting redundancies (see 16c).

16a Eliminating wordy sentence structures

Wordy sentence structures make writing seem abstract and dull. Whenever possible, revise to achieve conciseness.

16a.1 Revising unnecessary expletive constructions

An **expletive construction** consists of *there* or *it* and a form of the VERB* *be* (*is, was, were*) placed before the SUBJECT in a sentence. In some contexts, an expletive construction can create anticipation and provide emphasis, but expletive constructions are often merely wordy. Removing the expletive and revising slightly eliminates wordiness.

NO **It was** on Friday that we missed class.
YES On Friday, we missed class.
YES We missed class on Friday.

NO **There was** a new teacher waiting for us.
YES A new teacher was waiting for us.

ESL NOTES: (1) The *it* in an expletive construction is not a pronoun referring to a specific antecedent. It is an "empty" word that fills the subject position in a sentence but does not function as the actual subject. The actual subject appears after the expletive construction: *It was the **teacher** who answered the question.* [A more concise version is *The*

---

*You can find the definition of a word printed in small capital letters (such as VERB) in the Terms Glossary toward the back of this handbook.

teacher answered the question.] (2) The *there* in an expletive construction does not designate a place. *There* + a form of *be* indicates only that something exists. Expletive constructions with *there* shift the sequence of the subject and verb in a sentence so that the actual subject appears after the expletive construction: ***There** are many **teachers** who can answer the question.* [A more concise version is *Many **teachers** can answer the question.*] ✦

16a.2 Revising unnecessary passive constructions

In the **active voice,** the subject of a sentence does the action named by the verb.

ACTIVE **Professor Higgins teaches** public speaking. [*Professor Higgins* is the subject, and he does the action: He *teaches.*]

In the **passive voice,** the subject of a sentence *receives* the action named by the verb.

PASSIVE **Public speaking is taught** by Professor Higgins. [*Public speaking* is the subject, which receives the action *taught.*]

The active voice adds liveliness and is more concise than the passive voice. The simplest way to revise from passive to active is to make the doer of the action the subject of the sentence. (In the passive, the doer of an action is usually identified in a PHRASE starting with *by*.)

NO Volunteer work **was done by the students** for extra credit in sociology. [The students are doers of the action, but they are not the subject of the sentence.]

YES **The students did** volunteer work for extra credit in sociology.

NO The new spending bill **was vetoed by the governor.** [The governor is the doer of the action, but the governor is not the subject of the sentence.]

YES **The governor vetoed** the new spending bill.

Sometimes, you can revise a sentence from passive to active by finding a new verb. This method works especially well when you want to keep the same subject.

PASSIVE **Britain was defeated** by the United States in the War of 1812.

ACTIVE **Britain lost** the War of 1812 to the United States.

PASSIVE Many **soldiers were stricken** with yellow fever.

ACTIVE Many **soldiers caught** yellow fever.

Writers sometimes, however, deliberately use the passive voice in sentence after sentence in the mistaken belief that it sounds "mature" or "academic."

TEACHING TIP

A computer style-checker can be a great help to writers revising their sentences, but writers cannot expect the computer program to edit their papers for them. Most style-checkers flag phrases, verbs, and nominalizations often associated with wordiness, imprecision, and other problems, but the writer must decide whether to revise a flagged sentence and how to revise it. Many programs are easy to customize to deal with the writer's habitual problems.

STATEWIDE TESTING

If you teach in a state that requires students to pass basic competency tests in English, see the free publications coordinated with this handbook: One is for the CLAST (Florida), and another is for the TASP Exam (Texas).

TEACHING TIP

In *Style: Ten Lessons in Clarity and Grace*, 4th ed. (New York: HarperCollins, 1994), Joseph M. Williams writes that "the first principle of clear writing" can be stated in two parts:

1. In the subjects of your sentences, name your cast of characters.

2. In the verbs of your sentences, name the crucial actions in which you involve those characters (9).

EXTRA EXERCISE

Rewrite each of the following groups of sentences as a single statement by reducing the information in one of them to a group of words that you can include in the other.

1. William Shakespeare had seven brothers and sisters. He was the third child.

2. He attended Stratford's free grammar school until he was about thirteen. Later, he apprenticed to a local tradesperson.

3. Anne Hathaway was eight years older than Shakespeare. He married her in 1582.

4. Their first child was born the next year. They named her Susanna.

5. In 1585, Anne bore twins. They were named Hamnet and Judith.

6. In 1597, Shakespeare moved from London back to Stratford. He bought a large house called New Place.

Answers to Extra Exercise

Answers will vary, but here are some possibilities.

1. William Shakespeare was the third of eight children.

2. He attended Stratford's free grammar school until he was about thirteen, when he was apprenticed to a local tradesperson.

3. Shakespeare married Anne Hathaway, who was eight years his senior, in 1582.

4. Susanna, their first child, was born the next year.

5. In 1585, Anne bore the twins Hamnet and Judith.

6. In 1597, Shakespeare moved back from London to New Place, a large house in Stratford.

NO One very important quality developed **by an individual** during a first job is self-reliance. This strength **was gained by me** when I **was allowed by my supervisor** to set up and conduct my own survey project.

YES Many individuals develop the very important quality of self-reliance during their first job. I gained this strength when my supervisor allowed me to set up and conduct my own survey project.

YES During a first job, many people develop self-reliance, as I did when my supervisor let me set up and conduct my own survey project.

Be particularly alert for passive-voice constructions that mislead readers by hiding information about who acts: *Cracks in the foundation of the structure* **had been found,** *but they* **were not considered** *serious.* Left out of the sentence is important information about who found the cracks and who decided that they were not serious.

Writers may sometimes have no choice but to use the passive voice, as when the doer of an action is unknown or when naming the doer would disrupt the focus of a sentence, as explained in sections 8n and 8o.

16a.3 Combining sentences and shortening clauses and phrases

As you revise, check your writing for wordiness. Often, you can combine sentences and shorten CLAUSES and phrases to be more concise.

Combining sentences

Look carefully at sets of sentences in your writing. You may be able to fit the information contained in one sentence into another sentence.

TWO SENTENCES	The *Titanic* was discovered seventy-three years after being sunk by an iceberg. The wreck was located in the Atlantic by a team of French and American scientists.
COMBINED SENTENCE	Seventy-three years after being sunk by an iceberg, the *Titanic* was located in the Atlantic by a team of French and American scientists.
TWO SENTENCES	The stern of the ship was missing, and external damage to the hull was visible. Otherwise, the *Titanic* seemed to be in excellent condition.
COMBINED SENTENCE	Aside from a missing stern and external damage to its hull, the *Titanic* seemed to be in excellent condition.

For more advice about combining sentences, see Chapter 17.

Shortening clauses

Keep your meaning clear when you reduce clauses. Removing words should never get in the way of clarity.

You can sometimes make an ADJECTIVE CLAUSE shorter by dropping the opening RELATIVE PRONOUN and verb.

The *Titanic*, **which was** a huge ocean liner, sank in 1912.

The *Titanic*, a huge ocean liner, sank in 1912.

Sometimes you can shorten a clause to a single word.

The scientists held a memorial service for the passengers and crew members **who had drowned.**

The scientists held a memorial service for the **drowned** passengers and crew members.

Sometimes you can use ELLIPTICAL CONSTRUCTIONS to shorten clauses. If you do, be careful that any omitted word is clearly implied (see 15e.1).

When they were confronted with disaster, some passengers behaved heroically, **while others behaved selfishly.**

Confronted with disaster, some passengers behaved heroically, **others selfishly.**

Shortening phrases

Sometimes you can reduce phrases to shorter phrases or to single words.

More than fifteen hundred **travelers on that voyage** died in the shipwreck.

More than fifteen hundred **passengers** died in the shipwreck.

Objects found inside the ship included **unbroken** bottles of wine and expensive **undamaged** china.

Found **undamaged** inside the ship were bottles of wine and expensive china.

16a.4 Using strong verbs and avoiding nouns formed from verbs

Strong verbs convey action directly. *Be* and *have* are not strong verbs because they do not convey much action; they also tend to create wordiness. When you revise weak verbs to strong ones, you can both increase the impact of your writing and reduce the number of words in your sentences.

TEACHING TIP

One way to demonstrate how conciseness is achieved is to show students how you as a writer work toward it in your own work. Telling a student "I always revise to eliminate wordiness" rarely works. Instead, you might try one of these two approaches:

1. Distribute copies of a first, messy draft and a final version of one of your current projects. Invite students to trace the changes you made as you took out unnecessary words and passages, wavered between synonyms, adjusted verb tenses, and so forth. If you are using an anthology of essays that includes facsimile pages from writers' early drafts, students can also look for changes there. Students are likely to take the process more seriously, however, if they see your work. A page from Keats or Faulkner is not as immediate as one from their own teacher's current project.

2. You might distribute three or four versions of a piece (each successively more concise) without noting their order of composition. Ask the students to guess which came earlier or later and explain how they know. This activity helps prove that revising for conciseness produces noticeable results.

WEAK VERB	The proposal before the city council **has to do with** locating the sewage treatment plant outside city limits.
STRONGER VERB	The proposal before the city council **suggests** locating the sewage treatment plant outside city limits.
STRONGER VERB	The proposal before the city council **argues against** locating the sewage treatment plant outside city limits.
WEAK VERBS	The board members **were of the opinion** that the revisions in the code **were not changes they could accept.**
STRONGER VERBS	The board members **said** that **they could not accept** the revisions in the code.

🛑 **ALERT:** When you revise, look carefully at verbs with the pattern *be* + ADJECTIVE + *of* (*be aware of, be capable of, be fearful of*). Many of these phrases can be replaced with one-word verbs: *I **envy*** [not *am envious of*] *the council president's ability to speak in public.* Always avoid certain of these phrases; for example, always use *appreciate* (not *be appreciative of*), *illustrate* (not *be illustrative of*), and *support* (not *be supportive of*).

NO	The council president **was supportive of** the council's attempts to lower property taxes.
YES	The council president **supported** the council's attempts to lower property taxes. ❗

When you look for weak verbs to revise, also look for **nominals** (nouns derived from verbs, usually by added suffixes such as *-ance*, *-ment*, or *-tion*). Turning a nominal back into a verb reduces words and increases impact.

NO	We **arranged for the establishment of** a student advisory committee.
YES	We **established** a student advisory committee.
NO	The building **had the appearance of** having been renovated.
YES	The building **appeared** to have been renovated.

16a.5 Using pronouns for conciseness

Replacing nouns with pronouns can reduce wordiness. When changing nouns to pronouns, be sure that each pronoun's ANTECEDENT is unambiguous (see 10a–10c) and that each pronoun agrees with its antecedents (see 11m–11p).

NO	Queen Elizabeth II served as a driver and mechanic in World War II. **Elizabeth** joined the Auxiliary Territorial Service in 1944, while **the future queen** was still a princess. Although **Princess Elizabeth** did not know how to drive, she quickly learned how to strip and repair many kinds of engines.

TEACHING TIP

In class, you might ask the students to exchange papers and look for unnecessary words. As a courtesy, you should notify students ahead of time that their classmates are going to read their work. You can structure this lesson in several ways:

1. Have pairs of students write directly on one another's papers. You can then collect the paragraphs, add your own comments, and return the material at the next class.

2. Have pairs or trios of students confer on papers one at a time and arrive at a consensus. You can circulate around the room, answering questions, and give credit for each paragraph completed.

3. Have authors number their lines in the margin. Ask students to pass their assignments to the left. The students write comments on a separate sheet of paper, keying each comment to line number. After five minutes, students sign their comments and pass the paragraphs and comment sheets to the left again. Repeat as time and class interest allow. At the end of the class, give the comment sheets to the authors. For homework, students can review the responses to their work and incorporate whichever comments they feel are valid. At the next class, you can collect the revised paragraphs and comment sheets.

YES Queen Elizabeth II served as a driver and mechanic in World War II. **She** joined the Auxiliary Territorial Service in 1944, while **she** was still a princess. Although **she** did not know how to drive, she quickly learned how to strip and repair many kinds of engines.

EXERCISE 16-1

Consulting section 16a, combine each set of sentences to eliminate wordy constructions.

EXAMPLE A creative idea, says psychologist Robert Epstein, can be like a rabbit. The rabbit runs by fast. We glimpse only the rabbit's ears or tail.

A creative idea, says psychologist Robert Epstein, can be like a rabbit that runs by so fast that we glimpse only its ears or tail.

1. There is evidence that suggests that there is only one difference between creative people and the rest of us. It is creative people who are always poised to capture the new ideas we might not catch right away.

2. Creative thinking has to do with seizing opportunities. Creative thinking has to do with staying alert. Creative thinking has to do with seeking challenges and pushing boundaries.

3. The goal is that the idea be caught first and that the idea be evaluated later. A fleeting thought is captured by the alert person by writing it down at once. The goal is not to worry whether the thought will have eventual value.

4. There is an important part of creativity, and that is daydreaming, which is an activity allowing thoughts to bubble up spontaneously. These creative thoughts surprise us with their freshness.

5. Creativity can be unlocked in us by our trying something different. It is possible to turn pictures sideways or upside down to see them in new ways. We can mold clay while we think about a writing problem that is difficult.

6. It is stressed by the psychologist Robert Epstein that there are many exciting advances in everything. The advances are in fields from astrophysics to car design to dance. The advances creatively combine ideas that are from widely different sources.

7. Epstein gave his students the assignment of a problem. The problem called for the retrieval of a Ping-Pong ball. It was located at the bottom of a vertical drainpipe that was sealed at the bottom.

8. Some of the tools that the students had been given by Epstein were too short to reach the ball. Other tools that the students had been given were too wide to fit into the pipe.

ANSWERS AND COVERAGE: EXERCISE 16-1

Answers will vary. Here is one set of possibilities.

1. Evidence suggests that the only difference between creative people and the rest of us is that they are always poised to capture the new ideas we might not catch right away. [16a.1, unnecessary expletives; 16a.5, using pronouns]

2. Creative thinking involves seizing opportunities, staying alert, seeking challenges, and pushing boundaries. [16a.4, using stronger verbs]

3. Because the goal is to catch the idea first and evaluate it later, the alert person captures a fleeting thought by writing it down at once without worrying about its eventual value. [16a.2, unnecessary passive; 16a.5, using pronouns; 16a.3, reducing phrases]

4. An important part of creativity is daydreaming, which allows thoughts to bubble up spontaneously and surprise us with their freshness. [16a.1, unnecessary expletive; 16a.3, reducing clauses]

5. We can sometimes unlock our creativity by trying something different, such as turning pictures sideways or upside down to see them in new ways or molding clay while thinking about a difficult writing problem. [16a.2, unnecessary passive; 16a.3, reducing clauses to phrases and phrases to words; 16a.1, unnecessary expletive]

6. Psychologist Robert Epstein stresses that many exciting advances in fields from astrophysics to car design to dance combine creative ideas from widely different sources. [16a.2, unnecessary passive; 16a.3, reducing clauses]

7. Epstein assigned his students the problem of retrieving a Ping-Pong ball at the sealed bottom of a vertical drainpipe. [16a.4, using strong verbs and avoiding nouns formed from verbs; 16a.3, reducing phrases to words and clauses to phrases]

8. Epstein gave the students tools that were too short to reach the ball or too wide to fit into the pipe. [16a.3, reducing phrases]

→

Answers and Coverage: Exercise 16-1 (continued)

9. Stumped at first, the students tried unsuccessfully to capture the ball with the tools before stepping back from the immediate situation, seeing the big picture, and thinking creatively. [16a.3, reducing clauses to phrases and reducing phrases to words]

10. The students poured water down the drainpipe, and the ball floated to the top, where they retrieved it. [16a.2, unnecessary passive; 16a.4, strong verbs; 16a.5, using pronouns]

TEACHING TIP

Since empty words and phrases occur with some frequency in documents people receive every day, you might want to ask students to bring a memo from work, an advertising brochure from the mail, or a quotation from a newspaper that demonstrates useless verbal padding. (You may wish to bar documents written by teachers or administrators on campus.) The examples can be used for group discussion and revision and then presented to the class in their original as well as their revised form.

TEACHING TIP

Provide students with wordy phrases that commonly inflate and obscure English prose; then, ask them to find more direct and effective replacements.

at this point in time	now
free up some space	make room
in the event that	if
my personal physician	my doctor
thunderstorm activity	thunderstorm
it is believed by many	many believe
head up a committee	head a committee
experience some discomfort	hurt
in order to	to
making an effort to	trying to

9. The students were stumped at first. The students tried unsuccessfully to capture the ball with the tools. Then, the students stepped back from the immediate situation. The students saw the big picture and began thinking creatively.

10. Water was poured down the drainpipe by the students. The ball achieved flotation and rose to the top. The ball was retrieved by the students there.

16b Eliminating unneeded words

For conciseness, eliminate unneeded words that clutter sentences. Also, revise imprecise language. Never let six inexact words take the place of one precise word.

When a writer tries to write very formally or tries to reach an assigned word limit, **padding** usually results. Sentences loaded with **deadwood** contain empty words and phrases that increase the word count but lack meaning. If you find deadwood, clear it away.

PADDED ~~In fact,~~ the television station ~~which is situated in the local area~~ has won ~~a great~~ many awards ~~as a result of its having been involved in the~~ coverage ~~of all kinds of~~ controversial issues.

CONCISE The local television station has won many awards for its coverage of controversial issues.

PADDED The bookstore ~~entered the order~~ for the books ~~that the instructor has said will be utilized in~~ the course ~~sequence.~~

CONCISE The bookstore ordered the books for the course.

Chart 92 lists many of the worst offenders among empty words and suggests revisions for them. Apply the same approach to similar items not listed.

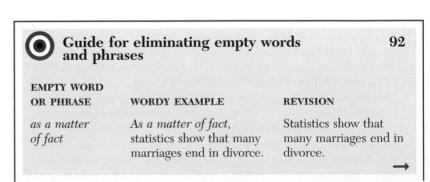

Guide for eliminating empty words and phrases		**92**
EMPTY WORD OR PHRASE	**WORDY EXAMPLE**	**REVISION**
as a matter of fact	*As a matter of fact,* statistics show that many marriages end in divorce.	Statistics show that many marriages end in divorce.

→

Guide for eliminating empty words and phrases *(continued)*   92

EMPTY WORD OR PHRASE	WORDY EXAMPLE	REVISION
due to the fact that	She cannot answer *due to the fact that* she is six days old.	She cannot answer because she is six days old.
in a very real sense	*In a very real sense,* they are heroes.	They are heroes.
factor	The project's final cost was an essential *factor* to consider.	The project's final cost was essential to consider.
in a . . . manner	The child spoke *in a* reluctant *manner.*	The child spoke reluctantly.
of a . . . nature, in nature	His comment was *of an* offensive *nature.* His comment was offensive *in nature.*	His comment was offensive.
type of	Gordon took a relaxing *type of* vacation.	Gordon took a relaxing vacation.
it seems	*It seems* that the union struck over health benefits.	The union struck over health benefits.
tendency	The team had a *tendency* to lose home games.	The team often lost home games.
in the process of	We are *in the process of* reviewing the proposal.	We are reviewing the proposal.
exist	The crime rate that *exists* is unacceptable.	The crime rate is unacceptable.
in light of the fact that	*In light of the fact that* jobs are scarce, I am going back to school.	Because jobs are scarce, I am going back to school.
for the purpose of	Work crews arrived *for the purpose of* fixing the potholes.	Work crews arrived to fix the potholes.

→

QUOTATION: ON WRITING

The language must be careful and must appear effortless. It must not sweat. It must suggest and be provocative at the same time.

—Toni Morrison

TEACHING TIP

Truman Capote, known for a prose style marked by clarity and lucidity, never relented in his efforts to delete everything that marred the lean simplicity of his work. In a book of essays published toward the end of his life, he included a description of an experience he had in a Moscow subway. To Capote's surprise, he recognized a man who had lived in Capote's apartment building in New York ten years earlier. Blind, crippled, and dignified, Mr. Jones never left his apartment but received a steady stream of visitors and telephone calls. Suddenly, he disappeared. Using the following excerpt from Capote's remembrance, you might ask students if they can delete any words, reduce any phrases, or otherwise revise the passage to be more concise.

—Ten years pass.

Now it is a zero-cold December afternoon, and I am in Moscow. I am riding in a subway car. There are only a few other passengers. One of them is a man sitting opposite me, a man wearing boots, a thick long coat and a Russian-style fur cap. He has bright eyes, blue as a peacock's.

After a doubtful instant, I simply stared, for even without the black glasses, there was no mistaking that lean distinctive face, those high cheekbones with the single scarlet star-shaped birthmark.

I was just about to cross the aisle and speak to him when the train pulled into a station, and Mr. Jones, on a pair of fine sturdy legs, stood up and strode out of the car. Swiftly, the train door closed behind him.

—Truman Capote,
Music for Chameleons

QUOTATION: ON WRITING

What is written without effort is in general read without pleasure.

—Samuel Johnson

ANSWERS: EXERCISE 16-2

Answers will vary. Phrases that could be eliminated or shortened are underlined. Check that students have revised words, capitalization, and punctuation appropriately in their sentences.

(1) <u>As a matter of fact,</u> <u>it seems as</u> <u>though</u> a great many folk beliefs that are popular are, <u>in a very real sense,</u> dead wrong. (2) For example, the American Academy of Ophthalmology <u>makes the</u> <u>statement that</u> reading in the dark will not <u>have the effect of</u> ruining a person's eyes. (3) <u>In the case of</u> spicy foods, specialists have proved that foods <u>of this sort</u> are not <u>necessarily</u> bad for the stomach, even for people who have been <u>treated as</u> ulcer patients. (4) What about our mothers' warning <u>that exists</u> about catching colds when we are <u>in the process of</u> becoming chilled? (5) <u>It is certainly quite true that</u> more people <u>have a tendency to</u> get sick in winter than <u>people do</u> in summer. (6) <u>It</u> <u>seems that</u> lower temperatures are not <u>the</u> <u>factor that</u> deserves the blame, however. (7) <u>In view of the fact that</u> cold weather often <u>has a tendency to</u> drive people indoors and <u>to</u> bring people together inside, <u>this factor has the appearance of</u> increasing our odds of infecting one another. (8) Finally, <u>there has been</u> a long-standing tradition <u>that states</u> that the full moon <u>has the effect on people of</u> making them crazy. (9) Investigations <u>that were</u> <u>made</u> by researchers <u>who were</u> tireless and careful <u>came to the ultimate conclusion</u> that <u>there is</u> no such relationship <u>in exis-</u> <u>tence.</u>

Guide for eliminating empty words and phrases (continued) 92

EMPTY WORD OR PHRASE	WORDY EXAMPLE	REVISION
in the case of	*In the case of* taxes, residents are furious.	Residents are furious about taxes.
in the event that	*In the event that* you are late, I will leave.	If you are late, I will leave.
the point I am trying to make	*The point I am trying to make* is that opinion is not fact.	Opinion is not fact.

EXERCISE 16-2

Consulting section 16b, eliminate unnecessary words or phrases.

EXAMPLE   Folk wisdom has a tendency to be untrue.
Folk wisdom is often untrue.

(1) As a matter of fact, it seems as though a great many folk beliefs that are popular are, in a very real sense, dead wrong. (2) For example, the American Academy of Ophthalmology makes the statement that reading in the dark will not have the effect of ruining a person's eyes. (3) In the case of spicy foods, specialists have proved that foods of this sort are not necessarily bad for the stomach, even for people who have been treated as ulcer patients. (4) What about our mothers' warning that exists about catching colds when we are in the process of becoming chilled? (5) It is certainly quite true that more people have a tendency to get sick in winter than people do in summer. (6) It seems that lower temperatures are not the factor that deserves the blame, however. (7) In view of the fact that cold weather often has a tendency to drive people indoors and to bring people together inside, this factor has the appearance of increasing our odds of infecting one another. (8) Finally, there has been a long-standing tradition that states that the full moon has the effect on people of making them crazy. (9) Investigations that were made by researchers who were tireless and careful came to the ultimate conclusion that there is no such relationship in existence.

16c Revising redundancies

Planned repetition can create a powerful rhythmic effect (see 19g). The dull drone of unplanned repetition, however, can bore a reader and prevent the delivery of your message. Unplanned repetition, called **redundancy,** says the same thing more than once.

Avoid redundant word pairs such as *each and every, one and only, forever and ever,* and *final and conclusive.* Other common redundancies are *perfectly clear, few* (or *many*) *in number, consensus of opinion,* and *reason . . . is because.*

NO Bringing the project to **final completion** three weeks early, the new manager earned our **respectful regard when the project was completed.**

YES **Completing the project** three weeks early, the new manager earned our **respect.**

YES The new manager earned our **respect** for **completing** the project three weeks early.

NO **Astonished,** the architect **circled around** the building **in amazement.**

YES **Astonished,** the architect **circled** the building.

YES The architect **circled** the building **in amazement.**

Notice how redundancies deaden a sentence's impact.

NO The council members **proposed a discussion** of the amendment, but **that proposal** was voted down **after they had discussed it for a while.**

YES The council members' **proposal to discuss** the amendment was **eventually** voted down.

NO The **consensus of opinion** among those of us who saw it **is that** the carton was **huge in size.**

YES Most of us who saw the carton **agree that** it was **huge.**

⊕ **ESL NOTE:** In all languages, words often carry an unspoken message—an *implied meaning*—that is assumed by native speakers of the language. Implied meaning can cause redundancy in writing. For example, *I sent an e-mail **by computer*** is redundant; in American English, to send an e-mail implies *by computer.* A good dictionary gives information about implied meaning of words (see the list of dictionaries in section 20a). *The American Heritage Dictionary,* Third Edition, for example, defines the verb *send* this way: "to dispatch, as by a communications medium: send a message by radio." ⊕

TEACHING TIP

In *Style: Ten Lessons in Clarity and Grace,* 4th ed. (New York: HarperCollins, 1994), Joseph M. Williams describes several sources of wordiness that students can look for in their writing. These sources include redundant pairs ("each and every," "hopes and desires"), redundant modifiers ("completely finish," "terrible tragedy"), belaboring the obvious, irrelevant detail, and unnecessary negatives ("not many" instead of "few," "did not remember" instead of "forgot").

ANSWERS: EXERCISE 16-3

Answers will vary. Here is one possibility.

(1) One such firm is the Campbell Soup Company, whose goal is to expand from a U.S. soup company into a global food force. (2) By the year 2000, Campbell hopes to receive half its revenues from foreign consumers. (3) The primary strategy for this change is expansion, and Campbell products are now being shipped from the United States to Asia, where the people consume large quantities of soup. (4) Campbell is also reworking its recipes, such as the recipes for its *flaki* soup that it ships to Poland and for its watercress and duck-gizzard soup that it ships to China, to appeal to certain ethnic groups. (5) The second strategy is acquisition, which has led Campbell to buy the majority of shares of an Australian company. (6) However, even with such strategies, food companies find that their products are among the most difficult to market worldwide because tastes depend on cultural preferences. (7) Also, global expansion leads to an increasing number of competitors. (8) However, since Campbell has reached a ceiling, it has no choice but to expand into a global market.

EXERCISE 16-3

Consulting section 16c, eliminate redundant words and phrases. Then, revise the paragraph so that it is concise.

EXAMPLE More North American companies that are based in the United States are attempting to enter global markets around the world.

More U.S.-based companies are attempting to enter global markets.

(1) One such firm is the Campbell Soup Company, whose goal is to expand from a U.S. soup company into a global food force extending beyond the fifty states. (2) By the year 2000, Campbell hopes to receive half its revenues from foreign consumers in other countries. (3) The primary and most important strategy for this change from the existing position is expansion, and Campbell products are now being shipped from the United States to Asia, where the people consume large quantities of soup. (4) Campbell is also reworking its recipes, such as the recipes for its *flaki* soup that it ships to Poland and for its watercress and duck-gizzard soup that it ships to China, in order to make soups different from the original recipe to appeal to certain ethnic groups. (5) Next, the second strategy is acquisition, which has led Campbell to buy the majority of shares of an Australian company. (6) However, even with such strategies, food companies find that their products are among the most difficult to market worldwide because tastes depend on worldwide cultural and ethnic preferences. (7) Also, global expansion leads to an increasing number of competitors, of which there are more and more each year. (8) However, since Campbell has reached an all-time high ceiling, it has no other choice but to expand and grow into a global market.

17

COORDINATION
AND SUBORDINATION

When you use the techniques of **coordination** and **subordination**, your writing communicates relationships between ideas gracefully. While you are DRAFTING, concentrate on getting your ideas onto paper. You can explore the full potential of coordination and subordination for enriching your writing style after you have your drafted ideas on paper and are ready to revise.

TWO IDEAS	The sky turned dark gray. The wind died suddenly.
COORDINATED VERSION	The sky turned dark gray, and the wind died suddenly.
SUBORDINATED VERSION	As the sky turned dark gray, the wind died suddenly. [The *wind* is the focus.]
SUBORDINATED VERSION	As the wind died suddenly, the sky turned dark gray. [The *sky* is the focus.]

COORDINATION

17a Understanding coordination

Coordination can produce harmony by bringing related elements together. Sections 17a through 17d explain coordination of INDEPENDENT CLAUSES. Coordinate sentences communicate balance in or sequence of ideas. You can apply the principles of coordinate sentences to the coordination of words and word groups within sentences. (See also the explanation of PARALLELISM in Chapter 18).

Patterns for **coordinate sentences,** also known as **compound sentences,** are shown in Chart 93. When you choose to coordinate sentences in your writing, keep the principles on page 322 in mind.

TEACHING TIP

Here is an alternate example and a discussion of how it illustrates the contrast between coordination and subordination.

> When we toss a handful of good-luck rice at newlyweds, we're gracing them with one of the world's most important and versatile foods.
>
> —Jack Denton Scott,
> "Rice: A Food for All Reasons"

This sentence mentions (1) the idea of tossing rice at a wedding and (2) the fact that rice is an essential grain with many uses. Scott wants to stress the importance of rice as food because he puts that information in the independent clause. Rice as a ceremonial custom gives an ironic context to the main idea, but according to the way the sentence is written, it is a less important idea.

If Scott had been writing on marriage customs, he could have used subordination to provide a different emphasis:

> Although rice is one of the world's most important and versatile foods, many Americans value it most as a good-luck symbol for newlyweds.

Here, the independent clause stresses the connection of rice with weddings, and the food value of rice is mentioned as a less central point.

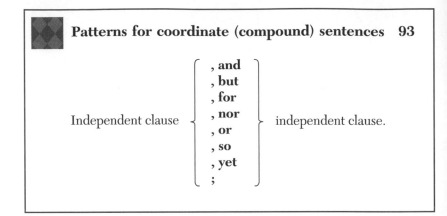

Patterns for coordinate (compound) sentences   93

Independent clause
- , and
- , but
- , for
- , nor
- , or
- , so
- , yet
- ;

independent clause.

- ■ A coordinate sentence consists of two grammatically equivalent independent clauses.
- ■ Coordinating independent clauses must be justified by the meaning that you want your sentence to communicate.
- ■ The independent clauses must be joined either by a **coordinating conjunction** (see Charts 93 and 94) or by a **semicolon** (see sections 25a and 25b).
- ■ The coordinating conjunction must accurately express the relationship between the ideas in the independent clauses (see Chart 94).
- ■ Coordinating more than two independent clauses calls for much care (see 17d.2 and 19b.2).

Coordinating conjunctions and the relationships they express   94

Relationship	Words
ADDITION	*and*
CONTRAST	*but, yet*
RESULT OR EFFECT	*so*
REASON OR CHOICE	*for*
CHOICE	*or*
NEGATIVE CHOICE	*nor*

❶ CONJUNCTION ALERT: Do not confuse coordinating conjunctions with CONJUNCTIVE ADVERBS such as *also, however,* and *therefore* (for a complete list, see Chart 51 in section 7f). When conjunctive adverbs connect independent clauses, they function as explained in 7f and 14e. **!**

❶ PUNCTUATION ALERT: You will never be wrong if you use a comma before a coordinating conjunction that joins two independent clauses (see 24a).

The sky turned dark gray**, and** the wind died suddenly.

The November morning had just begun**, but** it looked like dusk. **!**

17b Using coordinate sentences to show relationships

Deliberately writing a string of short sentences can create impact. In most cases, however, a series of short sentences fails to communicate relationships among ideas. Coordination can help you avoid writing a series of short sentences that have unclear relationships.

> **UNCLEAR**   We decided not to go to class. We planned to get the notes. Everyone else had the same plan. Most of us ended up failing the quiz.
>
> **CLEAR**   We decided not to go to class, **but** we planned to get the notes. Everyone else had the same plan, **so** most of us ended up failing the quiz.

Overuse of coordination, however, can bore readers with its unbroken rhythm (see 17d.2). For another technique to help you avoid an unwanted series of short sentences, see the discussion of subordination in sections 17e through 17i.

17c Using coordinate sentences for effect

Coordinate sentences can help you effectively communicate an unfolding of events.

> The first semester of my junior year at Princeton University is a disaster, **and** my grades show it. D's and F's predominate, **and** a note from the dean puts me on academic probation. Flunk one more course, **and** I'm out.
>
> —John A. Phillips and David Michaels, "Mushroom: The Story of an A-Bomb Kid"

F. Scott Fitzgerald, a U.S. writer of fiction and screenplays, often used coordination to achieve dramatic effect. In the following passage, coordination underlines the contrasts that Fitzgerald draws:

TEACHING TIP

You might want to ask your students to consider these two versions of the same passage from the opening of the twenty-second chapter of Genesis, marking the instances of coordination and subordination, then considering the differences in style and meaning that result. The first, from the King James translation of 1611, uses coordination heavily; the second, from the Revised Standard Version of 1971, uses much less.

King James Version

And it came to pass after these things, that God did tempt Abraham, and said unto him, Abraham: and he said, Behold, here I am. And he said, Take now thy son, thine only son Isaac, whom thou lovest, and get thee into the land of Moriah; and offer him there for a burnt offering upon one of the mountains which I will tell thee of. And Abraham rose up early in the morning, and saddled his ass, and took two of his young men with him, and Isaac his son, and clave the wood for the burnt offering, and rose up, and went unto the place of which God had told him. Then on the third day Abraham lifted up his eyes, and saw the place afar off. And Abraham said unto his young men, Abide ye here with the ass; and I and the lad will go yonder and worship, and come again to you. And Abraham took the wood for the burnt offering, and laid it upon Isaac his son; and he took the fire in his hand, and a knife; and they went both of them together.

→

Teaching Tip (continued)
Revised Standard Version

After these things God tested Abraham, and said to him, "Abraham!" And he said, "Here am I." He said, "Take your son, your only son Isaac, whom you love, and go to the land of Moriah, and offer him there as a burnt offering upon one of the mountains of which I shall tell you." So Abraham rose early in the morning, saddled his ass, and took two of his young men with him, and his son Isaac; and he cut the wood for the burnt offering, and arose and went to the place of which God had told him. On the third day Abraham lifted up his eyes, and saw the place afar off. Then Abraham said to his young men, "Stay here with the ass; I and the lad will go yonder and worship, and come again to you." And Abraham took the wood of the burnt offering, and laid it on Isaac his son; and he took in his hand the fire and the knife. So they went both of them together.

ADDITIONAL EXAMPLE:
EXCESSIVE COORDINATION

Soap operas have earned a bad name, and they don't always deserve it. Some people may watch too many programs, or some people may take the plots too seriously, but that does not make the programs themselves unworthy. Years ago the soap opera viewer was regarded as unintelligent, but today studies show that many professionals take time each day to relax with their favorite continuing story. Some hospitals tell patients to watch soap operas to pass the time, or therapists sometimes urge their emotionally disturbed patients to watch certain programs. Later the patients discuss the characters' problems, and therapists encourage the patients to relate those problems to their own, and often the patients are helped by this process.

—Emily Gordon

It was a hidden Broadway restaurant in the dead of night, **and** a brilliant and mysterious group of society people, diplomats, and members of the underworld were there. A few minutes ago the sparkling wine had been flowing, **and** a girl had been dancing gaily upon a table, **but** now the whole crowd were hushed and breathless.

—F. Scott Fitzgerald, "The Freshest Boy"

17d Avoiding the misuse of coordination

17d.1 Avoiding illogical coordination

Illogical coordination puts unrelated ideas together in a sentence. Readers expect one part of a coordinate construction to lead logically to the other.

> **NO** Computers came into common use in the 1970s, and they sometimes made costly errors.

The statement in each independent clause is true, but the ideas are not related closely enough. The date computers became commonly used is unrelated to their making errors. The two ideas should not be coordinated. Here are ideas that do coordinate logically.

> **YES** Computers came into common use in the 1970s, and they are now indispensable for conducting business.
>
> **YES** Modern computer systems are often very complex, and they sometimes make costly errors.

17d.2 Avoiding the overuse of coordination

Overused coordination creates writing that reads as if the writer simply wrote down whatever came into his or her head. Readers become impatient with "babble" and quickly lose interest. Be sure to check that your intended meaning justifies the use of coordination. In the *yes* version that follows, the sentences deliver their meanings clearly.

> **NO** Dinosaurs could have disappeared for many reasons, and one theory holds that the climate suddenly became cold, and another theory suggests that a sudden shower of meteors and asteroids hit the earth, so the impact created a huge dust cloud that caused a false winter. The winter lasted for years, and the dinosaurs died, for most of the vegetation they lived on died out.
>
> **YES** Dinosaurs could have disappeared for many reasons. One theory holds that the climate suddenly became cold, and another suggests that a sudden shower of meteors and asteroids hit the earth. The impact created a huge dust cloud that caused a false winter. The winter lasted for years, killing most of the vegetation that the dinosaurs used for food.

When writers do not feature important ideas more prominently than others, the cause is often the overuse of coordination. Such overuse makes the writing seem to drone on monotonously. In the *yes* version that follows, some ideas are kept separate and some are put into a coordinate sentence. (For another way to revise overused coordination, see the discussion of SUBORDINATION in sections 17e through 17h.)

NO   Laughter seems to help healing, so many doctors are prescribing humor for their patients, and some hospitals are doing the same. Comedians have donated their time to several California hospitals, and the nurses in one large hospital in Texas have been trained to tell each patient a joke a day.

YES   Laughter seems to help healing. Many doctors and hospitals are prescribing humor for their patients. Comedians have donated their time to several California hospitals, and the nurses in one large hospital in Texas have been asked to tell each patient a joke a day.

🌐 **ESL NOTE:** If your instructor tells you that your sentences are too long and complex, practice limiting them. Follow the advice of many ESL teachers: Revise any sentence containing a combination of more than three independent and dependent clauses. ◑

EXERCISE 17-1

Consulting sections 17a through 17d, revise these sentences to eliminate illogical or overused coordination. If you think a sentence needs no revision, circle its number.

EXAMPLE   Fencing, once a form of combat, has become a competitive sport worldwide, and today's fencers disapprove of those who identify fencing with fighting.

Fencing, once a form of combat, has become a competitive sport worldwide, *but* today's fencers disapprove of those who identify fencing with fighting.

1. As depicted in movies, fencing sometimes appears to be reckless swordplay, and fencing requires precision, coordination, and strategy.

2. The first fencing competitions in the fourteenth century were small, and because it was very popular, fencing was one of the few sports included in the first modern Olympic Games in 1896, and fencing has been part of the Olympics ever since then.

3. Fencing equipment includes a mask, a padded jacket, a glove, and one of three weapons—foil, epee, or saber—and a fencer's technique and targets differ depending on the weapon used and the fencer's experience.

ANSWERS AND COVERAGE: EXERCISE 17-1

Answers will vary somewhat. Here is one set of possibilities.

1. As depicted in movies, fencing sometimes appears to be reckless swordplay, but fencing requires precision, coordination, and strategy. [17d.1, illogical]

2. The first fencing competitions in the fourteenth century were small, and because it was very popular, fencing was one of the few sports included in the first modern Olympic Games in 1896. Fencing has been part of the Olympics ever since then. [17d.2, overused]

3. Fencing equipment includes a mask, a padded jacket, a glove, and one of three weapons—foil, epee, or saber. A fencer's technique and targets differ depending on the weapon used and the fencer's experience. [17d.2, overused]

➡

4. Correct

5. The object of fencing is to be the first to touch the opponent five times. A "president," who is sometimes assisted by a number of judges, officiates at competitions. [17d.1, illogical]

ANSWERS: EXERCISE 17-2

Answers will vary somewhat. Students have to choose ideas best given to effective compounding. They are to choose which ideas seem to have equal weight and could therefore be contained in compound sentences. Their final version should have no more than two compound sentences—all other sentences should be left as they are.

Searching for a job is a challenging task, <u>but</u> if done correctly, your search can result in a satisfying position that could lead to advancement. Job hunting involves many strategies. They begin with your analysis of career objectives. First, taking an inventory of your personal interests and skills is essential. Many hours of the day are spent at work, <u>so</u> often, jobs do not provide opportunities to explore those interests. Equally important is making an inventory of your strengths and weaknesses. These two inventories will allow you to choose a career path that suits your personality. They help you discover what you need to achieve personal happiness. Arriving for an interview after having completed such a personal analysis puts you one step ahead of the other interviewees, because it demonstrates to potential employers a unique element of motivation.

4. Generally, a fencer specializes in one of the three weapons, but some competitors are equally skilled with all three.
5. The object of fencing is to be the first to touch the opponent five times, and a "president," who is sometimes assisted by a number of judges, officiates at competitions.

EXERCISE 17-2

Consulting sections 17a through 17d, revise this paragraph. Decide which ideas seem to have equal weight and could therefore be contained in compound sentences. Your final version should have no more than two compound sentences—all other sentences should be left as they are.

Searching for a job is a challenging task. If done correctly, your search can result in a satisfying position that could lead to advancement. Job hunting involves many strategies. They begin with your analysis of career objectives. First, taking an inventory of your personal interests and skills is essential. Many hours of the day are spent at work. Often, jobs do not provide opportunities to explore those interests. Equally important is making an inventory of your strengths and weaknesses. These two inventories will allow you to choose a career path that suits your personality. They help you discover what you need to achieve personal happiness. Arriving for an interview after having completed such a personal analysis puts you one step ahead of the other interviewees, because it demonstrates to potential employers a unique element of motivation.

SUBORDINATION

17e Understanding subordination

Subordination expresses the relative importance of ideas in a sentence by making a less important idea grammatically dependent on or secondary to a more important one. Sections 17e through 17h explain subordination: The more important idea appears in the **independent clause**—a group of words that can stand alone as a complete grammatical unit; the subordinated idea appears in the **dependent clause**—a group of words that cannot stand alone as a complete grammatical unit. The information you choose to subordinate depends on the meaning that you want a sentence to deliver.

Major patterns of subordination with dependent clauses are shown in Chart 95. Two types of dependent clauses are *adverb clauses* and *adjective clauses* (see Chart 95). An **adverb clause** is a dependent clause that starts with a **subordinating conjunction.** Each subordinating conjunction has a specific meaning that expresses a relationship between the dependent clause and the independent clause, as shown in Chart 96 on page 328.

An **adjective clause** is a dependent clause that can start with a RELATIVE PRONOUN (*who, which, that*), a RELATIVE ADVERB (such as *where*), or a PREPOSITION before a "relative" word (for example, *to whom, above which*).

 Patterns of subordination with dependent clauses   **95**

Sentences with Adverb Clauses

- **Adverb clause,** independent clause.
  After the sky grew dark, the wind died suddenly.

- Independent clause, **adverb clause.**
  Birds stopped singing, **as they do during an eclipse.**

- Independent clause **adverb clause.**
  The shops closed **before the storm began.**

Sentences with Adjective Clauses

- Independent clause **restrictive (essential)* adjective clause.**
  The weather forecasts warned of a storm **that might bring a thirty-inch snowfall.**

- Independent clause, **nonrestrictive (nonessential)* adjective clause.**
  Spring is the season for tornadoes, **which rapidly whirl their destructive columns of air.**

- Beginning of independent clause **restrictive (essential)* adjective clause** end of independent clause.
  Anyone **who lives through a tornado** recalls the experience.

- Beginning of independent clause, **nonrestrictive (nonessential)* adjective clause,** end of independent clause.
  The sky, **which had been clear,** was turning gray.

*For an explanation of restrictive (essential) and nonrestrictive (nonessential) elements, see section 24e.

Subordinating conjunctions and the relationships they express   96

Relationship	Words
TIME	*after, before, once, since, until, when, whenever, while*
REASON OR CAUSE	*as, because, since*
RESULT OR EFFECT	*in order that, so, so that, that*
CONDITION	*if even, if, provided that, unless*
CONTRAST	*although, even though, though, whereas*
LOCATION	*where, wherever*
CHOICE	*rather than, than, whether*

17f Choosing the subordinate conjunction appropriate to your meaning

Subordinating conjunctions express relationships between major and minor ideas in sentences (see Chart 96). Consider the influence of the subordinating conjunction in each of the following sentences.

After you have handed your report in, you cannot make any changes in it. [time]

Because you have handed your report in, you cannot make any changes in it. [reason]

Unless you have handed your report in, you cannot make any changes in it. [condition]

Although you have handed your report in, you can make changes in it. [contrast]

I want to read your report **so that I can evaluate it.** [purpose]

Since you handed in your report, three more people have handed in theirs. [time]

Since I have seen the report, I can comment on it. [cause]

17g Using subordination to show relationships

Subordination directs your reader's attention to the idea in the INDEPENDENT CLAUSE while using the idea in the DEPENDENT CLAUSE to provide context and support. Consider these examples (dependent clauses are in boldface).

As soon as I saw the elephant, I knew with perfect certainty that I ought not to shoot it.

—George Orwell, "Shooting an Elephant"

If they are very lucky, the passengers may catch a glimpse of dolphins playfully breaking water near the ship.

—Elizabeth Gray, student

Subordination usually communicates relationships among ideas more effectively than a group of separate sentences does.

UNCLEAR	In 1888, two cowboys had to fight a dangerous Colorado snowstorm. They were looking for cattle. They came to a canyon. They saw outlines of buildings through the snow. Survival then seemed certain.
CLEAR	In 1888, two cowboys had to fight a dangerous Colorado snowstorm **while they were looking for cattle. When they came to a canyon,** they saw outlines of buildings through the snow. Survival then seemed certain.

In the clear version, the first four short sentences have been combined into two COMPLEX SENTENCES. The last sentence, which is left short, now makes a stronger impact.

EXERCISE 17-3

Consulting sections 17e through 17g, combine each pair of sentences, using an adverb clause to subordinate one idea. Then, revise each sentence so that the adverb clause becomes the independent clause. Refer to the list of subordinating conjunctions in Chart 96.

EXAMPLE   Shoes can be colorful, glamorous, or even witty. They are meant to protect the foot from some of the dangers of walking.

a. *Although shoes can be colorful, glamorous, or even witty, they are meant to protect the foot from some of the dangers of walking.*

b. *Although shoes are meant to protect the foot from some of the dangers of walking, they can be colorful, glamorous, or even witty.*

1. Sandals are worn primarily to protect the sole of the foot. They are also worn for comfort and style.
2. Ornamentation was added to sandals worn by ancient peoples. Footwear became a stylish article of clothing.

QUOTATION: ON WRITING

Blot out, correct, insert, refine,
Enlarge, diminish, interline;
Be mindful, when invention fails,
To scratch your head, and bite your
  nails.

—Jonathan Swift

ANSWERS: EXERCISE 17-3

Answers will vary. Here is one set of possibilities.

1. a. Although sandals are worn primarily to protect the sole of the foot, they are also worn for comfort and style.

b. Whereas they are also worn for comfort and style, sandals are worn primarily to protect the sole of the foot.

2. a. After ornamentation was added to sandals worn by ancient peoples, footwear became a stylish article of clothing.

b. When footwear became a stylish article of clothing, ornamentation was added to sandals worn by ancient people.

3. a. Although sandalmakers were constrained by certain requirements in ancient Egyptian society, they had to cater to their clients' fashion whims.

b. Because they had to cater to their clients' fashion whims, sandalmakers were constrained by certain requirements in ancient Egyptian society.

→

Answers: Exercise 17-3 (continued)

4. a. For example, when the nobility demanded sandals with turned-up toes, peasants were expected to wear sandals with rounded or pointed toes.

b. For example, whereas peasants were expected to wear sandals with rounded or pointed toes, the nobility demanded sandals with turned-up toes.

5. a. As clothing had to be made from available materials, ancient Egyptian sandals were made of leather, woven palm leaves, or papyrus stalks.

b. Clothing had to be made from available materials, so ancient Egyptian sandals were made of leather, woven palm leaves, or papyrus stalks.

ANSWERS: EXERCISE 17-4

Having students compare and discuss the differences in emphasis between the answers to each item may help them clarify their understanding of the differences.

1. a. An ancient Greek law *that* allowed voters to banish politicians from their city asked citizens to write the name of an unpopular politician on their ballots.

b. An ancient Greek law *that* asked citizens to write the name of an unpopular politician on their ballots allowed voters to banish politicians from their city.

2. a. A voter *who* was filling out a ballot when Aristides the Just walked by needed help in spelling *Aristides*.

b. A voter *who* needed help in spelling *Aristides* was filling out a ballot when Aristides the Just walked by.

3. a. Aristides, *who* knew the voter did not recognize him, asked why the voter wanted to banish that particular politician.

b. Aristides, *who* asked why the voter wanted to banish that particular politician, knew the voter did not recognize him.

4. a. The voter, *who* said he resented hearing someone called "the Just" all the time, handed Aristides his ballot.

3. Sandalmakers were constrained by certain requirements in ancient Egyptian society. They had to cater to their clients' fashion whims.

4. For example, the nobility demanded sandals with turned-up toes. Peasants were expected to wear sandals with rounded or pointed toes.

5. Clothing had to be made from available materials. Ancient Egyptian sandals were made of leather, woven palm leaves, or papyrus stalks.

EXERCISE 17-4

Consulting sections 17e through 17g, combine each pair of sentences, using an adjective clause to make one idea subordinate to the other. Then, revise each sentence so that the adjective clause becomes the independent clause. Use the relative pronoun given in parentheses.

EXAMPLE Aristides was an ancient Greek politician famous for his honesty and judgment. He was known as Aristides the Just. (who)

a. Aristides, *who was an ancient Greek politician famous for his honesty and judgment*, was known as Aristides the Just.

b. Aristides, *who was known as Aristides the Just*, was an ancient Greek politician famous for his honesty and judgment.

1. An ancient Greek law allowed voters to banish politicians from their city. It asked citizens to write the name of an unpopular politician on their ballots. (that)

2. A voter was filling out a ballot when Aristides the Just walked by. The voter needed help in spelling *Aristides*. (who)

3. Aristides knew the voter did not recognize him. He asked why the voter wanted to banish that particular politician. (who)

4. The voter said he resented hearing someone called "the Just" all the time. He handed Aristides his ballot. (who)

5. Aristides' reaction demonstrated that the nickname "the Just" was well deserved. His reaction was to write his own name on the voter's ballot even though that person's vote helped banish Aristides. (which)

17h Avoiding the misuse of subordination

17h.1 Avoiding illogical subordination

Subordination is illogical when the SUBORDINATING CONJUNCTION does not make the relationship between the INDEPENDENT CLAUSE and the DEPENDENT CLAUSE clear (see Chart 96). The following sentence is illogical.

NO   **Because** Beethoven was deaf when he wrote his final symphonies, they are musical masterpieces. [*Because* implies, illogically, that Beethoven's deafness caused him to write symphonic masterpieces.]

Revising from *because* to *although* creates logical subordination.

YES   **Although** Beethoven was deaf when he wrote his final symphonies, they are musical masterpieces. [*Although* implies that the symphonies are masterpieces despite Beethoven's deafness.]

17h.2 Avoiding the overuse of subordination

Overused subordination crowds too many images or ideas together, making readers lose track of your intended message. If you have used more than two subordinating conjunctions or RELATIVE PRONOUNS in a sentence, question closely whether your meaning is clear.

NO   A new technique for eye surgery, which is supposed to correct nearsightedness, which previously could be corrected only by glasses, has been developed, although many doctors do not approve of it because it can create unstable eyesight.

YES   A new technique for eye surgery, which is supposed to correct nearsightedness, has been developed. Previously, nearsightedness could be corrected only by glasses. Because the surgery can create unstable eyesight, many doctors do not approve of it, however.

In the *yes* version, the first sentence has a RELATIVE CLAUSE, the second is a SIMPLE SENTENCE, and the third has a dependent clause starting with *because*. Some words have been moved to new positions. The revision communicates its message more clearly because it provides a variety of sentence structures (see 19a) while avoiding the clutter of overused subordination.

EXERCISE 17-5

Consulting section 17h, correct illogical or excessive subordination in this paragraph. As you revise, use not only some short sentences but also some correctly constructed adverb clauses. Also, apply the principles of coordination discussed in sections 17a through 17d, if you wish.

Because too many young ape mothers in zoos were rejecting or abusing their infants, zookeepers decided to stop their usual practice of separating mother and infant from the rest of the ape community, which was done so that the infant would supposedly be safe from

Answers: Exercise 17-3 (continued)

b. The voter, *who* handed Aristides his ballot, said he resented hearing someone called "the Just" all the time.

5. a. Aristides' reaction, *which* demonstrated that the nickname "the Just" was well deserved, was to write his own name on the voter's ballot even though that person's vote helped banish Aristides.

b. Aristides' reaction, *which* was to write his own name on the voter's ballot even though that person's vote helped banish Aristides, demonstrated that the nickname "the Just" was well deserved.

ANSWERS AND COVERAGE: EXERCISE 17-5

Each sentence contains illogical and overused subordination. Answers will vary considerably. Here is one possibility.

Because too many young ape mothers in zoos were rejecting or abusing their infants, zookeepers decided to stop their usual practice of separating mother and infant from the rest of the ape community. This practice was done so that the infant would supposedly be safe from harm from other apes. In the new arrangement, group settings were established that included older, experienced, loving ape mothers, as well as other infants and young mothers. The abusive mothers could learn from good role models how to love and care for their infants, and each mother would have child-rearing support from the equivalent of aunts and cousins. The experiment was successful. When some pediatricians, who are doctors who specialize in child care, tried a similar program for abusive human mothers, it worked well even though the human mothers took far longer than the ape mothers to learn and use good mothering techniques.

ANSWERS: EXERCISE 17-6

Answers will vary. Here is one set of possibilities.

1. Owl pellets are the latest teaching tool in biology classrooms around the country because they provide an alternative to dissecting frogs and other animals.
2. Inside the pellets are the remains of the owl's nightly meal, which include beautifully cleaned hummingbird skulls, rat skeletons, and lots of bird feathers.
3. The owl pellet market has been cornered by companies in New York, California, and Washington that distribute pellets to thousands of biology classrooms all over the world.
4. Company workers scour barns and the ground under trees where owls nest to pick up the pellets, which sell for $1 each.
5. The owl pellet business may have a short future because the rural areas of the United States are vanishing. Old barns are being bulldozed. When all the barns are torn down, the owls will be gone, too.

ANSWERS: EXERCISE 17-7

Students use a topic of their own to imitate the styles of three different examples shown in this chapter. Imitation has a proud tradition as a learning tool. The classic rhetoricians said that versatility in style

harm from other apes. In the new arrangement, group settings were established that included older, experienced, loving ape mothers as well as other infants and young mothers so that the abusive mothers could learn from good role models how to love and care for their infants and so that each mother would have child-rearing support from the equivalent of aunts and cousins. The experiment was successful, and some pediatricians, who are doctors who specialize in child care, tried a similar program for abusive human mothers, which worked well even though the human mothers took far longer than the ape mothers to learn and use good mothering techniques.

17i Balancing subordination and coordination

Coordination and subordination used together can enhance each other.

When two Americans look searchingly into each other's eyes, emotions are heightened, **and** the relationship is tipped toward greater intimacy.

—Flora Davis, "How to Read Body Language"

By varying sentence types, you can improve your ability to emphasize key points in your writing. Consider the following paragraph, which demonstrates a good balance in the use of coordination and subordination. It contains COMPOUND SENTENCES (see 17a–17d), sentences that consist of DEPENDENT and INDEPENDENT CLAUSES (see 17e–17h), and SIMPLE SENTENCES.

When I was growing up, I lived on a farm just across the field from my grandmother. My parents were busy trying to raise six children and to establish their struggling dairy farm. It was nice to have Grandma so close. **While my parents were providing the necessities of life,** my patient grandmother gave her time to her shy, young granddaughter. I always enjoyed going with Grandma and collecting the eggs that her chickens had just laid. Usually, she knew which chickens would peck, **and** she was careful to let me gather the eggs from the less hostile ones.

—Patricia Mapes, student

When you vary your sentence types, be careful to avoid using both a coordinate and a subordinate conjunction to express one relationship.

NO	**Although** the story was well-written, **but** it was too unbelievable.
YES	**Although** the story was well-written, it was too unbelievable.
YES	The story was well-written, **but** it was too unbelievable.

EXERCISE 17-6

Consulting all sections of this chapter, use subordination and coordination to combine these sets of short, choppy sentences.

EXAMPLE   Owls cannot digest the bones and fur of the mice and birds they eat. They cough up a furry pellet every day.

Because owls cannot digest the bones and fur of the mice and birds they eat, they cough up a furry pellet every day.

1. Owl pellets are the latest teaching tool in biology classrooms around the country. The pellets provide an alternative to dissecting frogs and other animals.

2. Inside the pellet are the remains of the owl's nightly meal. They include beautifully cleaned hummingbird skulls, rat skeletons, and lots of bird feathers.

3. The owl pellet market has been cornered by companies in New York, California, and Washington. These companies distribute pellets to thousands of biology classrooms all over the world.

4. Company workers scour barns and the ground under trees where owls nest to pick up the pellets. The pellets sell for $1 each.

5. The owl pellet business may have a short future. The rural areas of the United States are vanishing. Old barns are being bulldozed. All the barns are torn down. The owls will be gone, too.

EXERCISE 17-7

Using topics you choose, imitate the style of three different examples shown in this chapter. Select from the quotations by Fitzgerald, Orwell, Gray, Davis, and Mapes.

EXERCISE 17-8

Consulting all sections of this chapter, revise this passage by using coordination and subordination.

   Few people have ever seen a manatee. Only about two thousand of these seagoing mammals are left in the world. In the South Pacific, manatees are known as dugongs. They are smaller than sea lions and bigger than seals. They bear an uncanny resemblance to humans. They are thought to be the source of sailors' mermaid legends. Researchers are trying to preserve and protect the dying manatee population in every way they can. Divers at the Sea World amusement park in Florida rescued one manatee female they named Fathom. She was severely injured, possibly by a boat's propeller. She would have died in the wild. She was unable to float or breathe properly. At Sea World, Fathom was given a tailor-made wet suit. She recovered nicely.

Answers: Exercise 17-7 (continued)

came from (1) a study of principles, (2) practice in writing, and (3) imitation of the practice of others. For a modern interpretation of classical rhetoric, see Edward P. J. Corbett, *Classical Rhetoric for the Modern Student* (New York: Oxford UP, 1990).

ANSWERS: EXERCISE 17-8

Answers may vary. Here are two possibilities that students might enjoy comparing with their own.

1. Few people have ever seen a manatee because only about two thousand of these seagoing mammals, known as dugongs in the South Pacific, are left in the world. Smaller than sea lions and bigger than seals, manatees bear an uncanny resemblance to humans, and they are thought to be the source of sailors' mermaid legends. Researchers are trying to preserve and protect the dying manatee population in every way they can. Divers at the Sea World amusement park in Florida rescued one manatee female they named Fathom. Severely injured, possibly from a boat's propeller, and unable to float or breathe properly, Fathom would have died in the wild. At Sea World, Fathom was given a tailor-made wet suit, and she recovered nicely.

2. Only about two thousand manatees are left in the world, and few people have ever seen one of these seagoing mammals. Known as dugongs in the South Pacific, manatees are smaller than sea lions and bigger than seals. Because manatees bear an uncanny resemblance to humans, they are thought to be the source of sailors' mermaid legends. Researchers are trying to preserve and protect the dying manatee population in every way they can. When divers at the Sea World amusement park in Florida rescued one manatee female they named Fathom, she was severely injured, possibly from a boat's propeller. Unable to float or breathe properly, she would have died in the wild. Fathom was given a tailor-made wet suit at Sea World, where she recovered nicely.

18
PARALLELISM

This chapter advises you how to make words and word groups parallel (18b through 18e) and how to use parallelism's grace and power to strengthen your writing (18f and 18g). It also explains parallelism in outlines and lists (18h).

Many writers attend to parallelism when they are REVISING. If you think while you are DRAFTING that your parallelism is faulty or that you can enhance your writing style by using parallelism, underline or highlight the material and keep your focus on getting ideas onto paper. When you revise, you can work on the places that you marked.

18a Understanding parallelism

Parallelism in writing, related to the concept of parallel lines in geometry, calls for the use of equivalent grammatical forms to express ideas of equal importance. An **equivalent grammatical form** is a word or group of words that matches—is parallel to—the structure of a corresponding word or group of words, as explained in Chart 97.

◉ **Parallel structures**   97

Parallel Words

Recommended exercise includes running, swimming, and cycling. [The *-ing* words are parallel in structure and equal in importance.]

Parallel Phrases

Exercise enables people to maintain healthy bodies and to handle mental pressures. [The *to* phrases are parallel in structure and equal in importance.]

→

Parallel structures *(continued)* **97**

Parallel Clauses

People exercise because they want to look healthy, because they need to have stamina, or because they hope to live longer. [The *because* clauses are parallel in structure and equal in importance.]

Also, when you are expressing ideas of equal weight in your writing, parallel sentence structures can echo that fact and offer you a writing style that uses balance and rhythm to help deliver your meaning.

> The deer often come to eat their grain, the wolves to destroy their sheep, the bears to kill their hogs, the foxes to catch their poultry. [The message of the multiple, accumulating assaults is echoed by the parallel structures.]
>
> —J. Hector St. Jean de Crèvecoeur, *Letters from an American Farmer*

18b Using words in parallel form

To achieve a graceful style, make words parallel by putting them in the same grammatical form. Using words in parallel form can also enhance the impact of meaning (see 18f and 18g).

NO The strikers had tried **pleading, threats,** and **shouting.**

YES The strikers had tried **pleading, threatening,** and **shouting.**

YES The strikers had tried **pleas, threats,** and **shouts.**

18c Using phrases and clauses in parallel form

To make word groups parallel, put them in the same grammatical form. Using PHRASES and CLAUSES in parallel form can enhance the impact of meaning (see 18f and 18g).

NO The committee members **read the petition, discussed its major points,** and **the unanimous decision was to ignore it.**

YES The committee members **read the petition, discussed its major points,** and **unanimously decided to ignore it.** [revised to parallel phrases]

TEACHING TIP

Classical rhetoric teaches that successful speaking or writing comes, in part, from the imitation of good examples. This imitation can take the form of copying passages verbatim or of imitating particular sentence patterns. Classical rhetoricians are not the only ones who have written about the benefits of imitation. Benjamin Franklin writes in his *Autobiography* (1771) of using essays in *The Spectator* as models for organization, sentence structure, and vocabulary. Malcolm X writes in his autobiography of the benefits he gained from simply copying the dictionary in longhand. Winston Churchill and Somerset Maugham also write of the lessons they learned by imitating written models. A possible first step in imitation is copying passages from favorite writers verbatim. This is not as brainless as it seems, for done properly, it enables students to observe the details of an author's style. For this exercise to succeed, students should follow these guidelines adapted from Edward P. J. Corbett, *Classical Rhetoric for the Modern Student* (New York: Oxford UP, 1990):

1. Students should read a piece through before beginning to copy it, to see the purpose and style of the whole. While working, they should read each sentence before beginning to write it. Once the passage has been completed, students should read their transcriptions again to "get a sense of the passage as a whole."

2. Students should copy for fifteen minutes per session. If they copy much longer, their minds will no longer focus on the work and the copying will become mechanical.

→

3. Students should copy by hand. Typing is too fast to allow students to see the qualities of a writer's style. Writing lets students work slowly enough to see the selection and placement of words and the lengths and types of sentences.

4. Students should copy from a variety of authors. If they concentrate on one author to the exclusion of others, they may end up aping a single style rather than getting the feel of a variety of styles.

5. Students should copy patiently and with care. Too much speed can make the exercise meaningless. One way of controlling speed is to require that work be legible.

A second kind of imitation exercise uses sentences as patterns. The students duplicate the *kind, number,* and *order* of clauses and phrases in the model. The aim of this exercise is not to achieve a word-for-word correspondence with the model but rather to achieve an awareness of the variety of sentence structures of which the English language is capable.

Parody can be an enjoyable imitation exercise for students. Writing a "restaurant review" of the cafeteria or a literary analysis of a comic book not only engages students in wordplay but also requires that they notice the stylistic and structural conventions of the model they are parodying.

NO **The signers heard** that their petition had not been granted, **they became** very upset, and then **staged** a protest demonstration.

YES **The signers heard** that their petition had not been granted, **they became** very upset, and then **they staged** a protest demonstration. [revised to parallel clauses]

YES **The signers heard** that their petition had not been granted, **became** very upset, and then **staged** a protest demonstration. [revised to parallel phrases]

18d Using parallel structures correctly with coordinating and correlative conjunctions and with *than* and *as*

18d.1 Using parallel forms with coordinating conjunctions

The **coordinating conjunctions** are *and, but, or, nor, for, yet,* and *so* (for the relationship each expresses, see Chart 94 in section 17a). To make elements joined by coordinating conjunctions parallel, put them in the same grammatical form.

NO **Love** and **being married** go together.

YES **Love** and **marriage** go together.

YES **Being in love** and **being married** go together.

18d.2 Using parallel forms with paired words (correlative conjunctions)

Correlative conjunctions are pairs of words such as *not only . . . but (also), either . . . or,* and *both . . . and* (for more, see 7h). To make elements joined by correlative conjunctions parallel, put them in the same grammatical form. As you check your writing, pay particular attention to where you place the first half of the pair.

NO Differing expectations for marriage **not only can lead to** disappointment **but also to** anger.

YES Differing expectations for marriage **not only can lead to** disappointment **but also can cause** anger.

—Norman DuBois, student

If the same verb applies to both parts, put the verb before the first part of the pair.

YES Differing expectations for marriage **can lead not only to** disappointment **but also to** anger.

18d.3 Using parallel forms with *than* and *as*

When you use *than* and *as* for comparisons, be sure that elements are parallel in grammatical form. Also, make sure that these comparisons are complete (see 15e.2).

NO   **Having a solid marriage** can be more satisfying **than the acquisition of wealth.**

YES **Having a solid marriage** can be more satisfying **than acquiring wealth.**

YES **A solid marriage** can be more satisfying **than wealth.**

—Eunice Fernandez, student

NO   A solid marriage can be **as satisfying,** if not **more satisfying than,** wealth.

YES A solid marriage can be **as satisfying as,** if not **more satisfying than,** wealth.

18e Repeating function words in parallel elements

In a series of two or more parallel elements, be consistent in the second and subsequent elements about repeating or omitting function words. These include ARTICLES (*the, a, an*), the *to* of the INFINITIVE (for example, *to love*), and PREPOSITIONS (for example, *of, in, about*). If you think that repeating such words clarifies your meaning or might help your reader catch the parallelism that you intend, use them.

NO   **To assign** unanswered letters their proper weight, **free** us from the expectations of others, **to give** us back to ourselves—here lies the power of self-respect.

YES **To assign** unanswered letters their proper weight, **to free** us from the expectations of others, **to give** us back to ourselves—here lies **the great, the singular** power of self-respect.

—Joan Didion, "On Self-Respect"

When you use *who, which,* or *that* to start a series of CLAUSES, either repeat *who, which,* or *that* consistently in all the clauses or omit it consistently from each clause after the first one.

I have in my own life a precious friend, a woman of 65 **who has** lived very hard, **who is** wise, **who listens** well, **who has been** where I am and can help me understand it, and **who represents** not only an ultimate ideal mother to me but also the person I'd like to be when I grow up.

—Judith Viorst, "Friends, Good Friends—and Such Good Friends"

TEACHING TIP

You may want to ask your students to identify the various techniques by which parallelism is set up in the following sentences.

1. Standing on a concrete jetty at seven-thirty of a drizzly morning, looking across the gray Hudson at the shore softened by fog, one can just make out an endless miniature procession of Manhattan-bound cars going down the ramp to the Lincoln Tunnel.

"Gray Manhattan," *The New Yorker*

2. There is a crazy restaurant in the south of France where you are expected to eat well and copiously, to drink to excess, to listen to music and perhaps to spin to it—and also to break up the joint before you leave.

—Richard Atcheson, *"Le Pirate"*

3. On one side of this line are They: the bribers, the cheaters, the chiselers, the swindlers, the extortioners. On the other side are We. . . .

—Marya Mannes, "The Thin Grey Line"

BACKGROUND

Martin Luther King Jr. (1929–1968) was a powerful and eloquent speaker and writer for the civil rights movement in the United States. His works include *Stride Toward Freedom* (1958), *Strength to Love* (1963), *Why We Can't Wait* (1964), and *Where Do We Go from Here: Chaos or Community* (1967), as well as his famous "I Have a Dream" speech, which he delivered to a crowd of over 250,000 people in 1963 at a massive civil rights demonstration in Washington, D.C.

Among his best-known writings is his "Letter from Birmingham Jail," which he wrote from prison in 1963 in response to a published statement by eight Alabama clergymen who called his activities "unwise and untimely." In "The *Other* Beauty of Martin Luther King, Jr.'s 'Letter from Birmingham Jail'" (*College Composition and Communication*, February 1981: 30–37), Mia Klein Anderson describes the musical, rhythmical effect of parallelism in King's powerful letter. King parallels clauses, nouns, verbs, adverbs, adjectives, and adjective-noun pairs throughout the letter. Using antithesis and parallelism, he juxtaposes contrasting ideas with an engaging rhythm. King often combines parallelism with deliberate repetition of a word or group of words at the start of successive clauses, a rhetorical figure called *anaphora*. "Martin Luther King, Jr., knew that his effectiveness in reaching his wider audience would come both from what he said and from how he said it," Anderson writes. "The words can reach the mind, but the music and imagination can reach the heart and soul" (36).

We looked into the bus, **which was painted** blue with orange daisies, **had** picnic benches instead of seats, and **showed** yellow curtains billowing out its windows.

—Kerrie Falk, student

18f Using parallel and balanced structures for impact

Parallel structures serve to emphasize the meaning that sentences deliver. **Deliberate, rhythmic repetition** of parallel word forms and word groups creates an effect of balance, reinforcing the impact of a message. (For information about misused repetition, see 16c.) Consider the impact of this famous passage:

> **Go back to** Mississippi, **go back to** Alabama, **go back to** South Carolina, **go back to** Georgia, **go back to** Louisiana, **go back to** the slums and ghettos of our northern cities, knowing that somehow this situation can and will be changed.
>
> —Martin Luther King Jr., "I Have a Dream"

If King had used only minimal or no parallelism, his message would have been weaker. An ordinary sentence would have been less effective: "Return to your homes in Mississippi, Alabama, South Carolina, Georgia, Louisiana, or the cities, and know that the situation will be changed." His structures reinforce the power of his message.

A **balanced sentence** presents contrasting content in two parallel structures, usually INDEPENDENT CLAUSES. A balanced sentence is a COORDINATE SENTENCE (see 17a), characterized by opposition in the meaning of the two structures, sometimes with one cast in the negative: *Mosquitos do not bite; they stab.* Consider the impact of this sentence:

> By night, the litter and desperation disappeared as the city's glittering lights came on; by day, the filth and despair reappeared as the sun rose.
>
> —Jennifer Kirk, student

Similarly, consider the impact of this famous sentence, which adds unusual word order (*ask not,* instead of *do not ask*) to its parallelism and balance.

> Ask not what your country can do for you, ask what you can do for your country.
>
> —John F. Kennedy

❶ **COMMA ALERT:** Authorities differ about using a comma or semicolon between the parts of a balanced sentence. In college, to avoid appearing to make the error of a comma splice (see Chapter 14), use a semicolon (or revise in some other way). ❗

18g Using parallel sentences for impact in longer passages

Parallel, balanced sentences in longer passages can create dramatic unity through carefully controlled repetition of words and word forms. Consider this rich passage of repeated words, concepts, and rhythms.

> You ask me what is **poverty**? **Listen** to me. Here I am, dirty, smelly, and with no "proper" underwear on and with the stench of my rotting teeth near you. I will tell you. **Listen** to me. **Listen** without pity. I cannot use your pity. **Listen** with understanding. Put yourself in my dirty, worn-out, ill-fitting shoes, and hear me.
>
> **Poverty** is getting up every morning from a dirt- and illness-stained mattress. The sheets have long since been used for diapers. **Poverty** is living in a **smell** that never leaves. This is a **smell** of urine, sour milk, and spoiling food sometimes joined with the strong **smell** of long-cooked onions. Onions are cheap. If you have **smelled** this **smell,** you did not know how it came. **It is the smell** of the outdoor privy. **It is the smell** of young children who cannot walk the long dark way in the night. **It is the smell** of the mattresses where years of "accidents" have happened. **It is the smell** of the milk which has gone sour because the refrigerator long has not worked, and it costs money to get it fixed. **It is the smell** of rotting garbage. I could bury it, but where is the shovel? Shovels cost money.
>
> —Jo Goodwin Parker, "What Is Poverty?"

EXERCISE 18-1

Reread the Jo Goodwin Parker passage. Then, consulting sections 18a through 18e, mark all the parallel elements in addition to those shown in boldface.

EXERCISE 18-2

Using topics you choose, imitate the writing style of three different passages shown in this chapter. Select from the quotations from Crèvecoeur, Didion, Viorst, King, Kennedy, and Parker.

EXERCISE 18-3

Consulting sections 18a through 18e, revise these sentences by putting appropriate information in parallel structures.

EXAMPLE   Difficult bosses not only affect their employees' performances but their private lives are affected as well.

Difficult bosses affect not only their employees' performances *but their private lives as well.*

1. According to psychologist Harry Levinson, the five main types of bad boss are the workaholic, the kind of person you would describe as bullying, a person who communicates badly, the jellyfish type, and someone who insists on perfection.

ANSWERS: EXERCISE 18-1

Elements of parallelism in Parker's passage not shown in boldface are: *Repetitions*: you, me, I, dirty (dirt), pity, onions, mattress(es), urine (privy, "accidents"), long, it, sour, rotting, shovels. *Paired words*: with / with. *Imperatives (mild commands)*: Listen, Put, hear. *Contrasts*: pity and understanding, with / without. *Words in a series*: my dirty, worn-out, ill-fitting shoes; smell of urine, sour milk, and spoiling food.

ANSWERS: EXERCISE 18-2

Students use topics of their own to imitate the parallel style of three of the passages shown in this chapter: by Crèvecoeur, Didion, Viorst, King, Kennedy, or Parker. Style imitation has a proud tradition as a learning tool. The classical rhetoricians said that versatility in style came from (1) a study of principles, (2) practice in writing, and (3) imitation of the practice of others. For a modern interpretation of classical rhetoric see Edward P. J. Corbett, *Classical Rhetoric for the Modern Student* (New York: Oxford UP, 1990).

ANSWERS AND COVERAGE: EXERCISE 18-3

Answers will vary. Here is one set of possibilities.

1. According to psychologist Harry Levinson, the five main types of bad boss are *the workaholic, the bully, the bad communicator, the jellyfish, and the perfectionist.* [18b, words]

Answers and Coverage: Exercise 18-3 (continued)

2. *To get ahead, to keep their self-respect, and simply to survive*, wise employees handle problem bosses with a variety of strategies. [18c, phrases]

3. To cope with a bad-tempered employer, workers can both *stand up for themselves and reason with a bullying boss.* [18d.2, correlative conjunctions]

4. Often, bad bosses communicate poorly or fail to calculate the impact of their personality on others; *good bosses listen carefully and are sensitive to others' responses.* [18f, parallel sentence structures]

5. Employees *who take the trouble to understand what makes their boss tick, who engage in some self-analysis, and who stay flexible* [18e, repeating parallel function words] are better prepared to cope with a difficult job environment than employees *who suffer in silence.* [18d.3, parallel form with *than*]

ANSWERS AND COVERAGE: EXERCISE 18-4

Answers may vary. Here is one set of possibilities.

1. A married couple *who met at Juniata College in Huntingdon, Pennsylvania*, and *who are both left-handed* have set up a scholarship for needy left-handed students attending Juniata. [18e, repeating function words]

2. Writers who specialize in humor bankroll a student humor writer at the University of Southern California in Los Angeles; a horse-racing association sponsors a student sportswriter at Vanderbilt University in Nashville, Tennessee. [18f, balanced sentence]

3. The Rochester Institute of Technology in New York State is choosing 150 students born on June 12, 1979. *It is granting each one $1,500 per year. It is awarding these grants to select students to honor its 150th anniversary*, which it celebrated on June 12, 1979. [18f, parallelism among sentences]

2. As a way of getting ahead, to keep their self-respect, and for simple survival, wise employees handle problem bosses with a variety of strategies.

3. To cope with a bad-tempered employer, workers can both stand up for themselves and reasoning with a bullying boss.

4. Often, bad bosses communicate poorly or fail to calculate the impact of their personality on others; being a careful listener and sensitivity to others' responses are qualities that good bosses possess.

5. Employees who take the trouble to understand what makes their boss tick, engage in some self-analysis, and staying flexible are better prepared to cope with a difficult job environment than suffering in silence like some employees.

EXERCISE 18-4

Consulting sections 18a through 18f, combine the sentences in each numbered item, using techniques of parallelism.

EXAMPLE   College scholarships are awarded not only for academic and athletic ability, but there are also scholarships that recognize unusual talents. Other scholarships even award accidents of birth, like left-handedness.

College scholarships are awarded not only for academic and athletic ability *but also for unusual talents and even for accidents of birth, like left-handedness.*

1. A married couple met at Juniata College in Huntingdon, Pennsylvania. They are both left-handed, and they have set up a scholarship for needy left-handed students attending Juniata.

2. Writers who specialize in humor bankroll a student humor writer at the University of Southern California in Los Angeles. A horse-racing association sponsors a student sportswriter. The student sportswriter must attend Vanderbilt University in Nashville, Tennessee.

3. The Rochester Institute of Technology in New York State is choosing 150 students born on June 12, 1979. Each one is to receive a grant of $1,500 per year. These awards are to be given to select students to honor the school's 150th anniversary, which was celebrated on June 12, 1979.

4. The College of Wooster in Ohio grants generous scholarships to students if they play the bagpipes, a musical instrument native to Scotland. Students playing the traditional Scottish drums and those who excel in Scottish folk dancing also qualify.

5. In return for their scholarships, Wooster's bagpipers must pipe for the school's football team. The terms of the scholarships also require the drummers to drum for the team. The dancers have to cheer the athletes from the sidelines.

EXERCISE 18-5

Find the parallel elements in the following examples. Then, use your own topics to imitate the parallelism in two of the examples.

1 Our earth is but a small star in a great universe. Yet of it we can make, if we choose, a planet unvexed by war, untroubled by hunger or fear, undivided by senseless distinctions of race, color, or theory.

—Stephen Vincent Benét

2 Some would recover [from polio] almost entirely. Some would die. Some would come through unable to move their legs, or unable to move arms and legs; some could move nothing but an arm, or nothing but a few fingers and their eyes. Some would leave the hospital with a cane, some with crutches, crutches and steel leg braces, or in wheelchairs—white-faced, shrunken, with frightened eyes, light blankets over their legs. Some would remain in an iron lung—a great, eighteen-hundred-pound, casket-like contraption, like the one in which the woman in the magic show (her head and feet sticking out of either end) is sawed in half.

—Charles L. Mee Jr., "The Summer Before Salk"

3 I am lonely only when I am overtired, when I have worked too long without a break, when for the time being I feel empty and need filling up. And I am lonely sometimes when I come back home after a lecture trip, when I have seen a lot of people and talked a lot, and am full to the brim with experience that needs to be sorted out.

—May Sarton, "The Rewards of a Solitary Life"

18h Using parallelism in outlines and lists

Items in formal outlines and lists must be parallel in grammar and structure. (For information about other issues of outline format and about how to develop an outline, see 2o.)

FORMAL OUTLINE NOT IN PARALLEL FORM

Reducing Traffic Fatalities

I. Stricter laws
  A. Top speed should be 50 mph on highways.
  B. Higher fines
  C. Requiring jail sentences for repeat offenders
II. The use of safety devices should be mandated by law.

Answers and Coverage: Exercise 18-4 (continued)

4. The College of Wooster in Ohio grants generous scholarships to students if they *play the Scottish bagpipes, play the traditional Scottish drums, or excel in Scottish folk dancing.* [18e, repeating phrases]

5. In return for their scholarships, Wooster's bagpipers must pipe for the school's football team, *the drummers must drum for the team, and the dancers must cheer the athletes* from the sidelines. [18e, parallelism among clauses]

ANSWERS: EXERCISE 18-5

The answers here list the examples' parallel elements.

1. a planet unvexed by war, untroubled by hunger or fear, undivided by senseless distinctions of race, color, or theory. [Some students may also list the parallel words *race, color, theory*.]

2. The clauses beginning with the word *some* are parallel.

3. The two clauses *I am lonely* are parallel, as are all the clauses beginning with *when*.

BACKGROUND

In *Style: Ten Lessons in Clarity and Grace*, 4th ed. (New York: HarperCollins, 1994), Joseph M. Williams points out that some nonparallel constructions are acceptable at times. Skilled writers often join a noun phrase with a *how* clause ("The debater knew the facts and how to use them to her best advantage") or an adjective or adverb with a prepositional phrase ("The young team played aggressively, intelligently, and with surprising poise"). Many editors and teachers, however, do not accept these constructions.

ADDITIONAL EXAMPLES

Because parallelism gives statements a stately, dignified sound, it appears often in official declarations, as in the following.

1. For the support of this declaration, with a firm reliance on the protection of Divine Providence, we mutually pledge to each other our Lives, our Fortunes, and our sacred Honor.

—The Declaration of Independence

2. It is rather for us to be here dedicated to the great task remaining before us—that from these honored dead we take increased devotion to that cause for which they gave the last full measure of devotion; that we here highly resolve that these dead shall not have died in vain; that this nation, under God, shall have a new birth of freedom; and that government of the people, by the people, for the people, shall not perish from the earth.

—Abraham Lincoln,
Gettysburg Address

3. We are saddened; we are stunned; we are perplexed.

—Earl Warren,
on the death of John Kennedy

ANSWERS AND COVERAGE: EXERCISE 18-6

Reducing Traffic Fatalities
I. Passing stricter speed laws
   A. Making 50 mph top speed on any highway
   B. Raising fine for first-time speeding offenders
   C. Requiring jail sentences for repeat offenders
II. Legislating installation of safety devices
   A. Requiring all automobiles to have safety belts in front and back seats
   B. Making seat belt use mandatory for all drivers
   C. Forcing auto manufacturers to offer airbags as an option in all cars

FORMAL OUTLINE IN PARALLEL FORM

Reducing Traffic Fatalities
I. **Passing** stricter speed laws
   A. **Making** 50 mph the top speed on highways
   B. **Raising** fines for speeding
   C. **Requiring** jail sentences for repeat offenders
II. **Mandating** by law the use of safety devices

Although a nonparallel outline might serve as an informal, scratch outline in the early stages of the writing process, only a parallel outline is acceptable as a final draft.

FORMAL LIST NOT IN PARALLEL FORM

Workaholics share these characteristics:
1. They are intense and driven.
2. Strong self-doubters
3. Labor is preferred to leisure by workaholics.

FORMAL LIST IN PARALLEL FORM

Workaholics share these characteristics:
1. **They are** intense and driven.
2. **They have** strong self-doubts.
3. **They prefer** labor to leisure.

EXERCISE 18-6

Consulting section 18h, revise this outline into parallel form.

Reducing Traffic Fatalities
I. Stricter laws
   A. Top speed on any highway should be 50 mph.
   B. Higher fines
   C. Repeat offenders sentenced to jail
II. Legislating installation of safety devices
   A. All automobiles should be required to have safety belts in both front and back seats.
   B. Making seat belt use mandatory for all drivers
   C. We should force auto manufacturers to offer airbags as an option in all cars.

19

VARIETY AND EMPHASIS

19a Understanding variety and emphasis

Your writing style has **variety** when your sentence lengths and patterns vary (see 19b and 19c). Your writing style is characterized by **emphasis** when your sentences are constructed to communicate the relative importance of their ideas. Strategies include choosing the subject of a sentence to highlight meaning (see 19d), adding MODIFIERS to basic sentences (see 19e), inverting standard word order (see 19f), and repeating important words or ideas (see 19g).

Consider the following passage, which successfully employs key techniques of variety and emphasis. The authors vary their sentence length (see 19b), include a variety of structures (see 19c), and use different kinds of modifiers in various positions (see 19e).

> Henri Poincaré, a famous mathematician who lived in the nineteenth century, devised an exercise in imagination to help people understand the relativity of measures. Imagine that one night while you were asleep everything in the universe became a thousand times larger than before. Remember this would include electrons, planets, all living creatures, your own body, and all the rulers and other measuring devices in the world. When you awoke, could you tell that anything had changed? Is there any experiment you could make to prove that some change had occurred? According to Poincaré there is no such experiment.
>
> —Judith and Herbert Kohl, *The View from the Oak*

Achieving variety and emphasis can move your writing beyond correctness to style and grace. Usually, the best time to apply the principles of variety and emphasis is while you are REVISING.

19b Varying sentence length

Variety in sentence length communicates clear distinctions among ideas. Such a style can help your readers understand the focus of your material. Also, such an approach helps you avoid the unbroken rhythm of sentences all the same length, which can bore readers and cause them to become inattentive.

19b.1 Revising strings of short sentences

Long strings of short sentences rarely establish relationships and levels of importance among ideas. Readers cannot easily make distinctions between major and minor points. Unless deliberately planned in a longer piece of writing for occasional impact (see 19b.3), strings of short sentences suggest that the writer has not thought about the material and decided what to emphasize. The resulting text tends to read like the writing of young children.

NO There is a legend. This legend is about a seventeenth-century Algonquin Indian. It says that he was inspired. He had an idea about popcorn. He transformed it into a gift. It was the first gift to a hostess in American history. He was invited to the Pilgrims' harvest meal. He brought along a bag of popcorn. This was a demonstration of good will. The occasion is honored to this day with Thanksgiving dinner.

YES According to legend, in the seventeenth century an inspired Algonquin transformed popcorn into the first hostess gift in history. Invited to the Pilgrims' harvest meal, the Indian brought along a bag of popcorn as a demonstration of good will. The occasion is honored today with Thanksgiving dinner.

—Patricia Linden, "Popcorn"

In the *yes* version, the sentence structures permit key ideas to be featured. The two versions use almost the same short last sentence, but because longer sentences lead up to it in the revised version, the short last sentence has more impact. In the *yes* version, note that ten sentences reduce to three and 74 words reduce to 47.

19b.2 Revising a string of compound sentences

A **compound sentence** consists of two or more INDEPENDENT CLAUSES. Too often, compound sentences string ideas together with *and* or *but* without consideration of the relationships among the ideas.

NO Science fiction writers are often thinkers, **and** they are often dreamers, **and** they let their imaginations wander. Jules Verne was such a writer, **and** he predicted space ships and atomic submarines, **but** most people did not believe airplanes were possible.

YES Science fiction writers are often thinkers and dreamers who let their imaginations wander. Jules Verne was one such writer. He predicted space ships and atomic submarines before most people believed airplanes were possible.

In the *yes* version, the relationships among the ideas are clear, and key ideas are featured. In the last sentence, a particularly obscure connection is clarified. For conciseness, one independent clause is reduced to a word, *dreamers;* another is reduced to a RELATIVE CLAUSE, *who let their imaginations wander;* another starts a new sentence, *He predicted . . . ;* and another is reduced to a SUBORDINATE CLAUSE, *before most people . . . possible.*

19b.3 Revising for a suitable mix of sentence lengths

To emphasize one idea among many others, you can express it in a sentence noticeably different in length or structure from the sentences surrounding it. Consider this passage, which carries its emphasis in one short sentence among longer ones.

> Today is one of those excellent January partly cloudies in which light chooses an unexpected landscape to trick out in gilt, and then shadow sweeps it away. **You know you are alive.** You take huge steps, trying to feel the planet's roundness arc between your feet. Kazantzakis says that when he was young he had a canary and a globe. When he freed the canary, it would perch on the globe and sing. All his life, wandering the earth, he felt as though he had a canary on top of his mind, singing.
> —Annie Dillard, *Pilgrim at Tinker Creek*

A long sentence among shorter ones is equally effective.

> Mistakes are not believed to be part of the normal behavior of a good machine. **If things go wrong, it must be a personal, human error, the result of fingering, tampering, a button getting stuck, someone hitting the wrong key.** The computer, at its normal best, is infallible. I wonder whether this can be true.
> —Lewis Thomas, "To Err Is Human"

EXERCISE 19-1

Consulting sections 19a and 19b, revise these sets of sentences to vary the sentence lengths effectively.

1. Biometeorology is a science. It examines the study of weather's unseen power over living things. The science concentrates on the effects of weather patterns on human behavior and health. Many researchers study these effects. They are attempting to find a connection between the two. One such researcher is William Ferdinand Peterson. He has spent the past 20 years collecting statistics and anecdotes. He wrote the book *The Patient and the Weather*. His research focuses on the invisible elements of air. These elements include passing fronts. These elements include falling barometric pressure. The elements include shifting wind directions.

2. The various changes in air elements related to the weather can occur simultaneously, and these changes may be the reason for

345

Teaching Tip (continued)

Evaluation	Professional	Student
G. Percentage of sentences that contain more than 10 words *over* the average sentence	____	____
H. Number of sentences that total 5 words or more *below* the average	____	____
I. Percentage of sentences that total 5 words or more below the average	____	____
J. Paragraph length: longest paragraph (in no. of sentences)	____	____
shortest paragraph (in no. of sentences)	____	____
average paragraph (in no. of sentences)	____	____

You might want to try Corbett's analysis on a piece that you have written and share the results with the class.

ANSWERS: EXERCISE 19-1

In this exercise, the first item has too many short sentences, the second too many compounds, and the third long and complicated sentences. Students will revise in various ways. Here is one set of possibilities.

1. Biometeorology, the science that studies weather's unseen power over living things, concentrates on the effects of weather patterns on human behavior and health. Many researchers are attempting to find a connection between the two. One such researcher, William Ferdinand Peterson, who has spent the past 20 years collecting statistics and anecdotes, wrote the

Answers: Exercise 19-1 (continued)

book *The Patient and the Weather*. His research focuses on the invisible elements of air, including passing fronts, falling barometric pressure, and shifting wind directions.

2. The various changes in air elements related to the weather can occur simultaneously. These changes may be the reason for mood swings and bad behavior among schoolchildren. They can even lead to bleeding ulcers and migraine headaches. There is a fine line between healthy change and change that is harmful, for such change can release toxic byproducts that worsen nearly every illness. The study of biometeorology began in Europe, which has extreme variations in weather. Biometeorologists there suggested a relationship between bone density and temperature. Hungarian scientists found an increase in gum inflammation with the arrival of warm fronts.

3. Feared winds and all their variations—from katabatic to chinook to Santa Ana—are frequently considered to be the cause of every illness that can be imagined. In Russia, high winds and the frequency of strokes seemed related; in Italy, southern winds and heart attacks seemed connected; and in Japan, there is a noticeable increase in asthma attacks whenever the wind changes direction.

mood swings and bad behavior among schoolchildren, and they can even lead to bleeding ulcers and migraine headaches. There is a fine line between healthy change and change that is harmful, for such change can release toxic byproducts, and these products worsen nearly every illness. The study of biometeorology began in Europe, which has extreme variations in weather, so biometeorologists there suggested a relationship between bone density and temperature, yet Hungarian scientists found an increase in gum inflammation with the arrival of warm fronts.

3.　　Feared winds and all their variations—from katabatic to chinook to Santa Ana—are frequently considered to be the cause of every illness that can be imagined by just about every human being in every country of the world. Whereas in Russia high winds and the frequency of strokes seemed related, in Italy southern winds and heart attacks seemed connected, while in Japan, researchers have noticed an increase in asthma attacks whenever the wind changes direction.

19c Using an occasional question, mild command, or exclamation

To vary sentence structure and to emphasize material, you can call on three alternative kinds of sentences. Most sentences in English are **declarative.** A declarative sentence makes a statement—it declares something. Declarative sentences offer an almost infinite variety of structures and patterns.

For variety, however, you may consider using the three alternative types. A sentence that asks a question is called **interrogative.** Occasional questions can help you involve readers. A sentence that issues a mild or strong command is called **imperative.** Occasional mild commands can gently urge your reader to think along with you. A sentence that makes an exclamation is called **exclamatory.** An occasional exclamatory sentence can make your writing more lively.

❶ **PUNCTUATION ALERT:** A mild command ends with a period. A strong command or an exclamation ends with an exclamation mark (see 23e). ❗

Consider the following paragraph, which uses the three kinds of sentence found most frequently in academic writing: declarative, interrogative, and imperative. (Exclamatory sentences are rare in serious writing, although the final sentence in this paragraph could have been treated as one.)

Imagine what people ate during the winter as little as seventy-five years ago. They ate food that was local, long-lasting, and dull, like acorn squash, turnips, and cabbage. Walk into an American supermarket in February and the world lies before you: grapes, melons, artichokes, fennel, lettuce, peppers, pistachios, dates, even strawberries, to say nothing of ice cream. Have you ever considered what a triumph of civilization it is to be able to buy a pound of chicken livers? If you lived on a farm and had to kill a chicken when you wanted to eat one, you wouldn't ever accumulate a pound of chicken livers.

—Phyllis Rose, "Shopping and Other Spiritual Adventures in America Today"

EXERCISE 19-2

The paragraph effectively varies sentence lengths and uses a question and a command. The result emphasizes the key points. Write an imitation of this paragraph, closely following all aspects except the topic. Choose your own topic.

EXAMPLE   *If your topic were gardens, your first sentence might be:* Why do most people plant tomatoes in their gardens when they know they will harvest many more tomatoes than the average family wants to eat in a whole year?

Why do most Americans spend $95 a year to operate their clothes dryers when nature provides free energy for the same task? Consider the humble clothesline and clothespins. They cost about $30 for a lifetime, and solar power is free, unlike an electric dryer, which can cost as much as $500. In an increasingly mechanized indoor life, people who hang their clothes on the line are obliged to notice the weather. Today is a perfect morning for drying, they think. Or will it rain this afternoon? Another line in the basement or spare room works well in rainy weather and in winter. Indoor drying has the further benefit of humidifying the house; twenty pounds of wet wash contributes about one gallon of water to the air.

19d Choosing the subject of a sentence according to your intended emphasis

The SUBJECT of a sentence establishes the focus for that sentence. As you write, each sentence's subject needs to reinforce the emphasis that you want your sentences to deliver.

Each of the following sentences, all of which are correct grammatically, contains the same information. Consider, however, how changes of the subject (and its VERB) influence meaning and impact.

Our study showed that 25 percent of college students' time is spent eating or sleeping. [Focus is on the study.]

College students eat or sleep 25 percent of the time, according to our study. [Focus is on the students.]

Eating or sleeping occupies 25 percent of college students' time, according to our study. [Focus is on eating and sleeping.]

Twenty-five percent of college students' time is spent eating or sleeping, according to our study. [Focus is on the time.]

19e Adding modifiers to basic sentences for variety and emphasis

Adding MODIFIERS to basic sentences can provide a rich variety of sentence patterns.

19e.1 Expanding basic sentences with modifiers

Sentences that consist only of a subject and a verb can sound flat unless you are using a very short sentence for its emphasis and dramatic effect among longer sentences (see 19b.3). If you want to avoid a very short sentence, you can expand the basic sentence as illustrated in Chart 98. Your decision to expand a basic sentence will depend on the focus of each sentence and how it works with its surrounding sentences.

◉ **Ways to expand a basic sentence**   98

BASIC SENTENCE	The river rose.
ADJECTIVE	The **swollen** river rose.
ADVERB	The river rose **dangerously.**
PREPOSITIONAL PHRASE	**In April,** the river rose **above its banks.**
PARTICIPIAL PHRASES	**Swollen by melting snow,** the river rose, **flooding the farmland.**
ABSOLUTE PHRASE	**Trees swirling away in the current,** the river rose.
ADVERB CLAUSE	**Because the snows had been heavy that winter,** the river rose.
ADJECTIVE CLAUSE	The river, **which runs through vital farmland,** rose.

EXERCISE 19-3

Consulting section 19e.1, expand each sentence by adding (a) an adjective, (b) an adverb, (c) a prepositional phrase, (d) a participial phrase, (e) an absolute phrase, (f) an adverb clause, and (g) an adjective clause.

1. We went to the fair.
2. The ride was full.
3. I won a basketball.
4. Rain poured from the sky.
5. Both of us got our clothes wet.

19e.2 Positioning modifiers to create variety and emphasis

Research on learning suggests that readers are more likely to retain the words and ideas placed at the very beginning or the very end of a sentence. They usually skim over the middle of a sentence, paying attention to it only enough to connect the sentences start and end. Although choices are unlimited for where to place modifiers, you often have options. Try to place a modifier according to the emphasis that you want to achieve. At the same time, be precise when you position a modifier so that you avoid the error of misplaced modifiers (see 15b).

A sentence that starts with a SUBJECT and VERB and then provides additional information with modifiers that appear after the subject and verb is called a **cumulative sentence.** The cumulative sentence is the most common sentence structure in English; it is called "cumulative" because information accumulates. Sometimes the cumulative sentence is referred to as a **loose sentence** because it lacks the tightly planned structure of other sentence varieties. Such sentences are easy to read because they reflect how humans receive and pass on information. They may not provide the impact of style, but they are very useful.

For greater impact, you can use a **periodic sentence,** also called a *climactic sentence.* It builds up to the period, reserving the main idea for the end of the sentence. It draws the reader in as it builds to its climax. Use periodic sentences only occasionally; overused, they lose their punch.

PERIODIC   At midnight last night, on the road from Las Vegas to Death Valley Junction, **a car hit a shoulder and turned over.**

—Joan Didion, "On Morality"

CUMULATIVE   **A car hit a shoulder and turned over** at midnight last night on the road from Las Vegas to Death Valley Junction.

ANSWERS AND COVERAGE: EXERCISE 19-3

Students are to expand each sentence by adding (a) an adjective, (b) an adverb, (c) a prepositional phrase, (d) a participial phrase, (e) an absolute phrase, (f) an adverb clause, and (g) an adjective clause. They can refer for guidance to the expansion techniques shown in Chart 98. Here is a possible set of answers for item 1:

a. We went to the *county* fair.

b. We went *happily* to the fair.

c. We went to the fair *in the park.*

d. *Tired of studying*, we went to the fair, *looking for a good time.*

e. *Textbooks left open on our desks*, we went to the fair.

f. *After we finished studying*, we went to the fair.

g. We went to the fair, *which had just opened.*

ADDITIONAL EXAMPLE

The following passage employs different sentence types. You may want to discuss with students the effect of the mixture.

> I froze when the voice said "Stop!" What did it want, I wondered, this voice that came from out of the shadows to my left? Although my knees were shaking, I hoped my voice would be steady. "What for?" I asked. "Because I said so, that's why. Don't go anywhere—yet." I didn't move, except that my eyes were almost popping out of my head trying to see the person with the voice. "Where's your car?" the voice asked. "Take me to it." "It's parked several blocks away," I objected. "Then go get it. Now!" "How do you know I'll come back?" I asked. "Because," the voice groaned, "I don't think you'd leave your best friend sitting in the street with a sprained ankle." "Well why didn't you say that in first place!" I shouted, then went to see if I could help Mike, the voice I thought I would know anywhere.
> —Emily Gordon

QUOTATION: ON WRITING

There is such an animal as a nonstylist, only they're not writers—they're typists.
—Truman Capote

Another technique for varying sentence structure is to start sentences with introductory words, PHRASES, or CLAUSES.

WORD   **Fortunately,** I taught myself to read before I had to face boring reading drills in school.
—Andrew Furman, student

PHRASE   **Along with cereal boxes and ketchup labels,** comic books were the primers that taught me how to read.
—Gloria Steinem

CLAUSE   **Long before I wrote stories,** I listened for stories.
—Eudora Welty, *One Writer's Beginnings*

Modifiers may appear in various positions within a sentence. Positioning modifiers offers you a chance to enhance your writing style with variety and emphasis. Here are sentences with the same modifiers in different positions. If you use this technique, take care to avoid placing modifiers in positions that create ambiguous meaning (see 15b.1).

Angrily, the physician slammed down the chart, **sternly** speaking to the patient.

The physician slammed down the chart **angrily,** speaking **sternly** to the patient.

The physician **angrily** slammed down the chart, speaking to the patient **sternly.**

❶ **PUNCTUATION ALERT:** For a discussion of commas with introductory material, see section 24b. ❗

EXERCISE 19-4

Consulting section 19e, combine each set of sentences by changing one sentence to a clause, phrase, or word that will modify the other sentence.

EXAMPLE   The ancestor of our pencil was the penicillum. The penicillum was a brush made of animal hairs that the Romans used for writing and drawing.

The ancestor of our pencil was the penicillum, *a brush made of animal hairs that the Romans used for writing and drawing.* [sentence changed to phrase]

1. These early writing implements were made of boar bristles; the hair of camels, badgers, and squirrels; and the down feathers of swans. This is according to the 1771 edition of the *Encyclopaedia Britannica.*

2. Graphite, a form of the element carbon, was to become a component of pencil lead. It would be the main component.

3. Cabinetmakers were producing the first version of the modern pencil by encasing strips of graphite in wood. This happened in the late 1600s.

ANSWERS AND COVERAGE: EXERCISE 19-4

Answers will vary. Here is one set of possibilities.

1. *According to the 1771 edition of the Encyclopaedia Britannica* [phrase], these early writing implements were made of boar bristles; the hair of camels, badgers, and squirrels; and the down feathers of swans.

2. Graphite, a form of the element carbon, was to become the *main* [word] component of pencil lead.

3. *In the late 1600s* [phrase], cabinetmakers were producing the first version of the modern pencil by encasing strips of graphite in wood.

→

4. They followed the sandwich-making principle. They sliced a strip of wood, cut a groove down the middle, glued the lead into the groove, and then glued the two halves together.

5. At one time, the ingredients of a fine pencil came from the geographically diverse areas of Siberia and Florida. Siberia is where the purest graphite was mined. Florida is where the best red cedar was grown.

6. When an acute shortage of southern red cedar developed in the United States during the early 1900s, pencil manufacturers bought old cedar fence posts. They were desperate.

7. The pencil makers had to substitute another kind of cedar. They dyed and perfumed it to match people's expectations of how a pencil should look and smell.

8. Pencils have had some unlikely promoters, such as the naturalist and writer Henry David Thoreau. He helped his father produce the highest-quality pencils in America during the 1840s.

9. The inventor Thomas Edison engaged a pencil factory to produce specially made stubby pencils just for him. He preferred short pencils.

10. The Scottish poet Robert Burns once lacked a pencil. He used his diamond ring to scratch verses on a windowpane.

19f Inverting standard word order

Standard word order in the English sentence places the SUBJECT before the VERB. Because this pattern is so common, it is set in people's minds, so any variation creates emphasis. **Inverted word order** places the verb before the subject. Used too often, inverted word order can be distracting; but used sparingly, it can be very effective.

STANDARD	**The mayor walked** in. **The governor walked** out.
INVERTED	In **walked the mayor.** Out **walked the governor.**
STANDARD	**Responsibilities begin** in dreams.
INVERTED	In dreams **begin responsibilities.**

—Delmore Schwartz, "In Dreams Begin Responsibilities"

19g Repeating important words or ideas to achieve emphasis

You can repeat some words to emphasize meaning, but choose the words carefully. Repeat words that contain a main idea or that use rhythm to focus attention on a main idea. Consider this passage, which uses deliberate repetition along with a variety of sentence lengths to deliver its meaning.

Answers and Coverage: Exercise 19-4 (continued)

4. *Following the sandwich-making principle,* [phrase] they sliced a strip of wood, cut a groove down the middle, glued the lead into the groove, and then glued the two halves together.

5. At one time, the ingredients of a fine pencil came from the geographically diverse areas of Siberia, *where the purest graphite was mined,* [clause] and Florida, *where the best red cedar was grown.* [clause]

6. When an acute shortage of southern red cedar developed in the United States during the early 1900s, *desperate* [word] pencil manufacturers bought old cedar fence posts.

7. The pencil makers had to substitute another kind of cedar, *so they dyed and perfumed it to match people's expectations of how a pencil should look and smell.* [clause]

8. Pencils have had some unlikely promoters, such as the naturalist and writer Henry David Thoreau, *who helped his father produce the highest-quality pencils in America during the 1840s.* [clause]

9. The inventor Thomas Edison engaged a pencil factory to produce specially made stubby pencils just for him *because he preferred short pencils.* [clause]

10. *Lacking a pencil,* [phrase] the Scottish poet Robert Burns once used his diamond ring to scratch verses on a windowpane.

Coal is **black** and it warms your house and cooks your food. The night is **black,** which has a moon, and a million stars, and is beautiful. Sleep is **black** which gives you rest, so you wake up **feeling good.** I am **black. I feel** very **good** this evening.

—Langston Hughes, "That Word *Black*"

Hughes repeats the word *black*, each time linking it to something related to joy and beauty. The rhythm that results from the deliberate repetition of *black* and *good* emphasizes Hughes's message and helps the reader remember it.

Use deliberate repetition sparingly, with central words, and only when your meaning justifies the technique. Consider this passage, which is the result of limited vocabulary and a dull, unvaried style. Although few synonyms exist for the words *insurance agent, car,* and *model,* some do, and pronouns can help. Also, the sentence structure has no variety.

NO   An insurance agent can be an excellent adviser when you want to buy a car. An insurance agent has records on most cars. An insurance agent knows which models tend to have most accidents. An insurance agent can tell you which models are the most expensive to repair if they are in a collision. An insurance agent can tell you which models are most likely to be stolen.

YES   If you are thinking of buying a new car, an insurance agent, who has complete records on most cars, can be an excellent adviser. For example, he or she knows which models are prone to accidents. Did you know that some car designs suffer more damage than others in a collision? If you want to know which cars crumple more than others and which are least expensive to repair, ask an insurance agent. Similarly, some models are more likely to be stolen, so find out from the person who specializes in dealing with claims.

EXERCISE 19-5

Consulting all sections of this chapter, revise this paragraph to achieve emphasis through varied sentence length and deliberate repetition. You can reduce or increase the number of sentences, and you can drop words to reduce unneeded repetition. Each writer's revision will vary somewhat, but try to include at least one question or exclamation (19c) and one instance of inverted word order (19f).

The chimney is one of civilization's great technological innovations. The chimney represents a major step up from a hole in the roof or a slit in the wall. The heating of houses was not an urgent problem in the warm climates of ancient Egypt and Mesopotamia. Scholars believed this until a palace was uncovered during a recent excavation of the great lost city of Mari on the upper Euphrates River in ancient

ANSWERS AND COVERAGE: EXERCISE 19-5

Answers will vary. One possible revision is shown here.

One of civilization's great technological innovations, [19e, sentence converted into appositive to modify] the chimney represents a major step up from a hole in the roof or a slit in the wall. *In the warm climates of ancient Egypt and Mesopotamia,* [19e.2, modifiers positioned for effect] the heating of houses was not an urgent problem. *So scholars believed* [19e.2, positioning modifiers for effect, with *this* changed to *so*] until a *four-thousand-year-old palace that was peppered with chimneys* was uncovered during a recent excavation of the great lost city of Mari on the upper Euphrates River in ancient Persia. [19b.1, short sentences combined] Along came the Romans two thousand years later. [19f, inverting standard word order] The Romans, *who* were [19b.2, sentence converted into relative clause] engineering geniuses, developed elaborate chimneys as part of their heating systems. *After the Roman empire fell in the fourth century A.D.,* nobody [19b.1, short sentences combined into one] from the former colonies knew how to make chimneys. For four centuries, western Europe had no chimneys. *How did chimneys finally get to western Europe?* [19c, revised to question] Nobody is quite sure. [19b.3, revised for short sentence] *A current theory holds that* around A.D. 800, chimneys were brought by Syrian and Egyptian traders *from the East.* [19b.3, short sentences combined into one long sentence]

Persia. The palace, which was four thousand years old, was peppered with chimneys. Two thousand years later, the Romans came along. The Romans were engineering geniuses. The Romans developed elaborate chimneys as part of their hot-air heating systems. The Roman empire declined in the fourth century A.D., After then, no one from the former colonies knew how to make chimneys. For four centuries, western Europe had no chimneys. So the simple question has always been how chimneys finally got to western Europe. Nobody is quite sure, but here is what a current theory holds. Around A.D. 800, chimneys were brought by Syrian and Egyptian traders. They were from the East.

EXERCISE 19-6

Consulting all sections of this chapter, use techniques of variety and emphasis to revise the following paragraph.

Huge caves known as the Carlsbad Caverns are hidden beneath the sands of New Mexico. The caverns contain a mysterious underground world. More than 20 miles of caves have been discovered. Miles more are found each year. The desert is above. In the desert, the sun shines. The desert is where the wind blows. Birds sing. Coyotes howl. Below in the caverns, no daylight penetrates. The air is cold and still. There are no winds or animal sounds. Such sounds do not disturb the silence. It is amazing to experience the contrast between the desert and the caves. Visitors to the caverns can see. Electric lights are placed there to illuminate the caves. The lights are also placed for dramatic effect. The lights reveal unusual rock formations. Spikes of rock hang from the ceiling. Tall, pointy rocks rise from the floor. Delicate sheets of thin rock are hanging like drapery. The slow drip of minerals through the caves' limestone roof formed them all. Some of the caves contain mysterious underground lakes. These caves echo with watery noises and glimmer with reflected light. Others are huge chambers, and their ceilings rise 200 feet. Not many people would have guessed that these caves beneath the desert originated as a coral reef in an ancient sea.

ANSWERS AND COVERAGE: EXERCISE 19-6

Answers will vary. This is a summary exercise, so it should reflect many of the techniques of variety and emphasis discussed in this chapter. Here is one answer; many others are possible.

Hidden beneath the sands of New Mexico, [19e.1, participial phrase to modify] the huge caves known as the Carlsbad Caverns contain a mysterious underground world. [19b.1, combined two short sentences] More than 20 miles of caves have been discovered, and miles more are found each year. [19b.3, revise for suitable mix by combining two sentences] In the desert above, the sun shines, the wind blows, birds sing, and coyotes howl. [19b.1, revise to avoid too many short sentences by combining] Below in the caverns, where no daylight penetrates, [19e.1, adjective clause to modify] the air is cold and still. No winds or animal sounds disturb the silence. [19b.3, revise for suitable mix by combining two sentences] The contrast between the desert and the caves is amazing! [19c, exclamation for variety] Visitors to the caverns can see because electric lights are placed there to illuminate the caves. [19e.1, adverb clause to modify] The lights, which are placed for dramatic effect, [19e.1, adjective clause to modify] reveal unusual rock formations. Spikes of rock hang from the ceiling, and tall, pointy rocks rise from the floor. [19b.3, combined sentences to vary sentence length] Hanging like drapery are delicate sheets of thin rock. [19f, inverted word order] All were formed by the slow drip of minerals through the caves' limestone roof. [19e.2, repositioned modifier *all* for emphasis] Some of the caves, which echo with watery noises and glimmer with reflected light, contain mysterious underground lakes. [19e.2, periodic sentence] Others are huge chambers whose ceilings rise 200 feet. [19e.1, adjective clause to modify] Who would have guessed that these caves beneath the desert originated as a coral reef in an ancient sea? [19c, question for variety]

20

UNDERSTANDING THE MEANING OF WORDS

Evolving over centuries into a rich language, American English reflects many cultures that have merged in our melting-pot society. The earliest varieties of American English can be traced from sixteenth-century Elizabethan English—the language of Shakespeare. As the United States expanded, so did American English. Vocabulary, spelling, and other changes from Elizabethan forms occurred. Distinctly American words originated colloquially—in spoken language—and words from all the cultures settling the United States became part of the language. Food names, for example, show how other languages and cultures loaned words to English. Africans brought the words *okra, gumbo,* and *goober* (peanut); Spanish and Latin American peoples contributed *tortilla, taco, burrito,* and *enchilada.* Greek gave us *pita,* Cantonese *chow,* and Japanese *sushi.* American English creates a truly international *smorgasbord,* a Swedish word meaning "a table bearing a wide variety of foods."

Etymology is the study of the origins and historical development of words, including changes in form and meaning. For example, *alphabet* comes from the names of the first two letters in Greek, *alpha* and *beta.* The meanings of some words change with time. For example, as W. Nelson Francis points out in *The English Language,* the word *nice* "has been used at one time or another in its 700-year history to mean . . . foolish, wanton, strange, lazy, coy, modest, fastidious, refined, precise, subtle, slender, critical, attentive, minutely accurate, dainty, appetizing, agreeable."

To use American English well, you want to be aware of the kinds of information that dictionaries offer (20a), to know how to choose exact words (20b), and to use strategies that actively build your vocabulary (20c).

20a Using dictionaries

Good dictionaries show how language has been used and is currently being used. Each dictionary entry gives the meaning of the word and much additional important information. Many dictionaries also include essays on the history and use of language.

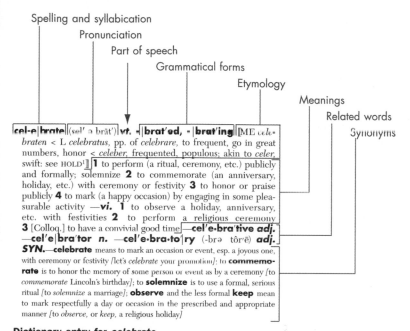

Spelling and syllabication
Pronunciation
Part of speech
Grammatical forms
Etymology
Meanings
Related words
Synonyms

cel·e|brate (sel′ə brāt′) **vt.** **-|brat′ed, -|brat′ing** [ME cele-braten < L celebratus, pp. of celebrare, to frequent, go in great numbers, honor < celeber, frequented, populous; akin to celer, swift: see HOLD¹] **1** to perform (a ritual, ceremony, etc.) publicly and formally; solemnize **2** to commemorate (an anniversary, holiday, etc.) with ceremony or festivity **3** to honor or praise publicly **4** to mark (a happy occasion) by engaging in some pleasurable activity —**vi.** **1** to observe a holiday, anniversary, etc. with festivities **2** to perform a religious ceremony **3** [Colloq.] to have a convivial good time —**cel′e|bra′tive adj.** —**cel′e|bra′tor n.** —**cel′e·bra·to′ry** (-brə tôr′ē) **adj.** **SYN.**—**celebrate** means to mark an occasion or event, esp. a joyous one, with ceremony or festivity [let's celebrate your promotion]; to **commemorate** is to honor the memory of some person or event as by a ceremony [to commemorate Lincoln's birthday]; to **solemnize** is to use a formal, serious ritual [to solemnize a marriage]; **observe** and the less formal **keep** mean to mark respectfully a day or occasion in the prescribed and appropriate manner [to observe, or keep, a religious holiday]

Dictionary entry for *celebrate*

20a.1 Understanding all parts of a dictionary entry

A dictionary entry usually includes items 1 through 11, and sometimes 12 and 13, in the list that starts below. As you use the list, consult the entry shown here for *celebrate*, from *Webster's New World Dictionary of American English*, Third College Edition.

1. **Spelling.** If more than one spelling is shown, the first is the most commonly used, and the others are acceptable.

    Celebrate has only one spelling.

2. **Word division.** Dots (or bars, in some dictionaries) separate the syllables of a word. Writers can hyphenate at syllables as long as the rules in section 22d are not violated. To help writers, *Webster's New World Dictionary*, Third College Edition, uses a hairline (a thin vertical line) to indicate any syllable break that should not be used for hyphenating.

    Ce·le|brate has three syllables: *cel, e,* and *brate.* This dictionary recommends hyphenating the word *cel-ebrate* but not *cele-brate.*

3. **Pronunciation.** The symbols in parentheses show pronunciation. If more than one pronunciation is given, the first is the most common, and the others are acceptable. A guide to the pronunciation of the symbols appears in the front of most dictionaries, and

WORD DERIVATION

The ancient Greeks felt that all foreigners were savages, speaking crude, primitive languages. *Barbarous* and *barbaric* come from the nonsense syllables the Greeks used in imitation of foreign speech: *barbar.*

TEACHING TIP

Many students are sufficiently unsure about alphabetical order to feel it necessary to repeat the entire alphabet to find out if *p* follows *m* or not. Their insecurity causes a number of problems; for example, it prevents them from using the guidewords in dictionaries. Since the ability to use alphabetical order is a great help in doing all research, you may want to ask students to sharpen their skills by alphabetizing the following words:

Out of Order	*Alphabetical Order*
1. implicate	1. antelope
2. bureau	2. bureau
3. panther	3. contemplate
4. contemplate	4. implicate
5. tarpaulin	5. implore
6. Ohio	6. McKinley
7. McKinley	7. M.D.
8. implore	8. Ohio
9. M.D.	9. panther
10. antelope	10. tarpaulin

A second activity that can help students improve their sense of alphabetical order asks them to think of a word that should come between pairs of words such as those listed below:

1. epicurean _____ equestrian
2. Massachusetts _____ material
3. slicker _____ slope
4. tribute _____ trio
5. bacon _____ bake

TEACHING TIP

Words dealing with cooking or food are often put to other uses. You can ask students to find the original meanings of the following words, then to write sentences in which they are used in situations that have nothing to do with food.

1. hodgepodge (a pot of beans, meat, and barley)
2. goulash (a Hungarian stew)
3. mishmash (an English stew dating back to the fifteenth century)
4. pastiche (a meat pie)
5. smorgasbord (a Swedish buffet)

TEACHING TIP

Students may find it interesting to discover that different dictionaries do not always provide the same information about specific words. To identify some differences (and even contradictions), you can ask students to bring to class their findings about the spelling, pronunciation, syllabification, etymology, and usage of the following words. Where differences appear, students can question and discuss the reasons for them.

1. gumbo
2. cab
3. broadcast
4. rhetoric
5. nachos

WORD DERIVATION

Georgia was named for King George II of England. *Virginia* was named for Elizabeth I, who was known as the Virgin Queen. Naming new territories after monarchs and their family members was a common practice among explorers who wanted to gain favor or give thanks for patronage.

some dictionaries provide a brief guide to the most common symbols at the bottom of pages.

Celebrate is pronounced *sel′ ə brāt.* The accent mark after the *l* shows that the stressed syllable is *sel.* The symbol ə, called a *schwa,* is pronounced "uh," as in *ago.* The line over the *a* indicates the long *a* sound, as in *ate.*

4. **Part of speech labels.** Abbreviations, explained in the front of the dictionary, indicate parts of speech. Many words can function as more than one part of speech.

Celebrate is a TRANSITIVE VERB (*vt.*), for which four definitions are given; it is also an INTRANSITIVE VERB (*vi.*), for which three definitions are given.

5. **Grammatical forms.** This information tells of variations in grammar: for a VERB, its principal parts and form variations; for a NOUN, its plural if formed other than by adding only *-s;* for an ADJECTIVE or ADVERB, its comparative and superlative forms, if formed with suffixes.

The principal parts of the verb *celebrate* are *celebrated* and *celebrating.*

6. **Etymology.** This information traces the way that the word has evolved through other languages over the years to become the word and meaning in current use.

Celebrate comes from a Middle English (*ME*) word that is derived from the Latin (*L*). The meaning evolved from the idea of "frequenting, going in great numbers, honoring," a meaning reflected by the first definition in the entry.

7. **Definitions.** If a word has more than one meaning, the definitions are numbered in most dictionaries from the oldest to the newest meaning. A few dictionaries start with the most common use.

The oldest meaning of *celebrate* is given first, and its most recent use is given last (item 4 in the *vt.* list and item 3 in the *vi.* list).

8. **Usage labels.** If the use of a word is special, a usage label explains how the word should be used. Chart 99 explains the most common usage labels in dictionaries.

The most recent meaning of *celebrate* as an intransitive verb (*vi.*) is colloquial. Therefore, such use is informal and probably should be avoided in academic writing.

9. **Field labels.** When a word applies to a specialized area of study, such as chemistry or law, an abbreviation alerts a reader to the specialized meaning. For example, along with its everyday meanings, the word *center* has specialized meanings in the fields of sports, mechanics, the military, and politics.

10. **Related words.** Words based on the defined word appear, with their part of speech, at the end of the definitions.

Words related to *celebrate* are *celebrative* (adjective), *celebrator* (noun), and *celebratory* (adjective).

11. **Synonyms and antonyms,** if any. **Synonyms** are words that are close in meaning. They are listed and their subtle differences are explained. Also, for each word in the list of synonyms, a cross-reference appears at that word's entry so that the reader can tell where to find the complete list. For example, at the entry *commemorate*, this information appears: **syn.** CELEBRATE. It means that synonyms for *commemorate* can be found at the entry for *celebrate*. **Antonyms** are words that are opposite in meaning to the word defined. Any antonyms are listed after any synonyms.

> *Celebrate* and four of its synonyms are listed and explained; it has no antonyms.

12. **Idioms,** if any. When the defined word is an IDIOM, either in itself or when combined with other words, it has a meaning that differs from its usual meaning. For example, in *Webster's New World Dictionary*, the entry for *ceiling* lists and defines the idiom *hit the ceiling*. If an idiom is considered slang or colloquial, a usage label (see item 8 on this list and section 20a.2) alerts the reader.

13. **Examples.** Some definitions include a sample phrase or sentence that illustrates the defined word in use.

20a.2 Understanding usage labels

Usage refers to the customary manner of using particular words or phrases. As a writer, you can refer to the **usage labels** in a dictionary to help you decide when a word is appropriate for use. For example, a word labeled *slang* usually is not suitable for academic writing unless you are writing about the word itself. A word labeled *poetic* is likely to be found in poetry, not in prose.

The concept of usage also applies to the customary manner of using certain words (for example, *among* versus *between*). For a list and explanation of such words, see the Usage Glossary toward the back of this handbook.

Usage labels		99
Label	**Definition**	**Example**
COLLOQUIAL	Characteristic of conversation and informal writing	*pa* [father] *ma* [mother]
SLANG	Not considered part of standard language but sometimes used in informal conversation	*whirlybird* [helicopter]

→

QUOTATION: ON WRITING

Many writers confess to observing certain professional superstitions which the non-writer would find absurd. Some break off a day's writing in mid-sentence, sure of how the sentence is to continue, so that the next day they can complete it, and thus find themselves in an already forward-moving phase of work. Others make a great fuss over having their materials arranged on their desks in exactly the same way throughout the writing of a work: the completed pages, the notes for those to come, the position of the dictionaries, the very direction of the lie of the bundle of pencils beside the typewriter, or the way the pen is pointing in its rack . . . all these are more than matters of simple convenience or efficiency. They signify continuity. They seem like a promise that what has gone well so far will continue to do so if the proper acts of propitiation are made.

—Paul Horgan

ANSWERS: EXERCISE 20-1

Answers will vary.

EXTRA EXERCISE B

List two synonyms for each of the following words. On the basis of information that you can find about them in a dictionary, explain the differences between the pairs of synonyms. (Answers will vary).

1. indulge
2. egotism
3. lazy
4. fame
5. friendly
6. frugal
7. red
8. good
9. govern
10. industry

WORD DERIVATION

New Mexico is a literal translation of the Spanish *Nuevo Méjico*. *Méjico* is the Spanish rendering of *Mexitli*, the name of an Aztec war god.

Usage labels *(continued)*		99
Label	**Definition**	**Example**
OBSOLETE	No longer used; occurred in earlier writing	*betimes* [promptly, quickly]
POETIC	Found in poetry or poetic prose	*o'er* [for *over*]
DIALECT	Used only in some geographical areas	*poke* [Southern: a bag or sack]

EXERCISE 20-1

Consulting sections 20a.1 and 20a.2, use a dictionary with entries that include a list of synonyms and some labels, as in the entry for *celebrate* on page 355. Then, write an explanation of each part, assuming that your audience is a student unfamiliar with such entries.

20a.3 Using unabridged dictionaries

Unabridged means "not shortened." Of the various kinds of dictionaries, unabridged dictionaries have the most extensive, accurate, complete, and scholarly entries. They give many examples of current uses and changes in meanings over time. They include infrequently used words that abridged dictionaries (see 20a.4) often omit.

The most comprehensive, authoritative unabridged dictionary of English is the *Oxford English Dictionary (OED)*. Its second edition has twenty volumes defining more than 616,500 words and terms. The *OED* traces each word's history, using quotations to illustrate changes in meaning and spelling over the life of the word. The second edition consists of three parts: (1) the first edition of the *OED*, which is largely unchanged; (2) the contents of the four supplements that accompanied the first edition; and (3) approximately 5,000 words or terms new to the second edition.

Its comprehensive historical information and examples about English words make the *OED* a specialized dictionary (20a.5) as well as an unabridged dictionary. The following small excerpt from the second edition's entry for *celebrate* shows the kinds of information that you can get from the *OED*. Compare it with the entry for *celebrate* on page 355 taken from *Webster's New World Dictionary of American English*, Third College Edition. In addition to the usual dictionary features, the *OED* offers a history of the word (*celebrate*'s first recorded use was in 1656). Note the historical examples of *celebrate* following its third meaning.

celebrate ('sɛlibreit), *v.* [f. prec., or on analogy of vbs. so
formed. See -ATE³.]
(**1656** BLOUNT *Glossogr.*, *Celebrate*, to frequent, to solemnize with
an Assembly of men, to make famous, also to keep a festival day or
other time with great solemnity.)

3. To observe with solemn rites (a day, festival, season); to
honour with religious ceremonies, festivities, or other
observances (an event, occasion). Also *absol.* (see quot.
1937).
    1560 BIBLE (Genev.) *Lev.* xxiii. 32 From euen to euen shall ye
celebrate [WYCL. halowe, COVERD. kepe] your Sabbath. **1591**
SHAKS. I *Hen. VI,* I. VI. 14 Feast and banquet in the open streets,
To celebrate the joy that God hath given us. **1672** DRYDEN *Conq.
Granada* 1. i, with Pomp and Sports my Love I celebrate. **1697** —
Virg. Georg. I. 466 Celebrate the mighty Mother's Day. **1737** N.
CLARKE *Hist. Bible* IX. (1840) I. 376 The Feast of Tabernacles
being then celebrating. **1841** Lane *Arab. Nts.* I. 71 The Minor
Festival . . is celebrated with more rejoicing than the other. **1929**
Randolph Enterprise (Elkins, W. Va.) 26 Sept. 3/2 [He] came over . .
Sunday night to celebrate a little. **1937** PARTRIDGE *Dict. Slang*
136/1 *Celebrate,* v.i., to drink in honour of an event or a person;
hence, to drink joyously. **1963** J. T. STORY *Something for Nothing* i.
40 It's Treasure's wedding day. Somebody's got to celebrate.

Sample entry from the *Oxford English Dictionary*

For most college students, *Webster's Third New International Dictionary of the English Language* provides any needed information. This
highly respected one-volume work has more than 470,000 entries and is
especially strong in new scientific and technical terms. It uses quotations
to show various meanings, and its definitions are given in chronological
order of their appearance in the language.

20a.4 Using abridged dictionaries

Abridged means "shortened." Abridged dictionaries contain the most
commonly used words. They are convenient in size and economical to buy,
and they serve as practical reference books for writers and readers. Many
good abridged dictionaries are referred to as "college" editions because
they serve the needs of most college students. Typical of these is *Webster's
New World Dictionary of American English,* Third College Edition, which
has more than 200,000 entries and gives detailed etymologies. Names of
people, places, abbreviations, and foreign expressions appear in the main
body of the work (rather than in appendixes). Definitions appear in chronological order of their acceptance into the language. *Webster's New World
Dictionary* has a contemporary American emphasis. It uses a star symbol
for Americanisms—words that first became part of the language in the
United States. It gives the origins of American place names (cities, states,
rivers, and so on). It supplies usage labels for many words and gives synonyms, often in lists that explain distinctions among closely related words.
In an appendix, punctuation, italics, numbers, capitalization, abbreviations,

WORD DERIVATION

Nevada is a shortening of the Spanish
Sierra Nevada ("snowy range"), a mountain range in eastern California.

WORD DERIVATION

The state of Pennsylvania is named after a
man and the local geography. *Sylvania*
means "wooded land" in Latin. The *Penn*
part is less clear. Some say that the *Penn*
is William Penn, the colonist to whom
King Charles II of England gave the land.
Others say that under orders from King
Charles, Penn named the land after his
own late father, an English admiral. In
either case, the admiral had died before
the king could repay a debt of 16,000
pounds. The king gave the land to William
Penn in settlement of the debt—and to
keep the religious activist out of England.

WORD DERIVATION

Rhode Island's etymology is a mystery.
There are two theories. According to one,
Italian explorer Giovanni da Verrazano saw
a resemblance between the island on
which the city of Newport is now located
and the Greek island of Rhodes. According to the second, Dutch explorers named
the area *Roode Eylandt* ("red island")
because of its red clay soil.

TEACHING TIP

You may want to ask students to work in
groups to research the origins of a slang
expression, a commonly used phrase, or a
regional expression of their own choice.
The results can take the form of an oral
report to the rest of the class.

WORD DERIVATION

Florida was named by explorer Ponce de
León. The name is Spanish for "abounding
in flowers."

BACKGROUND

Oxford University publishes the *Oxford English Dictionary*, commonly known as the *OED*. The idea for the first edition came from a paper delivered in 1857 to Britain's Philological Society by Richard Trench, Dean of Westminster; it was titled "On Some Deficiencies in Our English Dictionaries." His concerns led the society to make plans for compiling a completely new dictionary that would include "every word occurring in the literature of the language." In 1859, Herbert Coleridge, a grandson of the poet, became editor of the new work, expecting to publish it in two years. After his untimely death, he was succeeded by Frederick J. Furnivall, who agreed to devote four or five years to producing the first part of the dictionary. Overburdened by work, Furnivall in 1876 turned over his duties to James Murray, who agreed to produce a dictionary of between 6,000 and 7,000 pages within ten years. Beginning with nearly two tons of materials collected by Furnivall, he made a public appeal for a thousand readers of English to assist with finding quotations for unusual as well as ordinary words. Working twelve to fifteen hours a day, with the help of his eleven children, Murray had, by 1894, completed sections for the letters *A, B, C,* and *D,* whereupon the work was first called *The Oxford English Dictionary*. Murray died in 1915 with one-sixth of the work unfinished. The completed dictionary emerged in 1928 after seventy years of work by a series of devoted researchers. Since that time, supplements to the original work have been published.

The latest edition combines the original *OED* and the supplements, which add 5,000 new words as well as revised, corrected, and updated information. Revision will continue, and new supplements will appear as time goes on. Meanwhile, the first edition is now available in a CD-ROM version that presents not only the full text of the *OED*, but also eight indexes.

and source documentation are discussed. Its introductory material includes essays on the English language and on etymology.

🌐 **ESL NOTE:** A useful dictionary for students who speak English as a second language is the *Dictionary of American English* published by Addison Wesley Longman. You can also find a list of specialized dictionaries in section 20a.5. ◆

20a.5   Using specialized dictionaries of English

A **specialized dictionary** focuses on a single area, such as *slang, word origins, synonyms, antonyms, usage,* or some other aspect of language. Most college libraries include all or some of the volumes listed here.

	SPECIALIZED DICTIONARIES
SYNONYMS	*New Roget's Thesaurus of the English Language in Dictionary Form*
USAGE	*Modern American Usage,* ed. Jacques Barzun
IDIOMS	*A Dictionary of American Idioms,* by Adam Makkai *Dictionary of English Idioms*
REGIONALISMS	*Dictionary of American Regional English,* ed. Frederic Cassidy
SLANG	*Dictionary of Slang and Unconventional English,* ed. Eric Partridge *Dictionary of American Slang,* ed. Harold Wentworth and Stuart Berg Flexner [out of print, but available in many libraries] *The Thesaurus of Slang,* by Esther Lewin and Albert E. Lewin *NTC's Dictionary of American Slang and Colloquial Expressions,* by Richard A. Spear
ETYMOLOGIES	*Dictionary of Word and Phrase Origins,* ed. William Morris and Mary Morris *Origins: A Short Etymological Dictionary of Modern English,* ed. Eric Partridge [out of print, but available in many libraries]

20a.6   Using CD-ROM dictionaries

Several major dictionaries are available on floppy disks or CD-ROMs, including *Merriam-Webster's Collegiate Dictionary, The Random House Dictionary, Webster's Unabridged Dictionary,* and both long and short versions of the *Oxford English Dictionary*.

20b Choosing exact words

The English language offers a wealth of words for a writer to choose from. **Diction,** the term for choice of words, affects the clarity and impact of the message that you want your sentences to deliver. As a writer, you want to use words that perfectly fit the particular context of each piece of writing and convey your exact meaning.

20b.1 Understanding denotation and connotation

When you look up a word in the dictionary to find out what it means, you are looking for its **denotation.** For example, the one denotation of the word *semester* is "a period of time, about eighteen weeks, that makes up part of a school or college year."

Readers expect words to be used according to their established meanings for their established functions. Exactness is essential. When you use a thesaurus or other dictionary of synonyms, be aware that subtle shades of meaning create distinctions among words that have the same general definition. These small differences in meaning allow you to be very precise in choosing just the right word, but they also oblige you to make sure that you know the precise meanings your words convey. For instance, describing a person famous for praiseworthy achievements in public life as *notorious* would be wrong. Although *notorious* means "well-known" and "publicly discussed"—which famous people are likely to be—the term also carries the meaning "unfavorably known or talked about." George Washington is *famous*, not *notorious*. Al Capone, by contrast, is *notorious*.

Here is another example. *Obdurate* means "not easily moved to pity or sympathy," and its synonyms include *inflexible, obstinate, stubborn,* and *hardened.* The synonym *hardened* for *obdurate,* however, might prompt someone unfamiliar with *obdurate* to use the word incorrectly.

NO   Footprints showed in the **obdurate** concrete.

Here are two correct uses of *obdurate:*

YES   The supervisor remained **obdurate** in refusing to accept excuses.

YES   My **obdurate** roommates will not let my pet boa constrictor live in the bathtub.

💻 **COMPUTER ALERT:** Be especially careful about using the thesaurus in your word-processing program. Unless you know the exact meaning of an offered synonym, as well as its part of speech, you may introduce a grammatical error or a "wrong word" error into your writing. For example, one word-processing program's thesaurus offers the choices *low, below, beneath,* and *subterranean* as synonyms for *deep* with the sense

TEACHING TIP

To underscore the importance of subtle shades of meaning and connotation, you might ask your students how they would react to each of the following statements. Once their egos are involved, students will quickly see that not all synonyms are equivalent.

You are wrong.
You are incorrect.
What you say is false.
You are inaccurate.
You are imprecise.
You are evil.
You are improper.
You are unethical.
You are unrighteous.
You are bad.
You are willfully misleading.

WORD DERIVATION

Louisiana comes from *La Louisianne*. The French, who controlled the Mississippi Valley before selling the area to the United States in 1803, had named the area after their king, Louis XIV.

ANSWERS AND COVERAGE: EXERCISE 20-2

The response to this exercise is likely to elicit much debate, given that shades of connotative meaning are often fairly personal. The following are some possible answers.

→

of "low (down, inside)." None of these words, however, could replace *deep* in many sentences, including this one: *Mine shaft number four is too **deep** [not too low, below, beneath, or subterranean] to be filled with sand or rocks.* ◘

Connotation refers to ideas implied by a word but not directly indicated. Connotations involve associations and emotional overtones that go beyond the definition of a word. For example, the word *home* usually evokes more emotion than its denotation "a dwelling place" or its synonym *house*. *Home* may have very pleasant connotations of warmth, security, the love of family. Or *home* may have unpleasant connotations of an institution for elderly or sick people. As a student writer, be aware of the potential of connotation to help your words deliver their meaning. Connotations are never completely fixed, for they can vary with different contexts for a word. Still, people can communicate effectively because most words have relatively stable connotations and denotations in most contexts.

Being sensitive to the differences between the denotation and connotation of a word is essential for critical thinking. Critical thinkers must first consider material at its literal level (see 5d.1). Doing so calls for dealing with the denotation of words. Next, critical thinkers must move to the inferential level (see 5d.2)—to what is implied but not explicitly stated. Connotations of words often carry the inferential message, as illustrated in Chart 100.

◉   **Comparing denotation and connotation**   **100**

SAMPLE WORD	DENOTATION	CONNOTATION
additive	an added substance	something unnatural and perhaps harmful, especially in food
cheap	inexpensive	of products, low quality; of people, stingy
nuclear meltdown	melting of fuel rods in a nuclear reactor, releasing dangerous radiation	specter of imminent death or eventual cancer; poisoning of food chain

---

EXERCISE 20-2

Consulting section 20b.1, list the words in each set under one of three headings: "Neutral" if you think it has no connotations; "Positive" if you think it has good connotations; "Negative" if you think it has bad connotations. If you think a word fits into more than one group, put it under each heading that applies, and be ready to explain your choices. If you are unsure of a word, consult your dictionary.

EXAMPLE   grand, big, bulky, significant, oversized

> *Neutral:* big; *Positive:* grand, significant; *Negative:* bulky, oversized

1. harmony, sound, racket, shriek, melody, music, noise, pitch, voice
2. talkative, articulate, chattering, eloquent, vocal, verbose, gossipy, fluent, gabby
3. decorative, beautiful, modern, ornate, overelaborate, dazzling, flashy, elegant, sparkling
4. long, lingering, enduring, continued, drawn-out, stretched, never-ending, unbreakable, incessant
5. calculating, shrewd, crafty, ingenious, keen, sensible, sly, smooth, underhanded

20b.2 Using specific and concrete language to bring life to general and abstract language

Specific words identify individual items in a group (*Oldsmobile, Honda, Ford*). **General** words relate to an overall group (*car*). **Concrete** words identify persons and things that can be perceived by the senses—seen, heard, tasted, felt, smelled (*the black padded vinyl dashboard of my car*). **Abstract** words denote qualities, concepts, relationships, acts, conditions, ideas (*transportation*).

As a writer, you want to choose words suitable for your writing purpose and your audience. Usually, specific and concrete words are livelier than general and abstract words. Whenever you choose to be general and abstract, be sure to supply enough specific, concrete details and examples to illustrate your generalizations and abstractions effectively. Consider how sentences with general words come to life when they are revised with words that refer to specifics.

GENERAL	My car has a great deal of power, and it is very quick.
SPECIFIC	My 220-horsepower Sportfire can go from zero to fifty in six seconds.
GENERAL	The car gets good gas mileage.
SPECIFIC	The Contempo gets about 35 mpg on the highway and 30 mpg in the city.
GENERAL	Her car is comfortable and easy to drive.
SPECIFIC	When she drives her new Prestigia on a five-hour trip, she arrives refreshed and does not need a long nap to recover, as she did when she drove her ten-year-old Upushme.

Specific language is not always preferable to general language, nor is concrete language always preferable to abstract language. Effective writing usually combines them. Consider the following from an effective essay comparing cars:

GENERAL AND SPECIFIC COMBINED

GENERAL SPECIFIC SPECIFIC GENERAL
My car, a **220-horsepower Sportfire,** is **quick.** It accelerates

SPECIFIC SPECIFIC SPECIFIC
from 0 to 50 miles per hour in **6 seconds**—but it gets only **18 miles**

SPECIFIC GENERAL GENERAL
per gallon. The **Contempo,** by contrast, gets **very good** gas **mileage:**

SPECIFIC GENERAL SPECIFIC GENERAL
about **35 mpg** in **highway driving** and **30 mpg** when **traffic**

SPECIFIC GENERAL SPECIFIC
is **bumper to bumper** or when **car trips** are **frequent and short.**

Do not overdo being specific and concrete. If you want to inform a nonspecialist reader about possible automobile fuels other than gasoline, do name the fuels and be very specific about their advantages and drawbacks. Do not go into a detailed, highly technical discussion of the chemical profiles of the fuels. Always base your choices on an awareness of your purpose for writing (see 1b) and your audience (see 1c).

EXERCISE 20-3

Consulting section 20b.2, revise the following paragraph by providing specific and concrete words and phrases to explain and enliven the ideas presented here in general and abstract language. As needed, you can revise these sentences to accommodate your changes in language.

> The house for rent was exactly what I wanted. It had trees on the lawn and a driveway for my car. It had a porch, and flowers grew near the doorway. I was thrilled that the rent was even less money than I had hoped to spend. The real estate broker said I could move in that very day. I called a friend, who owned a truck, and asked him to help me move in. We got started that afternoon and almost finished unpacking all the boxes by that evening.

20c Increasing your vocabulary

The benefits of increasing your vocabulary are many. The more words you know, the more easily and the faster you can read. A large, rich

ANSWER: EXERCISE 20-3

Because of the many possibilities for rewording posed by this exercise, the answers are likely to vary widely. Students may enjoy comparing the different choices they have made. The important principle for revision is that the new versions should have a high degree of specificity and concreteness. Here is an example of an acceptable response.

The brick two-story colonial was exactly what I wanted to rent. It had three white birch trees spread out across the green lawn and a long, narrow driveway for my new Honda sedan. It had a porch with a set of oak chairs and a coffee table, and yellow and pink tulips grew on either side of the walkway leading up to the red front door. I was thrilled that the rent was even $400 less per month than I had been willing to spend. The friendly real estate broker said I could move my furniture into the house that very day. I called an old friend, who owned a four-wheel-drive Jeep Cherokee, and asked him to help me move all my belongings from my one-bedroom apartment. We got started around 1 o'clock in the afternoon and had almost finished unpacking the dozens of boxes by 9:30 that same evening.

vocabulary also helps you understand ideas and communicate them clearly and effectively in your writing. Use the techniques described in Chart 101.

 Techniques for building your vocabulary   **101**

To Find Words

■ Use a highlighter pen to mark all unfamiliar words in your own textbooks and other reading material. Then, define the words in the margin so that you can study the meaning in context. Use context clues (see 20c.2) to figure out definitions, or look up the words in a dictionary. Write each word and its definitions on an index card or in a notebook.

■ Listen carefully to learn how speakers use the language. Jot down new words to look up later. Write each word and its definitions on an index card or in a notebook.

To Study Words

■ Select some words to study each week. Put the date next to the word so that you can keep track of your goals. Whenever you look up a word in your dictionary, put a small checkmark next to it. When you accumulate three checkmarks next to a word, it is time to learn that word.

■ Set aside time each day to study your selected words. Carry your cards or notebook to study in spare moments each day.

■ Use mnemonics (see 22b) to help you memorize words. Set a goal of learning eight to ten new words a week. Use the words in your writing and, when possible, in conversation.

■ Go back to words from previous weeks, whenever possible. List any words you have not learned well. Study them again, and use them.

20c.1 Knowing prefixes and suffixes

Knowing common prefixes and suffixes is an excellent way to learn to decode unfamiliar words and increase your vocabulary.

Prefixes are syllables in front of a **root** word that modify its meaning. *Ante-* (before) placed before the root *bellum* (war) gives *antebellum*, which means "before the war." In American English, *antebellum* refers to the time before the Civil War. Common prefixes in English are listed in Chart 102.

EXTRA EXERCISE D

Be prepared to discuss differences in the connotations of the following pairs of words.

1. passive, shy
2. giggle, snicker
3. buddy, cohort
4. brave, foolhardy
5. wise, intelligent

TEACHING TIP

Knowledge of prefixes and suffixes can help students figure out the meanings of many words. If this skill is coupled with the ability to recognize root words, however, many students' power to decipher new words can increase dramatically. Fundamentally, a root word is a base to which prefixes and suffixes can be added. For example, *-graph* (from the Greek *graphos*, "to write") refers to something that writes or records, as in *telegraph* or *graphite*, or to something written, as in *paragraph* or the *graphic arts*; *graphology* is the study of handwriting.

Here are a few of the most common Greek and Latin roots, their meanings, and a sample word built from each root.

LATIN

aequus	equal (equivalent)
amare, amatum	to love (amiable)
dicere, dictum	to say, to speak (diction)
manus	hand (manuscript)
omnis	all (omnipotent)
portare, portatum	to carry (porter)
scribere, scriptum	to write (scribble)
sentire, sensum	to feel (sense)
spirare, spiratum	to breathe (inspiration)
verbum	word (verb)

→

GREEK

bios	life (biology)
chronos	time (chronology)
gamos	marriage (bigamy)
geo-	earth (geology)
krates (-crat)	member of a group (democrat)
metron	to measure (thermometer)
pathos	suffering, feeling, (sympathy)
phobos	fear (agoraphobia)
photos	light (photograph)
podos	foot (tripod)

EXTRA EXERCISE E

Using the following prefixes, devise new words, being prepared to explain their meaning.

1. inter-
2. ante-
3. anti-
4. post-
5. uni-

BACKGROUND

Over time, words change their meanings in several different ways. In *The Story of Our Language* (New York: Doubleday, 1962), Henry Alexander points out that a word may undergo a widening, in which it expands its range of meaning and is applied to new situations; a narrowing, by which it comes to refer to only a portion of the idea or objects it originally covered; a lowering of meaning, wherein it takes on pejorative aspects; and a raising of meaning, by which it loses its unpleasant associations and acquires more positive ones. For example, *meat* has undergone a narrowing of meaning; it originally referred to all kinds of food, but now denotes what was earlier called *flesh*. The word *hussy*, with its contemporary uncomplimentary meaning, has experienced a lowering; it originally denoted a housewife.

⊙ Common prefixes 102

PREFIX	MEANING	EXAMPLE
ante-	before	antebellum
anti-	against	antiballistic
auto-	self	autobiography
contra-	against	contradict
dis-	not	disagree
extra-	more	extraordinary
hyper-	more	hyperactive
il-	not	illegal
im-	not	immoral
in-	not	inadequate
inter-	between	interpersonal
intra-	inside	intravenous
ir-	not	irresponsible
mal-	poor	malnutrition
mis-	wrongly, badly	misunderstood
mono-	one	monopoly
non-	not	noninvolvement
poly-	many	polygamy
post-	after	postscript
pre-	before	prehistoric
re-	back	return
retro-	back	retroactive
semi-	half	semicircle
sub-	under	submissive
super-	more	supersonic
trans-	across	transportation
ultra-	more	ultraconservative
un-	not	unhappy
uni-	one	uniform

Suffixes are syllables added to the end of a root word that modify its meaning. For example, *excite* is formed by adding the prefix *ex-* (out) to the past participle of *ciere* (to summon). It has various forms when suffixes are added: *excited, exciting, excitedly, excitement*. The suffix often signals the part of speech of a word. Common suffixes in English are listed in Chart 103.

🎯 Common suffixes 103

SUFFIX	MEANING	EXAMPLES
Nouns		
-dom	state or domain	*freedom, officialdom*
-hood	state or condition	*childhood, brotherhood*
-ness	state or quality	*kindness, dampness*
-ship	state or rank	*friendship, chairmanship*
-tion	act	*calculation*
-tude	state	*solitude*
Verbs		
-ate	to become or form	*integrate, ulcerate*
-fy	to make	*unify, liquefy*
-ize	to make, act, or process	*computerize, theorize, rubberize*
Adjectives		
-able	capable or worthy of	*comfortable*
-ate	full of	*fortunate*
-ful	full of	*tactful*
-ible	capable or worthy of	*divisible*
-less	without	*penniless*
-ous	full of	*pompous*
-y	full of	*gloomy*

EXERCISE 20-4

Consulting section 20c.1, add a prefix to each italicized word to match the definition given. Use a dictionary if necessary.

EXAMPLE   not a *citizen* = noncitizen

1. not *possible*
2. *examine* again
3. poor *function*
4. between *states*
5. not *reversible*
6. half *conscious*
7. *stated* incorrectly
8. not *believable*
9. *conceived* before
10. more *sensitive*

EXTRA EXERCISE F

Working in groups and without a dictionary, compile a list of as many words as you can think of that begin with the following prefixes. How does the prefix affect the meaning of each of the words on your list? The group with the longest list can be declared the winner.

1. mono-
2. retro-
3. contra-
4. sub-
5. pre-
6. auto-
7. super-
8. un-
9. re-
10. poly-

EXTRA EXERCISE G

Working in groups and without a dictionary, compile a list of as many words as you can think of that end with the suffixes in Chart 103. What does the suffix tell you about the meaning of each word?

ANSWERS AND COVERAGE: EXERCISE 20-4

1. impossible [*im-*]
2. reexamine [*re-*]
3. malfunction [*mal-*]
4. interstate [*inter-*]
5. irreversible [*ir-*]
6. semiconscious [*semi-*]
7. misstated [*mis-*]
8. unbelievable [*un-*]
9. preconceived [*pre-*]
10. hypersensitive [*hyper-*]

ANSWERS AND COVERAGE: EXERCISE 20-5

1. childless [-*less*, adjective]
2. objectify [-*ify*, verb]
3. solidify [-*ify*, verb]
4. harmonize [-*ize*, verb]
5. kinship [-*ship*, noun]
6. touchable [-*able*, adjective]
7. hopeless [-*less*, adjective]
8. merciful [-*ful*, adjective]
9. bachelorhood [-*hood*, noun]
10. compassionate [-*ate*, adjective]

EXERCISE 20-5

Consulting section 20c.1, add a suffix to each italicized word to match the definition given. Notice that the form of the word should change to match the exact definition. Consult a dictionary to verify your spelling.

EXAMPLE   act of *communicating* = communication

1. lacking *children*
2. to make *objective*
3. to make *solid*
4. to make *harmony*
5. state of being *kin*
6. capable of being *touched*
7. without *hope*
8. full of *mercy*
9. state of being a *bachelor*
10. full of *compassion*

20c.2 Using context clues to figure out word meanings

Familiar words that surround an unknown word can give you hints about the meaning of the new word. Such context clues include four main types.

1. **Restatement context clue.** You can figure out an unknown word when a word you know repeats the meaning: *He jumped into the* **fray** *and enjoyed every minute of the fight. Fray* means "fight." Sometimes, a restatement is set off by punctuation. For example, parentheses contain a definition in this sentence: *Fatty deposits on artery walls combine with calcium compounds to cause* **arteriosclerosis** *(hardening of the arteries).* Sometimes, a technical term is set off by punctuation after its definition is given. For example, dashes set off a term after it is defined in this sentence: *The upper left part of the heart—the left* **atrium**—*receives blood returning from circulation.*

2. **Contrast context clue.** You can figure out an unknown word when an opposite or contrast is presented: *We feared that the new prime minister would be a* **menace** *to society, but she turned out to be a great peacemaker. Menace* means "threat"; the contrast that explains *menace* is *but she turned out to be a great peacemaker.* As you read, watch for words that express contrast (such as *but, however, nevertheless;* for a complete list, see Chart 25 in 4d.1).

3. **Example context clue.** You can figure out an unfamiliar word when an example or illustration relating to the word is given: *They were* **conscientious** *workers, making sure that everything was done correctly and precisely.* A dictionary defines *conscientious* as "motivated by a desire to do what is right." The words *done correctly and precisely* are close to that meaning.

4. **General-sense context clue.** You can use an entire passage to get a general sense of difficult words: *Nearly forty million Americans are overweight; obesity has become an* **epidemic**. Chances are good that *epidemic* refers to something happening to many people. Sometimes, a general-sense context clue will not reveal a word's exact denotation. For example, you might guess that *epidemic* indicates a widespread threat, but you might miss the connection of the word *epidemic* with the concept of disease. Interpreting the meaning of a word from the general sense carries the risk of allowing subtle variations that distinguish one word from another to slip by. You might want, therefore, to check the exact definition in a dictionary.

BACKGROUND

The roots of the *Dictionary of American Regional English (DARE)* go back to 1889 and the founding of the American Dialect Society. The society's purpose was to sponsor and record data for an American dialect dictionary. It had its own journal, which continues today as *The Publication of the American Dialect Society*. Compilation of a master file of entries for the dictionary began in 1917, and the society participated along the way in several other, smaller dialect dictionaries (the incomplete *Linguistic Atlas of the United States and Canada* and the *American Dialect Dictionary* [1944]).

In 1963, the society appointed Frederic G. Cassidy (editor of *The Dictionary of Jamaican English*) the *DARE* editor. He and his staff had at their disposal a hundred years of accumulated scholarship: the files of the American Dialect Society, linguistic and folklore journals, regional publications, diaries and other materials in library archives, records of folk speech, historical dictionaries, and linguistic atlases.

Astonishingly, Cassidy chose to go beyond the written word, and the *DARE* benefits from five years of original fieldwork aimed at finding out how people speak in their daily lives. Eighty-two trained field-workers, most of them graduate students in linguistics or the history of English, went across the United States conducting personal interviews.

The 2,777 informants represented 1,002 communities across the United States. The informants were chosen to create a balance of male and female, city and country, black and white, North and South. However, in order to preserve vanishing words, about two-thirds of the informants were sixty years old or older. Each questionnaire contained 1,847 questions. One questionnaire was filled in for each community. In some cases, one informant answered all the questions; in others, the questions were divided among a number of informants. The field-workers also brought back 1,843 tape recordings of conversations: a total of two million oral responses and 900 hours of tape recordings.

21
UNDERSTANDING THE EFFECT OF WORDS

As words communicate meaning (see Chapter 20), they have an effect on the people reading or hearing them. As a writer, you want to choose words carefully. Sometimes, the choices available to you are clearly either right or wrong, but often the choices are subtle. The guidelines discussed in this chapter can help you make good choices: using the right level of formality (see 21a.1), using edited American English (see 21a.2), avoiding slang or inappropriate colloquial words or regional words (see 21a.3), avoiding slanted language (see 21a.4), avoiding sexist language (see 21b), using figurative language appropriately (see 21c), avoiding clichés (see 21d), and avoiding artificial language (see 21e).

21a Using appropriate language

Using appropriate language means paying close attention to TONE (see 1d) and DICTION (see 20b). As a writer, you want the words you use to communicate your meaning as clearly and effectively as possible. Your choice of words and your sentence styles (see Chapters 16–19) work together to create your individual writing style.

21a.1 Using appropriate levels of formality

Informal and highly formal levels of writing differ clearly in tone. They use different vocabulary and sentence structures. Tone in writing indicates the attitude of the writer toward the subject and toward the audience. Tone may be highly formal, informal, or somewhere in between.

Different tones are appropriate for different AUDIENCES, different subjects, and different PURPOSES. An informal tone occurs in casual conversation or letters to friends. A highly formal tone, in contrast, occurs in sermons and proclamations.

Informal language, which creates a casual tone, may include slang, colloquialisms, and regionalisms (see 21a.3). Informal writing often includes sentence fragments (see Chapter 13), contractions, and other forms that approximate casual speech. **Medium-level language** uses general English, it is neither too casual nor too scholarly. Unlike informal language, medium-level language is acceptable for academic writing. This level uses standard vocabulary (for example, *learn* instead of *wise up*), conventional sentence structure, and few or no contractions. **Formal language** uses a multisyllabic Latinate vocabulary (*edify* instead of *teach*) and often stylistic flourishes such as extended or complex FIGURES OF SPEECH. Academic writing, along with most writing for general audiences, should range from medium to somewhat formal levels of language.

INFORMAL	Stars? Wow! They're, like, made of gas!
MEDIUM	Gas clouds slowly changed into stars.
FORMAL	The condensations of gas spun their slow gravitational pirouettes, slowly transmogrifying gas cloud into star.

—Carl Sagan, "Starfolk: A Fable"

The informal example would be appropriate in a letter to a close friend or in a journal. The writer's attitude toward the subject is playful and humorous; the word choice and sentence structure assume great familiarity between writer and reader. The medium example would be appropriate in most academic and professional situations. The writer's attitude toward the subject is serious and straightforward. The formal example works for readers with interest in and knowledge of scientific phenomena.

21a.2 Using edited American English for academic writing

The language standards that you are expected to use in academic writing are those of **edited American English,** the accepted written language of a book like this handbook or a magazine like *U.S. News and World Report* or *National Geographic*. Edited English is not a fancy dialect for the elite. It is a practical form of the language that educated people use. Such language conforms to widely established rules of grammar, sentence structure, punctuation, and spelling. Advertising language and other writing intended to appeal to a large and diverse audience may ignore conventional usage. Thus, you may see written English that varies from the standard. Such published departures from edited American English are not appropriate in academic writing, however.

21a.3 Avoiding slang and colloquial or regional language for most academic writing

Slang consists of coined words and new meanings attached to established terms. Slang words and phrases usually pass out of use quickly, although occasionally they become accepted into standard usage. A reasonable guideline is to reserve slang for very informal situations. At no time does slang communicate accurate meanings in academic or business writing. **Colloquial language** is characteristic of casual conversation and informal writing—for example, *the student flunked chemistry* instead of *the student failed chemistry*.

Regional language (also called *dialectal language*) is specific to certain geographical areas. A *dragonfly* is a *snake feeder* in parts of Delaware, a *darning needle* in parts of Michigan, and a *snake doctor* or an *ear sewer* in parts of the southern United States. Dialects are different from slang because dialectical differences reflect geographical regions and socioeconomic status. Using a dialect when writing for the general reading public tends to shut some people out of the communication. Except when dialect is the topic of the writing, academic writing rarely accommodates dialect well.

Although slang, colloquial words, and regional language are effective for communicating in various environments, they are usually not appropriate for academic writing. Replacing them in your college writing allows you to communicate clearly with the large number of people who speak and write in medium or somewhat formal levels of language (see 21a.1).

21a.4 Avoiding slanted language

To communicate clearly, choose words that convince your audience of your fairness as a writer. When you are writing about a subject on which you hold strong opinions, it is easy to slip into biased or emotionally loaded language. Such **slanted language** usually does not convince a careful reader to agree with your point. Instead, it makes the reader wary or hostile. For example, suppose you are arguing against the practice of scientific experimentation on animals. If you use language such as "laboratory Frankensteins" who "routinely and viciously maim helpless kittens and puppies," you are using slanted language. You want to use words that make your side of an issue the more convincing one. Once you start using slanted, biased language, readers feel manipulated rather than reasoned with.

21b Avoiding sexist language

Sexist language assigns roles or characteristics to people on the basis of gender. Most women and men today feel that sexist language unfairly discriminates against both sexes. Sexist language inaccurately assumes that all nurses and homemakers are female (and therefore refers to them as "she") and all physicians and wage earners are male (and therefore refers to them as "he"). One of the most widespread occurrences of sexist language is the use of the pronoun *he* to refer to someone whose sex is unknown or irrelevant. Although tradition holds that *he* is correct in such situations, using only masculine pronouns to represent the human species excludes women and thereby distorts reality.

TEACHING TIP

Discussions about slanted language make students more aware of biased writing. A logical follow-up assignment is to ask them to be alert to loaded diction in news articles and television broadcasts. Examples are particularly abundant during an election year. The words and phrases students collect can be the basis of another lesson, this one specific and close to home.

If you want to avoid sexist language in your writing, follow the guidelines in Chart 104. Also, avoid demeaning, outdated stereotypes or assumptions, such as *women are bad drivers* or *men cannot cook* and *all children have two parents*. Do not describe women's looks, clothes, or age unless you do the same for men. Do not use a title for one spouse but the first name for the other spouse: *Phil Miller* [not *Mr. Miller*] and his wife, Jeannette, travel on separate planes or Jeannette and Phil Miller live in Idaho.

◉ **How to avoid sexist language**   **104**

- Avoid using only the masculine pronoun to refer to males and females together. Use a pair of pronouns.

  NO   A doctor has little time to read outside **his** specialty.

  YES A doctor has little time to read outside **his or her** specialty.

  The *he or she* construction acts as a singular pronoun, and it therefore calls for a singular verb when it serves as the subject of a sentence. Try to avoid using the *he or she* construction, especially more than once in a sentence or in consecutive sentences. Revising into the plural may be a better solution:

  NO   A successful doctor knows that **he** has to work long hours.

  YES Successful doctors know that **they** have to work long hours.

  You may also recast a sentence to omit the gender-specific pronoun.

  NO   Everyone hopes that **he or she** will win the scholarship.

  YES Everyone hopes to win the scholarship.

- Avoid using *man* when both men and women are intended in the meaning.

  NO   **Man** is a social animal.

  YES **People** are social animals.

  NO   Dogs are **man's** best friend.

  YES Dogs are **humans'** best friends.

  YES Dogs are **people's** best friends.

  YES Dogs are **our** best friends.

  →

373

TEACHING TIP

If you have any doubts about whether encouraging nonsexist language is worth the effort, consider this passage from the introduction to "Guidelines for Nonsexist Use of Language in NCTE [National Council of Teachers of English] Publications":

"Sexism" may be defined as words or actions that arbitrarily assign roles or characteristics to people on the basis of sex. Originally used to refer to practices that discriminated against women, the term now includes any usage that unfairly delimits the aspirations or attributes of either sex. Neither men nor women can reach their full potential when men are conditioned to be only aggressive, analytical, and active and women are conditioned to be only submissive, emotional, and passive. The man who cannot cry and the woman who cannot command are equally victims of their socialization.

Language plays a central role in socialization, for it helps teach children the roles that are expected of them. Through language, children conceptualize their ideas and feelings about themselves and their world. Thought and action are reflected in words, and words in turn condition how a person thinks and acts. Eliminating sexist language will not eliminate sexist conduct, but as the language is liberated from sexist usages and assumptions, women and men will begin to share more equal, active, caring roles.

TEACHING TIP

In addition to the techniques given in Chart 104, here are a few more tactics.

1. When appropriate, use the first person or the second person.

NO *A person should always keep an eye on his luggage in airports.*

YES *I should always keep my eye on my luggage in airports.*

YES *We should always keep an eye on our luggage in airports.*

YES *Keep an eye on your luggage in airports.*

→

2. Repeat a noun or use a synonym in place of the troublesome pronoun.

NO *A preoccupied traveler is an easy target for thieves, who can pick his pocket in a second.*

YES *A preoccupied traveler is an easy target for thieves, who pick a traveler's pocket in a second.*

YES *A preoccupied traveler is an easy target for thieves, who can pick a tourist's pocket in a second.*

3. Use *who.*

NO *A traveler has little to worry about, if he stays alert.*

YES *A traveler who stays alert has little to worry about.*

ANSWERS: EXERCISE 21-1

Answers will vary. Here are some possible nonsexist versions.

1. Many of humanity's most important inventions are found not in scientific laboratories but in the home.

2. Among these inventions are the many home appliances that were designed in the early 1900s to simplify housework.

3. Every homemaker should be grateful to the inventors of labor-saving appliances such as vacuum cleaners, washing machines, and water heaters.

How to avoid sexist language *(continued)* 104

■ Avoid stereotyping jobs and roles by gender when both men and women are included.

NO		**YES**	
chairman		chair, chairperson	
policeman		police officer	
businessman		businessperson, business executive	
statesman		diplomat, prime minister, statesperson	

NO teacher . . . **she;** principal . . . **he**

YES teachers . . . **they;** principals . . . **they**

■ Avoid expressions that seem to exclude either sex.

NO	**YES**
mankind	humanity
the common man	the average person
man-sized sandwich	huge sandwich
old wives' tale	superstition

■ Avoid using demeaning and patronizing labels.

NO	**YES**
lady lawyer	lawyer
male nurse	nurse
gal Friday	assistant
coed	student

NO My **girl** will send it.

YES My **secretary** will send it.

YES **Ida Morea** will send it.

EXERCISE 21-1

Consulting section 21b, revise the following sentences by changing sexist language to nonsexist language.

1. Many of man's most important inventions are found not in scientific laboratories but in the home.
2. Among these inventions are the many home appliances that were designed in the early 1900s to simplify women's housework.
3. Every housewife should be grateful to the inventors of labor-saving appliances such as vacuum cleaners, washing machines, and water heaters.

4. Before such appliances became available, a family was fortunate if the husband could afford to hire a cleaning lady or a maid to help with the housework.

5. Otherwise, each family member had tasks to do that could include washing his clothes by hand or carrying hot water for bathing up or down the stairs.

6. Once family members were freed from these difficult duties early in the twentieth century, women had more time to spend with their children.

7. Also, now everyone in the household had more time for his favorite pastimes and hobbies.

8. None of the inventors of modern home appliances could have guessed what far-reaching effects his inventions would have on our society.

9. Every worker, from laborer to businessman, could return each day to a house where there was not nearly as much heavy housework waiting to be done.

10. Even more important, with less housework to do, women could now leave the home to take jobs as office girls and sometimes even lady doctors and lawyers.

21c Using figurative language

Figurative language uses words for more than their literal meanings. They are not merely decorative, however. Figurative language enhances meaning. It makes comparisons and connections that draw on one idea or image to explain another, as shown in Chart 105.

⊙ **Types of figurative language**   **105**

ANALOGY

A comparison of similar traits between dissimilar things (An analogy can range from one sentence to a paragraph to an entire essay; see 4f.8.)

A cheetah sprinting across the dry plains after its prey, the base runner dashed for home plate.

IRONY

The use of words to suggest the opposite of their usual sense

Told that the car repair would cost $2,000 and take at least two weeks, she said, "Oh, that's just great."

→

375

BACKGROUND

In "Writing and the Strategic Use of Metaphor" (*Teaching English in the Two-Year College*, May 1995: 110–115), Kristie S. Fleckenstein describes how she uses a structured approach to teaching metaphor. She explains how this work helps students better control their writing and find joy in writing.

TEACHING TIP

Sports have been a fertile field for metaphor in America. You might remind your students of these common metaphors. What does each mean within its sport? What does each mean in a general context? You might also ask students if they can add to the lists or start lists for other sports or interests. Many metaphors listed here are discussed in Tim Considine's "Starting from Scratch" (*New York Times*, June 8, 1985).

Soccer: kick off, get the ball rolling
Baseball: right off the bat, off base, touch base with, go to bat for, out in left field, drop the ball
Football: huddle, chalk talk, a flag on the play, all-American
Boxing: answer the bell, a low blow, hitting below the belt, on the ropes

ANSWERS AND COVERAGE: EXERCISE 21-2

1. mixed metaphor
2. simile

Types of figurative language *(continued)*   105

METAPHOR

A comparison between otherwise dissimilar things without using the word *like* or *as* (Avoid the error of a mixed metaphor, explained in the text.)	The rush-hour traffic bled out of all the city's major arteries.
OVERSTATEMENT (HYPERBOLE) Deliberate exaggeration for emphasis	The poet Andrew Marvell said that praising his love's eyes and forehead could take one hundred years.
PERSONIFICATION The assignment of a human trait to a nonhuman thing	The book begged to be read.
SIMILE A direct comparison between otherwise dissimilar things, using the word *like* or *as*	Langston Hughes said that a deferred dream dries up like a raisin in the sun.
UNDERSTATEMENT Deliberate restraint for emphasis	It gets a little warm when the temperature reaches 105 degrees.

As you use figurative language, be sure to avoid mixed metaphors. A **mixed metaphor** blends images that do not work well together.

> **NO** When she graduated, her spirits soared, but they have gone steadily downhill ever since.

> **YES** When she graduated, she was delighted, but she has steadily become less cheerful.

EXERCISE 21-2

Consulting section 21c, identify each figure of speech. Also, revise any mixed metaphors.

1. We stand with one foot in the twentieth century while we set sail on the sea of a new era in the twenty-first.
2. Having spent the whole day on the beach, he came home as red as a lobster.

3. If I eat one more bite of that chocolate cake, I'll explode.

4. What I love best about you is that you use all the hot water every time you take a shower.

5. The daisies nodded their heads in the hot sun.

6. Beginning to testify in the courtroom, the defendant was as nervous as a long-tailed cat in a roomful of rocking chairs.

7. Think of the environment as a human body, where small problems in one part do not much affect other parts, any more than a paper cut causes most of us more than an instant's pain and a heartfelt "Ouch!" Problems throughout a system like the air or the oceans, however—say, pollution building up beyond the system's ability to cleanse itself—can kill the entire organism just as surely as cholesterol building up in arteries can kill you or me.

8. The actor displayed the entire range of human emotions from A to B.

9. My heart stopped when I opened the gift my parents gave me.

10. Our supervisor said that reorganizing the department according to our recommendations would be trading a headache for an upset stomach.

21d Avoiding clichés

A **cliché** is a worn-out expression that has lost its capacity to communicate effectively. Many clichés are similes or metaphors, once clever but now overused and therefore flat: *dead as a doornail, gentle as a lamb, straight as an arrow.* If you have heard a certain expression over and over again, so has your reader. If you cannot think of a way to rephrase a cliché, drop the phrase entirely.

Be aware that English is full of frequently used word groups that are not clichés (for example, *up and down* and *in and out*). Common patterns are not clichés and need not be avoided.

EXERCISE 21-3

Consulting section 21d, revise these clichés. Use the idea in each cliché for a sentence of your own in plain English.

1. The bottom line is that Carl either raises his grade point average or finds himself in hot water.

2. Carl's grandfather says, "When the going gets tough, the tough get going."

3. Carl may not be the most brilliant engineering major who ever came down the pike, but he has plenty of get-up-and-go.

4. When they were handing out persistence, Carl was first in line.

5. The $64,000 question is, Will Carl make it safe and sound, or will the college drop him like a hot potato?

Answers and Coverage: Exercise 21-2 (continued)

3. overstatement
4. irony
5. personification
6. simile
7. analogy
8. irony
9. overstatement
10. metaphor

TEACHING TIP

Because language varies from one geographical area to another, students who have lived in several different parts of the country often know expressions that are used in one region but not in another. Other members of a class may find it interesting to hear some of those regionalisms, afterward compiling a list of words and phrases peculiar to their own area.

ANSWERS AND COVERAGE: EXERCISE 21-3

Answers will vary. Here is one set of possibilities.

1. Carl either raises his grade point average or risks probation.

2. Carl's grandfather says that difficult problems inspire strong people to come up with solutions.

3. Carl makes up with energy what he lacks in intelligence.

4. Persistence is one of Carl's most notable traits.

5. The central question is, Will Carl pass or fail college?

21e Avoiding artificial language

Sometimes, student writers think that fancy words and complicated sentence structures make writing impressive. Experienced writers, however, work hard to communicate as clearly and directly as they can. As a student writer, try to make your writing as accessible as possible to your readers. Of course, extremely complex ideas or subject areas may require complex terms or phrases to explain them, but in general, the simpler the language, the more likely your readers will understand it.

21e.1 Avoiding pretentious language

Pretentious language is showy, calling undue attention to itself with overly complex sentences and words of many syllables. Avoid writing big words used for their own sake. Overblown words and sentences are likely to obscure your message.

NO As I alighted from my vehicle, my clothing became besmirched with filth. [*Translation:* My coat got dirty as I got out of my car.]

NO I loathe his penchant for ostentatiously flaunting recently acquired haberdashery accoutrements. [*Translation:* I hate it when he tries to show off his new clothes.]

21e.2 Avoiding unnecessary jargon

Jargon is the specialized vocabulary of a particular group. Jargon uses words that an outsider might not understand. Specialized language evolves in every field: professions, academic disciplines (see Chapters 36–38), business, hobbies. As you write, consider your PURPOSE and AUDIENCE to decide whether a word is jargon in the context of your material. For example, a football fan easily understands a sportswriter's use of words such as *punt* and *safety,* but they are jargon to people unfamiliar with football. Avoid using jargon unnecessarily. When you must use jargon for a general audience, be sure to explain the specialized meanings.

This example, showing specialized language used appropriately, is from a college textbook. The writers assume that students know to look up or figure out the meaning of *eutrophicates, terrestrial,* and *eutrophic.*

> As the lake eutrophicates, it gradually fills until the entire lake will be converted into a terrestrial community. Eutrophic changes (or eutrophication) is the nutritional enrichment of the water, promoting the growth of aquatic plants.
>
> —Davis and Solomon, *The World of Biology*

21e.3 Avoiding euphemisms

Euphemisms attempt to avoid the harsh reality of truth by using more pleasant-sounding, "tactful" words. The word *euphemism* comes from the Greek meaning "words of good omen" (*eu-*, "good" + *pheme*, "voice").

Euphemisms are sometimes necessary for tact in social situations (using *passed away* instead of *died*, for example). In other situations, euphemisms drain meaning from truthful writing. Unnecessary euphemisms might describe socially unacceptable behavior (for example, *Johnny has a wonderfully vivid imagination* instead of *Johnny lies*). Unnecessary euphemisms might try to hide unpleasant facts (*She is between assignments* instead of *She lost her job*).

21e.4 Avoiding doublespeak

Doublespeak is artificial, evasive language. It aims to distort and deceive. For example, many automobile dealerships today refer to used cars as "preowned cars" or "previously distinguished cars." One major corporation described its notice that laid off five thousand workers as a "career alternative enhancement package." The Pentagon has used "collateral damage" for the unintended killing of innocent civilians in war.

To use doublespeak is to try to hide the truth, an unethical practice that seeks to control people's thoughts. So severe has the doublespeak problem become in our society that the National Council of Teachers of English yearly announces a Doublespeak Award to the "best" example of language that purposely misleads. A recent nominee for the award went to a foreign government for calling hostages "foreign guests" whose guards are "hosts." An award went to a member of the United States Congress for saying that Congress "did not raise taxes" but rather "sought new revenues." Such misuses of language have devastating social and political consequences in a free society. As a writer, always use language truthfully. Avoid using doublespeak.

21e.5 Avoiding bureaucratic language

Bureaucratic language is stuffy and overblown.

NO   You can include a page that also contains an Include instruction. The page including the Include instruction is included when you paginate the document but the included text referred to in its Include instruction is not included.

The irony in this example is that the writer seems to be trying to communicate very precisely, but nothing is communicated. Bureaucratic language (or *bureaucratese,* the word coined to describe the style) is marked by unnecessary complexity and is therefore meaningless.

QUOTATION: ON WRITING

People seldom write simply to be clear. . . . Pure prose is as rare as pure virtue, and for the same reasons.

—Richard A. Lanham

ANSWERS AND COVERAGE: EXERCISE 21-4

Answers will vary. Here is one set of possibilities.

1. Socializing on the job is not allowed. [bureaucratic language]

2. The sign in the window called it a used teddy bear. [doublespeak]

3. Shortly after Mrs. Harriman died, Mr. Harriman moved to Florida to be near his son and daughter-in-law and their new baby. [euphemism]

4. Your best friend, I've heard, is going to marry her boyfriend. [pretentious language]

5. My brother told a lie. [pretentious language]

6. An individual's systems of thinking and feeling are at the center of his or her personality. [jargon]

7. He told the police officer that the car accident happened because he sneezed and couldn't see the other driver coming. [doublespeak]

8. When the negotiation is finished, we will be in a better position. [jargon, pretentious language]

9. The trash has piled up because the trash collectors were on strike last month. [pretentious language, euphemism]

10. Full-time employees who have worked at the company for five years can participate in the savings program. [bureaucratic language]

EXERCISE 21-4

Consulting section 21e, revise these examples of pretentious language, jargon, euphemism, doublespeak, and bureaucratic language.

1. In-house employee interaction of a nonbusiness nature is disallowed.

2. The sign in the window called it a preloved teddy bear.

3. Shortly after Mrs. Harriman went to her reward, Mr. Harriman moved to Florida to be near his son and daughter-in-law and their bundle of joy.

4. Your dearest, closest acquaintance, it has been circulated through rumor, is entering into matrimony with her current beloved.

5. My male sibling concocted a tale that was entirely fallacious.

6. An individual's cognitive and affective domains are at the center of his or her personality.

7. He told the police officer that the unanticipated collision occurred as the result of a sudden, involuntary explosive action from his nose and mouth that caused him momentarily to close his eyes, which act prevented him from seeing the other motorist's automobile.

8. When the finalization of this negotiation comes through, it will clarify our position in a positive manner.

9. The refuse has accumulated because the sanitation engineers were on strike last month.

10. Employees who are employed by the company for no less than five years in a full-time capacity fulfill the eligibility requirements for participation in the company's savings program.

22

SPELLING AND HYPHENATION

QUOTATION: ON WRITING

Bad spellers of the world, untie!
—Anonymous graffiti writer

You might be surprised to know this about good spellers: They do not always remember how to spell every word they write, but they are very skilled at sensing when they should check the spelling of a word. Try, therefore, not to ignore your quiet inner voice that doubts a spelling; listen to it and look up the word. At the same time, do not allow spelling doubts to interrupt the flow of your writing during DRAFTING (see 3b). Underline or circle words you want to check, and go back to them when you are EDITING your writing (see 3d).

How do you look up a word in the dictionary if you do not know how to spell it? If you know the first few letters, find the general area for the word and browse for it. If you do not know how a word begins, try to find it listed in a thesaurus under an easy-to-spell synonym. When you are writing on a computer, you can usually use a program that checks spelling. Be careful, though, to proofread for spelling errors that result when you substitute another correctly spelled word for the word that you intend (for example, *whole* if you mean *hole*).

As you spell, be aware that the various origins and ways English-speaking people pronounce words make it almost impossible to rely solely on pronunciation to spell a word. What you can rely on is a system of proofreading and spelling rules.

22a Eliminating careless spelling errors

Many spelling errors are the result of illegible handwriting, slips of the pen, or typographical mistakes. Catching "typos" requires especially careful proofreading, using the techniques in Chart 106.

◉ **Techniques for proofreading for spelling**   **106**

- Slow down your reading speed so that you can concentrate on individual letters of words rather than on the meaning of the words.

➡

BACKGROUND

The earliest writing systems were developed not much more than six thousand years ago to meet the needs of increasingly complex cultures. In particular, the Egyptians and Babylonians contrived ways of recording their sacred records, commercial transactions, and royal decrees by pictographs—drawings that attempted to convey a general idea by visually reproducing the major elements in it. Writing can be said to have begun when a method for making a linguistic statement of the facts was devised. The earliest of such systems did not make use of the *phonology*, or sounds of language. Instead, they used signs to represent *morphemes* (roots and affixes). Chinese is the only language that continues to use this system exclusively. The Egyptians and other ancient Middle Eastern cultures based their writing systems on the sounds of the syllables that made up words. Alphabetic writing was invented by the peoples of the Eastern Mediterranean. At first, they used only consonants, depending on readers to fill in the vowels as well as to supply such information as intonation and stress. When the Greeks adopted a Semitic alphabet, they used the characters for consonant sounds that did not exist in Greek to represent vowels. That tradition is the basis of all modern alphabets used in the West today.

STATEWIDE TESTING

If you teach in a state that requires students to pass basic competency tests in English, see the free publications coordinated with this handbook: One is for the CLAST (Florida), and another is for the TASP Exam (Texas).

WORDS OFTEN MISSPELLED

Throughout this chapter, we present lists of commonly misspelled words, organized in the following categories: double consonants, word endings (suffixes), unstressed syllables, *ei/ie*, silent letters and blended sounds, and other commonly misspelled words. It's a good idea to assign words for study in groups of twenty-five at a time.

Double Consonants

accommodate	committee	missile
accompanied	controlled	occasion
accomplish	different	occurred
accordion	disappear	parallel
accustomed	disappoint	processes
address	disapprove	quizzes
annihilate	efficient	satellite
appoint	equipped	stepped
appreciate	fulfill	succeed
appropriate	happened	suppose
arrest	harass	surround
bulletin	interrupt	tyranny
commercial	mirror	villain

Word Endings (Suffixes)

acceptable	basically
accessible	beautiful
accidentally	beginning
accuracy	beneficial
acreage	biggest
actually	bureaucracy
admission	business
affectionately	calculator
aggression	carrying
announcement	changeable
apparent	changing
appearance	characteristic
approximately	Christianity
arguing	commitment
argument	competent
assassination	competition
attendance	completely
barbarous	confident

> **Techniques for proofreading for spelling** *(continued)* **106**
>
> - Stay within your "visual span," the number of letters you can identify with a single glance (for most people, about six letters).
> - Put a ruler or large index card under each line as you proofread, to focus your concentration and vision.
> - Read each paragraph in reverse, from the last sentence to the first. This method helps prevent your being distracted by the meaning of the material.

22b Spelling homonyms and commonly confused words

Homonyms are words that sound exactly like others (*its, it's; morning, mourning*). Further, many words sound so much alike that they are often confused with each other. A comprehensive list appears in Chart 107 (also, the most common sets are included in the Usage Glossary at the back of this handbook).

One source of confusion not covered by this list is "swallowed" pronunciation. For example, if a speaker fails to pronounce the letter *-d* at the end of words ("swallows" it), a writer may put down *use to, suppose to,* or *prejudice* when *used to, supposed to,* or *prejudiced* is required.

Another source of confusion is expressions that are always written as two words, not one: for example, *all right* (not *alright*) and *a lot* (not *alot*).

The best way to remember how to distinguish between homonyms and between other commonly confused words is to use memory devices (**mnemonics**). For example, if you have trouble with the two homonyms *stationary* and *stationery*, try this: *Stationary* means *stay* (*a* is in both), and to use *stationery*, you need a *pen* or a *pencil* (*e* is in both).

> ⊙ **Homonyms and commonly confused words** **107**
>
> Abbreviations used: *n.* noun, *v.* verb, *adj.* adjective.
>
> - *accept* to receive
>   *except* excluding
> - *advice* recommendation
>   *advise* to recommend
> - *affect* to influence (*v.*); emotional response (*n.*)
>   *effect* result (*n.*); to bring about (*v.*) →

Homonyms and commonly confused words *(continued)*

107

- *aisle*   space between rows
  isle   island
- *allude*   to refer indirectly
  elude   to avoid
- *allusion*   indirect reference
  illusion   false idea, misleading appearance
- *already*   by this time
  all ready   fully prepared
- *altar*   sacred platform or place
  alter   to change
- *altogether*   thoroughly
  all together   everyone or everything in one place
- *are*   plural form of *be*
  hour   sixty minutes
  our   plural form of *my*
- *ascent*   the act of rising or climbing
  assent   consent
- *assistance*   help
  assistants   helpers
- *bare*   nude, unadorned
  bear   to carry (*v.*); an animal (*n.*)
- *board*   piece of wood
  bored   uninterested
- *breath*   air taken in
  breathe   to take in air
- *brake*   device for stopping
  break   to destroy, split into pieces
- *buy*   to purchase
  by   next to, through the agency of
- *capital*   major city
  capitol   government building
- *choose*   to pick
  chose   past tense of *choose*
- *cite*   to point out, name
  sight   vision
  site   place, location
- *clothes*   garments
  cloths   pieces of fabric

→

Words Often Misspelled *(continued)*

consistent	idiosyncrasy
continuous	ignorant
convenient	illogical
coolly	imaginary
criticism	immediately
criticize	immensely
cruelty	incalculable
curiosity	incidentally
decision	incredible
definitely	independent
description	indispensable
desirable	individually
desperate	influential
despicable	innocuous
disastrous	insurance
discussion	intelligent
dormitory	interference
easily	irrelevant
elaborately	irresistible
entirely	irritated
environment	likelihood
equipment	listening
especially	liveliest
evidently	livelihood
existence	lying
experiment	magnificent
explanation	maintenance
extremely	manageable
finally	management
financially	marriage
generally	meanness
government	mischievous
governor	mysterious
guidance	narrative
happily	naturally
hindrance	necessary
hoping	noticeable
humorous	noticing
hungry	nuisance
hurriedly	numerous
hypocrisy	occasionally
ideally	occurrence

→

Words Often Misspelled *(continued)*

occurring	repetition
official	representative
omission	resemblance
omitting	ridiculous
opponent	scarcity
opportunity	scenery
opposite	secretary
oppression	senseless
optimism	shining
ordinarily	shrubbery
originally	significant
particularly	simply
peaceable	sincerely
peculiar	skiing
performance	strenuous
permanence	stubbornness
permissible	studying
politician	suburban
possession	succession
practicality	sufficient
predominant	summary
preparation	superintendent
prevalent	supersede
prisoner	suppress
probably	surely
professor	susceptible
prominent	suspicious
pronunciation	swimming
publicly	technical
pursuing	temporary
questionnaire	tendency
rarity	tragedy
reality	tremendous
realize	truce
really	unanimous
recession	unconscious
recommend	undoubtedly
referring	usage
regulate	using
rehearsal	usually
religious	valuable
remembrance	various

Homonyms and commonly confused words *(continued)*   107

- *coarse* — rough
  course — path; series of lectures
- *complement* — something that completes
  compliment — praise, flattery
- *conscience* — sense of morality
  conscious — awake, aware
- *council* — governing body
  counsel — advice
- *dairy* — farm where milk is produced
  diary — personal journal
- *decent* — respectable
  descent — downward movement
  dissent — disagreement
- *desert* — to abandon (*v.*); dry, sandy area (*n.*)
  dessert — final, sweet course in a meal
- *device* — a plan; an implement
  devise — to create
- *die* — to lose life (*v.*) (*dying*); one of a pair of dice (*n.*)
  dye — to change the color of something (*dyeing*)
- *dominant* — commanding, controlling
  dominate — to control
- *elicit* — to draw out
  illicit — illegal
- *eminent* — prominent
  immanent — living within; inherent
  imminent — about to happen
- *ensure* — to guarantee, protect
  insure — to buy or provide insurance
- *envelop* — to surround
  envelope — container for a letter or other papers
- *fair* — light in color; just, honest
  fare — money for transportation; food
- *faze* — to confuse or embarrass
  phase — stage of development
- *formally* — conventionally, with ceremony
  formerly — previously

➙

Homonyms and commonly confused words *(continued)* 107

- *forth* — forward
  fourth — next after *third*
- *gorilla* — animal
  guerrilla — rebel soldier
- *hear* — to sense sound by ear
  here — in this place
- *hole* — opening
  whole — complete; an entire thing
- *human* — relating to the species *Homo sapiens*
  humane — compassionate
- *its* — possessive form of *it*
  it's — contraction of *it is*
- *know* — to comprehend
  no — negative
- *later* — after a time
  latter — second one of two things
- *lead* — heavy metal substance (*n*); to guide (*v.*)
  led — past tense of *lead*
- *lightening* — making lighter
  lightning — storm-related electricity
- *loose* — unbound, not tightly fastened
  lose — to misplace
- *maybe* — perhaps
  may be — might be
- *meat* — animal flesh
  meet — to encounter
- *miner* — person who works in a mine
  minor — under age; of little importance
- *moral* — distinguishing right from wrong (*adj.*); lesson (*n.*)
  morale — attitude, outlook
- *of* — from; belonging to
  off — away from; not turned on
- *passed* — past tense of *pass*
  past — at a previous time
- *patience* — forbearance
  patients — people under medical care

→

Words Often Misspelled *(continued)*

vegetable — visible
vengeance — writing
violence — written

TEACHING TIP

A sophisticated relative of the spelling test is the dictation exercise. Passages can be created to test student ability to spell, punctuate, or capitalize. Here is a sample dictation passage aimed at testing whether students can distinguish among homonyms and commonly confused words. The context gives students clues to which word is intended (much as the sentences normally given as part of a spelling test do); at the same time, the paragraph format is more interesting than random illustrative sentences. (Homonyms and commonly confused words are in italics.)

The institution of marriage has received *its* share of public attention over the past few years. Rising divorce rates, *seen* as a symptom of a troubled society, have *led* people to question why some marriages *break* up and others succeed. One reason may be that the *effect* of courtship is to cause the bride and groom to *lose sight* of reality. Researchers *cite* evidence that some couples are *too* unrealistic. They *proceed* to the *altar* carrying romantic *illusions* about themselves, each other, and marriage itself. Having grown accustomed to *compliments* and *presents*, they find themselves walking down the *aisle* expecting a lifetime of romantic bliss to follow. The groom may assume that his bride is an *angel*, and she may *choose* to think of him as a *knight* on a white horse. They may fail to realize that one expects to *dominate* rather than *complement* the other or that he lacks *patience* and she is not as *quiet* as she seems. *They're* reluctant to look at the *whole* situation until *later*, when they *are* called on to *accept* the serious responsibilities of marriage. The best *advice*, of course, is for husbands and wives to live by *principles* that *lead* them to treat each other *respectfully*, *lightening* each other's troubles and acknowledging each other's *rights*.

QUOTATION: ON WRITING

English orthography satisfies all the requirements of the canons of reputability under the law of conspicuous waste. It is archaic, cumbrous, and ineffective; its acquisition consumes much time and effort; failure to acquire it is easy of detection.

—Thorstein Veblen

TEACHING TIP

Much of the recent research on spelling improvements stresses the importance of using as many of the senses as possible during word study. You may want to suggest to students that they try to improve their visual memory by writing a word in the air, using a finger to make the troublesome letters especially large. Ask them to try to imagine a word as if it were on an outdoor movie screen. Then they can try to write the word mentally in "longhand." The auditory sense can be invoked by making exaggerated pronunciations. That is, the speaker emphasizes the problem portion of a word when saying it. For example, the person who habitually leaves off the final -*d* of *used* should practice pronouncing the word as "you said." The kinesthetic and tactile senses are combined when a writer records a problem word on paper using a different kind of medium to write the difficult spots, changing from a ballpoint pen, for instance, to a crayon. This technique can include a visual element if the student puts the problem letters in red or some other bright color.

Homonyms and commonly confused words (*continued*)   107

■ *peace*	absence of fighting
piece	part of a whole; musical arrangement
■ *personal*	intimate
personnel	employees
■ *plain*	simple, unadorned
plane	to shave wood (*v.*); aircraft (*n.*)
■ *pore*	to read intently (*v.*); opening in the skin (*n.*)
pour	to dump water
■ *precede*	to come before
proceed	to continue
■ *presence*	being at hand; attendance at a place or in something
presents	gifts
■ *principal*	foremost (*adj.*); school head (*n.*)
principle	moral conviction, basic truth
■ *quiet*	silent, calm
quite	very
■ *rain*	water drops falling to earth (*n.*); to fall like rain (*v.*)
reign	to rule
rein	strap to guide or control an animal (*n.*); to guide or control (*v.*)
■ *raise*	to lift up
raze	to tear down
■ *respectfully*	with respect
respectively	in that order
■ *right*	correct; opposite of *left* (*adj.*); claim or privilege (*n.*)
rite	ritual
write	to put words on paper
■ *road*	path
rode	past tense of *ride*
■ *scene*	place of an action; segment of a play
seen	viewed
■ *sense*	perception, understanding
since	from the time of; because
■ *stationary*	standing still
stationery	writing paper
■ *than*	in comparison with; besides
then	at that time; next; therefore

→

Homonyms and commonly confused words *(continued)* 107

■	*their*	possessive form of *they*
	there	in that place
	they're	contraction of *they are*
■	*threw*	past tense of *throw*
	through	finished; into and out of
	thorough	complete
■	*to*	toward
	too	also; excessively
	two	number following *one*
■	*waist*	midsection of the body
	waste	discarded material (*n.*); to squander, fail to use up (*v.*)
■	*weak*	not strong
	week	seven days
■	*weather*	climatic condition
	whether	if
■	*where*	in which place
	were	past tense of *be*
■	*which*	relative pronoun
	witch	female sorcerer
■	*who's*	contraction of *who is*
	whose	possessive form of *who*
■	*yore*	times long past
	your	possessive form of *you*
	you're	contraction of *you are*

EXERCISE 22-1

Consulting section 22b, circle the appropriate homonym or commonly confused word of each group in parentheses.

Imagine that you (are, our) standing in the middle of a busy sidewalk, with a worried look on (your, you're, yore) face. In your hand (your, you're, yore) holding a map, (which, witch) you are puzzling over. If that happened in (real, reel) life, (its, it's) almost certain that within (to, too, two) or three minutes a passerby would ask if you (where, were) lost and would offer you (assistance, assistants). That helpful passerby, (buy, by) taking a (personal, personnel) interest in your problem, is displaying a quality known as empathy—the ability

LANGUAGE HISTORY

During the period of colonization, English continued to expand. From Native American words we took *tomahawk, wigwam, squaw,* and place names, such as *Nebraska, Allegheny, Kentucky, Seattle,* and *Dakota.* From spoken Spanish in the New World: *mustang, ranch, patio, bonanza, rodeo, vigilante, sombrero.* From words arrived from India: *thug, loot, pajamas, bandana.* From German words: *kindergarten, semester, delicatessen, frankfurter, hamburger.*

Borrowing continues unabated. Recent borrowings have come from Italian (*casino, malaria, studio*); Spanish (*cigar, canyon, cafeteria*); German (*pumpernickel, iceberg, protein*); Slavic (*pogrom, soviet, robot*); Arabic (*genie, candy, safari*); Hebrew (*hallelujah, kosher*); Persian (*spinach, lilac, bazaar*); Tibeto-Chinese (*tea, ketchup*); and Japanese (*zen, karate*). Over the centuries, the Anglo-Saxons' vocabulary of 50,000 words has expanded to more than 600,000 words. Irregular spellings are the price we pay for this acquired richness and flexibility.

ANSWERS: EXERCISE 22-1

Imagine that you *are* standing in the middle of a busy sidewalk, with a worried look on *your* face. In your hand *you're* holding a map, *which* you are puzzling over. If that happened in *real* life, *it's* almost certain that within *two* or three minutes a passerby would ask if you *were* lost and would offer you *assistance.* That helpful passerby, *by* taking a *personal* interest in your problem, is displaying a quality known as empathy—the ability *to* put oneself in another person's place. Some researchers claim that empathy is an instinct that *human* beings share with many other animals. Other scientists wonder *whether* empathy is instead a *conscious moral* choice that people make. Whatever explanation for the origin *of* empathy is *right,* such empathy generally has a positive *effect*—especially if *you're* a person who *may be too* lost to *know where to* turn.

WORDS OFTEN MISSPELLED

ei/ie

achievement	conscientious	relief
apiece	eighth	relieve
atheist	foreign	review
belief	forfeit	seize
believed	height	view
ceiling	leisure	weird
chief	lenient	
conceited	niece	
conceive	receive	

Unstressed Syllables (including syllables frequently not pronounced)

adolescent	delicate
alcohol	despair
amateur	destroy
analysis	develop
angel	disease
apology	dispel
article	divide
aspirin	divine
average	ecstasy
bargain	embarrass
boundary	enemy
cafeteria	escape
calendar	everything
category	exercise
cemetery	family
census	favorite
certain	grammar
challenge	heroes
channel	holiday
children	hundred
chocolate	imagine
chosen	imitate
coarsely	integrate
concentrate	interest
controversial	introduce
curious	laboratory
decorate	liable

→

(to, too, two) put yourself in another person's place. Some researchers claim that empathy is an instinct that (human, humane) beings share with many other animals. Other scientists wonder (weather, whether) empathy is instead a (conscience, conscious) (moral, morale) choice that people make. Whatever explanation for the origin (of, off) empathy is (right, rite, write), such empathy generally has a positive (affect, effect)—especially if (your, you're, yore) a person who (maybe, may be) (to, too, two) lost to (know, no) (where, were) (to, too, two) turn.

22c Using spelling rules for plurals, suffixes, and *ie*, *ei* words

The rules in Chart 108 will help you spell plurals, add suffixes, and spell words that contain *ie* or *ei* combinations.

◉ Spelling rules for plurals, suffixes, and *ie*, *ei* words   **108**

Plurals

- **Adding -s or -es**: Most plurals are formed by adding *-s*, including words that end in "hard" *-ch* (sounding like *k*): *leg, legs; shoe, shoes; stomach, stomachs.* For words ending in *-s, -sh, -x, -z,* or "soft" *-ch* (as in *beach*), add *-es* to the singular: *beach, beaches; tax, taxes; coach, coaches.*

- **Words ending in -o**: Add *-s* if the *-o* is preceded by a vowel (*radio, radios; cameo, cameos*). Add *-es* if the *-o* is preceded by a consonant (*potato, potatoes*). A few words can be pluralized either way: *cargo, volcano, tornado, zero.*

- **Words ending in -f or -fe**: Some *-f* and *-fe* words are made plural by adding *-s: belief, beliefs.* Others require changing *-f* or *-fe* to *-ves: life, lives; leaf, leaves.* Words ending in *-ff* or *-ffe* simply add *-s: staff, staffs; giraffe, giraffes.*

- **Compound words:** For most compound words, add *-s* or *-es* at the end of the last word: *checkbooks, player-coaches.* For a few, the word to make plural is not the last one: *sister-in-law, sisters-in-law; attorney general, attorneys general.* (For hyphenating compound words, see Chart 110 in 22d.2.)

- **Internal changes and endings other than -s**: A few words change internally or add endings other than *-s* to become plural: *foot, feet; man, men; mouse, mice; child, children.*

→

Spelling rules for plurals, suffixes, and *ie*, *ei* words (*continued*)   **108**

- **Foreign words:** Plurals other than *-s* or *-es* are listed in good dictionaries. In general, for many Latin words ending in *-um*, form plurals by changing *-um* to *-a*: *curriculum, curricula; datum, data; medium, media; stratum, strata.* For Latin words that end in *-us*, the plural is often *-i*: *alumnus, alumni; syllabus, syllabi.* For Greek *-on* words, the plural is often *-a*: *criterion, criteria; phenomenon, phenomena.*

- **One-form words:** A few spellings are the same for the singular and plural: *deer, elk, quail.* The differences are conveyed by adding words, not endings: *one deer, nine deer.*

Suffixes

- **-y words:** If the letter before the final *y* is a consonant, change the *y* to *i* unless the suffix begins with an *i* (for example, *-ing*): *fry, fried, frying.* If the letter before the *-y* is a vowel, keep the final *y*: *employ, employed, employing.* These rules do not apply to irregular verbs (see Chart 62 in section 8d).

- **-e words:** Drop a final *e* when the suffix begins with a vowel unless doing so would cause confusion (for example, *be + ing* does not become *bing*): *require, requiring; like, liking.* Keep the final *e* when the suffix begins with a consonant: *require, requirement; like, likely.* Exceptions include *argument, judgment,* and *truly.*

- **Words that double a final letter:** If the final letter is a consonant, double it only if it passes all three of these tests: (1) its last two letters are a vowel followed by a consonant, (2) it has one syllable or is accented on the last syllable, and (3) the suffix begins with a vowel: *drop, dropped; begin, beginning; forget, forgetful, forgettable.*

- **-cede, -ceed, -sede words:** Only one word ends in *-sede*: *supersede.* Three words end in *-ceed*: *exceed, proceed, succeed.* All other English words whose endings sound like "seed" end in *-cede*: *concede, intercede, precede.*

- **-ally and -ly words:** The suffixes *-ally* and *-ly* turn words into ADVERBS. For words ending in *-ic*, add *-ally*: *logically, statistically.* Otherwise, add *-ly*: *quickly, sharply.* (The only exception is *public, publicly.*)

- **-ance, -ence, and -ible, -able:** No consistent rules govern words with these suffixes. The best advice is, when in doubt, look it up. →

Words Often Misspelled (continued)

luxury	reproduce
magazine	resources
manual	restaurant
mathematics	sacrifice
medicine	saxophone
miniature	sentence
participle	separate
perhaps	several
persuade	sheriff
physical	similar
pigeon	sophomore
pitiful	specimen
pleasant	sponsor
poison	statistics
practical	strategy
prepare	surprise
privilege	temperature
propaganda	therefore
pumpkin	thorough
purpose	tobacco
pursue	together
pursuit	tomorrow
quandary	typical
rebel	vitamins
recognize	Wednesday
regular	woman
remember	women

> ⊙ **Spelling rules for plurals, suffixes, and *ie, ei* words** *(continued)*   **108**
>
> **The *ie, ei* Rule**
>
> ■ The old rhyme for *ie* and *ei* is usually true:
>
> *I* before *e* [bel**ie**ve, f**ie**ld, gr**ie**f]
> Except after *c* [c**ei**ling, conc**ei**t],
> Or when sounded like *ay* [**ei**ght, v**ei**n],
> As in *neighbor* and *weigh*.
>
> ■ You may want to memorize these major exceptions:
>
> ***ie:***   consc**ie**nce, financ**ie**r, sc**ie**nce, spec**ie**s
> ***ei:***   **ei**ther, n**ei**ther, l**ei**sure, s**ei**ze, counterf**ei**t, for**ei**gn, forf**ei**t, sl**ei**ght, w**ei**rd

ANSWERS: EXERCISE 22-2

1. scarves
2. species
3. rodeos
4. moose
5. leeches
6. curricula
7. logs
8. fathers-in-law
9. phenomena
10. wolves
11. nachos
12. fungi
13. lives
14. push-ups
15. theses

ANSWERS: EXERCISE 22-3

1. **(a)** profitable
   (b) reproducible
   (c) controllable
   (d) coercible
   (e) recognizable

2. **(a)** luxuriance
   (b) prudence
   (c) deviance
   (d) resistance
   (e) independence

EXERCISE 22-2

Consulting Chart 108, form the plurals of these words.

1. scarf	6. curriculum	11. nacho
2. species	7. log	12. fungus
3. rodeo	8. father-in-law	13. life
4. moose	9. phenomenon	14. push-up
5. leech	10. wolf	15. thesis

EXERCISE 22-3

Consulting Chart 108 and a dictionary, follow the directions for each group of words.

1. Add *-able* or *-ible*: (a) profit; (b) reproduce; (c) control; (d) coerce; (e) recognize.
2. Add *-ance* or *-ence*: (a) luxuri _____ ; (b) prud _____ ; (c) devi _____ ; (d) resist _____ ; (e) independ _____ .
3. Drop the final *e* as needed: (a) true + ly; (b) joke + ing; (c) fortunate + ly; (d) appease + ing; (e) appease + ment.
4. Change the final *y* to *i* as needed: (a) happy + ness; (b) pry + ed; (c) pry + ing; (d) dry + ly; (e) beautify + ing.

→

5. Double the final consonant as needed: (a) commit + ed; (b) commit + ment; (c) drop + ed; (d) occur + ed; (e) regret + ful.

6. Insert *ie* or *ei* correctly: (a) rel _____ f; (b) ach _____ ve; (c) w _____ rd; (d) n _____ ce; (e) dec _____ ve.

22d Using hyphens correctly

22d.1 Hyphenating at the end of a line

Unless the last word on a line would use up most of the right margin of your paper, do not divide it. If you must divide a word, try not to divide the last word on the first line of a paper, the last word in a paragraph, or the last word on a page. When you have to hyphenate, break the word only between syllables, using the guidelines in Chart 109. If you are unsure of how to divide a word into syllables, consult a dictionary (see 20a.1).

● Guidelines for end-of-line hyphenation   109

■ Do not divide very short words, one syllable words, or words pronounced as one syllable.

NO	we-alth	en-vy	scream-ed
YES	wealth	envy	screamed

■ Do not leave or carry over only one or two letters.

NO	a-live	tax-i	he-licopter	helicopt-er
YES	alive	taxi	heli-copter	helicop-ter

■ Divide words only between syllables.

NO	proc-eed
YES	pro-ceed

■ Always follow the rules governing double consonants.

NO	ful-lness	omitt-ing	asp-halt
YES	full-ness	omit-ting	as-phalt

■ Divide hyphenated words after the hyphen, if possible, rather than at any other point.

NO	self-con-scious	good-look-ing report
YES	self-conscious	good-looking report

Answers: Exercise 22-3 (continued)

3. (a) truly
   (b) joking
   (c) fortunately
   (d) appeasing
   (e) appeasement

4. (a) happiness
   (b) pried
   (c) prying
   (d) dryly
   (e) beautifying

5. (a) committed
   (b) commitment
   (c) dropped
   (d) occurred
   (e) regretful

6. (a) relief
   (b) achieve
   (c) weird
   (d) niece
   (e) deceive

TEACHING TIP

Because the hyphenation of compound words tends to change over time, students are sometimes uncertain whether to use hyphens with them or not. Words used consecutively over a considerable period of time often move closer together through hyphenation and may later become a single word. *Steamboat*, for example, was once written *steam boat*, then *steam-boat*, and finally one unhyphenated word. *Wristwatch* was, earlier, *wrist watch* and later *wrist-watch*. To be sure of current usage, students need to use a dictionary.

BACKGROUND

A single missing hyphen cost U.S. citizens $18.5 million in 1962. *Mariner I*, a U.S. space exploration rocket, went off course and had to be destroyed. The reason: a missing hyphen in its computer-run flight program.

WORDS OFTEN MISSPELLED

Silent Letters and Blended Sounds

acquainted	muscle
acquire	pamphlet
condemn	psychology
contradict	quantity
courteous	receipt
crowd	reminisce
dealt	rhythm
descend	safety
distinct	sandwich
empty	schedule
fascinate	sergeant
February	shoulder
foresee	source
foretell	souvenir
gauge	straight
group	strength
gruesome	stretch
guaranteed	strict
guard	technique
initiative	themselves
instead	though
knowledge	thought
length	through
library	trouble
meant	twelfth
mortgage	vacuum

22d.2 Hyphenating prefixes, suffixes, compound words, and numbers

Prefixes and **suffixes** are syllables attached to root words. **Compound words** use two or more words together to express one concept. Some prefixes and suffixes are hyphenated; others are not. Compound words can be separate words (*night shift*), hyphenated words (*tractor-trailer*), or one word (*handbook*). Chart 110 gives basic guidelines for word hyphenation.

⊙ Hyphenating prefixes, suffixes, compound words, and numbers   **110**

Prefixes and Suffixes

- Use hyphens after the prefixes *all-*, *ex-*, *quasi-*, and *self-*.
  - **YES** all-inclusive   self-reliant

- Do not use a hyphen when *self* is a root word, not a prefix.
  - **NO** self-ishness   self-less
  - **YES** selfishness   selfless

- Use a hyphen to avoid a distracting string of letters.
  - **NO** antiintellectual   belllike   prooutsourcing
  - **YES** anti-intellectual   bell-like   pro-outsourcing

- Use a hyphen before the suffix *-elect*.
  - **NO** presidentelect
  - **YES** president-elect

- Use a hyphen when a prefix or suffix is added to a numeral or to a word that starts with a capital letter.
  - **NO** post1950s   proAmerican   Rembrandtlike
  - **YES** post-1950   pro-American   Rembrandt-like

- Use a hyphen between a prefix and a compound word.
  - **NO** antigun control
  - **YES** anti-gun control

- Use a hyphen to prevent confusion in meaning or pronunciation.
  - **YES** re-dress ("dress again")   redress ("set right")
  - **YES** un-ionize ("remove the ions")   unionize ("form a union")

→

Hyphenating prefixes, suffixes, compound words, and numbers *(continued)*   110

■ Use a hyphen when two or more prefixes apply to one root word.

| **YES** | pre- and post-war eras   two-, three-, or four-year program |

Compound Words

■ Use a hyphen for most compound modifiers that precede the noun. Do not use a hyphen for most compound modifiers after the noun.

| **YES** | well-researched report | report is well researched |
| **YES** | two-inch clearance | clearance of two inches |

■ Use a hyphen between compound nouns joining two units of measure.

| **YES** | light-year   kilowatt-hour   foot-pound |

■ You do not need to use a hyphen when a compound modifier starts with an *-ly* adverb.

| **YES** | happily married couple   loosely tied package |

■ Do not use a hyphen when a compound modifier beginning with an *adverb* is in the comparative or superlative form.

| **NO** | more-significant factors | least-welcome guest |
| **YES** | more significant factors | least welcome guest |

■ Do use a hyphen when a compound modifier beginning with an *adjective* is in the comparative or superlative form.

| **NO** | better fitting shoes | longest lasting relief |
| **YES** | better-fitting shoes | longest-lasting relief |

■ Do not use a hyphen when a compound modifier is a foreign phrase.

| **YES** | post hoc fallacies |

■ Do not use a hyphen with a possessive compound modifier.

| **NO** | a full-week's work | eight-hours' pay |
| **YES** | a full week's work | eight hours' pay |

Spelled-Out Numbers

■ Use a hyphen between two-word numbers from twenty-one through ninety-nine.

| **YES** | thirty-five   two hundred thirty-five |

→

WORDS OFTEN MISSPELLED

Other Commonly Misspelled Words

absence	material
across	mere
always	minutes
among	morning
ancestry	nevertheless
anxiety	nineteen
anywhere	ninety
authentic	ninth
awkward	nuclear
bachelor	omit
benefited	opinion
birthday	paid
compel	parole
consensus	pastime
cylinder	penetrate
defer	pertain
disagree	phase
disturb	prairie
exceed	pretty
expense	prevail
familiar	restaurant
forty	science
forward	speak
furniture	speech
grandeur	temperature
hesitate	until
hypocrite	vicious
intercede	wherever
laid	whether
license	wholly

QUOTATION: ON WRITING

This morning I deleted the hyphen from "hell-bound" and made it one word; this afternoon I redivided it and restored the hyphen.

—Edwin Arlington Robinson

Hyphenating prefixes, suffixes, compound words, and numbers (*continued*)   **110**

- Use a hyphen in a compound-word modifier formed from a number and a word.

  YES   fifty-minute class   three-to-one odds
         [also *50-minute class*]   [also *3-to-1 odds*]

- Use a hyphen between the numerator and the denominator of two-word fractions.

  YES   one-half   two-fifths   seven-tenths

---

❶ ALERT: Use figures rather than words for any fraction that needs more than two words to express. If you cannot use figures (for example, if you cannot rearrange a sentence that starts with a multiword fraction), use hyphens between the words of the numerator's number and the words of the denominator's number but not between the numerator and the denominator: two one-hundredths (2/100), thirty-three ten-thousandths (33/10,000). **!**

ANSWERS AND COVERAGE: EXERCISE 22-4

1. all-powerful [*all-* prefixes hyphenated]

2. Comparison-and-contrast [hyphenated compound]; more agile [no hyphen with *more*]

3. boldly striped [no hyphen after *-ly* adverb]; underbody [*under-* prefix spelled closed]

4. eleven feet [no double digits]; one-quarter [fraction]; five hundred [no double digits]

5. self-confident [*self-* prefix hyphenated]

6. village destroyer [open compound]; into [closed compound]

7. terror-stricken [hyphenated compound]

8. spring-loaded [hyphenated compound]; poisoned arrows [not a compound]

9. cattle killers [open compound]

10. animal shows [open compound]; pro-animal [*pro-* prefix hyphenated before vowel]

EXERCISE 22-4

Consulting section 22d, write in each blank the correct form of the words in parentheses according to the way they are used in the sentence.

1. The tiger is (all powerful) _____ in the cat family.
2. (Comparison and contrast) _____ studies of tigers and lions show that the tiger is the (more agile) _____ and powerful.
3. The tiger's body is a (boldly striped) _____ yellow, with a white (under body) _____ .
4. The tiger's maximum length is about (eleven feet) _____ , about (one quarter) _____ of which is accounted for by its tail, and its maximum weight is up to (five hundred) _____ pounds.
5. The Bengal tiger, the largest of the family, is aggressive and (self confident) _____ .
6. In India, where the Bengal is called a (village destroyer) _____ , it has a reputation for going (in to) _____ villages to hunt for food.
7. Entire villages have been temporarily abandoned by (terror stricken) _____ people who have seen a Bengal tiger nearby.
8. Villagers seek to protect their homes by destroying tigers with traps, (spring loaded) _____ guns, and (poisoned arrows) _____ .

9. Bengal tigers are also called (cattle killers) _____ , although they attack domestic animals only when they cannot find wild ones.

10. Many people who do not live near a zoo get to see tigers only in (animal shows) _____ , although (pro animal) _____ activists try to prevent tigers' being used this way.

EXERCISE 22-5

The following paragraph contains twelve misspelled or incorrectly hyphenated words. Circle the words, correct them, and match them to a section in this chapter. If the error does not fall under any particular section, describe the cause of the error in your own words.

An invitation arrived last week in a beautyful, crisp white envelop. I knew rite away it was a peace of important mail, unlike all the junk mail I usually recieve. It seemed that the local chapter of the Falcon Club of America wanted to hear my thoughts on American car collecting. The prospect of giving a speech through me into a nervous frenzy as I tryed to prepare at the last minute—getting a haircut, memorizing my notes, practiceing in front of my freinds—all designed to insure that I would not humiliate myself publically. As it turned out, my heart-ache was pointless. The club really just wanted the opportunity to inspect my navy blue 1965 Ford Falcon.

ANSWERS AND COVERAGE: EXERCISE 22-5

Incorrect	Correct
beautyful	beautiful [22c, Chart 108]
envelop	envelope [22b, Chart 107]
rite	right [22b, Chart 107]
peace	piece [22b, Chart 107]
recieve	receive [22c, Chart 108]
through	threw [22b, Chart 107]
tryed	tried [22c, Chart 108]
practiceing	practicing [22c, Chart 108]
freinds	friends [22c, Chart 108]
insure	ensure [Usage Glossary]
publically	publicly [22c, Chart 108]
heart-ache	heartache [22c, Chart 110]

PART FOUR

USING PUNCTUATION AND MECHANICS

Part Four explains how to use punctuation and mechanics according to currently accepted practice. As you use Chapters 23 through 30, remember that punctuation and mechanics are tools that exist to help you deliver your message clearly and effectively to your readers.

23
PERIODS, QUESTION MARKS, AND EXCLAMATION POINTS

Periods, question marks, and exclamation points are known as **end punctuation** because they occur at the end of sentences.

I love you**.** Do you love me**?** I love you**!**

PERIOD

23a Using a period at the end of a statement, a mild command, or an indirect question

Unless a sentence asks a DIRECT QUESTION* (see 23c) or issues a strong command or emphatic declaration (see 23e), it ends with a **period.**

STATEMENT
A journey of a thousand miles must begin with a single step.
   —Lao-tsu, *The Way of Lao-tsu*

MILD COMMAND
Put a gram of boldness into everything you do.
   —Baltasar Gracian

INDIRECT QUESTION
I asked if they wanted to climb Mt. Everest. [A direct question would end with a question mark: I asked, "*Do you want to climb Mt. Everest?*"]

23b Using periods with most abbreviations

Most **abbreviations** call for periods, but some do not. Typical abbreviations with periods include *Mt., St., Dr., Mr., Ms., Mrs., Ph.D., M.D., R.N., a.m.,* and *p.m.* (For complete information about using *a.m.* and

---

*You can find the definition of a word printed in small capital letters (such as DIRECT QUESTION) in the Terms Glossary toward the end of this handbook.

p.m., see section 30h.) The word *professor* is ordinarily spelled out, not abbreviated. Abbreviations without periods include the names of some organizations and government agencies (such as CBS and NASA). For more about using abbreviations, see sections 30h and 30i.

> **Ms.** Yuan, who works at **NASA,** lectured to **Dr.** Garcia's physics class at 9:30 **a.m.**

❶ **PUNCTUATION ALERT:** When the period of an abbreviation falls at the end of a sentence that calls for a period, the period also serves to end the sentence. Put a sentence-ending question mark or exclamation point, however, after the period of the abbreviation.

> The phone rang at 4:00 **a.m.**
> How embarrassing to dial a wrong number at 4:00 **a.m.!**
> Who would call at 4:00 **a.m.?!**

QUESTION MARK

23c Using a question mark after a direct question

A **direct question** asks a question and ends with a **question mark.** In contrast, an **indirect question** reports a question and ends with a period (see 23a).

> How many attempts have been made to climb Mt. Everest? [An indirect question would be *The tourist wanted to know how many attempts had been made to climb Mt. Everest.*]

❶ **PUNCTUATION ALERT:** Do not combine a question mark with a comma, a period, or an exclamation point.

> **NO** She asked, "How are you?."
> **YES** She asked, "How are you?"!

Questions in a series are each followed by a question mark, whether or not each question is a complete sentence.

> After the fierce storm had passed, the mountain climbers debated what to do next. Turn back? Move on? Rest for a while?

❶ **CAPITALIZATION ALERT:** When questions in a series are not complete sentences, you can choose to capitalize the first letter or not, as long as you are consistent in each piece of writing. !

When a request is phrased as a question to achieve a polite tone, it does not always require a question mark:

> Would you please send me a copy.

23d Using a question mark in parentheses

When a date or number is unknown or doubtful even after your very best research, you can use *(?)*.

Mary Astell, an English author who wrote pamphlets on women's rights, was born in 1666 **(?)** and died in 1731.

The word *about* is often a graceful substitute for *(?)*: *Mary Astell was born about 1666.*

Do not use *(?)* to communicate that you are unsure of information.

NO   It will rain **(?)** today.

YES   It might rain today.

Also, your choice of words, not *(?)*, should communicate irony or sarcasm.

NO   Having the flu is a delightful **(?)** experience.

YES   Having the flu is not exactly a pleasant experience.

EXCLAMATION POINT

23e Using an exclamation point for a strong command or an emphatic declaration

An **exclamation point** can end a strong command or an emphatic declaration. A strong command gives a very firm order: *Look out behind you!* An emphatic declaration makes a shocking or surprising statement: *There's been an accident!*

PUNCTUATION ALERT: Do not combine an exclamation point with a comma, a period, or a question mark.

NO   "There's been an accident**!,**" cried my mother.

YES   "There's been an accident**!**" cried my mother. **!**

23f Avoiding the overuse of exclamation points

In academic writing, your words, rather than exclamation points, should communicate the strength of your message. Reserve exclamation points for occasional emphatic dialogue. Use them only very rarely for a short emphatic declaration within a longer passage.

When we were in Nepal, we tried each day to see Mt. Everest. But each day we failed to see it. Clouds defeated us**!** The summit never emerged from a heavy overcast.

If you use exclamation points too often in academic writing, your reader will think that your judgment of urgency is exaggerated.

NO   Mountain climbing can be dangerous! You must know correct procedures! You must have the proper equipment. Take rope! Wear spiked boots!

YES   Mountain climbing can be dangerous. Without knowing correct procedures, climbers quickly can turn an outing into a disaster. The proper equipment includes rope and spiked boots.

Your choice of words, not *(!)*, should communicate amazement or sarcasm.

NO   At 29,141 feet *(!)*, Mt. Everest is the world's highest mountain. I heard that Chris *(!)* wants to climb it.

YES   At a majestic but staggering 29,141 feet, Mt. Everest is the world's highest mountain. Yet Chris, amazingly, wants to climb it.

EXERCISE 23-1

Consulting sections 23a through 23f, insert any needed periods, quotation marks, and exclamation points. Also delete any unneeded ones.

EXAMPLE   Have you ever crossed a wide river or a deep canyon on a huge bridge that towered over the landscape.

           Have you ever crossed a wide river or a deep canyon on a huge bridge that towered over the landscape?

1. The first (?) modern bridge was the one built over the Severn River in England in 1781.
2. The fact that it was built out of cast-iron girders might explain why engineers today still call it a "modern" bridge?
3. Earlier bridges had been built from wood or stone!
4. Wooden bridges, however, often burned down when struck by lightning
5. The engineer who designed the Severn Bridge used cast-iron girders because iron was a lightweight (!) substitute for stone.
6. "Why would anyone prefer lightweight materials for building a sturdy bridge" is a question you may ask?
7. Strong but light building materials allow a bridge to stand on the fewest possible supports, a building technique that looks graceful and keeps costs down!
8. In the 1930s, people wondered if the graceful, narrow bridges that were being built were safe because such bridges often swayed in the wind?

QUOTATION: ON WRITING

Punctuation: what is it, after all, but another way of cutting up time, creating or negating relationships, telling words when to take a rest, when to get on with their relentless stories, when to catch their breath?

—Karen Elizabeth Gordon

ANSWERS AND COVERAGE: EXERCISE 23-1

1. Possibly the first modern bridge was the one built over the Severn River in England in 1781. [23d, question mark deleted and *Possibly* inserted]

2. The fact that it was built out of cast-iron girders might explain why engineers today still call it a "modern" bridge. [23a, question mark deleted and replaced with period]

3. Earlier bridges had been built from wood or stone. [23e, exclamation point deleted and replaced with period]

4. Wooden bridges, however, often burned down when struck by lightning. [23a, period added]

5. The engineer who designed the Severn Bridge used cast-iron girders because iron was a lightweight substitute for stone. [23e, exclamation point deleted]

6. "Why would anyone prefer lightweight materials for building a sturdy bridge?" is a question you may ask. [23c, question mark added to actual question; 23a, question mark deleted and replaced with period]

7. Strong but light building materials allow a bridge to stand on the fewest possible supports, a building technique that looks graceful and keeps costs down. [23e, exclamation point deleted and replaced with period]

8. In the 1930s, people wondered if the graceful, narrow bridges that were being built were safe because such bridges often swayed in the wind. [23a, question mark deleted and replaced with period]

→

Answers and Coverage: Exercise 23-1 (continued)

9. One of them, the Tacoma Narrows Bridge in Washington State, surprised no one when it began to twist in a windstorm (the date was Nov. 7, 1940). [23d, question mark deleted; 23a, period added to abbreviation]

10. But everyone was shocked when the wind ripped the bridge apart in just a few minutes! [23e, acceptable exclamation point]

ANSWERS: EXERCISE 23-2

Bill Gates, the billionaire founder of Microsoft Corp., recently expanded his empire by buying time itself! He completed the deal when he purchased the 16 million images of the Bettmann Archive, the company that controls the largest collection of historical photographs in existence. Otto Bettmann had started the company that bears his name with some of his father's photographs. The elder Bettmann had been a surgeon in Germany who put together a small file of scientific illustrations and X-rays. When the son was forced to flee Germany in the 1930s, he packed the photographs in two trunks and brought them to the United States with him. How did this small, unpromising file of scientific images grow into the world's largest collection of photographs? Over the years, Otto took some photos himself, but he also bought the pictures of retiring photographers and other collectors. In this way he managed to build a library whose images provide a photographic history of the twentieth century. Gates's purchase of this collection thus puts him in a unique position: He now owns the past!

9. One of them, the Tacoma Narrows Bridge in Washington State, surprised no one (?) when it began to twist in a windstorm (the date was Nov 7, 1940).

10. But everyone was shocked when the wind ripped the bridge apart in just a few minutes!

EXERCISE 23-2

Insert needed periods, question marks, and exclamation points.

Bill Gates, the billionaire founder of Microsoft Corp, recently expanded his empire by buying time itself He completed the deal when he purchased the 16 million (!) images of the Bettmann Archive, the company that controls the largest collection of historical photographs in existence Otto Bettmann had started the company that bears his name with some of his father's photographs The elder Bettmann had been a surgeon in Germany who put together a small file of scientific illustrations and X-rays When the son was forced to flee Germany in the 1930s, he packed the photographs in two trunks and brought them to the United States with him How did this small, unpromising file of scientific images grow into the world's largest collection of photographs Over the years, Otto took some photos himself, but he also bought the pictures of retiring photographers and other collectors In this way he managed to build a library whose images provide a photographic history of the twentieth century Gates's purchase of this collection thus puts him in a unique position: He now owns the past

24

COMMAS

Commas are the most frequently used marks of punctuation. Commas occur twice as often as all other marks of punctuation combined. Comma rules are many: A comma must be used in certain places, it must not be used in other places, and it is optional in still other places. This chapter will help you sort through the various rules and uses of commas: before a COORDINATING CONJUNCTION linking INDEPENDENT CLAUSES (see 24a); after an INTRODUCTORY CLAUSE, PHRASE, or word (24b); to separate items in a series (24c); to separate COORDINATE ADJECTIVES (24d); with NONRESTRICTIVE (nonessential) elements (24e); with parenthetical and TRANSITIONAL EXPRESSIONS, contrasts, words of DIRECT ADDRESS, and TAG SENTENCES (24f); with quoted words (24g); in names, dates, addresses, and numbers (24h); to clarify meaning (24i); and to avoid misuse or overuse (24j).

The comma serves to group and separate sentence parts, improving clarity for readers. Consider the clarity of the following paragraph, which contains all needed punctuation except commas.

> **NO** Among publishers typographical errors known as "typos" are an embarrassing fact of life. In spite of careful editing reviews and multiple readings few books are perfect upon publication. Soon after a book reaches bookstores, reports of errors embarrassments to authors and editors alike start to come in. Everyone laughed therefore although no one thought it was funny when an English textbook was published with this line: "Proofread your writing carefullly."

Here is the same paragraph with commas included.

> **YES** Among publishers, typographical errors, known as "typos," are an embarrassing fact of life. In spite of careful editing, reviews, and multiple readings, few books are perfect upon publication. Soon after a book reaches bookstores, reports of errors, embarrassments to authors and editors alike, start to come in. Everyone laughed, therefore, although no one thought it was funny, when an English textbook was published with this line: "Proofread your writing carefullly."

EXTRA EXERCISE A

Insert commas before coordinating conjunctions that separate independent clauses.

1. England, Scotland, and Wales are located on the same island.

2. Wales is located on the western peninsula of the island and England and Scotland occupy the rest of it.

3. It is bounded on the east by the North Sea and on the south by the English Channel.

4. The Teutonic invaders of the fifth century had to struggle with native Britons for possession of the island for the Romans had virtually abandoned the island by that time.

5. Britain is the proper name of the whole island but England is the political name of the part conquered by the Angles.

6. Neither the Jutes nor the Saxons moved north for they chose to settle in what is today Kent or moved on to Sussex, Wessex, and Essex.

7. The Scots were actually the people of Ireland yet a small colony they established in the northern part of the island eventually gave it its name.

8. The Norman Conquest of Britain was begun under William the Conqueror and was continued by his sons.

9. With few exceptions, all the existing shires of England had been established at the time of the Norman Conquest but the boundaries were not always exactly the same as they are now.

10. Since the eleventh century, the map of Britain has remained little changed yet the reins of power have shifted many times.

→

In the *yes* paragraph, the meaning is clear. Each comma in it is used for a specific reason according to a comma rule.

Avoid two practices that can get writers into trouble with commas: (1) As you write, do not insert a comma just because you happen to pause to think. (2) As you reread your writing, do not insert commas according to your personal habits of pausing. Although a comma may alert a reader to a slight pause, pausing is not a reliable guide for writers, because people's breathing rhythms, accents, and thinking spans vary greatly.

24a Using a comma before a coordinating conjunction that links independent clauses

When a **coordinating conjunction** (*and, but, for, or, nor, so,* or *yet*) links INDEPENDENT CLAUSES, use a comma before the coordinating conjunction (see Chart 111).

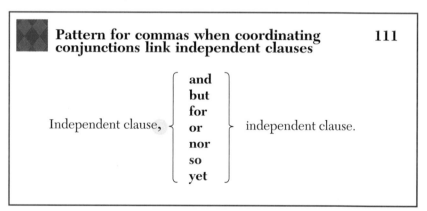

Pattern for commas when coordinating conjunctions link independent clauses   **111**

Independent clause, { and / but / for / or / nor / so / yet } independent clause.

The sky turned dark gray, **and** the wind died suddenly.

The November morning had just begun, **but** it looked like dusk.

Shopkeepers closed their stores early, **for** they wanted to get home.

Soon high winds would start, **or** thick snow would begin silently.

Farmers had no time to continue harvesting, **nor** could they round up their animals in distant fields.

The firehouse whistle blew four times, **so** everyone knew a blizzard was closing in.

People on the road tried to reach safety, **yet** a few unlucky ones were stranded.

When two independent clauses in a sentence are very short, some authorities omit the comma before the coordinating conjunction. You will never be wrong, however, and you avoid the risk of error, if you always use a comma in academic writing.

❶ COMMA CAUTION: Do not put a comma after a coordinating conjunction that links independent clauses.

NO The sky turned dark gray **and,** the wind died suddenly.
YES The sky turned dark gray**, and** the wind died suddenly. **!**

❶ COMMA CAUTION: Do not use a comma when a coordinating conjunction links only words, PHRASES, or DEPENDENT CLAUSES. However, do use commas to separate each of three or more items in a series (see 24c).

NO Learning a new language demands **time, and patience.**
[Two words linked by *and* use no comma.]

YES Learning a new language demands **time and patience.**

NO Each language has **a beauty of its own, and forms of expression** which are duplicated nowhere else. [Two phrases linked by *and* use no comma.]

YES Each language has **a beauty of its own and forms of expression** which are duplicated nowhere else.
—Margaret Mead, "Unispeak" **!**

❶ COMMA CAUTION: Do not use a comma to separate independent clauses unless they are linked by a coordinating conjunction. If you use such a comma, you will create the error known as a comma splice (see 14c).

NO Five inches of snow fell in two hours**,** one inch of ice built up when the snow turned to freezing rain. [Alone, the comma creates a comma splice. A coordinating conjunction must follow the comma.]

YES Five inches of snow fell in two hours**, and** one inch of ice built up when the snow turned to freezing rain. [The coordinating conjunction *and* links the two independent clauses.]

YES Five inches of snow fell in two hours**.** One inch of ice built up when the snow turned to freezing rain. [Independent clauses can become two separate sentences.] **!**

When independent clauses containing other commas are linked by a coordinating conjunction, you can choose to use a semicolon in place of the comma that would come right before the coordinating conjunction (see 25b). Base your decision on what would help your reader understand the material most easily.

Because temperatures remained low all winter, the snow could not melt until spring**; and** some people felt that they would never see grass again.

ANSWERS: EXERCISE 24-1

Answers may vary slightly. Here is one set of possibilities.

1. Immigrants from Eastern Europe came to New York City, and they sold meat patties in stands all over the city to hungry passersby.

2. The patties were too messy to carry around, so some German sailors on shore leave asked that the meat patties be placed on soft rolls of bread.

3. The combination of meat and bread came to be known as hamburger, for the German sailors named the portable snack after their hometown of Hamburg.

4. The hamburger went national in 1903 at the United States Louisiana Purchase Exposition in St. Louis, and it was an instant success.

5. A patty served with no roll and on a plate is not a true hamburger, nor can a true hamburger be any shape but round.

6. Many burger lovers pile onions and pickles on their hamburgers and smother them with ketchup, yet others insist the only authentic hamburger is served plain.

7. Some cooks put a slice of cheese on their burger, or they place slices of bacon on top for a special treat.

8. Some people prefer not to eat red meat, but U.S. cooks used only beef until a decade ago.

9. People not willing to eat beef missed their burgers, so a variety of ingredients are now available for making different kinds of burgers.

10. Most supermarkets carry the ingredients for turkey burgers and pork burgers, and some also carry ground tofu for tofu burgers.

EXERCISE 24-1

Consulting section 24a, combine each pair of sentences using the coordinating conjunction shown in parentheses. Rearrange words when necessary. Insert commas before coordinating conjunctions that separate independent clauses.

EXAMPLE   Sailors in U.S. ports put chopped meat patties between slices of bread at the turn of the century. An American classic was born. (and)

Sailors in U.S. ports put chopped meat patties between slices of bread at the turn of the century, **and** an American classic was born.

1. Immigrants from eastern Europe came to New York City. They sold meat patties in stands all over the city to hungry passersby. (and)

2. The patties were too messy to carry around. Some German sailors on shore leave asked that the meat patties be placed on soft rolls of bread. (so)

3. The combination of meat and bread came to be known as a hamburger. The German sailors named the portable snack after their hometown of Hamburg. (for)

4. The hamburger went national in 1903 at the United States Louisiana Purchase Exposition in St. Louis. It was an instant success. (and)

5. A patty served with no roll and on a plate is not a true hamburger. A true hamburger cannot be any shape but round. (nor)

6. Many burger lovers pile onions and pickles on their hamburgers and smother them with ketchup. Others insist the only authentic hamburger is served plain. (yet)

7. Some cooks put a slice of cheese on their burger. They place slices of bacon on top for a special treat. (or)

8. Some people prefer not to eat red meat. U.S. cooks used only beef until a decade ago. (but)

9. People not willing to eat beef missed their burgers. A variety of ingredients are now available for making different kinds of burgers. (so)

10. Most supermarkets carry the ingredients for turkey burgers and pork burgers. Some also carry tofu for tofu burgers. (and)

24b Using a comma after an introductory clause, phrase, or word

Use a comma to signal the end of an introductory element and the beginning of an INDEPENDENT CLAUSE (see Chart 112).

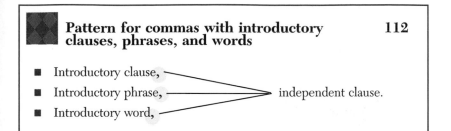

> **Pattern for commas with introductory clauses, phrases, and words**   112
>
> - Introductory clause,
> - Introductory phrase,   independent clause.
> - Introductory word,

Some authorities omit the comma when an introductory element is very short and the sentence is clear without a comma. However, in academic writing, you will never be wrong if you use a comma after an introductory element.

24b.1 Using a comma after an introductory adverb clause

An **adverb clause** is a DEPENDENT CLAUSE (see 7o.2). It cannot stand alone as an independent unit because it starts with a subordinating conjunction (for example, *although, because, if;* for a complete list, see 7h). When an adverb clause comes before an independent clause, use a comma after the adverb clause.

> **When it comes to eating,** you can sometimes help yourself more by helping yourself less.
>
> —Richard Armour

24b.2 Using a comma after an introductory phrase

A **phrase** is a group of words (see 7n) that cannot stand alone as a sentence. When a phrase comes before an independent clause, use a comma after the phrase.

PREPOSITIONAL PHRASE	**Between 1544 and 1689,** sugar refineries appeared in London and New York.
PAST-PARTICIPIAL PHRASE	**Obtained mainly from sugar cane and sugar beets,** sugar is also developed from the sap of maple trees.
PRESENT-PARTICIPIAL PHRASE	**Beginning in infancy,** we develop lifelong tastes for sweet foods.
INFINITIVE PHRASE	**To satisfy a craving for ice cream,** even timid people sometimes brave midnight streets.
ABSOLUTE PHRASE	**Eating being enjoyable,** we tend to eat more than we need for fuel.

TEACHING TIP

A surprising number of students, especially those inexperienced with academic writing, tend to equate writing ability with knowledge of spelling and rules for the comma. (Not all students who have these ideas admit them freely, but often such notions emerge on anonymous questionnaires or in teacher-student conferences.) You might deal with this misperception about comma rules in a variety of ways. First, you can put commas in their place by referring to the writing process, especially the different concerns that occupy a writer during drafting, revision, and editing—students can reread Chapters 2 and 3 to refresh their memories about these activities. Second, you can invite students to circle any comma in their writing about which they have a question—or any spot where they have not written a comma and have a question—and to jot the question in the margin. This helps students avoid getting snagged on commas while at the same time allowing them to get answers to their questions when you return their work. You will likely find that students have used most commas correctly (a fact that when pointed out enhances students' confidence) and that you can organize the areas of confusion and thus clarify them for the students. Finally, after students have studied topics such as coordination, subordination, parallelism, and variety and emphasis, you can offer a tutorial review of commas—and students will be happy to discover how much they already know.

TEACHING TIP

Unless they are set off by commas, some adverbs that double as propositions are likely to cause confusion when placed before the subject of a sentence. You can advise students to apply common sense to avoid confusion. This issue is discussed in section 13b.

NO Below the submarine checked the water for mines. [Was something below the submarine?]

YES Below, the submarine checked the water for mines.

NO After the crew expected to escort the president's ship. [Then what?]

YES After, the crew expected to escort the president's ship.

ANSWERS: EXERCISE 24-2

1. snack, Kellogg's
2. sugar, it
3. after, his
4. market, the
5. Correct

24b.3 Using a comma after introductory words

Introductory words include **transitional expressions** and **conjunctive adverbs.** These words carry messages of relationships between ideas in sentences and paragraphs. Transitional expressions include *for example* and *in addition* (for a complete list, see Chart 25 in section 4d.1). Conjunctive adverbs include *therefore* and *however* (for a complete list, see Chart 51 in section 7f). When these introductory words appear at the beginning of a sentence, most writers follow them with a comma.

> **For example,** fructose is fruit sugar that is metabolized as a blood sugar.

❶ **COMMA CAUTION:** A comma after a single introductory word has recently, in some contexts, been dropped. In most academic writing, however, this comma is still required. Ask your instructor what is required in each class. If the choice is yours, be consistent in each piece of writing. ❗

Interjections are introductory words that convey surprise or other emotions. Use a comma after an interjection at the beginning of a sentence:

> **Oh,** we did not realize that you are allergic to cats.
> **Yes,** your sneezing worries me.

❶ **PUNCTUATION ALERT:** Use a comma both before and after a transitional expression, conjunctive adverb, or interjection that falls within a sentence. Also, use a comma before such words that fall at the end of a sentence. ❗

EXERCISE 24-2

Consulting section 24b, insert commas where needed after introductory words, phrases, and clauses. If a sentence is correct, circle its number.

EXAMPLE   In 1876 Dr. John Kellogg created a precooked food made of dried wheat for the patients at his vegetarian health institute in Battle Creek, Michigan.

In 1876, Dr. John Kellogg created a precooked food made of dried wheat for the patients at his vegetarian health institute in Battle Creek, Michigan.

(1) Although he meant it to serve as a between-meals snack Kellogg's new "cereal" was quickly put to other uses. (2) Eaten with milk and sugar it became a popular breakfast food from coast to coast. (3) Not long after his brother Will Kellogg created cornflakes. (4) As other types of cereal such as shredded wheat and puffed rice flooded the market the American breakfast took on its present identity. (5) Other reasons besides perceived health benefits accounted for the sudden popularity of packaged dry food at the turn

of the twentieth century. (6) To save time in the morning the growing population of office workers abandoned heavy cooked breakfasts for quick "convenience" foods. (7) By 1900 the improvement of food preservation techniques and the introduction of railroad refrigerator cars had radically changed breakfast choices in the United States. (8) For the first time perishable food could be transported across North America without spoiling. (9) When the benefits of vitamin C were discovered in 1913 orange juice and grapefruits were added to the breakfast menu. (10) Consequently today's balanced breakfast consists of a glass of juice along with a bowl of cereal and milk.

EXERCISE 24-3

Consulting section 24b, combine each set of sentences into one sentence that starts according to the directions in parentheses. You can add, delete, and rearrange words as needed. Be sure to use commas after introductory elements in the combined sentences.

EXAMPLE   The term *cyberspace* was introduced in the 1970s by the science fiction writer William Gibson. The idea of a total electronic environment seemed highly fanciful. (clause beginning *when*)

When the term cyberspace was introduced in the 1970s by the science fiction writer William Gibson, the idea of a total electronic environment seemed highly fanciful.

1. It began as a flight of sheer fantasy. Virtual reality is turning out to be one of the most versatile technological applications of this century. (clause beginning *although*)
2. Computer-generated environments are now known as "virtual reality." Computer-generated environments now have many important applications ranging from medicine and space exploration to entertainment. (phrase beginning *now known*)
3. Surgeons can use virtual scalpels to practice difficult operations. They can predict their effects on the patient's total body system. (begin with *for example*)
4. Astronauts have been using virtual reality space walks to train themselves to function in the demanding zero-gravity environment of orbiting space satellites. They have been using virtual reality recently. (begin with *recently*)
5. You can also enter the world of virtual reality for entertainment. You can use a glove and a specially equipped helmet. (phrase beginning *to enter*)
6. The computer operator punches a few keys on the computer in a virtual reality room. She transports you into a colorful make-believe world. (phrase beginning *by punching*)

Answers: Exercise 24-2 (continued)

   6. morning, the
   7. 1900, the
   8. time, perishable
   9. 1913, orange
  10. Consequently, today's

ANSWERS AND COVERAGE: EXERCISE 24-3

Answers may vary, but the following versions are possibilities.

   1. Although it began as a flight of sheer fantasy, virtual reality is turning out to be one of the most versatile technological applications of this century. [adverb clause]

   2. Now known as "virtual reality," computer-generated environments have many important applications ranging from medicine and space exploration to entertainment. [participial phrase]

   3. For example, surgeons can use virtual scalpels to practice difficult operations and predict their effects on the patient's total body system. [introductory words—transitional expression]

   4. Recently, astronauts have been using virtual reality space walks to train themselves to function in the demanding zero-gravity environment of orbiting space satellites. [introductory word—transitional expression]

   5. To enter the world of virtual reality for entertainment, you can use a glove and a specially equipped helmet. [infinitive phrase]

   6. By punching a few keys on the computer in a virtual reality room, the computer operator transports you into a colorful make-believe world. [prepositional phrase]

→

Answers and Coverage: Exercise 24-3
(continued)

7. While two tiny television screens in the helmet's visor provide startlingly realistic three-dimensional vision, you can interact with objects in the virtual world by moving your glove. [adverb clause]

8. Looking up at the deep blue sky, you see a large prehistoric bird soaring above your head. [participial phrase]

9. Under your feet, the ground quakes and splits and becomes an ocean with a shark circling nearby. [prepositional phrase]

10. Fortunately, you can repel the shark with your virtual spear, and you will not be hurt if he attacks. [introductory word—conjunctive adverb]

7. Two tiny television screens in the helmet's visor provide startlingly realistic three-dimensional vision. You can interact with objects in the virtual world by moving your glove. (clause beginning *while*)

8. You look up at the deep blue sky. You see a large prehistoric bird soaring above your head. (phrase beginning *looking*)

9. The ground quakes and splits under your feet. It becomes an ocean with a shark circling nearby. (begin with *under your feet*)

10. You can repel the shark with your virtual spear. You will not be hurt if it attacks. (begin with *fortunately*)

24c Using commas to separate items in a series

A **series** is a group of three or more elements—words, PHRASES, or CLAUSES—that match in grammatical form as well as in importance in the same sentence. The items in a series should be separated by commas, as shown in Chart 113.

Pattern for commas in a series   113

- word, word, and word
- phrase, phrase, and phrase
- clause, clause, and clause

- word, word, word
- phrase, phrase, phrase
- clause, clause, clause

Marriage requires **sexual, financial, and emotional** discipline.
—Anne Roiphe, "Why Marriages Fail"

Culture is a way of **thinking, feeling, believing.**
—Clyde Kluckhohn, *Mirror for Man*

My love of flying goes back to those early days **of roller skates, of swings, of bicycles.**
—Teresa Wiggins, student

We have been taught **that children develop by ages and stages, that the steps are pretty much the same for everybody, and that to grow out of the limited behavior of childhood, we must climb them all.**
—Gail Sheehy, *Passages*

Some authorities omit the comma before the coordinating conjunction between the last two items of a series. I recommend using this comma, for omitting it can distort meaning and confuse a reader.

When the items in a series contain commas or other punctuation, separate them with semicolons instead of commas (see 25d). This practice ensures that your sentence will deliver the meaning you intend.

> If it's a bakery, they have to sell cake; if it's a photography shop, they have to develop film; **and** if it's a dry-goods store, they have to sell warm underwear.
>
> —Art Buchwald, "Birth Control for Banks"

Numbered or lettered lists within a sentence are items in a series. Use commas (or semicolons if the items themselves contain commas) to separate them when there are three or more items.

> To file your insurance claim, please enclose (1) a letter requesting payment, (2) a police report about the robbery, and (3) proof of purchase of the items you say are missing.

❶ COMMA CAUTION: Do not use a comma before the first item or after the last item in a series unless a different rule makes it necessary.

NO	Many artists, writers, and composers, have indulged in daydreaming.
YES	Many artists, writers, and composers have indulged in daydreaming.
NO	Such dreamers include, Miró, Debussy, Dostoevsky, and Dickinson.
YES	Such dreamers include Miró, Debussy, Beethoven, Tolstoy, and Dickinson.
YES	Such dreamers include, of course, Miró, Debussy, Dostoevsky, and Dickinson. [The comma after *of course* is, like the one before it, necessary to set off the phrase from the rest of the sentence; see 24f.] ❗

EXERCISE 24-4

Consulting section 24c, insert commas to separate items in a series. If a sentence needs no commas, circle its number.

EXAMPLE In the fertile Kentucky mountain country of the late 1700s deer elk and black bears were abundant.

In the fertile Kentucky mountain country of the late 1700s, deer, elk, and black bears were abundant.

1. Rabbits squirrels raccoons and other small game were so common that they were simply taken for granted by the Shawnees Cherokees and European pioneers who settled there.

BACKGROUND

The placement of a comma can have important consequences. Consider these examples:

1. A comma once saved a man's life. Czar Alexander III had signed a death warrant reading: "Pardon impossible, to be sent to Siberia." Being sent to Siberia inevitably led to death. However, Czarina Maria Fyodorovna saved the man by altering the message to read: "Pardon, impossible to be sent to Siberia."

2. Elizabeth Langmore (Letters, *Time*, July 4, 1988) points out how very different it is to ask, "Have you seen the elephant eating Tom?" and "Have you seen the elephant eating, Tom?"

3. In the same publication, Grover Reynolds points out the difference between "Woman without her man has no reason for living," and "Woman: without her, man has no reason for living."

4. In another letter to *Time*, Leslie Bryant asks readers to decipher "That that is is that that is not is not is that it is." With commas and periods, it reads "That that is, is. That that is not, is not. Is that it? It is."

ANSWERS: EXERCISE 24-4

1. Rabbits, squirrels, raccoons, and other small game; Shawnees, Cherokees, and European pioneers ➜

2. An alert observer noted that wild turkeys were so fat that the branches of trees could not hold their weight buffalo tracks were wide as highways and everybody wore a cap made of raccoon skin.

3. The farmers followed close on the heels of the hunters trappers and scouts despite the difficulties of making their way through a wilderness of vertical mountains overgrown forests and lush meadows.

4. The year 1788 marked the beginning of a mass migration of farmers from Virginia North Carolina Pennsylvania and other long-settled areas over the mountains to Kentucky.

5. Kentucky had so many new inhabitants in five short years that it became the first "western" state to be admitted to the Union.

24d Using a comma to separate coordinate adjectives

Coordinate adjectives are two or more ADJECTIVES that equally modify a NOUN. Separate coordinate adjectives with a comma, as shown in Chart 114, unless the coordinate adjectives are joined by *and.* Do not use a comma to separate noncoordinate adjectives.

Pattern for commas with coordinate adjectives   **114**

coordinate adjective, coordinate adjective noun

COORDINATE ADJECTIVES

The **huge, restless** crowd waited for the concert to begin. [Both *huge* and *restless* modify *crowd,* so a comma is used.]

The audience cheered when the **pulsating, rhythmic** music filled the stadium. [Both *pulsating* and *rhythmic* modify *music.*]

CUMULATIVE (NONCOORDINATE) ADJECTIVES

The concert featured **several new** bands. [*New* modifies *bands,* but *several* modifies *new bands,* so no comma is used.]

Each had a **distinctive musical** style. [*Musical* modifies *style,* but *distinctive* modifies *musical style,* so no comma is used.]

If you are not sure whether adjectives need a comma between them, use the tests for coordinate adjectives in Chart 115.

🎯 **Tests for coordinate adjectives**   **115**

If either test given here works, the adjectives are coordinate and need a comma between them.

- Can the order of the adjectives be reversed without changing the meaning or creating nonsense? If yes, use a comma.

  NO The concert featured **new several** bands. (Only *several new* makes sense.)

  YES The **huge, restless** (or **restless, huge**) crowd waited for the concert to begin.

  NO Each had a **musical distinctive** style. (Only *distinctive musical* makes sense.)

  YES The audience cheered happily as the **rhythmic, pulsating** (or **pulsating, rhythmic**) music filled the stadium.

- Can the word *and* be inserted between the adjectives? If yes, use a comma.

  NO The concert featured **new and several** bands.

  YES The **huge and restless** crowd waited.

❗ **COMMA CAUTION:** Do not put a comma after a final coordinate adjective and the noun it modifies. **!**

EXERCISE 24-5

Consulting section 24d, insert commas to separate coordinate adjectives. If a sentence needs no commas, circle its number.

EXAMPLE   The lively bright bird known as the parakeet was first imported to England from Australia in 1840.

The lively**,** bright bird known as the parakeet was first imported to England from Australia in 1840.

1. Small colorful parakeets were among the best-loved pets of the nineteenth century.
2. No upper-class British parlor was considered fashionable without a cage of several singing parakeets.
3. Parakeets are small sturdy parrots who use their strong curved beaks for husking seeds.
4. Their feet have two toes pointing forward and two toes pointing backward, a highly unusual feature that makes for effortless efficient climbing—even in a cage.

ANSWERS: EXERCISE 24-5

1. small, colorful
2. Correct
3. small, sturdy; strong, curved
4. effortless, efficient
5. short, simple

TEACHING TIP

The words *restrictive* and *nonrestrictive* are being replaced in many classrooms with the word *essential* and *nonessential*. For this reason, this chapter uses the more grammatically descriptive terms and then gives in parentheses the terms more accessible to nongrammarians. No matter what words you use in your teaching, the concept of restriction is a helpful one for students to understand. To illustrate this concept, you might focus on the differences between the words *the* and *a* in these sentences, as they affect restriction and the role of the commas:

> I took the bus, which made many stops, to get here.

> I took a bus that made many stops to get here.

ADDITIONAL EXAMPLES

Restrictive Clauses and Phrases

1. People *who travel abroad* should be willing to alter their eating habits.

2. Tours *that make dining decisions for travelers* sometimes provide surprises.

3. Diners *with conservative tastes* are sometimes offended.

4. For example, the evening meal *in Spain* is usually served after 9 p.m.

5. The restaurant *where I often had dinner in Madrid* was never filled until after 10.

Nonrestrictive Clauses and Phrases

1. My aunt, *who often travels abroad*, enjoys experimenting with unusual foods.

2. Holiday Tours, *which makes all the dining decisions for its travelers*, provides too few surprises for her.

3. Her tastes, *after her many excursions to exotic places*, are still adventuresome.

4. For example, eating in Spain, *which is always a late-evening affair*, is one of her favorite excursions.

5. Las Tres Encinas, *where she often dines when she is in Madrid*, is never filled until after 10 p.m.

5. Some parakeet owners report that their birds are able to speak a few short simple words after some persistent coaching.

24e Using commas to set off nonrestrictive (nonessential) elements but no commas with restrictive (essential) elements

The most complicated comma decisions are those related to **restrictive (essential)** elements and **nonrestrictive (nonessential)** elements. The comma rules themselves are easy; the difficult part is understanding the meanings of *restrictive, essential, nonrestrictive,* and *nonessential*. Use Chart 116 to become familiar with the meaning of these terms. Then apply the definitions as you analyze what message you want each of your sentences to deliver.

⊙ Definitions of *restrictive* and *nonrestrictive*　　116

Restrictive

A restrictive element contains information essential for the reader to understand the full meaning of the word or words that it modifies. It limits ("restricts") what it modifies. Commas are not needed.

> Some states retest drivers **who are over age sixty-five** to check their driving competency.

The RELATIVE CLAUSE *who are over age sixty-five* limits the word *drivers* so that a reader understands which drivers are being retested (not all drivers, only those over age sixty-five). Therefore, *who are over age sixty-five* is restrictive. Commas are not needed.

Nonrestrictive

A nonrestrictive element is not essential for a reader to understand the full meaning of word or words that it modifies. It describes but does not limit (does not "restrict") what it modifies. Commas are needed.

> My parents, **who are both over age sixty-five,** took a defensive driving course last year.

The RELATIVE CLAUSE *who are both over age sixty-five* describes *my parents*, but it is not essential to a reader's understanding which parents took a defensive driving course last year. Therefore, *who are both over age sixty-five* is nonrestrictive. Commas are needed.

RESTRICTIVE ELEMENTS

Some people **in my neighborhood** enjoy jogging. [The reader needs the information *in my neighborhood* to know which people enjoy jogging. The information is essential, so commas are not used.]

Some people **who are in excellent physical condition** enjoy jogging. [The reader needs the information *who are in excellent physical condition* to know which people enjoy jogging. The information is essential, so commas are not used.]

The agricultural scientist **Wendy Singh** has helped develop a new fertilization technique. [The appositive *Wendy Singh* is essential in identifying exactly which agricultural scientist has developed the new fertilization technique, so it is not set off with commas.]

NONRESTRICTIVE ELEMENTS

An energetic person, Anna Hom enjoys jogging. [Without knowing that Anna Hom is energetic, you can understand that she enjoys jogging. *An energetic person* is not essential information, so it is set off with a comma.]

Anna Hom**, who is in excellent physical condition,** enjoys jogging. You can understand that Anna Hom enjoys jogging without knowing about her physical condition. [*Who is in excellent physical condition* is thus not essential information, so commas are used.]

Anna Hom enjoys jogging, **which is also Adam's favorite pastime**. [You can understand that Anna Hom enjoys jogging without knowing about Adam's favorite pastime. *Which is also Adam's favorite pastime* is thus not essential information, so commas are used.]

The agricultural scientist**, a new breed of farmer,** controls the farming environment. [The appositive *a new breed of farmer* is not essential in identifying who controls the farming equipment, so it is set off with commas.]

Once you understand the concepts of *restrictive, essential, nonrestrictive,* and *nonessential,* use Chart 117 to learn the patterns for commas with nonrestrictive (nonessential) elements.

Patterns for commas with nonrestrictive elements   **117**

- **Nonrestrictive element,** independent clause.
- Beginning of independent clause, **nonrestrictive element,** end of independent clause.
- Independent clause, **nonrestrictive element.**

EXTRA EXERCISE B

Circle unnecessary commas and add needed commas where restrictive and nonrestrictive phrases, clauses, and appositives appear in the following sentences.

1. Elizabeth II, who is queen of the United Kingdom, was born in London in 1926.

2. She is the elder daughter of King George VI and Queen Consort Elizabeth who is now known as the Queen Mother.

3. Her education administered at home by private tutors covered a wide variety of subjects.

4. She was married, at Westminster Abbey to Philip Mountbatten, who was formerly Prince Philip of Greece.

5. He was created Duke of Edinburgh, with all the rights and privileges of the title, on the eve of the marriage.

6. Prince Charles Elizabeth's first child was born on November 14, 1948.

7. Princess Anne the second child was born on August 15, 1950.

8. Elizabeth's father George VI died in 1952.

9. She was crowned, queen of England, in Westminster Abbey a historic site on June 2, 1953.

10. Prince Charles, now himself a parent, thus became, the heir apparent.

Answers to Extra Exercise B

1. Correct

2. Elizabeth, who

3. education, administered; tutors, covered

4. married at

5. Correct

6. Charles, Elizabeth's first child, was

7. Anne, the second child, was

8. father, George VI, died

9. crowned queen of England in Westminster Abbey, a historic site, on

10. became the

❶ **COMMA CAUTION:** Remember, a restrictive element contains essential information, so do not set it off from the rest of the sentence with commas. ❗

ANSWERS AND COVERAGE: EXERCISE 24-6

1. The design of ordinary North American homes includes features originally invented for the wealthy, who often had different uses for them. [nonrestrictive relative clause]

2. Large front doors, often approached by a set of stairs, were first invented so that noble families could show off as they walked in and out of their houses. [nonrestrictive participial phrase]

3. Wide indoor staircases, which originated in the palaces of fifteenth-century Italy, are now found in many large suburban homes. [nonrestrictive relative clause]

4. In Italian palaces, those staircases led to the ballrooms and dining rooms of the second floor, called the "noble floor" because only the upper classes used it. [nonrestrictive participial phrase]

5. Correct [restrictive relative clause]

6. The two silent film stars who built Pickfair, a Hollywood mansion of the 1920s, created a sensation by including the first-ever private movie theater in their new home. [nonrestrictive appositive]

7. The typical family today, which owns a stereo and a VCR, is able to outdo Pickfair in the quality and variety of its home entertainment. [nonrestrictive relative clause]

8. Although today's homes often imitate the wealthy mansions of the past, one important exception is the family kitchen, unknown in the aristocratic home. [nonrestrictive participial phrase]

9. In wealthy households of old, the kitchen, a drab working room, was used only by the servants for cooking. [nonrestrictive appositive]

10. Today, the kitchen, the main gathering place in many homes, is used by both rich and poor families for cooking as well as for eating and conversing. [nonrestrictive appositive]

EXERCISE 24-6

Consulting section 24e and using your knowledge of restrictive and nonrestrictive clauses and phrases, insert commas as needed. If a sentence is correct, circle its number.

EXAMPLE   In today's suburban houses, many features including front doors imitate parts of the huge aristocratic mansions of past centuries.

In today's suburban houses, many features**,** *including front doors***,** imitate parts of the huge aristocratic mansions of past centuries.

1. The design of ordinary North American homes includes features originally invented for the wealthy who often had different uses for them.

2. Large front doors often approached by a set of stairs were first invented so that noble families could show off as they walked in and out of their houses.

3. Wide indoor staircases which originated in the palaces of fifteenth-century Italy are now found in many large suburban homes.

4. In Italian palaces, those staircases led to the ballrooms and dining rooms of the second floor called the "noble floor" because only the upper classes used it.

5. People today who select the latest entertainment features are also following the lead of the ultra-wealthy in earlier times.

6. The two silent film stars who built Pickfair a Hollywood mansion of the 1920s created a sensation by including the first-ever private movie theater in their new home.

7. The typical family today which owns a stereo and a VCR is able to outdo Pickfair in the quality and variety of its home entertainment.

8. Although today's homes often imitate the wealthy mansions of the past, one important exception is the family kitchen unknown in the aristocratic home.

9. In wealthy households of old, the kitchen a drab working room was used only by the servants for cooking.

10. Today, the kitchen the main gathering place in many homes is used by both rich and poor families for cooking as well as for eating and conversing.

24f Using commas to set off transitional and parenthetical expressions, contrasts, words of direct address, and tag sentences

Words, PHRASES, or CLAUSES that interrupt a sentence but do not change its essential meaning should be set off, usually with commas. (Dashes or parentheses can also set material off; see sections 29a and 29b.)

Conjunctive adverbs such as *however* and *therefore* (for a complete list, see Chart 51 in section 7f) and **transitional expressions** such as *for example* and *in addition* (for a complete list, see Chart 25 in section 4d.1) can express connections within sentences. When they do, set them off with commas.

Therefore, the American Midwest is considered the world's breadbasket.

California and Florida**, for example,** are important food producers.

❶ **COMMA CAUTION:** Use a semicolon or a period—not a comma—before the conjunctive adverb or a transitional expression that falls between independent clauses. If you use a comma, you will create the error known as a comma splice (see Chapter 14). ❗

Parenthetical expressions are "asides." They add information to sentences. Set them off with commas.

American farmers**, according to U.S. government figures,** export more wheat than they sell at home.

A major drought**, sad to say,** reduces wheat crops drastically.

Expressions of contrast describe something by stating what it is not. Set them off with commas.

Feeding the world's population is a serious**, though not intractable,** problem.

We must work against world hunger continuously**, not merely when emergencies develop**.

Words of **direct address** indicate the person or group spoken to. Set them off with commas.

Join me**, brothers and sisters,** to end hunger.

Your contribution to the Relief Fund**, Steve,** will help us greatly.

Tag sentences consist of a VERB, a PRONOUN, and often the word *not*, often as part of a CONTRACTION. Set off tag sentences with commas. If the tag sentence is a question, end it with a question mark.

People's response to the announcement of a blood shortage was impressive**, wasn't it?**

People will give blood regularly**, I hope.**

417

ANSWERS AND COVERAGE: EXERCISE 24-7

Answers may vary slightly. Here is one set of possibilities.

1. Inability to write, some say, [parenthetical expression] stems from lack of discipline and a tendency to procrastinate.

2. Therefore, [transitional word] according to this thinking, [parenthetical expression] the only way to overcome writer's block is to exert more willpower.

3. But writer's block can be a complex psychological event that happens to conscientious and hardworking people, not just the procrastinators. [expression of contrast]

4. Strange as it may seem, [parenthetical phrase] such people are often unconsciously rebelling against their own self-tyranny and rigid standards of perfection.

5. If I told you, my fellow writer, [direct address] that all it takes to start writing again is to quit punishing yourself, you would think I was crazy, wouldn't you? [tag sentence]

BACKGROUND

Here is the complete poem by William Blake quoted in section 24g.

The Clod and the Pebble
"Love seeketh not itself to please,
Nor for itself hath any care,
But for another gives its ease,
And builds a Heaven in Hell's despair."

So sung a little Clod of Clay
Trodden with the cattle's feet,
But a Pebble of the brook
Warbled out these metres meet:

"Love seeketh only self to please,
To bind another to its delight,
Joys in another's loss of ease,
And builds a Hell in Heaven's despite."

EXERCISE 24-7

Consulting section 24f, add necessary commas to set off transitional, parenthetical, and contrasting elements, words of direct address, and tag sentences. Adjust end punctuation as necessary.

EXAMPLE   Writer's block it seems to me is a misunderstood phenomenon.
Writer's block**,** *it seems to me***,** is a misunderstood phenomenon.

1. Inability to write some say stems from lack of discipline and a tendency to procrastinate.
2. Therefore according to this thinking the only way to overcome writer's block is to exert more willpower.
3. But writer's block can be a complex psychological event that happens to conscientious and hardworking people not just the procrastinators.
4. Strange as it may seem such people are often unconsciously rebelling against their own self-tyranny and rigid standards of perfection.
5. If I told you my fellow writer that all it takes to start writing again is to quit punishing yourself you would think I was crazy wouldn't you.

24g   Using commas to set off quoted words from explanatory words

Use a comma to set off quoted words from other words in the same sentence. This rule holds whether the explanatory words come before, between, or after the quoted words (see Chart 118).

Patterns for commas with quoted words   **118**

- Explanatory words, "Quoted words."
- "Quoted words," explanatory words.
- "Quoted words begin," explanatory words, "quoted words continue."

Speaking of ideal love**,** **the poet William Blake wrote,** "Love seeketh not itself to please."

"My love is a fever**,**" **said William Shakespeare** about love's passion.

"I love no love**,**" **proclaimed poet Mary Coleridge,** "but thee."

This use of commas is especially important in communicating conversations or other DIRECT DISCOURSE. Be aware, however, that if the quoted words are used as a grammatical part of your sentence, as is often the case in phrases with *that* and *as*, they should *not* be set off with commas. (For information on using capital letters in quotations, see section 30c.)

Shakespeare also wrote that "Love's not Time's fool."

The duke describes the duchess as being "too soon made glad."

Shaw's quip "Love is a gross exaggeration of the difference between one person and everybody else" delights me.

Sometimes, words a person has spoken or written are reported, not given as an exact quotation. Such words are called **indirect discourse.** Often, indirect discourse includes the word *that* before the reported words. Do not use a comma after *that* in indirect discourse.

Shakespeare also wrote that people should be true to themselves.

⬤ **COMMA CAUTION:** When quoted words end with a question mark or an exclamation point, keep that punctuation even if explanatory words follow.

QUOTED WORDS	*"O Romeo! Romeo!"*
NO	"O Romeo! Romeo**!,**" called Juliet as she stood at her window.
NO	"O Romeo! Romeo**,**" called Juliet as she stood at her window.
YES	"O Romeo! Romeo**!**" called Juliet as she stood at her window.
QUOTED WORDS	*"Wherefore art thou Romeo?"*
NO	"Wherefore art thou Romeo**?,**" continued Juliet as she yearned for her newfound love.
NO	"Wherefore art thou Romeo**,**" continued Juliet as she yearned for her newfound love.
YES	"Wherefore art thou Romeo**?**" continued Juliet as she yearned for her newfound love. **!**

EXERCISE 24-8

Consulting section 24g, punctuate the following dialogue correctly. If a sentence is correct, circle its number.

EXAMPLE   "Can you tell me just one thing?," asked the tourist.

"Can you tell me just one thing**?**" asked the tourist.

1. "I'm happy to answer any questions you have" said the rancher to the tourist.

QUOTATION: ON WRITING

I have performed the necessary butchery. Here is the bleeding corpse.

—Henry James,
following a request to cut three lines
from a 5,000-word article

BACKGROUND

Here is the complete poem by Mary Coleridge quoted in section 24g.

My True Love Hath My Heart
and I Have His

None ever was in love with me but grief.
   She wooed me from the day that I was
    born;
She stole my playthings first, the jealous
   thief,
   And left me there forlorn.

The birds that in my garden would have
   sung,
   She scared away with her unending
    moan;
She slew my lovers too when I was
   young,
   And left me there alone.

Grief, I have cursed thee often—now at
   last
   To hate thy name I am no longer free;
Caught in thy bony arms and prisoned
   fast,
   I love no love but thee.

ANSWERS AND COVERAGE: EXERCISE 24-8

1. "I'm happy to answer any questions you have," said the rancher to the tourist. [explanatory words at the end of a quotation]

QUOTATION: ON WRITING

The most important sentence in a good book is the first one; it will contain the organic seed from which all that follows will grow.

—Paul Horgan

2. "Well, then" said the tourist "I'd like to know how you make ends meet on such a tiny ranch."

3. "Do you see that man leaning against the shed over there?" asked the rancher, pointing with a twig.

4. The rancher continued "He works for me, but I don't pay him any money. Instead, I have promised him that after two years of work, he will own the ranch."

5. "Then, I'll work for him, and in two more years, the ranch will be mine again," said the rancher with a smile.

24h Using commas in dates, names, addresses, correspondence, and numbers according to accepted practice

When you write dates, names, addresses, correspondence, and numbers, be sure to use commas according to accepted practice as shown in Charts 119 through 122.

● Rules for commas with dates 119

- Use a comma between the date and the year: **July 20,** 1969.

- Use a comma between the day and the date: **Sunday,** July 20.

- Within a sentence, use a comma on both sides of the year in a full date.

  YES Everyone wanted to be near a television set on July 20, **1969,** to watch the lunar landing.

- Do not use a comma in a date that contains the month with only a day or the month with only a year. Also, do not use a comma in a date that contains only the season and year.

  YES The major news story during **July 1969** was the moon landing; news coverage was especially heavy on **July 21.**

- An inverted date takes no commas: **20 July 1969.**

  YES People stayed near their television sets on **20 July 1969** to watch the moon landing.

◉ Rules for commas with names, places, and addresses 120

- When an abbreviated academic degree (M.D., Ph.D.) comes after a person's name, use a comma between the name and the title—**Rosa Gonzales, M.D.**—and also after the title if it is followed by the rest of the sentence.

  YES The jury listened closely to the expert testimony of **Rosa Gonzales, M.D.,** last week.

- When an indicator of birth order or succession (*Sr., Jr., III, IV*) follows a name, no comma is necessary: **Martin Luther King Jr.**; **Henry Ford II**; **King Edward VI**.

- When you invert a person's name, use a comma to separate the last name from the first: **Troyka,** David.

- Use a comma to separate the names of a city and state: **Philadelphia, Pennsylvania.** If the city and state fall within a sentence, use a comma after the state as well, unless the state name ends the sentence and so is followed by a period, a question mark, or an exclamation point.

  YES The Liberty Bell has been on display in **Philadelphia, Pennsylvania,** for many years.

- When you write a complete address as part of a sentence, use a comma to separate all the items, with the exception of the state and ZIP code. The ZIP code follows the two-letter postal abbreviation for the state after a space but no comma.

  YES I wrote to **Mr. U. Lern, 10-01 Rule Road, Upper Saddle River, NJ 07458,** for the instruction manual.

◉ Rules for commas in correspondence 121

- For the opening of an informal letter, use a comma.

  Dear Betty,

  For the opening of a business or formal letter, use a colon (:).

- For the close of a letter, use a comma.

  Sincerely yours,   **Best regards,**

  Love,   **Very truly yours,**

QUOTATION: ON WRITING

Students who have learned to be careful about commas understandably "write around" the problem. Sentence-combining exercises not only illustrate how punctuation organizes sentence elements for a reader but also how to solve punctuation problems which for years have limited a student's range of syntactic options. Furthermore, the exercises sometimes expose misunderstood punctuation rules discussed in previous English classes . . . [and] grammatical labels [that] sometimes create punctuation problems. Sentence combining allows teachers to dispense with terminology altogether or, if they wish, to name constructions *after* students have practiced them.

—Erica Lindemann

ANSWERS AND COVERAGE: EXERCISE 24-9

1. Made by the noted German director Wim Wenders, *Paris, Texas* [comma after city in title] was set in an actual town in Lamar County, Texas, [comma after county and state] with a population of 24,699. [comma with numbers]

2. Correct

3. The custom of naming little towns in the United States after cosmopolitan urban centers in the Old World has resulted in such places as Athens, Georgia, and St. Petersburg, Florida. [commas after cities]

⊙ Rules for commas with numbers   122

■ Counting from the right, put a comma after every three digits in numbers with more than four digits.

72,867   **156,567,066**

■ A comma is optional in most four-digit numbers. Use a consistent style within a given piece of writing.

$1776   **$1,776**

1776 miles   **1,776** miles

1776 potatoes   **1,776** potatoes

■ Do not use a comma in a four-digit year: **1990** (a year of five digits or more gets a comma: **25,000** B.C.); in an address of four digits or more: **12161** Dean Drive; or in a page number of four digits or more: see page **1338**

■ Use a comma to separate related measurements written as words: **five feet, four inches**

■ Use a comma to separate a scene from an act in a play: **act 2, scene 4**

■ Use a comma to separate a reference to a page from a reference to a line: **page 10, line 6**

EXERCISE 24-9

Consulting section 24h, insert commas where they are needed. If a sentence is correct, circle its number.

EXAMPLE   On June 1 1984 the small German-French production company Road Movies released a feature film called *Paris Texas.*

On June 1**,** 1984**,** the small German-French production company Road Movies released a feature film called *Paris**,** Texas.*

1. Made by the noted German director Wim Wenders, *Paris Texas* was set in an actual town in Lamar County Texas with a population of 24699.

2. The movie's title was clearly intended to play off the slightly more famous Paris in France.

3. The custom of naming little towns in the United States after cosmopolitan urban centers in the Old World resulted in such places as Athens Georgia and St. Petersburg Florida.

→

4. As of December 31 1990 the American St. Petersburg had 238629 citizens and the American Athens had 45734.

5. By comparison, St. Petersburg Russia and Athens Greece have populations of approximately 4 million and 1 million, respectively.

24i Using commas to clarify meaning

Sometimes, a comma can clarify the meaning of a sentence, even though no other rule calls for one. Often, revising the sentence is a better solution than relying on a comma.

NO	Of the gymnastic team's twenty five were injured.
YES	Of the gymnastic team's twenty, five were injured.
YES	Of twenty on the gymnastic team, five were injured.

NO	Those who can practice many hours a day.
YES	Those who can, practice many hours a day.

NO	George dressed and performed for the sellout crowd.
YES	George dressed, and performed for the sellout crowd.
YES	After George dressed, he performed for the sellout crowd.

EXERCISE 24-10

Consulting section 24i, insert commas to prevent misreading. If a sentence is correct, circle its number.

EXAMPLE   When hunting owls use both vision and hearing.
　　　　　　When hunting, owls use both vision and hearing.

1. Flying at night owls get around by consulting a mental "map" of their surroundings.
2. During the daylight hours, those healthy owls who can fly over their territories and create such a map using their eyes and ears.
3. A team of scientists has given owls distorting eyeglasses to make them relearn this mental map.
4. The bespectacled owl scientists find wears its glasses as contentedly as humans.
5. In a short time after they have produced a new mental map using their glasses the owls once again can fly and chase small rodents across the ground.

24j Avoiding misuse of the comma

Using commas correctly helps you deliver your meaning to your reader. As a writer, you frequently have to make decisions about whether

Unlike the period, question mark, exclamation [point], colon, dash, and parentheses, the comma has no clear special quality. . . . It is not a terminal marking like the period, a specialized coordinating mark like the semicolon, or an anticipatory mark like the colon. Even the dash, which comes nearest the comma in variety of uses, has a characteristic quality, and all the points except the dash have a much more limited number of uses. The comma may be used alone or in pairs; it may stand between coordinate expressions or may separate expressions of different grammatical rank; it may set off a group for emphasis or clearness even when the grammatical relation is close.

— George Summey Jr.

BACKGROUND

The power of the comma was demonstrated a few years ago at a Republican National Convention. An item proposed for the party platform read, "The Convention opposes any form of tax increase which would hurt the economy." Someone called for the addition of a comma, so that the item would read, "The Convention opposes any form of tax increase, which would hurt the economy."

That comma was a reflection of the conservative economic position of its proposer. In the first version of the sentence, *which* begins a restrictive clause. The author of the proposal was talking only of harmful tax increases and implying that nonharmful increases would be acceptable. In the second version, *which* begins a nonrestrictive clause. This author saw all tax increases as harmful.

a comma is needed. If, as you are DRAFTING, you are in doubt about a comma, insert and circle it clearly so that you can go back to it later when you are REVISING and can think about whether it is correct. Throughout this chapter, most sections that discuss correct use of the comma include a comma caution to alert you to related misuse of the comma. This section summarizes those cautions and cites other frequent misuses of the comma.

Because the comma occurs so frequently, advice against overusing it sometimes clashes with a rule requiring it. In such cases, follow the rule that requires the comma.

> The town of Kitty Hawk, North Carolina, attracts thousands of tourists each year. [Although the comma after *North Carolina* separates the subject and verb, it is required because the state is set off from the city and from the rest of the sentence; see section 24h.]

24j.1 Avoiding misuse of a comma with coordinating conjunctions

Section 24a discusses the correct use of commas with sentences joined by COORDINATING CONJUNCTIONS. Do not put a comma *after* a coordinating conjunction that joins two INDEPENDENT CLAUSES unless another rule makes it necessary. Also, do not use commas to separate two items joined with a coordinating conjunction.

NO	The sky was dark gray **and,** it looked like dusk.
YES	The sky was dark gray**, and** it looked like dusk.

NO	**The moon, and the stars** were shining last night.
YES	**The moon and the stars** were shining last night.

24j.2 Avoiding misuse of a comma with subordinating conjunctions and prepositions

Do not put a comma *after* a SUBORDINATING CONJUNCTION or a PREPOSITION unless another rule makes it necessary.

NO	**Although, the storm brought high winds,** it did no damage.
YES	**Although the storm brought high winds,** it did no damage.

NO	The storm did no damage **although, it brought high winds.**
YES	The storm did no damage **although it brought high winds.**

NO	People expected worse **between, the high winds and the heavy downpour.**
YES	People expected worse **between the high winds and the heavy downpour.**

24j.3 Avoiding misuse of commas to separate items

Section 24c discusses the correct use of commas with items in a series. Do not use a comma *before the first* or *after the last* item in a series, unless another rule makes it necessary.

NO The gymnasium was decorated with**, red, white, and blue ribbons** for the Fourth of July

NO The gymnasium was decorated with **red, white, and blue, ribbons** for the Fourth of July.

YES The gymnasium was decorated with **red, white, and blue ribbons** for the Fourth of July.

Section 24d discusses the correct use of commas with COORDINATE ADJECTIVES. Do not put a comma *after* the final coordinate adjective and the noun it modifies. Also, do not use a comma between noncoordinate adjectives.

NO The **huge, restless,** crowd waited.

YES The **huge, restless** crowd waited.

NO The concert featured **several, new** bands.

YES The concert featured **several new** bands.

24j.4 Avoiding misuse of commas with restrictive elements

Section 24e discusses the correct use of commas with RESTRICTIVE (essential) ELEMENTS and NONRESTRICTIVE (nonessential) ELEMENTS. Do not use a comma to set off a restrictive (essential) element from the rest of a sentence.

NO Vegetables**, stir-fried in a wok,** are uniquely crisp and flavorful. [The information about being stir-fried in a wok is essential, so it is not set off with commas.]

YES Vegetables **stir-fried in a wok** are uniquely crisp and flavorful.

24j.5 Avoiding misuse of commas with quotations

Section 24g discusses the correct use of commas with quoted material. Do not use a comma to set off INDIRECT DISCOURSE (often signaled by *that* or *as*).

NO Jon **said that,** he likes stir-fried vegetables.

YES Jon **said that he likes stir-fried vegetables.**

YES Jon **said, "I like stir-fried vegetables."**

ANSWERS AND COVERAGE: EXERCISE 24-11

1. In the 1920s, [keep: introductory phrase] the Harlem Renaissance [omit: do not separate subject from its verb, 24j.6] was not confined to New York City; Harlem was only one of several [omit: comma between noncoordinate adjectives or modifiers, 24j.3] African-American urban districts where the arts flourished during this decade.

2. Black urban singers began to attract a national audience, and [omit: comma after coordinating conjunction, 24j.1; position between independent clauses] Harlem surpassed Broadway in the originality of its musical revues, poetry, and fiction. [keep: commas to separate items, 25j.3]

3. One of the leading poets of the Harlem Renaissance [omit: do not separate subject from its verb, 24j.6] was Claude McKay, who [keep: nonrestrictive clause] arrived in the United States from Jamaica in 1912 at the age of twenty-three.

4. He studied briefly at Booker T. Washington's [omit: noncoordinating adjectives or modifiers] famous Tuskegee Institute in Alabama.

5. In 1917, [keep: introductory phrase] he moved to Harlem, [keep: nonrestrictive clause, 24j.4] where he published his first poem.

24j.6 Avoiding use of a comma to separate a subject from its verb, a verb from its object, and a preposition from its object

NO The brothers **Wright, made** their first successful airplane flights on December 17, 1903. [As a rule, do not let a comma separate a subject from its verb.]

YES The brothers **Wright made** their first successful airplane flights on December 17, 1903.

NO These inventors enthusiastically **tackled, the problems** of powered flight and aerodynamics. [As a rule, do not let a comma separate a verb from its object.]

YES These inventors enthusiastically **tackled the problems** of powered flight and aerodynamics.

NO Airplane hobbyists visit Kitty Hawk's flight museum **from, all over the world.** [As a rule, do not let a comma separate a preposition from its object.]

YES Airplane hobbyists visit Kitty Hawk's flight museum **from all over the world.**

EXERCISE 24-11

Some commas have been deliberately misused in these sentences. Consulting 24j and the other sections in this chapter that are referred to in 24j, delete unneeded commas. If a sentence is correct, circle its number.

EXAMPLE   Large U.S. cities experienced a cultural flowering during the 1920s, and nurtured a diversity of cultures.

Large U.S. cities experienced a cultural flowering during the 1920s and nurtured a diversity of cultures.

1. In the 1920s, the Harlem Renaissance, was not confined to New York City; Harlem was only one of several, African-American urban districts where the arts flourished during this decade.

2. Black urban singers began to attract a national audience and, Harlem surpassed Broadway in the originality of its musical revues, poetry, and fiction.

3. One of the leading poets of the Harlem Renaissance, was Claude McKay, who arrived in the United States from Jamaica in 1912 at the age of twenty-three.

4. He studied briefly at Booker T. Washington's, famous Tuskegee Institute in Alabama.

5. In 1917, he moved to Harlem, where he published his first poem.

6. McKay said that, poetry was his vehicle of protest, and he wrote his 1919 poem "If We Must Die" in response to, the race riots of that year.

→

7. In fact, Harlem was a neighborhood seething in revolt, and racial pride.
8. Marcus Garvey, and his Universal Negro Improvement Association sought to transport blacks to, a new and better life in Africa.
9. Garvey, who was born in Jamaica like Claude McKay, was one of the first people, who taught African Americans that black is beautiful.
10. The Harlem Renaissance continued through 1945, when writers from Langston Hughes and Richard Wright to Zora Neale Hurston and Margaret Walker launched their great literary careers.

Answers and Coverage: Exercise 24-11 (continued)

6. McKay said that [omit: comma in indirect discourse, 24j.5] poetry was his vehicle of protest, and [keep: comma linking independent clauses, 24a] he wrote his 1919 poem "If We Must Die" in response to [omit: do not separate a preposition from its object, 24j.6] the race riots of that year.

7. In fact, [keep: introductory phrase] Harlem was a neighborhood seething in revolt [omit: coordinating conjunction joining two nouns, 24j.1] and racial pride.

8. Marcus Garvey [omit: coordinating conjunction joining two nouns, 24j.1] and his Universal Negro Improvement Association sought to transport blacks to [omit: do not separate a preposition from its object, 24j.6] a new and better life in Africa.

9. Garvey, who was born in Jamaica like Claude McKay, [keep: nonrestrictive clause] was one of the first people [omit: restrictive clause] who taught African Americans that black is beautiful.

10. The Harlem Renaissance continued through 1945, [keep: nonrestrictive clause] when writers from Langston Hughes and Richard Wright to Zora Neale Hurston and Margaret Walker launched their great literary careers.

25
SEMICOLONS

25a Using a semicolon between closely related independent clauses

When INDEPENDENT CLAUSES are clearly related in meaning, you can choose to separate them with a semicolon instead of a period. Your choice depends on the meaning you want your material to deliver. A period signals a more complete separation of the independent clauses than a semicolon does (see Chart 123).

Semicolon pattern I   123

Independent clause; independent clause.

This is my husband's second marriage; it's the first for me.
>   —Ruth Sidel, "Marion Deluca"

Our Constitution is in actual operation; everything appears to promise that it will last; but in this world nothing is certain but death and taxes.
>   —Benjamin Franklin, letter to M. Leroy (1789)

❶ **COMMA CAUTION:** Do not use only a comma between independent clauses, or you will create the error known as a comma splice (see Chapter 14). ❗

25b Using a semicolon before a coordinating conjunction that joins independent clauses containing commas

When a **coordinating conjunction** (*and, but, or, nor, for, so, yet*) links INDEPENDENT CLAUSES, use a comma to separate them (see 24a). There is only one exception: When one of the independent clauses

428

already contains a comma, you can help your reader see your coordination of independent clauses better if you substitute a semicolon for the comma (see Chart 124).

 Semicolon pattern II 124

- Independent clause, one that contains a comma; coordinating conjunction followed by independent clause.

- Independent clause; coordinating conjunction followed by independent clause, one that contains a comma.

- Independent clause, one that contains a comma; coordinating conjunction followed by independent clause, one that contains a comma.

When the peacock has presented his back, the spectator will usually begin to walk around him to get a front view; but the peacock will continue to turn so that no front view is possible.

—Flannery O'Connor, "The King of the Birds"

For anything worth having, one must pay the price; and the price is always work, patience, love, self-sacrifice.

—John Burroughs

25c Using a semicolon when conjunctive adverbs or other transitional expressions connect independent clauses

You can choose to use a semicolon between two INDEPENDENT CLAUSES when the second clause begins with a **conjunctive adverb** (*therefore, however;* for a complete list, see Chart 51 in section 7f) or other **transitional expression** (*in fact, as a result;* for a complete list, see Chart 25 in section 4d.1). Your other choice is to use a period, creating two sentences (see Chart 125).

 Semicolon pattern III 125

- Independent clause; conjunctive adverb, independent clause.

- Independent clause; transitional expression, independent clause.

ADDITIONAL EXAMPLES

1. Each year, people from all over the world visit the Tower of London; for centuries, it served as a prison for famous persons who were deemed to be enemies of the crown.

2. The tower is located in the borough of Stepney; it covers about eighteen acres.

3. The central portion, called the White Tower, was begun in 1078; it was modernized by the architect Christopher Wren.

4. The Beauchamp Tower has ninety-one inscriptions of prisoners in it; the Bloody Tower served as the prison of Sir Walter Raleigh, who wrote an incomplete history of the world during his stay there in 1614.

5. The place of execution within the walls was Tower Green; Anne Boleyn was beheaded there in 1536.

BACKGROUND

Beginning in the eighth century, the inverted semicolon served as a pause somewhere between a comma and a colon. After about seven hundred years of use, it was discarded. The semicolon as it is known today dates from the seventeenth century.

ADDITIONAL EXAMPLES

1. Black varieties of the leopard are common in humid parts of India; however, they are rare in Africa.

2. Leopards prey on monkeys, birds, and reptiles; consequently, they must hunt both in trees and on the ground.

3. A leopard begins its meal by tearing at the forequarters of its prey; in contrast, the tiger starts with the hindquarters of its victim.

4. One Indian leopard was alleged to have killed two hundred human beings in two years before it was shot; similarly, a leopard in Ceylon used to lie in wait for passersby on a main road.

5. The leopard's roar of belligerence is different from its mating call; nevertheless, both sound fierce to the human ear.

The average annual rainfall in Death Valley is about two inches; **nevertheless,** hundreds of plant and animal species survive and even thrive there.

Patient photographers have spent years recording desert life cycles; **as a result,** all of us have watched bare sand flower after a spring storm.

🛇 **COMMA ALERTS:** (1) Do not use *only* a comma between independent clauses connected by a conjunctive adverb or other words of transition, or you will create the error known as a comma splice; see Chapter 14. (2) Use a comma after a conjunctive adverb or a transitional expression that begins an independent clause; some writers omit the comma after short words, such as *then, next,* or *soon.* ❗

25d Using a semicolon with items in a series that are long or contain commas

When a sentence contains a series of long PHRASES or CLAUSES or ones that contain commas, separate the items with semicolons, not commas. Doing this allows your reader to read more easily, not having to stop to figure out where one item ends and the next begins (see Chart 126). (For information on using commas in a series, see section 24c.)

◆ Semicolon pattern IV	126

Independent clause containing a series of items, any of which contain a comma; another item in the series; and another item in the series.

Functioning as assistant chefs, the students chopped onions, green peppers, and parsley; sliced chicken and duck meat into strips; started a broth simmering; and filled a large, low copper pan with oil before the head chef stepped to the stove.

25e Avoiding misuse of the semicolon

25e.1 Not using a semicolon after an introductory phrase or between a dependent clause and an independent clause

This misuse creates the error known as a fragment; see Chapter 13.

NO   Once opened; the computer lab will be well used.
YES   Once opened, the computer lab will be well used.

NO	Although the new computers had arrived at the college**;** the computer lab was still being built.
YES	Although the new computers had arrived at the college**,** the computer lab was still being built.

25e.2 Not using a semicolon to introduce a list

To introduce a list, use a colon, never a semicolon.

NO	The newscast featured three major stories**;** the latest pictures of Uranus, a speech by the president, and a series of brush fires in Nevada.
YES	The newscast featured three major stories**:** the latest pictures of Uranus, a speech by the president, and a series of brush fires in Nevada.

❶ **PUNCTUATION ALERT:** If the words introducing the list do not form an INDEPENDENT CLAUSE, use no punctuation at all to introduce the list (see 26a and 26d): *The newscast featured the latest pictures of Uranus, a speech by the president, and a series of brush fires in Nevada.* **!**

EXERCISE 25-1

Consulting all sections of this chapter, insert semicolons where they are needed, and change any incorrectly used semicolons to correct punctuation. If a sentence is correct, circle its number.

EXAMPLE Writers at a magazine wondered whether people are honest nowadays, they designed an experiment to find out.

Writers at a magazine wondered whether people are honest nowadays**;** they designed an experiment to find out.

1. If you find a lost wallet, you may consider yourself lucky, if you return the wallet along with all the cash in it, you are acting honestly.
2. Writers at a magazine tested people's honesty by pretending to lose their wallets, people who returned a wallet with all the money in it passed the test.
3. The writers tried this experiment in many different neighborhoods, all in all, they left 120 wallets in twelve cities, towns, and suburbs across the country.
4. One writer would stop in a public place and tie a shoelace while intentionally letting the wallet slip out of a pocket, meanwhile, a colleague kept watch from a distance.

ANSWERS AND COVERAGE: EXERCISE 25-1

1. If you find a lost wallet, you may consider yourself lucky; if you return the wallet along with all the cash in it, you are acting honestly. [25a, closely related independent clauses]

2. Writers at a magazine tested people's honesty by pretending to lose their wallets; people who returned a wallet with all the money in it passed the test. [25a, closely related independent clauses]

3. The writers tried this experiment in many different neighborhoods; all in all, they left 120 wallet in twelve cities, town, and suburbs across the country. [25c, transitional expression connecting independent clauses]

4. One writer would stop in a public place and tie a shoelace while intentionally letting the wallet slip out of a pocket; meanwhile, a colleague kept watch from a distance. [25c, conjunctive adverb connecting independent clauses]

→

Answers and Coverage: Exercise 25-1 (continued)

5. Every wallet contained the following items: [25e.2, list introduced by colon, not semicolon] $50 cash; business cards and grocery lists to make the wallet look authentic; and an identification card with a phone number, so that the person who found the wallet could telephone its owner and offer to return the money. [25d, between comma-containing items in a series]

6. Many people called that telephone number or handed in the wallet to police, although others simply walked off with the money. [25e.1, use a comma, not a semicolon, to separate a dependent clause from an independent clause]

7. In a run-down part of one town, a man quickly scooped up the wallet he found on a sidewalk, putting it into his pocket; but the man, who looked as if he could use the money, went straight to the nearest police station with the wallet. [25b, coordinating conjunction joining independent clauses containing commas]

8. A middle-aged woman pushing a baby stroller in a large suburb spotted one wallet, examined its contents, and got into her Cadillac; she unexpectedly kept the wallet. [25a, closely related independent clauses]

9. Correct

10. People interviewed by the magazine often expected younger people to be less honest than their elders; however, younger people in the wallet test had the same "honesty score" as older people—exactly 67 percent. [25c, conjunctive adverb connecting independent clauses]

ANSWERS: EXERCISE 25-2

1. This defiant stand against bigotry by a single African-American woman made Parks one of the most respected civil rights leaders of the 1950s; now in her eighties, she has not lost her pep.

2. Parks still remains extremely active in the quest for improved race relations; in fact, she frequently travels to advocate

5. Every wallet contained the following items; $50 cash, business cards and grocery lists to make the wallet look authentic, and an identification card with a phone number, so that the person who found the wallet could telephone its owner and offer to return the money.

6. Many people called that telephone number or handed in the wallet to police; although others simply walked off with the money.

7. In a run-down part of one town, a man quickly scooped up the wallet he found on a sidewalk, putting it into his pocket, but the man, who looked as if he could use the money, went straight to the nearest police station with the wallet.

8. A middle-aged woman pushing a baby stroller in a large suburb spotted one wallet, examined its contents, and got into her Cadillac, she unexpectedly kept the wallet.

9. Wallets were returned with all the money in them 67 percent of the time, but small towns usually had more returns than most cities or suburbs.

10. People interviewed by the magazine often expected younger people to be less honest than their elders, however, younger people in the wallet test had the same "honesty score" as older people—exactly 67 percent.

EXERCISE 25-2

Combine each set of sentences into one sentence containing two independent clauses. Use a semicolon between the two clauses. You may add, omit, revise, and rearrange words. Try to use all the patterns in this chapter. More than one revision may be correct, so be ready to explain the reasoning behind your decisions.

EXAMPLE   Rosa Parks's refusal to move to the back of a bus in Montgomery, Alabama, in 1955 sparked the modern civil rights movement. Her action led to the greatest social revolution in U.S. history.

Rosa Parks's refusal to move to the back of a bus in Montgomery, Alabama, in 1955 sparked the modern civil rights movement; her action led to the greatest social revolution in U.S. history.

1. This defiant stand against bigotry by a single African-American woman made Parks one of the most respected civil rights leaders of the 1950s. Now in her eighties, she has not lost her pep.

2. Parks still remains active in the quest for improved race relations. Parks frequently travels to advocate equality. She devotes much of her time to an organization that she helped found, one that aids

young students in their pursuit of an education. And she has written two autobiographical books.

3. Parks neither sought nor expected the popularity that her defiance brought her. Nevertheless, she enjoys the idea that people consider her the "mother of the civil rights movement."

4. Parks continually tries to spread her message to the people of the world, as she did when she embarked on a 381-day tour throughout the United States and many foreign countries in 1996. She advised her audiences to come together to coexist peacefully. She told them to live as one.

5. The message heard in 1955 echoes today as strongly as it did then because of one enthusiastic, honored, and respected woman. The message Rosa Parks has brought to the world is sure to outlast each generation that hears it.

A *colon* (in Greek, *kōlon*) was originally a person's or an animal's limb. As such, it came to be used to refer to a portion of a strophe in choral dancing, then to a division in prosody, and later to a principal clause in a sentence. Finally, it became the sign marking the breathing space at the end of a clause.

Historically, the colon as a mark of punctuation was preceded by the semicolon, but in English it had more use than the semicolon until the nineteenth century, when it was employed almost solely as a mark of anticipation. It began to regain prestige with the publication of Fowler's *Dictionary of Modern English Usage* in 1926 and has experienced increased usage since that time.

QUOTATION: ON WRITING

The colon is usually a mark of addition or expectation, with emphasis on a following explanation, list, table, or quotation. With formal words (*as follows* or the like) it raps for attention; with easy wording it is little more formal than the somewhat lighter semicolon. It is not a series or balancing point like the semicolon; it seems to say "Watch carefully what comes next."

—George Summey Jr.

26
COLONS

26a Using a colon after an independent clause to introduce a list, an appositive, or a quotation

As you write, you can use a colon to introduce statements that summarize, restate, or explain what is said in an INDEPENDENT CLAUSE (see Chart 127). (For the use of colons in documenting sources, see sections 33c and 33d.)

 Colon pattern I   **127**

- Independent clause: list.

- Independent clause: appositive.

- Independent clause: "Quoted words."

To introduce a list, use a colon only when the words before the colon are an independent clause. After phrases such as *the following* or *as follows,* a colon is usually required. A colon is not called for with the words *such as* or *including* (see 26d).

LISTED ITEMS

If you really want to lose weight, you need give up only three things: breakfast, lunch, and dinner.

The students demanded the following: an expanded menu in the cafeteria, improved janitorial services, and more up-to-date textbooks.

A colon can introduce an **appositive**—a word or words that rename a NOUN or PRONOUN—but only if the introductory words are an independent clause.

APPOSITIVE

Only a cat would approve of one old-fashioned remedy for cuts: a lotion of catnip, butter, and sugar. [*A lotion of catnip, butter, and sugar* renames *old-fashioned remedy*.]

To introduce a quotation, use a colon only if the words before the colon are an independent clause. Use a comma, not a colon, if the words before the colon are not an independent clause (see 24b).

QUOTATION

The little boy in *E.T.* did say something neat: "How do you explain school to a higher intelligence?"

— George F. Will, "Well, *I* Don't Love You, E.T."

❶ QUOTATION ALERT: In a paper using MLA format, a quotation of more than four lines must be set off and all lines indented (see 28a). **!**

26b Using a colon between two independent clauses

When the first INDEPENDENT CLAUSE explains or summarizes the second independent clause, you can choose to use a colon to separate them (see Chart 120).

 Colon pattern II   **128**

Independent clause: Independent clause.

---

❶ CAPITALIZATION ALERT: You can use a capital letter or a lowercase letter for the first word of an independent clause that follows a colon. Whichever you choose, be consistent in each piece of writing. A capital letter is used in this handbook.

We will never forget the first time we made dinner at home together: **He** got stomach poisoning and for four days was too sick to go to work.

— Lisa Baladendrum, student **!**

26c Using a colon to format standard material

TITLE AND SUBTITLE

A Brief History of Time: From the Big Bang to Black Holes

QUOTATION: ON WRITING

When we are very young, we tend to regard the ability to use a colon much as a budding pianist regards the ability to play with crossed hands: many of us, when we are older, regard it as a proof of literary skill, maturity, even of sophistication: and many, whether young, not so young, or old, employ it gauchely, haphazardly, or at best inconsistently.

—Eric Partridge

ADDITIONAL EXAMPLES

To introduce quotations, summaries, and lists:

1. Alice Roosevelt Longworth's colorful reputation is exemplified by this remark: "I have a simple philosophy. Fill what's empty. Empty what's full. And scratch where it itches."

2. Greek mythology comprises the description of the gods and the various stories told about them: it is a series of narratives depicting their personalities, functions, and relationships.

3. Zeus, the supreme god of the Greeks, served in a number of capacities: weather god, sender of rain and lightning, and ruler over the other gods.

To separate material:

1. Eric Partridge is the author of *You Have a Point There: A Guide to Punctuation and Its Allies* as well as *Usage and Abusage: A Guide to Good English.*

2. I will cite the work in the bibliography as follows:

O'Connor, Flannery. "The Life You Save May Be Your Own." *The Realm of Fiction: Seventy-Four Stories.* Ed. James B. Hall and Elizabeth Hall. 3rd ed. New York: McGraw, 1977. 479–88.

3. To: Professor Jill Alexander
From: Professor Max Gregorian
Re: Selection of textbooks

HOURS, MINUTES, AND SECONDS
The plane took off at 7:15 p.m.
The track star passed the halfway point at 1:23.02.

In the military, hours and minutes are written without colons (and always use four digits):

The staff meeting originally scheduled for Tuesday at **0930** will be held Tuesday at **1430** instead.

CHAPTERS AND VERSES OF THE BIBLE
Psalms 23:1–3
Luke 3:13

MEMO FORM
To: Dean Kristen Olivero
From: Professor Daniel Black
Re: Student Work-Study Program

SALUTATION OF FORMAL OR BUSINESS LETTER
Dear Dr. Jewell:

26d Avoiding misuse of the colon

A complete INDEPENDENT CLAUSE must come before a colon, except with "standard material" as explained in section 26c. If you have not written an independent clause before it, do not use a colon.

NO The cook bought: eggs, milk, cheese, and bread.
YES The cook bought eggs, milk, cheese, and bread.

The words *such as, including, like,* and *consists of* do not signal the need for a colon after them. They call for a comma *before* them if they introduce nonrestrictive material (see 24e).

NO The health board discussed many problems **such as:** poor water quality, aging sewage treatment systems, and the lack of an alternate water supplies. [No colon is needed after *such as.*]

YES The health board discussed many problems**, such as** poor water quality, an aging sewage treatment system, and the lack of an alternate water supply. [A comma is needed before *such as* because the information following the expression is not restrictive; it is simply illustrative.]

YES The health board discussed many problems: poor water quality, aging sewage treatment systems, and lack of an alternate water supplies. [If *such as* is dropped; the colon is correct.]

Do not use a colon to separate a PHRASE or DEPENDENT CLAUSE from an independent clause. Use a comma when the dependent clause comes before the independent clause (see 24b).

NO   Day after day: the drought dragged on.

YES   Day after day, the drought dragged on.

NO   After the drought ended: the farmers celebrated.

YES   After the drought ended, the farmers celebrated.

EXERCISE 26-1

Consulting all sections of this chapter, insert colons where they are needed and delete unnecessary ones. If a sentence is correct, circle its number.

EXAMPLE   The twentieth century has seen a flowering of Irish literature, W. B. Yeats, G. B. Shaw, Samuel Beckett, and Seamus Heaney have all won the Nobel Prize in literature.

The twentieth century has seen a flowering of Irish literature: W. B. Yeats, G. B. Shaw, Samuel Beckett, and Seamus Heaney have all won the Nobel Prize in literature.

1. People who work the night shift are typically deprived of essential sleep, an average of nine hours a week.
2. The Iroquois of the Great Lakes region lived in fortified villages and cultivated: corn, beans, and squash.
3. Five nations originally formed the Iroquois Confederacy: the Mohawk, the Oneida, the Onondaga, the Cayuga, and the Seneca.
4. Later, these five Iroquois nations were joined by: the Tuscarora.
5. Shouting: "Come back!" Jason watched the vehicle speed down the highway.
6. When a runner breaks through that unavoidable wall of exhaustion, a very different feeling sets in; an intense sense of well-being known as the "runner's high."
7. However: the "runner's high" soon disappears.
8. Two new nations were born on the same day in 1947, India and Pakistan achieved their independence from Britain at midnight on August 15.
9. To   Instructors

   From   The Dean of Instruction

   Re   Classroom Assignments
10. Nothing except a hurricane could have kept Lisa from the appointment she had made with Donald for 800 p.m.; unfortunately, that night there was a hurricane.

26d   Colons

Answers and Coverage: Exercise 26-1 (continued)

11. ones: cars [26a, list]

12. *Aman: The Story* [26c, separate title and subtitle]

13. motto: "The [26a, quotation]

14. of teaching [26a, not an independent clause]

15. singer: the great [26a, appositive]

11. At age sixteen, George's interests were the usual ones, cars, music videos, and dating.

12. Like many people who have never learned to read or write, the woman who told her life story in *Aman; The Story of a Somali Girl* was able to remember an astonishing number of events in precise detail.

13. The Greek philosopher Socrates took these words as his motto, "The unexamined life is not worth living."

14. Socrates was executed after being found guilty of: teaching young people new ideas.

15. The voice coming from the radio could belong to only one singer; the great jazz singer Ella Fitzgerald.

27

APOSTROPHES

STATEWIDE TESTING

If you teach in a state that requires students to pass basic competency tests in English, see the free publications coordinated with this handbook: One is for the CLAST (Florida), and another is for the TASP Exam (Texas).

The apostrophe plays three roles: It helps form the possessive of nouns and some pronouns; it stands for one or more omitted letters; and it can be used to help form the plurals of letters and numerals. It does *not* help form plurals of nouns or the possessive case of personal pronouns.

WHAT ELSE?

The *Prentice Hall/Simon & Schuster Transparencies for Writers*, written by Duncan Carter, is a set of clear transparencies that cover many topics. It is available free of charge to adopters of this handbook. Ask your Prentice Hall representative.

27a Using an apostrophe to form the possessive case of nouns and indefinite pronouns

The **possessive case** communicates ownership or close relationship.

OWNERSHIP	the writer's pen
CLOSE RELATIONSHIPS	the novel's plot

Possession in NOUNS and certain INDEFINITE PRONOUNS can be communicated by PHRASES beginning with *of* (*comments of the instructor, comments of Professor Montana*) or by an apostrophe in combination with an *s* (*instructor's comments*).

27a.1 Adding 's to show possession when nouns and indefinite pronouns do not end in s

The **dean's** duties included working closely with the resident assistants. [*Dean* is a singular noun not ending in *s*.]

In one more year, I will receive my **bachelor's** degree. [*Bachelor* is a singular noun not ending in *s*.]

They care about their **children's** futures. [*Children* is a plural noun not ending in *s*.]

An **indefinite pronoun** refers to nonspecific persons or things (for example, *any, few, someone, no one;* see sections 7b and 11g).

The accident was really **no one's** fault. [*No one* is an indefinite pronoun not ending in *s*.]

The questions that follow this brief paragraph are designed to point out how much information about the situation has been provided by the apostrophes. You may want to use the questions in a class discussion of apostrophe usage.

The jury's deliberations were over. Charles's lawsuit had at last come to an end. The defendants' lawyers seemed calm as they waited, but the prosecuting attorney's hands twitched with nervousness. Charles's and Robert's businesses would be either ruined or saved by the verdict of the court. Charles and his family's holdings would be seriously affected. The judge's face was impassive as he addressed the jury about its verdict. The jury foreman's voice trembled as he began to speak.

1. Does the writer think of the jury as a single body or as individuals?

2. Is there one defendant, or are there several?

3. Is there one prosecuting attorney, or are there several?

4. Do Charles and Robert own businesses together or separately?

5. Does Charles share in his family's holdings?

6. Why is there no apostrophe in *its verdict*?

7. Why do the words *jury's* (first sentence), *judge's* (next to last sentence), and *foreman's* (last sentence) end in *'s*?

Answers to Extra Exercise A

1. as a single body

2. several

3. one

4. separately

5. yes

6. The personal pronoun is possessive without an apostrophe.

7. Each word is a singular noun that does not end in *s*.

27a.2 Adding 's to show possession when singular nouns end in s

Most academic writers use *'s* to show possession when singular nouns end in *s*, although some writers prefer to use only the apostrophe. Be consistent in each piece of writing. This handbook uses *'s*.

That **business's** system for handling complaints is inefficient.

Chris's ordeal ended.

Lee **Jones's** insurance is expensive.

When adding *'s* could lead to tongue-twisting pronunciation, practice varies. All writers use the apostrophe. Some writers do not add the *s* (for an example, see *Aristides'* on page 330); others do.

Charles **Dickens's** story "A Christmas Carol" is a classic tale.

27a.3 Using only an apostrophe to show possession when a plural noun ends in s

The **boys'** statements were recorded.

The newspapers have publicized several **medicines'** severe side effects.

Three **months'** maternity leave is in the **workers'** contract.

27a.4 Adding 's to the last word in singular compound words and phrases

His **mother-in-law's** corporation just bought out a competitor.

The **tennis player's** strategy was brilliant.

They wanted to hear **somebody else's** interpretation of the rule.

27a.5 Adding 's to only the last noun in joint or group possession

Olga and Joanne's books are valuable. [Olga and Joanne own the books together.]

Anne Smith and Glen Smith's article on solar heating interests me. [Anne Smith and Glen Smith wrote the article together.]

27a.6 Adding 's to each noun in individual possession

Olga's and Joanne's books are valuable. [Olga and Joanne each own some of the valuable books, but they do not own the books together.]

After the fire, **the doctor's and the lawyer's** offices had to be rebuilt. [The doctor and the lawyer had separate offices.]

❶ **APOSTROPHE CAUTION:** Do not use an apostrophe to indicate the plural form of a noun. Use *'s* only to indicate possession. ❗

27b Not using an apostrophe with the possessive forms of personal pronouns

Some pronouns have specific possessive forms that do not include an apostrophe. Do not confuse them with contractions, as explained in section 27c.

PRONOUN	POSSESSIVE FORMS
he	his
she	her, hers
it	its
we	our, ours
you	your, yours
they	their, theirs
who	whose

Be alert to *it's* and *its*, *you're* and *your*, and *who's* and *whose*, which are frequently confused. *It's* stands for *it is*; *its* is a personal pronoun showing possession. *You're* stands for *you are*; *your* is a personal pronoun showing possession. *Who's* stands for *who is*; *whose* is a personal pronoun showing possession.

> **NO** The government has to balance **it's** budget.
> **YES** The government has to balance **its** budget.
> **NO** The professor **who's** class was canceled is at a meeting of birdwatchers.
> **YES** The professor **whose** class was canceled is at a meeting of birdwatchers.

❶ **APOSTROPHE ALERT:** Do not use an apostrophe with a personal pronoun in the possessive case: *its* [not *it's*], *hers* [not *hers'* or *her's*], *their* [not *theirs'* or *their's*]. ❗

27c Using an apostrophe to show omitted letters or numbers in contractions

Contractions are words from which one or more letters have been intentionally omitted and in which apostrophes are inserted to signal the omission. Contractions are common in speaking and in informal writing.

QUOTATION: ON WRITING

It's my experience that very few writers, young or old, are really seeking advice when they give out their work to be read. They want support; they want someone to say, "Good job."

—John Irving

EXTRA EXERCISE B

You may want to see if students can identify all the unnecessary and misplaced apostrophes in the following paragraph.

(1) A good cook stay's busy doing many tasks that make cooking possible. (2) The oven's interior must be cleaned, the pots' and pans' scrubbed, and the knives sharpened. (3) Once the kitchen is tidy, the grocery list's have to be made and menu's planned. (4) Then comes the shopping so that the pantry's shelves will be full. (5) When the chopping and stirring actually begin, most cook's pleasure begins. (6) The aromas' that come from the kitchen are a sign that someone is having a good time.

Coverage for Extra Exercise B

1. stay's [error for *stays*: present-tense verb]
2. oven's [correct: possessive singular noun]; pots', pans' [errors for *pots, pans:* nonpossessive plural nouns]
3. list's, menu's [errors for *lists, menus:* nonpossessive plural nouns]
4. pantry's [correct: possessive singular noun]
5. cook's [error for *cooks':* possessive plural noun]
6. aromas' [error for *aromas:* nonpossessive plural noun]

In college, some readers dislike them as being too informal, while other readers think contractions are useful if the TONE calls for them. Check with your instructor before using contractions in your academic writing. A major exception is *o'clock* (which stands for *of the clock,* an expression no longer in common use).

SOME COMMON CONTRACTIONS

aren't = are not	*she's* = she is
can't = cannot	*there's* = there is
didn't = did not	*they're* = they are
don't = do not	*wasn't* = was not
he's = he is	*we're* = we are
it's = it is	*weren't* = were not
I'd = I would, I had	*we've* = we have
I'm = I am	*who's* = who is
isn't = is not	*won't* = will not
let's = let us	*you're* = you are

If you omit the first two numerals in a year, use an apostrophe. Avoid contraction of dates in academic writing.

They moved from Vermont to Florida after the blizzard of '78.

27d Using 's to form plurals of letters, numerals, symbols, and words when used as terms

Some writers use *'s* to form plurals of letters, numerals, years, symbols, and words used as terms. Others use *s* alone. Either style is acceptable as long as it is used consistently throughout a piece of writing. In this handbook, I do not use an apostrophe in such plurals.

Billie always has trouble printing **W's.**	Billie always has trouble printing **Ws.**
The address includes six **6's.**	The address includes six **6s.**
This trend should continue through the **1990's.**	This trend should continue through the **1990s.**
She ended the letter with a series of **X's** and **O's.**	She ended the letter with a series of **Xs** and **Os.**
The *for's* were all misspelled as *four's.*	The *fors* were all misspelled as *fours.*

❶ UNDERLINING ALERT: As shown in the following examples, always underline (or use italic type for) letters, numbers, and words that are being discussed as words. If you write a plural, do *not* underline (or use italics for) the *'s* or *s*.

```
Many first-graders find writing 8's and pronouncing
eight's hard.
```

```
Many first-graders find writing 8s and pronouncing
eights hard.❗
```

27e Avoiding misuse of the apostrophe

Beware of inserting apostrophes where they do not belong. Chart 129 lists the major causes for apostrophe errors. Some writers frequently make the same apostrophe error again and again. Learn yours, if any, and work consciously on avoiding them.

◉ Leading causes of apostrophe errors   **129**

■ Do not use an apostrophe with the present-tense verb form.

NO   Cholesterol **play's** an important role in how long we live.
YES Cholesterol **plays** an important role in how long we live.

■ Do not add an apostrophe at the end of a nonpossessive noun ending in *s*.

NO   Medical **studies'** reveal that cholesterol is the primary cause of coronary heart disease.
YES Medical **studies** reveal that cholesterol is the primary cause of coronary heart disease.

■ Use an apostrophe after the *s* in the possessive plural of a noun.

NO   The medical community is seeking more information from **doctor's** investigations into heart disease.
YES The medical community is seeking more information from **doctors'** investigations into heart disease.

■ Do not use an apostrophe to form a nonpossessive plural.

NO   **Team's** of doctors are trying to predict who might be most harmed by cholesterol.
YES **Teams** of doctors are trying to predict who might be most harmed by cholesterol.

ANSWERS: EXERCISE 27-1

1. product's; consumers'

2. people's; product's

3. box's; product user's; shopper's

4. Arm & Hammer's; Tide's

5. Heinz's; Coca-Cola's

6. company's; adult female's; adult males'; children's; teenagers'

7. marketing business's; consumers'; companies'

8. test takers'; Gross's; Sylvester Stallone's; Oprah Winfrey's; someone else's

9. companies'; Gross's; image makers'

10. Sports teams'; specialists'; teams'

EXERCISE 27-1

Consulting sections 27a and 27e, rewrite these sentences to insert 's or an apostrophe alone to make the words in parentheses show possession. Delete the parentheses.

EXAMPLE Each box, can, and bottle that shoppers see on a (supermarket) shelves has been designed to appeal to their emotions.

Each box, can, and bottle that shoppers see on a *supermarket's* shelves has been designed to appeal to their emotions.

1. A commercial (product) manufacturer designs its packages to appeal to (consumers) emotions through color and design.
2. Marketing specialists have learned that (people) beliefs about a (product) quality are influenced by their emotional response to the design of its package.
3. Circles and ovals appearing on a (box) design supposedly increase a (product user) feelings of comfort, while bold patterns and colors attract a (shopper) attention.
4. Using both circles and bold designs in (Arm & Hammer) and (Tide) logos produces both these effects on consumers.
5. (Heinz) familiar ketchup bottle and (Coca-Cola) famous label achieve the same effects by combining a bright color with an old-fashioned, "comfortable" design.
6. Often, a (company) marketing consultants will custom-design products to appeal to the supposedly "typical" (adult female) emotions or to (adult males), (children), or (teenagers) feelings.
7. One of the (marketing business) leading consultants, Stan Gross, tests (consumers) emotional reactions to (companies) products and their packages by asking consumers to associate products with well-known personalities.
8. Thus, (test takers) responses to (Gross) questions might reveal that a particular laundry detergent has (Sylvester Stallone) toughness, (Oprah Winfrey) determination, or (someone else) sparkling personality.
9. Manufacturing (companies) products are not the only products whose images rely on (Gross) and other corporate (image makers) advice.
10. (Sports teams) owners also use marketing (specialists) ideas in designing their (teams) images, as anyone who has seen the unforgettable angry bull logo of the Chicago Bulls basketball team will agree.

EXERCISE 27-2

Consulting sections 27a, 27b, and 27e, rewrite these sentences so that each contains a possessive noun.

EXAMPLE Early visitors to Greenland wrote about an unusual custom of the Eskimos of that island.

Early visitors to Greenland wrote about an unusual custom of *that island's Eskimos.*

1. The Eskimos of Greenland used to settle disputes by insulting each other in public.
2. Each of two people involved in a dispute would sing insulting songs about the faults of the other.
3. The other members of the tribe joined in the singing and decided whose insults were the funniest and the most embarrassing.
4. After the decision of the tribe members determined the winner in the dispute, the winner and the loser made up.
5. Similar customs, intended to keep the peace among all the members of the community, were also found in medieval Europe, the ancient Arab world, and early China.

EXERCISE 27-3

Consulting all sections of this chapter, correct any errors in the use of apostrophes in the paragraph.

(1) "Ive just got too many things to do" is an excuse used by many procrastinator's. (2) Perhaps, its true, the day is unusually busy. (3) Perhaps its a hopeless effort to try to start a new project youve been dreading for weeks. (4) There are solution's for procrastinators, however, that are almost guaranteed to work. (5) Psychologist M. Susan Roberts suggests' using stress management techniques. (6) She says that the best techniques' all involve some physical exercise. (7) Even individuals who's lifestyle's are filled with work and relationships need to fit exercise into their weekly routines. (8) Dr. Roberts study also proves that breaking down large, unappealing tasks into smaller, less overwhelming tasks is effective for getting started. (9) Similarly, psychologist Jane Burka believes that breaking jobs down into slice's of fifteen minutes each or simply narrowing goals makes the impossible task seem possible. (10) Many expert's also recommend creating a "to do" list. (11) Items on a list, whether theyre made for the day or the week, can be crossed off as they are completed. (12) Lists' make it easy to prioritize and visually see what has or hasnt been accomplished. (13) Simple technique's like these allow

ANSWERS: EXERCISE 27-2

1. Greenland's Eskimos used to settle disputes by insulting each other in public.
2. Each of two people involved in a dispute would sing insulting songs about the other's faults.
3. The tribe's other members joined in the singing and decided whose insults were the funniest and the most embarrassing.
4. After the tribe members' decision determined the winner in the dispute, the winner and the loser made up.
5. Similar customs, intended to keep the peace among all the community's members, were also found in medieval Europe, the ancient Arab world, and early China.

ANSWERS: EXERCISE 27-3

(1) "*I've* just got too many things to do" is an excuse used by many *procrastinators*. (2) Perhaps, *it's* true, the day is unusually busy. (3) Perhaps *it's* a hopeless effort to try to start a new project *you've* been dreading for weeks. (4) There are *solutions* for procrastinators, however, that are almost guaranteed to work. (5) Psychologist M. Susan Roberts *suggests* using stress management techniques. (6) She says that the best *techniques* all involve some physical exercise. (7) Even individuals *whose lifestyles* are filled with work and relationships need to fit exercise into their weekly routines. (8) Dr. *Roberts's* study also proves that breaking down large, unappealing tasks into smaller, less overwhelming tasks is effective for getting started. (9) Similarly, psychologist Jane Burka believes that breaking jobs down into *slices* of fifteen minutes each or simply narrowing goals makes the impossible task seem possible. (10) Many *experts* also recommend creating a "to do" list. (11) Items on a list, whether *they're* made for the day or the week, can be crossed off as they are completed. (12) *Lists* make it easy to prioritize and visually see what has or *hasn't* been accomplished. (13) Simple *techniques* like these allow *procrastinators* to

→

procrastinators' to relieve themselves of last-minute anxieties and to relax without feeling guilty. (14) At the completion of a job, the right to relax is their's to enjoy.

EXERCISE 27-4

Consulting all sections of this chapter, correct any errors in the use of apostrophes in the paragraph.

(1) Depending on the sensitivity of their taste bud's, people can be divided into three groups. (2) The first of these group's is called supertasters, the second regular tasters, and the third nontasters. (3) For supertasters, sugar taste's sweeter, coffee seem's more bitter, and chili pepper's are hotter than for other people. (4) Nontasters dont lack all sense of taste; their sense of taste is just weaker than other peoples. (5) The scientists' who study taste have actually learned how to count the number of taste buds on a persons tongue. (6) Their studies' show that differences in taste sensitivity are genetic in origin and that two-third's of supertasters are women.

Answers: Exercise 27-3 (continued)
relieve themselves of last-minute anxieties and to relax without feeling guilty. (14) At the completion of a job, the right to relax is *theirs* to enjoy.

ANSWERS: EXERCISE 27-4

(1) Depending on the sensitivity of their taste *buds*, people can be divided into three groups. (2) The first of these *groups* is called supertasters, the second regular tasters, and the third nontasters. (3) For supertasters, sugar *tastes* sweeter, coffee *seems* more bitter, and chili *peppers* are hotter than for other people. (4) Nontasters *don't* lack all sense of taste; their sense of taste is just weaker than other *people's*. (5) The *scientists* who study taste have actually learned how to count the number of taste buds on a *person's* tongue. (6) Their *studies* show that differences in taste sensitivity are genetic in origin and that *two-thirds* of supertasters are women.

28

QUOTATION MARKS

Most commonly, quotation marks enclose **direct quotations**—spoken or written words from an outside source (see 28a). Quotation marks also set off some titles (see 28b), and they can call attention to words used in special senses (see 28c).

Always use quotation marks in pairs: one set to open and another set to close. Be especially careful not to forget to use the second (closing) quotation mark. Double quotation marks (" ") are standard. Single quotation marks (' ') are used only for quotation marks within quotation marks as explained in section 28a.2. In print, opening and closing quotation marks differ slightly, but they usually look identical on a typewriter. Examples of both print and typewritten quotation marks appear in this chapter. (For using quotation marks with brackets, see section 29c; for use with ellipsis points, see 29d; and for use with the slash, see 29e. For commas with quoted words, see section 24g, and for capital letters with quotations, see 30c.)

28a Using quotation marks to enclose short direct quotations

Direct quotations are exact words from a print or nonprint source. When you use a quotation, always check carefully that you have recorded it precisely as it appeared in the original (see 31c.1).

A quotation is considered short if it can be typed or handwritten to occupy no more than four lines on a page. Use double quotation marks at the start and finish of a short quotation. Longer quotations are usually set off ("displayed") by indenting all lines to form a block of text. Do not enclose displayed quotations in quotation marks. The requirements for the length of displayed quotations varies with different documentation styles (discussed in Chapter 33). For guidance, see pages 549–550 for MLA style, the one used in most English courses. See pages 581–582 for APA style. The examples in this chapter are in MLA style.

QUOTATION: ON WRITING

Like italics and hyphens, quotation marks are to be used as sparingly as possible. They should light the way, not darken it.
—Eric Partridge

STATEWIDE TESTING

If you teach in a state that requires students to pass basic competency tests in English, see the free publications coordinated with this handbook: One is for the CLAST (Florida), and another is for the TASP Exam (Texas).

BACKGROUND

Quotation marks did not come into use until the seventeenth century. Before then, quotations and direct speech were simply tagged with comments such as *he said* to set them off. Early use of marks to indicate quoted matter included arrowheads in the margin of the manuscript and double commas placed before a sentence of quoted matter; later, the double commas were used to enclose quotations. The scholarly printer Theodore Low De Vinne lamented the decision of English printers to refuse the French form of marking quotations (a reversible mark that occupies the middle of the type face), since he found it more aesthetically pleasing than the one they adopted, that of a pair of reversed commas for the beginning of a quotation and a pair of apostrophes for its closing.

When punctuation was first employed, it was in the role of the handmaid of prose; later the handmaid was transformed by the pedants into a harsh-faced chaperone, pervertedly ingenious in the contriving of stiff regulations and starched rules of decorum; now, happily, she is content to act as an auxiliary to the writer and as a guide to the reader.

—Harold Herd

TEACHING TIP

You might point out to your students that typewriter face is used in section 28a so that writers can see how such material should look on their typed papers. All material is double-spaced. A short quotation is "run in" with the writer's prose; a long quotation is displayed. For additional examples in typewriter face, you might direct your students' attention to the student research paper in Chapter 34. In particular, you might point out that paragraphs are indented five spaces and displayed quotations are indented ten spaces for all lines.

TEACHING TIP

Many students think that they are not plagiarizing as long as they use quotation marks to indicate material taken from an outside source. These students do not realize that they must also document the source. You might find it useful, therefore, to take some time to explain documentation and the use of parenthetical citations, which may be unfamiliar to students inexperienced in writing research papers. You might also explain that the placement of the parenthetical citation depends on the length of the quotation. If the quotation is "run in," the citation comes before the period; if the quotation is displayed, the citation comes after the period.

❶ DOCUMENTATION ALERT: Whether a quotation is one word or occupies many lines, you must always document its source; see Chapter 33. **!**

SHORT QUOTATIONS

```
Hall explains the practicality of close conversational
distances: "If you are interested in something, your
pupils dilate; if I say something you don't like, they
tend to contract" (47).

Personal space "moves with us, expanding and contracting
according to the situation in which we find ourselves"
(Fisher, Bell, and Baum 149).
```

Any quotation marks that appear in the original source should also be used in a long (displayed) quotation.

LONG QUOTATION (MORE THAN FOUR LINES)

```
Robert Sommer, an environmental psychologist, uses
literary and personal analogies to describe personal
space:

          Like the porcupines in Schopenhauer's fable,
          people like to be close enough to obtain warmth
          and comradeship but far enough away to avoid
          pricking one another. Personal space . . . has
          been likened to a snail shell, a soap bubble,
          an aura, and "breathing room." (26)
```

❶ PUNCTUATION ALERT: In MLA documentation style, the period goes after the parenthetical reference for a "short" quotation, but for a displayed quotation, the period goes before the parenthetical reference. **!**

28a.1 Using quotation marks for quotations within quotations

In a short quotation, when you quote words that themselves contain quotation marks, use single quotation marks in place of the double ones. This is because the doubles have to be used for the whole quotation. In a "displayed" quotation, use the double quotation marks shown in the original.

ORIGINAL SOURCE

Personal space . . . has been likened to a snail shell, a soap bubble, an aura, and "breathing room."

—Robert Sommer, *Personal Space: The Behavioral Bases of Design*, p. 26

**SINGLE QUOTATION MARKS WITHIN DOUBLE QUOTATION MARKS
(IN A SHORT QUOTATION)**

Robert Sommer, an environmental psychologist, compares personal space to "a snail shell, a soap bubble, an aura, and 'breathing room'" (26).

28a.2 Using quotation marks for dialogue and for short quotations of poetry

A quotation of poetry is short if it is no more than three lines of the poem. As with short prose quotations, use double quotation marks to enclose the material. If you quote more than one line of poetry, use a slash with one space on each side to show the line divisions (see 29e).

> As Auden wittily defined personal space, "some thirty inches from my nose / The frontier of my person goes. . . ."

🛇 **CAPITALIZATION ALERT:** When you quote lines of poetry, follow the capitalization of your source. ❗

Dialogue, also called **direct discourse,** is the speakers' words. Whether you are reporting the words of a real speaker or making up dialogue in a short story, use quotation marks to let your reader know which words belong to the speaker and which words do not. Use double quotation marks at the beginning and end of a speaker's words, and start a new paragraph each time the speaker changes.

> "I don't know how you can see to drive," she said.
>
> "Maybe you should put on your glasses."
>
> "Putting on my glasses would help you to see?"
>
> "Not me; you," Macon said. "You're focused on the windshield instead of the road."
>
> —Anne Tyler, *The Accidental Tourist*

🛇 **ALERT:** If one speaker's words require you to use two or more paragraphs, do this: Use double opening quotation marks at the start of each paragraphs but do not use closing double quotation marks until the end of the last quoted paragraph. ❗

Indirect discourse reports what a speaker said. In contrast, direct discourse presents a speaker's exact words. Note that the difference between direct and indirect discourse is not only a matter of punctuation; pronouns and verb tenses differ as well. Do not enclose indirect discourse in quotation marks.

DIRECT DISCOURSE (DIALOGUE)

The mayor said, "I intend to veto that bill."

INDIRECT DISCOURSE

The mayor said that he intended to veto that bill.

QUOTATION: ON WRITING

Manuscript: Something submitted in haste and returned at leisure.

—Oliver Herford

TEACHING TIP

You may want to divide the class into groups of three or four, asking two members of each group to assume the role of a particular person or type of person. Giving one of them an opening statement that is likely to generate a dialogue, you can ask the two to engage in a conversation with each other. When they have finished, the group can write what they heard, first as direct discourse and then as indirect discourse. The first writing can take the form of a short play; the second, a short story.

TEACHING TIP

One pleasant way to review the use of quotation marks is to have students "translate" passages of indirect discourse found in short stories into dialogues. Alternatively, students can be given a short scene from a play they enjoy and asked first to rewrite it as if it were a chapter in a short story. They can set the scene and present the dialogue as conversation, following the conventions of the short story rather than those of the play. Then they can rewrite the scene using indirect discourse in all the conversations.

ANSWERS AND COVERAGE: EXERCISE 28-1

1. In his autobiography, the cartoon character Homer Simpson wrote, "When I say 'Doh!' I mean 'Doh!' " [quoted words within a quotation]

2. "Homework," said the professor, "is the key to capturing the knowledge of a day's lecture." [interrupted direct discourse]

3. The folk song warns, "He's going away for to stay a little while," and then it promises, "But he's coming back if he goes ten thousand mile." [opening and closing quotation marks needed]

4. Richard Hugo begins one of his poems with a unique description of women: "You started it all. You are lovely, / We look at you and we flow." [short poetry quotation]

5. In her book *Lying*, Sissella Bok comments that "the 'whole truth' has seemed so obviously unattainable to some as to cause them to despair of human communication in general." [quotation within quotation; closing quotation marks needed]

6. "Ah, why should life all labor be?" asked Alfred, Lord Tennyson. [opening and closing quotation marks needed]

7. The book review called the novel "a thrilling and unforgettable adventure" that is sure to become a "summer smash." [closing quotation marks needed]

8. "In nearly 90 percent of cases," the brochure said, "the women who have taken our self-defense course are able to escape a dangerous situation." [interrupted direct discourse]

9. A new health report announces, "The elderly may be able to bolster their ability to fight infection with 200 mg of vitamin E daily." [closing quotation mark needed]

10. Correct

ANSWERS AND COVERAGE: EXERCISE 28-2

1. The doctor was told, "You'll find your patient on the set of *Side Effects*. It's a new television series that takes place in a hospital." [from indirect to direct discourse]

EXERCISE 28-1

Consulting section 28a, correct the use of double and single quotation marks. All other punctuation related to the quotations is correct here. If a sentence is correct, circle its number.

EXAMPLE   It was Edward Moore who coined the phrase This is adding insult to injury.

It was Edward Moore who coined the phrase *"This is adding insult to injury."*

1. In his autobiography, the cartoon character Homer Simpson wrote, "When I say "Doh!" I mean "Doh!"

2. "Homework, said the professor, is the key to capturing the knowledge of a day's lecture."

3. The folk song warns, He's going away for to stay a little while, and then it promises, But he's coming back if he goes ten thousand mile.

4. Richard Hugo begins one of his poems with a unique description of women: You started it all. You are lovely, / We look at you and we flow.

5. In her book *Lying*, Sissela Bok comments that "the "whole truth" has seemed so obviously unattainable to some as to cause them to despair of human communication in general.

6. Ah, why should life all labor be? asked Alfred, Lord Tennyson.

7. The book review called the novel "a thrilling and unforgettable adventure" that is sure to become a "summer smash.

8. In nearly 90 percent of cases, the brochure said, the women who have taken our self-defense course are able to escape a dangerous situation.

9. A new health report announces, "The elderly may be able to bolster their ability to fight infection with 200 mg of vitamin E daily.

10. "Be confident that you can complete any task," said the orator, "especially at its beginning."

EXERCISE 28-2

Consulting section 28a, decide whether each sentence is direct or indirect discourse. Then, rewrite each sentence in the other form. Be sure to make any changes needed for grammatical accuracy. With direct discourse, you can put the speaker's words either before or after your explanatory words referring to the speaker.

EXAMPLE   A medical doctor told some newspaper reporters that he was called into a television studio one day to treat a sick actor.

A medical doctor told some newspaper reporters, "I was called into a television studio one day to treat a sick actor."

1. The doctor was told that he would find his patient on the set of *Side Effects*, a new television series that takes place in a hospital.

2. On his arrival at the television studio, the doctor announced, "I'm Dr. Gatley, and I'm looking for *Side Effects*."

3. The studio security guard asked him if he didn't mean to say that he was auditioning for the part of Dr. Gatley in *Side Effects*.

4. The visitor insisted that he really was Dr. Gatley.

5. The surprised security guard replied, "I like your attitude. With self-confidence like that, you're sure to go far in television."

28b Using quotation marks to enclose the titles of short works

When you refer to certain short works by their titles, enclose the titles in quotation marks (other works, usually longer, are underlined; see section 30f). These works include short stories, essays, poems, articles from periodicals, pamphlets, brochures, song titles, and individual episodes of television or radio series.

❶ **ALERT:** Do not put the title of your own paper in quotation marks when you place it on a title page or at the top of a page (see 28d). ❗

What is the rhyme scheme of Andrew Marvell's "Delight in Disorder." [poem]

Have you read "Young Goodman Brown"? [short story]

The best source I found is "The Myth of Political Consultants." [magazine article]

"Shooting an Elephant" describes George Orwell's experiences in Burma. [essay]

A few titles are neither underlined nor enclosed in quotation marks. (For useful lists showing how to present titles, see Chart 130 in section 30e and Chart 131 in section 30f).

❶ **UNDERLINING ALERT:** Underlining in typed or handwritten papers signals words that would appear in *italic type* if the paper were to be typeset or printed on some computer systems. (Printed books, magazines, newspapers, and similar documents are "typeset.") If you use a computer that can produce italic type, you can choose either underlining or italics as long as you are consistent in each piece of writing. ❗

EXERCISE 28-3

Consulting section 28b, correct any quotation mark errors. If a sentence is correct, circle its number.

1. Bharati Mukherjee describes a visitor from India who resents being treated as an exotic object in her short story The Lady from Lucknow.

Answers and Coverage: Exercise 28-2 (continued)

2. On his arrival at the television studio, the doctor announced that he was Dr. Gatley and that he was looking for *Side Effects*. [from direct to indirect discourse]

3. "Don't you mean to say that you are auditioning for the part of Dr. Gatley in *Side Effects*?" the studio security guard asked him. [from indirect to direct discourse]

4. The visitor insisted, "I really am Dr. Gatley." [from indirect to direct discourse]

5. The surprised security guard replied that he liked the man's attitude and that with self-confidence like that, the man was sure to go far in television. [from direct to indirect discourse]

TEACHING TIP

Lewis Thomas objects to the misuse and overuse of quotation marks in ordinary prose. He cites advertising as a prime culprit in the practice. You might want to ask students to bring to class examples of questionable uses of quotation marks that they find in stores, newspapers, billboards, and other advertising spaces. What point was the advertiser trying to make by using quotation marks? Was the advertiser successful?

ANSWERS AND COVERAGE: EXERCISE 28-3

1. Bharati Mukherjee describes a visitor from India who resents being treated as an exotic object in her short story "The Lady from Lucknow." [title of short story]

Answers and Coverage: Exercise 28-3 (continued)

2. Although his poem "The Red Wheelbarrow" contains only sixteen words, William Carlos Williams creates in it both a strong visual image and a sense of mystery. [title of poem]

3. With her soulful singing and relaxed gestures, Billie Holiday gave a bare television studio the atmosphere of a smoky jazz club in "The Sound of Jazz," which was broadcast in 1957 as an episode of the television series *The Seven Lively Arts.* [television episode]

4. Woody Guthrie wrote "This Land Is Your Land" as both a hymn to a vast continent and a song of protest against the selfish misuse of its resources. [song title]

5. In her essay "The Imagination of Disaster," Susan Sontag writes that viewers of disaster movies like to see how these movies succeed in "making a mess"—especially if the mess includes the make-believe destruction of a big city. [essay title; closing quotation marks needed]

QUOTATION: ON WRITING

If we had to say what writing is, we would have to define it essentially as an act of courage.

—Cynthia Ozick

2. Although his poem The Red Wheelbarrow contains only sixteen words, William Carlos Williams creates in it both a strong visual image and a sense of mystery.

3. With her soulful singing and relaxed gestures, Billie Holiday gave a bare television studio the atmosphere of a smoky jazz club in The Sound of Jazz, which was broadcast in 1957 as an episode of the television series *The Seven Lively Arts.*

4. Woody Guthrie wrote This Land Is Your Land as both a hymn to a vast continent and a song of protest against the selfish misuse of its resources.

5. In her essay "The Imagination of Disaster, Susan Sontag writes that viewers of disaster movies like to see how these movies succeed in "making a mess"—especially if the mess includes the make-believe destruction of a big city.

28c Using quotation marks for words used in special senses or for special purposes

Writers sometimes enclose in quotation marks words or phrases meant ironically or in some other nonliteral way.

The proposed tax "reform" is actually a tax increase.

Writers sometimes put technical terms in quotation marks and define them the first time they are used. No quotation marks are used once such terms have been introduced and defined.

"Plagiarism"—the undocumented use of another person's words or ideas—can result in expulsion. Plagiarism is a serious offense.

The translation of a word should be placed in quotation marks; the word or phrase being translated should be underlined to indicate italics.

My grandfather usually ended arguments with <u>de gustibus non disputandum est</u> ("there is no disputing about tastes").

Words being referred to as words can be either enclosed in quotation marks or underlined. Follow consistent practice throughout a paper.

NO Many people confuse affect and effect.

YES Many people confuse "affect" and "effect."

YES Many people confuse <u>affect</u> and <u>effect</u>.

28d Avoiding the misuse of quotation marks

Writers sometimes enclose in quotation marks words that they are uncomfortable about using, such as slang in academic writing or an intentional cliché. The best advice is not to use language you sense is inappropriate to your AUDIENCE or PURPOSE, so quotation marks are not an issue: Take the time to find accurate, appropriate, and fresh words instead.

NO   They "eat like birds" in public, but they "stuff their faces" in private.

YES   They eat very little in public, but they consume enormous amounts of food in private.

Do not enclose a word in quotation marks merely to call attention to it.

NO   "Plagiarism" can result in expulsion.

YES   Plagiarism can result in expulsion.

When you write your paper's title at the top of a page or on a title page, do not enclose it in quotation marks or underline it. The only exception is if the title of your paper refers to another title or a word that requires setting off in quotation marks.

NO   "The Elderly in Nursing Homes: A Case Study"

YES   The Elderly in Nursing Homes: A Case Study

NO   Character Development in Shirley Jackson's Story The Lottery

YES   Character Development in Shirley Jackson's Story "The Lottery"

A nickname does not need quotation marks unless you use the nickname along with the full name. When a person's nickname is widely known, you do not have to give both the nickname and the full name. For example, use *Senator Ted Kennedy* or *Senator Edward Kennedy*, whichever is appropriate to your AUDIENCE and PURPOSE; writing *Senator Edward "Ted" Kennedy* is not necessary.

EXERCISE 28-4

Consulting sections 28c and 28d, correct any incorrect use of quotation marks. If a sentence is correct, circle its number.

EXAMPLE   *Bossa nova*, Portuguese for new wave, is the name of both a dance and a musical style originating in Brazil.

Bossa nova, Portuguese for "new wave," is the name of both a dance and a musical style originating in Brazil.

1. To Freud, the "superego" is the part of the personality that makes moral demands on a person. The "superego" is the third of Freud's three subconscious personality elements.

2. Although many people believe the old adage "Where there's a will, there's a way," psychologists say that to get results, willingness must be combined with ability and effort.

3. "Observation" and "empathy" are two of the chief qualities that mark the work of the Dutch painter Rembrandt.

BACKGROUND

Classical Greek and Latin manuscripts usually had no word separation, but in inscriptions and nonliterary works, dots or apostrophes were often used to set off individual words. The custom of separating words by spacing was used off and on, beginning in the seventh century, becoming systematic only in the eleventh.

ADDITIONAL EXAMPLES

1. Virginia Woolf was a member of the "Bloomsbury group," the name taken from the district of London in which she and her sister lived after the death of their father.

2. She was the author of many short stories, essays, and sketches, such as "The Mark on the Wall."

3. She was an early user of "stream of consciousness" writing.

4. Have you read her long essay called "A Room of One's Own"?

ANSWERS AND COVERAGE: EXERCISE 28-4

1. To Freud, the "superego" is the part of the personality that makes moral demands on a person. The superego is the third of Freud's three subconscious personality elements. [28c, no quotation marks for the second use of a technical term]

2. Correct

3. Observation and empathy are two of the chief qualities that mark the work of the Dutch painter Rembrandt. [28d, misuse of quotation marks to call attention to words]

→

4. *Casbah*, an Arabic word meaning "fortress," is the name given to the oldest part of many North African cities. [28c, translation of a term]

5. *Flammable and inflammable* [or "Flammable" and "inflammable"] are a curious pair of words that once had the same meaning but today are often considered opposites. [28c, consistent treatment needed]

QUOTATION: ON WRITING

How to read writers on writing: With respect, amusement, and skepticism. They will contradict one another—as they should—for each writer brings an individual history to the writing task. There is no single theology here.

—Donald M. Murray

ANSWERS AND COVERAGE: EXERCISE 28-5

1. Dying in a shabby hotel room, the witty writer Oscar Wilde supposedly said, "Either that wallpaper goes, or I do." [period always placed inside closing quotation marks]

4. *Casbah*, an Arabic word meaning fortress, is the name given to the oldest part of many North African cities.

5. "Flammable" and *inflammable* are a curious pair of words that once had the same meaning but today are often considered opposites.

28e Using quotation marks with other punctuation

COMMAS AND PERIODS WITH QUOTATION MARKS

Rebecca enjoyed F. Scott Fitzgerald's story "The Freshest Boy," so she was eager to read his novels. [comma before closing quotation mark]

Jessica said, "Don't stand so far away from me." [comma before opening quotation mark (see also 24g); period before closing quotation mark]

Edward T. Hall coined the word "proxemia." [period before closing quotation mark]

SEMICOLONS AND COLONS WITH QUOTATION MARKS

We have to know each culture's standard for "how close is close": No one wants to offend. [Colon follows closing quotation mark.]

Computers offer businesses "opportunities that never existed before"; some workers disagree. [Semicolon follows closing quotation mark.]

QUESTION MARKS, EXCLAMATION POINTS, AND DASHES WITH QUOTATION MARKS

If these punctuation marks belong to the words enclosed in quotation marks, put them inside the quotation marks.

"Did I Hear You Call My Name?" was the winning song.

"I've won the lottery!" Arielle shouted.

"Who's there? Why don't you ans—"

If a question mark, an exclamation point, or a dash does not belong to the material being quoted, put the punctuation outside the quotation marks.

Have you read Nikki Giovanni's poem "Knoxville, Tennessee"?

If only I could write a story like David Wallace's "Girl with Curious Hair"!

Weak excuses—a classic is "I have to visit my grandparents"—change little from year to year.

EXERCISE 28-5

Consulting sections 28b and 28e, correct any errors in quotation marks and other punctuation with quotation marks. If a sentence is correct, circle its number.

1. Dying in a shabby hotel room, the witty writer Oscar Wilde supposedly said, "Either that wallpaper goes, or I do".

2. Was it personal experience that led the Russian novelist Tolstoy to write, "All happy families resemble one another, but each unhappy family is unhappy in its own way?"

3. In his poem A Supermarket in California, Allen Ginsberg addresses the dead poet Walt Whitman, asking him, Where are we going, Walt Whitman? The doors close / in an hour. Which way does your beard point tonight?

4. Toni Morrison made this reply to the claim that "art that has a political message cannot be good art:" She said that "the best art is political" and that her aim was to create art that was "unquestionably political" and beautiful at the same time.

5. Benjamin Franklin's strange question—"What is the use of a newborn child? —"was his response to someone who doubted the usefulness of new inventions.

This chapter explains the uses of the dash (see 29a), parentheses (see 29b), brackets (see 29c), ellipsis points (see 29d), and the slash (see 29e).

DASH

29a Using the dash

The dash, or a pair of dashes, lets you interrupt a sentence's structure to add information. Such interruptions can fall in the middle or at the end of a sentence. Use dashes sparingly—if you do use them—so that their impact is not diluted by overexposure.

In typed papers, make a dash by hitting the hyphen key twice (--). Do not put a space before, between, or after the hyphens. In print, the dash is an unbroken line that is approximately the length of two hyphens joined together (—). In handwritten papers, make a dash slightly longer than a hyphen, using one unbroken line.

29a.1 Using a dash or dashes to emphasize an example, a definition, an appositive, or a contrast

EXAMPLE

The care-takers—those who are helpers, nurturers, teachers, mothers—are still systematically devalued.

—Ellen Goodman, "Just Woman's Work?"

DEFINITION

Although the emphasis at the school was mainly language—speaking, reading, writing—the lessons always began with an exercise in politeness.

—Elizabeth Wong, *Fifth Chinese Daughter*

APPOSITIVE

Two of the strongest animals in the jungle are vegetarians—the elephant and the gorilla.

—Dick Gregory, *The Shadow That Scares Me*

CONTRAST

Tampering with time brought most of the house tumbling down, and it was this that made Einstein's work so important—and controversial.

—Banesh Hoffmann, "My Friend, Albert Einstein"

Always place the words that you set off in dashes next to or near the words they explain. Otherwise, the interruption will confuse your reader.

NO The current argument is—one that parents, faculty, students, and coaches all debate fiercely—whether athletes should have to meet minimum academic standards to play their sports.

YES The current argument—one that parents, faculty, students, and coaches all debate fiercely—is whether athletes should have to meet minimum academic standards to play their sports.

29a.2 Using a dash or dashes to emphasize an "aside"

Asides are writers' comments within the structure of a sentence or a paragraph. In writing meant to seem objective, asides help writers convey their personal views. Consider your PURPOSE and AUDIENCE when deciding whether to insert an aside.

Television showed us the war. It showed us the war in a way that was—if you chose to watch television, at least—unavoidable.

—Nora Ephron, *Scribble Scribble*

🔴 **PUNCTUATION ALERTS:** (1) If the words within a pair of dashes would take a question mark or an exclamation point if they were a separate sentence, use that punctuation before the second dash: *A first date—do you remember?—stays in the memory forever.* (2) Do not use commas, semicolons, or periods next to dashes. When such a possibility comes up, revise the sentence to avoid it. (3) Do not enclose dashes in quotation marks except when the words require them: *Many of George Orwell's essays—"A Hanging," for example—draw on his experiences as a civil servant. "Shooting an Elephant"—another Orwell essay—appears in many anthologies.* ❗

EXERCISE 29-1

Consulting section 29a, write a sentence about the italicized subject. In your sentence, use dashes to set off the contrast, appositive, aside, example, or definition called for.

EXAMPLE (*health,* definition)

Anorexia nervosa—an eating disorder characterized by an aversion to eating and an obsession with losing weight—is extremely common among young female gymnasts and ballet dancers.

1. (*television program,* contrast)
2. (*politician,* appositive)
3. (*food,* aside)
4. (*music,* example)
5. (*recreational sport,* definition)

Additional Examples: Dash (continued)

Contrast

It's not right or wrong—it's just fattening.

An Aside

If you choose to vote for that candidate—and I don't care whether you do or not—then you have put yourself in the conservative camp.

Broken-Off Speech

"It's not that I don't love you, Tom, it's just that—"

QUOTATION: ON WRITING

The dash has been described as the interruption, the mark of abruptness, the sob, the stammer, and the mark of ignorance. The last name—which might be equally well applied to the comma as crude writers use it—records the fact that the uninformed mistake the dash for an all-purpose mark for every possible occasion.

—George Summey Jr.

QUOTATION: ON WRITING

Surely the unnecessary profusion of straight lines, particularly on a printed page, is offensive to good taste, is an index of the *dasher's* profound ignorance of the art of punctuation, and, so far from helping to bring out the sense of an author, is better adapted for turning into nonsense some of his finest passages.

—John Wilson

ANSWERS AND COVERAGE: EXERCISE 29-1

Answers will vary. When checking them, make sure that the instructions were followed.

QUOTATION: ON WRITING

[The dash] is a comfortable punctuation mark since even the most rigorous critic can seldom claim that any particular example of it is a misuse. Its overuse is its greatest danger, and the writer who can't resist dashes may be suspected of uncoordinated thinking.

—Cornelia Evans and Bergen Evans

ADDITIONAL EXAMPLES: PARENTHESES

Explanations
Most Americans try to be honest about filing their income tax returns (no matter how much it hurts to pay).

Examples
Many modern zoos (such as the Santa Barbara Zoo) try to present the animals so that young children can easily see them.

Asides
House plants are subject to bug infestations (at least mine are) that require special treatment if the attack is to be repelled.

Numbers and Letters
There are five basic ingredients in a good gumbo: (1) a roux, (2) chopped vegetables, (3) water, (4) seafood or chicken, and (5) seasonings.

Numerical Repetition
A freshman is required to take twelve (12) hours of course work to be in regular status.

Expression of Doubt
We have $900 (?) in the bank.

PARENTHESES

29b Using parentheses

Parentheses allow writers to interrupt a sentence's structure to add information of many kinds. Parentheses are like dashes in this function of setting off extra or interrupting words. Unlike dashes, which tend to make interruptions stand out, parentheses tend to deemphasize what they enclose. Use parentheses sparingly, because their overuse can be very distracting for readers.

29b.1 Using parentheses to enclose interrupting words

EXPLANATION

After they've finished with the pantry, the medicine cabinet, and the attic, they will throw out the red geranium (too many leaves), sell the dog (too many fleas), and send the children off to boarding school (too many scuffmarks on the hardwood floors).

—Suzanne Britt, "Neat People vs. Sloppy People"

In *division* (also known as *partition*) a subject commonly thought of as a single unit is reduced to its separate parts.

—David Skwire, *Writing with a Thesis*

EXAMPLE

Though other cities (Dresden, for instance) had been utterly destroyed in World War II, never before had a single weapon been responsible for such destruction.

—Laurence Behrens and Leonard J. Rosen,
Writing and Reading Across the Curriculum

ASIDE

The older girls (non-graduates, of course) were assigned the task of making refreshments for the night's festivities.

—Maya Angelou, *I Know Why the Caged Bird Sings*

The sheer decibel level of the noise around us is not enough to make us cranky, irritable, or aggressive. (It can, however, affect our mental and physical health, which is another matter.)

—Carol Tavris, *Anger: The Misunderstood Emotion*

29b.2 Using parentheses for certain numbers and letters of listed items

When you number listed items within a sentence, enclose the numbers (or letters) in parentheses.

Four items are on the agenda for tonight's meeting: (1) current membership figures, (2) current treasury figures, (3) the budget for renovations, and (4) the campaign for soliciting additional public contributions.

❶ PUNCTUATION ALERTS: (1) Use a colon before a list only if the list is preceded by an INDEPENDENT CLAUSE; see 26a and 26b. (2) You can use commas or semicolons to separate items in a list that falls within a sentence, as long as you are consistent within a piece of writing. When any item itself contains punctuation, use a semicolon to separate the items so that your material is easily read. **❗**

In legal and some business writing, you can use parentheses to enclose a numeral that repeats a spelled-out number.

The monthly rent is three hundred fifty dollars ($350).

Your order of fifteen (15) gross was shipped today.

29b.3 Using other punctuation with parentheses

Do not put a comma before an opening parenthesis. If what comes before the parenthetical material requires a comma, place that comma after the closing parenthesis.

NO Although clearly different from my favorite film**,** (*The Wizard of Oz*) *Gone with the Wind* is an important film worth studying.

YES Although clearly different from my favorite film (*The Wizard of Oz*)**,** *Gone with the Wind* is an important film worth studying.

You can use a question mark or an exclamation point with parenthetical words that occur within the structure of a sentence.

Looking for clues (what did we expect to find**?**) wasted four days.

A complete sentence enclosed in parentheses sometimes stands alone and sometimes falls within the structure of another sentence. Those that stand alone start with a capital letter and end with a period. Those that fall within the structure of another sentence do not start with a capital and do not end with a period.

NO Looking for his car keys (He had left them at my sister's house**.**) wasted an entire hour.

YES Looking for his car keys wasted an entire hour**.** (He had left them at my sister's house**.**)

YES Looking for his car keys (he had left them at my sister's house) wasted an entire hour.

EXAMPLES: PARENTHESES WITH OTHER PUNCTUATION

When eating at a formal restaurant (such as Chez Marcelle), a man is expected to wear a coat and tie.

Although the rain kept falling (and the river rising!), we decided to wait for the rescue boat instead of striking out on our own.

Casablanca has become a favorite film of many people too young to have seen it when it was originally released (or to have seen Bogart and Bergman in their other films).

BACKGROUND

Literally, *parenthesis* indicates "an insertion beside" the basic meaning of the sentence. (The term applies to both the insertion itself and either of the punctuation marks used to surround it.) The Greek from which it comes (by way of Medieval Latin) is composed of *para*, "beside"; *en*, "in"; and *thesis*, "placing, position," from *tithenai*, "to place or put." Hence, a parenthesis is a thought placed beside the principal meaning.

Place quotation marks to enclose words that require them, but do not use quotation marks around parentheses that come before or after those words.

NO   Alberta Hunter **"(Down Hearted Blues)"** is better known for her jazz singing than for her poetry.

YES   Alberta Hunter **("Down Hearted Blues")** is better known for her jazz singing than for her poetry.

EXERCISE 29-2

Consulting section 29b, supply needed or useful parentheses.

EXAMPLE   The world's largest and only? camel hospital was set up by the Israeli government in 1978.

           The world's largest **(***and only?***)** camel hospital was set up by the Israeli government in 1978.

1. Railroad entrepreneur George Francis Train his real name dreamed of creating a chain of great cities across the country connected by his Union Pacific Railroad.

2. Nowadays, you can order almost anything clothing, toys, greeting cards, and even meat through mail-order catalogs.

3. W. C. Fields offered two pieces of advice on job hunting: 1 never show up for an interview in bare feet, and 2 do not read your prospective employer's mail while he is questioning you about your qualifications.

4. Patients who pretend to have ailments are known to doctors as "Munchausens" after Baron Karl Friedrich Hieronymus von Münchhausen he was a German army officer who had a reputation for wild and unbelievable tales.

5. The questions raised by the return of Hong Kong to China Will the former British colony continue its remarkable economic growth? What benefits will flow to China? Can China allow Hong Kong to keep its distinctive way of life? will be answered only with the passage of time.

BRACKETS

29c   Using brackets

29c.1   Using brackets to enclose words you insert into quotations

When you work quoted words into your own sentences (see 31c.4), you may have to change the form of a word or two to make the quoted words fit into the structure of your sentence. Enclose any changes you make in brackets. (The examples with brackets in this section use MLA style of parenthetical references; see section 33c.1.)

ANSWERS AND COVERAGE: EXERCISE 29-2

1. Railroad entrepreneur George Francis Train (his real name) dreamed of creating a chain of great cities across the country connected by his Union Pacific Railroad. [29b.1, interruptive aside]

2. Nowadays, you can order almost anything (clothing, toys, greeting cards, and even meat) through mail-order catalogs. [29b.1, interruptive examples]

3. W. C. Fields offered two pieces of advice on job hunting: (1) never show up for an interview in bare feet, and (2) do not read your prospective employer's mail while he is questioning you about your qualifications. [29b.2, numbers of listed items]

4. Patients who pretend to have ailments are known to doctors as "Munchausens" after Baron Karl Friedrich Hieronymus von Münchhausen. (He was a German army officer who had a reputation for wild and unbelievable tales.) [29b.1, interruptive explanation]

5. The questions raised by the return of Hong Kong to China (Will the former British colony continue its remarkable economic growth? What benefits will flow to China? Can China allow Hong Kong to keep its distinctive way of life?) will be answered only with the passage of time. [29b.1, interruptive examples; 29b.3, punctuation with parentheses]

ORIGINAL SOURCE

Surprisingly, this trend is almost reversed in Italy, where males interact closer and display significantly more contact than do male/female dyads and female couples.

—Robert Shuter, "A Field Study of Nonverbal Communication in Germany, Italy, and the United States," p. 305

QUOTATION WITH BRACKETS

Although German and American men stand farthest apart and touch each other the least, Shuter reported "this trend [to be] almost reversed in Italy" (305).

Enclose your words in brackets if you need to add explanations and clarifications to quoted material.

ORIGINAL SOURCE

This sort of information seems trivial, but it does affect international understanding. Imagine, for example, a business conference between an American and an Arab.

—Charles G. Morris, *Psychology: An Introduction,* p. 516

QUOTATION WITH BRACKETS

"This sort of information [about personal space] seems trivial, but it does affect international understanding" (Morris 516).

Now and then you may find that an author or a typesetter has made a mistake in something you want to quote—a wrong date, a misspelled word, an error of fact. You cannot change another writer's words, but you want your readers to know that the error was in the original work, not introduced by you during research or printing. To show that you have indeed quoted accurately, insert the Latin word *sic,* in brackets, right after the error. Meaning "so" or "thus," *sic* in brackets tells a reader, "It is thus in the original."

The building inspector's report mentioned an unintended consequence of doubling the amount of floor space: "With that much extra room per person, the tennants [*sic*] would sublet."

29c.2 Using brackets to enclose very brief parenthetical material inside parentheses

The expression (first used in *A Fable for Critics* [1848] by James R. Lowell) was popularized in the early twentieth century by Ella Wheeler Wilcox.

QUOTATION: ON WRITING

The author must keep his mouth shut when his work starts to speak.

—Friedrich Nietzsche

ADDITIONAL EXAMPLES: BRACKETS

Insertion of Words

Describing the end of grief, Marjorie Waters wrote, "[It] was a homecoming, a returning to myself made sweeter by the long separation."

To be reasonably comfortable for even short walks outdoors [in Moscow during the winter] it is necessary to wear coats of natural fur.

—Leona P. Schecter, "Moscow"

We hold these truths to be self-evident, that all men are created equal, that they are endowed by their Creator with certain unalienable Rights, that among these are Life, Liberty and the pursuit of Happiness.

—Declaration of Independence

Brief Parenthetical Material Inside Parentheses

The Declaration of Independence (subtitled "The Unanimous Declaration of the Thirteen United States of America" [and published by Congress in 1776]) is an eloquent assertion of human rights.

QUOTATION: ON WRITING

Speech is highly elliptical. It would scarcely be endurable otherwise. Ellipsis is indispensable to the writer or speaker who wants to be brief and pithy, but it can easily cause confusion and obscurity and must be used with skill.

—Cornelia Evans and Bergen Evans

ADDITIONAL EXAMPLES: ELLIPSIS POINTS

Give me liberty or . . . death!
—Patrick Henry

As a recommendation for raising children in the future, Elizabeth Janeway urges "the establishment of enriching and exciting child-care facilities at industrial plants, commercial centers, educational establishments . . . ."

In a comment about Dashiell Hammett, Lillian Hellman says, "He had made up honor early in his life and stuck with his rules . . ." (*An Unfinished Woman* 126), and then she cites examples of that honor from his own acts.

BACKGROUND

Ellipsis is the descendant of one of the classical rhetorician's schemes of omission, the deliberate dropping of a word or words that are readily implied by the context. In *Classical Rhetoric for the Modern Student*, 3rd ed. (New York: Oxford UP, 1990), Edward P. J. Corbett points out that ellipsis can be "an artful and arresting means of securing economy of expression. We must see to it, however, that the understood words are grammatically compatible."

ELLIPSIS POINTS

29d Using ellipsis points

Ellipsis means "omission." **Ellipsis points**—a set of three spaced dots (use the period key on a keyboard or a typewriter)—are used to show that you have left out some of the words in material you are quoting.

ORIGINAL SOURCE

Personal space is not necessarily spherical in shape, nor does it extend equally in all directions. (People are able to tolerate closer presence of a stranger at their sides than directly in front.) It has been likened to a snail shell, a soap bubble, an aura, and "breathing room."

—Robert Sommer, *Personal Space: The Behavioral Bases of Design*, p. 26

Ellipsis points signal readers that you have left out some of the source's words. If you are quoting a phrase without omitting any words between the first and the last in your quote, you do not need to use ellipsis points.

QUOTATION WITHOUT ELLIPSIS

Describing how personal space varies, Sommer says that it "is not necessarily spherical," for it does not "extend equally in all directions" (26).

If you do omit any of the original source's words between the first and the last word you quote, use ellipsis points at each omission.

QUOTATION WITH ELLIPSIS

Other descriptions of personal space include a "shell . . . and 'breathing room' " (Sommer 26).

🛇 PUNCTUATION ALERT: When you omit words from a source you are quoting, omit punctuation that accompanies the omitted words unless it correctly punctuates your sentence.

Other descriptions of personal space include a "shell . . . and 'breathing room' " (Sommer 26). [comma omitted after *shell*]

Other descriptions of personal space include a "shell, . . . a . . . bubble, . . . and 'breathing room' " (Sommer 26). [commas kept after *shell* and *bubble* to separate three items in a series]❗

In two situations, you must use a fourth dot—a sentence-ending period—along with the ellipsis points.

1. When an ellipsis comes at the end of your sentence, add a sentence-ending period before the three dots.

   Sommer goes on to say that people have described personal space as "a snail shell, a soap bubble, an aura. . . ."

🛇 DOCUMENTATION ALERT: In MLA documentation style, if a parenthetical reference is needed, the sentence-ending period goes in a different spot, following the parenthetical reference.

Sommer goes on to say that people have described personal space as "a snail shell, a soap bubble, an aura . . . " (26). ❗

2. When you omit a sentence or more from a source's words and the quoted words before and after the omission are INDEPENDENT CLAUSES, use a sentence-ending period before the ellipsis points.

Using similes to define its dimensions, Sommer explains that "personal space is not necessarily spherical in shape. . . . It has been likened to a snail shell, a soap bubble, an aura, and 'breathing room' " (26).

These rules apply to omissions of words from both prose and poetry. If you omit a line or more from poetry, however, use a full line of spaced dots.

ORIGINAL SOURCE

Sing a song of sixpence,
A pocket full of rye.
Four and twenty blackbirds
Baked in a pie.
When the pie was opened,
The birds began to sing.
Wasn't that a pleasant dish
To set before the king?

QUOTATION WITH LINES OMITTED

Sing a song of sixpence,
A pocket full of rye.
Four and twenty blackbirds
Baked in a pie.
. . . .
Wasn't that a pleasant dish
To set before the king?

SLASH

29e Using the slash

The **slash** (/) is a diagonal line, also called a *virgule* or *solidus*.

29e.1 Using the slash to separate quoted lines of poetry

If you quote more than three lines of a poem in writing, set the poetry off with space and indent as you would a prose quotation of more than four lines (see 28a). For three lines or less, use a sentence format and enclose the poetry lines in quotation marks, with a slash to divide one line from the next. Leave a space on each side of the slash.

QUOTATION: ON WRITING

Punctuation is the art of dividing a written composition into sentences, or parts of sentences, by points or stops, for the purpose of marking the different pauses which the sense, and an accurate pronunciation require.

—Lindley Murray (1794)

QUOTATION: ON WRITING

In the camp, this meant committing my verse—many thousands of lines—to memory. To help me with this I improvised decimal counting beads and, in transit prisons, broke up matchsticks and used the fragments as tallies. As I approached the end of my sentence I grew more confident of my powers of memory, and began writing down and memorizing prose—dialogue at first, but then, bit by bit, whole densely written passages. My memory found room for them! It worked. But more and more of my time—in the end as much as one week every month—went into the regular repetition of all I had memorized.

—Aleksandr Solzhenitsyn

Consider the beginning of Anne Sexton's poem "Words": "Be careful of words, / even the miraculous ones."

Capitalize and punctuate each line as it is in the original, with this exception: End your sentence with a period if the quoted line of poetry does not have other end punctuation. If your quotation ends before the end of the line, use ellipsis points (see 29d).

29e.2 Using the slash for numerical fractions in typed manuscripts

If you have to type numerical fractions, use the slash (with no space before or after the slash) to separate numerator and denominator. In mixed numbers, leave a space between the whole number and its fraction: *1/16, 1 2/3, 2/5, 3 7/8.* (For advice on using spelled-out and numerical forms of numbers, see section 30l.)

29e.3 Using the slash for *and/or*

Try not to use word combinations like *and/or* for writing in the humanities. In academic disciplines where use of such combinations is acceptable, separate the words with a slash. Leave no space before or after the slash. In the humanities, listing both alternatives in normal sentence structure is usually better than separating choices with a slash.

NO   The best quality of reproduction comes from 35-mm slides/direct-positive films.

YES   The best quality of reproduction comes from 35-mm slides or direct-positive films.

EXERCISE 29-3

Consulting all sections in this chapter, supply needed dashes, parentheses, brackets, ellipsis points, and slashes. If a sentence is correct as written, circle its number. In some sentences, you can choose between dashes and parentheses; when you make your choice, be ready to explain it.

EXAMPLE   Two tiny islands in the English Channel Jersey and Guernsey have breeds of cows named after them.

                Two tiny islands in the English Channel—*Jersey and Guernsey*—have breeds of cows named after them.

1. In *The Color Purple* a successful movie as well as a novel, Alice Walker explores the relationships between women and men in traditional African-American culture.

2. If we change our thoughts, we can change our moods: 1 Get up and go. When you most feel like moping, do something anything. Try

cleaning up a drawer. 2 Reach out. Make contact with people you care about. 3 Start smiling. Studies show that people send the same signals to their nervous system when they smile as they do when they are genuinely happy.

3. A series of resolutions was passed 11–0 with one council member abstaining calling on the mayor and the district attorney to improve safety conditions and step up law enforcement on the city buses.

4. All the really interesting desserts ice cream, chocolate fudge cake, pumpkin pie with whipped cream are fattening, unfortunately.

5. Thunder is caused when the flash of lightning heats the air around it to temperatures up to 30,000°F 16,666°C.

6. Christina Rossetti wonders if the end of a life also means the end of love in a poem that opens with these two lines: "When I am dead, my dearest, Sing no sad songs for me."

7. After the internationally famous racehorse Dan Patch died suddenly from a weak heart, his devoted owner, Will Savage, died of the same condition a mere 32 1/2 hours later.

8. In his famous letter from the Birmingham jail on April 16, 1963, Martin Luther King Jr. wrote: "You the eight clergymen who had urged him not to hold a protest deplore the demonstrations taking place in Birmingham."

9. The world's most expensive doll house sold for $256,000 at a 1978 London auction contains sixteen rooms, a working chamber organ, and a silver clothes press but no toilet.

10. The person renting this apartment agrees to pay five hundred fifty dollars $550 per month in rent; a monthly supplement of two hundred twenty-five dollars $225 is payable if that person is the owner of a drum set or an electric guitar.

EXERCISE 29-4

Follow the directions for each item. Consulting sections 29a, 29b, 29d, and 29e, use dashes, parentheses, ellipsis points, and slashes as needed.

EXAMPLE   Write a sentence using dashes that exclaims about getting something right.

I tried and failed, I tried and failed again—and then I did it!

1. Write a sentence that quotes only three lines of the following sonnet by William Shakespeare:

Let me not to the marriage of true minds
Admit impediments. Love is not love
Which alters when it alteration finds,
Or bends with the remover to remove.

Answers and Coverage: Exercise 29-3 (continued)

3. A series of resolutions was passed 11–0 (with one council member abstaining) calling on the mayor and the district attorney to improve safety conditions and set up law enforcement on city buses. [29b.1, parentheses for interruptive explanation]

4. All the really interesting desserts—ice cream, chocolate fudge cake, pumpkin pie with whipped cream—are fattening. [29a.1, dashes for interruptive example]

5. Thunder is caused when the flash of lightning heats the air around it to temperatures up to 30,000°F (16,666°C). [29b.2, numbers]

6. Christina Rossetti wonders if the end of life also means the end of love in a poem that opens with these two lines: "When I am dead, my dearest, / Sing no sad songs for me." [29e.1, slash between lines of quoted poetry]

7. Correct

8. In his famous letter from the Birmingham jail on April 16, 1963, Martin Luther King Jr. wrote: "You [the eight clergymen who had urged him not to hold a protest] deplore the demonstrations taking place in Birmingham." [29c.1, brackets for words inserted into quotation]

9. The world's most expensive doll house (sold for $256,000 at a 1978 London auction) [29b.1, interruptive explanation] contains sixteen rooms, a working chamber organ, and a silver clothes press—but no toilet. [29a.1, contrast]

10. The person renting this apartment agrees to pay five hundred fifty dollars ($550) per month in rent; a monthly supplement of two hundred twenty-five dollars ($225) is payable if that person is the owner of a drum set of an electric guitar. [29b.2, repetition of a spelled-out number]

ANSWERS: EXERCISE 29-4

Answers will vary greatly. When checking them, make sure that the directions were followed.

Answers: Exercise 29-4 (continued)

1. any three lines of the poem—with quotation marks and with slash marks between the first and second and between the second and third lines—in a sentence

2. parentheses to enclose a brief example in a sentence

3. dashes to set off a definition in a sentence

4. parentheses to enclose the numbers 1–4 that label a list within a sentence

5. ellipsis points to indicate an omission from a quotation, with the meaning of the whole still clear

O, no! it is an ever-fixèd mark
That looks on tempests and is never shaken;
It is the star to every wand'ring bark,
Whose worth's unknown, although his height be taken.
Love's not Time's fool, though rosy lips and cheeks
Within his bending sickle's compass come;
Love alters not with his brief hours and weeks,
But bears it out even to the edge of doom.
　　If this be error, and upon me proved,
　　I never writ, nor no man ever loved.

2. Write a sentence in which you use parentheses to enclose a brief example.

3. Write a sentence in which you use dashes to set off a definition.

4. Write a sentence that includes a list of four numbered items.

5. Quote a few sentences from a source. Choose one from which you can omit a few words without losing meaning. Correctly indicate the omission. At the end, give the source of the quotation.

30

CAPITALS, ITALICS, ABBREVIATIONS, AND NUMBERS

CAPITALS

30a Capitalizing the first word of a sentence

Always capitalize the first letter of the first word in a sentence: *Records show that four inches of snow fell last year.* If you write a series of questions that are not complete sentences, you can choose whether or not to use a capital letter. Whichever practice you choose, be consistent throughout a piece of writing. If the questions in the series are complete sentences, start each with a capital letter, of course.

> **YES** What facial feature would most people change if they could? Their eyes? Their ears? Their mouth?
>
> **YES** What facial feature would most people change if they could? their eyes? their ears? their mouth?

If you write a complete sentence after a colon (see 26b), you can choose whether or not to use a capital letter. Whichever practice you choose, be consistent throughout a piece of writing. In this handbook, I use a capital letter to start a sentence after a colon.

A complete sentence enclosed in parentheses sometimes stands alone and sometimes falls within the structure of another sentence (see section 29b.3). Those that stand alone start with a capital letter and end with a period. Those that fall within the structure of another sentence do not start with a capital letter and do not end with a period, but you can use a final question mark or exclamation point (see 29b.3).

> I did not know till years later that they called it the Cuban Missile Crisis. But I remember Castro. (We called him Castor Oil and were awed by his beard.) We might not have worried so much (what would the Communists want with our small New Hampshire town?) except that we lived 10 miles from an air base.
>
> —Joyce Maynard, "An 18-Year-Old Looks Back on Life"

30b Capitalizing listed items

A **run-in list** is one in which the items are worked into the structure of a sentence or a paragraph, rather than each item starting on a new line. When the items in a run-in list are complete sentences, capitalize the first letter of each item. When the items in a run-in list are not complete sentences, begin each with a lowercase letter.

> **YES** We found three reasons for the delay: (1) Bad weather held up delivery of materials. (2) Poor scheduling created confusion. (3) Improper machine maintenance caused an equipment failure.

> **YES** The reasons for the delay were (1) bad weather, (2) poor scheduling, and (3) equipment failure.

A **displayed list** is one in which each item starts on a new line. If the items are sentences, capitalize the first letter. If the items are not sentences, you can choose whether or not to use a capital letter. Whichever you choose, be consistent in each piece of writing.

PARALLELISM ALERT: Make list items parallel in structure. For example, if one item is a sentence, use sentences for all the items (see 18h). **!**

In a **formal outline** (see 2o), you need to start each item with a capital letter.

30c Capitalizing the first letter of an introduced quotation

If you use quoted words within the structure of your own sentence, do not capitalize the first quoted word.

> Mrs. Enriquez says that when students visit a country whose language they are trying to learn, they "absorb a good accent with the food."

If the words in your sentence serve only to introduce quoted words or if you are directly quoting speech, capitalize the first letter of the quoted words if it is capitalized in the original.

> Mrs. Enriquez says, "Students should always visit a country when they want to learn its language. They'll absorb a good accent with the food."

Do not capitalize the continuation of a one-sentence quotation within your sentence, and do not capitalize a partial quotation.

> "Of course," she continued with a smile, "the accent lasts longer than the food."

> Mrs. Enriquez told me that the best way "to absorb a good accent" is to live in the language's country and to eat its food.

30d Capitalizing *I* and *O*

Always capitalize the PRONOUN *I*, no matter where it falls in a sentence or in a group of words or when it stands alone: *I love you, even though I do not want to marry you.* Always capitalize the INTERJECTION *O: You are, O my fair love, a burning fever.* Do not capitalize the interjection *oh* unless it starts a sentence or is capitalized in material that you are quoting.

30e Capitalizing nouns and adjectives according to standard practice

Capitalize **proper nouns** (nouns that name specific people, places, and things): *Mexico, Rome.* Also capitalize **proper adjectives** (adjectives formed from proper nouns): *a Mexican entrepreneur, the Roman street.* Do not capitalize articles (*the, a, an*) accompanying proper nouns or proper adjectives.

A proper noun or adjective sometimes takes on a "common" meaning, losing its very specific "proper" associations. When this happens, the word loses its capital letter as well: *french fries, pasteurize.*

Many common nouns are capitalized when names or titles are added to them. For example, *lake* is not ordinarily capitalized, but when a specific name is added, it is: *Lake Mead.*

In your reading, expect sometimes to see capitalized words that this book says not to capitalize. How writers capitalize can sometimes depend on AUDIENCE and PURPOSE. For example, a corporation's written communications usually use *the Board of Directors* and *the Company,* not *the board of directors* and *the company.* Similarly, the administrators of your school might write *the Faculty* and *the College* or *the University,* words you would not capitalize in a paper. In specific contexts, adapt to the situation.

Chart 130 is a capitalization guide. If what you need is not in the guide, seek out a similar item and apply what is listed to your need. Also, for information about using capital letters in addresses on envelopes, see section 39a.

⊙ **Capitalization guide**   **130**

	CAPITALS	LOWERCASE LETTERS
NAMES	Mother Teresa (*also,* used as names: Mother, Dad, Mom, Pa, etc.)	my mother (*relationship*)
	Doc Holliday	the doctor (*role*) →

30e Capitals, Italics, Abbreviations, and Numbers

EXTRA EXERCISE A

To point out the importance of capitalization, you might want to give your students a paragraph that has been typed with only lowercase letters. Then ask them to sort out the sentences and meaning, placing capital letters where they are needed. Here is a paragraph you can use. (The words set in italic type are the ones that should be capitalized.)

drugs are one of the techniques of *western* therapy of which we are most proud. *however*, drugs are used by healers in other cultures as well. *rauwulfia* root, for example, which was introduced into *western* psychiatry in the 1950s as reserpine, a major tranquilizer, has been used in *india* for centuries as a tranquilizer and has also been in wide use in *west africa* for many years. *another* example is shock therapy. *when* electric shock therapy was introduced by *cerletti* in the 1930s, he was not aware that it had been used in some cultures for up to 4,000 years. *the* technique of applying electrical eels to the head of a patient is referred to in the writings of *aristotle*, *pliny*, and *plutarch*. *what* kinds of results do therapists in other cultures—witch doctors—achieve? *a canadian* psychiatrist, *dr. raymond prince*, spent 17 months studying 46 *nigerian* witch doctors and judged that the therapeutic results were about equal to those obtained in *north american* clinics and hospitals.

—Edwin Fuller Torrey,
The Mind Game

Capitalization guide (continued) 130

	CAPITALS	LOWERCASE LETTERS
TITLES	President Truman	the president
	Democrat (*party member*)	democrat (*believer in democracy*)
	Representative Patsy Mink	the congressional representative
	Senator Mark Hatfield	the senator
	Queen Elizabeth II	the queen
GROUPS OF HUMANITY	Caucasian (*race*)	white (*also* White)
	Negro (*race*)	black (*also* Black)
	Hispanic, African American (*ethnic group*)	
	Jew, Catholic, Protestant, Buddhist (*religious affiliation*)	
ORGANIZATIONS	Congress	congressional
	the Ohio State Supreme Court	the state supreme court
	the Republican Party	the party
	National Gypsum Company	the company
PLACES	Los Angeles	the city
	the South (*region*)	turn south (*direction*)
	Main Street	the street
	Atlantic Ocean	the ocean
	the Black Hills	the hills
BUILDINGS	the Capitol (*in Washington, D.C.*)	the state capitol
	Ace High School	the high school
	China West Café	the restaurant
	Highland Hospital	the hospital
SCIENTIFIC TERMS	Earth (*as one of the planets*)	the earth (*otherwise*)
	the Milky Way	the galaxy
		the moon, the sun
	Streptococcus aureus	a streptococcal infection
	Gresham's law	the theory of relativity

470

Capitalization guide *(continued)* 130

	CAPITALS	LOWERCASE LETTERS
LANGUAGES	Spanish	
NATIONALITIES	Chinese	
SCHOOL COURSES	Chemistry 342	a chemistry course my English class
NAMES OF SPECIFIC THINGS	the *Boston Globe* *Time* Purdue University Heinz ketchup a Dodge Cobra	the newspaper the magazine the university ketchup a car
TIMES AND SEASONS	Friday August	spring, summer, fall, autumn, winter
HISTORICAL PERIODS	World War II the Great Depression (*of the 1930s*) the Reformation	the war the depression (*any economic depression*) an era, an age the eighteenth century fifth-century manuscripts the civil rights movement
RELIGIOUS TERMS	God Buddhism the Torah the Koran the Bible	a god, a goddess a religion
LETTER PARTS	Dear Ms. Tauber: Sincerely, Yours truly,	
TITLES OF PUBLISHED AND RELEASED MATERIAL	"The Lottery" *A History of the United States to 1877* *Jazz on Ice*	[Capitalize the first letter of the first word and all other words word except ARTICLES, short PREPOSITIONS, and short CONJUNCTIONS.]
ACRONYMS AND INITIALISMS	NATO FBI AFL-CIO UCLA NAACP IBM	

→

TEACHING TIP

You might find that students overcapitalize in their writing. Comparison can be a useful tool in getting them to distinguish between common and proper nouns. First, review the basic rule: Proper (capitalized) nouns are the official names of specific people, places, or things; common (uncapitalized) nouns refer more generally to people, places, or things. Then give students pairs of noun phrases, one of which contains a proper noun and one a common noun. Omit all capitals. Ask students to identify and capitalize the proper noun: *president Washington, the president of the country; hunter high school, the high school band; a new car, a cadillac seville; psychological testing, psychology 101.* Augment this list with pairs representing your students' most common errors.

Your students will probably find this rather easy because contrast highlights the specific nouns. The next step can be to make up or edit a paragraph to eliminate all capital letters except those that begin sentences. Ask students to capitalize the first letters of all proper nouns. Upon completion, you might have students exchange papers and discuss the correct answers. Then, students can correct one another's exercises, and you can collect the papers to review or record grades.

TEACHING TIP

To draw students' attention to standard (and perhaps nonstandard) capitalization practice, you may want to ask them to bring to class examples from advertising and newspapers that demonstrate the use of capital letters for a variety of purposes. The examples can be the basis for discussing reasons for using capital letters and the effectiveness with which they are used.

ANSWERS: EXERCISE 30-1

Each word requiring a capital letter is italicized.

1. When the philosopher Bertrand Russell was asked if he would be willing to die for his beliefs, he replied, "*Of* course not. After all, *I* may be wrong."

2. In 1910, the U.S. *Congress* passed a law banning tall buildings in Washington, *D.C.*, so that the city's monuments could be seen from any direction.

3. Do travelers crossing the *Atlantic* gain or lose five hours if they cross the ocean from west to east?

4. You will find St. Luke's *Hospital* at the corner of *Sixteenth Avenue* and Elm *Street*.

5. "Please hurry, driver," pleaded Dorothy, "or we'll be late for the start of the *Bolshoi Ballet*!"

6. The fine art course taught by *Professor* Sanzio accepts only students who already have credits in *Fine Art* 101 and Renaissance *Studies* 211.

7. For years, a *European* travel guide written by Arthur Frommer (it advised tourists on how to live on five dollars a day) could be found in the backpacks and suitcases of thousands of travelers.

8. The *North Pole* is surrounded by an icy sea; the *South Pole* lies in the middle of a frozen landmass, the continent known as *Antarctica*. [lowercase *north pole* and *south pole* also acceptable]

9. Lovers of Mexican-*American* food know that there is more to that cuisine than just tacos, enchiladas, and sauces made with chili peppers.

Capitalization guide *(continued)* 130

	CAPITALS	LOWERCASE LETTERS
SOFTWARE	Microsoft Word WordPerfect	[Capitalize software names as shown in the program documentation. Do not underline these titles or enclose them in quotation marks.]
ADJECTIVES DERIVED FROM CAPITALIZED TERMS	Victorian Midwestern Indo-European	biblical transatlantic alpine

EXERCISE 30-1

Consulting sections 30a through 30e, add capital letters as needed.

1. When the philosopher Bertrand Russell was asked if he would be willing to die for his beliefs, he replied, "of course not. After all, i may be wrong."

2. In 1910, the U.S. congress passed a law banning tall buildings in Washington, d.c., so that the city's monuments could be seen from any direction.

3. Do travelers crossing the atlantic gain or lose five hours if they cross the ocean from west to east?

4. You will find St. Luke's hospital at the corner of sixteenth avenue and Elm street.

5. "Please hurry, driver," pleaded Dorothy, "or we'll be late for the start of the bolshoi ballet!"

6. The fine art course taught by professor Sanzio accepts only students who already have credits in fine art 101 and Renaissance studies 211.

7. For years, a european travel guide written by Arthur Frommer (it advised tourists on how to live on five dollars a day) could be found in the backpacks and suitcases of thousands of travelers.

8. The north pole is surrounded by an icy sea; the south pole lies in the middle of a frozen landmass, the continent known as antarctica.

9. Lovers of Mexican-american food know that there is more to that cuisine than just tacos, enchiladas, and sauces made with chili peppers.

10. A prince named Siddhārtha Gautama, who became known as the buddha ("the Enlightened One"), taught a philosophy that evolved in india into the buddhist religion.

→ 472

11. At one point in the action, the script calls for the "assembled multitudes" to break into shouts of "hail, o merciful queen Tanya!"

12. How should we think of the start of the french revolution? Was it the best of times? the worst of times? a time of indecision, perhaps?

13. According to the chapter "the making of a new world," among those credited with the discovery of the Americas before Columbus are (1) the vikings, (2) various groups of european fishermen and whalers, and (3) the peoples who crossed the Bering strait to Alaska in prehistoric times.

14. People who are accustomed to one of the lovely and powerful English translations of the bible sometimes forget that the bible was not originally written in English.

15. The organization of african unity (OAU) was founded in 1962, when many african nations were winning their independence.

ITALICS (UNDERLINING)

In printed material, **roman type** is the standard; type that slants to the right is called **italic.** Material that is underlined when typewritten or written by hand appears in italics when printed.

ROMAN	Catch-22
ITALIC	*Catch-22*
UNDERLINED	Catch-22

30f Using standard practice for underlining titles and other words, letters, or numbers

Chart 131 provides a guide for making decisions about whether or not to underline. If what you need is not listed, apply what is listed to your need according to your best judgment.

⊙ Guide to underlining   131

Titles

UNDERLINE	DO NOT UNDERLINE
The Bell Jar [a novel]	your own paper's title
Death of a Salesman [a play]	
Collected Works of O. Henry [a book]	"The Last Leaf" [one story in the book]
	→

BACKGROUND

The three basic type forms are gothic, old-style roman, and modern roman. (There are many variations of these basic ones.) Italic type is a companion form of modern roman, one that is lighter and slopes to the right. The earliest type forms were based on contemporary manuscript hands, for the printer was replacing the scribe. The old-style roman form reached its zenith in the fifteenth century, and in 1501, Aldus Manutius of Venice produced and used the first italic form in the printing of a series of Latin texts, the first volume of which was called *Aldine Virgil*. The "modern" roman form, the kind of type most used in Western publishing today, originated about 1693 with Philippe Grandjean. Benjamin Franklin was responsible for introducing a variety of roman type, designed by William Caslon, to the American colonies. The Declaration of Independence was printed using it. The early type founders were artists who were concerned about the aesthetics of their typefaces. In the nineteenth century, however, emphasis shifted from artistry to quantity, and attention to the beauty of printed letters suffered a decline.

ADDITIONAL EXAMPLES

Can your students cite the rule governing the following italicized words?

1. *Hamlet* is still one of the world's most frequently produced plays.

2. Several magazines, such as *Life* and the *Saturday Evening Post*, have significantly changed their format in recent years.

3. Some people prefer to keep up with current events by watching *CBS Evening News* instead of reading *USA Today*.

4. The reruns of *Star Trek* continue to attract viewers.

5. The *Challenger* disaster will be long remembered.

6. My grandfather always told me, "Mind your *p*'s and *q*'s, young man!"

→

474

Guide to underlining (continued)   131

UNDERLINE	DO NOT UNDERLINE
<u>Simon & Schuster Handbook for Writers</u> [a book]	"Writing Research" [one chapter in the book]
<u>Contexts for Composition</u> [a collection of essays]	"Science and Ethics" [one essay in the collection]
<u>The Iliad</u> [a book-length poem]	"Nothing Gold Can Stay" [a short poem]
<u>The African Queen</u> [a film]	
<u>Scientific American</u> [a magazine]	"The Molecules of Life" [an article in a magazine]
<u>The Barber of Seville</u> [title of an opera]	
<u>Symphonie Fantastique</u> [title of a long musical work]	Concerto in B-flat Minor [identification of a musical work by form, number, and key; use neither quotation marks nor underlining]
<u>Twilight Zone</u> [a television series]	"Terror at 30,000 Feet" [an episode of a television series]
<u>The Best of Bob Dylan</u> [a tape or CD]	"Mr. Tambourine Man" [a song or a single selection on a tape or CD]
	Lotus 1-2-3 [Software program names are neither underlined nor enclosed in quotation marks.]
the <u>Los Angeles Times</u> [a newspaper]*	

Other Words

UNDERLINE	DO NOT UNDERLINE
the <u>Intrepid</u> [a ship; do not underline preceding initials like *U.S.S.* or *H.M.S.*]	aircraft carrier [a general class of ship]
<u>Voyager 2</u> [names of specific aircraft, spacecraft, and satellites]	Boeing 747 [general names shared by classes of aircraft, spacecraft, and satellites]

*Even if *The* is part of the title printed on a newspaper, do not use a capital letter and do not underline it in your writing. In MLA and CM documentation, omit the word *The*. In APA and CBE documentation, keep *The*.]

→

Guide to underlining *(continued)*   **131**

UNDERLINE	DO NOT UNDERLINE
<u>summa cum laude</u> [term in a language other than English]	burrito, chutzpah [widely used and commonly understood words from languages other than English]
What does <u>our</u> imply? [a word referred to as such]	
the <u>ABC</u>s; confusing <u>3</u>s and <u>8</u>s [letters and numbers referred to as themselves]	

🖳 **COMPUTER ALERT:** In e-mail and other online communications, if underlining is impossible, some writers use an underscore before the first letter and after the last letter of a title. ◙

30g Underlining sparingly for special emphasis

Professional writers sometimes use italics to clarify a meaning or stress a point.

> Many people we *think* are powerful turn out on closer examination to be merely frightened and anxious.
>
> —Michael Korda, *Power!*

In academic writing, however, try to rely on choice of words and sentence structures to convey emphasis.

EXERCISE 30-2

Consulting section 30f, eliminate unneeded underlining and quotation marks, and add needed underlining. Correct capitalization as necessary.

1. The article on "The Banjo" in the Encyclopaedia Britannica calls it "America's only national instrument," explaining that it combines features from older African-American and European string instruments.

2. An artist who decorates holes in the street pavement and then photographs them was featured in a <u>Public Television</u> documentary called "They Shoot Potholes, Don't They?"

3. The writer of a humor column at a newspaper called The Globe and Mail described an imaginary paper called The Mop and Pail, where things were just slightly more ridiculous than in real life.

Additional Examples (continued)

7. The literary works of the *fin de siècle* were shocking to many readers.

8. English has borrowed many words from other languages, including *chauffeur*, *taco*, and *moccasin*.

9. *The Red Badge of Courage* is a modern epic.

10. The *Titanic* was thought to be invulnerable.

EXTRA EXERCISE B

What is the difference in meaning suggested by the following changes in the italicized words?

1. **a.** Six different bodies compose the United Nations.
   b. Six different bodies compose the *United Nations*.

2. **a.** All members of the UN can send *five* representatives to the General Assembly.
   b. All members of the UN can send five representatives to the *General Assembly*.

3. **a.** The *primary* responsibility of the Security Council is to maintain international peace and security.
   b. The primary responsibility of the Security Council is to maintain *international* peace and security.

ANSWERS AND COVERAGE: EXERCISE 30-2

1. The article on the banjo [quotation marks not needed because title is not cited] in the <u>Encyclopaedia Britannica</u> [underline title of book] calls it "America's only national instrument," explaining that it combines features from older African-American and European string instruments.

2. An artist who decorates holes in the street pavement and then photographs them was featured in a Public Television [omit underlining with proper noun (television network)] documentary called "They Shoot Potholes, Don't They?"

➡

3. The writer of a humor column at a newspaper called the <u>Globe and Mail</u> described an imaginary paper called the <u>Mop and Pail</u> where things were just slightly more ridiculous than in real life. [underline name of a newspaper (do not include *the*)]

4. Experiments carried out by the spacecrafts <u>Viking 1</u> and <u>Viking 2</u> [underline names of specific spacecraft] on the surface of Mars [omit quotation marks with proper noun (planet)] looked for signs of life on that planet.

5. <u>Porgy and Bess,</u> [underline title of a long musical works] the folk opera by George and Ira Gershwin and Du Bose Heyward, introduced the haunting song "Summertime." [use quotation marks with title of a song]

6. Marlon Brando persuaded the director of the film <u>The Godfather</u> [underline title of film] to let him play the elderly Don Corleone [omit underlining with proper noun] by auditioning with his cheeks stuffed with cotton and mumbling his lines hoarsely.

7. The Arabic [omit underlining with proper noun] word <u>salaam</u> and the Hebrew word <u>shalom</u> [underline foreign words] remind us that these two languages are closely related.

8. Of all the actors who have played James Bond, [omit underlining with proper noun] Sean Connery, who originated the role, is probably the most memorable.

9. When a small business chooses a name beginning with the letter <u>a</u> [underline letters used as themselves] repeated four times, as in AAAAbco Auto Body, we can be sure its marketing plan includes being noticed at the start of the telephone directory.

10. Ezra Pound's seventeen-syllable poem "In a Station of the Metro" [use quotation marks for titles of short poems] was inspired by a type of Japanese poem called <u>haiku</u>. [underline foreign word]

4. Experiments carried out by the spacecrafts Viking 1 and Viking 2 on the surface of "Mars" looked for signs of life on that planet.

5. "Porgy and Bess," the folk opera by George and Ira Gershwin and Du Bose Heyward, introduced the haunting song <u>Summertime</u>.

6. Marlon Brando persuaded the director of the film The Godfather to let him play the elderly <u>Don Corleone</u> by auditioning with his cheeks stuffed with cotton and mumbling his lines hoarsely.

7. The <u>Arabic</u> word "salaam" and the <u>Hebrew</u> word "shalom" remind us that these two languages are closely related.

8. Of all the actors who have played <u>James Bond</u>, Sean Connery, who originated the role, is probably the most memorable.

9. When a small business chooses a name beginning with the letter a repeated four times, as in AAAAbco Auto Body, we can be sure its marketing plan includes being noticed at the start of the telephone directory.

10. Ezra Pound's seventeen-syllable poem <u>In a Station of the Metro</u> was inspired by a type of Japanese poem called "haiku."

ABBREVIATIONS

30h Using abbreviations with time and symbols

Some abbreviations are standard in all writing circumstances. In some situations, you may have a choice about whether or not to abbreviate or spell out a word. Choose what seems suited to your PURPOSE for writing and your AUDIENCE, and be consistent in each piece of writing.

❶ PUNCTUATION ALERT: Most abbreviations call for periods: *Mr., R.N., a.m.* Acronyms generally do not, including names of organizations, government agencies, and postal service abbreviations (see 23b): *IBM, FBI, AZ.* When the period of an abbreviation falls at the end of a sentence, that period serves also to end the sentence. ❗

Time

The abbreviations *a.m. (A.M.)* and *p.m. (P.M.)* can be used only with exact times, such as *7:15 A.M., 7:15 a.m.; 3:47 P.M., 3:47 p.m.* You can choose to use capital or lowercase letters, as long as you are consistent in each piece of writing.

❶ USAGE ALERT: Use *a.m.* and *p.m.* only with numbers indicating time. Do not use them instead of the words *morning, evening,* and *night.* ❗

In abbreviations for years, A.D. precedes the year: *A.D. 977.* Conversely, B.C. (or B.C.E.) follows the year: *12 B.C. (or 12 B.C.E.).*

Symbols

Symbols are rarely used in papers written for courses in the humanities, although they are used for special needs such as charts or tables. In the sciences, however, symbols can be appropriate in a paper.

In the humanities, spell out the words *percent* and *cent* in your sentences rather than using symbols. However, you can use a dollar sign with specific dollar amounts: *$23 billion, $7.85.* Let common sense and your readers' needs guide you.

30i Using abbreviations with titles, names and terms, and addresses

Titles

Use either a title of address before a name (***Dr.** Daniel Klausner*) or an academic degree after a name (*Daniel Klausner, **Ph.D.***); do not use both. Because *Jr., Sr., II, III,* and the like are considered part of the name, they can be used with both titles of address and academic degree abbreviations: *Dr. Martin Luther King Jr.; Arthur Wax Sr., M.D.* (The title *Professor* is usually not abbreviated.)

⓿ COMMA ALERT: When you use an academic degree after a person's name, insert a comma both before it and after (unless it falls at the end of a sentence): *Carla Gooden, LL.D., is our guest speaker. Our guest speaker is Carla Gooden, LL.D.* Commas are no longer used to set off *Jr.* and *Sr.* (see 24h). ❗

Names and terms

If you use a long name or term frequently in a paper, you may abbreviate it using these guidelines: The first time, give the full term, with the abbreviation in parentheses immediately after the spelled-out form. After that, you can use the abbreviation alone.

Spain voted to continue as a member of the **North Atlantic Treaty Organization (NATO),** to the surprise of other **NATO** members.

You can abbreviate *U.S.* as a modifier (*the U.S. ski team*), but spell out the words *United States* when you use it as a noun.

> **NO**   The **U.S.** has many different climates.
> **YES**   The **United States** has many different climates.

Addresses

If you include a full address, including the ZIP code, in the body of a paper, use the postal abbreviation for the state name (see Chart 132). Spell out any other combination of a city and a state or a state by itself.

EXTRA EXERCISE C

You may want to organize your class into competing teams, giving each in turn a postal abbreviation to which a member is to respond by naming a city in that state. For example, an acceptable answer for a player who is given the abbreviation MN would be Minneapolis. When a player cannot answer, the abbreviation is given to a player on the other team.

⊙ **Postal abbreviations** 132

AL	Alabama	MT	Montana
AK	Alaska	NE	Nebraska
AZ	Arizona	NV	Nevada
AR	Arkansas	NH	New Hampshire
CA	California	NJ	New Jersey
CO	Colorado	NM	New Mexico
CT	Connecticut	NY	New York
DE	Delaware	NC	North Carolina
DC	District of Columbia	ND	North Dakota
FL	Florida	OH	Ohio
GA	Georgia	OK	Oklahoma
HI	Hawaii	OR	Oregon
ID	Idaho	PA	Pennsylvania
IL	Illinois	RI	Rhode Island
IN	Indiana	SC	South Carolina
IA	Iowa	SD	South Dakota
KS	Kansas	TN	Tennessee
KY	Kentucky	TX	Texas
LA	Louisiana	UT	Utah
ME	Maine	VT	Vermont
MD	Maryland	VA	Virginia
MA	Massachusetts	WA	Washington (state)
MI	Michigan	WV	West Virginia
MN	Minnesota	WI	Wisconsin
MS	Mississippi	WY	Wyoming
MO	Missouri		

❶ **COMMA ALERT:** When writing city and state without a ZIP code, use a comma before *and* after the state.

NO   Portland, OR, is much larger than Portland, ME.

YES   Portland, Oregon, is much larger than Portland, Maine.

YES   The Portland located in Oregon is much larger than the Portland located in Maine. ❗

30j Using abbreviations in documentation according to standard practice

Documentation involves identifying the source of any text or other material that you quote (see 31c), paraphrase (see 31d), or summarize (see 31e). Styles of documentation vary among the disciplines. Different documentation styles are discussed in Chapter 33. Charts 133 and 134 list scholarly abbreviations that you may want to use in your writing and documentation (and to help you understand your reading).

⊙ Common scholarly abbreviations 133

anon.	anonymous	**i.e.**	that is
b.	born	**ms., mss.**	manuscript, manuscripts
c. *or* ©	copyright	**n.b.**	note carefully
c. *or* **ca.**	about (with dates)	**n.d.**	no date (of publication, for a book)
cf.	compare		
col., cols.	column, columns	**p., pp.**	page, pages
d.	died	**pref.**	preface
ed., eds.	edited by, editors	**rept.**	report, reported by
e.g.	for example	**sec., secs.**	section, sections
esp.	especially	**v.** *or* **vs.**	versus (legal case)
et al.	and others	**vol., vols.**	volume, volumes
ff.	and the following pages		

⊙ Month abbreviations used in MLA-style documentation 134

Jan.	January	**May**	(none)	**Sept.**	September
Feb.	February	**June**	(none)	**Oct.**	October
Mar.	March	**July**	(none)	**Nov.**	November
Apr.	April	**Aug.**	August	**Dec.**	December

BACKGROUND

During the administration of President Franklin D. Roosevelt, a number of new government agencies became known by their initials. The Tennessee Valley Authority, for example, was called the TVA, and the National Industrial Recovery Act was the NIRA. World War II strengthened the policy of using initials without periods, and since that time it has been common practice to use an abbreviation without periods in place of some proper names, such as the UN (United Nations), USC (University of Southern California), the NYPD (New York Police Department), and DDT (dichlorodiphenyl-trichloroethane).

TEACHING TIP

You might want to refer your students to section 23b for a discussion of the use of periods with abbreviations.

TEACHING TIP

The letters *B.C.* follow a date, whereas the letters *A.D.* precede a date. William Safire reports that a plaque left on the moon by the first Americans to land there reads: "July 1969, A.D." He further reports that at the time he was a speechwriter at the White House and he approved the wording. He writes:

> In a century or so, I hope some descendant of mine will take a sharp stylus on some weekend rocket to the moon and, while awaiting a transfer rocket to Mars, will draw a little circle around the A.D and put an arrow placing it in front of the word *July*. This will show that human beings in the early days of space were grammatically fallible; that mankind (since changed to *humankind*, but you can leave it the old way on the plaque, Junior) is forever editing, and that a little precision is a dangerous thing.
> —William Safire, "On Language"

ANSWERS: EXERCISE 30-3

1. Both her father and her brother were named William, so friends of the family called her brother "Junior."

2. Medical doctors are amazed at the low rate of heart disease in France, a country where both cigarette smoking is popular and the people eat rich foods.

3. A college professor has compiled a list of books that he insists every educated person in the United States should read.

4. Although she took her college degree in a technical field, Charlene made a point of getting as many liberal arts credits as she could.

5. The Hudson River, which separates New York from New Jersey, is only a mile wide, but some people in New York City speak of New Jersey as if it were on another planet.

6. Graham knew instantly from Lucinda's accent that she came from the Massachusetts coast and couldn't possibly be a native of North Dakota as she claimed.

7. The National Association of Colored People (NAACP), one of the first civil rights organizations, celebrated its eightieth anniversary by holding a dinner in Washington, D.C., to which all members were invited.

8. Dozens of hours and thousands of dollars later, the contractors finally extended the driveway to the main road, a mere four feet away.

9. President Jimmy Carter was said to be a workaholic, but his successor, Ronald Reagan, reputedly took a nap every afternoon.

10. In August, the secretary of the home-owners' association addressed a twelve-page letter to the attention of everyone whose front lawn had more than four dandelions growing on it.

30k   Using *etc.*

The abbreviation *etc.* is from Latin *et cetera,* which means "and the rest." Do not use *etc.* when writing for courses in the humanities. Some commonly accepted substitutes are *and the like, and so on,* and *and so forth.* Even better is to use a more concrete verbal description.

> **NO**   We were asked to bring paper plates, plastic forks, etc., to the picnic.
>
> **YES**   We asked to bring paper plates, plastic forks, and other disposable table items to the picnic.

❶ PUNCTUATION ALERT: Note that a comma is used after *etc.* but not after any of its substitutes. **!**

EXERCISE 30-3

Consulting sections 30h, 30i, and 30j, revise this material so that abbreviations are used correctly.

1. Both her father and brother were named Wm., so friends of the family called her brother "Jr."

2. Medical drs. are amazed at the low rate of heart disease in France, a country where both cigarette smoking is popular and the people eat rich foods.

3. A college prof. has compiled a list of bks. that he insists every educated person in the U.S. should read.

4. Although she took her coll. degree in a tech. field, Charlene made a point of getting as many lib. arts credits as she could.

5. The Hudson R., which separates NY from NJ, is only a mi. wide, but some people in NYC speak of NJ as if it were on another planet.

6. Graham knew instantly from Lucinda's accent that she came from the MA coast and couldn't possibly be a native of N. Dakota as she claimed.

7. The National Association for the Advancement of Colored People (NAACP), one of the first civil rights orgs., celebrated its eightieth anniversary by holding a dinner in Washington, D.C., to which all members were invited.

8. Dozens of hrs. and thousands of $ later, the contractors finally extended the driveway to the main rd., a mere four ft. away.

9. Pres. J. Carter was said to be a workaholic, but his successor, R. Reagan, reputedly took a nap every p.m.

10. In Aug., the sec. of the homeowners' assoc. addressed a 12-p. letter to the attn. of everyone whose front lawn had more than four dandelions growing on it.

NUMBERS

30l Using spelled-out numbers

Depending on how often numbers occur in your paper and what they refer to, you will need to choose whether to express the numbers in words or numerals. The guidelines given here reflect those in the *MLA Handbook for Writers of Research Papers,* Fourth Edition, which focuses on writing in the humanities. For other disciplines, follow the guidelines on using words or numbers in their style manuals. If you are unsure of the guidelines to follow, ask your instructor.

You might decide to reserve numerals for some categories of numbers and words for other categories. Do not mix spelled-out numbers and figures in a paper when they both refer to the same thing.

> **NO** In **four** days, our volunteers increased from **five** to **eight** to **17** to **233.**

> **YES** In **four** days, our volunteers increased from **5** to **8** to **17** to **233.** [All the numbers referring to volunteers are given in figures, but *four* is still spelled out because it refers to a different entity, days.]

⚫ **HYPHENATION ALERT:** Use a hyphen between the spelled-out two-word numbers from *twenty-one* through *ninety-nine* (see 22d.2). ❗

If you use numbers fairly frequently in a paper, spell out the numbers from *one* to *nine* but use numerals for *10* and above.

In the humanities, never start a sentence with a figure; spell out the number. Also try to revise a sentence so that the number does not come first. Practice varies in other disciplines, so consult their manuals (see Chapter 33).

> **Three hundred seventy-five dollars** per credit is the tuition rate for nonresidents.

> The tuition rate for nonresidents is **$375** per credit.

If you are using specific numbers often in a paper (temperatures in a paper about climate, percentages, or any specific measurements of time, distance, or other quantities), use numerals. If you give an approximation, spell out the numbers: *About **five inches** of snow fell.*

30m Using numbers according to standard practice

Standard practice requires figures in many uses of specific numbers and amounts, as shown in Chart 135.

TEACHING TIP

William Safire, essayist on language for the *New York Times*, pointed out in his column of April 23, 1986, that practice varies greatly on how to write *noon* or *midnight* when the number 12 is involved. Some people use 12:00 a.m. for midnight, while others use 12:00 p.m. The same is true for noon. Safire suggests using 12 *noon* and 12 *midnight* for greater clarity.

ANSWERS AND COVERAGE: EXERCISE 30-4

1. At 5:15 p.m. (*or* 5:15 P.M.), the nearly empty city streets suddenly filled with thousands of commuters. [time]

2. Of the 40,000 entries in the *Concise Oxford Dictionary*, only 31 begin with the letter *x*. (*Or* Of the forty thousand entries in the *Concise Oxford Dictionary*, only thirty-one begin with the letter *x*.) [consistency with numbers over 10]

3. A tarantula spider can survive for two years and three months, on average, without eating any food. [words and figures mixed]

4. By the end of act 1, scene 5, Romeo and Juliet have met, and from then on, they are at the mercy of their unhappy fate. [act and scene]

5. Sound travels through the air at a speed of 1,089 feet per second, but in water, it travels 450 percent faster, at 4,859 feet per second. [statistics expressed with mixed figures and words]

6. Twenty-one years old and unhappily married, Cleopatra met the middle-aged Julius Caesar in 48 B.C.E. [sentence opened with figures; year expressed in words]

◉ Guide for using specific numbers 135

DATES	August 6, 1941; 1732–1845; 34 B.C. to A.D. 230
ADDRESSES	10 Downing Street 237 North 8th Street Export Falls, MN 92025
TIMES	8:09 A.M.; 6:00 p.m.; six o'clock [not *6 o'clock*]; four in the afternoon or 4 P.M. [not *four p.m.*]
DECIMALS AND FRACTIONS	5:55; 98.6; 3.1416; 7/8; 12 1/4 three-quarters [not *3-quarters*]; one-half
CHAPTERS AND PAGES	Chapter 27, page 245
SCORES AND STATISTICS	a 6–0 score; a 5 to 3 ratio; 29 percent
IDENTIFICATION NUMBERS	94.4 on the FM dial; call (212) 555-0000
MEASUREMENTS	2 feet; 67.8 miles per hour; 1.5 gallons; 2 level teaspoons; 3 liters; 8-1/2-by-11-inch paper
ACT, SCENE, AND LINE NUMBERS	act 2, scene 2 [or *act II, scene ii*], lines 75–79
TEMPERATURES	40°F; 4°C
MONEY	$1.2 billion; $3.41; 25 cents

EXERCISE 30-4

Consulting sections 30l and 30m, revise this material so that the numbers are in correct form, either spelled out or in figures.

1. At five fifteen p.m., the nearly empty city streets suddenly filled with 1000's of commuters.
2. Of the forty thousand entries in the *Concise Oxford Dictionary*, only 31 begin with the letter *x*.
3. A tarantula spider can survive for two years and 3 months on average without eating any food.
4. By the end of act one, scene five, Romeo and Juliet have met, and from then on, they are at the mercy of their unhappy fate.

5. Sound travels through the air at a speed of 1,089 feet per second, but in water, it travels four hundred and fifty percent faster, at 4,859 feet per second.

6. 21 years old and unhappily married, Cleopatra met the middle-aged Julius Caesar in forty-eight B.C.E.

7. 3/4 of all the people in the world who die from the bite of a snake each year have been bitten by a king cobra.

8. Among human beings, the ratio of female to male births is one hundred to 105, which means that, on average, for every one hundred baby girls born, there are one hundred and five baby boys.

9. An adult blue whale can weigh one hundred tons, which is the combined weight of 30 elephants; to get that big, a young blue whale gains over seven-point-five pounds an hour.

10. On the morning of August thirteenth, nineteen hundred thirty, 3 huge meteorites smashed into the Amazonian jungle.

11. 1 hour of bicycling at five and one-half miles per hour consumes two hundred and ten calories.

12. 2 out of every 5 people who have ever lived on earth are alive today, according to 1 estimate.

13. As they dug up the ancient city of Jericho, archeologist Kathleen Kenyon and her crew sweated through many days when the temperature was at least 90 degrees.

14. The house everyone thought was haunted, the one at six hundred and fifty-three Oak Street, stood empty for 8 months, awaiting a purchaser willing to pay its price of six hundred forty-nine thousand dollars.

15. The 1912 sinking of the *Titanic,* in which one thousand five hundred and three people drowned, is widely known, but few people seem to remember that more than 3,000 people lost their lives aboard the ferryboat *Doña Paz* when it hit an oil tanker in the Philippines in 1987.

Answers and Coverage: Exercise 30-4 (continued)

7. Three-quarters (*or* Three-fourths) of all the people in the world who die from the bite of a snake each year have been bitten by a king cobra. [fraction]

8. Among human beings, the ratio of female to male births in 100 to 105, which means that, on average, for every 100 baby girls born, there are one 105 baby boys. [words and figures mixed in statistics]

9. An adult blue whale can weigh 100 tons, which is the combined weight of 30 elephants; to get that big, a young blue whale gains over 7.5 pounds an hour. (Because *7.5 pounds* must be expressed in figures, figures must also used for the weight of the adult whale, but *thirty elephants* would also be correct.) [numbers over 10 expressed in words and figures; decimal]

10. On the morning of August 13, 1930, three huge meteorites smashed into the Amazonian jungle. [date expressed in words]

11. One hour of bicycling at 5½ miles per hour consumes 210 calories. [sentence opened with figures; measurements expressed in words]

12. Two out of every five people who have ever lived on earth are alive today, according to one estimate. [sentence opened with figures; numbers below 10 in nontechnical writing]

13. As they dug up the ancient city of Jericho, archaeologist Kathleen Kenyon and her crew sweated through many days when the temperature was at least ninety degrees. [occasional, approximate use of numbers 10 and above]

14. The house everyone thought was haunted, the one at 653 Oak Street, stood empty for eight months, awaiting a purchaser willing to pay its price of $649,000. [address; number below 10; money]

15. The 1912 sinking of the *Titanic,* in which 1,503 people drowned, is widely known, but few people seem to remember that more than 3,000 people lost their lives aboard the ferryboat *Doña Paz* when it hit an oil tanker in the Philippines in 1987. [numbers over 10 expressed in words and figures]

PART FIVE

WRITING RESEARCH

Writing research involves, first, conducting research and, then, writing a paper based on that research. Chapters 31 through 35 explain how to avoid plagiarism, plan research topics, find and evaluate sources, write a paper based on your synthesis of those sources, and document your sources correctly.

31

USING SOURCES: AVOIDING PLAGIARISM AND QUOTING, PARAPHRASING, AND SUMMARIZING

Sources, often called *outside sources,* are materials that provide information and from which you often learn something you did not know before. Outside sources include books, articles, people, television and radio, and online databases. Research paper assignments require you to use critical thinking to analyze, summarize, and mostly synthesize (see 5f) one or more sources. Using outside sources effectively and efficiently takes practice, so allow yourself time to become familiar with what is involved. The more you follow the guidelines in Chart 136, the more you will succeed.

◉ **Guidelines for using outside sources in your writing**　　　　**136**

1. Apply the concepts and skills of thinking critically (see 5a–5b), reading critically (see 5c–5f), and writing critically (see 5h–5k).

2. Avoid PLAGIARISM* by always crediting the source for any ideas and words not your own.

3. Use documentation (see Chapter 33) to credit sources accurately and completely.

4. Know how and when to use these techniques for incorporating material from sources into your own writing:

   ■ **Quotation:** the exact words of a source set off in quotation marks (see 31c)

　　　　　　　　　　　　　　　　　　　　　　　　→

---

*You can find the definition of a word printed in small capital letters (such as PLAGIARISM) in the Terms Glossary toward the end of this handbook.

<table>
<tr><td>

Guidelines for using outside sources in your writing *(continued)*
   136

- **Paraphrase:** a detailed restatement of someone else's statement expressed in your own words and your own sentence structures (see 31d)
- **Summary:** a condensed statement of the main points of someone else's passage expressed in your own words and sentence structure (see 31e)

</td></tr>
</table>

31a Avoiding plagiarism

To **plagiarize** is to present another person's words or ideas as if they were your own. Plagiarism is like stealing. The word *plagiarize* comes from the Latin word for kidnapper and literary thief. Plagiarism is a serious offense that can be grounds for failing a course or expulsion from a college. Plagiarism can be intentional, as when you submit as your own work a paper you did not write. Plagiarism is also intentional when you deliberately incorporate the work of other people into your writing without using documentation to acknowledge those sources. Plagiarism can also be unintentional—but no less serious an offense—if you are unaware of what must be acknowledged and how to do so with documentation.

31a.1 Knowing what not to document

When you write a paper that draws on outside sources, you are not expected to document common knowledge (if there is any on your topic) or your own thinking about the subject.

Common knowledge

You do not have to document **common knowledge.** Common knowledge is information that most educated people know, although they might need to remind themselves of certain facts by looking up information in a reference book. For example, it is common knowledge that the U.S. space program included moon landings. Even though you might have to look in a reference book to recall that Neil Armstrong was the first person to set foot on the moon on July 20, 1969, those facts are common knowledge and do not have to be documented. You move into the realm of research and the need to document as soon as you get into less commonly known details about the moon landing: the duration of the stay on the moon, the size and capabilities of the spaceship, what the astronauts ate during their journey, and similar details. If you feel that

than those who received such instruction from just a few of their teachers.

Only 47 percent of the students questioned understood, when they were seniors in high school, how to write an unplagiarized report. Among the untrained students, some felt that putting ideas into their own words and providing a bibliography (no parenthetical references or footnotes) was sufficient. Others felt that copying was fine provided that they supplied footnotes, parenthetical references, or a bibliography (no quotation marks). Almost 6 percent had no idea what *plagiarism* meant. Not surprisingly, over 60 percent of the students in these groups reported having copied high school reports.

Some students, however, consciously plagiarize to receive higher grades, and you may want to devote class time to a discussion of the ethics of plagiarism. To start the discussion, you might report that in a survey of 150 freshmen at Indiana University, Barry M. Kroll found that most students regarded plagiarism as a violation of one's responsibility to do one's own work, as a failure to give authors just credit for their work, or as theft of someone's ideas. Few students, however, identified deliberate plagiarism as lying, fraud, or a betrayal of trust—issues, Kroll believes, that students should be asked to consider in a class discussion.

QUOTATION: ON WRITING

Adam was the only man who, when he said a good thing, knew that nobody had said it before him.

—Mark Twain

TEACHING TIP

To give your students practice in notetaking before they are assigned research paper topics, you might distribute copies of a newspaper or magazine article on a popular subject and ask your students to take notes in support of a particular thesis.

Once they (and you) are sure of their skills, the students can move on to more complex issues with confidence, but at first keeping to popular subjects will help interest students.

Encourage students to paraphrase, summarize, and quote as they feel necessary and to take as many (or as few) notes as they feel would be useful in supporting a thesis. Then, collect their notes and distribute copies of all or some sets of notes. As a class (or in groups), discuss the notes one set at a time.

1. Do all the notes support the thesis?
2. Are paraphrases accurate?
3. Are summaries accurate?
4. Are quotations appropriate and accurate?
5. Are quoted words within paraphrases and summaries placed in quotation marks?
6. Would any material be better presented in a different kind of note?

TEACHING TIP: PLAGIARISM

ESL students may have more problems than native speakers understanding the concept of plagiarism. In many cultures, copying and memorizing are respected forms of learning. Originality and creativity are not valued as highly in all cultures as they are in the United States, where uniqueness in many forms (fashion, language, behavior) is often prized. ESL students may say they understand rather than question anything the teacher explains; therefore, difficult, culture-bound concepts like plagiarism may have to be explained and demonstrated repeatedly.

you are walking a thin line between knowledge held in common and knowledge learned from research, be safe and document.

Sometimes, of course, a research paper does not happen to contain common knowledge. For example, Lisa Laver, whose research paper appears in Chapter 34, had only very general common knowledge about the broad topic of intelligence. She had even less knowledge of her narrowed topic of "newer theories for defining intelligence." Laver's research paper consists of a little of her common knowledge, much she summarizes and synthesizes from outside sources, and some of her own thinking based on what she learned from her research.

Your own thinking

You do not have to document **your own thinking** about your subject. As you conduct your research, you learn new material by building on your prior knowledge—what you already know. You are expected to think about that new material, using the sequence for critical thinking explained in Chapter 5, especially Chart 30. When you synthesize what you have learned from outside sources, you are engaging in your own thinking. Carefully watch the line: When in doubt, document.

Be particularly careful not to allow plagiarism to slip into your research paper's THESIS STATEMENT or TOPIC SENTENCES. It is plagiarism to put a source's main idea into your words and pass that off as yours in your thesis statement or topic sentences. Similarly, it is plagiarism to combine the main ideas of several sources, put them into your own words, and pass that off as your own idea. Your thesis statement and topic sentences must reflect your synthesis of what you have learned from outside sources. Notice how Lisa Laver relied on synthesis and her own thinking in her research paper, presented in Chapter 34.

EXAMPLES OF LAVER'S OWN THINKING

- The thesis statement: paragraph 1
- Synthesis used for most topic sentences (which start all paragraphs except 1 and 10)
- Comments or opinion: opening sentence of paragraph 6 and entire concluding paragraph
- Transitional sentences: opening sentences of paragraphs 2, 3, 4, 8, 9, and 10
- Conclusion: paragraph 11

31a.2 Knowing what to document

What should you document? Everything that is not common knowledge or your own thinking (see 31a.1). Document any material from an outside source that you quote (see 31c), paraphrase (see 31d), or summarize (see 31e). Never forget that writing the exact words of others or the ideas of others in your own words means that you must document.

Careful notetaking is the key to preventing plagiarism. As you conduct research using outside sources, use these widely used techniques that help researchers avoid plagiarism.

PLAGIARISM PREVENTION WHILE TAKING NOTES

■ **Record complete documentation information.** Become entirely familiar with the DOCUMENTATION STYLE you will need in your paper (see 31b). If you are not sure of exactly which style to use, ask your instructor.

Next, make a master guide for the specific information your documentation style requires for each type of source. Check for your style's requirements, shown in Chapter 33. Focus especially on the examples (with identifying labels) in Chart 152 for MLA style, Chart 153 for APA style, Chart 154 for CM style, Chart 155 for CBE style.

Web pages used in your paper require the same level of documentation as a book or a journal. The thoughts and ideas of the author are presented on the Web page and must be acknowledged as another person's work even if the format is less formal than more traditional sources. Because many Web pages are actually self published and have no editor to ensure quality control or to insist on a standard format, you may have to look throughout an entire Web site to find and identify all the components needed for proper documentation. If all the elements of the needed documentation cannot be found, you may have to reconsider whether the particular Web page meets the criteria for a good research source (see Chart 147 in section 32f.3). If it does not, it may have to be discarded or other sources may have to be used to verify the information.

Drawing on your master guide, write a bibliography card for each source. Record all the information for the type of source. Also, record any information you need to locate the source again (see 33b).

■ **Record documentation information as you go along.** Never forget to write down complete, detailed documentation facts. Use your clearest, most readable handwriting. When you write a research paper, your chances of unintentional plagiarism decrease sharply if you can easily figure out from your notes the exact source and its information. Never expect to relocate a source later—it may be unavailable, or you may not be able to recall where you found it.

■ **Use a consistent notetaking system.** Never expect to reconstruct from memory what came from the source and what is the result of your own thinking. Always use different colors of ink or a clear coding system to keep three things separate: (1) paraphrased or

EXTRA EXERCISE A

Which of the following statements should be documented, and which need not be documented?

1. The Declaration of Independence was issued in 1776.

2. The sediments on the ocean floor are the accumulation of silt carried by rivers to the sea, volcanic dust, coastal sands, and discarded shells of living creatures.

3. Levi Strauss, the inventor of blue jeans, came to the United States from Germany in 1848.

4. Coca-Cola is a popular soft drink all around the world.

5. According to Germaine Greer, the reason few women artists have achieved greatness is that they have historically internalized their oppression, thereby draining the energy required for creative work.

6. The United States is a substantially less secure society today than it was forty years ago.

→

7. The Olympic Games are held every four years.

8. The initials GDP stand for the term *gross domestic product*.

9. As a society we should read poetry because it makes us live more fully and live more deeply.

10. Henry David Thoreau lived at Walden Pond for two years.

Answers to Extra Exercise A

1. No. Common knowledge.

2. Yes. Not common knowledge.

3. Not necessary. Can be found in a general encyclopedia.

4. No. Common knowledge.

5. Yes. Opinion of someone besides the writer.

6. No, if opinion of the writer. Yes, if opinion of someone besides the writer.

7. No. Common knowledge.

8. No. Common knowledge.

9. No, if opinion of the writer. Yes, if opinion of someone besides the writer.

10. Not necessary. Can be found in a general encyclopedia.

BACKGROUND

In a lively, ironic article, "Collaboration or Plagiarism: Cheating Is in the Eye of the Beholder" (*Dialogue*, Fall 1993: 6–27), Geraldine McNenny and Duane Roen address the controversies that often surround collaboration in academic settings. They also provide an extensive and useful bibliography.

QUOTATION: ON WRITING

I've never discussed my writing with others much, but I don't believe it can do any harm. I don't think that there's any risk that ideas or materials will evaporate.

—Aldous Huxley

summarized source material, (2) quotations from a source, and (3) your own thoughts. For quotations, many professional writers use oversize quotation marks so that they are certain they will see them later.

31b Understanding the concept of documentation

Documentation means acknowledging your sources by giving full and accurate information so that readers can find your sources if they choose to. This information includes the author, title, publication information or electronic accessing information, and related facts. Whenever you quote (see 31c), paraphrase (see 31d), or summarize (see 31e), you must document your source correctly according to the DOCUMENTATION STYLE you are using.

Documentation styles vary among the academic disciplines. When you write using outside sources, ask your instructor which documentation style you are expected to use. Chapter 33 explains and illustrates four documentation styles. Each style is identified for easy reference by a colored bar on the outer edge of the pages: a red bar for Modern Language Association (MLA) style, a blue bar for American Psychological Association (APA) style, a green bar for Chicago Manual (CM) style, and a gray bar for Council of Biology Editors (CBE) style.

31c Using quotations effectively

Quotations are the exact words of a source set off in quotation marks (see 28a). Quotations are not paraphrases (see 31d) or summaries (see 31e), techniques to use when you present your sources' ideas in your words. One advantage to quotations is that they allow your reader to encounter your source's words directly. Consult Chart 137 for guidelines when using quotations.

⊙ **Guidelines for using quotations**   **137**

1. Use quotations from authorities in your subject to *support* what you say. Do not use quotations as your THESIS STATEMENT or TOPIC SENTENCES.

2. Select quotations that fit your message.

3. Choose a quotation only if one or more of the following apply:

   ■ its language is particularly appropriate or distinctive   →

> **Guidelines for using quotations** *(continued)* **137**
>
> - its idea is particularly hard to paraphrase accurately
> - the authority of the source is especially important to support your material
> - the source's words are open to more than one interpretation, so your reader needs to see the original
>
> 4. Do not use quotations in more than a quarter of your paper; rely mostly on paraphrase and summary.
> 5. Quote accurately.
> 6. Integrate quotations smoothly into your prose (see 31c.4), paying special attention to the verbs that help you do so effectively (see 31f).
> 7. **Avoid plagiarism** (see 31a). Always document your source. Enclose quotations of four lines or fewer in quotation marks. Even if you use part of an entire quotation in your paper, use quotation marks to signal that all the words enclosed in them are words quoted directly from a source. (See 28a.1 for quotations of five or more lines.)

Two conflicting demands confront you when you use quotations in your writing. Along with the effect and support of quotations, you also want your writing to be coherent and readable. You might seem to gain authority by quoting experts on your topic, but if you use too many quotations, you lose coherence as well as control of your own paper. If more than a quarter of your paper consists of quotations, you may have written what some people call a "Scotch tape special." Having too many quotations gives readers—including instructors—the impression that you have not synthesized (see 5f) what your sources say. You are letting other people do your talking. Therefore, use quotations sparingly. When you draw on support from an authority, rely mostly on paraphrase (see 31d) and summary (see 31e).

31c.1 Quoting accurately

When using quotations, be very careful to quote each source exactly. Always check your quotations against the originals—and then recheck. Mistakes are extremely easy to make when you are copying from a source, especially in transferring from your notes into your paper. When practical, photocopy a source's words you think you might want to quote. (There is one danger in photocopying; see section 32j.2.) Mark off on the copy the exact place that caught your attention as a possible quotation; otherwise, you might forget your impressions and waste time trying to reconstruct your thought processes.

QUOTATION: ON WRITING

Why can't somebody give us a list of things that everybody thinks and nobody says, and another list of things that everybody says and nobody thinks?

—Oliver Wendell Holmes

TEACHING TIP

In the belief that most students who plagiarize from their sources do so because they don't know how to avoid the problem, Kathleen Mouton has devised a technique that can be demonstrated in class to help students avoid taking notes that are too close to the words of the source. She suggests that instructors ask students to read a short, informative passage of material and then put it away and make notes from memory. Students can check afterward to make sure that facts (such as dates and names) are correct. With larger amounts of material, students can stop frequently to make their notes, still being careful not to look at the source while recording the note.

QUOTATION: ON WRITING

The wisdom of the wise and the experience of the ages are perpetuated by quotations.

—Benjamin Disraeli

Often you have to add a word or words to a quotation so that it fits in with your prose: Always put those added words in brackets (see 29c). Also, make sure your added words do not distort the original meaning of the quotation. The following quotation is taken from original material shown in section 31d.2. The bracketed material replaces the word *he* in the original quotation; this helps the reader understand what was clear in the context of the original source but is not clear when quoted in isolation. The bracketed information supplies words to clarify the material.

> "If you hail from western Europe, you will find that [the person you are talking to] is at roughly fingertip distance from you" (Morris 131).*

If you delete a portion of a quotation, indicate the omission with ellipsis points (see 29d). When using ellipsis points, make sure that the remaining words accurately reflect the source's meaning. Also, check that your omission does not create an awkward sentence structure.

ORIGINAL

Like the porcupines in Schopenhauer's fable, people like to be close enough to obtain warmth and comradeship but far enough away to avoid pricking one another. Personal space is not necessarily spherical in shape, nor does it extend equally in all directions. (People are able to tolerate closer presence of a stranger at their sides than directly in front of them.) It has been likened to a snail shell, a soap bubble, an aura, and "breathing room" (Sommer 26).

WITH ELLIPSES

Like the porcupines in Schopenhauer's fable, people like to be close enough to obtain warmth and comradeship but far enough away to avoid pricking one another. Personal space . . . has been likened to a snail shell . . . (Sommer 26).

31c.2 Selecting quotations from accepted authorities that fit your meaning

Quotations from authorities on your subject can bring credibility to your discussion. However, you must be able to justify every quotation you decide to use. If you are unsure whether to quote, follow the criteria in Chart 137, item 3. If you decide not to quote, either paraphrase (see 31d) or summarize (see 31e) the material. For example, Lisa Laver, author of the student research paper in Chapter 34 about definitions of intelligence, quoted Daniel Goleman because he is an accepted authority on her topic. (See Chart 146 in Section 32f.3.)

Equally important, use a quotation only if its words fit your context. Never force a quotation to fit your material because most readers can quickly discern the manipulation. Also, if you have to hunt for a quotation

*Source information is in MLA style throughout this chapter (see 33c).

simply because you want to include a particular authority's words, chances are that the quotation will seem forced or tacked on.

31c.3 Keeping long quotations to a minimum

When you use a quotation, your purpose is to supply evidence or support for your paper. Do not use a quotation to reconstruct someone else's argument. When a quotation is very long, you might be making this error. Also, if you need to present a complicated argument in detail and thus quote long passages, make absolutely sure every word in the quotation counts. Edit out irrelevant parts (using ellipsis points to indicate deleted material; see 31c.1). Otherwise, your readers may skip over the long quotation—and your instructor will assume that you did not want to take the time to paraphrase (see 31d) or summarize (see 31e) the material.

⊘ **FORMAT ALERT:** For instructions on how to format the layout of a prose quotation more than four lines long (or more than three quoted lines of poetry) in MLA style, see pages 549–550. For formatting more than 40 quoted words in APA style, see pages 581–582. ❗

31c.4 Integrating quotations smoothly into your prose

When you use quotations, you must integrate them smoothly into your sentences to avoid choppy, incoherent sentences in which quotations do not mesh with the grammar, style, or logic of your prose. Consider these examples based on the original material in section 31c.1.

NO   Sommer says personal space for people "like the porcupines in Schopenhauer's fable, people like to be close enough to obtain warmth and comradeship but far enough away to avoid pricking one another" (26). [grammar problem]

YES   Concerning personal space, Sommer says that "like the porcupines in Schopenhauer's fable, people like to be close enough to obtain warmth and comradeship but far enough away to avoid pricking one another" (26).

Perhaps the biggest complaint instructors have about student research papers is that sometimes quotations are simply stuck in without any reason for their inclusion. Without context-setting information, the reader cannot know how the writer connects the quotation with its surroundings. When words are placed between quotation marks, they take on special significance concerning message as well as language.

Also, make sure your readers know who said the quoted words; otherwise, you have used *disembodied quotations* (some instructors call them "ghost quotations"). Quotation marks set off someone else's words, but they tell the reader nothing about who is being quoted and why. Your prose and documentation must do that.

EXTRA EXERCISE B

Practice working quotations smoothly into your own writing by devising introductions to the following statements. (Answers will vary.)

1. "Boys and girls grow up in different worlds, but we think we're in the same one, so we judge each other's behavior by the standards of our own."
—Deborah Tannen,
You Just Don't Understand: Men and Women in Conversation

2. "Science does not aim at establishing immutable truths and eternal dogmas: its aim is to approach the truth by successive approximations, without claiming that at any stage final and complete accuracy has been achieved."
—Bertrand Russell,
The ABC of Relativity

3. "Femininity, in essence, is a romantic sentiment, a nostalgic tradition of imposed limitations."
—Susan Brownmiller,
"Femininity"

4. "In books I've read since I was young I've searched for heroines who could serve as ideals, as models, as possibilities."
—Judith Viorst,
"How Books Helped Shape My Life"

5. "Every gift we give carries with it our idea of what a present is. Perhaps it expresses our personality; perhaps, on the contrary, it is what we believe the recipient really wants, a choice based on careful listening for the slightest hint of what he longs for or needs or should have, even though he may not realize it."
—Margaret Mead and Rhoda Metraux,
"The Gift of Autonomy"

A quotation should almost never begin a paragraph. Rely on your own TOPIC SENTENCE to begin. Then you can use the quotation if it supports or extends what you have said.

Citing the author's name and the title of the work as you introduce a quotation helps create a context for the quotation. Moreover, if the author is noteworthy, you give additional authority to your message by referring to his or her credentials as part of this introduction. Consider the following treatments of source material:

SOURCE

Hall, Edward T. *The Hidden Dimension.* New York: Doubleday, 1966: 171.

ORIGINAL MATERIAL

Therefore, people from different cultures, when interpreting each other's behavior, often misinterpret the relationship, the activity, or the emotions.

QUOTATION USING AUTHOR'S NAME

Edward T. Hall claims that "people from different cultures, when interpreting each other's behavior, often misinterpret the relationship, the activity, or the emotions" (171).

QUOTATION USING AUTHOR'S NAME AND SOURCE TITLE

Edward T. Hall claims in *The Hidden Dimension* that "people from different cultures, when interpreting each other's behavior, often misinterpret the relationship, the activity, or the emotions" (171).

QUOTATION USING AUTHOR'S NAME, CREDENTIALS, AND SOURCE TITLE

Edward T. Hall, an anthropologist who was a pioneer in the study of personal space, claims in *The Hidden Dimension* that "people from different cultures, when interpreting each other's behavior, often misinterpret the relationship, the activity, or the emotions" (171).

Occasionally, quotations speak for themselves, but at times they do not. Usually, the words you are quoting are part of a larger piece, and you know the connection that the quotation has to the original material. Your reader may puzzle over why you included the quotation, so a brief introductory remark provides the needed information.

QUOTATION USING AUTHOR'S NAME AND INTRODUCTORY ANALYSIS

Anthropologist Edward T. Hall believes that people from different societies perceive personal space in varying ways, claiming that "people from different cultures, when interpreting each other's behavior, often misinterpret the relationship, the activity, or the emotions" (171).

Another technique for fitting a quotation into your own writing involves interrupting the quotation with your own words. (Remember that if you insert your own words *within* the quotation, you must put those words between brackets; see section 29c.)

"Therefore," claims Edward T. Hall, "people from different cultures, when interpreting each other's behavior, often misinterpret the relationship, the activity, or the emotions" (171).

❶ **ALERT:** After using an author's full name in the first reference, you can use the author's last name only in subsequent references, unless another source has that same last name. **!**

EXERCISE 31-1

Read the original material, from "Avoiding the Hazards of Drowsy Driving" by Jane E. Brody in the *New York Times*, December 21, 1994, page C10. Then, evaluate the passages that show unacceptable uses of quotations. Describe the problems, and then revise each passage. End the quotations with this MLA parenthetical reference: (Brody C10).

ORIGINAL MATERIAL

It may lack the drama of drunken driving, but drowsy driving is even more common and can be just as deadly. Mix it with even one alcoholic drink and you have an asleep-at-the-wheel cocktail in the making.

With holiday preparations and celebrations prompting millions to cheat on sleep and then drive, often after a drink, the risk of dozing off behind the wheel is greater than ever. Even at quieter and more sober times, about 40 percent of adults are shortchanged on sleep and in danger of being lulled into slumber by humming tires on a dark road.

Compounding the problem is a growing fear of stopping to nap at highway rest areas, which in some states have become high-crime areas. In many states, rest areas are too small or too far apart to meet the needs of all the sleepy drivers.

UNACCEPTABLE USES OF QUOTATIONS

1. Many hazards on the road are caused by sleepy drivers. "The risk of dozing off behind the wheel is greater than ever" (Brody C10).

2. Researchers have determined that "it may lack the drama of drunken driving, but drowsy driving can be just as deadly" (Brody C10).

3. With studies showing that fully 40 percent of all adults suffer from a lack of sleep at all times, "being lulled into slumber by humming tires on a dark road" (Brody C10).

4. In the past, weary drivers would often stop at highway rest areas to nap, but the future may bring some changes. If current trends continue, such rest areas "in some states have become high-crime areas" (Brody C10) that drivers will shun with increasing frequency.

QUOTATION: ON WRITING

Usually I try to be there by six. Everything has been taken off the walls so that there's nothing to arrest my sight. On the bed I have *Roget's Thesaurus*, a dictionary, a Bible, and a deck of playing cards.

—Toni Morrison

ANSWERS AND COVERAGE: EXERCISE 31-1

1. *Analysis:* quotation does not relate clearly to the sentence it follows. A traditional introduction to the quotation is needed. *Acceptable version* (answers will vary): Many hazards on the road are caused by sleepy drivers. When a driver is short on sleep or has had some alcohol, "the risk of dozing off behind the wheel is greater than ever" (Brody C10).

2. *Analysis:* Quotation omits several words but does not indicate where material has been deleted. *Acceptable version* (answers will vary): Researchers have determined that "it may lack the drama of drunken driving, but drowsy driving . . . can be just as deadly" (Brody C10).

3. *Analysis:* Sentence is grammatically incorrect. The quotation does not fit with the rest of the sentence. Words need to be added so that the information flows smoothly. *Acceptable version* (answers will vary): With studies showing that fully 40 percent of all adults suffer from a lack of sleep at all times, drivers are constantly at risk of "being lulled into slumber by humming tires on a dark road" (Brody C10).

4. *Analysis:* Tense of the verb in the quotation is incorrect. Brackets can be used to change the tense of the verb in the quotation so that it is grammatically correct. *Acceptable version* (answers will vary): In the past, weary drivers would often stop at highway rest areas to nap, but the future may bring some changes. If current trends continue, such rest areas "in some states [will] become high-crime areas" (Brody C10) that drivers will shun with increasing frequency.

→

Answers and Coverage: Exercise 31-1 (continued)

5. *Analysis:* Quotation is inaccurate. The word "too" before the word "far" is omitted, and the word "just" is added. *Acceptable version* (answers will vary): But even when drivers consider rest stops to be safe, often such areas are "too small or too far apart to meet the needs of all the sleepy drivers" (Brody C10).

ANSWERS: EXERCISE 31-2

1. Answers will vary; one possibility follows:

Because genetic research is becoming increasingly important, scientists are seeking twins who are willing to participate in experiments either for pay or as volunteers. The Twins Foundation is confident that researchers will find the subjects they need because "there are approximately 4.5 million twin individuals in the United States alone, and about 70,000 more are born each year" (Begley 84).

2. Answers will vary; one possibility follows:

It is becoming increasingly difficult to ensure that large-scale testing will be taken honestly. For example, in New York State, students stole copies of the Regents exam, and because of their actions "1,200 principals received instructions from the State Education Commissioner to look for *unusual scoring patterns* that would show that students had the answers beforehand" (Robbins 12).

3. Answers will vary.

5. But even when drivers consider rest stops to be safe, often such areas are "just too small or far apart to meet the needs of all the sleepy drivers" (Brody C10).

EXERCISE 31-2

1. For a paper describing how and why twins make important contributions to scientific research, write a three- to four-sentence passage that includes your own words and a quotation from this material. After the quoted words, use this parenthetical reference: (Begley 84).

> For over a century twins have been used to study how genes make people what they are. Because they share precisely the same genes but live in different surroundings under different influences, identical twins reared apart are helping science sort out which qualities of body and mind are shaped by our genes, and which by upbringing. Researchers needn't worry about running out of subjects: according to the Twins Foundation, there are approximately 4.5 million twin individuals in the United States alone, and about 70,000 more are born each year.
>
> —Sharon Begley, "Twins"

2. For a paper arguing that it is difficult, if not impossible, to ensure honesty in large-scale testing, quote from the Robbins material in Exercise 31.6. Be sure to include at least one numerical statistic in your quotation.

3. Write a three- to four-sentence passage that includes your own words and a quotation from a source you are using for a paper assigned in one of your courses. If you have no such assignment, choose any material suitable for a college-level paper. Your instructor might request a photocopy of the material from which you are quoting.

31d Paraphrasing accurately

When you **paraphrase,** you precisely restate in your own words a passage written (or spoken) by another person. A paraphrase is more detailed and longer than a summary (see 31e). A paraphrase is a parallel text, one that goes alongside an original writing. Your paraphrases offer an account of what an authority says, not in the original words but in yours.

As a bonus, the process of writing a paraphrase can help you untangle difficult passages and come to understand them. Paraphrasing forces you to read closely and to extract precise meaning from complex passages. Consult the guidelines for writing a paraphrase in Chart 138.

⊙ **Guidelines for writing a paraphrase** 138

1. Say what the source says, but no more.
2. Emphasize what the source emphasizes.
3. Use your own words, phrasing, and sentence structure to restate the message. If certain synonyms are awkward, quote the material—but resort to quotation only occasionally.
4. Read over your sentences to make sure that they do not distort the source's meaning.
5. Expect your material to be as long as, and possibly longer than, the original.
6. Use verbs effectively to help you integrate paraphrases smoothly into your prose (see 31f).
7. **Avoid plagiarism** (see 31a).
8. As you take notes, record all documentation facts about your source so that you can acknowledge your source accurately and avoid plagiarism.

31d.1 Completely restating material in your own words

When you paraphrase, restate the material—and no more. Do not skip points. Do not guess at meaning. Do not insert your own opinions or interpretations. If the source's words trigger your own thinking, preserve your thought right away because you might not recall it later. But beware: Make sure your thoughts are physically separate from your paraphrase—in the margin, in a different color ink, circled, or clearly differentiated in some other way.

As you paraphrase, use your own words; otherwise you will be quoting. Use your own sentence structures. You can use synonyms, but sometimes synonyms or substitute phrases are not advisable. Consider how each synonym fits into the flow of your sentence. For example, for a basic concept such as *people,* the use of *Homo sapiens* might make the material seem strained. In paraphrasing, the farther you get from the original phrasing, the more likely you are to sound like yourself. Don't be surprised to find that when you change language and sentence structure, you might also have to change punctuation, VERB TENSE, and VOICE. When you finish, read over your paraphrase to check that it makes sense and does not distort the meaning of the source.

BACKGROUND

Only in the past century has the paraphrase been taught mainly for research. For two thousand years, the paraphrase was an important exercise for developing style and teaching structure. In his *Institutio Oratoria* (A.D. 95), Roman educator Quintilian described a curriculum in which young boys began paraphrasing simple stories such as Aesop's fables and, as they grew older, were required to paraphrase longer and more complex texts by great writers. Quintilian believed that paraphrasing also improved students' appreciation for great writing and their ability to critique their own work.

EXTRA EXERCISE C

Working in small groups or in pairs, students can learn good techniques of paraphrasing by trying to find acceptable synonyms for key words in a passage. The italicized words and phrases in the following excerpts can be used for the exercise.

1. It is clear that between what a man calls (a) *"me"* and what he simply calls (b) *"mine,"* the line is difficult to draw. We (c) *feel and act* about certain things that are ours very much as we (c) *feel and act* about ourselves. . . . In its widest possible sense, a man's Self is the sum total of all that he can call his, not only his (d) *body* and his (e) *psychic powers,* but his (f) *clothes* and his (g) *house,* his (h) *wife and his children,* his (i) *ancestors* and his (j) *friends,* his (k) *reputation* and his (l) *works,* his (m) *land and horses and yacht and bank account.* If they (n) *wax and prosper,* he feels triumphant, if they (o) *dwindle and die away,* he feels (p) *cast down*—not necessarily in the same degree for each thing, but in much the same way for all.

—William James,
Principles of Psychology

2. Subject to (a) *infinite variables* of winds and currents, of (b) *supply and demand,* of crops and markets, trade has a way of (c) *carving its own paths* not always obedient to (d) *the mercantilist faith.* The faith →

(e) *was embodied* in Britain's Navigation Act, enacted under Oliver Cromwell in 1651 in the interests of the (f) *rising middle class* and the industrial towns and major trading ports—the so-called Cinque Ports, so long (g) *influential* in British history. Aimed specifically at the Dutch to protect British trade against its (h) *most dangerous rival*, the Act raised (i) *a wall of customs duties*, and permitted (j) *transshipment of goods* only in British (k) *bottoms* calling at British ports. The natural result had been (l) *maritime war* with Holland and (m) *bitter resentment* of customs duties in the Colonies, feeding the (n) *spirit of rebellion* which led to the American war. For Britain, the expense of fighting the Dutch and trying to (o) *suppress the American revolt* was more costly than anything that could be gained by the trade laws, causing (p) *higher taxes* at home and their natural consequence, a rise in (q) *domestic disaffection*. That was not the least of Britain's (r) *afflictions* in her (s) *embattled time.*
— Barbara W. Tuchman,
The First Salute

Answers to Extra Exercise C

Answers will vary, but here are possible responses.

1. (a) myself, (b) my people and my things, (c) respond to and behave, (d) physical substance, (e) spiritual capacities, (f) dress, (g) home, (h) family, (i) lineage, (j) favored companions, (k) general character estimation by others, (l) accomplishments, (m) possessions, (n) increase and thrive, (o) decrease and disappear, (p) undone.

2. (a) unlimited possibilities, (b) resources and desires, (c) going its own way, (d) commercial assumptions, (e) was contained, (f) growing bourgeois class, (g) a force, (h) greatest enemy, (i) tariff barriers, (j) transfer of merchandise, (k) ships, (l) naval battles, (m) animosity, (n) defiant temper, (o) put down the American revolution, (p) greater levies, (q) discontent among the people, (r) ills, (s) period of struggle.

31d.2 Avoiding plagiarism when you paraphrase

You must **avoid plagiarism** (see 31a) when you paraphrase. Even though a paraphrase is not a direct quotation, you must use DOCUMEN-TATION to credit your source. Also, you must reword your source material, not merely change a few words. Compare the following passages.

SOURCE

Morris, Desmond. *Manwatching.* New York: Abrams, 1977: 131.

ORIGINAL

Unfortunately, different countries have different ideas about exactly how close is close. It is easy enough to test your own "space reaction": when you are talking to someone in the street or in any open space, reach out with your arm and see where the nearest point on his body comes. If you hail from western Europe, you will find that he is at roughly fingertip distance from you. In other words, as you reach out, your fingertips will just about make contact with his shoulder. If you come from eastern Europe, you will find you are standing at "wrist distance." If you come from the Mediterranean region, you will find that you are much closer to your companion, at little more than "elbow distance."

UNACCEPTABLE PARAPHRASE (UNDERLINED WORDS ARE PLAGIARIZED)

Regrettably, different nations think differently about <u>exactly how close is close</u>. Test yourself: <u>When you are talking to someone in the street or in any open space</u>, stretch your arm out to measure how close that person is to you. If you are from western Europe, you will find that <u>your fingertips will just about make contact with the person's shoulder</u>. If you are from eastern Europe, your wrist will reach the person's shoulder. If you are from <u>the Mediterranean region, you will find that you are much closer to your companion</u>, when your elbow will reach that person's shoulder (Morris 131).

ACCEPTABLE PARAPHRASE

According to Morris, people from different nations think that "close" means different things. You can easily see what your reaction is to how close to you people stand by reaching out the length of your arm to measure how close someone is as the two of you talk. When people from western Europe stand on the street and talk together, the space between them is the distance it would take one person's fingertips to reach to the other person's shoulder. People from eastern Europe converse at a wrist-to-shoulder distance. People from the Mediterranean, however, prefer an elbow-to-shoulder distance (131).

The first attempt to paraphrase is not acceptable. All that the writer has done is simply change a few words. What remains is plagiarized because the passage keeps most of the original's language, has the same sentence structure, and uses no quotation marks. The documentation is correct, but its accuracy does not make up for the unacceptable paraphrasing.

The second paraphrase is acceptable. It captures the essence of the original in the student's own words. Also, starting the paraphrase with the words "According to Morris" signals readers where the paraphrase begins, just as the parenthetical page references signals its end.

EXERCISE 31-3

Read the original material, a paragraph from "Teenagers Called Shrewd Judge of Risk" by Daniel Goleman in the *New York Times,* March 2, 1993, page C1. Then, read the unacceptable paraphrase. Point out each example of plagiarism. Finally, write your own paraphrase, starting it with words naming Goleman and ending it with this parenthetical reference: (C1).

ORIGINAL MATERIAL

In trying to help teenagers deal more successfully with the perils they face, psychologists are undertaking a search to better understand the ways adolescents think and view their world. In the process, the research is challenging many common assumptions about teenagers that have long guided parents, educators and policy makers.

UNACCEPTABLE (PLAGIARIZED) PARAPHRASE

In helping teenagers cope with the hardships they face, psychologists are striving to understand the way teenagers think and look at the world. In the process, psychologists are raising questions about the traditional beliefs held by parents, teachers, and others who help teenagers (Goleman C1).

EXERCISE 31-4

1. For a paper on economic conditions in Third World countries, paraphrase this paragraph. Start with words mentioning the authors: Ehrenreich and Fuentes. End with this parenthetical reference: (87).

For many Third World women, electronics is a prestige occupation, at least compared to other kinds of factory work. They are unlikely to know that in the United States the National Institute on Occupational Safety and Health (NIOSH) has placed electronics on its select list of high health-risk industries using the greatest number of toxic substances. If electronics assembly work is risky here, it is doubly so in countries where there is no equivalent of NIOSH to even issue warnings. In many plants toxic chemicals and solvents sit in open containers, filling the work area with fumes that can literally knock you out.

—Barbara Ehrenreich and Annette Fuentes, "Life on the Global Assembly Line"

2. Write a paraphrase of a paragraph of at least 150 words from one of the sources you are using for a paper assigned in one of your courses. If you have no such assignment, choose any material suitable for a college-level paper. Your instructor may request that you submit a photocopy of the original material to accompany your paraphrase.

ANSWERS AND COVERAGE: EXERCISE 31-3

Analysis: Paraphrase is unacceptable because it uses many words and phrases from the original. Also, both sentences use the same sentence structure as the originals. *Acceptable paraphrase* (answers will vary): According to Goleman, teenagers, whose lives are filled with daily difficulties, can be helped by scientists who study teenagers' thinking processes and the ways in which these processes affect a teen's point of view. Psychologists today embrace this approach and are looking for ways to understand young people's patterns of thought. These researchers are making interesting discoveries, and some of their new theories call into question many traditional assumptions that older role models and policy makers have traditionally relied on when trying to assist teens (C1).

ANSWERS: EXERCISE 31-4

1. Answers will vary; here is one acceptable paraphrase:

Ehrenreich and Fuentes tell about women in underdeveloped or emerging countries who frequently regard working with electronics as giving them higher status than other assembly line work. Most of these women are unaware that the electronics occupation may pose significant threats to their physical well-being. They have no way of knowing that the National Institute on Occupational Safety and Health (NIOSH) has identified electronics plants in the United States as employing the largest amount of poison materials that may have a negative effect on workers' health in any industry. Certainly, the dangers here in the United States are twice as threatening when they exist in Third World nations, which have no organization like NIOSH to act as watchdog. In underdeveloped countries, the air in factories is often polluted with toxic vapors that arise from poisonous materials that are stored in uncovered vessels. The gas created by these chemicals and other substances is strong enough to make a worker lose consciousness (87).

2. Answers will vary.

EXTRA EXERCISE D

EXTRA EXERCISE D

Following the guidelines for writing a summary, summarize one of the following paragraphs.

1. The Elizabethan Age takes its name from the queen who reigned over England and Ireland from 1558 to 1603. Elizabeth I was an intelligent and gifted ruler, managing for decades to escape political disasters at home and abroad. Always an insightful judge of character, she achieved her success in large part because of her tendency to make use of the shrewdest people around her. However, her clear awareness of what she wanted and why she wanted it sometimes led her to go her own way, using a variety of means to reach the ends she desired. She was on occasion devious, even false, but she managed to outwit her opposition time after time. As a result, it was a glorious time in the history of Britain, for under her rule, the nation rose from a relatively weak position among the nations of Europe to the highest rank. England's power and success grew rapidly in the sixteenth century, leaving it, at Elizabeth's death, a leader in navigation and exploration, in literary productivity—particularly in the drama—and in colonization of the New World.

2. When she died in 1986, Georgia O'Keeffe the person generated almost as much interest among the public as Georgia O'Keeffe the artist. Sometimes, she was thought of as the wife and often-photographed model of Alfred Stieglitz, but more often, she was pictured as a romantic recluse who, when she grew older, moved increasingly away from the world of art critics and historians and closer to the rugged but exotic New Mexico countryside and culture. In the long run, however, it will be for her art that she will be best remembered. Some viewers admire her abstractions; others, her figurative works. Even those who disagree about the relative quality of her paintings agree that her art is memorable, clear, and strong. She painted with a dis-

→ 500

31e Summarizing accurately

A **summary** reviews the main points of a passage and gets at the gist of what an author or speaker says. A summary condenses the essentials of someone else's thought into a few statements. Summaries and paraphrases (see 31d) differ in one primary way: A summary is much shorter than a paraphrase and provides only the main point in the original source. Consult the guidelines for writing a summary in Chart 139.

◎ **Guidelines for writing a summary**   **139**

1. Identify the main points, and condense them without losing the essence of the material.
2. Use your own words to condense the message.
3. Keep your summary short.
4. Use verbs effectively to integrate summaries into your prose (see 31f).
5. **Avoid plagiarism** (see 31a).
6. As you take notes, record all documentation facts about your source so that you can acknowledge your source accurately and avoid plagiarism.

Summarizing forces you to read closely and to comprehend clearly. You can learn the material by writing summaries because that process helps lock information in your memory. Summarizing is probably the most frequently used technique for taking notes and for incorporating sources into papers.

Here is a summary based on the original material in section 31d.2. Compare it with the acceptable paraphrase in that section.

SUMMARY

Expected amounts of space between people when they are talking differs among cultures: In general, people from western Europe prefer fingertip to shoulder distance, from eastern Europe, wrist to shoulder, and from the Mediterranean, elbow to shoulder (Morris 131).

31e.1 Isolating the main points and condensing without losing meaning

A summary captures the entire sense of a passage in very little space, so you must read through all the content before you write. Then, isolate the main points by asking these questions: What is the subject? What is the central message on the subject? A summary excludes more than it includes, so you must make substantial deletions. A summary should reduce the original by at least half.

As you summarize, you trace a line of thought. Doing this involves deleting less central ideas and sometimes transposing certain points into an order more suited to summary. In summarizing a longer original—say, ten pages or more—you may find it helpful first to divide the original into subsections and summarize each. Then, group your subsection summaries and use them as the basis for further condensing the material into a final summary. You will likely have to revise a summary more than once. Always make sure that a summary accurately reflects the source and its emphases.

Condensing information into a table is another option for summarizing, particularly when you are working with numerical data. (For an example, see the student research paper in Chapter 34: Table 1 summarizes many pages of a source.)

As you summarize, you may be tempted to interpret something the author says or make a judgment about the value of the author's point. Your own opinions do not belong in a summary, but do jot them down immediately so that you can recall your reactions later. Be sure to place your own ideas in your notes so that they are physically separate from your summary: in the margin, in a different color ink, circled, or otherwise made very different-looking.

31e.2 Avoiding plagiarism when you summarize

Even though a summary is not a direct quotation, you must use DOCUMENTATION to credit your source. Also, you must use your own words. Compare the following passages.

SOURCE
Hall, Edward T. *The Hidden Dimension*. New York: Doubleday, 1966: 109.

ORIGINAL
The general failure to grasp the significance of the many elements that contribute to man's sense of space may be due to two mistaken notions: (1) that for every effect there is a single and identifiable cause; and (2) that man's boundary begins and ends with his skin. If we can rid ourselves of the need for a single explanation, and if we can think of man as surrounded by a series of expanding and contracting fields which provide information of many kinds, we shall begin to see him in an entirely different light. We can then begin to learn about human behavior, including personality types. . . . Concepts such as these are not always easy to grasp, because most of the distance-sensing process occurs outside the awareness. We sense other people as close or distant, but we cannot always put our finger on what it is that enables us to characterize them as such. So many different things are happening at once it is difficult to sort out the sources of information on which we base our reactions.

501

TEACHING TIP

Sometimes students fall into the habit of using summaries to take notes, forgetting that they can also be used in developing the thesis of a paper. You may find it helpful to remind students that when they want to introduce ideas from sources but have no need to use direct quotation, summaries are a useful strategy to employ. In them, the writer can provide unusual facts, background information, and even other points of view regarding the subject. When summaries are used in this way, however, it is important to make sure that they fit smoothly and easily into the text. A series of unconnected summaries will not make an effective piece of writing.

ANSWERS AND COVERAGE: EXERCISE 31-5

Analysis: Summary is unacceptable because it uses many words and phrases from the original. *Acceptable summary* (answers will vary): Eyre and Eyre say that having an honest relationship with your own children is essential for demonstrating the importance of honesty in every relationship. They advise talking with children openly and honestly, without white lies or evasions. By following an honest parent's example, children learn that being honest not only applies to them but also to others with whom they come into contact (42).

ANSWERS: EXERCISE 31-6

1. Answers will vary, but here is one possible summary.

According to Robbins, a cloud hangs over testing programs because of an increase in cheating, as when students in New York State sold the state Regents examination in advance. This led to warnings that educators should watch for student scores that appear in unusual patterns (12).

UNACCEPTABLE SUMMARY (UNDERLINED WORDS ARE PLAGIARIZED)

<u>Concepts such as</u> identifying causes and determining boundaries <u>are not always easy to grasp</u> (Hall 109).

ACCEPTABLE SUMMARY

Hall writes that human beings make the mistake of thinking that an event has a "single and identifiable cause" and that people are limited by the boundaries of their bodies. Most people are unaware that they have a sense of interpersonal space, which contributes to their reactions to other people (109).

The unacceptable summary does not isolate the main point, and it plagiarizes by using almost all language used in the source.

The second summary is acceptable because it not only isolates the main idea but also recasts it in the student's words. One phrase ("single and identifiable cause") is borrowed, but it is set off in quotation marks. No one would charge this student with plagiarism. Also, starting the summary with the words "Hall writes that" signals readers where the summary begins, just as the parenthetical page reference signals its end.

EXERCISE 31-5

Read the original paragraph from *Teaching Your Children Values* by Linda Eyre and Richard Eyre, published by Simon & Schuster in 1993, page 42. Then, read the unacceptable summary. Point out each example of plagiarism. Finally, write your own summary, starting it with a phrase mentioning Eyre and Eyre and ending it with this parenthetical reference: (42).

ORIGINAL MATERIAL

Be completely honest with your children. This will show them how always applicable the principle is and will demonstrate your commitment to it. Answer their questions truthfully and candidly unless it is a question that is off-limits, and then tell them simply and honestly why you won't answer it. Never let them hear you tell little "convenient lies" on the phone and never ask them to tell one for you ("My mommy isn't home"). Don't exaggerate. Don't threaten to do things you don't really intend to do.

UNACCEPTABLE SUMMARY

It is best to be completely honest with your children in every situation that is not off limits; do not exaggerate, threaten children, or ask them to tell little convenient lies for you. This approach will clearly demonstrate to them that the idea of honesty is always applied to every situation and relationship (Eyre and Eyre 42).

EXERCISE 31-6

1. Summarize the paragraph at the top of page 503. Start your summary by mentioning the author: Robbins. End with this parenthetical reference: (12).

More and more states are requiring students to pass competency tests in order to receive their high school diplomas. And many educators fear that an increase in the use of state exams will lead to a corresponding rise in cheating. They cite the case of students in New York State who faced criminal misdemeanor charges for possessing and selling advance copies of state Regents examinations. Approximately 600,000 students take the Regents exams. And it proved impossible to determine how many of them had seen the stolen tests. As a result, 1,200 principals received instructions from the State Education Commissioner to look for *unusual scoring patterns* that would show that students had the answers beforehand. This put a cloud over the test program.

—Stacia Robbins, "Honesty: Is It Going out of Style?"

2. Write a summary of your paraphrase of the Ehrenreich and Fuentes material in Exercise 31-4. Use the parenthetical reference given there.

3. Write a summary of a source you are using for a paper assigned in one of your courses, or select material suitable for a college-level paper. Your instructor may request that you submit a photocopy of the original material with your summary.

31f Using verbs effectively to integrate source material into your prose

The verbs listed in Chart 140 help you work quotations, paraphrases, and summaries smoothly into your writing. Some of these verbs imply your position toward the source material (for example, *argue, complain, concede, deny, grant, insist,* and *reveal*); others are neutral (*comment, describe, explain, note, say,* and *write*). (The student research papers presented in Chapters 34, 35, and 38 provide many good examples of such verb use.)

⊙ **Verbs useful for integrating quotations,**   **140**
paraphrases, and summaries

agree	complain	emphasize	note	see
analyze	concede	explain	observe	show
argue	conclude	find	offer	speculate
ask	consider	grant	point out	state
assert	contend	illustrate	refute	suggest
believe	declare	imply	report	suppose
claim	deny	insist	reveal	think
comment	describe	maintain	say	write

32

THE PROCESSES OF RESEARCH WRITING

32a Understanding research writing

Research writing involves you in three processes: conducting research, understanding the results of your research, and writing a paper on your understanding. These processes are interwoven throughout your research project. All three processes roll ahead and circle back according to what unfolds as you work. To help you, I cover each process in this chapter. Also, you can rely on the more general writing explanations in the earlier chapters of this handbook.

For example, the **writing process** for a research paper resembles the process of writing for all academic papers (see Chapters 1–4). Using research simply adds one more dimension. In PLANNING the paper, you choose a suitable research topic; refine that topic into a research question; use a search strategy to locate, understand, and evaluate sources; and take notes. In DRAFTING and REVISING the paper, you present your SYNTHESIS (see 5b and 5f) of the material you found during your search. Then you support your synthesis by quoting, paraphrasing, and summarizing your sources (see Chapter 31). At all stages of research writing, be sure to consult Chapter 5 so that you can apply the principles of critical thinking.

Although few research paper assignments are phrased as questions, research writing means that you must search to find answers. Regarding research as a quest for an answer gives you focus: You cannot know whether you have found useful material unless you know what you are looking for.

Research questions, whether stated or implied, and the strategies needed to answer them vary widely. Your purpose might be to present and explain information: "How does penicillin destroy bacteria?" Or your purpose might be to argue one side of an issue: "Is Congress more important than the Supreme Court in setting social policy?" To find answers, you SYNTHESIZE material from various sources in an attempt to understand.

Attempt is an important word in relation to research. Some research questions lead to a final, definitive answer, but some do not. In the preceding paragraph, the question about penicillin leads to a definitive answer (you describe how the antibiotic penicillin destroys the cell walls of some bacteria), so your writing has to be INFORMATIVE. The question about social policy has no definitive answer, but rather, it invites you to present an informed opinion based on information and opinions gathered from your research; so your writing has to be PERSUASIVE.

Research can be an engrossing, creative activity. By gathering information, analyzing its separate elements, and composing a synthesis of them, you come to know your subject deeply. The act of writing can help you make fresh connections and gain unexpected insights. Equally important, you can sample the pleasures of being a self-reliant learner, someone with the self-discipline and intellectual resources to track down, absorb, and synthesize information independently. If you feel overwhelmed by the prospect of research writing, you are not alone. Many researchers, inexperienced and experienced, have such feelings. My best advice is to break research writing into the series of steps described in this chapter so that the project becomes far less intimidating.

32b Scheduling for research writing

Research writing takes time. The key to your successfully completing a research project is to plan ahead and budget your time intelligently. As soon as you get a research paper assignment, work out a time schedule for finishing each step. The schedule in Chart 141 lists typical research steps (the section of this handbook where each step is discussed is indicated in parentheses.) No two research paper projects are alike, so adapt the schedule to your needs. You might need only one day for some steps but two weeks for others. Be flexible, but always keep your eye on the calendar. The more you use a time schedule, the better you will handle research projects efficiently.

⊙ Sample schedule for a research project 141

Assignment received _____

Planning **Finish By (Date)**

1. Start a research log (32c). _____
2. Choose a topic suitable for research (32d). _____
3. Draft a preliminary research question (32r). _____
4. Decide on my purpose and audience (32e). _____
5. Gather needed equipment (32f.1). _____
6. Learn how to evaluate sources (32f.3). _____
7. Decide what documentation style to use (32f.4). _____

→

History (continued)

extensive footnotes, and charts and diagrams. Faculty regarded students as "apprentices" in a profession, and the thesis was an opportunity for students to develop the investigative skills needed to become experts in their fields and to learn to address readers in their professions. The research paper soon moved into lower-level courses, and by 1931, high school students were often required to write a term paper in their junior or senior year.

Research paper instruction began to be offered in freshman composition courses in the 1920s. By the early 1980s, according to James E. Ford and Dennis R. Perry ("Research Paper Instruction in the Undergraduate Writing Program," *College English*, December 1982: 825–831), 84 percent of freshman writing programs and 40 percent of advanced composition programs were teaching the research paper, and the research paper was a requirement in 78 percent of the freshman programs and 42 percent of the advanced programs.

QUOTATION: ON RESEARCH

Research is a way of life dedicated to discovery.

—Anonymous

QUOTATION: ON WRITING

Though old the thought and oft exprest,
'Tis his at last who says it best.
                    —James Russell Lowell

TEACHING TIP

Saying something original based on several sources is an imposing challenge for most students. Many instead treat the research paper as a knowledge-telling exercise in which they restate what they have read. The research paper becomes a string of quotations, paraphrases, and summaries that drown out the student's voice, lack purpose and focus, and often invite plagiarism. According to Margaret Kantz ("Helping Students Use Textual Sources Persuasively," *College English* January 1990: 74–91), "Writing an original persuasive argument based on sources requires students to apply material to a problem or to use it to answer a question, rather than simply to repeat it or evaluate it" (78). But students "have learned to see texts statically, as descriptions of truths, instead of as arguments" (79). This view encourages students simply to collect facts into a research paper in the belief that the facts will settle any disagreements and reveal the truth. Kantz recommends that teachers encourage students to regard the research paper and its sources "as existing to solve problems" (84). Students should try to understand what the author of a source was trying to accomplish and what audience was being addressed. They should treat facts as claims that could be challenged or interpreted differently. And they should write their research paper to solve a problem or answer a question for a particular audience.

Sample schedule for a research project *(continued)*   **141**

Researching   **Finish By (Date)**

8. Start with a "search strategy"—but remember I might modify it (32h).   _____

9. Decide what types of research I need:

   a. field research (32g)?   _____

   b. interview (32q)?   _____

   c. print and/or electronic sources (32k–32p)?   _____

10. If 9a or 9b, schedule tasks and appointments (32g or 32q).   _____

11. If 9c, consult Library of Congress Subject Headings

   a. to get library call numbers (32m).   _____

   b. to begin list of headings and key words (32i).   _____

12. Consult reference works:

   a. general (32k).   _____

   b. specialized (32l).   _____

13. Consult book catalog and books (32m).   _____

14. Consult periodicals (32n).   _____

15. Decide whether to use electronic sources: tapes, CD-ROMs, etc. (32o.1).   _____

16. Decide whether to use online sources: World Wide Web (32o.2).   _____

Writing

17. Draft a preliminary thesis statement and expect to revise it (32r).   _____

18. Outline as required (32s).   _____

19. Draft paper (32t).   _____

20. Use correct in-text (parenthetical) citations (33c).   _____

21. Revise paper (32t).   _____

22. Compile a final list of Works Cited (33c.2).   _____

Assignment due _____

32c Using a research log

A **research log** is like a diary. It becomes a record of your research process, especially your evolving thoughts about your work. Start a research log as soon as you get your assignment. Use a separate notebook for the log, one that you can take with you wherever you conduct research. If you use a laptop, start a separate folder for your research log. Begin by entering the schedule (see 32b) you intend to follow.

Although much of your research log will never find its way into your research paper itself, you can use its pages to enhance your efficiency. A well-kept log traces your line of reasoning as your project evolves, tells where you ended each work session, and suggests what your next steps should be. Such a record means much less wasted time retracing a research path or reconstructing your thinking.

After all, college students are expected to focus on many separate courses all at the same time. A research log also helps you "think on paper," especially when you use the critical thinking sequence of Chart 30 in section 5b. Writing in your log helps you discover insights that only the physical act of writing makes possible. Excerpts from the research log shown here are by Lisa Laver, the student whose research paper, about multiple intelligences, appears in Chapter 34.

EXCERPTS FROM LISA LAVER'S RESEARCH LOG

Oct 19: Looked for "intelligence" in Library of Congress Subject Headings (LCSH) located in the reference collection. Figured LCSH was one book. Wrong. Four in alpha order, and each is huge and heavy. Found nothing. Ready to give up. Remembered to relax and let myself browse a little. Paid off. Found "intellect." Started going through the listing and writing down key words, especially ones marked with NT for "narrowed topic."

Nov. 8: Ready to try online sources. In the computer lab, I used Netscape to start my search, and its home page lists choices of browsers. I chose Yahoo because I have used it to look up sports scores. Searched for 15 minutes but found nothing on "multiple intelligences." Asked the reference librarian for advice. She said Yahoo is only for very general topics. For specific topics, she suggested AltaVista. In minutes I found tons of sites and sources. What a relief.

QUOTATION: ON WRITING

The longer I write, the more important I believe it is to write the first draft as fast as possible. In drafting, I push myself so I am at the edge of discomfort. . . . Later, it will be time for consideration and reconsideration, slow, careful revision and editing. But on the first draft I have to achieve velocity, just as you do if you want the bike to balance.

—Donald M. Murray

HISTORY

In the early 1980s, James E. Ford and Dennis R. Perry ("Research Paper Instruction in the Undergraduate Writing Program," *College English*, December 1982: 825–831) reported:

> Research paper instruction is currently being offered in 84.09% of freshman composition programs and in 40.03% of advanced composition programs. In general this high level of occurrence is fairly uniform in all types and sizes of institutions and in all regions of the country. There is, however, a slight tendency for research paper instruction to decrease as the size of the school increases (down to 71.06% in the large schools). Also, occurrence is highest in the Rocky Mountain region (91.66%) and . . . lowest on the Pacific coast (72.40%). Instruction in the research paper is required in 78.11% of freshman composition programs offering it and 42.35% of advanced writing programs where it is offered. Although 4.16% of the schools not offering instruction in the research paper at the basic level indicated their reason for omitting it as "faculty think it unnecessary," the most common reason given for not offering it came under the "other" category, checked by 12.12%. About half of these (that is, about 6% of the total respondents) said the course was already too full to allow time for such instruction. . . . No institution surveyed had eliminated a research paper requirement during the past five years and only two now have plans to do away with it. (827)

32d Choosing and narrowing a topic for research writing

Instructors assign topics for research papers in various ways. Some assign the specific topic. Others assign a general subject area and expect you to narrow it to a topic that can be researched within the constraints of time and length imposed by the assignment. Still other instructors expect you to choose a topic on your own.

When you have free choice of a topic, always choose a topic worthy of research writing. Above all, the topic must give you full opportunity to demonstrate your ability to think critically (see Chapter 5), especially to use SYNTHESIS. What if you develop what some students call a "research topic block"? First, know you can overcome it. Second, force yourself to stay calm. Only then can you think clearly. Next, force yourself to get started by using the suggestions presented in Chart 142. What if you have an assigned topic in a general subject area but you are not sure how to narrow the subject area into a topic appropriate for a research paper? Use the guidelines in Chart 143.

⊙ Ways to find ideas for research 142

Before you settle on an idea, "test" it by using Chart 143.

- **Get ready.** Carry a pocket-size notebook and a pencil or pen at all times. Ideas have a way of popping into your mind when you least expect them. Jot down your thought immediately to prevent its slipping away.

- **Think actively.** Do not rush through material. Take the time to use the techniques for gathering ideas you know from using sections 2d through 2m of this handbook.

- **Conquer writing block.** Feeling overwhelmed can cause a writing block. Avoid thinking about all the steps in a research project at once. Take it one step at a time.

- **Browse through textbooks.** Pick a field that interests you and look over a textbook or two (in the bookstore, borrow from a friend, see if any are on reserve at your library's reserve desk). Search for an area that catches your interest and read about it.

- **Look over the Library of Congress Subject Headings.** The multivolume LCSH lists every single topic (and the call number of the books on each topic) covered by books copyrighted by the U.S. federal government. You can find it in the reference collection of any library. Often, it is kept close at hand by librarians at the main reference desk, so you might have to ask to look at it (see 32i). ➝

Ways to find ideas for research *(continued)*   142

- **Browse general encyclopedias.** Topics range over many subjects, but the articles give only a general sense of each subject. They can be in book form, CD-ROM, or online. Each article is a beginning, but only that (see 32k).
- **Browse specialized encyclopedias.** Each different book focuses on a specific area (social science, history, philosophy, natural sciences, etc.), and its articles or chapters treat topics in some depth. Most selections mention names of major figures in the field and can help you start your list of headings and key words. They can be in book form, CD-ROM, or online (see 32l).
- **Look through books.** Stroll in the open stacks, if your library has them. If your library has closed stacks or if you'd rather not walk around, look through your library's book catalog (see 32m).

◉ Choosing a workable topic for a research   143 paper

1. **Expect to consider various topics before making your final choice.** Consult Chart 142 for specific ways to find ideas. Avoid rushing; give yourself time to think. Keep your mind open to flashes of insight and to alternative ideas. Conversely, avoid allowing indecision to block you.

2. **Be practical.** Plan to do the work within the established time limit and paper length. Be sure that sufficient resources on your topic are available and accessible to you.

3. **Choose a topic worth researching.** Trivial topics prevent you from doing what student researchers are expected to do—use critical thinking: Investigate related ideas; analyze, summarize, and interpret them; SYNTHESIZE complex, perhaps conflicting, concepts; and assess them critically (see Chapter 5).

4. **Try to select a topic that interests you.** Know that your topic will be a companion for a while, sometimes most of a semester. Select a topic that arouses your interest and allows you the pleasure of satisfying your intellectual curiosity.

5. **Narrow the topic sufficiently.** Avoid topics that are too broad, such as "communication" or even "nonverbal communication." Conversely, avoid topics that are too narrow to allow a suitable mix of generalizations and specific details.

→

History (continued)

Ford and Perry also say:

> Not surprisingly, research paper instruction is offered more in freshman programs (50.56%) during the second semester of the freshman year, but it also is included in a significant number of courses offered during the first semester (41.57%). It is a feature in both semesters at 15.17% of the institutions. Such instruction on the advanced level most often comes during the sophomore year (63.83%), but it is common also during the junior year (46.81%). . . . Whenever it is offered, research paper instruction constitutes, on the average, a very considerable 34.66% of one basic course and 36.71% of an advanced course. (828)

QUOTATION: ON RESEARCH

The search should take place because somebody needs to find out something or wants to satisfy an itch of curiosity as insistent as athlete's foot.

                              Ken Macrorie

TEACHING TIP

Students usually write more effective research papers if they formulate a tentative thesis after they have read and taken notes on a wide selection of sources but well before they begin drafting the paper, according to Sandra Stotsky ("On Developing Independent Critical Thinking: What We Can Learn from Studies of the Research Process," *Written Communication*, April 1991: 193–212). "Finding a focus, or controlling idea," Stotsky suggests, "may well depend on how much information is gathered in an initial search process and how students organize and evaluate their initial notes. Categorizing, organizing, recategorizing, and reorganizing may be the most significant generative activities in the search process" (207).

Choosing a workable topic for a research paper *(continued)*   **143**

6. **Perhaps confer briefly with a professor in your field of interest.** Ask whether you have narrowed your topic sufficiently and productively. Also, ask for the names of the major books and authorities on your topic.

"Intelligence" was the general subject area assigned to Lisa Laver, the student whose research paper appears in Chapter 34. Her instructor required a paper of 1,800 to 2,000 words to be written in six weeks based on about a dozen sources. To get started, Laver borrowed a textbook from a friend. It was called *Introduction to Psychology,* and it contained a chapter on intelligence. She browsed through it. That browsing helped Laver become familiar with the many general aspects of human intelligence. To narrow her search, Laver looked up the term *intelligence* in the Library of Congress Subject Headings (LCSH). She discovered several subdivisions under *intellect* (see section 32i for what she saw in the LCSH). She then went to specialized reference books for more information. A full narrative of Laver's research process starts Chapter 34. That narrative explains how Laver's research question became "Can there be only one way of describing human intelligence?" The flowchart on page 511 illustrates Laver's process of narrowing her topic.

Although each decision seems to flow smoothly from the one before, the process is rarely neat and tidy. It looks clear-cut only at the end of your thinking, searching, considering alternatives, and choosing. Most likely, you will back out of dead ends and make some sharp turns as you find a suitable path to your research question. To help clarify your thinking, try flowcharting your decision process as you go along.

32e   Determining the purpose and audience for your research paper

The question that guides your research process helps you determine whether the **purpose** of your paper is INFORMATIVE or PERSUASIVE. If your research question asks for facts, information, and explanation, your purpose is to inform. For example, "How have theories of intelligence changed over time?" requires an answer that calls for informative writing. If your research question asks for an informed opinion based on information and other evidence that leads to presenting various contrasting views, your purpose is to persuade. For example, "Why should

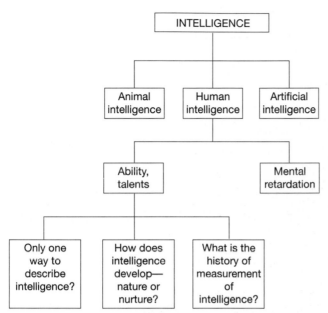

Flowchart of Lisa Laver's Narrowing Process

people be aware of new theories about intelligence?" calls for persuasive writing. Your paper's purpose might shift during your research process, as Lisa Laver's did (see Chapter 34). Remain open-minded as you work, but never forget that you must determine your writing purpose before you get too far along.

The **audience** for your college writing is primarily, but perhaps not exclusively, your instructor (see section 1c). When you think of writing for your instructor, remember that he or she plays two roles: a surrogate for the general reading public or a specialized reader as well as a person responsible for judging how well you have understood your material and the forms for presenting it. Sometimes, the audience for a research paper includes other people—students in your class or perhaps specialists on your topic. Your sense of your readers' expertise on your topic helps you make decisions about content, specific details in explanations, and word choice.

32f Preparing to undertake research

32f.1 Gathering equipment needed for research

Experienced researchers use equipment that helps them work efficiently. Gather the materials listed in Chart 144. For efficiency's sake, keep these materials in a separate place so that you can find them easily.

HISTORY

During the Middle Ages, the libraries of Western Europe were affiliated with religious houses and cathedrals. The few private libraries belonged to bishops. The clergy were the only people who could read, and the church maintained the tradition of schools and libraries. These religious libraries were quite small by twentieth-century standards. The largest (at Canterbury and Bury St. Edmunds) had two thousand volumes each, but libraries of only a few hundred volumes were the rule. The libraries contained theological and biblical works, law books, classical texts, and medical and historical works. Contemporary histories, written in monasteries, remain the best records of what happened during the period. In the thirteenth and fourteenth centuries, the rise of the new universities, the rediscovery of Aristotle (from Arabic), and the position of the friars as university teachers undermined the dominance of the monastic libraries. Although the university libraries were not open to undergraduates, the Franciscan friars opened their own libraries (some still survive in England). They printed small, portable books that contrasted with the bulky illuminated manuscripts of the monasteries. The monastic libraries of England were destroyed in 1536–1540 (during Henry VIII's reign), and their books were dispersed. In 1550, university libraries, schools, and churches were purged. Many treasures saved during the thousand years of the Dark Ages were lost.

Medieval libraries were apparently noisier than libraries today. Silent reading was not a common practice until the Renaissance. Until then, most people mumbled as they read. Small private enclosures called *carrels* were invented so that readers would not disturb other people in the library with their noise.

◉ **Basic equipment for conducting research**   **144**

1. A copy of your assignment.
2. This handbook. Refer to sections 32j and 33b when you make bibliography cards. (Write down bibliographic information while you have your sources in hand; that is easier than trying to find them again and wastes no time.)
3. A separate notebook for your research log (see 32c).
4. Index cards: one color for taking notes and a second color for bibliographic data. Cards give you flexibility in moving information around. Use a separate index card for each source. Also, use a separate index card for each new idea in a source.
5. Pens with different-colored ink, to color code. (Pencils smudge.) Or use self-sticking dots or different-colored paper clips.
6. Coins for the library's copy machines or printers for downloading CD-ROM or online sources.
7. Floppy disks (if the library allows downloading to disk).
8. A small stapler and rubber bands to help you organize and control your index cards and other papers.
9. A separate book bag for you to check out books from the library. Librarians joke about researchers with wheelbarrows. You might need a backpack.

If you use index cards, color coding can help your research process greatly. Colors allow you to group categories of information. Use one color of index cards for notes and another color for bibliographic information. Going further, especially if you are writing a long paper with many sources, you might use one color pen or paper clips for your notes, a second color for quotations (see 31c), a third color for paraphrases and summaries (see 31d and 31e), and a fourth for each synthesis of sources and your personal thoughts.

If you use a computer, be sure to use separate folders for your research log, your notes, and your bibliographical facts. To differentiate among categories of information, use a separate font in the same way you would use colors for index cards, as just described.

32f.2 Learning how the library is organized

Almost all libraries in the United States and Canada are organized around the same principles for grouping information. But few college libraries have similar physical layouts, so be sure to take the time to walk around until you feel comfortable and confident there.

Public and community libraries often provide additional sources for researchers, but their mission is more general and nonacademic.

Some college libraries provide in-class tours for English courses; some offer individual training sessions; and most offer informative, free fliers to help students learn the library layout and resources. To use your library efficiently, try to know the answers to the questions in Chart 145.

 Checklist for touring a library   **145**

1. Where is the **general reference** collection? (You cannot check out reference books, so plan time to use them in the library.)
2. Where is the **special reference** collection? (These books are valuable for narrowing a subject area into a research topic.)
3. Is the **book catalog** computerized or on cards? (Some libraries use cards for older books and computer systems for newer acquisitions). If computerized, how does the system work?
4. What **periodical indexes** does the library have? (These are lists of articles in journals and magazines, grouped by subject areas.)
5. How are the library's collection of **journals and magazines** stored? Most libraries keep separate issues of periodicals published in the past year on display; older ones may be have been put in binders and shelved. If journals and magazines may be accessed through the computer, how does the system work?
6. Are the **book and journal stacks** open (you can go to the shelves and browse) or closed (you must request each item by filling out a form to hand to library personnel.)
7. Does the library have any **special collections** such as newspapers on microfilm, local historical works, or state and federal government documents?
8. Does the library make available **access to the Internet?** Sometimes, such access is available in a college's computer center. (See 32f.3.)
9. If you use a computer at home or in your dormitory, can you gain **access to the library's computerized systems** with it?

32f.3 Preparing to evaluate sources

A **source** can be a book, an article, a World Wide Web page, a CD-ROM, a videotape, or any other form of communication. Sources are rarely of equal value. Your research can be ruined unless you apply the criteria for evaluating research material given in Charts 146 and 147. Do not rush. Evaluate each source with a cold, critical eye.

TEACHING TIP

The Web page "Evaluating Web Resources" is at <http://www.science.widener.edu/~withers/webeval.htm>. It gives several separate checklists to identify and evaluate five of the most common types of Web pages: advocacy, business/marketing, news, informational, and personal. This site is written by librarians experienced in using and teaching about the Web and is on the home page of Widener University.

TEACHING TIP

In "How the Web Destroys the Quality of Students' Research Papers," (*Chronicle of Higher Education*, August 15, 1997: A44), David Rothenberg points out: "It's easy to spot a research paper that is based primarily on information collected from the Web. First, the bibliography cites no books, just articles and pointers to places in that virtual land somewhere off any map_. Then a strange preponderance of material in the bibliography is curiously out of date_Another clue is the beautiful pictures and graphs that are inserted neatly into the body of the student's text_.bear[ing] little relation to the precise subject of the paper_Accompanying them are unattributed quotes_" Rothenberg's point that the Web is "only a pale, two-dimensional version of a real library" supports the need for students to use extra care in selecting Web pages and not to neglect library resources.

514

Criteria for evaluating print and online sources for research   146

1. **Is it authoritative?** You can consider a source authoritative if it is mentioned repeatedly by respected references such as encyclopedias, textbooks, articles in academic journals, bibliographies, electronic indexes on CD-ROM, online databases, and conversations with experts. Also, look for the author's name in bibliographies at the end of journal articles on your topic.

   ONLINE ALERT: For an online source, answer these questions:
   - Is the author named? Are credentials listed for the author? (Look for an academic degree, an e-mail address at an academic or other institution, a credentials page, a list of publications. The last part of an e-mail address can be informative: .edu is an address at an educational site, .gov is an address at a government site, and .com is an address at a commercial or business site.)
   - Is the author an authority in reputable print sources?
   - Do you recognize the author as an authority from other online research into your subject?❗

2. **Is it reliable?** You can consider material reliable when it is published in academic journals (see 32n.2), by university presses, or by publishers that specialize in scholarly books. Material published in newspapers, general-readership magazines, and by large commercial publishers may be reliable, but be sure to cross-check names and facts whenever possible. Material obtained online may be unreliable (see Chart 147).

   ONLINE ALERT: For an online source, answer these questions:
   - Why does the information exist? Who gains from it? Why was it written? Why was it put on the Internet? Are you asked to take action of any kind? (If yes, the source is likely to be an advocate for a point of view or a particular stance and thus subjective or even biased.)
   - Is the material dated? Is the date or update recent? No date may mean unreliable.
   - Does the author give an e-mail address for questions or comments? If not, doubt reliability.
   - Are any links active, authoritative, up-to-date, and reliable?❗

3. **Is it well known?** Check several reliable sources to see if the same information appears.

→

Criteria for evaluating print and online sources for research *(continued)*   146

4. **Is it well supported?** Check that each source supports the given assertions or information with sufficient evidence (see 5h). If the material expresses the author's point of view but adds little evidence to back up that position, reject the source.

5. **Is its tone balanced?** Read a source using critical thinking (see 5b–5h). If the TONE (see 1d) is unbiased and the reasoning is logical, the source is probably balanced.

6. **Is it current?** Check that the information is up-to-date. A source's being current can be important because sometimes long-accepted information is replaced or modified by new research. Check indexes to journals or online databases to see if anything newer has come along.

⊙ **Researcher beware: Reliability of information obtained online**   147

- **Junk mail:** The name says it all. Do not trust.
- **Chat rooms:** Not reliable. Informal settings in which anyone can claim to be anyone.
- **USENET groups, discussion groups, bulletin boards, mailing lists:** Groups share knowledge on a topic by networking with others. Topics can range from the silly to the serious. Try to verify the authority of the participants and the information they share by using Chart 146.
- **World Wide Web sites:** Many Web sites are useful for research, but the quality of their contents varies tremendously. Some are personal pages. Some are advertisements. Use special scrutiny; judge each site thoroughly using Chart 146.

As you evaluate sources, remember the difference between a **primary source** and a **secondary source.** Secondary sources report, describe, comment on, or analyze someone else's work. As a result, the information comes to you secondhand. It is influenced by the intermediary between you and that someone else. Consulting secondary sources gives you the opportunity to understand what scholars and other experts believe about your subject. Primary sources include original works, first-hand reports of observations and research, novels, poems, short stories, autobiographies, and diaries. When you use primary sources, no one comes between you and the author's own words. This fact adds to a source's reliability. Note also that you create a primary source yourself when you conduct primary research such as field research (see 32g), including observation, survey, or interview or a scientific experiment.

32f.4 Determining your documentation style

Documentation style refers to a specific system for providing publication information about each source you use in a research paper. Documentation styles vary among the disciplines. The **Modern Language Association (MLA)** has developed a style often used in English and other courses in the humanities (see 33c). The **American Psychological Association (APA)** has developed a style often used in the social sciences (see 33d). **Chicago Manual (CM)** style is used in some of the humanities and other disciplines (see 33e). The **Council of Biology Editors (CBE)** style is used in the life and physical sciences and in mathematics (see 33f).

Before you start searching for sources, know what documentation style you need to use. (If your assignment does not specify a documentation style, ask your instructor which to use.) Then, as you take notes on each source, you will know precisely what sorts of information your documentation style demands so you will write down the correct, full facts from the start.

32g Deciding whether to conduct field research

Field research is primary research. It involves going "into the field" to observe, survey, interview, or engage in other activities. Field research yields original data. It becomes a PRIMARY SOURCE.

If you intend to do field research, plan time to gather the data or information you need, to analyze what you have gathered, and to synthesize it with any other material (see 5b and 5f). Also, allow extra time if you want to interview an expert on your topic because many steps are needed. First, gain enough control of your topic to know who the authorities are and whom you would like to interview. Have your research question in clear focus so that you can ask worthwhile questions of an expert during the interview. For detailed information about conducting an interview, see section 32q.

If you want to survey a group of people on an issue your topic involves, allow time to write, reflect on, and revise a questionnaire. Provide time to test the questionnaire on a few people, using only those you intend not to include in your survey. Revise any ineffective or ambiguous questions. For detailed information on creating a questionnaire, see Chart 159 in section 38a.

If you need tickets to an event such as a concert or a play, plan ahead. Be ready to suggest alternate dates if you cannot get your first choice. If you need to visit a museum, do so right away so that you can go back again as needed.

Field research often involves events that cannot be revisited. Expect to record detailed information during an observation or interview. You can decide later whether to use the information. If conditions make it impossible to take notes (for example, darkness in a performance hall), the instant you have an opportunity, find a quiet place and write down notes as fully as you can.

Later, as you look over your notes, decide what is important. Field research conditions usually make selective notetaking difficult, so go over your notes while your memory is fresh to highlight major categories of information. Take the opportunity to fill in details.

Remember to document your sources for field research. Interviews and some performances involve other persons' words, which must be documented if you use them. For spoken words, use the guidelines in Chapter 31 for documenting quotations, paraphrases, and summaries. If your own work is included, mention that fact in your paper and create an entry for it for your list of works cited at the end of your paper.

32h Using a search strategy for conducting research

A **search strategy** is an organized procedure that leads you step by step from general to specific sources. These sources help you answer your research question (see 32a). You can judge your search to be productive when it leads you to useful sources and allows you to compile a **working bibliography.** A working bibliography is a list of possible sources that relate to your research question. Eventually, some of them may not be usable for your research paper, so a working bibliography needs to be about twice as long as the list of sources that you actually use in your finished research paper. If your assignment asks for a minimum of ten to twelve sources, your working bibliography should contain no fewer than twenty to twenty-five items.

Planning a strategy for your search is crucial. When you search for sources according to a plan, you can avoid feeling either at a loss for useful sources or overwhelmed by a seemingly limitless choice of sources. An effective search strategy structures your work so that you do not mistake activity for productivity. Spending days in the library to locate anything even remotely related to a topic is as fruitless as it is exhausting. No two research processes are exactly alike. Expect to be guided by your needs as you adapt the search strategies explained in this chapter. Know

BACKGROUND

In "Strategy for a Cross-Disciplinary Research Paper" (*Teaching English in the Two Year College,* May 1992: 136–138), Marilyn D. Jensen describes a process for original research that requires interviewing an expert before beginning library research.

HISTORY

Benjamin Franklin organized the Library Company of Philadelphia in 1731. It was the first American subscription library. Its original purpose was to provide ready access to books for members of the Junto Club, a public service group to which Franklin belonged. Franklin himself said that he spent time at the library almost daily, learning foreign languages or reading for general knowledge.

Until the founding of the Library Company, there were few public libraries in the American colonies. The earliest one was the library of Harvard College, founded in 1638 with around four hundred volumes bequeathed by John Harvard. Libraries were established at Yale and at William and Mary around 1700. In the Southern colonies the Reverend Thomas Bray (1656–1730), working by appointment of the Bishop of London as commissary of the Anglican Church, established parochial libraries. In 1876, a report titled *Public Libraries in the United States* stated: "So far as is known, there were, in 1776, twenty-nine public libraries in the thirteen American colonies, and they numbered altogether 45,623 volumes; in the year 1800 the number of libraries had increased to forty-nine, and the number of volumes to about 80,000." The Library of Congress, which contains over 72 million pieces of material (among them 16.5 million books and 31 million manuscripts), was begun by Congress in 1800 with a budget of $5,000.

also that no search strategy is rarely as tidy as it seems when described. Real life is more messy—and more interesting—than a flowchart or plan.

One useful search strategy is the **expert method.** You start by reading or interviewing an expert in the field. Another is the **chaining method.** It uses reference books and bibliographies from current articles to link to additional sources. A third strategy is the **layering method.** It layers information gathered from general sources to increasingly specific sources. The layering method is especially useful for anyone researching in an unfamiliar field. Lisa Laver, whose research paper is shown in Chapter 34, started with the layering method and soon combined it with the chaining method.

Both the layering strategy and the chaining strategy move from general to specialized reference materials as they uncover the most credible authors and sources. Each time you locate a useful source about your topic, try to use it to find other sources to help you answer your research question.

As soon as you begin to learn background information and possible author names, you can be more productive as you search in the book catalogs, periodical indexes, and CD-ROM and online computer databases accessed with search engines. Try to complete this phase of the research project as soon as possible after you get the assignment. Discovering early in the process which sources are available allows you time to find those that are hard to locate, to use interlibrary loan, and to wait for other people to return books that you want.

32i Using the LCSH and compiling a list of subject headings and key words

The Library of Congress Subject Headings (LCSH) is a multivolume catalog available online or in book form in the reference section of the library. It lists subject headings only; authors and titles are not included. Beginning a search strategy with the LCSH helps you see how a subject is broken down. It also guides you to narrow your topic (see 32d). Lisa Laver, whose research paper appears in Chapter 34, looked in the LCSH for *intelligence,* which led her to the heading *intellect.* She found the excerpt shown on the next page. In addition to the subject headings, the LCSH gives other headings that can lead to additional sources.

Researchers use the LCSH to find subject headings and key words. **Subject headings** are categories describing the content of books and periodical articles. Libraries arrange their collections based on subject headings. **Key words,** sometimes called *descriptors* or *identifiers,* are the main words that appear in the title, abstract, or full-text source. Key words can be used to search most book catalogs, periodical indexes, CD-ROMs, and Web sites. When using key words, chances are you will come up with a large or even overwhelming number of citations. Not all of what has turned up will be relevant to your topic. For example, the topic "nuclear

Intellect
        [BF431-BF433 (Psychology)]
    UF   Human intelligence
            Intelligence
            Mind
    BT   Ability
            Psychology
    RT   Knowledge, Theory of
            Mental retardation
            Thought and thinking
    SA   *subdivision* Intelligence levels *under*
                classes of persons and ethnic groups
    NT   Age and intelligence
            Cognitive styles
            Creation (Literary, artistic, etc.)
            Heart beat and intelligence
            Imagination
            Logic
            Memory
            Mental efficiency
            Motor ability and intelligence
            Perception
            Reason
            Self-organizing systems
            Social intelligence
            Stupidity
            Wisdom

Excerpt from Library of Congress Subject Headings

energy" is identified with various headings or key words: *energy, nuclear; atomic energy; energy, atomic; nuclear power; power, nuclear;* and so on. You have to "break the code" to figure out what words identify the category you are seeking in each source. Expect to use a "try and see" approach. Do not get discouraged. If you are totally stumped, ask for help. Keep an ongoing list in your research log of subject headings and key words that do and do not work for your topic. This practice helps you progress efficiently. (For using key words for online searches, see 32o.)

32j Understanding how to take notes

Your research process includes taking notes as you consult sources. Notetaking has two phases. First, you write preliminary bibliography and summary cards when you think you have located a useful source for your working bibliography. Second, once you have moved from a general search

USING COLLABORATION

Group members may divide subject matter areas or source materials. For example, in an essay on automobile exhaust pollution, dividing by subject matter might send one student to look up "regulation," another to investigate "industry response," and another to search for "testing results." Dividing by source might send one student to a business database, another to periodical indexes, and another to a library's catalog. By dividing the work and pooling information, students can gain a broader perspective on their topics and compose better-balanced papers.

BACKGROUND

In "A Pedagogy to Address Plagiarism" (*College Composition and Communication*, December 1993: 509–514), Elaine E. Whitaker describes a hands-on exercise that leads to students to understand both the practical and philosophical issues related to academic integrity.

EXTRA EXERCISE A

To practice methods of preventing unconscious plagiarism, paraphrase or summarize the following paragraphs. (Answers will vary.)

1. Jane Austen, an English novelist, was born in 1775 the daughter of the Reverend George Austen, rector of Steventon and Deane, and Cassandra Leigh Austen. She was the youngest of seven children. Her childhood at Steventon was quiet, domestic, and moderately studious. Much of her spare time was spent in writing, mostly for her own amusement. In 1801, the family moved to Bath. After the death of her father in 1805, she settled in Chawton, where she remained until shortly before her death.

2. Jane Austen began writing stories at an early age and by the time she was twenty-two had completed one of her best-known novels, *Pride and Prejudice*. Other works for which she is remembered include *Sense and Sensibility* and *Northanger Abbey*, which was published by her family after her death. The novels were not especially popular in Austen's lifetime, but today they are regarded as among the best novels in the English language. Although her people are neither intellectual nor heroic and her plots are not elaborate, her skill at storytelling and drawing characters continues to please her readers.

3. On the map, Mexico resembles a great funnel, or rather, a cornucopia, with its widest part towards the north and its smallest end twisting to the south and east, meeting there the sudden expansion of the Maya area. There are few regions in the world with such a diverse geography as we find within this area—Mexico is not one, but many countries. All the climatic extremes of our globe are found, from arctic cold near the summits of the highest volcanoes to the Turkish-bath atmosphere of the coastal jungle. Merely to pass from one valley to another is to enter a markedly different ecological zone.

—Michael D. Coe,
Mexico, p. 12

to actually reading the sources with the most potential, you write content notes. **Notetaking** is a decision-making process. The criteria in Chart 146 in section 32f can help you decide if a particular source is worthy of notetaking—or photocopying or printing out from the computer. Even if the source does not appear to be useful, keep your preliminary bibliography card with the title, author, date, and call number; Uniform Resource Locator (URL), or Internet address, for a Web page; or journal source. Add a message to yourself about why you rejected it. What seems useless one day might have potential if you later revise the focus of your paper.

32j.1 Taking preliminary notes

As you find usable sources, write bibliography cards for them immediately while you have each source in front of you (see 33b). Record the information exactly as it will be listed in your finished paper in the documentation style that your instructor has specified (see 32f.4). Doing this can save endless hours of work and frustration later on, because when you are ready to compile the list of sources you have referred to in your paper, you have only to put the cards in alphabetical order and type directly from them.

Also, each time you find a potentially useful source, summarize it briefly at the bottom of its bibliography card according to the criteria for evaluating sources in Chart 146. An evaluation might read: "This article is by one of the most credible authors writing about my subject" or "Although this book is old, it has good background information and gives good definitions and interesting historical data" or "This article was published only two months ago—it appeared in a scholarly journal and answers my research question perfectly!" or "This Web page has pertinent information, but I must check whether the author is really an authority on the subject." Such evaluative statements provide direction later for your reading and for further notetaking.

32j.2 Taking content notes

In **content notes,** record information and ideas that relate specifically to your paper. Also, record any understanding you have gained from your reading, using a different color ink for quotations (see 31c), paraphrases and summaries (see 31d and 31e), and your syntheses (see 5b–5f). Always try to sort major information from minor information as it relates to your topic.

Think of taking content notes as a survey process to find out what is available on a particular subject before you commit to extensive reading and notetaking. For this process, set aside more than two to three hours to search on a given subject, write information in your research log, and begin to create a listing of available useful materials on your topic. If you feel comfortable in the early stages of searching that your topic is going to work, begin to photocopy useful material and make preliminary note cards as you go along. Use your bibliography cards to learn specific author names and sources. Notetaking helps you in three ways: first, to understand and narrow your topic; second, to find answers to your research question; and third, to help you guard against plagiarism. The third matter is so important that Chapter 31 is devoted to **avoiding plagiarism** (see 31b) and to the skills of quoting (see 31c), paraphrasing (see 31d), and summarizing (see 31e). To plagiarize is to steal someone else's words and pass them off as your own. To avoid the risk of plagiarism, take notes so that you can always tell what is your own thinking and what belongs to a source. Using pens of different colors helps.

Use index cards for content notes. In contrast to pages in a notebook, cards provide flexibility for organizing and moving around material to use in writing your paper. Put a heading on each index card that shows a precise link to one of your bibliography cards (see 33b). Include in your content notes the source's title and the number of the page or pages from which you are taking notes. Never put notes from more than one source on the same index card. If your notes on a source require more than one index card, number the cards sequentially (if you need two cards, use "1 of 2" for the first card and "2 of 2" for the second card on that same source). If you take notes on more than one idea or topic from a particular source, start a new card for each new area of information. Also, describe the type of note on the card: quotation, paraphrase, or summary.

A summary note card written by Lisa Laver, the student whose paper is in Chapter 34, is shown below. The full title of the article by Gray and Viens is "The Theory of Multiple Intelligences." Laver put full information about this source in her working bibliography. On the content cards for the Gray and Viens article, Laver used a shortened form of the title. She also noted page numbers and whether the information was a quotation, paraphrase, or summary.

Gray and Viens. "The theory of,"
p. 22.

Summary:
Evidence that intelligence is pluralistic.

Note Card Summarizing a Source

Extra Exercise A (continued)

4. In 1773 we know that [Francisco] Goya was in Madrid, where he married Josefa Bayeau, the sister of the painter who had introduced him into Madrid society. His first important chance was a commission for a series of cartoons for tapestries, which Mengs (possibly advised by Bayeau, who had acquired a certain reputation and had become part of a group of young academic painters, which included his brothers) commissioned for the Royal Tapestry Factory at Santa Barbara. It was an important opportunity because it meant that Goya was admitted to court circles; in addition this kind of work allowed him great freedom in his choice of subject matter and of technique. Perhaps most important of all, the sketchy nature of the cartoon medium spared Goya the necessity of "finishing" his work. His style was slow to mature; until now he had displayed a dextrous hand but had shown no signs of genius.

—Margherita Abbaruzzese,
Goya, p. 5

BACKGROUND

Some very famous people have been librarians. A few of them may even have helped students with research papers.

- German diplomat and philosopher mathematician Gottfried von Leibniz (1646–1716) served two terms as a librarian.
- British philosopher, economist, and historian David Hume (1711–1776) spent five years as a librarian at the Library of the Faculty of the Advocates at Edinburgh while writing his *History of England*.
- The infamous Casanova (1725–1798) served as a private librarian to royalty for thirteen years at the end of his life.
- Pope Pius XI (1857–1939) spent nineteen years at the Ambrosian Library in Milan, where he then served as chief librarian. In 1911, he began reorganizing and updating the Vatican Library and four years later was named its prefect. He became pope in 1922.
- Archibald MacLeish (1892–1982), poet, playwright, assistant secretary of state, and three-time winner of the Pulitzer Prize served as Librarian of Congress under Franklin D. Roosevelt.
- Mao Zedong (1893–1976) was at one time assistant to the chief librarian of the University of Beijing.
- Longtime Federal Bureau of Investigation chief J. Edgar Hoover (1895–1964) was a messenger and cataloger at the Library of Congress as a young man.

Urbina, 1330

A review of the 1921 and 1986 surveys shows that the definitions proposed have become considerably more sophisticated and suggests that, as the field of psychology has expanded, the views of experts on intelligence may have grown farther apart. The reader of the 1986 work is left with the clear impression that intelligence is such a multifaceted concept that no single quality can define it and no single task or series of tasks can capture it completely. Moreover, it is clear that in order to unravel the qualities that produce intelligent behavior one must look not only at individuals and their skills but also at the requirements of the systems in which people find themselves. In other words, intelligence cannot be defined in a vacuum.

maybe quote this?

Photocopy of a Source, with Annotations

Photocopying or downloading from a CD-ROM or an online database can save you time. Having a copy of articles, book chapters, or Web pages in your research file can be useful. Such copies allow you to check your paraphrases and your quotes for accuracy. Having a copy of the source also allows you to make certain you have not inadvertently plagiarized (see 31a). Also, some instructors require that students submit copies of any material used for research. Be sure to label each photocopied or downloaded source with the author's name and other bibliographic information so you can prepare a bibliography card (see 32j.1 and 33b). Always underline the section that caught your eye and write why. Many students use the photocopy or download when they write their content notes.

32k Using reference works

The reference book and CD-ROM collection in the library is the starting point for many research studies. This collection is also one of the best places to learn the search words (subject headings and key words; see 32i) that are so critical to successful research.

Most widely used reference works are available in computerized versions, usually CD-ROMs. Many libraries give students on-site access to computer-based dictionaries, thesauruses, encyclopedias, bibliographies, and even atlases; some libraries allow off-site access to some resources. Almanacs and statistical works on computer are often kept more up-to-date than their printed counterparts and can often present information in several different ways. If you use full-text material from a CD-ROM or an online database, in addition to the basic bibliographic information, be sure to note on your card the title of the product, the producer, and whether it was a CD-ROM (include the copyright date) or an online source (include the date you used it). You will need this information for your works cited page. Be sure to check with a librarian to make sure you have used the best source in the best format for your subject.

General reference

The works in this collection are interdisciplinary; they provide basic summaries on vast amounts of information.

General encyclopedias

General encyclopedia articles can help you get started but usually are not suitable as major sources for college-level papers. Articles in general encyclopedias such as the *Encyclopaedia Britannica* summarize information about a wide variety of subjects. The articles can give you background information and authors' names. General encyclopedias are not the place to look for information on recent events or current research, although sometimes controversies about the field are summarized. Many articles end with a brief bibliography of major works on the subject, which may lead you to the authors' names and their most current works. To locate the information, start with the index volume, which will give you volume and page numbers related to your topic. The letters *bib* at the end of an index listing mean that the article contains a bibliography and so might be worth checking. If you cannot find what you are looking for, try alternative headings or key words. One-volume general encyclopedias, such as the *New Columbia Encyclopedia* or the *Random House Encyclopedia,* may cover subjects very briefly. For college-level work, these sources are useful only for you to see whether a general subject area interests you enough for further research.

Almanacs, yearbooks, fact books

Almanacs—books such as the *World Almanac and Book of Facts*—briefly present a year's events and data in government, politics, sports, economics, demographics, and many other categories. *Facts on File* covers world events in a weekly digest and in an annual one-volume yearbook. The annual *Statistical Abstract of the United States* contains a wealth of data about the United States. *Demographic Yearbook* and *United Nations Statistical Yearbook* carry worldwide data. (Other specialized yearbooks and handbooks are named in section 32l.) These reference books provide additional resources for key word lists as well as give statistical data that can verify or support the problem you may be investigating.

Atlases

Atlases contain maps—and remember that seas and skies and even other planets have been mapped. These comprehensive sources, many

BACKGROUND

The Guinness Book of Records was founded as a result of the curiosity of Sir Hugh Beaver, the managing director of the Arthur Guinness, Son and Co. brewery. One day in 1954, Sir Hugh went bird hunting. He shot at some plovers—and missed. He started wondering if plovers were the fastest game birds, and he tried to satisfy his curiosity in the encyclopedia. Neither it nor any other reference work had the answer.

As a result, Sir Hugh decided that people needed a book that would accurately list record sizes, speeds, and durations. His plan was to have a copy of the book in every pub that sold Guinness stout, as an aid in settling bets. He set about finding someone to compile such a book, and one of his executives recommended the McWhirter brothers. Trivia history was made.

Norris and Ross McWhirter, identical twin sons of a newspaper writer, had grown up around newspapers, magazines, and reference books. Their childhood hobby had been to collect information of the very type Sir Hugh was seeking. They had frequently found contradictions in their sources, and so as adults they had founded a company to verify these statistics and to "supply facts and figures to newspapers, yearbooks, encyclopedias, and advertisers."

Four months after Sir Hugh interviewed them, the McWhirters published the first book in the series. The 198-page bet-settler became England's all-time nonfiction best-seller in only four months. Immediately, readers began submitting their own fantastic facts. The McWhirters collected and checked these submissions, and soon an updated volume was on the way. Norris and Ross McWhirter served as coeditors until 1975.

of which have been computerized, contain much geographical information: topography, climates, populations, migrations, natural resources, crops, and so on.

Dictionaries

Dictionaries define words and terms (see Chapter 20). In addition to general dictionaries, specialized dictionaries exist in many academic disciplines to define words and phrases specific to a field (see 32l).

Biographical reference works

Biographical reference books give brief factual information about famous people. They are good places to find dates and brief listings of major events or accomplishments in noted people's lives. (Do not confuse these works with full-length biographies or bestseller accounts about noted people.) Various *Who's Who* series cover noteworthy people. *Current Biography: Who's News and Why* is published monthly, with six-month and annual cumulative editions. The *Dictionary of American Biography* and *Webster's Biographical Dictionary* are also widely available. These sources, as well as specialized biographical reference works on famous people in various fields, also list Nobel and Pulitzer prizewinners.

Sometimes a source you use will have a corporate author; you may be able to find additional information in the *Encyclopedia of Associations.*

Because of the many different biographical sources, you may want to ask a librarian for assistance in locating biographical references.

Bibliographies

Bibliographies list books. *Books in Print* lists all books that are available through their publishers and certain other sources in the United States. This multivolume work classifies its entries by author name, title, and general subject headings, but it does not describe a book's content. The database *WorldCat,* available through FirstSearch, lists all the book holdings in most U.S. and some international libraries. It does not describe a book's contents, but it does list the subject headings assigned by librarians to categorize the subjects covered by the book.

The *Book Review Digest* excerpts book reviews that have appeared in major newspapers and magazines. These excerpts of critics' opinions can help you evaluate a source (see 32f.3). This digest is published every year. The reviews appear in the volume that corresponds either to the year a book was published or to the one immediately following. The *Book Review Index* lists where reviews have appeared but does not carry the actual reviews. Other book reviews are available in specialized areas.

Consulting specialized bibliographies—ones that list many books on a particular subject—can be very helpful in your research process (see 32l). Annotated or critical bibliographies describe and evaluate the works that they list and are therefore especially useful.

321 Using specialized reference works

Specialized or subject encyclopedias, which provide more authoritative and specific information than general reference works, are usually appropriate for college-level research. As you work with the layering strategy (see 32h) in your search for sources, you will soon need to become more focused in your research. The specialized reference collection can assist you at this point. It is an area many students overlook in their preliminary searches. Specialized encyclopedias usually contain short summaries that introduce you to the controversies, the experts, and the key words for searching that are specific to your topic. Be sure to look for authors' names in the article or in the bibliography so that you can begin to accumulate a list of credible authors. Those names become especially valuable as you search book and periodical catalogs. You may wish to photocopy articles you find and, in particular, any bibliographies that are listed. You will want to start your notetaking process with these sources. Here are the titles of some commonly used specialized materials, categorized by subject area.

BUSINESS AND ECONOMICS

A Dictionary of Economics
Encyclopedia of Advertising
Encyclopedia of Banking and Finance
Handbook of Modern Marketing

FINE ARTS

Crowell's Handbook of World Opera
International Cyclopedia of Music and Musicians
New Grove Dictionary of Music and Musicians
Oxford Companion to Art

HISTORY

Dictionary of American Biography
Encyclopedia of American History
An Encyclopedia of World History
New Cambridge Modern History

LITERATURE

Cassell's Encyclopedia of World Literature
Dictionary of Literary Biography
A Dictionary of Literary Terms

HISTORY

Libraries are as old as recorded history. In fact, they were the repository of the records of past civilizations. In what was ancient Mesopotamia, for example, temples and princely houses have been excavated that held thousands of clay tablets inscribed with epic poems, liturgic and magic texts, and commercial records. The palace of Ashurbanipal, who reigned from 668–633 B.C. in Nineveh, has provided tablets bearing stamps of ownership, catchwords, and sometimes source and place indications, thereby testifying to the existence of a well-developed cataloging system. In Egypt, every temple had its library and school. Although the Egyptian collections were made on papyrus (and thus have been found mostly in graves and tombs rather than in temples), the content was similar. Much has been lost, but records often remain. In the temple at Edfu, for instance, a full catalog of all the hieratical works the library contained was incised on the walls, bearing witness to what was once there.

HISTORY

Under the strong influence of the Renaissance, Italy became the center of book collecting in the Western world. Florence was one of the major trading cities, because of the support of the princes, who served as patrons to scholars who searched for lost treasures of Greek and Latin literature. The scholars' efforts were in large measure responsible for transmitting classical learning to a new age through the works they found, translated, recopied, and sold. Among the princes of that time, Cosimo de Medici (1389–1464) is especially notable for building the Medici Library, the first public library in Europe to have been opened since the Romans. The Medicis invested $15 million from 1434 to 1469, collecting and commissioning copies of manuscripts. The collection acquired under their patronage, especially that of Cosimo and his successor, Lorenzo the Magnificent (1449–1492), are now housed in the Laurentian and National libraries of Florence.

QUOTATION: ON RESEARCH

Research is the ability to investigate systematically and truly all that comes under your observation in life.

—Marcus Aurelius

HISTORY

One of the most famous libraries of antiquity was the one at Alexandria, founded by Ptolemy I (c. 323–285 B.C.) and greatly augmented by his son Ptolemy II Philadelphus (c. 285–247 B.C.) and his grandson Ptolemy III Euergetes (c. 247–221 B.C.). Manuscripts were imported from all parts of Greece and Asia, resulting in holdings that are estimated to have been as high as 700,000 papyrus rolls during the time of Julius Caesar (100–44 B.C.). Because of its riches, leading scholars of the Hellenistic world were drawn to it, resulting in a flurry of scholarly activity. Books were edited into a standard format, and systems of punctuation and accents were introduced. Textual scholarship, revisions of books to incorporate new knowledge, and the writing of new books went on constantly. Most of the books have been lost. Only works that were widely copied and distributed have managed to survive. As the political importance of Alexandria waned, the library suffered from neglect. Finally, in A.D. 270, much of it was razed, and a good part of the rest was destroyed by fire a century later.

HISTORY

Abdul Kassem Ismael (938–995), Grand Vizier of Persia, had a library of 117,000 volumes. When he traveled, he took his books along—all of them. He had four hundred camels trained to walk in order; the books they carried remained in strict alphabetical sequence. His camel drivers doubled as librarians.

MLA International Bibliography of Books and Articles on the Modern Languages and Literature

Oxford Companion to American Literature

Oxford Companion to English Literature

PHILOSOPHY AND RELIGION

Dictionary of the Bible

Eastern Definitions: A Short Encyclopedia of Religions of the Orient

Encyclopedia of Philosophy

Encyclopedia of Religion

POLITICAL SCIENCE

Foreign Affairs Bibliography

Political Handbook and Atlas of the World

Political Science Bibliographies

SCIENCE AND TECHNOLOGY

Encyclopedia of Chemistry

Encyclopedia of Computer Science and Technology

Encyclopedia of Physics

Encyclopedia of the Biological Sciences

Larousse Encyclopedia of Animal Life

McGraw-Hill Encyclopedia of Science and Technology

SOCIAL SCIENCES

Dictionary of Anthropology

Dictionary of Education

Encyclopedia of Psychology

International Encyclopedia of the Social Sciences

FILM, TELEVISION, THEATER

International Encyclopedia of Film

International Television Almanac

Oxford Companion to the Theatre

One Hundred Greatest Films

❶ **ALERTS:** (1) Very specific one-volume works are not listed here. For example, in the social sciences you would also find the *Encyclopedia of Divorce*, the *Encyclopedia of Aging*, and the *Encyclopedic Dictionary of Psychology*. (2) New specialized reference works are published throughout the year. Always know the call number for your subject area, and browse the reference collection to see if any new special reference works have become available in your library. !

32m Using a library's book catalog

A library's online book catalog can typically be accessed in four ways in the library: by author, by title, by subject, and by key word. To use the subject headings, you must use the correct words as search keys (see 32i). Usually, these are the ones listed in the Library of Congress Subject Headings. If you type in your heading only to have "nothing on this subject" appear on the computer screen, ask a reference librarian to help you, or try another key word. Many libraries are connected electronically to other libraries' book catalogs, giving you access to the holdings of those libraries. Some states link all their state colleges and universities into one system. Some libraries through the Internet connect to colleges and universities outside their state systems. Librarians can request materials from other libraries through interlibrary loan.

Each entry in a book catalog contains much useful information. The call number is most important. Be sure to copy it down exactly as it appears, with all numbers, letters, and decimal points. The call number tells where the book is located in the stacks. If you are researching in a library with open stacks (you can go where books are shelved), the call number leads you to the area in the library where all books on the same subject can be found. Being there can help you search for various sources, even though some books might have been checked out and other books might be at the reserve desk. The call number is also crucial in a library with closed stacks (you fill in a call slip, hand it in at the call desk, and wait for the book to arrive). If you fill in the wrong number or an incomplete number, your wait will be in vain. On your preliminary bibliography cards, be sure to write down all call number information to make it easier to locate your books and periodicals. You can see an example of an online book catalog key search on page 528.

Additional subject headings are found at the end of the catalog entry. These are the additional subjects covered in the book you are investigating. They can be valuable hints for further searching. If your library has a card catalog in drawers for all or part of its collection, you will find the same type of information, but you will not need key words for access.

32n Using periodicals

Periodicals are magazines and journals published at set intervals during the year. The key to using periodicals is to consult **indexes to periodicals** first. The indexes allow articles published in periodicals to be searched by subject and author.

list of
search results

search
term

detailed
information
for first entry
in the list
of results

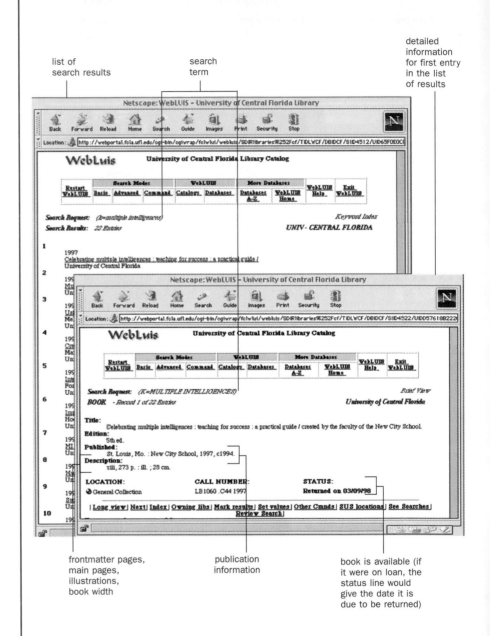

frontmatter pages,
main pages,
illustrations,
book width

publication
information

book is available (if
it were on loan, the
status line would
give the date it is
due to be returned)

Example of an Online Book Catalog Key Search (formats may differ)

Indexes are updated frequently and packaged in a variety of ways. They are often available in all three of the following formats: print index, CD-ROM index, and online index.

❶ ALERT: Pick the correct index for your subject. If your library only has the print version of the best index for your subject, use it. The fact than an index is on a computer does not necessarily make it the best index. Choosing the wrong index will cause you to miss the best sources for your paper. **❗**

32n.1 Using general indexes to periodicals

General indexes list articles in magazines and newspapers. Headings and key words on the same subject vary among indexes, so think of every possible way to look up the information you seek. Large libraries have many general indexes, among them these major ones:

- The *New York Times Index* catalogs all articles that have been printed in this encyclopedic newspaper since 1851.

- *Newsbank* covers over five hundred newspapers from around the United States. It has full-text coverage from 1993 on, and reproductions of the articles from 1980–1992 are stored on microfiche.

- The *Readers' Guide to Periodical Literature* is the most widely used index to over one hundred magazines and journals for general (rather than specialized) readers. This index does not include scholarly journals, so its uses are often very limited for college-level research. It can be useful for getting a broad overview and for thinking of ways to narrow a subject. Lisa Laver used the *Readers' Guide* in the initial stages of working on her research paper, presented in Chapter 34.

- *Academic Abstracts* and *Info-Trace* are general indexes available only online. Although they sometimes list scholarly articles and journals, the majority of these listings serve broad general subjects. These indexes allow printing out of the information on the screen; some articles are available in full text.

32n.2 Using specialized indexes to periodicals

Specialized indexes are much more helpful than general indexes for most college-level research. Specialized indexes help a researcher become a specialist in a particular topic. These indexes list articles published in academic and professional periodicals. Many specialized indexes carry an abstract, or summary, of each listed article. Here is a sampling of specialized indexes:

Business and Economics
Business Periodicals Index

HISTORY

The first general index of magazine articles was *Poole's Index of Periodical Literature*, which lists articles from the years 1802 through 1906 and is still a valuable reference tool. The idea for *Poole's Index* originated in the 1840s when a college student from Yale, William Frederick Poole, noticed that the many periodicals in the Yale library were going unused because people could not find the articles they wanted except by going through the journals one by one. Poole decided to scan the periodicals himself, compile a list of articles, and organize the list under subject headings. At first, he wrote out a single copy, which he shared with others, but the demand for the list was so great that Poole published it in 1848. For many years, Poole updated and expanded the index himself, until 1876, when he asked the American Library Association to sponsor the index and assign fifty librarians from across the United States to the project. Receiving no pay, each librarian went through a list of assigned magazines to record and classify the articles and then sent this information to Poole for the next volume of the index.

BACKGROUND

According to Curtis and Bernhardt, computers and the information explosion are changing the nature of indexing. Books and articles increasingly are indexed by title and keywords instead of by subject. Subject indexing requires readers to scan and classify each item for the index and is a slower, more expensive process than indexing by title and keywords, which can be done by computers. The process of having readers scan and classify makes it difficult and more expensive for indexes to adjust to the present rapid increase in journals and the development of new subject areas. Curtis and Bernhardt argue that the new emphasis on titles and keywords in indexes and computer searches means that writing teachers and students need to give more attention to composing titles.

ABI-Inform

Humanities and Fine Arts

Art Index

Essay and General Literature Index

Humanities Index

MLA International Bibliography of Books and Articles in the Modern Languages and Literatures

Music Index

Medicine and Nursing

Cumulative Index of Nursing and Allied Health Literature (CINAHL)

Medline (online only)

Religion and History

Religious Index

Historical Abstracts

America: History and Life

Social Science

Education Index

Psychological Abstracts

Social Science Index

PAIS (Public Affairs Information Service)

Science and Technology

General Science Index

Applied Science and Technology Index

Biological Abstracts

Biological and Agricultural Index

On page 531, there is a search from *PsycFirst* (the online version of *Psychological Abstracts*) that Lisa Laver, whose research paper appears in Chapter 34, used in her research on multiple intelligences.

Few libraries subscribe to all the periodicals listed in specialized indexes. Most libraries have a list of the periodicals they carry; ask at the reference desk.

Although it may not be possible to locate every article you find listed in the indexes, the interlibrary loan system (generally free of charge) or document delivery (generally at a cost to the student) allows you to request articles from other locations. Also, if the library has Internet access to other library collections, use it (see 32o.2)

list of search results

opening screen
for *PsycFirst*

detailed information
about one source in
the list of results

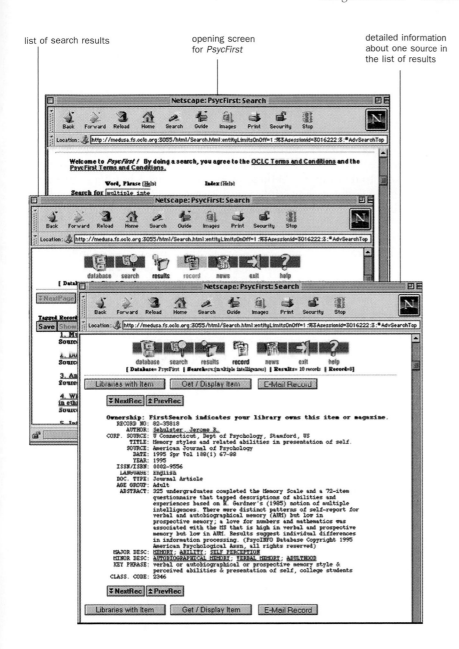

Three Screens from a Search of *PsycFirst* (online version of *Psychological Abstracts*) for Sources on Multiple Intelligences

32n.3 Searching computerized periodical indexes

Computerized indexes to periodicals allow you to search for articles by subject. Choose the most useful to you by checking with the librarian or consulting your library's handbook. It may not be immediately obvious that your library owns a particular database because it could be on a "gateway screen" on the library's book catalog, listed on a menu screen with other titles, or accessed under a network of databases like Dialog (more than two hundred different databases) or FirstSearch (60 databases). When you use a database, check the help screen (usually the F1 key) to determine whether you can use subject headings. If subject heading searches are possible, consult section 32i. If there is no subject heading access or if you do not find enough articles, use key words.

The help screen of each database is a lifeline. You waste time in a key word search unless you know such terms as *Boolean operators* and whether "truncation" and "phrase searching" are supported in the database you are using. The help screen will tell you. This information varies from database to database, so check before you start.

Boolean operators allow you to connect key words. The most common connectors are AND and OR. If your topic is "curfews for teenagers," keying in *teens AND curfews* would narrow your search by finding articles in which *both* search words appear. By contrast, keying in *teens OR adolescents* would expand the search by including synonyms or related words.

A **phrase search,** using a specific phrase enclosed in quotation marks, allows you to limit your search exclusively to articles that contain that phrase. This is especially useful for proper nouns or unique series of words, such as "The Sun Also Rises" or "American Medical Association."

Truncation symbols allow variations of a root word to be searched. The most common symbols used are ? (to stand for one character) and * (to stand for one or more characters). Used carefully, truncating words will cut down the number of times you need to conduct a search. For example, a search of *teen** will bring back articles containing the words *teens, teenage, teenager, teenagers,* and other variations.

32o Using electronic resources

32o.1 Knowing about online and CD-ROM databases

Electronic databases include bibliographic files of articles, reports, and—less often—books. Each item in these databases provides information about title, author, and publisher. If a database catalogs articles from scholarly journals, the entry might also provide an abstract, or summary, of the material. Once you locate an entry that seems promising for your research, however, you must then track down the source itself. Some databases, including ERIC and *Newsbank,* provide the full texts of cited articles on microfiche. With such a system, each citation contains an abstract as well as a catalog number (for example, ERIC ED 139 580), which allows you to look up the microfiche (ask a librarian where this is stored) that contains the entire article. ERIC is also online.

Key words are essential for searching electronic databases, some of which contain as many as one hundred million references. You must therefore choose which databases will be most helpful before you can begin to search. The Dialog Information System, one of the largest databases, is a compilation of over two hundred smaller databases in the humanities, the social sciences, business, science and technology, medicine, economics, and current events. Restrict your search to one database at a time. A reference librarian can usually help you choose the databases best suited to your research, but first, you must be able to provide a very specific description of your research.

Electronic databases may be online (such as Dialog) or on CD-ROM. CD-ROM is cheaper and easier to use—an inexperienced user may follow simple on-screen instructions to search for entries. In contrast, online systems must often be used by trained librarians. Online databases require the library to pay a fee for the time used and the number of entries requested, and your library may pass the fee on to you when you use such a system. Find out whether the service is free for students and, if not, what the charge is. (Some charges are $1 or more per entry). Narrowing your search with key words is important to avoid having to pay for a list of useless sources.

Recently, many databases previously available only online have been transferred to CD-ROM. The most popular databases on the Dialog system (such as the business, psychology, and scientific databases) are now available in this format. CD-ROM databases tend to be smaller than those online and are updated less frequently.

32o.2 Knowing about the Internet

The **Internet** is a network linking computers at universities, research centers, government facilities, and businesses around the world. People with personal computers, modems, and a connecting service can also access the Internet. Nicknamed the "information highway," the Internet contains vast numbers of databases that offer a wide variety of information, from company reports, statistical information, and copies of speeches to treaties and government documents. **Gophers** are menus of databases that can be accessed through the Internet. As a researcher, you can use gopher menus to do subject searches.

Also, the Internet enables e-mail, bulletin boards, and other public access between individuals. It contains numerous discussion groups and newsgroups that you can browse or query.

The **World Wide Web** is the easiest way to get into the Internet. You use a personal computer, modem, and a connecting service to access the

TEACHING TIP

The computer is the best place to learn about the Web and the Net. If additional tutorials are needed, select Yahoo, then select the subdivision "Computers and Internet," then "Internet," then "World Wide Web," then "Information and Documentation," and finally "Beginner's Guides." By selecting one of these sites, the beginner can become more familiar with the Web. (Although this process looks cumbersome on paper, it is only several quick mouse clicks on the Web, and it is a good illustration of the hierarchical structure of Yahoo.)

TEACHING TIP

When the URL is typed in, most browsers will automatically add the first part of the address. For example, <http://www.yahoo.com> can be typed as <yahoo.com>.

Web. Access is often provided for students at the library, computer center, or dorm. The Web presents information in words, pictures, and audio and video formats and links documents together, allowing you to explore related concepts. To learn how to use the Web, go to a Web-connected computer and type in this URL (the angle brackets are *not* part of the URL): <http//:www.newbie-u.com/web/welcome2.html> for an excellent tutorial on gathering material on the Web.

The Web is organized around pages (called *Web pages*) that are linked together. The main page is called the *home page,* and it acts as table of contents to all the Web pages linked together—which are in turn known collectively as the *Web site. Web page* and *Web site* are sometimes used interchangeably.

The term *page* is not comparable to a printed page. On the Web, a page can be a picture or a few words or a hundred screens of text. One Web page on a computer in New York may provide links to a dozen different computers in other states or countries.

In conducting research, once you have narrowed your topic, the best way to find material on the Web is to use a search engine like AltaVista. *Search engines* allow you to type in key words and find Web pages containing those words. Any computer you use to access the Web has to have a browser software program such as Netscape Navigator or Microsoft Internet Explorer. An icon or the tool bar will lead you to the various search engines. See Chart 148 for hints on using search engines.

See an example of search using AltaVista on pages 536–537.

◉ **Using online search engines**   **148**

1. Always check the help screen on the search engine you want to use. Like the rest of the Web, the search engines add or change features frequently.

2. The overall lack of organization makes the Web difficult to search efficiently. AltaVista supports only key word searching. When you enter your key words, AltaVista searches millions of pages and brings back everything with those key words. You may need to revise your search several times that the results are not overwhelming. Keep trying to narrow your key words.

3. Be sure to type a key word or words in the ranking window even if it is a duplicate from the window above. If you do not, the search is returned in random order, and the most important source may be last.

4. If possible, limit the date range. This date refers to when the page was added or revised on the Web and may or may not be the same as the copyright date.

→

> **Using online search engines** (*continued*) 148
>
> 5. When you find a source that is useful, be sure to go to the tool-bar at the top of the screen and click on Bookmarks (or Favorites) and then click on "add." This allows you to return to a good source easily by opening Bookmarks and double-clicking on the Web page you want to look at again.
> 6. Use AltaVista or similar engines only when you have a very specific, narrow topic with unique keywords. If you enter a general topic in AltaVista, you will be overwhelmed with thousands of returns. If this happens, switch to a subject directory like Yahoo (you may have to type *yahoo.com* in the search window) and try reentering the general topic in Yahoo.

32p Using the government documents collection

United States government publications are available in astounding variety. Information is available on population figures, weather patterns, agriculture, national parks, education, welfare, and many other topics. Government document collections are available in reference libraries throughout the country. Ask your reference librarian if your library contains government publications; if it does not, ask what library nearest you houses them.

Also, you can order government publications that are not available to you through your library system by consulting one of the directories listed here. Many of these publications are available at the Web site "Thomas: Legislative Information on the Web," available at <http://thomas.loc.gov/>. Ask a reference librarian for the best way to find the publications you need.

- The *Monthly Catalog of United States Government Publications* is an up-to-date listing of all offerings. Items are cataloged according to subject.
- *American Statistics Index (ASI)* is published in two volumes: the index, which catalogs all statistical documents produced by government departments, and the *Abstracts,* which gives concise summaries of the contents of the documents.
- The *Congressional Information Service (CIS)* indexes all papers produced by U.S. congressional panels and committees. These documents include the texts of hearings (for example, testimony about the plight of the homeless) and reports (for example, a comparative study of temporary shelters for the homeless.)

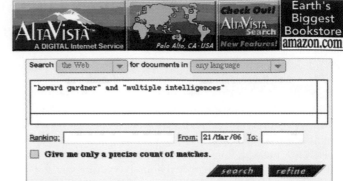

About 1376 documents match your query.

1. No Title
Ambiguity A sermon by Rev. John E. Gibbons. When people come to me for advice about their marriage or their teenagers - subjects, by the way, in which I...
http://www.ultranet.com/~fpbedfcs/sermons/ambiguit.htm - size 17K - 30-Jun-96 - English

2. The Role of Multiple Intelligences... - Page 5
I F U N G   L U > T A B L E   O F   C O N T E N T S > C H A P T E R one | two | three | four | five | appendix. the...
http://web.mit.edu/ild/www/Thesis/thesis05.htm - size 4K - 20-Jun-97 - English

3. Academic Support Center, MU (Media Library Subject List - Education: Administr
Media Library · University of Missouri-Columbia · 505 East Stewart Road · Columbia, MO 65211 Telephone:...
http://www.missouri.edu/~asrwww/newmsg/s358500.htm - size 23K - 2-Jun-97 - English

4. No Title
Elizabeth's capricious courtyard of. ... Cerebral Calisthenics ... New Yorker at heart... Elizabeth Marrin -- Originally from Long Island (The island is...
http://www.mit.edu:8001/people/caprice/self.html - size 5K - 7-Mar-97 - English

5. Amazon.com - Query Results
Amazon.com. Your Search Results for: the subjects include "Intellect" Eyes works while you play. Eyes sends you e-mail every time a new book is released...
http://www.amazon.com/exec/obidos/Subject=Intellect#/1483-1457404-659010 - size 39K - 15-Aug-97 - English

6. No Title
ALL KINDS Of SMARTS: MULTIPLE INTELLIGENCE THEORY IN ACTION Kids are smart in all kinds of ways. Howard Gardner of Harvard University has identified seven.
http://www.tier.net/users/mv23/smarts.htm - size 2K - 20-Feb-96 - English

7. Kamehameha Schools Bishop Estate
MEET THE TRUSTEES Kamehameha Schools Bishop Estate is governed by a board of five trustees selected by the justices of the Hawaii Supreme Court, acting as.
http://users.aol.com/luke214/ksbu2.html - size 16K - 3-Jun-96 - English

8. index
160; Pittsburgh Humanities Index. PHI is a public service intended for the centralized promotion of speeches, lectures, forums, luncheons and like events..
http://www.concentric.net/~ph-index/april.html - size 11K - 2-Jun-97 - English

9. CIM - Issues in Arts Education
ISSUES IN ARTS EDUCATION: Toward the 21st Century. HOWARD GARDNER, Ph.D. Harvard University. Commencement Address to The Cleveland Institute of Music, May..
http://www.cwru.edu/CIMPREP/ISSUES.HTM - size 18K - 14-Aug-97 - English

10. Gifted Definition
Introduces and discusses what gifted means when one talks about gifted children.
http://ourworld.compuserve.com/homepages/humanicfidefn.htm - size 6K - 17-Aug-97 - English

Results of an AltaVista Simple Search: 1376 Documents Found

Search the Web ▼ for documents in any language ▼

```
"multiple intelligences" and "howard gardner"
```

Ranking: naturalist   From: 01/jan/95 To:

☐ **Give me only a precise count of matches.**

search   refine

Help . Preferences . New Search . Simple Search

Click to find related books at Amazon.com.
About 88 documents match your query.

1. **The Toolroom: Article: Bruce Campbell: The Naturalist Intelligence**
   Elevator | Text Elevator | Home | Tool Room. The Naturalist Intelligence By: Bruce Campbell Dr Howard Gardner added the Naturalist Intelligence to his...
   📄 *http://www.cyberspace.com/~buildine/article_eightintel.html* - size 7K - 18-Mar-97 - English

2. **MCAD@ Advisor Spring 1997**
   THE MCAD. ® ADVISOR. Spring 1997. A Message from the President... It was wonderful to meet with so many talented educators at our annual SRS...
   📄 *http://www.xxxxx.com/advisor3.html* - size 18K - 1-Jul-97 - English

3. **Tapping Into Mental Abilities**
   Tapping Into Mental Abilities. From Parent Journal, Summer 1997. Mindy Kornhaber is a researcher at Harvard Project Zero. She investigates how...
   📄 *http://www.penn-schwab/din.cus/pj/97sum1.html* - size 10K - 17-Jul-97 - English

4. **WSSDA News-Gardner:re: two intelligences**
   Harvard professor reveals two distinct new intelligences. BALTIMORE, May 27, 1997 Howard Gardner of Harvard University, famous among educators for his...
   📄 *http://www.wssda.cus/News/Hawygardner.htm* - size 4K - 23-Jul-97 - English

5. **SITE97-Theory**
   Theory. Section Editors: Jerry D. Price, University of Houston Caroline M. Crawford, University of Houston Ruth Gannon Cook, University of Houston. This...
   📄 *http://www.uno.edu/~edca/site97/23-th.htm* - size 226K - 23-Aug-97 - English

6. **The Toolroom: Multiple Intelligences Theory: An Interview With Howard Gardner**
   Elevator | Text Elevator | Home | Tool Room. The Naturalist Intelligence by Thomas Hoerr. This article first appeared in Mindshift Connection, a...
   📄 *http://www.newhorizons.cus/trm_hoerrmi.html* - size 11K - 4-Sep-97 - English

7. **Educational Leadership September 1997 abstracts**
   Home |Publications |Educational Leadership |Abstracts| September 1997 Educational Leadership Abstracts. In New South Wales: The Brain-Flex Project...
   📄 *http://www.ascd.cus/pubs/el/sep97/sept97.html* - size 21K - 27-Aug-97 - English

8. **Zephyr Press -- Mindshift Connection--Multiple Intelligences**
   An Interview with HOWARD GARDNER--This is the man who started it all in 1983 with the publication of
   📄 *http://www.zephyrpress.com/gardner.htm* - size 8K - 25-Aug-97 - English

9. **GIFTED EDUCATION PRESS**
   GIFTED EDUCATION PRESS. 10201 YUMA COURT. P.O. BOX 1586. MANASSAS, VA 20108. Telephone: 703-369-5017. E-Mail Address: mdfish@cais.com. Publisher of Books..
   📄 *http://www.cais.com/gep/index.html* - size 6K - 14-Jun-97 - English

10. **defined**
    Multiple Intelligences. What Is It? What Does It Mean? Howard Gardner was the pioneer who first

Results of an AltaVista "Refined Search" (limited to sources including the word *naturalist* and from 1995 to the present): 88 Documents Found

QUOTATION: ON RESEARCH

You should always collect more material than you will eventually use. Every article is strong in proportion to the surplus of details from which you can choose the few that will serve you best—if you don't go on gathering facts forever. At some point you must decide to stop researching and start writing.

—William Zinsser

32q Interviewing an expert

An expert can often offer valuable information, points of view concerning your topic, or advice. The faculty at your college or nearby colleges have special expertise about many topics. Corporations and professional organizations can often suggest experts in many fields; a customer service department or public relations office is a good place to begin. Public officials are sometimes available for interviews. Many federal and state government offices have employees who specialize in providing information to the public. If your topic relates to an event that your family or friends experienced, they qualify as experts.

If you think you might want to interview other people, plan ahead. It takes time to set up appointments and fit your research needs into other people's schedules. You may not always be granted the interviews you seek, but many people remember their own experiences doing academic research and try to help. If you are following the layering strategy, conduct an interview only after you have solid control of your topic. The layering strategy leads you from the most general to the most specific sources on your topic, and you gradually become an expert on your research question. Wait to interview an expert until you have a solid foundation of knowledge about your topic and you know the specific focus your paper is going to take. Do not expect an interview with an expert to save you the work of researching your topic.

Know why you are interviewing the person and what you want to know. Ask questions that elicit information, not merely a yes or no answer. Be constructive; avoid language that conveys bias or a hostile attitude. Keep in mind the following basic rules to follow in arranging an interview:

1. Call for an appointment during office hours.
2. Ask permission to use a tape recorder at the time you make the appointment.
3. Be on time for the interview.
4. If you are tape-recording, know your equipment and have it ready when you arrive. Set it up and leave it running until the end of the interview. (Avoid periodic checks to see if it is running.)
5. Go to the appointment prepared with specific questions. The more you know about the subject already, the more specific your questions can be.
6. Pace the interview to the time you have been allotted. Be courteous and appreciative, and be prepared to leave promptly at the end of your appointment time.
7. Ask permission to use quotes in your paper.
8. If a secretary or other assistant set up the interview for you, thank that person at the end of the interview.

9. Follow up an interview, no matter how short, with a brief thank-you note. A note is not just polite; it helps pave the way for the next student who might ask for an interview.

10. After the interview, allow yourself time to fill in any notes you didn't have time to finish. Write a bibliography entry, and summarize and evaluate your experience on note cards. Recognize that no one is ever totally unbiased and that an expert may have a slanted point of view in line with vested interests.

For details about creating and using questionnaires to gather research data, see section 38a.

32r Drafting a thesis statement for a research paper

Drafting a **thesis statement** for a research paper is the beginning of the transition between the research process and the writing process. A thesis statement in a research paper is like the thesis statement in any essay: It sets out the central theme (see section 2n, especially Chart 12). Any paper must fulfill the promise of its thesis statement. Because readers expect unified material, the theme of the thesis must be sustained throughout a research paper.

Most researchers draft a preliminary thesis statement before or during their research process. They expect that they will revise the thesis somewhat after their research because they know that the sources they will consult will enlarge their knowledge of their subject. Other researchers draft a thesis statement after the research process.

No matter when you draft your thesis statement, expect to write many alternatives. Your goal is to draft the thesis carefully so that it delivers the message you intend. In writing a revised thesis statement, take charge of your material. Reread your research log (see 32c). Reread your notes (see 32j). Look for categories of information. Rearrange your note cards into logical groupings. Begin to impose a structure on your material. As you draft a thesis statement, remember that one of your major responsibilities in a research paper is to support the thesis. Be sure that the material you gathered during the research process offers effective support. If it does not, revise your thesis statement, conduct further research, or do both.

Lisa Laver, whose research paper appears in Chapter 34, drafted two different preliminary thesis statements before she composed one that worked well with her material.

FIRST PRELIMINARY THESIS STATEMENT

There is more than one way of describing human intelligence. [Laver saw this as too close to her research question (Can there be only one way of describing intelligence?) and too broad to prepare readers for the main message of her paper.]

EXTRA EXERCISE B

For each of the following subjects, devise a narrowed topic, then a research question, followed by a thesis statement, noting its purpose.

1. Fishing
2. Large families
3. Retirement communities
4. Competitive swimming
5. Study habits
6. Current clothing styles
7. Contemporary American novels
8. Olympics
9. Professional football
10. Diets

NEXT PRELIMINARY THESIS STATEMENT

The intelligence quotient (IQ) test used today do not measure all aspects of human intelligence. [Laver liked this better but rejected it because it put too much emphasis on IQ tests when her focus was the complexity of human intelligence.]

FINAL THESIS STATEMENT

Human intelligence results from a complex interaction of the riches of many abilities, only a few of which are taken into account by intelligence quotient (IQ) tests widely used today. [Laver felt this got closer to her message; she then checked it to make sure it also satisfied the criteria for a thesis statement listed in Chart 12 in section 2n.]

As you revise your thesis statement, go back to the research question that guided your research process (see 32a). Your thesis statement should be one answer to the question. Here are examples of subjects narrowed to topics, focused into research questions, and then cast as thesis statements.

SUBJECT	*Rain forests*
TOPIC	The importance of rain forests
RESEARCH QUESTION	What is the importance of rain forests?
INFORMATIVE THESIS STATEMENT	Rain forests provide the human race with many irreplaceable resources.
PERSUASIVE THESIS STATEMENT	Rain forests must be preserved because they offer the human race many irreplaceable resources.
SUBJECT	*Nonverbal communication*
TOPIC	Personal space
RESEARCH QUESTION	How do standards for personal space differ among cultures?
INFORMATIVE THESIS STATEMENT	Everyone has expectations concerning the use of personal space, but accepted distances for that space are determined by each person's culture.
PERSUASIVE THESIS STATEMENT	To prevent intercultural misunderstandings, people must be aware of cultural differences in standards for personal space.
SUBJECT	*Smoking*
TOPIC	Curing nicotine addiction
RESEARCH QUESTION	Are new approaches being used to cure nicotine addiction?

INFORMATIVE THESIS STATEMENT	Some approaches to curing nicotine addiction are themselves addictive.
PERSUASIVE THESIS STATEMENT	Because some methods of curing addiction are themselves addictive, doctors should prescribe them with caution.

32s Outlining a research paper

Some instructors require an outline of a research paper. To begin organizing your material for an outline, you might write an **informal outline.** Group the subcategories in your material until you are ready to write a formal outline.

A **formal outline** should be in the form discussed in section 2o. Head it with the paper's THESIS STATEMENT. You can use a **topic outline** (a format that requires words or phrases for each item) or a **sentence outline** (a format that requires full sentences for each item). Do not mix the two types. A sentence outline of a student's research paper is presented in see Chapter 34.

32t Drafting and revising a research paper

Drafting and revising a research paper have much in common with the writing processes for writing any type of paper (see Chapters 2 and 3). But more is demanded. You must demonstrate that you have followed the research steps in this chapter. You must demonstrate an understanding of the information you have found, and you must organize for effective presentation. You must integrate sources into your writing without plagiarizing (see 31a) by properly using the techniques of quotation (see 31c), paraphrase (see 31d), and summary (see 31e). You must use parenthetical references (see 33a) to document your sources. These many special demands require that you allow ample time for drafting, thinking, redrafting, and rethinking.

Expect to write a number of drafts of your research paper. Successive drafts help you gain authority over the information that you have learned from your research. The **first draft** is your initial attempt to structure your notes into a unified whole. It is also a chance to discover new insights and fresh connections. Only the act of writing makes such discovery possible. A first draft is a rough draft. It is a prelude to later work at revising and polishing. Chart 149 suggests some alternative ways to write the first draft of a research paper.

TEACHING TIP

Since the processes of drafting and revising vary from one writer to another, students may gain insight into their own processes by interviewing one another about how they approach these stages of writing a research paper. They can base their interviews on the following questions.

1. Do you organize your note cards in piles?

2. Do you work with your notes in front of you?

3. Do you write the first draft without referring to your note cards?

4. Is your first draft a complete draft?

5. When do you insert parenthetical references?

6. Is your first draft composed slowly and carefully or quickly and sketchily?

7. Do you proceed immediately to a second draft, or do you let some time elapse between drafting and revising?

8. Do you show your work to other people for responses and suggestions?

◉ **Suggestions for drafting a research paper**　　149

- Some researchers work with their notes in front of them. They use the organized piles made for drafting a thesis statement (see 32r) and for outlining (see 32s). They spread out each pile and work according to the categories of information that have emerged from their material. They proceed from one pile to the next. They expect this process to take time, but they are assured of a first draft that includes much of the results of their research.

- Some researchers gather all their information and then set it aside to write a **partial first draft**, a quickly written first attempt at getting the material under control. Writing this way helps researchers get a broad view of the material. The second step is to go back and write a **complete first draft** with research notes at hand. The researchers go over their partial draft slowly to correct information, add material left out, and insert in-text references (see Chapter 33).

- Some researchers write their first draft quickly to get words down on paper when they feel "stuck" about what to say next. When they have a clear idea of how to proceed, they slow down and use their notes. These researchers draw on their experiences with gathering ideas (see 2d through 2j), shaping ideas (see 2k), getting started (see 3a), and drafting (see 3b).

- Some researchers photocopy their first drafts and cut up the paper to move paragraphs and sentences around. If a new order suggests itself, the researchers tape the paper together in its new form. Researchers who have access to a computer will find this process considerably easier.

Second and subsequent drafts result from reading your first draft critically and revising it. If possible, get some distance from your material by taking a break of a few days (or a few hours, if you are pressed for time). Then, reread your first draft and think how it can be improved. You might also ask friends or classmates to read it and react.

As you work, pay attention to any uneasy feelings you have that hint at the need to rethink or rework your material. Experienced writers expect to revise; they know that writing is really rewriting. Research papers are among the most demanding composing assignments, and most writers have to revise their drafts more than a few times. As you revise, consult Charts 19 and 20 in section 3c to remind yourself of general principles of writing. Also, consult the revision checklist in Chart 150 designed especially for a research paper.

Revision checklist for a research paper   150

If the answer to any question in the list is no, revise your draft.

1. Does the introductory paragraph lead effectively into the material (see 4g)?
2. Are you fulfilling the promise of the thesis statement (see 32r)?
3. Do the ideas follow from one another?
4. Do you stay on the topic?
5. Are important questions answered?
6. Do you avoid bogging down the paper with irrelevant or insignificant information?
7. Do you avoid leaving gaps in information?
8. Have you integrated source material without plagiarizing (see 31a)?
9. Have you used quotations, paraphrases, and summaries well (see Chapter 31)?
10. Have you used parenthetical references (see 33c.1 and 33d.1) correctly, and is each tied in with a source listed in the list of works cited at the end of the paper (see 33c.3 and 33d.3)?
11. Have you used correct documentation forms (see Chapter 33)?
12. Does the concluding paragraph end the material effectively (see 4g)?

The **final draft** shows that you have revised well. It also shows that you have edited (see 3d) and proofread (see 3e) for correct grammar, spelling, and punctuation. No amount of careful research and good writing can make up for a sloppy manuscript. If your instructor accepts handwritten papers, use ruled white paper that has not been torn out of a spiral notebook. (If at all possible, however, type your work because it will present itself better.) Use black or blue ink and write very legibly.

A case study of the writing of an MLA-style research paper, including a narrative of the writing process in action, and a sample student research paper are presented in Chapter 34. A case study and a sample student research paper using APA style are presented in Chapter 35.

The term *bibliography* is derived from two Greek roots. The first is *biblia,* the plural form of the word meaning "book" or "papyrus," so named after the Phoenician city *Byblos* (now Jubayl), from which papyrus was exported. *Biblia* has been responsible for many words in the English language dealing with books. For example, a *biblioclast* is a destroyer of books, and a *bibliognost* is someone who is knowledgeable about books. A *bibliolater* is a lover of books. A *bibliopegist* is a bookbinder.

The second Greek root is *graphos,* meaning "to write." At one time, *bibliography* meant "the writing of books," but in the seventeenth century the term came to meaning "writing about books." At the same time, *bibliography* began to receive wide usage in Latin and began to replace such words as *catalogus* and *bibliotheca* in the titles of bibliographies, the making of which became increasingly important as bibliographers struggled to devise some type of organization for keeping track of the flood of publications that resulted from the invention of printing. Nevertheless, the term *bibliography* was not included in Samuel Johnson's dictionary of 1755 and was not found in the *Encyclopaedia Britannica* until its third edition in 1797. According to the *Oxford English Dictionary,* not until the early nineteenth century was the word *bibliography* first used to refer to "the systematic description and history of books, their authorship, printing, publication, editions, etc." or to a book about such matters.

TEACHING TIP

Students often wonder why they need to be scrupulous in their documentation of information, sometimes thinking of the process as just another pointless but difficult exercise devised by the teacher. It may help them understand the demands of documentation if you point out the reasons behind it. You will probably think of additional reasons, but here are some that you might find useful.

33

DOCUMENTING IN MLA, APA, CM, AND CBE STYLES

When you write a research paper, you must **document** your sources. If you do not, you are plagiarizing, which is a serious offense (see 31a). The purpose of documenting sources is to inform your reader of the exact sources from which you have taken information. To prepare to document, you want to create a working bibliography (see 33b) to keep careful track of all the sources on which you take notes. In your research paper itself, you are expected to use the style of documentation required by your instructor. Four major styles are presented in this chapter.

33a Understanding the concept of documentation

Documentation involves marking the exact place in a paper where source material has been used and presenting bibliographic information (for example, a book's author, title, year of publication, publisher, and any other required information). Although *bibliography* literally means "description of books," for your research projects you might find yourself compiling a list of sources that includes live interviews, CDs, online information, and films, as well as books and articles.

Bibliographic information is given in a **list of sources** at the end of the paper or in bibliographic notes. When a list of sources includes only the sources actually referred to in a paper, it is titled " Works Cited" or "References." A source list that includes all the works a writer looks at, not just those referred to in the paper, is headed "Works Consulted," "Bibliography," or "References."

Four documentation styles are featured in this chapter. Never mix documentation styles. The style used most frequently in the humanities was developed by the **Modern Language Association (MLA)**. It is a **parenthetical citation system** that calls for a source name and page reference to be entered at each place you use a source in your paper. Also, at the end of your paper, you include a Works Cited list giving full bibliographic details about each cited source. For full coverage of MLA documentation and editorial style, see the fourth edition of the *MLA Handbook for Writers of Research Papers* by Joseph Gibaldi (1995) and new MLA guidelines for certain online sources at the MLA's Web site (see page 546 for the URL). For coverage of MLA documentation in this handbook, see section 33c.

The documentation style used in most social sciences was developed by the **American Psychological Association (APA)**. It is a parenthetical citation system that calls for a source name and a publication year, and sometimes a page reference, to be entered at each place you use a source in your paper. Also, at the end of your paper, you include a References list of all cited and recoverable sources. (A **recoverable source** is one that a reader can expect to be able to locate, like a book, and unlike a personal letter.) For full coverage of APA documentation and editorial style, see the fourth edition of the *Publication Manual of the American Psychological Association* (1994) and the APA Web site (see page 546 for the URL). For coverage of APA documentation in this handbook, see section 33d.

A third style, also used in the humanities and other disciplines, is described in the style manual of the University of Chicago Press and is known as **Chicago Manual (CM)** style. The *Chicago Manual of Style* describes two quite different documentation systems: (1) a name-year parenthetical citation system and References list similar to APA's and (2) a system using **bibliographic notes** containing full source information. (A separate list of references is usually unnecessary with bibliographic notes.) For coverage of the CM bibliographic note style of documentation as described in the fourteenth edition of *The Chicago Manual of Style* (1993), see section 33e.

The **Council of Biology Editors (CBE)** has compiled a manual of editorial style and documentation guidelines for mathematics, the physical sciences, and the life sciences, titled *Scientific Style and Format*. In it, the CBE describes two documentation systems: (1) a **name-year parenthetical citation system** and References list and (2) as covered in this handbook, a **numbered reference system** using numbers in the paper to cite a source and a numbered list of references giving full bibliographic details for each source. For coverage of CBE recommendations for citing sources in a paper and for a References list as described in the sixth edition of *The CBE Manual for Authors, Editors, and Publishers* (1994), see section 33f.

Documenting electronic sources is a developing art and science. Changes and refinements can happen so fast that no printed handbook can keep up. Luckily, your computer can help you document electronic sources correctly. The MLA, the APA, and the University of Chicago Press maintain frequently updated Web sites. At the MLA and APA main sites, you can find documentation information and style FAQs (frequently asked questions and their answers). At the Chicago site, go to the FAQ. Also, at English Central, a Prentice Hall Web site, you can find links to up-to-date information about several styles of documentation.

BACKGROUND

As commonly used, the term *bibliography* sometimes refers to a science, sometimes to an art, and sometimes to the product of the art. As a science, it is an organized body of knowledge dealing with all aspects of books, both as physical objects and as the expression of ideas. Bibliography as an art consists of the techniques for finding, organizing, and presenting information about books. The bibliography that is produced by that art is a systematic listing of books that share common characteristics.

The objectives of bibliography may be analytical or systematic. Analytical bibliography tries to discover information about authorship, publication, and derivation of a text. Systematic bibliography produces systematic lists of books. The result is many different kinds of bibliographies. For example, bibliographies may be critical (critically appraising the books they list), current or retrospective, comprehensive or selective, annotated or not, enumerative (presenting an inventory) or subject-oriented (presenting content). In all their varied forms, they provide the modern researcher with valuable assistance in finding out where to look to learn what is already known about a subject.

TEACHING TIP

Older documentation styles often called for the use of abbreviations, many of them in Latin. Although current style manuals have dropped most of the abbreviated terms, your students may need to know what the terms mean when they appear in articles encountered in the course of doing research. Students should be cautioned not to use them in their own papers unless you, another instructor, or their style manual asks them to do so. Some of the more common ones appear in Chart 133 in section 30j.

MLA	http://www.mla.org
APA	http://www.apa.org
CHICAGO MANUAL	http://www.press.uchicago.edu/Misc/Chicago/cmos.faq.html
PRENTICE HALL'S ENGLISH CENTRAL	http://www.prenhall.com/english

Careful, responsible documentation is an academic obligation. To help you fulfill this obligation, this handbook presents MLA, APA, CM, and CBE documentation guidelines in separate sections, each with a different identifying color bar down the outside of the pages. Chart 151 tells where in this handbook you can find information on each style.

⊙ **Where to find the MLA, APA, CM, and CBE   151 information you need**

MLA Style: Red Bar on Pages 547–580, Section 33c

- MLA parenthetical citations: 33c.1
- Guidelines for compiling an MLA-style Works Cited list (Chart 152); 33c.2
- Directory of MLA Works Cited list models: 33c.3
- Content or other notes with MLA parenthetical documentation: 33c.4

APA Style: Blue Bar on Pages 580–603, Section 33d

- APA in-text style and parenthetical citations: 33d.1
- Guidelines for compiling an APA-style References list (Chart 153): 33d.2
- Directory of APA References list models: 33d.3
- Abstracts and notes: 33d.4

CM Style: Green Bar on Pages 603–615, Section 33e

- Guidelines for compiling CM-style bibliographic notes (Chart 154): 33e.1
- Directory of CM-style bibliographic notes and References models: 33e.2

CBE Style: Gray Bar on Pages 615–622, Section 33f

- Guidelines for compiling a CBE-style References list (Chart 155): 33f.1
- Directory of CBE-style References list models: 33f.2

33b Creating a working bibliography

To create a working bibliography, write out a bibliography card for every source you take notes on. Include all the information you need to fulfill the requirements of the documentation style you are using. Also, for each card on a library source, write the call number in the upper left corner, being careful to copy it exactly. (Note that magazines and journals may not have call numbers.) If you conduct research at more than one library, also note on the card the library where you found each source.

Be especially vigilant with online sources. In the upper left corner of the bibliography card for each online source, write the URL, being careful to copy it exactly. Include on the bibliography card for each online source the date on which you access the material. Because online sources may be updated periodically, documentation for an online source must include both any date related to the source (such as the most recent update, if any, for a Web source) and the date you access the material. If you download the source, use the date you download as the access date, even if you take notes on it later. If you take notes from the screen, use the date you take notes.

When the time comes to compile bibliographic information for your research paper, you can easily arrange your bibliography cards in the order required by your documentation style (for example, in alphabetical order for an MLA-style Works Cited list). The bibliography cards shown here are for two sources Lisa Laver found when she was doing research for the paper in Chapter 34.

153 - G

Gardner, Howard.
Frames of Mind: The Theory of Multiple Intelligences

New York: Basic Books, 1993.

Bibliography Card: Book

http://www.apa.org/monitor/neuralb.html

Azar, Beth
Working out builds the mind's muscles.
APA Monitor, July 1996.
Access date: July 18, 1996.

Bibliography Card: Online Source

33c Using MLA-style documentation

In Modern Language Association (MLA) documentation, you use a two-part system to document any source that you quote, paraphrase, or summarize.

1. Within the body of the paper, use in-text citations, as described in section 33c.1.

2. At the end of the paper, provide a list of sources titled "Works Cited"; see sections 33c.2 and 33c.3.

(For information about using notes for additional content or for extensive citations of sources when you are using MLA-style parenthetical citations, see section 33c.4.)

33c.1 Citing sources in the body of a paper in MLA style

For most in-text citations, wherever you use ideas or information you have found in a source, you give a name or a title (whichever is the first information in the source's entry in the Works Cited list) to identify the source. You also give page numbers to show the exact location in the source of the material you are using. In your sentences that set the context for your use of source material, try to include author names and, when relevant, credentials of authors who are authorities. In such cases, the only part of a citation to put in parentheses is the page number. If you cannot incorporate author names into your sentences, give them as part of the parenthetical citation. In a parenthetical citation, use one space between an author name (or title) and page number; do not use a comma or other punctuation between name and page number.

🛈 **MLA FORMAT ALERT:** Position a parenthetical citation at the end of the material it refers to, preferably at the end of a sentence, if that is not too far away from the material. At the end of a sentence, place a parenthetical reference before the sentence's end punctuation. ❗

The examples in this section show how to handle various parenthetical citations in the body of your paper. Remember, however, that you can usually integrate the names and titles of sources into your sentences.

1. Citing a Paraphrased or Summarized Source—MLA

According to Brent Staples, IQ tests give scientists little insight into intelligence (293). [Author name cited in text; page number cited in parentheses.]

In "The IQ Cult," journalist Brent Staples states that IQ tests give scientists little insight into intelligence (293). [Title of source, author name, and author credentials cited in text; page number cited in parentheses.]

IQ tests give scientists little insight into intelligence (Staples 293). [Author name and page number cited in parentheses.]

2. Citing the Source of a Short Quotation—MLA

If it is true that "thoughts, emotions, imagination and predispositions occur concurrently . . . [and] interact with other brain processes" (Caine and Caine 66), it is easy to understand why "whatever [intelligence] might be, paper and pencil tests aren't the tenth of it" (Staples 293).

🟡 **MLA FORMAT ALERT:** When a quotation is no longer than four hand-written or typed lines, enclose the quoted words in quotation marks to distinguish them from your own words in the sentence. Place the parentheses after the closing quotation mark but before sentence-ending punctuation. If a quotation ends with an exclamation point or a question mark, however, put that punctuation mark before the closing quotation mark, put the parenthetical citation next, and then put a period after the parenthetical citation.

Coles asks, "What binds together a Mormon banker in Utah with his brother, or other coreligionists in Illinois or Massachusetts?" (2).

3. Citing the Source of a Long Quotation—MLA

Gray and Viens explain how, by tapping into a student's highly developed spatial-mechanical intelligence, one teacher can bolster a student's poor writing skills:

> The teacher asked that during "journal time" Jacob create a tool dictionary to be used as a resource in the mechanical learning center. After several entries in which he drew and described tools and other materials, Jacob confidently moved on to writing about other things of import to him, such as his brothers and a recent birthday party. Rather than shy away from all things linguistic--he previously had refused any task requiring a pencil--Jacob became invested in journal writing. (23-24)

🟡 **MLA FORMAT ALERT:** When a quotation is longer than four handwritten or typed lines, do not put quotation marks around the quoted words. Instead, set the quoted words off from your own words by indenting each line of the quotation. In a typed paper, use a ten-space indent for each line of a quotation longer than four lines. If you are handwriting or

---

QUOTATION: ON WRITING

An original writer is not one who imitates no one but one whom no one can imitate.
—François-René de Chateaubriand

EXTRA EXERCISE A

Devise parenthetical references for the following quotation, paraphrase, and summary. The source is provided at the end of each selection.

1. "If indeed we note in [Thomas Carlyle's] writings those passages in which the words and rhythms are most resonant, and the accent falls with the strongest emphasis, we shall find they are the expression of the cosmic wonder and terror which formed the darkly flaming background of all his thoughts." (Logan Pearsall Smith, "Thomas Carlyle: The Rembrandt of English Prose," *Reperusals and Re-Collections*, Harcourt, Brace and Company, 1936, p. 115.)

2. Ethologists study the traits that distinguish a group—a group of people or a group of animals. They try to discover how the group usually acts by observing its members in their natural surroundings, and to understand their behavior by testing it, when possible, in the laboratory. (Sally Carrighar, "Ethology," from *Wild Heritage*, Houghton Mifflin Company, 1965, pp. 174–175.)

Answers to Extra Exercise A
1. (Smith 115).
2. (Carrighar 174-75).

using a computer, indent each line of the quotation one inch. Put one space after the last punctuation mark of the quotation, and then put in the parenthetical citation. For other examples of long quotations, see Lisa Laver's research paper in Chapter 34. ❗

4. Citing One Author—MLA

Give an author's name as it appears on the source: for a book, on the title page; for an article, directly below the title or at the end of the article. Many nonprint sources also name an author; for a CD, cassette, tape, or software, for example, check the printed sleeve or cover. For an online source, identify the author exactly as identified online.

```
One test asks four-year-olds to choose between one
marshmallow now or two marshmallows later (Gibbs 60).
```

5. Citing Two or Three Authors—MLA

Give the names in the same order as in the source. Spell out *and*. For three authors, use commas to separate the authors' names.

```
As children get older, they begin to express several
different kinds of intelligence (Todd and Taylor 23).
```

```
Another measure of emotional intelligence is the success of
inter- and intrapersonal relationships (Voigt, Dees, and
Prigoff 14).
```

6. Citing More Than Three Authors—MLA

With three or more authors, you can name them all or use the first author's name only, followed by *et al.*, either in a parenthetical reference or in your sentence. Do not underline *et al.* No period follows *et,* but do use a period after *al.*

❶ USAGE ALERT: The abbreviation *et al.* stands for "and others"; when an author's name followed by *et al.* is a subject, use a plural verb. ❗

```
Carter et al. have found that emotional security varies
depending on the circumstances of the social interaction
(158).
```

```
Emotional security varies depending on the circumstances of
the social interaction (Carter et al. 158). ❗
```

7. Citing More Than One Source by an Author—MLA

When you use two or more sources by an author, include the relevant title in each citation. In parenthetical citations, use a shortened version of the title. For example, in a paper using as sources two of Howard Gardner's works, *Frames of Mind: The Theory of Multiple Intelligences* and "Reflections on Multiple Intelligences: Myths and Messages," parenthetical citations use *Frames* and "Reflections." Shorten the titles as much as possible, keeping them unambiguous to readers and starting them with the word by which you alphabetize the works in Works Cited. Separate the author's name and the title with a comma, but do not use punctuation between the title and page number.

```
Although it seems straightforward to think of multiple
intelligences as multiple approaches to learning (Gardner,
Frames 60-61), an intelligence is not a learning style
(Gardner, "Reflections" 202-203).
```

When you incorporate the title into your own sentences, you can omit a subtitle, but do not shorten it more than that.

8. Citing Two or More Authors with the Same Last Name—MLA

Use each author's first and last name in each citation, whether in your sentences or in parenthetical citations.

```
According to Anne Cates, psychologists can predict how
empathetic an adult will be from his or her behavior
at age two (41), but other researchers disagree (Tyrone
Cates 171).
```

9. Citing a Work with a Group or Corporate Author—MLA

When a corporation or other group is named as the author of a source you want to cite, use the corporate name just as you would an individual's name.

```
In a five-year study, the Boston Women's Health Collective
reported that these tests are usually unreliable (11).
```

```
A five-year study shows that these tests are usually
unreliable (Boston Women's Health Collective 11).
```

10. Citing a Work by Title—MLA

If no author is named, use the title in citations. In your own sentences, use the full main title and omit a subtitle, if any. For parenthetical citations, shorten the title as much as possible (making sure that the shortened version refers unambiguously to the correct source), and always make the first word the one by which you alphabetize it. The following citation is to an article fully titled "Are You a Day or Night Person?"

QUOTATION: ON WRITING

Beginning to write, you discover what you have to write about.

—Kit Reed

```
The "morning lark" and "night owl" connotations are
typically used to categorize the human extremes ("Are You"
11).
```

11. Citing a Multivolume Work—MLA

When you cite more than one volume of a multivolume work, include the relevant volume number in each citation. (In the Works Cited list, list the multivolume work once and give the total number of volumes; see item 9 in the Works Cited examples in 33c.3.) Give the volume number first, followed by a colon and one space, followed by the page number(s).

```
By 1900, the Amazon forest dwellers had been exposed to
these viruses (Rand 3: 202).
```

```
Rand believes that forest dwellers in Borneo escaped illness
from retroviruses until the 1960s (4: 518-19).
```

12. Citing Material from a Novel, Play, or Poem—MLA

When you cite material from literary works, providing part, chapter, act, scene, canto, stanza, or line numbers usually help readers trying to locate what you refer to more than page numbers do. Unless your instructor tells you not to, use arabic numerals for these references, even if the literary work uses roman numerals.

For novels that use them, give part and/or chapter numbers after page numbers. Use a semicolon after the page number but a comma to separate a part from a chapter.

```
Flannery O'Connor describes one character in The Violent
Bear It Away as "divided in two--a violent and a rational
self" (139; pt. 2, ch. 6).
```

For plays that use them, give act, scene, and/or line numbers. Use periods between these numbers.

```
Among the most quoted of Shakespeare's lines is Hamlet's
soliloquy beginning "To be, or not to be: that is the
question" (3.1.56).
```

For poems and plays that use them, give canto, stanza, and/or line numbers. Use periods between these numbers.

```
In "To Autumn," Keats's most melancholy image occurs in the
lines "Then in a wailful choir the small gnats mourn /
Among the river swallows" (3.27-28).
```

❶ **MLA ABBREVIATION ALERT:** Because the typed or typeset abbreviation for *line* (*l.*, plural *ll.*) can be misread as the numeral 1, the *MLA Handbook* advises beginning your first reference to lines with the word *line* (or *lines*). After the first citation, omit the word and just give the numbers. !

13. Citing a Work in an Anthology or Other Collection—MLA

You may want to cite a work you have read in a book that contains many works by various authors and that was compiled or edited by someone other than the person you are citing. For example, suppose you want to cite "When in Rome," by Mari Evans, which you have read in a literature text by Pamela Annas and Robert Rosen. Use Evans's name and the title of her work in the in-text citation and as the first block of information for the entry in the Works Cited list (see item 11 in section 33c.3).

```
In "When in Rome," Mari Evans uses parentheses to enclose
lines expressing the houseworker's thoughts as her employer
offers lunch, as in the first stanza's "(an egg / or soup /
. . . there ain't no meat)" (688-89).
```

14. Citing an Indirect Source—MLA

When you want to quote words that you found quoted in someone else's work, put the name of the person whose words you are quoting into your own sentence. Indicate the work where you found the quotation either in your sentence or in a parenthetical citation beginning with *qtd. in.*

🚫 **RESEARCH ALERT:** When it is possible to do so, find the primary source for words that you want to quote rather than taking a quotation from a secondary source.

```
Martin Scorsese acknowledges the link between himself and
his films: "I realize that all my life, I've been an
outsider. I splatter bits of myself all over the screen"
(qtd. in Giannetti and Eyman 397).
```

```
Giannetti and Eyman quote Martin Scorsese as acknowledging
the link between himself and his films: "I realize that all
my life, I've been an outsider. I splatter bits of myself
all over the screen" (397). !
```

15. Citing Two or More Sources in One Reference—MLA

If more than one source has contributed to an idea, opinion, or fact in your paper, acknowledge all of them. In a parenthetical citation, separate each block of information with a semicolon followed by one space.

```
Once researchers agreed that multiple intelligences existed,
their next step was to try to measure or define them (West
17; Arturi 477; Gibbs 68).
```

QUOTATION: ON WRITING

There is no way to write unless you read, and read a lot.

—Walter J. Ong

Because long parenthetical citations can disturb the flow of your paper, consider using an endnote or footnote for citing multiple sources; see section 33c.4.

16. Citing an Entire Work—MLA

References to an entire work usually fit best into your own sentences.

```
In Frames of Mind, Gardner proposes a revolutionary
expansion of our understanding of human intelligence.
```

17. Citing an Electronic Source with a Name or Title and Page Numbers—MLA

The principles that govern in-text citations of electronic sources are exactly the same as the ones that apply to books, articles, letters, interviews, or any other source you get information from on paper or in person. You put in your own sentences or in parenthetical references enough information for a reader to be able to locate full information about the source in the Works Cited list.

When an electronically accessed source identifies its author, use the author's name for in-text citations. If an electronic source does not name the author, use its title for in-text citations and for the first block of information in that source's Works Cited entry. (See item 10 in this section for an example of a work cited by its title and for advice about shortening a title for an in-text citation.)

When an electronic source has page numbers, use them exactly as you would the page numbers of a print source.

18. Citing an Electronic Source That Numbers Paragraphs—MLA

When an electronic source has numbered paragraphs (instead of page numbers), use them for in-text references as you would page numbers, with two differences: (1) Use a comma followed by one space after the name (or title), and (2) use the abbreviation *par.* for a reference to one paragraph or *pars.* for a reference to more than one paragraph, followed by the numbers of the paragraphs you are citing.

```
Artists seem to be haunted by the fear that psychoanalysis
might destroy creativity while it reconstructs personality
(Francis, pars. 22—25).
```

19. Citing an Electronic Source Without Page or Paragraph Numbers—MLA

Many online sources do not number pages or paragraphs. In the Works Cited entry for such a source, include the abbreviation *n. pag.* ("no pagination"). This abbreviation serves to explain to readers why in-text references to this source do not cite page numbers. Here are two examples referring to "The Naturalist Intelligence," by Thomas Hoerr, a Web site without page numbers or paragraph numbers.

```
Meriwether Lewis, the legendary explorer of the United
States' Northwest Territory, certainly possessed the
naturalist intelligence (Hoerr).
```

```
Thomas Hoerr mentions Meriwether Lewis, the legendary
explorer of the United States' Northwest Territory, as
someone who possessed the naturalist intelligence.
```

33c.2 Compiling an MLA-style Works Cited list

In MLA documentation, in-text citations must be accompanied by a list of all the sources referred to in your paper. In a Works Cited list, include only the sources from which you quote, paraphrase, or summarize. Do not include sources that you have consulted but do not refer to in the paper unless your instructor asks for a Works Consulted list (which follows the same format as a Works Cited list). Chart 152 gives general information about a Works Cited list. It includes new information about MLA editorial style and a new documentation model—of a source found on the World Wide Web—from the MLA Web site.

⊙ **Guidelines for compiling an MLA-style**   **152**
Works Cited list

■ **TITLE**
   Works Cited

■ **PLACEMENT OF LIST**
   Start a new page numbered sequentially with the rest of the paper, after Notes pages, if any.

■ **CONTENT AND FORMAT**
   Include all sources quoted from, paraphrased, or summarized in your paper. Start each entry on a new line and at the regular left margin. If the entry uses more than one line, indent all lines but the first five spaces (or one-half inch) from the left margin. Double-space all lines.

■ **SPACING AFTER PUNCTUATION**
   On its Web site,* the MLA explains that computer type fonts have influenced may users of MLA style to leave one space

*See page 546 for the URL.   →

Guidelines for compiling an MLA-style Works Cited list *(continued)*   **152**

rather than two spaces after punctuation at the ends of sentences. The *MLA Handbook* and the *MLA Style Manual* use one space. Either style is acceptable, so do whichever your instructor prefers.

Put one space after a comma or a colon.

■ **ARRANGEMENT OF ENTRIES**

Alphabetize by author's last name. If no author is named, alphabetize by the title's first significant word (not *A, An,* or *The*).

■ **AUTHORS' NAMES**

Use first names and middle names or middle initials, if any, as given in the source. Do not reduce to initials any name that is given in full. For one author or the first-named author in multiauthor works, give the last name first. Use the word *and* with two or more authors. List multiple authors in the order given in the source. Use a comma between the first author's last and first names and after each complete author name except the last. After the last author name, use a period: `Fein, Ethel Andrea, Bert Griggs, and Delaware Rogash.`

Include *Jr., Sr., II, III,* but do not include other titles and degrees before or after a name. For example, an entry for a work by Edward Meep, III, M.D., and Sir Feeney Bolton, would start like this: `Meep, Edward, III, and Feeney Bolton.`

■ **CAPITALIZATION OF TITLES**

Capitalize all major words in titles.

■ **SPECIAL TREATMENT OF TITLES**

Use quotation marks around titles of shorter works (poems, short stories, essays, articles). On the MLA Web site, the MLA states that although computers can create italic type, in student papers underlined roman type may be more exact. Check which style your instructor prefers. Underline titles of longer works (books, names of newspapers or journals containing cited articles). For underlining, use an unbroken line like this (unless you use software that underlines only with a broken line, like this).

When a book title includes the title of another work that is usually underlined (such as a novel, play, or long poem), do not underline the incorporated title: `Decoding Jane Eyre.`

→

Guidelines for compiling an MLA-style Works Cited list *(continued)*   152

If the incorporated title is usually enclosed in quotation marks (such as a short story or short poem), keep the quotation marks and underline the complete title of the book (do not underline the period): <u>Theme and Form in "I Shall Laugh Purely."</u>

Drop *A, An,* or *The* as the first word of a periodical title.

■ **PLACE OF PUBLICATION**

If several cities are listed for the place of publication, give only the first. If a U.S. city name alone would be ambiguous, also give the state's two-letter postal abbreviation (see Chart 132 in section 30i). For an unfamiliar city outside the United States, include an abbreviated country name or an abbreviated Canadian province name.

■ **PUBLISHER**

Use shortened names as long as they are clear: *Prentice* for *Prentice Hall, Simon* for *Simon & Schuster.* For university presses, use the capital letters *U* and *P* (without periods): Oxford UP; U of Chicago P.

■ **PUBLICATION MONTH ABBREVIATIONS**

Abbreviate all publication months except *May, June,* and *July.* Use the first three letters followed by a period (see Chart 134 in section 30j): Dec., Feb.

■ **PARAGRAPH NUMBERS IN ELECTRONIC SOURCES**

For electronic sources that number paragraphs instead of pages, give the total number of paragraphs followed by the abbreviation *pars.:* 77 pars.

■ **PAGE RANGES**

Give the page range—the starting page number and the ending page number, connected by a hyphen—of any paginated electronic source and any paginated print source that is part of a longer work (for example, a chapter in a book, an article in a journal). A range indicates that the cited work is on those pages and all pages in between. If that is not the case, use the style shown next for discontinuous pages. In either case, use numerals only, without the word *page* or *pages* or the abbreviation *p.* or *pp.*

Use the full second number through 99. Above that, use only the last two digits for the second number unless it would be unclear: 103–04 is clear, but 567–602 requires full numbers.

→

QUOTATION: ON WRITING

Vigorous writing is concise. A sentence should contain no unnecessary words, a paragraph no unnecessary sentences, for the same reason that a drawing should have no unnecessary lines and a machine no unnecessary parts. This requires not that the writer makes all his sentences short, or that he avoid all detail and treat his subjects only in outline, but that every word tell.

—William Strunk

MLA MLA MLA MLA MLA MLA MLA MLA MLA MLA MLA MLA MLA MLA MLA

QUOTATION: ON WRITING

I write the first draft quickly. This is most often done in longhand. I simply fill up the pages as rapidly as I can. In some cases, there's a kind of personal shorthand, notes to myself for what I will do later when I come back to it.

—Raymond Carver

Guidelines for compiling an MLA-style Works Cited list *(continued)* 152

■ **DISCONTINUOUS PAGES**

Use the starting page number followed by a plus sign (+): 32+.

■ **WORKS CITED ENTRIES: BOOKS**

Citations for books have three main parts: author, title, and publication information (place of publication, publisher, and date of publication).

AUTHOR   TITLE   PUBLICATION INFORMATION

Didion, Joan. <u>Salvador</u>. New York: Simon, 1983.

■ **WORKS CITED ENTRIES: PRINT ARTICLES**

Citations for periodical articles contain three major parts: author, title of article, and publication information (usually periodical title, volume number, year of publication, and page range).

AUTHOR   ARTICLE TITLE

Shuter, Robert. "A Field Study of Nonverbal

Communication in Germany, Italy, and the United

JOURNAL TITLE

States." <u>Communication Monographs</u>

PUBLICATION INFORMATION

44 (1977): 298–305.

ARTICLE TITLE   JOURNAL TITLE   PUBLICATION INFORMATION

"A Start." <u>New Republic</u> 2 May 1994: 7+.

■ **WORKS CITED ENTRIES: SOURCES FROM THE WORLD WIDE WEB—NEW**

On its Web site, the MLA sets out a system for documenting sources found on the World Wide Web. This system also applies to FTP and Gopher sites. Citations of these sources contain as much of the following information as you can find: author, title, publication information about a print version if there is one, publication information about the online source, the date you accessed the material, and the URL (electronic address). For →

Guidelines for compiling an MLA-style Works Cited list *(continued)* 152

these sources, the URL is required in the Works Cited entry. The URL, enclosed in angle brackets <like these>, comes after the access date and before the period at the end of the entry. Here is an entry for an article in a scientific news journal that appears only on the Web.

```
  ARTICLE AUTHOR              ARTICLE TITLE
Lewis, Ricki. "Chronobiology Researchers Say Their

                          PUBLICATION    PUBLICATION
                             TITLE       INFORMATION
  Field's Time Has Come." Scientist 9.24 (1995):

        ACCESS DATE              URL
  14. 30 Dec. 1997 <http://www.the-scientist.

  library.upenn.edu/yr1995/dec/chrono_951211.html>.
```

■ **WORKS CITED ENTRIES: "PORTABLE" AND ONLINE* SOURCES WITHOUT URLs**

Citations for electronic sources that do not have URLs contain at least six major parts: author, publication information, title of database, publication medium, name of vendor or computer service, and electronic publication date (add access date if different). Electronic versions of sources that also appear in print start with information about the print version. Here is an entry for a journal article accessed through a computer service; it also has a print version.

```
                TITLE OF         PUBLICATION INFORMATION
 ARTICLE TITLE  PRINT JOURNAL       FOR PRINT JOURNAL
"A Start." New Republic (2 May 1994): n. pag.

 ELECTRONIC
 PUBLICATION    COMPUTER        ACCESS
 MEDIUM         NETWORK         DATE
 Online. America Online. 21 Apr. 1996.
```

*The word *online* is not hyphenated in MLA style or the style of this *Handbook*.

→

QUOTATION: ON WRITING

When you first start writing—and I think it's true for a lot of beginning writers—you're scared to death that if you don't get that sentence right that minute it's never going to show up again. And it isn't. But it doesn't matter—another one will, and it'll probably be better. And I don't mind writing badly for a couple of days because I know I can fix it—and fix it again and again and again, and it will be better.

—Toni Morrison

MLA MLA MLA MLA MLA MLA MLA MLA MLA MLA MLA MLA MLA MLA MLA MLA

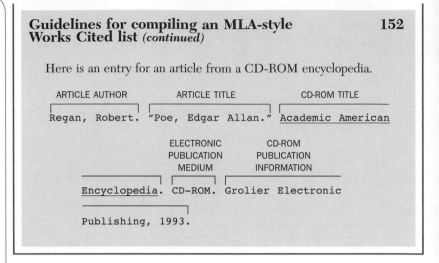

Guidelines for compiling an MLA-style Works Cited list *(continued)* **152**

Here is an entry for an article from a CD-ROM encyclopedia.

ARTICLE AUTHOR · ARTICLE TITLE · CD-ROM TITLE

Regan, Robert. "Poe, Edgar Allan." Academic American

ELECTRONIC PUBLICATION MEDIUM · CD-ROM PUBLICATION INFORMATION

Encyclopedia. CD-ROM. Grolier Electronic

Publishing, 1993.

33c.3 Following models for an MLA-style Works Cited list

Directory

PRINT SOURCES: BOOKS

1. Book by One Author—MLA
2. Book by Two or Three Authors—MLA
3. Book by More Than Three Authors—MLA
4. Two or More Books by the Same Author(s)—MLA
5. Book by Group or Corporate Author—MLA
6. Book with No Author Named—MLA
7. Book with an Author and an Editor—MLA
8. Translation—MLA
9. Work in Several Volumes or Parts—MLA
10. Anthology or Collection—MLA
11. One Selection from an Anthology or Collection—MLA
12. More Than One Selection from an Anthology or Collection—MLA
13. Signed Article in a Reference Book—MLA
14. Unsigned Article in a Reference Book—MLA
15. Edition—MLA
16. Introduction, Preface, Foreword, or Afterword—MLA
17. Unpublished Dissertation—MLA

QUOTATION: ON WRITING

I put a piece of paper under my pillow, and when I could not sleep I wrote in the dark.
—Henry David Thoreau

49. Work in More Than One Publication Medium—MLA
50. Online: Article from a Newspaper with a Print Version—MLA
51. Online: Article from a Magazine with a Print Version—MLA
52. Online: Material with No Print Version—MLA
53. Online: Material from an Electronic Newsletter—MLA
54. Online: Public Message—MLA—*NEW*
55. Online: E-Mail—MLA—*NEW*
56. Online: Article from a Newspaper on the Web—MLA—*NEW*
57. Online: Interview from a Magazine on the Web with a Print Version—MLA—*NEW*
58. Online: Article from a Journal Available Only on the Web—MLA—*NEW*
59. Online: Electronic Text on the Web—MLA—*NEW*
60. Online: Organization Home Page—MLA—*NEW*
61. Online: Personal Home Page—MLA—*NEW*
62. Online: FTP Site—MLA—*NEW*
63. Online: Gopher Site—MLA—*NEW*
64. Online: Synchronous Communication—MLA—*NEW*

Print sources: Books

1. Book by One Author—MLA

Mayle, Peter. <u>A Dog's Life</u>. New York: Knopf, 1995.

2. Book by Two or Three Authors—MLA

Smith, Richard J., and Mark Gibbs. <u>Navigating the Internet</u>. Indianapolis: Sams, 1994.

3. Book by More Than Three Authors—MLA

Cameron, Deborah, et al. <u>Researching Language: Issues of Power and Method</u>. London: Routledge, 1992.

4. Two or More Books by the Same Author(s)—MLA

Waller, R. J. <u>The Bridges of Madison County</u>. New York: Warner, 1992.

---. <u>Old Songs in a New Café</u>. New York: Warner, 1994.

---. <u>Slow Waltz in Cedar Bend</u>. New York: Warner, 1993.

Arrange an author's multiple entries alphabetically by title.

5. Book by Group or Corporate Author—MLA

Environmental Defense Fund. <u>Recycling and Incineration:</u>
    <u>Evaluating the Choice</u>. Washington: Island, 1990.

American Psychological Association. <u>Publication Manual of</u>
    <u>the American Psychological Association</u>. 4th ed.
    Washington: APA, 1994.

6. Book with No Author Named—MLA

<u>The Chicago Manual of Style</u>. 14th ed. Chicago: U of Chicago
    P, 1993.

7. Book with an Author and an Editor—MLA

If your focus is on Eudora Welty as the author of the reviews in *A Writer's Eye* and your paper refers to her or her words, put her name first in the Works Cited entry:

Welty, Eudora. <u>A Writer's Eye: Collected Book Reviews</u>.
    Ed. Pearl A. McHaney. Jackson: UP of Mississippi,
    1994.

If your focus is on Pearl A. McHaney's work as the editor of this collection of reviews and your paper refers to her or her words, put her name first in the Works Cited entry:

McHaney, Pearl A., ed. <u>A Writer's Eye: Collected Book</u>
    <u>Reviews</u>. By Eudora Welty. Jackson: UP of Mississippi,
    1994.

8. Translation—MLA

Dostoevsky, Fyodor. <u>Devils</u>. Trans. Michael R. Katz. Oxford:
    Oxford UP, 1992.

9. Work in Several Volumes or Parts—MLA

When you use more than one volume of a multivolume work, after the title give the total number of volumes. In each parenthetical citation, give both volume and page numbers (see item 11 in section 33c.1).

Rand, Enid. <u>Virology</u>. 5 vols. Philadelphia: Lippincott,
    1979.

When you use only one volume, instead of the total number of volumes, give the number of the volume you used. In parenthetical citations, give page numbers only; do not repeat the volume number.

QUOTATION: ON READING

In a very real sense, people who have read good literature have lived more than people who cannot or will not read. . . . It is not true that we have only one life to live; if we can read, we can live as many more lives and as many kinds of lives as we wish.

—S. I. Hayakawa

```
Rand, Enid. Virology. Vol. 2. Philadelphia: Lippincott,
    1979.
```

When you use only one volume of a multivolume work in which each volume is titled separately, you can list it as you would any book, using its individual title and not referring to the rest of the volumes.

```
Goldman, L. H., Cloria L. Cronin, and Ada Aharoni. Saul
    Bellow: A Mosaic. New York: Lang, 1992.
```

If you want to include information about the set of volumes, put it after the basic information about the volume you used.

```
Goldman, L. H., Cloria L. Cronin, and Ada Aharoni. Saul
    Bellow: A Mosaic. New York: Lang, 1992. Vol. 2 of
    Twentieth-Century American Jewish Writers. 14 vols.
```

10. Anthology or Collection—MLA

When your paper is about a collection of works rather than about the individual selections in an anthology or collection, use this form. Also see item 15.

```
Elliott, Emory, et al., eds. American Literature: A Prentice
    Hall Anthology. Concise ed. Englewood Cliffs: Prentice,
    1991.
```

11. One Selection from an Anthology or Collection—MLA

```
Franklin, Benjamin. "An Address to the Public." American
    Literature: A Prentice Hall Anthology. Concise ed. Ed.
    Emory Elliott et al. Englewood Cliffs: Prentice, 1991.
    173-74.
```

12. More Than One Selection from an Anthology or Collection—MLA

When you use more than one selection from one anthology, in the Works Cited list you can give one entry for the anthology and separate brief entries for each selection cited from the anthology. This plan is more efficient than using the form shown in item 11 for each selection you use. Give full details about the anthology or edited collection, with the editor's name as the first item of information. For each selection cited in your paper, give the name of the selection's author and title. End this information with a period, and then give the name that starts the entry for the anthology and inclusive pages on which the specific selection falls. For citations in your paper, use the name of the author of the selection, not the editor of the anthology. The following entries show first an entry for an anthology followed by entries for two selections in the anthology. Readers looking at the Glück and Ortiz entries are directed to the Roberts and Jacobs entry for full information about the anthology and see that the cited material is on pages 634 and 1082, respectively.

Roberts, Edgar V., and Henry E. Jacobs. <u>Literature: An</u>
<u>Introduction to Reading and Writing</u>, 5th ed. Upper
Saddle River, NJ: Prentice, 1998.

Glück, Louise. "Snowdrops." Roberts and Jacobs. 634.

Ortiz, Simon J. "A Story of How a Wall Stands." Roberts and
Jacobs. 1082.

13. Signed Article in a Reference Book—MLA

Sax, Joseph L. "Environmental Law." <u>The Encyclopedia</u>
<u>Americana</u>. 1994 ed.

Alphabetically arranged collections such as the encyclopedias in this model and the next one do not require page numbers.

14. Unsigned Article in a Reference Book—MLA

"Russia." <u>Encyclopaedia Britannica</u>. 1994 ed.

15. Edition—MLA

When a book is in some edition other than the first, the edition number appears on the title page. Include this information after the title. Use *2nd ed., 3rd ed., Rev. ed.* (for *revised edition*), and so on. Put a period after *ed.*, which also acts as the period at the end of the information block.

Walker, Robert S. <u>AIDS Today, Tomorrow: An Introduction to</u>
<u>the HIV Epidemic in America</u>. 2nd ed. Atlantic
Highlands, NJ: Humanities, 1994.

Books are also "editions" when an editor has made an important contribution, such as in selecting works and writing background material about them for an anthology. In this sort of edition, the editor's name (or editors' names) comes first. Also see item 10.

Lantolf, James P., and Gabriela Appel, eds. <u>Vygotskian</u>
<u>Approaches to Second Language Research</u>. Norwood, NJ:
Ablex, 1994.

Spear, Thomas, and Richard Waller, eds. <u>Being Masai:</u>
<u>Ethnicity and Identity in East Africa</u>. Athens: Ohio UP,
1993.

QUOTATION: ON WRITING

Writer's block is a natural affliction. Writers who have never experienced it have something wrong with them. It means there isn't enough friction—that they aren't making enough of an effort to reconcile the contradictions of life. All you get is a sweet monotonous flow. Writer's block is nothing to commit suicide over. It simply indicates some imbalance between your experience and your art, and I think that's constructive.

—Stanley Kunitz

16. Introduction, Preface, Foreword, or Afterword—MLA

When you cite an introduction, preface, foreword, afterword, or appendix, give first the name of the person who wrote it. Then, give the name of the cited part, capitalizing it and using a period after it; do not underline it or put it in quotation marks. Next, give the title of the book. If the preface, introduction, foreword, afterword, or appendix was written by someone other than the author of the book, write the word *By* and the name of the book's author(s), in normal order. If the book's author(s) wrote the part you are citing, after *By* repeat only the last name or names. After publication information, give inclusive page numbers. If a cited preface or introduction uses roman numerals for page numbers, use roman numerals.

Diamond, Jared. Foreword. <u>Wild Forests Conservation Biology and Public Policy</u>. By William S. Alverson, Walter Kuhlmann, and Donald M. Waller. Washington: Island, 1994. iv.

Carter, Carol. Introduction. <u>Majoring in the Rest of Your Life</u>. By Carter. New York: Noonday-Farrar, 1990. 1—7.

17. Unpublished Dissertation—MLA

Black, Laurel Johnson. "Language, Power, and Gender in Student-Teacher Conferences." Diss. Miami U, 1993.

18. Reprint of an Older Book—MLA

A republished book may be the paperback version of a book originally published as a hardbound, or it may be the reissue of a book. Republishing information can be found on the copyright page. Give the date of the original version before the publication information for the version you used.

Melville, Herman. <u>Moby Dick, or The Whale</u>. 1851. New York: Modern Library, 1992.

19. Book in a Series—MLA

Give the book title, underlined, after the author name. Put the series title, neither underlined nor in quotation marks, after the book title.

Rothman, Hal. <u>On Rims and Ridges: The Los Alamos Area since 1880</u>. Twentieth-Century American West. Lincoln: U of Nebraska P, 1992.

20. Book with a Title Within a Title—MLA

When a book title includes the title of another work that is usually underlined (such as a novel, play, or long poem), do not underline the incorporated title. When a book title includes a title enclosed in quotation marks (such as of a short story or most poems), keep the quotation marks and underline the entire title.

```
Hayes, Kevin J., ed. The Critical Response to Herman
     Melville's Moby Dick. Westport: Greenwood, 1994.
```

21. Government Publication—MLA

For most government publications, use the name of the government as the first information unit (such as United States). If no author is named, give the name of the branch of government or the government agency next (such as Dept. of State or Cong. House).

```
United States. Dept. of the Interior. Minerals
     Management Service. Minerals Revenues, 1992: Report
     on Receipts from Federal and Indian Leases. Washington:
     GPO, 1993.

United States. Dept. of Commerce. National Oceanic and
     Atmospheric Administration. COSPAS-SARSAT Search and
     Rescue Satellite System. Washington: GPO, 1988.

United States. Dept. of Labor. Bureau of Labor Statistics.
     Consumer Expenditure Survey, 1990-91 (Bulletin 2425).
     Washington: GPO, 1993.
```

For citations from the *Congressional Record,* just give the abbreviation *Cong. Rec.,* the date, and page numbers.

```
Cong. Rec. 26 Nov. 1993: 3050-51.
```

22. Published Proceedings of a Conference—MLA

```
Pavlyshyn, Marko, and J. E. M. Clarke, eds. Ukraine in the
     1990s. Proc. of the First Conference of the Ukrainian
     Studies Association of Australia. Melbourne: Monash U,
     1992.
```

If the title of the publication of the conference proceedings does not include the name and location of the conference, give that information after the title.

QUOTATION: ON WRITING

I don't think that writer's block exists really. I think that when you're trying to do something prematurely, it just won't come. Certain subjects just need time, as I've learned over and over again. You've got to wait before you write about them.
—Joyce Carol Oates

Print sources: Articles and other short documents

23. Signed Article from a Daily Newspaper—MLA

Steinberg, Jacques. "Love, Peace, Money, Lawsuits." New York
       Times 12 May 1995: B1.

24. Editorial, Letter to the Editor, or Review—MLA

"Patching Up Health Care." Editorial. New York Times 17
       July 1994, natl. ed., sec. 4: 16.

Turkel, Stanley. Letter. New York Times 3 July 1993: A18.

Doniger, Wendy. "Shackled to the Past." Rev. of Gerald's
       Game by Stephen King. New York Times Book Review 16
       Aug. 1992: 3.

25. Unsigned Article from a Daily Newspaper—MLA

"Gene Is Shown to Block the Spread of Prostate Cancer in
       Mice." New York Times 12 May 1995: A17.

26. Signed Article from a Weekly or Biweekly Magazine or Newspaper—MLA

Rosen, Jeffrey. "Is Affirmative Action Doomed?" New Republic
       17 Oct. 1994: 25+.

   The Rosen article appears on pages 25–30, 34, and 35; the + sign
indicates that it runs on noncontinuous pages, starting on page 25.

27. Signed Article from a Monthly or Bimonthly Periodical—MLA

Came, Barry. "Policing Haiti." Maclean's Oct. 1994: 20—22.

Bell, Jim. "Kingdom Come: Canada's Inuit Finally May Be
       Getting Their Own Homeland, but at What Price?"
       Earthwatch Sept.—Oct. 1994: 10—11.

28. Unsigned Article from a Weekly or Monthly Periodical—MLA

"The March Almanac." Atlantic Monthly 16 Mar. 1994: 16.

29. Article from a Collection of Reprinted Articles—MLA

Brumberg, Abraham. "Russia after Perestroika." New York
       Review of Books 27 June 1991: 53—62. Rpt. in Russian
       and Soviet History. Ed. Alexander Dallin. Vol. 14 of
       The Gorbachev Era. New York: Garland, 1992. 300-320.

30. Article from a SIRS Collection of Reprinted Articles—MLA

Social Issues Resources Series (SIRS) articles are looseleaf collections of reprints from many sources. Give information about the original publication before the information about the article's publication in SIRS. Use the abbreviation *Art.* before the SIRS article number.

```
Curver, Philip C. "Lighting in the 21st Century." Futurist
    Jan. Fob. 1989: 25+. Energy. Ed. Eleanor Goldstein.
    Vol. 4. Boca Raton: SIRS, 1990. Art. 84.
```

31. Article in a Journal with Continuous Pagination—MLA

A journal that pages continuously throughout a volume (usually one year's publications) does not begin each issue with page 1. If the first issue in the volume ends on page 160, for example, the second issue starts on page 161. A reader who has the volume number, the year, and the page numbers can locate the correct issue of a continuously paged journal. Give the volume number in arabic numerals (without an abbreviation before it such as *vol.* or *Vol.*) immediately after the journal name. Include the year in parentheses. Give inclusive page numbers unless the article is not printed on consecutive pages; in that case, give the article's first page number followed by a plus sign (+).

```
La Follette, M. C. "The Politics of Research Misconduct:
    Congressional Oversight, Universities, and Science."
    Journal of Higher Education 65 (1994): 261-85.
```

32. Article in a Journal That Pages Each Issue Separately—MLA

If each issue in a year's issues of a scholarly journal starts on page 1, give an issue number after the volume number. Use arabic numerals. Separate the two numbers with a period with no space before or after the period. For example, in the model, 30.10 signifies that the Hancock article is in volume 30, issue 10 of *IEEE Spectrum*.

```
Hancock, D. "Prototyping the Hubble Fix." IEEE Spectrum
    30.10 (1993): 34-39.
```

If a journal uses issue numbers but not volume numbers, give the issue number after the journal name.

33. Abstract from a Collection of Abstracts—MLA

To cite an abstract, first give information for the full work: the author's name, the title of the article, and publication information about the full article. If a reader could not know that the cited material is an abstract, write the word *Abstract*, not underlined, followed by a period.

MLA MLA MLA MLA MLA MLA MLA MLA MLA MLA MLA MLA

QUOTATION: ON WRITING

A great writer creates a world of his own and his readers are proud to live in it. A lesser writer may entice them in for a moment, but soon he will watch them filing out.

—Cyril Connolly

EXTRA EXERCISE B

Using the following information, compile a Works Cited list following MLA style.

1. *Abraham Lincoln: The Man Behind the Myths*, by Stephen B. Oates. Harper & Row, Publishers, New York, Cambridge, Philadelphia, San Francisco, London, Mexico City, São Paulo, and Sydney, 1984.

2. Barbara W. Tuchman. *Practicing History*. Alfred A. Knopf, Inc. Copyright 1936, 1959, 1966, 1974, 1981. New York.

3. *Time's Arrow, Time's Cycle: Myth and Metaphor in the Discovery of Geological Time*. Stephen Jay Gould. Harvard University Press, Cambridge, Massachusetts. 1987.

4. T. C. Smout. *A Century of the Scottish People, 1830–1950*. New Haven and London. 1986, Yale University Press.

5. Thomas J. Peters and Robert H. Waterman Jr. *In Search of Excellence*. Harper & Row, Publishers, New York, 1982.

6. *The Man Who Mistook His Wife for a Hat, and Other Clinical Tales*. Oliver Sacks. New York. Summit Books. "The Autist Artist." No year of publication listed. Pages 204 through 223.

7. *The Rise and Fall of the House of Medici*. 1974. Penguin Books. New York. By Christopher Hibbert.

8. *Capote: A Biography*. 1988. Simon & Schuster. New York. Gerald Clarke.

→

Give publication information about the collection of abstracts. For abstracts identified by item numbers rather than page numbers, use the word *item* before the item number.

Marcus, Hazel R., and Shinobu Kitayamo. "Culture and the Self: Implications for Cognition, Emotion, and Motivation." <u>Psychological Review</u> 88 (1991): 224–53. <u>Psychological Abstracts</u> 78 (1991): item 23878.

34. Published and Unpublished Letters—MLA

If you cite a letter from a published source, name the author of the letter first. Identify the letter as such, and give its date, if available. Then, give publication information.

Lapidus, Jackie. Letter to her mother. 12 Nov. 1975. <u>Between Ourselves: Letters between Mothers and Daughters</u>. Ed. Karen Payne. Boston: Houghton, 1983. 323–26.

If you cite a personal letter that is not in a published source, give the letter writer's name as author, and put *Letter to the author* after the letter writer's name. Then, give the date on the letter.

Reilly, Gary Edward. Letter to the author. 26 Dec. 1994.

You can document electronic mail in a similar way.

Putnam, Christopher. E-mail to the author. 6 June 1996.

35. Map or Chart—MLA

<u>Russia and Post-Soviet Republics</u>. Map. Moscow: Mapping Production Assn., 1992.

Nonprint sources

36. Interview—MLA

Friedman, Randi. Telephone interview. 30 June 1992.

For a face-to-face interview, use *Personal interview* instead of *Telephone interview*. For a published interview, give the name of the interviewed person first, identify the source as an interview, and then give details as for any published source: author (preceded by the word *By*), title, publication details.

For a radio or television interview, give the name of the interviewed person first, the name of the interviewer next, and then information about the program on which the interview was broadcast.

Kennan, George F. Interview with Robert MacNeil. <u>MacNeil/</u>
<u>Lehrer NewsHour</u>. PBS. WGBH, Boston. 22 Aug. 1991.

37. Lecture, Speech, or Address—MLA

Clinton, William J. Address. World Youth Day Conf. Denver,
12 Aug. 1993.

38. Film or Videotape—MLA

<u>A World of Gestures: Cultural and Nonverbal Communication</u>.
Writ.-Dir. David Archer. U of California Extension
Media Center, 1992.

39. Recording—MLA

In a citation of a recording, put first the information important to
your use of the source. Here is an entry with the focus on the director
of the choral group.

De la Cuesta, Ismael Fernando, dir. Benedictine Monks of
Santo Domingo de Silos. <u>Chant</u>. Angel, 1994.

If the use of this source in the paper focused on the performers and
the music, the entry would look like this:

Benedictine Monks of Santo Domingo de Silos. <u>Chant</u>. Dir.
Ismael Fernando de la Cuesta. Angel, 1994.

If you are citing a recording in some medium other than a compact
disk, name the medium. To cite a specific song, give the song title in
quotation marks before the title of the recording.

Springsteen, Bruce. "Local Hero." <u>Lucky Town</u>. Audiocassette.
Columbia, 1992.

40. Live Performance—MLA

<u>Song of a Mockingbird</u>. By Susan J. Whitenight. Prod. Randal
King. Utah Valley State Coll. Theater, Orem. 28 Nov.
1994.

41. Work of Art or Musical Composition—MLA

For musical compositions, give composer and title of work. Underline the title of an opera, ballet, or descriptive word title for music. But
if a composition is identified only by musical form, number, and key, do
not underline it and do not put it in quotation marks. The entries for
Schubert show two ways of identifying the same composition.

Answers to Extra Exercise B
Works Cited

Clarke, Gerald. *Capote: A Biography.*
New York: Simon, 1988.

Gould, Stephen Jay. *Time's Arrow, Time's
Cycle: Myth and Metaphor in the
Discovery of Geological Time.*
Cambridge: Harvard UP, 1987.

Hibbert, Christopher. *The Rise and Fall
of the House of Medici.* New York:
Penguin, 1974.

Oates, Stephen B. *Abraham Lincoln: The
Man Behind the Myths.* New York:
Harper, 1984.

Peters, Thomas J., and Robert H.
Waterman Jr. *In Search of
Excellence.* New York: Harper, 1982.

Sacks, Oliver. "The Autist Artist." *The
Man Who Mistook His Wife for a
Hat, and Other Clinical Tales.* New
York: Summit, n.d.

Smout, T. C. *A Century of the Scottish
People, 1830–1950.* New Haven: Yale
UP, 1986.

Tuchman, Barbara W. *Practicing History.*
New York: Knopf, 1981.

MLA MLA MLA MLA MLA MLA MLA MLA MLA MLA MLA MLA

PORTFOLIOS DEFINED

Portfolios offer an effective, interactive learning strategy and assessment tool that raises students' abilities and motivation to assume responsibility for learning. Portfolios require that students go beyond merely keeping a writing folder as a work bin that does little more than house a number of grades to be averaged. Instead, portfolios should become a collection of work that profiles a student's commitment and achievement. To create such a profile appropriately, the student must be included in the selection of content, the basis for the selection, the guideline for evaluation, and ongoing self-reflection. This process is properly identified as authentic or performance assessment because it relies on what the student actually produces in a given situation. The power of the process lies in students' ability to see patterns of behaviors in their work, set independent goals, and monitor their own growth.

Portfolios will and should be as varied and diverse as the teachers and students creating them because they arise directly out of the needs and the instruction delivered to meet the needs of the class or program. This flexibility is a major strength of portfolio assessment; however, there are characteristics or guidelines that make the process distinctive. All portfolios should include work created over time, work selected by the instructor, work selected by the student, and an in-depth explanation or analysis in which the student justifies how and why the included work represents effort, progress, and achievement.

THREE-PHASE PROGRAM, DIAGNOSTIC, WORKING, AND DISPLAY PORTFOLIOS

Although the individuality and flexibility of portfolios are their chief benefits, sometimes the process of managing the paperwork seems overwhelming. To avoid the helter-skelter stress associated with portfolios, a three-phase portfolio template →

Cassatt, Mary. <u>Five o'Clock Tea</u>. Museum of Fine Arts, Boston.

Gershwin, George. <u>Porgy and Bess</u>.

Schubert, Franz. Symphony no. 8 in B minor.

Schubert, Franz. <u>Unfinished Symphony</u>.

42. Radio or Television Program—MLA

For programs that title both the series and each episode, give the episode title first in quotation marks, and then give the series title underlined. If your use of the program focuses on a participant (such as a performer, writer, or director), give that name first, an abbreviated indication of that person's role (*perf., writ., dir.*), and then the programming information. Include the network, the local station and its city, and the date of the broadcast.

"The Homecoming." <u>Frontline</u>. PBS. WNYC, New York. 25 Apr. 1995.

Electronic sources

The objectives for documenting electronic sources are the same as those for print sources: giving information so that a reader understands what sources you have used and can find those sources that are generally available. Guidelines in the 1995 edition of the *MLA Handbook for Writers of Research,* now supplemented by new information on the MLA Web site,* describe the information you need for Works Cited entries for electronic sources. You need to distinguish between electronic sources that are "portable" (CD-ROMs and diskettes, for example) and online sources. You need to give information about the print version of any electronic source that has a print version. And you need to give the electronic address, or URL, for any online source that has one.

Here is a list of the basic information to provide for an electronic source: name of author (if any), publication information for a print version (if any), database title, publication medium (CD-ROM, for example), name of the producer (for portable sources), computer network or service (for online sources), electronic publication date (portable) or access date (online), and URL (if any).

To see the differences in an entry for a portable and an online source, compare items 43 and 44. They show a Works Cited entry for the same abstract from *Psychological Abstracts.* Item 43 documents the source accessed through PsycLIT, a CD-ROM version, and item 44 documents online access via the computer service CompuServe to the same source in the online database, named PsycINFO.

*See page 546 for the URL.

43. CD-ROM Database: Abstract with a Print Version—MLA

Marcus, Hazel R., and Shinobu Kitayamo. "Culture and the
    Self: Implications for Cognition, Emotion, and
    Motivation." Psychological Abstracts 78 (1991): item
    23878. PsycLIT. CD-ROM. SilverPlatter. Sept. 1991.

This model shows a portable database of information that also appears in a print version and that is updated from time to time. The information units for such a source start with the print version, followed by information about the electronic version. This source is an abstract from *Psychological Abstracts.* The information following the title *Psychological Abstracts* is the volume number and year and the item number of the abstract in the print version. PsycLIT is the name of the CD-ROM database, and SilverPlatter is the name of the producer of the CD-ROM. The database was issued in September 1991. Compare this entry with item 44, for this source accessed online.

44. Online Database: Abstract with a Print Version—MLA

Marcus, Hazel R., and Shinobu Kitayamo. "Culture and the
    Self: Implications for Cognition, Emotion, and
    Motivation." Psychological Abstracts 78 (1991): item
    23878. PsycINFO. Online. CompuServe. 10 Oct. 1991.

This entry is for the same abstract from *Psychological Abstracts* shown in item 43 but accessed online. This model notes PsycINFO, the name of the online database, where item 43 notes PsycLIT, the name of the CD-ROM database. It uses *Online* where the model in item 43 uses *CD-ROM.* Access was through a computer service, so this model uses *CompuServe* where item 43 uses *SilverPlatter.* In both entries, 78 is the volume number of the print version of *Psychological Abstracts,* and item 23878 is the abstract number in the print version. The date on which the abstract was accessed is October 10, 1991.

45. CD-ROM: Article from a Magazine with a Print Version—MLA

"The Price Is Right." Time 20 Jan. 1992: 38. Time Man of
    the Year. CD-ROM. Compact Publishing 1993.

The information common to both the CD-ROM version and the print version comes first. After the publication date for the print version comes a colon, followed by the page number for the print version, 38. The title of the CD-ROM is *Time Man of the Year,* its producer is Compact Publishing, Inc., and its copyright year is 1993. Underline both the title of the print publication and the title of the CD-ROM.

Portfolios *(continued)*

should allow for sensible implementation and yet maintain the diversity of instructional and learning needs. This is just one approach that has proved workable; feel free to design your own program.

Diagnostic Portfolio (Weeks 1–4)
This portfolio is created during the early weeks of the term through the assembly of all early work, which could include everything from in-class and formal writing assignments to journal entries to text and class notes. The whole point of this phase is to provide a clear, written record of the student's current abilities and commitment. This means that students must reflect (in a cover essay) on the implications of their work by analyzing their grades and teachers' comments to set individual goals to be fulfilled throughout the remainder of the semester. This process is a modified application of the scientific method (see Chart 160).

Working Portfolio (Weeks 5–13)
This portfolio contains *all* the work produced during the semester (except, of course, for the work already housed in the Diagnostic Portfolio): all formal and informal writing assignments, all prewriting and drafts, and any independent work on individual needs identified in the Diagnostic Portfolio such as grammar remediation. The Working Portfolio could also contain all work associated with the research project, such as bibliography and note cards and photocopies of articles. The purpose of this phase in the portfolio process is to document progress and commitment and the relationship between the two. This does, indeed, profile time on task. In fact, this is the phase that clearly illustrates the relationship between quantity and quality of work.

Display Portfolio (Weeks 14–16)
This portfolio contains best works only. Therefore, the only pieces in this phase will be clean, polished drafts of writing

→

Portfolios (continued)

produced and chronicled in the previous portfolio phases. The only new work in this section will be the final reflection essay that discusses in depth the student's achievement and establishes the evidence of the grade desired by the student. This discussion should include references to the work contained in both of the other portfolios.

SHARPENING THE LISTENING-READING-WRITING CONNECTION

Portfolios offer a structured, systematic "reading in the content course" approach. Indeed, the success of portfolio assessment rests in the comforting roots of its pedagogy, the synergistic relationship among listening, reading, and writing. Understanding this fundamental connection as used in portfolio assessment will make for effective and exciting results. Foster student's critical reading skills by asking them to pay attention to the purpose of each assignment, your feedback, and the textbook's information. For example, the Diagnostic Portfolio not only establishes preexisting abilities and becomes a measuring tool for future growth and reflection but also quickly establishes the ongoing connection among listening, reading, and writing.

Using a variety of early-semester learning activities—such as in-class and take-home writing assignments, teacher feedback and scores, interest and behavior inventories, a diagnostic grammar test, and class notes—ask students to discuss their strengths and needs by providing a set of reflective questions (see "Student Reflection" on pages 576–578). Once the student has identified an individual list of needs, require a textbook recognizance for the solutions for each problem, and have the student create a study plan based on the pages required to study, projected amount of time needed to study, and ways to measure mastery of *each* skill need. Notice that the student has had to actually *read* teacher

46. CD-ROM: Selection from a Book with a Print Version—MLA

"Prehistoric Humans: Earliest Homo Sapiens." Guinness Book
    of Records, London: 1994. Guinness Publishing, 1994.
    Guinness Multimedia Disk of Records, 1994 ed. Vers.
    2.0. CD-ROM. Danbury, CT: Grolier Electronic
    Publishing, 1994.

The information about the book version ends after the publisher and year and information about the CD-ROM version begins. *Vers. 2.0* signals that this CD-ROM is updated periodically; the producer changes version numbers rather than giving update dates.

47. CD-ROM: Material with No Print Version—MLA

"Spanish Dance." Encarta, 1994 ed. CD-ROM. Redmond:
    Microsoft, 1993.

Encarta is a CD-ROM encyclopedia with no print version. "Spanish Dance" is the title of an article in this encyclopedia.

48. CD-ROM: Nonperiodical Publication—MLA

Wick, James, and Dave Jackson. Wayzata World Factbook, 1993
    ed. CD-ROM. Wayzata, MN: Wayzata Technology, 1992.

When authors are named, treat the names as for a print publication.

World Atlas MPC. Vers. 3.2. CD-ROM. Novato: Software
    Toolworks, 1992.

49. Work in More Than One Publication Medium—MLA

Some sources come in more than one medium: a book and a CD, a disk and a video, a CD and a laserdisk. As for other electronic sources, give as much information as available, separating it into information blocks for each medium.

Clarke, David James, IV. Novell's CNE Study Guide. Book.
    Network Support Encyclopedia. CD-ROM. Alameda: Sybex,
    1994.

This book and this CD-ROM come together. They have different titles, but the publication information—*Alameda: Sybex, 1994*—applies to both.

Diskettes and magnetic tape are two other "portable" electronic media. For them, use the same kinds and patterns of information shown for CD-ROMs, except write *Diskette* or *Magnetic tape* for the publication medium.

50. Online: Article from a Newspaper with a Print Version—MLA

```
Johnson, Dirk. "For Many Americans, Nothing but Blue Skies."
     New York Times 14 Jan. 1998. New York Times on America
     Online. America Online. 14 Dec. 1998.
```

Although there is a print version of the *New York Times,* the online version does not provide information about where the Johnson article appears in the print version. *New York Times on America Online* is the name of the database, which was accessed through the computer service America Online. The date *14 Jan. 1998* at the end tells when the article was accessed. See item 56 for an article from an online newspaper on the Web.

51. Online: Article from a Magazine with a Print Version—MLA

```
"Homeowners Insurance." Consumer Reports Oct. 1993: n. pag.
     Online. CompuServe. 5 May 1995.
```

When an online source does not show page numbers even though a source has a print version, at the end of the information about the print version, put *n. pag.,* an abbreviation meaning "no pagination." This abbreviation in a Works Cited entry signals readers why page numbers are not given in parenthetical references to the source in your paper.

52. Online: Material with No Print Version—MLA

```
"Athenian-Spartan Rivalry." Academic American Encyclopedia.
     Online. CompuServe. 3 Feb. 1995.
```

53. Online: Material from an Electronic Newsletter—MLA

```
"Microsoft Licenses OSM Technology from Henter-Joyce."
     Microsoft WinNews Electronic Newsletter 2.6 (1 May
     1995): n. pag. Online. Internet. 15 May 1995.
```

The numerals *2.6* mean volume 2, number 6 of this electronic newsletter.

54. Online: Public Message—MLA—*NEW*

Be careful about using an online posting as a source. Some posts contain cutting-edge information from experts; some contain trash. To cite one, give the author name (if any), title of the message from the *Subject* line, and then *Online posting.* Then, give the date of the message, the name of the group or list, the access date, and location information.

```
Descher, Robert. "Ballooning Lessons." Online posting. 21
     Apr. 1997. Student Aviation Newsgroup. 1 June 1997
     <rec.aviation.students>.
```

Portfolios (continued)

comments, survey the textbook, establish prior knowledge, and use inference, prediction, and time management skills.

INSTRUCTOR FEEDBACK IN THE USE OF PORTFOLIO ASSESSMENT

Too often, teachers hold on to information that students really need. Portfolio assessment can be a tool to communicate this very information in a nonthreatening and motivational manner. Instructor feedback is a valuable communication opportunity. Generally speaking, feedback comes to the student in one of two ways: grades and teacher comments. Too often, students ignore the comments and are angered or discouraged by the grades. The portfolio process can help students make insightful connections between the two.

INDIVIDUAL ASSIGNMENTS

First, be sure that feedback never corrects the mistake but only identifies it. Use correction symbols (see "Response Symbols" at the back of this book) to identify the error; then ask students to look up the rule, pull the faulty sentence out of context for a grammar exercise, and explain why the rule applies and how to fix the error. In this way, feedback becomes an opportunity for a reflective journal entry.

If the paper is holistically scored, the score itself becomes the feedback, and students should be provided with a rubric or definition of what that score represents. The student is then required to analyze, in a reflective journal entry, the reasons the paper received the score it did, in addition to the ways in which the paper could be rewritten to improve it. Both holistic and trait scoring should then allow the student to *read the audience* by responding to the implications of the feedback.

PORTFOLIO FEEDBACK

Regardless of the kind of portfolio you implement, the scoring process can be a valuable opportunity to further the dialogue

→

Portfolios (continued)

between student and instructor, and it can be accomplished rather quickly with a score sheet. Simply identify beforehand (this is an excellent occasion to include the class's participation) the traits and characteristics you expect to observe at each grade level; then, create a checklist for each of those characteristics. Be sure to leave room for a section marked "Comments" for individual explanations of your score as needed. In this way, the scoring of portfolios can be a quick, holistic approach that provides meaningful feedback to the student.

PORTFOLIO SCORES

If you decide to use the three-phase portfolio, you have available three separate but distinct scores reflecting specific skills, strategies, and achievement that can be translated into percentages. Some instructors prefer to weight specific assignments within each portfolio. This weighted value can be included in the assessment score sheet. Again, the purpose of portfolios is to showcase the process as well as the product, so you want to create a scoring system that clearly and efficiently communicates your values.

STUDENT REFLECTION

The most crucial step in portfolio assessment is training students to think about their own work and instructor response to that work. This training occurs through the use of teacher-generated reflective questions about individual assignments as well as collections of assignments as in a portfolio. That means that these questions can be used to introduce or review concepts, track progress, and justify achievement. The following questions serve as models that can be adapted to fit the individual needs of a group, program, or student; actual questions should come from the teacher's observation of obstacles to achievement. Therefore, any of the charts in the tinted boxes can be turned into reflective journal entries to focus the student on an immediate and apparent need,

55. Online: E-Mail—MLA—*NEW*

Thompson, Jim. "Bob Martin's Address." E-mail to June Cain. 11 Nov. 1997.

Items 56–64 show new MLA Works Cited forms for online Web, FTP, and Gopher sources, as well as an MLA-style form for synchronous communication (MOOs and MUDs). What makes these Works Cited entries different from those for other online sources is the URL. If an online source has a URL, include it in angle brackets <like these> after the access date. Put the period ending the Works Cited entry after the angle bracket on the right of the URL.

You may not be able to find all the information suggested for a Web-source Works Cited entry. If you cannot find what you need on the page you are using, look for a *Home* button, and check on the page it takes you to (see page 577).

56. Online: Article from a Newspaper on the Web—MLA—*NEW*

Lewis, Ricki. "Chronobiology Researchers Say Their Field's Time Has Come." Scientist 9.24 (1995): 14. 30 Dec. 1997 <http://www.the-scientist.library.upenn.edu/ yr1995/dec/chrono_951211.html>.

The Scientist is an online newspaper with no print version. The volume, issue, and page number—9, 24, and 14—were at the end of the article. Also look at item 50 for an article from a newspaper with a print version, accessed through a computer service.

57. Online: Interview from a Magazine on the Web with a Print Version—MLA—*NEW*

Kincaid, Jamaica. Interview. "Jamaica Kincaid Hates Happy Endings." By Marilyn Snell. Mother Jones. Sept.—Oct. 1997. 15 Jan. 1998 <http://www.mojones.com/ mother_jones/SO97/snell.html>.

The name of the person interviewed comes first. *Mother Jones* is the print magazine's title. The interview, conducted by Marilyn Snell, appeared in the September–October issue of *Mother Jones*. The article is archived on the Web at the given URL.

58. Online: Article from a Journal Available Only on the Web—MLA—*NEW*

Anderson, Virginia. "The Usual Suspects." Computers, Writing, Rhetoric and Literature 2.1 (1996): 25 pars. 15 Jan. 1998 <http://www.cwrl.utexas.edu/~cwrl/v2nl/ v.anderson/anderson.html>.

A Modular Approach to Teaching the World Wide Web

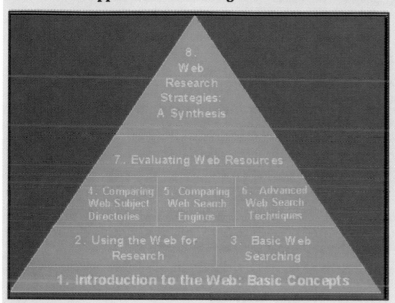

8.
Web
Research
Strategies:
A Synthesis

7. Evaluating Web Resources

4. Comparing Web Subject Directories 5. Comparing Web Search Engines 6. Advanced Web Search Techniques

2. Using the Web for Research 3. Basic Web Searching

1. Introduction to the Web: Basic Concepts

Introduction to the Web: Basic Concepts | Using the Web for Research | Basic Web Searching | Comparing Web Subject Directories | Comparing Web Search Engines | Advanced Web Search Techniques | Evaluating Web Resources | Web Research Strategies: A Synthesis

This pyramid consists of **eight self-contained modules** which can be used for Web instruction.

- **Modules 1 through 3** provide basic tools for using the Web.
- **Modules 4 through 8** build upon the foundation set forth in the first three modules.
- The modules, intended for classroom use, can be used individually or in combination and may be modified as appropriate, depending on the needs of the audience.
- Each module includes:
  - Goals for the lesson module.
  - Teaching materials to accompany the lesson module.
  - Suggested methods for teaching the module.

These materials were designed by Mike Powell, Marsha Tate, and Jan Alexander, Reference Librarians at the Wolfgram Memorial Library, Widener University. The teaching pyramid and the eight modules provide the basis for a *President's Showcase of Ideas* poster session at the June, 1997 American Library Association Conference in San Francisco.

Copyright Widener University 1997
J. Alexander, J. Powell & M. A. Tate: March 1997
Date Mounted on Server: March 1997
Last Revised: 30 May 1997

typical places to look for information you need for documentation

Finding Documentation Information on a Web Page

Portfolios (continued)

yet the best source for reflective questions is the behavior of the students in both cognitive and affective domains.

Reflective Questions for Diagnostic Portfolios

Describe your current writing process.

Has your writing process changed in any way?

How long do you spend writing an essay?

In what ways do you use your textbook?

What information learned in class has helped you the most so far?

What do you like or dislike about writing?

Which is your strongest piece of writing (in-class or take-home) and why?

What is the relationship between your performance on the grammar test and your writing scores?

Based on the grammar test and teacher feedback, what do you need to study?

How many pages in the handbook do these skills cover?

How long do you think you need to study each skill?

How will you measure your mastery of these skills?

What is your plan of study?

How will you use your textbooks?

What is your greatest strength as a writer?

Reflective Questions for Working and Display Portfolios

Describe your current writing process and the ways in which it has changed from the beginning of the semester.

In what ways did your Diagnostic Portfolio indicate your needed improvement?

How did you ensure mastery of these skills and concepts?

→

Portfolios (continued)

How does the Display Portfolio reflect the goals set in the Diagnostic Portfolio?

How does the Display Portfolio reflect the effort exhibited in the Working Portfolio?

Why did you choose these pieces for your Display Portfolio?

How do they represent growth?

Summarize your learning—just what have you learned, and how do your portfolios reflect this learning?

What do you still need to learn?

If you did not achieve certain diagnostic goals, explain how you will ensure mastery of these needs in the next level of study.

What grade do these portfolios indicate you have earned? Explain your judgment.

For cover letters and journal entries, reflection will be an ongoing informal process much as for a journal entry; however, formal self-assessment is the cornerstone of the portfolio. In the three-phase portfolio approach, there are two cover letters: one included the Diagnostic Portfolio and one included in the Display Portfolio. These are formal and should be polished, best works. This is an excellent opportunity to incorporate business writing skills.

PORTFOLIO HINTS

To ensure the maximum benefit of portfolio assessment, the following guidelines may be helpful.

What Students Should Do

- Date and label everything. Dating and labeling will show when and where success occurred.
- Reflect frequently. Students have to learn how to think, so they need frequent practice in written reflection. Also, individual reflections become the prewrites for the cover letters.

59. Online: Electronic Text on the Web—MLA—*NEW*

```
Herodotus. The History of Herodotus. Trans. George
     Rawlinson. The Internet Classics Archive. Ed. Daniel C.
     Stevenson. 11 Jan. 1998. Massachusetts Institute of
     Technology. 17 Jan. 1998 <http://classics.mit.edu/
     Herodotus/history.sum.html>.
```

This is the kind of Works Cited entry you are likely to need if you do research into literary works in archives you can access through the Web. Herodotus is the author of the work titled *The History of Herodotus. Trans.* stands for "Translated by." The database in which this work was found—its title underlined, just like the title of the work—is *The Internet Classics Archive*, a database "sponsored" by the Massachusetts Institute of Technology. The date of January 11, 1998, appeared on the home page of *The Internet Classics Archive* as the date of the most recent update. The text was accessed on January 17, 1998.

60. Online: Organization Home Page—MLA—*NEW*

```
"LEARN@PZ." Project Zero. Home page. Harvard Graduate School
     of Education. 17 Jan. 1998 <http://pzweb.harvard.edu/
     default.htm>.
```

LEARN@PZ is the title of the home page for *Project Zero*, sponsored by the Harvard Graduate School of Education.

61. Online: Personal Home Page—MLA—*NEW*

```
Hunter-Kilmer, Melissa. Home page. 15 Feb. 1996. 17 Jan.
     1998 <http://www.idsonline.com/userweb/phantom/
     index.htm>.
```

62. Online: FTP Site—MLA—*NEW*

```
Beck, Alan. "Glass, a Fractal gif." 2 July 1994.
     Archive ftp.sunet.se. Swedish University Network
     SUNET. 13 Jan. 1998 <ftp://ftp.sunet.se/pub/
     pictures/fractals/>.
```

Alan Beck created the graphic image titled "Glass, a Fractal gif." The image is stored (archived) at *ftp.sunet.se*. This archive of graphic images is sponsored by and stored in the Swedish University network SUNET. The URL is for the specific image. MLA's new guidelines call for the URL of FTP-archived material to be given in angle brackets after the access date.

MLA MLA MLA MLA MLA MLA MLA MLA MLA MLA MLA MLA MLA MLA

63. Online: Gopher Site—MLA—*NEW*

"Petshop." Transcribed by Bret Shefter 28 Mar. 1986, rev.
   Malcolm Dickinson 3 Apr. 1986. From <u>Monty Python's</u>
   <u>Flying Circus</u> and <u>And Now for Something Completely</u>
   <u>Different</u>. <u>The Monty Python Gopher</u>. 13 Jan. 1998
   <gopher://gopher.ocf.berkeley.edu/00.Library/
   Monty_Python/petshop%09%09%2B>.

This entry is for a script titled "Petshop," used in two Monty Python productions and archived in *The Monty Python Gopher* (the underlined titled). The Gopher site is a collection of the text of *Monty Python* scripts transcribed from tapings of television shows. No information appears about the writers of the scripts, performance dates, performers, or other information you would have if the script were printed in a book or if you saw it performed. For an electronic source like this one, give whatever useful information you can find, such as the name of the original transcriber and the person who revised the first transcript. Be sure to include the URL as you would for a source you found on the Web. MLA's new guidelines call for the URL of Gopher-archived material to be given in angle brackets after the access date.

64. Online: Synchronous Communication—MLA-type—*NEW*

The MLA has not announced a format for real-time computer-mediated communications (MUDs and MOOs). As for the senders of e-mail and other online postings, the person you communicate with in a MUD or a MOO is not necessarily who he or she claims to be, thus making that person a possibly unreliable source of information. If, knowing that, you use such communications in your paper, you can use the form here for your Works Cited list.

Bleck, Bradley. DaMOO. "Virtual First Year Composition:
   Distance Education, the Internet, and World Wide Web."
   8 June 1997. California State University Northridge. 27
   Feb. 1998 <http://DaMOO.csun.edu/CW/brad.html>.

This Works Cited entry cites Bradley Bleck as the speaker in the MOO session. For a parenthetical in-text reference, use (Bleck).

33c.4 Using content or bibliographic notes in MLA style

In MLA style, footnotes or endnotes serve two specific purposes: (1) You can use them for content (ideas and information) that does not fit into your paper but is still worth relating, and (2) you can use them for bibliographic information that would intrude if you were to include it in your text.

Portfolios (continued)

- Revise and resubmit work frequently. Students need to see that work does improve with effort. To minimize your workload, encourage peer editing of drafts, and use holistic scoring and rubrics whenever possible.

What Instructors Might Need to Do

- Encourage cross-curriculum connections. Students too often don't understand that writing is a tool for success in other courses. If possible, allow students to submit work required in other classes along with reflections discussing the impact of their writing instruction in other academic situations.
- Publish rubrics for the portfolio itself. Students need to understand the criteria, so short paragraphs describing an A, B, C, D, or F portfolio should enhance success. These standards may include criteria about work habits as well as the work product (timeliness, neatness, etc.).
- Require a specified length for the cover letters to ensure in depth details.
- Clarify the relationship between the cover essays and the portfolios. For the process offered here, there are only two cover letters: one placed in the Diagnostic Portfolio and one placed in the Display Portfolio (which actually discusses the work in all three portfolio phases).
- Confer frequently with the student and the student's portfolio. These conferences don't have to take much time because of the evidence of the student's work. Be sure to have the student take notes of any advice given during the conference as a portfolio entry.
- Place the workload on the student whenever possible. The more work students do, the more they learn.

RESEARCH: PORTFOLIO APPROACHES AND ACTIVITIES

The research project offers a sound opportunity for a task-oriented, self-contained portfolio or a rich selection for a program or class portfolio. Obviously, the research process requires the student to synthesize multiple correlate skills and concepts. By carefully dating, labeling, and reflecting on this sophisticated reading and writing task, students can see, refine, and deepen learning before, during, and after various strategic stages of the process. The pivotal components of portfolio assessment that delineate it from traditional assessments are student reflection and input. Students must assume the responsibility of creating and defending the meaning and quality of the learning taking place.

Reading-Writing Connection

Place the responsibility for learning by reiterating the reading-writing connection. The technical aspects of the research format and the density of the instructional material strain the functional and textual reading abilities of many students. Well-guided reflection can activate reading strategies such as previewing, skimming, and questioning and provide dated portfolio entries.

Provide five to ten minutes of class time for the students to skim the entire chapter and to record impressionistic responses to the following prompts: Record your first reaction to this material. What seems clear to you? What confuses you? Which sections seem most important and why? Write out five questions, and rank them from dumb to important. How much time do you need to study this chapter to understand the material and why? When will you do this studying?

Using the Reporter's Questions in Reflecting and Researching

Keep the instructional responsibility on the student by using the tinted charts as the basis of reflective informal journals.

TEXT OF PAPER

Eudora Welty's literary biography, <u>One Writer's Beginnings</u>, shows us how both the inner world of self and the outer world of family and place form a writer's imagination.[1]

CONTENT NOTE—MLA

[1] Welty, who values her privacy, has resisted investigation of her life. However, at the age of seventy-four, she chose to present her own autobiographical reflections in a series of lectures at Harvard University.

TEXT OF PAPER

Barbara Randolph believes that enthusiasm is contagious (65).[1] Many psychologists have found that panic, fear, and rage spread more quickly in crowds than positive emotions do, however.

BIBLIOGRAPHIC NOTE—MLA

[1] Others who agree with Randolph include Thurman 21, 84, 155; Kelley 421–25; and Brookes 65–76.

❶ MLA FORMAT ALERT: Place a note number at the end of a sentence, if possible. Put it after any punctuation mark except the dash. Do not put any space before a note number, and put one space after it. In typed papers, raise the note number a little above the line of words. In word-processing programs, use superscript numbers. **❗**

To see more examples of MLA-style content notes and the page format for endnotes, see the student research paper in section 34b.

33d Using APA-style documentation

The American Psychological Association (APA) endorses a name-year parenthetical reference documentation system that is used in its journals and has come to be used by students in the social sciences and some other disciplines. APA in-text citations alert readers to material you have used from outside sources. These citations function with an alphabetical References list at the end of your paper containing information that enables readers to retrieve the sources you have quoted from (see 31c), paraphrased (see 31d), or summarized (see 31e).

33d.1 Citing sources in the body of a paper in APA style

In-text citations identify a source by a name (usually an author name) and a year (for copyrighted sources, usually the copyright year). You can often incorporate the relevant name, and sometimes the year, into your sentence. Otherwise, put this information in parentheses, placing the parenthetical reference so that a reader knows exactly what it refers to and is distracted by it as little as possible.

The APA *Publication Manual* recommends that if you refer to a work more than once in a paragraph, you give the author name and date the first time that you mention the work, and then give only the name after that. There is one exception: If you are citing two or more works by the same author, each citation must include the date so that a reader knows which work is being cited.

APA style requires page numbers for direct quotations only (not for paraphrases or summaries).* However, some instructors expect page references for any use made of sources, so find out your instructor's preference. Put page numbers in parentheses, using the abbreviation *p.* before a single page number and *pp.* when the material you are citing falls on more than one page. Item 1 below, Citing a Paraphrased or Summarized Source—APA, shows citations of a paraphrased source both using and omitting the page number.

1. Citing a Paraphrased or Summarized Source—APA

People from the Mediterranean prefer an elbow-to-shoulder distance from each other (Morris, 1977). [Name and date cited in parentheses.]

Desmond Morris (1977, p. 131) notes that people from the Mediterranean prefer an elbow-to-shoulder distance from each other. [Name cited in text, date and page cited in parentheses.]

2. Citing the Source of a Short Quotation—APA

A recent report of reductions in SAD-related "depression in 87 percent of patients" (Binkley, 1990, p. 203) reverses the findings of earlier studies. [Name, date, and page reference in parentheses immediately following the quotation.]

Binkley reports reductions in SAD-related "depression in 87 percent of patients" (1990, p. 203). [Name incorporated into the words introducing the quotation and date and page number in parentheses immediately following the quotation.]

---

*When a source is no more than one page long, the page number is included in information about the source in the References list. Therefore, it is unnecessary to repeat the page number in the in-text citation.

Research: Portfolios (continued)

For example, certain items in Chart 141 in section 32b, combined with the exemplified research log in section 32c, provide excellent roots for reflective questions and answers.

Item 2 "Choose a topic suitable for research," could be presented as a two- to three-minute class opener to establish prior knowledge and preview the lesson in the following manner: What would be a suitable topic for research and why? What topics would you like to learn and read about? Does this topic have two sides? Which side do you presently support and why?

Item 6 "Learn how to evaluate sources," could yield a subsequent set of questions: Where would information on this topic likely to be found? Who would be best qualified to offer an opinion and why? How many different types of sources might be available? Where and how could you locate these sources?

This procedural model yields as many questions for lively class discussion and quiet written reflection as you have time for in your curriculum. Choose your own focus and create questions that help students connect the function, form, and processes of learning activities to knowledge.

Research Portfolio: Task-Oriented, Self-Contained Profile of a Student Researcher

The following information can be quickly and easily translated into a research portfolio overview handout. Such a handout provides the student with a reference document throughout the learning and assessment process. However, many of the question, reflection, and writing activities may be assigned in an ongoing fashion through daily, informal journals that can, by design, preview, reinforce, or review specific steps in the research process. To reinforce the relationship among reading, listening, speaking, and writing, try scheduling some time for small group and whole class discussion as talk-aloud reflections. Sponsor a "hallway bull session" in class;

Research: Portfolios (continued)

just remind students to record their questions and understandings.

Before research begins, establish prior knowledge and stimulate learning readiness by asking students to record reflections in any or all of the following ways: Briefly describe your research history—how many times have you researched? How will information already learned in this class help in the research process? What are the purposes of research? What was the required documentation style? Describe your success with the process. Describe your struggles with the process. Describe your preferred method of research.

As research proceeds, encourage students to track and document every minute spent on research by dating and recording reflections on any or all of the following topics (you may wish to reword these prompts in language appropriate for your student audience):

- Concepts: What is the value of your topic—who cares or needs to know about it? What is its value to the audience? What are the inherent biases for or against the topic? What propaganda techniques are used by opposing sides of this topic, if any, and how are they employed? Record and describe new understandings or changed views as you research. What action, if any, do you want from your reader?

- Procedures: Date and record questions that occur to you as you listen to instruction and lectures, hunt for proper formats in the textbook, create bibliography and note cards, and then apply the style rules to your paper. Date, record and label answers to your questions as you learn them. Using as a model Chart 141 in section 32b, present your own step-by-step research process. Discuss why you might implement your own adaptations of textbook- or lecture-given procedures. This procedure can be quickly refined into an additional five minutes of quickly written reflections that create a daily record of the attention you are giving to your studies. →

3. Formatting a Long Quotation and Citing Its Source—APA

Incorporate a direct quotation of fewer than 40 words into your own sentence and enclose it in quotation marks. Place the parenthetical citation after the closing quotation mark and, if the quotation falls at the end of the sentence, before the sentence-ending punctuation. When you use a quotation longer than 40 words, set it off from your own words by starting it on a new line and indenting each line of the quotation five spaces from the left margin. Do not enclose it in quotation marks. Place the parenthetical citation two spaces after the end punctuation of the last sentence.

DISPLAYED QUOTATION (40 OR MORE WORDS)

```
Jet lag, with its characteristic fatigue and irregular sleep
patterns, is a common problem among those who travel great
distances by jet airplane to different time zones:
     Jet lag syndrome is the inability of the internal
     body rhythm to rapidly resynchronize after sudden
     shifts in the timing. For a variety of reasons, the
     system attempts to maintain stability and resist
     temporal change. Consequently, complete adjustment
     can often be delayed for several days--sometimes for a
     week--after arrival at one's destination. (Bonner,
     1991, p. 72)
Interestingly, this research shows that the number of flying
hours is not the cause of jet lag.
```

The following examples show how to handle parenthetical citations for various sources. Remember, though, that you often can introduce source names, including titles when necessary, and sometimes even years in your own sentences.

4. Citing One Author—APA

```
One of his questions is "What binds together a Mormon
banker in Utah with his brother, or other coreligionists in
Illinois or Massachusetts?" (Coles, 1993, p. 2).
```

In a parenthetical reference in APA style, a comma and a space separate a name from a year and a year from a page reference. (Examples 1 through 4 also show citations of works by one author.)

5. Citing Two Authors—APA

If a work has two authors, give both names in each citation.

APA APA APA APA APA APA APA APA APA APA APA APA APA

One report describes 2,123 occurrences (Krait & Cooper, 1994).

The results Krait and Cooper (1994) report would not support the conclusions Davis and Sherman (1992) draw in their review of the literature.

When citing two (or more) authors, use an ampersand (&) between the (final) two names in parenthetical references, but write out the word *and* for references in your own sentence.

6. Citing Three, Four, or Five Authors—APA

For three, four, or five authors, use all the authors' last names in the first reference. In all subsequent references, use only the first author's last name followed by *et al.*

FIRST REFERENCE

In one anthology, 35% of the selections had not been anthologized before (Elliott, Kerber, Litz, & Martin, 1992).

SUBSEQUENT REFERENCE

Elliott et al. (1992) include 17 authors whose work has never been anthologized.

7. Citing Six or More Authors—APA

For six or more authors, use the name of the first author followed by *et al.* for all references, including the first.

8. Citing Author(s) with Two or More Works in the Same Year—APA

If you use more than one source written in the same year by the same author(s), alphabetize the works by their titles for the References list, and assign letters in alphabetical order to the years—(1996a), (1996b), (1996c). Use the year-letter combination in parenthetical references. Note that a citation of two or more of such works lists the years in alphabetical order.

Most recently, Jones (1996c) draws new conclusions from the results of 17 sets of experiments (Jones, 1996a, 1996b).

9. Citing Two or More Authors with the Same Last Name—APA

Include first initials for every in-text citation of authors who share a last name. Use the initials appearing in the Reference list.

R. A. Smith (1997) and C. Smith (1989) both confirm these results.

Research: Portfolios (continued)

- Technology: Date, record, and label the ways in which technology enhanced or complicated your work. Do you have access to a computer or word processor? How often and in what ways do you use the library's or learning center's computerized databases? How often and in what ways do you use the Internet? Discuss the ease or frustration of your experiences. What are the greatest benefits of computers in the research writing process?

Once research concludes, ask students to determine the value of their work by assigning themselves a grade and then defending that grade through a formal reflective summary and synthesis of learning activities, growth, and mastery. Remember, the following questions only serve as models; experiment and create your own questions that mirror your instructional emphasis

- Concepts: Readdress relevant questions asked before research began with the intent to demonstrate dynamic understanding. Also include a discussion about things you still need to learn as evidenced in the portfolio: In what ways would you improve your use of the research process? This paper? What still confuses you? Based on feedback and grades, what do you still need to learn? How would you do so, if given the chance? Record and reflect on the connections between research and writing strategies learned earlier in the term. For example, discuss the way in which the use of verbs helped you integrate source material into your prose (see 31f and 32c).
- Procedures: Discuss the effectiveness of note and bibliography cards (see 32j.2 and 33b). In what way does your portfolio reflect the use and value of your various sources (32f.1)? Describe your search strategy and its success (32h). Discuss why you implemented your own adaptations of textbook- or lecture-given

procedures. How have research skills developed study skills? How are these skills relevant to other courses, life, or career?

- Technology: What new technological knowledge or skills did you gain? What are the pitfalls or limitations of technology?

Creating a Research Process Profile

This approach allows students to showcase their growing understanding and mastery of the research process. Encourage students to chronicle the research process through a show-and-tell technical report that demonstrates skills and applications and discusses procedural decisions and the impact of those decisions. Consider, for example, the following series of steps and journal reflections:

1. Create a registry that logs and tracks sources (see 32f and Chart 144).

2. Create and catalog bibliography cards (33b).

3. Provide sample photocopies or printouts of sources.

4. Use these to identify and highlight possible ideas for note cards.

5. Create and label note cards (32j.2).

6. Reclassify cards into outline order (32s).

7. Write a draft from the note cards rearranged into outline order (32t).

8. Complete the writing process.

9. Write an informal research summary reflection. It should describe your individual adaptations or variations from the expected procedures; describe the relationship between steps in the procedure; discuss challenges, understandings, and rewards met through this process; and discuss the specific new knowledge and fact versus opinion, authoritative sources, notetaking, and synthesis skills. In what way does this profile prove your mastery and the grade you seek? (See Chart 149 for a model that can be adapted. A sample sentence may read, "This researcher worked with her notes in front of her.")

These results have been confirmed independently (C. Smith, 1989; R. A. Smith, 1997).

10. Citing a Group or Corporate Author—APA

If you use a source in which the "author" is a corporation, agency, or group, an in-text reference gives that name as author. Use the full name in each citation unless an abbreviated version of the name is likely to be familiar to your audience. In that case, use the full name and give its abbreviation at the first citation; then, use the abbreviation for subsequent citations.

This exploration will continue into the 21st century (National Aeronautics and Space Administration [NASA], 1996).

In subsequent citations, you can then use the abbreviated form.

11. Citing Works by Title—APA

If no author is named, use a shortened form of the title in citations. Ignoring *A, An,* or *The,* make the first word the one by which you alphabetize the title in the References. The following citation is to an article fully titled "Are You a Day or Night Person?"

The "morning lark" and "night owl" connotations are typically used to categorize the human extremes ("Are You," 1989).

12. Citing More Than One Source in a Parenthetical Reference—APA

If more than one source has contributed to an idea or opinion in your paper, cite the sources alphabetically in one set of parentheses; separate each block of information with a semicolon.

Conceptions of personal space vary among cultures (Morris, 1977; Worchel & Cooper, 1983).

13. Citing a Personal Communication, Including E-Mail—APA

Telephone calls, personal letters, interviews, and e-mail messages are "personal communications" that your readers do not have access to. Acknowledge personal communications in parenthetical references, but do not include them in your References list. Because it is impossible to know whether e-mail was written by the person who claims to have written it, be careful about using e-mail as source material.

Recalling his first summer at camp, one person said, "The proximity of 12 other kids made me--an only child with older, quiet parents--frantic for the entire eight weeks" (A. Weiss, personal communication, January 12, 1996).

14. Citing Graphics—APA

If you include in your paper a graphic from another source, give a note in the text at the bottom of the table or graphic crediting the original author and the copyright holder. Here are examples of two source lines, one for a graphic from an article, the other for a graphic from a book. (If you plan to publish your document, you will need permission from the copyright holder to reproduce the table or graphic. You will also have to add a line such as *Reprinted* [or *Adapted*] *with permission.*)

GRAPHIC FROM AN ARTICLE

Note. From "Bridge over Troubled Waters? Connecting Research and Pedagogy in Composition and Business/Technical Communication," by J. Allen, 1992, Technical Communication Quarterly, 1(4), p. 9. Copyright 1992 by the Association of Teachers of Technical Writing.

GRAPHIC FROM A BOOK

Note. From How to Lower Your Fat Thermostat: The No-Diet Reprogramming Plan for Lifelong Weight Control (p. 74), by D. Remington, A. G. Fisher, and E. Parent, 1983, Provo, UT: Vitality House International. Copyright 1983 by Vitality House International.

33d.2 Compiling an APA-style References list

In APA documentation, in-text citations must be supported by a list of the sources referred to in your paper. Include in this References list the "recoverable" sources that you quote from, paraphrase, or summarize. A **recoverable source** is one that another person could retrieve with reasonable effort. Do not include in the References list any source not available to others, such as personal letters and other personal communications. (To alert readers to your use of such sources, you use a parenthetical citation marking the source as a personal communication; see, for example, item 34 about personal interviews.) Chart 153 summarizes information about the References list.

⊙ **Guidelines for compiling an APA-style References list**   **153**

■ **TITLE**

References

■ **PLACEMENT OF LIST**

Start a new page numbered sequentially with the rest of the paper, after Notes pages, if any.

➡

Research: Portfolios (continued)

10. Write a formal draft of the research reflection.

Creating a Research Skill Profile

This variation of the show-and-tell technical approach allows students to showcase and illustrate the relationship between building individual skills and the final product. Encourage students to target independent and individual needs and demonstrate goal setting, time on task, growing understanding, and, ultimately, mastery. Once the need is targeted, chronicle growth by creating a series of reflections based on the following steps:

1. Create a self-monitoring log or registry for daily work.

2. Survey instruction and feedback (scores and comments), and write a list of things you need to know to earn the desired grade (needs will run the gamut from time management to grammar to computer skills).

3. Locate print resources that address each item on the need-to-know list (take note of textbooks, libraries, learning centers), and set up a study system.

4. Locate nonprint resources that address each need to know (take note of computer software, tutors, peers, teacher conferences).

5. Set up a time line study schedule.

6. Create and organize print copies of each study session.

7. Label each study session with date, time spent on task, and purpose of task.

8. After each study session (or periodically), write an application reflection discussing how the information studied will improve research writing. Remember, voluminous practice produces skill, so reflect and write often.

9. As mastery of an individual skill is achieved, make a significant registry entry as proof or evidence of growth and reward.

10. Upon completion of the research project, write a final informal self-assessment

➡

Research: Portfolios (continued)

defending the value of your studies and the worth of your new information. Assign yourself a grade, and give evidence to support the worth of that judgment.

11. Write a final, formal draft to submit with the registry.

Portfolio Assessment as Action Research

Portfolios are wonderful research resources in themselves. Based on a shared curriculum and the sound pedagogy of self-monitoring for comprehension, the portfolio can be designed to explore specific contextual learning issues. For example, the ESL student or any special student population may be able to articulate successful study strategies that might be of benefit to other students. Sometimes, the complex issues surrounding testing and assessment clash with the instructional program or student needs; portfolios may offer a method of tracing and assessing these complex issues.

- *Portfolio research empowers teachers.* Remember that this reflective learning strategy will empower you, the instructor; quick, holistic reads and scores will provide a valuable and authentic tracking record of comprehension. The implications in research are numerous. For example, you may wish to document your own program's effectiveness by tracking the characteristics of the students' reflections, portfolio products, and grades to traditional or objective measurements such as GPA or standardized tests scores. Or if you want to track your teaching effectiveness in strategic lessons to ensure mastery, student reflections offer sound primary documents on which to base such assessments. Also, students reflect teacher values; if you ask meaningful questions that interest you, students will respond in kind.

- *Portfolio research empowers students.* The foundation skill of self-monitoring by creating a series of responses to

---

**Guidelines for compiling an APA-style
References list** *(continued)* **153**

- **CONTENTS AND FORMAT**

  Include all quoted, paraphrased, or summarized sources in your paper that are not personal communications, unless your instructor tells you to include all the references you have consulted, not just those you have referred to. Start each entry on a new line, and double-space all lines. At its Web site (see page 546 for the URL), the APA suggests that whether to use style 1 or 2 is a matter of instructor preference, so check which of the following indent styles your instructor wants you to use:

  1. First line of each entry indented, other lines full width. This style is shown in the APA manual. Indent the first line of each entry five to seven spaces (or one default tab, which is about an inch in most word-processing programs). If an entry has more than one line, make all lines after the first full width.

         Shuter, R. (1977). A field study of nonverbal
     communication in Germany, Italy, and the United
     States. <u>Communication Monographs, 44,</u> 298—305.

  2. First line of each entry full width, other lines indented. This "hanging indent" style makes source names and dates prominent. Type the first line of each entry full width, and indent an entry's subsequent lines five to seven spaces (or one tab).

     Shuter, R. (1977). A field study of nonverbal
         communication in Germany, Italy, and the
         United States. <u>Communication Monographs, 44,</u>
         298—305.

- **SPACING AFTER PUNCTUATION**

  The 1994 APA manual calls for one space after most punctuation marks: periods at the ends of information units in references (and at the ends of sentences in your paper), commas, semicolons, and colons (except in ratios in your paper [2:1, 100:1]).

- **ARRANGEMENT OF ENTRIES**

  Alphabetize by author's last name. If no author is named, alphabetize by the first significant word (not *A, An,* or *The*) in the title of the work.

Guidelines for compiling an APA-style References list *(continued)* 153

- **AUTHORS' NAMES**

  Use last names, first initials, and middle initials if any. Reverse the order for all author names, and use an ampersand (&) between the second-to-last and last authors: Mills, J. F., & Holahan, R. H.

  Give names in the order in which they appear on the work (title page of book, usually under title of article or other printed work). Use a comma between the first author's last name and first initial and after each complete author name except the last. After the last author name, use a period.

- **DATE**

  Put date information after name information, enclosing it in parentheses and using a period followed by one space after the closing parenthesis.

  For books, articles in journals that have volume numbers, and many other print and nonprint sources, the year of publication or production is the date to use. For articles from most magazines and newspapers, use the year followed by a comma and then the exact date appearing on the issue. Individual entries in section 32d.3 show how much information to give for various sources.

- **CAPITALIZATION OF TITLES**

  For books, capitalize the first word, the first word after a colon between a title and subtitle, and any proper nouns. For names of journals and proceedings of meetings, capitalize the first word, all nouns and adjectives, and any other words five or more letters long.

- **SPECIAL TREATMENT OF TITLES**

  Use no special treatment for titles of shorter works (poems, short stories, essays, articles). Underline titles of longer works (books, names of newspapers or journals containing cited articles). For underlining, use an unbroken line if possible. Check with your instructor before using italic type in place of underlining.

  Do not drop *A*, *An*, or *The* from the titles of periodicals (such as newspapers, magazines, and journals).

- **FORM DESCRIPTION**

  When a source is not a book or an article, a statement about its form is often useful for a reader who wants to retrieve the source. Enclose such form information in brackets, and include it

  ➡

Research: Portfolios (continued)

teacher prompts allows students the opportunity to teach themselves to see and solve problems. Sometimes, the very act of talking or writing through a problem provides insight or solution. Therefore, this ongoing self-assessment is of particular benefit to students who come to the college writing class with unrealistic expectations or scant preparation. Students eagerly accept the challenge to prove themselves by justifying the impact of mistakes or immaturity, then demonstrating the outcomes of changed behavior based on reflection and goal setting. In this sense, students will be studying themselves by observing, documenting, and explaining their behavior, your instruction, and feedback. However, the talented, gifted student also benefits through this process. Again and again, talented students exceed expectations and offer creative, stimulating models for peers.

Portfolio Hint

The student is the key. The student is the very center of instruction and, therefore, must demonstrate a strong work ethic to substantiate learning. Too many teachers fear assigning numerous writing assignments because of the volume of scoring. We all know that students do not do much work if the assignment is not to be graded. However, four components of portfolios fuel their success: clearly communicated standards, holistic scoring, organized independent work (homework), and student reflection. Student success courses warn students that for every hour spent in class, students must also spend three hours out of class working independently. Portfolios give that out-of-class work a framework that helps illuminate the relationship between work and knowledge. So give some class time early in the term to train students in reflection and journal writing, and then encourage them to assume full responsibility; expect them to do this, and they will!

BACKGROUND

Until the middle of the fifteenth century, the only books available to Europeans were handwritten manuscripts, which were costly and often inaccurate. The development of printing made books available to the common people for the first time.

The major breakthrough in the history of printing was the invention of movable type, the making of a stamp for each letter on a separate base so that the letters could be assembled to form a page. Although this system was already known in China and Korea (where it was little used because of the large number of Chinese characters and the lack of suitable ink), its discovery in Europe was made independently. Credit for the European development is given to Johann Gutenberg (c. 1400–1468). Although his "Gutenberg Bible," printed in 1455, was not his first printed work, it is his most famous one.

Today, it is often remarked that the world is going through another printing revolution. With the availability of copying machines, memory typewriters, word processing computer programs, and a variety of desktop printers, methods of producing printed material have undergone another major shift. Whereas only a few years ago having a document printed meant handing it over to a professional printer, today it is likely to be produced on equipment readily available in most offices and many homes.

Guidelines for compiling an APA-style References list *(continued)* 153

after the title and before the period at the end of the block of title information. Do not underline it. Electronically accessed sources should always have a form statement—for example, `[On-line]*` or `[CD-ROM]`. Also see items 41–49.

■ **PUBLISHER**

Use the full name of the publisher, but drop *Co., Inc., Publishers,* and the like. Retain *Books* or *Press.*

■ **PLACE OF PUBLICATION**

For publishers in the United States, give city and state (use the two-letter postal abbreviations listed in Chart 132 in section 30i) for all but the largest U.S. cities (such as Boston, Chicago, Los Angeles, and New York). For other countries, give city and country. However, if the state or country is mentioned in the publisher's name, omit it after the name of the city.

■ **PUBLICATION MONTH ABBREVIATIONS**

Do not abbreviate publication months.

■ **PAGE NUMBERS**

Use all digits, omitting none. *Only* for references to parts of books or material in newspapers, use *p.* and *pp.* before page numbers. List all discontinuous pages, with numbers separated by commas: `pp. 32, 44–45, 47–49, 53.`

■ **REFERENCES ENTRIES: BOOKS**

Citations for books have four main parts: author, date, title, and publication information (place of publication and publisher).

AUTHOR	DATE	TITLE
Didion, J.	(1977).	A book of common prayer.

PUBLICATION INFORMATION

New York: Simon & Schuster.

■ **REFERENCES ENTRIES: ARTICLES**

Citations for periodical articles contain four major parts: author, date, title of article, and publication information (usually, the periodical title, volume number, and page numbers).

*The word *online* is hyphenated in APA style, but not in MLA style or the style of this *Handbook.* →

Guidelines for compiling an APA-style References list *(continued)*   153

AUTHOR	DATE	ARTICLE TITLE

Shuter, R. (1977). A field study of nonverbal

communication in Germany, Italy, and the United

	PERIODICAL TITLE	VOLUME NUMBER	PAGE NUMBERS

States. Communication Monographs, 44, 298—305.

■ REFERENCES ENTRIES: ELECTRONIC SOURCES

The APA recommends giving information for print forms of sources when print and electronic forms are the same. For Web, FTP, and Gopher sources, give a *Retrieved from* statement with access date and URL. The basic elements of an electronically accessed source include author(s), date, title and form description (such as [On-line] or [CD-ROM]), periodical title and other information about a print version, producer and database name for a CD-ROM, retrieval statement with access date, and URL for sources that have them. Unlike MLA style, APA style *does not* enclose URLs in angle brackets.

Here are two typical entries for electronic sources. The first is for an abstract on CD-ROM, and the second is for a newspaper article found on the World Wide Web.

AUTHORS	DATE

Marcus, H. F., & Kitayamo, S. (1991).

ARTICLE TITLE

Culture and the self: Implications for group dynamics.

FORM DESCRIPTION	JOURNAL TITLE AND PUBLICATION INFORMATION

[CD-ROM]. Psychological Review, 88(2), 224, 253.

LOCATION INFORMATION

Abstract from: SilverPlatter File: PsycLIT Item:

78-23878

→

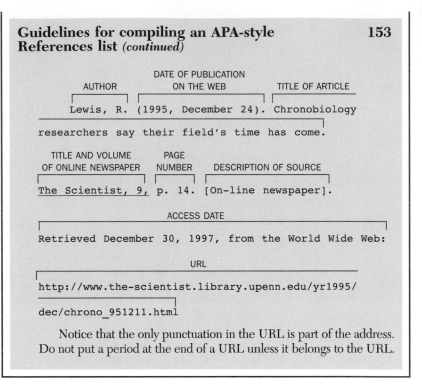

Guidelines for compiling an APA-style References list (*continued*) **153**

```
              DATE OF PUBLICATION
   AUTHOR        ON THE WEB        TITLE OF ARTICLE
   Lewis, R. (1995, December 24). Chronobiology
researchers say their field's time has come.

   TITLE AND VOLUME     PAGE
   OF ONLINE NEWSPAPER   NUMBER   DESCRIPTION OF SOURCE
   The Scientist, 9, p. 14. [On-line newspaper].

                    ACCESS DATE
   Retrieved December 30, 1997, from the World Wide Web:

                       URL
   http://www.the-scientist.library.upenn.edu/yr1995/
   dec/chrono_951211.html
```

Notice that the only punctuation in the URL is part of the address. Do not put a period at the end of a URL unless it belongs to the URL.

33d.3 Following models for an APA-style References list

Directory

PRINT SOURCES: BOOKS

1. Book by One Author—APA
2. Book by Two Authors—APA
3. Book by Three or More Authors—APA
4. Two or More Books by the Same Author(s)—APA
5. Book by Group or Corporate Author—APA
6. Book with No Author Named—APA
7. Book with an Author and an Editor—APA
8. Translation—APA
9. Work in Several Volumes or Parts—APA
10. Anthology or Edited Book—APA
11. One Selection from an Anthology or Edited Book—APA

QUOTATION: ON WRITING

We do not write in order to be understood; we write in order to understand.

—C. Day-Lewis

43. Online: Announcement Posted on the Web—APA—*NEW*
44. Online: Material from an FTP Site—APA—*NEW*
45. Online: Material from a Gopher Site—APA—*NEW*
46. Online Document Without a Print Version—APA
47. Computer Software—APA
48. Abstract on CD-ROM—APA
49. Information Services: ERIC and Newsbank—APA

Print sources: Books

1. Book by One Author—APA

Schaller, G. B. (1993). <u>The last panda.</u> Chicago: University of Chicago Press.

2. Book by Two Authors—APA

Smith, R. J., & Gibbs, M. (1994). <u>Navigating the Internet.</u> Indianapolis, IN: Sams.

3. Book by Three or More Authors—APA

McMahan, E., Day, S., & Funk, R. (1993). <u>Nine short novels by American women.</u> New York: St. Martin's Press.

Cameron, D., Frazer, E., Harvey, P., Rampton, M. B. H., & Richardson, K. (1992). <u>Researching language: Issues of power and method.</u> London: Routledge.

In an APA References list, include the last names and initials of all authors, even though in your paper you use only the first author's name when a work has six or more authors.

4. Two or More Books by the Same Author(s)—APA

Waller, R. J. (1992). <u>The bridges of Madison County.</u> New York: Warner Books.

Waller, R. J. (1993). <u>Slow waltz in Cedar Bend.</u> New York: Warner Books.

Waller, R. J. (1994). <u>Old songs in a new café.</u> New York: Warner Books.

Repeat the author name(s) for each entry. Arrange the entries by date, from least recent to most recent. To cite two or more works by the same author(s) in the same year, arrange those entries in alphabetical order by title, and then assign a letter to the year for each (for example, 1993a, 1993b, 1993c). In parenthetical citations, the letter following the year distinguishes one same-year source from another.

5. Book by Group or Corporate Author—APA

Environmental Defense Fund. (1990). <u>Recycling and incineration: Evaluating the choice.</u> Washington, DC: Island.

American Psychological Association. (1994). <u>Publication manual of the American Psychological Association</u> (4th ed.). Washington, DC: Author.

When a book is in an edition other than the first, include the edition number in parentheses after the title. Put the period at the end of the block of title information after the closing parenthesis (see also item 6).

6. Book with No Author Named—APA

<u>The Chicago manual of style</u> (14th ed.). (1993). Chicago: University of Chicago Press.

In your paper, use a shortened version of the title in parenthetical references (drop *A*, *An*, or *The* from a shortened title). Underline the words you use for a book title, and capitalize each significant word, even ones that start with lowercase letters in the References list: (Chicago Manual, 1993).

7. Book with an Author and an Editor—APA

Welty, E. (1994). <u>A writer's eye: Collected book reviews</u> (P. A. McHaney, Ed.). Jackson: University Press of Mississippi.

In an APA References list, always capitalize the abbreviation *Ed.* when it stands for *Editor* (or *Editors*). (Use a lowercase letter when *ed.* stands for *edition*, as in *Rev. ed.* or *2nd ed.*)

Note that the state abbreviation is omitted if the state is mentioned in the publisher's name.

8. Translation—APA

Dostoevsky, F. (1992). <u>Devils</u> (M. R. Katz, Trans.). Oxford, England: Oxford University Press.

9. Work in Several Volumes or Parts—APA

Rand, E. (1979). <u>Virology</u> (Vols. 1–5). Philadelphia: Lippincott.

QUOTATION: ON WRITING

[The writing process] is sort of like when you've got no electricity and you've gotten up in the middle of the night to find the bathroom, feeling your way along in the dark. I can't hardly tell you what I do because I really don't know.

—Carolyn Chute

Goldman, L. H., Cronin, C. L., & Aharoni, A. (1992). Twentieth-century American Jewish writers: Vol. 2. Saul Bellow: A mosaic. New York: Lang.

10. Anthology or Edited Book—APA

Lantolf, J. P., & Appel, G. (Eds.). (1994). Vygotskian approaches to second language research. Norwood, NJ: Ablex.

Spear, T., & Waller, R. (Eds.). (1993). Being Masai: Ethnicity and identity in East Africa. Athens: Ohio University Press.

11. One Selection from an Anthology or Edited Book—APA

Savitch, W. J. (1991). Infinity is in the eye of the beholder. In C. Georgopoulos & R. Ishihara (Eds.), Interdisciplinary approaches to language: Essays in honor of S. Y. Kuroda (pp. 487—500). Boston: Kluwer Academic.

12. Two Selections from One Anthology or Edited Book—APA

Blank, C. (Ed.). (1992). Language and civilization: A concerted profusion of essays and studies in honor of Otto Hietsch. Frankfurt-am-Main, Germany: Lang.

Middleton, M. (1992). A note on computer jargon. In C. Blank (Ed.), Language and civilization: A concerted profusion of essays and studies in honor of Otto Hietsch (pp. 732—739). Frankfurt-am-Main, Germany: Lang.

Give full publication information in each entry, whether for a selection or for the whole work. In selection entries, after the title of the main work, enclose page numbers for the selection in parentheses, followed by a period. In the main entry, the first information unit is the name of the editor or compiler of the collection. In an entry for each selection entry, the first unit is the name of the author of the selection.

13. Signed Article in a Reference Book—APA

Sax, J. L. (1994). Environmental law. In The encyclopedia Americana (International ed., Vol. 10, p. 488). Danbury, CT: Grolier.

14. Unsigned Article in a Reference Book—APA

    Russia. (1994). In <u>The new encyclopaedia Britannica</u>
(15th ed., Vol. 10, pp. 253–255). Chicago: Encyclopaedia
Britannica.

15. Edition—APA

    Walker, R. S. (1994). <u>AIDS today, tomorrow: An
introduction to the HIV epidemic in America</u> (2nd ed.).
Atlantic Highlands, NJ: Humanities Press.

16. Introduction, Preface, Foreword, or Afterword—APA

If the part of the book you are citing was written by the person who wrote the book, do the entry as you would for the entire work, with the following exceptions: If the part you are citing has a title, give it, without quotation marks or underlining, after the year (for example, a chapter title or the word *Preface, Foreword, Introduction, Afterword,* or *Appendix*). Then, give the title of the book, followed by parentheses enclosing the page numbers of the cited part and ending with a period after the closing parenthesis. Then, give publication information.

    Troyka, L. Q. (1999). Preface for ESL students. In
<u>Simon & Schuster handbook for writers</u> (5th ed., pp.
718–719). Upper Saddle River, NJ: Prentice Hall.

Page numbers can follow an edition number or a volume number in one set of parentheses; use a comma between the sets of information.

If the part you are citing does not have a special title, do the entry as you would for any book, but include page numbers in parentheses after the title. If the part you are citing was written by someone other than the person(s) who wrote the book, first give the name of the person who wrote the part, then give the date, and then give the title of the part. Then, write the word *In* followed by the name(s) of the book's author(s) or editor(s) in normal order, not reversed. Then, give the title of the book, page numbers of the relevant part in parentheses, and publication information.

    Diamond, J. (1994). Foreword. In W. S. Alverson,
W. Kuhlmann, & D. M. Waller, <u>Wild forests conservation
biology and public policy (p. iv).</u> Washington, DC: Island
Press.

17. Unpublished Dissertation or Essay—APA

    Black, L. J. (1993). <u>Language, power, and gender in
student-teacher conferences.</u> Unpublished doctoral
dissertation, Miami University, Oxford, OH.

EXTRA EXERCISE C

Using the same sources that appeared in Extra Exercise B, compile a References list, following APA style.

Answers to Extra Exercise C

References

Clarke, G. (1988). *Capote: A biography*. New York: Simon & Schuster.

Gould, S. J. (1987). *Time's arrow, time's cycle: Myth and metaphor in the discovery of geological time*. Cambridge, MA: Harvard University Press.

Hibbert, C. (1974). *The rise and fall of the House of Medici*. New York: Penguin Books.

Oates, S. B. (1984). *Abraham Lincoln: The man behind the myths*. New York: Harper & Row.

Peters, T. J., & Waterman, R. H., Jr. (1982). *In search of excellence*. New York: Harper & Row.

Sacks, O. (n.d.). The autist artist. In *The man who mistook his wife for a hat, and other clinical tales* (pp. 204–223). New York: Summit Books.

Smout, T. C. (1986). *A century of the Scottish people, 1830–1950*. New Haven, CT: Yale University Press.

Tuchman, B. W. (1981). *Practicing history*. New York: Knopf.

Stafford, K. M. (1993, January). Trapped in death and enchantment: The liminal space of women in three classical ballets. Paper presented at the annual meeting of the American Comparative Literature Association Graduate Student Conference, Riverside, CA.

18. Reprint of an Older Book—APA

Melville, H. (1992). Moby Dick, or The whale. New York: Modern Library. (Original work published 1851)

In the text, the citation would read Melville (1851/1992).

19. Book in a Series—APA

Rothman, H. (1992). On rims and ridges: The Los Alamos area since 1880. Twentieth-century American West. Lincoln: University of Nebraska Press.

20. Book with a Title Within a Title—APA

Hayes, K. J. (Ed.). (1994). The critical response to Herman Melville's Moby Dick. Westport, CT: Greenwood Press.

21. Government Publication—APA

Calvert, K. (1993, November 26). Speech to the 103rd Congress. Congressional Record, 139(168) 3050–3051.

National Oceanic and Atmospheric Administration. (1988). COSPAS-SARSAT search and rescue satellite system. Washington, DC: U.S. Government Printing Office.

National Education Association. (1992). 1991–92 estimates of school statistics as provided by the state departments of education. West Haven, CT: NEA Professional Library.

22. Published Proceedings of a Conference—APA

Pavlyshyn, M., & Clarke, J. E. M. (Eds.). (1992). Ukraine in the 1990s: Proceedings of the first conference of the Ukrainian Studies Association of Australia. Melbourne: Monash University.

Print sources: Articles and other short documents

23. Article from a Daily Newspaper—APA

Broad, W. J. (1994, November 21). Nuclear roulette for Russia: Burying uncontained waste. The New York Times, p. A1.

24. Editorial, Letter to the Editor, or Review—APA

Patching up health care. (1994, July 17). [Editorial]. The New York Times, sec. 4, p. 16.

Turkel, S. (1993, July 3). [Letter to the editor]. The New York Times, p. A18.

Doniger, W. (1992, August 16). Shackled to the past. [Review of Gerald's Game]. The New York Times Book Review, p. 3.

Form descriptions—[Editorial], [Letter to the editor], [Review of Gerald's Game]—are enclosed in brackets because they are words that the person who used the sources inserted into the title information (see 29c.1). Do not put the titles of special documents or of parts of works in brackets (see item 16).

25. Unsigned Article from a Daily Newspaper—APA

Gene is shown to block the spread of prostate cancer in mice. (1995, May 12). The New York Times, p. A17.

26. Article from a Weekly or Biweekly Periodical—APA

Rosen, J. (1994, October 17). Is affirmative action doomed? The New Republic, 25–30, 34–35.

Only when a periodical is a newspaper, use *p.* or *pp.* before page numbers.

27. Article from a Monthly or Bimonthly Periodical—APA

Came, B. (1994, October). Policing Haiti. Maclean's, 20–22.

Bell, J. (1992, September/October). Kingdom come: Canada's Inuit finally may be getting their own homeland, but at what price? Earthwatch, 10–11.

597

28. Unsigned Article from a Weekly or Monthly Periodical—APA

The March almanac. (1994, March 16). <u>Atlantic Monthly,</u> 16.

29. Article from a SIRS Collection of Reprinted Articles—APA

Curver, P. C. (1990). Lighting in the 21st century. In E. Goldstein (Ed.), <u>Social Issues Resources Series: Vol. 4. Energy</u> (art. 84). Boca Raton, FL: Social Issues Resources.

30. Article in a Journal with Continuous Pagination—APA

La Follette, M. C. (1994). The politics of research misconduct: Congressional oversight, universities, and science. <u>Journal of Higher Education, 65,</u> 261—285.

31. Article in a Journal That Pages Each Issue Separately—APA

Hancock, D. (1993). Prototyping the Hubble fix. <u>IEEE Spectrum, 30</u>(10), 34—39.

32. Letter—APA

Orlyansky, V. (1991). Letter to the Soviet president. In R. McKay (Ed.), <u>Letters to Gorbachev: Life in Russia through the postbag of "argumenty i fakty"</u> (pp. 120—121). London: Michael Joseph.

An unpublished letter is not available to your readers. Treat it as a personal communication, acknowledging it in a parenthetical reference in your paper but not including it in the References list.

33. Map or Chart—APA

<u>Russia and Post-Soviet republics</u> [Map]. (1992). Moscow: Mapping Production Association.

Nonprint sources

34. Interview—APA

A personal interview is not available to your readers. Treat it as a personal communication, acknowledging it in a parenthetical reference in your paper but not including it in the References list.

Randi Friedman (personal communication, June 30, 1992) endorses this view.

35. Lecture, Speech, or Address—APA

A live lecture, speech, or address is not available to your readers. Acknowledge it in a parenthetical reference in your paper, but do not include it in your References list.

36. Film or Videotape—APA

Archer, D. (Writer and Director). (1992). A world of gestures: Cultural and nonverbal communication [Videotape]. Berkeley: University of California Extension Media Center.

37. Recording—APA

The Benedictine Monks of Santo Dimingo de Silos. (1994). Chant [CD] (I. F. de la Cuesta, Director; Recording No. CDC 724355513823). Madrid, Spain: Angel Records.

38. Live Performance—APA

A live performance is not available to your readers. Acknowledge it in a parenthetical reference in your paper, but do not include it in the References list.

39. Work of Art—APA

Hatcher, B. Seer [Artwork]. Provo, UT: Brigham Young University Art Museum.

40. Radio or Television Program—APA

MacNeil, R. (Interviewer). (1991, August 22). [Interview with G. F. Kennan]. The MacNeil/Lehrer NewsHour (Program 4144). New York and Washington, DC: Public Broadcasting Service.

Electronic sources

Items 41–45 show how to document material from the World Wide Web and FTP and Gopher sites for an APA-style References list. These References entries are based on new APA guidelines at the APA Web site (see page 546 for the URL). Items 46–49 show how to document from other electronic sources. For electronic sources not covered here, the APA manual suggests consulting the current edition of Li and Crane's *Electronic Style: A Guide to Citing Electronic Information.*

QUOTATION: ON WRITING

No tears in the writer, no tears in the reader. No surprise for the writer, no surprise for the reader.

—Robert Frost

41. Online*: Article from a Newspaper on the Web—APA

    Lewis, R. (1995, December 24). Chronobiology
researchers say their field's time has come. The Scientist,
9, p. 14 [On-line newspaper]. Retrieved December 30, 1997,
from the World Wide Web: http://www.the-scientist.library.
upenn.edu/yr1995/dec/chrono_951211.html

Notice especially the description of the source in square brackets—[On-line newspaper]*—and the URL, which is *not* enclosed in angle brackets. Be careful not to put any punctuation, such as a period, at the end of the entry unless it belongs to the URL.

42. Online: Article from a Journal or Magazine on the Web—APA—*NEW*

    Broydo, L. (1998, January 13—18). The clean cleaner
cover-up. Mother Jones, January/February 1998. Mother Jones
the Mojo Wire. [Magazine, selected stories on-line].
Retrieved January 15, 1998, from the World Wide Web:
http://www.mojones.com/mother_jones/JF98/homeplanet.html

The first underlined title, *Mother Jones,* and the date *January/February 1998* refer to the print magazine. The rest of the References entry refers to the Web material.

43. Online: Announcement Posted on the Web—APA—*NEW*

    National Institute of Mental Health. (1997, May 15).
Mammalian clock gene closed. [Press release posted on the
World Wide Web]. Bethesda, MD: Author. Retrieved December
30, 1997, from the World Wide Web: http://www.nimh/gov/
events/prnorth.htm

For a source of this kind, the person who wrote the press release may not be named as author, so use the organization issuing the announcement as the author. In the press release's title, the word *clock* was in italics. Because underlining indicates that this title would otherwise be in italics, *clock* is not underlined.

44. Online: Material from an FTP Site—APA—*NEW*

    Beck, A. (1994, July 2). Glass, a fractal gif. [On-line
graphic]. Swedish University Network SUNET. Retrieved
January 17, 1998: ftp://ftp.sunet.se/pub/pictures/fractals/

*Note that in MLA style and the style of this *Handbook,* the word *online* is not hyphenated, but it is hyphenated in the APA style.

APA APA APA APA APA APA APA APA APA APA APA

APA suggests documenting FTP sources, like this one, and Gopher sources, like the one in item 45, as you would Web sources, including the URL at the end of the *Retrieved* statement.

45. Online: Material from a Gopher Site—APA—*NEW*

```
    The undertaker. (1986, May 4). [On-line script].
Retrieved September 13, 1997: gopher://gopher.ocf.
berkeley.edu/00.Library/Monty_Python/undertaker
```

This script stored at a Gopher site is the text only, transcribed from tapes. No information about authors, performers, performances, and so on, is given, so the References entry gives title, date at the site, description of the material, the access date, and the URL.

46. Online Document Without a Print Version—APA

```
    Wallach, D. S. (1993, September 22). FAQ: Typing
injuries (2/5): General Info. [On-line]. Available FTP:
rtfm.mit.edu   Directory: pub/usenet/news.answers   File:
typing-injury-faq/general.z
```

Avoid end punctuation after the availability, directory, and file statements because extra punctuation marks can be mistaken for part of the address. Separate these statements with one extra space.

47. Computer Software—APA

```
    Transparent Language Presentation Program (Version 2.0
for Windows) [Computer software]. (1994). Hollis, NH:
Transparent Language.
```

48. Abstract on CD-ROM—APA

```
    Marcus, H. F., & Kitayamo, S. (1991). Culture and the
self: Implications for group dynamics [CD-ROM].
Psychological Review, 88(2), 224, 253. Abstract from:
SilverPlatter   File: PsycLIT   Item: 78-23878
```

49. Information Services: ERIC and Newsbank—APA

```
    Chiang, L. H. (1993). Beyond the language: Native
Americans' nonverbal communication. (ERIC Document
Reproduction Service No. ED 368 540).

    Wenzell, R. (1990). Businesses prepare for a more
diverse work force. (Newsbank Document Reproduction Service
No. EMP 27:D12).
```

QUOTATION: ON WRITING

Writing comes more easily if you have something to say.

—Sholem Asch

APA
APA
APA
APA
APA
APA

33d.4 Writing an abstract and using notes in APA style

You may be asked to include an **abstract** at the start of a paper you prepare in APA style. An abstract, as described in the 1994 edition of the *Publication Manual of the American Psychological Association*, is "a brief, comprehensive summary" (p. 8). Make this summary accurate, objective, and exact.

❶ **APA FORMAT ALERT:** If you include an abstract in an APA-style paper, put it on page 2, a separate page after the title page. For an example of an abstract, see the student paper on biological clocks in section 35b. ❗

Content notes can be used in APA-style papers for additional relevant information that cannot be worked effectively into the text discussion. Use consecutive arabic numerals for note numbers, both within your paper and on a separate page following the last text page of your paper. Use the heading *Notes* on this page, number it with your paper, and double-space the notes themselves.

CM
CM
CM
CM
CM
CM
CM

33e Using CM-style documentation

The style manual of the University of Chicago Press endorses two styles of documentation. One is a "name-year" style, similar to the APA's system, using in-text citations that direct readers to an alphabetical References list containing full bibliographic details about each source. Parenthetical references commonly contain an author name and a publication year, separated by a space but no punctuation: `(English 1995)`.

The other style of CM (for *Chicago Manual*) documentation is a note system often used in the disciplines of English, the humanities, and history; that is the style presented here. The CM note system gives complete bibliographic information within a footnote or endnote the first time a source is cited. If that source is cited again, less information is given because the source has already been fully described. A separate bibliography is usually unnecessary.

TEXT

```
Welty also makes this point.¹
```

NOTE

```
    1. Eudora Welty, One Writer's Beginnings (Cambridge:
Harvard University Press, 1984), 17.
```

Notes may be either at the end of a paper (endnotes) or at the foot of the page on which a citation falls (footnotes). Endnotes are usually easier to format, especially if you are handwriting or typing your paper. Popular word-processing programs can format either endnotes or footnotes easily.

Section 33e focuses on the CM bibliographic note system of documentation. In case you are asked to provide a separate bibliography, models of various bibliography entries are shown as well. For complete coverage of bibliography entries in CM style, see Chapter 15 of *The Chicago Manual of Style*, 14th edition.

33e.1 Creating CM-style bibliographic notes

Chart 154 gives general guidelines for the content and format of CM-style bibliographic notes.

⊙ **Guidelines for compiling CM-style**   **154**
bibliographic notes

■ **TITLE**

For endnotes, Notes, on a new page numbered sequentially with the rest of the paper, after the last text page of the paper. (Footnotes appear at the bottom of pages where sources are cited.)

■ **FORMAT**

Place endnotes after the text of your paper, on a separate page headed Notes. Center the word *Notes* about an inch from the top of the page. Double-space after the word *Notes*. Single-space the notes themselves. Indent each note's first line three characters (or one tab space in your word-processing program); do not indent a note's subsequent lines.

In the body of your paper, use raised (superscript) arabic numerals for the note numbers. Note numbers should be positioned after any punctuation marks except the dash, preferably at the end of a sentence. On the Notes page, number and note should be the same type size; the number is not raised, and a period should follow it. (Not all word-processing programs allow you to observe these guidelines.)

■ **SPACING AFTER PUNCTUATION**

Use one space.

■ **ARRANGEMENT OF NOTES**

Arrange notes in numerical order.

■ **AUTHORS' NAMES**

Give the name in standard (not inverted) order, with names and initials as given in the original source. Use the word *and* between (the last) two authors.

→

QUOTATION: ON WRITING

Get up very early and get going at once; in fact, work first and wash afterwards.

—W. H. Auden

CM
CM
CM
CM
CM
CM
CM
CM
CM
CM
CM
CM
CM

Guidelines for compiling CM-style bibliographic notes *(continued)* 154

■ **CAPITALIZATION OF TITLES**

Capitalize the first word, the last word, and all intervening words except articles (*a, an, the*), coordinating conjunctions (*and, but, or, for, nor*), and prepositions, no matter how long they are.

■ **SPECIAL TREATMENT OF TITLES**

Underline the titles of long works, and use quotation marks around the titles of shorter works.

Omit *A, An,* and *The* from the titles of newspapers and periodicals. If the city of publication is not part of a newspaper title, add it before the title and treat it as part of the name: `Newark Star-Ledger`. The name of the state, where useful for clarity, may be added in parentheses: `Newark (N.J.) Star-Ledger`.

■ **PUBLICATION INFORMATION**

Enclose publication information in parentheses. Use a colon and one space after the city of publication. If it is unclear what state or country the city is in, follow the city with a comma, insert the standard (*not* postal) abbreviation for the state or country, and end with a colon and one space. Give complete publishers' names or abbreviate them according to standard abbreviations in *Books in Print.* Omit *Co., Inc.,* and *Ltd.* Do not omit *Books* or *Press.*

Do not abbreviate publication months.

■ **PAGE NUMBERS**

List all page numbers. In ranges of numbers, the second number shows only the parts of the first number that are different: 75–6, 100–2, 295–303, 750–75.

■ **SECOND CITATIONS**

After giving full bibliographic information in the first note citing a source, subsequent citations can be brief. In short papers, author name(s) and a page reference are usually sufficient information. If you have used more than one work by the author(s), give a shortened title as well.

■ **CONTENT NOTES**

Try to avoid using content notes. If you must use one or two, make them footnotes and use symbols (* and † are standard) rather than numbers. You can repeat these footnote symbols on every page.

→

Guidelines for compiling CM-style bibliographic notes *(continued)* 154

■ **BIBLIOGRAPHIC NOTES: BOOKS**

Citations for books include the author, title, publication information, and page numbers if applicable. Note 1 here is for the first citation of a book; note 5 is for its second citation in a paper that cites two works by Welty, *One Writer's Beginnings* and "A Worn Path."

```
           AUTHOR                   TITLE
       ┌──────────┐     ┌──────────────────────────┐
   1. Eudora Welty, One Writer's Beginnings


                                                PAGE
               PUBLICATION INFORMATION         NUMBER
       ┌────────────────────────────────────┐  ┌──┐
   (Cambridge: Harvard University Press, 1984),  15.


   5. Welty, One, 21.
```

■ **BIBLIOGRAPHIC NOTES: ARTICLES**

Citations for articles include the author, article title, journal title, volume number, year, and page numbers. Note 1 shows the first citation of an article, and note 5 shows the second citation for the article in a paper citing only one work by these authors.

```
                          AUTHORS
       ┌────────────────────────────────────────────┐
   1. D. D. Cochran, W. Daniel Hale, and Christine P.

                           ARTICLE TITLE
   ┌──┐ ┌──────────────────────────────────────────┐
   Hissam, "Personal Space Requirements in Indoor versus

                                       VOLUME
                        JOURNAL TITLE   NUMBER
   ┌──────────────────┐ ┌─────────────┐ ┌──┐
   Outdoor Locations," Journal of Psychology  117

            PAGE
    YEAR   NUMBERS
   ┌────┐  ┌──────┐
   (1984):  132-3.


   5. Cochran, Hale, and Hissam, 133.
```

BACKGROUND

Nicolás Antonio (1617–1684) is credited with the creation of modern bibliography and the shaping of literary history into a scholarly discipline. His *Bibliotheca Hispana* is an index in Latin of Old World and New World Spanish writers after 1500. It also contains a history of earlier Spanish literature.

QUOTATION: ON WRITING

To write you have to set up a routine, to promise yourself that you will write. Just state in a loud voice that you will write so many pages a day, or write for so many hours a day. Keep the number of pages or hours within reason, and don't be upset if a day slips by. Start again; pick up the routine. Don't look for results. Just write, easily, quietly.

—Janwillem van de Wetering

33e.2 Following models for CM-style documentation

Directory

PRINT SOURCES: BOOKS

1. Book by One Author—CM
2. Book by Two or Three Authors—CM
3. Book by More Than Three Authors—CM
4. Multiple Citation of a Single Source—CM
5. Book by Group or Corporate Author—CM
6. Book with No Author Named—CM
7. Book with an Author and an Editor—CM
8. Translation—CM
9. Work in Several Volumes or Parts—CM
10. One Selection from an Anthology or Edited Book—CM
11. Two Selections from One Anthology or Edited Book—CM
12. Signed Article in a Reference Book—CM
13. Unsigned Article in a Reference Book—CM
14. Edition—CM
15. Anthology or Edited Book—CM
16. Introduction, Preface, Foreword, or Afterword—CM
17. Unpublished Dissertation or Essay—CM
18. Reprint of an Older Book—CM
19. Book in a Series—CM
20. Book with a Title Within a Title—CM
21. Secondary Source—CM
22. Government Publication—CM
23. Published Proceedings of a Conference—CM

PRINT SOURCES: ARTICLES

24. Article from a Daily Newspaper—CM
25. Editorial, Letter to the Editor, or Review—CM
26. Unsigned Article from a Daily Newspaper—CM
27. Article from a Weekly or Biweekly Periodical—CM
28. Article from a Monthly or Bimonthly Periodical—CM
29. Unsigned Article from a Weekly or Monthly Periodical—CM
30. Article from a Collection of Reprinted Articles—CM

31. Article in a Journal with Continuous Pagination—CM

32. Article in a Journal That Pages Each Issue Separately—CM

NONPRINT SOURCES

33. Personal Interview—CM

34. Letter—CM

35. Film or Videotape—CM

36. Recording—CM

ELECTRONIC SOURCES

37. Computer Software—CM

38. ERIC Information Service—CM

39. Electronic Document—CM

Print sources: Books

1. Book by One Author—CM

    1. George B. Schaller, <u>The Last Panda</u> (Chicago:
University of Chicago Press, 1993).

    2. Giuliana Prata, M. D., <u>A Systematic Harpoon into
Family Games: Preventive Interventions in Therapy</u> (New York:
Brunner/Mazel, 1990).

Here are the Bibliography entries should you need to prepare one.
(Entries are arranged alphabetically.)

Prata, Giuliana, M. D. A <u>Systematic Harpoon into Family
    Games: Preventive Interventions in Therapy.</u> New York:
    Brunner/Mazel, 1990.

Schaller, George B. <u>The Last Panda.</u> Chicago: University of
    Chicago Press, 1993.

2. Book by Two or Three Authors—CM

    1. Elizabeth McMahan, Susan Day, and Robert Funk, <u>Nine
Short Novels by American Women</u> (New York: St. Martin's
Press, 1993).

    2. Richard J. Smith and Mark Gibbs, <u>Navigating the
Internet</u> (Indianapolis: Sams, 1994).

Here are the Bibliography entries.

McMahan, Elizabeth, Susan Day, and Robert Funk. <u>Nine Short
    Novels by American Women.</u> New York: St. Martin's Press,
    1993.

Smith, Richard J., and Mark Gibbs. <u>Navigating the Internet.</u>
    Indianapolis: Sams, 1994.

CM
CM
CM
CM
CM
CM
CM
CM
CM
CM

QUOTATION: ON WRITING

An author arrives at a good style when his language performs what is required of it without shyness.

—Cyril Connolly

3. Book by More Than Three Authors—CM

1. Deborah Cameron et al., <u>Researching Language: Issues of Power and Method</u> (London: Routledge, 1992).

Here is the Bibliography entry.

Cameron, Deborah, et al. <u>Researching Language: Issues of Power and Method.</u> London: Routledge, 1992.

4. Multiple Citation of a Single Source—CM

Second and subsequent notes use shortened forms (see Chart 154). *Ibid.* can be used when the information in a note is exactly the same as the information in the immediately preceding note. If only the page references differ in two successive notes, you can use *Ibid.* with the respective pages.

2. Schaller, 33.

3. Ibid., 37.

5. Book by Group or Corporate Author—CM

1. Environmental Defense Fund, <u>Recycling and Incineration: Evaluating the Choices</u> (Washington, D.C.: Island Press, 1990).

2. American Psychological Association, <u>Publication Manual of the American Psychological Association,</u> 4th ed. (Washington, D.C.: American Psychological Association, 1994).

Here are the Bibliography entries.

American Psychological Association. <u>Publication Manual of the American Psychological Association,</u> 4th ed. Washington, D.C.: American Psychological Association, 1994.

Environmental Defense Fund. <u>Recycling and Incineration: Evaluating the Choice.</u> Washington, D.C.: Island Press, 1990.

6. Book with No Author Named—CM

1. <u>The Chicago Manual of Style,</u> 14th ed. (Chicago: University of Chicago Press, 1993).

7. Book with an Author and an Editor—CM

If the focus in your paper is on Welty and her reviews, use this form:

1. Eudora Welty, <u>A Writer's Eye: Collected Book Reviews,</u> ed. Pearl Amelia McHaney (Jackson: University Press of Mississippi, 1994).

If your focus is on McHaney's work as editor, use this form:

1. Pearl Amelia McHaney, ed., <u>A Writer's Eye: Collected Book Reviews,</u> by Eudora Welty (Jackson: University Press of Mississippi, 1994).

Here are the Bibliography entries. Parenthetical citations use the name that begins the entry.

McHaney, Pearl Amelia, ed. <u>A Writer's Eye: Collected Book Reviews,</u> by Eudora Welty. Jackson: University Press of Mississippi, 1994.

Welty, Eudora. <u>A Writer's Eye: Collected Book Reviews.</u> Edited by Pearl Amelia McHaney. Jackson: University Press of Mississippi, 1994.

8. Translation—CM

1. Fyodor Dostoevsky, <u>Devils,</u> trans. Michael R. Katz (Oxford: Oxford University Press, 1992).

Here is the Bibliography entry.

Dostoevsky, Fyodor. <u>Devils.</u> Translated by Michael R. Katz. Oxford: Oxford University Press, 1992.

9. Work in Several Volumes or Parts—CM

1. L. H. Goldman, Cloria L. Cronin, and Ada Aharoni, <u>Saul Bellow: A Mosaic,</u> vol. 2 of <u>Twentieth-Century American Jewish Writers</u> (New York: Lang, 1992).

10. One Selection from an Anthology or Edited Book—CM

1. Walter J. Savitch, "Infinity Is in the Eye of the Beholder," in <u>Interdisciplinary Approaches to Language: Essays in Honor of S. Y. Kuroda,</u> ed. Carol Georgopoulos and Roberta Ishihara (Boston: Kluwer Academic, 1991), 487–500.

11. Two Selections from One Anthology or Edited Book—CM

If you cite two or more selections from the same anthology or edited book, give complete bibliographical information in the first note for each selection.

12. Signed Article in a Reference Book—CM

1. Joseph L. Sax, "Environmental Law," in <u>Encyclopedia Americana,</u> international ed., 1994.

QUOTATION: ON WRITING

I have tried simply to write the best I can; sometimes I have good luck and write better than I can.

—Ernest Hemingway

13. Unsigned Article in a Reference Book—CM

1. <u>Encyclopaedia Britannica,</u> 15th ed., s.v. "Russia."

14. Edition—CM

1. Robert Searles Walker, <u>AIDS Today, Tomorrow: An Introduction to the HIV Epidemic in America,</u> 2nd ed. (Atlantic Highlands, N.J.: Humanities Press, 1994).

15. Anthology or Edited Book—CM

1. James P. Lantolf and Gabriela Appel, eds., <u>Vygotskian Approaches to Second Language Research</u> (Norwood, N.J.: Ablex, 1994).

16. Introduction, Preface, Foreword, or Afterword—CM

1. Jared Diamond, foreword to <u>Wild Forests Conservation Biology and Public Policy,</u> by William S. Alverson, Walter Kuhlmann, and Donald M. Waller (Washington, D.C.: Island Press, 1994).

17. Unpublished Dissertation or Essay—CM

1. Laurel Johnson Black, "Language, Power, and Gender in Student-Teacher Conferences" (Ph.D. diss., Miami University, 1993), 122–34.

State the author's name first, the title in quotation marks (not underlined), then a description of the work (such as *Ph.D. diss.* or *master's thesis*), then the degree-granting institution, and the date.

18. Reprint of an Older Book—CM

1. Herman Melville, <u>Moby Dick, or The Whale</u> (1851; reprint, New York: Modern Library, 1992).

19. Book in a Series—CM

1. Hal Rothman, <u>On Rims and Ridges: The Los Alamos Area since 1880,</u> vol. 2 of <u>Twentieth-Century American West</u> (Lincoln: University of Nebraska Press, 1992).

20. Book with a Title Within a Title—CM

1. Kevin J. Hayes, ed., <u>The Critical Response to Herman Melville's</u> Moby Dick (Westport, Conn.: Greenwood Press, 1994).

21. Secondary Source—CM

When you quote one person's words, having found them in another person's work, give information as fully as you can about both sources. Note 1 shows the form when the focus of your citation is Mary Wollstonecraft's words. If your focus is on what Shrodes, Finestone, and Shugrue have to say about Wollstonecraft's words, handle the information as shown in note 2.

1. Mary Wollstonecraft, A Vindication of the Rights of Woman (1792), quoted in Caroline Shrodes, Harry Finestone, and Michael Shugrue, The Conscious Reader, 4th ed. (New York: Macmillan, 1988), 282.

2. Caroline Shrodes, Harry Finestone, and Michael Shugrue, The Conscious Reader, 4th ed. (New York: Macmillan, 1988), 282, quoting Mary Wollstonecraft, A Vindication of the Rights of Woman (1792).

22. Government Publication—CM

1. House, Representative Ken Calvert speaking on the Endangered Species Act, 103rd Cong., 1st sess., Congressional Record (26 November 1993), 139, pt. 168:3050—1.

2. House, Subcommittee on Housing and Community Development of the Committee on Banking, Finance, and Urban Affairs, Basic Laws on Housing and Community Development, revised through September 30, 1991, Public Laws 102—109 (Washington, D.C: GPO, 1991).

3. U.S. Department of Commerce, National Oceanic and Atmospheric Administration, COSPAS-SARSAT Search and Rescue Satellite System (Washington, D.C.: GPO, 1988).

4. National Education Association, 1991—92 Estimates of School Statistics as Provided by the State Departments of Education, developed under contract with N.I.E., U.S. Department of Education (West Haven, Conn.: NEA Professional Library, 1992).

When a government department, bureau, agency, or committee produces a document, cite that group as the author. *GPO* stands for Government Printing Office.

23. Published Proceedings of a Conference—CM

1. Marko Pavlyshyn and J. E. M. Clarke, eds., Ukraine in the 1990s: Proceedings of the First Conference of the Ukrainian Studies Association of Australia (Melbourne: Monash University, 1992).

Here is the Bibliography entry.

Pavlyshyn, Marko, and J. E. M. Clarke, eds. <u>Ukraine in the
1990s: Proceedings of the First Conference of the
Ukrainian Studies Association of Australia.</u> Melbourne:
Monash University, 1992.

Print sources: Articles

24. Article from a Daily Newspaper—CM

1. William J. Broad, "Nuclear Roulette for Russia:
Burying Uncontained Waste," <u>New York Times,</u> 21 November
1994, sec. A, p. 1.

Here is the Bibliography entry.

Broad, William J. "Nuclear Roulette for Russia: Burying
Uncontained Waste." <u>New York Times,</u> 21 November 1994,
sec. A, p. 1.

25. Editorial, Letter to the Editor, or Review—CM

1. "Patching Up Health Care," editorial, <u>New York Times,</u>
17 July 1994, sec. 4, p. 16.

2. Stanley Turkel, letter, <u>New York Times,</u> 3 July 1993,
sec. 4, p. 18.

3. Wendy Doniger, "Shackled to the Past," review of
<u>Gerald's Game,</u> by Stephen King, <u>New York Times Book Review,</u>
16 August 1992, p. 3.

Here are the Bibliography entries.

"Patching Up Health Care." Editorial. <u>New York Times,</u> 17
July 1994, sec. 4, p. 16.

Turkel, Stanley. Letter. <u>New York Times,</u> 3 July 1993,
sec. 4, p. 18.

Doniger, Wendy. "Shackled to the Past." Review of <u>Gerald's
Game,</u> by Stephen King. <u>New York Times Book Review,</u> 16
August 1992, p. 3.

26. Unsigned Article from a Daily Newspaper—CM

1. "Gene Is Shown to Block the Spread of Prostate Cancer
in Mice," <u>New York Times,</u> 12 May 1995, sec. A, p. 17.

27. Article from a Weekly or Biweekly Magazine or Newspaper—CM

1. Jeffrey Rosen, "Is Affirmative Action Doomed?" <u>New
Republic,</u> 17 October 1994, 25—30, 34—35.

Here is the Bibliography entry.

Rosen, Jeffrey. "Is Affirmative Action Doomed?" <u>New
    Republic,</u> 17 October 1994, 25–30, 34–35.

28. Article from a Monthly or Bimonthly Periodical—CM

1. Jim Bell, "Kingdom Come: Canada's Inuit Finally May
Be Getting Their Own Homeland, but at What Price?"
<u>Earthwatch,</u> September–October 1992, 10–11.

Here is the Bibliography entry.

Bell, Jim. Kingdom Come: Canada's Inuit Finally May Be
    Getting Their Own Homeland, but at What Price?"
    <u>Earthwatch,</u> September–October 1992, 10–11.

29. Unsigned Article from a Weekly or Monthly Periodical—CM

1. "The March Almanac," <u>Atlantic Monthly,</u> March 1994,
16.

30. Article from a Collection of Reprinted Articles—CM

1. Abraham Brumberg, "Russia after Perestroika," in <u>The
Gorbachev Era,</u> vol. 14 of <u>Articles on Russian and Soviet
History</u> (New York: Garland, 1992)

31. Article in a Journal with Continuous Pagination—CM

1. Marcel C. La Follette, "The Politics of Research
Misconduct: Congressional Oversight, Universities,
and Science," <u>Journal of Higher Education</u> 65 (1994):
261–85.

Here is the Bibliography entry.

La Follette, Marcel C. "The Politics of Research Misconduct:
    Congressional Oversight, Universities, and Science."
    <u>Journal of Higher</u> Education 65 (1994): 261–85.

32. Article in a Journal That Pages Each Issue Separately—CM

1. Dennis Hancock, "Prototyping the Hubble Fix," <u>IEEE
Spectrum</u> 30, no. 10 (1993): 34–9.

Nonprint sources

33. Personal Interview—CM

For an unpublished interview, give the name of the interviewee, identify the interviewer, and then give location and date.

1. Randi Friedman, interview by author, Ames, Iowa, 30
June 1992.

34. Letter—CM

Treat a published letter like any other published document. For an unpublished letter, give the name of the writer, the name of the recipient, and the date of the letter.

    1. Gary Edward Reilly, letter to author, 26 December
    1994.

35. Film or Videotape—CM

    1. Dane Archer, A World of Gestures: Cultural and
    Nonverbal Communication (Berkeley: University of California
    Extension Media Center, 1992), videocassette.

Here is the Bibliography entry.

    Archer, Dane. A World of Gestures: Cultural and Nonverbal
        Communication. Berkeley: University of California
        Extension Media Center, 1992, videocassette.

36. Recording—CM

    1. Benedictine Monks of Santo Domingo de Silos. Chant.
    Ismael Fernandes de la Cuesta, dir. Angel CDC 724355513823.

Electronic sources

37. Computer Software—CM

    1. Transparent Language Presentation Program Version 2.0
    for Windows, Transparent Language, Hollis, N.H.

Here is the Bibliography entry.

    Transparent Language Presentation Program Version 2.0 for
        Windows. Transparent Language, Hollis, N.H.

38. ERIC Information Service—CM

    1. Linda H. Chiang. Beyond the Language: Native
    Americans' Nonverbal Communication (Anderson, Ind.: Midwest
    Association of Teachers of Educational Psychology, 1993).
    ERIC, ED 368540.

Here is the Bibliography entry.

    Chiang. Linda H. Beyond the Language: Native Americans'
        Nonverbal Communication. Anderson, IN: Midwest
        Association of Teachers of Educational Psychology,
        1993. ERIC, ED 368540.

39. Electronic Documents—CM

At its Web site (see page 546 for the URL), the University of Chicago Press promises complete coverage of electronic sources in its new edition, due in 2007. Until then, it endorses documentation guidelines of the International Standards Organization (ISO) for electronic sources. Check the Web site from time to time. Like the MLA and the APA, the University of Chicago Press may post guidelines there before it publishes a new manual.

For electronic sources, the units of information are author(s), if any; title; database medium; information about a print version; access or update dates; item or access numbers, if any; paging or other description of length, if any; and location information. The ISO recommends putting information about the database medium, access dates, and length in brackets.

```
1. Dan S. Wallach, "FAQ: Typing Injuries (2/5): General
Info.," in typing-injury-faq/general.z [USENET newsgroup],
1993_[cited 14 November 1993]; available from mail-server
@ rtfm.mit.edu; INTERNET
```

33f Using CBE-style documentation

In its 1994 style manual, *Scientific Style and Format*, the Council of Biology Editors (CBE) endorses two documentation systems widely used in mathematics and the physical and life sciences. The first system uses name-year parenthetical citations in the text of a paper together with a References list that gives full bibliographic information for each source. The second system uses numbers to mark references to sources in the paper. These numbers correlate with a numbered References list that gives full bibliographic information for each source.

Each of these styles uses a slightly different format for entries in the References list. With the name-date parenthetical system, a name and a date are the first two units of information in each References entry. When in-text citations are numbers referring to the numbered entries in the References list, the first two units of information in References entries are usually a name and title.

This handbook focuses mainly on CBE's numbered reference system. Here is the way it works:

- The first time you cite a particular source in your paper, assign it a number in sequence, starting with 1.

- In your References list, list and number the entries in their order of appearance in your paper, starting with 1.

The CBE recommends using superscript numbers for marking source citations in your paper, although numbers in parentheses are also acceptable. Here is a brief example showing two sources cited in a paper and a References list arranged in citation sequence.

IN-TEXT CITATIONS

Sybesma[1] insists that this behavior occurs periodically, but Crowder[2] claims never to have observed it.

REFERENCES LIST

1. Sybesma C. An introduction to biophysics. New York: Academic Press; 1977. 648 p.

2. Crowder W. Seashore life between the tides. New York: Dodd, Mead & Co.; 1931. New York: Dover Publications Reprint; 1975. 372 p.

Each citation of Sybesma's *Introduction to Biophysics* is followed by a superscript 1, and each citation of Crowder's *Seashore Life* is followed by a superscript 2 in this paper.

33f.1 Compiling a CBE-style References list

Chart 155 gives general guidelines for a CBE-style References list.

⊙ **Guidelines for compiling a CBE-style Reference list**   155

■ **TITLE**

References or Cited References

■ **PLACEMENT OF LIST**

Start a new page numbered sequentially with the rest of the paper.

■ **CONTENT AND FORMAT**

Include all sources quoted from, paraphrased, or summarized in your paper. Center the title about one inch from the top of the page. Start each entry on a new line. Put the number followed by a space at the regular left margin. If an entry takes more than one line, indent the second and all other lines. The CBE does not specify an indent; unless your instructor specifies an indent, you can use five characters (typewritten papers) or one-half inch (papers prepared on a computer). Double-space each entry and between entries.

→

Guidelines for compiling a CBE-style Reference list *(continued)*   155

■ **SPACING AFTER PUNCTUATION**

Follow the spacing shown in the models in section 33f.2.

■ **ARRANGEMENT OF ENTRIES**

Sequence the entries in the order that you cite the sources in your paper.

■ **AUTHORS' NAMES**

Invert all author names, giving the last name first. You can give first names or use only initials of first and middle names. If you use initials, do not use a period or a space between first and middle initials. Use a comma to separate the names of multiple authors identified by initials; if you use full first names, use a semicolon. Do not use *and* or &. Place a period after the last author's name.

■ **CAPITALIZATION OF TITLES**

Capitalize a title's first word and any proper nouns. Do not capitalize the first word of a subtitle unless it is a proper noun.

Capitalize the titles of academic journals. If the title of a periodical is one word, give it in full; otherwise, abbreviate it according to recommendations established by the *American National Standard for Abbreviations of Titles of Periodicals*.

Capitalize a newspaper title's major words, giving the full title, including a beginning *A*, *An*, or *The*.

■ **SPECIAL TREATMENT OF TITLES**

Do not underline titles or enclose them in quotation marks.

■ **PLACE OF PUBLICATION**

Use a colon after the city of publication. Add a state postal abbreviation (see Chart 132 in section 30i) or a country name to a city that might be ambiguous—for example, `Springfield (VA)` or `Nijmegen (Netherlands)`.

■ **PUBLISHER**

Give publishers' names in full, including *Co., Inc., Press, Ltd.,* and so on. Use a semicolon after the publisher's name.

■ **PUBLICATION MONTH ABBREVIATIONS**

Abbreviate publication months as shown in Chart 134 in section 30j, but omit the period.

→

QUOTATION: ON WRITING

There is no one right way. Each of us finds a way that works for him. But there is a wrong way. The wrong way is to finish your writing day with no more words on paper than when you began. Writers write.

—Robert B. Parker

Guidelines for compiling a CBE-style 155
Reference list *(continued)*

■ **INCLUSIVE PAGE NUMBERS**

Shorten the second number as much as possible while keeping it unambiguous—for example, 233–4 for 233 to 234; 233–44 for 233 to 244; 233–304. Use the abbreviation *p* without a period or underlining with designations of pages. Follow the guidelines in the models.

■ **DISCONTINUOUS PAGE NUMBERS**

Give the full numbers of all discontinuous pages, preceding the first number with the *p* abbreviation and separating successive numbers or ranges with a comma.

■ **TOTAL PAGE NUMBERS**

When citing an entire book, give as the last information unit the total number of pages, followed by the abbreviation *p* and a period.

■ **REFERENCES ENTRY: BOOK**

Citations for books usually list author(s), title, publication information, and pages (either total pages when citing an entire work or inclusive pages for citing part of a book). Each unit of information ends with a period.

```
1. Stacy RW, Williams DT, Worden RE, McMorris
   RO. Essentials of biological and medical sciences.
   New York: McGraw-Hill Book Company, Inc.; 1955.
   727 p.
```

■ **REFERENCES ENTRY: ARTICLE**

Citations for articles usually list author(s), article title, and journal name and publication information, each section followed by a period. *Sci Am* is the abbreviated form of *Scientific American*. The volume number is 269, and the issue number, in parentheses, is (3).

```
1. Weissman IL, Cooper MD. How the immune system
   develops. Sci Am 1993 Mar;269(3):65—71.
```

33f.2 Following models for a CBE-style reference list

Directory

PRINT SOURCES: BOOKS

1. Book by One Author—CBE

2. Book by More than One Author—CBE

3. Book by Group or Corporate Author—CBE

4. Anthology or Edited Book—CBE

5. One Selection or Chapter from an Anthology or Edited Book—CBE

6. All Volumes of a Multivolume Work—CBE

7. Unpublished Dissertation or Thesis—CBE

PRINT SOURCES: ARTICLES

8. Published Article from Conference Proceedings—CBE

9. Signed Newspaper Article—CBE

10. Unsigned Newspaper Article—CBE

11. Article in a Journal with Continuous Pagination—CBE

12. Article in a Journal That Pages Each Issue Separately—CBE

13. Journal Article on Discontinuous Pages—CBE

14. Entire Issue of a Journal—CBE

OTHER SOURCES

15. Slide Set—CBE

16. Electronic Sources—CBE

Print sources: Books

1. Book by One Author—CBE

1. Hawking SW. Black holes and baby universes and other essays. New York: Bantam Books; 1993. 320 p.

Use one space but no punctuation between an author's last name and the initial of the first name. Do not put punctuation or a space between a first and a middle initial.

QUOTATION: ON WRITING

Some authors type their works, but I cannot do that. Writing is tied up with the hand, almost with a special nerve.

—Graham Greene

2. Book by More Than One Author—CBE

1. Wegzyn S, Gille J-C, Vidal P. Developmental systems: at the crossroads of system theory, computer science, and genetic engineering. New York: Springer-Verlag; 1990. 595 p.

3. Book by Group or Corporate Author—CBE

1. Chemical Rubber Company. Handbook of laboratory safety. 3rd ed. Boca Raton (FL): CRC Press; 1990. 1352 p.

Use the two-letter postal abbreviation for the state (see Chart 132 in section 30i), enclosed in parentheses, after the name of a city that might be unfamiliar to your readers.

4. Anthology or Edited Book—CBE

1. Heermann B, Hummel S, editors. Ancient DNA: recovery and analysis of genetic material from paleontological, archeological, museum, medical, and forensic specimens. New York: Springer-Verlag; 1994. 1029 p.

5. One Selection or Chapter from an Anthology or Edited Book—CBE

1. Basov NG, Feoktistov LP, Senatsky YV. Laser driver for inertial confinement fusion. In: Brueckner, KA, editor. Research trends in physics: inertial confinement fusion. New York: American Institute of Physics; 1992: p 24—37.

6. All Volumes of a Multivolume Work—CBE

1. Crane FL, Morre DJ, Low HE, editors. Oxidoreduction at the plasma membrane: relation to growth and transport. Boca Raton (FL): CRC Press; 1991. 2 vol.

7. Unpublished Dissertation or Thesis—CBE

1. Baykul MC. Using ballistic electron emission microscopy to investigate the metal-vacuum interface. [dissertation]. Orem (UT): Polytechnic University; 1993. 111 p.

Print sources: Articles

8. Published Article from Conference Proceedings—CBE

1. Tsang CP, Bellgard MI. Sequence generation using
   a network of Boltzmann machines. In: Tsang CP,
   editor. Proceedings of the 4th Australian Joint
   Conference on Artificial Intelligence; 1990 Nov 8–11;
   Perth, Australia. Singapore: World Scientific; 1990:
   p 224–33.

9. Signed Newspaper Article—CBE

1. Hoke F. Gene therapy: clinical gains yield a wealth of
   research opportunities. Scientist 1993 Oct 4;Sect A:1,
   5, 7.

   Sect stands for *Section.*

10. Unsigned Newspaper Article—CBE

1. [Anonymous]. Irish urge postgame caution. USA Today 1993
   Nov 12; Sect C:2.

11. Article in a Journal with Continuous Pagination—CBE

1. Scott ML, Fredrickson RJ, Moorhead BB. Characteristics
   of old-growth forests associated with northern spotted
   owls in Olympic National Park. J Wildlf Mgt
   1993;57:315–21.

   Give only the volume number before the page numbers.

12. Article in a Journal That Pages Each Issue Separately—CBE

1. Weissman IL, Cooper MD. How the immune system develops.
   Sci Am 1993 Mar;269(3):65–71.

   Give both the volume number and the issue number (here, 269 is the
   volume number and 3 is the issue number). *Sci Am* is the abbreviation
   for *Scientific American* based on the standards established by the *American
   National Standard for Abbreviations of Titles of Periodicals.*

13. Journal Article on Discontinuous Pages—CBE

1. Richards FM. The protein folding problem. Sci Am 1991
   Nov;246(1):54–7, 60–6.

14. Entire Issue of a Journal—CBE

1. Whales in a modern world: a symposium held in London, November 1988. Mamm Rev 1990 Jan;20(9).

November 1988, the date of the symposium, is part of the title of the issue in this case.

Other sources

15. Slide Set—CBE

1. Human parasitology [slides]. Chicago: American Society of Clinical Pathologists Press; 1990: color. Accompanied by: guide.

16. Electronic Sources—CBE

In general, to cite electronic sources, start with a statement of the type of document, and then give the information you would give for a print version. Then, give information that would help a reader to locate the electronic source. End with a date: your access date for online sources or the date of the update you used for CD-ROM databases that are updated periodically.

34

CASE STUDY:
A STUDENT WRITING
AN MLA RESEARCH PAPER

WEB SITE

English Central is Prentice Hall's Web site for English instructors and their students. English Central offers much general information about English, hyperlinks to interesting and important sites for students and instructors of English composition and literature, and sites for Prentice Hall's major English textbooks. At the Troyka Web site, you will find supplementary resources and activities. These include quotations (twenty-five, with suggestions to students for using them to stimulate writing), practice exercises on key topics, other sample student essays, e-mail contact with the author, and an invitation to students to submit model essays (for Chapters 3 or 6), model paragraphs (for Chapter 4), model research papers (for Chapter 34), and model literature papers (for Chapter 37).

This chapter presents a case study of a student, Lisa Laver, going through the processes of conducting research and writing a paper based on her findings. Section 34a narrates the processes. Section 34b shows the final draft of Laver's paper, along with commentary on its key elements. The commentary includes **process notes** explaining many of Laver's decisions during her writing process.

Lisa Laver was given this assignment for a research paper: Write a research paper on the general subject of intelligence. The paper should be 1,800 to 2,000 words long and should be based on a variety of sources. The final paper is due in six weeks. Interim deadlines for parts of the work will be announced. To complete this assignment, you need to engage in three interrelated processes: conducting research, understanding the results of that research, and writing a paper based on the first two processes. Consult the *Simon & Schuster Handbook for Writers,* Fifth Edition, especially Chapter 32, which gives you practical, step-by-step guidance on what this assignment entails.

34a Observing the processes of researching and writing an MLA-style research paper

Lisa Laver was eager to plan her research schedule so that she could budget her time and not end up in a panic of time pressure. She knew from experience that she would likely have the most trouble in the first stages of her research process as she narrowed her topic and began to look for useful sources. She resolved to face the challenge calmly and patiently as she went along.

The general topic assigned was "intelligence." Laver realized that she had to face many steps to narrow it to a **topic suitable for a research paper** (see 32d). Collecting possible **subject headings** and **key words** was her first step. She went to the library reference desk to use the Library of Congress Subject Headings (LCSH) books (see 32i). She found nothing under "intelligence" but browsed a bit and found "intellect" as a main category. Its library call number, the code to lead her to all books on the subject, had a range from BF431 to BF433. She wrote down *intellect* and its call numbers in her **research log** (see 32c). She had taken the first step for this project.

Laver then examined the subentries at "intellect" in the LCSH and found the listing "human intelligence," which appealed to her as a direction to take. Then, Laver looked at the LCSH headings preceded by the code NT (meaning "narrowed topic"). In her research log, she listed all the NT headings as possible key words. Looking up a few of them, she soon became overwhelmed with the variety of directions she could take. She decided to try another route.

With the call numbers and key words in hand, Laver looked at **specialized reference books** (see 32l) with call numbers in the range BF431–BF433 (the call numbers she had found in the LCSH). In Volume 3 of *Survey of Social Science: Psychology Series,* she found an article called "Intelligence: Definition and Theoretical Models." This proved to be Laver's first big break.

As she read the survey article, Laver's interest was captured by material on a concept of intelligence developed fairly recently by Howard Gardner of Harvard University. She wrote down Gardner's name as a possible **authority** (see 32f.3). Gardner states that human intelligence is not what people think of as IQ. He believes IQ is a limited concept because it draws on only one or two inborn human abilities. According to Gardner, the totality of human intelligence results from the interaction of eight "intelligences." Laver decided that she would pursue this topic if she could determine that Gardner was a credible authority on the subject of intelligence.

To start checking on Gardner, Laver looked in the *Columbia Encyclopedia,* a **general reference book** she was familiar with from high school. Under "intelligence," Laver found Gardner and his concept of multiple intelligences mentioned. This gave her hope, so next she looked in the library's **book catalog** (see 32m) under the name "Gardner." She was delighted to find several books by him on the subject of multiple intelligences. One of them, *Frames of Mind,* became a major source on her topic. She then started writing out **bibliography cards** (32j and 33b).

Because Gardner's work with the concept of multiple intelligences had started twenty years earlier, Laver realized that she would have to rely heavily on journals and online sources. The periodicals indexes at Laver's college library were on CD-ROM. Using the key word "multiple intelligences," she quickly found a number of journal articles with titles indicating that they had good potential as sources for her research. Laver was able to locate some of the articles in journals that the library had available in print. Others Laver located online using the AltaVista search engine (see 32o). Each article named Gardner as a major authority.

As Laver read, checked the credibility of her sources, and found additional useful sources, she was at first somewhat skeptical of the concept of multiple intelligences. All her life, she had heard that intelligence was defined by IQ, which was measured by a test. In fact, she had wondered what her IQ and the IQs of her family and friends were. The more Laver thought about what she was reading, the more open she felt to the possibility of changing her viewpoint. This led Laver to form her **research question** (see 32a): "Can there be only one way of describing intelligence?"

As she researched further, Laver saw references to the work of Salovey and Mayer. These names led Laver to material on "emotional intelligence," a concept that encompassed in great detail two of Gardner's eight intelligences: interpersonal and intrapersonal. Laver remembered seeing her parents reading a book by Daniel Goleman titled *Emotional Intelligence.* Browsing through it, she saw that it drew heavily on Salovey and Mayer's work as well as Gardner's. Laver decided to include Salovey and Mayer's work in her paper.

After taking notes, Laver was ready to draft her research paper. Thinking about her purpose, Laver concluded that she should *inform* her readers about the concept of multiple intelligences. (For a discussion of the informative purpose, see section 1b.2). Soon after she started her second draft, however, Laver realized that her paper lacked a *focus*—a reason for her wanting to explain what she had learned. She decided to include her rationale for why the topic of multiple intelligences was worth writing about: She felt that the concept held benefits especially for students and also for the general population.

As Laver wrote, she used her **note cards** carefully to make sure she always knew when she was quoting a source and when she was summarizing. She made sure to put in the correct in-text documentation (see 33c.1) for each source. She also kept a **working bibliography** (see 32h) so that she would be ready to list each one of her sources in the Works Cited list (see 33c.2 and 33c.3) at the end of her paper. By the time Laver came to the final draft of her research paper, she decided to drop a few sources because they repeated what others whom she considered better authorities had said.

Laver struggled with her concluding paragraph. She wanted to assert her conviction that the ideas of Gardner, Salovey and Mayer, and Goleman relating to human intelligence held great promise. At first, she lacked the confidence to state her position outright; after a while, the strength of her convictions overrode her hesitancy. Here is an early draft of Laver's concluding paragraph, which you can compare to the one in her final draft that appears in section 34b.

> Today, there is no longer a single definition of
> intelligence. Scientists have found new ways of describing human

TEACHING TIP

You may want to point out to students that symbols, such as #, %, ¢, +, and = should not be used in the body of a paper, although they often appear in graphs and tables. The dollar sign ($) can be used anywhere when accompanied by figures.

intelligence and seeing it in operation. Educators, in turn, can use those findings to give students more avenues to school success and, as a result, to greater self-esteem.

34b Analyzing an MLA-style research paper

Lisa Laver followed MLA style for format decisions on this paper.

Separate Title Page

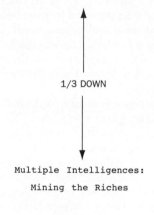

1/3 DOWN

Multiple Intelligences:

Mining the Riches

TITLE: DOUBLE-SPACE IF MORE THAN ONE LINE

by

Lisa Laver

BY ON SEPARATE LINE; DOUBLE-SPACE TO NAME

COURSE, SECTION	English 101, Section A1
INSTRUCTOR	Professor Jill
DATE SUBMITTED	10 December 2000

1"

Title page and first page of essay with a title page. If your instructor requires a title page, you can use the format and types of information shown opposite for Lisa Laver's title page. Then, on page 1 of your paper, put your last name followed by a space followed by the numeral 1 in the upper right corner, 1/2 inch below the top edge of the page. Double-space below this heading, and then type the paper's title, centering it. Double-space after the title, and then start your paper, indenting the first line of each paragraph five characters. If you are using a computer rather than a typewriter, format for double line spacing and 1/2-inch tabs for indents.

First page without a title page. If your instructor does not require a title page, follow MLA format style, shown below, for the first page of your paper.

First Page for a Paper Without a Title Page

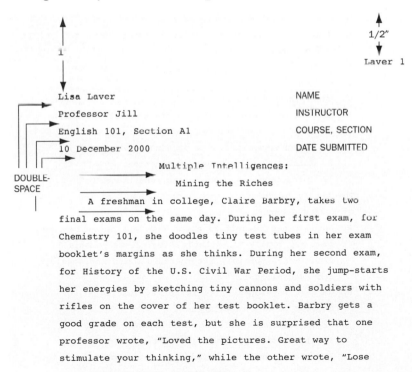

Laver 1

Lisa Laver — NAME
Professor Jill — INSTRUCTOR
English 101, Section A1 — COURSE, SECTION
10 December 2000 — DATE SUBMITTED

DOUBLE-SPACE

Multiple Intelligences:

Mining the Riches

A freshman in college, Claire Barbry, takes two final exams on the same day. During her first exam, for Chemistry 101, she doodles tiny test tubes in her exam booklet's margins as she thinks. During her second exam, for History of the U.S. Civil War Period, she jump-starts her energies by sketching tiny cannons and soldiers with rifles on the cover of her test booklet. Barbry gets a good grade on each test, but she is surprised that one professor wrote, "Loved the pictures. Great way to stimulate your thinking," while the other wrote, "Lose

BACKGROUND

A direct title tells exactly what the essay will be about. An indirect title hints at the essay's topic. In either case, it stands alone, not as part of the body of the essay. (See 3c.2.)

627

BACKGROUND

A formal outline (see 2o) follows conventions concerning content and format that ensure that relationships among ideas are clear and that the content is orderly. In a topic outline, each item is only a word or a phrase. In a sentence outline, each item is a complete sentence.

1/2″

Laver ii

    4. It must be supported by experimental and
       psychological tasks.
  C. MI theory has affected educational practices.
    1. One school reports an example of using one
       intelligence to encourage development of another.
    2. Another school reports using a variety of
       intelligences to study American history.
V. Other researchers have developed the concept of
 emotional intelligence.
  A. Emotional intelligence builds on two of Gardner's
    eight intelligences.
    1. Interpersonal intelligence is one.
    2. Intrapersonal intelligence is the other.
  B. Salovey and Mayer did pioneering work in the area.
  C. Daniel Goleman wrote a best-selling book on the subject.

Name and page-number heading. Except for a separate title page, give each page of a paper you prepare according to MLA format guidelines a heading in the upper right corner 1/2 inch below the top edge of the paper. Use your last name, followed by a space, followed by the page number. Number pages that come before your essay begins, such as outline pages, with lowercase roman numerals (see Lisa Laver's outline on pages 628–629). Use arabic numeral 1 on the page on which your essay begins, and then number each page consecutively through to the last page of Works Cited.

Outline. Laver's instructor required a formal outline in the final draft of each student's research paper. To format her outline, Laver referred to sections 2o and 32s in this handbook. In the name–page number line in the upper right corner, she used lowercase roman numerals for the page numbers, a conventional way of showing that the outline comes before the first page of the essay itself. She double-spaced below the name-number heading and then centered the word *Outline*. She double-spaced and then typed the words *Thesis statement* at the left margin, underlining them. The thesis statement in the outline matches the last sentence of the first paragraph of her paper.

Laver used a **sentence outline,** not a topic outline (see 2o). To reflect the organization of her paper, she divided the material in the outline into five major parts, numbered I, II, III, IV, and V. The main items in each part are marked A, B, C. When a main item went into more detail, she used 1, 2, 3, and so on, for the new level of information.

BACKGROUND

In "Scoring Peers' Papers: Teaching Audience Awareness and Generating Enthusiasm," (*Teaching English in the Two Year College,* December 1993: 300–305), Sharon Albert and Kathryn Ring explain a teaching process that asks students from two classes to grade each others' papers. While the identity of individual graders and writers remain anonymous, students develop the sense of writing to a real audience rather than simply to their instructor.

QUOTATION: ON WRITING

Since long before the invention of universities, not to mention university programs in creative writing, authors have acquired their authority in four main ways—first, by paying a certain sort of attention to the experience of life as well as merely undergoing it; second, by paying a certain sort of attention to the works of their great and less great predecessors in the medium of written language, as well as merely reading them; third, by practicing that medium themselves, usually a *lot* (Charles Newman, the writer and critic, declares that the first prerequisite for aspiring writers is sufficient motor control to keep their pens moving left to right, line after line, hour after hour, day after day, and I would add year after year, decade after decade); and fourth, by offering their apprentice work for discussion and criticism by one or several of their impassioned peers, or by some more experienced hand or by both.

—John Barth

Laver 1

Multiple Intelligences: A

Mining the Riches

1   A freshman in college, Claire Barbry, takes two   B
final exams on the same day. During her first exam, for
Chemistry 101, she doodles tiny test tubes in her exam
booklet's margins as she thinks. During her second exam,
for History of the U.S. Civil War Period, she jump-starts
her energies by sketching tiny cannons and soldiers with
rifles on the cover of her test booklet. Barbry gets a
good grade on each test, but she is surprised that one
professor wrote, "Loved the pictures. Great way to
stimulate your thinking," while the other wrote, "Lose
those pictures. They waste your time." Barbry knew her
second professor was wrong. By drawing, Barbry had been
consciously applying discoveries from research into the
psychology of brain functioning. She knew that school
success can increase greatly when students tap into their
talents not usually associated with academic work. Human
intelligence results from a complex interaction of the   C
riches of many abilities, only a few of which are taken
into account by intelligence quotient (IQ) tests widely
used today.

2   A context for such an assertion can be found by
briefly reviewing the history of defining and testing
human intelligence. Interest in the topic dates back   D, E
to the nineteenth century. Sir Francis Galton attempted
in the late 1800s to create a test that supported his
view that mental ability is determined solely by
heredity. His assumption and the test he wrote were never
widely accepted. However, building on Galton's notion
that intelligence levels could actually be tested,

→

630

COMMENTARY

A. **Title.** Laver uses her title to prepare her readers for the paper's major theme (multiple intelligences) and central focus (that the concept offers rich possibilities). ❶ **PROCESS NOTE:** Laver drafted a few titles as she was revising. She started with "Everyone Is Smart in Some Way," but that oversimplified the point. She later tried and rejected "Evolving Theories of Human Intelligence" because she was not writing a historical survey of human intelligence theories but rather a discussion of such theories of more recent interest. ❗

B. **Introductory device.** Laver tells this anecdote, which is based on the experience of one of her friends, because she feels it illustrates her point dramatically.

C. **Thesis statement.** The last sentence of Laver's introductory paragraph is her thesis statement. In writing it, she wants to prepare her readers, in more detail than her title does, for the message she wants to deliver. ❶ **PROCESS NOTE:** Laver tried out a few thesis statements as she moved from early to later drafts, each time trying to get closer to her central message. For evolving versions of this thesis statement, see 32r. ❗

D. ❶ **PROCESS NOTE:** In an earlier draft of this paper, Laver wrote four paragraphs about the history of definitions and measurements of human intelligence. Then, as she read over her draft, she realized that her coverage of history should not consume nearly a third of her paper when her central goal was to discuss in some detail a new theory of great potential. For this final draft, Laver condenses the history into one paragraph. ❗

E. **Summary.** In her final draft, Laver condenses her historical information from four paragraphs to one. To do so, she summarizes the information to cover only the major events that relate to the central message of her paper. All the historical background information ends up in Laver's second paragraph.

QUOTATION: ON WRITING

There mark what ills the scholar's life
    assail:
Toil, envy, want, the patron, and the goal.
        —Samuel Johnson

Laver 2

Alfred Binet in 1905 wrote the first reasonably practical
intelligence test. He did so at the request of the French
government, which wanted schools to place students with
similar ability levels together in classes. In 1916, a
significant revision of Binet's test was undertaken at
Stanford University, and the test was renamed the
Stanford-Binet Intelligence Test ("History"). This test,   F
which has been updated every few decades since 1916, is
designed to measure only two abilities: to compute
numbers and to think in structured patterns. The
Stanford-Binet Intelligence Test introduced such
innovations as "scaling" and "standardizing" of scores.
By applying a formula, the test can be used to compare
one person's score to the scores of other people of the
same age who answered the same questions across the
United States ("Intelligence").

3   The Stanford-Binet Intelligence Test, and   G
others like it, caught on quickly with the public.
People liked the idea that a single number could
supposedly define someone's intelligence. Today, IQ tests
have become hugely respected, although some experts   H
discount them. Indeed, the notion that a single number
can describe a person's intelligence seems firmly fixed
in people's thinking about intelligence today. Many
people want to know the exact number of their IQ. When
IQ tests are given in school, students and parents are
rarely told the outcome, yet many people manage to find
out their scores or pay to retake the test privately.
Then, they carry their IQ number for the rest of their
lives, either as a secret burden when the score is not
as high as they had hoped or as a badge of honor allowed

→

COMMENTARY

F. **Using an online encyclopedia.** Laver needed to make sure that her reference source, *Grolier's Multimedia Encyclopedia,* cited by the parenthetical reference ("History"), is a reliable, respected collection of information. She decided to ask her college's librarian how to determine whether a specific encyclopedia is considered a reliable source. The librarian suggested that Laver read some reviews of CD-ROM and online encyclopedias. Laver learned that such reviews appear fairly often in computer magazines as well as in library journals. She searched those sources and quickly located an encyclopedia review article that compared five different CD-ROM and online encyclopedias (including *Grolier's Multimedia*). After reading the review and finding that *Grolier's* is a reliable source, Laver felt confident about the material it contained.

G. **Topic sentences.** Laver composed her topic sentences to begin most of her paragraphs. She felt that they provided a useful guide to her line of reasoning and presentation of information.

H. **Using her own thinking.** Laver had learned this information through personal experience. As she was growing up, she had heard people talking about IQ tests and scores. She had even wondered at times about whether her IQ was high or low. But as she progressed through high school and met all kinds of people with all sorts of different abilities, she began to suspect that intelligence involved more than what one IQ test could measure. Laver does not use sources to support this section because it is drawn from her own knowledge.

BACKGROUND

In "Making a Place for Music in Basic Writing" (*Journal of Basic Writing*, Fall 1995: 31–37), Sarah Coprich Johnson offers a specific application to enhance learning of one of Howard Gardner's eight multiple intelligences.

Laver 3

sometimes "accidentally to slip out" during conversations. According to Anemona Hartocollis, public respect for IQ testing is so deeply ingrained that some parents expect their preschoolers, usually at age three, to take the Stanford-Binet Intelligence Test. These parents know that scores alone will determine whether their children qualify for one of the limited openings at prestigious prekindergarten schools. Parents who have their very young children tested--and there are many--are highly competitive and often insist that much of their children's time be spent on activities and games that are supposed to prepare them for the test (B1).

I, J

4   Opponents of such a worshipful emphasis on IQ scores say its overuse is a disaster. One such opponent, Brent Staples, argues in "The IQ Cult": "Most scientists concede that they don't really know what 'intelligence' is. Whatever it might be, paper and pencil tests aren't the tenth of it" (293). Experiences like Claire Barbry's on the day of her two final exams help to show that today's IQ tests are indeed severely limited and their underlying assumptions can actually hamper a student's success in school. A review of a 1986 survey of definitions of intelligence in scholarly publications reveals that the reader "is left with the clear impression that intelligence is such a multifaceted concept that no single quality can define it and no single task or series of tasks can capture it completely" (Urbina 1330).

K

L

M

5   To everyone's benefit, the last twenty years of brain research have inspired broader theories of human intelligence that are getting increasingly respectful attention. Caine and Caine, summarizing a number

→

634

COMMENTARY

I. **Incorporating a very current source.** 🟠 **PROCESS NOTE:** The morning that Laver was planning to edit her final draft of this paper, she saw, to her surprise, an article in that day's *New York Times* about the Stanford-Binet test being given to three-year-old children. The issues of the accuracy of IQ testing and the prestige of high scores were a major part of the article. Because the information in the article provided strong, timely support for this section of her paper, Laver decided, even though it would take her a little extra writing time, to integrate the article into her paper. ❗

J. **Marking the extent of a paraphrase.** To ensure that readers of her paper know precisely where the paraphrase starts, Laver puts the author's name at the beginning: "According to Anemona Hartocollis. . . ." The page number, in parentheses, marks the end of the paraphrase: (B1).

K. **Quotation from a source.** This is Laver's first quotation from a source. (Before this, she has paraphrased or summarized her sources.) She decided to use the quotation because she felt that its down-to-earth language would reinforce her message. In addition, she believed that the prestige of the well-respected journalist Brent Staples, who often writes on issues of race and class, would bring greater authority to the point she wanted to make.

L. 🟠 **PROCESS NOTE:** Laver mentions Barbry again to show the explicit relationship between the anecdote in her introductory paragraph and the message of paragraph 4; she again mentions Barbry in paragraph 11. ❗

M. **Major source.** Laver considers the Urbina material a major source. She had found the essay in the specialized reference book that was located within the call-number range for "intellect" that she had found in the Library of Congress Subject Headings (LCSH). The essay, listed in the Works Cited at the end of Laver's paper, introduced Laver to the concept of "multiple intelligences," the topic of her paper, and to the name Howard Gardner, the main authority on that topic.

QUOTATION: ON WRITING

The wastepaper basket is the writer's best friend.

—Isaac Bashevis Singer

QUOTATION: ON WRITING

Writing represents a unique mode of learning—not merely valuable, not merely special, but unique.

—Janet Emig

of recent studies into the nature of intelligence, urge that educators enlarge their concepts of learning and of teaching to move beyond simplistic IQ scores. Caine and Caine, however, do not claim that all new theories of diversity in intelligences are equally valid. For example, one new theory, considered "the answer" for a short time, held that each person's brain consists of two hemispheres, one of which is dominant: The right side controls creative, artistic talents, and the left side controls logical, language-based talents (67). By now, expanded and more widely accepted theories, based on careful research, show that the human brain continuously performs many functions simultaneously:

> Thought, emotions, imagination, and predisposition occur concurrently. They interact with other brain processes such as health maintenance and the expansion of general social and cultural knowledge. (66)

6   The researcher who has had the strongest impact on theories of human intelligence is Howard Gardner. In 1979, he was a junior member of a research team at the Harvard Graduate School of Education that investigated human potential and cognition. That experience, along with his years of additional research as a developmental psychologist, led Gardner to theorize that humans possess many different intelligences. In his book Frames of Mind, Gardner strives to disprove the idea that human intelligence consists of only one or two abilities. He offers his alternative: the theory of multiple intelligences (MI). This theory, Gardner explains, calls into question an idea that many people learn "explicitly (from psychology or educational texts)

N

O

P

→

636

COMMENTARY

N. ❶ **PROCESS NOTE:** Laver debated about including the information that the "answer" had once rested almost entirely on the theory of right brain/left brain dominance. (Today, it is only one part of some intelligence theories, and it is ignored in others.) On the one hand, she worried that it might be off the topic; on the other hand, she felt that her paper needed to reflect a little of the scholarly debates that go on concerning descriptions of human intelligence, so she decided to include it. ❗

O. **Use of quotations.** Laver knew that quotations lend authority to research papers but that too many quotations suggest that the writer has not synthesized (see 5f) or summarized (see 31e) the material. Here, Laver quoted because she found the authors' word choice and writing style particularly effective.

P. **Major source.** Howard Gardner is the psychologist who originated the theory of multiple intelligences. Laver decided that the central section of her paper should focus on Gardner and his work. She found his discussions of his theories of his book *Frames of Mind* and in the work of other people who refer to Gardner as the top authority.

QUOTATION: ON WRITING

QUOTATION: ON WRITING

You must learn to write rather than be a writer. Write as well as you can. Don't think of what is wanted, what is popular, what will sell. Write what you want, and write as well as you can.

—Margery Sharp

Laver 5

or implicitly (by living in a culture with a strong but possibly circumscribed view of intelligence)" (5). At first, in 1983, Gardner delineated seven intelligences: musical, bodily-kinesthetic, logical-mathematical, linguistic, spatial, interpersonal, and intrapersonal (<u>Frames</u> 73—76). Later, in 1995, he added an eighth intelligence to his list: naturalistic (Campbell). Table 1 defines the characteristics of each intellgience and then describes behaviors typical of a person with such an intelligence. The only two intelligences that traditional IQ tests measure are logical-mathematical and linguistic.

Q

R

S

T

Table 1

Gardner's Eight Intelligences

Type of Intelligence	Definition	Behavior
Musical	Refers to musical ability, perhaps from a biological advantage. Requires the use of symbols that are read, heard internally, and interpreted to create harmonic melody.	Person enjoys listening to music; expresses eagerness to learn from music and musicians; responds to music by conducting, performing, and/or dancing.
Bodily-kinesthetic	Refers to physical skill, including the ability to play sports, expressing emotions in dance, or otherwise displaying masterful use of the body.	Person enjoys touching and exploring objects; learns best by direct involvement and participation; displays skill in acting, athletics, and dance.
Logical-mathematical	Necessitates problem solving and synthesizing a solution in one's mind before actually articulating it.	Person enjoys logical problem solving and complex operations such as calculus, physics, and computer programming; likes to study the concepts of quantity and time.

→

638

COMMENTARY

Q. ❶ **PROCESS NOTE:** Laver almost made a serious error as a researcher as she was searching for information about Howard Gardner's theory of multiple intelligences. Early in her online research process, she found a Web site featuring a photograph of Gardner along with information about a videotape on his theories. At first, Laver was thrilled to have found something online about Gardner. But when she applied the information in Charts 146 and 147 in section 32f.3 for evaluating sources, she discovered that (1) the information was two years old and included only seven of the eight intelligences Gardner had identified; (2) the material was presented by a commercial enterprise that wanted to sell the videotape; and (3) the many misspellings showed that the material had not been issued by a professionally responsible group. She put the material aside and looked for more credible sources. ❗

R. **Online source.** Campbell is a source that Laver found on the World Wide Web. Because Campbell's article does not have page numbers, Laver cannot give a page reference for her information. In the Works Cited entry at the end of her paper, Laver includes complete information according to new MLA guidelines for documenting World Wide Web sources, including the URL enclosed in angle brackets.

S. **Table.** Table 1 is a condensation of information that Laver at first took eight paragraphs to write. She found them boring to write and dull to read. As a result, she decided to present the material in a table because she felt it would be more concise and useful in this form.

T. **Parallelism.** In early drafts, Laver wrote out the information as it came to mind. For her final draft, however, Laver knew she needed to use parallel structures for the items in each column. In the *Definition* column, she started each definition with a verb in the present tense. In the *Behavior* column, she started each explanation with the words "Person enjoys."

QUOTATION: ON WRITING

Whenever citizens are seen routinely as enemies of their own government, writers are routinely seen to be the most dangerous enemies.

—E. L. Doctorow

Laver 6

Table 1 Gardner's Eight Intelligences, <u>continued</u>   U

Type of
Intelligence   Definition   Behavior

Type of Intelligence	Definition	Behavior
Linguistic	Encompasses the ability to master language by comprehending words and the desire to use them effectively and in a variety of ways to form grammatically correct and well-styled sentences.	Person enjoys and responds to the rhythm and variety of language; listens and reads well with the ability to comprehend, summarize, and interpret ideas.
Spatial	Refers to the capacity to visualize objects without experiencing their actual existence and to recognize people, places, and fine detail.	Person enjoys navigating self and objects through space; produces mental imagery; thinks in pictures and visualizes detail; perceives space from multiple perspectives.
Interpersonal	Involves the ability to interact well with others, seek out or follow leadership, encourage human interaction, and enhance each individual's place in society.	Person enjoys relating and interacting with others to form social relationships; communicates well verbally and nonverbally; recognizes and appreciates diverse perceptions on social and other issues.
Intrapersonal	Involves knowledge of the inner self, including the ability to use feelings and emotions as a rationale for one's behavior.	Person enjoys opportunities to explore the inner self; tends not to conform to popular opinion or peer pressure; works independently to discover meaning in experiences and thoughts.

→

COMMENTARY

U. **Format of table.** Laver had to make some decisions about formatting this table. Advice in the *MLA Handbook for Writers of Research Papers*, 4th edition, states that tables should be double-spaced. She tried that out, but the table took up six pages, overwhelming the rest of her paper. She decided to single-space the table.

Laver followed MLA guidelines by positioning the table title at the left margin and putting a broken line above and below the column headings.

She decided to repeat the table number and title, followed by the word *continued*, underlined. She repeated the column headings on the second and third pages of the table. (The *MLA Handbook* does not include guidelines for tables longer than one page, leaving format decisions for such tables up to the writer.)

Laver 7

```
Table 1  Gardner's Eight Intelligences, continued
-------------------------------------------------------
Type of
Intelligence   Definition            Behavior
-------------------------------------------------------

Naturalistic   Refers to the ability  Person enjoys
               to observe, understand, doing experiments
               and organize patterns  in nature,
               in nature; involves    learning names of
               interest in collecting natural objects,
               and sorting natural    classifying and
               objects.               labeling articles
                                      from nature, and
                                      recognizing small
                                      changes in nature.
-------------------------------------------------------
```

Source: Based on Howard Gardner, <u>Frames of Mind: The Theory of Multiple Intelligences</u> (New York: Basic, 1993) and Thomas Hoerr, "The Naturalist Intelligence," <http://www.newhorizons.org/trm_hoerrmi.html>.

V

7   Gardner has established criteria by which to judge whether an ability deserves to be categorized as an "intelligence" that confers

> a set of skills of problem solving--enabling the individual <u>to resolve genuine problems or difficulties</u> [author's emphasis] that he or she encounters and laying the groundwork for the acquisition of new knowledge. (<u>Frames</u> 60—61)

W

These criteria include a specific, identifiable location in the brain; identifiable stages of development; specific new skills as development progresses; a "core set of operations," or specific ways of processing specific kinds of information; an evolutionary reason for existing; and being measurable or testable (Hoerr, "Naturalist").

8   Although MI theory emerged from research in psychology, educators--and their students--have begun to adopt the concept. Teachers using Gardner's ideas and methods are demonstrating that when students who do not usually do well in school are encouraged,

→

COMMENTARY

V. **More on format of table.** Following MLA style, Laver uses a broken line at the end of the information in the table.

For the source line, she includes information about Gardner's *Frames of Mind*, a print book, and Thomas Hoerr's "The Naturalist Intelligence," a source from the World Wide Web. She gives the URL in angle brackets, as in the Works Cited entry.

W. **Author's emphasis.** Laver knows that when underlining (or italic type) appears in a quotation, it may not be clear who is doing the emphasizing. It is prudent to insert [author's emphasis] or [emphasis added], between brackets, the standard way to insert information into quotations.

QUOTATION: ON WRITING

Each paragraph almost discovers the paragraph it precedes. When I end one paragraph I know it must lead to another.

—Roger Rosenblatt

Laver 8

and taught how, to tap the rich mine of their other intelligences to learn traditional classroom tasks, the students succeed. Specific illustrations are easy to find in reports from teachers. For example, a teacher drew on the highly developed spatial-mechanical intelligence of Jacob, a first-grader who refused to take part in writing activities.

X

> The teacher asked that during "journal time" Jacob create a tool dictionary to be used as a resource in the mechanical learning center. After several entries in which he drew and described tools and other materials, Jacob confidently moved on to writing about other things of import to him, such as his brothers and a recent birthday party. Rather than shy away from all things linguistic--he had previously refused any task requiring a pencil--Jacob became invested in journal writing. (Gray and Viens 23–24)

Y

9   Traditional theory asks, "Is this student intelligent?" MI theory allows Jacob's teacher to ask a more rewarding question: "In what way is this student intelligent?" and "How can I use his strongest intelligence to help him develop other abilities?" (Hoerr, "Focusing").

10   Another illustration comes from a class of high school students studying American history. Dealing with the Expansion Era, from the late eighteenth century to the middle of the nineteenth century, students get an assignment to choose a topic from a list prepared by the teacher, to research the topic, and to respond to the topic by using what they have learned about MI theory.

→

COMMENTARY

X. **Specific examples.** Laver knows that well-chosen specific examples can be clarifying and confirming illustrations of a point. Of the many examples she finds during her research, she chooses the ones here and in paragraph 10 because she finds them memorable and convincing.

Y. **Displayed quotation.** Because the quotation by Gray and Viens is more than four lines long, MLA style calls for it to be "displayed." This means that the quotation must have all lines in a "block" indented from the left margin. For a paper prepared on a typewriter, each line should be indented ten characters on the left. For a paper prepared on a computer, each line should be indented 1 inch (or one tab) from the left margin.

QUOTATION: ON WRITING

Sometimes I organize a piece so carefully that I will not only know the general thought I want to end with, I will write the last sentence before having written anything else. This sentence will contain all of the feeling of a piece unwritten, but I know it will be there and almost always I'm right.

—Roger Rosenblatt

QUOTATION: ON WRITING

There are no dull subjects. There are only dull writers.

—H. L. Mencken

Students choose a format that allows them to use their strongest intelligence so that they can come to know really well the history they are studying. The projects in this class included writing and performing a skit about the Lewis and Clark Expedition (linguistic and interpersonal intelligences); painting watercolors of birds and other wildlife for a project on John J. Audubon (visual-spatial intelligence); creating a working telegraph (logical-mathematical and bodily-kinesthetic intelligences); giving a eulogy of Davy Crockett (interpersonal intelligence); and taking on the role of a historical figure and speaking to the class "in character" (intrapersonal, linguistic, and interpersonal intelligences). Their teacher found that her students gained self-knowledge along with their American history. Because of this teacher's awareness of and ability to engage her students' multiple intelligences, those students feel "that they will be valued for their unique qualities, that they can succeed in their own way, and that they can have a successful future" (Lambert).

Clearly, whether students adopt the concepts of multiple intelligences on their own, as Barbry did, or work on them together with teachers, a new chance exists for more students to excel in school and eventually in their jobs and lives. Interestingly, many people in the general public are beginning to become interested in the concept of multiple intelligences. For example, strong popular interest recently emerged concerning two of Gardner's intelligences: interpersonal and intrapersonal. Starting

COMMENTARY

Z. ❶ **PROCESS NOTE:** In earlier drafts, Laver used full sentences for the information shown in parentheses here. This section of the paper seemed too long and wordy, so she condensed the material. Here is an excerpt from an earlier draft:

```
    One class project was to write and perform a skit about
the Lewis and Clark Expedition. This drew on linguistic and
interpersonal intelligences. Another was to paint watercolors
of birds and other wildlife for a project on John J. Audubon.
This drew on visual-spatial intelligence.
```
❗

QUOTATION: ON WRITING

In every real sense, the writer writes in order to teach himself, to understand himself, to satisfy himself; the publishing of the ideas is a curious anticlimax.

—Alfred Kazin

Laver 10

with the 1990 publication of their journal article   AA
"Emotional Intelligence," Peter Salovey and John Mayer
led the way among scientists to a substantial expansion
of Gardner's concepts of interpersonal and intrapersonal
intelligences. Salovey and Mayer avoid overusing
technical language and so make their ideas more generally
accessible. For example, here is their straightforward
definition of emotional intelligence: "the ability to
monitor one's own feelings and emotions, to discriminate
among them, and to use this information to guide one's
thinking and actions" [author's emphasis] (189). In 1995
a general-audience "pop psychology" book, Emotional
Intelligence, became an immediate best-seller upon
publication and remained one for many months. Its author,
Daniel Goleman, a journalist and writer, fleshes out
Gardner's concepts of interpersonal and intrapersonal
intelligences. But he also emphasizes the close
interaction between them and the other intelligences that
Gardner has identified:

> These two minds, the emotional and the
> rational, operate in tight harmony for
> the most part, intertwining their very
> different ways of knowing to guide us through
> the world. Ordinarily there is a balance
> between emotional and rational minds, with
> emotion feeding into and informing the
> operations of the rational mind, and the
> rational mind refining and sometimes vetoing
> the inputs of the emotions. (9)

12   Goleman, drawing mainly from the work of Salovey and
Mayer and a few others, asked Gardner his reaction

COMMENTARY

AA. ❶ **PROCESS NOTE:** Serendipity (which means "luck, happenstance") led Laver to discover the work of Salovey and Mayer and of Goleman. A while before she wrote her paper, she had seen the title *Emotional Intelligence* on a book that her parents were reading. It had been recommended by friends who liked to read best-sellers. As Laver was learning about Gardner's concepts of different types of intelligence, the Goleman book popped into her mind, and so she checked it out of the library. It turned out to be an excellent source, and its bibliography led her to the very useful scholarly article by Salovey and Mayer. ❗

QUOTATION: ON WRITING

Had I known the answer to any of these questions, I would never have needed to write.

—Joan Didion

BACKGROUND

Ellipsis is the omission of words from a quotation. Three spaced dots, known as *ellipsis points*, are used to show that some of the original writer's words have been left out. If an omission occurs at the beginning of a quotation, ellipsis points are not needed to show the omission. They are also unnecessary at the end of a quotation as long as the sentence in which it occurs is complete. (See 29d.)

Laver 11

to the new public interest in emotional abilities. Gardner said he applauded the interest as a balance to trends in his work. He said that he tended to focus more on cognition,

> yet when I first wrote about the personal
> intelligences, I was [author's emphasis]
> talking about emotion . . . but as it evolved in
> practice, the theory of multiple intelligences
> has evolved to focus more on cognition--that
> is, awareness of one's mental processes--
> "rather than on the full range of emotional
> abilities." (41)

13   Additional new discoveries about the brain and human intelligence will likely emerge as scientists continue their investigations. In turn, changes in public attitudes toward IQ scores are likely to follow. Most educators and the members of the general public will begin to accept the idea that human intelligence is far-ranging, involving much more than the logical-mathematical intelligence and, to a lesser extent, the linguistic intelligence that IQ tests claim to measure. The greatest benefit will be that more students can start to excel in all subjects through avenues built on talents not traditionally valued in schools. In turn, those students can enjoy the greater self-esteem that leads to better personal and family lives and to more satisfying jobs.

BB

→

COMMENTARY

BB. **Concluding paragraph.** Laver decides to end her paper with her opinion coupled with a call for awareness and a prediction for the future.

QUOTATION: ON WRITING

He that will write well in any tongue must follow this counsel of Aristotle: to speak as the common people do, to think as wise men do.

—Roger Ascham

Works Cited   CC

Caine, Renate Nummela, and Geoffrey Caine. "Understanding   DD
     a Brain-Based Approach to Learning and Teaching."
     <u>Educational Leadership</u> 48 (1990): 66–70.
Campbell, Bruce. "The Naturalist Intelligence." <u>The</u>   EE
     <u>Building Tool Room</u>. Home page. 10 Oct. 1997
     <http://www.newhorizons.org/article_eightintel.html>.
Gardner, Howard. <u>Frames of Mind: The Theory of Multiple</u>   FF
     <u>Intelligences</u>. New York: Basic, 1993.
---. "Reflections on Multiple Intelligences: Myths and   GG
     Messages." <u>Phi Delta Kappan</u> 77 (1995): 200–09.
Goleman, Daniel. <u>Emotional Intelligence</u>. New York:
     Bantam, 1995.
Gray, James, and Julie Viens. "The Theory of Multiple
     Intelligences: Understanding Cognitive Diversity in
     School." <u>National Forum: Phi Kappa Phi Journal</u> 74
     (1994): 22–25.
Hartocollis, Anemona. "The Big Test Comes Early." <u>New</u>   HH
     <u>York Times</u> 12 Dec. 1997, late ed.: B1+.
"History of Intelligence." <u>Grolier Multimedia</u>   II
     <u>Encyclopedia</u>. Online. America Online. 12 Dec.
     1997.
Hoerr, Thomas. "Focusing on the Personal Intelligences   JJ
     as a Basis for Success." <u>NASSP Bulletin</u> 80.583
     (1996): n.pag. <u>Periodical Abstracts</u>. Online.
     FirstSearch. 4 Oct. 1997.
---. "The Naturalist Intelligence." <u>The Building Tool</u>
     <u>Room</u>. Home page. 10 Oct. 1997.
     <http://www.newhorizons.org/trm_hoerrmi.html>.

➜

COMMENTARY

CC. **General format.** Laver provides an alphabetically arranged list of all the sources referred to in the paper. It is headed "Works Cited" and follows MLA documentation style (see 33c). Entries are alphabetized by each author's last name; if no author's name is given, the work's title is the first information unit and is alphabetized by its first word (excluding *A, An,* or *The*). Any entry more than one line long has a five-space (or 1/2-inch) indent for each line after the first. Double-spacing is used within and between entries.

DD. **Journal article by two authors.** The name of the first author is inverted (last name, first name, middle name, if any), but the name of the second is not. Article title is in quotation marks, and journal title is underlined. Volume, year (in parentheses), and page numbers are given. (The same format is used for the entries for Gray and Viens and for Salovey and Mayer.)

EE. **Article published on a professional site on the World Wide Web.** Author's name is inverted. Article title is in quotation marks. Title of the professional site is underlined, and the site is identified as a home page. The access date is followed by the URL enclosed in angle brackets. (The same format is used for another source found on the World Wide Web, the second entry for Hoerr.)

FF. **Book by one author.** Author's name is inverted. Title is underlined. Publisher is identified in as brief a form as possible.

GG. **Second work by an author.** Three hyphens followed by a period indicate that the author is the same as in the preceding entry. Multiple works by the same author are listed in alphabetical order by title. (This device is also used for the second entry for Hoerr.)

HH. **Article in a daily newspaper.** Article title is in quotation marks. Name of newspaper is underlined. Date of newspaper is given as day, abbreviated month, and year, followed by a colon and inclusive page numbers.

II. **Unsigned article in an online encyclopedia.** Entry is alphabetized by article title, which is given first, in quotation marks. Encyclopedia name is underlined. *Online* indicates that the encyclopedia was found online (not on the World Wide Web). America Online is the computer service through which it was accessed, on the date given last.

JJ. **Abstract accessed online.** After the author's name, the title of the work is in quotation marks, followed by the name of the original publication (*NASSP Bulletin*), underlined; its volume, issue number, and year; and, after the colon, the abbreviation *n.pag.* to indicate that the online version is unpaged. The title of the database

QUOTATION: ON WRITING

I'm not alone when I'm writing—the language itself, like a kind of trampoline, is there helping me.

—William Stafford

Laver 13

"Intelligence." <u>Columbia Encyclopedia</u>. 1963 ed.   KK

Lambert, Endy Ecklund. "From Crockett to Tubman:

    Investigating Historical Perspectives." <u>Educational</u>

    <u>Leadership</u> 55 (1997): n.pag. <u>Periodical Abstracts</u>.

    Online. FirstSearch. 5 Oct. 1997.

Salovey, Peter, and John D. Mayer. "Emotional

    Intelligence." <u>Imagination, Cognition and Personality</u>

    9 (1989—90): 185—211.

Staples, Brent. "The IQ Cult." <u>The Bell Curve Debate:</u>   LL

    <u>History, Documents, Opinions</u>. Ed. Russell Jacoby and

    Naomi Glauberman. New York: Times, 1995. 293—95.

Urbina, Susana P. "Intelligence: Definition and   MM

    Theoretical Models." <u>Survey of Social Science:</u>

    <u>Psychology Series</u>. Ed. Frank Magill. Vol. 3.

    Pasadena: Salem, 1994. 1328—33.

COMMENTARY

Abstract accessed online *(continued)*

Periodical Abstracts, is underlined. FirstSearch is the service by which *Periodical Abstracts* was accessed on the date given last. (This format is also used for the entry for Lambert.)

KK. **Unsigned article in a print encyclopedia.** Entry is alphabetized by article title, given first in quotation marks. Encyclopedia title is underlined. No publication information is required for familiar reference books, other than the edition number or the year of publication. When articles are arranged in alphabetical order, as they are in this encyclopedia, no page numbers need be given.

LL. **Essay in an edited book.** Name of essay author is given first, followed by essay title in quotation marks. Title of the book is underlined. Abbreviation *Ed.* (for "Edited by") is followed by the names of the editors in regular order. Publication information is given in briefest form, and page range uses last two digits of the second number.

MM. **Signed article in a multivolume reference work.** Author of article is followed by title of article in quotation marks. Title of book is underlined. Abbreviation *Ed.* (for "Edited by") is followed by the editor's name in regular order. Volume numbers use arabic numerals, even if the volumes are numbered with roman numerals. Publication information is followed by inclusive page numbers for the article.

QUOTATION: ON WRITING

Writing represents a unique mode of learning—not merely valuable, not merely special, but unique.... Writing serves learning uniquely because writing as process-and-product possesses a cluster of attributes that correspond uniquely to certain powerful learning strategies.

—Janet Emig

TEACHING TIP

You might want to explain that formats are of major importance in many disciplines other than English composition. The formats constitute "genres" that readers expect. The formats ease communication because readers know where to look for specific information: background, data, conclusions.

35

CASE STUDY: A STUDENT WRITING AN APA RESEARCH PAPER

This chapter presents a student research paper written in the DOCUMENTATION STYLE of the American Psychological Association (APA). Section 35a discusses the researching (see Chapter 32), planning (see Chapter 2), drafting (see 3b and 32t), and revising (see 3c and 32t) processes of the student, Carlos Velez. Section 35b shows the final draft of the paper, including its abstract.

> **Carlos Velez was given this assignment for a research paper in a course called Introduction to Psychology:** Write a research paper of 1,800 to 2,000 words about an unconscious process in humans. For guidance, refer to the *Simon & Schuster Handbook for Writers,* Fifth Edition, Chapters 31 through 33. Use the documentation style of the American Psychological Association (APA) explained in Chapter 33. Your topic and working bibliography are due in two weeks. An early draft of your paper is due two weeks later (try to get it close to what you hope will be your last draft, so that comments from me and your peers can concretely help you write an excellent final draft). Your final draft is due one week after the early draft is returned to you with comments.

35a Observing the processes of researching and writing an APA-style research paper

After Carlos Velez read his assignment, he started **planning** by listing various unconscious processes in humans so that he could pick one most interesting to him. Referring to his class notes and the textbook from his psychology course, he found these topics: sleep, dreams, insomnia, biological clocks, daydreams, hypnosis, and meditation. He favored biological clocks because of his experiences with jet lag whenever he traveled between his home in California (in the Pacific Time Zone) and his grandparents' home in Puerto Rico (in the Atlantic Time Zone, where it is four hours later).

Velez then checked to see whether the library at his college had enough sources useful for research on biological clocks. He was pleased to find books, journal articles, magazine and newspaper articles, and even a videotape of a Public Broadcasting System program on the subject. So that he could compile a working bibliography (see 33b) and, at the same time, try to find an approach to the topic suitable for a paper of 1,800 to 2,000 words, Velez began to read and take notes (see 32j). He saw entire books about biological clocks, so he realized that he would need to narrow the topic (see 32d) sufficiently to shape a THESIS STATEMENT (see 2n and 32r). The narrowing process worried him because he had been told in other college courses that his topics for research papers were too broad. He was determined this time to avoid that same problem.

The working bibliography that Velez submitted consisted of twenty-six sources, though he had read and rejected about six others (he knew that this represented real progress for him). He did not intend to use them all in his paper, but he wanted them available as he wrote his early drafts. Not surprisingly, his instructor urged him to reduce the list once drafting began; otherwise, Velez would risk writing too little about too much. He redoubled his efforts to read even more critically to evaluate his sources (see 5e and 32f.3) and weed out material. He got his list down to nineteen sources, took detailed notes (see 32j) on each, and began to group his material into emerging subtopics.

To start **drafting** his paper, Velez spread his note cards around him for easy reference, but he felt somewhat overwhelmed by the amount of information at hand, and he wrote only a few sentences. To break through, he decided to write a "discovery draft" (see 3b) to see what he had absorbed from his reading and notetaking. That very rough draft became his vehicle for many things, including creating an effective thesis statement, inserting source information according to APA documentation style, and checking the logical arrangement of his material.

Revising for Velez started with his thesis statement, a process that helped him further narrow his focus. He started with "Biological clocks are fascinating," which expressed his feelings but said nothing of substance. His next version served well as he revised his discovery draft into a true first draft: "Biological clocks, our unconscious timekeepers, affect our lives in many ways including compatibility in marriage, family life, jet travel, work schedules, illnesses, medical treatments, and the

QUOTATION: ON WRITING

Writing is thinking on paper. Anyone who thinks clearly should be able to write clearly—about any subject at all.
—William Zinsser

space program." That version proved to Velez that he was covering too much for an 1,800- to 2,000-word research paper, and he wanted to drop material. He decided first to inform his readers about the phenomenon of biological clocks and then to discuss the effects of those clocks on people's alertness in the morning and later in the day, on travelers on jet airplanes, and on workers' performance. For his final draft, Velez used this more focused thesis statement: "Biological clocks, which are a significant feature of human design, greatly affect personal and professional lifestyles."

Using APA documentation style made Velez attend very closely to the details of correct parenthetical references (see 33d.1) within his paper and a correct References list (see 33d.2 and 33d.3) at the end. Because he had used MLA documentation style in other courses, he made sure not to confuse the two styles. For example, he saw that APA-style parenthetical citations require a page reference for a quotation but not for a paraphrase or summary (whereas MLA style requires a page reference for all three). For format and style details of the References list at the end of his paper, he found Chart 153 in section 33d.2 especially helpful.

As Velez checked the logical arrangement of his material, he realized that because he had dropped some aspects of biological clocks when he finally narrowed his topic sufficiently, he needed a little more depth about the aspects that he was retaining. A few hours at the computer led him to what he needed, including examples about baseball players and emergency room physicians. Velez learned from his research experiences the difference between researching a topic too broadly (and therefore gathering too many sources for the assignment) and researching a few aspects of a topic in depth by focusing on selected sources. His final draft, which appears in 35b, draws on sixteen sources, a number that is down considerably from the twenty-six with which he started.

Part of Velez's title page and abstract page are shown opposite. For guidelines on writing an abstract, see section 33d.4.

35b Looking at the final draft of an APA-style research paper

```
                    Biological Clocks    1  ◄— 1″ —►


                 Biological Clocks:
            The Body's Internal Timepieces
                    Carlos Velez
```

APA-style Title Page

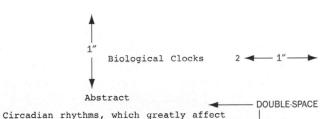

```
                    Biological Clocks    2  ◄— 1″ —►

                        Abstract              ◄— DOUBLE-SPACE
            Circadian rhythms, which greatly affect
        human lives, often suffer disruptions in
        technological societies, resulting in such
        disorders as jet lag syndrome and seasonal
        affective disorder (SAD). With growing
        scientific awareness of both natural circadian
        cycles and the effects of disturbances of
        these cycles, individuals are learning how to
        control some negative effects.
```

APA-style Abstract Page

QUOTATION: ON WRITING

It is by sitting down to write every morning that one becomes a writer. Those who do not do this remain amateurs.
—Gerald Brenan

Biological Clocks:

The Body's Internal Timepieces

Life in modern, technological societies is built around timepieces. People set clocks on radios, microwave ovens, VCRs, and electric coffee makers. Students respond to bells that start and end the school day as well as divide it into blocks of time. Almost everyone relies on clocks to manage time well. While carefully managing the minutes and hours each day, individuals are often encouraged or forced by current styles of family and work life to violate another kind of time: their body's time. Biological clocks, which are also known as circadian cycles, are a significant feature of human design that greatly affect personal and professional lifestyles.

The term circadian, which is Latin for "about a day," describes the rhythms of people's internal biological clocks. Circadian cycles are in tune with external time cycles such as the 24-hour period of the earth's daily rotation as signaled by the rising and setting of the sun. In fact, says William Schwartz, professor of neurobiology and a researcher in the field of chronobiology (the study of circadian rhythms), "All such biological clocks are adaptations to life on a rotating world" (Lewis, 1995, p. 14). Usually, humans set their biological clocks by seeing these cycles of daylight and darkness. Carefully designed studies conducted in caves or similar environments that let researchers control light and darkness have shown that most people create cycles slightly over 24 hours when they are not exposed to natural cycles of day and night (Allis & Haederle, 1989; Enright, 1980). Human perception of the external day-night cycle affects the production and release of a brain hormone, melatonin, which is important in initiating and regulating the sleep-wake cycle, as Alfred Lewy and other scientists at the National Institutes of Health in Bethesda, Maryland, have found (Winfree, 1987).

➜

An individual's lifestyle reflects that person's own circadian cycle. Scientists group people as "larks" or "owls" based on whether individuals are more efficient in the morning or at night. The idea behind the labels is that "in nature certain animals are diurnal, active during the light period; others are nocturnal, active at night. The 'morning lark' and 'night owl' connotations typically are used to categorize the human extremes" ("Are You," 1989, p. 11).

"Larks" who must stay up late at night and "owls" who must awaken early in the morning experience mild versions of the disturbances, called "jet lag," that time-zone travelers often encounter. Jet lag, which is characterized by fatigue and irregular sleep patterns, results from disruption of circadian rhythms, a common problem among those who travel great distances by jet airplane to different time zones:

> Jet lag syndrome is the inability of the internal
> body rhythm to rapidly resynchronize after sudden
> shifts in the timing. For a variety of reasons, the
> system attempts to maintain stability and resist
> temporal change. Consequently, complete adjustment
> can often be delayed for several days--sometimes for
> a week--after arrival at one's destination. (Bonner,
> 1991, p. 72)

Interestingly, research shows that the number of flying hours is not the cause of jet lag. Rather, "the number, rate, and direction of time-zone changes are the critical factors in determining the extent and degree of jet lag symptoms," according to Richard Coleman (1986, p. 67) in <u>Wide Awake at 3 a.m.: By Choice or by Chance?</u> Eastbound travelers find it harder than westbound travelers to adjust.

Proof of this theory can be found in the national pastime, baseball. Three researchers analyzed win-lose records to discover whether jet lag affected baseball players'

→

Biological Clocks   5

performance (Recht, Lew, & Schwartz, 1995). They focused on the records of teams in the eastern and western United States over a period of 3 years. If a visiting team did not have to travel through any time zones, it lost 54% of the time. If the visiting team had traveled from east to west, it lost 56.2% of the time. But if the visitors had traveled from west to east, the home team beat the visitors 62.9% of the time.

Besides people who experience jet lag, another group that suffers greatly from biological-clock disruptions consists of people whose livelihoods depend on erratic schedules. This situation affects 20 to 30 million U.S. workers whose work schedules differ from the usual morning starting time and afternoon or early evening ending time (Weiss, 1989). Charles Czeisler, director of the Center for Circadian and Sleep Disorders at Brigham and Woman's Hospital in Boston, reports that 27% of the U.S. workforce does shift work (Binkley, 1990). Shift work can mean, for example, working from 7:00 a.m. to 3:00 p.m. for 6 weeks, from 3:00 p.m. to 11:00 p.m. for 6 weeks, and from 11:00 p.m. to 7:00 a.m. for 6 weeks. Many shift workers endure stomach and intestinal-tract disorders, and, on average, they have a three times higher risk of heart disease than non-shift workers (Bingham, 1989). In a 1989 report to the American Association for the Advancement of Science, Czeisler states that "police officers, [medical] interns, and many others who work nights perform poorly and are involved in more on-the-job accidents than their daytime counterparts" (Binkley, 1990, p. 26).

Other researchers confirm that safety is at risk during late-shift hours (Chollar, 1989). In a study of 28 medical interns observed during late-night shifts over a 1-year period, 25% admitted to falling asleep while talking on the phone, and 34% had at least one accident or near-accident during that period (Weiss, 1989). Investigations into the Challenger Shuttle explosion and the nuclear-reactor disasters at Three Mile Island and Chernobyl reveal critical errors made by people undergoing the combined stresses of lack of sleep and unusual work schedules (Toufexis, 1989).

Emergency room physicians experience these two stresses all the time. Their professional group, the American College of Emergency Physicians (ACEP), after investigating circadian rhythms and shift work, drafted a formal policy statement, approved by ACEP's Board of Directors in 1994. The policy calls for "shifts . . . consistent with circadian principles" to prevent "burnout" and keep emergency physicians from leaving the field, as well as to enable them to take the best care of patients (Thomas, 1996).

If jet lag and circadian disruptions caused by shift work are obvious ways to upset a biological clock, a less obvious disruption is increasingly recognized as a medical problem: the disorder known as seasonal affective disorder (SAD). Table 1 lists some of the major symptoms of SAD.

Table 1

Common Symptoms of Seasonal Affective Disorder

Sadness	Later waking
Anxiety	Increased sleep time
Decreased physical activity	Interrupted, unrefreshing sleep
Irritability	Daytime drowsiness
Increased appetite	Decreased sexual drive
Craving for carbohydrates	Menstrual problems
Weight gain	Work problems
Earlier onset of sleep	Interpersonal problems

Note. From The Clockwork Sparrow (p. 204), by S. Binkley, 1990, Englewood Cliffs, NJ: Prentice Hall. Copyright 1990 by Prentice Hall.

SAD appears to be related to the short daylight (photoperiod) of winter in the temperate zones of the northern and southern hemispheres. The phenomenon of SAD not only

→

illustrates the important role of circadian rhythms but also dramatically proves that an understanding of circadian principles can help scientists improve the lives of people who experience disruptions of their biological clocks. Binkley claims that exposure to bright light for periods of up to 2 hours a day during the short-photoperiod days of winter reduces SAD-related "depression in 87 percent of patients . . . within a few days; relapses followed" (pp. 203–204) when light treatment ended.

Lengthening a person's exposure to bright light can also help combat the effects of jet lag and shift work. Specific suggestions for using light to help reset a jet traveler's biological clock include "a late-afternoon golf game or early-morning walk"; for night-shift workers, staying in the dark during the day and being in artificial light that mimics daylight at night are helpful (Mayo Clinic, 1997).

Establishing work schedules more sensitive to biological clocks can increase a sense of well-being and reduce certain safety hazards. A group of police officers in Philadelphia were studied while on modified shift schedules (Locitzer, 1989; Toufexis, 1989). These officers changed between day shifts and night shifts less frequently than they had on former shift schedules; they rotated forward rather than backward in time; and they worked 4 rather than 6 consecutive days. Officers reported 40% fewer patrol car accidents and decreased use of drugs or alcohol to get to sleep. Overall, the police officers preferred the modified shift schedules. Charles Czeisler, who conducted the study, summarizes the importance of these results: "When schedules are introduced that take into account the properties of the human circadian system, subjective estimates of work schedule satisfaction and health improve, personnel turnover decreases, and worker productivity increases" (Locitzer, 1989).

Biological Clocks   8

Scientists like Charles Czeisler are helping individuals live harmoniously with their biological clocks. Growing awareness of the effects of such situations as shift work and travel across time zones is one significant step toward control. The use of light to manipulate the body's sense of time is another. As more people become aware of how circadian rhythms affect lifestyles, the day might soon come when we can fully control our biological clocks instead of their controlling us.

QUOTATION: ON READING

If we encounter a man of rare intellect, we should ask him what books he reads.
—Ralph Waldo Emerson

QUOTATION: ON READING

A book is like a garden carried in the pocket.

—Chinese proverb

References

Allis, T., & Haederle, M. (1989, June 12). Ace in the hole: Stefania Follini never caved in. People, 52.

Are you a day or night person? (1989, March 4). USA Today, 11.

Bingham, R. (Writer and Director). (1989, June 10). The time of our lives [Television production]. Los Angeles: KCET Public Television of Southern California.

Binkley, S. (1990). The clockwork sparrow. Englewood Cliffs, NJ: Prentice Hall.

Bonner, P. (1991, July). Travel rhythms. Sky Magazine, 72—73, 76—77.

Chollar, S., (1989, November). Safe solutions for night work. Psychology Today, 26.

Coleman, R. (1986). Wide awake at 3:00 a.m.: By choice or by chance? New York: Freeman.

Enright, J. T. (1980). The timing of sleep and wakefulness. Berlin: Springer-Verlag.

Lewis, R. (1995, December 24). Chronobiology researchers say their field's time has come. The Scientist, 9, 14 [On-line newspaper]. Retrieved December 30, 1997, from the World Wide Web: http://www.the-scientist.library.upenn.edu/yr1995/dec/chrono_951211.html

Locitzer, K. (1989, July/August). Are you out of sync with each other? Psychology Today, 66.

Mayo Clinic. (1997, December 30). Tricks to try when you're out of sync. Mayo Health Oasis [On-line newsletter]. Originally published in Mayo Clinic Health Letter, March 1995. Retrieved December 30, 1997, from the World Wide Web: http://www.mayohealth.org/mayo/9503/htm/sync_sb.htm

Recht, L., Lew, R., & Schwartz, W. (1995, October 19). Baseball teams beaten by jet lag [Letter]. Nature, 377, 583.

→

Biological Clocks   10

Thomas, H. (1996). Circadian rhythms and shift work [American College of Emergency Physicians policy resource and education paper posted on the World Wide Web]. ACEP Online. Retrieved December 30, 1997, from the World Wide Web: http://www.acep.org/POLICY/PR004166.HTM

Toufexis, A. (1989, June 5). The times of your life. Time, 66—67.

Weiss, R. (1989, January 21). Safety gets short shrift on long night shift. Science News, 37.

Winfree, A. (1987). The timing of biological clocks. New York: Freeman.

PART SIX

WRITING ACROSS THE CURRICULUM

When you write for different disciplines, you become familiar with the perspectives and assumptions that underlie each discipline. Part Six compares and contrasts various disciplines to help you respond effectively to the major types of writing assignments each discipline involves. The information in Part Six is a resource for your entire college career and beyond.

BACKGROUND

In "Using Feedback Groups and an Editorial Board in a WAC Classroom" (*Teaching English in the Two-Year College*, February 1996: 57–63), Dave Healy and Murray Jensen explain how science instructors can collaborate to incorporate "real-world experiences" into course content.

BACKGROUND

In "Evolving Paradigms: WAC and the Rhetoric of Inquiry" (*College Composition and Communication*, October 1994: 369–380), Judy Kirscht, Rhonda Levine, and John Reiff describe their emphasis on "*how* knowledge has been constructed as well as *what* that knowledge is."

36

COMPARING THE DISCIPLINES

The humanities, the social sciences, and the natural sciences each have their own perspectives on the world. Each of the disciplines also has its own philosophies about academic thought and research. To understand some of the differences among the disciplines, consider these three quite different paragraphs about a mountain.

HUMANITIES

The mountain stands above all that surrounds it. Giant timbers—part of a collage of evergreen and deciduous trees—conceal the expansive mountain's slope, where cattle once grazed. At the base of the mountain, a cool stream flows over rocks of all sizes, colors, and shapes. Next to the outer bank of the stream stands a shingled farmhouse, desolate, yet suggesting its active past. Unfortunately, the peaceful scene is interrupted by billboards and chairlifts, landmarks of a modern, fast-paced life.

SOCIAL SCIENCES

Among the favorite pastimes of American city dwellers is the "return to nature." Many outdoor enthusiasts hope to enjoy a scenic trip to the mountains, only to be disappointed. They know they have arrived at the mountain that they have traveled hundreds of miles to see because huge billboards are directing them to its base. As they look up the mountain, dozens of people are riding over the treetops in a chairlift, littering the slope with paper cups and food wrappers. At the base of the mountain stands the inevitable refreshment stand, found at virtually all American tourist attractions. Land developers consider such commercialization a way to preserve and utilize natural resources, but environmentalists are appalled.

NATURAL SCIENCES

The mountain rises approximately 5,600 feet above sea level. The underlying rock is igneous, of volcanic origin, composed primarily of granites and feldspars. Three distinct biological communities are present on the mountain. The community at the top of the mountain is alpine, dominated by very short grasses and forbs. At middle altitudes, the community is a typical northern boreal coniferous forest community, and at the base and lower altitudes, deciduous forest is the dominant community.

This community has, however, been highly affected by agricultural development along the river at its base and by recreational development.

These examples illustrate that each discipline has its perspective and emphasis. The paragraph written for the humanities describes the mountain from the individual perspective of the writer—a perspective both personal and yet representative of a general human response. The paragraph written for the social sciences focuses on the behavior of people as a group. The paragraph written for the natural sciences reports observations of natural phenomena.

As you study and write in each of the academic disciplines, you can experience alternate ways of thinking. As you come to know the habits of mind that characterize each discipline, you can develop specialized vocabularies to participate in the conversations of each discipline. As the range of your perspectives grows, you gain lifelong access to the major benefit of a college education. No matter what differences exist among the academic disciplines, all subject areas interconnect and overlap. Chart 156 lists similarities and differences.

 Similarities and differences in writing across the disciplines **156**

Similarities

1. Consider your purpose, audience, and tone (see Chapters 1–2).
2. Use the writing process to plan, shape, draft, revise, edit, and proofread (see Chapters 2–3).
3. Develop a thesis (see Chapters 2–3).
4. Arrange and organize your ideas (see Chapter 2).
5. Use supporting evidence see (Chapters 2–4).
6. Develop paragraphs thoroughly (see Chapter 4).
7. Critically read, think, synthesize, and write (see Chapter 5).
8. Avoid confusing summary with synthesis (see Chapter 5).
9. Reason well; use good logic (see Chapter 5).
10. Write effective sentences (see Chapters 16–19).
11. Argue well (see Chapter 6).
12. Choose words well (see Chapters 20–21).
13. Use correct grammar (see Chapters 7–15).
14. Spell correctly (see Chapter 22).
15. Use correct punctuation and mechanics (see Chapters 23–30). →

WRITING ACROSS THE CURRICULUM: PORTFOLIO APPROACHES AND ACTIVITIES

Literacy is ultimately the student's responsibility. The instructional cycle is complete only to the degree that the student can translate information into a skill or tool. Portfolios offer a process through which students can transfer what they have learned in a writing course to other courses. By identifying, organizing, and reflecting on the various writing and reading activities necessary to master a course, students learn connections between curricula that exceed what can be taught.

Scoring Issues

Scoring a content portfolio (an application of Writing Across the Curriculum) can be as simple as assigning a percentage as if it were an independent project. Even 10 percent of a final college grade will provide an incentive to make the process work. However, truthfully, the more the process is valued and weighted, the more the student pays attention to the process. Holistic scoring, accompanied with published rubrics and eventually even sample student portfolios, makes the process surprisingly manageable. However, checklists and point systems for individual entries work just as well. In fact, the great strength of portfolio assessment is that the instructor is free to choose weights and values. A portfolio is a means to an end, a framework to house learning, a way to connect learning to assessment.

Reading-Writing-Listening Connection

Understanding the interdependence of lecture, reading, notetaking, test taking, and essay writing marks a mature student. Portfolios can become a system of tracking and communicating that connection, thereby nurturing this maturity. Ideally, success will demonstrate itself in measurable ways such as quizzes and tests scores, reading speed, and organizational and time management skills. →

Portfolio (continued)

Students need to develop inferential, interpretive reading skills. These critical thinking skills, the cornerstone of portfolios, are recorded by careful student notetaking.

Notetaking: A Portfolio Activity That Records Reading-Writing-Listening Skills

Take time to recommend notetaking strategies. Provide visual models for students. Present an outline of the daily lesson in an overhead as you present a lecture, or divide the board into vertical sections with headings such as "Question," "Answers," and "Applications" to guide small group work. Reward good notetakers with warm-up, open-note quizzes as a bridge between lessons (an excellent portfolio entry or series of entries).

Creating a Content Portfolio

1. Establish prior knowledge and current needs: Use informal journal writing.

a. Preview the course: Read syllabus, mark calendar for important due dates.

b. Review prior experience: Identify barriers (consider everything from time management and reading and writing skills to the specialized vocabulary or jargon of the course (see 36d).

c. Recognize your audience: Consider the instructor; carefully record instructor's opinions and preferences (see 36c).

d. Identify resources—library, learning centers, tutors, instructor office hours.

2. Set temporary goals and activities for study sessions: Use a formal essay.

a. Keep written records of all activities in and out of class; use a notetaking system for academic research (see 32g and 32j.2) and for self-study and class notes (Chapter 5).

b. Reflect frequently: What did I learn? How will this help? What is its relevance? Its importance?

c. Label and organize everything: Date, type, and purpose of assignment.

Similarities and differences in writing across the disciplines *(continued)*	156

Differences

1. Conduct primary research and use sources for secondary research in each discipline (see 36a).
2. Select a style of documentation appropriate to each discipline (see 36a and Chapter 33).
3. Follow manuscript format requirements in each discipline (see 36c).
4. Use specialized language as needed for each discipline (see 36d).

For example, in a humanities class, you might read *Lives of a Cell*, by Lewis Thomas, a collection of essays about science and nature written by a noted physician and author. As you consider the art of the writer, you will also be thinking deeply about biology and other sciences.

36a Conducting primary research and using sources for secondary research in each discipline

Primary sources offer you firsthand exposure to information, offering you the exciting experience of discovering material on your own. But research methods differ among the disciplines when primary sources are used. In the humanities, existing documents are primary sources; the task of the researcher is to analyze and interpret these primary sources. Typical primary source material for humanities research could be a poem by Dylan Thomas, the floor plans of Egyptian pyramids, or early drafts of music manuscripts. In the social and natural sciences, primary research entails the design and undertaking of experiments involving direct observation. The task of the researcher in the social and natural sciences is to conduct experiments or to read the firsthand reports of experiments and studies by the people who conducted them.

Secondary sources—articles and books that draw on primary sources—are important but are not firsthand reports. In the humanities, secondary sources offer analysis and interpretation; the author of a secondary source steps between you and the primary sources. In the social and natural sciences, secondary sources summarize and then synthesize findings and draw parallels that offer new insights.

36b Selecting a style of documentation appropriate to each discipline

Writers use **documentation** to give credit to the sources they have used. A writer who does not credit a source is guilty of PLAGIARISM*—a serious academic offense (see 31a). Styles of documentation differ among the disciplines.

In the humanities, most fields use the DOCUMENTATION STYLE of the Modern Language Association (MLA), as explained and illustrated in section 33c. The student research paper in Chapter 34 and the student literary analysis in Chapter 37 use MLA documentation style. CM (Chicago Manual) style is sometimes used in the humanities; it is described in section 33e. In the social sciences, most fields use the documentation style of the American Psychological Association (APA), as explained and illustrated in section 33d. The student research paper in Chapter 35 uses APA documentation style. In the natural sciences, documentation styles vary widely; consult sections 33f and 38g for more information.

36c Following manuscript format requirements in each discipline

One reflection of the differences among disciplines is the different formats sometimes expected for written material. These formats have evolved to communicate a writer's purpose, to emphasize content by eliminating distracting variations in format, and to make the reader's work easier. Writing in the humanities uses set formats less often, although writing is always expected to be well organized and logically presented. Writing in the social and natural sciences often calls for set formats for specific types of writing, as explained in Chapter 38.

36d Using specialized language as needed for each discipline

Specialized language is often referred to as **jargon.** Jargon can help people who are specialists communicate easily with each other in a kind of "verbal shorthand." When specialized material is communicated to the general reading public, however, such jargon must be defined so that everyone understands the message. At all times, jargon that is unnecessarily obscure or overblown (see 21e.2) must be avoided in all writing.

*You can find the definition of a word printed in small capital letters (such as PLAGIARISM) in the Terms Glossary toward the end of this handbook.

Portfolio (continued)

Set up sections as needed: class notes, reading log, research project, test previews, reviews and repairs, and so on.

3. Adjust goals as necessary and continue reflective study process. Identify and comment on successes and growth as they occur.

4. Reflect in final, formal writing. Always justify learning by synthesizing and summarizing (see 5f and 5g). Prove you deserve the grade you want (5h).

Test Repairs:
Refining Self-Monitoring

Essay and objective testing offers rich insights into student progress. The more involved students are in the evaluation of their progress, the more significant their progress seems to be. Interestingly, tests also offer the valuable opportunity to learn through failure. Low scores and missed test items show students where their weaknesses lie. Only the student can say for sure what type of weakness the miss indicates. The reflective nature of portfolios encourages students to explore why they performed as they did, how they might change, and the impact of that change once it occurs and is tracked.

Objective tests are a necessity in many content courses. These tests are often seen as separate and unrelated to writing skills. Yet the connection, though underlying, is potent. Objective testing is an assessment of reading and listening comprehension. Obviously, written language (a lecture is merely a flower from this root) has been encountered. The strain is now placed on inferential and contextual reading. Essay tests bear down on whole language skills and create a literacy pressure cooker. Tests test testing skills as well as content knowledge. This portfolio approach allows students to study themselves; writing becomes a reflective study tool in every curriculum, even math.

Remember to use a good notetaking system (review Chapter 5). →

673

Portfolio (continued)

1. Before the test: Write a summary of how you prepared for the test and how well prepared you feel. Predict test questions and score. Prepare your test-taking strategy (see 40c).

2. During the test: Read instructions carefully. Immediately record any information you fear you may forget. Manage your time. Relax. Note trouble questions for review.

3. Immediately after the test: Write a summary of how well you did, what you think you might have missed and why, and a prediction of your score. Try to remember and record key phrases and verbs from test items. Analyze the questions to reveal instructor's emphasis, biases, or preferences (see 40a and 40b).

4. When you receive your scored test: Review missed questions and search for correct answers. Write why you answered incorrectly and justify the correct answer. Then, write a study plan for the next exam.

All disciplines use specialized language to some extent. Specialized terms in the social and natural sciences are generally more technical than those in the humanities. The more important that exactness is to a discipline, the more likely that many words will have specialized meanings. For example, consider the word *niche.* It has two generally known meanings: "a place particularly suitable to the person or thing in it" and "a hollowed space in a wall for a statue or vase." *Niche* in the natural sciences, however, has a very specialized meaning: "the set of environmental conditions—climate, food sources, water supply, enemies—that permit an organism or species to survive."

❶ **USAGE ALERT:** Many writers in scientific disciplines make a habit of writing in the passive voice. Yet style manuals for scientific writing agree with the advice you will find in section 8o of this handbook: Use the active voice except for purposes best fulfilled by the passive. For more information, see section 2.06 of the *Publication Manual of the American Psychological Association*, Fourth Edition. ❗

37

WRITING ABOUT LITERATURE

WEB SITE

English Central is Prentice Hall's Web site for English instructors and their students. English Central offers much general information about English, hyperlinks to interesting and important sites for students and instructors of English composition and literature, and sites for Prentice Hall's major English textbooks. At the Troyka Web site, you will find supplementary resources and activities. These include quotations (twenty-five, with suggestions to students for using them to stimulate writing), practice exercises on key topics, other sample student essays, e-mail contact with the author, and an invitation to students to submit model essays (for Chapters 3 or 6), model paragraphs (for Chapter 4), model research papers (for Chapter 34), and model literature papers (for Chapter 37).

Literature, which includes **fiction** (novels and stories), **drama** (plays and scripts), and **poetry** (poems and lyrics), has developed from age-old human impulses to discover and communicate meaning by telling stories, reenacting events, and singing or chanting.

37a Understanding methods of inquiry into literature

All questions about literature require that you read a literary work closely (see 5e.2). Some questions then ask you to deal with the material on a literal level (see 5d.1). You might be asked to explain the meaning of a passage in a novel or to describe the historical events that took place when the work was being written.

Other questions call for inferential reasoning (see 5d.2) and evaluative thinking (see 5d.3). You might be asked to discuss the effect of sound or rhythm or rhyme in a poem or to compare and contrast characters in two plays by a particular playwright. As you write, keep in mind the principles of critical thinking, especially the vastly important differences between summary and synthesis (see 5b and 5f). Unlike inquiry called for by many other disciplines, literary inquiry sometimes includes asking you to describe your response or reaction to a work of literature after a close, careful reading.

In each case, your answers must reflect knowledge of the work and must be thorough, well-reasoned, and well-supported with evidence.

37b Understanding purposes and practices in writing about literature

37b.1 Using first and third person appropriately

Instructors often require students to use the **first person** (*I, we, our*) only when writing about their personal point of view evaluations. They then want students to use the **third person** (*he, she, it, they*) for other content. Those rules are becoming less rigid, so be sure to ask about your instructor's requirements.

WHAT ELSE?

Strategies and Resources is a free 400-page book written especially for instructors who adopt this handbook. It offers a "primer for students" on reading and writing about literature and includes definitions, samples of student writing, and the complete text of "The Necklace" by Guy de Maupassant.

37b.2 Using verbs in the present tense and the past tense correctly when writing about literature

Have you ever wondered what verb tense to use when writing about literature? Use the PRESENT TENSE when you describe or discuss a literary work or any of its elements: *George Henderson* [a character] ***takes*** *control of the action and **tells** the other characters when they may speak.* The present tense is also correct for discussing what the author has done in a specific work: *Because Susan Glaspell* [the author] ***excludes*** *Minnie and John Wright from the stage as speaking characters, she **forces** her audience to learn about them through the words of others.*

Use a PAST-TENSE VERB to discuss historical events or biographical information: *Susan Glaspell **was** a social activist who **was** strongly **influenced** by the chaotic events of the early twentieth century.*

37b.3 Using your own ideas and using secondary sources

Some assignments call only for your own ideas about the subject of your essay. Other assignments ask you to support your ideas with **secondary sources.** Secondary sources include books and articles in which an expert discusses material related to your topic. You can locate secondary sources by using the research process discussed in Chapter 32.

So that no reader mistakes someone else's ideas as your own, always document your sources (see 31b and Chapter 33). Otherwise, you are guilty of PLAGIARISM (see 31a). Also, work material from secondary sources gracefully into your writing, using the techniques of quotation (see 31c), paraphrase (see 31d), and summary (see 31e).

37c Using documentation style for writing about literature

You are required to credit your sources by using DOCUMENTATION. Many literature instructors require their students to use the DOCUMENTATION STYLE of the Modern Language Association (MLA), an organization of scholars and teachers of language and literature. MLA documentation style is described in section 33c. Two other documentation styles sometimes required in the humanities are that of the American Psychological Association (APA), presented in section 33d, and that of the University of Chicago Press, known as CM style, presented in section 33e.

37d Writing different types of papers about literature

Before you write about a literary work, read the work closely. Your readers can tell easily when you leave out details that are central to your message. To read closely, use your understanding of the reading process (see 5d) and engage in critical reading (see 5e).

WHAT ELSE?

Strategies and Resources, a 400-page book provided free to faculty who use this handbook, offers specific, practical ways to "stimulate students to carry out deeper and more methodical explorations of literacy works."

37d.1 Writing reaction papers

In a paper in which you react to a work of literature, you might answer a central question that the work made you think about, criticize a point of view in the work, or present a problem that you see in the work. For example, you might write about why you did or did not enjoy reading the work, how it does or does not relate to your personal experience or to your view of life, or what it made you think about. You can focus on the entire work or on part of it. As evidence for your reactions, use quotations from the work.

37d.2 Writing book reports

A book report first informs readers about the content of a book, using **summary** (see 5f and 31e). This summary is followed by your discussion of the purpose and significance of the book, the structure of the book, and who might be most interested in the book. When you discuss the significance of the book, try to relate it to your field of study. For example, if the book is a classic in children's literature, your focus for a literature class would differ somewhat from your focus for a course in psychology or education.

37d.3 Writing interpretations

An **interpretation** discusses one of two things: either what you think the author means by the work or what the work means personally to you. As you write an interpretation paper, keep an eye on the questions in Chart 157.

⊙ Questions for an interpretation paper   **157**

1. What is the theme of the work?
2. How are particular parts of the work related to the theme?
3. If patterns exist in various elements of the work, what do they mean?
4. What message does the author convey through the use of major aspects of the work, listed in Chart 158?
5. Why does the work end as it does?

BACKGROUND

In "A Student-Written Syllabus for Second-Semester English Composition" (*Teaching English in the Two-Year College*, February 1994: 27–32), Amber Dahlin explains that her sophomore composition students in Alaska designed their class reading list in a literature anthology, and as the semester progressed, so did the students' skills in critical reading and general metacognitive analysis.

37d.4 Writing analyses

Analysis is the examination of the relationship of a whole to its parts. In a literary analysis, you are expected to discuss your ideas and insights about a work of fiction, poetry, or drama. Your ideas and insights come from the thinking you do, the patterns you see, and the connections you make when you look at various aspects of the work (see Chart 158). To get to know the work well and to gather ideas for your analysis, read the work thoroughly, again and again, looking for patterns. Write notes as you go along so that you have a record of two important resources for your writing: the patterns you find in the material and your thinking about the patterns and their meaning to the whole work.

⊙ Major aspects of literary works to analyze	158
PLOT	The events and their sequence
THEME	Central idea or message
STRUCTURE	Organization and relationship of parts to each other and to the whole
CHARACTERIZATION	Traits, thoughts, and actions of the people in the plot
SETTING	Time and place of the action
POINT OF VIEW	Perspective or position from which the material is presented—sometimes by a narrator or a main character
STYLE	How words and sentence structures present the material
IMAGERY	Pictures created by the words (similes, metaphors, figurative language; see Chart 105 in section 21c)
TONE	Attitude of the author toward the subject of the work—and sometimes toward the reader—expressed through choice of words and imagery
FIGURE OF SPEECH	Nonliteral use of words, as in metaphor and simile, for enhanced vividness or effect
SYMBOLISM	Meaning beneath the surface of the words and images
RHYTHM	Beat, meter
RHYME	Repetition of similar sounds for their auditory effect

37e Three case studies of students writing about literature

This section includes three student essays of literary analysis. Two do not use secondary sources (see 37e.1 and 37e.2), and one does use them (see 37e.3). All three essays use MLA documentation style (see sections 33c and 37c).

37e.1 Student essay interpreting a plot element in a short story

The following essay interprets a plot element in Edgar Allan Poe's story "The Tell-Tale Heart."

Born in 1809, Edgar Allan Poe was an important American journalist, poet, and fiction writer. In his short, dramatic life, Poe gambled, drank, lived in terrible poverty, saw his young wife die of tuberculosis, and died himself under mysterious circumstances at age forty. He also created the detective novel and wrote brilliant, often bizarre short stories that still stimulate readers' imaginations.

When Valerie Cuneo read Poe's "Tell-Tale Heart," first published in 1843, she was fascinated by one of the plot elements: the sound of a beating heart that compels the narrator of the story to commit a murder and then to confess it to the police. In the following paper, Cuneo discusses her interpretation of the source of the heartbeat.

Cuneo 1

The Sound of a Murderous Heart

In Edgar Allan Poe's short story "The Tell-Tale Heart," several interpretations are possible as to the source of the beating heart that causes the narrator-murderer to reveal himself to the police. The noise could simply be a product of the narrator's obviously deranged mind. Or perhaps the murder victim's spirit lingers, heart beating, to exact revenge upon the narrator. Although either of these interpretations is possible, most of the evidence in the story suggests that the inescapable beating heart that haunts the narrator is his own.

The interpretation that the heartbeat stems from some kind of auditory hallucination is flawed. The narrator is clearly insane--his killing a kind old man because of an

BACKGROUND

In "Using Reader-Response in a College Literature Class" (*Teaching English in the Two-Year College*, May 1995: 136–140), Derek Soles presents specific techniques to help students enjoy poetry in literature classes.

➔

679

"Evil Eye" demonstrates this--and his psychotic behavior is more than sufficient cause for readers to question his truthfulness. Even so, nowhere else in the story does the narrator imagine things that do not exist. Nor is it likely that he would intentionally attempt to mislead us since the narrative is a confessional monologue through which he tries to explain and justify his actions. He himself describes his "disease" as a heightening of his senses, not of his imagination. Moreover, his highly detailed account of the events surrounding the murder seems to support this claim. Near the end of the story, he refutes the notion that he is inventing the sound in his mind when he says, "I found that the noise was not within my ears" (792). Although the narrator's reliability is questionable, there seems to be no reason to doubt this particular observation.

Interpreting the heartbeat as the victim's ghostly retaliation against the narrator also presents difficulties. Perhaps most important, when the narrator first hears the heart, the old man is still alive. The structure of the story also argues against the retaliation interpretation. Poe uses the first-person point of view to give readers immediate access to the narrator's strange thought processes, a choice that suggests the story is a form of psychological study. If "The Tell-Tale Heart" were truly a ghost story, it would probably be told in the third person, and it would more fully develop the character of the old man and explore his relationship with the narrator. If the heartbeat that torments the narrator is his own, however, these inconsistencies are avoided.

The strongest evidence that the tell-tale heart is really the narrator's is the timing of the heartbeat. Although it is the driving force behind the entire story, the narrator hears the beating heart only twice. In both of these instances, he is under immense physical and psychological stress--times when his own heart would be pounding. The narrator first hears the heartbeat with the

→

Cuneo 3

shock of realizing that he has accidentally awakened his
intended victim:

> Meantime the hellish tattoo of the heart
> increased. It grew quicker and quicker, and
> louder every instant. The old man's terror must
> have been extreme! It grew louder, I say,
> louder every moment!--do you mark me well? I
> have told you that I am nervous: so I am. And
> now at the dead hour of the night, amid the
> dreadful silence of that old house, so strange
> a noise as this excited me to uncontrollable
> terror. (791)

As the narrator's anxiety increases, so does the
volume and frequency of the sound, an event easily
explained if the heartbeat is his own. Also, the sound of
the heart persists even after the old man is dead, fading
slowly into the background, as the murderer's own
heartbeat would after his short, violent struggle with
the old man. This reasoning can also explain why the
narrator did not hear the heart on any of the seven
previous nights when he looked into the old man's
bedchamber. Because the old man slept and the "Evil Eye"
was closed, no action was necessary (according to the
narrator-murderer's twisted logic), and, therefore, he
did not experience the rush of adrenaline that set his
heart pounding on the fatal eighth visit.

The heart also follows a predictable pattern at the
end of the story when the police officers come to
investigate a neighbor's report of the dying old man's
scream. In this encounter, the narrator's initial calm
slowly gives way to irritation and fear. As he becomes
increasingly agitated, he begins to hear the heart again.
The narrator clearly identifies it as the same sound he
heard previously, as shown by the almost word-for-word
repetition of the language he uses to describe it,
calling it "a low, dull, quick sound--much such a sound

→

<u>as a watch makes when enveloped in cotton</u>" [Poe's emphasis]

(792). As the narrator-murderer focuses his attention on the

sound, which ultimately overrides all else, his panic

escalates until, ironically, he is betrayed by the very

senses that he boasted about at the start of the story.

Work Cited

Poe, Edgar Allan. "The Tell-Tale Heart." <u>American Literature:</u>

<u>A Prentice Hall Anthology</u>. Vol. 1. Ed. Emory Elliott,

Linda K. Kerber, A. Walton Litz, and Terence Martin.

Englewood Cliffs: Prentice, 1991. 789–92.

37e.2 Student essay analyzing the characters in a drama

The following essay analyzes actions and interactions of the male and female characters in *Trifles*, a one-act play written by Susan Glaspell (1882–1948). Glaspell was a feminist and social activist who wrote many plays for the Provincetown Players, a theater company she cofounded in Cape Cod, Massachusetts. She wrote *Trifles* in 1916, four years before women were allowed to vote in the United States. In 1917, Glaspell rewrote *Trifles* as the short story "A Jury of Her Peers." In both versions of the work, two married couples and the county attorney gather at a farmhouse where a taciturn farmer has been murdered, apparently by his wife. The five characters try to discover a motive for the murder. In doing so, they reveal much about gender roles in marriage and in the larger society.

After reading *Trifles*, Peter Wong said to his instructor, "No male today could get away with saying some of the things the men in that play say." The instructor encouraged Wong to analyze that reaction.

Gender Loyalties: A Theme in <u>Trifles</u>

Susan Glaspell's play <u>Trifles</u> is a study of character

even though the two characters most central to the drama

never appear on stage. By excluding Minnie and John Wright

→

Form in literature is an arousing and fulfillment of desires. A work has form insofar as one part of it leads a reader to anticipate another part, to be gratified by the sequence.

—Kenneth Burke

from the stage as speaking characters, Glaspell forces us to
learn about them through the observations and recollections
of the group visiting the farmhouse where the murders of
Minnie Wright's canary and of John Wright took place. By
indirectly rounding out her main characters, Glaspell
invites us to view them not merely as individuals but also
as representatives in a conflict between the sexes. This
conflict grows throughout the play as characters' emotions
and sympathies become increasingly polarized and oriented in
favor of their own gender. From this perspective, each of
the male characters can be seen to stand for the larger
political, legal, and domestic power structures that drive
Minnie Wright to kill her husband.

George Henderson's speaking the first line of the play
is no accident. Although his power stems from his position
as county attorney, Henderson represents the political, more
than the legal, sphere. With a job similar to a district
attorney's today, he is quite powerful even though he is
the youngest person present. He takes control of the action,
telling the other characters when to speak and when not to
and directing the men in their search for evidence that
will establish a motive for the murder. As the person in
charge of the investigation, George Henderson orders the
other characters about. Mrs. Peters acknowledges his skill
at oratory when she predicts that Minnie Wright will be
convicted in the wake of his "sarcastic" cross-examination
(speech 63).

Glaspell reveals much of the conflict in the play
through the heated (but civil) exchanges between George
Henderson and Mrs. Hale. His behavior (according to the
stage directions, that of a gallant young politician) does
not mask his belittling of Minnie Wright and of women in
general:

> COUNTY ATTORNEY. I guess before we're through she
> may have something more serious than preserves
> to worry about.

→

> HALE. Well, women are used to worrying over
>   trifles. [<u>The two women move a little closer</u>
>   <u>together</u>.]
> COUNTY ATTORNEY. [<u>With the gallantry of a young</u>
>   <u>politician</u>.] And yet, for all their worries,
>   what would we do without the ladies? [<u>The women</u>
>   <u>do not unbend. He goes to the sink, takes a</u>
>   <u>dipperful of water from the pail, and pouring</u>
>   <u>it into a basin, washes his hands. Starts to</u>
>   <u>wipe them on the roller-towel, turns it for a</u>
>   <u>cleaner place</u>.] Dirty towels! [<u>Kicks his foot</u>
>   <u>against the pans under the sink</u>.] Not much of a
>   housekeeper, would you say, ladies? (speeches
>   29—31)

As this excerpt shows, George Henderson seems to hold
that a woman's place is in the kitchen, even when she is
locked up miles away in the county jail. He shows so much
emotion at the discovery of dirty towels in the kitchen
that it is almost as if he has found a real piece of
evidence that he can use to convict Minnie Wright, instead
of an irrelevant strip of cloth. It is apparent that his
own sense of self-importance and prejudicial views of women
are distracting him from his real business at the farmhouse.

Sheriff Henry Peters, as his title suggests,
represents the legal power structure. Like the county
attorney, Henry Peters is also quick to dismiss the
"trifles" that his wife and Mrs. Hale spend their time
discussing while the men conduct a physical search of the
premises. His response to the attorney's asking whether he
is absolutely certain that the downstairs contains no
relevant clues to the motive for the murder is a curt
"Nothing here but kitchen things" (speech 25). Ironically,
the women are able to reconstruct the entire murder,
including the motive, by beginning their inquiries with
these same "kitchen things." Sheriff Peters and the other
men all completely miss the unfinished quilt,

→

the bird cage, and the dead bird's body. When the sheriff overhears the women talking about the quilt, his instinctive reaction is to ridicule them, saying, "They wonder if she was going to quilt it or just knot it!" (speech 73). Of course, the fact that Minnie Wright was going to knot the quilt is probably the single most important piece of evidence that the group could uncover, since John Wright was strangled with what we deduce is a quilting knot. Although he understands the law, the sheriff seems to know very little about people, and this prevents him from ever cracking this case. His blindness is made clear when he chuckles his assent to the county attorney's observation that Mrs. Peters is literally "married to the law" (speech 145) and therefore beyond suspicion of trying to hinder the case against Minnie Wright. This assumption is completely wrong, for Mrs. Peters joins Mrs. Hale in suppressing the evidence and lying to the men.

Rounding out the male characters is Lewis Hale, a husband and farmer who represents the domestic sphere. Although Lewis Hale may not be an ideal individual, he provides a strong foil for John Wright's character. We might expect Lewis Hale, as Mrs. Hale's spouse, to be a good (or at least a tolerable) person, and, on the whole, he is. Although he, too, misses the significance of the "trifles" in the kitchen and mocks the activities of his wife and Mrs. Peters, he seems less eager than the other men to punish Minnie Wright--possibly because he knew John Wright better than they did. Lewis Hale is clearly reluctant to provide evidence against Minnie Wright when he speaks of her behavior after he discovers the body:

> HALE. She moved from that chair to this one over
>   here [Pointing to a small chair in the corner.]
>   and just sat there with her hands held together
>   and looking down. I got a feeling that I ought
>   to make some conversation, so I said I had come

in to see if John wanted to put in a telephone, and at that she started to laugh, and then she stopped and looked at me--scared. [The county attorney, who has had his notebook out, makes a note.] I dunno, maybe it wasn't scared. I wouldn't like to say it was . . . (speech 23)

Lewis Hale is the only man who tries to bring up the incompatibility of the Wrights' marriage, citing John Wright's dislike for conversation and adding, "I didn't know if what his wife wanted made much difference to John--" (speech 9), but George Henderson cuts him off before he can pursue this any further. Lewis Hale is a personable and talkative man--not at all like John Wright, whom Mrs. Hale likens to "a raw wind that gets to the bone" (speech 103). Lewis Hale is a social being who wants to communicate with the people around him, as his desire for a telephone party line indicates. The Hales' functional marriage shows that gender differences need not be insurmountable, but it also serves to highlight the truly devastating effect that a completely incompatible union can have on two people's lives. Mrs. Hale reminds us that even a marriage that "works" can be dehumanizing:

> MRS. HALE. I might have known she needed help! I know how things can be--for women. I tell you it's queer, Mrs. Peters. We live close together and we live far apart. We all go through the same things--it's all just a different kind of the same thing. (speech 136)

The great irony of the drama is that the women are able to accomplish what the men cannot: They establish the motive for the murder. They find evidence suggesting that John Wright viciously killed his wife's canary--her sole companion through long days of work around the house. More important, they recognize the damaging nature of a marriage based on the unequal status of the participants. Mrs. Hale and Mrs. Peters decide not to help the case against Minnie

Wong 6

Wright, not because her husband killed a bird, but because he isolated her, made her life miserable for years, and cruelly destroyed her one source of comfort. Without hope of help from the various misogynistic, paternalistic, and uncomprehending political, legal, and domestic power structures surrounding her, Minnie Wright took the law into her own hands. As the characters of George Henderson, Henry Peters, and Lewis Hale demonstrate, she clearly could not expect understanding from the men of her community.

Wong 7

Work Cited

Glaspell, Susan. <u>Trifles</u>. <u>Literature: An Introduction to Reading and Writing</u>. 4th ed. Ed. Edgar V. Roberts and Henry E. Jacobs. Englewood Cliffs: Prentice, 1995. 1038—48.

37e.3 Student research paper analyzing two poems

The following essay is a literary analysis that uses secondary sources. Born in 1889 on the Caribbean island of Jamaica, Claude McKay moved to the United States in 1910 and became a highly respected poet. Paule Cheek chose to write about Claude McKay's nontraditional use of a very traditional poetic form, the sonnet. A sonnet has fourteen rhyming lines and develops one idea. In secondary sources, Cheek found information about McKay's life that she felt gave her further insights into both the structure and the meaning of McKay's sonnets "The White City" and "In Bondage."

Cheek 1

Words in Bondage: Claude McKay's
Use of the Sonnet Form in Two Poems
The sonnet has remained one of the central poetic forms of Western tradition for centuries. This fourteen-line form is easy to learn but difficult to master. With

→

its fixed rhyme schemes, number of lines, and meter, the sonnet form forces writers to be doubly creative while working within it. Many poets over the years have modified or varied the sonnet form, playing upon its conventions to keep it vibrant and original. One such writer was Jamaican-born Claude McKay (1889—1948).

The Jamaica of McKay's childhood was very different from turn-of-the-century America. Slavery had ended there in the 1830s, and McKay was able to grow up "in a society whose population was overwhelmingly black and largely free of the overt white oppression which constricted the lives of black Americans in the United States during this same period" (Cooper, Passion 5—6). This background could not have prepared McKay for what he encountered when he moved to America in his twenties. Lynchings, still common at that time, were on the rise, and during the Red Scare of 1919, there were dozens of racially motivated riots in major cities throughout the country. Thousands of homes were destroyed in these riots, and several black men were tortured and burned at the stake (Cooper, Claude McKay 97). McKay responded to these atrocities by raising an outraged cry of protest in his poems. In two of his sonnets from this period, "The White City" and "In Bondage," we can see McKay's mastery of the form and his skillful use of irony in the call for social change.

McKay's choice of the sonnet form as the vehicle for his protest poetry at first seems strange. Since his message was a radical one, we might expect that the form of his poetry would be revolutionary. Instead, McKay gives us sonnets--a poetic form that dates back to the early sixteenth century and was originally intended to be used exclusively for love poems. Critic James R. Giles notes that this choice

> is not really surprising, since McKay's Jamaican
> education and reading had been based firmly upon
> the major British poets. From the point quite
> early in his life when he began to think of

→

himself as a poet, his models were such major
English writers as William Shakespeare, John
Milton, William Wordsworth. He thus was committed
from the beginning to the poetry which he had
initially been taught to admire. (44)

McKay published both "The White City" and "In Bondage"
in 1922, and they are similar in many ways. Like most
sonnets, each has fourteen lines and is in iambic
pentameter. The diction is extremely elevated. For example,
this quatrain from "In Bondage" is almost Elizabethan in its
word choice and order:

> For life is greater than the thousand wars
> Men wage for it in their insatiate lust,
> And will remain like the eternal stars,
> When all that shines to-day is drift and dust.
> (8–12)

If this level of diction is reminiscent of
Shakespeare, it is no accident. Both poems employ the
English sonnet rhyme scheme (a b a b c d c d e f e f
g g) and division into three quatrains and a closing
couplet. McKay introduces a touch of his own, however.
Although the English sonnet form calls for the "thematic
turn" to fall at the closing couplet, McKay defies
convention. He incorporates two turns into each sonnet
instead of one. This allows him to use the first "mini-
turn" to further develop the initial theme set forth in the
first eight lines while dramatically bringing the poem to a
conclusion with a forcefully ironic turn in the closing
couplet. Specifically, in "The White City," McKay uses the
additional turn to interrupt his description of his
"Passion" with a vision of "a mighty city through the mist"
(9). In "In Bondage," he uses the additional turn to
justify his desire to escape the violent existence that
society has imposed on his people.

McKay also demonstrates his poetic ability through his
choice of words within his customized sonnets. Consider the
opening of "In Bondage":

→

689

> I would be wandering in distant fields
>
> Where man, and bird, and beast, lives leisurely,
>
> And the old earth is kind, and ever yields
>
> Her goodly gifts to all her children free;
>
> Where life is fairer, lighter, less demanding,
>
> And boys and girls have time and space for play
>
> Before they come to years of understanding--
>
> Somewhere I would be singing, far away. (1—8)

The conditional power of <u>would</u> in the first line, coupled with the alliterative <u>wandering</u>, subtly charms us into a relaxed, almost dreamlike state in which the poet can lead us gently through the rest of the poem. The commas in the second line force us to check our progress to a "leisurely" crawl, mirroring the people and animals that the line describes. By the time we reach the eighth line, we are probably ready to join the poet in this land of "somewhere . . . far away."

Then, this optimistic bubble is violently burst by the closing couplet:

> But I am bound with you in your mean graves,
>
> O black men, simple slaves of ruthless slaves.
>
> (13—14)

In "The White City," McKay again surprises us. This time, he does so by turning the traditional love sonnet upside down; instead of depicting a life made unendurable through an overpowering love, McKay shows us a life made bearable through a sustaining hate:

> I will not toy with it nor bend an inch.
>
> Deep in the secret chambers of my heart
>
> I muse my life-long hate, and without flinch
>
> I bear it nobly as I live my part.
>
> My being would be a skeleton, a shell,
>
> If this dark Passion that fills my every mood,
>
> And makes my heaven in the white world's hell,
>
> Did not forever feed me vital blood. (1—8)

If it were not for the presence of "life-long hate" in line three, this opening would easily pass as part of a

→

conventional love sonnet. The emotion comes from "deep in the secret chambers" of the speaker's heart (2), it allows him to transcend "the white world's hell" (7), and it is a defining "Passion." Once again, however, McKay uses the couplet to defy our expectations by making it plain that he has used the form of the love sonnet only for ironic effect: "The tides, the wharves, the dens I contemplate, / Are sweet like wanton loves because I hate" (13—14).

McKay's impressive poetic ability made him a master of the sonnet form. His language could at times rival even Shakespeare's, and his creativity allowed him to adapt the sonnet to his own ends. His ironic genius is revealed in his use of one of Western society's most elevated poetic forms in order to critique that same society. McKay once described himself as "a man who was bitter because he loved, who was both right and wrong because he hated the things that destroyed love, who tried to give back to others a little of what he had got from them . . . " (Barksdale and Kinnamon 491). As these two sonnets show, McKay gave back very much indeed.

Works Cited

Barksdale, Richard, and Kenneth Kinnamon, eds. Black Writers of America: A Comprehensive Anthology. New York: Macmillan, 1972.

Cooper, Wayne F. Claude McKay: Rebel Sojourner in the Harlem Renaissance. Baton Rouge: Louisiana State UP, 1987.

---, ed. The Passion of Claude McKay. New York: Schocken, 1973.

Giles, James R. Claude McKay. Boston: Twayne, 1976.

McKay, Claude. "In Bondage." Literature: An Introduction to Reading and Writing. 4th ed. Ed. Edgar V. Roberts and Henry E. Jacobs. Englewood Cliffs: Prentice, 1995. 772—73.

---, "The White City." Literature: An Introduction to Reading and Writing. 4th ed. Ed. Edgar V. Roberts and Henry E. Jacobs. Englewood Cliffs: Prentice, 1995. 967.

38

WRITING IN THE SOCIAL SCIENCES AND NATURAL SCIENCES

SOCIAL SCIENCES

38a Understanding ways of gathering information in the social sciences

The **social sciences** focus on the behavior of people as individuals and in groups. The social sciences include disciplines such as economics, education, geography, political science, psychology, and sociology. At some colleges, history is included in the social sciences; at others, it is part of the humanities.

Observation is a common method for inquiry in the social sciences. To make observations, use whatever tools or equipment you might need: writing utensils, sketching materials, tape recorders, cameras. As you observe, take complete and accurate notes. In a report of your observations, tell what tools or equipment you used, because your method might have influenced what you saw (for example, your taking photographs may make people act differently than usual).

Interviewing is another common method of inquiry that social scientists use. Interviews are useful for gathering people's opinions and impressions of events. If you interview, remember that interviews are not always a completely reliable way to gather factual information, because people's memories are not precise or people prefer to present themselves in the best light. If your only source of factors is interviews, try to interview as many people as possible so that you can cross-check the information.

❶ NOTETAKING ALERTS: (1) If you use abbreviations to speed your note-taking, be sure to write down what they stand for so that you will be able to understand them later when you write up your observations. (2) Before you interview anyone, master any equipment you might need to use so that mechanical problems do not intrude on the interview process (see 32q). ❗

Questionnaires are also a useful method of inquiry in the social sciences. To write questions for a questionnaire, use the guidelines in Chart 159. When you give people a questionnaire, be sure to ask enough people so that you do not reach conclusions based on too small a sample of responses.

> ⊙ **Guidelines for writing questions for a questionnaire**   **159**
>
> 1. Define what you want to find out, and then write questions that will elicit the information you seek.
> 2. Phrase questions so that they are easy to understand.
> 3. Use appropriate language (see 21a), and avoid artificial language (see 21e).
> 4. Be aware that how you phrase your questions will determine whether the answers that you get truly reflect what people are thinking. Make sure that your choice of words does not imply what you want to hear.
> 5. Avoid questions that invite one-word answers about complex matters that call for a range of responses.
> 6. Test a draft of the questionnaire on a small group of people before you use it. If any question is misinterpreted or hard to understand, revise and retest it.

38b   Understanding writing purposes and practices in the social sciences

Summary and **synthesis** (see 5f) are fundamental and important strategies for analytical writing in the social sciences.

Analysis (see 4f.6 and 5a) helps social scientists write about problems and their solutions. For example, an economist writing about financial troubles in a major automobile company might start by breaking the situation into parts: analyzing employee salaries and benefits, the selling price of cars, and the costs of doing business. Next, the economist might show how these parts relate to the financial health of the whole company. Finally, the economist might suggest how specific changes would help solve the company's financial problems.

Social scientists often also use **analogy** (see 4f.8) to make unfamiliar ideas clear. When an unfamiliar idea is compared to one that is more familiar, the unfamiliar idea becomes easier to understand. For example, sociologists may talk of the "culture shock" that some people feel when they enter a new society. The sociologists might compare this shock to the reaction of someone suddenly being moved hundreds of years into the future or the past.

WAC PORTFOLIOS IN THE NATURAL AND SOCIAL SCIENCES

Portfolios can be presented as case studies of individuals or groups or as collaborative research projects. Teachers (their scores and feedback) become experts with authoritative opinions.

Portfolios can also foreshadow the kinds of writing expected in the field. Written summaries of readings of trade journals, observation logs that apply theory and concepts to the learning environment, questionnaires, and interviews all make for diverse and powerful portfolio entries. The following questions should serve as models for student reflection (see 38b and 38d; these types of questions can be applied before, during, or after learning by simply adjusting the tense of the verb).

> What was the purpose of this study?
> What did you expect to learn or prove?
> What barriers or obstacles did you encounter?
> How did you overcome them?
> What kinds of unexpected understandings did you encounter?
> What types of writing did you read?
> What types of papers did you chose to write and why?

One of the most exciting ways to present writing across the curriculum is to have students apply the scientific method (see Chart 160 in Section 38e) and the science report (Chart 161 in section 38h.1) to the formal, final reflective essay in the portfolio assessment process. In this way, students combine objective and subjective, primary and secondary, literal and inferential, and creative and critical thinking and communication skills. This is truly a bridge between skills and whole language, writing, and content courses.

Social scientists are particularly careful to **define their terms** when they write, especially when they discuss complex social issues. For example, if you are writing a paper on substance abuse in the medical profession, you must first define what you mean by the terms *substance abuse* and *medical profession.* Does *substance* mean alcohol and drugs or only drugs? How do you measure *abuse?* By *medical profession,* do you mean nurses or only doctors? Without defining such terms, you confuse readers or lead them to wrong conclusions.

In college courses in the social sciences, using the first person (*I, we, our*) is acceptable, but only to write about your reactions and experiences. Your goal is usually to be a neutral observer, so most of the time writers use the third person (*he, she, it, one, they*). Some writing in the social sciences overuses the passive voice (see 8n and 8o). Style manuals for the social sciences, however, recommend the active voice whenever possible.

38c Using documentation style in the social sciences

If you use SOURCES when writing about the social sciences, you must credit these sources by using DOCUMENTATION. The most commonly used DOCUMENTATION STYLE in the social sciences is that of the American Psychological Association (APA). APA documentation style uses parenthetical references in the body of a paper and a References list at the end of a paper. APA documentation style is described in detail in section 33d. You can find a sample student research paper using APA documentation style in Chapter 35.

The Chicago Manual (CM) style of documentation is sometimes used in the social sciences. CM bibliographic note style is described in detail in section 33e.

38d Writing different types of papers in the social sciences

Case studies and research papers are the two major types of papers written in the social sciences.

38d.1 Writing case studies in the social sciences

A **case study** is an intensive study of one group or individual. If you write a case study, describe situations as a neutral observer. Refrain from interpreting them unless your assignment says that you can add your interpretation after your report. Also, always differentiate between fact and opinion (see 5d.3). For example, you may observe nursing home patients lying in bed on their sides facing the door. Describe exactly what you see: If you interpret or read into this observation that patients are lonely and are watching the door for visitors, you could be wrong. Perhaps medicines are injected in the right hip, and patients are more comfortable lying on their left side, which just happens to put them in a position facing the door. Such work requires field research (see 32g).

A case study is usually presented in a relatively fixed format, but the specific parts and their order vary. Most case studies contain the following components: (1) basic identifying information about the individual or group, (2) a history of the individual or group, (3) observations of the individual's or group's behavior, and (4) conclusions and perhaps recommendations as a result of the observations.

38d.2 Writing research papers in the social sciences

Research papers in the social sciences can be based on your field research (see 38d.1 on case studies and 38a on interviews and questionnaires). Also, research papers can require that you consult **secondary sources** (see 32l on using specialized reference books and 32n.2 on using specialized indexes). These sources are usually articles and books that report, summarize, and otherwise discuss the findings of other people's research. You can find a sample of a student research paper using secondary sources written for an introductory psychology course in Chapter 35.

NATURAL SCIENCES

38e Understanding ways of gathering information in the sciences

The **natural sciences** include disciplines such as astronomy, biology, chemistry, geology, and physics. The sciences focus on natural phenomena. Scientists form and test hypotheses. They do this to explain cause and effect (see 5i) as systematically and objectively as possible.

The **scientific method,** commonly used in the sciences to make discoveries, is a procedure for gathering information related to a specific hypothesis. The scientific method is the cornerstone of all inquiry in the sciences. Guidelines for using the scientific method are presented in Chart 160.

⊙ **Guidelines for using the scientific method   160**

1. Formulate a tentative explanation—known as a **hypothesis**—for a scientific phenomenon. Be as specific as possible.

2. Read and summarize previously published information related to your hypothesis.

→

> **Guidelines for using the scientific**   **160**
> **method** *(continued)*
>
> 3. Plan and outline a method of investigation to uncover the information needed to test your hypothesis.
> 4. Experiment, exactly following the investigative procedures you have outlined.
> 5. Observe closely the results of the experiment, and write notes carefully.
> 6. Analyze the results. If they prove the hypothesis to be false, rework the investigation and begin again. If the results confirm the hypothesis, say so.
> 7. Write a report of your research. At the end, you might suggest additional hypotheses that might be investigated.

38f   Understanding writing purposes and practices in the natural sciences

Because scientists usually write to inform their audiences about factual information, summary and synthesis are fundamental, important techniques (see 5f).

Exactness is extremely important in scientific writing. Readers expect precise descriptions of procedures and findings, free of personal biases. Scientists expect to be able to *replicate*—repeat step by step—the experiment or process the researcher carried out and get the same outcome.

Completeness is as important as exactness in scientific writing. Without complete information, a reader can misunderstand the writer's message and reach a wrong conclusion. For example, a researcher investigating how plants grow in different types of soil needs to report all these facts: an analysis of each soil type, the amount of daylight exposure for each plant, the soil's moisture content, the type and amount of fertilizer used, and all other related facts. By including all this information, the researcher tells the reader how the conclusion in the written report was arrived at. Specifically, in the soil example just described, plant growth turns out to depend on a combination of soil type, fertilizer, and watering.

Because science writing depends largely on objective observation, rather than subjective comments, scientists generally avoid using the first person (*I, we, our*) in their writing. Another reason to avoid the first person is that the sciences generally focus on the experiment rather than on the person doing the experimenting.

When writing for the sciences, you are often expected to follow fixed formats, which are designed to summarize a project and present its results efficiently. In your report, organize the information to achieve clarity and precision. Writers in the sciences sometimes use charts, graphs, tables, diagrams, and other illustrations to present material. In fact, illustrations can sometimes explain complex material more clearly than words can.

38g Using documentation style in the natural sciences

If you use SECONDARY SOURCES when you write about the sciences, you are required to credit your sources by using DOCUMENTATION. DOCUMENTATION STYLES in the various sciences differ somewhat. Ask your instructor which style you should use.

The Council of Biology Editors (CBE) has compiled style and documentation guidelines for the life sciences, the physical sciences, and mathematics in *Scientific Style and Format: The CBE Manual for Authors, Editors, and Publishers*, Sixth Edition (1994). CBE documentation guidelines are described in section 33f.

38h Writing different types of papers in the natural sciences

Two major types of papers in the sciences are reports and reviews.

38h.1 Writing science reports

Science reports tell about observations and experiments. Such reports may also be called *laboratory reports* when they describe laboratory experiments. Formal reports feature the eight elements identified in Chart 161. Less formal reports, which are sometimes assigned in introductory college courses, might not include an abstract or a review of the literature. Ask your instructor which sections to include in your report.

◉ **Parts of a science report** 161

1. **Title.** This is a precise description of what your report is about.
2. **Abstract.** This is a short overview of the report.
3. **Introduction.** This section states the purpose behind your research and presents the hypothesis. Any needed background information and a review of the literature appear here.
4. **Methods and Materials.** This section describes the equipment, material, and procedures used.

→

Parts of a science report *(continued)*   **161**

5. **Results.** This section provides the information obtained from your efforts. Charts, graphs, and photographs help present the data.

6. **Discussion.** This section presents your interpretation and evaluation of the results. Did your efforts support your hypothesis? If not, can you suggest why not? Use concrete evidence in discussing your results.

7. **Conclusion.** This section lists conclusions about the hypothesis and the outcomes of your efforts, with particular attention given to any theoretical implications that can be drawn from your work. Be specific in suggesting further research.

8. **References Cited.** This list presents references cited in the review of the literature, if any. Its format conforms to the requirements of the documentation style in the particular science.

An Experiment to Predict Vestigial Wings

in an F2 <u>Drosophila</u> Population

INTRODUCTION

The purpose of this experiment was to observe second filial generation (F2) wing structures in <u>Drosophila</u>. The hypothesis was that abnormalities in vestigial wing structures would follow predicted genetic patterns.

METHODS AND MATERIALS

On February 7, four <u>Drosophila</u> (P1) were observed. Observation was made possible by etherizing the parents (after separating them from their larvae), placing them on a white card, and observing them under a dissecting microscope. The observations were recorded on a chart.

On February 14, the larvae taken from the parents on February 7 had developed to adults (F1), and they were

→

observed using the same methods as on February 7. The observations were recorded on the chart.

On February 19, the second filial generation (F2) was supposed to be observed. This was impossible because they did not hatch. The record chart had to be discontinued.

RESULTS

No observations of F2 were possible. For the F1 population, according to the prediction, no members should have had vestigial wings. According to the observations, however, some members of F1 did have vestigial wings.

[DISCUSSION SECTION OMITTED]

CONCLUSIONS

Two explanations are possible to explain vestigial wings in the F1 population. Perhaps members from F2 were present from the F1 generation. This is doubtful since the incubation period is 10 days and the time between observations was only 8 days. A second possible explanation is that the genotype of the male P1 was not homozygous (WW, indicating that both genes were for normal wings) but rather heterozygous (Ww). If this were true, the following would be the first filial products in a 1:1 ratio:

$$P_1 \quad Ww \; X \; ww$$
$$F_1 \quad Ww \; ww$$

Thus, the possibility for vestigial wings would exist. The problem remains, however, that the ratio was not 2:1 (i.e., 24 normal to 12 abnormal). One explanation could be that the total number was not large enough to extract an average.

The hypothesis concerning predicted genetic patterns in F2 could not be confirmed because the F2 generation did not hatch. This experiment should be repeated to get F2 data. A larger F1 sample should be used to see if the F1 findings reported here are repeated.

38h.2 Writing science reviews

A **science review** is a paper discussing published information on a scientific topic or issue. The purpose of the review is **summary:** to assemble for readers all the current knowledge about the topic or issue.

Sometimes, the purpose of a science review is **synthesis:** to suggest a new interpretation of the old material. Reinterpretation combines the older views with new and more complete or more compelling information. In such reviews, the writer must present evidence to persuade readers that the new interpretation is valid.

If you are required to write a science review, (1) choose a very limited scientific issue currently being researched; (2) use information that is current—the more recently published the articles, books, and journals you consult, the better; (3) accurately paraphrase and summarize material (see 31d and 31e); and (4) document your sources (see Chapter 33). If your review runs longer than two or three pages, you might want to use headings to help your reader understand the organization and idea progression of your paper. See Chapter 32 for advice on finding sources.

39

BUSINESS WRITING

Business writing starts where writing in all other disciplines does: thinking about your purpose (see 1b) and your audience (see 1c). This chapter explains how to write business letters (see 39a), job application letters (see 39b), and résumés (see 39c). As you write for business, use the guidelines listed in Chart 162.

> ◉ **Guidelines for business writing** 162
>
> - Consider your audience's needs and expectations.
> - Show that you understand the purpose for a business communication and the context in which it takes place.
> - Put essential information first.
> - Make your points clearly and directly.
> - Use conventional formats.

39a Writing and formatting a business letter

Business letters are written to give information, to build goodwill, or to establish a foundation for discussions or transactions. Experts in business and government agree that the letters likely to get results are short, simple, direct, and human. Here is good, basic advice: (1) Call the person by name, (2) tell what your letter is about in the first paragraph, (3) be honest, (4) be clear and specific, (5) use correct English, (6) be positive and natural, and (7) edit ruthlessly.

For business letters, use the guidelines in Chart 163 and the format on page 703. To avoid sexist language in the salutation of your letter, use the guidelines in Chart 164. For a business envelope, see page 707.

WEB SITE

English Central is Prentice Hall's Web site for English instructors and their students. English Central offers much general information about English, hyperlinks to interesting and important sites for students and instructors of English composition and literature, and sites for Prentice Hall's major English textbooks. At the Troyka Web site, you will find supplementary resources and activities. These include quotations (twenty-five, with suggestions to students for using them to stimulate writing), practice exercises on key topics, other sample student essays, e-mail contact with the author, and an invitation to students to submit model essays (for Chapters 3 or 6), model paragraphs (for Chapter 4), model research papers (for Chapter 34), and model literature papers (for Chapter 37).

WHAT ELSE?

Strategies and Resources is a free 400-page book written especially for instructors who adopt this handbook. It discusses in detail the teaching of workplace and business writing and includes many examples of business letters and memos, résumés, and proposals and reports.

⊙ **Guidelines for business letters** **163**

LETTERHEAD	If printed stationery is not available, type the company name and address centered at top of white 8 1/2-by-11-inch paper.
DATE	Put the date at the left margin under the letterhead, when typing in block form as shown in the example. When using paragraph indentations, type the date so that it ends at the right margin.
INSIDE ADDRESS	Direct your letter to a specific person. Be accurate in spelling the name and the address. If unsure of your information, telephone and ask questions of a secretary or other assistant.
SUBJECT LINE	Place at the left margin. In a few, concise words, state the letter's subject.
SALUTATION	Use a first name only if you personally know the person. Otherwise, use *Mr.* or *Ms.* or whatever title is applicable with the person's last name. Avoid sexist language.
CLOSING	*Sincerely* or *Sincerely yours* is generally appropriate, unless you know the person very well and wish to use *Best regards* or a similarly casual expression. Leave about four lines for your signature.
NAME LINES	Type your full name and title below your signature. The title can be on the same line as your name or the line below it.
SECOND PAGE	Head a second page with three items of information: the name of the person or company to which your letter is addressed, the number 2 or *page 2*, and the date. Place the information on three lines at the top left margin or on one line spaced across the top of the page.

LETTERHEAD	**AlphaOmega Industries, Inc.** 123456 Motor Parkway Fresh Hills, CA 91999
DATE	December 28, 2000
INSIDE ADDRESS	Ron R. London, Sales Director Seasonal Products Corp. 5000 Seasonal Place Wiscasset, ME 04321
SUBJECT LINE	Subject: Spring Promotional Effort
SALUTATION	Dear Ron:
MESSAGE	Since we talked last week, I have completed plans for the spring promotion of the products that we market jointly. AlphaOmega and Seasonal Products should begin a direct mailing of the enclosed brochure on January 28. I have secured several mailing lists that contain the names of people who have a positive economic profile for our products. The profile and the outline of the lists are attached. Do you have additional approaches for the promotion? I would like to meet with you on January 6 to work out the details of the project. Please let me know if a meeting next week at your office accommodates your schedule.
CLOSING	Sincerely,
NAME, TITLE	*Alan Stone* Alan Stone Director of Special Promotions
WRITER'S/ TYPIST'S INITIALS	AS/kw
COURTESY COPY	cc: Yolanda Lane, Vice President, Marketing
ENCLOSURES	Encl: brochure, outline of mailing lists, customer profile

Business Letter Format

WAC SAMPLE ACTIVITIES

The following suggestions are just a few ways in which writing teachers can help students see the connection between freshman English and other courses.

Assign a mini-collaborative research project using the procedures outlined in Charts 14, 142, 143, and 160. Require students to create the project and reserve a certain percentage of the final score for the reflective portfolio record-keeping process. Make students track and reflect on their learning process.

Combine business writing formats such as business letters and résumés (see 39a–39c) with literature or content course topics. For example, ask students to create a résumé based on the biography of a significant author, inventor, or leader. Or reward students for creating real-life documents such as letters to the editor or to a federal, state, or local politician. These documents, along with any reciprocal communication, become substantial portfolio entries documenting commitment and mastery.

⊙ **Guidelines for writing a nonsexist**   **164**
salutation

You may want to send a business letter but not know the specific person to whom it should be addressed. Use the following steps to prepare a salutation.

1. Telephone the company to which you are sending the letter. State your reason for sending the letter, and ask for the name of the person who should receive it.

2. Use a first name only if you know the person. Otherwise, use *Mr.* or *Ms.* or an applicable title. Avoid a sexist opening such as *Dear Sir.*

3. If you cannot find out the name of the person who should read your letter, use a generic title.

> **NO**   Dear Sir: [obviously sexist]
>
>   Dear Madam/Sir or Dear Sir or Madam: [few women want to be addressed as "Madam"]
>
> **YES**   Dear Personnel Officer:
>
>   Dear IBM Sales Manager:

In addressing an envelope, remember that the best-written letter means nothing if it does not reach its destination. Whenever possible, type rather than handwrite an envelope. In the illustration on page 707, you will see the U.S. Postal Service guidelines for addressing envelopes so that they can be processed by machine. (Envelopes that must be sorted by hand may take longer to be delivered.)

39b   Writing and formatting a job application letter

Chart 165 gives guidelines for a job application letter. A sample job application letter appears on page 706.

⊙ **Guidelines for job application letters**	**165**

YOUR ADDRESS	Type your address in block style as you would on an envelope. Use as your address (with a ZIP code) a place where you can be reached by letter.
DATE	Put the date below your address. Make sure that you mail the letter on either the same day or the next day; a delayed mailing can imply lack of planning.
INSIDE ADDRESS	Direct your letter to a specific person. Telephone the company to find out the name of the person to whom you are writing. Be accurate. A misspelled name can offend the receiver. A wrong address usually results in a lost letter.
SALUTATION	Be accurate. No one likes to see his or her name misspelled. In replying to an ad that gives only a post office box number, omit the salutation and start your opening paragraph directly below the inside address. To avoid sexist language, use Chart 164.
INTRODUCTORY PARAGRAPH	State your purpose for writing and your source of information about the job.
BODY	Interest the reader in the skills and talents you offer by mentioning whatever experience you have that relates to the specific job. Mention your enclosed résumé, but do not summarize it.
CLOSING PARAGRAPH	Suggest an interview, stating that you will call to make arrangements.
CLOSING	*Sincerely* or *Sincerely yours* is generally appropriate.
NAME	Type your full name below your signature. Leave about four lines for your signature.
ENCLOSURES	If you are enclosing any material with your letter, type *Encl:* and briefly list the items.

WHAT ELSE?

Strategies and Resources, a 400-page book provided free to faculty who use this handbook, offers specific, practical ways to apply this statement: "Writing skills that have previously been only marginally palatable take on the allure of real life when they are taught using documents from the world of business."

UNIVERSITY OF TEXAS AT ARLINGTON
422 Broward
Arlington, TX 75016

May 15, 2000

Ms. Rebecca Clemens, Director of Human Resources
Taleno, Ward Marketing, Inc.
1471 Summit Boulevard
Houston, TX 78211

Dear Ms. Clemens:

I am answering Taleno, Ward's advertisement for a marketing trainee in today's *Houston Chronicle*.

Marketing has been one of the emphases of my course work here at the University of Texas, Arlington, as you will see on my enclosed résumé. This past year, I gained some practical experience as well when I developed marketing techniques that helped turn my typing service into a busy and profitable small business.

Successfully marketing the typing service (with fliers, advertisements in college publications, and even a two-for-one promotion) has made me a very enthusiastic novice. I can think of no better way to become a professional than by working for Taleno, Ward.

I will be here at the Arlington campus through August 1. You can reach me by phone at (713) 555-1976. Unless I hear from you before, I'll call on May 25 about setting up an interview.

Sincerely yours,

Lee Franco

Lee Franco

Encl: Résumé

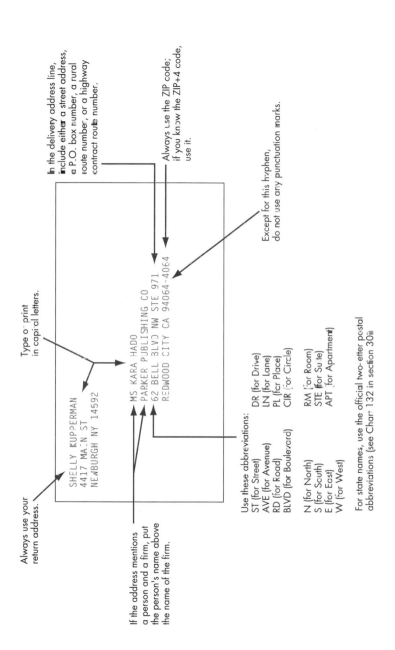

In the delivery address line, include either a street address, a P.O. box number, a rural route number, or a highway contract route number.

Always use the ZIP code; if you know the ZIP+4 code, use it.

Except for this hyphen, do not use any punctuation marks.

Type or print in capital letters.

Always use your return address.

If the address mentions a person and a firm, put the person's name above the name of the firm.

SHELLY KUPPERMAN
4417 MAIN ST
NEWBURGH NY 14592

MS KARA HADO
PARKER PUBLISHING CO
62 BELL BLVD NW STE 971
REDWOOD CITY CA 94064-4064

Use these abbreviations:
ST (for Street)
AVE (for Avenue)
RD (for Road)
BLVD (for Boulevard)

N (for North)
S (for South)
E (for East)
W (for West)

DR (for Drive)
LN (for Lane)
PL (for Place)
CIR (for Circle)

RM (for Room)
STE (for Suite)
APT (for Apartment)

For state names, use the official two-letter postal abbreviations (see Chart 132 in section 30iii

U.S. Postal Service Guidelines for Business Envelope Format

39c   Writing and formatting a résumé

A **résumé** is an easy-to-read, factual document that presents your qualifications for employment. All résumés cover certain standard items: name, address, phone number; education; past experience; skills and talents; publications, awards, honors, membership in professional organizations; and a list of references or a statement that they are "available upon request."

A résumé gives you an opportunity to present a positive picture of yourself to a prospective employer. Employers understand that college students may have limited experience in the business world. Think of headings that allow you to emphasize your strengths. For example, if you have never done paid work, do not use "Business Experience." You can use "Work Experience" if you have done volunteer or other unpaid work. If the experience you offer an employer is that you have run school or social events, you might use "Organizational Experience." If your greatest strength is your academic record, put your educational achievements first.

You may choose to arrange your résumé in *emphatic* order, with the most important information first and the least important last. Or you may choose to arrange information in *chronological* (time) order, a sequence that is good for showing a steady work history or solid progress in a particular field. Lee Franco's résumé, which was sent with the job application letter on page 706, is on page 709. It uses emphatic order. Stephen Schmit's résumé, on page 710, uses chronological order.

When you are applying for a specific job, modify your basic résumé to emphasize your qualifications for that job. Lee Franco added the "Marketing Trainee" heading and the statement about relevant experience for becoming a marketing trainee to her basic résumé and positioned the "Marketing Experience" section first. These modifications help send a message that Franco's qualifications for the marketing trainee position are better than other applicants'. If you keep your résumé on computer, you can easily tailor it to specific job opportunities.

Your résumé usually has to fulfill only one purpose: It has to convince the person who first looks at it to put it into the "Call for an interview" pile rather than into the wastebasket. To do that best, a résumé should be eye-catching and informative, and it should make its readers think, "We should talk to this person—seems like someone who would be an asset to our business."

MARKETING TRAINEE

LEE FRANCO
University of Texas at Arlington
422 Broward
Arlington, TX 75016
(713) 555-1976

The experience I acquired marketing my typing service provided me with a good practical background for a position as a marketing trainee.

MARKETING EXPERIENCE (program for campus typing service)

> Increased annual business income by $2,300 by evaluating typing-service capabilities, analyzing the market, and drawing up and implementing a marketing plan. Produced a two-color flier, designed print ads and wrote copy, developed and ran a special promotion. August 19XX to February 19XX

BUSINESS EXPERIENCE

> Type-Right Typing Service: Ran campus typing service for two years. Duties included word processing (Word, WordPerfect), proofreading, billing and other financial record keeping (Excel), and customer contact. August 19XX to present.

> Archer & Archer Advertising: Worked as general assistant in the copy department under direct supervision of John Allen, Director. Duties included proofreading, filing, direct client contact. June 19XX to August 19XX.

ADDITIONAL EXPERIENCE

> Coordinated the student employment service at Hawthorne High School, Baton Rouge, Louisiana. Duties included contacting students to fill jobs with local employers, arranging interviews, and writing follow-up reports on placements.

EDUCATION

> University of Texas, Arlington
> B.A. May 2000, Psychology, Marketing

EXTRACURRICULAR

> Marketing Club, Computer Graphics Society

References available upon request.

Emphatic Résumé

STEPHEN L. SCHMIT
5230 St. Stephens Street
Boston, MA 02188
(617) 555-8165

CAREER QUALIFICATIONS   Technical writer trained in preparation of manuals, catalogs, and instructional materials. Experienced in writing computer documentation containing syntax formats.

WORK EXPERIENCE   *Northeastern University, Boston,* Reading and Writing Specialist, English Language Center, March–July 19XX, January–March 19XX.
Created individual lesson plans for each student assigned to the Reading and Writing Laboratory and developed materials for use in laboratory programs. Ran the laboratory for approximately 100 students 20 hours a week. Kept all records of students' work and prepared written and oral reports on student progress and laboratory operations.

Tutor of Foreign Students, September 19XX–present. Integrated foreign students into a large urban school and community and was a positive role model educationally and socially.

W. M. Mercer, Inc., Boston, September–December 19XX. Data processing and general office duties. Created and implemented a CRT search system for office personnel.

SPECIAL SKILLS   C programming language; Word, WordPerfect, Lotus 1-2-3, Excel.

EDUCATION   Northeastern University, Boston, Bachelor of Arts, June 2000.

Concentration: English with minors in Economics and Technical Communications.

Activities: Selected to serve on the Residence Judicial Board, a faculty-staff-student group adjudicating residence hall disputes; *Northeastern News* reporter; Northeastern Yearbook staff.

Chronological Résumé

40
WRITING UNDER PRESSURE

WEB SITE

English Central is Prentice Hall's Web site for English instructors and their students. English Central offers much general information about English, hyperlinks to interesting and important sites for students and instructors of English composition and literature, and sites for Prentice Hall's major English textbooks. At the Troyka Web site, you will find supplementary resources and activities. These include quotations (twenty-five, with suggestions to students for using them to stimulate writing), practice exercises on key topics, other sample student essays, e-mail contact with the author, and an invitation to students to submit model essays (for Chapters 3 or 6), model paragraphs (for Chapter 4), model research papers (for Chapter 34), and model literature papers (for Chapter 37).

The demands of writing under pressure can sometimes seem overwhelming, but if you break the challenge into small, sequential steps and then focus on each step in turn, you can succeed. When you write under the pressure of time constraints, you are expected to write as completely and clearly as possible. If you tend to freeze under pressure, force yourself to take some slow, deep breaths and use a relaxation technique such as counting backward from ten. When you turn to the task, remember to break the whole into parts so that the process is easier to work through.

Writing answers for essay tests is one of the most important writing tasks that you face in college. Essay tests are common in all disciplines, including the natural sciences. Essay tests demand that you recall information and also put assorted pieces of that information into contexts that lead to generalizations you can support. Essay tests give you the chance to synthesize and apply your knowledge, helping your instructor determine what you have learned.

40a Understanding cue words and key words

Most essay questions contain what is sometimes called a **cue word**, a word of direction that tells what the content of your answer is expected to emphasize. Knowing the major cue words and their meanings can increase your ability to plan efficiently and to write effectively. Be guided by the list of cue words and sample essay test questions in Chart 166.

◉ **Cue words found in questions for essay tests**   **166**

■ *Analyze* **means to separate something into parts and then discuss the parts and their meanings.**

Analyze Socrates' discussion of "good life" and "good death." →

711

BACKGROUND

In "An Apologia for the Timed Impromptu Essay Test" (*College Composition and Communication*, February 1995: 30–45), Edward M. White discusses the value of essay tests, with all their disadvantages, over other forms of language testing.

Cue words found in questions for essay tests *(continued)*   **166**

- *Clarify* **means to make clear, often by giving a definition of a key term and by using examples to illustrate it.**
  Clarify T. S. Eliot's idea of tradition.

- *Classify* **means to arrange into groups on the basis of shared characteristics.**
  Classify the different types of antipredator adaptations.

- *Compare and contrast* **means to show similarities and differences.**
  Compare and contrast the reproductive cycles of a moss and a flowering plant.

- *Criticize* **means to give your opinion concerning the good points and bad points of something.**
  Criticize the architectural function of modern football stadiums.

- *Define* **means to state precisely what something is and thereby to differentiate it from similar things.**
  Define the term "yellow press."

- *Describe* **means to explain features to make clear an object, procedure, or event.**
  Describe the chain of events that constitutes the movement of a sensory impulse along a nerve fiber.

- *Discuss* **means to consider as many elements as possible concerning an issue or event.**
  Discuss the effects of television viewing on modern attitudes toward violence.

- *Evaluate* **means to give your opinion about the importance of something.**
  Evaluate Margaret Mead's contribution to anthropology studies.

- *Explain* **means to make clear or intelligible something that needs to be understood or interpreted.**
  Explain how the amount of carbon dioxide in the blood regulates rates of heartbeat and breathing.

- *Illustrate* **means to give examples of something.**
  Illustrate the use of symbolism in Richard Wright's novel *Native Son*.

→

Cue words found in questions for essay tests *(continued)* 166

- *Interpret* **means to explain the meaning of something.**

  Give your interpretation of Maxine Kumin's poem "Beans."

- *Justify* **means to show or prove that something is valid or correct.**

  Justify the existence of labor unions in today's economy.

- *Prove* **means to present evidence that cannot be refuted logically or with other evidence.**

  Prove that smoking is a major cause of lung cancer.

- *Relate* **means to show the connections between two or more things.**

  Relate increases in specific crimes in 1932–1933 to the prevailing economic conditions.

- *Review* **means to evaluate or summarize something critically.**

  Review the structural arrangements in proteins to explain the meaning of the term "polypeptide."

- *Show* **means to point out or demonstrate something.**

  Show what effects pesticides have on the production of wheat.

- *Summarize* **means to identify the major points of something.**

  Summarize the major benefits of compulsory education.

- *Support* **means to argue in favor of something.**

  Support the position that destruction of rain forests is endangering the planet.

Each essay question also has one or more key words that tell you the information, topics, and ideas you are to write about. For example, in the question "Criticize the architectural function of the modern football stadium," the cue word is *criticize*, and the key words are *architectural function* and *football stadium*. To answer the question successfully, you must define *architectural function*, then describe the typical modern football stadium (mentioning major variations when important), and then discuss how well the typical modern football stadium fits your definition of *architectural function*.

BACKGROUND

In "Toward a New Theory of Writing Assessment" (*College Composition and Communication*, December 1996: 549–566), Brian Huot explores a theory of writing assessment "based on our understandings about the nature of language, written communication, and its teaching."

40b Writing effective responses to essay test questions

An effective response to an essay test question is complete and logically organized. Here are two answers to the question "Classify the different types of antipredator adaptations." The first one is successful; the second is not. The sentences are numbered for your reference, and they are explained in the text.

ANSWER 1

(1) Although many antipredator adaptations have evolved in the animal kingdom, all can be classified into four major categories according to the prey's response to the predator. (2) The first category is hiding techniques. (3) These techniques include cryptic coloration and behavior in which the prey assumes characteristics of an inanimate object or part of a plant. (4) The second category is early enemy detection. (5) The prey responds to alarm signals from like prey or other kinds of prey before the enemy can get too close. (6) Evasion of the pursuing predator is the third category. (7) Prey that move erratically or in a compact group are displaying this technique. (8) The fourth category is active repulsion of the predator. (9) The prey kills, injures, or sickens the predator, establishing that it represents danger to the predator.

ANSWER 2

(1) Antipredator adaptations are the development of the capabilities to reduce the risk of attack from a predator without too much change in the life-supporting activities of the prey. (2) There are many different types of antipredator adaptations. (3) One type is camouflage, hiding from the predator by cryptic coloration or imitation of plant parts. (4) An example of this type of antipredator adaptation is the praying mantis. (5) A second type is the defense used by monarch butterflies, a chemical protection that makes some birds ill after eating the butterfly. (6) This protection may injure the bird by causing it to vomit, and it can educate the bird against eating other butterflies. (7) Detection and evasion are also antipredator adaptations.

Here is an explanation of what happens, sentence by sentence, in the two answers to the question about antipredator adaptations.

SENTENCE	ANSWER 1	ANSWER 2
1	Sets up classification system and gives number of categories based on key word	Defines key word
2	Names first category	Throwaway sentence— accomplishes nothing

SENTENCE	ANSWER 1	ANSWER 2
3	Defines first category	Names and defines first category
4	Names second category	Gives an example for first category
5	Defines second category	Gives an example for second (unnamed) category
6	Names third category	Continues to explain example
7	Defines third category	Names two categories
8	Names fourth category	
9	Defines fourth category	

Answer 1 sets about immediately answering the question by introducing a classification system as called for by the cue word *classify*. Answer 2, by contrast, defines the key word, a waste of time on a test that will be read by an audience of specialists. Answer 1 is tightly organized, easy to follow, and to the point. Answer 2 rambles, never names the four categories, and says more around the subject than on it.

40c Using strategies when writing under pressure

If you use specific strategies when writing under pressure, you can be more comfortable and your writing will likely be more effective. As you use the strategies listed in Chart 167, remember that your purpose in answering questions is to show what you know in a clear, direct, and well-organized way. When you are studying for an essay exam, write out one-sentence summaries of major areas of information. This technique helps fix the ideas in your mind, and a summary sentence may become a thesis sentence for an essay answer.

⊙ **Strategies for writing essay tests**   **167**

1. Do not start writing immediately.
2. If the test has two or more questions, read them all at the start. Determine whether you are supposed to answer all the questions. Doing this gives you a sense of how to budget your time either by dividing it equally or by allotting more time for some questions than for others. If you have a choice, select questions about which you know the most and can write about most completely in the time limit.

→

Strategies for writing essay tests *(continued)*   **167**

3. Analyze each question that you answer by underlining the cue words and key words (see 40a) to determine exactly what the question asks.

4. Use the writing process as much as possible within the constraints of the time limit. Try to allot time to plan and revise. For a one-hour test on one question, take about ten minutes to jot down preliminary ideas about content and organization, and save ten minutes to reread, revise, and edit your answer. If you are suddenly pressed for time—but try to avoid this—consider skipping a question that you cannot answer well or a question that counts less toward your total score. If you feel blocked, try freewriting (see 2f) to get your hand and your thoughts moving.

5. Support any generalizations with specifics (see 4c about using the formula RENNS for being specific).

6. Beware of going off the topic. Respond to the cue words and key words in the question, and do not try to reshape the question to conform to what you might prefer to write about. Remember, your reader expects a clear line of presentation and reasoning that answers the stated question.

The more you use the strategies in the chart and adapt them to your personal needs, the better you will use them to your advantage. Try to practice them, make up questions that might be on your test, and time yourself as you write the answers. Doing this offers you another benefit: If you study by anticipating possible questions and writing out the answers, you will be very well prepared if one or two of them show up on the test.

ANSWERS: EXERCISE 40-1

Answers will vary.

EXERCISE 40-1

Look back at an essay that you have written under time pressure. Read it over and decide whether you would change the content of your answer or the strategies you used as you were writing under pressure. List these specific strategies, and if you think they were useful, add them to Chart 167.

PART SEVEN

WRITING WHEN ENGLISH IS A SECOND LANGUAGE

Preface for ESL Students

When English is your second language, you face the special challenge of needing to learn characteristics of English that native-born writers take for granted. Part Seven begins with a special ESL preface to set the context for your using the rest of Part Seven, which explains the features of English that tend to give non-native writers the most trouble. As you use Chapters 41 through 46, remember that learning to write English involves much more than studying separate features. As for writers in any language, the more time you spend actually writing, the faster you can become a fluent writer.

PREFACE FOR ESL STUDENTS

Do you sometimes worry when you write in English? If you ever do worry about your English writing, let me assure you that you have much in common with me and with many U.S. college students. But as an ESL writer, you face a special challenge because you must attend to every word, every phrase, every sentence, and every paragraph in a way that native speakers of English do not.

You may be reassured to know that any errors you make as an ESL writer indicate that you are progressing through necessary stages of second-language development. Eventually, when you have passed through all the stages that all language learners must, you should be a proficient writer of English.

Unfortunately, there are no shortcuts. As with progress in speaking, listening, and reading comprehension in a new language, passing through the various stages of language development takes time. Some students have more available time than others, and some students have a home or study environment that enables faster learning of a new language. However, no matter how fast a language skill is learned, all the stages of language development must be experienced. Just as most adults make mistakes when they learn to play a new sport or a musical instrument, few people write fluently and without error when they compose a first draft of a piece of writing. In fact, only rarely have even the most noted and experienced writers ever written something perfectly the first time.

What can you do to progress as quickly as possible from one writing stage to another? You might start by trying to remember what school writing is like in your first language. Try to recall how ideas are presented in writing in your native language, especially when information has to be explained and when a matter of opinion has to be argued.

In recalling the typical style of school writing in your native language, compare it with what you are learning about writing style in American English. For example, most college writing in the United States has a very direct, straightforward basic structure. In a typical essay or research paper, the reader expects to find a THESIS STATEMENT,* which clearly states the overall message of the piece of writing, by the end of the first or second paragraph. Usually, each paragraph that follows relates directly to the thesis statement and starts with a sentence, called a TOPIC SENTENCE, that tells the point of the paragraph. The rest of each paragraph usually supports the point by using reasons, examples, and other specific details. The final paragraph brings the essay or research paper to a reasonable, logical conclusion.

*You can find the definition of a word printed in small capital letters (such as THESIS STATEMENT) in the Terms Glossary toward the back of this handbook.

This handbook contains many examples of writing by U.S. college students. For essays, see sections 3f, 6i, and 37e. For research papers, see Chapters 34 and 35 and section 37e. Also, this handbook explains paragraph structures typically expected in U.S. college writing; see Chapter 4. By the way, these typical academic structures do not apply to novels, plays, poems, or articles in most newspapers and magazines published in the United States.

Writing structures typical of your native language probably differ from those in the United States. Always honor your culture's writing traditions and structures, for they reflect the richness of your heritage. At the same time, try to adapt to and practice the academic writing style characteristic of the United States. Later, when you are writing fluently, your college instructors likely will encourage you to practice other American English writing styles that are less common and that allow greater liberty in organization and expression.

Over the past twenty years, many interesting observations have been made about the distinctive variations in school writing styles among people of different cultures and language groups. Research about these contrasts is ongoing, so scholars hesitate to generalize about them. Even so, interesting differences seem to exist. For example, many Spanish-speaking students feel that U.S. school writing lacks the sort of traditional introductory background observations that Spanish-language writing usually includes, yet U.S. composition teachers will often mark such introductory material as wordy or not sufficiently relevant to the central point of an essay or research paper. Traditional French school essays usually begin with a series of points that are discussed in the body of the essay and then repeated in reverse order in the conclusion. Japanese school writing customarily begins with references to nature. In some African nations, a ceremonial, formal opening is expected to start school writing as an expression of respect for the reader. As a person, I greatly enjoy discovering the rich variations in the writing traditions of the many cultures of the world. As a teacher, however, my responsibility is to explain the expectations in the United States.

The ESL chapters following this special ESL preface are designed to help you focus on errors that many ESL writers make. I hope that Chapters 41 through 46 can be of great use to you.

I also hope that the rest of this handbook will become your trusted companion. Throughout its pages, ESL Notes and various kinds of Alerts present information in related contexts that can help you as you acquire American English-language writing skills. A directory of selected ESL Notes and Alerts follows on page 720 to help you find ones that may be especially useful to you.

Lynn Quitman Troyka

DIRECTORY OF SELECTED ESL NOTES AND ALERTS

41
SINGULARS AND PLURALS

HOW TO USE CHAPTER 41 EFFECTIVELY

1. Use this chapter together with these handbook sections:
   - 7a NOUNS
   - 8c -*s* form of VERBS
   - 11a–11l SUBJECT-VERB AGREEMENT
   - 12f nouns as MODIFIERS

2. Remember that throughout this handbook, you can find the definitions of words printed in SMALL CAPITAL LETTERS in the Terms Glossary.

3. Use **cross-references** (often given in parentheses) to find full explanations of key concepts.

This chapter can help you choose between using SINGULAR (one) and PLURAL (more than one). Section 41a discusses the concept of COUNT and NONCOUNT NOUNS. Section 41b discusses DETERMINERS and nouns. Section 41c discusses particularly confusing instances of the choice between singular and plural. Section 41d discusses some nouns with irregular plural forms.

41a Understanding the concept of count and noncount nouns

Count nouns name items that can be counted: *radio, street, idea, fingernail.* Count nouns can be SINGULAR or PLURAL.

Noncount nouns name things that are thought of as a whole and not split into separate, countable parts: *rice, knowledge, traffic.* There are two important rules to remember about noncount nouns: (1) They are never preceded by *a* or *an,* and (2) they are never plural. Chart 168 lists eleven categories of uncountable items, giving examples in each category.

WHAT ELSE?

Strategies and Resources, a 400-page book provided free to faculty who use this handbook, offers specific, practical ways to help students whose first language is not English. It first

examines cultural issues that make studying in the United States a challenging situation for many international students and suggests ways in which a composition teacher can integrate international students into the classroom. It also discusses some of the general concerns in cross-cultural education and provides insights into the differing perspectives of international students. The second section describes some of the difficulties new international students may have in speaking and listening. It discusses classroom activities that have proved useful in helping ESL students improve their listening comprehension and speaking abilities. The third section looks more specifically at writing pedagogy for the ESL student, covering such issues as understanding differences in rhetorical expectations of native and nonnative students, handling errors in ESL student's writing, and adapting pedagogical techniques like peer review and collaborative writing to a class including nonnative students (189).

> ◉ **Uncountable items**   **168**
>
> | | |
> |---|---|
> | **GROUPS OF SIMILAR ITEMS** | clothing, equipment, furniture, jewelry, junk, luggage, mail, money, stuff, traffic, vocabulary |
> | **ABSTRACTIONS** | advice, equality, fun, health, ignorance, information, knowledge, news, peace, pollution, respect |
> | **LIQUIDS** | blood, coffee, gasoline, water |
> | **GASES** | air, helium, oxygen, smog, smoke, steam |
> | **MATERIALS** | aluminum, cloth, cotton, ice, wood |
> | **FOOD** | beef, bread, butter, macaroni, meat, pork |
> | **PARTICLES OR GRAINS** | dirt, dust, hair, rice, salt, wheat |
> | **SPORTS, GAMES, ACTIVITIES** | chess, homework, housework, reading, sailing, soccer |
> | **LANGUAGES** | Arabic, Chinese, Japanese, Spanish |
> | **FIELDS OF STUDY** | biology, computer science, history, literature, math |
> | **EVENTS IN NATURE** | electricity, heat, humidity, moonlight, rain, snow, sunshine, thunder, weather |

Some nouns can be countable or uncountable, depending on their meaning in a sentence. Most of these nouns name things that can be meant either individually or as "wholes" made up of individual parts.

> **COUNT**   You have a **hair** on your sleeve. [In this sentence, *hair* is meant as an individual, countable item.]
>
> **NONCOUNT**   Kioko has black **hair.** [In this sentence, all the strands of *hair* are referred to as a whole.]
>
> **COUNT**   The **rains** were late last year. [In this sentence, *rains* is meant as individual, countable occurrences of rain.]
>
> **NONCOUNT**   The **rain** is soaking the garden. [In this sentence, all the particles of *rain* are referred to as a whole.]

When you are editing your writing (see Chapter 3), be sure that you have not added a plural *-s* to any noncount nouns, for they are always singular in form.

❶ VERB ALERT: Be sure to use a singular verb with any noncount noun that functions as a SUBJECT in a CLAUSE. **❗**

To check whether a noun is count or noncount, look it up in a dictionary such as the *Longman Dictionary of American English.* In this dictionary, count nouns are indicated by [C], and noncount nouns are indicated by [U] (for "uncountable"). Nouns that have both count and noncount meanings are marked [C;U].

41b Using determiners with singular and plural nouns

Determiners, also called *expressions of quantity,* are used to tell how much or how many with reference to nouns. Other names for determiners include *limiting adjectives, noun markers,* and ARTICLES. (For information about articles—the words *a, an,* and *the*—see Chapter 42.)

Choosing the right determiner with a noun can depend on whether the noun is noncount or count (see 41a). For count nouns, you must also decide whether the noun is singular or plural. Chart 169 lists many determiners and the kinds of nouns that they can accompany.

⊙ **Determiners to use with count and noncount nouns**   **169**

Group 1: Determiners for Singular Count Nouns

With every **singular count noun,** always use one of the determiners listed in Group 1.

a, an, the	**a house**	**an egg**	**the car**
one, any, some, every, each, either, neither, another, the other	**any house**	**each egg**	**another car**
my, our, your, his, her, its, their, nouns with *'s* or *s'*	**your house**	**its egg**	**Connie's car**
this, that	**this house**	**that egg**	**this car**
one, no, the first, the second, etc.	**one house**	**no egg**	**the fifth car**

Group 2: Determiners for Plural Count Nouns

All the determiners listed in Group 2 can be used with **plural count nouns.** Plural count nouns can also be used without determiners, as discussed in section 42b.

→

WEB SITE

English Central is Prentice Hall's Web site for English instructors and their students. English Central offers much general information about English, hyperlinks to interesting and important sites for students and instructors of English composition and literature, and sites for Prentice Hall's major English textbooks. At the Troyka Web site, you will find supplementary resources and activities. These include quotations (twenty-five, with suggestions to students for using them to stimulate writing), practice exercises on key topics, other sample student essays, e-mail contact with the author, and an invitation to students to submit model essays (for Chapters 3 or 6), model paragraphs (for Chapter 4), model research papers (for Chapter 34), and model literature papers (for Chapter 37).

Determiners to use with count and noncount nouns (*continued*)   **169**

Group 2: Determiners for Plural Count Nouns

the	the bicycles	the rooms	the ideas
some, any, both, many, more, most, few, fewer, the fewest, a number of, other, several, all, all the, a lot of	some bicycles	many rooms	all ideas
my, our, your, his, her, its, their, nouns with *'s or s'*	our bicycles	her rooms	student's ideas
these, those	these bicycles	those rooms	these ideas
no, two, three, etc.; *the first, the second, the third,* etc.	no bicycles	four rooms	the first ideas

Group 3: Determiners for Noncount Nouns

All the determiners listed in Group 3 can be used with noncount nouns (always singular). Noncount nouns can also be used without determiners, as discussed in section 42b.

the	the rice	the rain	the pride
some, any, much, more, most, other, the other, little, less, the least, enough, all, all the, a lot of	enough rice	a lot of rain	more pride
my, our, your, his, her, its, their, nouns with *'s or s'*	their rice	India's rain	your pride
this, that	this rice	that rain	this pride
no, the first, the second, the third, etc.	no rice	the first rain	no pride

❶ **USAGE ALERT:** The phrases *a few* and *a little* convey the meaning "some": *I have **a few** rare books* means "I have *some* rare books." *They are worth **a little** money* means "They are worth *some* money."

Without the word *a*, the words *few* and *little* convey the meaning "almost none": I have **few** [or *very few*] *books* means "I have *almost no* books." *They are worth **little** money* means "They are worth *almost no* money." **!**

41c Using *one of*, nouns as adjectives, and *states* in names or titles

One of *constructions*

One of constructions include *one of the* and a NOUN or *one of* followed by an ADJECTIVE-noun combination (*one of my hats, one of those ideas*). Always use a plural noun as the OBJECT when you use *one of the* with a noun or *one of* with an adjective-noun combination.

> **NO** *One of the **reason** to live here is the beach.*
>
> **YES** *One of the **reasons** to live here is the beach.*
>
> **NO** *One of her best **friend** has moved away.*
>
> **YES** *One of her best **friends** has moved away.*

The VERB in these constructions is always singular because it agrees with the singular *one*, not with the plural noun: ***One** of the most important inventions of the twentieth century **is** [not are] television.*
For advice about verb forms that go with *one of the . . . who* constructions, see section 11j.

Nouns used as adjectives

ADJECTIVES in English do not have plural forms. When you use an adjective with a plural noun, make the noun plural but not the adjective: *the **green** [not greens] leaves.* Be especially careful when you use as a modifier a word that can also function as a noun.

The bird's wingspan is ten inches. [*Inches* is functioning as a noun.]

The bird has a ten-inch wingspan. [*Inch* is functioning as a modifier.]

Do not add *-s* (or *-es*) to the adjective even when it is modifying a plural noun or pronoun.

> **NO** Many **Americans** students are basketball fans.
>
> **YES** Many **American** students are basketball fans.

Names or titles that include the word *states*

States is a plural word. However, names such as *United States* or *Organization of American States* refer to singular things—one country and one organization, even though made up of many states. When *states*

725

is part of a name or title referring to one thing, the name is a singular noun and therefore requires a singular verb.

> **NO**   The **United States have** a large entertainment industry.
>
> **NO**   The **United State has** a large entertainment industry.
>
> **YES**   The **United States has** a large entertainment industry.

41d   Using nouns with irregular plurals

Some English nouns have irregularly spelled plurals. In addition to those discussed in Chart 108 in section 22c, here are others that often cause difficulties.

Plurals of foreign nouns and other irregular nouns

Whenever you are unsure whether a noun is plural, look it up in a dictionary. If no plural is given for a singular noun, add -*s* to form the plural.

Many nouns from other languages that are used unchanged in English have only one plural. If two plurals are listed in the dictionary, look carefully for differences in meaning. Some words, for example, keep the plural form from the original language for scientific usage and have another English-form plural for nonscientific contexts: *formula, formulae, formulas; appendix, appendices, appendixes; index, indices, indexes; medium, media, mediums; cactus, cacti, cactuses; fungus, fungi, funguses.*

Words from Latin that end in -*is* in their singular form become plural by substituting -*es: parenthesis, parentheses; thesis, theses; oasis, oases.*

Other words

Medical terms for diseases involving an inflammation end in -*itis: tonsillitis, appendicitis.* They are always singular.

The word *news,* although it ends in *s,* is always singular: *The **news is** encouraging.* The words *people, police,* and *clergy* are always plural even though they do not end in *s: The **police are** prepared.*

EXERCISE 41-1

Consulting all sections of this chapter, select the correct choice from the words in parentheses and write it in the blank.

EXAMPLE   At the beginning of every school year, all (student, students) **students** can expect (homework, homeworks) **homework** that teaches them about the toll-free No Bully hot line.

1. One of the main (reason, reasons) _____ for such a hot line is the change in tempers and violent capacities of (American, Americans) _____ students.

ANSWERS AND COVERAGE: EXERCISE 41-1

1. reasons [41c, plural object with *one of*]; American [41c, singular for noun used as adjective]

2. Because students are often bullied by a fellow classmate when outside the classroom, it is important that they receive (information, informations) _____ about how to react when confronted by such a threat.

3. Many a child in the (United State, United States) _____ is in danger not only of being teased and taunted by others but also of being the victim of a crime in which (blood, bloods) _____ is spilled, like assault or robbery.

4. Because (many, much) _____ classrooms are unsupervised after school hours, this (time, times) _____ is especially dangerous.

5. In a moment of danger, (ignorance, ignorances) _____ can be deadly, so the No Bully hot line was set up to give students (advice, advices) _____ on how to handle bullies and other threatening situations.

EXERCISE 41-2

Consulting all sections of this chapter, select the correct choice from the words in parentheses and write it in the blank.

EXAMPLE   Because of their innate (intelligence, intelligences) **intelligence,** many (pet, pets) **pets** can often be very protective of the humans they love.

1. One of the most frightening (animal, animals) _____ is a poisonous (rattlesnake, rattlesnakes) _____—but not to Partner, a twelve-year-old retriever.

2. Longtime friends Nick and Ross, both eight years old, were chopping down a tree for a campfire when a (six foot, six-feet) _____ rattlesnake fell from a branch.

3. Partner leaped over (dirt, dirts) _____ and (leave, leaves) _____ to get to the poisonous snake, which he attacked and shook feverishly.

4. Verle, Nick's father and Partner's owner, was (many, much) _____ yards away when he heard the racket, and he rushed over just in time to see the rattler sink its fangs into Partner's nose.

5. Within minutes, the rattler was killed by a bystander, and Partner, who showed a lot of (courage, courages) _____ and has now recovered, has become one of the best (friend, friends) _____ Nick and Ross could hope for.

Answers and Coverage: Exercise 41-1 (continued)

2. information [41a, singular for noncount nouns]

3. United States [41c, *States* plural in *United States*]; blood [41a, singular for noncount nouns]

4. many [41b, *many* the correct determiner with the plural count noun *classrooms*]; time [41b, singular for count noun after the determiner *this*]

5. ignorance [41a, singular for noncount nouns]; advice [41a, singular for noncount nouns]

ANSWERS AND COVERAGE: EXERCISE 41-2

1. animals [41c, plural object, with *one of*]; rattlesnake [41b, singular for count noun used after the determiner *a*]

2. six-foot [41c, singular for noun used as adjective]

3. dirt [41a, singular for noncount nouns]; leaves [41a, plural for count nouns]

4. many [41b, *many* the correct determiner with the plural count noun *yards*]

5. courage [41a, singular for noncount nouns]; friends [41c, plural object with *one of*]

42

ARTICLES

HOW TO USE CHAPTER 42 EFFECTIVELY
1. Use this chapter together with these handbook sections:
   - 7a ARTICLES and NOUNS
   - 41a SINGULARS and PLURALS with COUNT and NONCOUNT NOUNS
   - 41b DETERMINERS with count and noncount nouns
2. Remember that throughout this handbook, you can find the definitions of words printed in SMALL CAPITAL LETTERS in the Terms Glossary.
3. Use **cross-references** (often given in parentheses) to find full explanations of key concepts.

This chapter gives you guidelines for using **articles.** Section 42a discusses using articles with singular count nouns. Section 42b discusses using articles with plural count nouns and with noncount nouns (which are always singular). Section 42c discusses using articles with PROPER NOUNS and with GERUNDS.

42a Using *a*, *an*, or *the* with singular count nouns

The words *a* and *an* are called **indefinite articles.** The word *the* is called the **definite article.** Articles are one type of DETERMINER. (For other determiners, see Chart 169 in section 41b.) Articles signal that a noun will follow and that any modifiers between the article and the noun refer to that noun.

a chair	**the** computer
a cold, metal chair	**the** lightning-fast computer

Every time you use a SINGULAR COUNT NOUN, a COMMON NOUN that names one countable item, the noun requires some kind of determiner; see Group 1 in Chart 169 (in 41b) for a list. To choose between *a* or *an* and *the*, you need to determine whether the noun is **specific** or **nonspecific.** A noun is considered specific when anyone who reads your writing can understand exactly and specifically to what item the noun is referring. If the noun refers to any of a number of identical items, it is nonspecific.

For nonspecific singular count nouns, use *a* (or *an*). When the singular noun is specific, use *the* or some other determiner. Chart 170 can help you decide when a singular count noun is specific and therefore requires *the*.

 When a singular count noun is specific   **170**
and requires *the*

- **Rule 1: A noun is specific and requires *the* when it names something unique or generally and unambiguously known.**

  The sun has risen above **the horizon.** [Because there is only one *sun* and only one *horizon*, these nouns are specific in the context of this sentence.]

- **Rule 2: A noun is specific and requires *the* when it names something used in a representative or abstract sense.**

  Benjamin Franklin favored **the turkey** as **the national bird** of the United States. [Because *turkey* and *national bird* are representative references rather than references to a particular turkey or bird, they are specific nouns in the context of this sentence.]

- **Rule 3: A noun is specific and requires *the* when it names something defined elsewhere in the same sentence or in an earlier sentence.**

  The ship *Savannah* was the first steam vessel to cross the Atlantic Ocean. [*Savannah* names a specific ship.]

  The carpet in my bedroom is new. [*In my bedroom* defines exactly which carpet is meant, so *carpet* is a specific noun in this context.]

  I have **a computer** in my office. **The computer** is often broken. [*Computer* is not specific in the first sentence, so it uses *a*. In the second sentence, *computer* has been made specific by the first sentence, so it uses *the*.]

- **Rule 4: A noun is specific and requires *the* when it names something that can be inferred from the context.**

  Monday, I had to call **the technician** to fix it. [*A technician* would be any of a number of individuals; *the technician* implies the same person has been called before, and so it is specific in this context.]

❶ **ALERT:** Use *an* before words that begin with a vowel sound. Use *a* before words that begin with a consonant sound. Go by the sound, not the spelling. For example, words that begin with *h* or *u* can have either a vowel or a consonant sound. Make the choice based on the sound of the first word after the article, even if that word is not the noun.

an idea	**a g**ood idea
an umbrella	**a u**seless umbrella
an honor	**a h**istory book **!**

One common exception affects Rule 3 in Chart 170. A noun may still require *a* (or *an*) after the first use if more information is added between the article and the noun: *I bought **a sweater** today. It was **a** (not *the*) **red sweater**.* (Your audience has been introduced to *a sweater* but not *a red sweater,* so *red sweater* is not yet specific in this context and cannot take *the.*) Other information may make the noun specific so that *the* is correct. For example, *It was **the red sweater that I saw in the store yesterday*** uses *the* because the *that* clause makes specific which red sweater is meant.

42b Using articles with plural nouns and with noncount nouns

With plural nouns and noncount nouns, you must decide whether to use *the* or to use no article at all. (For guidelines about using DETER-MINERS other than articles with nouns, see Chart 169 in section 41b.) What you learned in section 42a about nonspecific and specific nouns can help you make the choice between using *the* or using no article. Chart 170 in section 42a explains when a singular count noun's meaning is specific and calls for *the.* Plural nouns and noncount nouns with specific meanings usually use *the* in the same circumstances. However, a plural noun or a noncount noun with a general or nonspecific meaning usually does not use *the.*

Geraldo grows **flowers** but not **vegetables** in his garden. He is thinking about planting **corn** sometime.

Plural nouns

A plural noun's meaning may be specific because it is widely known.

The oceans are being damaged by pollution. [Because there is only one possible meaning for *oceans*—the oceans on the earth—it is correct to use *the.* This example is related to Rule 1 in Chart 170.]

A plural noun's meaning may also be made specific by a word, PHRASE, or CLAUSE in the same sentence.

Geraldo sold **the daisies from last year's garden** to the florist. [Because the phrase *from last year's garden* makes *daisies* specific, *the* is correct. This example is related to Rule 3 in Chart 170.]

A plural noun's meaning usually becomes specific by being used in an earlier sentence.

Geraldo planted **tulips** this year. **The tulips** will bloom in April. [*Tulips* is used in a general sense in the first sentence, without *the*. Because the first sentence makes *tulips* specific, *the tulips* is correct in the second sentence. This example is related to Rule 3 in Chart 170.]

A plural noun's meaning may be made specific by the context.

Geraldo fertilized **the bulbs** when he planted them last October. [In the context of the sentences about tulips, *bulbs* is understood as a synonym for *tulips,* which makes it specific and calls for *the*. This example is related to Rule 4 in Chart 170.]

Noncount nouns

Noncount nouns are always singular in form (see 41a). Like plural nouns, noncount nouns use either *the* or no article. When a noncount noun's meaning is specific, use *the* before it. If its meaning is general or nonspecific, do not use *the*.

Kalinda served us **rice**. She flavored **the rice** with curry. [*Rice* is a noncount noun. This example is related to Rule 3 in Chart 170. By the second sentence, *rice* has become specific, so *the* is used.]

Kalinda served us **the rice that she had flavored with curry.** [*Rice* is a noncount noun. This example is related to Rule 3 in Chart 170. *Rice* is made specific by the clause *that she had flavored with curry,* so *the* is used.]

Generalizations with plural or noncount nouns

Rule 2 in Chart 170 tells you to use *the* with singular count nouns used in a general sense. With generalizations using plural or noncount nouns, omit *the*.

| NO | The tulips are the flowers that grow from the bulbs. |
| YES | Tulips are flowers that grow from bulbs. |

| NO | The dogs require more care than the cats do. |
| YES | Dogs require more care than cats do. |

42c Using *the* with proper nouns and with gerunds

Proper nouns

Proper nouns name specific people, places, or things (see 7a). Most proper nouns do not require ARTICLES: *We visited **Lake Mead** with **Asha** and **Larry**.* As shown in Chart 171, however, certain types of proper nouns do require *the*.

◉ **Proper nouns that use *the*** 171

- **Nouns with the pattern *the . . . of . . .***

  the United States **of** America   **the** Fourth **of** July

  the Republic **of** Mexico   **the** University **of** Paris

- **Plural proper nouns**

  the United Arab Emirates

  the Johnsons

  the Rocky Mountains [*but* Mount Fuji]

  the Chicago Bulls

  the Falkland Islands [*but* Long Island]

  the Great Lakes [*but* Lake Louise]

- **Collective proper nouns (nouns that name a group)**

  the Modern Language Association

  the Society of Friends

- **Some (but not all) geographical features**

  the Amazon   **the** Gobi Desert   **the** Indian Ocean

- **Two countries and one city**

  the Congo   **the** Sudan   **the** Hague [capital of the Netherlands]

Gerunds

Gerunds are present participles (the *-ing* form of VERBS) used as nouns: ***Skating** is challenging.* Gerunds are usually not preceded by *the*.

> **NO**   **The constructing** new bridges is necessary to improve traffic flow.

> **YES**   **Constructing** new bridges is necessary to improve traffic flow.

Use *the* before a gerund when two conditions are met: (1) The gerund is used in a specific sense (see 42a), and (2) the gerund does not have a DIRECT OBJECT.

NO **The designing** fabric is a fine art. [*Fabric* is a direct object of *designing,* so *the* should not be used.]

YES **Designing** fabric is a fine art. [*Designing* is a gerund, so *the* is not used.]

YES **The designing of** fabric is a fine art. [*The* is used because *fabric* is the OBJECT OF THE PREPOSITION *of* and *designing* is meant in a specific sense.]

EXERCISE 42-1

Consulting all sections of this chapter, select the correct choice from the words in parentheses and write it in the blank.

EXAMPLE   Be forewarned: (A, An, The) **The** camera as we know it may soon be obsolete.

1. At (a, an, the) _____ dawn of (a, an, the) _____ twenty-first century comes (a, an, the) _____ invention so advanced that it may completely rid (a, an, the) _____ United States of America of every camera that had come before it.

2. (A, An, The) _____ digital camera, which allows photos to appear on (a, an, the) _____ computer monitor, takes up virtual space, not physical space.

3. As (a, an, the) _____ result, if you see (a, an, the) _____ bad photo on (a, an, the) _____ screen, you can simply erase (a, an, the) _____ poor photo to make room for (a, an, the) _____ new one.

4. With this new technology, (a, an, the) _____ aunt can even e-mail photos to her niece or nephew, or she can put them on (a, an, the) _____ Web page.

5. Digital cameras also allow people to alter (a, an, the) _____ appearance of people or things, which, according to many critics, is (a, an, the) _____ chief disadvantage of (a, an, the) _____ digital camera.

ANSWERS AND COVERAGE: EXERCISE 42-1

1. *the* dawn of *the* twenty-first century [Rule 1, widely understood meaning of singular count nouns]; *an* invention [42a, nonspecific use of a singular count noun]; *the* United States of America [42c, proper nouns that use *the*]

2. *The* digital camera [Rule 2, representative use of singular count noun]; *a* computer monitor [42a, nonspecific use of singular count noun]

3. *a* result [42a, nonspecific use of singular count noun]; *a* bad photo [42a, nonspecific use of a singular noun]; *the* screen [Rule 2, noun is specific in representative sense]; *the* poor photo [Rule 3, singular count noun defined elsewhere in same sentence]

4. *an* aunt, *a* Web page [42a, nonspecific use of singular count nouns, *a* or *an* depending on sound]

5. *the* appearance [Rule 2, representative use of singular noun]; *the* chief disadvantage [Rule 1, singular count noun]; *the* digital camera [Rule 2, representive use of singular noun]

ANSWERS AND COVERAGE: EXERCISE 42-2

1. *a* good idea, *an* antibacterial property [42a, nonspecific uses of singular count nouns, *a* or *an* depending on sound]

2. to treat burns [42b, omit article with generalization about the plural *burns*]; *the* skin [Rule 2, representative use of singular count noun]; *the* healing process [Rule 1, widely understood meaning of singular count nouns]

3. *the* pain [Rules 1 and 4, wide comprehension of noun's meaning and the context make use specific]

4. *a* person [42a, nonspecific use of singular count noun, *a* before a consonant sound]; *the* least painful . . . burn [Rule 3, singular count noun made specific by the words *less painful* and *scarred*]

5. *the* burn [Rule 2, representative use of singular count noun]; *the* first person [Rule 3, singular count noun made specific by the word *first*]

EXERCISE 42-2

Consulting all sections of this chapter, select the correct choice from the words in parentheses and write it in the blank. If no article is needed, leave the blank empty.

EXAMPLE   For (a, an, the) _____ years, people have worked under (a, an, the) **the** assumption that (a, an, the) **the** best remedy for (a, an, the) **a** burn is butter.

1. This kind of treatment seems to be (a, an, the) _____ good idea because butter looks and feels like ointment, but butter doesn't contain (a, an, the) _____ antibacterial property like ointment does.

2. In using butter to treat (a, an, the) _____ burns, you are coating (a, an, the) _____ skin with debris that must be removed later to keep it from interfering with (a, a, the) _____ healing process.

3. In actuality, cold water without ice will not only ease (a, an, the) _____ pain but also prevent scarring and further damage.

4. In fact, (a, an, the) _____ person who keeps the finger submerged for at least several minutes and as long as half an hour will have (a, an, the) _____ least painful or scarred burn, according to doctors.

5. However, if (a, an, the) _____ burn is serious, (a, an, the) _____ first person to be consulted should be a doctor.

43

WORD ORDER

HOW TO USE CHAPTER 43 EFFECTIVELY

1. Use this chapter together with these handbook sections:
   - 7j–7p SENTENCE types and patterns
   - 7e ADJECTIVES
   - 7f ADVERBS
   - 7m MODIFIERS
   - 11f VERBS in inverted word order
   - 7o CLAUSES

2. Remember that throughout this handbook, you can find the definitions of words printed in SMALL CAPITAL LETTERS in the Terms Glossary.

3. Use **cross-references** (often given in parentheses) to find full explanations of key concepts.

This chapter can help you with several issues of word order in sentences. Section 43a discusses standard word order for English sentences and important variations. Section 43b discusses the placement of adjectives. Section 43c discusses the placement of adverbs.

43a Understanding standard and inverted word order in sentences

In **standard word order,** the most common pattern for declarative sentences in English, the SUBJECT comes before the VERB. (To understand these concepts more fully, review sections 7k–7o.)

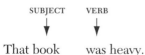

SUBJECT   VERB

That book   was heavy.

With **inverted word order,** the MAIN VERB or an AUXILIARY VERB comes before the subject. The most common use of inverted word order in English is in forming direct questions. Questions that can be answered "yes" or "no" begin with a form of *be* used as a main verb, with an auxiliary verb (*be, do, have*), or with a modal auxiliary (*can, should, will,* and others; see Chapter 46).

Questions that can be answered "yes" or "no"

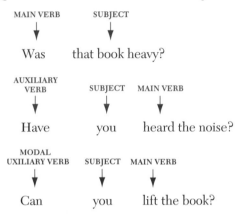

To form a yes/no question with a verb other than *be* as the main verb and when there is no auxiliary or modal as part of a verb phrase, use the appropriate form of the auxiliary verb *do.*

A question that begins with a question-forming word like *why, when, where,* or *how* cannot be answered "yes" or "no": **Why** *did the book fall?* Some kind of information must be provided to answer such a question; the answer cannot be simply "yes" or "no." Information is needed to answer: for example, *It was too heavy for me.*

Information questions: Inverted order

Most information questions follow the same rules of inverted word order as yes/no questions.

QUESTION WORD	MAIN VERB	SUBJECT
↓	↓	↓
Why	is	that book open?

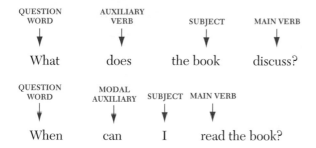

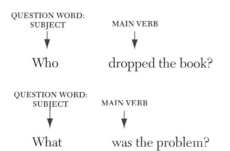

Information questions: Standard order

When *who* or *what* functions as the subject in a question, use standard word order.

ALERT: When a question has more than one auxiliary verb, put the subject after the first auxiliary verb.

FIRST AUXILIARY	SUBJECT	SECOND AUXILIARY	MAIN VERB
↓	↓	↓	↓
Would	you	have	replaced the book?**!**

The same rules apply to emphatic exclamations: ***Was*** *that book heavy!* ***Did*** *she enjoy that book!*

Negatives

When you use negatives such as *never, hardly ever, seldom, rarely, not only,* or *nor* to start a clause, use inverted order. These sentence pairs show the differences.

I have never seen a more exciting movie. [standard order]

Never have I seen a more exciting movie. [inverted order]

She is not only a talented artist **but also** an excellent musician.

Not only is she a talented artist, **but she is also** an excellent musician.

737

I didn't like the book, and **my husband didn't either.**

I didn't like the book, and **neither did my husband.**

❶**USAGE ALERT:** With indirect questions, use standard word order: *She asked* **how I dropped the book** (not *She asked* **how did I drop** *the book*). ❗

❶**STYLE ALERT:** Word order deliberately inverted can be effective, when used sparingly, to create emphasis in a sentence that is neither a question nor an exclamation (also see 19f). ❗

43b Understanding the placement of adjectives

Adjectives modify—describe or limit—NOUNS, PRONOUNS, and word groups that function as nouns (see 7e). In English, an adjective comes directly before the noun it describes. However, when more than one adjective describes the same noun, several sequences may be possible. Chart 172 shows the most common order for positioning several adjectives.

◉ **Word order for more than one adjective   172**

1. **Determiners, if any:** *a, an, the, my, your, Jan's, this, that, these, those,* and so on

2. **Expressions of order, including ordinal numbers, if any:** *first, second, third, next, last, final,* and so on

3. **Expressions of quantity, including cardinal (counting) numbers, if any:** *one, two, three, few, each, every, some,* and so on

4. **Adjectives of judgment or opinion, if any:** *pretty, happy, ugly, sad, interesting, boring,* and so on

5. **Adjectives of size or shape, if any:** *big, small, short, round, square,* and so on

6. **Adjectives of age or condition, if any:** *new, young, broken, dirty, shiny,* and so on

7. **Adjectives of color, if any:** *red, green blue,* and so on

8. **Adjectives that can also be used as nouns, if any:** *French, Protestant, metal, cotton,* and so on

9. **The noun**

1	2	3	4	5	6	7	8	9
a		few		tiny		red		ants
the	last	six					Thai	carvings
my			fine		old		oak	table

43c Understanding the placement of adverbs

Adverbs modify—describe or limit—VERBS, ADJECTIVES, other adverbs, or entire sentences (see 7f). Adverbs may be positioned first, in the middle, or last in clauses. Chart 173 summarizes adverb types, what they tell about the words they modify, and where each type can be placed.

⊙ **Types of adverbs and where to position them   173**

ADVERBS OF MANNER	■ describe *how* something is done	Nick **carefully** groomed the dog.
	■ are usually in middle or last position	Nick groomed the dog **carefully.**
ADVERBS OF TIME	■ describe *when* or *how long* about an event	**First,** he shampooed the dog.
	■ are usually in first or last position	He shampooed the dog **first.**
	■ include *just, still, already,* and similar adverbs, which are usually in middle position	He had **already** brushed the dog's coat.
ADVERBS OF FREQUENCY	■ describe *how often* an event takes place	Nick has **never** been bitten by a dog.
	■ are usually in middle position	
	■ are in first position when they modify an entire sentence (see "Sentence adverbs" on page 740)	**Occasionally,** he is scratched while shampooing a cat.
ADVERBS OF DEGREE OR EMPHASIS	■ describe *how much* or *to what extent* about other modifiers	Nick is **extremely** calm around animals. [*Extremely* modifies *calm.*]
	■ are directly before the word they modify	
	■ include *only,* which is easy to misplace (see 15b.1)	→

Types of adverbs and where to position them   173
(continued)

SENTENCE ADVERBS	■ modify the entire sentence rather than just one word or a few words ■ include transitional words and expressions (see 4d.1), as well as such expressions as *maybe, probably, possibly, fortunately, unfortunately,* and *incredibly* ■ are in first position	**Incredibly,** he was once asked to groom a rat.

🛇 **USAGE ALERT:** Do not let an adverb separate a verb from its DIRECT OBJECT or INDIRECT OBJECT (see section 15b.3). ❗

EXERCISE 43-1

Consulting all sections of this chapter, find and correct any errors in word order.

1. For two hundred years almost, the North Pacific humpback whales have returned to the tropic waters of Hawaii.
2. Why they are returning to these particular waters year after year?
3. The humpbacks do not accidentally arrive in Hawaiian waters; they are precise extremely in searching for this specific location, where they gather to complete their breeding rituals.
4. The whales first to arrive are sighted sometime in late November, after completing a 3,000-mile journey.
5. The humpbacks last to migrate to Hawaii arrive by December late or January early.

EXERCISE 43-2

Consulting all sections of this chapter, find and correct any errors in word order.

1. A beautiful few flowers began to bloom in my garden this week.
2. A neighbor asked me, "You did grow all these yourself?"
3. "Yes," I replied, "the roses are my favorite husband's, but my favorite are the tulips."
4. My neighbor, who extremely was impressed with my gardening efforts, decided to grow some flowers of her own.
5. Weeks later, as I strolled by her house, I saw her planting happily seeds from her favorite type of plant—petunias.

ANSWERS AND COVERAGE: EXERCISE 43-1

1. For almost two hundred years [43c, adverb of degree is positioned before the words it modifies, *two hundred years*]
2. Why are they returning [43a, inverted word order for questions, form of *be* precedes subject]
3. are extremely precise [43c, adverb of degree or emphasis precedes the word it modifies, *precise*]
4. The first whales [43b, expression of order follows determiner *the* but precedes all other modifiers (if any) and the noun]
5. The last humpbacks; by late December or early January [43b, expressions of order precede the words they modify]

ANSWERS AND COVERAGE: EXERCISE 43-2

1. A few beautiful flowers [43b, expressions of quantity precede adjectives or opinion]
2. Did you grow [43a, inverted word order for questions, form of *do* precedes subject]
3. my husband's favorite [43b, determiner precedes descriptive adjective, *favorite*]
4. was extremely impressed [43c, adverb of degree is positioned before the word it modifies, *impressed*]
5. her happily planting seeds [43c, adverb of manner is positioned before the word it modifies, *planting*]

44

PREPOSITIONS

HOW TO USE CHAPTER 44 EFFECTIVELY

1. Use this chapter together with these handbook sections:
   - 7g PREPOSITIONS
   - 21a using appropriate language
2. Remember that throughout this handbook, you can find the definitions of words printed in SMALL CAPITAL LETTERS in the Terms Glossary.
3. Use **cross-references** (often given in parentheses) to find full explanations of key concepts.

Prepositions function with other words in PREPOSITIONAL PHRASES. Prepositional phrases usually indicate *where* (direction or location), *how* (by what means or in what way), or *when* (at what time or how long) about the words they modify.

This chapter can help you with several uses of prepositions, which function in combination with other words in ways that are often idiomatic. An idiom's meaning differs from the literal meaning of each individual word (see 20a). For example, the word *break* usually refers to shattering, but the sentence *Yao-Ming **broke into** a smile* means that a smile appeared on Yao-Ming's face. Knowing which preposition to use in a specific context takes much experience reading, listening to, and speaking the language. A dictionary like the *Longman Dictionary of Contemporary English* or the *Oxford Advanced Learner's Dictionary* can be especially helpful when you need to find the correct preposition to use in cases not covered by this chapter. Section 44a lists many common prepositions. Section 44b discusses prepositions with some expressions of time and place. Section 44c discusses combinations of verbs and prepositions called PHRASAL VERBS. Section 44d discusses common expressions using prepositions.

44a Recognizing prepositions

Chart 174 on the next page shows many common prepositions.

◉ **Common prepositions** 174

about	before	except for	near	through
above	behind	excepting	next	throughout
according to	below	for	of	till
across	beneath	from	off	to
after	beside	in	on	toward
against	between	in addition to	onto	under
along	beyond	in back of	on top of	underneath
along with	but	in case of	out	unlike
among	by	in front of	out of	until
apart from	by means of	in place of	outside	up
around	concerning	inside	over	upon
as	despite	in spite of	past	up to
as for	down	instead of	regarding	with
at	during	into	round	within
because of	except	like	since	without

44b Using prepositions with expressions of time and place

Chart 175 shows how to use the prepositions *in, at,* and *on* to deliver some common kinds of information about time and place. The chart, however, does not cover every preposition that indicates time or place, nor does it cover all uses of *in, at,* and *on*. Also, the chart does not include expressions that operate outside the general rules. (Both these sentences are correct: *You ride **in** the car* and *You ride **on** the bus.*)

◉ **Using *in, at,* and *on* to show time and place** 175

Time

■ ***in* a year or a month** (*during* is also correct but less common)

    in 1995   **in** May

■ ***in* a period of time**

    in a few months (seconds, days, years)

→

Using *in*, *at*, and *on* to show time and place *(continued)*   175

- ■ *in* **a period of the day**

  in the morning (afternoon, evening)

  in the daytime (morning, evening) *but* **at** night

- ■ *on* **a specific day**

  on Friday   **on** my birthday

- ■ *at* **a specific time or period of time**

  at noon   **at** 2:00   **at** dawn   **at** nightfall

  at takeoff (the time a plane leaves)

  at breakfast (the time a specific meal takes place)

Place

- ■ *in* **a location surrounded by something else**

  in the province of Alberta   **in** the kitchen

  in Utah   **in** the apartment

  in downtown Bombay   **in** the bathtub

- ■ *at* **a specific location**

  at your house   **at** the bank

  at the corner of Third Avenue and Main Street

- ■ *on* **a surface**

  on page 20

  on the second floor *but* **in** the attic *or* **in** the basement

  on Washington Street

  on the mezzanine

  on street level

44c Using prepositions in phrasal verbs

Phrasal verbs, also called *two-word verbs* and *three-word verbs,* are VERBS that combine with prepositions to deliver their meaning.

In some phrasal verbs, the verb and the preposition should not be separated by other words: ***Look at*** *the moon* [not ***Look*** *the moon* ***at***]. In **separable phrasal verbs,** other words in the sentence can separate the verb and the preposition without interfering with meaning: *I **threw away** my homework* is as correct as *I **threw** my homework **away.***

Here is a list of some common phrasal verbs. The ones that cannot be separated are marked with an asterisk (*).

SELECTED PHRASAL VERBS

ask out	get along with*	look into
break down	get back	look out for*
bring about	get off*	look over
call back	go over*	make up
drop off	hand in	run across*
figure out	keep up with*	speak to*
fill out	leave out	speak with*
fill up	look after*	throw away
find out	look around	throw out

Position a PRONOUN OBJECT between the words of a separable phrasal verb: *I threw **it** away.* Also, you can position an object PHRASE of several words between the parts of a separable phrasal verb: *I threw **my research paper** away.* However, when the object is a CLAUSE, do not let it separate the parts of the phrasal verb: *I threw away **all the papers that I wrote last year.***

Many phrasal verbs are informal and are used more in speaking than in writing. For academic writing, a more formal verb may be more appropriate than a phrasal verb. In a research paper, for example, *propose* or *suggest* might be better choices than *come up with.* For academic writing, acceptable phrasal verbs include *believe in, benefit from, concentrate on, consist of, depend on, dream of* (or *dream about*), *insist on, participate in, prepare for,* and *stare at.* None of these phrasal verbs can be separated.

EXERCISE 44-1

Consulting the preceding sections of this chapter and using the list of phrasal verbs in section 44c, write a one- or two-paragraph description of a typical day at work or school in which you use at least five phrasal verbs. After checking a dictionary, revise your writing, substituting for the phrasal verbs any more formal verbs that you think might be more appropriate for academic writing.

44d Using prepositions in common expressions

In many common expressions, different prepositions convey great differences in meaning. For example, four prepositions can be used with the verb *agree* to create five different meanings.

agree to = to give consent: *I cannot **agree to** my buying you a new car.*

agree about = to arrive at a satisfactory understanding: *We **agree about** your needing a car.*

agree on = to arrive at a satisfactory understanding: *You and the seller must **agree on** a price for the car.*

agree with = to have the same opinion: *I **agree with** you that you need a car.*

agree with = be suitable or healthful: *The idea of having such a major expense does not **agree with me.***

You can find entire books filled with English expressions that include prepositions. The following list shows a few that you are likely to use often.

SELECTED EXPRESSIONS WITH PREPOSITIONS

ability in	different from	involved with [*someone*]
access to	faith in	knowledge of
accustomed to	familiar with	made of
afraid of	famous for	married to
angry with *or* at	frightened by	opposed to
authority on	happy with	patient with
aware of	in charge of	proud of
based on	independent of	reason for
capable of	in favor of	related to
certain of	influence on *or* over	suspicious of
confidence in	interested in	time for
dependent on	involved in [*something*]	tired of

45

GERUNDS, INFINITIVES, AND PARTICIPLES

HOW TO USE CHAPTER 45 EFFECTIVELY

1. Use this chapter together with these handbook sections:
   - 7d VERBALS
   - 11a SUBJECT-VERB AGREEMENT
   - 7k–7l SUBJECTS and OBJECTS
   - 18a–18c PARALLELISM
   - 8b PRINCIPAL PARTS of verbs

2. Remember that throughout this handbook, you can find the definitions of words printed in SMALL CAPITAL LETTERS in the Terms Glossary.

3. Use **cross-references** (often given in parentheses) to find full explanations of key concepts.

Participles are VERB forms (see 8b). A verb's *-ing* form is its **present participle.** The *-ed* form of a regular verb is its **past participle;** irregular verbs form their past participles in various ways (for example, *bend, bent; eat, eaten; think, thought*—for a complete list, see Chart 62 in section 8d). Participles can function as ADJECTIVES (*a **smiling** face, a **closed** book*).

A verb's *-ing* form can also function as a NOUN (***Sneezing** spreads colds*), which is called a **gerund.** Another verb form, the **infinitive,** can also function as a noun. An infinitive is a verb's simple or base form, usually preceded by the word *to* (*We want everyone **to smile***). Verb forms—participles, gerunds, and infinitives—functioning as nouns or modifiers are called **verbals,** as explained in section 7d.

This chapter can help you make the right choices among verbals. Section 45a discusses gerunds and infinitives used as subjects. Section 45b discusses verbs that are followed by gerunds, not infinitives. Section 45c discusses verbs that are followed by infinitives, not gerunds. Section 45d discusses meaning changes that depend on whether certain verbs are followed by a gerund or by an infinitive. Section 45e explains that meaning does not change for certain sense verbs no matter whether they are followed by a gerund or an infinitive. Section 45f discusses differences in meaning between the present-participle form and the past-participle form of some modifiers.

45a Using gerunds and infinitives as subjects

Gerunds are used more commonly than infinitives as subjects. Sometimes, however, either is acceptable.

Choosing the right health club is important.

To choose the right health club is important.

❶ VERB ALERT: When a gerund or an infinitive is used alone as a subject, it is singular and requires a singular verb. When two or more gerunds or infinitives create a COMPOUND SUBJECT, they require a plural verb. (See sections 7k and 11d.)❗

45b Using a gerund, not an infinitive, as an object after certain verbs

Some verbs must be followed by GERUNDS used as DIRECT OBJECTS. Other verbs must be followed by infinitives. Still other verbs can be followed by either a gerund or an infinitive. (A few verbs can change meaning depending on whether they are followed by a gerund or an infinitive; see section 45d.) Chart 176 lists common verbs that must be followed by gerunds, not infinitives.

Yuri **considered** *calling* [not *to call*] the mayor.

He **was having trouble** *getting* [not *to get*] a work permit.

Yuri's boss **recommended** *taking* [not *to take*] an interpreter to the permit agency.

◉ Verbs and expressions that must be followed by gerunds　　**176**

acknowledge	detest	mind
admit	discuss	object to
advise	dislike	postpone
anticipate	dream about	practice
appreciate	enjoy	put off
avoid	escape	quit

➡

747

> **Verbs and expressions that must be followed by gerunds** *(continued)* 176
>
> | | | |
> |---|---|---|
> | cannot bear | evade | recall |
> | cannot help | favor | recommend |
> | cannot resist | finish | regret |
> | complain about | give up | resent |
> | consider | have trouble | resist |
> | consist of | imagine | risk |
> | contemplate | include | suggest |
> | defer from | insist on | talk about |
> | delay | keep (on) | tolerate |
> | deny | mention | understand |

Gerund after go

Go is usually followed by an infinitive: *We can **go to see*** [not *go seeing*] *a movie tonight.* Sometimes, however, *go* is followed by a gerund in phrases such as *go swimming, go fishing, go shopping,* and *go driving: I will **go shopping*** [not *go to shop*] *after work.*

Gerund after be + complement + preposition

Many common expressions use a form of the verb *be* plus a COMPLEMENT plus a PREPOSITION. In such expressions, use a gerund, not an infinitive, after the preposition. Here is a list of some of the most frequently used expressions in this pattern.

SELECTED EXPRESSIONS USING *BE* **+ COMPLEMENT + PREPOSITION**

be (get) accustomed to	be interested in
be angry about	be prepared for
be bored with	be responsible for
be capable of	be tired of
be committed to	be (get) used to
be excited about	be worried about

We **are excited about** *voting* [not *to vote*] in the next election.

Who **will be responsible for** *locating* [not *to locate*] our polling place?

❶ **USAGE ALERT:** Always use a gerund, not an infinitive, as the object of a preposition. Be especially careful when the word *to* is functioning as a preposition in a phrasal verb (see 44c): *We are committed **to changing*** [not *to change*] *the rules.* ❗

45c Using an infinitive, not a gerund, as an object after certain verbs

Chart 177 lists selected common verbs and expressions that must be followed by INFINITIVES, not GERUNDS, as OBJECTS.

She **wanted *to go*** [not *wanted going*] to the lecture.

Only three people **decided *to question*** [not *decided questioning*] the speaker.

◉ **Verbs and expressions that must be followed by infinitives**   177

afford	claim	hope	promise
agree	consent	intend	refuse
aim	decide	know how	seem
appear	decline	learn	struggle
arrange	demand	like	tend
ask	deserve	manage	threaten
attempt	do not care	mean	volunteer
be left	expect	offer	vote
beg	fail	plan	wait
cannot afford	give permission	prepare	want
care	hesitate	pretend	would like

Infinitives after be + *complement*

Gerunds are common in constructions that use forms of the verb *be*, a COMPLEMENT, and a PREPOSITION (see 45b). However, use an infinitive, not a gerund, when *be* plus a complement is not followed by a preposition.

We **are eager *to go*** [not *going*] camping.

I **am ready *to sleep*** [not *sleeping*] in a tent.

Infinitives to indicate purpose

Use an infinitive in expressions that indicate purpose: *I read a book* **to learn** *more about Mayan culture.* This sentence means "I read a book for the purpose of learning more about Mayan culture." *To learn* delivers the idea of purpose more concisely (see Chapter 16) than expressions such as *so that I can* or *in order to.*

Infinitives with the first, the last, the one

Use an infinitive after the expressions *the first, the last,* and *the one: Nina is the first* **to arrive** [not *arriving*] *and the last* **to leave** [not *leaving*] *every day.*

Unmarked infinitives

Infinitives used without the word *to* are called **unmarked infinitives** or **bare infinitives.** An unmarked infinitive may be hard to recognize because it is not preceded by *to.* Some common verbs followed by unmarked infinitives are *feel, have, hear, let, listen to, look at, make* (meaning "compel"), *notice, see,* and *watch.*

> Please let me **take** [not *to take*] you to lunch. [unmarked infinitive]
>
> I want **to take** you to lunch. [marked infinitive]
>
> I can have Kara **drive** [not *to drive*] us. [unmarked infinitive]
>
> I will ask Kara **to drive** us. [marked infinitive]

The verb *help* can be followed by either a marked or an unmarked infinitive. Either is correct: *Help me* **put** [or **to put**] *this box in the car.*

❶ **USAGE ALERT:** Be careful to use parallel structure (see Chapter 18) correctly when you use two or more gerunds or infinitives after verbs. If two or more VERBAL OBJECTS follow one verb, put the verbals into the same form.

> **NO**   We went **sailing** and **to scuba dive.**
>
> **YES**   We went **sailing** and **scuba diving.**

> **NO**   We heard the wind **blow** and the waves **crashing.**
>
> **YES**   We heard the wind **blow** and the waves **crash.**
>
> **YES**   We heard the wind **blowing** and the waves **crashing.**

Conversely, if you are using verbal objects with COMPOUND PREDICATES, be sure to use the kind of verbal that each verb requires.

> **NO**   We enjoyed **scuba diving** but do not plan **sailing** again.
> [*Enjoyed* requires a gerund object, and *plan* requires an infinitive object; see Charts 176 and 177.]
>
> **YES**   We enjoyed **scuba diving** but do not plan **to sail** again. ❗

45d Knowing how meaning changes when certain verbs are followed by a gerund or an infinitive as an object

With stop

The verb *stop* followed by a GERUND means "finish, quit." *Stop* followed by an infinitive means "interrupt one activity to begin another."

We **stopped** *eating.* [We finished our meal.]

We **stopped** *to eat.* [We stopped another activity, such as driving, in order to eat.]

With remember *and* forget

The verb *remember* followed by an infinitive means "not to forget to do something": *I must* **remember to talk** *with Isa. Remember* followed by a gerund means "recall a memory": *I* **remember talking** *in my sleep last night.*

The verb *forget* followed by an infinitive means "fail to do something": *If you* **forget to put** *a stamp on that letter, it will be returned. Forget* followed by a gerund means "do something and not recall it": *I* **forget having put** *the stamps in the refrigerator.*

With try

The verb *try* followed by an infinitive means "make an effort": *I* **tried to find** *your jacket.* Followed by a gerund, *try* means "experiment with": *I* **tried jogging** *but found it too difficult.*

45e Understanding that meaning does not change whether a gerund or an infinitive follows certain sense verbs

Sense VERBS include words such as *see, notice, hear, observe, watch, feel, listen to,* and *look at.* The meaning of these verbs is usually not affected whether they are followed by a GERUND or by an INFINITIVE as an OBJECT. *I* **saw** *the water* **rise** and *I* **saw** *the water* **rising** both have the same meaning in American English.

EXERCISE 45-1

Consulting sections 45b, 45c, 45d, and 45e, write the correct form of the verbal object (either a gerund or an infinitive) for each verb in parentheses.

EXAMPLE   People like (think) **to think** that they have a good memory, but everybody shows signs of forgetfulness from time to time.

751

ANSWERS AND COVERAGE: EXERCISE 45-1

1. riding [45b, gerund after preposition]

2. take [45c, unmarked infinitive with *let*]

3. to bring [45c, infinitive following *force*]

4. to walk [45c, infinitive following *need*]

5. Stepping [45a, gerund as subject]

6. losing [45a, gerund after *be* + complement *angry* + preposition *about*]

7. reunite *or* to reunite [45c, marked or unmarked infinitive with *help*]

8. to call [45c, infinitive following *tend*]

9. leaving [45b, gerund used with *acknowledge*]

10. answering, identifying [45b, gerund used after preposition *by*]

1. Think about (ride) _____ the railroad to work on a rainy Monday morning.
2. The comfortable reclining seats let passengers (take) _____ a relaxing nap on the way to work.
3. Because of the rain, commuters are forced (bring) _____ an umbrella and a raincoat, along with their usual traveling items.
4. Once they reach their destination, passengers forget that they need their umbrellas and raincoats (walk) _____ the few blocks to work.
5. (Step) _____ out into the rain makes them suddenly realize that they've left their umbrellas and raincoats on the train, which has already left the station.
6. However, they need not be angry about (lose) _____ the forgotten item.
7. Many railroads have lost and found offices that help (reunite) _____ the rightful owners with their lost possessions.
8. After losing a possession, passengers tend (call) _____ the lost and found office in search of the missing article.
9. Some commuters even acknowledge (leave) _____ gifts, false teeth, wooden legs, and bicycles aboard the train.
10. Most times, people can claim their possessions either by (answer) _____ a few questions to ensure proper ownership or by (identify) _____ the lost item.

45f Choosing between *-ing* and *-ed* forms for adjectives

Deciding whether to use the *-ing* form (PRESENT PARTICIPLE) or the *-ed* form (PAST PARTICIPLE of a regular VERB) as an ADJECTIVE in a specific sentence can be difficult. For example, *I am **amused*** and *I am **amusing*** are both correct in English, but their meanings are very different. To make the right choice, decide whether the modified NOUN or PRONOUN is causing or experiencing what the participle describes.

Use a present participle (*-ing*) to modify a noun or pronoun that is the agent or the cause of the action.

> Mica described your **interesting** plan. [The noun *plan* causes what its modifier describes—interest; so *interesting* is correct.]

> I find your plan **exciting**. [The noun *plan* causes what its modifier describes—excitement; so *exciting* is correct.]

Use a past participle (*-ed* in regular verbs) to modify a noun or pronoun that experiences or receives whatever the modifier describes.

An **interested** committee wants to hear your plan. [The noun *committee* experiences what its modifier describes—interest; so *interested* is correct.]

Excited by your plan, they called a board meeting. [The pronoun *they* experiences what its modifier describes—excitement; so *excited* is correct.]

Here are frequently used participles that convey very different meanings, depending on whether the *-ed* or the *-ing* form is used.

amused, amusing	frightened, frightening
annoyed, annoying	insulted, insulting
appalled, appalling	offended, offending
bored, boring	overwhelmed, overwhelming
confused, confusing	pleased, pleasing
depressed, depressing	reassured, reassuring
disgusted, disgusting	satisfied, satisfying
fascinated, fascinating	shocked, shocking

EXERCISE 45-2

Consulting section 45f, choose the correct participle.

EXAMPLE   It can be a (satisfied, satisfying) **satisfying** experience to learn about the lives of artists.

1. Artist Frida Kahlo led an (interested, interesting) _____ life.
2. When Kahlo was eighteen, (horrified, horrifying) _____ observers saw her (injured, injuring) _____ in a streetcar accident.
3. A (disappointed, disappointing) _____ Kahlo had to abandon her plan to study medicine.
4. Instead, she began to create paintings filled with (disturbed, disturbing) _____ images.
5. Some art critics consider Kahlo's paintings to be (fascinated, fascinating) _____ works of art even though many people find them (overwhelmed, overwhelming) _____.

EXERCISE 45-3

Consulting section 45f, choose the correct participle.

EXAMPLE   Learning about the career of a favorite actor or actress is always an (interested, interesting) **interesting** exercise.

1. Canadian Jim Carrey is an actor-comedian with a very (fascinated, fascinating) _____ history.
2. (Raised, Raising) _____ by his parents in southern Ontario, Carrey grew up in one of the most media-rich areas in North America.

Answers and Coverage: Exercise 45-3 (continued)

3. surprising [news conveys rather than experiences surprise]

4. disappointed [Carrey experiences rather than causes disappointment]; canceled [the TV series experiences rather than causes the cancellation]

5. amusing [appearances cause rather than experience amusement]

ANSWERS AND COVERAGE: EXERCISE 45-4

1. interesting [information conveys rather than experiences interest]

2. unsettling [passage conveys rather than experiences the sensation of being unsettled]

3. frightened [ostriches experience rather than convey fright]

4. hunted [ostrich experiences rather than causes the hunt]

5. threatened [ostriches experience rather than convey a threat]; frightening [opponent conveys rather than experiences fright]

3. Biographies reveal the (surprised, surprising) _____ news that this bright and talented student dropped out of school during the tenth grade.

4. After relocating to Los Angeles in the 1980s, the (disappointed, disappointing) _____ Carrey discovered the difficulties of acting after his first (canceled, canceling) _____ TV series left him briefly out of work.

5. Carrey's career skyrocketed with his (amused, amusing) _____ appearances on *In Living Color*, a TV show that led to numerous box office hits like *Ace Ventura: Pet Detective* and *The Mask*.

EXERCISE 45-4

Consulting section 45f, choose the correct participle.

EXAMPLE   Studying popular myths that turn out to be false can be a (fascinated, fascinating) **fascinating** experience.

1. While doing research for a paper about birds, I discovered some (interested, interesting) _____ information about ostriches.

2. I encountered an (unsettled, unsettling) _____ passage in a book, which said that ostriches do not, in fact, stick their heads into the sand for protection when they feel fear.

3. This myth about (frightened, frightening) _____ ostriches began among the ancient Arabs and has since been passed on by many reputable writers.

4. In reality, an ostrich does not have to do something as useless as bury its head in the sand when a predator approaches, because a (hunted, hunting) _____ ostrich can reach speeds of nearly 35 miles an hour and can thus outrun most other animals.

5. A (threatened, threatening) _____ ostrich can also kick its way out of most dangerous situations with its powerful legs, and with its 8-foot-tall frame, it presents itself as a (frightened, frightening) _____ opponent.

46

MODAL AUXILIARY VERBS

HOW TO USE CHAPTER 46 EFFECTIVELY

1. Use this chapter together with these handbook sections:
   - 7c recognizing VERBS
   - 8e AUXILIARY VERBS
   - 8g verb TENSE
   - 8j PROGRESSIVE TENSES
   - 8l–8m SUBJUNCTIVE MOOD
2. Remember that throughout this handbook, you can find the definitions of words printed in SMALL CAPITAL LETTERS in the Terms Glossary.
3. Use **cross-references** (often given in parentheses) to find full explanations of key concepts.

    Auxiliary verbs are known as *helping verbs* because adding an auxiliary verb to a MAIN VERB helps the main verb convey additional information (see 8e). For example, the auxiliary verb *do* is important in turning sentences into questions. *You have to sleep* becomes a question when *do* is added: *Do you have to sleep?* The most common auxiliary verbs are forms of *be, have,* and *do.* Charts 63 and 64 in section 8e list the forms of these three verbs.

    Modal auxiliary verbs are one type of auxiliary verb. They include *can, could, may, might, should, had better, must, will, would,* and others discussed in this chapter. Modals differ from *be, have,* and *do* used as auxiliary verbs in the ways discussed in Chart 178.

◉ **Modals and their differences from other auxiliary verbs**   **178**

- Modals in the present future are always followed by the simple form of a main verb: *I might **go** tomorrow.*

→

> **Modals and their differences**   178
> **from other auxiliary verbs** *(continued)*
>
> ■ One-word modals have no *-s* ending in the third-person singular: *She **could** go with me, you **could** go with me, they **could** go with me.* (The two-word modal *have to* changes form to agree with its subject: *I **have to** leave, she **has to** leave.*) Auxiliary verbs other than modals usually change form for third-person singular: *I **do** want to go, he **does** want to go.*
>
> ■ Some modals change form in the past. Others (*should, would, must,* which convey probability, and *ought to*) use *have* + a past participle. *I **can** do it* becomes *I **could** do it* in past-tense clauses about ability. *I **could** do it* becomes *I **could have done** it* in clauses about possibility.
>
> ■ Modals convey meaning about ability, advisability, necessity, possibility, and other conditions: For example, *I can go* means "I am able to go." Modals do not describe actual occurrences.

This chapter can help you use modals to convey shades of meaning. Section 46a discusses using modals to convey ability, necessity, advisability, possibility, and probability. Section 46b discusses using modals to convey preferences, plans or obligations, and past habits. Section 46c introduces modals in the PASSIVE VOICE.

46a Conveying ability, necessity, advisability, possibility, and probability with modals

Conveying ability

The modal *can* conveys ability now (in the present), and *could* conveys ability before (in the past). These words deliver the meaning of "able to." For the future, use *will be able to.*

> We **can** work late tonight. [*Can* conveys present ability.]
>
> I **could** work late last night, too. [*Could* conveys past ability.]
>
> I **will be able to** work late next Monday. [*Will be able* is the future tense; *will* here is not a modal.]

Adding *not* between a modal and the main verb makes the CLAUSE negative: *We **cannot** work late tonight; I **could not** work late last night; I **will not** be able to work late next Monday.*

❶ **USAGE ALERT:** You will often see negative forms of modals turned into CONTRACTIONS: *can't, couldn't, won't, wouldn't,* and others. Because contractions are considered informal usage by some instructors, you will never be wrong if you avoid them in academic writing except when you are reproducing spoken words. ❗

Conveying necessity

The modals *must* and *have to* convey a need to do something. Both *must* and *have to* are followed by the simple form of the main verb. In the present tense, *have to* changes form to agree with its subject.

You **must** leave before midnight.

She **has to** leave when I leave.

In the past tense, *must* is never used to express necessity. Instead, use *had to.*

> **PRESENT TENSE**   We **must** study today. We **have to** study today.
>
> **PAST TENSE**   We **had to** [not *must*] take a test yesterday.

The negative forms of *must* and *have to* also have different meanings. *Must not* conveys that something is forbidden; *do not have to* conveys that something is not necessary.

You **must not** sit there. [Sitting there is forbidden.]

You **do not have to** sit there. [Sitting there is not necessary.]

Conveying advisability or the notion of a good idea

The modals *should* and *ought to* express the idea that doing the action of the main verb is advisable or is a good idea.

You **should** go to class tomorrow morning.

In the past tense, *should* and *ought to* convey regret or knowing something through hindsight. They mean that good advice was not taken.

You **should have** gone to class yesterday.

I **ought to have** called my sister yesterday.

The modal *had better* delivers the meaning of good advice or warning or threat. It does not change form for tense.

You **had better** see the doctor before your cough gets worse.

Need to is often used to express strong advice, too. Its past-tense form is *needed to.*

You **need to** take better care of yourself. You **needed to** listen.

Conveying possibility

The modals *may, might,* and *could* can be used to convey an idea of possibility or likelihood.

We **may** become hungry before long.

We **could** eat lunch at the diner next door.

The past-tense forms for *may, might,* and *could* use these words followed by *have* and the past participle of the main verb.

I **could have studied** French in high school, but I studied Spanish instead.

Conveying probability

In addition to conveying the idea of necessity (see page 757), the modal auxiliary verb *must* can also convey probability or likelihood. It means that a well-informed guess is being made.

Marisa **must** be a talented actress. She has been chosen to play the lead role in the school play.

When *must* conveys probability, the past tense is *must have* plus the past participle of the main verb.

I did not see Boris at the party; he **must have left** early.

**ANSWERS AND COVERAGE:
EXERCISE 46-1**

1. had to *or* needed to [either past-tense form of modal auxiliary is acceptable]

2. should have *or* ought to have [either past-tense form of modal auxiliary is acceptable]

3. could [past-tense form of modal auxiliary]

4. must/could/might/may have [any of the past-tense forms for conveying possibility and making a guess is acceptable]

5. should have *or* ought to have [either past-tense form of modal auxiliary is acceptable]

EXERCISE 46-1

Consulting section 46a, fill in the blanks with the past-tense modal that expresses the meaning given in parentheses.

EXAMPLE I (advisability) **should have** gone straight to the doctor the instant I felt a cold coming on.

1. Since I (necessity, no choice) _____ work late this past Monday, I could not get to the doctor's office before it closed.

2. I (advisability) _____ fallen asleep after dinner, but I stayed awake for a while instead.

3. Even after I finally got into bed, I (ability) _____ not relax.

4. I (making a guess) _____ not _____ heard the alarm the next morning, because I overslept nearly two hours.

5. When I finally arrived at work, my boss came into my office and said, "Julie, you (necessity) _____ stayed home and rested if you are sick."

46b Conveying preferences, plans, and past habits with modals

Conveying preferences

The modal *would rather* expresses a preference. *Would rather,* the PRESENT TENSE, is used with the SIMPLE FORM of the MAIN VERB, and *would rather have,* the PAST TENSE, is used with the PAST PARTICIPLE of the main verb.

> We **would rather see** a comedy than a mystery.

> Carlos **would rather have stayed** home last night.

Conveying plan or obligation

A form of *be* followed by *supposed to* and the simple form of a main verb delivers a meaning of something planned or of an obligation.

> I **was supposed to meet** them at the bus stop.

Conveying past habit

The modals *used to* and *would* express the idea that something happened repeatedly in the past.

> I **used to** hate going to the dentist.

> I **would** dread every single visit.

🛈 USAGE ALERT: Both *used to* and *would* can be used to express repeated actions in the past, but *would* cannot be used for a situation that lasted for a period of time in the past.

> **NO** I **would** live in Arizona.

> **YES** I **used to** live in Arizona. **❗**

46c Recognizing modals in the passive voice

Modals use the ACTIVE VOICE, as shown in sections 46a and 46b. In the active voice, the subject does the action expressed in the MAIN VERB (see 8n and 8o).

Modals can also use the PASSIVE VOICE. In the passive voice, the doer of the main verb's action is either unexpressed or is expressed as an OBJECT in a PREPOSITIONAL PHRASE starting with the word *by.*

> **PASSIVE** The waterfront **can be seen** from my window.

> **ACTIVE** I **can see** the waterfront from my window.

PASSIVE	The tax form **must be signed** by the person who fills it out.
ACTIVE	The person who fills out the tax form **must sign** it.

ANSWERS AND COVERAGE: EXERCISE 46-2

1. had to *or* needed to [either past-tense form of modal auxiliary is acceptable]

2. should have *or* ought to have [either past-tense form of modal auxiliary is acceptable]

3. could [past-tense form of modal auxiliary]

4. must/could/might/may have [any of the past-tense forms for conveying possibility and making a guess is acceptable]

5. should have *or* ought to have [either past-tense form of modal auxiliary is acceptable]

ANSWERS AND COVERAGE: EXERCISE 46-3

1. ought to have [45a, correct form for modal auxiliary expressing advisability]

2. must have rained [46a, correct form for past-tense modal auxiliary expressing likelihood]

3. might not have been [46a, correct form for past-tense modal auxiliary expressing likelihood or possibility]

4. should have been [46c, passive modal auxiliary with *Pedro* receiving the action of the verb]

5. should not [46a, correct form for expressing negative advisability rather than negative ability]

EXERCISE 46-2

Consulting section 46a, fill in the blanks with the past-tense modal auxiliary that expresses the meaning given in the parentheses.

EXAMPLE   I (advisability) **should have** waited for a rainy afternoon to visit the Empire State Building.

1. Since I (necessity, no choice) _____ work all week, Sunday was my only free day to visit the Empire State Building.

2. I (advisability) _____ known that because it was a such a clear, beautiful day, everyone else would want to visit this New York City landmark, too.

3. The lines for the elevator were terribly long, and even though I am physically fit, I (ability) _____ not possibly climb the eighty-six flights of stairs to the observation deck near the top of the building.

4. The other visitors to the Empire State Building (probability) _____ noticed how impatient I was becoming by the look on my face.

5. Then I heard the security guard say to the woman on line ahead of me, "You (advice, good idea) _____ come yesterday. Because of the light drizzle, hardly anyone was here."

EXERCISE 46-3

Consulting all sections of this chapter, select the correct choice from the words in parentheses and write it in the blank.

EXAMPLE   When I was younger, I (would, used to) **used to** love to go bicycle riding.

1. You (ought to have, ought have) _____ called yesterday as you had promised you would.

2. Judging by the size of the puddles in the street outside, it (must rained, must have rained) _____ all night long.

3. Ingrid (must not have, might not have been) _____ as early for the interview as she claims she was.

4. After all the studying he did, Pedro (should have, should have been) _____ less frightened by the exam.

5. I have to go home early today, although I really (cannot, should not) _____ leave before the end of the day because of all the work I have to do.

EXERCISE 46-4

Consulting all sections of this chapter, select the correct choice from the words in parentheses and write it in the blank.

EXAMPLE We (must have, must) **must** study this afternoon.

1. Unfortunately, I (should not, cannot) _____ go to the movies with you because I have to take care of my brother tonight.

2. Juan (would have, would have been) _____ nominated class valedictorian if he had not moved to another city.

3. You (ought not have, ought not to have) _____ arrived while the meeting was still in progress.

4. Louise (must be, must have been) _____ sick to miss the party last week.

5. Had you not called in advance, you (may not have, may not have been) _____ aware of the traffic on the expressway.

ANSWERS AND COVERAGE: EXERCISE 46-4

1. cannot [46a, correct form for expressing negative ability rather than negative advisability]

2. would have been [46c, passive modal auxiliary with *Juan* receiving the action of the verb]

3. ought not to have [46a, correct form for past-tense modal auxiliary expressing advisability]

4. must have been [46a, correct form for past-tense modal auxiliary expressing possibility or likelihood]

5. may not have been [46a, correct form for past-tense modal auxiliary expressing possibility or likelihood]

USAGE GLOSSARY

This usage glossary presents the customary manner of using particular words and phrases. "Customary manner," however, is not as firm in practice as the term implies. Usage standards change. If you think a word's usage might differ from what you read here, consult a dictionary published more recently than this book.

As used here, *informal* indicates that the word or phrase occurs commonly in speech but should be avoided in academic writing. *Nonstandard* indicates that the word or phrase should not be used in standard spoken English or in writing.

Some commonly confused words appear in this Usage Glossary. For an extensive list of homonyms and other commonly confused words, see section 22b. Parts of speech, sentence structures, and other grammatical terms mentioned in this Usage Glossary are defined in the Terms Glossary, which follows this Usage Glossary.

a, an Use *a* before words beginning with consonants (*a dog, a grade, a hole*) or consonant sounds (*a one-day sale, a European*). American English uses *a,* not *an,* with words starting with a pronounced *h* (*a* [*not* an] *historical event*).

accept, except *Accept* means "agree to; receive." As a verb, *except* means "exclude, leave out"; as a preposition, *except* means "leaving out":

- **Except** [preposition] for one detail, the workers were ready to **accept** [verb] management's offer: They wanted the no-smoking rule **excepted** [verb] from the contract.

advice, advise *Advice,* a noun, means "recommendation"; *advise,* a verb, means "recommend; give advice":

- My **advice** is to do what your physician **advises**.

affect, effect As a verb, *affect* means "cause a change in; influence" (*affect* also functions as a noun in the discipline of psychology). As a noun, *effect* means "result or conclusion"; as a verb, it means "bring about":

- Many groups **effected** [verb] amplification changes at their concerts after discovering that high decibel levels **affected** [verb] their hearing. Many fans still choose to ignore sound's harmful **effects**.

763

aggravate, irritate *Aggravate* is used colloquially to mean "irritate." Use *aggravate* to mean "intensify; make worse." Use *irritate* to mean "annoy; make impatient."

ain't Nonstandard contraction for *am not, is not,* and *are not.*

all ready, already *Already* means "before; by this time"; *all ready* means "completely prepared":

- The ballplayers were **all ready**, and the manager had **already** given the lineup card to the umpire.

all right Two words, never one (not *alright*).

all together, altogether *All together* means "in a group, in unison"; *altogether* means "entirely, thoroughly":

- The judge decided it was **altogether** absurd to expect the jurors to stay **all together** in one hotel room.

allude, elude *Allude* means "refer to indirectly or casually"; *elude* means "escape notice":

- They were **alluding** to budget cuts when they said that "constraints beyond our control enabled the suspect to **elude** us."

allusion, illusion An *allusion* is an indirect reference to something; an *illusion* is a false impression or idea.

a lot Informal for *a great deal* or *a great many*; avoid it in academic writing.

a.m., p.m. Use only with numbers, not as substitutes for the words *morning, afternoon,* or *evening*:

- We will arrive **in the afternoon** [*not* in the p.m.], and we have to leave no later than **8:00 a.m.**

among, between Use *between* for two items and *among* for three or more items:

- My roommates and I discussed **among** ourselves the choice **between** staying in school and getting full-time jobs.

amount, number Use *amount* for uncountable things (*wealth, work, corn, happiness*); use *number* for countable items:

- The **amount** of rice to cook depends on the **number** of dinner guests.

and/or Appropriate in business and legal writing when either or both items it connects can apply:

- This process is quicker if you have a modem **and/or** a fax machine.

In the humanities, you should usually express alternatives in words:

- This process is quicker if you have a modem, a fax machine, or both.

anymore   Use *anymore* with the meaning "now, any longer" in negative statements or questions only:

- No one knits **anymore**.

For positive statements, use an adverb such as *now*:

- Summers are so hot **now** [*not* anymore] that holding yarn is unbearable.

anyplace   Informal for *any place* or *anywhere*.

anyways, anywheres   Nonstandard for *anyway, anywhere*.

apt, likely, liable   *Apt* and *likely* are used interchangeably. Strictly, *apt* indicates a tendency or inclination:

- Allen is **apt** to leave early on Friday.

Likely indicates a reasonable expectation or greater certainty than apt:

- I will **likely** go with him to the party.

Liable denotes legal responsibility or implies unpleasant consequences:

- Maggy and Gabriel are **liable** to be angry if neither of us shows up.

as, like, as if, as though   Use *as*, not *like*, as a subordinating conjunction introducing a clause:

- This hamburger tastes good, **as** [*not* like] a hamburger should.

Use *as if* (or *as though*), not *like*, to introduce a subjunctive or other conditional clause:

- That hamburger tastes **as if** [*not* like] it had been on the grill all day.

As and *like* can both function as prepositions in comparisons. Use *like* to suggest a point of similarity or an area of resemblance, but not complete likeness, between nouns or pronouns:

- Mexico, **like** [*not* as] Argentina, belongs to the United Nations.

Use *as* to show equivalence:

- Beryl acted **as** [*not* like] the moderator of our panel.

Also, if the items are in prepositional phrases, use *as* even if you are suggesting only one point of similarity:

- In Mexico, **as** [*not* like] in Argentina, Spanish is the main language.

assure, ensure, insure *Assure* means "promise, convince"; *ensure* means "make certain or secure"; *insure* means "indemnify or guarantee against loss" and is reserved for financial or legal certainty, as in insurance:

- The agent **assured** me that he could **insure** my rollerblades but that only I could **ensure** that my elbows and knees would outlast the skates.

as to Avoid as a substitute for *about*:

- They answered questions **about** [*not* as to] their safety record.

awful, awfully The adjective *awful* means "causing fear." Avoid it as a substitute for intensifiers such as *very* or *extremely*. In academic writing, also avoid the informal usage of the adverb *awfully* for *very* or *extremely*.

a while, awhile *Awhile* is an adverb; it modifies verbs. In all other circumstances, *a while* (article + noun) is called for: *in a while, after a while, for a while.*

bad, badly *Bad* is an adjective; use it after linking verbs. (Remember that verbs like *feel* and *smell* can function as either linking verbs or action verbs.) *Badly* is an adverb and is nonstandard after linking verbs; see section 12d:

- Farmers feel **bad** because a **bad** drought has **badly** damaged the crops.

been, being *Been* is the past participle of the verb *be*; *being* is the present participle of *be*, used in the progressive form:

- You **are being** [*not* You being] silly if you think I believe you **have been** [*not* you been] to Sumatra.

being as, being that Nonstandard for *because* or *since*:

- We forfeited the game **because** [*not* being as *or* being that] our goalie has appendicitis.

beside, besides *Beside* is a preposition meaning "next to, to the side of":

- She stood **beside** the new car, insisting that she would drive.

As a preposition, *besides* means "other than, in addition to":

- No one **besides** her had a driver's license.

As an adverb, *besides* means "also, moreover":

- **Besides**, she owned the car.

better, had better   Used in place of *had better*, *better* is informal:

- We **had better** [*not* We better] be careful.

breath, breathe   *Breath* is a noun; *breathe* is a verb.

bring, take   Use *bring* for movement from a distant place to a near place or toward the speaker; use *take* for movement from a near place or from the speaker to a distant place:

- If you **bring** a leash when you come to my house, you can **take** Vicious to the vet.

but, however, yet   Use *but*, *however*, or *yet* alone, not in combination with each other:

- The economy is strong, **but** [*not* but yet *or* but however] unemployment is high.

calculate, figure, reckon   Informal or regional for *estimate*, *imagine*, *expect*, *think*, and similar words.

can, may   *Can* signifies ability or capacity; *may* requests or grants permission. In negative statements, however, *can* is acceptable in place of *may*:

- You **cannot** [*or* You **may not**] leave yet.

can't hardly, can't scarcely   Nonstandard double negatives. Avoid.

censor, censure   The verb *censor* means "delete objectionable material; judge"; *censure* means "condemn; reprimand officially."

chairman, chairperson, chair   Many writers and speakers prefer the gender-neutral terms *chairperson* and *chair* to *chairman*; *chair* is more commonly used than *chairperson*.

choose, chose   *Choose* is the simple form of the verb; *chose* is the past-tense form:

- I **chose** the movie last week, so you **choose** it tonight.

cloth, clothe   *Cloth* is a noun meaning "fabric"; *clothe* is a verb meaning "cover with garments or fabric; dress."

complement, compliment *Complement* means "bring to perfection, go well with; complete"; *compliment* means "praise; flatter":

- They **complimented** us on the design of our experiment, saying that it **complemented** work done twenty years ago.

conscience, conscious The noun *conscience* means "a sense of right and wrong"; the adjective *conscious* means "being aware or awake."

consensus of opinion Redundant; use *consensus* only.

continual(ly), continuous(ly) *Continual* means "occurring repeatedly"; *continuous* means "going on without interruption":

- Intravenous fluids were given **continuously** for three days after surgery; nurses were **continually** hooking up new bottles of saline.

couple, couple of Nonstandard for *a few* or *several*:

- Rest for **a few** [*not* a couple *or* a couple of] minutes.

data Plural of *datum*, a rarely used word. Common usage treats *data* as a collective noun (see 11h) that can take a singular or plural verb.

different from, different than *Different from* is preferred for formal writing; *different than* is common in speech.

disinterested, uninterested *Disinterested* means "impartial"; *uninterested* means "indifferent; not concerned with."

don't A contraction for *do not*, but not for *does not (doesn't)*:

- She **doesn't** [*not* don't] like crowds.

emigrate from, immigrate to *Emigrate from* means "leave one country to live in another"; *immigrate to* means "enter a country to live there."

enthused Nonstandard substituting for the adjective *enthusiastic*:

- Are you **enthusiastic** [*not* enthused] about seeing that movie?

etc. Abbreviation for the Latin *et cetera*, meaning "and the rest." For writing in the humanities, avoid in-text use of *etc.*; acceptable substitutes are *and the like, and so on, and so forth.*

everyday, every day The adjective *everyday* means "daily" or "usual" and modifies nouns; *every day* is an adjective-noun combination, which functions as a subject or object:

- I missed the bus **every day** last week. Being late for work has become an **everyday** occurrence.

everywheres Nonstandard for *everywhere*. Avoid.

explicit, implicit *Explicit* means "stated or expressed"; *implicit* means "implied, suggested":

- The warning on cigarette packs is **explicit**: "Smoking is dangerous to health." The **implicit** message is "Don't smoke."

farther, further Although many writers reserve *farther* for geographical distances and *further* for all other cases, current usage treats them as interchangeable.

fewer, less Use *fewer* for anything that can be counted (count nouns): ***fewer** dollars*, ***fewer** fleas*, ***fewer** haircuts*. Use *less* with collective or other noncount nouns: ***less** money*, ***less** scratching*, ***less** hair*.

fine, find *Fine* can be a noun or an adjective:

- She risked a $100 **fine** when she parked her **fine** new car in a reserved space.

Find is the simple form of the verb:

- We **find** new evidence each day.

former, latter When two items are referred to, *former* signifies the first one and *latter* signifies the second. Do not use *former* and *latter* for references to more than two items.

go, say *Go* is nonstandard for *say, says,* or *said*:

- After he stepped on my hand, he **said** [*not* he goes], "Your hand was in my way."

gone, went *Gone* is the past participle of *go*; *went* is the past tense of *go*:

- They **went** [*not* gone] to the concert after Ira **had gone** [*not* had went] home.

good and Nonstandard intensifier:

- They were tired [*not* good and tired].

good, well *Good* is an adjective: ***good** idea*. Using it as an adverb is nonstandard. *Well* is the equivalent adverb: *run **well*** [*not* run good].

got, have *Got* is nonstandard in place of *have*:

- What do we **have** [*not* got] for supper?

have, of Use *have*, not *of*, after such verbs as *could*, *should*, *would*, *might*, and *must*:

- You should **have** [*not* should of] called first.

have got, have got to Avoid using *have got* when *have* alone delivers your meaning:

- I **have** [*not* have got] two more sources to read.

Avoid *have got to* for *must*:

- I **must** [*not* have got to] turn in a preliminary thesis statement by Monday.

hopefully An adverb meaning "with hope, in a hopeful manner" or "it is hoped that," *hopefully* can modify a verb, an adjective, or another adverb:

- They waited **hopefully** for the plane to land.

Hopefully is commonly used as a sentence modifier with the meaning "I hope," but you should avoid this usage in academic writing:

- I **hope** [*not* Hopefully] the plane will land safely.

if, whether Use either *if* or *whether* at the start of a noun clause:

- I don't know **if** [*or* **whether**] I want to dance with you.

In conditional clauses, use *whether* (or *whether or not*) when alternatives are expressed or implied:

- I will dance with you **whether or not** I like the music.
- I will dance with you **whether** the next song is fast or slow.

Use *if* in a conditional clause that does not express or imply alternatives:

- **If** you promise not to step on my feet, I will dance with you.

imply, infer *Imply* means "hint at or suggest without stating outright"; *infer* means "draw a conclusion from what is being expressed." A writer or speaker *implies*; a reader or listener *infers*:

- When the governor **implied** that she would not seek reelection, reporters **inferred** that she hoped to run for vice president.

incredible, incredulous *Incredible* means "extraordinary; beyond belief"; *incredulous* means "skeptical; unable or unwilling to believe." A person would be *incredulous* in response to finding something *incredible*:

- Listeners were **incredulous** as the freed hostages described the **incredible** hardships they had experienced.

inside of, outside of Nonstandard for *inside* or *outside*:

- She waited **outside** [*not* outside of] the dormitory.

Also, *inside of* meaning "in less than" in time references is an Americanism inappropriate for academic writing;

- I changed clothes **in less than** [*not* inside of] ten minutes.

irregardless Nonstandard for *regardless*. Avoid.

is when, is where Avoid these constructions in giving definitions:

- Defensive driving **involves** drivers' staying alert [*not* is when drivers stay alert] to avoid accidents that other drivers might cause.

its, it's *Its* is a personal pronoun in the possessive case:

- The dog buried **its** bone.

It's is a contraction of *it is* or *it has*:

- **It's** a hot day; **it's** seemed hotter than usual because the humidity is high.

kind, sort Use *this* or *that* with these singular nouns; use *these* or *those* with the plural nouns *kinds* and *sorts*. Also, do not use *a* or *an* after *kind of* or *sort of*:

- You should drink **these kinds** of fluids [*not* this kind of fluids] on this **sort of** [*not* sort of a] day.

kind of, sort of Informal as adverbs meaning "in a way; somewhat":

- The hikers were **somewhat** [*not* kind of] dehydrated by the time they got back to camp.

later, latter *Later* means "after some time; subsequently"; *latter* refers to the second of two:

- The college library stays open **later** than the town library; also, the **latter** is closed on weekends.

lay, lie *Lay (laying, laid)* means "place or put something," usually on something else, and needs a direct object; *lie (lying, lay, lain)*, meaning "recline," does not take a direct object; see section 8f. Substituting *lay* for *lie* is nonstandard:

- **Lay** [*not* lie] the blanket down, and then **lay** the babies on it so they can **lie** [*not* lay] in the shade.

leave, let *Leave* means "depart"; *let* means "allow, permit." *Leave* is nonstandard for *let*:

- **Let** [*not* Leave] me use your car tonight.

lots, lots of, a lot of Informal for *many*, *much*, *a great deal*:

- **Many** [*not* A lot of] bees were in the hive.

may be, maybe *May be* is a verb phrase; *maybe* is an adverb:

- Our team **may be** tired, but **maybe** we can win anyway.

media Plural of *medium*, but common usage sometimes pairs it with a singular verb. In most cases, a more specific word is preferable:

- **Television reporters** [*not* The media] offend viewers by shouting questions at grief-stricken people.

morale, moral *Morale* is a noun meaning "a mental state relating to courage, confidence, or enthusiasm." As a noun, *moral* means "ethical lesson implied or taught by a story or event"; as an adjective, moral means "ethical":

- One **moral** to draw from corporate downsizings is that overstressed employees suffer from low **morale**. Under such stress, sometimes even employees with high **moral** standards steal time, supplies, or products from their employers.

most Nonstandard for *almost*:

- **Almost** [*not* Most] all the dancers agree.

Most is correct as the superlative form of an adjective *(some, more, most)*:

- **Most** dancers agree.

Most also creates the superlative form of adverbs and some adjectives: **most** *suddenly*, **most** *important*.

Ms. A woman's title free of reference to marital status, equivalent to *Mr.* for men.

nowheres Nonstandard for *nowhere*. Avoid.

off of Nonstandard for *off*:

- Don't fall **off** [*not* off of] the piano.

OK, O.K., okay All three forms are acceptable in informal writing. In academic writing, try to express meaning more specifically:

- The weather was **satisfactory** [*not* OK] for the race.

on account of Wordy; use *because* or *because of*:

- **Because of** [*not* On account of] the high humidity, paper jams occur in the photocopier.

percent, percentage Use *percent* with specific numbers: *two percent*, *95 percent*. Use *percentage* when descriptive words accompany amounts that have been expressed as percentages:

- About 47 **percent** of the eligible U.S. population votes regularly; but when presidential elections are excluded, the **percentage** [*not* percent] of voters in the population drops sharply.

plus Nonstandard as a substitute for *and*:

- The band has three concerts in Hungary, **and** [*not* plus] it will tour Poland for a month.

Nonstandard as well as a substitute for *also, in addition, moreover*:

- **Also** [*not* Plus], it may be booked to do one concert in Vienna.

precede, proceed *Precede* means "go before"; *proceed* means "advance, go on, undertake, carry on":

- **Preceded** by elephants and tigers, the clowns **proceeded** into the tent.

pretty Informal qualifying word; use *rather, quite, somewhat*, or *very* in academic writing:

- The flu epidemic was **quite** [*not* pretty] severe.

principal, principle *Principle* means "a basic truth or rule." As a noun, *principal* means "chief person; main or original amount"; as an adjective, *principal* means "most important":

- During assembly, the **principal** said, "A **principal** value in this society is the **principle** of free speech."

raise, rise *Raise (raised, raising)* needs a direct object; *rise (rose, risen, rising)* does not take a direct object. Using these verbs interchangeably is nonstandard:

- What if the angry mob **rises** [*not* raises] up to rebel?

rarely ever Informal; in academic writing, use *rarely* or *hardly ever*:

- The groups **rarely** [*not* rarely ever] meet, so they **hardly ever** interact.

real, really Nonstandard intensifiers.

reason is because Redundant; use *reason is that*:

- One **reason** we moved away **is that** [*not* is because] we changed jobs.

reason why Redundant; use either *reason* or *why*:

- I still do not know **the reason that** [*not* the reason why] they left home.
- I still do not know **why** they left home.

regarding, in regard to, with regard to Too stiff or wordy for most writing purposes; use *about*, *concerning*, or *for*:

- What should I do **about** [*not* with regard to] dropping this course?

respective, respectively The adjective *respective* relates the noun it modifies to two or more individual persons or things; the adverb *respectively* refers to a second set of items in a sequence established by a preceding set of items:

- After the fire drill, Dr. Pan and Dr. Moll returned to their **respective** offices, on the second and third floors, **respectively**. [Dr. Pan has an office on the second floor; Dr. Moll has an office on the third floor.]

Do not confuse *respective* and *respectively* with *respectful* and *respectfully*, which refer to showing regard for or honor to something or someone.

right Colloquial intensifier; use *quite*, *very*, *extremely*, or a similar word for most purposes:

- You did **very** [*not* right] well on the quiz.

seen Past participle of *see (see, saw, seen)*, *seen* is a nonstandard substitute for the past-tense form, *saw*. As a verb, *seen* must be used with an auxiliary verb:

- Last night, I **saw** [*not* seen] the show that you **had seen** in Florida.

set, sit *Set (set, setting)* means "put in place, position, put down" and must have a direct object. *Sit (sat, sitting)* means "be seated." *Set* is nonstandard as a substitute for *sit*:

- Sue **set** [*not* sat] the sandwiches beside the salad, made Spot **sit** [*not* set] down, and then **sat** [*not* set] on the sofa.

shall, will *Shall* was once used with *I* or *we* for future-tense verbs, and *will* was used with all other persons (**We shall** *leave Monday, and **he will***

leave Thursday); but *will* is commonly used for all persons now. Similarly, distinctions were once made between *shall* and *should*. *Should* is much more common with all persons now.

- **Should** [*or* **Shall**] I get your jacket?

should, would Use *should* to express condition or obligation:

- If you **should** see them, tell them that they **should** practice what they preach.

Use *would* to express wishes, conditions, or habitual actions:

- If you **would** buy a VCR for me, I **would** tape all the football games for you.

sometime, sometimes, some time The adverb *sometime* means "at an unspecified time"; the adverb *sometimes* means "now and then"; *some time* is an adjective-noun combination meaning "an amount or span of time":

- **Sometime** next year we have to take qualifying exams. I **sometimes** worry about finding **some time** to study for them.

stationary, stationery *Stationary* means "not moving"; *stationery* refers to paper and related writing products.

such Informal intensifier; avoid it in academic writing unless it precedes a noun introducing a *that* clause:

- That play got **terrible** [*not* such bad] reviews. It was **such** a dull drama **that** it closed after one performance.

supposed to, used to The final -*d* is essential:

- We were **supposed to** [*not* suppose to] leave early. I **used to** [*not* use to] wake up as soon as the alarm rang.

sure Nonstandard for *surely* or *certainly*:

- I was **certainly** [*not* sure] surprised at the results.

than, then *Than* indicates comparison:

- One is smaller **than** two.

Then relates to time:

- I tripped and **then** fell.

that there, them there, this here, these here Nonstandard for *that*, *them*, *this*, and *these*, respectively.

that, which Use *that* with restrictive (essential) clauses only; *which* can be used with both restrictive and nonrestrictive clauses, but many writers use *which* for nonrestrictive clauses only:

- The house **that** [*or* **which**] Jack built is on Beanstalk Street, **which** [*not* that] runs past the reservoir.

their, there, they're *Their* is a possessive; *there* means "in that place" or is part of an expletive construction; *they're* is a contraction of *they are*:

- **They're** going to **their** accounting class in the building over **there** behind the library. **There** are twelve sections of Accounting 101.

theirself, theirselves, themself Nonstandard for *themselves*. Do not use.

them Nonstandard for *these* or *those*:

Buy **those** [*not* them] strawberries.

thusly Nonstandard for *thus*.

till, until Both are acceptable; avoid the contracted form *'til* in academic writing.

to, too, two *To* is a preposition; *too* is an adverb meaning "also; more than enough"; *two* is the number:

- When you go **to** Chicago, visit the Art Institute. Go **to** Harry Caray's for dinner, **too**. It won't be **too** expensive because **two** people can share an entree.

toward, towards Both are acceptable; *toward* is more common.

try and, sure and Nonstandard for *try to* and *sure to*:

- If you **try to** [*not* try and] find a summer job, be **sure to** [*not* sure and] list on your résumé all the software programs you can use.

type Nonstandard for *type of*:

- Use that **type of** [*not* type] glue on plastic.

unique An absolute adjective; use it without *more*, *most*, or other qualifiers, or use a different adjective:

- Solar heating is **uncommon** [*not* rather unique] in the Northeast. In only one home in Vermont, a **unique** [*not* very unique] heating system uses hydrogen for fuel.

wait on Informal for *wait for*; appropriate in the context of persons giving service to others:

- I had to **wait** a half hour for that clerk to **wait on** me.

where Nonstandard for *that*:

- I read **that** [*not* where] Michael Jordan might retire from basketball again.

where . . . at Redundant; drop *at*:

- **Where** is your **house** [*not* house at]?

-wise The suffix *-wise* means "in a manner, direction, or position." Be careful not to attach *-wise* indiscriminately to create new words rather than using good words that already exist. When in doubt, check your dictionary to be sure that a *-wise* word you want to use is acceptable.

your, you're *Your* is a possessive; *you're* is the contraction of *you are*:

- **You're** generous to share **your** break time with us.

TERMS GLOSSARY

This glossary defines important terms used in this handbook, including the ones that are printed in SMALL CAPITAL LETTERS. Many of these glossary entries end with parenthetical references to the handbook section(s) or chapter(s) where the specific term is most fully discussed.

absolute phrase A phrase containing a subject and a participle that modifies an entire sentence (7n).

- **The semester** [subject] **being** [present participle of *be*] **over,** the campus looks deserted.

abstract noun A noun that names things not knowable through the five senses: *idea, respect*. (7a)

active voice An attribute of verbs showing that the action or condition expressed in the verb is done by the subject, in contrast with the passive voice, which conveys that the action or condition of the verb is done to the subject. (8n–8o)

adjective A word that describes or limits (modifies) a noun, a pronoun, or a word group functioning as a noun: *silly, three*. (Chapter 12)

adjective clause A dependent clause, also known as a *relative clause*. An adjective clause modifies a preceding noun or pronoun and begins with a relative word (such as *who, which, that*, or *where*) that relates the clause to the noun or pronoun it modifies. Also see *clause*. (7o.2)

adverb A word that describes or limits (modifies) verbs, adjectives, other adverbs, phrases, or clauses: *loudly, very, nevertheless, there*. (Chapter 12)

adverb clause A dependent clause beginning with a subordinating conjunction that establishes the relationship in meaning between the adverb clause and its independent clause. An adverb clause modifies the independent clause's verb or the entire independent clause. Also see *clause, conjunction*. (7o.2)

agreement The required match of number and person between a subject and verb or a pronoun and antecedent. A pronoun that expresses gender must match its antecedent in gender also. (Chapter 11)

analogy An explanation of the unfamiliar in terms of the familiar. Like a simile, an analogy compares things not normally associated with each other; but unlike a simile, an analogy does not use *like* or *as* in making the comparison. Analogy is also a rhetorical strategy for developing paragraphs. (4f.8, 21c)

analysis A process of critical thinking that divides a whole into its component parts in order to understand how the parts interrelate. Sometimes called *division*, analysis is also a rhetorical strategy for developing paragraphs. (Chapter 5, 4f.6)

antecedent The noun or pronoun to which a pronoun refers. (Chapter 10, 11m–11r)

antonym A word opposite in meaning to another word. (20a)

APA style See *documentation style.*

appositive A word or group of words that renames a preceding noun or noun phrase: *my favorite month,* **October**. (7m.3)

argument A rhetorical attempt to convince others to agree with a position about a topic open to debate. (1b, 6)

articles Also called *determiners* or *noun markers*, articles are the words *a, an,* and *the*. *A* and *an* are indefinite articles, and *the* is a definite article; also see *determiner*. (7a, Chapter 42)

assertion A statement. In developing a thesis statement, an assertion is a sentence that makes a statement and expresses a point of view about a topic. (2n)

audience The readers to whom a piece of writing is directed. (1c)

auxiliary verb Also known as a *helping verb*, an auxiliary verb is a form of *be, do, have, can, may, will,* or certain other verbs, that combines with a main verb to help it express tense, mood, and voice. Also see *modal auxiliary verb*. (8e)

base form See *simple form.*

bibliography A list of information about sources. (Chapter 33)

brainstorming Listing all ideas that come to mind on a topic and then grouping the ideas by patterns that emerge. (2g)

case The form of a noun or pronoun in a specific context that shows whether it is functioning as a subject, an object, or a possessive. In modern English, nouns change form in the possessive case only (*city* = form for subjective and objective cases; *city's* = possessive-case form). Also see *pronoun case*. (Chapter 9)

cause and effect The relationship between outcomes (effects) and the reasons for them (causes). Cause-and-effect analysis is a rhetorical strategy for developing paragraphs. (5i, 5k, 4f.9)

chronological order Also called *time order*, an arrangement of information according to time sequence; an organizing strategy for sentences, paragraphs, and longer pieces of writing. (4e)

citation Information to identify a source referred to in a piece of writing. Also see *documentation*. (Chapters 31 and 33)

clause A group of words containing a subject and a predicate. A clause that delivers full meaning is called an *independent* (or *main*) *clause*. A clause that lacks full meaning by itself is called a *dependent* (or *subordinate*) *clause*. Also see *adjective clause, adverb clause, nonrestrictive element, noun clause, restrictive element*. (7o)

cliché An overused, worn-out phrase that has lost its capacity to communicate effectively: *flat as Kansas, ripe old age*. (21d)

climactic order Sometimes called *emphatic order*, climactic order is an arrangement of ideas or other kinds of information from least important to most important. (4e)

clustering See *mapping*.

coherence The clear progression from one idea to another using transitional expressions, pronouns, selective repetition, or parallelism to make connections between ideas. (4d)

collective noun A noun that names a group of people or things: *family, committee*. (11h, 11r)

comma fault See *comma splice*.

comma splice The error that occurs when only a comma connects two independent clauses. (Chapter 13)

common noun A noun that names a general group, place, person, or thing: *dog, house*. (7a)

comparative The form of a descriptive adjective or adverb that expresses a different degree of intensity between two: *bluer, less blue; more easily, less easily*. Also see *positive, superlative*. (12e)

comparison and contrast A rhetorical strategy for organizing and developing paragraphs by discussing a subject's similarities (*comparison*) and differences (*contrast*). (4f.7)

complement An element after a verb that completes the predicate, such as a direct object after an action verb or a noun or adjective after a linking verb. Also see *object complement, predicate adjective, predicate nominative, subject complement.*

complete predicate See *predicate.*

complete subject See *subject.*

complex sentence See *sentence types.*

compound predicate See *predicate.*

compound sentence See *sentence types.*

compound subject See *subject.*

concrete noun A noun naming things that can be seen, touched, heard, smelled, or tasted: *smoke, sidewalk.* (7a)

conjunction A word that connects or otherwise establishes a relationship between two or more words, phrases, or clauses. Also see *coordinating conjunction, correlative conjunction, subordinating conjunction.*

conjunctive adverb An adverb, such as *therefore* or *meanwhile,* that communicates a logical connection in meaning.

coordinating conjunction A conjunction that joins two or more grammatically equivalent structures: *and, or, for, nor, but, so, yet.*

coordination The use of grammatically equivalent forms to show a balance or sequence of ideas. (17a–17d)

correlative conjunction A pair of words that joins equivalent grammatical structures, including *both . . . and, either . . . or, neither . . . nor, not only . . . but* (or *but also*).

count noun A noun that names items that can be counted: *radio, street, idea, fingernail.* (41a–41b, 42a–42b)

critical response Formally, an essay summarizing a source's central point or main idea and then presenting the writer's synthesized reactions in response. (5g)

cumulative sentence The most common structure for a sentence, with the subject and verb first, followed by modifiers adding details; also called a *loose sentence.* (19e)

dangling modifier A modifier that attaches its meaning illogically, either because it is closer to another noun or pronoun than to its true subject or because its true subject is not expressed in the sentence. (15c)

declarative sentence A sentence that makes a statement: *Sky diving is exciting.* Also see *exclamatory sentence, imperative sentence, interrogative sentence.*

deduction The process of reasoning from general claims to a specific instance. (5j.2)

definite article See *articles.*

demonstrative pronoun A pronoun that points out the antecedent: *this, these; that, those.*

denotation The dictionary definition of a word. (20a)

dependent clause A clause that cannot stand alone as an independent grammatical unit. Also see *adjective clause, adverb clause, noun clause.*

descriptive adjective An adjective that describes the condition or properties of the noun it modifies and (except for a very few such as *dead* and *unique*) has comparative and superlative forms: *flat, flatter, flattest.*

descriptive adverb An adverb that describes the condition or properties of whatever it modifies and that has comparative and superlative forms: *happily, more happily, most happily.*

determiner A word or word group, traditionally identified as an adjective, that limits a noun by telling how much or how many about it. Also called *expression of quantity, limiting adjective,* or *noun marker.* (41b, 42)

diction Word choice. (Chapters 20 and 21)

direct address Words naming a person or group being spoken to. Written words of direct address are set off by commas. (24f)

- The answer, **my friends,** lies with you. Go with them, **Gene.**

direct discourse In writing, words that repeat speech or conversation exactly and so are enclosed in quotation marks.

direct object A noun or pronoun or group of words functioning as a noun that receives the action (completes the meaning) of a transitive verb. (7l)

direct question A sentence that asks a question and ends with a question mark: *Are you going?*

direct quotation See *quotation*.

documentation The acknowledgment of someone else's words and ideas used in any piece of writing by giving full and accurate information about the person whose words were used and where those words were found. For example, for a print source, documentation usually includes names of all authors, title of the source, place and date of publication, and related information. (Chapters 31 and 33)

documentation style A system for providing information about the source of words, information, and ideas quoted, paraphrased, or summarized from some source other than the writer. Documentation styles discussed in this handbook are *MLA, APA, CM,* and *CBE*. (33)

double negative A nonstandard negation using two negative modifiers rather than one. (12c)

drafting A part of the writing process in which writers compose ideas in sentences and paragraphs. (3b)

edited American English English language use that conforms to established rules of grammar, sentence structure, punctuation, and spelling; also called *standard English*. (21a.2)

editing A part of the writing process in which writers check the technical correctness of grammar, spelling, punctuation, and mechanics. (3d)

elliptical construction A sentence structure that deliberately omits words expressed elsewhere or that can be inferred from the context.

euphemism Language that attempts to blunt certain realities by speaking of them in "nice" or "tactful" words. (21e)

evidence Facts, data, examples, and opinions of others used to support assertions and conclusions.

exclamatory sentence A sentence beginning with *What* or *How* that expresses strong feeling: *What a ridiculous statement!*

expletive The phrase *there is (are), there was (were), it is,* or *it was* at the beginning of a clause, changing structure and postponing the subject:

- **It is** Mars that we hope to reach [*compare* We hope to reach Mars].

expository writing See *informative writing*.

expression of quantity See *determiner*.

faulty predication A grammatically illogical combination of subject and predicate. (15d.2)

finite verb A verb form that shows tense, mood, voice, person, and number while expressing an action, occurrence, or state of being.

first person See *person*.

freewriting Writing nonstop for a period of time to generate ideas by free association of thoughts. Focused freewriting may start with a set topic or may build on one sentence taken from earlier freewriting. (2f)

fused sentence See *run-together sentence*.

future perfect progressive tense The form of the future perfect tense that describes an action or condition ongoing until some specific future time: *I will have been talking*.

future perfect tense The tense indicating that an action will have been completed or a condition will have ended by a specified point in the future: *I will have talked*.

future progressive tense The form of the future tense showing that a future action will continue for some time: *I will be talking*.

future tense The form of a verb, made with the simple form and either *shall* or *will*, expressing an action yet to be taken or a condition not yet experienced: *I will talk*.

gender Concerning languages, the classification of words as masculine, feminine, or neutral. In English, a few pronouns show changes in gender in third-person singular: *he, him, his; she, her, hers; it, its, its*. A few nouns naming roles change form to show gender difference: *prince, princess,* for example. (11q, 21b)

gerund A present participle functioning as a noun: **Walking** is good exercise. Also see *verbal*.

gerund phrase A gerund, with its modifiers and objects, that functions as a subject or an object. (7n)

helping verb See *auxiliary verb*.

homonyms Words spelled differently that sound alike: *to, too, two*. (22b)

idiom A word, phrase, or other construction that has a different meaning from its usual meaning:

  ■ He lost his head. She hit the ceiling.

illogical predication See *faulty predication.*

imperative mood The mood that expresses commands and direct requests, using the simple form of the verb and often implying but not expressing the subject, you: *Go.* (8l)

imperative sentence A sentence that gives a command:

- Go to the corner to buy me a newspaper.

indefinite article See *articles, determiner.*

indefinite pronoun A pronoun, such as *all, anyone, each,* and *others,* that refers to a nonspecific person or thing. (11p)

independent clause A clause that can stand alone as an independent grammatical unit. (7o.1)

indicative mood The mood of verbs used for statements about real things or highly likely ones:

- I think Grace is arriving today. (8l)

indirect discourse Reported speech or conversation that does not use the exact structure of the original and so is not enclosed in quotation marks. (15a.4)

indirect object A noun or pronoun or group of words functioning as a noun that tells to whom or for whom the action expressed by a transitive verb was done. (7l)

indirect question A sentence that reports a question and ends with a period:

- I asked if you are leaving.

indirect quotation See *quotation.*

induction The reasoning process of arriving at general principles from particular facts or instances. (5j.1)

infinitive A verbal made of the simple form of a verb and usually, but not always, *to* that functions as a noun, adjective, or adverb.

infinitive phrase An infinitive, with its modifiers and object, that functions as a noun, adjective, or adverb.

informal language Word choice that creates a tone appropriate for casual writing or speaking. (21a.1)

informative writing Writing that gives information and, when necessary, explains it; also known as *expository writing*. (1b)

intensive pronoun A pronoun that ends in *-self* and that intensifies its antecedent:

- Vida **himself** argued against it.

interjection An emotion-conveying word that is treated as a sentence, starting with a capital letter and ending with an exclamation point or a period: *Oh! Ouch!*

Internet A vast, international network of computers. An online server allows individuals to access information on the network and view it on their own computer. Also simply called the *Net*.

interrogative pronoun A pronoun, such as *whose* or *what*, that implies a question:

- **Who** called?

interrogative sentence A sentence that asks a direct question:

- Did you see that?

intransitive verb A verb that does not take a direct object. (8f)

invention techniques Ways of gathering ideas for writing. (Chapter 2)

inverted word order In contrast to standard order, the main verb or an auxiliary verb comes before the subject in inverted word order. Most questions and some exclamations use inverted word order. (19f)

irony Words used to imply the opposite of their usual meaning. (21c)

irregular verb A verb that forms the past tense and past participle in some way other than by adding *-ed* or *-d*. (8d)

jargon A particular field's or group's specialized vocabulary that a general reader is unlikely to understand. (21e)

levels of formality Word choices and sentence structures reflecting various degrees of formality of language. A formal level is used for ceremonial and other occasions when stylistic flourishes are appropriate. A medium level, neither too formal nor too casual, is acceptable for most academic writing. (21a.1)

levels of generality Various degrees of specificity used in organizing information or ideas, as when moving from the most general to the most specific. (2l)

limiting adjective See *determiner*.

linking verb A main verb that links a subject with a subject complement that renames or describes the subject. Linking verbs convey a state of being, relate to the senses, or indicate a condition. (8a)

logical fallacies Flaws in reasoning that lead to illogical statements. (5k)

loose sentence See *cumulative sentence*.

main clause See *independent clause*.

main verb A verb that expresses action, occurrence, or state of being and that shows mood, tense, voice, number, and person. (Chapter 8)

mapping An invention technique based on thinking about a topic and its increasingly specific subdivisions; also known as *clustering* or *webbing*. (2i)

mechanics Conventions governing matters such as the use of capital letters, italics, abbreviations, and numbers. (Chapter 30)

metaphor A comparison implying similarity between two things; a metaphor does not use words such as *like* or *as*, which are used in a simile and which make a comparison explicit: *a mop of hair* (compare the simile *hair like a mop*). (21c)

misplaced modifier Describing or limiting words that are wrongly positioned in a sentence so that their message is either illogical or relates to the wrong word or words. (15b)

mixed construction A sentence that unintentionally changes from one grammatical structure to another, incompatible one, so that the meaning is garbled. (15d)

mixed metaphors Incongruously combined images. (21c)

MLA style See *documentation style*.

modal auxiliary verb A group of auxiliary verbs that add information such as a sense of needing, wanting, or having to do something or a sense of possibility, likelihood, obligation, permission, or ability. (Chapter 46)

modifier A word or group of words functioning as an adjective or adverb to describe or limit another word or word group. (Chapter 12, 19e)

mood The attribute of verbs showing a speaker's or writer's attitude toward the action by the way verbs are used. English has three moods: imperative, indicative, and subjunctive. Also see *imperative mood, indicative mood, subjunctive mood*. (8l–8m)

787

Net See *Internet*.

noncount noun A noun that names things that cannot be counted: *water, time*. (Chapters 41 and 42)

nonessential element See *nonrestrictive element*.

nonrestrictive element A descriptive word, phrase, or dependent clause that provides information not essential to understanding the basic message of the element it modifies and so is set off by commas. Also see *restrictive element*. (24e)

nonsexist language See *sexist language*.

nonstandard Language usage other than edited American English. Also see *edited American English*. (21a.2)

noun A word that names a person, place, thing, or idea. Nouns function as subjects, objects, or complements.

noun clause A dependent clause that functions as a subject, object, or complement. (7o.2)

noun complement See *complement*.

noun determiner See *determiner*.

noun phrase A noun and its modifiers functioning as a subject, object, or complement. (7n)

number The attribute of some words indicating whether they refer to one (singular) or more than one (plural).

object A noun, pronoun, or group of words functioning as a noun or pronoun that receives the action of a verb (direct object); tells to whom or for whom something is done (indirect object); or completes the meaning of a preposition (object of a preposition). (7l)

object complement A noun or adjective renaming or describing a direct object after a few verbs including *call, consider, name, elect,* and *think*:

   ■ I call some joggers **fanatics**.

objective case The case of a noun or pronoun functioning as a direct or indirect object or object of a preposition or of a verbal. A few pronouns change form to show case (*him, her, whom*). Also see *case*. (Chapter 9)

paragraph A group of sentences that work together to develop a unit of thought. (Chapter 4)

paragraph development Using specific, concrete details (RENNS) to support a generalization in a paragraph; rhetorical strategies for arranging and organizing paragraphs. (4f)

parallelism The use of equivalent grammatical forms or matching sentence structures to express equivalent ideas. (18)

paraphrase A restatement of someone else's ideas in language and sentence structure different from those of the original. (31d)

parenthetical documentation See *parenthetical reference*.

parenthetical reference Information enclosed in parentheses following quoted, paraphrased, or summarized material from a source to alert readers to the use of material from a specific source. Parenthetical references function together with a list of bibliographic information about each source used in a paper to document the writer's use of sources. (33c.1, 33d.1)

participial phrase A phrase that contains a present participle or a past participle and any modifiers and that functions as an adjective. Also see *verbal*.

passive construction See *passive voice*.

passive voice The form of a verb in which the subject is acted on; if the subject is mentioned in the sentence, it usually appears as the object of the preposition *by*:

- **I was frightened by** the thunder. [Compare the active-voice version *The thunder **frightened me.**]*

The passive voice emphasizes the action, in contrast to the active voice, which emphasizes the doer of the action. (8n–8o)

past participle The third principal part of a verb, formed in regular verbs, like the past tense, by adding *-d* or *-ed* to the simple form. In irregular verbs, it often differs from the simple form and the past tense: *break, broke, broken.* (8b)

past perfect progressive tense The past perfect tense form that describes an ongoing condition in the past that has been ended by something stated in the sentence: *I had been talking.*

past perfect tense The tense that describes a condition or action that started in the past, continued for a while, and then ended in the past: *I had talked.*

past progressive tense The past tense form that shows the continuing nature of a past action: *I was talking.*

past-tense form The second principal part of a verb, in regular verbs formed by adding -*d* or -*ed* to the simple form. In irregular verbs, the past tense may change in several ways from the simple form. (8b, 8d)

perfect tenses The three tenses—the present perfect (*I have talked*), the past perfect (*I had talked*), and the future perfect (*I will have talked*)— that help show complex time relationships between two clauses. (8i)

periodic sentence A sentence that begins with modifiers and ends with the independent clause, thus postponing the main idea—and the emphasis—for the end; also called a *climactic sentence*. (19e)

person The attribute of nouns and pronouns showing who or what acts or experiences an action. *First person* is the one speaking (*I, we*); *second person* is the one being spoken to (*you, you*); and *third person* is the person or thing spoken about (*he, she, it, they*). All nouns are third person.

personal pronoun A pronoun that refers to people or things, such as *I, you, them, it*.

persuasive writing Writing that seeks to convince the reader about a matter of opinion. (1b, Chapter 6)

phrasal verb A verb that combines with one or more prepositions to deliver its meaning: *ask out, look into*. (44c)

phrase A group of related words that does not contain a subject and predicate and thus cannot stand alone as an independent grammatical unit. A phrase functions as a noun, verb, or modifier. (7n)

plagiarism A writer's presenting another person's words or ideas without giving credit to that person. Documentation systems allow writers to give proper credit to sources in ways recognized by scholarly communities. Plagiarism is a serious offense, a form of intellectual dishonesty that can lead to course failure or expulsion. (Chapter 31)

planning An early part of the writing process in which writers gather ideas. Along with shaping, planning is sometimes called *prewriting*. (Chapter 2)

plural See *number*.

positive The form of an adjective or adverb when no comparison is being expressed: *blue, easily*. Also see *comparative, superlative*. (12e)

possessive case The case of a noun or pronoun that shows ownership or possession. Also see *case*. (9, 27a–27d)

predicate The part of a sentence that contains the verb and tells what the subject is doing or experiencing or what is being done to the subject. A *simple predicate* contains only the main verb and any auxiliary verbs. A *complete predicate* contains the verb, its modifiers, objects, and other related words. A *compound predicate* contains two or more verbs and their objects and modifiers, if any. (7k)

predicate adjective An adjective used as a subject complement:

- That tree is **leafy**.

predicate nominative A noun or pronoun used as a subject complement:

- That tree is a **maple**.

premises In a deductive argument expressed as a syllogism, statements presenting the conditions of the argument from which the conclusion must follow. (5j)

preposition A word that conveys a relationship, often of space or time, between the noun or pronoun following it and other words in the sentence. The noun or pronoun following a preposition is called its *object*. (7g, Chapter 44)

prepositional phrase See *phrase, preposition*.

present participle A verb's *ing* form. Used with auxiliary verbs, present participles function as main verbs. Used without auxiliary verbs, present participles function as nouns or adjectives. (8b, 7d)

present perfect progressive tense The present perfect tense form that describes something ongoing in the past that is likely to continue into the future: *I have been talking*.

present perfect tense The tense indicating that an action or its effects, begun or perhaps completed in the past, continue into the present: *I had talked*.

present progressive tense The present tense form of the verb that indicates something taking place at the time it is written or spoken about: *I am talking*.

present tense The tense that describes what is happening, what is true at the moment, and what is consistently true. It uses the simple form (*I talk*) and the *-s* form in the third person singular (*he, she, it talks*). (8h)

prewriting All activities in the writing process before drafting. See *planning, shaping*. (Chapter 2)

primary sources Firsthand work: write-ups of experiments and observations by the researchers who conducted them; taped accounts, interviews, and newspaper accounts by direct observers; autobiographies, diaries, and journals; expressive works (poems, plays, fiction, essays); also known as *primary evidence*. Also see *secondary source*. (5h, 32g)

progressive forms Verb forms made in all tenses with the present participle and forms of the verb *be* as an auxiliary. Progressive forms show that an action, occurrence, or state of being is ongoing. (8j)

pronoun A word that takes the place of a noun and functions in the same ways that nouns do. Types of pronouns are *demonstrative, indefinite, intensive, interrogative, personal, reciprocal, reflexive,* and *relative*. The word (or words) a pronoun replaces is called its *antecedent*. (Chapters 9 and 10, 11m–11r)

pronoun-antecedent agreement The match in expressing number and person—and for personal pronouns, gender as well—required between a pronoun and its antecedent. (11m–11r)

pronoun case The way a pronoun changes form to reflect its use as the agent of action *(subjective case)*, the thing being acted upon *(objective case)*, or the thing showing ownership *(possessive case)*. (Chapter 9)

pronoun reference The relationship between a pronoun and its antecedent. (Chapter 10)

proofreading Reading a final draft to find and correct any spelling or mechanics mistakes, typing errors, or handwriting illegibility; the final step of the writing process. (3e)

proper adjective An adjective formed from a proper noun: *Victorian, American*.

proper noun A noun that names specific people, places, or things and is always capitalized: *Michael Stipe, Buick*.

purpose The goal or aim of a piece of writing: to express oneself, to provide information, to persuade, or to create a literary work. (1b)

quotation Repeating or reporting another person's words. Direct quotation repeats another's words exactly and encloses them in quotation marks. Indirect quotation reports another's words without quotation marks except around any words repeated exactly from the source. Both direct and indirect quotation require documentation of the source to avoid plagiarism. Also see *direct discourse, indirect discourse*. (28a, 31c)

reciprocal pronoun The pronouns *each other* and *one another* referring to individual parts of a plural antecedent:

- We respect **each other**.

References In many documentation styles, including APA, the title of a list of sources cited in a research paper or other written work. (33d, 33e, 33f)

reflexive pronoun A pronoun that ends in *-self* and that reflects back to its antecedent:

- They claim to support **themselves**.

regular verb A verb that forms its past tense and past participle by adding *-ed* or *-d* to the simple form. Most English verbs are regular. (8d)

relative adverb An adverb that introduces an adjective clause:

- The lot **where** I usually park my car was full.

relative clause See *adjective clause*.

relative pronoun A pronoun, such as *who, which, that, whom,* or *whoever,* that introduces an adjective clause or sometimes a noun clause.

restrictive clause A dependent clause that gives information necessary to distinguish whatever it modifies from others in the same category. In contrast to a nonrestrictive clause, a restrictive clause is not set off with commas. (24e)

restrictive element A word, phrase, or dependent clause that provides information essential to the understanding of the element it modifies. In contrast to a nonrestrictive element, a restrictive element is not set off with commas. (24e)

revision A part of the writing process in which writers evaluate their rough drafts and, based on their assessments, rewrite by adding, cutting, replacing, moving, and often totally recasting material. (3c)

rhetoric The area of discourse that focuses on arrangement of ideas and choice of words as a reflection of both the writer's purpose and the writer's sense of audience. (Chapter 1)

rhetorical strategies In writing, various techniques for presenting ideas to deliver a writer's intended message with clarity and impact. Reflecting typical patterns of human thought, rhetorical strategies include arrangements such as chronological and climactic order; stylistic techniques such as parallelism and planned repetition; and patterns for organizing and developing writing such as description and definition. (4)

Rogerian argument An argument technique adapted from the principles of communication developed by psychologist Carl Rogers. (6c)

run-together (run-on) sentence The error of running independent clauses together without the required punctuation that marks them as complete units. (Chapter 14)

secondary source A source that reports, analyzes, discusses, reviews, or otherwise deals with the work of someone else, as opposed to a primary source, which is someone's original work or firsthand report. A reliable secondary source should be the work of a person with appropriate credentials, should appear in a respected publication or other medium, should be current, and should be well-reasoned. (5h, 32g)

second person See *person*.

sentence See *sentence types*.

sentence fragment A portion of a sentence that is punctuated as though it were a complete sentence. (Chapter 13)

sentence types A grammatical classification of sentences by the kinds of clauses they contain. A *simple sentence* consists of one independent clause. A *complex sentence* contains one independent clause and one or more dependent clauses. A *compound-complex sentence* contains at least two independent clauses and one or more dependent clauses. A *compound sentence* contains two or more independent clauses joined by a coordinating conjunction. Sentences are also classified by their grammatical function; see *declarative sentence, exclamatory sentence, imperative sentence, interrogative sentence*. (7j, 7p)

sexist language Language that unfairly or unnecessarily assigns roles or characteristics to people on the basis of gender. Language that avoids gender stereotyping is called *nonsexist language*. (21b, 11q)

shaping An early part of the writing process in which writers consider ways to organize their material. Along with planning, shaping is sometimes called *prewriting*. (Chapter 2)

simile A comparison, using *like* or *as*, of otherwise dissimilar things. (21c)

simple form The form of the verb that shows action, occurrence, or state of being taking place in the present. It is used in the singular for first and second person and in the plural for first, second, and third person. It is also the first principal part of a verb. The simple form is also known as the *dictionary form* or *base form*. (8b)

simple predicate See *predicate*.

simple sentence See *sentence types*.

simple subject See *subject*.

simple tenses The present, past, and future tenses, which divide time into present, past, and future. (8h)

singular See *number*

slang Coined words and new meanings for existing words, which quickly pass in and out of use; not appropriate for most academic writing. (21a.3)

source A book, article, document, other work, or person providing information. (1e, Chapters 31, 32 and 33)

split infinitive One or more words coming between the two words of an infinitive. (15b.2)

standard English See *edited American English*.

standard word order The most common order for words in English sentences: The subject comes before the predicate.

subject The word or group of words in a sentence that acts, is acted upon, or is described by the verb. A *simple subject* includes only the noun or pronoun. A *complete subject* includes the noun or pronoun and all its modifiers. A *compound subject* includes two or more nouns or pronouns and their modifiers. (7k)

subject complement A noun or adjective that follows a linking verb, renaming or describing the subject of the sentence; also called a *predicate nominative*. (7m.1)

subjective case The case of the noun or pronoun functioning as a subject. Also see *case*. (Chapter 9)

subject-verb agreement The required match between a subject and verb in expressing number and person. (11a–11l)

subjunctive mood A verb mood that expresses wishes, recommendations, indirect requests, speculations, and conditional statements. (8l–8m)

■ I wish you **were** here.

subordinate clause See *dependent clause*.

subordinating conjunction A conjunction that introduces an adverbial clause and expresses a relationship between the idea in it and the idea in the independent clause. (7h)

subordination The use of grammatical structures to reflect the relative importance of ideas. A sentence with logically subordinated information expresses the most important information in the independent clause and less important information in dependent clauses or phrases. (17a–17d)

summary A brief version of the main message or central point of a passage or other discourse; a critical thinking activity preceding synthesis. (5f, 31e)

superlative The form of an adjective or adverb that expresses comparison among three or more things: *bluest, least blue; most easily, least easily.* (12e)

syllogism The structure of a deductive argument expressed in two premises and a conclusion. The first premise is a generalized assumption or statement of fact. The second premise is a different assumption or statement of fact based on evidence. The conclusion is also a specific instance that follows logically from the premises. (5j)

synonym A word that is very close in meaning to another word. (20a)

synthesis A component of critical thinking in which material that has been summarized, analyzed, and interpreted is connected to what is already known (one's prior knowledge) or to what has been learned from other authorities. (5b, 5f)

tag question An inverted verb-pronoun combination added to the end of a sentence, creating a question, that asks the audience to agree with the assertion in the first part of the sentence:

- You know what a tag question is, **don't you?**

A tag question is set off from the rest of the sentence with a comma. (24f)

tag sentence See *tag question.*

tense The time at which the action of the verb occurs: the present, the past, or the future. (8g–8k)

tense sequence In sentences that have more than one clause, the accurate matching of verbs to reflect logical time relationships. (8k)

thesis statement A statement of an essay's central theme that makes clear the main idea, the writer's purpose, the focus of the topic, and perhaps the organizational pattern. (2n)

third person See *person.*

tone The writer's attitude toward his or her material and reader, especially as reflected by word choice. (1d)

topic The subject of discourse.

topic sentence The sentence that expresses the main idea of a paragraph. A topic sentence may be implied, not stated. (4b.3)

Toulmin model for argument A model that defines the essential parts of an argument as the *claim* (or *main point*), the *support* (or *evidence*), and the *warrants* (or *assumptions behind the main point*). (6e)

transition The connection of one idea to another in discourse. Useful strategies for creating transitions include transitional expressions, parallelism, and planned repetition of key words and phrases. (4d)

transitional expressions Words and phrases that signal connections among ideas and create coherence. (4d.1)

transitive verb A verb that must be followed by a direct object. (8f)

unity The clear and logical relationship between the main idea of a paragraph and the evidence supporting the main idea. (4b)

URL The uniform resource locator, the address of a specific Web page.

usage A customary way of using language. (Chapter 21, Usage Glossary)

valid Correctly and rationally derived; applied to a deductive argument whose conclusion follows logically from the premises. Validity applies to structure of an argument, not its truth. (5j)

verb Any word that shows action or occurrence or describes a state of being. Verbs change form to convey time *(tense)*, attitude *(mood)*, and role of the subject *(voice)*. Verbs occur in the predicate of a clause and can be in verb phrases, which may consist of a main verb, auxiliary verbs, and modifiers. Verbs can be described as *transitive* or *intransitive*, depending on whether they take a direct object. (Chapter 8)

verbal A verb part functioning as a noun, adjective, or adverb. Verbals include *infinitives, present participles* (functioning as adjectives), *gerunds* (present participles functioning as nouns), and *past participles*. (7d)

verbal phrase A group of words that contains a verbal (an infinitive, participle, or gerund) and its modifiers.

verb phrase A main verb, any auxiliary verbs, and any modifiers.

voice An attribute of verbs showing whether the subject acts *(active voice)* or is acted on *(passive voice)*. (8n–8o)

Web See *World Wide Web*.

webbing See *mapping*.

Web page On the Internet, a file of information. Such a file is not related in length to a printed page, as it may be a paragraph or many screens long.

World Wide Web A user-friendly computer network used to access information in the form of text, graphics, and sound on the Internet. Also simply called the *Web*.

Works Cited In MLA documentation style, the title of a list of all sources cited in a research paper or other written work. (33c.2–33c.3)

writing process Stages of writing in which a writer gathers and shapes ideas, organizes material, expresses those ideas in a rough draft, evaluates the draft and revises it, edits the writing for technical errors, and proofreads it for typographical accuracy and legibility. The stages often overlap. See *planning, shaping, drafting, revision, editing, proofreading*. (Chapters 1, 2, and 3)

INDEX

List of Charts

List of Charts (*continued*)

List of Charts (*continued*)

RESPONSE SYMBOLS

Here are two lists of symbols your instructor might write on your papers. The first list shows traditional correction symbols; the second list shows complimentary symbols. You can find material related to each item by consulting the handbook sections or chapters given.

Correction Symbols

ab	abbreviation error, **23b, 30h-30k**	pro ref	pronoun reference error, **10**
ad	adjective or adverb error, **12**	pro agr	pronoun agreement error, **11m-11r**
agr	agreement error, **11**	pe	punctuation error, **23-29**
ca	case error, **9**	ref	pronoun reference error, **10**
cap	needs capital letter, **30a-30e**	rep	repetitious (redundant), **16c**
cl	avoid cliché, **21d**	rt	run-together sentence, **14**
coh	needs coherence, **4d**	shift	shift, **15a**
coord	faulty coordination, **17a-17d**	sl	avoid slang, **21a-3**
cs	comma splice, **14**	sp	spelling error, **22**
dev	needs development, **4a, 4c, 4f**	subord	faulty subordination, **17e-17h**
dm	dangling modifier, **15c**	sxt	sexist language use, **11q, 21b**
e	needs exact language, **20b**	t	verb tense error, **8g-8k**
emph	needs emphasis, **19**	trans	needs transition, **4d.1, 4d.5**
frag	sentence fragment, **13**	u	needs unity, **4b, 4c**
hyph	hyphenation error, **22d**	us	usage error, **Usage Glossary**
Inc	incomplete sentence, **15e**	v	verb form error, **8b-8f**
ital	italics (underlining) error, **30f-30g**	v agr	verb agreement error, **11a-11l**
		var	needs sentence variety, **19**
k	awkward construction, **15, 16, 21e**	w	wordy, **16**
		wc	word choice error, **20, 21**
lc	needs lowercase letter, **30a-30e**	ww	wrong word, **20, 21**
mixed	mixed construction, **15d**	∧	insert
mm	misplaced modifier, **15b**	ℯ	delete
num	number use error, **30l-30m**	∼	transpose
¶	start new paragraph, **4**	#	space needed
no ¶	do not start new paragraph, **4**	◡	close up
//	parallelism, **18**	?	meaning unclear
pl	plural error, **22c**		

Complimentary Symbols

gd coh	good coherence, **4d**	gd th	good thesis statement, **2n, 3c.2, 6b, 32r**
gd coord	good coordination, **17a-17c**	gd trans	good transitions, **4d.1, 4d.5**
gd dev	good development, **4c, 4f**	gd ts	good topic sentence, **4a, 4b**
gd log	good logic, **5j-5k**	gd u	good unity, **4b, 4c**
gd //	good parallelism, **18**	gd var	good sentence variety, **19**
gd rea	good reasoning, **5i-5k**	gd wc	good word choice, **20, 21**
gd rev	good revising, **3c**	gd wp1	good writing process, **1, 2, 3**
gd sub	good subordination, **17e-17g**		

HOW TO FIND INFORMATION
IN THIS HANDBOOK

You can use your *Simon and Schuster Handbook for Writers* as a reference book, just as you use a dictionary or an encyclopedia. At each step, use one or more suggestions to find the information you want.

STEP 1: Use lists to decide where to go.
- Scan the Overview of Contents (on inside front cover).
- Scan the longer Contents that starts on page iii.
- Scan the Index at the back of the book for a detailed alphabetical list of all major and minor topics.
- Scan the List of Charts that highlight and summarize all major subjects.

STEP 2: Locate the number that leads to the information you seek.
- Find a chapter number.
- Find a number-letter combination for a chapter section and its rule or guiding principle.
- Find a chart number.
- Find a page number.

STEP 3: Check elements on each page, illustrated on the opposite page, to confirm where you are in the book.
- Look at the top of each page for the color bar that identifies the part.
- Look for the shortened title at the top of each page (left page for chapter title and right page for section title).
- Look for a section's number-letter combination in white inside a blue rectangle.
- Look for a chart title and number.
- Look for a page number at the bottom of the page.

STEP 4: Locate and read the information you need. Use special features, illustrated on the opposite page, to help you.
- Use cross-references to related key concepts.
- Find the definition for any word printed in small capital letters in the Terms Glossary at the back of the book.
- Use ⊕ALERTS !, ⊕ ESL NOTES ⊕, and ▣ COMPUTER TIPS ▣ for pointers about related matters of usage, grammar, punctuation, and writing.